American Casebook Series
Hornbook Series and Basic Legal Texts
Nutshell Series

of

WEST PUBLISHING COMPANY
P.O. Box 64526
St. Paul, Minnesota 55164-0526

ACCOUNTING

Faris' Accounting and Law in a Nutshell, 377 pages, 1984 (Text)

Fiflis, Kripke and Foster's Teaching Materials on Accounting for Business Lawyers, 3rd Ed., 838 pages, 1984 (Casebook)

Siegel and Siegel's Accounting and Financial Disclosure: A Guide to Basic Concepts, 259 pages, 1983 (Text)

ADMINISTRATIVE LAW

Davis' Cases, Text and Problems on Administrative Law, 6th Ed., 683 pages, 1977 (Casebook)

Davis' Basic Text on Administrative Law, 3rd Ed., 617 pages, 1972 (Text)

Davis' Police Discretion, 176 pages, 1975 (Text)

Gellhorn and Boyer's Administrative Law and Process in a Nutshell, 2nd Ed., 445 pages, 1981 (Text)

Mashaw and Merrill's Cases and Materials on Administrative Law–The American Public Law System, 2nd Ed., 975 pages, 1985 (Casebook)

Robinson, Gellhorn and Bruff's The Administrative Process, 2nd Ed., 959 pages, 1980, with 1983 Supplement (Casebook)

ADMIRALTY

Healy and Sharpe's Cases and Materials on Admiralty, 875 pages, 1974 (Casebook)

Maraist's Admiralty in a Nutshell, 390 pages, 1983 (Text)

Sohn and Gustafson's Law of the Sea in a Nutshell, 264 pages, 1984 (Text)

AGENCY—PARTNERSHIP

Fessler's Alternatives to Incorporation for Persons in Quest of Profit, 258 pages, 1980 (Casebook)

AGENCY—PARTNERSHIP—Continued

Henn's Cases and Materials on Agency, Partnership and Other Unincorporated Business Enterprises, 2nd Ed., 733 pages, 1985 (Casebook)

Reuschlein and Gregory's Hornbook on the Law of Agency and Partnership, 625 pages, 1979, with 1981 pocket part (Text)

Seavey, Reuschlein and Hall's Cases on Agency and Partnership, 599 pages, 1962 (Casebook)

Selected Corporation and Partnership Statutes and Forms, approximately 555 pages, 1985

Steffen and Kerr's Cases and Materials on Agency-Partnership, 4th Ed., 859 pages, 1980 (Casebook)

Steffen's Agency-Partnership in a Nutshell, 364 pages, 1977 (Text)

AGRICULTURAL LAW

Meyer, Pedersen, Thorson and Davidson's Agricultural Law: Cases and Materials, 931 pages, 1985 (Casebook)

AMERICAN INDIAN LAW

Canby's American Indian Law in a Nutshell, 288 pages, 1981 (Text)

Getches, Rosenfelt and Wilkinson's Cases on Federal Indian Law, 660 pages, 1979, with 1983 Supplement (Casebook)

ANTITRUST LAW

Gellhorn's Antitrust Law and Economics in a Nutshell, 2nd Ed., 425 pages, 1981 (Text)

Gifford and Raskind's Cases and Materials on Antitrust, 694 pages, 1983 with 1985 Supplement (Casebook)

Hovenkamp's Economics and Federal Antitrust Law, Student Ed., 414 pages, 1985 (Text)

List current as of April, 1985

T7202—1g

LAW SCHOOL PUBLICATIONS—Continued

ANTITRUST LAW—Continued

Oppenheim, Weston and McCarthy's Cases and Comments on Federal Antitrust Laws, 4th Ed., 1168 pages, 1981 with 1985 Supplement (Casebook)

Posner and Easterbrook's Cases and Economic Notes on Antitrust, 2nd Ed., 1077 pages, 1981, with 1984-85 Supplement (Casebook)

Sullivan's Hornbook of the Law of Antitrust, 886 pages, 1977 (Text)

See also Regulated Industries, Trade Regulation

ART LAW

DuBoff's Art Law in a Nutshell, 335 pages, 1984 (Text)

BANKING LAW

Lovett's Banking and Financial Institutions in a Nutshell, 409 pages, 1984 (Text)

Symons and White's Teaching Materials on Banking Law, 2nd Ed., 993 pages, 1984 (Casebook)

BUSINESS PLANNING

Epstein and Scheinfeld's Teaching Materials on Business Reorganization Under the Bankruptcy Code, 216 pages, 1980 (Casebook)

Painter's Problems and Materials in Business Planning, 2nd Ed., 1008 pages, 1984 (Casebook)

Selected Securities and Business Planning Statutes, Rules and Forms, 470 pages, 1985

CIVIL PROCEDURE

Casad's Res Judicata in a Nutshell, 310 pages, 1976 (text)

Cound, Friedenthal, Miller and Sexton's Cases and Materials on Civil Procedure, 4th Ed., approximately 1147 pages, 1985 with 1985 Supplement (Casebook)

Ehrenzweig, Louisell and Hazard's Jurisdiction in a Nutshell, 4th Ed., 232 pages, 1980 (Text)

Federal Rules of Civil-Appellate-Criminal Procedure—West Law School Edition, approximately 500 pages, 1985

Friedenthal, Kane and Miller's Hornbook on Civil Procedure, Student Edition, approximately 870 pages, 1985 (Text)

Hodges, Jones and Elliott's Cases and Materials on Texas Trial and Appellate Procedure, 2nd Ed., 745 pages, 1974 (Casebook)

Hodges, Jones and Elliott's Cases and Materials on the Judicial Process Prior to Trial in Texas, 2nd Ed., 871 pages, 1977 (Casebook)

Kane's Civil Procedure in a Nutshell, 271 pages, 1979 (Text)

CIVIL PROCEDURE—Continued

Karlen's Procedure Before Trial in a Nutshell, 258 pages, 1972 (Text)

Karlen, Meisenholder, Stevens and Vestal's Cases on Civil Procedure, 923 pages, 1975 (Casebook)

Koffler and Reppy's Hornbook on Common Law Pleading, 663 pages, 1969 (Text)

Marcus and Sherman's Complex Litigation—Cases and Materials on Advanced Civil Procedure, approximately 900 pages, 1985 (Casebook)

Park's Computer-Aided Exercises on Civil Procedure, 2nd Ed., 167 pages, 1983 (Coursebook)

Siegel's Hornbook on New York Practice, 1011 pages, 1978 with 1985 Pocket Part (Text)

See also Federal Jurisdiction and Procedure

CIVIL RIGHTS

Abernathy's Cases and Materials on Civil Rights, 660 pages, 1980 (Casebook)

Cohen's Cases on the Law of Deprivation of Liberty: A Study in Social Control, 755 pages, 1980 (Casebook)

Lockhart, Kamisar and Choper's Cases on Constitutional Rights and Liberties, 5th Ed., 1298 pages plus Appendix, 1981, with 1985 Supplement (Casebook)—reprint from Lockhart, et al. Cases on Constitutional Law, 5th Ed., 1980

Vieira's Civil Rights in a Nutshell, 279 pages, 1978 (Text)

COMMERCIAL LAW

Bailey's Secured Transactions in a Nutshell, 2nd Ed., 391 pages, 1981 (Text)

Epstein and Martin's Basic Uniform Commercial Code Teaching Materials, 2nd Ed., 667 pages, 1983 (Casebook)

Henson's Hornbook on Secured Transactions Under the U.C.C., 2nd Ed., 504 pages, 1979 with 1979 P.P. (Text)

Murray's Commercial Law, Problems and Materials, 366 pages, 1975 (Coursebook)

Nordstrom and Clovis' Problems and Materials on Commercial Paper, 458 pages, 1972 (Casebook)

Nordstrom and Lattin's Problems and Materials on Sales and Secured Transactions, 809 pages, 1968 (Casebook)

Nordstrom, Murray and Clovis' Problems and Materials on Sales, 515 pages, 1982 (Casebook)

Selected Commercial Statutes, 1389 pages, 1985

Speidel, Summers and White's Teaching Materials on Commercial and Consumer Law, 3rd Ed., 1490 pages, 1981 (Casebook)

Stockton's Sales in a Nutshell, 2nd Ed., 370 pages, 1981 (Text)

II

LAW SCHOOL PUBLICATIONS—Continued

COMMERCIAL LAW—Continued

Stone's Uniform Commercial Code in a Nutshell, 2nd Ed., 516 pages, 1984 (Text)

Uniform Commercial Code, Official Text with Comments, 994 pages, 1978

UCC Article 9, Reprint from 1962 Code, 128 pages, 1976

UCC Article 9, 1972 Amendments, 304 pages, 1978

Weber and Speidel's Commercial Paper in a Nutshell, 3rd Ed., 404 pages, 1982 (Text)

White and Summers' Hornbook on the Uniform Commercial Code, 2nd Ed., 1250 pages, 1980 (Text)

COMMUNITY PROPERTY

Mennell's Community Property in a Nutshell, 447 pages, 1982 (Text)

Verrall and Bird's Cases and Materials on California Community Property, 4th Ed., 549 pages, 1983 (Casebook)

COMPARATIVE LAW

Barton, Gibbs, Li and Merryman's Law in Radically Different Cultures, 960 pages, 1983 (Casebook)

Glendon, Gordon and Osakive's Comparative Legal Traditions: Text, Materials and Cases on the Civil Law, Common Law, and Socialist Law Traditions, approximately 1190 pages, 1985 (Casebook)

Glendon, Gordon, and Osakwe's Comparative Legal Traditions in a Nutshell, 402 pages, 1982 (Text)

Langbein's Comparative Criminal Procedure: Germany, 172 pages, 1977 (Casebook)

COMPUTERS AND LAW

Mason's An Introduction to the Use of Computers in Law, 223 pages, 1984 (Text)

CONFLICT OF LAWS

Cramton, Currie and Kay's Cases-Comments-Questions on Conflict of Laws, 3rd Ed., 1026 pages, 1981 (Casebook)

Scoles and Hay's Hornbook on Conflict of Laws, Student Ed., 1085 pages, 1982 (Text)

Scoles and Weintraub's Cases and Materials on Conflict of Laws, 2nd Ed., 966 pages, 1972, with 1978 Supplement (Casebook)

Siegel's Conflicts in a Nutshell, 469 pages, 1982 (Text)

Engdahl's Constitutional Power in a Nutshell: Federal and State, 411 pages, 1974 (Text)

Lockhart, Kamisar and Choper's Cases-Comments-Questions on Constitutional Law, 5th Ed., 1705 pages plus Appendix, 1980, with 1985 Supplement (Casebook)

CONFLICT OF LAWS—Continued

Lockhart, Kamisar and Choper's Cases-Comments-Questions on the American Constitution, 5th Ed., 1185 pages plus Appendix, 1981, with 1985 Supplement (Casebook)—reprint from Lockhart, et al. Cases on Constitutional Law, 5th Ed., 1980

Manning's The Law of Church-State Relations in a Nutshell, 305 pages, 1981 (Text)

Miller's Presidential Power in a Nutshell, 328 pages, 1977 (Text)

CONSTITUTIONAL LAW

Nowak, Rotunda and Young's Hornbook on Constitutional Law, 2nd Ed., Student Ed., 1172 pages, 1983 (Text)

Rotunda's Modern Constitutional Law: Cases and Notes, 2nd Ed., approximately 1055 pages, 1985, with 1985 Supplement (Casebook)

Williams' Constitutional Analysis in a Nutshell, 388 pages, 1979 (Text)

See also Civil Rights

CONSUMER LAW

Epstein and Nickles' Consumer Law in a Nutshell, 2nd Ed., 418 pages, 1981 (Text)

McCall's Consumer Protection, Cases, Notes and Materials, 594 pages, 1977, with 1977 Statutory Supplement (Casebook)

Selected Commercial Statutes, 1389 pages, 1985

Spanogle and Rohner's Cases and Materials on Consumer Law, 693 pages, 1979, with 1982 Supplement (Casebook)

See also Commercial Law

CONTRACTS

Calamari & Perillo's Cases and Problems on Contracts, 1061 pages, 1978 (Casebook)

Calamari and Perillo's Hornbook on Contracts, 2nd Ed., 878 pages, 1977 (Text)

Corbin's Text on Contracts, One Volume Student Edition, 1224 pages, 1952 (Text)

Fessler and Loiseaux's Cases and Materials on Contracts, 837 pages, 1982 (Casebook)

Freedman's Cases and Materials on Contracts, 658 pages, 1973 (Casebook)

Friedman's Contract Remedies in a Nutshell, 323 pages, 1981 (Text)

Fuller and Eisenberg's Cases on Basic Contract Law, 4th Ed., 1203 pages, 1981 (Casebook)

Hamilton, Rau and Weintraub's Cases and Materials on Contracts, 830 pages, 1984 (Casebook)

Jackson and Bollinger's Cases on Contract Law in Modern Society, 2nd Ed., 1329 pages, 1980 (Casebook)

Keyes' Government Contracts in a Nutshell, 423 pages, 1979 (Text)

LAW SCHOOL PUBLICATIONS—Continued

CONTRACTS—Continued

Reitz's Cases on Contracts as Basic Commercial Law, 763 pages, 1975 (Casebook)

Schaber and Rohwer's Contracts in a Nutshell, 2nd Ed., 425 pages, 1984 (Text)

COPYRIGHT

See Patent and Copyright Law

CORPORATIONS

Hamilton's Cases on Corporations—Including Partnerships and Limited Partnerships, 2nd Ed., 1108 pages, 1981, with 1981 Statutory Supplement and 1985 Supplement (Casebook)

Hamilton's Law of Corporations in a Nutshell, 379 pages, 1980 (Text)

Henn's Cases on Corporations, 1279 pages, 1974, with 1980 Supplement (Casebook)

Henn and Alexander's Hornbook on Corporations, 3rd Ed., Student Ed., 1371 pages, 1983 (Text)

Jennings and Buxbaum's Cases and Materials on Corporations, 5th Ed., 1180 pages, 1979 (Casebook)

Selected Corporation and Partnership Statutes, Regulations and Forms, 555 pages, 1985

Solomon, Stevenson and Schwartz' Materials and Problems on Corporations: Law and Policy, 1172 pages, 1982 with 1984 Supplement (Casebook)

CORPORATE FINANCE

Hamilton's Cases and Materials on Corporate Finance, 895 pages, 1984 (Casebook)

CORRECTIONS

Krantz's Cases and Materials on the Law of Corrections and Prisoners' Rights, 2nd Ed., 735 pages, 1981, with 1982 Supplement (Casebook)

Krantz's Law of Corrections and Prisoners' Rights in a Nutshell, 2nd Ed., 384 pages, 1983 (Text)

Popper's Post-Conviction Remedies in a Nutshell, 360 pages, 1978 (Text)

Robbins' Cases and Materials on Post Conviction Remedies, 506 pages, 1982 (Casebook)

Rubin's Law of Criminal Corrections, 2nd Ed., 873 pages, 1973, with 1978 Supplement (Text)

CREDITOR'S RIGHTS

Bankruptcy Code, Rules and Forms, Law School and C.L.E. Ed., 602 pages, 1984

Epstein's Debtor-Creditor Law in a Nutshell, 2nd Ed., 324 pages, 1980 (Text)

Epstein and Landers' Debtors and Creditors: Cases and Materials, 2nd Ed., 689 pages, 1982 (Casebook)

CREDITOR'S RIGHTS—Continued

Epstein and Sheinfeld's Teaching Materials on Business Reorganization Under the Bankruptcy Code, 216 pages, 1980 (Casebook)

LoPucki's Player's Manual for the Debtor-Creditor Game, 123 pages, 1985 (Coursebook)

Riesenfeld's Cases and Materials on Creditors' Remedies and Debtors' Protection, 3rd Ed., 810 pages, 1979 with 1979 Statutory Supplement and 1981 Case Supplement (Casebook)

White's Bankruptcy and Creditor's Rights: Cases and Materials, 812 pages, 1985 (Casebook)

CRIMINAL LAW AND CRIMINAL PROCEDURE

Cohen and Gobert's Problems in Criminal Law, 297 pages, 1976 (Problem book)

Davis' Police Discretion, 176 pages, 1975 (Text)

Dix and Sharlot's Cases and Materials on Criminal Law, 2nd Ed., 771 pages, 1979 (Casebook)

Federal Rules of Civil-Appellate-Criminal Procedure—West Law School Edition, approximately 500 pages, 1985

Grano's Problems in Criminal Procedure, 2nd Ed., 176 pages, 1981 (Problem book)

Israel and LaFave's Criminal Procedure in a Nutshell, 3rd Ed., 438 pages, 1980 (Text)

Johnson's Cases, Materials and Text on Substantive Criminal Law in its Procedural Context, 3rd Ed., approximately 750 pages, 1985 (Casebook)

Kamisar, LaFave and Israel's Cases, Comments and Questions on Modern Criminal Procedure, 5th ed., 1635 pages plus Appendix, 1980 with 1985 Supplement (Casebook)

Kamisar, LaFave and Israel's Cases, Comments and Questions on Basic Criminal Procedure, 5th Ed., 869 pages, 1980 with 1985 Supplement (Casebook)—reprint from Kamisar, et al. Modern Criminal Procedure, 5th ed., 1980

LaFave's Modern Criminal Law: Cases, Comments and Questions, 789 pages, 1978 (Casebook)

LaFave and Israel's Hornbook on Criminal Procedure, Student Ed., 1142 pages, 1985 (Text)

LaFave and Scott's Hornbook on Criminal Law, 763 pages, 1972 (Text)

Langbein's Comparative Criminal Procedure: Germany, 172 pages, 1977 (Casebook)

Loewy's Criminal Law in a Nutshell, 302 pages, 1975 (Text)

LAW SCHOOL PUBLICATIONS—Continued

CRIMINAL LAW AND CRIMINAL PROCEDURE—Continued

Saltzburg's American Criminal Procedure, Cases and Commentary, 2nd Ed., 1193 pages, 1985 with 1985 Supplement (Casebook)

Uviller's The Processes of Criminal Justice: Investigation and Adjudication, 2nd Ed., 1384 pages, 1979 with 1979 Statutory Supplement and 1983 Update (Casebook)

Uviller's The Processes of Criminal Justice: Adjudication, 2nd Ed., 730 pages, 1979. Soft-cover reprint from Uviller's The Processes of Criminal Justice: Investigation and Adjudication, 2nd Ed. (Casebook)

Uviller's The Processes of Criminal Justice: Investigation, 2nd Ed., 655 pages, 1979. Soft-cover reprint from Uviller's The Processes of Criminal Justice: Investigation and Adjudication, 2nd Ed. (Casebook)

Vorenberg's Cases on Criminal Law and Procedure, 2nd Ed., 1088 pages, 1981 with 1985 Supplement (Casebook)

See also Corrections, Juvenile Justice

DECEDENTS ESTATES

See Trusts and Estates

DOMESTIC RELATIONS

Clark's Cases and Problems on Domestic Relations, 3rd Ed., 1153 pages, 1980 (Casebook)

Clark's Hornbook on Domestic Relations, 754 pages, 1968 (Text)

Krause's Cases and Materials on Family Law, 2nd Ed., 1221 pages, 1983 (Casebook)

Krause's Family Law in a Nutshell, 400 pages, 1977 (Text)

Krauskopf's Cases on Property Division at Marriage Dissolution, 250 pages, 1984 (Casebook)

ECONOMICS, LAW AND

Goetz' Cases and Materials on Law and Economics, 547 pages, 1984 (Casebook)

Manne's The Economics of Legal Relationships—Readings in the Theory of Property Rights, 660 pages, 1975 (Text)

See also Antitrust, Regulated Industries

EDUCATION LAW

Alexander and Alexander's The Law of Schools, Students and Teachers in a Nutshell, 409 pages, 1984 (Text)

Morris' The Constitution and American Education, 2nd Ed., 992 pages, 1980 (Casebook)

EMPLOYMENT DISCRIMINATION

Player's Cases and Materials on Employment Discrimination Law, 2nd Ed., 782 pages, 1984 (Casebook)

Player's Federal Law of Employment Discrimination in a Nutshell, 2nd Ed., 402 pages, 1981 (Text)

See also Women and the Law

ENERGY LAW

Rodgers' Cases and Materials on Energy and Natural Resources Law, 2nd Ed., 877 pages, 1983 (Casebook)

Selected Environmental Law Statutes, 786 pages, 1985

Tomain's Energy Law in a Nutshell, 338 pages, 1981 (Text)

See also Natural Resources Law, Environmental Law, Oil and Gas, Water Law

ENVIRONMENTAL LAW

Bonine and McGarity's Cases and Materials on the Law of Environment and Pollution, 1076 pages, 1984 (Casebook)

Findley and Farber's Cases and Materials on Environmental Law, 2nd Ed., approximately 800 pages, 1985 (Casebook)

Findley and Farber's Environmental Law in a Nutshell, 343 pages, 1983 (Text)

Rodgers' Hornbook on Environmental Law, 956 pages, 1977 with 1984 pocket part (Text)

Selected Environmental Law Statutes, 786 pages, 1985

See also Energy Law, Natural Resources Law, Water Law

EQUITY

See Remedies

ESTATES

See Trusts and Estates

ESTATE PLANNING

Kurtz' Cases, Materials and Problems on Family Estate Planning, 853 pages, 1983 (Casebook)

Lynn's Introduction to Estate Planning, in a Nutshell, 3rd Ed., 370 pages, 1983 (Text)

See also Taxation

EVIDENCE

Broun and Meisenholder's Problems in Evidence, 2nd Ed., 304 pages, 1981 (Problem book)

Cleary and Strong's Cases, Materials and Problems on Evidence, 3rd Ed., 1143 pages, 1981 (Casebook)

Federal Rules of Evidence for United States Courts and Magistrates, 337 pages, 1984

Graham's Federal Rules of Evidence in a Nutshell, 429 pages, 1981 (Text)

LAW SCHOOL PUBLICATIONS—Continued

EVIDENCE—Continued

Kimball's Programmed Materials on Problems in Evidence, 380 pages, 1978 (Problem book)

Lempert and Saltzburg's A Modern Approach to Evidence: Text, Problems, Transcripts and Cases, 2nd Ed., 1296 pages, 1983 (Casebook)

Lilly's Introduction to the Law of Evidence, 486 pages, 1978 (Text)

McCormick, Elliott and Sutton's Cases and Materials on Evidence, 5th Ed., 1212 pages, 1981 (Casebook)

McCormick's Hornbook on Evidence, 3rd Ed., Student Ed., 1155 pages, 1984 (Text)

Rothstein's Evidence, State and Federal Rules in a Nutshell, 2nd Ed., 514 pages, 1981 (Text)

Saltzburg's Evidence Supplement: Rules, Statutes, Commentary, 245 pages, 1980 (Casebook Supplement)

FEDERAL JURISDICTION AND PROCEDURE

Currie's Cases and Materials on Federal Courts, 3rd Ed., 1042 pages, 1982 (Casebook)

Currie's Federal Jurisdiction in a Nutshell, 2nd Ed., 258 pages, 1981 (Text)

Federal Rules of Civil-Appellate-Criminal Procedure—West Law School Edition, approximately 500 pages, 1985

Forrester and Moye's Cases and Materials on Federal Jurisdiction and Procedure, 3rd Ed., 917 pages, 1977 with 1981 Supplement (Casebook)

Redish's Cases, Comments and Questions on Federal Courts, 878 pages, 1985 (Casebook)

Vetri and Merrill's Federal Courts, Problems and Materials, 2nd Ed., 232 pages, 1984 (Problem Book)

Wright's Hornbook on Federal Courts, 4th Ed., Student Ed., 870 pages, 1983 (Text)

FUTURE INTERESTS

See Trusts and Estates

IMMIGRATION LAW

Aleinikoff and Martin's Immigration Process and Policy, approximately 950 pages, 1985 (Casebook)

Weissbrodt's Immigration Law and Procedure in a Nutshell, 345 pages, 1984 (Text)

INDIAN LAW

See American Indian Law

INSURANCE

Dobbyn's Insurance Law in a Nutshell, 281 pages, 1981 (Text)

Keeton's Cases on Basic Insurance Law, 2nd Ed., 1086 pages, 1977

INSURANCE—Continued

Keeton's Basic Text on Insurance Law, 712 pages, 1971 (Text)

Keeton's Case Supplement to Keeton's Basic Text on Insurance Law, 334 pages, 1978 (Casebook)

Keeton's Programmed Problems in Insurance Law, 243 pages, 1972 (Text Supplement)

York and Whelan's Cases, Materials and Problems on Insurance Law, 715 pages, 1982, with 1985 Supplement (Casebook)

INTERNATIONAL LAW

Henkin, Pugh, Schachter and Smit's Cases and Materials on International Law, 2nd Ed., 1152 pages, 1980, with Documents Supplement (Casebook)

Jackson's Legal Problems of International Economic Relations, 1097 pages, 1977, with Documents Supplement (Casebook)

Kirgis' International Organizations in Their Legal Setting, 1016 pages, 1977, with 1981 Supplement (Casebook)

Weston, Falk and D'Amato's International Law and World Order—A Problem Oriented Coursebook, 1195 pages, 1980, with Documents Supplement (Casebook)

Wilson's International Business Transactions in a Nutshell, 2nd Ed., 476 pages, 1984 (Text)

INTERVIEWING AND COUNSELING

Binder and Price's Interviewing and Counseling, 232 pages, 1977 (Text)

Shaffer's Interviewing and Counseling in a Nutshell, 353 pages, 1976 (Text)

INTRODUCTION TO LAW

Dobbyn's So You Want to go to Law School, Revised First Edition, 206 pages, 1976 (Text)

Hegland's Introduction to the Study and Practice of Law in a Nutshell, 418 pages, 1983 (Text)

Kinyon's Introduction to Law Study and Law Examinations in a Nutshell, 389 pages, 1971 (Text)

See also Legal Method and Legal System

JUDICIAL ADMINISTRATION

Carrington, Meador and Rosenberg's Justice on Appeal, 263 pages, 1976 (Casebook)

Nelson's Cases and Materials on Judicial Administration and the Administration of Justice, 1032 pages, 1974 (Casebook)

JURISPRUDENCE

Christie's Text and Readings on Jurisprudence—The Philosophy of Law, 1056 pages, 1973 (Casebook)

LAW SCHOOL PUBLICATIONS—Continued

JUVENILE JUSTICE
Fox's Cases and Materials on Modern Juvenile Justice, 2nd Ed., 960 pages, 1981 (Casebook)

Fox's Juvenile Courts in a Nutshell, 3rd Ed., 291 pages, 1984 (Text)

LABOR LAW
Gorman's Basic Text on Labor Law—Unionization and Collective Bargaining, 914 pages, 1976 (Text)

Leslie's Labor Law in a Nutshell, 403 pages, 1979 (Text)

Nolan's Labor Arbitration Law and Practice in a Nutshell, 358 pages, 1979 (Text)

Oberer, Hanslowe and Andersen's Cases and Materials on Labor Law—Collective Bargaining in a Free Society, 2nd Ed., 1168 pages, 1979, with 1979 Statutory Supplement and 1982 Case Supplement (Casebook)

See also Employment Discrimination, Social Legislation

LAND FINANCE
See Real Estate Transactions

LAND USE
Hagman's Cases on Public Planning and Control of Urban and Land Development, 2nd Ed., 1301 pages, 1980 (Casebook)

Hagman's Hornbook on Urban Planning and Land Development Control Law, 706 pages, 1971 (Text)

Wright and Gitelman's Cases and Materials on Land Use, 3rd Ed., 1300 pages, 1982 (Casebook)

Wright and Wright's Land Use in a Nutshell, 2nd Ed., approximately 350 pages (Text)

LEGAL HISTORY
Presser and Zainaldin's Cases on Law and American History, 855 pages, 1980 (Casebook)

See also Legal Method and Legal System

LEGAL METHOD AND LEGAL SYSTEM
Aldisert's Readings, Materials and Cases in the Judicial Process, 948 pages, 1976 (Casebook)

Berch and Berch's Introduction to Legal Method and Process, 550 pages, 1985 (Casebook)

Bodenheimer, Oakley and Love's Readings and Cases on an Introduction to the Anglo-American Legal System, 161 pages, 1980 (Casebook)

Davies and Lawry's Institutions and Methods of the Law—Introductory Teaching Materials, 547 pages, 1982 (Casebook)

Dvorkin, Himmelstein and Lesnick's Becoming a Lawyer: A Humanistic Perspective on Legal Education and Professionalism, 211 pages, 1981 (Text)

LEGAL METHOD AND LEGAL SYSTEM—Continued
Fryer and Orentlicher's Cases and Materials on Legal Method and Legal System, 1043 pages, 1967 (Casebook)

Greenberg's Judicial Process and Social Change, 666 pages, 1977 (Coursebook)

Kelso and Kelso's Studying Law: An Introduction, 587 pages, 1984 (Coursebook)

Kempin's Historical Introduction to Anglo-American Law in a Nutshell, 2nd Ed., 280 pages, 1973 (Text)

Kimball's Historical Introduction to the Legal System, 610 pages, 1966 (Casebook)

Murphy's Cases and Materials on Introduction to Law—Legal Process and Procedure, 772 pages, 1977 (Casebook)

Reynolds' Judicial Process in a Nutshell, 292 pages, 1980 (Text)

See also Legal Research and Writing

LEGAL PROFESSION
Aronson, Devine and Fisch's Problems, Cases and Materials on Professional Responsibility, 745 pages, 1985 (Casebook)

Aronson and Weckstein's Professional Responsibility in a Nutshell, 399 pages, 1980 (Text)

Mellinkoff's The Conscience of a Lawyer, 304 pages, 1973 (Text)

Mellinkoff's Lawyers and the System of Justice, 983 pages, 1976 (Casebook)

Pirsig and Kirwin's Cases and Materials on Professional Responsibility, 4th Ed., 603 pages, 1984 (Casebook)

Schwartz and Wydick's Problems in Legal Ethics, 285 pages, 1983 (Casebook)

Selected Statutes, Rules and Standards on the Legal Profession, 276 pages, Revised 1984

Smith's Preventing Legal Malpractice, 142 pages, 1981 (Text)

Wolfram's Hornbook on Professional Responsibility, Student Edition, approximately 950 pages (Text)

LEGAL RESEARCH AND WRITING
Cohen's Legal Research in a Nutshell, 4th Ed., 450 pages, 1985 (Text)

Cohen and Berring's How to Find the Law, 8th Ed., 790 pages, 1983. Problem book by Foster and Kelly available (Casebook)

Cohen and Berring's Finding the Law, 8th Ed., Abridged Ed., 556 pages, 1984 (Casebook)

Dickerson's Materials on Legal Drafting, 425 pages, 1981 (Casebook)

Felsenfeld and Siegel's Writing Contracts in Plain English, 290 pages, 1981 (Text)

Gopen's Writing From a Legal Perspective, 225 pages, 1981 (Text)

Mellinkoff's Legal Writing—Sense and Nonsense, 242 pages, 1982 (Text)

LAW SCHOOL PUBLICATIONS—Continued

LEGAL RESEARCH AND WRITING—Continued

Rombauer's Legal Problem Solving—Analysis, Research and Writing, 4th Ed., 424 pages, 1983 (Coursebook)

Squires and Rombauer's Legal Writing in a Nutshell, 294 pages, 1982 (Text)

Statsky's Legal Research, Writing and Analysis, 2nd Ed., 167 pages, 1982 (Coursebook)

Statsky's Legislative Analysis: How to Use Statutes and Regulations, 2nd Ed., 217 pages, 1984 (Text)

Statsky and Wernet's Case Analysis and Fundamentals of Legal Writing, 2nd Ed., 441 pages, 1984 (Text)

Teply's Programmed Materials on Legal Research and Citation, 334 pages, 1982. Student Library Exercises available (Coursebook)

Weihofen's Legal Writing Style, 2nd Ed., 332 pages, 1980 (Text)

LEGISLATION

Davies' Legislative Law and Process in a Nutshell, 279 pages, 1975 (Text)

Nutting and Dickerson's Cases and Materials on Legislation, 5th Ed., 744 pages, 1978 (Casebook)

Statsky's Legislative Analysis: How to Use Statutes and Regulations, 2nd Ed., 217 pages, 1984 (Text)

LOCAL GOVERNMENT

McCarthy's Local Government Law in a Nutshell, 2nd Ed., 404 pages, 1983 (Text)

Michelman and Sandalow's Cases-Comments-Questions on Government in Urban Areas, 1216 pages, 1970, with 1972 Supplement (Casebook)

Reynolds' Hornbook on Local Government Law, 860 pages, 1982 (Text)

Valente's Cases and Materials on Local Government Law, 2nd Ed., 980 pages, 1980 with 1982 Supplement (Casebook)

MASS COMMUNICATION LAW

Gillmor and Barron's Cases and Comment on Mass Communication Law, 4th Ed., 1076 pages, 1984 (Casebook)

Ginsburg's Regulation of Broadcasting: Law and Policy Towards Radio, Television and Cable Communications, 741 pages, 1979, with 1983 Supplement (Casebook)

Zuckman and Gayne's Mass Communications Law in a Nutshell, 2nd Ed., 473 pages, 1983 (Text)

MEDICINE, LAW AND

King's The Law of Medical Malpractice in a Nutshell, 340 pages, 1977 (Text)

Shapiro and Spece's Problems, Cases and Materials on Bioethics and Law, 892 pages, 1981 (Casebook)

MEDICINE, LAW AND—Continued

Sharpe, Fiscina and Head's Cases on Law and Medicine, 882 pages, 1978 (Casebook)

MILITARY LAW

Shanor and Terrell's Military Law in a Nutshell, 378 pages, 1980 (Text)

MORTGAGES

See Real Estate Transactions

NATURAL RESOURCES LAW

Laito's Cases and Materials on Natural Resources Law, approximately 930 pages, 1985 (Casebook)

See also Energy Law, Environmental Law, Oil and Gas, Water Law

NEGOTIATION

Edwards and White's Problems, Readings and Materials on the Lawyer as a Negotiator, 484 pages, 1977 (Casebook)

Williams' Legal Negotiation and Settlement, 207 pages, 1983 (Coursebook)

OFFICE PRACTICE

Hegland's Trial and Practice Skills in a Nutshell, 346 pages, 1978 (Text)

Strong and Clark's Law Office Management, 424 pages, 1974 (Casebook)

See also Computers and Law, Interviewing and Counseling, Negotiation

OIL AND GAS

Hemingway's Hornbook on Oil and Gas, 2nd Ed., Student Ed., 543 pages, 1983 (Text)

Huie, Woodward and Smith's Cases and Materials on Oil and Gas, 2nd Ed., 955 pages, 1972 (Casebook)

Lowe's Oil and Gas Law in a Nutshell, 443 pages, 1983 (Text)

See also Energy and Natural Resources Law

PARTNERSHIP

See Agency—Partnership

PATENT AND COPYRIGHT LAW

Choate and Francis' Cases and Materials on Patent Law, 2nd Ed., 1110 pages, 1981 (Casebook)

Miller and Davis' Intellectual Property—Patents, Trademarks and Copyright in a Nutshell, 428 pages, 1983 (Text)

Nimmer's Cases on Copyright and Other Aspects of Entertainment Litigation, 3rd Ed., approximately 1000 pages, 1985 (Casebook)

POVERTY LAW

Brudno's Poverty, Inequality, and the Law: Cases-Commentary-Analysis, 934 pages, 1976 (Casebook)

LAW SCHOOL PUBLICATIONS—Continued

POVERTY LAW—Continued

LaFrance, Schroeder, Bennett and Boyd's Hornbook on Law of the Poor, 558 pages, 1973 (Text)

See also Social Legislation

PRODUCTS LIABILITY

Noel and Phillips' Cases on Products Liability, 2nd Ed., 821 pages, 1982 (Casebook)

Noel and Phillips' Products Liability in a Nutshell, 2nd Ed., 341 pages, 1981 (Text)

PROPERTY

Aigler, Smith and Tefft's Cases on Property, 2 volumes, 1339 pages, 1960 (Casebook)

Bernhardt's Real Property in a Nutshell, 2nd Ed., 448 pages, 1981 (Text)

Boyer's Survey of the Law of Property, 766 pages, 1981 (Text)

Browder, Cunningham and Smith's Cases on Basic Property Law, 4th Ed., 1431 pages, 1984 (Casebook)

Bruce, Ely and Bostick's Cases and Materials on Modern Property Law, 1004 pages, 1984 (Casebook)

Burby's Hornbook on Real Property, 3rd Ed., 490 pages, 1965 (Text)

Burke's Personal Property in a Nutshell, 322 pages, 1983 (Text)

Chused's A Modern Approach to Property: Cases-Notes-Materials, 1069 pages, 1978 with 1980 Supplement (Casebook)

Cohen's Materials for a Basic Course in Property, 526 pages, 1978 (Casebook)

Cunningham, Stoebuck and Whitman's Hornbook on the Law of Property, Student Ed., 916 pages, 1984 (Text)

Donahue, Kauper and Martin's Cases on Property, 2nd Ed., 1362 pages, 1983 (Casebook)

Hill's Landlord and Tenant Law in a Nutshell, 319 pages, 1979 (Text)

Moynihan's Introduction to Real Property, 254 pages, 1962 (Text)

Uniform Land Transactions Act, Uniform Simplification of Land Transfers Act, Uniform Condominium Act, 1977 Official Text with Comments, 462 pages, 1978

See also Real Estate Transactions, Land Use

PSYCHIATRY, LAW AND

Reisner's Law and the Mental Health System, Civil and Criminal Aspects, 696 pages, 1985 (Casebooks)

REAL ESTATE TRANSACTIONS

Bruce's Real Estate Finance in a Nutshell, 2nd Ed., 262 pages, 1985 (Text)

Maxwell, Riesenfeld, Hetland and Warren's Cases on California Security Transactions in Land, 3rd Ed., 728 pages, 1984 (Casebook)

REAL ESTATE TRANSACTIONS—Continued

Nelson and Whitman's Cases on Real Estate Transfer, Finance and Development, 2nd Ed., 1114 pages, 1981, with 1983 Supplement (Casebook)

Nelson and Whitman's Hornbook on Real Estate Finance Law, 2nd Ed., Standard Ed., approximately 900 pages, 1985 (Text)

Osborne's Cases and Materials on Secured Transactions, 559 pages, 1967 (Casebook)

REGULATED INDUSTRIES

Gellhorn and Pierce's Regulated Industries in a Nutshell, 394 pages, 1982 (Text)

Morgan, Harrison and Verkuil's Cases and Materials on Economic Regulation of Business, 2nd Ed., 670 pages, 1985 (Casebook)

Pozen's Financial Institutions: Cases, Materials and Problems on Investment Management, 844 pages, 1978 (Casebook)

See also Mass Communication Law, Banking Law

REMEDIES

Dobbs' Hornbook on Remedies, 1067 pages, 1973 (Text)

Dobbs' Problems in Remedies, 137 pages, 1974 (Problem book)

Dobbyn's Injunctions in a Nutshell, 264 pages, 1974 (Text)

Friedman's Contract Remedies in a Nutshell, 323 pages, 1981 (Text)

Leavell, Love and Nelson's Cases and Materials on Equitable Remedies and Restitution, 3rd Ed., 704 pages, 1980 (Casebook)

McCormick's Hornbook on Damages, 811 pages, 1935 (Text)

O'Connell's Remedies in a Nutshell, 2nd Ed., 325 pages, 1985 (Text)

York, Bauman and Rendleman's Cases and Materials on Remedies, 4th Ed., approximately 1025 pages, 1985 (Casebook)

REVIEW MATERIALS

Ballantine's Problems

Black Letter Series

Smith's Review Series

West's Review Covering Multistate Subjects

SECURITIES REGULATION

Hazen's Hornbook on The Law of Securities Regulation, Student Ed., 739 pages, 1985 (Text)

Ratner's Securities Regulation: Materials for a Basic Course, 2nd Ed., 1050 pages, 1980 with 1982 Supplement (Casebook)

Ratner's Securities Regulation in a Nutshell, 2nd Ed., 322 pages, 1982 (Text)

LAW SCHOOL PUBLICATIONS—Continued

SECURITIES REGULATION—Continued

Selected Securities and Business Planning Statutes, Rules and Forms, 470 pages, 1985

SOCIAL LEGISLATION

Hood and Hardy's Workers' Compensation and Employee Protection Laws in a Nutshell, 274 pages, 1984 (Text)

LaFrance's Welfare Law: Structure and Entitlement in a Nutshell, 455 pages, 1979 (Text)

Malone, Plant and Little's Cases on Workers' Compensation and Employment Rights, 2nd Ed., 951 pages, 1980 (Casebook)

See also Poverty Law

TAXATION

Dodge's Cases and Materials on Federal Income Taxation, approximately 825 pages, 1985 (Casebook)

Dodge's Federal Taxation of Estates, Trusts and Gifts: Principles and Planning, 771 pages, 1981 with 1982 Supplement (Casebook)

Garbis and Struntz' Cases and Materials on Tax Procedure and Tax Fraud, 829 pages, 1982 with 1984 Supplement (Casebook)

Gunn's Cases and Materials on Federal Income Taxation of Individuals, 785 pages, 1981 with 1985 Supplement (Casebook)

Hellerstein and Hellerstein's Cases on State and Local Taxation, 4th Ed., 1041 pages, 1978 with 1982 Supplement (Casebook)

Kahn and Gann's Corporate Taxation and Taxation of Partnerships and Partners, 2nd Ed., 1204 pages, 1985 (Casebook)

Kragen and McNulty's Cases and Materials on Federal Income Taxation: Individuals, Corporations, Partnerships, 4th Ed., approximately 1200 pages, 1985 (Casebook)

McNulty's Federal Estate and Gift Taxation in a Nutshell, 3rd Ed., 509 pages, 1983 (Text)

McNulty's Federal Income Taxation of Individuals in a Nutshell, 3rd Ed., 487 pages, 1983 (Text)

Posin's Hornbook on Federal Income Taxation of Individuals, Student Ed., 491 pages, 1983 with 1985 pocket part (Text)

Rice and Solomon's Problems and Materials in Federal Income Taxation, 3rd Ed., 670 pages, 1979 (Casebook)

Rose and Raskind's Advanced Federal Income Taxation: Corporate Transactions—Cases, Materials and Problems, 955 pages, 1978 (Casebook)

Selected Federal Taxation Statutes and Regulations, approximately 1300 pages, 1985

Sobeloff and Weidenbruch's Federal Income Taxation of Corporations and Stockholders in a Nutshell, 362 pages, 1981 (Text)

TORTS

Christie's Cases and Materials on the Law of Torts, 1264 pages, 1983 (Casebook)

Dobbs' Torts and Compensation—Personal Accountability and Social Responsibility for Injury, 955 pages, 1985 (Casebook)

Green, Pedrick, Rahl, Thode, Hawkins, Smith and Treece's Cases and Materials on Torts, 2nd Ed., 1360 pages, 1977 (Casebook)

Green, Pedrick, Rahl, Thode, Hawkins, Smith, and Treece's Advanced Torts: Injuries to Business, Political and Family Interests, 2nd Ed., 544 pages, 1977 (Casebook)—reprint from Green, et al. Cases and Materials on Torts, 2nd Ed., 1977

Keeton, Keeton, Sargentich and Steiner's Cases and Materials on Torts, and Accident Law, 1360 pages, 1983 (Casebook)

Kionka's Torts in a Nutshell: Injuries to Persons and Property, 434 pages, 1977 (Text)

Malone's Torts in a Nutshell: Injuries to Family, Social and Trade Relations, 358 pages, 1979 (Text)

Prosser and Keeton's Hornbook on Torts, 5th Ed., Student Ed., 1286 pages, 1984 (Text)

Shapo's Cases on Tort and Compensation Law, 1244 pages, 1976 (Casebook)

See also Products Liability

TRADE REGULATION

McManis' Unfair Trade Practices in a Nutshell, 444 pages, 1982 (Text)

Oppenheim, Weston, Maggs and Schechter's Cases and Materials on Unfair Trade Practices and Consumer Protection, 4th Ed., 1038 pages, 1983 (Casebook)

See also Antitrust, Regulated Industries

TRIAL AND APPELLATE ADVOCACY

Appellate Advocacy, Handbook of, 249 pages, 1980 (Text)

Bergman's Trial Advocacy in a Nutshell, 402 pages, 1979 (Text)

Binder and Bergman's Fact Investigation: From Hypothesis to Proof, 354 pages, 1984 (Coursebook)

Goldberg's The First Trial (Where Do I Sit?, What Do I Say?) in a Nutshell, 396 pages, 1982 (Text)

Haydock, Herr and Stempel's, Fundamentals of Pre-Trial Litigation, 768 pages, 1985 (Casebook)

Hegland's Trial and Practice Skills in a Nutshell, 346 pages, 1978 (Text)

Hornstein's Appellate Advocacy in a Nutshell, 325 pages, 1984 (Text)

Jeans' Handbook on Trial Advocacy, Student Ed., 473 pages, 1975 (Text)

McElhaney's Effective Litigation, 457 pages, 1974 (Casebook)

LAW SCHOOL PUBLICATIONS—Continued

TRIAL AND APPELLATE ADVOCACY—Continued

Nolan's Cases and Materials on Trial Practice, 518 pages, 1981 (Casebook)

Parnell and Shellhaas' Cases, Exercises and Problems for Trial Advocacy, 171 pages, 1982 (Coursebook)

Sonsteng, Haydock and Boyd's The Trialbook: A Total System for Preparation and Presentation of a Case, Student Ed., 404 pages, 1984 (Coursebook)

TRUSTS AND ESTATES

Atkinson's Hornbook on Wills, 2nd Ed., 975 pages, 1953 (Text)

Averill's Uniform Probate Code in a Nutshell, 425 pages, 1978 (Text)

Bogert's Hornbook on Trusts, 5th Ed., 726 pages, 1973 (Text)

Clark, Lusky and Murphy's Cases and Materials on Gratuitous Transfers, 3rd Ed., approximately 1200 pages, 1985 (Casebook)

Gulliver's Cases and Materials on Future Interests, 624 pages, 1959 (Casebook)

Gulliver's Introduction to the Law of Future Interests, 87 pages, 1959 (Casebook)—reprint from Gulliver's Cases and Materials on Future Interests, 1959

McGovern's Cases and Materials on Wills, Trusts and Future Interests: An Introduction to Estate Planning, 750 pages, 1983 (Casebook)

Mennell's Cases and Materials on California Decedent's Estates, 566 pages, 1973 (Casebook)

Mennell's Wills and Trusts in a Nutshell, 392 pages, 1979 (Text)

TRUSTS AND ESTATES—Continued

Powell's The Law of Future Interests in California, 91 pages, 1980 (Text)

Simes' Hornbook on Future Interests, 2nd Ed., 355 pages, 1966 (Text)

Turrentine's Cases and Text on Wills and Administration, 2nd Ed., 483 pages, 1962 (Casebook)

Uniform Probate Code, 5th Ed., Official Text With Comments, 384 pages, 1977

Waggoner's Future Interests in a Nutshell, 361 pages, 1981 (Text)

WATER LAW

Getches' Water Law in a Nutshell, 439 pages, 1984 (Text)

Trelease's Cases and Materials on Water Law, 3rd Ed., 833 pages, 1979, with 1984 Supplement (Casebook)

See also Energy Law, Natural Resources Law, Environmental Law

WILLS

See Trusts and Estates

WOMEN AND THE LAW

Kay's Text, Cases and Materials on Sex-Based Discrimination, 2nd Ed., 1045 pages, 1981, with 1983 Supplement (Casebook)

Thomas' Sex Discrimination in a Nutshell, 399 pages, 1982 (Text)

See also Employment Discrimination

WORKERS' COMPENSATION

See Social Legislation

ADVISORY BOARD
AMERICAN CASEBOOK SERIES
HORNBOOK SERIES AND BASIC LEGAL TEXTS
NUTSHELL SERIES AND BLACK LETTER SERIES

JOHN A. BAUMAN
Professor of Law
University of California, Los Angeles

CURTIS J. BERGER
Professor of Law
Columbia University School of Law

JESSE H. CHOPER
Dean and Professor of Law
University of California, Berkeley

DAVID P. CURRIE
Professor of Law
University of Chicago

DAVID G. EPSTEIN
Dean and Professor of Law
Emory University

ERNEST GELLHORN
Dean and Professor of Law
Case Western Reserve University

YALE KAMISAR
Professor of Law
University of Michigan

WAYNE R. LaFAVE
Professor of Law
University of Illinois

RICHARD C. MAXWELL
Professor of Law
Duke University

ARTHUR R. MILLER
Professor of Law
Harvard University

JAMES J. WHITE
Professor of Law
University of Michigan

CHARLES ALAN WRIGHT
Professor of Law
University of Texas

CASES AND MATERIALS ON
COPYRIGHT
And Other Aspects of ENTERTAINMENT LITIGATION
Including Unfair Competition, Defamation, Privacy
ILLUSTRATED
Third Edition

By

Melville B. Nimmer

Professor of Law
University of California, Los Angeles

AMERICAN CASEBOOK SERIES

WEST PUBLISHING CO.
ST. PAUL, MINN., 1985

COPYRIGHT © 1971, 1979 By WEST PUBLISHING CO.
COPYRIGHT © 1985 By WEST PUBLISHING CO.
50 West Kellogg Boulevard
P.O. Box 64526
St. Paul, Minnesota 55164-0526

All rights reserved

Printed in the United States of America

Library of Congress Cataloging in Publication Data

Nimmer, Melville B.
  Cases & materials on copyright and other aspects of entertainment litigation illustrated.

  (American casebook series)
  Rev. ed. of: Cases and materials on copyright and other aspects of law pertaining to literary, musical, and artistic works. 2nd ed. 1979.
  Includes index.
  1. Copyright—United States—Cases. I. Nimmer, Melville B. Cases and materials on copyright and other aspects of law pertaining to literary, musical, and artistic works. II. Title. III. Title: Cases and materials on copyright and other aspects of entertainment litigation illustrated. IV. Series.
KF2993.N54 1985   346.7304'82   85-7206
                        347.306482

ISBN 0-314-90275-9

*For
Gloria,
Becca and Paul,
Larry and Melissa,
David and Marcia*

Preface to the Third Edition

The current update of the statutory and case materials speaks for itself, and requires no further comment. It may be added, however, that the ambivalence which I have previously expressed (see Preface to the First Edition) as to the phrase "entertainment law" continues. That phrase has gained a wider acceptance both in the profession and in academia. Increasingly, it has come to refer to the form and substance of contractual arrangements within the entertainment industries. In this sense entertainment law refers to deal making. A course devoted to this subject matter might more accurately be referred to as Entertainment Transactions. In contrast, the subject matter of this work deals with the substantive causes of action likely to arise in the entertainment context in the absence of an applicable contract. This may be referred to as Entertainment Litigation. To be sure, breach of contract in an entertainment context may also be viewed as entertainment litigation. But for pedagogical reasons it seems best to leave such problems to courses in contract law. The above is by way of explanation of the new subtitle of this work, which employs the phrase entertainment litigation.

I should like to incorporate by reference and repeat here the acknowledgments and thanks contained in the Prefaces to the first two editions. In addition, I wish to thank Wayne Williams, UCLA Law Class of '84, for his valuable research assistance. Finally, my thanks to my secretary, Margaret Kiever, who as usual proved invaluable, in helping to obtain the new illustrations, and generally in putting everything together.

MELVILLE B. NIMMER

Los Angeles, California
May, 1985

*

Preface to the Second Edition

The long-heralded general revision of the copyright law has at last become a reality. The Copyright Act of 1976 was enacted on October 19, 1976, and for most purposes became effective on January 1, 1978. This first general revision of copyright law since 1909 obviously required a profound reworking of this casebook, hence the present second edition. Preparation of this edition offered the pedagogical challenge of how to deal in a casebook with a body of law so new as to lack almost any cases. It is believed that an in-depth understanding of many of the new provisions in the Copyright Act of 1976 may be attained through the combination of notes, problems, and questions which are contained herein. Of course, many of the pre-1978 cases are included in this edition because they remain relevant to an understanding of the new law. In addition, some older cases are retained even if the substantive law which they expound has been repealed. This is done not out of antiquarian interest, but because the law of these cases resulted in many works having been injected into the public domain. Once a work enters the public domain it is ineligible for further copyright protection under the current Act even if that aspect of the pre-1978 law which caused the work to be injected into the public domain has itself been repealed by the Act of 1976. Such older cases therefore retain a very practical significance for the lawyer presently dealing with works which were first created pre-1978.

This edition also up-dates judicial developments both in copyright, and in those other areas of entertainment law which form the subject matter of this casebook. Such developments have been particularly notable with respect to First Amendment aspects of the law of defamation and the right of privacy. Perhaps, most striking of all is the rapidly increasing judicial recognition of the right of publicity. The chapter divisions have been somewhat altered. Authors' moral rights, for example, are now treated in a separate chapter. So too is the general question of federal preemption. The defamation and privacy cases have been re-ordered so that each substantive area is treated separately.

One innovation contained in this edition is the addition of numerous pictures illustrating many of the cases. It is believed that many of these pictures contribute to a fuller understanding of the bases for the courts' decisions. Even where this may not be true, the illustrations are pedagogically useful in that they help to flesh out and make more vivid the facts before the courts.

Special thanks are due to Matthew Bender & Co. for permission to reproduce here a number of passages from the 1978 edition of Nimmer on Copyright. I am grateful to Mary Moline and to Robert Kunstadt for their respective efforts in locating certain of the illustrations contained herein. The abbreviation "H.Rep." will be found throughout the copyright chapters in this casebook. This refers to H.R.Rep. No. 94–1476, 94th Cong., 2d Sess. (1976).

The cartoons by Bion Smalley at pages 382 and 406 reprinted by permission of the American Library Association from "Living in the Gap of Ambiguity; An Attorney's Advice to Librarians on the Copyright Law" by Lewis I. Flacks, in American Libraries, May, 1977, pp. 249 and 255, copyright © 1977 by the American Library Association.

MELVILLE B. NIMMER

Los Angeles, California
June, 1979

Preface to the First Edition

The practice of law, no matter how specialized, is never limited to the subject matter of any one of the traditional conceptual branches of law. There is no such thing as a "contracts lawyer" or a "procedure lawyer" or a "conflicts lawyer". Even those whose practice is devoted to particular fields, such as taxation, patents, personal injury, and criminal law, soon find that the "seamless web" cliche about the law is quite accurate. Still, the conceptual branches of law often do constitute convenient boundaries in determining the subject matter of law school courses. Where feasible, however, it seems obviously desirable for a given law school offering to cut across conceptual boundaries so as to encompass the primary related fields in a given commercial or industrial context. This casebook is an attempt to do just that for the student who may find himself in a practice consisting mainly of clients who write or publish books, magazines, or newspapers, or who are connected with the legitimate stage, motion pictures, radio or television, or who are in the fields of the musical or graphic arts. Neither legal terminology nor the English language contains a term to encompass the legal substance of these diverse, but related, endeavors. The best we have is the phrase "entertainment law". It is not an entirely satisfactory designation since ordinarily one does not think, for example, of book publishing or the graphic arts as forms of "entertainment". Still, "entertainment law" seems to be increasingly accepted as descriptive of the general field.

Basic contract law is, of course, vital to the entertainment lawyer, and on occasion he will enter diverse other areas of the law. But in the main, in his day to day work, apart from contract law, his practice is confined to the substantive areas of law explored in this casebook. There is an obvious utility in dealing with these areas in a single course. Real life facts are not conceptually air-tight. A given work may, for example, raise questions of copyright, unfair competition, right of privacy, and defamation. Advice to the client will require an understanding of all of these fields, and of the manner in which they interact. Copyright is, however, the heart of entertainment law, though it and the other areas of law encompassed in this casebook, have non-entertainment components. It is the entertainment aspects that are here treated in greatest depth. Some instructors may wish to limit a given semester or quarter offering to copyright alone, and perhaps devote a second semester or quarter to the non-copyright aspects of entertainment law, as contained in Chapters Nine through Twelve. Such a dual offering could be designated, as it is at U.C.L.A., Entertainment Law I and II.

A word as to editing technique. Although I have deleted extraneous portions of the judicial opinions that are here reproduced, I have avoided the sort of tightly digested extract of opinions found in many casebooks. The digested opinion seems to me to be pedagogically unsound. Either an opinion should be read as an opinion, with all the ambiguity and limitations inherent therein, or the principles contained in a case may be synthesized and generalized in textual material. The digested opinion serves neither of these purposes. It is, moreover, an unreal and misleading law school device that has no counterpart in the research necessary in actual practice. As to textual material, although there is a somewhat substantial amount of it contained herein, I think it is a mistake for a given work to attempt to be both a casebook and a treatise. It is unlikely to be satisfactory as either. The primary reliance here is on the reading of cases. This is not to denigrate the importance of treatises and other textual material, and references to such materials may be found throughout. But with all that has been said against the case method in recent years, it remains a fact that the practicing lawyer worth his salt when faced with a problem reads the cases, and not merely what others have said about the cases. No less should be expected of students.

Acknowledgment and thanks are due to Matthew Bender & Co. who have permitted extensive portions of Nimmer on Copyright to appear herein. Thanks for permission to reproduce materials are also due to The American Law Institute, the California Law Review, Law and Contemporary Problems, and the Columbia Law Review.

MELVILLE B. NIMMER

Los Angeles, California
June, 1971

Summary of Contents

	Page
PREFACE TO THE THIRD EDITION	xvii
PREFACE TO THE SECOND EDITION	xix
PREFACE TO THE FIRST EDITION	xxi
TABLE OF ILLUSTRATIONS	xxxv
TABLE OF CASES	xxxvii

Chapter One. The Subject Matter of Copyright 1

- A. Originality 1
- B. Fixation in a Tangible Medium of Expression 30
- C. Works of Authorship 40

Chapter Two. Publication 127

- A. General Publication Distinguished From Limited Publication 130
- B. Distribution of Phonorecords 140
- C. Performances 150
- D. Exhibition of Works of Art 158
- E. Publication of Derivative Works 161

Chapter Three. Formalities 171

- A. Notice 171
- B. Registration and Deposit 186
- C. The Manufacturing Clause 193

Chapter Four. The Nature of the Rights Protected by Copyright 197

- A. The Reproduction Right 197
- B. The Distribution Right 208
- C. The Performance Right 214
- D. The Display Right 238

Chapter Five. Duration and Renewal of Copyright 240

- A. Duration 240
- B. Renewal of Copyright 245

	Page
Chapter Six. Transfers of Copyright	277
A. Indivisibility	278
B. Recordation	289
C. Copyright Distinct From the Tangible Object	298
D. Determination of Media to Which Licenses Apply	302
Chapter Seven. Infringement Actions	316
A. Jurisdiction	316
B. Copying	322
C. The Defense of Fair Use	366
D. The Defense of the First Amendment	426
Chapter Eight. Copyright Remedies	431
A. Defendant's Profits	432
B. Statutory Damages	441
C. Attorney's Fee	445
Chapter Nine. Federal Preemption of State Law	451
A. Preemption Pre–1978	451
B. Preemption Under the Current Copyright Act	475
Chapter Ten. Author's Moral Rights	479
A. Distortion	480
B. The Right to Prevent Use of an Author's Name	503
C. The Right to Require Use of an Author's Name	513
D. Droit de Suite	520
Chapter Eleven. Unfair Competition	524
A. News	524
B. Titles	542
C. Characters	559
Chapter Twelve. The Protection of Ideas by Express or Implied Contract	566
Chapter Thirteen. Defamation	595
A. Nature of the Injury	597
B. Identification	622
C. First Amendment Defense	640

Page

Chapter Fourteen. Right of Privacy—Public Disclosure of Private Facts 704
- A. The Nature of the Injury 704
- B. Identification 742
- C. First Amendment Defense 751

Chapter Fifteen. Right of Privacy—False Light 781
- A. Nature of Injury 781
- B. First Amendment Defense 792

Chapter Sixteen. Right of Publicity 828
- A. The Nature of Injury 828
- B. First Amendment Defense 858

Appendices

App.
- A. The Constitutional Provision Respecting Copyright 894
- B. The Copyright Act of 1976 895
- C. The Copyright Act of 1909 as Incorporated in the United States Code 972
- D. Parallel Reference Tables Showing Disposition of Sections of Act of March 4, 1909 as Amended (1947) in Title 17, U.S.C. (Pre–1978) 998
- E. Fair Use (Harper & Row, Publishers, Inc. v. Nation Enterprises) 1000

INDEX 1019

Table of Contents

	Page
Preface to the Third Edition	xvii
Preface to the Second Edition	xix
Preface to the First Edition	xxi
Table of Illustrations	xxxv
Table of Cases	xxxvii

Chapter One. The Subject Matter of Copyright 1
- A. Originality 1
  - *Introductory Note* 1
  - *Bleistein v. Donaldson Lithographing Co.* 2
  - *Note—Copyrightability of Advertisements* 6
  - *Burrow-Giles Lithographic Co. v. Sarony* 7
  - *Alfred Bell & Co. v. Catalda Fine Arts* 13
  - *Gracen v. Bradford Exchange* 19
  - *Lee v. Runge* 24
  - *Note—The Purpose of Copyright* 28
  - *Note—The Meaning of "Science and Useful Arts"* 29
- B. Fixation in a Tangible Medium of Expression 30
  - 1. Statutory Copyright 30
    - *Note* 30
  - 2. Common Law Copyright 32
    - *Note on Preemption and Fixation* 32
    - *Hemingway v. Random House, Inc.* 33
    - *Note* 40
- C. Works of Authorship 40
  - *Note—The Scope of "Works of Authorship"* 40
  - 1. Photographs 41
    - *Time, Inc. v. Bernard Geis Associates* 41
  - 2. Factual Works 49
    - *Hoehling v. Universal City Studios, Inc.* 49
  - 3. Works of Applied Art 56
    - *Mazer v. Stein* 56
    - *Esquire, Inc. v. Ringer* 61
    - *Kieselstein-Cord v. Accessories by Pearl, Inc.* 69
  - 4. Characters 74
    - *Warner Bros. Pictures v. Columbia Broadcasting System* 74
    - *Walt Disney Productions v. The Air Pirates* 80
    - *Warner Brothers Inc. v. American Broadcasting Companies, Inc.* 85

	Page
C. Works of Authorship—Continued	
5. Sound Recordings	93
Note	*93*
6. Derivative Works and Compilations	96
Note	*96*
Stodart v. Mutual Film Corp.	*97*
G. Ricordi & Co. v. Paramount Pictures, Inc.	*99*
Leon v. Pacific Telephone & Telegraph Co.	*103*
7. Works of Utility	108
Baker v. Selden	*108*
Morrissey v. Procter & Gamble Co.	*113*
8. Computer Programs	115
Apple Computer, Inc. v. Franklin Computer Corp.	*115*
Note—Final Report of the National Commission on New Technological Uses of Copyrighted Works (CONTU)	*124*
Chapter Two. Publication	**127**
Note—The Significance of Publication in the Law of Copyright	*127*
A. General Publication Distinguished From Limited Publication	130
Bell v. Combined Registry Co.	*130*
White v. Kimmell	*135*
B. Distribution of Phonorecords	140
Rosette v. Rainbo Record Mfg. Corp.	*140*
C. Performances	150
King v. Mister Maestro, Inc.	*150*
D. Exhibition of Works of Art	158
American Tobacco Co. v. Werckmeister	*158*
E. Publication of Derivative Works	161
O'Neill v. General Film Co.	*161*
Chapter Three. Formalities	**171**
A. Notice	171
Note	*173*
Wrench v. Universal Pictures Co.	*174*
Heim v. Universal Pictures Co.	*181*
B. Registration and Deposit	186
Washingtonian Pub. Co. v. Pearson	*186*
Note—Deposit Distinguished From Registration	*192*

	Page
C. The Manufacturing Clause	193
1. The Manufacturing Clause Under the Copyright Act of 1976	193
2. The Manufacturing Clause Under the Copyright Act of 1909	194
Hoffenberg v. Kaminstein	*194*

Chapter Four. The Nature of the Rights Protected by Copyright ... 197

Note—The Copying Requirement and Other Limitations on the Rights of the Copyright Owner ... *197*

A. The Reproduction Right ... 197
    White-Smith Music Co. v. Apollo Co. ... *197*
    Gross v. Seligman ... *203*

B. The Distribution Right ... 208
    United States v. Atherton ... *208*

C. The Performance Right ... 214
    1. The Requirement That the Performance Be Public ... 214
        Note ... *214*
        Columbia Pictures Industries, Inc. v. Redd Horne Inc. ... *216*
    2. The Requirement That the Performance Be for Profit ... 221
        Note ... *221*
        Herbert v. Shanley ... *222*
        Note ... *225*
    3. Performing Rights Societies ... 229
        Note ... *229*
        The Robert Sigwood Group Ltd. v. Sperber ... *231*

D. The Display Right ... 238

Chapter Five. Duration and Renewal of Copyright ... 240

A. Duration ... 240
B. Renewal of Copyright ... 245
    Note—The Rationale of the Renewal Concept ... *245*
    1. Who Is Entitled to Claim Renewal? ... 247
        De Sylva v. Ballentine ... *247*
    2. Assignability of Renewal ... 253
        Fred Fisher Music Co. v. M. Witmark & Sons ... *253*
        Rohauer v. Killiam Shows, Inc. ... *263*

Chapter Six. Transfers of Copyright ... 277

Note—Employment For Hire—Constitutional Limitations ... *277*

		Page
A.	Indivisibility	278
	Note	278
	Goodis v. United Artists Television, Inc.	281
	Note	288
B.	Recordation	289
	Vidor v. Serlin	289
	Group Publishers v. Winchell	293
C.	Copyright Distinct From the Tangible Object	298
	Pushman v. New York Graphic Society	298
	New York General Business Law, Secs. 223, 224	301
D.	Determination of Media to Which Licenses Apply	302
	Bartsch v. Metro-Goldwyn-Mayer, Inc.	302
	Goodis v. United Artists Television, Inc.	308

Chapter Seven. Infringement Actions — 316

A.	Jurisdiction	316
	T.B. Harms Co. v. Eliscu	316
B.	Copying	322
	1. Access	322
	Selle v. Gibb	322
	2. Similarity	331
	Nichols v. Universal Pictures Corp.	331
	Sheldon v. Metro-Goldwyn Pictures Corp.	338
	Sid & Marty Krofft Television Productions, Inc. v. McDonald's Corp.	348
	Musto v. Meyer	359
C.	The Defense of Fair Use	366
	Note	366
	Benny v. Loew's Inc.	368
	Walt Disney Productions v. The Air Pirates	374
	Elsmere Music, Inc. v. National Broadcasting Co.	378
	Wihtol v. Crow	385
	Note—Teacher Photocopying Guidelines	389
	The Williams & Wilkins Co. v. The United States	392
	Time, Inc. v. Bernard Geis Associates	406
	Sony Corporation of America v. Universal City Studios, Inc.	407
D.	The Defense of the First Amendment	426
	Sid & Marty Krofft Television Productions, Inc. v. McDonald's Corp.	426

Chapter Eight. Copyright Remedies — 431

Note—The Relationship Between Actual Damages, Defendant's Profits, and Statutory Damages 431

		Page
A.	Defendant's Profits	432
	Sheldon v. Metro-Goldwyn Corp.	*432*
B.	Statutory Damages	441
	F.W. Woolworth Co. v. Contemporary Arts, Inc.	*441*
C.	Attorney's Fee	445
	Cloth v. Hyman	*445*
	Note—The Copyright Royalty Tribunal	*449*

Chapter Nine. Federal Preemption of State Law — 451

Introductory Note — *451*

A. Preemption Pre-1978 — 451
 Sears, Roebuck & Co. v. Stiffel Co. — *451*
 Compco Corp. v. Day-Brite Lighting, Inc. — *456*
 Goldstein v. California — *459*

B. Preemption Under the Current Copyright Act — 475
 Note—The Legislative History of Sections 301(b)(3) — *475*

Chapter Ten. Author's Moral Rights — 479

Note—The Scope of Moral Rights — *479*

A. Distortion — 480
 Granz v. Harris — *480*
 Gilliam v. American Broadcasting Companies, Inc. — *485*
 Note—Artists' Moral Rights in California and New York — *497*
 Edgar Rice Burroughs, Inc. v. Metro-Goldwyn-Mayer, Inc. — *498*

B. The Right to Prevent Use of an Author's Name — 503
 1. Truthful Attribution — 503
  Williams v. Weisser — *503*
  Shostakovich v. Twentieth Century-Fox Film Corp. — *505*
 2. False Attribution — 509
  Clevenger v. Baker, Voorhis & Co. — *509*
  Note—What Constitutes False Attribution? — *512*

C. The Right to Require Use of an Author's Name — 513
 Smith v. Montoro — *513*

D. Droit de Suite — 520
 Note—The Nature of the Droit de Suite — *520*

TABLE OF CONTENTS

	Page
Chapter Eleven. Unfair Competition	524
A. News	524
International News Service v. Associated Press	*524*
B. Titles	542
Jackson v. Universal International Pictures	*542*
Kirkland v. National Broadcasting Co., Inc.	*549*
Capital Films Corp. v. Charles Fries Production, Inc.	*555*
C. Characters	559
Warner Bros. Pictures, Inc. v. Columbia Broadcasting System, Inc.	*559*
Dallas Cowboy Cheerleaders, Inc. v. Pussycat Cinema, Ltd.	*560*
Edgar Rice Burroughs, Inc. v. Charlton Publications, Inc.	*564*
Chapter Twelve. The Protection of Ideas by Express or Implied Contract	566
Donahue v. ZIV Television Programs, Inc.	*566*
Blaustein v. Burton	*582*
Yadkoe v. Fields	*588*
Chapter Thirteen. Defamation	595
Note—Aspects of Defamation Not Directly Related to Literary and Artistic Works	*595*
A. Nature of the Injury	597
Restatement of Torts, Sec. 559	*597*
Peck v. Tribune Co.	*598*
Kelly v. Loew's Inc.	*600*
Burton v. Crowell Pub. Co.	*617*
B. Identification	622
Kelly v. Loew's Inc.	*622*
Youssoupoff v. Metro-Goldwyn-Mayer Pictures, Ltd.	*623*
Bindrim v. Mitchell	*634*
C. First Amendment Defense	640
New York Times Co. v. Sullivan	*640*
Note—The Balancing of Interests in New York Times Co. v. Sullivan	*649*
Gertz v. Robert Welch, Inc.	*654*
Time, Inc. v. Firestone	*670*
Street v. National Broadcasting Co.	*688*

	Page
Chapter Fourteen. Right of Privacy—Public Disclosure of Private Facts	704
A. The Nature of the Injury	704
Restatement of Torts § 867	704
Melvin v. Reid	705
Bernstein v. National Broadcasting Co.	710
Gill v. Hearst Publishing Co.	726
Mau v. Rio Grande Oil, Inc.	733
Johnson v. Evening Star Newspaper Co.	734
DeSalvo v. Twentieth Century-Fox Film Corp.	735
B. Identification	742
Levey v. Warner Bros. Pictures	742
Toscani v. Hersey	746
Bernstein v. National Broadcasting Co.	749
C. First Amendment Defense	751
Cox Broadcasting Corp. v. Cohn	751
Briscoe v. Reader's Digest Association	761
Virgil v. Time, Inc.	773
Chapter Fifteen. Right of Privacy—False Light	781
A. Nature of the Injury	781
Restatement (Second) of Torts § 652E	781
Kerby v. Hal Roach Studios	781
Strickler v. National Broadcasting Co.	787
Restatement (Second) of Torts § 652E	789
Spahn v. Julian Messner, Inc.	790
B. First Amendment Defense	792
Time, Inc. v. Hill	792
Note—The Right to Speak From Times to Time: First Amendment Theory Applied to Libel and Misapplied to Privacy by Nimmer	808
Spahn v. Julian Messner, Inc.	816
Leopold v. Levin	821
Chapter Sixteen. Right of Publicity	828
A. The Nature of the Injury	828
Haelan Laboratories, Inc. v. Topps Chewing Gum, Inc.	828
Note—The Right of Publicity	832
Restatement (Second) of Torts § 652C	842
California Civil Code § 3344	842
Factors, Etc., Inc. v. Pro Arts, Inc.	844
Note—Descendibility of the Right of Publicity	852
California Civil Code Sec. 990	854

TABLE OF CONTENTS

		Page
B.	First Amendment Defense	858
	Zacchini v. Scripps-Howard Broadcasting Co.	858
	Hicks v. Casablanca Records	871
	Guglielmi v. Spelling-Goldberg Productions	879
	Eastwood v. Superior Court	881

Appendices

App.		
A.	The Constitutional Provision Respecting Copyright	894
B.	The Copyright Act of 1976	895
C.	The Copyright Act of 1909 as Incorporated in the United States Code	972
D.	Parallel Reference Tables Showing Disposition of Sections of Act of March 4, 1909 as Amended (1947) in Title 17, U.S.C. (Pre-1978)	998
E.	Fair Use (Harper & Row, Publishers, Inc. v. Nation Enterprises)	1000

INDEX 1019

Table of Illustrations

	Page
Two of the plaintiffs' circus posters in *Bleistein*	3
The Portrait of Oscar Wilde by Napoleon Sarony	9
The Wizard of Oz: Miss Gracen's painting and a scene from the MGM film	21
A. E. Hotchner and Ernest Hemingway	34
John Kennedy in Dallas: upper left a frame from the Zapruder film, upper right a sketch from "Six Seconds in Dallas"	41
The Hindenburg: an artist's depiction of a scene from the Universal film	50
One of the statuettes in *Mazer v. Stein*	57
One of Esquire's lighting fixtures	62
The Vaquero buckle, the Winchester buckle	70
Humphrey Bogart as Sam Spade in the Warner Bros. film, holding the Maltese Falcon	76
Mickey Mouse	81
A reproduction of the Introduction from Selden's Condensed Ledger	109
Desiderata: an unauthorized poster reproduction of the Ehrman poem	131
Martin Luther King, Jr. delivering his *I Have a Dream* speech	151
Plaintiff James O'Neill (father of playwright Eugene O'Neill) in the role of the Count of Monte Cristo	162
Complainant's *Grace of Youth*, defendant's *Cherry Ripe*	204
Plaintiff Victor Herbert, well-known composer, and founder of the American Society of Composers, Authors and Publishers (ASCAP)	223
A scene from the Universal film *Jesus Christ Superstar*	232
Rudolph Valentino and co-star in *Son of the Sheik*	265
The Bee Gees	323
A scene from the defendant's motion picture, *The Cohens and The Kellys*	332
Joan Crawford and co-star in defendant's *Letty Lynton*	339
Dr. Watson (Robert Duvall), Sherlock Holmes (Nicol Williamson) and Dr. Freud (Alan Arkin) in a scene from the Universal motion picture *The Seven-Per-Cent-Solution*	361
"What is 'fair use'?"	367
Charles Boyer and Ingrid Bergman in plaintiff's *Gas Light*	370
The Air Pirates' version of Mickey and Minnie	376
Self-Service Copier (a cartoon by Bion Smalley)	393

TABLE OF ILLUSTRATIONS

Page

A commentary on the contributory infringement issue in *Sony* published after the Court of Appeals decision, and before the Supreme Court reversal	407
Tarzan, The Ape Man, the 1932 version (left) and the 1959 version (right)	500
Plaintiff Dmitry Shostakovich	506
One of defendant's advertisements in *Smith v. Montoro*	514
Dallas Cowboys Cheerleaders	560
Defendants Elizabeth Taylor (Mrs. Burton) and Richard Burton in *The Taming of the Shrew*	583
W. C. Fields in *You Can't Cheat an Honest Man*	589
Lt. Ryan (John Wayne), Lt. Davis (Donna Reed), and Lt. Brickley (Robert Montgomery) in defendant's motion picture *They Were Expendable*	601
"Get a Lift With a Camel": the plaintiff as shown in the advertisement in defendant's magazine	618
Princess Natasha (Diana Wynyard), the Czarina (Ethel Barrymore) and Rasputin (Lionel Barrymore) in defendant's motion picture *Rasputin, the Mad Monk*	624
The offending advertisement in *New York Times Co. v. Sullivan*	641
The Scottsboro defendants together with the sheriff (extreme left) and their attorney Samuel Leibowitz. Inset: Victoria Price Street as she appeared in 1933 at the second Scottsboro trial	689
A scene from *The Red Kimono*	706
The disputed photograph of the Gills	727
Appearing in the original *Topper* motion picture: Topper (Roland Young), George Kerby (Cary Grant), and Marion Kerby (Constance Bennett)	783
Time, Inc. v. Hill: FEVERISH FATHER cleverly foists off unloaded gun on the leader (Paul Newman), saves his son and family	793
Time, Inc. v. Hill: DARING DAUGHTER (Patricia Peardon) bites hand of youngest convict (George Grizzard), makes him drop gun	793
The disputed Pro Arts poster of Elvis Presley	846
Hugo Zacchini performing his "human cannonball" act	859
The National Enquirer article concerning Clint Eastwood	882

Table of Cases

The principal cases are in italic type. Cases cited or discussed are in roman type. References are to pages.

Abrams v. United States, 650
Acme Screen Co. v. Pebbles, 836
Affiliated Music Enterprises, Inc. v. Sesac, Inc., 231
Alden-Rochelle, Inc. v. ASCAP, 231
Alfred Bell & Co. Ltd. v. Catalda Fine Arts, 13, 19, 23, 28, 49, 440, 441
American Broadcasting Co. v. Wahl, 837
American International Pictures, Inc. v. Foreman, 213
American Tobacco Co. v. Werckmeister, 158, 161
Ansehl v. Puritan Pharmaceutical Co., 6, 7
Apple Computer, Inc. v. Franklin Computer Corporation, 115
ASCAP, United States v., 230
Atherton, United States v., 208, 213
Aviation Guide Co. v. American Aviation Associates, Inc., 449

B. & B. Auto Supply Co. v. Plesser, 448
Bailey v. Alabama, 277
Bailie v. Fisher, 6
Baker v. Selden, 108, 113, 123
Barber v. Time, Inc., 811, 816
Barr v. Matteo, 653
Bartok v. Boosey & Hawkes, Inc., 246
Bartsch v. Metro-Goldwyn-Mayer, Inc., 102, 302, 308
Bates v. Arizona, 871
Batlin & Son, Inc. v. Snyder, 23
Battaglia v. Adams, 813
Bazemore v. Savannah Hospital, 811
Beacon Looms, Inc. v. S. Lichtenberg & Co., 173
Bell v. Combined Registry Co., 130
Benny v. Loew's Incorporated, 368
Bernstein v. National Broadcasting Co., 710, 725, *749*
Bindrim v. Mitchell, 634
Binns v. Vitagraph Co. of America, 725
Black Press Inc. v. Public Bldg. Comm'n of Chicago, 30, 161, 281
Blaustein v. Burton, 581, *582*

Bleistein v. Donaldson Lithographing Co., 2, 7, 29, 39, 205
Brink v. Griffith, 810
Briscoe v. Reader's Digest Association, 761, 772
Broadcast Music, Inc., United States v., 230
Broadcast Music, Inc. v. Walters, 215
Buck v. Duncan, 225
Buck v. Gallagher, 231
Buck v. Harton, 231
Buck v. Jewell-LaSalle Realty Co., 215, 225, 226, 227, 228, 229
Burrow-Giles Lithographic Co. v. Sarony, 7, 13
Burton v. Crowell Publishing Co., 617

Canadian Admiral Corp. v. Rediffusion, Inc., 30
Canessa v. J.I. Kislak, Inc., 733
Cantrell v. Forest City Publishing Co., 807
Capital Films Corporation v. Charles Fries Productions, Inc., 555
Capitol Records, Inc. v. Erickson, 95, 477
Capitol Records, Inc. v. Greatest Records, Inc., 95
Capitol Records, Inc. v. Mercury Records Corp., 30, 31, 95
Capitol Records, Inc. v. Spies, 95
Cason v. Baskin, 835
Classic Film Museum Inc. v. Warner Brothers, Inc., 170
Clemens v. Belford, Clark & Co., 512
Clevenger v. Baker, Voorhis & Co., 509
Cloth v. Hyman, 445
Coffey v. Midland Broadcasting Co., 596
Columbia Broadcasting Sys., Inc. v. AS-CAP, 231
Columbia Broadcasting System, Inc. v. Cartridge City, Limited, 95
Columbia Broadcasting System, Inc. v. Custom Recording Co., 95
Columbia Broadcasting Sys., Inc. v. DeCosta, 30
Columbia Broadcasting System, Inc. v. Newman, 95

TABLE OF CASES

Columbia Broadcasting System, Inc. v. Spies, 95
Columbia Broadcasting System, Inc. v. Teleprompter Corp., 227
Columbia Pictures Corp. v. Krasna, 330
Columbia Pictures Industries, Inc. v. Redd Horne, Inc., 216
Compco Corp. v. Day-Brite Lighting, Inc., *456*, 458, 475, 565, 814
Comptone Co. Ltd. v. Rayex Corp., 7
Consumers Union of United States v. Hobart, 7
Continental Optical Co. v. Reed, 810
Cooper, In re, 555
Corcoran v. Montgomery Ward & Co., 202
Corliss v. E. W. Walker Co., 839
County of (see name of county)
Cox Broadcasting Corp. v. Cohn, 751, 761, 772
Crimi v. Rutgers Presbyterian Church, 479
Curtis Publishing Co. v. Butts, 649, 652, 653, 654, 733

Daily Times Democrat v. Graham, 733, 734, 810
Dallas Cowboy Cheerleaders, Inc. v. Pussycat Cinema, Limited, 560
Dam v. Kirke La Shelle Co., 279, 281
Davis v. E.I. du Pont de Nemours & Co., 180
Day Brite Lighting Inc. v. Sta-Brite Manufacturing Co., 7
DC Comics, Inc. v. Filmation Associates, 565
De Sylva v. Ballentine, Guardian, 247, 252
DeCosta v. Columbia Broadcasting Sys., Inc., 30
Dellar v. Samuel Goldwyn, Inc., 366
DeSalvo v. Twentieth Century-Fox Film Corp., 735, 742
Desny v. Wilder, 580, 581, 582, 588
Deutsch v. Felton, 7
Donahue v. Ziv Television Programs, Inc., 566, 581, 582, 588
Donaldson v. Beckett, 40
Du Puy v. Post Tel. Co., 1
Duchess Music Corp. v. Stern, 206

E.H. Tate Co. v. Jiffy Enterprises, 6
Eastwood v. Superior Court, 881
Ed Brawley, Inc. v. Gaffney, 279, 280
Edgar Rice Burroughs, Inc. v. Charlton Publications, Inc., 564
Edgar Rice Burroughs, Inc. v. Metro-Goldwyn-Mayer, Inc., 313, 498
Edward Thompson Co. v. American Law Book Co., 1

Eisenschiml v. Fawcett Publications, Inc., 366
Elsmere Music, Inc. v. National Broadcasting Co., 378, 384
Encore Music Publishers, Inc. v. London Film Prods., Inc., 230
Erie R.R. v. Tompkins, 541
Esquire, Inc. v. Ringer, 61, 68, 69, 73, 74
Estate of (see name of estate)

F.W. Woolworth Co. v. Contemporary Arts, Inc., 441
Factors Etc., Inc. v. Pro Arts, Inc., 844, 851, 852, 853, 854, 881
Fairfield v. American Photocopy Equipment Co., 810, 813
Farmers Education and Coop. Union of America v. WDAY, Inc., 596
Feeney v. Young, 811
Field v. True Comics, Inc., 280
Fields v. Commissioner, 279
First Fin. Marketing Servs. Group, Inc. v. Field Promotions, Inc., 279, 280
Fisher Music Co. v. Witmark, 246
Fisk v. Fisk, 837
Ford v. Charles E. Blaney Amusement Co., 281
Foreign & Domestic Music Corp. v. Licht, 230
Fortnightly Corp. v. United Artists Television, Inc., 226, 227, 228, 229
Fox Film Corp. v. Dayal, 28
Fred Fisher Music Co. v. M. Witmark & Sons, 246, 253
Fredrick Chusid & Co. v. Marshall Leeman & Co., 581

G. & C. Merriam Co. v. Syndicate Pub. Co., 549
G. Rocordi & Co. v. Paramount Pictures, Inc., 99, 276
Gardenia Flowers, Inc. v. Joseph Markovits, Inc., 6
Garrison v. Louisiana, 649, 651, 653
Gason v. Baskin, 810
Gate City Record Service Co. v. Custom Recording Co., 95
Gautier v. Pro-Football, Inc., 733, 810, 833, 836, 840, 841
Geisel v. Poynter Prods., Inc., 281, 512
Gershwin Publishing Corp. v. Columbia Artists Management, Inc., 215
Gertz v. Robert Welch, Inc., 653, *654*, 670, 687, 703, 807
Gibbs v. Buck, 231
Gill v. Hearst Publishing Co., 726, 733

TABLE OF CASES

Gilliam v. American Broadcasting Companies, Inc., 479, *485,* 496
Gladys Music, Inc. v. Arch Music Co., 1
Goldberg v. Ideal Publishing Corp., 813
Golden West Melodies, Inc. v. Capitol Records, Inc., 322
Goldsmith v. Commissioner, 279
Goldstein v. California, 30, 31, 32, 33, 94, 95, *459,* 475
Goldwyn Pictures Corp. v. Howells Sales Co., 279, 280
Goodis v. United Artists Television, Inc., 79, 181, 280, *281,* 308
Gordon v. Warner Bros. Pictures Inc., 559
Gracen v. Bradford Exchange, 19, 23
Graham v. John Deere Co., 29
Granz v. Harris, 479, *480*
Greater Recording Co. v. Stambler, 95
Greenbie v. Noble, 280
Griffin v. Medical Society, 811
Griswold v. Connecticut, 809
Gross v. Seligman, 203
Groucho Marx Productions, Inc. v. Day and Night Co., 854
Group Publishers v. Winchell, 293, 297
Grove Press, Inc. v. Greenleaf Publishing Co., 102
Guglielmi v. Spelling-Goldberg Productions, 853, 854, *879*

H.M. Kolbe Co. Inc. v. Armgus Textile Co., Inc., 448
Haelan Laboratories, Inc. v. Topps Chewing Gum, Inc., 828, 833, 835, 839, 841, 851
Hanna Manufacturing Co. v. Hillerich & Bradsby, 835
Harper & Bros. v. Kalem Co., 31
Harper & Row, Publishers, Inc. v. Nation Enterprises, 1000
Harris v. Coca-Cola Co., 246
Hartmann v. Winchell, 596
Heim v. Universal Pictures Co., 181, 330
Hemingway v. Random House, Inc., 33, 158
Henreid v. Four Star Television, 581
Herbert v. Shanley, 222
Hiawatha Card Co. v. Colourpicture Publishers, Inc., 279
Hicks v. Casablanca Records, 854, *871, 878*
Hirshon v. United Artists Corp., 279
Hoehling v. Universal City Studios, Inc., 49, 56
Hoffenberg v. Kaminstein, 194, 195
Holdredge v. Knight Publishing Corp., 366, 367
Holmberg v. Armbrecht, 851
Howe Scale Co. v. Wyckoff, Seamans & Benedict, 837

Hubco Data Products Corp. v. Management Assistance Inc., 139
Hubbard v. Journal Pub. Co., 816

Ilyin v. Avon Publications, 280
In re (see name of party)
Inter-City Press Inc. v. Siegfried, 7
International News Service v. Associated Press, 476, *524,* 838
International Telephone and Telegraph Corp. v. General Telephone and Electronics Corp., 851

J.L. Mott Iron Works v. Clow, 6
Jackson v. Universal International Pictures, 542
James v. Screen Gems, Inc., 710
Jansen v. Hilo Packing Co., 834
Jeffreys v. Boosey, 279
Jerry Vogel Music Co. v. Edward B. Marks Music Corp., 253
Jewelers Circular Publishing Co. v. Keystone, 13
Johnson v. Evening Star Newspaper Co., 734, 735
Jones v. Supreme Music Corp., 330

Kalem Co. v. Harper Bros., 30
Kaplan v. Fox Film Corp., 281
Kelly v. Johnson Publishing Co., 810
Kelly v. Loew's Inc., 600, *622, 633,* 648
Kerby v. Hal Roach Studios, 781
Kieselstein-Cord v. Accessories by Pearl, Inc., 69, 73, 74
Kimberly Corp. v. Hartley Pen Co., 852
King v. Mister Maestro, Inc., 150, 158
King Features Syndicate Inc. v. Bouve, 193
Kirkland v. National Broadcasting Co., Inc., 549, 554
Klasmer v. Baltimore Football, Inc., 180
Klauber Bros., Inc. v. Westchester Lace Works, Inc., 280
Krisel v. Duran, 581

L. Batlin & Son, Inc. v. Snyder, 19
Lane v. F.W. Woolworth Co., 834
Laskowitz v. Marie Designer Inc., 7
Lawrence v. Ylla, 836
Lear, Inc. v. Adkins, 582
Lee v. Runge, 24, 28
Leigh v. Barnhart, 281
Leigh v. Gerber, 281
Leo Feist, Inc. v. Apollo Records, 449
Leon v. Pacific Telephone & Telegraph Co., 103
Leopold v. Levin, 821, 826, 827
Lerner v. Club Wander In, Inc., 214

TABLE OF CASES

Lerner v. Schectman, 215
Levey v. Warner Brothers Pictures, 742
Liberty/UA Inc. v. Eastern Tape Corp., 95
Lin-Brook Builders Hardware v. Gertler, 7
Litwin v. Maddux, 549
Local Trademarks, Inc. v. Powers, 280
Loftus v. Greenwich Lithographing, 834
Lugosi v. Universal Pictures, 353, 851, 852, 854

McAndrews v. Roy, 811
M.M. Business Forms Corp. v. Uarco, Inc., 1
M. Witmark & Sons v. Jensen, 230, 231
M. Witmark & Sons v. Pastime Amusement Co., 279
M. Witmark and Sons v. Standard Music Roll, 448
M. Witmark & Sons v. Tremont Social & Athletic Club, 214
Mager, People v., 653
Maheu v. Hughes Tool Co., 670
Mail & Express Co. v. Life Publishing Co., 281
Mann v. Columbia Pictures, Inc., 581
Maritote v. Desilu Productions, Inc., 710
Marks Music Corp. v. Borst Music Pub. Co., 253
Marks Music Corp. v. C.K. Harris Publishing Co., 263
Marsh v. Buck, 231
Martin v. F.I.Y. Theatre Co., 834
Martin Luther King, Jr., Center for Social Change, Inc. v. American Heritage Products, Inc., 852
Marvin Worth Productions v. Superior Films Corp., 384
Masline v. New York N.H. & H.R. Co., 581
Mathews Conveyer Co. v. Palmer-Bee Co., 366
Mau v. Rio Grande Oil, Inc., 733, 734, 735, 811
Maysville Transit Co. v. Ort, 836
Mazer v. Stein, 28, *56,* 69, 74, 113
Melvin v. Reid, 705, 709, 710, 761
Memphis Development Foundation v. Factors Etc., Inc., 852
Mercury Record Productions Inc. v. Economic Consultants, Inc., 95
Meredith Corp. v. Harper & Row, Publishers, Inc., 366
Metro-Goldwyn-Mayer Distrib. Corp. v. Wyatt, 214, 215
Metropolitan Opera Ass'n v. Wagner-Nichols Recorder Corp., 838
Meyers v. United States Camera Publishing Corp., 811

Mifflin v. R.H. White Co., 281
Miller Music Corp. v. Daniels, 262
Minniear v. Tors, 581
Misbourne Pictures Ltd. v. Johnson, 279
Modern Aids Inc. v. R.H. Macy & Co., 7
Morrissey v. Procter & Gamble Co., 113, 115
Morse v. Fields, 330
Morseburg v. Balyon, 522
Musto v. Meyer, 359, 366
Myers v. Afro-American Publishing Co., 811

Nathan v. Monthly Review Press, Inc., 280
National Broadcasting Co. v. Nance, 95
National Comics Publications, Inc. v. Fawcett Publications, Inc., 180
National Security Secrets v. Free Speech, 213
New Fiction Publishing Co. v. Star Co., 279, 280
New York Times Co. v. Sullivan, 512, 596, *640,* 648, 649, 650, 651, 652, 653, 654, 670, 688, 703, 773, 807, 808, 810, 811, 814, 816
New York Tribune, Inc. v. Otis & Co., 366
Nichols v. Universal Pictures Corporation, 74, 79, *331*
Norbay Music, Inc. v. King Records, Inc., 208

O'Brien v. Pabst Sales Co., 834
Oliver v. Saint Germain Foundation, 140
Olmstead v. United States, 809
Oma v. Hillman Periodical Inc., 834
O'Neill v. General Film Co., 161, 170
O'Neill Developments, Inc. v. Galen Kilburn, Inc., 173
Orgel v. Clark Boardman Co., Ltd., 440d

Paine v. Electrical Research Prods., Inc., 230
Palm Tavern, Inc. v. ASCAP, 231
Paramount Pictures, Inc. v. Leader Press, Inc., 834, 837, 839
Patterson v. Century Productions, 202
Pavesich v. New England Life Ins. Co., 834
Peay v. Curtis Publishing Co., 815, 833
Peck v. Tribune Co., 598
People v. _____ **(see opposing party)**
Pittsburgh Athletic Co. v. KQV Broadcasting Co., 31
Presley, Estate of v. Russen, 852
Press v. Walker, 652
Public Ledger v. New York Times, 280
Puddu v. Buonamici Statuary, Inc., 1
Pushman v. New York Graphic Society, 297, 302

TABLE OF CASES xli

Radio Corp. of America v. Premier Albums, Inc., 95
Redmond v. Columbia Pictures Corp., 834
Reed v. Real Detective Publishing Co., 810, 815, 833
Remick Music Corp. v. Interstate Hotel Co. of Nebraska, 1, 231
Riggs Optical Co. v. Riggs, 836
Robert Stigwood Group Limited v. Sperber, 230, *231*
Roberts v. Meyers, 279
Rohauer v. Killiam Shows, Inc., 103, *263,* 276
Rohmer v. Commissioner, 279
Rose v. Bourne, Inc., 262, 449
Rosenblatt v. Baer, 646, 653, 654
Rosenbloom v. Metromedia, Inc., 688
Rosette v. Rainbo Record Manufacturing Corp., 140, 149
Rossiter v. Vogel, 262

Sam Fox Publishing Co. v. United States, 231
Sam Spade case, 79, 84
Samuel v. Curtis Pub. Co., 733
Scherr v. Universal Match Corp., 277, 278
Scholz Homes v. Maddox, 113
Schwartz v. Broadcast Music, Inc., 231
Scutt v. Bassett, 836
Sears Roebuck & Co. v. Stiffel Co., 451, 458, 475, 565, 814
Selle v. Gibb, 322, 330, 331
Semler v. Ultem Publications, 834
Shapiro, Bernstein & Co. v. 4636 So. Vermont Ave., Inc., 449
Shapiro, Bernstein & Co., Inc. v. Gabor, 322
Sheldon v. Metro-Goldwyn Pictures Corp., 19, *338,* 367, 389, *432*
Shipman v. RKO, 367
Shor v. Billingsley, 596
Shostakovich v. Twentieth Century-Fox Film Corp., 479, *505*
Shubert v. Columbia Pictures Corp., 836
Shultz, United States v., 93
Sid & Marty Krofft Television Productions, Inc. v. McDonald's Corp., 84, *348,* 359, 366, 426, 430, 445
Sidis v. F-R Publishing Corp., 815
Sinclair v. Postal Telegraph and Cable Co., 834, 835
Smith v. Montoro, 513, 520
Smith v. Suratt, 840
Society of European Stage Authors & Composers v. New York Hotel Statler Co., 215

Sony Corporation of America v. Universal City Studios, Inc., 406, *407,* 426
Sorenson v. Wood, 596
Southwestern Cable Co., United States v., 226
Spahn v. Julian Messner, Inc., 725, *790,* 808, 813, 815, *816,* 826
Stephano v. News Group Publications, Inc., 854
Stephens v. Howells Sales Co., 280
Stodart v. Mutual Film Corp., 97
Stone & McCarrick v. Dugan Piano Co., 7
Street v. National Broadcasting Co., 688, 703
Strickler v. National Broadcasting Co., 733, 787, 789, 810, 813
Surgical Supply Services Inc. v. Adler, 7

T.B. Harms Company v. Eliscu, 316
Taylor v. Washington, 231
Teleprompter Corp. v. Columbia Broadcasting Sys., Inc., 227, 228, 229
Tennessee Fabricating Co. v. Moultrie Mfg. Co., 368
Themo v. New England Newspaper Publishing Co., 810
Time-Incorporated v. Bernard Geis Associates, 41, 115, 158, 366, *406,* 430
Time, Inc. v. Firestone, 670, 687, 688
Time, Inc. v. Hill, 786, 792, *807,* 808, 809, 812, 813, 814, 815, 826, 871
Tomlin v. Walt Disney Production, 564
Toscani v. Hersey, 746
Trust Co. Bank v. MGM/UA Entertainment Co., 79
Twentieth Century-Fox Film Corp. v. Stonesifer, 366
Twentieth Century Music Corp. v. Aiken, 214, 228, 229

United Artists Records, Inc. v. Eastern Tape Corp., 95
United States v. ———— (see opposing party)
Universal Athletic Sales Co. v. Salkeld, 1
University of Notre Dame v. Twentieth Century-Fox Film Corp., 623, 878

Vacheron Watches Inc. v. Benrus Watch Co., 191
Vargas v. Esquire, Inc., 479
Vassar College v. Loose-Wiles Biscuit Co., 836
Ventura, County of v. Blackburn, 279
Venus Music Corp. v. Mills Music Inc., 263
Vidor v. Serlin, 289
Virgil v. Time, Inc., 773

TABLE OF CASES

Walt Disney Productions v. Alaska Television Network, Inc., 202
Walt Disney Productions v. The Air Pirates, 80, 84, 374, 749
Walt Disney Productions, Inc. v. Souvaine Selective Pictures, 559
Waring v. Dunlea, 95
Waring v. WDAS Broadcasting Station, Inc., 95
Warner Brothers Inc. v. American Broadcasting Companies, Inc., 85, 384
Warner Brothers Pictures v. Columbia Broadcasting System, 74, *496,* 559
Washington Post Co. v. Keogh, 653
Washingtonian Publishing Co. v. Pearson, 186, 190, 193
Waterman v. Mackenzie, 279
Watson v. Buck, 231
Weitzenkorn v. Lesser, 582
Wheaton v. Peters, 40
White v. Kimmell, 135, 139, 158
White-Smith Music Publishing Co. v. Apollo Co., 30, *197,* 202
White-Smith Music Publishing Co. v. Goff, 246
Whitney v. California, 649, 650

Widenski v. Shapiro, Bernstein & Co., 280
Wihtol v. Crow, 385, 389, 405, 406
Williams v. Weisser, 503, 509, 512
Williams & Wilkins Co. v. United States, 392, 405, 406
Willpat Productions, Inc. v. Sigma III Corp., 548
Wise, United States v., 213
Wodehouse, Commissioner v., 279
Women's Mutual Benefit Society v. Catholic Society Feminine, 836
Wood v. Lucy, Lady Duff Gordon, 839
Woodman of the World Life Ins. Soc'y v. ASCAP, 231
Wrench v. Universal Pictures Co., 174, 180, 181

Yadkoe v. Fields, 588
Young v. Greneker Studios, 834
Young v. That Was The Week That Was, 710
Youssoupoff v. Metro-Goldwyn-Mayer Pictures, Limited, 623, 648

Zacchini v. Scripps-Howard Broadcasting Co., 851, *858,* 871

CASES AND MATERIALS ON
COPYRIGHT

And Other Aspects of ENTERTAINMENT LITIGATION
Including Unfair Competition, Defamation, Privacy
ILLUSTRATED

*

Chapter One

THE SUBJECT MATTER OF COPYRIGHT

A. ORIGINALITY

Introductory Note *

Copyright protection subsists only in *original* works of authorship."[1] But what constitutes an "original" work? The Copyright Act leaves this term undefined, and the House Report explained the omission as follows:

> The phrase 'original works of authorship,' which is purposely left undefined, is intended to incorporate without change the standard of originality established by the courts under the present [1909] copyright statute.[2]

The 1909 Act neither defined originality, nor even expressly required that a work be "original" in order to command protection. However, the courts uniformly inferred the requirement[3] from the fact that copyright protection may only be claimed by "authors," or their successors in interest.[4] It was reasoned that since an author is "the beginner * * * or first mover of anything * * * creator, originator" it follows that a work is not the product of an author unless the work is original.[5]

It is necessary, then, to turn to prior case law in order to understand the meaning of "originality" under the current Act.

---

* Nimmer on Copyright, § 2.01. (This is the first of a number of Notes taken from Nimmer on Copyright, published with the consent of Matthew Bender & Co. In most instances the text is slightly revised, and citations either partially or wholly omitted.)

1. 17 U.S.C.A. § 102(a) (emphasis added).

2. H.Rep., p. 51.

3. See e.g., Du Puy v. Post Tel. Co., 210 F. 883 (3d Cir.1914); Edward Thompson Co. v. American Law Book Co., 122 F. 922 (2d Cir.1903); Puddu v. Buonamici Statuary, Inc., 450 F.2d 401 (2d Cir.1971) (Treatise cited); M.M. Business Forms Corp. v. Uarco, Inc., 472 F.2d 1137 (6th Cir.1973) (Treatise cited). A statement in Universal Athletic Sales Co. v. Salkeld, 511 F.2d 904, 908 (3d Cir.1975), is either erroneous or contains a typographical error ("It is true that originality is not a prerequisite of copyright * * *").

4. See 17 U.S.C.A. § 9 (1909 Act), and Gladys Music, Inc. v. Arch Music Co., 150 U.S.P.Q. 26 (S.D.N.Y.1966).

5. Remick Music Corp. v. Interstate Hotel Co. of Nebraska, 58 F.Supp. 523 (D.C. Neb.1944).

BLEISTEIN v. DONALDSON LITHOGRAPHING CO.

Supreme Court of the United States, 1903.
188 U.S. 239, 23 S.Ct. 298, 47 L.Ed. 460.

Mr. Justice Holmes delivered the opinion of the court.

This case comes here from the United States Circuit Court of Appeals for the Sixth Circuit by writ of error. It is an action brought by the plaintiffs in error to recover the penalties prescribed for infringements of copyrights. Rev.Stat. §§ 4952, 4956, 4965, amended by act of March 3, 1891, c. 565, 26 Stat. 1109, and act of March 2, 1895, c. 194, 28 Stat. 965. The alleged infringements consisted in the copying in reduced form of three chromolithographs prepared by employés of the plaintiffs for advertisements of a circus owned by one Wallace. Each of the three contained a portrait of Wallace in the corner and lettering bearing some slight relation to the scheme of decoration, indicating the subject of the design and the fact that the reality was to be seen at the circus. One of the designs was of an ordinary ballet, one of a number of men and women, described as the Stirk family, performing on bicycles, and one of groups of men and women whitened to represent statues. The Circuit Court directed a verdict for the defendant on the ground that the chromolithographs were not within the protection of the copyright law, and this ruling was sustained by the Circuit Court of Appeals. Courier Lithographing Co. v. Donaldson Lithographing Co., 104 Fed.Rep. 993.

There was evidence warranting the inference that the designs belonged to the plaintiffs, they having been produced by persons employed and paid by the plaintiffs in their establishment to make those very things.

Finally, there was evidence that the pictures were copyrighted before publication. There may be a question whether the use by the defendant for Wallace was not lawful within the terms of the contract with Wallace, or a more general one as to what rights the plaintiffs reserved. But we cannot pass upon these questions as matter of law; they will be for the jury when the case is tried again, and therefore we come at once to the ground of decision in the courts below. That ground was not found in any variance between pleading and proof, such as was put forward in argument, but in the nature and purpose of the designs.

We shall do no more than mention the suggestion that painting and engraving unless for a mechanical end are not among the useful arts, the progress of which Congress is empowered by the Constitution to promote. The Constitution does not limit the useful to that which satisfies immediate bodily needs. Burrow-Giles Lithographic Co. v. Sarony, 111 U.S. 53. It is obvious also that the plaintiffs' case is not affected by the fact, if it be one, that the pictures represent actual groups—visible things. They seem from the testimony to have been composed from hints or description, not from sight of a performance.

Two of the plaintiffs' posters in *Bleistein*.

But even if they had been drawn from the life, that fact would not deprive them of protection. The opposite proposition would mean that a portrait by Velasquez or Whistler was common property because others might try their hand on the same face. Others are free to copy the original. They are not free to copy the copy. Blunt v. Patten, 2 Paine, 397, 400. See Kelly v. Morris, L.R. 1 Eq. 697; Morris v. Wright, L.R. 5 Ch. 279. The copy is the personal reaction of an individual upon nature. Personality always contains something unique. It expresses its singularity even in handwriting, and a very modest grade of art has in it something irreducible, which is one man's alone. That something he may copyright unless there is a restriction in the words of the act.

If there is a restriction it is not to be found in the limited pretensions of these particular works. The least pretentious picture has more originality in it than directories and the like, which may be copyrighted. Drone, Copyright, 153. See Henderson v. Tomkins, 60 Fed.Rep. 758, 765. The amount of training required for humbler efforts than those before us is well indicated by Ruskin. "If any young person, after being taught what is, in polite circles, called 'drawing,' will try to copy the commonest piece of real *work,*—suppose a lithograph on the title page of a new opera air, or a woodcut in the cheapest illustrated newspaper of the day—they will find themselves entirely beaten." Elements of Drawing, 1st ed. 3. There is no reason to doubt that these prints in their *ensemble* and in all their details, in their design and particular combinations of figures, lines and colors, are the original work of the plaintiffs' designer. If it be necessary, there is express testimony to that effect. It would be pressing the defendant's right to the verge, if not beyond, to leave the question of originality to the jury upon the evidence in this case, as was done in Hegeman v. Springer, 110 Fed.Rep. 374.

We assume that the construction of Rev.Stat. § 4952, allowing a copyright to the "author, inventor, designer, or proprietor * * * of any engraving, cut, print * * * [or] chromo" is affected by the act of 1874, c. 301, § 3, 18 Stat. 78, 79. That section provides that "in the construction of this act the words 'engraving,' 'cut' and 'print' shall be applied only to pictorial illustrations or works connected with the fine arts." We see no reason for taking the words "connected with the fine arts" as qualifying anything except the word "works," but it would not change our decision if we should assume further that they also qualified "pictorial illustrations," as the defendant contends.

These chromolithographs are "pictorial illustrations." The word "illustrations" does not mean that they must illustrate the text of a book, and that the etchings of Rembrandt or Steinla's engraving of the Madonna di San Sisto could not be protected to-day if any man were able to produce them. Again, the act however construed, does not mean that ordinary posters are not good enough to be considered within its scope. The antithesis to "illustrations or works connected with the fine arts" is not works of little merit or of humble degree, or illustrations addressed to the less educated classes; it is "prints or labels designed to be used for any other articles of manufacture." Certainly works are not the less connected with the fine arts because their pictorial quality attracts the crowd and therefore gives them a real use—if use means to increase trade and to help to make money. A picture is none the less a picture and none the less a subject of copyright that it is used for an advertisement. And if pictures may be used to advertise soap, or the theatre, or monthly magazines, as they are, they may be used to advertise a circus. Of course, the ballet is as legitimate a subject for illustration as any other. A rule cannot be laid down that would excommunicate the paintings of Degas.

Finally, the special adaptation of these pictures to the advertisement of the Wallace shows does not prevent a copyright. That may be a circumstance for the jury to consider in determining the extent of Mr. Wallace's rights, but it is not a bar. Moreover, on the evidence, such prints are used by less pretentious exhibitions when those for whom they were prepared have given them up.

It would be a dangerous undertaking for persons trained only to the law to constitute themselves final judges of the worth of pictorial illustrations, outside of the narrowest and most obvious limits. At the one extreme some works of genius would be sure to miss appreciation. Their very novelty would make them repulsive until the public had learned the new language in which their author spoke. It may be more than doubted, for instance, whether the etchings of Goya or the paintings of Manet would have been sure of protection when seen for the first time. At the other end, copyright would be denied to pictures which appealed to a public less educated than the judge. Yet if they command the interest of any public, they have a commercial value—it would be bold to say that they have not an aesthetic and educational value—and the taste of any public is not to be treated with contempt. It is an ultimate fact for the moment, whatever may be our hopes for a change. That these pictures had their worth and their success is sufficiently shown by the desire to reproduce them without regard to the plaintiffs' rights. See Henderson v. Tomkins, 60 Fed.Rep. 758, 765. We are of opinion that there was evidence that the plaintiffs have rights entitled to the protection of the law.

The judgment of the Circuit Court of Appeals is reversed; the judgment of the Circuit Court is also reversed and the cause remanded to that court with directions to set aside the verdict and grant a new trial.

MR. JUSTICE HARLAN, with whom concurred MR. JUSTICE MCKENNA, dissenting.

Judges Lurton, Day and Severens, of the Circuit Court of Appeals, concurred in affirming the judgment of the District Court. Their views were thus expressed in an opinion delivered by Judge Lurton: "What we hold is this: That if a chromo, lithograph, or other print, engraving, or picture has no other use than that of a mere advertisement, and no value aside from this function, it would not be promotive of the useful arts, within the meaning of the constitutional provision, to protect the 'author' in the exclusive use thereof, and the copyright statute should not be construed as including such a publication, if any other construction is admissible. If a mere label simply designating or describing an article to which it is attached, and which has no value separated from the article, does not come within the constitutional clause upon the subject of copyright, it must follow that a pictorial illustration designed and useful only as an advertisement, and having no intrinsic value other than its function as an advertisement, must be equally without the obvious meaning of the Constitution. * * * "

MR. JUSTICE MCKENNA authorizes me to say that he also dissents.

Questions

1. Like so many of Justice Holmes' phrases, there are frequent quotations of the passage: "Others are free to copy the original. They are not free to copy the copy." What does it mean? What does it *not* mean? Does it mean that an original oil painting may be freely copied, and that only the copying of reproductions of the painting will constitute copyright infringement?

2. Do you agree that "it would be a dangerous undertaking for persons trained only to the law to constitute themselves final judges of the worth of pictorial illustrations, outside of the narrowest and most obvious limits"? Is the same true of verbal as well as pictorial works? Should there be "narrow" and "obvious" limits within which a court may properly determine the "worth" of a work for purposes of denying copyright protection? Can you think of an example of a work falling within such limits? What about the phrase "Apply hook to wall"? See E.H. Tate Co. v. Jiffy Enterprises, 16 F.R.D. 571 (E.D.Pa. 1954). Consider "a cardboard star with a circular center bearing the photograph of an entertainer, upon which is superimposed a transparent phonograph record from which the voice of the pictured person may be heard. The cardboard has two flaps, which, when folded back, enable it to stand for display." Should this be regarded as copyrightable? See Bailie v. Fisher, 258 F.2d 425 (D.C.Cir.1958). Is there a requirement of minimal creativity in addition to the requirement of originality in order to qualify for copyright?

3. Should a different standard of creativity be applied to a work of art from that applied to the other works? Does a work of art differ from other works in that by definition it requires creativity? See Gardenia Flowers, Inc. v. Joseph Markovits, Inc., 280 F.Supp. 776 (S.D.N.Y.1968); Nimmer on Copyright, § 2.08[B][1].

Note [*]

Copyrightability of Advertisements

Under an earlier view copyright protection was denied for advertisements on the ground that they lack artistic merit [1] and some few cases under the 1909

---

[*] Nimmer on Copyright, § 2.08[G][4].

[1] J.L. Mott Iron Works v. Clow, 82 Fed. 316 (7th Cir.1897); see cases collected in Ansehl v. Puritan Pharmaceutical Co., 61 F.2d 131 (8th Cir.1932).

Act persisted in this view.[2] The prevailing rule, however, unquestionably accords copyright protection to advertisements.[3] This doctrine can be directly traced to Mr. Justice Holmes' opinion in the *Bleistein* case. It is interesting to recall, however, that copyright was there recognized not because the works were advertisements, but because they were found to be copyrightable pictures which happened to be used as advertisements. Thus Justice Holmes stated:

> "A picture is none the less a picture, and none the less a subject of copyright, that it is used for an advertisement."

Moreover, the *Bleistein* opinion seems to suggest that no copyright protection may be claimed for commercial prints and labels. Nevertheless the basic rationale of the *Bleistein* opinion—that any minimal expression of originality will suffice—does justify the protection of the most humble forms of literary and artistic expression. That such expression is intended for advertising purposes does not negate its protectability. It has been held that a mere listing of goods and prices together with the name and address of the seller, but with little more, is devoid of even the minimal elements of creativity and originality required for copyright protection.[4] Protection may be denied on the ground that the content is dictated solely by functional considerations.[5] Most courts however, would probably find the work a protectible compilation.

The copyright in an advertisement, as is generally true of any copyrightable work, will protect not only against a literal word for word copying, but also against a substantial but non-literal copying.[6] However, at least one court has departed to some extent from general rules of copyright liability by denying copyright protection to an advertisement which it found to be false in content.[7]

Collateral References

Derenberg, *Commercial Prints and Labels,* 49 Yale L.J. 1212 (1940);

Kupferman, *Copyright Protection for Commercial Prints and Labels,* 33 So.Calif.Law Rev. 163 (1960).

Nimmer on Copyright, § 2.08[G].

BURROW–GILES LITHOGRAPHIC CO. v. SARONY

Supreme Court of the United States, 1884.
111 U.S. 53, 4 S.Ct. 279, 28 L.Ed. 349.

MILLER, J. This is a writ of error to the circuit court for the southern district of New York. Plaintiff is a lithographer, and defendant a photographer, with large business in those lines in the city of New York. The suit was commenced by an action at law in which

---

2. Laskowitz v. Marie Designer Inc., 119 F.Supp. 541 (S.D.Calif.1954); cf. Inter-City Press Inc. v. Siegfried, 172 F.Supp. 37 (W.D.Mo.1958).

3. Lin-Brook Builders Hardware v. Gertler, 352 F.2d 298 (9th Cir.1965); Modern Aids Inc. v. R.H. Macy & Co., 264 F.2d 93 (2d Cir.1959); Comptone Co. Ltd. v. Rayex Corp., 251 F.2d 487 (2d Cir.1958); Day Brite Lighting Inc. v. Sta-Brite Manufacturing Co., 308 F.2d 377 (5th Cir.1962).

4. Surgical Supply Service Inc. v. Adler, 206 F.Supp. 564 (E.D.Pa.1962).

5. See Consumers Union of U.S. v. Hobart, 199 F.Supp. 860 (S.D.N.Y.1961).

6. Ansehl v. Puritan Pharmaceutical Co., 61 F.2d 131 (8th Cir.1932).

7. Stone & McCarrick v. Dugan Piano Co., 220 Fed. 837 (5th Cir.1915); cf. Deutsch v. Felton, 27 F.Supp. 895 (E.D.N.Y.1939).

Sarony was plaintiff and the lithographic company was defendant, the plaintiff charging the defendant with violating his copyright in regard to a photograph, the title of which is "Oscar Wilde, No. 18." A jury being waived, the court made a finding of facts on which a judgment in favor of the plaintiff was rendered for the sum of $600 for the plates and 85,000 copies sold and exposed to sale, and $10 for copies found in his possession, as penalties under section 4965 of the Revised Statutes. * * * the two assignments of error in this court by plaintiff in error are: (1) That the court below decided that congress had and has the constitutional right to protect photographs and negatives thereof by copyright. The second assignment related to the sufficiency of the words "Copyright, 1882, by N. Sarony," in the photographs, as a notice of the copyright of Napoleon Sarony, under the act of congress on that subject.

With regard to this latter question it is enough to say that the object of the statute is to give notice of the copyright to the public by placing upon each copy, in some visible shape, the name of the author, the existence of the claim of exclusive right, and the date at which this right was obtained. This notice is sufficiently given by the words "Copyright, 1882, by N. Sarony," found on each copy of the photograph. It clearly shows that a copyright is asserted, the date of which is 1882, and if the name Sarony alone was used, it would be a sufficient designation of the author until it is shown that there is some other Sarony. When, in addition to this, the initial letter of the Christian name Napoleon is also given, the notice is complete.

The constitutional question is not free from difficulty. The eighth section of the first article of the constitution is the great repository of the powers of congress, and by the eighth clause of that section congress is authorized "to promote the progress of science and useful arts, by securing, for limited times to authors and inventors the exclusive right to their respective writings and discoveries." The argument here is that a photograph is not a writing nor the production of an author. Under the acts of congress designed to give effect to this section, the persons who are to be benefited are divided into two classes—authors and inventors. The monopoly which is granted to the former is called a copyright: that given to the latter, letters patent, or, in the familiar language of the present day, *patent-right*. We have then copyright and patent-right, and it is the first of these under which plaintiff asserts a claim for relief. It is insisted, in argument, that a photograph being a reproduction, on paper, of the exact features of some natural object, or of some person, is not a writing of which the producer is the author. Section 4952 of the Revised Statutes places photographs in the same class as things which may be copyrighted with "books, maps, charts, dramatic or musical compositions, engravings, cuts, prints, paintings, drawings, statues, statuary, and models or designs intended to be perfected as works of the fine arts." "According to the practice of legislation in England and America, (says JUDGE BOUVIER, 2 Law Dict. 363), the copyright is confined to the exclusive right secured to the

The Portrait of Oscar Wilde by Napoleon Sarony

author or proprietor of a writing or drawing which may be multiplied by the arts of printing in any of its branches."

The first congress of the United States, sitting immediately after the formation of the constitution, enacted that the "author or authors of any map, chart, book, or books, being a citizen or resident of the United States, shall have the sole right and liberty of printing, reprinting, publishing, and vending the same for the period of fourteen years from the recording of the title thereof in the clerk's office, as afterwards directed." 1 St. p. 124, § 1. This statute not only makes maps and charts subjects of copyright, but mentions them before books in the order of designation. The second section of an act to amend this act, approved April 29, 1802, (2 St. 171), enacts that from the first day of January thereafter he who shall invent and design, engrave, etch, or work, or from his own works shall cause to be designed and engraved, etched, or worked, any historical or other print or prints, shall have the same exclusive right for the term of 14 years from recording the title thereof as prescribed by law.

By the first section of the act of February 3, 1831, 4 St. 436, entitled "An act to amend the several acts respecting copyright, musical compositions, and cuts, in connection with prints and engravings," are added, and the period of protection is extended to 28 years. The caption or title of this act uses the word "copyright" for the first time in the legislation of congress.

The construction placed upon the constitution by the first act of 1790 and the act of 1802, by the men who were contemporary with its formation, many of whom were members of the convention which framed it, is of itself entitled to very great weight, and when it is remembered that the rights thus established have not been disputed during a period of nearly a century, it is almost conclusive. Unless, therefore, photographs can be distinguished in the classification of this point from the maps, charts, designs, engravings, etchings, cuts, and other prints, it is difficult to see why congress cannot make them the subject of copyright as well as the others. These statutes certainly answer the objection that books only, or writing, in the limited sense of a book and its author, are within the constitutional provision. Both these words are susceptible of a more enlarged definition than this. An author in that sense is "he to whom anything owes its origin; originator; maker; one who completes a work of science or literature." Worcester. So, also, no one would now claim that the word "writing" in this clause of the constitution, though the only word used as to subjects in regard to which authors are to be secured, is limited to the actual script of the author, and excludes books and all other printed matter. By writings in that clause is meant the literary productions of those authors, and congress very properly has declared these to include all forms of writing, printing, engravings, etchings, etc., by which the ideas in the mind of the author are given visible expression. The only reason why photographs were not included in the extended list in the act of 1802 is, probably, that they did not exist, as photography, as an art, was then unknown, and the scientific principle on which it rests, and the chemicals and machinery by which it is operated, have all been discovered long since that statute was enacted. Nor is it supposed that the framers of the constitution did not understand the nature of copyright and the objects to which it was commonly applied, for copyright, as the exclusive right of a man to the production of his own genius or intellect, existed in England at that time, and the contest in the English courts, finally decided, by a very close vote in the house of lords, whether the statute of 8 Anne, c. 19, which authorized copyright for a limited time, was a restraint to that extent on the common law or not, was then recent. It had attracted much attention, as the judgment of the king's bench, delivered by LORD MANSFIELD, holding it was not such a restraint, in Millar v. Taylor, 4 Burr. 2303, decided in 1769, was overruled on appeal in the house of lords in 1774. Id. 2408. In this and other cases the whole question of the exclusive right to literary and intellectual productions had been freely discussed.

We entertain no doubt that the constitution is broad enough to cover an act authorizing copyright of photographs, so far as they are representatives of original intellectual conceptions of the author.

But it is said that an engraving, a painting, a print, does embody the intellectual conception of its author, in which there is novelty, invention, originality, and therefore comes within the purpose of the constitution in securing its exclusive use or sale to its author, while a photograph is the mere mechanical reproduction of the physical features or outlines of some object, animate or inanimate, and involves no originality of thought or any novelty in the intellectual operation connected with its visible reproduction in shape of a picture. That while the effect of light on the prepared plate may have been a discovery in the production of these pictures, and patents could properly be obtained for the combination of the chemicals, for their application to the paper or other surface, for all the machinery by which the light reflected from the object was thrown on the prepared plate, and for all the improvements in this machinery, and in the materials, the remainder of the process is merely mechanical, with no place for novelty, invention, or originality. It is simply the manual operation, by the use of these instruments and preparations, of transferring to the plate the visible representation of some existing object, the accuracy of this representation being its highest merit. This may be true in regard to the ordinary production of a photograph, and that in such case a copyright is no protection. On the question as thus stated we decide nothing.

In regard, however, to the kindred subject of patents for invention, they cannot, by law, be issued to the inventor until the novelty, the utility, and the actual discovery or invention by the claimant have been established by proof before the commissioner of patents; and when he has secured such a patent, and undertakes to obtain redress for a violation of his right in a court of law, the question of invention, of novelty, of originality is always open to examination. Our copyright system has no such provision for previous examination by a proper tribunal as to the originality of the book, map, or other matter offered for copyright. A deposit of two copies of the article or work with the librarian of congress, with the name of the author and its title page, is all that is necessary to secure a copyright. It is therefore much more important that when the supposed author sues for a violation of his copyright, the existence of those facts of originality, of intellectual production, of thought, and conception on the part of the author should be proved than in the case of a patent-right. In the case before us we think this has been done.

The third finding of facts says, in regard to the photograph in question, that it is a "useful, new, harmonious, characteristic, and graceful picture, and that plaintiff made the same * * * entirely from his own original mental conception, to which he gave visible form by posing the said Oscar Wilde in front of the camera, selecting and arranging the costume, draperies, and other various accessories in said photograph, arranging the subject so as to present graceful outlines, arranging and disposing the light and shade, suggesting and evoking the desired expression, and from such disposition, arrangement, or representation, made entirely by plaintiff, he produced the picture in suit." These findings, we think, show this photograph to be an original work of art, the product of plaintiff's intellectual invention, of which plaintiff is the author, and of a class of inventions for which the constitution intended that congress should secure to him the exclusive right to use, publish, and sell, as it has done by section 4952 of the Revised Statutes.

The question here presented is one of first impression under our constitution, but an instructive case of the same class is that of Nottage v. Jackson, 11 Q.B.Div. 627, decided in that court on appeal, August, 1883. The first section of the act of 25 & 26, Vict. c. 68, authorizes the *author* of a photograph, upon making registry of it under the copyright act of 1882, to have a monopoly of its reproduction and multiplication during the life of the author. The plaintiffs in that case described themselves as the authors of the photograph which was pirated in the registration of it. It appeared that they had arranged with the captain of the Australian cricketers to take a photograph of the whole team in a group, and they sent one of the artists in their employ from London to some country town to do it. The question in the case was whether the plaintiffs, who owned the establishment in London, where the photographs were made from the negative, and were sold, and who had the negative taken by one of their men, were the authors, or the man who, for their benefit, took the negative. It was held that the latter was the author, and the action failed, because plaintiffs had described themselves as authors. Brett, M.R., said, in regard to who was the author: "The nearest I can come to is that it is the person who effectively is as near as he can be the cause of the picture which is produced; that is, the person who has superintended the arrangement, who has actually formed the picture by putting the persons in position, and arranging the place where the people are to be—the man who is the effective cause of that." LORD JUSTICE COTTON said: "In my opinion, 'author' involves originating, making, producing, as the inventive or master mind, the thing which is to be protected, whether it be a drawing, or a painting, or a photograph;" and LORD JUSTICE BOWEN says that photography is to be treated for the purposes of the act as an art, and the author is the man who really represents, creates, or gives effect to the idea, fancy, or imagination. The appeal of plaintiffs from the original judgment against them was accordingly dismissed.

These views of the nature of authorship and of originality, intellectual creation, and right to protection, confirm what we have already said.

The judgment of the circuit court is accordingly affirmed.

Questions

1. In Jewelers' Circular Publishing Co. v. Keystone, 274 F. 932 (S.D.N.Y. 1921) Judge Learned Hand suggested that the ambiguous status in which *Burrow-Giles* left "the ordinary production of a photograph" was clarified by the subsequent enactment of the 1909 Copyright Act, wherein under Sec. 5(j) photographs were recognized as copyrightable "without regard to the degree of 'personality' which enters into them." What is wrong with this argument? For further on the copyrightability of photographs, see Time, Inc. v. Bernard Geis Associates, infra.

2. Under the court's reasoning in *Burrow-Giles*, should a phonograph record be regarded as a "writing" in the constitutional sense? If so, how can you explain the court's reference to "visible" expression? On the constitutional status of phonograph records, see Goldstein v. California, infra.

3. Are works of sculpture "writings" in the constitutional sense? See Mazer v. Stein, infra. Could you argue, under the reasoning of *Burrow-Giles*, that sculptural works are not "writings"?

ALFRED BELL & CO. v. CATALDA FINE ARTS

United States Court of Appeals, Second Circuit, 1951.
191 F.2d 99.

["The plaintiff, a British print producer and dealer, member of the Fine Arts Guild, copyrighted in the United States eight mezzotint engravings of old masters produced at its order by three mezzotint engravers * * *. Concededly the subjects of the eight engravings are paintings by other persons than the mezzotint engravers, all of them being well-known paintings executed in the late eighteenth or early nineteenth centuries and all now in the public domain. The mezzotint method lends itself to a fairly realistic reproduction of oil paintings. It is a tedious process requiring skill and patience and is, therefore, rather expensive compared with modern color photographic processes * * * the mezzotint engraving process is performed by first rocking a copper plate, that is, drawing across the plate under pressure a hand tool having many fine and closely spaced teeth. The tool is drawn across the plate many times in various directions so that the plate is roughened by the process. The outlines of the engraving are then placed upon the plate either by tracing with carbon paper from a photograph of the original work which it is desired to reproduce in this medium or by a tracing taken from such a photograph on gelatine sheets transferred to the copper plate by rubbing carbon black or some similar substance in the lines of the tracing on the gelatine sheet and transferring of them by pressing the sheet upon the copper plate. With the image on the roughened plate the engraver then scrapes with a hand tool the picture upon the plate, obtaining light and shade effects by the depth of the scraping of the roughened plate or ground."] *

Before CHASE, CLARK and FRANK, CIRCUIT JUDGES.

FRANK, CIRCUIT JUDGE.

1. Congressional power to authorize both patents and copyrights is contained in Article 1, § 8 of the Constitution.[1] In passing on the validity of patents, the Supreme Court recurrently insists that this constitutional provision governs. On this basis, pointing to the Supreme Court's consequent requirement that, to be valid, a patent must disclose a high degree of uniqueness, ingenuity and inventiveness, the defendants assert that the same requirement constitutionally governs copyrights. As several sections of the Copyright Act—e.g., those authorizing copyrights of "reproductions of works of art," maps, and compilations—plainly dispense with any such high standard, defendants are, in effect, attacking the constitutionality of those sections. But the very language of the Constitution differentiates (a) "authors" and their "writings" from (b) "inventors" and their "discoveries." Those who penned the Constitution,[2] of course, knew the difference. The pre-revolutionary English statutes had made the distinction.[3] In 1783,

---

* This statement of facts is taken from Alfred Bell & Co. v. Catalda Fine Arts, 74 F.Supp. 973 (S.D.N.Y.1947).

1. "To promote the Progress of Science and useful Arts, by securing for limited Times to Authors and Inventors the exclusive Right to their respective Writings and Discoveries".

2. Many of them were themselves authors.

3. The Act of Anne 8, c. 19, was entitled "An Act for the encouraging of learning, by vesting of the copies of printed books in the authors or purchasers of such copies, during the times therein mentioned."

The previous history shows the source of the word "copyright." See 1 Laddas, The International Protection of Literary and Artistic Property (1938) 15:

"In England, the royal grants of privilege to print certain books were not copyrights. They were not granted to encourage learning or for the benefit of authors; they were commercial monopolies, licenses to tradesmen to follow their calling. As gradually monopolies became unpopular, the printers sought to base their claims on other grounds, and called the 'right of copy' not a monopoly, but a property right. The Stationers Company had a register in which its members entered the titles of the works they were privileged to print. A custom developed by which members refrained from printing the books which stood on the register in the name of another. Thus members respected each other's 'copy,' as it was called, and there grew up a trade recognition of 'the right of copy' or copyright. This right was subsequently embodied in a by-law of the Stationers Company. The entry in the register was regarded as a record of the rights of the individual named, and it was assumed that possession of a manuscript carried with it the right to print copies." See also Sheavyn, The Literary Profession in the Elizabethan Age (1909) 52–53, 64–65, 70–71, 76–80.

the Continental Congress had passed a resolution recommending that the several states enact legislation to "secure" to authors the "copyright" of their books.[4] Twelve of the thirteen states (in 1783–1786) enacted such statutes.[5] Those of Connecticut and North Carolina covered books, pamphlets, maps, and charts.[6]

Moreover, in 1790, in the year after the adoption of the Constitution, the first Congress enacted two statutes, separately dealing with patents and copyrights. The patent statute, enacted April 10, 1790, 1 Stat. 109, provided that patents should issue only if the Secretary of State, Secretary of War and the Attorney General, or any two of them "shall deem the invention or discovery sufficiently useful and important"; the applicant for a patent was obliged to file a specification "so particular" as "to distinguish the invention or discovery from other things before known and used * * * "; the patent was to constitute *prima facie* evidence that the patentee was "the first and true inventor or * * * discoverer * * * of the thing so specified."[7] The Copyright Act, enacted May 31, 1790, 1 Stat. 124, covered "maps, charts, and books". A printed copy of the title of any map, chart or book was to be recorded in the Clerk's office of the District Court, and a copy of the map, chart or book was to be delivered to the Secretary of State within six months after publication. Twelve years later, Congress in 1802, 2 Stat. 171, added, to matters that might be copyrighted, engravings, etchings and prints.

Thus legislators peculiarly familiar with the purpose of the Constitutional grant, by statute, imposed far less exacting standards in the case of copyrights. They authorized the copyrighting of a mere map which, patently, calls for no considerable uniqueness. They exacted far more from an inventor. And, while they demanded that an official should be satisfied as to the character of an invention before a patent issued, they made no such demand in respect of a copyright. * * * Accordingly, the Constitution, as so interpreted, recognizes that the standards for patents and copyrights are basically different.

The defendants' contention apparently results from the ambiguity of the word "original." It may mean startling, novel or unusual, a marked departure from the past. Obviously this is not what is meant when one speaks of "the original package," or the "original bill," or (in

---

4. See Bulletin No. 3 (1900) of Library of Congress. Copyright Office.

5. Ibid. 11–31.

6. It is of interest that the statutes of Connecticut, South Carolina, Georgia and New York contained this provision: If on the complaint of a person, a court found that the author or proprietor had neglected to furnish the public with sufficient editions of a copyrighted work, or had offered the work for sale at an unreasonable price, the court should enter an order requiring the offering, within a reasonable time, of a sufficient number at a reasonable price determined by the court; if there was non-compliance, the court was authorized to give the complainant a license to publish the work in such numbers and on such terms as the court deemed just and reasonable. The North Carolina statute was somewhat similar in this respect.

7. See Jefferson's remarks on the strict criteria of invention used by the Secretarial "patent board," in a letter of August 13, 1813, to Isaac McPherson, reprinted in Padover, The Complete Jefferson (1943) 1011 at 1016.

connection with the "best evidence" rule) an "original" document; none of those things is highly unusual in creativeness. "Original" in reference to a copyrighted work means that the particular work "owes its origin" to the "author."[8] No large measure of novelty is necessary. Said the Supreme Court in Baker v. Selden, 101 U.S. 99, 102–103, 25 L.Ed. 841: "The copyright of the book, if not pirated from other works, would be valid without regard to the novelty, or want of novelty, of its subject-matter. The novelty of the art or thing described or explained has nothing to do with the validity of the copyright. * * *"

In Bleistein v. Donaldson Lithographing Co., 188 U.S. 239, 250, 252, 23 S.Ct. 298, 47 L.Ed. 460, the Supreme Court cited with approval Henderson v. Tompkins, C.C., 60 F. 758, where it was said, 60 F. at page 764: "There is a *very broad distinction between what is implied in the word 'author,' found in the constitution, and the word 'inventor'. The latter carries an implication which excludes the results of only ordinary skill, while nothing of this is necessarily involved in the former. * * *"[9]

It is clear, then, that nothing in the Constitution commands that copyrighted matter be strikingly unique or novel. Accordingly, we were not ignoring the Constitution when we stated that a "copy of something in the public domain" will support a copyright if it is a "distinguishable variation";[10] or when we rejected the contention that "like a patent, a copyrighted work must be not only original, but new", adding, "That is not * * * the law as is obvious in the case of maps or compendia, where later works will necessarily be anticipated."[11] All that is needed to satisfy both the Constitution and the statute is that the "author" contributed something more than a "merely trivial" variation, something recognizably "his own."[12] Originality in this context "means little more than a prohibition of actual copying."[13] No matter how poor artistically the "author's" addition, it is enough if it be his own. Bleistein v. Donaldson Lithographing Co., 188 U.S. 239, 250, 23 S.Ct. 298, 47 L.Ed. 460.

On that account, we have often distinguished between the limited protection accorded a copyright owner and the extensive protection

8. Burrow-Giles Lithographic Co. v. Sarony, 111 U.S. 53, 57–58, 4 S.Ct. 279, 281, 28 L.Ed. 349.

9. Emphasis added.

10. Gerlach-Barklow Co. v. Morris & Bendien, 2 Cir., 23 F.2d 159, 161.

11. Sheldon v. Metro-Goldwyn Pictures Corp., 2 Cir., 81 F.2d 49, 53. See also Ricker v. General Electric Co., 2 Cir., 162 F.2d 141, 142.

12. Chamberlin v. Uris Sales Corp., 2 Cir., 150 F.2d 512; cf. Gross v. Seligman, 2 Cir., 212 F. 930.

13. Hoague-Sprague Corp. v. Frank C. Meyer, Inc., D.C.N.Y., 31 F.2d 583, 586. See also as to photographs Judge Learned Hand in Jewelers Circular Publishing Co. v. Keystone Pub. Co., D.C.N.Y., 274 F. 932, 934.

The English doctrine is the same. See Copinger, The Law of Copyrights (7th ed. 1936) 40–44: "Neither original thought nor original research is essential"; he quotes the English courts to the effect that the statute "does not require that the expression must be in an original or novel form, but that the work must not be copied from another work—that it should originate from the author," but only that "though it may be neither novel or ingenious, [it] is the claimant's original work in that it originates from him, and is not copied."

granted a patent owner. So we have held that "independent reproduction of a copyrighted * * * work is not infringement",[14] whereas it is *vis a vis* a patent. Correlative with the greater immunity of a patentee is the doctrine of anticipation which does not apply to copyrights: The alleged inventor is chargeable with full knowledge of all the prior art, although in fact he may be utterly ignorant of it. The "author" is entitled to a copyright if he independently contrived a work completely identical with what went before; similarly, although he obtains a valid copyright, he has no right to prevent another from publishing a work identical with his, if not copied from his. A patentee, unlike a copyrightee, must not merely produce something "original"; he must also be "the first inventor or discoverer."[15] "Hence it is possible to have a plurality of valid copyrights directed to closely identical or even identical works. Moreover, none of them, if independently arrived at without copying, will constitute an infringement of the copyright of the others."[16]

The difference between patents and copyrights is neatly illustrated in the design patent cases.[17] We have held that such a patent is invalid unless it involves "a step beyond the prior art", including what is termed "inventive genius." A.C. Gilbert Co. v. Shemitz, 2 Cir., 45 F.2d 98, 99. We have noted that, as in all patents, there must be a substantial advance over the prior art. Neufeld-Furst & Co. v. Jay-Day Frocks, 2 Cir., 112 F.2d 715, 716. We have suggested that relief for designers could be obtained if they were permitted to copyright their designs, and that, until there is an amendment to the copyright statute, "new designs are open to all, unless their production demands some salient ability." Nat Lewis Purses v. Carole Bags, 2 Cir., 83 F.2d 475, 476. We have noted that if designers obtained such a statute, it would give them "a more limited protection and for that reason easier to obtain. * * *" White v. Leanore Frocks, Inc., 2 Cir., 120 F.2d 113, 115.[18]

2. We consider untenable defendants' suggestion that plaintiff's mezzotints could not validly be copyrighted because they are reproductions of works in the public domain. Not only does the Act include "Reproductions of a work of art",[19] but—while prohibiting a copyright of "the original text of any work * * * in the public domain"[20]—it explicitly provides for the copyrighting of "translations, or other versions of works in the public domain".[21] The mezzotints were such

---

14. Arnstein v. Edward B. Marks Music Corp., 2 Cir., 82 F.2d 275; Ricker v. General Electric Co., 2 Cir., 162 F.2d 141, 142.

15. See Admur, Copyright Law and Practice (1936) 70.

16. Id.

17. 35 U.S.C.A. § 73 requires that for a design patent the design shall be "not known or used by others in this country before" the "invention thereof, and not * * described in any printed publication in this or any foreign country before" the "invention thereof."

18. See also Stein v. Export Lamp Co., 7 Cir., 188 F.2d 611, 612–613.

19. 17 U.S.C. § 5.

20. 17 U.S.C. § 8 (formerly § 7).

21. 17 U.S.C. § 7 (formerly § 6).

See Judge Learned Hand in Fred Fisher, Inc. v. Dillingham, D.C., 298 F. 145, 150–151: "Take, for example, two faithful com-

"versions." They "originated" with those who made them, and—on the trial judge's findings well supported by the evidence—amply met the standards imposed by the Constitution and the statute.[22] There is evidence that they were not intended to, and did not, imitate the paintings they reproduced. But even if their substantial departures from the paintings were inadvertent, the copyrights would be valid.[23] A copyist's bad eyesight or defective musculature, or a shock caused by a clap of thunder, may yield sufficiently distinguishable variations.[24] Having hit upon such a variation unintentionally, the "author" may adopt it as his and copyright it.[25]

pilations or translations. While it may be rare that they should be identical, obviously even that is possible over substantial parts. It could not be maintained that the earlier version destroyed the copyright of the later, and yet, if copyright be analogous to patents, this must result. Certainly, the labor of the second translator or compiler is not lost, so he do [sic] not use the work of the first.

"Directories constitute a familiar instance of such compilations. No one doubts that two directories, independently made, are each entitled to copyright, regardless of their similarity, even though it amount to identity. Each being the result of original work, the second will be protected, quite regardless of its lack of novelty. But the best instance is in the case of maps. Here, if each be faithful, identity is inevitable, because each seeks only to set down the same facts in precisely the same relations to each other. So far as each is successful, each will be exactly the same. While I know no case which involves the point, Bowker says on page 255 (Copyright, Its History and Law):

"'Two map makers, collecting at first hand, would naturally make the same map, and each would equally be entitled to copyright. In this respect copyright law differs from patent law, where a first use bars others from the same field.'"

Judge Hand there also said at page 150 of 298 F.: "Any subsequent person is, of course, free to use all works in the public domain as sources for his compositions. No later work, though original, can take that from him. But there is no reason in justice or law why he should not be compelled to resort to the earlier works themselves, or why he should be free to use the composition of another, who himself has not borrowed. If he claims the rights of the public, let him use them; he picks the brains of the copyright owner as much, whether his original composition be old or new. The defendant's concern lest the public should be shut off from the use of works in the public domain is therefore illusory; no one suggests it. That domain is open to all who tread it; not to those who invade the closes of others, however similar."

22. See Copinger, The Law of Copyrights (7th ed. 1936) 46: "Again, an engraver is almost invariably a copyist, but although his work may infringe copyright in the original painting if made without the consent of the owner of the copyright therein, his work may still be original in the sense that he has employed skill and judgment in its production. He produces the resemblance he is desirous of obtaining by means very different from those employed by the painter or draughtsman from whom he copies: means which require great labour and talent. The engraver produces his effects by the management of light and shade, or, as the term of his art expresses it, the *chiarooscuro*. The due degrees of light and shade are produced by different lines and dots; he who is the engraver must decide on the choice of the different lines or dots for himself, and on his choice depends the success of his print."

23. See Kallen, Art and Freedom (1942) 977 to the effect that "the beauty of the human singing voice, as the western convention of music hears it, depends upon a physiological dysfunction of the vocal cords. * * *"

Plutarch tells this story: A painter, enraged because he could not depict the foam that filled a horse's mouth from champing at the bit, threw a sponge at his painting; the sponge splashed against the wall—and achieved the desired result.

24. Cf. Chamberlin v. Uris Sales Corp., 2 Cir., 150 F.2d 512 note 4.

25. Consider inadvertent errors in a translation. Compare cases holding that a patentable invention may stem from an accidental discovery. See, e.g., Radiator Specialty Co. v. Buhot, 3 Cir., 39 F.2d 373, 376; Nichols v. Minnesota Mining & Mfg. Co., 4 Cir., 109 F.2d 162, 165; New Wrinkle v.

Accordingly, defendants' arguments about the public domain become irrelevant. They could be relevant only in their bearing on the issue of infringement, i.e., whether the defendants copied the mezzotints.[26] But on the findings, again well grounded in the evidence, we see no possible doubt that defendants, who did deliberately copy the mezzotints, are infringers. For a copyright confers the exclusive right to copy the copyrighted work—a right not to have others copy it. Nor were the copyrights lost because of the reproduction of the mezzotints in catalogues.[27] * * *

Questions

1. In Sheldon v. Metro-Goldwyn Pictures Corp., infra, Judge Learned Hand, with his characteristic felicity of phrase, articulated the principle of copyright originality as follows:

" * * * if by some magic a man who had never known it were to compose anew Keats' Ode On a Grecian Urn, he would be an 'author', and, if he copyrighted it, others might not copy that poem, though they might of course copy Keats."

Suppose, however, that the same man had copied verbatim the first two stanzas of Keats' poem, and then without copying added his own latter two stanzas. If then another person saw this resulting poem, and copied from it only the first two stanzas would this constitute copyright infringement? See the discussion of Derivative Works infra.

2. Given the concept of originality as formulated in *Alfred Bell*, if in a copyright infringement action the defendant attempts to introduce evidence of one or more works substantially similar to that of the plaintiff's which were written prior to the time when plaintiff wrote his work, should such evidence be excluded as irrelevant? Admitting that plaintiff need not prove novelty, but only originality, on what issues might such evidence be relevant?

3. Suppose that a work is copied without distinguishable variation from a prior work, but that the making of the copy required qualities of special skill, training and knowledge, and independent judgment upon the part of the copyist. Should such a copy be regarded as an original work, capable of qualifying for its own copyright? See L. Batlin & Son, Inc. v. Snyder, 536 F.2d 486 (2d Cir.1976).

GRACEN v. BRADFORD EXCHANGE

United States Court of Appeals, Seventh Circuit, 1983.
698 F.2d 300.

Before BAUER and POSNER, CIRCUIT JUDGES, and HOFFMAN, SENIOR DISTRICT JUDGE.

POSNER, CIRCUIT JUDGE.

This appeal brings up to us questions of some novelty, at least in this circuit, regarding implied copyright licenses and the required originality for copyrighting a derivative work.

In 1939 MGM produced and copyrighted the movie "The Wizard of Oz." The central character in the movie, Dorothy, was played by Judy

---

Fritz, D.C.W.D.N.Y., 45 F.Supp. 108, 117; Byerley v. Sun Co., 3 Cir., 184 F. 455, 456–457.

Many great scientific discoveries have resulted from accidents, e.g., the galvanic circuit and the x-ray.

26. Sheldon v. Metro-Goldyn Pictures Corp., 2 Cir., 81 F.2d 49, 54; Detective Comics, Inc. v. Bruns Publications, 2 Cir., 111 F.2d 432, 433.

27. Gerlach-Barklow Co. v. Morris & Bendien, 2 Cir., 23 F.2d 159, 163; Basevi v. Edward O'Toole Co., D.C., 26 F.Supp. 41, 49.

Garland. The copyright was renewed by MGM in 1966 and is conceded, at least for purposes of this case, to be valid and in effect today. In 1976 MGM licensed Bradford Exchange to use characters and scenes from the movie in a series of collectors' plates. Bradford invited several artists to submit paintings of Dorothy as played by Judy Garland, with the understanding that the artist who submitted the best painting would be offered a contract for the entire series. Bradford supplied each artist with photographs from the movie and with instructions for the painting that included the following: "We do want *your* interpretation of these images, but your interpretation must evoke all the warm feeling the people have for the film and its actors. So, *your* Judy/Dorothy must be very recognizable as everybody's Judy/Dorothy."

Jorie Gracen, an employee in Bradford's order-processing department, was permitted to join the competition. From photographs and her recollections of the movie (which she had seen several times) she made a painting of Dorothy as played by Judy Garland; Figure 1 at the end of this opinion is a reproduction of a photograph of Miss Gracen's painting (an inadequate one, because the original is in color). Bradford exhibited it along with the other contestants' paintings in a shopping center. The passersby liked Miss Gracen's the best, and Bradford pronounced her the winner of the competition and offered her a contract to do the series, as well as paying her, as apparently it paid each of the other contestants, $200. But she did not like the contract terms and refused to sign, and Bradford turned to another artist, James Auckland, who had not been one of the original contestants. He signed a contract to do the series and Bradford gave him Miss Gracen's painting to help him in doing his painting of Dorothy. The record does not indicate who has her painting now.

Gracen's counsel describes Auckland's painting of Dorothy as a "piratical copy" of her painting. Bradford could easily have refuted this charge, if it is false, by attaching to its motion for summary judgment a photograph of its Dorothy plate, but it did not, and for purposes of this appeal we must assume that the plate is a copy of Miss Gracen's painting. This is not an absurd supposition. Bradford, at least at first, was rapturous about Miss Gracen's painting of Dorothy. It called Miss Gracen "a true prodigy." It said that hers "was the one painting that conveyed the essence of Judy's character in the film * * * the painting that left everybody saying, 'That's Judy in Oz.'" Auckland's deposition states that Bradford gave him her painting with directions to "clean it up," which he understood to mean: do the same thing but make it "a little more professional."

* * *

Auckland completed the series, and the plates were manufactured and sold. But Miss Gracen meanwhile had obtained copyright registrations on her painting and drawings, and in 1978 she brought this action for copyright infringement against MGM, Bradford, Auckland, and the manufacturer of the plates. * * *

The district court granted summary judgment against Miss Gracen. * * * It held that she could not copyright her painting and drawings because they were not original.

Sec. A ORIGINALITY 21

Miss Gracen's painting

A scene from the MGM film

* * *

Miss Gracen reminds us that judges can make fools of themselves pronouncing on aesthetic matters. But artistic originality is not the same thing as the legal concept of originality in the Copyright Act. Artistic originality indeed might inhere in a detail, a nuance, a shading too small to be apprehended by a judge. A contemporary school of art known as "Super Realism" attempts with some success to make paintings that are indistinguishable to the eye from color photographs. See Super Realism: A Critical Anthology (Battcock ed. 1975). These paintings command high prices; buyers must find something original in them. Much Northern European painting of the Renaissance is meticulously representational, see, e.g., Gombrich, The Story of Art 178–80 (13th ed. 1978), and therefore in a sense—but not an aesthetic sense—less "original" than Cubism or Abstract Expressionism. A portrait is not unoriginal for being a good likeness.

But especially as applied to derivative works, the concept of originality in copyright law has as one would expect a legal rather than aesthetic function—to prevent overlapping claims. See L. Batlin & Son, Inc. v. Snyder, supra, 536 F.2d at 491–92. Suppose Artist A produces a reproduction of the Mona Lisa, a painting in the public domain, which differs slightly from the original. B also makes a reproduction of the Mona Lisa. A, who has copyrighted his derivative work, sues B for infringement. B's defense is that he was copying the original, not A's reproduction. But if the difference between the original and A's reproduction is slight, the difference between A's and B's reproductions will also be slight, so that if B had access to A's reproductions the trier of fact will be hard-pressed to decide whether B was copying A or copying the Mona Lisa itself. Miss Gracen's drawings illustrate the problem. They are very similar both to the photographs from the movie and to the plates designed by Auckland. Auckland's affidavit establishes that he did not copy or even see her drawings. But suppose he had seen them. Then it would be very hard to determine whether he had been copying the movie stills, as he was authorized to do, or copying her drawings.

The painting of Dorothy presents a harder question. A comparison of Figures 1 and 2 reveals perceptible differences. A painting (except, perhaps, one by a member of the Super Realist school mentioned earlier) is never identical to the subject painted, whether the subject is a photograph, a still life, a landscape, or a model, because most painters cannot and do not want to achieve a photographic likeness of their subject. Nevertheless, if the differences between Miss Gracen's painting of Dorothy and the photograph of Judy Garland as Dorothy were sufficient to make the painting original in the eyes of the law, then a painting by an Auckland also striving, as per his commission, to produce something "very recognizable as everybody's Judy/Dorothy" would look like the Gracen painting, to which he had access; and it would be difficult for the trier of fact to decide whether Auckland had copied her painting or the original movie stills. True, the background in Miss Gracen's painting differs from that in Figure 2, but it is drawn from the movie set. We do not consider a picture created by superimposing one copyrighted photographic image on another to be "original" —always bearing in mind that the purpose of the term in copyright law is not to guide aesthetic judgments but to assure a sufficiently gross difference between the underlying and the derivative work to avoid entangling subsequent artists depicting the underlying work in copyright problems.

We are speaking, however, only of the requirement of originality in derivative works. If a painter paints from life, no court is going to hold that his painting is not copyrightable because it is an exact photographic likeness. If that were the rule photographs could not be copyrighted—the photographs of Judy Garland in "The Wizard of Oz," for example—but of course they can be, 1 Nimmer on Copyright § 2.08[E] (1982). The requirement of originality is significant chiefly in connection with derivative works, where if interpreted too liberally it would paradoxically inhibit rather than promote the creation of such works by giving the first creator a considerable power to interfere with the creation of subsequent derivative works from the same underlying work.

Justice Holmes' famous opinion in Bleistein v. Donaldson Lithographing Co., 188 U.S. 239, 23 S.Ct. 298, 47 L.Ed. 460 (1903), heavily relied on by Miss Gracen, is thus not in point. The issue was whether lithographs of a circus were copyrightable under a statute (no longer in force) that confined copyright to works "connected with the fine arts." Holmes' opinion is a warning against using aesthetic criteria to answer the question. If Miss Gracen had painted Judy Garland from life, her painting would be copyrightable even if we thought it *kitsch;* but a derivative work must be substantially different from the underlying work to be copyrightable. This is the test of L. Batlin & Son, Inc. v. Snyder, supra, 536 F.2d at 491, a decision of the Second Circuit—the nation's premier copyright court—sitting en banc. Earlier Second Circuit cases discussed in *Batlin* that suggest a more liberal test must be considered superseded.

We agree with the district court that under the test of *Batlin* Miss Gracen's painting, whatever its artistic merit, is not an original derivative work within the meaning of the Copyright Act. Admittedly this is a harder case than Durham Industries, Inc. v. Tomy Corp., [630 F.2d 905 (2d Cir.1980)] heavily relied on by the defendants. The underlying works in that case were Mickey Mouse and other Walt Disney cartoon characters, and the derivative works were plastic reproductions of them. Since the cartoon characters are extremely simple drawings, the reproductions were exact, differing only in the medium. The plastic Mickey and its cartoon original look more alike than Judy Garland's Dorothy and Miss Gracen's painting. But we do not think the difference is enough to allow her to copyright her painting even if, as we very much doubt, she was authorized by Bradford to do so.

The judgment dismissing the complaint is therefore affirmed. * *

Questions

1. Does the Gracen painting, when compared with the MGM photograph, constitute a "distinguishable variation" that is more than "merely trivial"? Was Judge Posner correct in concluding that the "distinguishable variation" test adopted in *Alfred Bell* had been "superseded" in the Second Circuit by L. Batlin & Son, Inc. v. Snyder, 536 F.2d 486 (2d Cir.1976)? The *Batlin* court did require "some substantial, not merely trivial originality," but further concluded that "a distinguishable variation" would suffice.

2. Do you agree with the *Gracen* court's rationale for its "substantially different" test? Is it true that the "distinguishable variation" test would

"paradoxically inhibit rather than promote the creation of [derivative] works by giving the first [derivative work] creator a considerable power to interfere with the creation of subsequent derivative works from the same underlying work"? In Judge Posner's Mona Lisa hypothetical, is it true that the "slight difference" in A's reproduction will necessarily be substantially similar to the "slight difference" in B's reproduction?

Collateral Reference

Nimmer on Copyright, § 3.03.

LEE v. RUNGE

Supreme Court of the United States, 1971.
404 U.S. 887, 92 S.Ct. 197, 30 L.Ed.2d 169.

The petition for a writ of certiorari is denied.

Mr. Justice Douglas, dissenting.

Petitioner infringed respondent's copyright and a verdict was rendered against her. Petitioner argued that because the congressional power over copyrights and patents stemmed from the same constitutional provision, they both should be governed by the same standard. Thus, petitioner contended that the copyright was invalid because the book in question lacked "novelty," but the Court of Appeals rejected this argument saying that the appropriate standard for a copyright was "originality" and that the respondent's book met this criteria.[1] The standard of copyrightability presents an important question concerning the scope of Congress' enumerated powers. It has not heretofore been decided by this Court[2] and, arguably, it was wrongly decided by the courts below.

In 1961, respondent published and copyrighted a book entitled Face Lifting by Exercise. This book explained how isometric facial exercises could be used to preserve the appearance of youth. It was based on respondent's study of anatomy, physical therapy and magazine and newspaper articles, but there is nothing in the record to indicate that

---

1. Runge v. Lee, 441 F.2d 579, 581 (C.A.9 1971):

"The standard of 'novelty' urged by appellants is applicable to patents, but not to copyrights. The copyright standard is one of 'originality':

"'The requirements for the "originality" necessary to support a copyright are modest. The author must have created the work by his own skill, labor and judgment, contributing something "recognizably his own" to prior treatments of the same subject. However, neither great novelty nor superior artistic quality is required.'" Quoting Doran v. Sunset House Dist. Corp., 197 F.Supp. 941, 944 (S.D.Cal.1961), aff'd 304 F.2d 251 (C.A.9 1962).

2. Mazer v. Stein, 347 U.S. 201, 74 S.Ct. 460, 98 L.Ed. 630, dealt only with the statutory standards for copyrightability because the constitutional questions were not raised until oral argument. Respondent's reliance upon *Mazer* as an expression of the constitutional standards, for copyrights is misplaced, therefore. Those cases in which we have considered the constitutional ramifications of the copyright power have not dealt with the standard of copyrightability. E.G., Bleistein v. Donaldson Lithographing Co., 188 U.S. 239, 23 S.Ct. 298, 47 L.Ed. 460; Burrow-Giles Lithographic Co. v. Sarony, 111 U.S. 53, 4 S.Ct. 279, 28 L.Ed. 349. See also Note, 68 Harv.L.Rev. 517 (1955).

the ideas it contained constituted anything more than "selecting the last piece to put into the last opening in a jig-saw puzzle." Sinclair & Carroll Co. v. Interchemical Corp., 325 U.S. 327, 335, 65 S.Ct. 1143, 1147, 89 L.Ed. 1644. It was merely a repetition of the existing state of the art. During 1962, petitioner was employed in respondent's beauty salon and we may assume that it was during this time that petitioner first read respondent's book and learned of respondent's facial exercises. In 1965, petitioner published The Joyce Lee Method of Scientific Facial Exercises. It contained a system of facial exercises strikingly similar to respondent's and, even though it was unquestionably expressed in petitioner's own language, we may safely conclude that it was based on respondent's book. An action for copyright infringement was made out, therefore, if the respondent's copyright was valid and if it embraced the ideas in her book.

The constitutional power over copyrights is found in the same clause that governs the issuance of patents: "The Congress shall have Power * * * To promote the Progress of Science and useful Arts, by securing for limited Times to Authors and Inventors the exclusive Right to their respective Writings and Discoveries." Art. I, § 8, cl. 8. Many of the same interests underlie both grants of power. The Federalist No. 43. While this Court has not had many occasions to consider the constitutional parameters of copyright power, we have indicated that the introductory clause, "To promote the Progress of Science and useful Arts," acts as a limit on Congress' power to grant monopolies through patents. In Graham v. John Deere Co., 383 U.S. 1, 5–6, 86 S.Ct. 684, 687–688, 15 L.Ed.2d 545, we said:

> The clause is both a grant of power and a limitation. This qualified authority, unlike the power often exercised in the Sixteenth and Seventeenth Centuries by the English Crown, is limited to the promotion of advances in the "useful arts." It was written against the backdrop of the practices eventually curtailed by the Statute of Monopolies of the Crown in granting monopolies to court favorites in goods or businesses which had long before been enjoyed by the public. The Congress in the exercise of the patent power may not overreach the restraints imposed by the stated constitutional purpose. Nor may it enlarge the patent monopoly without regard to the innovation, advancement or social benefit gained thereby. Moreover, Congress may not authorize the issuance of patents whose effects are to restrict free access to materials already available. Innovation, advancement, and things which add to the sum of the useful knowledge are inherent requisites in a patent system which by constitutional command must "promote the Progress of * * * the useful Arts." This is the *standard* expressed in the Constitution and it may not be ignored. And it is in this light that patent "validity requires reference to a standard written into the Constitution." (Citations omitted.)

In Mazer v. Stein, 347 U.S. 201, 219, 74 S.Ct. 460, 471, we indicated that the copyright power is also governed by this same introductory phrase: "The economic philosophy behind the clause empowering Congress to grant patents and copyrights is the conviction that encouragement of individual effort by personal gain is the best way to advance public welfare through the talents of authors and inventors in 'Science and useful Arts.'" See also Bleistein v. Donaldson Lithographing Co., 188 U.S. 239, 249, 23 S.Ct. 298. In other contexts, we have also shown that patents and copyrights stand on the same footing. E.g., United States v. Paramount Pictures, 334 U.S. 131, 158, 68 S.Ct. 915, 929, 92 L.Ed. 1260; Sheldon v. Metro-Goldwyn Pictures Corp., 309 U.S. 390, 401, 60 S.Ct. 681, 684, 84 L.Ed. 825. No reason can be offered why we should depart from the plain import of this grant of congressional power and apply more lenient constitutional standards to copyrights than to patents.[3] Indeed, for reasons which will later be considered, a copyright may have to meet greater constitutional standards for validity than a patent. The limitations set forth in Graham v. John Deere Co., therefore, apply with at least equal force to copyrights. Cf. Burrow-Giles Lithographic Co. v. Sarony, 111 U.S. 53, 59, 4 S.Ct. 279, 281, 28 L.Ed. 349.

An author's "Writing" or an inventor's "Discovery" can, in the constitutional sense, only extend to that which is his own. It may not be broadened to include matters within the public domain. The congressional power to grant monopolies for "Writings and Discoveries" is likewise limited to that which accomplishes the stated purpose of promoting "the Progress of Science and useful Arts." No distinction is made in the constitutional language between copyrights and patents and I would not create one by judicial gloss. Where, as here, a writer has published a book which compiles and applies information available to all men, should that writer have a monopoly on the ideas in that book through a copyright issued merely because the words used were the author's own?

Patents which did not serve the broad goals of furthering scientific advancement and bettering the lot of mankind (Great Atlantic & Pacific Tea Co. v. Supermarket, 340 U.S. 147, 154–155, 71 S.Ct. 127, 131, 95 L.Ed. 162, concurring opinion) have been held invalid because they lacked utility, did no more than combine existing inventions, were obvious to someone schooled in the art, or sought to monopolize ideas within the public domain. Graham v. John Deere Co., supra; Great Atlantic & Pacific Tea Co. v. Supermarket Equipment Corp., supra; Hotchkiss v. Greenwood, 11 How. 248, 13 L.Ed. 683. It is not obvious that respondent's system of facial exercises was patentable under these standards. It arguably amounted to nothing more than an application of existing knowledge based upon sources available to all men. We have repeatedly held that patents so devoid of novelty were invalid. To

---

3. Statutory support for the distinction made by the courts below is, at best, flimsy. It is true that the standards of "novelty," 35 U.S.C. § 102, and "non-obviousness," 35 U.S.C. § 103, are embodied in the patent statutes. "Originality," however, is not set forth in the copyright laws as a sufficient measure of copyrightability and it owes its development solely to the courts. E.g., Du Puy v. Post Telegram Co., 210 F. 883 (C.A.3 1914); Edward Thompson Co. v. American Law Book Co., 122 F. 922 (C.A.2 1903). A longstanding, but erroneous, pattern of statutory interpretation may not be spared from the force of a constitutional mandate by reason of its longevity. Erie R. Co. v. Tompkins, 304 U.S. 64, 58 S.Ct. 817, 82 L.Ed. 1188.

create a monopoly under the copyright power which would not be available under the patent power would be to betray the common birthright of all men at the altar of hollow formalisms.

The application of the constitutional standard of "novelty" will not "invalidate the copyright in a substantial portion of all literary works, where novelty as distinguished from originality is a very rare commodity," as one commentator has suggested.[4] If Johann Spies' Historia von Dr. Johann Fausten, Christopher Marlowe's The Tragical History of Dr. Faustus, Goethe's Faust and all the other countless operatic, symphonic, dramatic and literary versions of the Faustian legend were published for the first time today, copyright protection could well be extended to all. "[A] copyright gives no exclusive right to the art disclosed; protection is given only to the expression of the idea—not the idea itself." Mazer v. Stein, supra, at 217, 74 S.Ct. 470. The manner in which the words or musical notes are combined to recount the Faustian legend could well satisfy the constitutional requirement of novelty even though the broad ideas they describe may be part of the public domain. This question is not before us in the present case, however, because the manner of expression used by petitioner was unquestionably her own and it was only the ideas of respondent that were used.[5]

Serious First Amendment questions would be raised if Congress' power over copyrights were construed to include the power to grant monopolies over certain ideas. See Nimmer, Does Copyright Abridge the First Amendment Guarantees of Free Speech and Press?, 17 U.C.L.A. L.Rev. 1180 (1970). The framers of the Bill of Rights added the guarantees of freedom of speech and of the press because they did not feel them to be sufficiently protected by the original Constitution. This liberty is necessary if we are to have free, open, and lively debate of political and social ideas. The "public interest in having the fullest information available on the murder of President Kennedy," for example, led one court to conclude that photographs of the assassination were not entitled to the full range of copyright protection. Time, Inc. v. Bernard Geis Assoc., 293 F.Supp. 130, 146 (S.D.N.Y.1968). The arena of public debate would be quiet, indeed, if a politician could copyright his speeches or a philosopher his treatises and thus obtain a monopoly on the ideas they contained. We should not construe the copyright laws to conflict so patently with the values that the First Amendment was designed to protect.

4. M. Nimmer on Copyright 33 n. 7a (1971). Professor Nimmer seems to have retreated somewhat from this view, however. Nimmer, Does Copyright Abridge the First Amendment Guarantees of Free Speech and Press?, 17 U.C.L.A.L.Rev. 1180 (1970). Even if it were assumed that the application of the "novelty" standard curtailed the monopoly afforded by the copyright, it has recently been demonstrated that this would not seriously affect the publishing industry nor would it disserve the interests underlying the copyright power. Breyer, The Uneasy Case for Copyright: A Study of Copyright in Books, Photocopies, and Computer Programs, 84 Harv.L.Rev. 281 (1970).

5. I recognize that if copyright protection prevented only literal copying, the clever plagiarist could avoid its sanctions by changing irrelevant words. Protecting the manner of expression, however, cannot be allowed to become the tail that wags the dog.

Application of the novelty standard does not require that a person whose literary work is used by another be left without a remedy. We deal here only with the extent of Congress' enumerated constitutional powers. Quite different questions would be raised by actions for unfair competition or conversion of a common law property interest. International News Service v. Associated Press, 248 U.S. 215, 39 S.Ct. 68, 63 L.Ed. 211. Similarly, different questions would be involved had Congress acted pursuant to other enumerated powers. Cf. Missouri v. Holland, 252 U.S. 416, 40 S.Ct. 382, 64 L.Ed. 641. The respondent's rights are limited to that which is necessary to "promote the Progress of Science and useful Arts." This requires a level of "novelty" which respondent arguably has not satisfied.

I would grant certiorari and set the case for argument.

Questions

1. If, as Justice Douglas indicates, the only similarity as between the plaintiff's and defendant's works was as to the facial exercises themselves, and not as to their manner of expression, is Douglas correct in suggesting that the plaintiff should not have prevailed? Can it ever constitute copyright infringement to copy the essence of a work if the verbatim word-for-word expression has not been copied? See Chapter Seven infra. What if that which is copied in essence but not word-for-word consists of factual rather than fictional material? See the Note on Factual Works at p. 50 infra.

2. Is Justice Douglas correct in concluding that a novelty standard would not invalidate any more copyrights than does an originality standard? Is he correct as to factual works (such as that involved in *Runge*), but incorrect as to fictional works?

3. Is Justice Douglas correct that "no reason can be offered why we should * * * apply more lenient constitutional standards to copyrights than to patents"? Re-read Judge Frank's opinion in Alfred Bell & Co. v. Catalda Fine Arts, supra.

Collateral Reference

Nimmer, *A Comment on the Douglas Dissent in Lee v. Runge,* 19 Bull.Cr. Soc. 68, Item 17 (1971).

Note [*]

The Purpose of Copyright

The primary purpose of copyright it is said is not to reward the author, but rather to secure "the general benefits derived by the public from the labors of authors."[1] The Supreme Court in Mazer v. Stein[2] stated the purpose as follows:

---

[*] Nimmer on Copyright, § 1.03[A].
[1] Fox Film Corp. v. Doyal, 286 U.S. 123, 127 (1932).
[2] This case is reproduced infra.

"The economic philosophy behind the clause empowering Congress to grant patents and copyrights is the conviction that encouragement of individual effort by personal gain is the best way to advance public welfare through the talents of authors and inventors in 'Science and useful Arts.'"

Thus the authorization to grant to individual authors the limited monopoly of copyright is predicated upon the dual premises that the public benefits from the creative activities of authors, and that the copyright monopoly is a necessary condition to the full realization of such creative activities. Implicit in this rationale is the assumption that in the absence of such public benefit the grant of a copyright monopoly to individuals would be unjustified. This appears to be consonant with the pervading public policy against according private economic monopolies in the absence of overriding countervailing considerations. Yet, one may well inquire as to whether the monopoly inherent in copyright requires any greater justification in terms of public welfare than does the monopoly which is an essential concomitant of any form of private property. This, of course, poses the philosophical issue as to whether copyright should be regarded as properly based upon the "natural right" concept fundamental (at least in origin) to the theory of private property. Are the fruits of an author's labor no less deserving of the privileges and status of "property" than are the more tangible creative efforts of other laborers, or are there countervailing policy considerations related to copyright that do not arise in connection with other forms of personal property? Does the First Amendment have a relevance in this connection? See *Nimmer on Freedom of Speech*, § 2.05[C][2]. Does Copyright Abridge the First Amendment Guarantees of Free Speech and Press? 17 UCLA Law Rev. 1180, 1193 (1970). For a fundamental challenge to the premises which underlie copyright, see Breyer, The Uneasy Case For Copyright: A Study of Copyright in Books, Photocopies, and Computer Programs, 84 Harv.Law Rev. 281 (1970). Cf. Tyerman, The Economic Rationale for Copyright Protection For Published Books: A Reply to Professor Breyer, 18 UCLA Law Rev. 1100 (1971); Breyer, Copyright: a Rejoinder, 20 UCLA Law Rev. 75 (1972).

Collateral References

Ladd, *The Harm of the Concept of Harm in Copyright*, 30 J. Copr. Soc'y 421 (1983).

Lange, *Recognizing the Public Domain*, 44 Law & Contemp. Probs. 147 (Autumn 1981).

The Meaning of "Science and Useful Arts" **

There is some confusion on whether "science" refers to the work of authors and "useful arts" to the product of inventors, or whether the relationship is reversed. Thus in Bleistein v. Donaldson Lithographing Co., supra, the Supreme Court indicated that it is the "useful arts" which are the subject of copyright legislation under the Constitution. More recently, however, in Graham v. John Deere Co., 383 U.S. 1 (1966), the Court treated the reference to "useful arts" as applicable to patents, and suggested agreement with DeWolf, An Outline of Copyright Law, p. 15 (1925), that in colonial usage "science" referred to the work of authors and "useful arts" to that of inventors. This position is further supported by the internal logic of the Constitutional clause,

---

** Nimmer on Copyright, § 1.03.

in that in both the phrases "authors and inventors" and "writings and discoveries" the reference to copyright precedes the reference to patents. It is reasonable to suppose that the same order was intended in the reference to "science and useful arts."

B. FIXATION IN A TANGIBLE MEDIUM OF EXPRESSION

1. Statutory Copyright

Note *

In order for works to be eligible for federal copyright (known as "statutory copyright"), they must be "fixed in any tangible medium of expression now known or later developed, from which they can be perceived, reproduced, or otherwise communicated, either directly or with the aid of a machine or device."[1] Fixation in tangible form is not merely a statutory condition to copyright. It is also a constitutional necessity. Although there are no decisions directly so holding,[2] it would seem that in order for a work to constitute a "writing" within the meaning of the constitutional clause authorizing federal copyright legislation, such work must be embodied in some tangible form.[3] If the word "writings" is to be given any meaning whatsoever, it must, at the very least, denote "some material form, capable of identification and having a more or less permanent endurance."[4] A work is not written if it is not recorded in some manner, and a record even in a broad generic sense, necessarily imports a tangible, as opposed to an evanescent, form.

From this, it must follow that a live television broadcast is not a writing and is therefore not *per se* eligible for federal copyright protection. Similarly the *performance* of a play, musical composition, or other work cannot in and of

---

* Nimmer on Copyright, §§ 1.08[C][2], 2.03[B].

1. 17 U.S.C.A. § 102(a).

2. But see the reference in Goldstein v. California, 412 U.S. 546 (1973) to "writings" as including "any *physical* rendering of the fruits of creative intellectual or aesthetic labor." (Emphasis added). See also Kalem Co. v. Harper Bros., 222 U.S. 55 (1911), and note the reference to "a physical object that can be made to reproduce" in dissenting opinion (but concurring on this point) by Judge Learned Hand in Capitol Records Inc. v. Mercury Records Corp., 221 F.2d 657, 664 (2d Cir.1955), and the reference to a "collocation of visible or audible points—of lines, colors, sounds or words." in concurring opinion by Mr. Justice Holmes in White Smith Music Publishing Co. v. Apollo Co., 209 U.S. 1, 19 (1908). See also Letter Edged in Black Press, Inc. v. Public Bldg. Comm'n of Chicago, 320 F.Supp. 1303 (N.D. Ill.1970).

3. Cf. Columbia Broadcasting Sys., Inc. v. DeCosta, infra, in which the court disagreed with this conclusion, stating that "while more precise limitations on 'writings' might be convenient in connection with a statutory scheme of registration and notice, we see no reason why Congress's [sic] power is so limited." The *DeCosta* court somewhat contradictorily stated that constitutional "writings" include "any concrete, describable manifestation of intellectual creation," adding that "to the extent that a creation may be ineffable, we think it ineligible for protection against copying *simpliciter* under either state or federal law." The suggestion that "writings" may include creations not in tangible form probably should be regarded as dictum in view of the court's determination in that case that the work for which protection was sought had been reduced to tangible form on cards distributed by the plaintiff. These cards, the court concluded, "were unquestionably 'writings' within the meaning of the copyright clause * * *."

4. Canadian Admiral Corp. v. Rediffusion, Inc. [1954] Can.Exch., 382, 383 (stated with reference to a copyrightable "work"). Cf. DeCosta v. Columbia Broadcasting Sys., Inc., 520 F.2d 499 (1st Cir.1975).

itself be regarded as a writing capable of copyright protection. This must be distinguished from a copyright owner's right to control performances of his validly copyrighted work. That is, a play, musical composition, or other work reduced to written form is, of course, a "writing" for which copyright protection may be secured. The congressional authority to grant to authors "the exclusive right" to their writings properly includes the authority to control performances of such writings.[5] However, the copyright as distinguished from the exclusive rights therein, attaches to tangible writings and not to evanescent performances.[6] This distinction becomes significant only when that which is being performed is not itself a writing. Thus, a live television broadcast of a baseball game is not capable of statutory copyright protection since neither the broadcast itself nor that which is being broadcast may be constituted a writing.[7] This is to be contrasted with a live television broadcast of a play or musical composition. In this instance the broadcast itself is still not a writing, but, since the work being broadcast is a writing, the authors' exclusive rights include the control of unauthorized broadcasts. The converse situation should also be noted. Thus, if a work which itself is not a writing (e.g., an athletic event, a parade, etc.) is broadcast or otherwise disseminated in a written form (e.g., motion picture film) then such writing itself may claim copyright protection. The copyright in such case lies in the manner of photographing or otherwise recording the event, although not in the event itself. Similarly, a phonograph recording of a performance will constitute a writing in a constitutional sense even though the performance itself is not a writing.[8]

In order to render live broadcasts protectible as "writings," the Copyright Act provides: "A work consisting of sounds, images, or both, that are being transmitted, is 'fixed' for purposes of this title if a fixation of the work is being made simultaneously with its transmission."[9] Since most television and many radio stations now customarily record their live broadcasts on video or audio tape simultaneously with the live transmission, the effect of the above provision would apparently render such broadcasts eligible for statutory copyright. But the issue is ultimately one of constitutional rather than of statutory dimension. If a live broadcast is not a constitutional "writing," notwithstanding its simultaneous recordation, then Congress has no power to render it such. Still, when the courts come to decide this issue, it seems probable that they will conclude that such simultaneous recordation satisfies the tangible form requirement for "writings." It is as if one who was dictating live into a tape recorder were overheard and copied at the moment of dictation. At that moment, the

---

5. See Harper & Bros. v. Kalem Co., 169 F. 61, 65 (2d Cir.1909).

6. In order to be "fixed" under the current Copyright Act, a work must be embodied in a copy or phonorecord in a manner which is "sufficiently permanent or stable to permit it to be perceived, reproduced or otherwise communicated for a period of more than transitory duration." 17 U.S. C.A. § 101. "The discussions on this point * * * further emphasized the need for a clear definition of 'fixation' that would exclude from the concept purely evanescent or transient reproductions such as those projected briefly on a screen, shown electronically on a television or other cathode ray tube, or captured momentarily in the 'memory' of a computer." H.R. No. 2237, 89th Cong., 2d Sess. p. 45 (1966), reporting on H.R. 4347, an earlier version of the current Copyright Act.

7. However, under certain circumstances the unauthorized reproduction of athletic events and similar "performances" may be prevented under a theory of unfair competition, or a related property right theory. See e.g., Pittsburgh Athletic Co. v. KQV Broadcasting Co., 24 F.Supp. 490 (W.D.Pa. 1938) and see Chapter Sixteen *infra*.

8. Goldstein v. California, 412 U.S. 546 (1973); Capitol Records, Inc. v. Mercury Record Corp., 221 F.2d 657 (2d Cir.1955).

9. 17 U.S.C.A. § 101.

material has become a "writing," even if copied simultaneously rather than a moment later.

Problem

Is the simultaneous recordation concept applicable not only to broadcasts and other transmissions, but also to face-to-face performances by live entertainers? May a nightclub musician obtain statutory copyright for his spontaneous improvisations by the device of simultaneously recording his live performance? That is, may such musician hold liable for copyright infringement a member of the audience who records or otherwise copies from the live performance?

See Nimmer on Copyright, § 1.08[C][2].

2. Common Law Copyright

A Note on Preemption and Fixation *

Until the advent of the Copyright Act of 1976, the American law of copyright had been the subject of a dichotomy between federal and state law. Unpublished works were automatically protected by state law, referred to somewhat inaccurately [1] as common law copyright. Such protection began at the moment of creation, and terminated upon publication, when common law copyright was lost.[2] Thereafter,[3] protection was available, if at all, only through federal, or as it is generally known, statutory copyright. The dichotomy between common law and statutory copyright was recognized by the Supreme Court in its first significant copyright decision, Wheaton v. Peters,[4] and was reaffirmed in one of the last copyright decisions rendered by that Court prior to enactment of the Act of 1976.[5] This dual form of copyright has now, for the most part, been terminated, by reason of federal preemption under Section 301(a) of the current Act. As of January 1, 1978, common law copyright ended for all works that are the subject of federal preemption.

The nature of such preemption is discussed in greater depth elsewhere in this casebook.[6] It is sufficient here to note that rights created under state law are the subject of preemption under Section 301(a) if two conditions coalesce. The rights themselves must be "equivalent" to those rights granted under Section 106 of the Copyright Act, and such rights must inhere in works which "come within the subject matter of copyright as specified by sections 102 and 103" of the Copyright Act. Since the rights under common law copyright are infringed by the acts of reproduction, performance and distribution, it may be concluded that they are, indeed, "equivalent" to statutory copyright. Thus, whether preemption occurs will turn on whether the other condition referred to above is satisfied. That relates to whether the "subject matter" of the works

---

* Nimmer on Copyright, § 2.02.

1. Protection for unpublished works in some states was predicated upon statute rather than common law.

2. See Chapter Two.

3. Under the 1909 Act, statutory copyright was also available for certain works by registration even prior to publication. It was optional with the copyright owner of such works as to whether he would retain common-law copyright while the work remained unpublished, or elect instead to claim statutory copyright, in which case common-law copyright was lost, although publication had not yet occurred.

4. 33 U.S. (8 Pet.) 591 (1834).

5. Goldstein v. California, 412 U.S. 546 (1973).

6. See Chapter Nine.

under the Copyright Act are the same as the subject matter of the works protected by common law copyright. For the most part, there is an identity of such subject matter, and to that extent common law copyright is terminated by preemption.[7] Any subject matter which does not constitute a "work of authorship" within the meaning of Sections 102 and 103 of the Copyright Act is clearly eligible for common law copyright. Of what categories such subject matter may consist is by no means clear, and is discussed elsewhere in this casebook.

Quite apart from the category of a work, any work which is not "fixed in a tangible medium of expression" is indisputably immune from federal preemption. This is true even if it otherwise constitutes a "work of authorship". This result is commanded by statutory provision,[8] as well as constitutional necessity. The states, therefore, have the power to protect via common law copyright "choreography that has never been filmed or notated, an extemporaneous speech, 'original works of authorship' communicated solely through conversations or live broadcasts, and a dramatic sketch or musical composition improvised or developed from memory and without being recorded or written down."[9] The states have such power because the constitutional requirement that a work be fixed in tangible form in order to constitute a "writing" is not, of course, applicable to common law copyright.[10]

But even if the Constitution does not require fixation for common law copyright, and there is no federal preemption of state law protecting unfixed works, this merely establishes that the states have the power to include unfixed works under the doctrine of common law copyright. There is the further question whether as a matter of law the states have elected to extend common law copyright to unfixed works. It is to that question to which we now turn.

HEMINGWAY v. RANDOM HOUSE, INC.

Court of Appeals of New York, 1969.
23 N.Y.2d 341, 296 N.Y.S.2d 771, 244 N.E.2d 250.

FULD, CHIEF JUDGE. On this appeal—involving an action brought by the Estate of the late Ernest Hemingway and his widow against the publisher and author of a book, entitled "Papa Hemingway"—we are called upon to decide primarily, whether conversations, at least those of a gifted and highly regarded writer, may become the subject of common law copyright, even though the speaker himself has not reduced his words to writing.

Hemingway died in 1961. During the last thirteen years of his life, a close friendship existed between him and A.E. Hotchner, a younger and far less well-known writer. Hotchner, who met Hemingway in the course of writing articles about him, became a favored drinking and traveling companion of the famous author, a frequent visitor to his home and the adapter of some of his works for motion pictures and television. During these years, Hemingway's conversation with Hotch-

---

7. This is now true regardless of whether or not such works have been published. See 17 U.S.C.A. § 301(a).

8. 17 U.S.C.A. § 301(a), (b)(1).

9. H.Rep., p. 131.

10. See Goldstein v. California, 412 U.S. 546 (1973) (limitations in the copyright clause of the Constitution not applicable to common law copyright).

ner, in which others sometimes took part, was filled with anecdote, reminiscence, literary opinion and revealing comment about actual

A. E. Hotchner and Ernest Hemingway

persons on whom some of Hemingway's fictional characters were based. Hotchner made careful notes of these conversations soon after they occurred, occasionally recording them on a portable tape recorder.

During Hemingway's lifetime, Hotchner wrote and published several articles about his friend in which he quoted some of this talk at length. Hemingway, far from objecting to this practice, approved of it. Indeed, the record reveals that other writers also quoted Hemingway's conversation without any objection from him, even when he was displeased with the articles themselves.

After Hemingway's death, Hotchner wrote "Papa Hemingway," drawing upon his notes and his recollections, and in 1966 it was published by the defendant Random House. Subtitled "a personal memoir," it is a serious and revealing biographical portrait of the world-renowned writer. Woven through the narrative, and giving the book much of its interest and character, are lengthy quotations from Hemingway's talk, as noted or remembered by Hotchner. Included also are two chapters on Hemingway's final illness and suicide in which Hotchner, writing of his friend with obvious feeling and sympathy, refers to events, and even to medical information, to which he was privy as an intimate of the family. Hemingway's widow, Mary, is mentioned frequently in the book, and is sometimes quoted, but only incidentally.

The complaint, which seeks an injunction and damages, alleges four causes of action. The first three, in which the Estate of Hemingway and his widow join as plaintiffs, are, briefly stated, (1) that "Papa Hemingway" consists, in the main, of literary matter composed by Hemingway in which he had a common law copyright; (2) that publication would constitute an unauthorized appropriation of Hemingway's work and would compete unfairly with his other literary creations; and (3) that Hotchner wrongfully used material which was imparted to him in the course of a confidential and fiduciary relationship with Hemingway. In the fourth cause of action, Mary Hemingway asserts that the book invades the right of privacy to which she herself is entitled under section 51 of the Civil Rights Law.

Following the filing of the defendants' answers, the plaintiffs moved for a preliminary injunction. The motion was denied (49 Misc.2d 726, 148 USPQ 618, aff'd 25 App.Div.2d 719), and the book was thereafter published. After its publication, the defendants sought and were granted summary judgment dismissing all four causes of action, 153 USPQ 871. The Appellate Division unanimously affirmed the resulting orders (without opinion) and granted the plaintiffs leave to appeal to this court.

Turning to the first cause of action we agree with the disposition made below but on a ground more narrow than that articulated by the court at Special Term. It is the position of the plaintiffs (under this court) that Hemingway was entitled to a common law copyright on the theory that his directly quoted comment, anecdote and opinion were his "literary creations," his "literary property," and that the defendant Hotchner's note-taking only performed the mechanics of recordation. And, in a somewhat different vein, it is argued that "[w]hat for Hemingway was oral one day would be or could become his written manuscript the next day," that his speech, constituting not just a statement of his ideas but the very form in which he conceived and expressed them, was as much the subject of common law copyright as what he might himself have committed to paper.

Common law copyright is the term applied to an author's proprietary interest in his literary or artistic creations before they have been made generally available to the public. It enables the author to exercise control over the first publication of his work or to prevent publication entirely—hence, its other name, the "right of first publication". Chamberlain v. Feldman, 300 N.Y. 135, 139, 84 USPQ 148, 149.[1] No cases deal directly with the question whether it extends to conversational speech and we begin, therefore, with a brief review of some relevant concepts in this area of law.

It must be acknowledged—as the defendants point out—that nearly a century ago, our court stated that common law copyright extended to " '[e]very new and innocent product of mental labor which has been *embodied in writing, or some other material form*' " Palmer v. DeWitt, 47 N.Y. 532, 537. (Emphasis supplied.) And, more recently, it has been said that "an author has no property right in his ideas unless * * given embodiment in a tangible form." O'Brien v. RKO Pictures, 68 F.Supp. 13, 14, 69 USPQ 367, 368. However, as a noted scholar in the field has observed, "the underlying rationale for common law copyright (i.e., the recognition that a property status should attach to the fruits of intellectual labor) is applicable regardless of whether such labor assumes tangible form." Nimmer, Copyright, p. 41. The principle that it is not the tangible embodiment of the author's work but the creation of the work itself which is protected, finds recognition in a number of ways in copyright law.

One example, with some relevance to the problem before us, is the treatment which the law has accorded to personal letters—a kind of half-conversation in written form. Although the paper upon which the letter is written belongs to the recipient, it is the author who has the right to publish them or to prevent their publication. See Baker v. Libbie, 210 Mass. 599, 605, 606. In the words of the Massachusetts court in the *Baker* case (210 Mass., at pp. 605–606), the author's right "is an interest in the intangible and impalpable thought and the particular verbal garments in which it has been clothed." Nor has speech itself been entirely without protection against reproduction for

---

1. Although common law copyright in an unpublished work lasts indefinitely, it is extinguished immediately upon publication of the work by the author. He must then rely, for his protection, upon Federal statutory copyright. See Nimmer, Copyright, sec. 11, pp. 38–42.2 and ch. 4, pp. 183 et seq. Section 2 of the Copyright Act (U.S.Code, tit. 17) expressly preserves the common law right in *unpublished* works against any implication that the field is preempted by the Federal statute.

publication. The public delivery of an address or a lecture or the performance of a play is not deemed a "publication," and, accordingly, it does not deprive the author of his common law copyright in its contents. See Ferris v. Frohman, 223 U.S. 424; King v. Mister Maestro, Inc., 224 F.Supp. 101, 106, 140 USPQ 366, 370; Palmer v. DeWitt, 47 N.Y. 532, 543, supra; see, also, Nimmer, Copyright, sec. 53, p. 208.

Letters, however—like plays and public addresses, written or not—have distinct, identifiable boundaries and they are, in most cases, only occasional products. Whatever difficulties attend the formulation of suitable rules for the enforcement of rights in such works, (see, e.g., Note, Personal Letters: In Need of a Law of Their Own, 44 Iowa L.Rev. 705), they are relatively manageable. However, conversational speech, the distinctive behavior of man, is quite another matter, and subjecting any part of it to the restraints of common law copyright presents unique problems.

One such problem—and it was stressed by the court at Special Term (Schweitzer, J.)[2]—is that of avoiding undue restraints on the freedoms of speech and press and, in particular, on the writers of history and of biographical works of the genre of Boswell's "Life of Johnson." The safeguarding of essential freedoms in this area is not without its complications. The indispensable right of the press to report on what people have *done,* or on what has *happened* to them or on what they have *said in public* (see Time, Inc., v. Hill, 385 U.S. 374; Curtis Publishing Co. v. Butts, 388 U.S. 130; Associated Press v. Walker, 388 U.S. 130) does not necessarily imply an unbounded freedom to publish whatever they may have *said in private conversation,* any more than it implies a freedom to copy and publish what people may have put down in *private writings.*

Copyright, both common law and statutory, rests on the assumption that there are forms of expression—limited in kind, to be sure—which should not be divulged to the public without the consent of their author. The purpose, far from being restrictive, is to encourage and protect intellectual labor. See Note, Copyright: Right to Common Law Copyright in Conversation of a Decedent, 67 Col.L.Rev. 366, 367, commenting on the decision denying the plaintiffs before us a preliminary injunction, 49 Misc.2d 726, 148 USPQ 618. The essential thrust of the First Amendment is to prohibit improper restraints on the *voluntary* public expression of ideas; it shields the man who wants to speak or publish when others wish him to be quiet. There is necessarily, and within suitably defined areas, a concomitant freedom *not* to speak publicly, one which serves the same ultimate end as freedom of speech in its affirmative aspect.

---

2. Another problem—also remarked by the court—is the difficulty of measuring the relative self-sufficiency of any one party's contributions to a conversation, although it may be, in the case of some kinds of dialogue or interview, that the difficulty would not be greater than in deciding other questions of degree, such as plagiarism. See e.g., Nichols v. Universal Pictures Corp., 45 F.2d 119, 7 USPQ 84.

The rules of common law copyright assure this freedom in the case of written material. However, speech is now easily captured by electronic devices and, consequently, we should be wary about excluding all possibility of protecting a *speaker's* right to decide when his words, uttered in private dialogue, may or may not be published at large. Conceivably, there may be limited and special situations in which an interlocutor brings forth oral statements from another party which both understand to be the unique intellectual product of the principal speaker, a product which would qualify for common law copyright if such statements were in writing. Concerning such problems, we express no opinion; we do no more than raise the questions, leaving them open for future consideration in cases which may present them more sharply than this one does.

On the appeal before us, the plaintiffs' claim to common law copyright may be disposed of more simply and on a more narrow ground.

The defendant Hotchner asserts—without contradiction in the papers before us—that Hemingway never suggested to him or to anyone else that he regarded his conversational remarks to be "literary creations" or that he was of a mind to restrict Hotchner's use of the notes and recordings which Hemingway knew him to be accumulating. On the contrary, as we have already observed, it had become a continuing practice, during Hemingway's lifetime, for Hotchner to write articles about Hemingway, consisting largely of quotations from the latter's conversation—and of all of this Hemingway approved. In these circumstances, authority to publish must be implied, thus negativing the reservation of any common law copyright.

Assuming, without deciding, that in a proper case a common law copyright in certain limited kinds of spoken dialogue might be recognized, it would, at the very least, be required that the speaker indicate that he intended to mark off the utterance in question from the ordinary stream of speech, that he meant to adopt it as a unique statement and that he wished to exercise control over its publication. In the conventional common law copyright situation, this indication is afforded by the creation of the manuscript itself. It would have to be evidenced in some other way if protection were ever to be accorded to some forms of conversational dialogue.

Such an indication is, of course, possible in the case of speech. It might, for example, be found in prefatory words or inferred from the circumstances in which the dialogue takes place.[3] Another way of formulating such a rule might be to say that, although, in the case of

---

3. This was the situation in Jenkins v. News Syndicate, Inc., 128 Misc. 284. The plaintiff alleged that she had had a conference with a newspaper editor in which she described in detail the proposed content of some articles she was requested to write. Later, she decided not to write them and the newspaper thereupon published an "interview" with her, precisely quoting much of her conversation with the editor. The court held that she had stated a cause of action for damages on the theory of common law copyright.

most intellectual products, the courts are reluctant to find that an author has "published," so as to lose his common law copyright (see Nimmer, Copyright, sec. 58.2, pp. 226–229), in the case of conversational speech—because of its unique nature—there should be a presumption that the speaker has not reserved any common law rights unless the contrary strongly appears. However, we need not carry such speculation further in the present case since the requisite conditions are plainly absent here.

For present purposes, it is enough to observe that Hemingway's words and conduct, far from making any such reservation, left no doubt of his willingness to permit Hotchner to draw freely on their conversation in writing about him and to publish such material. What we have said disposes of the plaintiffs' claim both to exclusive and to joint copyright and we need not further consider this aspect of the case. It follows, therefore, that the courts below were eminently correct in dismissing the first cause of action. * * *

[The dismissals of the other causes of action were also affirmed.]

Questions

1. Does the court *hold* that Hemingway had no common law copyright in his oral statements, or that he licensed the copyright therein to Hotchner?

2. Assuming Hemingway had not consented, would it have made any difference in the determination of Hotchner's liability whether in the book Hemingway's words were transcribed verbatim or were paraphrased by Hotchner? Would that distinction be significant on the question of whether Hotchner can claim copyright in such words?

3. Do you agree with the Court's suggested rule as to when speech not reduced to written form should be able to claim common law copyright protection? Does this rule conflict with the principle underlying Bleistein v. Donaldson, supra? Should the suggested rule be applicable to all sounds, including music, formal speeches, etc., not reduced to tangible form, or should it be limited to "conversational remarks"?

4. Which is to be preferred, the rule suggested in the Hemingway case or the rule now adopted in California? California Civil Code, Section 980(a)(1) provides:

> "The author of any original work of authorship that is not fixed in any tangible medium of expression has an exclusive ownership in the representation or expression thereof as against all persons except one who originally and independently creates the same or similar work. A work shall be considered not fixed when it is not embodied in a tangible medium of expression or when its embodiment in a tangible medium of expression is not sufficiently permanent or stable to permit it to be perceived, reproduced, or otherwise communicated for a period of more than transitory duration, either directly or with the aid of a machine or device."

Collateral References

Dunlap, "Copyright Protection for Oral Works", 20 Bull.Cr.Soc. 285 (1973).

Nimmer on Copyright, § 2.02.

Nelson, "Jazz and Copyright: A Study in Improvised Protection", 21 Copyright Law Symposium (ASCAP), p. 35 (1974).

Note

For a discussion of the early development of common law copyright see the analysis of the famous English case, Donaldson v. Beckett, 4 Burr. 2408 (1774 H.L.), and the first significant U.S. Supreme Court copyright case, Wheaton v. Peters, 33 U.S. (8 Pet.) 591, 8 L.Ed. 1055 (1834), in Nimmer on Copyright, § 4.02. For a full discussion of early copyright history see Patterson, Copyright In Historical Perspective (Vanderbilt Univ.Press 1968).

C. WORKS OF AUTHORSHIP

Note *

The Scope of "Works of Authorship"

Under Section 102(a) of the Copyright Act only "works of authorship" are eligible for copyright. But what are "works of authorship"? It is clear that this phrase is not intended to be coextensive with an author's "writings" in the constitutional sense. That is, Congress has elected not to exercise its full authority to provide for copyright protection of all "writings".[1] On the other hand, it is also clear that "works of authorship" are not necessarily limited to the seven broad categories of works listed under Section 102(a).[2] The House Report explicitly states that these categories are "'illustrative and not limitative,' and * * * do not necessarily exhaust the scope of 'original works of authorship' that the bill is intended to protect."[3] But, if "works of authorship" are neither so broad as to encompass all constitutional "writings," nor so narrow as to be confined to the seven broad categories enumerated in Section 102(a), how is one to delineate the scope of such works? The House Report states that the phrase "works of authorship" is "purposely left undefined."[4] A flexible definition was intended that would neither "freeze the scope of copyrightable subject matter at the present stage of communications technology or * * * allow unlimited expansion into areas completely outside the present congressional intent."[5] What manner of works may be said to be "completely outside the present congressional intent"? Neither the Copyright Act, nor the accompanying Committee Reports answer this question. We turn now to a consideration of certain types of works for which at least a measure of copyright protection has been afforded, but which present particular problems.

---

* Nimmer on Copyright, § 2.03[A].

1. "In using the phrase 'original works of authorship,' rather than 'all the writings of the author' now in section 4 of the [1909] statute, the committee's purpose is to avoid exhausting the constitutional power of Congress to legislate in this field * * *" H.Rep., p. 51.

2. These are: (1) literary works; (2) musical works, including any accompanying words; (3) dramatic works, including any accompanying music; (4) pantomimes and choreographic works; (5) pictorial, graphic and sculptural works; (6) motion pictures and other audio-visual works; and (7) sound recordings.

3. H.Rep., p. 53.

4. H.Rep., p. 51.

5. Id.

1. Photographs

TIME INCORPORATED v. BERNARD GEIS ASSOCIATES

United States District Court, Southern District of New York, 1968.
293 F.Supp. 130.

WYATT, DISTRICT JUDGE. This is a motion by plaintiff for summary judgment "interlocutory in character" on the issue of liability alone, as authorized by Rule 56(c) of the Federal Rules of Civil Procedure.

Time Incorporated (Time Inc.), the plaintiff, is a corporation which, among other things, publishes "Life", "Time" and "Fortune" magazines; it also publishes books; and it has "Broadcast divisions" the operations of which are not explained but presumably involve radio or television broadcasting or both. The events in suit principally concern "Life" magazine, which is an activity or division of Time Inc. and is not a separate corporation. For simplicity, however, the word "Life" is hereafter often used in describing or in referring to events when the more technically correct expression would be "Time Inc.", the plaintiff.

When President Kennedy was killed in Dallas on November 22, 1963, Abraham Zapruder, a Dallas dress manufacturer, was by sheer happenstance at the scene taking home movie pictures with his camera. His film—an historic document and undoubtedly the most important photographic evidence concerning the fatal shots—was bought a few days later by Life; parts of the film were printed in several issues of the magazine. As to these issues and their contents (including, of course, the Zapruder pictures) and as to the film itself, Life has complied with all provisions of the Copyright Act (17 U.S.C. § 1 and following; the Act).

Upper left a frame from the Zapruder film. Upper right a sketch from "Six Seconds in Dallas".

Defendant Thompson has written a book, "Six Seconds in Dallas" (the Book), which is a study of the assassination. It is a serious, thoughtful and impressive analysis of the evidence * * *.

In the memorandum submitted for defendants, it is asserted that they are entitled to summary judgment but, if found not so entitled, that there should be a trial of the issue whether plaintiff consented to use of the sketches in the Book. If defendants are entitled to summary judgment, it may properly be granted by the Court even without a written or formal motion. 6 Moore's Federal Practice (2d ed.) 2241–2246.

There is no genuine issue as to any material fact on the issue of liability alone. Some of the questions of law, ably argued on both sides, are difficult. The conclusion is that there must be summary judgment for defendants.

The facts are almost entirely established beyond any dispute and without any dispute, except as expressly noted in the following recital.

On November 22, Zapruder decided to make a motion picture film of the President passing by. He had an 8 millimeter color home movie camera with a "telephoto" lens. At first he thought to take the pictures from his office in an office building at 501 Elm Street, at the corner of Elm and Houston Streets where the President's car would make a left turn from Houston into Elm Street. Then he felt he could get better pictures on the ground, so he went down with several others from his office and walked along Elm Street toward a triple underpass trying to pick the best spot for his camera. He tried several places and finally settled on a pedestal of concrete about 4 feet high on a slope; from this point he could look up Elm Street away from the underpass and see the corner where the left turn would be made, after which the President's car would come toward and pass directly in front of him on its way to the underpass; it was a "superb spot" for his pictures. He tried out the camera, felt that he was not steady, and then had his receptionist come up on the pedestal and steady him while he ran the camera.

The procession came into view and with the speed control at "Run" (about 18 frames per second) Zapruder started his camera, not knowing the horror it would record. When the car came close to Zapruder, there were the sudden shots and the reactions of those in the car—all caught on Zapruder's color film.

On the same day—November 22—Zapruder had the original color film developed and three color copies made from the original film.

(There are about 480 frames in the Zapruder film, of which 140 show the immediate events of the shooting and 40 are relevant to the shots themselves. While working with the film, agents of the Secret Service or of the Federal Bureau of Investigation identified each frame with a number, beginning with "1" for the frame showing the lead motorcycles coming into view on Houston Street and continuing the numbers in sequence for the frames following; these numbers have since been used to identify the frames.)

On the same or the next day, Zapruder in his Dallas office turned over two copies of the film to the Secret Service, specifying that it was strictly for government use and not to be shown to newspapers or magazines because he expected to sell the film.

Life then negotiated with Zapruder and on November 25 by written agreement bought the original and all three copies of the film (two of which were noted as then in the possession of the Secret Service) and all rights therein, for $150,000 to be paid in yearly instalments of $25,000.

In its next edition (cover date November 29, 1963) Life featured some 30 of the Zapruder frames, calling them a "remarkable and exclusive series". Doubtless because of time pressure, the frames were in black and white.

Life published on December 7, 1963 a special "John F. Kennedy Memorial Edition". This featured 9 enlarged Zapruder frames in color, telling how they came to be taken and how they recorded the tragic sequence "with appalling clarity".

President Johnson on November 29, 1963 appointed a Commission with Chief Justice Warren as Chairman (the Commission) to investigate the killing of President Kennedy. This Commission on September 24, 1964 submitted its lengthy report (the Warren Report) and all the evidence before it.

The Commission made extensive use of the Zapruder film, and placed great reliance on it, as evidenced in the Report (for example, pp. 97, 98–115). Six of the Zapruder frames are shown in the body of the Report (at pp. 100–103, 108, 114) and some 160 Zapruder frames are included (in volume XVIII) in the Exhibits of the Commission printed and submitted with the Report. * * *

There appears to be no privilege for the United States to use copyrighted material without the consent of the owner. A statute (28 U.S.C. § 1498(b)) gives a remedy in the Court of Claims for copyright infringement by the United States. Another statute (17 U.S.C. § 8) provides that publication by the government of copyrighted material does not cause any "abridgment" of the copyright and does not authorize "any use * * * of such copyright material without the consent of the copyright proprietor."

Life did in fact consent to use by the Commission of the Zapruder film and to its reproduction in the Report, provided a usual notice of copyright was given. Apparently this proviso was disregarded by the Commission.

Shortly after the submission of the Report, Life featured it in an issue (cover date, October 2, 1964) with a cover containing enlargements in color of five Zapruder frames. The text for the article on the Report was by a member of the Commission. The Zapruder film was described as "one of the most important pieces of evidence to come before the * * Commission". Eight Zapruder frames, enlarged and in color were printed alongside the text. * * *

On May 15, 1967, Life registered the Zapruder film in the Copyright office as an unpublished "motion picture other than a photoplay". 17 U.S.C. § 5(m); 37 C.F.R. § 202.15. The three issues of Life magazine in which Zapruder frames appeared had earlier been registered in the Copyright office as "periodicals". 17 U.S.C. § 5(b); 37 C.F.R. § 202.5. The Memorial Edition had been registered in the Copyright office as a book. 17 U.S.C. § 5(a); 37 C.F.R. § 202.4.

The three weekly issues of Life and its Memorial Edition, each containing Zapruder frames, had a total distribution of over 23,750,000 copies. Weekly issues of Life, published outside the United States and containing Zapruder frames, had a circulation of over 3 million copies.

It is undisputed that Life complied with all provisions of the Copyright Act and that, if the Zapruder pictures are properly the subject of copyright, Life secured statutory copyrights for them.

* * *

On or about June 22, [Bernard Geis] Associates offered to pay Life a royalty equal to the profits from publication of the Book in return for permission to use specified Zapruder frames in the Book. This offer was refused by Life.

Having failed to secure permission from Life to use the Zapruder pictures, Thompson and the other defendants (presumably with the advice of counsel) concluded that they would copy certain frames anyway. Doubtless having in mind the probability of an action for infringement, defendants did not reproduce photographically any Zapruder frames but employed an "artist" to make copies in charcoal by means of a "rendering" or "sketch". It is said that the artist was paid $1550.

Beginning November 18, 1967, Associates has been publishing and Random House, Inc. has been distributing the Book.

The Book relies heavily on the Zapruder pictures.

No Zapruder frame is reproduced in its entirety but whatever parts of any frame were considered significant by Thompson, these were reproduced.

Significant parts of 22 copyrighted frames are reproduced in the Book. * * *

The so-called "sketches" in the Book as listed above are in fact copies, as is readily apparent by comparison with the Zapruder frames involved, copies of all of which have been submitted. The "artist" has simply copied the original in charcoal with no creativity or originality whatever. * * *

It must be determined if there is a valid copyright in the Zapruder pictures. As noted, all requirements of the Copyright Act have been met. The question remains whether the pictures are properly the subject of copyright.

It is said for defendants that the pictures are simply records of what took place, without any "elements" personal to Zapruder, and that "news" cannot be the subject of copyright.

The Zapruder pictures are "photographs" of an event. The Copyright Act provides (17 U.S.C. §§ 4, 5(j)) that "Photographs" may be the subject matter of copyright. If this were all to be considered, it would seem clear that the pictures here were properly copyrighted because Congress has expressly made photographs the subject of copyright, without any limitation.

The copyright provision for photographs first appeared in an Act of July 8, 1870, which became Section 4952 of the Revised Statutes and is now Section 5(j) of Title 17 of the Code.

This provision first came before the Supreme Court in Burrow-Giles Lithographic Co. v. Sarony, 111 U.S. 53, 4 S.Ct. 279, 28 L.Ed. 349 (1884). The question was whether a studio photograph of Oscar Wilde could be the subject of copyright. It was assumed that Section 4952 applied to *all* photographs. The argument was made, however, that Congress could not constitutionally do so because photographs are not "writings" of which the photographers are "authors", as the quoted words are used in the Constitution (Art. I, § 8, cl. 8). The argument was that photographs were "merely mechanical" and involved no "novelty, invention or originality" (111 U.S. at 59, 4 S.Ct. at 279). The Supreme Court declined to say whether copyright could constitutionally be granted to "the ordinary production of a photograph" (111 U.S. at 59, 4 S.Ct. at 282). It found that the photograph in suit had involved the posing of the subject and a choice of costume, background, etc. The Court held that the photograph was a writing of which the photographer was the author and that the Congress could constitutionally make such photograph the subject of copyright. This left open whether an ordinary photograph of a real life object could constitutionally be a proper subject of copyright.

The question was again before the Supreme Court in Bleistein v. Donaldson Lithographing Co., 188 U.S. 239, 23 S.Ct. 298, 47 L.Ed. 460 (1903). The works were chromolithographs (pictures printed by a special process) of certain groups performing in a circus. The Court, by Mr. Justice Holmes, held that such pictures had been constitutionally made subjects of copyright. The Court found it "obvious" that the result could not be affected by the fact that the pictures represented "actual groups—visible things" and that such pictures "drawn from the life" (as opposed to a "composed" subject) could be copyrighted. In this connection, the Court declared: "Others are free to copy the original. They are not free to copy the copy." (188 U.S. at 249, 23 S.Ct. at 299). And later: "The least pretentious picture has more originality in it than directories and the like, which may be copyrighted" (188 U.S. at 250, 23 S.Ct. at 300).

Judge Learned Hand believed that any photograph could be the subject of copyright because in *Bleistein* the Supreme Court had ruled that "no photograph, however simple, can be unaffected by the personal influence of the author, and no two will be absolutely alike." Jewelers Circular Publishing Co. v. Keystone Pub. Co., 274 Fed. 932, 934 (S.D.N.Y. 1921), affirmed 281 Fed. 83 (2d Cir.1922). Judge Hand in the same opinion said:

> * * * under section 5(j) photographs are protected, without regard to the degree of "personality" which enters into them. At least there has been no case since 1909 in which that has been held to be a condition. The suggestion that the Constitution might not include all photographs seems to me overstrained. Therefore, even if the cuts be deemed only photographs, which in these supposed cases they are, still I think that they and the illustrations made from them may be protected.

Mr. Justice Brandeis, in a dissenting opinion, stated: "The mere record of isolated happenings, whether in words or by photographs not involving artistic skill, are denied [copyright] protection". International News Service v. Associated Press, 248 U.S. 215, 254, 39 S.Ct. 68, 78, 63 L.Ed.2d 211 (1918; the "Associated Press" case). The reference to photographs was not necessary to the point being made and in any event it seems clear that Mr. Justice Brandeis was mistaken. None of the cases cited to support his statement had anything to do with photographs, other than *Bleistein* and *Burrow-Giles,* which have already been considered.

The commentators, or at least most of them, have concluded that any photograph may be the subject of copyright.

For example, Nimmer on Copyright, page 99, after explaining that the conclusion of Judge Learned Hand has become "the prevailing view", goes on to say:

> * * * any (or as will be indicated below, almost any) photograph may claim the necessary originality to support a copyright merely by virtue of the photographers' personal choice of subject matter, angle of photograph, lighting and determination of the precise time when the photograph is to be taken. Thus a photograph of the New York Public Library was held to exhibit the necessary originality.

The exceptions indicated by Nimmer's parenthetical "almost any" are not relevant in the case at bar.

A law review article has dealt with this question in part as follows (Gorman, Copyright Protection for the Collection and Representation of Facts, 76 Harv.L.Rev. 1569, 1597–1598 (1963):

> There is, no doubt, some element of personality—the choice of subject, the framing of it in the camera viewer, the decision when to shoot—in the taking of a snapshot. * * * its visual appeal, its partaking of the nature of artistic work, seems to have deterred courts from sitting as critics on the degree of artistic merit, skill, or effort embodied in a photograph. Another reason for granting copyright protection to the simple photograph is the familiar saw which tells us that one picture is worth a thousand words. If it can be as instructive as a lengthily written description of the same scene,

a photograph advances our knowledge of the useful arts and sciences and enhances our understanding of historical occurrences and natural events, just as much as does the written description. If the latter can be copyrighted because in pursuance of the constitutional purpose, why not photographs too, no matter how studied or how extemporaneous they may be?

* * * there is little difficulty today in deciding that a photograph has ample originality to be copyrighted. * * *

There are very few decisions dealing with photographs of real life objects, apparently because their copyright protection has been assumed.

There was an interesting case in this Court some fifty years ago. The question was whether a photograph of a street scene showing the Public Library on Fifth Avenue could be the subject of copyright. The decision upheld the copyright, saying among other things (Pagano v. Beseler Co., 234 Fed. 963, 964 (2 Cir.1916):

It undoubtedly requires originality to determine just when to take the photograph, so as to bring out the proper setting for both animate and inanimate objects, with the adjunctive features of light, shade, position, etc.

Thus, if Zapruder had made his pictures at a point in time before the shooting, he would clearly have been entitled to copyright. On what principle can it be denied because of the tragic event it records?

The defendants argue that "news cannot be copyrighted" citing the *Associated Press* case and National Tel. News Co. v. Western Union, 119 Fed. 294, 60 L.R.A. 805 (7th Cir.1902).

Defendants are perfectly correct in their contention. A news event may not be copyrighted, as the cited cases hold. Life claims no copyright in the news element of the event but only in the particular form of record made by Zapruder.

The *Associated Press* case involved news articles (words) and not photographs. The *Associated Press* case did not involve copyrighted material but the Court discussed news articles as subjects of copyright. The Court carefully distinguished between the "news element," the "substance of the information" on the one hand, and "the particular form or collocation of words in which the writer has communicated it" (248 U.S. at 234, 39 S.Ct. at 70) on the other. The latter, the "particular form", was recognized as a proper subject of copyright, the Court saying (248 U.S. at 234, 39 S.Ct. at 70):

No doubt news articles often possess a literary quality, and are the subject of literary property at the common law; nor do we question that such an article, as a literary production, is the subject of copyright by the terms of the act as it now stands.

It is said for defendants that the pictures cannot be copyrighted because of "lack of creativity."

This argument has already been dealt with in the discussion just above.

Any photograph reflects "the personal influence of the author, and no two will be absolutely alike," to use the words of Judge Learned Hand.

The Zapruder pictures in fact have many elements of creativity. Among other things, Zapruder selected the kind of camera (movies, not snapshots), the kind of film (color), the kind of lens (telephoto), the area in which the pictures were to be taken, the time they were to be taken, and (after testing several sites) the spot on which the camera would be operated.

It is said for defendants that aside from all else the Zapruder pictures could not be copyrighted because of the "doctrine" of a recent decision, Morrissey v. Procter & Gamble Co., 379 F.2d 675 (1st Cir.1967). This "doctrine" is here invoked to avoid an "oligopoly of the facts of the assassination of President Kennedy".

The *Morrissey* case involved the rules of a sales promotion contest. The substance of the contest itself was found not to be copyrightable. It was also found that there was a very limited number of ways in which the rules could be expressed. If the rules were made the subject of copyright, then the uncopyrighted substance of the contest would be appropriated by the owner of the rules copyright. The Court declined to extend copyright protection to the rules.

Such a decision can have no possible application here. Life claims no copyright in the events at Dallas. They can be freely set forth in speech, in books, in pictures, in music, and in every other form of expression. All that Life claims is a copyright in the particular form of expression of the Zapruder film. If this be "oligopoly", it is specifically conferred by the Copyright Act and for any relief address must be to the Congress and not to this Court.

Life has a valid copyright in the Zapruder film.

As already noted, the so-called "sketches" in the Book are in fact copies of the copyrighted film. That they were done in charcoal by an "artist" is of no moment. As put in Nimmer on Copyright, page 98:

> It is of course, fundamental, that copyright in a work protects against unauthorized copying not only in the original medium in which the work was produced, but also in any other medium as well. Thus copyright in a photograph will preclude unauthorized copying by drawing or in any other form, as well as by photographic reproduction.

There is thus an infringement by defendants unless the use of the copyrighted material in the Book is a "fair use" outside the limits of copyright protection. * * *

[The Court then found for the defendants on the issue of fair use, and accordingly granted them summary judgment. This aspect of the case is discussed at p. 431 infra.]

Questions

1. Suppose Zapruder had "selected the kind of camera (movies, not snapshots), the kind of film (color), [and] the kind of lens (telephoto)", but contrary

to the court's findings, he copied from another photographer who had preceded him (and who was taking black and white snapshots with an ordinary lens) "the area in which the pictures were to be taken, the time they were to be taken, and * * * the spot on which the camera would be operated." Could Zapruder then claim originality in the resulting home movies?

2. If one makes a photograph of a painting which is itself in the public domain, may copyright be claimed in the photograph? Recall Alfred Bell & Co. v. Catalda Fine Arts, supra. Suppose one makes a photograph of a photograph. Is the second photograph "original" for copyright purposes? Doesn't such a process require a knowledgable choice of camera, film, and lighting? Is the second photograph a "distinguishable variation" from the first within the meaning of the *Alfred Bell* case? Can one claim copyright in a Xerox reproduction of a public domain pictorial work?

3. Suppose the defendants in their book had described in words rather than by sketches President Kennedy's posture and demeanor before and immediately after the shots were fired, and suppose defendants acknowledged that this information could only be learned from an examination of the Zapruder film. Could Life claim that its copyright in the film extended to such a verbal description? What does it mean that "copyright in a work protects against unauthorized copying not only in the original medium in which the work was produced, but also in any other medium as well"?

4. Under the Copyright Act of 1976 is a photograph a graphic work, protectible under § 102(a)(5), or is it an audiovisual work, protectible under § 102(a)(6)? Compare the definitions of "pictorial, graphic, and sculptural works" and "audiovisual works" in § 101. Is there any substantive significance as to whether a photograph falls under one or the other such classification?

Collateral Reference

Nimmer on Copyright, § 2.08[E].

2. *Factual Works*

HOEHLING v. UNIVERSAL CITY STUDIOS, INC.

United States Court of Appeals, Second Circuit, 1980.
618 F.2d 972.

Before KAUFMAN, CHIEF JUDGE, TIMBERS, CIRCUIT JUDGE, and WERKER, DISTRICT JUDGE.

IRVING R. KAUFMAN, CHIEF JUDGE:

A grant of copyright in a published work secures for its author a limited monopoly over the expression it contains. The copyright provides a financial incentive to those who would add to the corpus of existing knowledge by creating original works. Nevertheless, the protection afforded the copyright holder has never extended to history, be it documented fact or explanatory hypothesis. The rationale for this doctrine is that the cause of knowledge is best served when history is the common property of all, and each generation remains free to draw upon the discoveries and insights of the past. Accordingly, the scope of copyright in historical accounts is narrow indeed, embracing no more than the author's original expression of particular facts and theories already in the public domain. As the case before us illustrates, absent wholesale usurpation of another's expression, claims of copyright infringement where works of history are at issue are rarely successful.

* * *

This litigation arises from three separate accounts of the triumphant introduction, last voyage, and tragic destruction of the Hindenburg, the colossal dirigible constructed in Germany during Hitler's reign. The zeppelin, the last and most sophisticated in a fleet of luxury airships, which punctually floated its wealthy passengers from the Third Reich to the United States, exploded into flames and disintegrated in 35 seconds as it hovered above the Lakehurst, New Jersey Naval Air Station at 7:25 p.m. on May 6, 1937. Thirty-six passengers and crew were killed but, fortunately, 52 persons survived. Official investigations conducted by both American and German authorities could ascertain no definitive cause of the disaster, but both suggested the plausibility of static electricity or St. Elmo's Fire, which could have ignited the highly explosive hydrogen that filled the airship. Throughout, the investigators refused to rule out the possibility of sabotage.

An artist's depiction of a scene from the Universal film.

©Universal Pictures

From the motion picture THE HINDENBURG (Univ.1975). Courtesy of Universal Pictures.

The destruction of the Hindenburg marked the concluding chapter in the chronicle of airship passenger service, for after the tragedy at Lakehurst, the Nazi regime permanently grounded the Graf Zeppelin I and discontinued its plan to construct an even larger dirigible, the Graf Zeppelin II.

The final pages of the airship's story marked the beginning of a series of journalistic, historical, and literary accounts devoted to the Hindenburg and its fate. Indeed, weeks of testimony by a plethora of witnesses before the official investigative panels provided fertile source material for would-be authors. Moreover, both the American and German Commissions issued official reports, detailing all that was then known of the tragedy. A number of newspaper and magazine articles had been written about the Hindenburg in 1936, its first year of trans-Atlantic service, and they, of course, multiplied manyfold after the crash. In addition, two passengers—Margaret Mather and Gertrud Adelt—published separate and detailed accounts of the voyage, C.E. Rosendahl, commander of the Lakehurst Naval Air Station and a pioneer in airship travel himself, wrote a book titled *What About the Airship?*, in which he endorsed the theory that the Hindenburg was the victim of sabotage. In 1957, Nelson Gidding, who would return to the subject of the Hindenburg some 20 years later, wrote an unpublished "treatment" for a motion picture based on the deliberate destruction of the airship. In that year as well, John Toland published *Ships in the Sky* which, in its seventeenth chapter, chronicled the last flight of the Hindenburg. In 1962, Dale Titler released *Wings of Mystery,* in which he too devoted a chapter to the Hindenburg.[1]

Appellant A.A. Hoehling published *Who Destroyed the Hindenburg?*, a full-length book based on his exhaustive research in 1962. Mr. Hoehling studied the investigative reports, consulted previously published articles and books, and conducted interviews with survivors of the crash as well as others who possessed information about the Hindenburg. His book is presented as a factual account, written in an objective, reportorial style.

The first half recounts the final crossing of the Hindenburg, from Sunday, May 2, when it left Frankfurt, to Thursday, May 6, when it exploded at Lakehurst. Hoehling describes the airship, its role as an instrument of propaganda in Nazi Germany, its passengers and crew, the danger of hydrogen, and the ominous threats received by German officials, warning that the Hindenburg would be destroyed. The second portion, headed *The Quest,* sets forth the progress of the official investigations, followed by an account of Hoehling's own research. In the final chapter, spanning eleven pages, Hoehling suggests that all proffered explanations of the explosion, save deliberate destruction, are

---

[1] Titler's account was published after the release of appellant's book. In an affidavit in this litigation, Titler states that he copied Hoehling's theory of sabotage. Hoehling, however, has never instituted a copyright action against Titler.

unconvincing. He concludes that the most likely saboteur is one Eric Spehl, a "rigger" on the Hindenburg crew who was killed at Lakehurst.

According to Hoehling, Spehl had motive, expertise, and opportunity to plant an explosive device, constructed of dry-cell batteries and a flashbulb, in "Gas Cell 4," the location of the initial explosion. An amateur photographer with access to flashbulbs, Spehl could have destroyed the Hindenburg to please his ladyfriend, a suspected communist dedicated to exploding the myth of Nazi invincibility.

Ten years later appellee Michael MacDonald Mooney published his book, *The Hindenburg*. Mooney's endeavor might be characterized as more literary than historical in its attempt to weave a number of symbolic themes through the actual events surrounding the tragedy. His dominant theme contrasts the natural beauty of the month of May, when the disaster occurred, with the cold, deliberate progress of "technology." The May theme is expressed not simply by the season, but also by the character of Spehl, portrayed as a sensitive artisan with needle and thread. The Hindenburg, in contrast, is the symbol of technology, as are its German creators and the Reich itself. The destruction is depicted as the ultimate triumph of nature over technology, as Spehl plants the bomb that ignites the hydrogen. Developing this theme from the outset, Mooney begins with an extended review of man's efforts to defy nature through flight, focusing on the evolution of the zeppelin. This story culminates in the construction of the Hindenburg, and the Nazis' claims of its indestructibility. Mooney then traces the fateful voyage, advising the reader almost immediately of Spehl's scheme. The book concludes with the airship's explosion.

Mooney acknowledges, in this case, that he consulted Hoehling's book, and that he relied on it for some details. He asserts that he first discovered the "Spehl-as-saboteur" theory when he read Titler's *Wings of Mystery*. Indeed, Titler concludes that Spehl was the saboteur, for essentially the reasons stated by Hoehling. Mooney also claims to have studied the complete National Archives and New York Times files concerning the Hindenburg, as well as all previously published material. Moreover, he traveled to Germany, visited Spehl's birthplace, and conducted a number of interviews with survivors.

After Mooney prepared an outline of his anticipated book, his publisher succeeded in negotiations to sell the motion picture rights to appellee Universal City Studios.[2] Universal then commissioned a screen story by writers Levinson and Link, best known for their television series, *Columbo*, in which a somewhat disheveled, but wise detective unravels artfully conceived murder mysteries. In their screen story, Levinson and Link created a Columbo-like character who endeavored to identify the saboteur on board the Hindenburg. Director

---

2. Mooney, his publishers, and Universal entered into an agreement under which (1) Universal acquired the film rights to Mooney's book, (2) Universal agreed to promote sales of the book, and (3) Mooney would receive a percentage fee, tied to sales of his book. Hoehling claims that because of this arrangement, Universal is vicariously liable if Mooney's book, but not the motion picture, is held to infringe his copyright. In view of our disposition of the appeal, however, we need not address this issue.

Robert Wise, however, was not satisfied with this version, and called upon Nelson Gidding to write a final screenplay. Gidding, it will be recalled, had engaged in preliminary work on a film about the Hindenburg almost twenty years earlier.

The Gidding screenplay follows what is known in the motion picture industry as a "Grand Hotel" formula, developing a number of fictional characters and subplots involving them. This formula has become standard fare in so-called "disaster" movies, which have enjoyed a certain popularity in recent years. In the film, which was released in late 1975, a rigger named "Boerth," who has an anti-Nazi ladyfriend, plans to destroy the airship in an effort to embarrass the Reich. Nazi officials, vaguely aware of sabotage threats, station a Luftwaffe intelligence officer on the zeppelin, loosely resembling a Colonel Erdmann who was aboard the Hindenburg. This character is portrayed as a likable fellow who soon discovers that Boerth is the saboteur. Boerth, however, convinces him that the Hindenburg should be destroyed and the two join forces, planning the explosion for several hours after the landing at Lakehurst, when no people would be on board. In Gidding's version, the airship is delayed by a storm, frantic efforts to defuse the bomb fail, and the Hindenburg is destroyed. The film's subplots involve other possible suspects, including a fictional countess who has had her estate expropriated by the Reich, two fictional confidence men wanted by New York City police, and an advertising executive rushing to close a business deal in America.

Upon learning of Universal's plans to release the film, Hoehling instituted this action against Universal for copyright infringement and common law unfair competition in the district court for the District of Columbia in October 1975. Judge Smith declined to issue an order restraining release of the film in December, and it was distributed throughout the nation.

* * *

Hoehling's principal claim is that both Mooney and Universal copied the essential plot of his book—i.e., Eric Spehl, influenced by his girlfriend, sabotaged the Hindenburg by placing a crude bomb in Gas Cell 4. In their briefs, and at oral argument, appellees have labored to convince us that their plots are not substantially similar to Hoehling's. While Hoehling's Spehl destroys the airship to please his communist girlfriend, Mooney's character is motivated by an aversion to the technological age. Universal's Boerth, on the other hand, is a fervent anti-fascist who enlists the support of a Luftwaffe colonel who, in turn, unsuccessfully attempts to defuse the bomb at the eleventh hour.

* * * [A]ppellees argue that Hoehling's plot is an "idea," and ideas are not copyrightable as a matter of law. See Sheldon v. Metro-Goldwyn Pictures Corp., 81 F.2d 49, 54 (2d Cir.), cert. denied, 298 U.S. 669, 56 S.Ct. 835, 80 L.Ed. 1392 (1936).

Hoehling, however, correctly rejoins that while ideas themselves are not subject to copyright, his "expression" of *his* idea is copyrightable. Id. at 54. He relies on Learned Hand's opinion in *Sheldon,* supra, at 50, holding that *Letty Lynton* infringed *Dishonored Lady* by copying its story of a woman who poisons her lover, and Augustus Hand's analysis in Detective Comics, Inc. v. Bruns Publications, Inc., 111 F.2d 432 (2d Cir.1940), concluding that the exploits of "Wonderman" infringed the copyright held by the creators of "Superman," the original indestructible man. Moreover, Hoehling asserts that, in both these cases, the line between "ideas" and "expression" is drawn, in the first instance, by the fact finder.

Sheldon and *Detective Comics,* however, dealt with works of fiction, where the distinction between an idea and its expression is especially elusive. But, where, as here, the idea at issue is an interpretation of an historical event, our cases hold that such interpretations are not copyrightable as a matter of law. In Rosemont Enterprises, Inc. v. Random House, Inc., 366 F.2d 303 (2d Cir.1966), cert. denied, 385 U.S. 1009, 87 S.Ct. 714, 17 L.Ed.2d 546 (1967), we held that the defendant's biography of Howard Hughes did not infringe an earlier biography of the reclusive alleged billionaire. Although the plots of the two works were necessarily similar, there could be no infringement because of the "public benefit in encouraging the development of historical and biographical works and their public distribution." Id. at 307; accord, Oxford Book Co. v. College Entrance Book Co., 98 F.2d 688 (2d Cir.1938). To avoid a chilling effect on authors who contemplate tackling an historical issue or event, broad latitude must be granted to subsequent authors who make use of historical subject matter, including theories or plots. Learned Hand counseled in Myers v. Mail & Express Co., 36 C.O.Bull. 478, 479 (S.D.N.Y.1919), "[t]here cannot be any such thing as copyright in the order of presentation of the facts, nor, indeed, in their selection." [5]

In the instant case, the hypothesis that Eric Spehl destroyed the Hindenburg is based entirely on the interpretation of historical facts, including Spehl's life, his girlfriend's anti-Nazi connections, the explosion's origin in Gas Cell 4, Spehl's duty station, discovery of a dry-cell battery among the wreckage, and rumors about Spehl's involvement dating from a 1938 Gestapo investigation. Such an historical interpretation, whether or not it originated with Mr. Hoehling, is not protected by his copyright and can be freely used by subsequent authors.

* * *

The same reasoning governs Hoehling's claim that a number of specific facts, ascertained through his personal research, were copied by appellees. The cases in this circuit, however, make clear that factual information is in the public domain. See, e.g., Rosemont Enterprises, Inc., supra, 366 F.2d at 309; Oxford Book Co., supra, 98 F.2d at 691.

---

5. This circuit has permitted extensive reliance on prior works of history. See, e.g., Gardner v. Nizer, 391 F.Supp. 940 (S.D.N.Y.1975) (the story of the Rosenberg trial not copyrightable); Fuld v. National Broadcasting Co., 390 F.Supp. 877 (S.D.N.Y.1975) ("Bugsy" Siegel's life story not copyrightable); Greenbie v. Noble, 151 F.Supp. 45 (S.D.N.Y.1957) (the life of Anna Carroll, a member of Lincoln's cabinet, not copyrightable). The commentators are in accord with this view. See, e.g., 1 Nimmer on Copyright § 2.11[A] (1979); Chafee, *Reflections on the Law of Copyright:* I, 45 Colum.L. Rev. 503, 511 (1945).

Each appellee had the right to "avail himself of the facts contained" in Hoehling's book and to "use such information, whether correct or incorrect, in his own literary work." Greenbie v. Noble, 151 F.Supp. 45, 67 (S.D.N.Y.1957). Accordingly, there is little consolation in relying on cases in other circuits holding that the fruits of original research are copyrightable. See, e.g., Toksvig v. Bruce Publications Corp., 181 F.2d 664, 667 (7th Cir.1950); Miller v. Universal City Studios, Inc., 460 F.Supp. 984 (S.D.Fla.1978).[a] Indeed, this circuit has clearly repudiated *Toksvig* and its progeny. In Rosemont Enterprises, Inc., supra, 366 F.2d at 310, we refused to "subscribe to the view that an author is absolutely precluded from saving time and effort by referring to and relying upon prior published material. * * * It is just such wasted effort that the proscription against the copyright of ideas and facts * * are designed to prevent." *Accord,* 1 Nimmer on Copyright § 2.11 (1979).

* * *

The remainder of Hoehling's claimed similarities relate to random duplications of phrases and sequences of events. For example, all three works contain a scene in a German beer hall, in which the airship's crew engages in revelry prior to the voyage. Other claimed similarities concern common German greetings of the period, such as "Heil Hitler," or songs, such as the German National anthem. These elements, however, are merely *scenes a faire*, that is, "incidents, characters or settings which are as a practical matter indispensable, or at least standard, in the treatment of a given topic." Alexander v. Haley, 460 F.Supp. at 45; *accord,* Bevan v. Columbia Broadcasting System, Inc., 329 F.Supp. 601, 607 (S.D.N.Y.1971). Because it is virtually impossible to write about a particular historical era or fictional theme without employing certain "stock" or standard literary devices, we have held that *scenes a faire* are not copyrightable as a matter of law. See Reyher v. Children's Television Workshop, 533 F.2d 87, 91 (2d Cir.), cert. denied, 429 U.S. 980, 97 S.Ct. 492, 50 L.Ed.2d 588 (1976).

* * *

In works devoted to historical subjects, it is our view that a second author may make significant use of prior work, so long as he does not bodily appropriate the expression of another. Rosemont Enterprises, Inc., supra, 366 F.2d at 310. This principle is justified by the fundamental policy undergirding the copyright laws—the encouragement of contributions to recorded knowledge. The "financial reward guaranteed to the copyright holder is but an incident of this general objective, rather than an end in itself." Berlin v. E.C. Publications, Inc., 329 F.2d 541, 543–44 (2d Cir.), cert. denied, 379 U.S. 822, 85 S.Ct. 46, 13 L.Ed.2d 33 (1964). Knowledge is expanded as well by granting new authors of historical works a relatively free hand to build upon the work of their predecessors.[7]

* * *

The judgment of the district court is affirmed.

a. Reversed, 650 F.2d 1365 (5th Cir. 1981).

7. We note that publication of Mooney's book and release of the motion picture re-

Questions

1. Although the destruction of the Hindenburg is clearly a "fact," and therefore not copyrightable, is the court correct in concluding that Hoehling's theory as to how and why such destruction occurred is also a "fact" incapable of copyright? When is a theory a "work of authorship," and when is it not? Should all theories as to what in fact occurred be treated as "facts"? Are all "facts" actually someone's theory as to what in fact occurred?

2. The dichotomy between unprotectible "idea" and protectible "expression" is discussed in Chapter Seven. In drawing the line between "idea" and "expression," what is the relevance of whether the material is fact or fiction?

3. In a biography, are the precise words said to have been uttered by the subject of the biography copyrightable by the author of the biography? Should it make any difference if it is an autobiography?

4. The *Hoehling* opinion finds unprotectible *scenes a faire,* defined as "incidents, characters or settings which are as a practical matter indispensable, or at least standard, in the treatment of a given topic." What if such incidents are "standard" but not "indispensable"? Recall the distinction between novelty and originality.

5. If a work is presented as factual, may the author later prove in an infringement action that the work was actually fictional in order to counter a defense that only "facts" were copied?

Collateral References

Gorman, *Copyright Protection for the Collection and Representation of Facts,* 76 Harv.Law Rev. 1569 (1963).

Gorman, *Fact or Fancy? The Implications for Copyright,* 29 Journal of the Copyright Society 560 (1982).

Denicola, *Copyright in the Collection of Facts: A Theory for the Protection of Nonfiction Literary Works,* 81 Colum.L.Rev. 516 (1981).

Ginsburg, *Sabotaging and Reconstructing History: A Comment on the Scope of Copyright Protection in Works of History after Hoehling v. Universal City Studios,* 29 J. Copr. Soc'y 647 (1982).

Nimmer on Copyright, § 2.11.

For further information on the copyrightability of factual materials, see *Harper & Row, Publishers, Inc. v. Nation Enterprises,* which may be found in Appendix E.

3. Works of Applied Art

MAZER v. STEIN

Supreme Court of the United States, 1954.
347 U.S. 201, 74 S.Ct. 460, 98 L.Ed. 630.

MR. JUSTICE REED delivered the opinion of the Court.

This case involves the validity of copyrights obtained by respondents for statuettes of male and female dancing figures made of

vived long dormant interest in the Hindenburg. As a result, Hoehling's book, which had been out of print for some time, was actually re-released after the film was featured in theaters across the country.

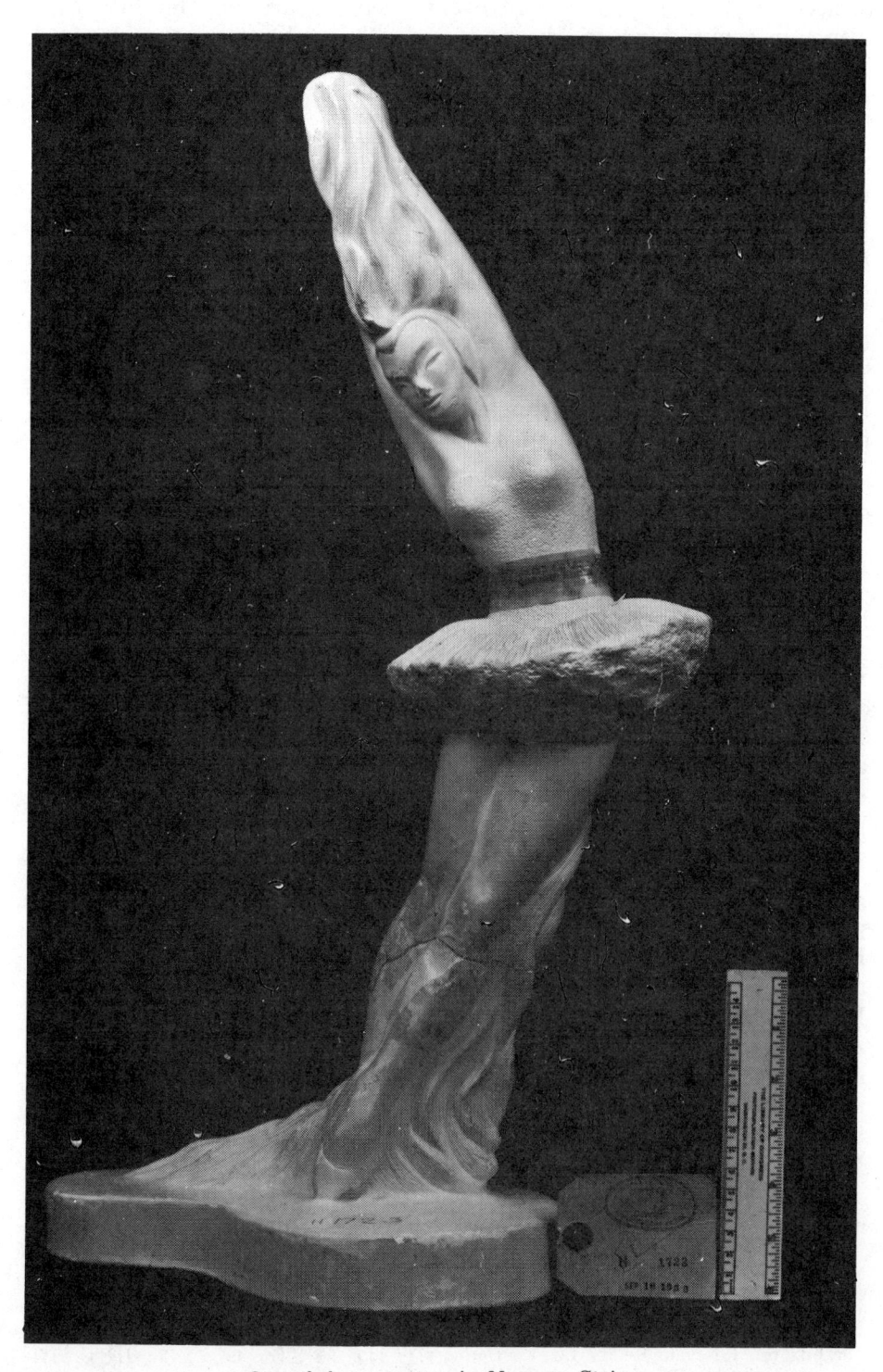

One of the statuettes in *Mazer v. Stein*.

semivitreous china. The controversy centers around the fact that although copyrighted as "works of art," the statuettes were intended for use and used as bases for table lamps, with electric wiring, sockets and lamp shades attached.

Respondents are partners in the manufacture and sale of electric lamps. One of the respondents created original works of sculpture in the form of human figures by traditional clay-model technique. From this model, a production mold for casting copies was made. The resulting statuettes, without any lamp components added, were submitted by the respondents to the Copyright Office for registration as "works of art" or reproductions thereof under § 5(g) or § 5(h) of the copyright law, and certificates of registration issued. * * *

Petitioners are partners and, like respondents, make and sell lamps. Without authorization, they copied the statuettes, embodied them in lamps and sold them.

* * * Petitioners in their petition for certiorari present a single question:

> Can statuettes be protected in the United States by copyright when the copyright applicant intended primarily to use the statuettes in the form of lamp bases to be made and sold in quantity and carried the intentions into effect?
>
> Stripped down to its essentials, the question presented is: Can a lamp manufacturer copyright his lamp bases?

The first paragraph accurately summarizes the issue. The last gives it a quirk that unjustifiably, we think, broadens the controversy. The case requires an answer, not as to a manufacturer's right to register a lamp base but as to an artist's right to copyright a work of art intended to be reproduced for lamp bases. * * *

* * * The constitutional power of Congress to confer copyright protection on works of art or their reproductions is not questioned.[5] Petitioners assume, as Congress has in its enactments and as do we, that the constitutional clause empowering legislation "To promote the Progress of Science and useful Arts, by securing for limited Times to Authors and Inventors the exclusive Right to their respective Writings and Discoveries," Art. I, § 8, cl. 8, includes within the term "Authors" the creator of a picture or a statue. The Court's consideration will be limited to the question presented by the petition for writ of certiorari. * * *

The practice of the Copyright Office, under the 1870 and 1874 Acts and before the 1909 Act, was to allow registration "as works of the fine

---

5. We do not reach for constitutional questions not raised by the parties. Chicago & G.T.R. Co. v. Wellman, 143 U.S. 339, 345, 12 S.Ct. 400, 402, 36 L.Ed. 176; New York ex rel. Rosevale Realty Co. v. Kleinert, 268 U.S. 646, 651, 45 S.Ct. 618, 619, 69 L.Ed. 1135; C.I.O. v. McAdory, 325 U.S. 472, 475, 65 S.Ct. 1395, 1397, 89 L.Ed. 1741. The fact that the issue was mentioned in argument does not bring the question properly before us. Herbring v. Lee, 280 U.S. 111, 117, 50 S.Ct. 49, 51, 74 L.Ed. 217.

* * *

arts" of articles of the same character as those of respondents now under challenge. * * *

* * * The current pertinent regulation, published in 37 CFR, 1949, § 202.8, reads thus:

> *Works of art (Class G)*—(a) *In General.* This class includes works of artistic craftsmanship, in so far as their form but not their mechanical or utilitarian aspects are concerned, such as artistic jewelry, enamels, glassware, and tapestries, as well as all works belonging to the fine arts, such as paintings, drawings and sculpture. * * *

So we have a contemporaneous and long-continued construction of the statutes by the agency charged to administer them that would allow the registration of such a statuette as is in question here.

* * *

The successive acts, the legislative history of the 1909 Act and the practice of the Copyright Office unite to show that "works of art" and "reproductions of works of art" are terms that were intended by Congress to include the authority to copyright these statuettes. Individual perception of the beautiful is too varied a power to permit a narrow or rigid concept of art. As a standard we can hardly do better than the words of the present Regulation, § 202.8, supra, naming the things that appertain to the arts. They must be original, that is, the author's tangible expression of his ideas. Compare Burrow-Giles Lithographic Co. v. Sarony, 111 U.S. 53, 59–60, 4 S.Ct. 279, 281–282, 28 L.Ed. 349. Such expression, whether meticulously delineating the model or mental image or conveying the meaning by modernistic form or color, is copyrightable. * * *

The conclusion that the statues here in issue may be copyrighted goes far to solve the question whether their intended reproduction as lamp stands bars or invalidates their registration. This depends solely on statutory interpretation. Congress may after publication protect by copyright any writing of an author. * * *

As we have held the statuettes here involved copyrightable, we need not decide the question of their patentability. Though other courts have passed upon the issue as to whether allowance by the election of the author or patentee of one bars a grant of the other, we do not. We do hold that the patentability of the statuettes, fitted as lamps or unfitted, does not bar copyright as works of art. Neither the Copyright Statute nor any other says that because a thing is patentable it may not be copyrighted. We should not so hold.

Unlike a patent, a copyright gives no exclusive right to the art disclosed; protection is given only to the expression of the idea—not the idea itself. Thus, in Baker v. Selden, 101 U.S. 99, 25 L.Ed. 841, the Court held that a copyrighted book on a peculiar system of bookkeeping was not infringed by a similar book using a similar plan which achieved similar results where the alleged infringer made a different arrangement of the columns and used different headings. * * * Absent copying there can be no infringement of copyright. Thus, respondents may not exclude others from using statuettes of human figures in table lamps; they may only prevent use of copies of their statuettes as such or as incorporated in some other article. Regulation § 202.8, supra, makes clear that artistic articles are protected in "form but not their mechanical or utilitarian aspects." See Stein v. Rosenthal, 103 F.Supp. 227, 231. The dichotomy of protection for the aesthetic is not beauty and utility but art for the copyright and the invention of original and ornamental design for design patents. We find nothing in the copyright statute to support the argument that the intended use or use in industry of an article eligible for copyright bars or invalidates its registration. We do not read such a limitation into the copyright law.

* * *

The economic philosophy behind the clause empowering Congress to grant patents and copyrights is the conviction that encouragement of individual effort by personal gain is the best way to advance public welfare through the talents of authors and inventors in "Science and useful Arts." Sacrificial days devoted to such creative activities deserve rewards commensurate with the services rendered.

Affirmed.

Opinion of MR. JUSTICE DOUGLAS, in which MR. JUSTICE BLACK concurs.

An important constitutional question underlies this case—a question which was stirred on oral argument but not treated in the briefs. It is whether these statuettes of dancing figures may be copyrighted. Congress has provided that "works of art," "models or designs for works of art," and "reproductions of a work of art" may be copyrighted (17 U.S.C.A. § 5); and the Court holds that these statuettes are included in the words "works of art." But may statuettes be granted the monopoly of the copyright?

Article I, § 8 of the Constitution grants Congress the power "To promote the Progress of Science and useful Arts, by securing for limited Times to Authors * * * the exclusive Right to their respective Writings. * * *" The power is thus circumscribed: it allows a monopoly to be granted only to "authors" for their "writings." Is a sculptor an "author" and is his statue a "writing" within the meaning of the Constitution? We have never decided the question.

Burrow-Giles Lithographic Co. v. Sarony, 111 U.S. 53, 4 S.Ct. 279, 28 L.Ed. 349, held that a photograph could be copyrighted.

Bleistein v. Donaldson Lithographing Co., 188 U.S. 239, 23 S.Ct. 298, 47 L.Ed. 460, held that chromolithographs to be used as advertisements for a circus were "pictorial illustrations" within the meaning of the copyright laws. Broad language was used in the latter case, "* * * a very modest grade of art has in it something irreducible, which is one man's alone. That something he may copyright unless there is a restriction in the words of the act." 188 U.S., at page 250, 23 S.Ct. at page 300. But the constitutional range of the meaning of "writings" in the field of art was not in issue either in the *Bleistein* case nor in

Woolworth Co. v. Contemporary Arts, 344 U.S. 228, recently here on a writ of certiorari limited to a question of damages.

At times the Court has on its own initiative considered and decided constitutional issues not raised, argued, or briefed by the parties. Such, for example, was the case of Continental Bank v. Rock Island R. Co., 294 U.S. 648, 667, 55 S.Ct. 595, 601, 79 L.Ed. 1110, in which the Court decided the constitutionality of § 77 of the Bankruptcy Act though the question was not noticed by any party. We could do the same here and decide the question here and now. This case, however, is not a pressing one, there being no urgency for a decision. Moreover, the constitutional materials are quite meager (see Fenning, The Origin of the Patent and Copyright Clause of the Constitution, 17 Geo.L.J. 109 (1929)); and much research is needed.

The interests involved in the category of "works of art," as used in the copyright law, are considerable. The Copyright Office has supplied us with a long list of such articles which have been copyrighted—statuettes, book ends, clocks, lamps, door knockers, candlesticks, inkstands, chandeliers, piggy banks, sundials, salt and pepper shakers, fish bowls, casseroles, and ash trays. Perhaps these are all "writings" in the constitutional sense. But to me at least, they are not obviously so. It is time that we came to the problem full face. I would accordingly put the case down for reargument.

ESQUIRE, INC. v. RINGER

United States Court of Appeals, District of Columbia Circuit, 1978.
591 F.2d 796.

Before BAZELON, LEVENTHAL and ROBINSON, CIRCUIT JUDGES.

Opinion for the Court filed by CIRCUIT JUDGE BAZELON.

Concurring opinion filed by CIRCUIT JUDGE LEVENTHAL.

BAZELON, CIRCUIT JUDGE:

This case presents the question whether the overall shape of certain outdoor lighting fixtures is eligible for copyright as a "work of art." The Register of Copyrights determined that the overall shape or configuration of such articles is not copyrightable. The district court disagreed, and issued a writ of mandamus directing the Register to enter the claim to copyright. Esquire, Inc. v. Ringer, 414 F.Supp. 939 (D.D.C.1976).[a] For the reasons expressed below, we reverse.

a. Judge Gesell in the district court, in describing the Esquire lighting fixtures, stated: "Surely they would satisfy a Gropius or a Brancusi far more than would a Rembrandt portrait, and to many they are much more artistic than some examples of sculpture found at such museums as the Corcoran or the Hirshhorn. Art through the ages has often served a utilitarian purpose. The Caryatids of the Acropolis or Cellini's exquisite saltcellar are two of many examples of traditional art serving such a purpose. There has always been a close link between art and science. The forms represented by Esquire's fixtures emphasize line and shape rather than the realistic or the ornate but it is not for the Register to reject them on artistic grounds * * * or because the form is accommodated to a utilitarian purpose * * * There cannot

I.

Although the issues involved are fairly complex, the facts may be briefly stated. Appellee, Esquire, Inc. (Esquire) submitted three applications to the Copyright Office for registration of what it described as "artistic design[s] for lighting fixture[s]." Photographs accompanying the applications showed stationary outdoor luminaries or floodlights, of contemporary design, with rounded or elliptically-shaped housings. The applications asserted that the designs were eligible for copyright protection as "works of art." 17 U.S.C. § 5(g).

The Register of Copyrights (Register) refused to register Esquire's claims to copyright. The principal reason given was that Copyright Office regulations, specifically 37 C.F.R. § 202.10(c) (1976), preclude registration of the design of a utilitarian article, such as lighting

One of Esquire's lighting fixtures.

be and there should not be any national standard of what constitutes art and the pleasing forms of the Esquire fixtures are entitled to the same recognition afforded more traditional sculpture." 414 F.Supp. at 941.

fixtures, "when all of the design elements * * * are directly related to the useful functions of the article. * * *" The fixtures, according to the Register's analysis, did not contain "elements, either alone or in combination, which are capable of independent existence as a copyrightable pictorial, graphic, or sculptural work apart from the utilitarian aspect." Esquire twice requested reconsideration of its copyright applications, and was twice refused.

Esquire then filed suit in the district court, seeking a writ of mandamus directing the Register to issue a certificate of copyright for its lighting fixture designs. This time, Esquire met with success. The court, per Judge Gesell, concluded that registration was compelled by Mazer v. Stein, 347 U.S. 201, 74 S.Ct. 460, 98 L.Ed. 630 (1954), where the Supreme Court upheld the copyright of statuettes intended to be mass-produced for use as table lamp bases. The district court reasoned that to uphold the issuance of the copyrights in *Mazer,* but deny Esquire's applications, would amount to affording certain copyright privileges to traditional works of art, but not to abstract, modern art forms. The court went on to find that "[t]he forms of the articles here in dispute are clearly art" and concluded that they were "entitled to the same recognition afforded more traditional sculpture." 414 F.Supp. at 941. The court also suggested that registration of Esquire's designs was compelled by prior "interpretative precedent." Id. This appeal followed.

The heart of the controversy in this case involves, in the district court's words, an "elusive semantic dispute" over the applicable regulation, 37 C.F.R. § 202.10(c). We have divided our analysis of this dispute into two parts: Part II considers whether the Register adopted a permissible interpretation of the regulation; Part III, whether the regulation, as interpreted, was properly applied to the facts presented by Esquire's applications.

II.

A.

Section 5(g) of the Copyright Act of 1909, 17 U.S.C. § 5(g), indicates that "[w]orks of art; models or designs for works of art" are eligible for copyright. The terse language of the statute is more fully elaborated in regulations drafted by the Register pursuant to Congressional authorization. The provision at issue, 37 C.F.R. § 202.10(c), provides as follows:

> (c) If the sole intrinsic function of an article is its utility, the fact that the article is unique and attractively shaped will not qualify it as a work of art. However, if the shape of a utilitarian article incorporates features, such as artistic sculpture, carving, or pictorial representation, which can be identified separately and are capable of existing independently as a work of art, such features will be eligible for registration.

The parties have advanced conflicting interpretations of § 202.-10(c). The Register interprets § 202.10(c) to bar copyright registration of the overall shape or configuration of a utilitarian article, no matter how aesthetically pleasing that shape or configuration may be. As support for this interpretation, the Register notes that the regulation limits copyright protection to features of a utilitarian article that "can be identified separately and are capable of existing independently as a work of art." The Register argues that this reading is required to enforce the congressional policy against copyrighting industrial designs, and that it is supported by the continued practice of the Copyright Office and by legislative history.

Esquire on the other hand, interprets § 202.10(c) to allow copyright registration for the overall shape or design of utilitarian articles as long as the shape or design satisfies the requirements appurtenant to works of art—originality and creativity. Esquire stresses that the first sentence of § 202.10(c) reads in its entirety, "If the *sole* intrinsic function of an article is its utility, the fact that the article is unique and attractively shaped will not qualify it as a work of art." Esquire maintains that it designed its lighting fixtures with the intent of creating "works of modernistic form sculpture," and therefore that their *sole* intrinsic function is not utility. Esquire also contends that the language of § 202.10(c) referring to "features * * * which can be identified separately and are capable of existing independently as a work of art" is not inconsistent with its interpretation. In effect, Esquire asserts that the shape of the lighting fixtures is the "feature" that makes them eligible for copyright as a work of art. Esquire argues that its reading of § 202.10(c) is required by the decisions of the Supreme Court in Mazer v. Stein, 347 U.S. 201, 74 S.Ct. 460, 98 L.Ed. 630 (1954) and Bleistein v. Donaldson Lithographing Co., 188 U.S. 239, 23 S.Ct. 298, 47 L.Ed. 460 (1903).

B.

We conclude that the Register has adopted a reasonable and well-supported interpretation of § 202.10(c).

The Register's interpretation of § 202.10(c) derives from the principle that industrial designs are not eligible for copyright. Congress has repeatedly rejected proposed legislation that would make copyright protection available for consumer or industrial products. Most recently, Congress deleted a proposed section from the Copyright Act of 1976 that would have "create[d] a new limited form of copyright protection for 'original' designs which are clearly a part of a useful article, regardless of whether such designs could stand by themselves, separate from the article itself." In rejecting proposed Title II, Congress noted the administration's concern that to make such designs eligible for copyright would be to create a "new monopoly" having obvious and significant anticompetitive effects.[15] The issues raised by Title II were

---

15. The Register's brief illustrates the problems involved in allowing copyright of the shape of utilitarian articles.

There are several economic considerations that Congress must weigh before deciding whether, for utilitarian articles,

left for further consideration in "more complete hearings" to follow the enactment of the 1976 Act.

In the Register's view, registration of the overall shape or configuration of utilitarian articles would lead to widespread copyright protection for industrial designs. The Register reasons that aesthetic considerations enter into the design of most useful objects. Thus, if overall shape or configuration can qualify as a "work of art," "the whole realm of consumer products—garments, toasters, refrigerators, furniture, bathtubs, automobiles, etc.—and industrial products designed to have aesthetic appeal—subway cars, computers, photocopying machines, typewriters, adding machines, etc.—must also qualify as works of art."

* * *

The regulation in question attempts to define the boundaries between copyrightable "works of art" and noncopyrightable industrial designs. This is an issue of longstanding concern to the Copyright Office, and is clearly a matter in which the Register has considerable expertise.

* * *

The Register's interpretation of § 202.10(c) finds further support in the legislative history of the recently enacted 1976 Copyright Act. Although not applicable to the case before us, the new Act was designed in part to codify and clarify many of the regulations promulgated under the 1909 Act, including those governing "works of art."[23] Thus, the

---

shape alone, no matter how aesthetically pleasing, is enough to warrant copyright protection. First, in the case of some utilitarian objects, like scissors or paper clips, shape is mandated by function. If one manufacturer were given the copyright to the design of such an article, it could completely prevent others from producing the same article. Second, consumer preference sometimes demands uniformity of shape for certain utilitarian articles, like stoves for instance. People simply expect and desire certain everyday useful articles to look the same particular way. Thus, to give one manufacturer the monopoly on such a shape would also be anticompetive [sic]. Third, insofar as geometric shapes are concerned, there are only a limited amount of basic shapes, such as circles, squares, rectangles and ellipses. These shapes are obviously in the public domain and accordingly it would be unfair to grant a monopoly on the use of any particular such shape, no matter how aesthetically well it was integrated into a utilitarian article.

Brief for Appellant at 18–19. See also Note, *Protection for the Artistic Aspects of Articles of Utility*, 72 Harv.L.Rev. 1520, 1532 (1959).

23. The former classification "works of art" has been reformulated as "pictorial, graphic, and sculptural works" under the new Act. 17 U.S.C. § 102(a)(5) (1976). Section 101 of the Act advises that works encompassed within this category

> include two-dimensional and three-dimensional works of fine, graphic, and applied art, photographs, prints and art reproductions, maps, globes, charts, technical drawings, diagrams, and models. Such works shall include *works of artistic craftsmanship insofar as their form but not their mechanical or utilitarian aspects are concerned;* the design of a useful article * * * shall be considered a pictorial, graphic, or sculptural work only if, and only to the extent that, *such design incorporates pictorial, graphic or sculptural features that can be identified separately from, and are capable of existing independently of, the utilitarian aspects of the article.*

17 U.S.C. § 101 (1976). The two italicized passages are drawn from 37 C.F.R. §§ 202.-10(a) and (c), respectively. Section 202.10(a) was expressly endorsed by the Supreme Court in Mazer v. Stein, 347 U.S. 201, 74 S.Ct. 460, 98 L.Ed. 630 (1954). The Committee on the Judiciary incorporated its language into "the definition of 'pictorial, graphic, and sculptural works' in an effort to make clearer the distinction between works of applied art protectable under the bill and industrial designs not subject to copyright protection." H.R.Rep. No. 1476, supra n. 13, at 54, U.S.Code Cong. & Admin.

1976 Act and its legislative history can be taken as an expression of congressional understanding of the scope of protection for utilitarian articles under the old regulations. "Subsequent legislation which declares the intent of an earlier law is not, of course, conclusive * * *. But the later law is entitled to weight when it comes to the problem of construction." Federal Housing Administration v. The Darlington, Inc., 358 U.S. 84, 90, 79 S.Ct. 141, 145, 3 L.Ed.2d 132 (1958).

The House Report indicates that the section of the 1976 Act governing "pictorial, graphic and sculptural works" was intended "to draw as clear a line as possible between copyrightable works of applied art and uncopyrighted works of industrial design." The Report illustrates the distinction in the following terms:

> * * * although the shape of an industrial product may be aesthetically satisfying and valuable, the Committee's intention is not to offer it copyright protection under the bill. Unless the shape of an automobile, airplane, ladies' dress, food processor, television set, or any other industrial product contains some element that, physically or conceptually, can be identified as separable from the utilitarian aspects of that article, the design would not be copyrighted under the bill. The test of separability and independence from "the utilitarian aspects of the article" does not depend upon the nature of the design—that is, <u>even if the appearance of an article is determined by esthetic (as opposed to functional) considerations, only elements, if any, which can be identified separately from the useful article as such are copyrightable</u>. And even if the three dimensional design contains some such element (for example, a carving on the back of a chair or a floral relief design on silver flatware), <u>copyright protection would extend only to that element, and would not cover the over-all configuration of the utilitarian article as such</u>.

H.Rep. No. 1476, 94th Cong., 2d Sess. 55 (1976), U.S.Code Cong. & Admin.News 1976, p. 5668 (emphasis added).

This excerpt is not entirely free from ambiguity. Esquire could arguably draw some support from the statement that a protectable element of a utilitarian article must be separable "physically *or conceptually*" from the utilitarian aspects of the design. But any possible ambiguity raised by this isolated reference disappears when the excerpt is considered in its entirety. The underscored passages indicate unequivocally that the overall design or configuration of a utilitarian object, even if it is determined by aesthetic as well as functional considerations, is not eligible for copyright. Thus the legislative history, taken as congressional understanding of existing law, reinforces the Register's position.

The legislative history of the 1976 Act also supports the Register's practice of ascribing little weight to the phrase "sole intrinsic function." As noted above, see TAN 11 supra, Esquire contends that as

News 1976, p. 5667. The second italicized passage "is an adaption of [§ 202.10(c)], added to the Copyright Office Regulations in the mid-1950's in an effort to implement the Supreme Court's decision in the *Mazer* case." Id. at 54–55, U.S.Code Cong. & Admin.News 1976, p. 5668.

long as the overall shape of a utilitarian article embodies *dual* intrinsic functions—aesthetic and utilitarian—that shape may qualify for registration. But the new Act includes a definition of "useful article," referred to by the House Report as "an adaptation" of the language of § 202.10(c), H.R.Rep. No. 1476, supra n. 13, at 54, U.S.Code Cong. & Admin.News 1976, p. 5668, which provides:

> A "useful article" is an article having *an* intrinsic utilitarian function that is not merely to portray the appearance of the article or to convey information.

17 U.S.C. § 101 (1976) (emphasis added). In deleting the modifier "sole" from the language taken from § 202.10(c), the draftsmen of the 1976 Act must have concluded that the definition of "useful article" would be more precise without this term. Moreover, Congress may have concluded that literal application of the phrase "sole intrinsic function" would create an unworkable standard. For as one commentator has observed, "[t]here are no two-dimensional works and few three-dimensional objects whose design is absolutely dictated by utilitarian considerations." [25]

C.

The district court basically ignored the foregoing considerations. Instead, it advanced two reasons for rejecting the Register's interpretation of § 202.10(c) as a matter of law. It concluded, first, that the Register's construction was inconsistent with the Supreme Court's decision in Mazer v. Stein, 347 U.S. 201, 79 S.Ct. 141, 3 L.Ed.2d 132 (1954). Second, it found that the Register's interpretation amounted to impermissible discrimination against abstract modern art. We respectfully disagree on both counts.

We are unable to join in the district court's broad reading of Mazer v. Stein, supra.[26] The principal issue in *Mazer* was whether objects that are concededly "works of art" can be copyrighted if incorporated into mass-produced utilitarian articles. * * *

The issue here—whether the overall shape of a utilitarian object is "an article eligible for copyright"—was not addressed in *Mazer*. In fact, under the Register's interpretation of § 202.10(c), the dancing figures considered in *Mazer* would clearly be copyrightable. The statuettes were undeniably capable of existing as a work of art independent of the utilitarian article into which they were incorporated. And they were clearly a "feature" segregable from the overall shape of the table lamps. There is thus no inconsistency between the copyright upheld in *Mazer* and the Register's interpretation of § 202.10(c) here.

---

25. Comment, *Copyright Protection for Mass-Produced, Commercial Products: A Review of the Developments Following Mazer v. Stein*, 38 U.Chi.L.Rev. 807, 812 (1971).

26. A number of authorities are in agreement that *Mazer* should not be read as opening the door to the inclusion of industrial designs under copyright law. See B. Kaplan, *An Unhurried View of Copyright* 55 (1968); 38 U.Chi.L.Rev. supra note 25, at 823; 72 Harv.L.Rev., supra, n. 15, at 1526.

The district court's second conclusion is somewhat problematical. The court found, in effect, that that Register's interpretation of § 202.10(c) amounted to impermissible discrimination against designs that "emphasize line and shape rather than the realistic or the ornate * * *." 414 F.Supp. at 941.

We agree with the district court that the Copyright Act does not enshrine a particular conception of what constitutes "art." Id.[27] As Justice Holmes noted in Bleistein v. Donaldson Lithographing Co., 188 U.S. 239, 251, 23 S.Ct. 298, 300, 47 L.Ed. 460 (1903), "[i]t would be a dangerous undertaking for persons trained only to the law to constitute themselves final judges of the worth of pictorial illustrations * * *." Neither the Constitution nor the Copyright Act authorizes the Copyright Office or the federal judiciary to serve as arbiters of national taste. These officials have no particular competence to assess the merits of one genre of art relative to another. And to allow them to assume such authority would be to risk stultifying the creativity and originality the copyright laws were expressly designed to encourage. Id. at 251–52, 23 S.Ct. 298; accord, Mazer v. Stein, supra at 214, 79 S.Ct. 141.

But in our view the present case does not offend the nondiscrimination principle recognized in *Bleistein*. *Bleistein* was concerned only with conscious bias against one form of art—in that case the popular art reflected in circus posters. Esquire's complaint, in effect, is that the Register's interpretation of § 202.10(c) places an inadvertent burden on a particular form of art, namely modern abstract sculpture. We may concede, for present purposes, that an interpretation of § 202.10(c) that bars copyright for the overall design or configuration of a utilitarian object will have a disproportionate impact on designs that exhibit the characteristics of abstract sculpture. But we can see no justification, at least in the circumstances of this case, for extending the nondiscrimination principle of *Bleistein* to include action having an unintentional, disproportionate impact on one style of artistic expression. Such an extension of the nondiscrimination principle would undermine other plainly legitimate goals of copyright law—in this case the congressional directive that copyright protection should not be afforded to industrial designs.

* * *

For the aforesaid reasons, the decision of the district court is Reversed.

Questions

1. Was the *Esquire* court correct in equating § 202.10(c) of the 1909 Act Regulations with the definition of "useful article" in Section 101 of the 1976 Act?

---

27. The House Report accompanying the 1976 Copyright Act reaffirms this principle. "[T]he definition of 'pictorial, graphic, and sculptural works' carries with it no implied criterion of artistic taste, aesthetic value, or intrinsic quality." H.R.Rep. No. 1476, supra n. 13, at 54, U.S.Code Cong. & Admin. News 1976, p. 5667.

2. If you had been representing the copyright claimant, what arguments might you have made in answer to the Register's arguments contained in the opinion at footnote 15?

3. Was the *Esquire* court's attempt to distinguish *Mazer* convincing? Were the dancing figures in the Mazer lamp "a 'feature' segregable from the overall shape of the table lamps"? Since the dancing figures constituted the lamp base, could the figures be physically removed without affecting "the overall shape of the table lamps"? How does that bear upon the *Esquire* court's conclusion that in order to be copyrightable the artistic aspect of a utilitarian work must be physically, not merely conceptually, separable?

Collateral References

Nimmer on Copyright, § 2.08[B][3].

KIESELSTEIN–CORD v. ACCESSORIES BY PEARL, INC.

United States Court of Appeals, Second Circuit, 1980.
632 F.2d 989.

Before OAKES and VAN GRAAFEILAND, CIRCUIT JUDGES, and WEINSTEIN, DISTRICT JUDGE.

OAKES, CIRCUIT JUDGE:

This case is on a razor's edge of copyright law. It involves belt buckles, utilitarian objects which as such are not copyrightable. But these are not ordinary buckles; they are sculptured designs cast in precious metals—decorative in nature and used as jewelry is, principally for ornamentation. We say "on a razor's edge" because the case requires us to draw a fine line under applicable copyright law and regulations. Drawing the line in favor of the appellant designer, we uphold the copyrights granted to him by the Copyright Office and reverse the district court's grant of summary judgment, 489 F.Supp. 732, in favor of the appellee, the copier of appellant's designs.

FACTS

Appellant Barry Kieselstein-Cord designs, manufactures exclusively by handcraftsmanship, and sells fashion accessories. To produce the two buckles in issue here, the "Winchester" and the "Vaquero," he worked from original renderings which he had conceived and sketched. He then carved by hand a waxen prototype of each of the works from which molds were made for casting the objects in gold and silver. Difficult to describe, the buckles are solid sculptured designs, in the words of district court Judge Goettel, "with rounded corners, a sculpted surface, * * * a rectangular cutout at one end for the belt attachment," and "several surface levels." The Vaquero gives the appearance of two curved grooves running diagonally across one corner of a modified rectangle and a third groove running across the opposite corner. On the Winchester buckle two parallel grooves cut horizontally across the center of a more tapered form, making a curving ridge which is completed by the tongue of the buckle. A smaller single curved groove flows diagonally across the corner above the tongue.

The Vaquero buckle, created in 1978, was part of a series of works that the designer testified was inspired by a book on design of the art nouveau school and the subsequent viewing of related architecture on a trip to Spain. The buckle was registered with the Copyright Office by appellant's counsel on March 3, 1980, with a publication date of June 1, 1978, as "jewelry," although the appellant's contribution was listed on the certificate as "original sculpture and design." Explaining why he named the earlier buckle design "Winchester," the designer said that he saw "in [his] mind's eye a correlation between the art nouveau period and the butt of an antique Winchester rifle" and then "pulled these elements together graphically." The registration, which is recorded on a form used for works of art, or models or designs for works of art, specifically describes the nature of the work as "sculpture."

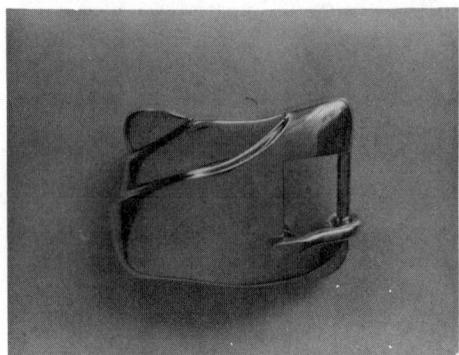

The Vaquero buckle.

The Winchester buckle.

The Winchester buckle in particular has had great success in the marketplace: more than 4,000 belts with Winchester buckles were sold from 1976 to early 1980, and in 1979 sales of the belts amounted to 95% of appellant's more than $300,000 in jewelry sales. A small women's size in silver with "double truncated triangle belt loops" sold, at the time this lawsuit commenced, at wholesale for $147.50 and a larger silver version for men sold at wholesale with loops for $662 and without loops for $465. Lighter-weight men's versions in silver wholesaled for $450 and $295, with and without loops respectively. The gold versions sold at wholesale from $1,200 to $6,000. A shortened version of the belt with the small Winchester buckle is sometimes worn around the neck or elsewhere on the body rather than around the waist. Sales of both buckles were made primarily in high fashion stores and jewelry stores, bringing recognition to appellant as a "designer." This recognition included a 1979 Coty American Fashion Critics' Award for his work in jewelry design as well as election in 1978 to the Council of Fashion Designers of America. Both the Winchester and the Vaquero buckles, donated by appellant after this lawsuit was commenced, have been accepted by the Metropolitan Museum of Art for its permanent collection.

As the court below found, appellee's buckles "appear to be line-for-line copies but are made of common metal rather than" precious metal. Appellee admitted to copying the Vaquero and selling its imitations, and to selling copies of the Winchester. Indeed some of the order blanks of appellee's customers specifically referred to "Barry K Copy," "BK copy," and even "Barry Kieselstein Knock-off." Thus the only legal questions for the court below were whether the articles may be protected under the copyright statutes and, if so, whether the copyrights were adequate under the laws. Having found that the copyrights were invalid—the Winchester under the Copyright Act of 1909, and the Vaquero under the 1976 Act [1]—because they "fail[ed] to satisfy the test of separability and independent existence of the artistic features, which is required under both statutes," * * *.

We * * * only reach the question whether the buckles may be copyrighted.

Discussion

We commence our discussion by noting that no claim has been made that the appellant's work here in question lacks originality or creativity, elements necessary for copyrighting works of art. See L. Batlin & Son, Inc. v. Snyder, 536 F.2d 486 (2d Cir.), cert. denied, 429 U.S. 857, 97 S.Ct. 156, 50 L.Ed.2d 135 (1976); Alfred Bell & Co. v. Catalda Fine Arts, Inc., 191 F.2d 99 (2d Cir.1951); 1 Nimmer on Copyright §§ 2.01, 2.08[B] (1980). The thrust of appellee's argument, as well as of the court's decision below, is that appellant's buckles are not copyrightable because they are "useful articles" with no "pictorial, graphic, or sculptural features that can be identified separately from, and are capable of existing independently of, the utilitarian aspects" of the buckles. The 1976 copyright statute does not provide for the copyrighting of useful articles except to the extent that their designs

---

1. The Winchester buckle was registered before the January 1, 1978, effective date of the Copyright Act of 1976.

incorporate artistic features that can be identified separately from the functional elements of the articles. See 17 U.S.C. §§ 101, 102. With respect to this question, the law adopts the language of the longstanding Copyright Office regulations, 37 C.F.R. § 202.10(c) (1977) * * * The regulations in turn were adopted in the mid-1950's, under the 1909 Act, in an effort to implement the Supreme Court's decision in Mazer v. Stein, 347 U.S. 201, 74 S.Ct. 460, 98 L.Ed. 630 (1954). * * * The Court in *Mazer,* it will be recalled, upheld the validity of copyrights obtained for statuettes of male and female dancing figures despite the fact that they were intended for use and used as bases for table lamps, with electric wiring, sockets, and lampshades attached. *Mazer* itself followed a "contemporaneous and long-continued construction" by the Copyright Office of the 1870 and 1874 Acts as well as of the 1909 Act, under which the case was decided. 347 U.S. at 211–13, 74 S.Ct. at 467. As Professor Nimmer points out, however, the Copyright Office's regulations in the mid-1950's that purported to "implement" this decision actually limited the Court's apparent open-ended extension of copyright protection to all aesthetically pleasing useful articles. See 1 Nimmer, supra, § 2.08[B], at 2–88 to 2–89.

Ultimately, as Professor Nimmer concludes, none of the authorities—the *Mazer* opinion, the old regulations, or the statute—offer any "ready answer to the line-drawing problem inherent in delineating the extent of copyright protection available for works of applied art." Id. at 2–89. Congress in the 1976 Act may have somewhat narrowed the sweep of the former regulations by defining a "useful article" as one with "*an* intrinsic utilitarian function," 17 U.S.C. § 101 (emphasis added), instead of one, in the words of the old regulations, with utility as its "*sole* intrinsic function," 37 C.F.R. § 202.10(c) (1977) (revoked Jan. 5, 1978, 43 Fed.Reg. 965, 966 (1978)) (emphasis added).

We are left nevertheless with the problem of determining when a pictorial, graphic, or sculptural feature "can be identified separately from, and [is] capable of existing independently of, the utilitarian aspects of the article," 17 U.S.C. § 101. This problem is particularly difficult because, according to the legislative history explored by the court below, such separability may occur either "physically or conceptually," *House Report* at 55, * * * Examples of conceptual separateness as an artistic notion may be found in many museums today and even in the great outdoors. Professor Nimmer cites Christo's "Running Fence" as an example of today's "conceptual art": it "did not contain sculptural features that were physically separable from the utilitarian aspects of the fence, but the whole point of the work was that the artistic aspects of the work were conceptually separable." 1 Nimmer, supra, § 2.08[B] at 2–94.

Appellee argues that the belt buckles are merely useful objects, which include decorative features that serve an aesthetic as well as a utilitarian purpose. And the copyright laws, appellee points out, were never intended to nor would the Constitution permit them to protect monopolies on useful articles. But appellee goes too far by further arguing that "copyrightability cannot adhere in the 'conceptual' separation of an artistic element." Brief for Defendant-Appellee at 17. This assertion flies in the face of the legislative intent as expressed in the House Report, which specifically refers to elements that "physically or conceptually, can be identified as separable from the utilitarian aspects of" a useful article. *House Report* at 55, [1976] U.S.Code Cong. & Admin.News at 5668.

We see in appellant's belt buckles conceptually separable sculptural elements, as apparently have the buckles' wearers who have used them as ornamentation for parts of the body other than the waist. The primary ornamental aspect of the Vaquero and Winchester buckles is conceptually separable from their subsidiary utilitarian function. * *

Appellant's designs are not, as the appellee suggests in an affidavit, mere variations of "the well-known western buckle." As both the expert witnesses for appellant testified and the Copyright Office's action implied, the buckles rise to the level of creative art. Indeed, body ornamentation has been an art form since the earliest days, as anyone who has seen the Tutankhamen or Scythian gold exhibits at the Metropolitan Museum will readily attest. The basic requirements of originality and creativity, which the two buckles satisfy and which all works of art must meet to be copyrighted, would take the vast majority of belt buckles wholly out of copyrightability. The Copyright Office continually engages in the drawing of lines between that which may be and that which may not be copyrighted. It will, so long as the statute remains in its present form, always be necessary to determine whether in a given case there is a physically or conceptually separable artistic sculpture or carving capable of existing independently as a work of art.

We reverse the grant of summary judgment to the appellee and remand the case for consideration of whether appellant has satisfied the copyright notice requirements.

WEINSTEIN, DISTRICT JUDGE (dissenting):

Questions

1. Is the *Esquire* decision reconcilable with the *Kieselstein-Cord* decision in its reasoning? In its result?

2. Assuming that conceptual separability, without physical separability, is sufficient to accord copyright in a work of applied art, what are the standards for determining the presence of conceptual separability? The House Report indicated that there is not even conceptual separability in the shape of the ordinary "automobile, ladies' [sic] dress, food processor, [and] television set." H.Rep., p. 55. How then may it be argued that there is conceptual separability in the *Kieselstein-Cord* belt buckles? How significant is the court's statement that "the buckles' wearers * * * have used them as ornamentation for parts of the body other than the waist"? Does this suggest a test of conceptual separability based upon the nature of consumer demand? Would anyone purchase an attractively shaped automobile if it did not have an engine?

3. Is copyright less justified and the inhibition on competition more pernicious, if the work depicts not a Balinese dancer, as in *Mazer*, but an abstract design as in *Esquire* and *Kieselstein-Cord?*

Collateral References

Nimmer on Copyright, § 2.08[B][3].

Denicola, *Applied Art and Industrial Design: A Suggested Approach to Copyright in Useful Articles*, 67 Minn.L.Rev. 707 (1983).

Reichman, *Design Protection in Domestic and Foreign Copyright Law: From the Berne Revision of 1948 to the Copyright Act of 1976*, 1983 Duke L.J. 1143 (1983).

4. *Characters*

JUDGE LEARNED HAND in Nichols v. Universal Pictures Corp., 45 F.2d 119, 121 (2d Cir.1930): " * * * we do not doubt that two plays may correspond in plot closely enough for infringement. How far that correspondence must go is another matter. Nor need we hold that the same may not be true as to the characters, quite independently of the 'plot' proper, though, as far as we know, such a case has never arisen. If Twelfth Night were copyrighted, it is quite possible that a second comer might so closely imitate Sir Toby Belch or Malvolio as to infringe, but it would not be enough that for one of his characters he cast a riotous knight who kept wassail to the discomfort of the household, or a vain and foppish steward who became amorous of his mistress. These would be no more than Shakespeare's 'ideas' in the play, as little capable of monopoly as Einstein's Doctrine of Relativity, or Darwin's theory of the Origin of Species. It follows that the less developed the characters, the less they can be copyrighted; that is the penalty an author must bear for marking them too indistinctly."

WARNER BROTHERS PICTURES v. COLUMBIA BROADCASTING SYSTEM

United States Court of Appeals, Ninth Circuit, 1954.
216 F.2d 945.

Before STEPHENS and FEE, CIRCUIT JUDGES, and CLARK, DISTRICT JUDGE.

STEPHENS, CIRCUIT JUDGE. Dashiell Hammett composed a mystery-detective story entitled "The Maltese Falcon" which was published serially, and each installment was copyrighted by the publisher. Subsequently, Alfred A. Knopf, Inc., entered into a contract with the author to publish the work in book form, Knopf published the book and, in accord with the terms of the contract, copyrighted it.

In 1930, after publication in book form and after publication of all installments of the first serial thereof, Knopf and Hammett, designated as "Owners", for a consideration of $8,500.00, granted certain defined rights in and to The Maltese Falcon (called "writings" in the agreement) to Warner Bros., as "Purchaser". Coincidentally, Knopf executed an instrument to Warner called "Assignment of Copyright" for a nominal consideration. The text of the "assignment" shows on its face that it is not an assignment of the copyright but that it is a grant to Warner of specified rights to the use of the writings in The Maltese Falcon. Both the contract between Hammett-Knopf and Warner, and the "assignment" from Knopf, purport to grant to Warner certain defined and detailed exclusive rights to the use of The Maltese Falcon "writings" in moving pictures, radio, and television.

By the common law, the author of a writing possesses the sole and exclusive right to publish it, but upon and after the first publication the writing may be published by anyone including the author, since the writing has gone into the public domain. Bobbs-Merrill Co. v. Straus, 1908, 210 U.S. 339, 28 S.Ct. 722, 52 L.Ed. 1086; Bobbs-Merrill Co. v. Straus, 2 Cir., 1908, 147 F. 15, 15 L.R.A.,N.S., 766; Harper & Bros. v. M.A. Donohue & Co., C.C.1905, 144 F. 491. The copyright statute extends the author's sole and exclusive right in accordance with its terms and provisions. Constitution of the United States, Art. I, § 8, Clause 8; Title 17 U.S.C.A.; Bobbs-Merrill Co. v. Straus, 1908, 210 U.S. 339, 28 S.Ct. 722, 52 L.Ed. 1086; Bobbs-Merrill Co. v. Straus, 2 Cir., 1908, 147 F. 15, 15 L.R.A.,N.S., 766. In other words, it reserves the writing from the public domain for the effective period of the copyright. What we have just said is what is meant by courts when they say: "When the copyright comes in, the common law right goes out."

No question as to the legality of the copyright on The Maltese Falcon or to its continuing effectiveness through all times in suit, or to its complete beneficial ownership by Hammett and Knopf together, is in issue. Therefore, at the effective moment of the grants by Hammett and Knopf to Warner, the latter became possessed of the sole and exclusive right to the writing which is within the copyright, less all limiting terms of the grants. The grants are limited to defined uses in motion picture, talking pictures, radio, and television.

It is claimed by Warner that it acquired the exclusive right to the use of the writing, The Maltese Falcon, including the individual characters and their names, together with the title, "The Maltese Falcon", in motion pictures, radio, and television. The use of the title is not in issue, since the grant to Warner specifically includes it.

It is the position of Hammett and the other defendants, all of whom claim some interest under him, that the rights acquired by Warner are those specifically mentioned in the conveying or granting instruments, and that the exclusive right to the use of the characters and/or their names were not mentioned as being granted; that the instruments, properly construed, do not convey any exclusive right to the use of characters with or without names, hence Hammett could use them in other stories. However, if, by reason of the silence in the instruments as to such claimed rights, the instruments should be held to be ambiguous on this point, the custom and practice demonstrate that such rights are not customarily parted with by authors, but that characters which are depicted in one detective story together with their names are customarily retained and used in the intricacies of subsequent but different tales.

Hammett did so use the characters with their names and did contract with others for such use. In 1946 he used The Maltese Falcon characters including Sam Spade, the detective and the leading charac-

Humphrey Bogart as Sam Spade in the Warner Bros. film, holding the Maltese Falcon.

ter in the Falcon, by name, and granted to third parties the sole and exclusive right, except their use in the Falcon, to use that character by name (later orally enlarged to include other characters of the Falcon) in radio, television, and motion pictures. Under such claimed rights, radio broadcasts of "Adventures of Sam Spade", including "The Kandy Tooth" were broadcast in weekly half-hour episodes from 1946 to 1950.

Warner claims infringement of copyright and "unfair use and competition" by such re-use and, as well, for infringement of parts of the story and the whole of the writing inclusive of characters and their names. Hammett and the other defendants deny infringement or unfair use and competition on any count, and Hammett requests the court to declare his rights in the premises. Knopf is a nominal party asking and claiming nothing, and is made a plaintiff under the right granted Warner in the Hammett-Knopf-Warner contract.

The trial court denied relief to Warner, declared Hammett's rights, and assessed costs against Warner, who appeals.

The instruments under which Warner claims were prepared by Warner Bros. Corporation which is a large, experienced moving picture producer. It would seem proper, therefore, to construe the instruments under the assumption that the claimant knew what it wanted and that in defining the items in the instruments which it desired and intended to take, it included all of the items it was contracting to take. We are of the opinion that since the use of characters and character names are nowhere specifically mentioned in the agreements, but that other items, including the title, "The Maltese Falcon", and their use are specifically mentioned as being granted, that the character rights with the names cannot be held to be within the grants, and that under the doctrine of *ejusdem generis,* general language cannot be held to include them. As was said in Phillip v. Jerome H. Remick & Co., S.D.N.Y., Op. No. 9,999, 1936, "Such doubt as there is should be resolved in favor of the composer. The clearest language is necessary to divest the author of the fruits of his labor. Such language is lacking here." See, also, Tobani v. Carl Fischer, Inc., 1942, 263 App.Div. 503, 507, 33 N.Y.S.2d 294, 299, affirmed 1942, 289 N.Y. 727, 46 N.E.2d 347.

The conclusion that these rights are not within the granting instruments is strongly buttressed by the fact that historically and presently detective fiction writers have and do carry the leading characters with their names and individualisms from one story into succeeding stories. This was the practice of Edgar Allen Poe, Sir Arthur Conan Doyle, and others; and in the last two decades of S.S. Van Dine, Earle Stanley Gardner, and others. The reader's interest thereby snowballs as new "capers" of the familiar characters are related in succeeding tales. If the intention of the contracting parties had been to avoid this practice which was a very valuable one to the author, it is hardly reasonable that it would be left to a general clause following specific grants. Another buttressing fact is that Hammett wrote and caused to be published in 1932, long after the Falcon agreements, three stories in which some of the leading characters of the Falcon were featured, and no objection was voiced by Warner. It is also of some note that the evidence shows that Columbia, long subsequent to the conveying instruments, dickered with Warner for the use of the Falcon on its "Suspense" radio program and, failing in its efforts, substituted "The Kandy Tooth" which uses the Falcon characters under license of Hammett. Warner made no claim against Columbia at or reasonably soon afterward. The conclusion we have come to, as to the intention of the parties, would seem to be in harmony with the fact that the purchase price paid by Warner was $8,500.00, which would seem inadequate compensation for the complete surrender of the characters made famous by the popular reception of the book, The Maltese Falcon; and that the intention of the parties, inclusive of the "Assignment", was not that Hammett should be deprived of using the Falcon characters in subsequently written stories, and that the contract, properly construed, does not deprive Hammett of their use.

Up to this point we have discussed the points at issue by construing the contract and by seeking the intention of the parties to it, and we have concluded that the parties never intended by their contract to buy and sell the future use of the personalities in the writing.

It will now be profitable to consider whether it was ever intended by the copyright statute that characters with their names should be under its protection.

The practice of writers to compose sequels to stories is old, and the copyright statute, though amended several times, has never specifically mentioned the point. It does not appear that it has ever been adjudicated, although it is mentioned in Nichols v. Universal Pictures Corp., 2 Cir., 1930, 45 F.2d 119. If Congress had intended that the sale of the right to publish a copyrighted story would foreclose the author's use of its characters in subsequent works for the life of the copyright, it would seem Congress would have made specific provision therefor. Authors work for the love of their art no more than other professional people work in other lines of work for the love of it. There is the financial motive as well. The characters of an author's imagination and the art of his descriptive talent, like a painter's or like a person with his penmanship, are always limited and always fall into limited patterns.[5] The restriction argued for is unreasonable, and would effect the very opposite of the statute's purpose which is to encourage the production of the arts.

---

5. "He must be a poor creature that does not often repeat himself. Imagine the author of the excellent piece of advice, 'Know thyself', never alluding to that sentiment again during the course of a protracted existence! Why, the truths a man carries about with him are his tools; and do you think a carpenter is bound to use the same plane but once to smooth a knotty board with, or to hang up his hammer after it has driven its first nail? I shall never repeat a conversation, but an idea, often. I shall use the same types when I like, but not commonly the same stereotypes. A thought is often original, though you have uttered it a hundred times. It has come to you over a new route, by a new and express train of associations." *The Autocrat of the Breakfast Table*, by O.W. Holmes, M.D., p. 9, reprint of original edition.

It is our conception of the area covered by the copyright statute that when a study of the two writings is made and it is plain from the study that one of them is not in fact the creation of the putative author, but instead has been copied in substantial part exactly or in transparent re-phrasing to produce essentially the story of the other writing, it infringes.

It is conceivable that the character really constitutes the story being told, but if the character is only the chessman in the game of telling the story he is not within the area of the protection afforded by the copyright. The subject is given consideration in the Nichols case, supra, 45 F.2d at page 121 of the citation. At page 122 of 45 F.2d of the same case the court remarks that the line between infringement and non-infringement is indefinite and may seem arbitrary when drawn; nevertheless it must be drawn. Nichols v. Universal Pictures Corp., 2 Cir., 1930, 45 F.2d 119. See Warner Bros. Pictures v. Majestic Pictures Corp., 2 Cir., 70 F.2d 310, 311.

We conclude that even if the Owners assigned their complete rights in the copyright to the Falcon, such assignment did not prevent the author from using the characters used therein, in other stories. The characters were vehicles for the story told, and the vehicles did not go with the sale of the story. * * *

Reversed and affirmed in part.

Questions

1. Does the Court in the instant case, popularly known as the *Sam Spade* case, follow the Learned Hand dicta in Nichols v. Universal?

2. Is the copyright portion of the *Sam Spade* opinion holding or dicta? Is this a meaningful distinction? For further on the contract issue, i.e., whether and when sequel rights are conveyed by contract, see Trust Co. Bank v. MGM/UA Entertainment Co., 593 F.Supp. 580 (N.D.Ga.1984) (sequel rights in *Gone With the Wind* not conveyed).

3. What would be an example of a character that "really constitutes the story being told" and is not merely a "chessman in the game of telling the story"?

4. Assuming the Sherlock Holmes stories were fully protected by copyright, should it constitute an act of copyright infringement for an unauthorized person to write new stories with Holmes and Dr. Watson as the principal characters? What if some of Conan Doyle's Holmes stories have entered the public domain, and others retain copyright protection, should it constitute copyright infringement (a) to copy the stories which are in the public domain?; (b) to copy the stories which retain copyright?; (c) to write new stories using the Holmes and Watson characters?

5. If the view espoused in the *Sam Spade* case were generally followed, how would it affect the value of television series? In this connection see Goodis v. United Artists Television, Inc., p. 308 infra.

Collateral References

Brylawski, "Protection of Characters—Sam Spade Revisited", 22 Bull.Cr. Soc. 77 (1974).

Nimmer on Copyright, § 2.12.

WALT DISNEY PRODUCTIONS v. THE AIR PIRATES

United States Court of Appeals, Ninth Circuit, 1978.
581 F.2d 751.

Before CHAMBERS, CUMMINGS * and ANDERSON, CIRCUIT JUDGES.

CUMMINGS, CIRCUIT JUDGE.

This case involves the admitted copying of plaintiff Walt Disney Productions' ("Disney") cartoon characters in defendants' adult "counter-culture" comic books. The present defendants are three individuals and two business entities operated by them. The complaint alleges that they infringed Disney copyrights, a Disney trademark and engaged in unfair competition, trade disparagement and interference with Disney's business. Disney sought injunctive relief, destruction of infringing materials, damages, costs and attorney's fees.

The district court awarded Disney a temporary restraining order and subsequently granted its motion for a preliminary injunction, simultaneously issuing an opinion reported in 345 F.Supp. 108 (N.D.Cal. 1972). As Judge Wollenberg noted in his opinion, the basic facts are undisputed. He found as follows (at 109–110):

Plaintiff holds valid copyrights on the various works noted in the first seven causes of action. The works protected by the copyrights comprise a series of cartoon drawings ranging from a single page to "book length." The cartoons depict the antics of characters created by plaintiff, with "balloons" over each of the characters' heads containing dialog. Cartoons are drawn to form a narrative.

According to plaintiff, defendants infringed Disney copyrights by copying the graphic depiction of over 17 characters. Two of the characters are represented as insects, and the others as animals endowed with human qualities. Each character has a recognizable image.

The individual defendants have participated in preparing and publishing two magazines of cartoons entitled "Air Pirates Funnies." The characters in defendants' magazines bear a marked similarity to those of plaintiff. The names given to defendants' characters are the same names used in plaintiff's copyrighted work. However, the themes of defendants' publications differ markedly from those of Disney. While Disney sought only to foster "an image of innocent delightfulness," defendants supposedly sought to convey an allegorical message of

---

* The Honorable Walter J. Cummings, United States Circuit Judge, Seventh Circuit, sitting by designation.

significance. Put politely by one commentator, the "Air Pirates" was "an 'underground' comic book which had placed several well-known Disney cartoon characters in incongruous settings where they engaged in activities clearly antithetical to the accepted Mickey Mouse world of scrubbed faces, bright smiles and happy endings." It centered around "a rather bawdy depiction of the Disney characters as active members of a free thinking, promiscuous, drug ingesting counterculture." Note, Parody, Copyrights and the First Amendment, 10 U.S.F.L.Rev. 564, 571, 582 (1976).

Mickey Mouse
Certified by the Ninth Circuit as a copyrightable character.

In awarding Disney a preliminary injunction, the district court held that Disney's graphic depictions were protectable under Section 3 of the then Copyright Act [7] as component parts of Disney's copyrighted work. Next, the defense of fair use was rejected because defendants had copied the substance of the Disney products. Finally, after balancing the competing interests of free speech and press versus "encouraging creation by protecting expression" of ideas as reflected in the Copyright Clause of the Constitution,[8] the district court held that the

---

7. Section 3 provided:

"The copyright provided by this title shall protect all the copyrightable component parts of the work copyrighted, and all matter therein in which copyright is already subsisting, but without extending the duration or scope of such copyright. The copyright upon composite works or periodicals shall give to the proprietor thereof all the rights in respect thereto which he would have if each part were individually copyrighted under this title."

8. Article I, § 8, Cl. 8, empowers the Congress

"To promote the Progress of Science and useful Arts, by securing for limited Times to Authors and Inventors the exclusive Right to their respective Writings and Discoveries."

First Amendment did not bar the issuance of a preliminary injunction (at 115–116).

Three years after granting the preliminary injunction, the district court granted summary judgment for plaintiff because the issues were "purely legal and ripe for decision" (R. 512). In its unreported summary judgment order, the court followed the rationale of its preliminary injunction opinion, adding that defendants' parody of Disney's copyrighted work without the consent of Disney "may not be achieved through outright copying of the original work" (R. 514). The court considered it immaterial that in some instances defendants used the challenged cartoon figures in different plots than Disney's or portrayed them with altered personalities, stating that "The test is whether the figures drawn by Defendants are substantial copies of the work of Plaintiff" (R. 515). The court concluded that defendants' challenged publications constituted trade[mark] infringements (concerning the Disney "Silly Symphony" trademark) and violated Disney's valid copyrights and that defendants were guilty of "unfair competition in the form of trade disparagement". In addition to granting Disney a permanent injunction, the court ordered defendants to deliver all infringing materials to Disney's counsel. Costs were awarded to Disney, and the amount of damages and reasonable attorney's fees to be paid to Disney was submitted to a magistrate for preliminary assessment. Only the question of defendants' liability is before us. We affirm as to copyright violation and reverse and remand as to the remainder.

I. Copyright Infringement

The issue that has attracted the most attention from the parties in this case is whether defendants' copies of the images of Disney's characters are infringements of Disney's copyright. In order to answer the subsidiary questions of whether Disney's characters are copyrightable and if so whether they were infringed, and whether defendants' infringement can be excused by the fair use defense or can be protected by the First Amendment, it is important to begin by noting what statute is controlling. In a post-argument letter, defendants claim that the Copyright Act of 1976, which took effect on January 1, 1978, must provide the controlling standards even though it became law after the entry of judgment below. See Bradley v. School Board of the City of Richmond, 416 U.S. 696, 711–721, 94 S.Ct. 2006, 40 L.Ed.2d 476. While this claim is based on a generally valid rule of law, that rule does not apply where there is a "statutory direction * * * to the contrary." Id. at 711, 94 S.Ct. 2006. The new Copyright Act expressly provides that all causes of action that arose under the Copyright Act before January 1, 1978, "shall be governed by title 17 as it existed when the cause of action arose." Public Law 94–553, 90 Stat. 2600 (Transitional and Supplementary Provisions § 112), reproduced in 17 U.S.C. § 501 note. Therefore to the extent the legal issues in this case are controlled by statute, the old Copyright Act governs.

Sec. C   WORKS OF AUTHORSHIP   83

A. Copyrightability

In some instances Disney's copyrights cover a book and others an entire strip of several cartoon panels. The fact that its characters are not the separate subject of a copyright does not preclude their protection, however, because Section 3 of the then Copyright Act provided that Disney's copyrights included protection for "all the copyrightable component parts of the work copyrighted" (note 7 supra).

The essence of defendants' argument is that characters are never copyrightable and therefore cannot in anyway constitute a copyrightable component part. That argument flies in the face of a series of cases dating back to 1914 that have held comic strip characters protectable under the old Copyright Act. See Detective Comics, Inc. v. Bruns Publications Inc., 111 F.2d 432 (2d Cir.1940); Fleischer Studios v. Freundlich, 73 F.2d 276 (2d Cir.1934), certiorari denied, 294 U.S. 717, 55 S.Ct. 516, 79 L.Ed. 1250; King Features Syndicate v. Fleischer, 299 F. 533 (2d Cir.1924); Detective Comics, Inc. v. Fox Publications Inc., 46 F.Supp. 872 (S.D.N.Y.1942); Hill v. Whalen & Martell, Inc., 220 F. 359 (S.D.N.Y.1914); 1 Nimmer on Copyright § 30.[9]

It is true that this Court's opinion in Warner Brothers Pictures v. Columbia Broadcasting System, 216 F.2d 945 (9th Cir.1954), certiorari denied, 348 U.S. 971, 75 S.Ct. 532, 99 L.Ed. 756, lends some support to the position that characters ordinarily are not copyrightable. There the mystery writer Dashiell Hammett and his publisher entered into a 1930 contract with Warner Brothers giving the movie production company copyright and various other rights to a "certain story * * * entitled Maltese Falcon" involving the fictional detective Sam Spade. In 1946, Hammett and other defendants used the Maltese Falcon characters in other writings, causing Warner Brothers to sue for copyright infringement and "unfair use and competition." After pointing out the sophisticated nature of the plaintiff, we construed the contracts between the parties and held:

> "We are of the opinion that since the use of characters and character names are nowhere specifically mentioned in the agreements [including the assignment of copyright instrument], but that other items, including the title, 'The Maltese Falcon', and their use are specifically mentioned as being granted [to Warner Brothers], that the character rights with the names cannot be held to be within the grants, and that under the doctrine of *ejusdem generis*, general language cannot be held to include them." (Footnote omitted.)

---

9. National Comics Publications v. Fawcett Publications, Inc., 191 F.2d 594 (2d Cir.1951), clarified 198 F.2d 927 (2d Cir. 1952), relied upon by defendants, deals more with copyright formalities than with copyrightability, and the copyrightability of a character was not in issue. To the extent that opinion discusses copyrightability, it indicates that copying details of comic strips constitutes infringement. 191 F.2d at 603. Contrary to defendants' contention, the opinion does not imply or indicate that protecting of characters would necessarily last for more than 56 years. See Section 3 of the then Copyright Act.

After so holding, Judge Stephens' opinion considered "whether it was ever intended by the copyright statute that characters with their names should be under its protection." [10] In that context he concluded that such a restriction on Hammett's future use of a character was unreasonable, at least when the characters were merely vehicles for the story and did not "really constitute" the story being told. Judge Stephens' reasons for that conclusion provide an important indication of the applicability of that conclusion to comic book characters as opposed to literary characters. In reasoning that characters "are always limited and always fall into limited patterns," Judge Stephens recognized that it is difficult to delineate distinctively a literary character. Cf. Nichols v. Universal Pictures Corp., 45 F.2d 119 (2d Cir.1930), certiorari denied, 282 U.S. 902, 51 S.Ct. 216, 75 L.Ed. 795. When the author can add a visual image, however, the difficulty is reduced. See generally 1 Nimmer on Copyright § 30. Put another way, while many literary characters may embody little more than an unprotected idea (see Sid & Marty Krofft Television v. McDonald's Corp., 562 F.2d 1157 (9th Cir.1977)), a comic book character, which has physical as well as conceptual qualities, is more likely to contain some unique elements of expression. Because comic book characters therefore are distinguishable from literary characters, the *Warner Brothers* language does not preclude protection of Disney's characters.[11] [That part of the court's opinion dealing with the defense of fair use is set forth at p. 374 infra.]

Questions

1. What constitutes a "comic book" character, which the *Air Pirates* court holds to be copyrightable, as compared with a "literary" character, as to which the *Sam Spade* opinion is left undisturbed? Does the "comic book" characterization apply to cartoon characters which appear other than in comic books? Does it include characters depicted by living actors dressed in "fanciful" costumes? See Sid & Marty Krofft Television Productions, Inc. v. McDonald's Corporation, infra.

2. Does the *Air Pirates* opinion render it easier or more difficult to argue that the exclusion of copyright protection for literary characters in *Sam Spade* was dicta?

---

10. Judge Wollenberg's opinion viewed this language as an alternate holding rather than dicta, rekindling an old dispute about the status of the language. See 1 Nimmer on Copyright § 30 n. 587. For the reasons that follow, either characterization of the language would not affect the result in this case.

11. Because this conclusion is sufficient to justify protection of the characters, we need not endorse the district court's conclusion that Disney's characters fell within the *Warner Brothers* exception for characters who "really constitute" the story. The district judge did not state which Disney stories were the basis of the protection for any character, nor did it state which characters were so protected. Apart from failing to recognize that this exception seems to be limited to a "story devoid of plot" (1 Nimmer on Copyright § 30), the district court's conclusion may have been based on the incorrect assumption that Disney's characters could be protected if together they constitute a whole story. Obviously the larger the group of characters that is selected, the easier it is to say that they "constitute" the entire story, particularly when only a general abstraction and not a particular story is analyzed.

3. What is the significance of the court's reliance upon Sec. 3 of the 1909 Act? Does the fact that Sec. 3 was not reenacted in so many words in the current Act require a reappraisal of character protection under the current Act? What is the impact of Sec. 103 of the current Act?

WARNER BROTHERS INC. v. AMERICAN BROADCASTING COMPANIES, INC.

United States Court of Appeals, Second Circuit, 1983.
720 F.2d 231.

Before MANSFIELD, MESKILL and NEWMAN, CIRCUIT JUDGES.

NEWMAN, CIRCUIT JUDGE:

The primary issue raised by this appeal is whether as a matter of law the fictional character Ralph Hinkley, the principal figure in a television series, "The Greatest American Hero," is not sufficiently similar to the fictional character Superman, the hero of comic books, television, and more recently films, so that claims of copyright infringement and unfair competition may be dismissed without consideration by a jury. * * *

Many of the significant facts are set out in our prior opinion affirming the denial of plaintiffs' motion for a preliminary injunction. Warner Bros. Inc. v. American Broadcasting Companies, Inc., 654 F.2d 204 (2d Cir.1981). Plaintiffs own the copyrights in various works embodying the character Superman and have thereby acquired copyright protection for the character itself. See Detective Comics, Inc. v. Bruns Publications, Inc., 111 F.2d 432 (2d Cir.1940). Since the creation of Superman in 1938, plaintiffs have exploited their rights with great success, portraying Superman in several media and licensing the character for a variety of merchandising purposes. Through plaintiffs' efforts, Superman has attained an extremely high degree of exposure and recognition.

In 1978, building on previous Superman works, plaintiff Warner Bros., Inc. released a motion picture entitled "Superman, The Movie" (*Superman I*) and more recently two sequels. Our prior opinion in this case summarizes the manner in which *Superman I* recounts the Superman legend:

> The character is depicted as a superhuman being from a fictional planet, Krypton, who was sent to earth to escape the fatal consequences of the imminent destruction of his planet. Superman is found by the Kents, a midwestern couple, who name the boy Clark and raise him as their son in a bucolic setting. The Kents instill in Clark a strong sense of moral conviction and faith in the "American way," and counsel the boy not to reveal his superhuman powers to anyone. Clark matures into a tall, well-built, dark-haired, and strikingly handsome young man. Ultimately, Clark leaves his pastoral home, finding himself drawn by a mysterious force to a place where he encounters the image of his deceased father, Jor-El. There, Jor-El informs him of his true identity and instructs him to use his superpowers to protect the world from evil. Clark emerges from his fantastic encounter with Jor-El wearing for the first time his Superman

costume—a skin-tight blue leotard with red briefs, boots and cape, and a large "S" emblazoned in red and gold upon the chest and cape.

Clark subsequently obtains a position as a reporter for the *Daily Planet*, but reveals his true identity to no one, assuming instead the appearance of a shy, bumbling, but well-intentioned young man. There he soon meets and becomes infatuated with a beautiful colleague, Lois Lane. Later he appears clad in his Superman regalia to perform amazing feats of strength and courage which immediately attract wide attention, acclaim, and the amorous interest of Lois Lane.

Superman is continually confronted by villains in all of his adventures, but eventually overcomes all evil opponents by exploiting his superpowers of self-propelled flight, imperviousness to bullets, blinding speed, X-ray vision, fantastic hearing, and seemingly immeasurable strength.

654 F.2d at 206.

In *Superman I* and in previous Superman works, Superman is portrayed as a brave, fearless hero, endowed with superhuman powers. His strength, speed, vision, and hearing far exceed the physical capabilities of mere mortals. He is impervious to bullets. In early works, Superman displayed extraordinary leaping ability, see Detective Comics, Inc. v. Bruns Publications, Inc., supra, 111 F.2d at 433; in later works this skill had become the power of flight, as Superman is regularly seen soaring through the sky, arms stretched ahead, then landing agilely on his feet ready for action. Superman engages in a series of exploits against assorted criminals and villains who pose threats not only to public safety but also to national security and even world peace. Regardless of his adversary, Superman always prevails.

Descriptions of Superman and lines of dialogue in the Superman works have become as well known as the Superman character. He is described as "faster than a speeding bullet," "more powerful than a locomotive," and "able to leap tall buildings in a single bound," and he always fights for "truth, justice, and the American way." From the early comic books continuing through the modern films, startled pedestrians have shouted, "Look! Up in the sky! * * * It's a bird! * * * It's a plane! * * * It's Superman!"

The substantial commercial success of *Superman I* and the attendant publicity prompted many requests for licenses permitting use of the Superman character in connection with the merchandising of toys, greeting cards, apparel, and other products. It also led ABC to seek a license for production of a television series about "Superboy" based on the early adventures of Superman. Plaintiffs, who were planning to make their own sequels and derivative works, refused ABC permission to proceed with its proposed project.

Unable to obtain this license, ABC assigned to Cannell, the principal of the third-party defendant production company, the task of creating a "pilot" program for a TV series involving a superhero. Cannell produced a program, and subsequently a weekly series, entitled "The Greatest American Hero" (*Hero*), which he described as being about "what happens when you [the average person] become Superman." *Hero's* protagonist, Ralph Hinkley, was given attributes intended to identify him as an "ordinary guy." Hinkley is portrayed as a young high school teacher attempting to cope with a recent divorce, a dispute over the custody of his son, and the strain that his domestic problems place upon his work and his relationship with his girlfriend. Although Hinkley is attractive, his physical appearance is not imposing: he is of medium height with a slight build and curly, somewhat unkempt, blond hair.

In the pilot show, as described on the prior appeal:

> Hinkley's van breaks down en route to a high school field trip in the desert. While walking along a road in search of help, Hinkley is nearly run over by an out-of-control automobile driven by Bill Maxwell, an American undercover agent. Maxwell has been searching the desert for his missing FBI partner who, unbeknownst to Maxwell, has been murdered by a band of extremists. Maxwell and Hinkley are suddenly approached by a brightly glowing spaceship from which descends the image of Maxwell's deceased partner. Hinkley is handed a magical caped costume—a red leotard with a tunic top, no boots, and a black cape—which, when worn, endows him with fantastic powers. Unfortunately, however, Hinkley loses the instruction book that accompanied the intergalactic gift and is left only with the verbal instruction that he should use his powers to save the world from self-destruction. Hinkley grudgingly accepts the mission after being importuned to do so by Maxwell.

654 F.2d at 206–07.

Hinkley's magical costume endows him with superhuman speed and strength, the ability to fly, imperviousness to bullets, and what Cannell calls "holographic vision," the power to perceive sights and sounds occurring out of his line of vision. Partly for lack of the instruction book that accompanied the costume and partly because some of his character traits remain dominant when he is wearing the suit, Hinkley as a superhero is not an unqualified success. He uses his superpowers awkwardly and fearfully. When flying, Hinkley shouts with fright and makes crash-landings, sometimes crumpling in a heap or skidding nearly out of control to a stop. Though protected from bullets by his costume, Hinkley cringes and cowers when shot at by villains.

* * *

The *Hero* series contains several visual effects and lines that inevitably call Superman to mind, sometimes by way of brief imitation, sometimes by mention of Superman or another character from the Superman works, and sometimes by humorous parodying or ironic twisting of well-known Superman phrases. Hinkley's suit invests him with most of Superman's powers, and the suit, like Superman's, is a tight-fitting leotard with a chest insignia and a cape. Their outfits differ in that Superman wears a blue leotard with red briefs, boots, and cape, while Hinkley's costume is a red leotard with a tunic top, no boots, and a black cape. In one scene, as Hinkley is running at super speed, smoke emerges from his footsteps, and the sound of a locomotive is heard. A similar scene occurs in *Superman I*, though even without seeing the movie it would be difficult not to be reminded by the *Hero* scene of Superman, who is regularly described as "more powerful than a locomotive." When Hinkley first views himself in a mirror holding his costume in front of him, he says, "It's a bird * * * it's a plane * * * it's Ralph Hinkley." The youngster, Jerry, watching Hinkley's unsuccessful first effort to fly, tells him, "Superman wouldn't do it that way." In a scene with his girlfriend, who is aware of the powers that come with the magic costume, Hinkley says, "Look at it this way * * * you're already one step up on Lois Lane. She never found out who Clark Kent really was."

* * * On December 16, 1981, the District Judge concluded that no reasonable jury could find that the parties' works were substantially similar and granted summary judgment to defendants on the entire copyright claim. * * *

The basic issues concerning the copyright infringement claim are whether the *Hero* and *Superman* works are substantially similar so as to support an inference of copying and whether the lack of substantial similarity is so clear as to fall outside the range of reasonably disputed fact questions requiring resolution by a jury. * * *

It is a fundamental objective of the copyright law to foster creativity. However, that law has the capacity both to augment and diminish the prospects for creativity. By assuring the author of an original work the exclusive benefits of whatever commercial success his or her work enjoys, the law obviously promotes creativity. At the same time, it can deter the creation of new works if authors are fearful that their creations will too readily be found to be substantially similar to preexisting works. The idea-expression dichotomy originated in the case law and is now codified in the statute, 17 U.S.C. § 102(b) (Supp. V 1981), in an effort to enable courts to adjust the tension between these competing effects of copyright protection. Though imprecise, it remains a useful analytic tool for separating infringing from non-infringing works, especially when the essence of the work sought to be protected is a story and the allegedly infringing work is accused of what Professor Nimmer calls "comprehensive nonliteral similarity," 3 Nimmer § 13.03[A][1], duplicating the "fundamental essence or structure" of a work, id. Confronting a claim of that sort, courts have often invoked Learned Hand's "abstractions" test,[6] or Professor Chaffee's "pattern" test.[7]

---

6. "Upon any work, and especially upon a play, a great number of patterns of increasing generality will fit equally well, as more and more of the incident is left out. The last may perhaps be no more than the most general statement of what the play is about, and at times consist only of its title; but there is a point in this series of abstractions where they are no longer protected, since otherwise the playwright could prevent the use of his 'ideas,' to which, apart from their expression, his property is never extended." Nichols v. Universal Pictures Corp., supra, 45 F.2d at 121.

7. "No doubt, the line does lie somewhere between the author's idea and the precise form in which he wrote it down. I like to say that the protection covers the 'pattern' of the work * * * the sequence of events, and the development of the interplay of characters." Chafee, *Reflections on the Law of Copyright*, 45 Colum.L.Rev. 503, 513–14 (1945).

When, as in this case, the claim concerns infringement of a character, rather than a story, the idea-expression distinction has proved to be especially elusive. In *Nichols,* Hand applied his "abstractions" test in determining that neither the plot nor the characters of "Abie's Irish Rose" were infringed by a similar play called "The Cohens and the Kellys." He noted that no case then decided had found infringement of a character described only by written word, although he recognized the possibility that a literary character could be sufficiently delineated to support a claim of infringement by a second comer, 45 F.2d at 121. Copyrightability of a literary character has on occasion been recognized, Burroughs v. Metro-Goldwyn-Mayer, Inc., 519 F.Supp. 388, 391 (S.D.N.Y.1981) (Tarzan), aff'd with issue expressly left open, 683 F.2d 610, 621 (2d Cir.1982). However, there has been no doubt that copyright protection is available for characters portrayed in cartoons, even before Nichols, e.g., King Features Syndicate v. Fleischer, 299 Fed. 533 (2d Cir.1924) (Barney Google's horse, Spark Plug); Hill v. Whalen & Martell, Inc., 220 F. 359 (S.D.N.Y.1914) (Mutt and Jeff); see also Empire City Amusement Co. v. Wilton, 134 F. 132 (C.C.D.Mass.1903) (Alphonse and Gaston) (claim sustained against demurrer), and after Nichols, e.g., Walt Disney Productions v. Air Pirates, 581 F.2d 751 (9th Cir.), cert. denied, 439 U.S. 1132, 99 S.Ct. 1054, 59 L.Ed.2d 94 (1978) (Mickey Mouse and other Disney characters); Detective Comics, Inc. v. Bruns Publications, Inc., supra (Superman); see 1 Nimmer § 2.12.

In determining whether a character in a second work infringes a cartoon character, courts have generally considered not only the visual resemblance but also the totality of the characters' attributes and traits. * * *

A somewhat paradoxical aspect of infringement disputes, especially pertinent to claims of character infringement, concerns the attention courts give both to similarities and differences in the two works at issue. Professor Nimmer categorically asserts as a proposition, "It is entirely immaterial that in many respects plaintiff's and defendant's works are dissimilar if in other respects similarity as to a substantial element of plaintiff's work can be shown." 3 Nimmer § 13.03[B] at 13–38. In Hand's pithy phrase, "[N]o plagiarist can excuse the wrong by showing how much of his work he did not pirate." Sheldon v. Metro-Goldwyn Pictures Corp., 81 F.2d 49, 56 (2d Cir.), cert. denied, 298 U.S. 669, 56 S.Ct. 835, 80 L.Ed. 1392 (1936). Yet Professor Nimmer also recognizes, as a second proposition, that "a defendant may legitimately avoid infringement by intentionally making sufficient changes in a work which would otherwise be regarded as substantially similar to that of the plaintiff's," 3 Nimmer § 13.03[B] at 13–38.1 to –38.2, a proposition we recognized on the prior appeal of this case, 654 F.2d at 211, and elsewhere, Eden Toys, Inc. v. Marshall Field & Co., supra, 675 F.2d at 501; Durham Industries, Inc. v. Tomy Corp., supra, 630 F.2d at 913 & n. 11. The two propositions are not facially inconsistent; the second proposition contemplates a work that *would be* substantially similar if its author had not made changes from the plaintiff's work.

Yet in practice the distinction between the two propositions has become somewhat blurred. We have observed that "numerous differences tend to undercut substantial similarity," id. at 913; see Herbert Rosenthal Jewelry Corp. v. Honora Jewelry Co., 509 F.2d 64, 65–66 (2d Cir.1974). This observation appears to go beyond Professor Nimmer's second proposition by emphasizing the significance of differences that do not necessarily change features of the plaintiff's work, but may be entirely additional. To that extent, the observation modifies the first proposition.

The tension between these two propositions perhaps results from their formulation in the context of literary works and their subsequent application to graphic and three-dimensional works. A story has a linear dimension: it begins, continues, and ends. If a defendant copies substantial portions of a plaintiff's sequence of events, he does not escape infringement by adding original episodes somewhere along the line. A graphic or three-dimensional work is created to be perceived as an entirety. Significant dissimilarities between two works of this sort inevitably lessen the similarity that would otherwise exist between the total perceptions of the two works. The graphic rendering of a character has aspects of both the linear, literary mode and the multi-dimensional total perception. What the character thinks, feels, says, and does and the descriptions conveyed by the author through the comments of other characters in the work episodically fill out a viewer's understanding of the character. At the same time, the visual perception of the character tends to create a dominant impression against which the similarity of a defendant's character may be readily compared, and significant differences readily noted.

Ultimately, care must be taken to draw the elusive distinction between a substantially similar character that infringes a copyrighted character despite slight differences in appearance, behavior, or traits, and a somewhat similar though non-infringing character whose appearance, behavior, or traits, and especially their combination, significantly differ from those of a copyrighted character, even though the second character is reminiscent of the first one. Stirring one's memory of a copyrighted character is not the same as appearing to be substantially similar to that character, and only the latter is infringement. See Ideal Toy Corp. v. Kenner Products Division of General Mills Fun Group, Inc., 443 F.Supp. 291, 305 (S.D.N.Y.1977).

An entirely separate issue of infringement, also posed by this case, concerns what Professor Nimmer calls "fragmented literal similarity," 3 Nimmer § 13.03[A][2], duplicating the exact or nearly exact wording of a fragment of the protected work, id. With respect to such claims, courts have invoked two distinct doctrines. First, a *de minimis* rule has been applied, allowing the literal copying of a small and usually insignificant portion of the plaintiff's work. See, e.g., G.R. Leonard & Co. v. Stack, 386 F.2d 38 (7th Cir.1967); Werlin v. Reader's Digest Ass'n, Inc., 528 F.Supp. 451, 463–64 (S.D.N.Y.1981). Second, under the "fair use" doctrine, codified in 17 U.S.C. § 107(2) (Supp. V 1981), courts have allowed the taking of words or phrases when adapted for use as commentary or parody, see, e.g., Elsmere Music, Inc. v. National Broadcasting Co., 623 F.2d 252 (2d Cir.1980) (per curiam); Berlin v. E.C. Publications, Inc., 329 F.2d 541 (2d Cir.), cert. denied, 379 U.S. 822, 85 S.Ct. 46, 13 L.Ed.2d 33 (1964).

* * * No matter how well known a copyrighted phrase becomes, its author is entitled to guard against its appropriation to promote the sale of commercial products. That doctrine enabled the proprietors of the Superman copyright to prevent a discount chain from using a television commercial that parodied well-known lines associated with Superman. D.C. Comics, Inc. v. Crazy Eddie, Inc., 205 U.S.P.Q. 1177 (S.D.N.Y.1979) ("Look! * * * Up in the sky! * * * It's a bird! * * * It's a plane * * * It's * * * Crazy Eddie!"). But an original work of authorship with elements of parody, though undoubtedly created in the hope of commercial success, stands on a different footing from the products of a discount chain. Whatever aesthetic appeal such a work may have results from the creativity that the copyright law is designed to promote. It is decidedly in the interests of creativity, not piracy, to permit authors to take well-known phrases and fragments from copyrighted works and add their own contributions of commentary or humor.

* * *

Applying these principles to this case, we conclude that Chief Judge Motley correctly entered summary judgment for the defendants on the claim of copyright infringement. Plaintiffs make no claim that the *Hero* pilot, subsequent episodes, or "promos" infringed the story of any Superman works. Their contention is that the *Hero* character, Ralph Hinkley, is substantially similar to Superman and that the *Hero* works impermissibly copied what plaintiffs call the "indicia" of Superman, a concept broad enough to include Superman's costume, his abilities, the well-known lines associated with him—in short, anything occurring in the *Hero* works that might remind a viewer of Superman.

The total perception of the Hinkley character is not substantially similar to that of Superman. On the contrary, it is profoundly different. Superman looks and acts like a brave, proud hero, who has dedicated his life to combating the forces of evil. Hinkley looks and acts like a timid, reluctant hero, who accepts his missions grudgingly and prefers to get on with his normal life. Superman performs his superhuman feats with skill, verve, and dash, clearly the master of his own destiny. Hinkley is perplexed by the superhuman powers his costume confers and uses them in a bumbling, comical fashion. In the genre of superheros, Hinkley follows Superman as, in the genre of detectives, Inspector Clouseau follows Sherlock Holmes.

However, we do not accept defendants' mode of analysis whereby every skill the two characters share is dismissed as an idea rather than a protected form of expression. That approach risks elimination of any copyright protection for a character, unless the allegedly infringing character looks and behaves exactly like the original. A character is an aggregation of the particular talents and traits his creator selected for him. That each one may be an idea does not diminish the expressive aspect of the combination. But just as similarity cannot be rejected by isolating as an idea each characteristic the characters have in common, it cannot be found when the total perception of all the ideas as expressed in each character is fundamentally different.

An infringement claim would surely be within the range of reasonable jury fact issues if a character strongly resembled Superman but displayed some trait inconsistent with the traditional Superman image. If a second comer endowed his character with Superman's general appearance, demeanor, and skills, but portrayed him in the service of the underworld, a jury would have to make the factual determination whether the second character was Superman gone astray or a new addition to the superhero genre. In this case, however, a reasonable jury could not conclude that Hinkley is substantially similar to the Superman character with only a change of name. The overall perception of the way Hinkley looks and acts marks him as a different, non-infringing character who simply has some of the superhuman traits popularized by the Superman character and now widely shared within the superhero genre.

* * *

That leaves for consideration on the infringement claim the use in the *Hero* episodes and "promos" of lines that either mention Superman and other characters from the Superman saga or incorporate phrases associated with Superman. The use of such lines is manifestly not infringement. In each instance the lines are used, not to create a similarity with the Superman works, but to highlight the differences, often to a humorous effect. Appellants acknowledge the contrasting point made by some of the *Hero* lines, but insist nevertheless that the point may not be appreciated by some of the viewers, especially young viewers who make up a significant share of the television audience for the *Hero* series. Appellants were prepared to offer expert testimony to show that some children would not perceive the negatives when the announcer says that Hinkley "may be unable to leap tall buildings in a single bound," "may be slower than a speeding bullet," and "may be less powerful than a locomotive." We do not doubt that some viewers may miss the point, but their misunderstanding does not establish infringement. Perhaps if *Hero* were a children's series, aired on Saturday mornings among the cartoon programs, we would have greater concern for the risk that lines intended to contrast Hinkley with Superman might be mistakenly understood to suggest that *Hero* was a Superman program. Cf. Ideal Toy Corp. v. Fab-Lu, Ltd., 261 F.Supp. 238, 241–42 (S.D.N.Y.1966) (children's perception of television commercial for dolls). But when a work is presented to a general audience of evening television viewers, the possible misperception of some young viewers cannot prevent that audience from seeing a program that will readily be recognized by the "average lay observer," Ideal Toy Corp. v. Fab-Lu Ltd., 360 F.2d 1021, 1022 (2d Cir.1966), as poking fun at, rather than copying, a copyrighted work.

* * *

The judgment of the District Court is affirmed.

Questions

1. Would the result in this case have been different if stories containing the Superman character had been first published in 1978 rather than 1938? Was there an unconscious tendency by the court to regard the Superman character as a folk-hero, like Robin Hood and Santa Claus, simply because of the public's long-standing familiarity with his attributes? Was there an unconscious assumption that a superhero will necessarily have the superpowers of self-propelled flight, imperviousness to bullets, blinding speed, X-ray vision, fantastic hearing and seemingly immeasurable strength? Does the fact that prior to "The Greatest American Hero" there had already been a number of other superheroes, also displaying most of these superpowers, tend to denigrate the claim of protection for Superman? Should it matter that these other superheroes' powers were also copied from Superman?

2. Do you agree with Judge Newman's conclusion that "differences that do not necessarily change features of the plaintiff's work, but may be entirely additional" should be considered in determining whether there is substantial similarity between the two works?

3. Should the Superman traits common to both plaintiff's and defendants' works be regarded as constituting merely unprotected "ideas" rather than protected "expression"?

5. Sound Recordings

Note *

Section 102(a)(7) of the Copyright Act provides that sound recordings may qualify for copyright protection. Sound recordings are defined as "works that result from the fixation of a series of musical, spoken, or other sounds, but not including the sounds accompanying a motion picture or other audiovisual work, regardless of the nature of the material objects, such as discs, tapes, or other phonorecords, in which they are embodied."[1] Thus, except with respect to a sound track integrated with an audiovisual work, a sound recording copyright may be claimed in the aggregate of sounds embodied in any tangible medium, including phonograph discs, open-reel tapes, cartridges, cassettes, player piano rolls, and other material objects in which sounds are fixed and can be communicated either directly or with the aid of machine or device. Of course, no statutory copyright may be claimed in sounds which are not embodied in a tangible medium.

Sound recordings first "fixed"[2] prior to February 15, 1972 are not subject to statutory copyright protection.[3] Why such an exclusion from federal coverage of this vast body of works? It is true that under the Sound Recording

---

* Nimmer on Copyright, § 2.10.

1. 17 U.S.C.A. § 101.

2. For the definition of "fixed" see 17 U.S.C.A. § 101.

3. 17 U.S.C.A. § 301(c). There is, however, a federal statute (18 U.S.C. § 2318) which forbids the transportation in interstate or foreign commerce of sound recordings bearing forged or counterfeit labels. See United States v. Shultz, 482 F.2d 1179 (6th Cir.1973). Sec. 2318 was amended so as to increase the penalties for its violation and to provide for forfeiture and destruction of counterfeit labels. 17 U.S.C.A., Transitional and Supplementary Provisions, § 111.

Amendment of 1971,[4] which first extended statutory copyright to sound recordings, only recordings fixed on or after February 15, 1972 were protected. But the Supreme Court in Goldstein v. California[5] held that under the 1909 Act there was no federal preemption of state law protection for pre-February 15, 1972 sound recordings. Thus, by reason of *Goldstein* it was clear under the 1909 Act, that common law copyright could be claimed in such pre-1972 sound recordings whether published or unpublished. Therefore, as of January 1, 1978, pre-1972 sound recordings had not (at least by reason of federal preemption) entered the public domain. If, then, one turns to Section 303 of the current Act, it would appear that pre-1972 sound recordings, like other works in common law copyright up to January 1, 1978, would as of that date be invested with statutory copyright protection. But such a result is precluded by Section 301(c) which provides: "Notwithstanding the provisions of section 303, no sound recording fixed before February 15, 1972 shall be subject to copyright under this title. * * *" Why this particular exclusion? It seems to have occurred almost inadvertently, and as a result of a misconception upon the part of the Department of Justice. The bill for general revision of the Copyright Act as introduced in the Senate at the beginning of the 94th Congress was substantially identical to S. 1361, which during the 93d Congress had been passed by the Senate, but not by the House of Representatives. Section 301, the preemption provision, in that bill did not exclude from the thrust of federal preemption sound recordings fixed prior to February 15, 1972. The Department of Justice expressed the fear that unless state law protection for such pre-1972 recordings were exempted from federal preemption, the result would be an "immediate resurgence of piracy of pre-February 15, 1972 sound recordings."[6] The Senate accepted this argument, and in order to meet it, added a new Section 301(b)(4), which expressly excluded from federal preemption, state laws with respect to "sound recordings fixed prior to February 15, 1972."[7] What both the Justice Department and the Senate overlooked was the fact that a resurgence of record piracy would not have resulted even if state record piracy laws were preempted for the reason that Section 303 of the bill in the form adopted by the Senate would have conferred statutory copyright upon all sound recordings (as well as other works of authorship) that had not theretofore entered the public domain. As indicated above, under the holding in *Goldstein,* pre-1972 sound recordings had not entered the public domain. Therefore, the Senate bill would have conferred statutory copyright on pre as well as post 1972 sound recordings. Thus, even if record piracy of pre-1972 sound recordings would no longer be prohibited by state law, it would have been prohibited by federal law. Although the stated reason for preservation of state record piracy laws as applied to pre-1972 recordings was erroneous, when the House came to consider the Senate bill, it retained this provision. But since state law protection for pre-1972 sound recordings was preserved, it became unnecessary also to confer federal statutory copyright protection for such recordings. Therefore, the House added a further amendment, which appears in the final Act, whereby pre-1972 sound recordings are excluded from coverage of statutory copyright.[8] In this manner, the Justice Department's mistaken belief that

---

4. Act of October 15, 1971 (P.L. 92–140, 85 Stat. 391), as amended by the Act of December 31, 1974 (P.L. 93–573, 88 Stat. 1873).

5. 412 U.S. 546 (1973). This case is set forth infra.

6. Quoted in H.Rep., p. 133.

7. S. 22, 94th Cong., 2d Sess. Sec. 301(b)(4).

8. 17 U.S.C.A. § 301(c).

pre-1972 sound recordings were excluded from statutory copyright under the general revision bill led to an amendment which validated that belief.

Although sound recordings fixed prior to February 15, 1972 are ineligible for statutory copyright, they are generally protected under state law.[9] Thus, a number of state court decisions have granted protection against unauthorized duplication of sound recordings (pejoratively referred to as "record piracy"). These decisions often have not invoked the label "common law copyright," but have rather been based either upon an asserted "property right,"[10] or upon a theory of unfair competition.[11] In addition, the laws of several states render record piracy a criminal offense.[12]

Questions

1. If the only tangible medium of expression in which a musical work is "fixed" is that of a phonorecord (see the definition of "phonorecord" in Sec. 101), is there a copyright under Sec. 102(a)(2), or Sec. 102(a)(7), or both? Who is the "author" of a musical work copyright? Who is the "author" of a sound recording copyright? See Nimmer on Copyright, § 2.10[A][2].

2. In Goldstein v. California, 412 U.S. 546 (1973), the Supreme Court held that common law copyright in pre-1972 sound recordings might endure in perpetuity without federal preemption. Has that rule been altered under the current Copyright Act? See Sec. 301(c).

---

9. See Cal.Civil Code, § 980(a)(2). For an extensive discussion of common law rights in sound recordings, see Ringer, The Unauthorized Duplication of Sound Recordings, U.S. Copyright Office Study No. 26.

10. Waring v. WDAS Broadcasting Station, Inc., 327 Pa. 433, 194 A. 631 (1937); Waring v. Dunlea, 26 F.Supp. 338 (E.D.N.C. 1939); Radio Corp. of America v. Premier Albums, Inc., 19 App.Div.2d 62, 240 N.Y. S.2d 955 (1963); Capitol Records Inc. v. Mercury Records Corp., 221 F.2d 657 (2d Cir.1955) (application of state law under diversity jurisdiction); Columbia Broadcasting System, Inc. v. Custom Recording Co., 174 U.S.P.Q. 309 (S.C.Sup.Ct.1972). See also United Artists Records, Inc. v. Eastern Tape Corp., 179 U.S.P.Q. 824 (N.C.Ct.App. 1973). Cf. Liberty/UA Inc. v. Eastern Tape Corp., 170 U.S.P.Q. 351 (N.C.Ct.App.1971).

11. Capitol Records, Inc. v. Erickson, 2 Cal.App.3d 526, 82 Cal.Rptr. 798 (1969); Capitol Records, Inc. v. Spies, 167 U.S.P.Q. 489 (Ill.App.1970); Columbia Broadcasting System, Inc. v. Spies, 167 U.S.P.Q. 492 (Ill. Cir.Ct.1970); Greater Recording Co. v. Stambler, 144 U.S.P.Q. 547 (N.Y.Sup.Ct. 1965); Columbia Broadcasting System, Inc. v. Cartridge City, Limited, 35 C.O.Bull. 87 (N.Y.Sup.Ct.1966); Capitol Records, Inc. v. Greatest Records Inc., 43 Misc.2d 878, 252 N.Y.S.2d 553 (1964); National Broadcasting Co. v. Nance, 506 S.W.2d 483, 182 U.S.P.Q. 285 (Mo.Ct.App.1974) (misappropriation form of unfair competition); Mercury Record Productions Inc. v. Economic Consultants, Inc., 64 Wis.2d 163, 183 U.S.P.Q. 358 (Wis.Sup.Ct.1974) (misappropriation form of unfair competition); Columbia Broadcasting System, Inc. v. Newman, 184 U.S.P.Q. 18 (D.D.C.N.M.1974) (misappropriation form of unfair competition). Cf. Gate City Record Service Co. v. Custom Recording Co., 176 U.S.P.Q. 20 (N.D.Ga.1972), affirmed 177 U.S.P.Q. 243 (5th Cir.1973) (plaintiff distributors of authorized recordings held to have no standing to sue unauthorized record duplicators).

12. See e.g., N.Y. Penal Law § 275(h); California Penal Code § 653h.

6. Derivative Works and Compilations

Note *

The Distinction Between a Derivative Work, a Compilation and a Collective Work

Section 103(a) of the Copyright Act provides that the subject matter of copyright includes compilations and derivative works. Section 101 defines a derivative work as:

> "a work based upon one or more pre-existing works, such as a translation, fictionalization, motion picture version, sound recording, art reproduction, abridgment, condensation, or any other form in which a work may be recast, transformed or adapted. A work consisting of editorial revisions, annotations, elaborations, or other modifications which, as a whole, represent an original work of authorship, is a 'derivative work.'"

A compilation is defined as:

> "a work formed by the collection and assembling of pre-existing materials or of data that are selected, coordinated, or arranged in such a way that the resulting work as a whole constitutes an original work of authorship. * *" [1]

The House Report explains the distinction between a "compilation" and a "derivative work" as follows:

> "A 'compilation' results from a process of selecting, bringing together, organizing, and arranging previously existing material of all kinds, regardless of whether the individual items in the material have been or ever could have been subject to copyright. A 'derivative work,' on the other hand, requires a process of recasting, transforming, or adapting 'one or more preexisting works * * *'." [2]

Thus, while a compilation consists merely of the selection and arrangement of pre-existing material without any internal changes in such material, a derivative work involves recasting or transformation, i.e., changes in the pre-existing material, whether or not it is juxtaposed in an arrangement with other pre-existing materials. A catalog constitutes a compilation, and a translation of a pre-existing work constitutes a derivative work.

There is a further distinction between a derivative work and a compilation in that the former by definition incorporates pre-existing "works," i.e., matter capable of protection by copyright, while the latter incorporates pre-existing "materials" or "data" which may or may not in itself be capable of being protected by copyright. Thus a collection of materials (if the combination is original) will be held protectible as a compilation regardless of whether such materials would be separately copyrightable.

Those compilations which consist of contributions which themselves constitute "works" capable of copyright are called collective works.[3] A collective work is defined as

---

* Nimmer on Copyright, §§ 3.01, 3.02.
1. 17 U.S.C.A. § 101.
2. H.Rep., p. 57.
3. "The term 'compilation' includes collective works." 17 U.S.C.A. § 101.

"a work, such as a periodical issue, anthology, or encyclopedia, in which a number of contributions, constituting separate and independent works in themselves, are assembled into a collective whole." [4]

A collective work more nearly resembles a derivative work than it does other forms of compilation. Both collective works and derivative works are based upon pre-existing works which are in themselves capable of copyright. The fact that the originality called for in a collective work consists of the collection and assembling of pre-existing works, while derivative work originality lies in the manner in which a pre-existing work is transformed would not appear to justify a difference in substantive treatment, and hence not require a terminological distinction. Collective works might well have been regarded as a form of derivative work, but that is not the terminology adopted by the drafters of the current Copyright Act.

STODART v. MUTUAL FILM CORP.

District Court, Southern District of New York, 1917.
249 F. 507.

LEARNED HAND, DISTRICT JUDGE. In this cause the plaintiff sues two moving picture companies for infringement of copyright of his play, "The Woodsman," by performance of the same upon the screen. It is conceded that in the year 1911 plaintiff composed a play by the title in question and secured its proper copyright under the statute in that case provided, and that the defendants have performed upon the screen a moving picture drama entitled "The Strength of Donald MacKenzie." The first question, therefore, is whether this picture is an infringement of the plaintiff's copyright.

The scene of the play is the north woods of Maine, and one of its supposed merits consists in the fact that it contains an atmosphere based upon the woods and life in the woods. The plot I need not consider in great detail. It is trite and conventional in the extreme, and its only claim to originality is in the setting of the scenes, all of which are out of doors and in the supposed local color. There is a simple-hearted and poetic hero, a north woods guide, who wins the heart of a person described as a society girl, whatever that may be. The latter, who is the heroine, is at the time of the play engaged to a villain, a rich person from the city, who supports himself out of the income of filthy and squalid tenements which are outside of the law. He is a typical villain, of unqualified rascally character, who, observing the tenderness of his lady for the heroic and poetic guide, employs the usual needy tool, and with him plots to compromise the lady and the hero in such a way as to make her suppose that the hero has intended her wrong. This he does by directing his tool, who is a half-breed Indian, to change a mark upon the trail upon which the lady and the hero are to start off on the morrow. The tool does as directed, the couple are lost in the woods, and a compromise is effected sufficient to disturb the susceptibilities of the respectable. The lady doubts her hero. An imbecile father at once assumes that the hero has attempted to seduce his daughter, and all looks black for the hero and bright for

---

4. 17 U.S.C.A. § 101.

the villain, as romance requires. The hero, however, induces the tool to repent upon the latter's deathbed, and he betrays the schemes of the villain, who is utterly confounded, and the couple live happily forever after.

The moving picture play is beyond question a direct copy from this plot almost in its entirety. The characters are the same. The hero is a woodsman guide with a turn for poetry, a strong father, and a poetic mother. The heroine is betrothed to a rascal in the city, who lives upon the income of foul and illegal tenements. The lady and the villain go with her father to the north woods of Maine, and there encounter the hero guide, for whom she develops a sentimental leaning, to the discomfiture of her betrothed. He thereupon suborns a half-breed villain to change the direction of a sign upon a trail upon which the lady and the hero are to leave on the morrow. The hero mistakes the trail by virtue of the sign, is compelled to spend the night with the lady in the open, to the great horror of all the respectable people who form the party and who go out in search of them. The hero's motives are at once misunderstood, both by the lady and by an imbecile father; the villain's tool is about to die from a wound, just as in the original; he repents and discloses the artifices of the villain, and the villain is thus exposed, to the eternal justification of the respectable nonentities. There are some incidents in the play which are not in the film, and some incidents in the film which are not in the play; but they are trivial and do not concern the plot. So far as infringement is concerned, the case needs no discussion.

[The defendant argues] that the play was in the public domain and was not entitled to protection. Nothing of the sort has been proved. The nearest approach is a play based upon Mr. Owen Davis' novelette, entitled "The Sentimental Lady," which was dramatized under the title "An Everyday Man." There are incidents in that play which are similar to those of the plaintiff's play. There is no reason to suppose one is copied from the other. The points of similarity are only these: That the scene takes place in the woods of the Adirondacks; that the lady and the hero are compromised by being left on a desert island for a short time. The hero, however, is not a poetic and romantic guide, but, strangely enough, a lawyer. The villain, who has nothing to do with illegal tenements, does not attempt to compromise his lady and the hero, so that the hero's motives shall be misconstrued; there is no change of the mark on the trail, no confession. There is nothing between the two but a similarity of incident, already mentioned. Now, incident is different from plot. It may be said that the incidents here are like those in the plaintiff's play, but that the plots are quite different, and the question here is of plot.

The defendant relies upon the case of London v. Biograph, 231 Fed. 696, 145 C.C.A. 582, in which Judge Lacombe held that, where the copyrighted plot was in the public domain, it could not be protected. This, of course, is true; but in that case it could be said that the supposed infringement was no nearer to the copyrighted plot than the

copyrighted plot was to the plots in the public domain. If that had been true in this case, the case would apply; but the defendants have copied the plaintiff's copyright much more nearly than that which resembles anything which is in the public domain. A man may take an old story and work it over, and if another copies, not only what is old, but what the author has added to it when he worked it up, the copyright is infringed. It cannot be a good copyright, in the broader sense that all features of the plot or the bare outlines of the plot can be protected; but it is a good copyright in so far as the embellishments and additions to the plot are new and have been contributed by the copyright. That is this case. Therefore * * * I overrule [this defense].
* * *

Questions

1. Did Judge Hand base his decision on the assumption that the plaintiff did not copy from either the Owen Davis novelette or the play based upon it, or would the defendant be liable in any event because it copied substantially all of the plaintiff's work, including material dissimilar to anything in the Davis works? Does Sec. 103(a) of the Copyright Act bear upon this question?

2. When great classics of past centuries are published in modern editions, with new introductions what, if anything, does the copyright in such works cover? See Sec. 103(b).

G. RICORDI & CO. v. PARAMOUNT PICTURES, INC.

United States Court of Appeals, Second Circuit, 1951.
189 F.2d 469.

Before L. HAND, CHIEF JUDGE, and SWAN, and FRANK, CIRCUIT JUDGES.

SWAN, CIRCUIT JUDGE. This is a suit for a declaratory judgment with respect to motion picture rights in the copyrighted opera "Madame Butterfly," the renewal copyright of which is owned solely by the plaintiff. Federal jurisdiction is claimed on diversity of citizenship, the plaintiff being a partnership composed of Italian citizens and the defendant a New York corporation. After answer, both parties moved for summary judgment upon the pleadings, affidavits and exhibits. The district court granted the plaintiff's motion and awarded a judgment declaring the plaintiff to be the exclusive owner of motion picture rights in the renewal copyright of the opera and enjoining the defendant from interfering with the plaintiff's exercise of such rights. The defendant has appealed.

There is no dispute as to the facts. In 1897 John Luther Long wrote a novel entitled "Madame Butterfly," which was published in the Century Magazine and copyrighted by the Century Company. In 1900 David Belasco, with the consent of the copyright owner, wrote a play based upon the novel and having the same title. The play was not copyrighted until 1917. In 1901 Long and Belasco made a contract with the plaintiff by which they gave it "the exclusive rights * * * to make a libretto for an Opera of his [Belasco's] dramatic version of

Madame Butterfly, founded on the original theme, written by Mr. John Luther Long * * * the said Libretto and all rights therein, dramatic or otherwise, to be the exclusive property of Messrs. G. Ricordi & Company for all countries of the world." It is upon this agreement that the plaintiff grounds its claim to motion picture rights in the world-famous opera, with music and lyrics by Puccini in collaboration with Giacosa Illica, which was copyrighted by the plaintiff in 1904, and of which the renewal copyright was acquired by the plaintiff from the son of Puccini.

The defendant does not deny that the plaintiff is the sole owner of the renewal copyright of the opera but it asserts that it owns the motion picture rights in the John Luther Long basic story and in the Belasco dramatic version thereof, and, consequently, if the plaintiff wishes to make a motion picture version of the opera, the defendant's consent must be obtained for the use of the Long novel and the Belasco play. Its primary contentions are two: (1) that the 1901 agreement of Long and Belasco with the plaintiff did not grant any motion picture rights; and (2) that in any event the expiration in 1925 of the copyright of Long's novel and the expiration in 1945 of the copyright of Belasco's play put an end to any exclusive license of the plaintiff to use the novel and the play for a motion picture version of the opera. Long had obtained in 1925 a renewal of the copyright on his novel and in 1932 his administrator granted to the defendant the motion picture rights therein. In the same year, 1932, the defendant obtained from the trustee under Belasco's will an assignment of the motion picture rights in Belasco's play. So far as appears there was no renewal of copyright in the play.

The district court was of opinion that the primary question for decision was whether the 1901 agreement granted to the plaintiff motion picture rights in the operatic version of the novel and of Belasco's dramatization of it. After an extensive review of the authorities, the court concluded that it did. The appellant argues strenuously that the court erred in so construing the agreement, but we do not find it necessary to decide this question. The right which Long had to make motion pictures of the story of his copyrighted novel did not extend beyond the term of the copyright; hence, if it be assumed that he assigned to the plaintiff any moving picture rights, they were necessarily similarly limited to the term of the copyright, unless the assignment included the right of renewal. It did not; the 1901 agreement made no allusion to renewal of copyright. In Fred Fisher Music Co. v. M. Whitmark & Sons, 318 U.S. 643, 63 S.Ct. 773, 87 L.Ed. 1055, which held that an author has power to assign his right of renewal during the term of the original copyright, no one suggested that rights assigned under the original copyright did not end with it, if nothing was said of renewal. We think they do. A copyright renewal creates a new estate, and the few cases which have dealt with the subject assert that the new estate is clear of all rights, interests or licenses granted under the original copyright. It is true that the expiration of Long's copyright of the novel did not affect the plaintiff's copyright of so much of the opera as was a "new work" and entitled to be independently copyrighted as such.[2] But the plaintiff has acquired no rights under Long's renewal of the copyright on his novel and the plaintiff's renewal copyright of the opera gives it rights only in the new matter which it added to the novel and the play. It follows that the plaintiff is not entitled to make general use of the novel for a motion picture version of Long's copyrighted story; it must be restricted to what was copyrightable as new matter in its operatic version.[3]

The next question is whether the plaintiff's right to make use of Belasco's play for a motion picture version thereof is similarly restricted to what was copyrightable as new matter in its operatic version. After Long's novel was copyrighted, Belasco was given permission—a license—to make use of the story for a play. Apparently the license was oral and its precise terms are not disclosed by the record. If it be assumed that the license gave Belasco any motion picture rights, they were necessarily limited to the term of the copyright of the novel. However, Belasco as author of the play had the common law rights of an author, which include the right to copyright it. This was done in 1917. By so doing the play was dedicated to the public except for the rights reserved by the copyright, for that is the condition upon the grant of any copyright. When the copyright expired, the play was property in the public demesne, since the record discloses no renewal of the copyright. Consequently, the exclusive motion picture rights in the play, which the trustee under Belasco's will assigned to the defendant by the 1932 agreement, expired in 1945 with the expiration of the copyright of the play. Thereafter the plaintiff was as free to use the play as was the defendant in making a motion picture version of the play.

However, the defendant still has the motion picture rights in the renewal copyright of Long's novel. Therefore it may assert, as it did, that the plaintiff cannot make general use of the story of the novel for a motion picture version of its opera; and, as already stated, the plaintiff is restricted to using what was copyrightable as new matter in its operatic version of the novel but is not so restricted in using the play which is now in public demesne. It scarcely need be added that the defendant, while free to use the novel and the play in making a motion picture, may not make use of the plaintiff's opera without its consent.

The remaining contentions of the parties have been examined and found without merit. Discussion of them is deemed unnecessary.

So much of the judgment as declares that the plaintiff is "the rightful owner and sole proprietor of the valid renewal copyright in the Opera entitled Madame Butterfly and of all rights and interest therein

---

2. The Act of 1947, 61 Stat. 652, 655, 17 U.S.C.A. § 7, formerly section 6 of the Act of 1909, 35 Stat. 1077. Edmonds v. Stern, 2 Cir., 248 F. 897.

3. See McCaleb v. Fox Film Corp., 5 Cir., 299 F. 48, 49; Glaser v. St. Elmo Co., Inc., C.C.S.D.N.Y., 175 F. 276, 277. The statute expressly provides that a copyright on a new work shall neither extend nor be construed to imply an exclusive right to use the original work from which the new work is derived. 17 U.S.C.A. § 7.

including the sole and exclusive motion picture rights" is affirmed. The injunction granted the plaintiff is too broad unless it be construed to forbid only such assertions of claims by the defendant as exceed those which the defendant is entitled to make as shown by the foregoing opinion. Accordingly the injunction is modified to conform to our opinion. Each party shall bear its own appellate costs and no attorney's fees are awarded to either party.

On Petition for Clarification

Paramount Pictures, Inc., asks for a clarification of that part of our opinion relating to the expiration and dedication of Belasco's copyright. We there said: "When the copyright expired, the play was property in the public demesne, since the record discloses no renewal of the copyright." What the petitioner desires is an express statement that only the new matter which Belasco's play added to Long's novel came into the public demesne upon the expiration of Belasco's copyright. It is implicit in the opinion as a whole that what is dedicated to the public as a condition of obtaining a copyright is only such matter as is copyrightable, but to avoid any possible cavil we will amend the above quoted sentence to read as follows: "When the copyright expired, the copyrightable new matter in the play was property in the public demesne, since the record discloses no renewal of the copyright".

Questions

1. During the renewal term of copyright in the Long novel, did Ricordi have the right to perform its opera on the stage? Would Paramount have standing to object to such a performance? Would anyone else?

2. Suppose the copyright in the Belasco play had been renewed, but that Paramount never acquired motion picture rights in the play for the renewal period, but did acquire motion picture rights in the Long novel for the renewal period. If Belasco had acquired from Long "exclusive dramatic rights" in the novel, would Paramount infringe Belasco's rights by producing during the renewal period a dramatic motion picture? Does the phrase "dramatic rights" include "dramatic motion picture rights"? See Bartsch v. Metro-Goldwyn-Mayer, Inc., p. 315 infra.

3. Suppose A wrote and copyrighted a novel in French, and then granted to B the exclusive English translation rights. Pursuant thereto B wrote and copyrighted an English translation of the novel. A applied for and obtained a renewal copyright in the original French version, but B neglected to obtain a renewal copyright in the English translation version. If thereafter C publishes copies of the English translation version, does he infringe either A's rights or B's rights? Cf. Grove Press, Inc. v. Greenleaf Publishing Co., 247 F.Supp. 518 (E.D.N.Y.1965).

4. Suppose Long had purported to grant to Ricordi operatic rights (including the right to perform the opera in motion pictures) for the renewal as well as the original term of copyright, but suppose further that Long died before such renewal rights vested in him. Would Ricordi have the right during the renewal term to perform the opera (either live or in motion pictures) without the

consent of the owners of the renewal rights in the Long novel? Bear this question in mind when you later consider Rohauer v. Killiam Shows, Inc., infra.

Collateral References

Brown, *The Widening Gyre: Are Derivative Works Getting Out of Hand?*, 3 Cardozo Arts & Ent. L.J. 1 (1984).

Goldstein, *Derivative Rights and Derivative Works in Copyright*, 30 J. Copr. Soc'y 209 (1983).

Jaszi, *When Works Collide: Derivative Motion Pictures, Underlying Rights, and the Public Interest*, 28 UCLA L.Rev. 715 (1981).

Nevins, *Doctrine of Copyright Ambush: Limitations on the Free Use of Public Domain Derivative Works*, 25 St. Louis U.L.J. 58 (1981).

LEON v. PACIFIC TELEPHONE & TELEGRAPH CO.

Circuit Court of Appeals, Ninth Circuit, 1937.
91 F.2d 484.

Before DENMAN, STEPHENS, and HEALY, CIRCUIT JUDGES.

DENMAN, CIRCUIT JUDGE. This is an appeal from a decree restraining infringement of copyright.

Appellee, Pacific Telephone & Telegraph Company, brought a suit in equity in the District Court to restrain appellants from infringement of appellee's copyright in the May, 1935, issues of appellee's San Francisco and East Bay telephone directories. The bill alleged the copyright duly issued covering these telephone books and set out that the defendants had infringed it by their publication of a "numerical telephone directory"—that is to say, they had taken the information contained in plaintiff's alphabetical directory and published it in rearranged form, classifying it according to "exchanges" or prefixes, and listing the numbers under each exchange in numerical consecutive order. The number was followed by the subscriber's name.

The bill prayed for temporary and permanent injunctions, damages and costs, and that the defendants be required to deliver up for destruction all the infringing copies as well as all plates, molds, matrices, or other means of making such infringing copies.

The defendants answered, denying the validity of the copyright and the charge of infringement, and also alleged that defendants' use of plaintiff's material was a "fair use" and hence not an infringement.

Trial was had and findings of fact and conclusions of law were made to this effect:

That since October, 1908, plaintiff had caused to be printed and distributed to its subscribers, at frequent intervals, alphabetical directories of the subscribers with their addresses and telephone numbers, all of which have been duly copyrighted, including the May, 1935, issues.

That the copyrights were valid.

That defendants had compiled, published, and sold to the public numeral directories entitled "Numerical Telephone Directory, San Francisco and other Cities and Towns, 1935–36" and "Numerical Telephone Directory, Oakland, Berkeley, Alameda, San Leandro, 1935," the same being compiled exclusively from the plaintiff's alphabetical directories.

That such action constituted infringement of the plaintiff's copyright.

That "The collection, editing, compilation, classification, arrangement, preparation of the material in said directories [by plaintiff] involved a large amount of detail and required great effort, discretion, judgment, painstaking care, skill, labor, accuracy, experience and authorship of high order. Said telephone directories were the sole and exclusive property of plaintiff, and plaintiff possessed the sole and exclusive literary and other rights therein, including the right to copy. Said directories constitute new and original literary works, and are the proper subject of copyright. Said copyrights are existing and plaintiff is the sole and exclusive owner, author and proprietor thereof."

The court entered a final decree permanently restraining the defendants from printing, publishing, selling, disposing of, etc., the infringing work; requiring them to deliver up for destruction all copies of the numerical directory and all plates, molds, matrices, or other means for making the directories, and awarding costs against them.

The appeal in this case raises three questions:

(1) Whether plaintiff has a valid copyright.

(2) Whether defendants' actions constituted an infringement.

* * *

(1) *Validity of the copyright.* That all formal steps necessary to perfect the copyright were taken is admitted by the defendants. Their contention here is that a directory represents nothing new or original and hence is not a proper subject of copyright. The District Court found otherwise, as the above quotation shows. Defendants introduced no evidence to contradict that finding. The plaintiff offered evidence as to how the 1935 directory was constructed. A person desiring telephone service, who was not listed in the previous directory, filled out an application card, and a telephone number was assigned to him. Then his name, address, and assigned number was typed on a slip of paper. Each page from the old directory was cut out and pasted on a sheet of paper and the new subscriber's slip was pasted alongside, preserving the alphabetical order. Subscribers in the old directory whose numbers had been discontinued, were penciled out of the page cut from the former volume. The paper sheets, with the penciling out of discontinued subscribers and the adjoining data on new subscribers were sent to the printer who made up a new page incorporating the changes.

The San Francisco listings of the directory alleged to be infringed totaled 160,266, and the East Bay listings 97,512. The total cost of producing these directories was $295,222. One hundred persons are regularly employed by plaintiff in its directory department.

It is obvious from this evidence that the business of getting out a directory is an expensive, complicated, well-organized endeavor, requiring skill, ingenuity, and original research. Unless the product of such activity is by its very nature not subject to copyright, plaintiff's directories are certainly entitled to copyright protection in the case at bar.

That a directory may be copyrighted is well settled. The principle is recognized in the statute (Act of March 4, 1909, c. 320, § 5, 35 Stat. 1076; 17 U.S.C.A. § 5):

The application for registration shall specify to which of the following classes the work in which copyright is claimed belongs:

> (a) Books, including composite and cyclopedic works, *directories*, gazetteers, and other compilations. (Italics supplied.)

A city directory may be copyrighted. Sampson & Murdock Co. v. Seaver-Radford Co. (C.C.A. 1) 140 F. 539, 542.

In Jeweler's Circular Pub. Co. v. Keystone Pub. Co., 281 F. 83, at page 88, 26 A.L.R. 571, the Circuit Court of Appeals for the Second Circuit held copyrightable a directory of jewelers' trade-marks:

> The right to copyright a book upon which one has expended labor in its preparation does not depend upon whether the materials which he has collected consist or not of matters which are publici juris, or whether such materials show literary skill or originality, either in thought or in language, or anything more than industrious collection. The man who goes through the streets of a town and puts down the names of each of the inhabitants, with their occupations and their street number, acquires material of which he is the author. He produces by his labor a meritorious composition, in which he may obtain a copyright, and thus obtain the exclusive right of multiplying copies of his work.

In Bleistein v. Donaldson Co., 188 U.S. 239, 250, 23 S.Ct. 298, 300, 47 L.Ed. 460, the court observed:

> The least pretentious picture has more originality in it than directories and the like, which may be copyrighted.

In National Tel. News Co. v. Western Union Tel. Co. (C.C.A. 7) 119 F. 294, 297, 60 L.R.A. 805, it was said:

> Little by little copyright has been extended to the literature of commerce, so that it now includes books that the old guild of authors would have disdained; catalogues, mathematical tables, statistics, designs, guidebooks, directories, and other works of similar character. Nothing, it would seem, evincing, in its makeup, that there has been underneath it, in some substantial way, the mind of a creator or originator, is now excluded.

Defendants seek to use this last case as an authority for their contention. The case holds that news printed by a teletype mechanism is not subject to copyright. This holding is of no help to defendants.

It must be concluded, in view of these decisions, that plaintiff's copyright is valid.

(2) *Infringement.* The defendants admit that they appropriated the material for their numerical directory from the plaintiff's copyrighted works. The only difference between the two directories is that that of the defendants omitted the listed parties' addresses and gave the rest of the information in inverted form. To take an example, the plaintiff's directory lists alphabetically,

>   Smith, John Joseph r 104 Chattanooga ATwater 3670.

The defendants' directory is divided into sections representing exchanges or prefixes. Under the Atwater section occurs the item

>   3670 Smith J.J.

It is not denied that this constitutes copying, nor do defendants contest the well-settled proposition that the owner of a copyright enjoys the exclusive right to multiply copies of his work. But the defendants assert that this copying in a rearranged form constitutes "fair use" of the protected material and hence is not an infringement.

It is not necessary in the case before us to discuss generally the question of what constitutes "fair use." Obviously, every publication copyrighted admits of many uses which do not constitute infringement. Counsel have not disclosed a single authority, nor have we been able to find one, which lends any support to the proposition that wholesale copying and publication of copyrighted material can ever be fair use. The defendants' contention in this regard rests entirely on the proposition that the numerical directory serves a different purpose than plaintiff's alphabetical directory.

The fact that plaintiff has not chosen to arrange its material in the inverted form used by appellants is no determinant of fair use. The inversion, without license, is not permitted merely because the holder of the copyright has not so used it. This is settled by the case of Fox Film Corporation v. Doyal, 286 U.S. 123, 127, 52 S.Ct. 546, 547, 76 L.Ed. 1010, where the Supreme Court said:

> The owner of the copyright, if he pleases, may refrain from vending or licensing and content himself with simply exercising the right to exclude others from using his property.

A like conclusion has been expressed by the courts of England. Weatherby & Sons v. International Horse Agency and Exchange, Ltd., [1910] 2 Ch. 297, 304; 79 L.J.Ch. 609. This case deals with the claimed infringement of the copyright of a stud book published periodically. The defendants made use of the material in this book and of another book which had originated a figure system for rating breeding race horses. The infringing work was a sort of combination of the two. The court said:

> Then it is said that the real and only test as to whether or not the defendants have made an unfair use of volume 21 of the Stud Book lies in the answer to the question whether there will be any competition between such volume and the defendant's book. * * * But, in my opinion, an unfair use may be made of one book in the preparation of another, even if there is no likelihood of competition between the former and the latter. After all

copyright is property, and an action will lie even if no damage be shown. In the present case there may not be much probability that any one will buy the defendants' book instead of volume 21 of the Stud Book, but the fact remains that in preparing this book the defendants have utilized, wholesale and without permission, lists prepared by the plaintiffs at much trouble and expense. In so doing they have appropriated the result of this labor and expense to their own use, and even if they have injured the plaintiffs in no other way, they have at any rate deprived them of the advantage, which their copyright conferred on them, of being able to publish such a book as the defendants' book at much less labor and expense than anyone else.

And in H. Blacklock & Co. v. C. Arthur Pearson, Ltd., [1915] 2 Ch. 276, 383, the court said:

* * * But in all events it appears to me that the defendants took a substantial portion of the list of names contained in the index to the plaintiffs' publication, thus without an exertion of their own getting the benefit of the labour and expense expended in compiling the list which formed the index to Bradshaw. * * * I come to the conclusion that what was done by the defendants was an infringement of the copyright of the plaintiffs. * * *

Questions

1. If you were writing the copyright law *de novo* would you include protection for directories?

2. What was Pacific Telephone's *original* contribution to its directory? Was it in the names and numbers themselves? Was it in the arrangement of the names and numbers? Is originality involved in listing names and numbers in alphabetical order?

3. If originality may be found in Pacific Telephone's arrangement of the names and numbers, did Leon copy that aspect of Pacific's work which was original? Is there infringement of a derivative work if that which is copied from it consists of non-original aspects of the work? See Sec. 103(b) of the Copyright Act.

4. If I spend ten years painstakingly exploring the stacks of the British Museum, and finally come upon a forgotten Shakespeare manuscript, may I claim a copyright in it? I may have demonstrated "great effort, discretion, judgment, painstaking care, skill, labor, accuracy, [and] experience" but have I also demonstrated "authorship"?

5. When is a work the product of a joint authorship? Is it necessary that several authors make their respective contributions contemporaneously in order to be able to claim as joint authors? (For the respective rights of joint authors see Nimmer on Copyright, §§ 6.08–6.12.) Is the later contribution by a second author a derivative work, in which the author of the first contribution is at most a licensee, or does the fusion of the earlier and later contributions create a "joint work", in which each author-contributor has an undivided interest? See Nimmer on Copyright, §§ 6.05–6.06.

Collateral References

Comment, *Accountability Among Co-Owners of Statutory Copyright*, 72 Harv.Law Rev. 1550 (1959);

Cary, *Joint Ownership of Copyrights,* Studies on Copyright 689 (Fisher ed. 1963) (Copyright Law Revision Study No. 12, 1958, U.S.Gov't Print.Off. 1960).

Nimmer on Copyright, § 3.04.

7. *Works of Utility*

BAKER v. SELDEN
Supreme Court of the United States, 1879.
101 U.S. 99, 11 Otto 99, 25 L.Ed. 841.

Mr. Justice Bradley delivered the opinion of the court.

Charles Selden, the testator of the complainant in this case, in the year 1859 took the requisite steps for obtaining the copyright of a book, entitled "Selden's Condensed Ledger, or Bookkeeping Simplified," the object of which was to exhibit and explain a peculiar system of bookkeeping. In 1860 and 1861, he took the copyright of several other books, containing additions to and improvements upon the said system. The bill of complaint was filed against the defendant, Baker, for an alleged infringement of these copyrights. The latter, in his answer, denied that Selden was the author or designer of the books, and denied the infringement charged, and contends on the argument that the matter alleged to be infringed is not a lawful subject of copyright.

The parties went into proofs, and the various books of the complainant, as well as those sold and used by the defendant, were exhibited before the examiner, and witnesses were examined on both sides. A decree was rendered for the complainant, and the defendant appealed.

The book or series of books of which the complainant claims the copyright consists of an introductory essay explaining the system of book-keeping referred to, to which are annexed certain forms or blanks, consisting of ruled lines, and headings, illustrating the system and showing how it is to be used and carried out in practice. This system effects the same results as book-keeping by double entry; but, by a peculiar arrangement of columns and headings, presents the entire operation, of a day, a week, or a month, on a single page, or on two pages facing each other, in an account-book. The defendant uses a similar plan so far as results are concerned; but makes a different arrangement of the columns, and uses different headings. If the complainant's testator had the exclusive right to the use of the system explained in his book, it would be difficult to contend that the defendant does not infringe it, notwithstanding the difference in his form of arrangement; but if it be assumed that the system is open to public use, it seems to be equally difficult to contend that the books made and sold by the defendant are a violation of the copyright of the complainant's book considered merely as a book explanatory of the system. Where the truths of a science or the methods of an art are the common property of the whole world, any author has the right to express the one, or explain and use the other, in his own way. As an author,

Sec. C   WORKS OF AUTHORSHIP   109

Selden explained the system in a particular way. It may be conceded that Baker makes and uses account-books arranged on substantially the

---

INTRODUCTION.

The new system of Book-keeping introduced by the accompanying illustrative forms, contain within themselves their own demonstration. The captions of the blank forms sufficiently indicate their uses without explanation. Utility and simplicity are united to as great an extent as is practicable, and they are carried much further than by any previous structure.

A correct record of business transactions is necessary in all systems of Book-keeping, consequently original explanatory entry is indispensable. For Governmental Accounts, this is amply provided for in the Forms of Record of the Auditor and Treasurer, which present a clear and concise exhibit of all Receipts and Disbursements in their respective departments, and of Distributions derived from Taxes, Appropriations, Profit and Loss or Transfers, Auditorial, Congressional or otherwise, as provided for by Law. With regard to the Condensing Books now known, viz: the Journal, which compacts preceding books in a comparatively small space, and the Ledger, which compacts the Journal, and until now regarded the extreme condensing book of accounts, they are superseded by the Condensed Ledger, which fully supplies their place, dispenses with the *absolute* necessity of an Index, and presents a continual Balance Sheet, determining its correctness the whole time, which important result an adept in Book-keeping will perceive at a glance. By my system of arrangement, the Departments of Auditor and Treasurer are completely counterparted, and no error can occur which is not susceptible of quick discovery, as the only *legitimate* difference in the accounts between them *must exist* in the Floating Orders.

The Condensed Ledger which shows only monthly postings of accounts, may answer for any other interval. The Reports may also embrace any period of time. Aggregates or Balances of accounts may be carried forward indiscriminately, at any period, without changing the result. Governments usually continue aggregates for the Fiscal Year, adopting only the balances at the commencement. Individuals may be governed by intervening settlements, or convenience.

Respecting the Mercantile Ledger, comprising *many* and various accounts, my Ledger as a re-condenser thereof, classifying those accounts under a *few* comprehensive titles, and indicating Financial Condition *instantly* is invaluable.

The author, though always desirous of promoting the public good, does not in this instance, disclaim a hope of pecuniary reward; to this end he has taken steps to secure his right to some personal compensation, for what he thinks, a valuable discovery. In addition to the copyright of this little book, he has applied for a patent right to cover the forms of the publication, and prevent their indiscriminate use by the public.

The above is a reproduction of the Introduction from Selden's Condensed Ledger. Note in particular the last paragraph.

same system; but the proof fails to show that he has violated the copyright of Selden's book, regarding the latter merely as an explanatory work; or that he has infringed Selden's right in any way, unless the latter became entitled to an exclusive right in the system.

The evidence of the complainant is principally directed to the object of showing that Baker uses the same system as that which is explained and illustrated in Selden's books. It becomes important, therefore, to determine whether, in obtaining the copyright of his books, he secured the exclusive right to the use of the system or method of book-keeping which the said books are intended to illustrate and explain. It is contended that he has secured such exclusive right, because no one can use the system without using substantially the same ruled lines and headings which he has appended to his books in illustration of it. In other words, it is contended that the ruled lines and headings, given to illustrate the system, are a part of the book, and, as such, are secured by the copyright; and that no one can make or use similar ruled lines and headings, or ruled lines and headings made and arranged on substantially the same system, without violating the copyright. And this is really the question to be decided in this case. Stated in another form, the question is, whether the exclusive property in a system of book-keeping can be claimed, under the law of copyright, by means of a book in which that system is explained? The complainant's bill, and the case made under it, are based on the hypothesis that it can be.

It cannot be pretended, and indeed it is not seriously urged, that the ruled lines of the complainant's account-book can be claimed under any special class of objects, other than books, named in the law of copyright existing in 1859. The law then in force was that of 1831, and specified only books, maps, charts, musical compositions, prints, and engravings. An account-book, consisting of ruled lines and blank columns, cannot be called by any of these names unless by that of a book.

There is no doubt that a work on the subject of book-keeping, though only explanatory of well-known systems, may be the subject of a copyright; but, then, it is claimed only as a book. Such a book may be explanatory either of old systems, or of an entirely new system; and, considered as a book, as the work of an author, conveying information on the subject of book-keeping, and containing detailed explanations of the art, it may be a very valuable acquisition to the practical knowledge of the community. But there is a clear distinction between the book, as such, and the art which it is intended to illustrate. The mere statement of the proposition is so evident, that it requires hardly any argument to support it. The same distinction may be predicated of every other art as well as that of book-keeping. A treatise on the composition and use of medicines, be they old or new; on the construction and use of ploughs, or watches, or churns; or on the mixture and application of colors for painting or dyeing; or on the mode of drawing lines to produce the effect of perspective,—would be the subject of copyright; but no one would contend that the copyright of the treatise would give the exclusive right to the art or manufacture described therein. The copyright of the book, if not pirated from other works, would be valid without regard to the novelty, or want of novelty, of its subject-matter. The novelty of the art or thing described or explained has nothing to do with the validity of the copyright. To give to the author of the book an exclusive property in the art described therein, when no examination of its novelty has ever been officially made, would be a surprise and a fraud upon the public. That is the province of letters-patent, not of copyright. The claim to an invention or discovery of an art or manufacture must be subjected to the examination of the Patent Office before an exclusive right therein can be obtained; and it can only be secured by a patent from the government.

The difference between the two things, letters-patent and copyright, may be illustrated by reference to the subjects just enumerated. Take the case of medicines. Certain mixtures are found to be of great value in the healing art. If the discoverer writes and publishes a book on the subject (as regular physicians generally do), he gains no exclusive right to the manufacture and sale of the medicine; he gives that to the public. If he desires to acquire such exclusive right, he must obtain a patent for the mixture as a new art, manufacture, or composition of matter. He may copyright his book, if he pleases; but that only secures to him the exclusive right of printing and publishing his book. So of all other inventions or discoveries.

The copyright of a book on perspective, no matter how many drawings and illustrations it may contain, gives no exclusive right to the modes of drawing described, though they may never have been known or used before. By publishing the book, without getting a patent for the art, the latter is given to the public. The fact that the art described in the book by illustrations of lines and figures which are reproduced in practice in the application of the art, makes no difference. Those illustrations are the mere language employed by the author to convey his ideas more clearly. Had he used words of description instead of diagrams (which merely stand in the place of words), there could not be the slightest doubt that others, applying the art to practical use, might lawfully draw the lines and diagrams which were in the author's mind, and which he thus described by words in his book.

The copyright of a work on mathematical science cannot give to the author an exclusive right to the methods of operation which he propounds, or to the diagrams which he employs to explain them, so as to prevent an engineer from using them whenever occasion requires. The very object of publishing a book on science or the useful arts is to communicate to the world the useful knowledge which it contains. But this object would be frustrated if the knowledge could not be used without incurring the guilt of piracy of the book. And where the art it teaches cannot be used without employing the methods and diagrams used to illustrate the book, or such as are similar to them, such methods and diagrams are to be considered as necessary incidents to the art, and given therewith to the public; not given for the purpose of publication in other works explanatory of the art, but for the purpose of practical application.

Of course, these observations are not intended to apply to ornamental designs, or pictorial illustrations addressed to the taste. Of these it may be said, that their form is their essence, and their object, the production of pleasure in their contemplation. This is their final end. They are as much the product of genius and the result of composition, as are the lines of the poet or the historian's periods. On the other hand, the teachings of science and the rules and methods of useful art have their final end in application and use; and this application and use are what the public derive from the publication of a book which teaches them. But as embodied and taught in a literary composition or book, their essence consists only in their statement. This alone is what is secured by the copyright. The use by another of the same methods of statement, whether in words or illustrations, in a book published for teaching the art, would undoubtedly be an infringement of the copyright.

Recurring to the case before us, we observe that Charles Selden, by his books, explained and described a peculiar system of book-keeping, and illustrated his method by means of ruled lines and blank columns, with proper headings on a page, or on successive pages. Now, whilst no one has a right to print or publish his book, or any material part thereof, as a book intended to convey instruction in the art, any person may practise and use the art itself which he has described and illustrated therein. The use of the art is a totally different thing from a publication of the book explaining it. The copyright of a book on book-keeping cannot secure the exclusive right to make, sell, and use account-books prepared upon the plan set forth in such book. Whether the art might or might not have been patented, is a question which is not before us. It was not patented, and is open and free to the use of the public. And, of course, in using the art, the ruled lines and headings of accounts must necessarily be used as incident to it.

The plausibility of the claim put forward by the complainant in this case arises from a confusion of ideas produced by the peculiar nature of the art described in the books which have been made the subject of copyright. In describing the art, the illustrations and diagrams employed happen to correspond more closely than usual with the actual work performed by the operator who uses the art. Those illustrations and diagrams consist of ruled lines and headings of accounts; and it is similar ruled lines and headings of accounts which, in the application of the art, the book-keeper makes with his pen, or the stationer with his press; whilst in most other cases the diagrams and illustrations can only be represented in concrete forms of wood, metal, stone, or some other physical embodiment. But the principle is the same in all. The description of the art in a book, though entitled to the benefit of copyright, lays no foundation for an exclusive claim to the art itself. The object of the one is explanation; the object of the other is use. The former may be secured by copyright. The latter can only be secured, if it can be secured at all, by letters-patent. * * *

The conclusion to which we have come is, that blank account-books are not the subject of copyright; and that the mere copyright of Selden's book did not confer upon him the exclusive right to make and use account-books, ruled and arranged as designated by him and described and illustrated in said book.

The decree of the Circuit Court must be reversed, and the cause remanded with instructions to dismiss the complainant's bill; and it is

So ordered.

Questions

1. Does the Copyright Act of 1976 continue the doctrine of Baker v. Selden? Nothing in the Act itself or the Committee Reports expressly allude to the doctrine, which is surprising given its importance under the 1909 Act. But note Sec. 113(b).

2. Did the Court hold that Baker's use of Selden's book was not an act prohibited by copyright, or that Selden's book was incapable of copyright protection?

3. Was Selden's contention that "no one can use the system without using substantially the same ruled lines and headings which he has appended to his books" factually accurate? Did Baker use "substantially the same ruled lines and headings"? Compare the explanation of the Baker v. Selden principle as re-stated in Mazer v. Stein, supra, with the *Baker* Court's own explanation.

4. If it is possible to use Selden's "system" without necessarily using his particular arrangement of ruled lines and headings, should he be able to claim copyright protection for such arrangement even if not for the "system"?

5. Architectural plans are said to be copyrightable as a form of "pictorial, graphic, or sculptural work". See H.Rep., p. 55. To what extent is such protection limited by the doctrine of Baker v. Selden? See Scholz Homes v. Maddox, 379 F.2d 84 (6th Cir.1967).

Collateral Reference

Nimmer on Copyright, § 2.18.

MORRISSEY v. PROCTER & GAMBLE CO.

United States Court of Appeals, First Circuit, 1967.
379 F.2d 675.

Before ALDRICH, CHIEF JUDGE, MCENTEE and COFFIN, CIRCUIT JUDGES.

ALDRICH, CHIEF JUDGE. This is an appeal from a summary judgment for the defendant. The plaintiff, Morrissey, is the copyright owner of a set of rules for a sales promotional contest of the "sweepstakes" type involving the social security numbers of the participants. Plaintiff alleges that the defendant, Procter & Gamble Company, infringed, by copying, almost precisely, Rule 1. In its motion for summary judgment, based upon affidavits and depositions, defendant denies that plaintiff's Rule 1 is copyrightable material, * * *

The * * * case raises a * * * difficult question. Before discussing it we recite plaintiff's Rule 1, and defendant's Rule 1, the italicizing in the latter being ours to note the defendant's variations or changes.

1. Entrants should print name, address and social security number on a boxtop, or a plain paper. Entries must be accompanied by * * * boxtop or by plain paper on which the name * * * is copied from any source. Official rules are explained on * * * packages or leaflets obtained from dealer. If you do not have a social security number you may use the name and number of any member of your immediate family living with you. Only the person named on the entry will be deemed an entrant and may qualify for prize.

Use the correct social security number belonging to the person named on entry * * * wrong number will be disqualified.

(Plaintiff's Rule)

1. Entrants should print name, address and *Social Security* number on a *Tide* boxtop, or *on* [a] plain paper. Entries must be accompanied by Tide boxtop (*any size*) or by plain paper on which the name 'Tide' is copied from any source. Official rules are *available* on Tide Sweepstakes packages, or *on* leaflets *at* Tide dealers, *or you can send a stamped, self-addressed envelope to:* Tide "Shopping Fling" Sweepstakes, P.O. Box 4459, Chicago 77, Illinois.

If you do not have a *Social Security* number, you may use the name and number of any member of your immediate family living with you. Only the person named on the entry will be deemed an entrant and may qualify for a prize.

Use the correct *Social Security* number, belonging to the person named on *the* entry—wrong numbers will be disqualified.

(Defendant's Rule)

The district court, following an earlier decision, Gaye v. Gillis, D.Mass., 1958, 167 F.Supp. 416, took the position that since the substance of the contest was not copyrightable, which is unquestionably correct, Baker v. Selden, 1879, 101 U.S. 99, 25 L.Ed. 841; Affiliated Enterprises v. Gruber, 1 Cir., 1936, 86 F.2d 958; Chamberlin v. Uris Sales Corp., 2 Cir., 1945, 150 F.2d 512, and the substance was relatively simple, it must follow that plaintiff's rule sprung directly from the substance and "contains no original creative authorship." 262 F.Supp. at 738. This does not follow. Copyright attaches to form of expression, and defendant's own proof, introduced to deluge the court on the issue of access, itself established that there was more than one way of expressing even this simple substance. Nor, in view of the almost precise similarity of the two rules, could defendant successfully invoke the principle of a stringent standard for showing infringement which some courts apply when the subject matter involved admits of little variation in form of expression. E.g., Dorsey v. Old Surety Life Ins. Co., 10 Cir., 1938, 98 F.2d 872, 874, 119 A.L.R. 1250 ("a showing of appropriation in the exact form or substantially so."); Continental Casualty Co. v. Beardsley, 2 Cir., 1958, 253 F.2d 702, 705, cert. denied, 358 U.S. 816, 79 S.Ct. 25, 3 L.Ed.2d 58 ("a stiff standard for proof of infringement.").

Nonetheless, we must hold for the defendant. When the uncopyrightable subject matter is very narrow, so that "the topic necessarily requires," Sampson & Murdock Co. v. Seaver-Radford Co., 1 Cir., 1905, 140 F. 539, 541; cf. Kaplan, An Unhurried View of Copyright, 64–65 (1967), if not only one form of expression, at best only a limited number, to permit copyrighting would mean that a party or parties, by copyrighting a mere handful of forms, could exhaust all possibilities of future use of the substance. In such circumstances it does not seem accurate to say that any particular form of expression comes from the subject matter. However, it is necessary to say that the subject matter would be appropriated by permitting the copyrighting of its expression. We cannot recognize copyright as a game of chess in which the public can be checkmated. Cf. Baker v. Selden, supra.

Upon examination the matters embraced in Rule 1 are so straightforward and simple that we find this limiting principle to be applicable. Furthermore, its operation need not await an attempt to copyright all possible forms. It cannot be only the last form of expression which is to be condemned, as completing defendant's exclusion from the substance. Rather, in these circumstances, we hold that copyright does not extend to the subject matter at all, and plaintiff cannot complain even if his particular expression was deliberately adopted.

Affirmed.

Questions

1. Try to write a contest rule that in substance contains all of the elements found in Morrissey's Rule 1 but that in form differs from both the Morrissey and Procter & Gamble versions. Can you do it? If you think you have succeeded, compare your version with those of the other members of the class. Are there more than "a mere handful" of different versions?

2. Return to Time, Inc. v. Bernard Geis Associates, p. 41 supra. Was that court correct in finding the *Morrissey* doctrine inapplicable?

8. *Computer Programs*

APPLE COMPUTER, INC. v. FRANKLIN COMPUTER CORPORATION

United States Court of Appeals, Third Circuit, 1983.
714 F.2d 1240.

Before HUNTER, HIGGINBOTHAM and SLOVITER, CIRCUIT JUDGES.

OPINION OF THE COURT

SLOVITER, CIRCUIT JUDGE.

* * *

Apple Computer, Inc. appeals from the district court's denial of a motion to preliminarily enjoin Franklin Computer Corp. from infringing the copyrights Apple holds on fourteen computer programs.

* * * Because we conclude that the district court proceeded under an erroneous view of the applicable law, we reverse the denial of the preliminary injunction and remand.

* * *

Apple, one of the computer industry leaders, * * * It presently manufactures Apple II computers and distributes over 150 programs. * * * One of the byproducts of Apple's success is the independent development by third parties of numerous computer programs which are designed to run on the Apple II computer.

Franklin, the defendant below, manufactures and sells the ACE 100 personal computer and at the time of the hearing employed about 75 people and had sold fewer than 1,000 computers. The ACE 100 was designed to be "Apple compatible," so that peripheral equipment and software developed for use with the Apple II computer could be used in conjunction with the ACE 100. Franklin's copying of Apple's operating system computer programs in an effort to achieve such compatibility precipitated this suit.

Like all computers both the Apple II and ACE 100 have a central processing unit (CPU) which is the integrated circuit that executes programs. In lay terms, the CPU does the work it is instructed to do. Those instructions are contained on computer programs.

There are three levels of computer language in which computer programs may be written.[2] High level language, such as the commonly used BASIC or FORTRAN, uses English words and symbols, and is relatively easy to learn and understand (e.g., "GO TO 40" tells the computer to skip intervening steps and go to the step at line 40). A somewhat lower level language is assembly language, which consists of alphanumeric labels (e.g., "ADC" means "add with carry"). Statements in high level language, and apparently also statements in assembly language, are referred to as written in "source code." The third, or lowest level computer language, is machine language, a binary language using two symbols, 0 and 1, to indicate an open or closed switch (e.g., "01101001" means, to the Apple, add two numbers and save the result). Statements in machine language are referred to as written in "object code."

The CPU can only follow instructions written in object code. However, programs are usually written in source code which is more intelligible to humans. Programs written in source code can be converted or translated by a "compiler" program into object code for use by the computer. Programs are generally distributed only in their object code version stored on a memory device.

---

2. Useful nontechnical descriptions of computer operations appear in Note, *Copyright Protection for Computer Programs In Read Only Memory Chips*, 11 Hofstra L.Rev. 329 (1982), and Note, *Copyright Protection of Computer Program Object Code*, 96 Harv.L.Rev. 1723 (1983).

A computer program can be stored or fixed on a variety of memory devices, two of which are of particular relevance for this case. The ROM (Read Only Memory) is an internal permanent memory device consisting of a semi-conductor "chip" which is incorporated into the circuitry of the computer. A program in object code is embedded on a ROM before it is incorporated in the computer. Information stored on a ROM can only be read, not erased or rewritten.[3] The ACE 100 apparently contains EPROMs (Erasable Programmable Read Only Memory) on which the stored information can be erased and the chip reprogrammed, but the district court found that for purposes of this proceeding, the difference between ROMs and EPROMs is inconsequential. 545 F.Supp. at 813 n. 3. The other device used for storing the programs at issue is a diskette or "floppy disk", an auxiliary memory device consisting of a flexible magnetic disk resembling a phonograph record, which can be inserted into the computer and from which data or instructions can be read.

Computer programs can be categorized by function as either application programs or operating system programs. Application programs usually perform a specific task for the computer user, such as word processing, checkbook balancing, or playing a game. In contrast, operating system programs generally manage the internal functions of the computer or facilitate use of application programs. The parties agree that the fourteen computer programs at issue in this suit are operating system programs.

* * *

Franklin's principal defense at the preliminary injunction hearing and before us is primarily a legal one, directed to its contention that the Apple operating system programs are not capable of copyright protection.

* * *

Copyrightability of a Computer Program Expressed in Object Code

Certain statements by the district court suggest that programs expressed in object code, as distinguished from source code, may not be the proper subject of copyright. We find no basis in the statute for any such concern. * * *

In 1976, after considerable study, Congress enacted a new copyright law to replace that which had governed since 1909. Act of October 19, 1976, Pub.L. No. 94–553, 90 Stat. 2541 (*codified at* 17 U.S.C. §§ 101 et seq.). Under the law, two primary requirements must be satisfied in order for a work to constitute copyrightable subject matter—it must be an "original wor[k] of authorship" and must be "fixed in [a] tangible medium of expression." 17 U.S.C. § 102(a). * * *

* * * The statute enumerates seven categories under "works of authorship" including "literary works", defined as follows:

---

3. In contrast to the permanent memory devices a RAM (Random Access Memory) is a chip on which volatile internal memory is stored which is erased when the computer's power is turned off.

> "Literary works" are works, other than audiovisual works, expressed in words, numbers, or other verbal or numerical symbols or indicia, regardless of the nature of the material objects, such as books, periodicals, manuscripts, phonorecords, film, tapes, disks, or cards, in which they are embodied.

17 U.S.C. § 101. A work is "fixed" in a tangible medium of expression when:

> its embodiment in a copy or phonorecord, by or under the authority of the author, is sufficiently permanent or stable to permit it to be perceived, reproduced, or otherwise communicated for a period of more than transitory duration. A work consisting of sounds, images, or both, that are being transmitted, is "fixed" for purposes of this title if a fixation of the work is being made simultaneously with its transmission.

Id.

Although section 102(a) does not expressly list computer programs as works of authorship, the legislative history suggests that programs were considered copyrightable as literary works. See H.R.Rep. No. 1476, 94th Cong., 2d Sess. 54, *reprinted in* 1976 U.S.Code Cong. & Ad.News 5659, 5667 ("'literary works' ... includes ... computer programs"). Because a Commission on New Technological Uses ("CONTU") had been created by Congress to study, *inter alia,* computer uses of copyrighted works, Pub.L. No. 93–573, § 201, 88 Stat. 1873 (1974), Congress enacted a status quo provision, section 117, in the 1976 Act concerning such computer uses pending the CONTU report and recommendations.[6]

The CONTU Final Report recommended that the copyright law be amended, *inter alia,* "to make it explicit that computer programs, to the extent that they embody an author's original creation, are proper subject matter of copyright." National Commission on New Technological Uses of Copyrighted Works, *Final Report* 1 (1979) [hereinafter CONTU Report]. CONTU recommended two changes relevant here: that section 117, the status quo provision, be repealed and replaced with a section limiting exclusive rights in computer programs so as "to ensure that rightful possessors of copies of computer programs may use or adapt these copies for their use," id.; and that a definition of computer program be added to section 101. Id. at 12. Congress adopted both changes. Act of Dec. 12, 1980, Pub.L. No. 96–517, § 10, 94 Stat. 3015, 3028. The revisions embodied CONTU's recommendations to clarify the law of copyright of computer software. H.R.Rep. No. 1307. * * *

The 1980 amendments added a definition of a computer program:

> A "computer program" is a set of statements or instructions to be used directly or indirectly in a computer in order to bring about a certain result.

---

6. Section 117 applied only to the scope of protection to be accorded copyrighted works when used in conjunction with a computer and not to the copyrightability of programs. H.R.Rep. No. 1476, at 116. * *

17 U.S.C. § 101. The amendments also substituted a new section 117 which provides that "it is not an infringement for the owner of a copy of a computer program to make or authorize the making of another copy or adaptation of that computer program" when necessary to "the utilization of the computer program" or "for archival purposes only." 17 U.S.C. § 117. The parties agree that this section is not implicated in the instant lawsuit. The language of the provision, however, by carving out an exception to the normal proscriptions against copying, clearly indicates that programs are copyrightable and are otherwise afforded copyright protection.

We considered the issue of copyright protection for a computer program in Williams Electronics, Inc. v. Artic International, Inc., and concluded that "the copyrightability of computer programs is firmly established after the 1980 amendment to the Copyright Act." 685 F.2d at 875. * * *

The district court here questioned whether copyright was to be limited to works "designed to be 'read' by a human reader [as distinguished from] read by an expert with a microscope and patience", 545 F.Supp. at 821. The suggestion that copyrightability depends on a communicative function to individuals stems from the early decision of White-Smith Music Publishing Co. v. Apollo Co., 209 U.S. 1, 28 S.Ct. 319, 52 L.Ed. 655 (1908), which held a piano roll was not a copy of the musical composition because it was not in a form others, except perhaps for a very expert few, could perceive. See 1 Nimmer on Copyright § 2.03[B][1] (1983). However, it is clear from the language of the 1976 Act and its legislative history that it was intended to obliterate distinctions engendered by *White-Smith*. * * *

Under the statute, copyright extends to works in any tangible means of expression "*from which they can be perceived,* reproduced, or otherwise communicated, either directly or *with the aid of a machine or device.*" 17 U.S.C. § 102(a) (emphasis added). Further, the definition of "computer program" adopted by Congress in the 1980 amendments is "sets of statements or instructions to be used *directly* or *indirectly* in a computer in order to bring about a certain result." 17 U.S.C. § 101 (emphasis added). As source code instructions must be translated into object code before the computer can act upon them, only instructions expressed in object code can be used "directly" by the computer. * * * This definition was adopted following the CONTU Report in which the majority clearly took the position that object codes are proper subjects of copyright. See CONTU Report at 21. The majority's conclusion was reached although confronted by a dissent based upon the theory that the "machine-control phase" of a program is not directed at a human audience. See CONTU Report at 28–30 (dissent of Commissioner Hersey).

* * *

The district court also expressed uncertainty as to whether a computer program in object code could be classified as a "literary work."[7] However, the category of "literary works", one of the seven

---

7. The district court stated that a programmer working directly in object code

copyrightable categories, is not confined to literature in the nature of Hemingway's *For Whom the Bell Tolls*. The definition of "literary works" in section 101 includes expression not only in words but also "numbers, or other * * * numerical symbols or indicia", thereby expanding the common usage of "literary works." Cf. Harcourt, Brace & World, Inc. v. Graphic Controls Corp., 329 F.Supp. 517, 523–24 (S.D.N.Y. 1971) (the symbols designating questions or response spaces on exam answer sheets held to be copyrightable "writings" under 1909 Act); Reiss v. National Quotation Bureau, Inc., 276 F. 717 (S.D.N.Y.1921) (code book of coined words designed for cable use copyrightable). Thus a computer program, whether in object code or source code, is a "literary work" and is protected from unauthorized copying, whether from its object or source code version. * * *

Copyrightability of a Computer Program Embedded on a ROM

Just as the district court's suggestion of a distinction between source code and object code was rejected by our opinion in *Williams* issued three days after the district court opinion, so also was its suggestion that embodiment of a computer program on a ROM, as distinguished from in a traditional writing, detracts from its copyrightability. In *Williams* we rejected the argument that "a computer program is not infringed when the program is loaded into electronic memory devices (ROMs) and used to control the activity of machines." 685 F.2d at 876. Defendant there had argued that there can be no copyright protection for the ROMs because they are utilitarian objects or machine parts. We held that the statutory requirement of "fixation", the manner in which the issue arises, is satisfied through the embodiment of the expression in the ROM devices. * * * Therefore we reaffirm that a computer program in object code embedded in a ROM chip is an appropriate subject of copyright. See also Note, *Copyright Protection of Computer Program Object Code*, 96 Harv.L.Rev. 1723 (1983); Note, *Copyright Protection for Computer Programs in Read Only Memory Chips*, 11 Hofstra L.Rev. 329 (1982).

* * *

Copyrightability of Computer Operating System Programs

We turn to the heart of Franklin's position on appeal which is that computer operating system programs, as distinguished from application programs, are not the proper subject of copyright "regardless of the language or medium in which they are fixed." * * *

Franklin contends that operating system programs are *per se* excluded from copyright protection under the express terms of section

---

appears to think more as a mathematician or engineer, that the process of constructing a chip is less a work of authorship than the product of engineering knowledge, and that it may be more apt to describe an encoded ROM as a pictorial three-dimensional object than as a literary work. 545 F.Supp. at 821–22. The district court's remarks relied in part on a quotation about "microcode", see id. at 821 n. 14; Apple introduced testimony that none of the works in suit contain "microcode." Moreover, Apple does not seek to protect the ROM's architecture but only the program encoded upon it.

102(b) of the Copyright Act, and under the precedent and underlying principles of Baker v. Selden, 101 U.S. 99, 25 L.Ed. 841 (1879). These separate grounds have substantial analytic overlap.

* * *

Franklin reads *Baker v. Selden* as "stand[ing] for several fundamental principles, each presenting * * * an insuperable obstacle to the copyrightability of Apple's operating systems." It states:

> *First, Baker* teaches that use of a system itself does not infringe a copyright on the description of the system. *Second, Baker* enunciates the rule that copyright does not extend to purely utilitarian works. *Finally, Baker* emphasizes that the copyright laws may not be used to obtain and hold a monopoly over an idea. In so doing, *Baker* highlights the principal difference between the copyright and patent laws—a difference that is highly pertinent in this case.

Section 102(b) of the Copyright Act, the other ground on which Franklin relies, appeared first in the 1976 version, long after the decision in *Baker v. Selden*. It provides:

> In no case does copyright protection for an original work of authorship extend to any idea, procedure, process, system, method of operation, concept, principle, or discovery, regardless of the form in which it is described, explained, illustrated, or embodied in such work.

It is apparent that section 102(b) codifies a substantial part of the holding and dictum of *Baker v. Selden*. See 1 Nimmer on Copyright § 2.18[D], at 2–207.

We turn to consider the two principal points of Franklin's argument.

1. "Process", "System" or "Method of Operation"

Franklin argues that an operating system program is either a "process", "system", or "method of operation" and hence uncopyrightable. Franklin correctly notes that underlying section 102(b) and many of the statements for which *Baker v. Selden* is cited is the distinction which must be made between property subject to the patent law, which protects discoveries, and that subject to copyright law, which protects the writings describing such discoveries. However, Franklin's argument misapplies that distinction in this case. Apple does not seek to copyright the method which instructs the computer to perform its operating functions but only the instructions themselves. The method would be protected, if at all, by the patent law, an issue as yet unresolved. See Diamond v. Diehr, 450 U.S. 175, 101 S.Ct. 1048, 67 L.Ed.2d 155 (1981).

Franklin's attack on operating system programs as "methods" or "processes" seems inconsistent with its concession that application programs are an appropriate subject of copyright. Both types of programs instruct the computer to do something. Therefore, it should make no difference for purposes of section 102(b) whether these instructions tell the computer to help prepare an income tax return (the task of an application program) or to translate a high level language program from source code into its binary language object code form (the task of an operating system program such as "Applesoft". * * * Since it is only the instructions which are protected, a "process" is no more involved because the instructions in an operating system program may be used to activate the operation of the computer than it would be if instructions were written in ordinary English in a manual which described the necessary steps to activate an intricate complicated machine. There is, therefore, no reason to afford any less copyright protection to the instructions in an operating system program than to the instructions in an application program.

Franklin's argument, receptively treated by the district court, that an operating system program is part of a machine mistakenly focuses on the physical characteristics of the instructions. But the medium is not the message. We have already considered and rejected aspects of this contention in the discussion of object code and ROM. The mere fact that the operating system program may be etched on a ROM does not make the program either a machine, part of a machine or its equivalent. Furthermore, as one of Franklin's witnesses testified, an operating system does not have to be permanently in the machine in ROM, but it may be on some other medium, such as a diskette or magnetic tape, where it could be readily transferred into the temporary memory space of the computer. In fact, some of the operating systems at issue were on diskette. As the CONTU majority stated,

> Programs should no more be considered machine parts than videotapes should be considered parts of projectors or phonorecords parts of sound reproduction equipment. * * * That the words of a program are used ultimately in the implementation of a process should in no way affect their copyrightability.

CONTU Report at 21.

Franklin also argues that the operating systems cannot be copyrighted because they are "purely utilitarian works" and that Apple is seeking to block the use of the art embodied in its operating systems. This argument stems from the following dictum in *Baker v. Selden:*

> The very object of publishing a book on science or the useful arts is to communicate to the world the useful knowledge which it contains. But this object would be frustrated if the knowledge could not be used without incurring the guilt of piracy of the book. And where the art it teaches cannot be used without employing the methods and diagrams used to illustrate the book, or such as are similar to them, such methods and diagrams are to be considered as necessary incidents to the art, and given therewith to the public; not given for the purpose of publication in other works explanatory of the art, but for the purpose of practical application.

101 U.S. at 103. We cannot accept the expansive reading given to this language by some courts, see, e.g., Taylor Instrument Companies v. Fawley-Brost Co., 139 F.2d 98 (7th Cir.1943), cert. denied, 321 U.S. 785, 64 S.Ct. 782, 88 L.Ed. 1076 (1944). In this respect we agree with the views expressed by Professor Nimmer in his treatise. See 1 Nimmer on Copyright § 2.18[C].

* * *

Idea/Expression Dichotomy

Franklin's other challenge to copyright of operating system programs relies on the line which is drawn between ideas and their expression. * * *

We * * * focus on whether the idea is capable of various modes of expression. If other programs can be written or created which perform the same function as an Apple's operating system program, then that program is an expression of the idea and hence copyrightable. In essence, this inquiry is no different than that made to determine whether the expression and idea have merged, which has been stated to occur where there are no or few other ways of expressing a particular idea. See, e.g., Morrissey v. Procter & Gamble Co., 379 F.2d 675, 678–79 (1st Cir.1967); Freedman v. Grolier Enterprises, Inc., 179 U.S. P.Q. 476, 478 (S.D.N.Y.1973) ("[c]opyright protection will not be given to a form of expression necessarily dictated by the underlying subject matter"); CONTU Report at 20.

The district court made no findings as to whether some or all of Apple's operating programs represent the only means of expression of the idea underlying them. Although there seems to be a concession by Franklin that at least some of the programs can be rewritten, we do not believe that the record on that issue is so clear that it can be decided at the appellate level. Therefore, if the issue is pressed on remand, the necessary finding can be made at that time.

* * *

In summary, Franklin's contentions that operating system programs are per se not copyrightable is unpersuasive. * * *

For the reasons set forth in this opinion, we will reverse the denial of the preliminary injunction and remand to the district court for further proceedings in accordance herewith.

Questions

1. Is the court correct in regarding computer programs as falling within the Section 102(a)(1) "literary works" classification?

2. Is the court correct in regarding the object code version of a computer program to be no less copyrightable than the source code version?

3. Is the court correct in regarding operating system programs to be no less copyrightable than application programs? What impact, if any, does the *Baker v. Selden* doctrine now have on the issue of computer program copyrightability?

Collateral Reference

Nimmer on Copyright, §§ 2.04[C], 2.18[J].

Note

FINAL REPORT OF THE NATIONAL COMMISSION ON NEW TECHNOLOGICAL USES OF COPYRIGHTED WORKS (CONTU)

Dissent of COMMISSIONER JOHN HERSEY.

This dissent from the Commission report on computer programs takes the view that copyright is an inappropriate, as well as unnecessary, way of protecting the usable forms of computer programs. Its main argument, briefly summarized, follows.

In the early stages of its development, the basic ideas and methods to be contained in a computer program are set down in written forms, and these will presumably be copyrightable with no change in the 1976 Act. But the program itself, in its mature and usable form, is a machine-control element, a mechanical device, which on constitutional grounds and for reasons of social policy ought not be copyrighted.

The view here is that the investment of creative effort in the devising of computer programs does warrant certain modes of protection for the resulting devices, but that these modes already exist or are about to be brought into being under other laws besides copyright; that the need for copyright protection of the machine phase of computer programs, quite apart from whether it is fitting, has not been demonstrated to this Commission; and that the social and economic effects of permitting copyright to stand alongside these other forms of protection would be, on balance, negative.

The heart of the argument lies in what flows from the distinction, raised above, between the written and mechanical forms of computer programs: admitting these devices to copyright would mark the first time copyright had ever covered a means of communication, not with the human mind and senses, but with machines.

Concurring opinion of COMMISSIONER NIMMER.

I concur in the Commission's opinion and in its recommendations regarding software. I do, however, share in a number of the doubts and concerns expressed in Commissioner Hersey's thoughtful dissenting opinion. What is most troubling about the Commission's recommendation of open-ended copyright protection for all computer software is its failure to articulate any rationale which would not equally justify copyright protection for the tangible expression of any and all original ideas (whether or not computer technology, business, or otherwise). If *literary works* are to be so broadly construed, the Copyright Act becomes a general misappropriation law, applicable as well in what has traditionally been regarded as the patent arena, and, indeed, also in other areas to which neither copyright nor patent law has previously extended. This poses a serious constitutional issue in that it is arguable that such an approach stretches the meaning of *authors* and *writings* as used in the Copyright Clause of the Constitution beyond the breaking point. Apart from the constitutional issues, it raises policy questions, the full implications of which remain murky at best. Still, at this time, knowing what we now know about the nature of the computer industry, its needs, and its potential for great contributions to the public welfare, I am prepared, on balance, to support the Commission's conclusions and recommendations.

At the same time I should like to suggest a possible line of demarcation which would distinguish between protectible and nonprotectible software in a manner more consistent with limiting such protection to the conventional copyright arena. This suggestion is made not because I recommend its immediate implementation, but rather because it may prove useful in the years to come if the Commission's recommendation for protection of all software should prove unduly restrictive. In such circumstances it may prove desirable to limit copyright protection for software to those computer programs which produce works which themselves qualify for copyright protection. A program designed for use with a data base, for example, would clearly be copyrightable since the resulting selection and arrangement of items from such data base would itself be copyrightable as a compilation. Thus, a program designed for use in conjunction with a legal information retrieval system would be copyrightable, since the resulting enumeration of cases on a given topic could claim copyright. A program designed for a computer game would be copyrightable because the output would itself constitute an audiovisual work. (For this purpose the fact that such audiovisual work is not fixed in a tangible medium of expression, and for that reason is ineligible for copyright protection should not invalidate the copyright in the computer program as long as the program itself is fixed in a tangible medium of expression.) On the other hand, programs which control the heating and air-conditioning in a building, or which determine the flow of fuel in an engine, or which control traffic signals would not be eligible for copyright because their operations do not result in copyrightable works. The fact that such a program might also provide for a printout of written instructions (which would be copyrightable) would only render protectible that particular aspect of such a program.

The distinction here suggested appears to me to be consistent with the recognized copyrightability of sound recordings. It sometimes has been argued that while printed instructions tell *how* to do work, computer programs actually *do* the work. But this is also true of sound recordings, which in a sense constitute a machine (the phonorecord) communicating with another machine (the record player). A sound recording contained in a phonorecord does not tell a record player *how* to make sounds which constitute a Cole Porter melody. Rather, it activates the record player in such manner as actually to create such a melody. But Commissioner Hersey has made another and most important distinction. "The direct product of a sound recording, when it is put in a record player, is the sound of music—the writing of the author in its audible form." The point is that the operation of the sound recording produces a musical work which itself is copyrightable. That is sufficient to render the sound recording itself copyrightable quite apart from the separate copyright in the musical work. This principle is directly analogical to the distinction suggested above with respect to computer programs.

Collateral References

Koenig, *Software Copyright: The Conflict Within CONTU,* 24 Bull. Copr. Soc'y 340 (1980).

Samuelson, *CONTU Revisited: The Case Against Copyright Protection For Computer Programs In Machine-Readable Form,* (1984) Duke L.J. 663.

See the discussion of the Semiconductor Chip Protection Act of 1984 in Nimmer on Copyright, Chapter 18.

Chapter Two

PUBLICATION

Note *

The Significance of Publication in the Law of Copyright

The concept of publication was of immense importance under the 1909 Act. It became a legal word of art, denoting a process much more esoteric than is suggested by the lay definition of the term. That it thus evolved was due largely to the American dichotomy between common law and statutory copyright, wherein the act of publication constituted the dividing line between the two systems of protection.

With the current Act's virtual abolition of common law copyright by federal preemption, the concept ceases to have the full significance it formerly possessed. Publication, nevertheless, continues to be important under the current Act. In analyzing its current significance, it is necessary to distinguish between publications occurring on or after January 1, 1978, and those occurring before. Not only will the legal consequences *under the current Act* vary depending upon whether a publication occurred before or after that date, but the very definition of publication may differ depending upon whether the acts said to constitute publication occurred prior to January 1, 1978.

[A]—The Significance of Publication Occurring on or After January 1, 1978

Whether or not a publication has occurred after the effective date of the current Act can be significant in each of the following contexts: (1) a copyright notice must appear on copies and phonorecords of works which have been "published;"[1] (2) the copyright notice which must appear on all such copies and phonorecords must include the year of first publication;[2] (3) the deposit requirement applies only to published works;[3] (4) unpublished works are protected under the current Act regardless of the nationality or domicile of the author,[4] while published works by foreign authors are protected only under certain prescribed circumstances;[5] (5) the term of copyright for anonymous and

---

* Nimmer on Copyright, §§ 4.01, 4.04.

1. 17 U.S.C.A. §§ 401(a); 402(a). Failure to observe this requirement could result in the invalidation of the copyright. See 17 U.S.C.A. § 405.

2. 17 U.S.C.A. §§ 401(b)(2); 402(b)(2).

3. 17 U.S.C.A. § 407(a), (d).

4. 17 U.S.C.A. § 104(a).

5. 17 U.S.C.A. § 104(b).

pseudonymous works, and works made for hire, is measured from the year of first publication; [6] (6) even where the usual term of the life of the author plus 50 years applies, the date of first publication may be significant in that 75 years after the first publication of such a work (or 100 years from creation if that is sooner) it may be presumed that the author has been dead for at least 50 years unless the Copyright Office records relating to the death of authors indicates the contrary; [7] (7) under the termination of transfers provisions relating to grants executed on or after January 1, 1978, if such a grant "covers" publication rights, the period during which it may be terminated is during the five year period beginning "thirty-five years from the date of publication under the grant or at the end of forty years from the date of execution of the grant, whichever ends earlier"; [8] (8) registration in the Copyright Office must occur within five years of first publication in order for the registration certificate to constitute prima facie evidence of the validity of the copyright; [9] (9) statutory damages and attorney's fees are available as to unpublished works only if registration preceded infringement, and as to published works only if registration either preceded infringement, or if registration occurred within three months after first publication; [10] (10) first publication abroad will under certain circumstances constitute an exemption from the manufacturing clause; [11] (11) the reproduction rights of libraries and archives will vary depending upon whether or not the work has been published; [12] (12) the performance exemption for dramatic works primarily directed to the blind may be invoked only ten years after publication of the work; [13] (13) the compulsory performance license for noncommercial broadcasting is applicable only to nondramatic musical works which have been published.[14]

[B]—The Significance Under the Current Act of Publication Having Occurred Prior to January 1, 1978

On January 1, 1978 common law copyright as to most works terminated by reason of federal preemption. Prior thereto common law copyright existed in a work from the moment of its creation, and continued unless and until the work was published.[15] But upon publication of a work prior to January 1, 1978 the owner's common law protection therein was lost, through a forfeiture imposed by law. For this reason common law copyright was often referred to as the right of first publication. Likewise, publication was generally a condition precedent to obtaining statutory protection under the 1909 Act, the duration of the copyright being measured from the date of first publication. Furthermore, the right to statutory protection might not be claimed in the first instance, or if once claimed would thereafter be lost if publication were made without observance of statutory formalities.

All of this was true under the 1909 Act. But of what significance are such pre-1978 acts of publication under the current Act? Their significance lies in

---

6. The term is 75 years from the year of first publication, or 100 years from creation, whichever expires first. 17 U.S.C.A. § 302(c).

7. 17 U.S.C.A. § 302(d), (e).

8. 17 U.S.C.A. § 203(a)(3).

9. 17 U.S.C.A. § 410(c).

10. 17 U.S.C.A. § 412.

11. 17 U.S.C.A. § 601(b)(7)(B).

12. 17 U.S.C.A. § 108(b), (c).

13. 17 U.S.C.A. § 110(9).

14. 17 U.S.C.A. § 118(b), (d).

15. Even if a work remained unpublished, it lost its common law copyright if it were registered for statutory copyright as an unpublished work under Sec. 12 of the 1909 Act. See Nimmer on Copyright, § 7.16[A][2].

the fact that in each such instance the act of publication may have resulted in a work being injected into the public domain under the law as it existed prior to January 1, 1978. If that occurred, it is of crucial relevance under the current Act for the reason that no work in the public domain prior to January 1, 1978 may be protected under the current Act.[16] Because some works created prior to 1978, if not theretofore injected into the public domain, will continue to be protected under statutory copyright until 75 years after publication,[17] or until 50 years after the author's death,[18] it will remain necessary at least until the year 2053, and in some instances thereafter,[19] to be concerned with whether an act of publication occurred prior to January 1, 1978.

Quite apart from the question of whether publication injected the work into the public domain, a pre-1978 publication continues to be relevant under the current Act for the purpose of determining when the initial copyright term ends, and the renewal term begins with respect to those works which under the current Act remain subject to the renewal provisions.[20]

[C]—The Definition of Publication

The current Copyright Act contains the following definition of "publication":

> "the distribution of copies [21] or phonorecords [22] of a work to the public by sale or other transfer of ownership, or by rental, lease, or lending. The offering to distribute copies or phonorecords to a group of persons for purposes of further distribution, public performance, or public display, constitutes publication. A public performance or display of a work does not of itself constitute publication." [23]

The Copyright Act of 1909 contained no such statutory definition, so that the courts were required to give meaning to the term through the accretion of case law. To what extent does the definition of "publication" in the current Act constitute a codification of such case law? Consider your answer to that question as you read the next series of cases.

---

16. 17 U.S.C.A. Trans. and Supp.Prov. § 103.

17. This assumes that the work was published with proper notice, or otherwise obtained statutory copyright as an unpublished work, prior to January 1, 1978, and was thereafter renewed.

18. This assumes that the work remained unpublished and protected by common law copyright until January 1, 1978.

19. If the life plus 50 term is applicable, and the author dies after 2003.

20. This is true only as to those works in which a pre-1978 statutory copyright was originally secured by publication with notice rather than by registration as an unpublished work.

21. " 'Copies' are material objects, other than phonorecords, in which a work is fixed by any method now known or later developed, and from which the work can be perceived, reproduced, or otherwise communicated, either directly or with the aid of a machine or device. The term 'copies' includes the material object, other than a phonorecord, in which the work is first fixed." 17 U.S.C.A. § 101.

22. " 'Phonorecords' are material objects in which sounds, other than those accompanying a motion picture or other audiovisual work, are fixed by any method now known or later developed, and from which the sounds can be perceived, reproduced, or otherwise communicated, either directly or with the aid of a machine or device. The term 'phonorecords' includes the material object in which the sounds are first fixed." 17 U.S.C.A. § 101.

23. 17 U.S.C.A. § 101.

Collateral Reference

Brylaski, *Publication: Its Role in Copyright Matters, Both Past and Present,* 31 J. Copr. Soc'y 507 (1984).

A. GENERAL PUBLICATION DISTINGUISHED FROM LIMITED PUBLICATION

BELL v. COMBINED REGISTRY CO.

United States District Court, Northern District of Illinois, 1975.
397 F.Supp. 1241.

FLAUM, DISTRICT JUDGE.

This is an action for copyright infringement arising out of the publication of a poem (herein referred to as "Desiderata") by defendant in the August, 1971, issue of *Success Unlimited Magazine.* The case has been submitted to the Court for decision on affidavits, depositions, exhibits, and memoranda. The following shall constitute the findings of fact and conclusions of law.

THE ISSUES

Plaintiff alleges that the poem (originally untitled) was written by Max Ehrman in Terre Haute, Indiana, in the early 1920s; Mr. Ehrman obtained a federal copyright (No. 962402) on the poem on January 3, 1927 under the name of "Indiana Publishing Company"; Mr. Ehrman bequeathed the copyright to his widow Bertha upon his death in 1945; Bertha Ehrman renewed the copyright in 1954; Bertha Ehrman bequeathed the copyright to her nephew Richmond Wight upon her death in 1962; Richmond Wight assigned the copyright for value to plaintiff in 1971. Plaintiff also claims that in 1948 Bertha Ehrman copyrighted a book entitled *The Poems of Max Ehrman* (copyright No. A28266) which included Desiderata; Bertha Ehrman assigned this copyright in the same year to Bruce Humphreys Inc. for value; in 1968 an assignment was made by the above assignee to plaintiff. Plaintiff claims that the copyrights are valid and have been infringed by defendant. He cites Bell v. Pro Arts Inc., 366 F.Supp. 474 (N.D.Ohio 1973), aff'd, 511 F.2d 451 (6th Cir.1975), in which his ownership and the validity of the instant copyrights were upheld. * * *

DEFENDANT'S ATTACKS ON THE COPYRIGHT

Defendant has raised the following issues by way of defense:

(1) was the copyright forfeited by acts of Max Ehrman in publishing the work without the requisite copyright notice?

(2) was the copyright abandoned by Max Ehrman?

(3) was the copyright forfeited by incorrect notice prior to the assignment to plaintiff?

(4) is the plaintiff estopped from asserting the copyright against defendant?

(5) is the plaintiff guilty of laches?

DESIDERATA

GO PLACIDLY AMID THE NOISE & HASTE, & REMEMBER WHAT PEACE THERE MAY BE IN SILENCE. AS FAR AS POSSIBLE WITHOUT surrender be on good terms with all persons. Speak your truth quietly & clearly; and listen to others, even the dull & ignorant; they too have their story. ❧ Avoid loud & aggressive persons, they are vexations to the spirit. If you compare yourself with others, you may become vain & bitter; for always there will be greater & lesser persons than yourself. Enjoy your achievements as well as your plans. ❧ Keep interested in your own career, however humble; it is a real possession in the changing fortunes of time. Exercise caution in your business affairs; for the world is full of trickery. But let this not blind you to what virtue there is; many persons strive for high ideals; and everywhere life is full of heroism. ❧ Be yourself. Especially, do not feign affection. Neither be cynical about love; for in the face of all aridity & disenchantment it is perennial as the grass. ❧ Take kindly the counsel of the years, gracefully surrendering the things of youth. Nurture strength of spirit to shield you in sudden misfortune. But do not distress yourself with imaginings. Many fears are born of fatigue & loneliness. Beyond a wholesome discipline, be gentle with yourself. ❧ You are a child of the universe, no less than the trees & the stars; you have a right to be here. And whether or not it is clear to you, no doubt the universe is unfolding as it should. ❧ Therefore be at peace with God, whatever you conceive Him to be, and whatever your labors & aspirations, in the noisy confusion of life keep peace with your soul. ❧ With all its sham, drudgery & broken dreams, it is still a beautiful world. Be careful. Strive to be happy. ❧ ❧

FOUND IN OLD SAINT PAUL'S CHURCH, BALTIMORE; DATED 1692

An unauthorized poster reproduction of the Ehrman poem.

It is helpful to define the terms forfeiture and abandonment. According to Nimmer on Copyrights,

> Despite imprecise usage in some of the cases, abandonment must be distinguished from forfeiture of copyrights. The latter occurs upon publication of the work without proper copyright notice and is effectuated by operation of law regardless of the intent of the copyright proprietor. Abandonment occurs only if there is an intent by the copyright proprietor to surrender rights in his work. Id. at Section 146, p. 656.6

Thus forfeiture presents a narrower technical question; abandonment is a more subjective determination.

The Facts

This case turns upon a reconstruction of events of many years ago. Some of the proof submitted by defendant consists of letters and newspaper articles from the 1930s and 1940s. This material is hearsay, for it is offered in an attempt to reconstruct the facts related in them. The court finds that these materials nevertheless are admissible under the "ancient documents" exception to the hearsay rule. As embodied in the Federal Rules of Evidence (effective July 1, 1975), the rule excepts from operation of the hearsay rule:

> Statements in a document in existence twenty years or more the authenticity of which is established. Rule 803(16)

It is fair to assume that the material offered by defendant is the best evidence available on the issues present. Insofar as plaintiff's objections go to the weight of the exhibits, they have been considered as the documents are evaluated.

As to the issues raised by the defendant, the court finds the following facts.

Mr. Max Ehrman was the author of the work now known as Desiderata. His diary states that the poem had its early formation in 1921. As he stated therein:

> I should like, if I could, to leave a humble gift * * *: a bit of chaste prose that had caught up some noble moods.

In 1927 he copyrighted the work under his business name—Indiana Publishing Company. In December of 1933, Mr. Ehrman used Desiderata as part of a Christmas greeting sent to friends. At least two of the recipients wrote back thanking him for the cards. Thereafter Mr. Ehrman received a letter from one Merrill Moore, dated July 20, 1942. Mr. Moore identified himself in the correspondence as a practicing psychiatrist presently on active duty with the U.S. Army. He explained his reasons for writing as follows:

> I think you should know that nearly every day of my life I use your very fine prose poem Desiderata in my work * * *. Here I have found your philosophy as useful and have used it considerably as part of the psychotherapy I am doing * * *. I must have given away a thousand copies in the last few years. A patient, a depressed woman, gave it to me once several years ago, with no name attached * * *.

Thereafter, several letters were exchanged between the men regarding Moore's use of the poem. On August 17, 1942, a Mr. Fuller wrote to Moore stating that a package containing autographed copies of the work had been sent a month earlier per Moore's request. By letter of October 5, 1942, Moore thanked Ehrman for the copies he had received and made the following statement:

> * * * I have distributed the beautiful copies which you sent me and want to thank you for them again. I know that I shall carry Desiderata with me and when I get there I shall have it multigraphed for distribution to the soldiers if you have no objection * * *.

Ehrman responded to this letter on November 3, 1942:

> Yes, of course, you may distribute multigraphed copies of Desiderata to the soldiers. I am happy to have at least this small part in your splendid work.

Additional correspondence from Moore to Ehrman dated Thanksgiving and November, 1944, stated:

> Also I use Desiderata liberally and always find it helpful. Like a panacea (it cures *everything*) it should be bottled and sold as Dr. EHRMANN'S MAJIC SOUL MEDICINE!!!

> and

> I am continuing to use your priceless prose poem in my work.

Several publications of that time carried stories of Moore's work and his use of Desiderata, see *Saturday Spectator,* "A Poet's Influence", December 15, 1945; *A.A.A.S. Bulletin,* "From the Netherlands East Indies", October, 1945; *DePauw Alumnus,* "Nationally Known Poet and Author Dies", Vol. X, November 1945.

Found in the Merrill Moore papers in the Library of Congress is a typed copy of Desiderata with the author's name under the title but no copyright notice.

The next chapter of this saga takes place in the 1950s. Sometime between September 1, 1952, and 1956 the Reverend Frederick Kates, serving as the dean of St. John's Cathedral in Spokane, Washington, came across a copy of Desiderata without a copyright notice. On June 1, 1956, Rev. Kates became rector of St. Paul's Church, Baltimore. This church had been founded in 1692. In 1957 Rev. Kates included the poem in the first edition of his book, *Between Dark and Dawn,* (The Upper Room 1957). During the lenten season of either 1959 or 1960 Rev. Kates included the poem on a sheet of devotional material he passed out to about 200 members of his congregation. At the top of the page of this handout containing the poem was the notation:

> Old St. Paul's Church, Baltimore A.D. 1692.

Reverend Kates also passed out copies of Desiderata at various other times until 1972. Seven editions of his book included the poem. In 1972 he was informed by his publisher that a copyright claim had been asserted.

Both parties agree that a great number of periodicals and commercial firms used Desiderata with the attribution "Old St. Paul's Church, Baltimore, A.D. 1692". The above was the source of such erroneous attribution.

In March of 1967 defendant published the poem in *Success Unlimited Magazine* with this attribution. Mr. Mandino, the officer of defendant in charge of content of the magazine, had received the poem from Father John O'Brien of the University of Notre Dame. Mr. Mandino then saw the poem in Equinox, its publisher stated that he had found the poem in India and that it had no known author. The poem was published again in the August 1971 edition of *Success Unlimited*. This suit was instituted based on this publication.

Forfeiture Issues

The copyright notice is required on material sought to be protected by the Copyright Act, see 17 U.S.C. § 10. A publication authorized on the copyright proprietor which fails to include the correct notice of copyright forfeits the copyright protection and places the material into the public domain. *Nimmer,* supra, § 82. Thus a proprietor who desires to preserve his legal monopoly must be vigilant in policing distributions of the work.

To produce a forfeiture of the copyright, the evidence must show: (1) that the poem was published, (2) that no correct notice appeared thereon. According to *Nimmer,* supra,

> * * * publication occurs when by consent of the copyright owner, the original or tangible copies of a work are sold, leased, loaned, given away, or otherwise made available to the general public * * * Id. § 49 pp. 194–195.

Defendant cites several instances which, it argues, produced a forfeiture of the Desiderata copyright. The most substantial of these instances, in the court's view, was the distribution of copies of the poem to U.S. troops in the Pacific by Merrill Moore during World War II. There can be no serious dispute that this distribution was a "publication" as defined by *Nimmer,* supra. By letter Max Ehrman expressly authorized the distribution, and copies of the work were distributed to many hundreds of men. What is critical is this factual issue: did the copies distributed by Merrill Moore include the required copyright notice? There is no direct evidence on this question. However, it is a fair inference that the distribution of the work through Merrill Moore was accomplished without the requisite copyright notice. All of the circumstances are consistent with such a conclusion, and inconsistent with a contrary one. The ambience of the exchange of letters between the two men was one of informality and cordiality. Permission to use the work was given gratuitously. Nowhere was a copyright or copyright notice mentioned. The lone copy of the poem found in the Merrill Moore papers did not have such a notice. Nor did the copy that Rev. Kates found some years later. The actions of Max Ehrman are not consonant with those of a copyright proprietor intent on protecting a commercial asset. Defendants have met the burden of showing that a forfeiture was more likely than not.

In the face of defendant's showing on the forfeiture issue, plaintiff has offered no evidence in rebuttal. A copyright owner has the duty to police all distributions of his work if he desires to preserve his legal monopoly. Indeed, most courts have imposed the burden of proof on the copyright proprietor in the first instance to demonstrate that he has placed the notice on all published copies. Defendant in the case at bar has established *prima facie* that a forfeiture took place. Plaintiff could definitively resolve the issue by producing a copy of the work which was distributed to the troops. It is not unreasonable to place upon a copyright proprietor this ultimate burden. An owner who desires to protect his copyright ordinarily preserves copies of all publications so that proof of notice is always available. Thus the inability of the present proprietor to produce a copy showing notice has substantive significance. In view of the evidence submitted by defendant, and the absence of any rebuttal by plaintiff, the court concludes that a forfeiture has been established by a preponderance of the evidence.

This finding that a forfeiture occurred during World War II means that the poem entered the public domain, and no valid copyright may now be asserted.

Defendant also contends that the work was forfeited when published in newspapers, and when plaintiff used his own name on a flyer sent to accused infringers. The evidence on these two issues is not, in the court's view, sufficient to show a forfeiture. * * *

For the foregoing reasons, judgment is entered for the defendant, Combined Registry Company.

Questions

1. Suppose that Merrill Moore had never distributed copies of Desiderata. Should the plaintiff's copyright in the work nevertheless have been held invalid by reason of the publication without notice by Reverend Kates? By reason of Max Ehrman's publication of the poem on Christmas greeting cards? Consider the answer to this latter question in connection with your reading of White v. Kimmell, infra.

2. If you were representing the plaintiff what arguments might you have made as to why the distribution of the poem by Moore without a proper notice affixed thereto did not inject the work into the public domain? What is the possible relevance of Section 8 of the 1909 Act? See the affirming opinion on appeal, 536 F.2d 164 (7th Cir.1976).

WHITE v. KIMMELL

United States Court of Appeals, Ninth Circuit, 1952.
193 F.2d 744.

Before STEPHENS and HEALY, CIRCUIT JUDGES and McCORMICK, DISTRICT JUDGE.

HEALY, CIRCUIT JUDGE.

Appellant sought a declaratory judgment that a manuscript entitled "Gaelic," authored by Stewart Edward White, and a certain book by the same author entitled "The Job of Living," based on the Gaelic manuscript and quoting from it, are in the public domain and may be quoted without infringement of the copyright claimed by appellee Kimmell or the common-law proprietary rights claimed by her in Gaelic. For convenience appellant will be referred to as the plaintiff, appellee Kimmell as the defendant, and Stewart Edward White as White.

Some preliminary attention should be given the nature of the Gaelic manuscript. Gaelic is supposedly the spirit of an individual who had departed this world and become an invisible nonmaterial entity. The work embodies communications from Gaelic, received chiefly by White's wife. The communications were written down by various individuals, and were subsequently, between about 1920 and 1930, reduced to manuscript form by White. The latter identified Gaelic as his and his wife's "nickname for what seemed to us a single and definite personality, apparently detailed to tell us what made the wheels go round."

Plaintiff's complaint avers that the Gaelic manuscript was abandoned by White to the general public by his reproducing and distributing copies himself and permitting others to do the same without limitation as to use or right to republish and without notice of claim of copyright. The defendant relies on a transfer to her by White of his interest in his work as establishing her exclusive right to quote from Gaelic. This transfer was made in October 1944, about two years before White's death.

The court found that the reproduction and distribution of the manuscript amounted to a limited and restricted publication only; that there was no general publication of it, and that the manuscript is not in the public domain. D.C., 94 F.Supp. 502. The sole issue here is whether these findings are justified by the evidence. We think they are not.

The testimony is not in conflict, although as will later appear, portions of it do exhibit contrasts. The following is a fair summary of the showing made on the part of the plaintiff: In the fall of 1933 mimeographed stencils of the Gaelic manuscript were cut and run off by a Mrs. Maguire, White's secretary, at the instance of White. Originally sixty or seventy copies were made. The secretary, at White's request, mailed out eighteen or twenty of them to a list of persons furnished her by White, together with a letter of transmittal. In this letter White stated in part that he had "finally made some extra copies of 'Gaelic' because so many of you wanted them. * * * I am glad to know of your interest, and I wish you to read it, to use it as you like, and pass it on to others, and for as long a time as you can. If you get through with it, you might return it to me to hand to someone else.

Otherwise, you are at liberty to keep it." Later, additional copies were mailed out by the secretary at the request of White with the same letter of transmittal. White left four or five copies with the secretary which she gave to friends or clients of hers who were interested in the manuscript. White was not acquainted with these persons. He at no time made any statement to the secretary or to anyone in her presence limiting the use of the Gaelic manuscript by persons receiving it. The distribution was not made to a group or association. A second run of forty or fifty copies was later made by the secretary. These were distributed by White in part to friends and in part to strangers who wrote him requesting a copy. No limitation was expressed by White to the donee as to the use which might be made of Gaelic. At the time of White's death, only two copies were found in his possession. He never sold a copy to anyone. So runs the testimony of the secretary.

Near the end of 1940 a witness, Margaret Oettinger of Palo Alto, wrote to White, whom she did not know, requesting a copy of Gaelic. When informed there were none left, she wrote asking permission to make mimeographed copies for herself. White wrote her that she was at liberty to do so. He did not in his correspondence or otherwise place any limitation on the persons among whom the manuscript might be circulated. Later Mrs. Oettinger wrote White asking permission to charge persons the cost of reproduction. Permission was granted. Mrs. Oettinger saw White on only two occasions. On the one occasion when the Gaelic manuscript was discussed, White told her that he had no objection to additional copies being made, and no limitations were placed on the amount to be charged nor to whom the manuscript was to be sold. It is clear that Mrs. Oettinger told White she wanted to distribute copies to some of her friends. It was understood that the charge was to cover the cost of materials. Mrs. Oettinger ran off three mimeographed sets of the manuscript, averaging about forty copies apiece. The first two sets were sold for $2.00 per copy and the last for $1.50. This witness testified that as time went on she sent copies to persons who were strangers to her, who said they had seen the manuscript somewhere and wanted a copy. These people were apparently strangers to White, also. Most of the people to whom she sold were referred to her by White or by appellee as a source from which copies could be obtained.

A Mrs. Jones testified to having purchased several copies of the manuscript from Mrs. Oettinger through correspondence, and to having paid for them. No restriction or limitation was placed on the use she could make of them. She sent the volumes to people who had asked her for them.

The defendant testified on her own behalf, as did also two other persons, namely a Mrs. Duce and a Mr. Stevens. The testimony of the latter two related to a time apparently not earlier than 1943. These three persons all said, in substance, that while they were given permission to reproduce or to distribute mimeographed copies of the Gaelic manuscript, they were cautioned by White to use extreme care not only as regards the persons given copies but also as regards the persons permitted even to see a copy. Their testimony, however, related entirely to their own activities and their own relations with White. None of it purported to have any bearing on the Oettinger publication or on the publication of the author himself.

White clearly did not wish to publish Gaelic as a conventionally printed book. Several reasons said to have been given by him are testified to—his wife's work in the field was more important and should have precedence; the work was not in proper form for a book; the "Invisibles" had instructed him not to print it.

The trial judge's opinion contains a comprehensive and concededly accurate survey of the judicial precedents relating to limited publication, and there would seem to be no justification for our duplicating his efforts in that direction. We adopt as a fair summary of the applicable principle his statement that a limited publication which communicates the contents of a manuscript to a definitely selected group and for a limited purpose, and without the right of diffusion, reproduction, distribution or sale, is considered a "limited publication," which does not result in loss of the author's common-law right to his manuscript; but that the circulation must be restricted both as to persons and purpose, or it can not be called a private or limited publication. The respect in which we are constrained to disagree with the judge is in the application of the stated legal principles to the facts of the case.

It appears to us that the court disregarded in large part vital and uncontradicted testimony, notably that of White's secretary and of Mrs. Oettinger. No mention is made of White's letter of transmittal, testified to by the secretary, which suggested unqualifiedly that the recipients of the copies of the manuscript pass it on to "others." Who these others might be, or what their philosophy, would necessarily be matters completely unknown to White. As to Oettinger, it seems to be implied by the court that actually she was permitted only to make copies under a strict limitation, whereas her testimony is unequivocal that no limitation was put on the number of copies she might turn out, and none on the persons to whom they would go. Eloquent of her freedom from restrictions is her testimony that on one occasion she sent a copy to a person who had seen a copy in a dentist's office and had written asking her for one. Her evidence conclusively indicates that some of the people to whom she sent copies were not friends or even acquaintances of White, of appellee, or of Mrs. Oettinger herself. Thus it can not be said, on the basis of this phase of the showing, that only friends of White, or "kindred spirits," got or were intended to get copies. Nobody seeking the mimeographed manuscript appears to have been asked for any sort of credentials. In a word, we are unable to see in this picture any definitely selected individuals or any limited, ascertained group or class to whom the communication was restricted.

Nor is it thought that the case is comparable to those involving publication of lecture notes, or the distribution of copies of a minister's sermon among the members of his congregation, or kindred cases relied on below. It is by such assimilation that the trial court endeavors to satisfy the criterion of the distribution being limited to a specific purpose. But White does not appear in the record as a teacher or as a propagandist endeavoring to persuade. He is not pictured as a man with a message. His only apparent purpose was to enable any persons interested to obtain a copy of the manuscript. No other motive is discernible. Such a purpose, we think, is too broadly general and indefinite to satisfy the test of a limited publication. Obviously only those interested or curious would take the trouble to ask for a copy, and a mere request seems to have been all that was necessary to obtain one.

The court stresses what is found to be White's intent not to publish generally, citing especially the statement in his letter to Mrs. Oettinger, reproduced in note 5 above [omitted], namely, that he had no objection whatever to the distribution of copies "provided, of course, it is not in published form." In the context of the case the phrase "in published form" could only mean in book form; and it is in that sense that White must have expected the recipient of the letter to understand it. White was of course quite familiar with the mimeographed distribution. One must in any event look at what he intended to do rather than at what he intended to be the legal consequence of his acts.

Another indication of the limited nature of the publication was thought below to be evidenced by the fact that not more than seventy-five copies were distributed. However, the record clearly shows that at least as many as two hundred copies were put in unrestricted circulation over the long period between 1933 and 1946. Through how many hands they passed among the members of the general public can only be surmised.

Judgment reversed.

Questions

1. Why may it be important under the current Copyright Act to determine whether a pre-1978 publication was "general" or "limited"? Is the doctrine of limited publication applicable to publications occurring after January 1, 1978? See Hubco Data Products Corp. v. Management Assistance Inc., 219 U.S.P.Q. 450 (D.Idaho 1983). Does the fact that common law copyright has been abolished make the answer to that question unimportant?

2. Under the principle stated in White v. Kimmell, should "the distribution of copies of a minister's sermon among the members of his congregation" be regarded as a general or a limited publication? Should it make a difference that the writer is a "teacher" or "a propagandist endeavoring to persuade"? Is there a difference between the sermon hypothetical and the case of a songwriter or author submitting a manuscript to a number of prospective publishers?

3. If pre-1978 a screenwriter sold to a motion picture producer his common law copyright in his unpublished screenplay, and in connection therewith delivered the manuscript of the screenplay to the producer, did a general publication occur? Why not?

4. The court concluded that White's expressed wish "not to publish generally" simply evidenced an intent not to publish in book form. Suppose White very clearly expressed an intent not to generally publish in the technical copyright sense, but he agreed to the specific disposition of the manuscript in the manner described in the opinion. Would this warrant a different result?

5. What argument might the plaintiff have made to the effect that the manuscript was in the public domain because it failed to evince any originality? Would the argument succeed? See Oliver v. Saint Germain Foundation, 41 F.Supp. 296 (S.D.Cal.1941) discussed in the note on Factual Works, supra.

Collateral Reference

Nimmer on Copyright, § 4.13.

B. DISTRIBUTION OF PHONORECORDS

ROSETTE v. RAINBO RECORD MANUFACTURING CORP.

United States District Court, S.D. New York, 1973.
354 F.Supp. 1183.

GURFEIN, DISTRICT JUDGE. The plaintiff in this action is the composer of children's songs which were either adapted by her from classic children's nursery rhymes or were original compositions. In her 42 count complaint she charges that the defendants infringed her copyrights by manufacturing and selling records containing thirty-three (33) compositions. Thirty-three counts are premised on statutory copyright claims; the remaining nine (Counts 19, 26, 28, 30, 32, 34, 36, 38 and 40) charge common law copyright infringements. Jurisdiction is alleged generally under 17 U.S.C. § 1 et seq. and under 28 U.S.C. § 1338(b). The plaintiff seeks injunctive and monetary relief, including treble damages and attorneys' fees.

The defendants deny that they have infringed the plaintiff's alleged statutory or common law copyright as set forth in the complaint. The defendants further contend, *inter alia,* that they are not proper defendants in this suit since Rainbo was merely a record presser and not a "manufacturer" within the meaning of 17 U.S.C. § 1(e).

The defendants seek dismissal of twenty counts on the ground of prior publication.[1] Nine of these are the common law counts and eleven are statutory copyright claims. Dismissal is sought of two counts, 41 and 42, on the ground that the plaintiff has failed to show ownership of the copyrights involved. The remaining eleven counts and all the other counts as well are said to be time barred by limitation and because the plaintiff allegedly failed to file notices of use until after the alleged infringements had occurred.

---

1. 13, 18, 19, 23, 25, 26, 27, 28, 29, 30, 31, 32, 33, 34, 35, 36, 37, 38, 39 and 40. The plaintiff concedes prior publication as to eighteen of these counts, contesting only counts 13 and 23 as to which she claims that no recording was released prior to registration. Because the defendants have failed to offer any proof of prior publication on counts 13 and 23, I find for the plaintiff on this matter.

A trial was held to the Court on October 10–11, 1972.

Facts

The plaintiff is a graduate of the Peabody Conservatory and a member of ASCAP. In 1949 she formed Lincoln Records Co., a corporation wholly owned by herself and her husband. The plaintiff testified at the trial and was the only witness on her behalf. Mrs. Rosette is the composer of the thirty-three compositions here at issue. The schedule showing the count of the complaint, the date of the copyright, the first recording date and the filing date of notice of use is set forth in the margin.[2]

The Defense of Prior Publication

The plaintiff admitted in her testimony that the compositions Chicken Licken (count 13); Pussy Cat, Pussy Cat (counts 18 and 19); Jack and the Beanstalk (count 23); Pinocchio (counts 25 and 26); Mary had a Little Lamb (counts 27 and 28); Ding Dong Bell (counts 29 and 30); Fiddle Dee Dee (counts 31 and 32); Goosy Goosy Gander (counts 33 and 34); Where has my Little Dog Gone (counts 35 and 36); Alice in Wonderland (counts 37 and 38); and Old King Cole (counts 39 and 40) were recorded, manufactured and continuously sold by the plaintiff and her company for many years before the plaintiff or her company obtained a statutory copyright of the compositions. Phonograph records of Chicken Licken and Jack and the Beanstalk were sold to the general public approximately one and one-half years before the date on which the copyrights were obtained, and the copyrights for Pinocchio, Mary had a Little Lamb, Ding Dong Bell, Fiddle Dee Dee, Goosy Goosy Gander, Where has my Little Dog Gone, Alice in Wonderland and Old King Cole, were obtained between ten and thirteen years after the recordings of these compositions were sold throughout the United States by the plaintiff and her companies. As to the other compositions whose recording date she recalled, the plaintiff testified that the recordings were not released until after the copyright registration had been secured. With respect to the compositions Old Mother Hubbard (count 5), Hobbledy Horse (count 8), The Weez Wump (count 14), The Pied Piper (count 15) and Little Red Hen (count 20), she could not recall the dates of recording but she believed that there could have been no prior publication of these compositions since it was her practice to register her compositions prior to their release on phonograph records. The defendants introduced no proof of prior sale of phonograph records with respect to any of the counts except those conceded by the plaintiff in her own testimony.

The Alleged Infringement

The plaintiff introduced into evidence fourteen long playing records and testified that she had purchased them about December 1964, give or take one year. According to Mrs. Rosette the Playtime Albums

---

2. The full schedule is omitted from the   published text.

numbered 106, 107, 108, 109, 111, 112, 116, 117 and 118 and the Carousel Albums numbered 806, 807, 808 and 812 contained exact duplications of her compositions which are the subject of this action and were in fact the same mechanical reproductions which she had authorized earlier. She testified that the names of the songs on these albums had been varied slightly in some cases.

The plaintiff also introduced the Schwann Long Playing Record Catalog for 1964 which enters records "only on authority of written or printed information sent to us by the manufacturer." That catalog listed for sale the Playtime albums numbered 106, 107, 108, 109, 111 and 112 referred to above.

The defendant Jack Brown is President of the defendant Rainbo Record Manufacturing Corporation. Together with the defendant Harold Markowitz he had formed the partnership Rainbo Record Company, also a defendant. Brown was the sole witness called by the defendants. * * *

I find as a fact that there was infringement by the defendants Rainbo and Brown of the plaintiff's compositions which are the subject of suit. * * *

The defendants raise an important issue, however, which has intrigued the law professors: whether the distribution of phonograph records without copyright registration is a publication that results in a loss of the common law copyright in the unpublished composition and is a dedication of the musical composition to the public.

Under the Copyright Law when a copyrighted work is reproduced mechanically it is protected, 17 U.S.C. § 1(e), and unauthorized manufacture, sale or use constitutes infringement of the copyright (17 U.S.C. § 101(e)). The Copyright Law also saves to the author or proprietor of an *unpublished* work the right, at common law or in equity, to prevent the copying, publication or use of such unpublished work without his consent and to obtain damages therefor (17 U.S.C. § 2).

The effect of the Copyright Act is "to secure to the author of a copyrighted play the sole right to its performance after it had been printed" Ferris v. Frohman, 223 U.S. 424, 435, 32 S.Ct. 263, 266, 56 L.Ed. 492 (1912). This applies to a musical composition as well. See Kaplan, Publication in Copyright Law, 103 U.Pa.L.Rev. 469, 473 (1955).

Thus, so long as the work is unpublished the author retains common law rights in the composition, including the sole right of its performance. On the other hand, if the author chooses to publish the work without meeting the requirements for statutory copyright he will lose his common law protection. See National Comics Publication v. Fawcett Publications, 191 F.2d 594 (2 Cir.1951).

Here the plaintiff did not publish some of her musical compositions as sheet music for sale to the public. She kept some of her musical manuscript in unpublished form but she, nevertheless, authorized the mechanical reproduction of such unpublished compositions on phonograph records. If she had lent an original manuscript to an orchestra for performance without publishing it as sheet music she would have retained her common law rights. See Mills Music v. Cromwell Music, 126 F.Supp. 54 (S.D.N.Y.1954); Patterson v. Century Productions, 93 F.2d 489 (2 Cir.1937). If she had published her composition as sheet music without getting statutory copyright protection she would have lost her rights in its performance. The question is whether the mechanical reproduction on a phonograph record of an otherwise *unpublished* composition itself constitutes publication so as to divest the author of common law rights.

The plaintiff contends that it is not publication but *performance* of an unpublished work. The defendants argue that the phonograph record is a copy of the composition and is also a publication because it is perpetuated and is not ephemeral like a stage performance.

On this modern version of a scholastic dialogue the law professors enjoy the disputation, but the judicial process must resolve the dispute one way or the other. See, e.g., Kaplan, supra; Nimmer, on Copyright §§ 50.1–50.2; also Tannenbaum, "Practical Problems in Copyright" in 7 Copyright Problems Analyzed (CCH 1952); Schulman, "Authors' Rights" Id. at 19; Burton, "Business Practices in the Copyright Field," Id. at 87.

The familiar tools of statutory construction, of precedent and its *ratio decidendi,* of the weight to be accorded *stare decisis* and of the vaguer notions of public interest in the face of claims to monopolize, all come into play. On the one hand there is distaste for the perpetual monopoly that sustaining common law rights unlimited in time involves. On the other, there is a strong reaction that precedent should be reliable rather than a trap for the unwary, particularly in a technical field where the lawyers, assumed to be learned, guide the hand of the untutored artist.

It may be noted, incidentally, that the Universal Copyright Convention (UCC) to which the United States is a party has clearly eliminated mechanical production on phonograph records as "publication." The Convention in Article VI defines publication as "the reproduction in tangible form and the general distribution to the public of copies of a work from which it can be read or otherwise visually perceived." Curiously the definition was reached not so much on a theoretical basis as on the belief shared by the conference "that according to the United States law the issuance of phonograph records does not amount to publication, and that an unpublished work remains unpublished. * *" It was believed that a contrary provision in the Convention would require an amendment of the United States Copyright Law unlikely to be accepted by Congress. Bogsch, Universal Copyright Convention, 83 (1958). Three of the four American delegates to the Conference in 1952 who participated in the drafting of the Convention are said to have stated the view that the sale of records is not a publication of the musical work involved.[4] And the practicing copyright bar has voiced

4. Arthur E. Farmer, "Report to Section of Patent, Trademark and Copyright Law of

its objection to relinquishing what they consider *stare decisis* so as to cast into the public domain thousands of works of popular and classical music, performances of which have been distributed on phonograph records without statutory copyright in reliance upon the rule of law that a distribution of phonograph records is not a publication.[5]

The distinction between sheet music, a literal copy of the original manuscript, and a mechanical reproduction of a musical composition originally came before the Supreme Court in the famous case of White-Smith Music Publishing Co. v. Apollo Co., 209 U.S. 1, 28 S.Ct. 319, 52 L.Ed. 655 (1908). There the Court held that a music roll for mechanical pianos did not constitute a "copy" of the recorded music and hence was not an infringement of it. From this result it was logical to conclude that if the infringing music roll was not a copy of the composition so as to cast its maker in liability, the creation of a music roll by the author himself would not make it a "copy" of his work and hence not a publication of it. The *White-Smith* result can also be rationalized as an opinion that mechanical reproduction is performance, like live performance, and is, therefore, not publication. The Court noted: "As the Act of Congress now stands we believe it does not include these records as copies or *publications* of the copyrighted music involved in these cases." 209 U.S. at 18, 28 S.Ct. at 323 (emphasis supplied). The Ninth Circuit in Corcoran v. Montgomery Ward & Co., 121 F.2d 572 (9 Cir.1941) seems to have specifically extended the *White-Smith* rule to phonograph records.

The Copyright Act was completely revised in 1909.

The impact of the *White-Smith* case was limited by the statutory provision in the 1909 Act that "[c]opyright may also be had of the works of an author, of which copies are not reproduced for sale, by the deposit, with claim of copyright, of one complete copy of such work if it be a lecture or similar production or a dramatic, musical, or dramatico-musical composition" (formerly Section 11 of the 1909 Act), 17 U.S.C. § 12. Thus, copyright protection was made available for *unpublished* musical compositions. And the sale of records of a musical composition registered under Section 11 of the Copyright Act will not terminate its copyright protection, Yacaubian v. Carroll, 74 U.S.P.Q. 257 (S.D.Cal. 1947) against unauthorized phonograph records. Shilkret v. Musicraft Records, 131 F.2d 929 (2 Cir.1942). But the Court of Appeals has not yet had occasion to consider the protection of unpublished musical compositions which rely on *common law rights* against unauthorized phonograph records. Section 2 of the Copyright Act recognizes the continued validity of common law rights in an "unpublished work" and

American Bar Association," September 15, 1952, at p. 11;

John Schulman, "A Realistic Treaty," The American Writer, Vol. 1, No. 218, at p. 23 (November, 1952);

Sydney M. Kaye, "Duration of Copyright and the Concept of Dedication," Bulletin of the Copyright Society of the U.S.A., Vol. 2, No. 4, p. 93, at pp. 95–96 (February, 1955).

5. Tannenbaum, supra; Schulman, supra; McDonald, "The Law of Broadcasting." Id. at 31; Burton, supra.

confirms the right of an author to prevent "[the] use of such unpublished work."

The 1909 Act was a comprehensive revision of the Copyright Law. As we have seen, the Supreme Court in *White-Smith* had previously ruled that the recordation of a musical composition by mechanical means did not make the record (piano roll) a "copy" of the composition. The drafters of the 1909 Act stated that "it is not the intention of the committee to extend the right of copyright to the mechanical reproductions themselves, but only to give the composer or copyright proprietor the control, in accordance with the provisions of the bill, of the manufacture and use of such devices." House Reports, 60th Cong.2d Sess.Vol. 1 (1909), p. 9. The provisions of the bill referred to included the now familiar compulsory licensing provision whereunder [for] the payment of a royalty of two cents per record anyone may use the copyrighted composition (§ 1(e)). The assumption remained, however, that the musical composition itself was a thing apart from its performance on a phonograph record.

In this light the Act provided for two different protections for the unpublished musical composition itself. First, a new statutory method of copyright was provided in Section 11 for *unpublished* works and second, common law rights were preserved in *unpublished* works. It has been held, however, that an author is not compelled to resort to a Section 11 copyright to avoid forfeiture of his common law rights. Nutt v. National Institute Inc. for the Imp. of Memory, 31 F.2d 236 (2 Cir.1929).

While that is true of the author of an unpublished manuscript it does not follow that it is also necessarily true of a composer of an unpublished composition who has chosen to make and sell phonograph records for which special provision has been made in the Copyright Act.

The Copyright Act does not define publication and it is true that generally a performance of an unpublished musical manuscript is not a publication. *Frohman,* supra. This accords with the expressed view of the Copyright Bar and the music industry that making a record of an unpublished composition is not a "publication." Their reliance is on accepted doctrines of copyright law.

It is small wonder then that a brief opinion by Judge Igoe in Shapiro, Bernstein & Co. v. Miracle Record Co., 91 F.Supp. 473 (N.D.Ill. 1950) raised the hackles of the Copyright Bar.[6] Judge Igoe, by way of dictum, expressed the view that the composer "abandoned his rights, if any, to a copyright by permitting his composition to be produced on phonograph records and sold some time before copyright" (91 F.Supp. at 475). Judge Igoe apparently rejected the view that "a record is nothing

---

6. The lament was loud and clear. Joseph A. McDonald in his lecture on "The Law of Broadcasting" in 7 Copyright Problems Analyzed, supra, at 46 relates: "I was quite cast down about that, and in all the beaneries where the copyright bar eats, you could overhear remarks such as 'Have you heard what Judge Igoe did? What can we do? Someone ought to try for a rehearing.' Et cetera, et cetera."

but a captured performance of the composition," see Kaplan, supra, at 480 and he made no mention of *White-Smith,* supra.[7]

In Mills Music v. Cromwell Music, 126 F.Supp. 54, 69–70 (S.D.N.Y. 1954) Judge Leibell considered a defense that plaintiff's assignors had "waived all rights in the musical composition and dedicated it to the public" (Id. at 57). Judge Leibell found that there was no such authorized manufacture and sale of records of "Tzena" by the plaintiff's assignors (Id. at 70). By the way of dictum, however, he expressed the view that "[t]he manufacture and sale of phonograph records in this country by a person or corporation duly authorized by Miron would have constituted a publication of his composition" (Id. at 69).

In McIntyre v. Double A-Music Corporation, 166 F.Supp. 681, 683 (S.D.Cal.1958) Judge Solomon found that the plaintiff's arrangement of a musical composition "was insufficient to qualify for either a common-law or a statutory copyright." By way of dictum, Judge Solomon expressed the view that the sale to the general public of hundreds of thousands of phonograph records of his arrangement "was a general publication of plaintiff's arrangement and destroyed whatever rights he had in the arrangement under the common law of copyrights." (Id. at 682).

None of the distinguished judges cited made any reference to *White-Smith* or the impact of the 1909 Act on its doctrine.

In this District, Judge Cooper has expressed a contrary view, also by way of dictum, that "a phonograph record is not a copy of a musical composition * * * nor is a sale of the record a 'publication' of the underlying composition." Nom Music, Inc. v. Kaslin, 227 F.Supp. 922, 926 (S.D.N.Y.1964), aff'd on other grounds, 343 F.2d 198 (2 Cir.1965).

This leaves us with the conviction that higher judicial authority has not passed directly on the point. It has remained since 1909 a bone of contention between the Copyright Bar and some of the law professors.

Section 2 of the Copyright Act was reenacted at the same time that phonograph recordings were themselves a current subject of debate. It would have been simple to carve out an exception to the protection of unpublished musical compositions for the production and sale of phonograph records otherwise covered by Section 1 and Section 11. This was not done.

The questions nevertheless confront us (1) whether the 1909 Act overruled *White-Smith* and made a phonograph record a "copy" or a "publication," and (2) whether the special statutory scheme involving phonograph records is a gloss on the scope of Section 2 of the Act.

---

7. The Second Circuit in RCA Mfg. Co., Inc. v. Whiteman, 114 F.2d 86, cert. denied, 311 U.S. 712, 61 S.Ct. 393, 85 L.Ed. 463 (2 Cir.1940) and Capitol Records, Inc. v. Mercury Records Corp., 221 F.2d 657 (2 Cir. 1955) dealt with *performer's* rights in phonograph records where the musical composition was not owned by the performer. That is a different question and does not deal with "publication" of an unpublished musical composition.

With regard to the first question it is difficult to rationalize accepted principles of copyright law to make performance of a composition a publication of the composition itself. The argument that the permanency of the recording makes it more than a mere performance is an argument that the Congress did not accept or it could easily have made such an enactment. And the Copyright Office had held that the phonograph record itself may not be registered under Section 11. C.F.R. 202.8(b).[8]

The difficult second question still remains. The common law right in the unpublished composition makes no requirement of notice of use of the musical composition on phonograph records by the composer or the copyright owner as is required under Section 1(e) where a statutory copyright has been obtained. This puts the statutory copyright owner at an apparent disadvantage, for if the statutory copyright owner fails to file his notice in the Copyright Office "any failure to file such notice shall be a complete defense to any suit, action or proceeding for any infringement of such copyright." (§ 1(e)). Can the States, by virtue of the common law, constitutionally impose a lesser requirement when copyright has been vested by the Constitution in the national Government? Must the impediments to the free exercise of the *statutory* copyright be held to limit the exploitation of the common law copyright to the same degree? A statutory construction that avoids a constitutional problem is desirable.

Judge Learned Hand, dissenting in *Capitol Records,* supra, had expressed misgivings about the power of the States "to follow their own notions as to when an author's right shall be unlimited both in *user* and in duration." 221 F.2d at 667 (emphasis supplied). Judge Hand's prophecy of 1955 became law in 1964 when the *Sears-Compco* doctrine was announced by the Supreme Court. In Sears, Roebuck & Co. v. Stiffel Company, 376 U.S. 225, 84 S.Ct. 784, 11 L.Ed.2d 661, and in Compco Corp. v. Day-Brite Lighting, Inc., 376 U.S. 234, 84 S.Ct. 779, 11 L.Ed.2d 669 (1964), the Court held that a State may not prohibit the copying of an article unprotected under the Federal patent laws. Justice Black, relying on the Supremacy Clause stated, "Just as a State cannot encroach upon the federal patent laws directly, it cannot, under some other law, such as that forbidding unfair competition, give protection of a kind that clashes with the objectives of the federal patent laws." 376 U.S. at 231, 84 S.Ct. at 789.

One might still have supposed that copyright law is different from patent law because Section 2 of the Copyright Act specifically recog-

---

8. While copyright registration by publication with notice of copyright (§ 10) requires the prompt deposit in the Copyright Office of two complete copies of the best edition, the Copyright Office Rules provided that "[a] phonograph record or other sound recording is not considered a copy of the compositions recorded on it, and is not acceptable for copyright registration." Rules and Regulations of the Copyright Office, 37 C.F.R. 202.8(b). A phonograph record is not a copy of the musical composition itself. But note that the Copyright Act was amended on October 15, 1971 to provide that sound recordings may now qualify for copyright protection. Pub.L. 92–140, 85 Stat. 391.

nizes common law rights which are State created rights. But the distinction is apparently not to be made. For Justice Black in the *Compco* case made it explicit that "Today we have held in Sears, Roebuck & Co. v. Stiffel Co., supra, that when an article is unprotected by a patent *or a copyright,* state law may not forbid others to copy that article. To forbid copying would interfere with the federal policy, found in Art. I, § 8, cl. 8, of the Constitution and in implementing federal statutes, of allowing free access to copy whatever the federal patent *and copyright* laws leave in the public domain." 376 U.S. at 237, 84 S.Ct. at 782 (emphasis supplied).

The failure of a copyright owner to file his notice of use in effect puts his composition into the public domain—at least from the time of use to the date of filing. Norbay Music, Inc. v. King Records, Inc., 290 F.2d 617 (2 Cir.1961). Cf. Biltmore Music Corp. v. Kittinger, 238 F.2d 373 (9 Cir.1956). During such time it would seem that granting protective rights under State law would be inconsistent with the Congressional policy of requiring notice by copyright owners to would-be users so that they in turn may protect themselves under the two-cent royalty provision by paying the royalty to the copyright owner (§§ 1(e), 101(e)).

To avoid the constitutional problem I think that the exception of Section 2 of the Copyright Law must be limited to exclude the sale of phonograph records from the protection given to the owner of an unpublished manuscript to the extent that the common law right exceeds the rights of statutory copyright owners. The conditions for use of the musical composition on phonograph records are so well defined in the comprehensive Copyright Act of 1909 that it is unlikely that the Congress intended that contradictory principles of State law should survive.[9]

This leads to the conclusion that the use of phonograph records without compliance with the Copyright Act bars claims for infringement not because the record is a "copy" or a "publication," but because any other interpretation leads to conflict with the Federal statutory scheme. Section 2 would still be read as applying to unpublished works protectible at common law including unpublished musical compositions where no mechanical recordings have been made.

---

9. Professor Nimmer has suggested a more complete divestment of the common law rights upon grounds with which I do not agree as appears from this opinion. His consideration of the *Sears-Compco* doctrine in relation to the problem at hand is, however, provocative and novel. See Nimmer, supra, § 59. His discussion of the effect of the 1971 Amendment to the Copyright Act (Pub.L. No. 92–140, 85 Stat. 391; 17 U.S.C. §§ 1, 5, 19, 20, 26, 101) on the *Sears-Compco* doctrine is interesting as well. Nimmer, Id. § 35.225. I incline to the view that Congress in the Sound Recording Amendment was concerned with *performance* on phonograph records and not with the musical composition itself as an unpublished work under State law. "The copyrighted work" is the "sound recording"—17 U.S.C. § 1(f) and the proviso that the Amended Copyright Act shall not be applied retroactively refers only to "sound recordings," i.e. the *performance* of musical works rather than the unpublished musical work. Pub.L. 92–140, 85 Stat. 392, § 3.

On the other hand the failure to file notice of use does not bar the copyright owner forever, *Norbay,* supra. By analogy then I hold that the sale of phonograph records is not a divestment of common law rights by publication but that it does inhibit suit against infringers until the statutory copyright is obtained and the notice of use is filed. Thereafter, applying the rule of *Norbay,* the statutory copyright owner may sue for subsequent infringement. This provides an accommodation to basic copyright *stare decisis* in preventing the loss of rights in the "unpublished" composition by an unintended dedication to the public while preserving the supremacy of the Federal copyright law and effecting its policy.

Applying this ruling to the facts, I find that the plaintiff may recover but only from the dates of her filing the respective notices of use. * * *

Questions

1. Does the current Copyright Act accept the *Rosette* rule that sale of phonograph records does not constitute publication of the work recorded therein?

2. If Mrs. Rosette had sold phonorecords of her musical works after January 1, 1978, would this have constituted a publication of such works? Would the Sec. 101 definition of "publication" in the current Act have required a different result in this case if such sales and the defendants' allegedly infringing conduct all occurred after January 1, 1978? Suppose the sales by plaintiff occurred pre-1978, but defendants' conduct occurred after January 1, 1978. Would the Sec. 101 definition of "publication" be applicable? Does 17 U.S.C.A., Transitional and Supplementary Provisions, § 112 mean that the Sec. 101 definition would apply? What is the effect of 17 U.S.C.A., Transitional and Supplementary Provisions, § 103?

3. Note that Judge Gurfein states the publication issue in two different ways: (1) "whether the distribution of phonograph records without copyright registration is a publication that results in a loss of the common law copyright in the unpublished composition * * *", and (2) "whether the mechanical reproduction on a phonograph record of an otherwise *unpublished* composition itself constitutes a publication so as to divest the author of common law rights." Are these simply different formulations of the same issue, or do they pose significantly different issues? Why does only issue (1) above present a difficult question?

4. Assuming Judge Gurfein's conclusion that a pre-1978 sale of phonograph records of a musical work does not constitute a publication of such work, how does he justify his conclusion that "the [1909] Copyright Act bars claims for [common law copyright] infringement" notwithstanding the preservation of common law copyright claims in unpublished works under Sec. 2 of the 1909 Act?

Collateral References

Kaplan, *Publication in Copyright Law: The Question of Phonograph Records,* 103 Univ.Penn.Law Rev. 469 (1955).

Nimmer on Copyright, § 4.05.

C. PERFORMANCES

KING v. MISTER MAESTRO, INC.

United States District Court, Southern District of New York, 1963.
224 F.Supp. 101.

WYATT, DISTRICT JUDGE. Plaintiff moves for a preliminary injunction restraining defendants from selling phonograph records of a speech by him or from otherwise infringing the copyright claimed for the speech. The action is for a permanent injunction, damages and an accounting.

Plaintiff is a citizen of Georgia. Defendant 20th Century-Fox Record Corporation is apparently a New York corporation although the amended complaint, if deemed to refer to it, would allege that it is a Delaware corporation. Defendant Mister Maestro, Inc. is alleged to be a New York corporation. The two defendants are each alleged to have their principal place of business in New York.

Jurisdiction rests on the fact that this action is one "arising" under an Act of Congress "relating to * * * copyrights" (28 U.S.C.A. § 1338(a)) but there is also diversity jurisdiction (28 U.S.C.A. § 1332(a)).

Plaintiff, a highly educated negro clergyman, has been also for some time a distinguished and effective leader in the movement to secure equal civil rights for negro citizens. As such he has developed a unique literary and oratorical style and has delivered lectures, sermons and addresses to large crowds in many parts of the nation.

On June 23, 1963 in an auditorium at Detroit, Dr. King made a speech to which he gave no title but in the course of which he used the words "I have a dream".

Thereafter an assembly or "march" for civil rights was planned for Washington on August 28, 1963. Dr. King was one of the organizers and was invited to deliver a speech. He wrote his speech from time to time between August 24 and August 28, 1963; it was finished about 4 o'clock in the morning of August 28. The speech contains some of the ideas and words of the Detroit speech, but is much longer and has a great deal not contained in the Detroit speech.

Dr. King had been asked by the organizing committee to furnish a "summary or excerpts" of his prepared speech, this for the purpose of being read and made available to the press at a press conference in the afternoon or evening of August 27, 1963. Dr. King could not and did not comply with this request because his speech was not finished in time. He did, however, in the morning of August 28 send his speech—substantially in the form later delivered—to the "press liaison personnel of the Washington office of the March on Washington Committee". Dr. King says that he did not intend his speech "to be generally distributed or generally made available to the public at large" but to be "specifically limited in use to assisting the press coverage of the March

Sec. C   **PERFORMANCES**   151

by the press". The intent of Dr. King is legally irrelevant; the question is solely with what he did. National Comics Publications v. Fawcett Publications, 191 F.2d 594 (2d Cir.1951). In fact, the speech was mimeographed as an "advance text" and put into a "press kit" (containing other material also) which was made available to the press

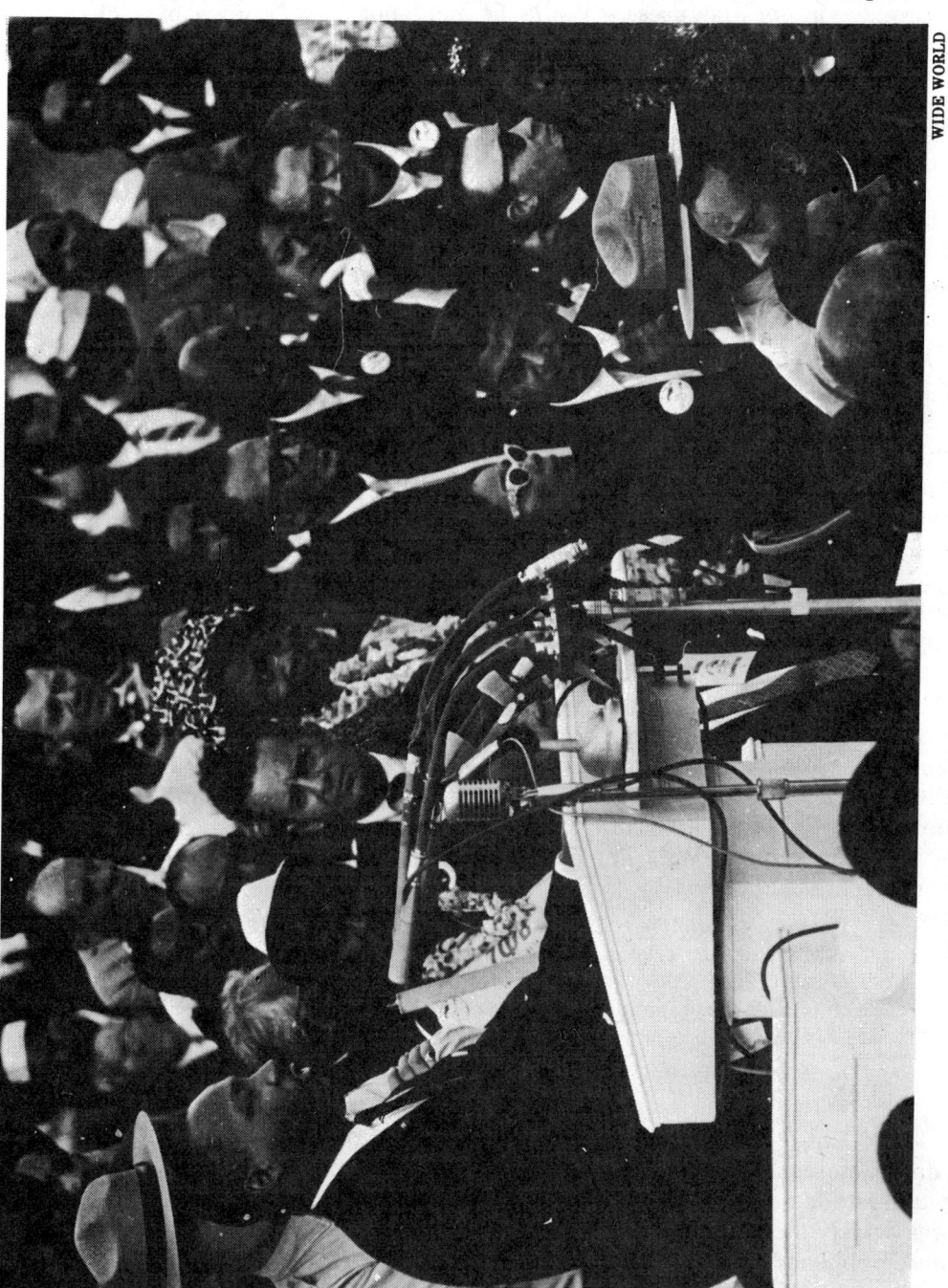

Martin Luther King delivering his *I Have a Dream* speech. (WIDE WORLD)

some time in advance of delivery of the speech. Dr. King says that this mimeographing and distribution as part of the press kit was without his "personal advance knowledge thereof or consent thereto".

Dr. King did deliver a copy of his speech to the press representatives of the organizing committee and apparently did not forbid its reproduction for the press. While he may not have known of such reproduction or have expressly consented to it, the use made of it seems natural and reasonable. The significant and important fact is that the copies of the speech were distributed *only to the press* and that this distribution took place only in the "press tent". Such is the showing made in the affidavit for defendants of the editor of Fox Movietone News who secured a copy of Dr. King's speech at the press tent on the morning of August 28. The only reasonable conclusion is that the distribution of copies of the speech was limited to the press. There is not even a suggestion that any copies were offered to, or made available to, the general public.

The "advance text" has no title and from this it seems that Dr. King had not given it a title.

In the afternoon of August 28, some 200,000 people gathered before the Lincoln Memorial in Washington for a "freedom" demonstration in behalf of civil rights for negro citizens. Among the speeches delivered was that by Dr. King.

Apparently it was Dr. King's speech which most stirred and impressed the crowd, especially his repetition of the words "I have a dream". The New York Times reported (August 29, 1963, page 16, column 1) that it was Dr. King "who ignited the crowd with words that might have been written by the sad, brooding man enshrined within" the Memorial; the Times then quoted from the speech its repetitions of the words "I have a dream". On the front page of The New York Times for August 29, 1963, there is a feature article (by James Reston, Chief of the Times' Washington Bureau) on Dr. King's speech under the headlines: "'I Have a Dream * * *' Peroration by Dr. King Sums Up A Day the Capital Will Remember". The flavor of the occasion is perhaps best expressed by this quotation from the article:

> "I have a dream" he cried again and again. And each time the dream was a promise out of our ancient articles of faith: phrases from the Constitution, lines from the great anthem of the nation, guarantees from the Bill of Rights, all ending with a vision that they might one day all come true. * * *
>
> Dr. King touched all the themes of the day, only better than anybody else.

Dr. King's speech (along with the speeches of others made at the same time) was broadcast by television and radio, recorded (sound and pictures) for newsreels, was later shown in movie houses, and of course was widely reported in the press. Excerpts from Dr. King's speech were published in many newspapers. The New York Post in its issue of September 1, 1963, published the complete text of the speech under the title "I Have A Dream * * *". The Post thereafter offered for sale reprints of the speech. Dr. King says that he has not consented in any way to such reprinting and sale of the speech and did not give to the Post any copy of his speech.

Defendant 20th Century-Fox Record Corporation and Movietonews, Inc. are subsidiaries of Twentieth Century Fox Film Corporation. Movietonews, Inc. produces a newsreel for movie theaters called "Fox Movietone News" and took pictures of and made a sound record of Dr. King's speech on August 28, 1963 and of the speeches made on the same occasion by five other speakers.

Defendant 20th Century-Fox Record Corporation made a phonograph record from the newsreel sound track of the speeches including that of Dr. King, and about September 18, 1963 began selling these records in a cover, with a picture from the newsreel film of the crowd in front of the Lincoln Memorial. The cover is entitled "Freedom March on Washington August 28, 1963" and states that the record is of the speeches made that day (including that of Dr. King) which were "recorded live by Fox Movietone News". The record has both the voice and the words of Dr. King. Sales of the record have continued.

Defendant Mister Maestro, Inc. made and is selling a somewhat similar record entitled "The March on Washington", which record does not on its cover or elsewhere refer to Dr. King. The record does contain, however, part or all of the speech of Dr. King as delivered by him in Washington; it has both the voice and the words of Dr. King.

Defendants are selling their records without the consent of Dr. King and of course without paying anything to him.

After the Washington speech, a phonograph record of some of Dr. King's speeches was offered for sale with his consent by Motown Record Corp. This record is in a cover entitled "The Great March to Freedom —Rev. Martin Luther King Speaks—Detroit June 23, 1963." This record does not contain the Washington speech; it does contain the much shorter Detroit speech under the title "I Have A Dream". Dr. King says that this title was given to the Detroit speech by Motown after it "saw the widespread public reception accorded said words when used in the text of my address to the March on Washington".

On September 30, 1963 Dr. King sent a copy of his speech to the Copyright Office for deposit and at the same time sent an application form for a certificate of registration of his claim to copyright. 17 U.S.C.A. §§ 11, 12, 207. The class to which the work was claimed to belong was Class C—"[l]ectures, sermons, addresses (prepared for oral delivery)". 17 U.S.C.A. § 5(c); 37 C.F.R. § 202.1. The "title of the work" was said to be "I Have A Dream". The claim to copyright was under 17 U.S.C.A. § 12, "works not reproduced for sale"—unpublished works.

The complaint was filed on October 4, 1963 and named three defendants—Mister Maestro, Inc., Twentieth Century Fox, Inc., and

Motown Record Corp. On the same day, Judge Bryan made an order to show cause bringing on the present motion.

Before the motion was heard, plaintiff served and later filed an amended complaint, naming only two defendants: Mister Maestro, Inc. and Twentieth Century Fox Film Corporation. By later stipulation, 20th Century-Fox Record Corporation was in effect substituted for Twentieth Century Fox Film Corporation as a defendant, the caption was amended accordingly, and references in the amended complaint to Twentieth Century Fox Film Corporation were deemed to be made to 20th Century-Fox Record Corporation.

While the file shows no return of service by the Marshal, counsel for defendants Mister Maestro, Inc. and 20th Century-Fox Record Corporation have appeared to oppose this motion and an affidavit on file shows that a copy of the summons and complaint were delivered to counsel for these two defendants and that counsel agreed to accept service. The two defendants are therefore before the Court and subject to its jurisdiction.

The motion was heard on October 8 and 9, 1963 and at that time no certificate of registration had issued.

Subsequently a Class C certificate was duly issued, showing receipt of the application therefor on October 2, 1963.

Dr. King then authorized publication of his speech in circular form, with notice of copyright. Copies were then sent to the Copyright Office for deposit and at the same time an application form was sent for a certificate of registration of the claim of Dr. King to copyright. 17 U.S.C.A. §§ 10, 11, 207. The class to which the work was claimed to belong was Class A—"books * * *". 17 U.S.C.A. § 5(a); 37 C.F.R. § 202.1. The claim to copyright was under 17 U.S.C.A. § 10, "publication of work with notice"—published works.

Subsequently a Class A certificate was duly issued, showing receipt of the application therefor on October 21, 1963.

There seems to be no real dispute as to the facts set forth. The application raises only questions of law and if these are decided for plaintiff, a preliminary injunction is appropriate and necessary.

As an original proposition, it seems unfair and unjust for defendants to use the voice and the words of Dr. King without his consent and for their own financial profit. Of course, decision cannot be made simply because of such a feeling. This is a Court of law which must look to legal principles established by the Congress and by higher Courts. But under the circumstances here present it does seem that defendants should demonstrate that their use of the voice and words of plaintiff is permitted by legal principles so established.

The general principles of law here involved are relatively simple; their application in some cases is difficult.

At common law there was a property right in an unpublished work but after publication there was no copyright protection.

Congress has provided copyright protection after publication on certain conditions and also on conditions has given such protection before publication, somewhat parallel to the common law property right which the legislation specifically recognizes.

Statutory copyright may be obtained for "[l]ectures, sermons, addresses (prepared for oral delivery)". 17 U.S.C.A. § 5(c). The copyright may be obtained before any publication of such works but as soon as publication occurs there must be compliance with the requirements as to published works. 17 U.S.C.A. §§ 10, 12. Ordinarily the public performance of a work—such as delivery of a speech or performance of a play—is not a publication.

Thus on general principles there is no reason why Dr. King could not obtain copyright protection under the laws of Congress for his speech.

The arguments for defendants must be considered.

It is first suggested that the speech was not sufficiently original to be the subject of copyright, because it was preceded by a similar speech of plaintiff in Detroit. It is doubtful that the rights of plaintiff would be lost even if the two speeches of plaintiff were exactly the same. But the argument is without merit in any event because the two speeches are sufficiently different in length, content and otherwise that the former does not destroy the originality for copyright purposes of the latter. Alfred Bell & Co. v. Catalda Fine Arts, 191 F.2d 99 (2d Cir.1951).

The substantial argument for defendants, and one which must be carefully considered, is that Dr. King lost any right to copyright protection because what he did in Washington placed the speech in the public domain (dedicated it to the public, as it is sometimes put) because it amounted to a publication without obtaining a copyright. There can be no copyright of any work in the public domain. 17 U.S.C.A. § 8.

Defendants stress the public nature of the delivery of the speech by Dr. King—the enormous crowd, the radio and television broadcasts, the movie newsreel pictures. The question is: was this a general publication of the speech so as to place it in the public domain?

The word "general" with respect to publication in this sense is of greatest significance. There can be a limited publication, which is a communication of the work to others under circumstances showing no dedication of the work to the public. A general publication is one which shows a dedication to the public so as to lose copyright.

The public exhibition of a painting without notice of copyright in a gallery the rules of which forbade copying is not a general publication. Werckmeister v. American Lithographic Co., 134 F. 321, 68 L.R.A. 591 (2d Cir.1904). In affirming in this case, the Supreme Court said: "One *or many* persons may be permitted to an examination under circumstances which show no intention to part with the property right, and it will remain unimpaired." (American Tobacco Company v. Werckmeister, 207 U.S. 284, at 299, 28 S.Ct. 72, at 77, 52 L.Ed. 208, emphasis supplied).

The public performance of a play is not a general publication. Ferris v. Frohman, 223 U.S. 424, 435, 32 S.Ct. 263, 56 L.Ed. 492 (1912).

The public delivery of lectures on a memory system is not a general publication. Nutt v. National Institute Incorporated for the Improvement of Memory, 31 F.2d 236 (2d Cir.1929).

The playing of a song in public is not a general publication of the work. Heim v. Universal Pictures Co., 154 F.2d 480 (2d Cir.1946).

The broadcast by radio of a script is not a general publication thereof. Uproar Co. v. National Broadcasting Co., 8 F.Supp. 358, 362 (D.Mass.1934).

The copyright statute itself plainly shows that "oral delivery" of an address is not a dedication to the public. Sections 5(c) and 12 (of Title 17 U.S.C.A.) taken together show that Congress intended copyright protection for "[l]ectures, sermons, addresses (prepared for oral delivery)" despite such "oral delivery".

It has never been suggested that the number of persons in the audience had any effect on the principle. The Supreme Court in the Werckmeister case, above, referred to "one or many". The Court in the Nutt case, above, used the expressions "publicly delivered", "public performance" and "public delivery", and finally stated that "the delivery of these lectures before audiences prior to copyrighting was limited publication" (31 F.2d at 238). Nothing whatever is said about the *size* of the "audiences".

A recognized authority in the field after an analysis of the principles and the cases states the criterion to be as follows (Nimmer, Copyright Publication, 56 Col.L.Rev. 185, 197 (1956)):

> This analysis suggests that a *sine qua non* of publication should be the acquisition by members of the public of a possessory interest in *tangible* copies of the work in question."

And elsewhere (195) the same author says:

> The principle that public performance does not constitute a publication of the work being performed is well established in the American law of copyright and, unlike the effect of the sale of phonograph records, is not the subject of any serious debate among copyright lawyers.

It should also be noted that in considering the questions of copyright in Public Affairs Associates, Inc. v. Rickover, 177 F.Supp. 601 (D.C.1960), reversed 109 U.S.App.D.C. 128, 284 F.2d 262 (1960), reversed 369 U.S. 111, 82 S.Ct. 580, 7 L.Ed.2d 604 (1962), none of the judges or justices paid any attention to the number of persons in the audiences addressed by Admiral Rickover.

The "oral delivery" of his speech by Dr. King, no matter how vast his audience, did not amount to a general publication of his literary work.

Defendants stress the delivery without copyright notice of an advance text of his speech and the distribution of it to the press. But within the concept of publication just examined, it is clear that this was a *limited*, as opposed to a general, publication. There is nothing to suggest that copies of the speech were ever offered to the *public;* the fact is clear that the "advance text" was given to the press only.

This is a very different situation from that in the Rickover case, above. In Rickover, there was "a wide distribution not only to the press but also to people generally who desired copies through interest in the subjects of the addresses"; the Admiral not only attempted "to secure publicity * * * through the channels of information" but went "beyond customary sources of press or broadcasting in distributing the addresses to any interested individual" (284 F.2d at 270). The Court of Appeals majority then expressed its conclusion (284 F.2d at 271):

> Since the distribution was not limited in any way to a particular group, no question exists in this case as to the extent of any limitation so as to avoid "publication" in the copyright sense. Anyone was welcome to a copy.
>
> Nor do we have any problem as to limited use of the addresses by the press for fair comment. The press was free to use the speeches in whole or in part for their news value. But such ephemeral use is far different from the unlimited distribution to anyone who was interested which is manifested by the agreed statement of facts. It is the complete absence of limitation on the use of the printed distributions by anyone at any time which destroyed the common law rights of the author.

These facts are not here present. Moreover, Judge Washington would have given Admiral Rickover protection in any event. He declared in his dissent (with which this Court is in agreement) as follows (284 F.2d at 273):

> Speeches of men in the forefront of public life are unique among literary products. Not only are they often works of considerable literary merit, but they may also be "news" of the first importance. As "news" they deserve the widest unfettered contemporaneous dissemination. Where, as here, an author seeks to advance this end by making copies of his speeches available to the press and other interested persons, he is serving the public's interest as well as his own. But insofar as they have a commercial value as literary works after their immediate news importance has passed, they belong appropriately to their creator. The public interest in the news value of the author's work may cut across or postpone his rights; but that is not to say that it extinguishes them.

The treatment of the Rickover case in the Supreme Court is not relevant here because the Supreme Court addressed itself primarily to procedure and to the position of the Admiral as an officer of the United States.

The conclusion seems plain that there was no general publication by Dr. King in making his speech available to the press. * * *

Questions

1. Does the current Copyright Act accept the rule adopted by the courts under the 1909 Act, and articulated in the *King* case, that public performance does not constitute publication?

2. The *King* court expressed agreement with the statement that "speeches of men in the forefront of public life are unique among literary products * * * as 'news' they deserve the widest unfettered contemporaneous dissemination." Does this mean that the principle that performance does not dedicate should be modified, or even not applied where the speech "performed" is one of this nature? Would it be feasible to provide that such a work is in the public domain while it remains "news", but may thereafter be recaptured by its author? Compare the views expressed in Hemingway v. Random House, Inc., and Time, Inc. v. Bernard Geis Associates, supra.

3. Do you agree that the distribution of printed copies of Dr. King's speech was a limited publication because it was distributed "only to the press"? Is this conclusion consistent with the concept of limited publication as expressed in White v. Kimmell, supra? Was there any express or implied limitation on the use which the press might make of the copies?

4. Did the defendants commence selling records of Dr. King's speech prior to the time that he obtained a statutory copyright? Should that make a difference in the disposition of the case?

5. What justification, if any, is there for the suggestion that "a *sine qua non* of publication should be the acquisition by members of the public of a possessory interest in *tangible* copies of the work in question"?

Collateral References

Selvin, *Should Performance Dedicate?*, 42 Calif.Law Rev. 40 (1954).

Nimmer on Copyright, § 4.08.

D. EXHIBITION OF WORKS OF ART

AMERICAN TOBACCO CO. v. WERCKMEISTER

Supreme Court of the United States, 1907.
207 U.S. 284, 28 S.Ct. 72, 52 L.Ed. 208.

This is a writ of error to the Circuit Court of Appeals for the Second Circuit, seeking reversal of a judgment affirming the judgment of the United States Circuit Court for the Southern District of New York in favor of the defendant in error, adjudging him to be entitled to the possession of 1196 sheets, each containing a copy of a certain picture called "Chorus," the same representing a company of gentlemen with filled glasses, singing in chorus. The painting was the work of an English artist, W. Dendy Sadler. The defendant in error claimed to be the owner of a copyright taken out under the laws of the United States.

The judgment was rendered under authority of § 4965, as amended March 2, 1895. 28 Stat. 965; 3 U.S.Comp.Stat. p. 3414.

In January, 1894, by agreement between the artist and Werckmeister, the defendant in error, it was agreed that the painting should be finished by March 1, and then sent to Werckmeister to be photographed and returned to Sadler in time to exhibit at the Royal Academy in 1894. The painting was sent to Werckmeister at Berlin, where it was received on March 8, 1894, and was returned to Sadler in London on March 22, 1894 * * *.

[On April 2, 1904 Sadler conveyed the copyright in the painting to Werckmeister.] After the painting was returned to London it was exhibited by Sadler at the exhibition of the Royal Academy at London, and was there on exhibition for about three months; the exhibition opening the first Monday of May and closing the first Monday of August, 1894. The exhibition was open to the public on week days from 8 a. m. to 7 p. m. upon the payment of the admission fee of one shilling, and during the last week was open evenings, the entrance charge being sixpence. There was a private view for the press on May 2, and on May 3 up to one o'clock, and the remainder of the day was for the Royal private view. There was also a general private view on May 4. The members and the associate members of the Royal Academy and the artists exhibiting at the exhibition and their families were entitled at all times to free admission, and they as well as the public visited the exhibition in large numbers.

During the time that the painting was shown at the exhibition it was not inscribed as a copyright, nor were any words thereon indicating a copyright, nor on the substance on which it was mounted, nor on the frame, as required by the copyright act (3 U.S.Comp.Stat., p. 3411), if the original painting is within the requirements of the law in this respect.

The painting while on exhibition was for sale at the Royal Academy, but with the copyright reserved, which reservation was entered in the gallery sale book. The by-laws of the Royal Academy provided "that no permission to copy works on exhibition shall on any account be granted." The reasons for the by-law, as it appears upon minutes of the Academy, are as follows:

> That so much property in copyright being entrusted to the guardianship of the Royal Academy, the council feel themselves compelled to disallow, in future, all copying within their walls from pictures sent for exhibition.

The photogravures of the painting were placed on sale in June, 1894, or in the autumn of 1894; those photogravures were inscribed with the notice of copyright.

Mr. Sadler, the artist, afterwards, in October, 1899, sold the painting to a Mr. Cotterel, residing in London, England, since which time, so far as has been shown, it has been hanging in the dining room of the house of that gentleman.

On June 20, 1902, Werckmeister commenced an action, by the service of a summons, against the American Tobacco Company, plaintiff in error, * * *

Mr. Justice Day, after making the foregoing statement, delivered the opinion of the court.

This case involves important questions under the copyright laws of the United States, upon which there has been diversity of view in the Federal courts. * * *

It is further contended that the exhibition in the Royal Gallery was such a publication of the painting as prevents the defendant in error from having the benefit of the copyright act. This question has been dealt with in a number of cases, and the result of the authorities establishes, we think, that it is only in cases where what is known as a general publication is shown, as distinguished from a limited publication under conditions which exclude the presumption that it was intended to be dedicated to the public, that the owner of the right of copyright is deprived of the benefit of the statutory provision.

Considering this feature of the case, it is well to remember that the property of the author or painter in his intellectual creation is absolute until he voluntarily parts with the same. One or many persons may be permitted to an examination under circumstances which show no intention to part with the property right, and it will remain unimpaired.

The subject was considered and the cases reviewed in the analogous case of Werckmeister v. The American Lithographic Company, 134 Fed.Rep. 321, in a full and comprehensive opinion by the late Circuit Judge Townsend, which leaves little to be added to the discussion.

The rule is thus stated in Slater on the Law of Copyright and Trademark (p. 92):

> It is a fundamental rule that to constitute publication there must be such a dissemination of the work of art itself among the public, as to justify the belief that it took place with the intention of rendering such work common property.

And that author instances as one of the occasions that does not amount to a general publication the exhibition of a work of art at a public exhibition where there are by-laws against copies, or where it is tacitly understood that no copying shall take place, and the public are admitted to view the painting on the implied understanding that no improper advantage will be taken of the privilege.

We think this doctrine is sound and the result of the best considered cases. In this case it appears that paintings are expressly entered at the gallery with copyrights reserved. There is no permission to copy; on the other hand, officers are present who rigidly enforce the requirements of the society that no copying shall take place.

Starting with the presumption that it is the author's right to withhold his property, or only to yield to a qualified and special inspection which shall not permit the public to acquire rights in it, we think the circumstances of this exhibition conclusively show that it was the purpose of the owner, entirely consistent with the acts done, not to permit such an inspection of his picture as would throw its use open to the public. We do not mean to say that the public exhibition of a painting or statue, where all might see and freely copy it, might not amount to publication within the statute, regardless of the artist's purpose or notice of reservation of rights which he takes no measure to protect. But such is not the present case, where the greatest care was taken to prevent copying. * * *

Finding no error in the judgment of the Circuit Court of Appeals, the same is

Affirmed.

Questions

1. If pre-1978 there were a public exhibition of a work of art without restrictions on copying, and without guards to prevent copying, did this constitute a publication of such work? See Letter Edged in Black Press, Inc. v. Public Building Commission of Chicago, 320 F.Supp. 1303 (N.D.Ill.1970), involving the public exhibition of a Picasso sculpture. If such an exhibition occurred after January 1, 1978, did the fact that there were no restrictions on copying render it a publication?

2. Should the fact that the painting in the *American Tobacco* case was offered for sale at the time it was exhibited at the Royal Gallery affect the result? Would this make a difference under the current Act? Note the following: "I would like to discuss * * * the meaning of the concept of 'publication' in the case of a work of art, such as a painting or statue, that exists in only one copy. It is not the committee's intention that such a work would be regarded as 'published' when the single existing copy is sold or offered for sale in the traditional way—for example, through an art dealer, gallery, or auction house. On the other hand, where the work has been made for reproduction in multiple copies—as in the case of fine prints such as lithographs—or where multiple reproductions of the prototype work are offered for purchase by the public—as in the case of castings from a statue or reproductions from a photograph or painting—publication would take place at the point when reproduced copies are publicly distributed or when, even if only one copy exists at that point, reproductions are offered for purchase by multiple members of the public." 122 Cong.Rec. H 10874–5 (daily ed. Sept. 22, 1976) (remarks of Rep. Kastenmeier, Chairman of the House Subcommittee which reported out the Copyright Act). Does this statement of legislative intent interpret or contradict the statutory text?

Collateral Reference

Nimmer on Copyright, § 4.09.

E. PUBLICATION OF DERIVATIVE WORKS

O'NEILL v. GENERAL FILM CO.

Supreme Court, Appellate Division, First Department, 1916.
171 A.D. 854, 157 N.Y.S. 1028.

LAUGHLIN, J. The plaintiff, claiming to own the literary rights as well as the performing rights in a dramatization of Alexander Dumas' novel, "The Count of Monte Cristo," by Charles Fechter, brought this suit in equity to enjoin the defendant from producing or exhibiting, or distributing for production and exhibition, on the stage or in any theater or place of amusement, any motion picture films containing in whole or in part any of the scenes, incidents, plot, or story of said novel as so dramatized, or any simulated or colorable imitation or adaptation thereof.

Dumas' novel was published in 1845. He wrote a dramatization thereof in French in 1848. There was a dramatization prior to 1870 in

Plaintiff James O'Neill (father of playwright Eugene O'Neill) in the role of the Count of Monte Cristo.

English, known as the "French-Lacy Dramatization." Charles Fechter, a Frenchman, wrote another English dramatization of the novel for Benjamin Webster, who was a celebrated actor and the manager of the Adelphi Theater, London, England, and it was publicly performed at that theater on or about the 19th of October, 1868; Webster playing the rôle of Noirtier, which was written expressly for him, and Fechter the rôle of Edmond Dantes, who becomes the Count of Monte Cristo. As a condition precedent to the issuance of a license to present the play, under the English statute regulating theaters (6 & 7 Vict. c. 68, § 12), a printed copy of this dramatization by Fechter was filed with the Lord Chamberlain of Her Majesty's Household on the 17th day of October, 1868, and such a license was duly issued. The London newspapers, including the Daily Telegraph, gave extended accounts of the play as thus presented.

According to the testimony of the plaintiff, Fechter thereafter came to the United States and appeared in the presentation of the play in the same rôle in various theaters in this country from 1873 until his death in 1879, and "produced it from the manuscript in his possession." The plaintiff also testified that in the year 1883 he was employed by John Stetson, who owned the Globe Theater, in Boston, Mass., to appear in the title rôle in the presentation of "Monte Cristo" in New York City, and that in the month of June, 1885, he purchased from Stetson for the consideration of $2,000 all of the right, title, and interest of the latter in the Fechter version of the Count of Monte Cristo, which Stetson claimed to have purchased from Arthur Cheney, and received from Stetson a bill of sale thereof and the typewritten manuscript, the title page of which is as follows:

Monte Cristo,
Arranged and Adapted Expressly for
Arthur Cheney, Esq.,
Proprietor and Manager of the
GLOBE THEATER, BOSTON, MASS.,

by

CHARLES FECHTER, ESQUIRE,
Under the Stage Direction of
Arthur Le Clercy.
First Representation

at

GLOBE THEATER, BOSTON, MASS.

on

Monday Evening, Sept. 12th, 1870,

and

Now the Property of
Mr. JOHN STETSON

of the

FIFTH AVENUE THEATER, NEW YORK,

and the

GLOBE THEATER, BOSTON, MASS.,
Who Has the Sole and Exclusive Right of Production for the
UNITED STATES AND CANADA.

It appears, by a comparison of this manuscript with the printed play filed with the Lord Chamberlain in London as aforesaid, that the play as originally written by Fechter had been abridged by the elimination of many parts for the purpose of shortening the production, but otherwise they are the same. The recitals on the title page of the plaintiff's manuscript of the play constitute the only evidence of the authorship thereof. The plaintiff testified that Fechter appeared in the play at the Globe Theater in Boston, of which Arthur Cheney was one of the proprietors, and that Cheney died prior to 1883.

The trial court found, in effect, that the defendant used the Fechter version in making a motion picture film for the production of Monte Cristo as a motion picture play. * * *

No evidence was offered on the part of the defendant with respect to the source from which the scenario used in making the motion picture was taken, and no explanation with respect thereto was offered. The trial court by consent witnessed a presentation of the motion picture photoplay as presented by defendant, and was thereby aided in determining the question of fact; but without the evidence thus taken by viewing the picture it is quite clear from the record that the motion picture photoplay presented by the defendant was prepared to a large extent from the Fechter dramatization, for many scenes and incidents are depicted therein which are either not found in the novel or in any other dramatization thereof, or in the order as presented by the Fechter dramatization and by defendant's films. In the novel Noirtier is the father of Villefort, and is an unimportant character in the story, and this is followed in the other dramatizations; but Fechter changed the character of Noirtier, making him the half-brother of Villefort and one of the leading characters in his dramatization, and this change is substantially followed in defendant's films. In the novel and the other dramatization, Albert is the son of Mercedes and Fernand. Fechter changed this character, making him the son of Mercedes and Dantes, and makes use of this change in a dramatic way near the end of his dramatization, where he has Mercedes prevent a duel between Albert and Dantes, by informing the latter that Albert is his son, and this incident is found in defendant's films. The scene at the end of the Fechter dramatization, in which Dantes kills his enemy, Danglars, in a duel, is original with Fechter, and is reproduced in the last picture in defendant's films. In the novel and the other dramatizations, after Dantes has substituted himself for the dead body of the Abbé in the burial sack, and has been thrown into the sea from the Chateau D'If, he extricates himself from the sack and swims to and climbs upon a rock or an island and thanks God for his deliverance. In the Fechter dramatization, after Dantes gains the rock, he exclaims:

> Saved! Mine, the treasures of Monte Cristo! The world is mine!

This is original with Fechter, although in the Dumas dramatization, after Dantes has visited the island of Monte Cristo and has found the buried treasure of Spada, of which the Abbé Faria had told him, he exclaims:

> Faria told the truth! The treasure of the Spadas is mine! The world is mine!

One of the pictorial posters used by Stetson to advertise performances of the play, at the time the plaintiff appeared in it for him, showed Dantes standing upon a rock in the sea, with the Chateau D'If in the distance, with his arms outstretched and the knife with which he freed himself from the sack in his hand, and underneath was printed the words, "The World is Mine!" In the presentation of defendant's photoplay, just following a picture showing Dantes in the sea freeing himself from the sack with the knife, were flashed on the screen the words "The World is Mine," and then followed a picture showing him emerging from the water and appearing on a rock with outstretched arms. It thus appears that the trial court was warranted by the evidence in finding that the defendant used the Fechter dramatization.

The next question to be considered is whether the Fechter dramatization was dedicated to the public, * * * by filing the printed copy with the Lord Chamberlain, or by the expiration of the statutory period of 42 years from the first public representation or performance in England. St. 5 & 6 Vict. c. 45, §§ 3 and 20. These statutory provisions gave protection to the *performing rights* in plays for the period provided for copyright in books, which was for the natural life of the author and for seven years after his death and until the expiration of 42 years from the first publication. Seven years after Fechter's death expired before the end of 42 years from the first public performance in 1868. The period during which the performing rights were protected expired in 1910. I am of opinion that there is no force in the argument that there was a dedication to the public by filing the printed copy of the play as stated, for that was a condition precedent, under the English statute regulating theaters, to the right to present a public performance of the play. St. 6 & 7 Vict. c. 68, §§ 12 and 13. * * *

The learned counsel for the appellant ingeniously argues that any one was at liberty to produce the play in England after the expiration of the statutory period during which the right *to produce* it was protected there, and that therefore it should be deemed that the play thereupon became dedicated to the public the world over. That would be giving effect here to the English law; and since, in so far as appears, there has been no publication of the play, and a public performance of it under our law is not a dedication (Palmer v. De Witt, supra; Ferris v. Frohman, supra), it cannot be held that any rights existing here during the period during which the statute was running in England have been lost by the expiration of the period of statutory protection there. It was held in Ferris v. Frohman, supra, on like facts, excepting that the statutory period of protection of the performing rights of the play under the English statute had not expired, that the common-law rights in the unpublished play here were in no manner affected by the English statute. Therefore it is quite clear that whatever rights existed have not been lost by filing the printed copy of the play with the Lord Chamberlain, or by the presentation of the play on the stage in England. * * * If the controversy were between the plaintiff and Fechter, or his representatives, and it appeared that Fechter made the dramatization and revision *in his own right,* it may well be that the evidence in the record now before the court would be insufficient to show that the title of the author had been acquired by the plaintiff; but the question here is whether the plaintiff has shown sufficient title as against a stranger to any right, title, or interest in the play, and in such case I think less evidence should suffice to establish a prima facie case.

The recitals on the title page of the manuscript of the play which Stetson assigned to the plaintiff, and Stetson's verbal declarations, and his allegation in the complaint in the action brought against Studley, are not competent evidence of the *source* of his title, either to the literary or to the performing right in the play; but they are, I think, competent evidence to characterize the title which he claimed by virtue of the manuscript of which he had possession, and constitute some evidence of title, not only to the manuscript, but to the play, and to the performing right. 3 Wigmore on Evidence, § 1779. See, also, 2 Wigmore on Evidence, §§ 1573, 1574, 1576; Jones on Evidence, par. 2, § 311, p. 702. The plaintiff evidently has presented the best evidence obtainable with respect to the ownership of this play, and it is in no manner impeached or controverted, and I am of opinion that it sufficiently shows title to enable him to maintain the action.

The evidence showed, and the trial court found, that the plaintiff and his assignor, Stetson, for the purpose of advertising performances of the play, took flashlight photographs of many of the important scenes and incidents of the play as represented on the stage, and reproduced therefrom pictorial posters and prints, and widely circulated and displayed them in show windows and on billboards and other public places in various parts of the United States. Counsel for appellant contends that this constituted a publication of the play, or of its important features, and that any one was thereafter at liberty to present the play with such features by motion pictures. The public presentation of a play is not a dedication thereof. Palmer v. De Witt, 47 N.Y. 532, 7 Am.Rep. 480. The public posting of posters and prints was merely incidental to the presentation of the play. The posters and prints did not tell the story of the play in connected form, or constitute a representation of the drama. See Kalem Co. v. Harper Bros., 222 U.S. 55–62, 32 Sup.Ct. 20, 56 L.Ed. 92, Ann.Cas.1913A, 1285. Such a publication in no sense constitutes a dedication to the public of the play or the performing right.

Counsel for appellant finally contends that in any event the complaint should have been dismissed for want of right in the plaintiff to equitable relief on November 18, 1912, when the action was commenced. The basis of his contention in this regard is the copyrighting by the Famous Players' Film Company, with the consent of the plaintiff, of a motion picture photoplay of the plaintiff's play, and the facts preceding it.

The plaintiff testified, and the trial court found, that on or before the 1st day of November, 1912, he made a contract with said Famous Players' Company for the making of a motion picture film "adapted to reproduce in motion pictures" the said drama "Monte Cristo"; that, for the purpose of making the pictures, plaintiff engaged a company of actors and actresses, who in costume and with the aid of scenery gave performances of the play before a high-speed camera, and that positive films have been prepared by said company with the consent of the plaintiff; that the plaintiff caused to be given through said company exhibitions of Monte Cristo in motion picture theaters with the aid of said positive films, and that said exhibitions were advertised and announced under the title "Monte Cristo"; that for the purpose of enabling said company to make said films and to give performances, plaintiff delivered the play to its stage director and assisted in making the films; that the films "adapted to reproduce in motion pictures said play" were released for distribution and circulation among exhibitors and motion picture theaters on the 1st day of November, 1912; that with the consent of the plaintiff said company secured copyright in said films "adapted to reproduce in motion pictures said play" on the 10th day of December, 1912; that to secure copyright in the motion picture photoplay "a description of said motion picture photoplay was filed in the office of the Register of Copyrights on the 16th day of December, 1912." The plaintiff testified in effect that his contract with the Famous Players' Company was in writing, but it was not offered in evidence; and the evidence with respect thereto goes only to the extent already stated.

By the steps taken by the plaintiff and by the Famous Players' Company under that contract, which culminated in copyrighting the motion picture films, it is quite clear. I think that the plaintiff parted with any common-law motion picture rights he had in the play, to the extent, at least, represented by the motion pictures thus taken and copyrighted; but whether all common-law motion picture rights with respect to scenes and incidents in the play not represented in the copyrighted motion pictures films, and not preserved by the substituted statutory right, have been abandoned or lost, is a question not free from difficulty and on which we find no precedent.

It is well settled that an author or an owner of a book or play, by publishing it, which is a condition precedent to obtaining a copyright, waives and abandons his common-law rights therein, and must thenceforth depend upon the statutory rights conferred by the acts of Congress, which give exclusive rights and provide for injunctive relief and damages, but those rights must be enforced in the federal courts. Caliga v. Inter-Ocean Newspaper Co., 157 Fed. 186, 84 C.C.A. 634, affirmed 215 U.S. 182, 30 Sup.Ct. 38, 54 L.Ed. 150; Jewelers' Mercantile Agency v. Jewelers' Pub. Co., 155 N.Y. 241, 49 N.E. 872, 41 L.R.A. 846, 63 Am.St.Rep. 666; Photo-Drama Motion Picture Co., Inc., v. Social Uplift Film Corporation, 220 Fed. 448, 137 C.C.A. 42; Act Cong. March 4, 1909, c. 320 (35 U.S. Statutes at Large, p. 1075), as amended by Act Cong. Aug. 24, 1912, c. 356 (37 U.S. Statutes at Large, p. 488) §§ 1, 23, 25, 26, 27, 34, 35, 36, 37, 38; Rev.St.U.S.1878, § 711; Judicial Code (Act March 3, 1911, c. 231) § 256, 36 Stat. 1100 (U.S.Comp.St.1913, § 1233). A photoplay taken from a book constitutes a dramatization of the author's work, which may be copyrighted. Kalem v. Harper Bros., 222 U.S. 55, 32 Sup.Ct. 20, 56 L.Ed. 92, Ann.Cas.1913A, 1285; Photo-Drama Motion Picture Co., Inc., v. Social Uplift Film Corporation, supra.

When a book or drama is dedicated to the public, any one may prepare and copyright a motion picture photoplay founded thereon; but such copyright will not give the owner thereof an *exclusive* right to the motion picture rights in the book or drama, for it has been held that, although any one is at liberty to translate or to dramatize a book that has become public property, no translator or dramatizer thereof can obtain an exclusive right to more than his own literary work in translating or dramatizing, and all others are free to do the same, provided they do not appropriate anything original in his work. Drone on Copyright, pp. 158, 159, 232, 433, 449, 458 and cases cited; Shook v. Rankin, 6 Biss. 477, 482, Fed.Cas. No. 12,804; Crowe v. Aiken, 2 Biss. 208, Fed.Cas. No. 3,441; Boucicault v. Wood, 2 Biss. 34, Fed.Cas. No. 1,693.

Where one owning an unpublished play and all rights therein in a foreign language and the work of a foreign author, which could not for that reason be copyrighted here, copyrights a translation thereof, or, having the dramatization rights, copyrights a drama, it has been held that he forfeits all rights save those preserved by the Copyright Law, and that others are free to translate or to dramatize the original work, provided they do not infringe upon the original work of translation in the copyrighted translation. Shook v. Rankin, supra. See Drone on Copyright, pp. 582–585. By publishing the translation or dramatization, which was required as a condition precedent to obtaining the copyright, the owner of the play or of the dramatization rights is deemed to have dedicated the entire play or dramatic rights to the public. In such case it may be presumed, I think, that the translation or dramatization was a substantial reproduction of the original work. Copyrighting a motion picture photoplay of an author's work, however, does not either necessarily or presumptively involve a dedication to the public of the motion picture rights with respect to *all* the scenes and incidents of the play; and in the case at bar, although the court has found that the copyrighted motion picture photoplay is adapted to present the plaintiff's play by motion pictures, yet it fairly appears that many scenes and incidents in the plaintiff's play, which have never otherwise been dedicated to the public, are not represented in the motion picture films which have been copyrighted.

The copyright of the motion picture photoplay by the Famous Players' Company does not under the law constitute a copyright of the plaintiff's play. The law does not require that the sources from which the pictures are taken be given either in the application for copyright, registration, or otherwise, and neither in the application for copyright registration nor in the description of the motion picture photoplay filed in the office of the Register of Copyrights, in the case at bar, is there any reference to the source from which the pictures were obtained. In this respect I think the copyright of a motion picture photoplay differs from the copyright of a book or drama, or of a translation. So far as shown by the evidence, the only right, title, or interest the plaintiff has parted with is such as was essential to obtaining the copyright, and all that he has authorized to be published, and was required to publish as a condition precedent to obtaining the copyright, were the titles and particular scenes and incidents photographed, together with a description thereof (section 11 of the Copyright Act); and I am of opinion that the dedication to the public should be deemed limited accordingly, and that no one is at liberty, without the consent of the plaintiff, to appropriate his unpublished play, excepting in so far as he has thus dedicated rights therein to the public. It may be that the scenes and incidents in the plaintiff's play, not published by the copyrighting, have no substantial value for motion picture photoplay purposes; but it is manifest that his right to present the play as he has done heretofore might be prejudicially affected if others were at liberty to present a motion picture photoplay founded in whole or in part on the unpublished scenes or incidents in his play.

The plaintiff, or the owner of the copyright, must seek redress for any infringement thereof in the federal courts; but the state courts have jurisdiction to enforce his reserved common-law rights. These views would require a modification of the decree by excluding from the scope of the injunction scenes and incidents of the plaintiff's play which have been copyrighted; but, if an injunction is to be issued at all, evidently a modification is not deemed material, and is not requested. Since, however, the plaintiff has not seen fit to defer action in the state court to enforce his remaining common-law rights until it has been decided in the federal courts to what extent the owner of the copyright is entitled to recover damages for the infringement of the copyright, and since it is not competent for a state court to decide that question, I am of opinion that the recovery of damages herein must be limited to the time the copyright was obtained.

It follows, therefore, that the judgment should be modified by limiting the recovery of damages to the 10th day of December, 1912, and, as thus modified, affirmed, without costs. Settle order on notice. All concur.

Questions

1. Under the Copyright Act of 1976 does publication of a derivative work constitute publication of the pre-existing work contained therein? What is the implication of Sec. 401(b)(2) in this regard?

2. Suppose the defendant in *O'Neill* had produced a stage play rather than a motion picture, but that the play did not contain any material taken from plaintiff's play other than that which had already appeared in the Famous Players' motion picture. Could plaintiff have prevailed in a common law copyright action? When the court in the instant case concluded that publication of the Famous Players' film had divested plaintiff of "common-law *motion picture* rights", was it implying that plaintiff still retained common law copyright with respect to stage performances, book publications, etc.? Was such a conclusion correct?

3. If publication of a derivative work, such as a motion picture, did not constitute publication of the underlying work contained therein, what would that mean as to the term of protection that would in fact be available for the derivative work?

4. Does the fact that a derivative work has entered the public domain necessarily mean that the preexisting work contained therein has also entered the public domain? Suppose that the motion picture "A Star Is Born" had been injected into the public domain by reason of an inadvertent failure to obtain a renewal copyright therein. Suppose further that the screenplay (i. e., the script) upon which the motion picture was based had never been separately published, and pre-1978 was not the subject of statutory copyright. Did the common law copyright in the screenplay survive the pre-1978 publication of the motion picture, so that Warner Brothers, which had purportedly purchased all rights in both the film and the underlying screenplay, could claim that the unlicensed performance of the (public domain) film constituted an infringement of its rights in the screenplay? See Classic Film Museum, Inc. v. Warner Brothers, Inc., 453 F.Supp. 852 (D.Me.1978), affirmed 597 F.2d 13 (1st Cir.1979). Alternatively, suppose that the motion picture "Pygmalion", based upon the George Bernard Shaw play of the same name, had been injected into the public domain by reason of a failure to renew the copyright in the film, but suppose further that the Shaw play had been the subject of statutory copyright prior to the publication of the film, and that the play had been properly renewed. May the copyright owner of the play prohibit the unauthorized performance of the public domain film? See Russell v. Price, 612 F.2d 1123 (9th Cir.1979).

Collateral Reference

Nimmer on Copyright, § 4.12.

Chapter Three

FORMALITIES

A. NOTICE

Note and Questions

The United States is virtually alone among the nations of the world in requiring a copyright notice. Within the United States ownership in other forms of real and personal property is not conditioned upon the placement of a notice identifying the owner. What is the justification for this singular requirement under American law? The House Report [1] identified four principal functions of copyright notice under the 1909 Act which it was suggested justified the continuance of the notice requirement under the current Act. These are:

"(1) [Notice] has the effect of placing in the public domain a substantial body of published material that no one is interested in copyrighting;

(2) It informs the public as to whether a particular work is copyrighted;

(3) It identifies the copyright owner; and

(4) It shows the date of publication."

It may be argued that none of these reasons fully justify the possible loss of copyright which (even under the more ameliorative provisions of the current Act) may result from the failure to observe the notice requirements. As you become familiar with the notice requirements, consider whether and to what extent they satisfy the above listed objectives.

In general, a copyright notice consists of the word "Copyright", or a prescribed variation thereof,[2] accompanied by the name of the copyright owner, and in most instances the notice must also include the year of first publication.

Question 1: Under the Copyright Act of 1976, when may the year of first publication be omitted from the copyright notice? See Sec. 401(b)(2). How does this differ from the Copyright Act of 1909? See Sec. 19 (1909 Act).

---

1. H.Rep., p. 143.
2. The notice required to be placed upon copies must contain either the word "Copyright," the abbreviation "Copr.," or the symbol ©. In the case of the notice required to be placed upon phonorecords, the symbol ℗ must be used, and neither the word "Copyright," nor any other substitute will suffice.

A notice is required only on copies and phonorecords which are published.[3] Moreover, the notice requirements are applicable only to such copies or phonorecords of a work as are published "by authority of the copyright owner".[4]

Question 2: Suppose copyright owner A licenses B to publish copies of his work, subject to the condition that all such copies bear a proper copyright notice. If B publishes copies without such a notice, will this trigger the consequences (discussed below) of a violation of the notice requirements? Has B published "by authority of the copyright owner"? Suppose the above condition is oral or implied rather than express and in writing—will this affect the determination of whether B's publication contrary to the condition is "by authority of the copyright owner"? Compare Sec. 405(a)(3) with Secs. 401(a) and 402(a).

As regards copies, a copyright notice must be "placed on all publicly distributed copies from which the work can be visually perceived, either directly or with the aid of a machine or device."[5]

Question 3: Is the qualification that the work must be "visually" perceived in order to trigger the requirement of notice on copies a meaningful limitation? If a work is aurally rather than visually perceived from a material object is not such object a "phonorecord" rather than a "copy"? Or are there some types of "copies" from which the work is aurally rather than visually perceived? What about a motion picture sound track? Is any copyright notice required on a motion picture film in order to protect the music and dialogue contained on its sound track?

The special notice required for sound recordings [6] must be placed on all publicly distributed phonorecords of the sound recording.[7]

Question 4: Recall the distinction between a musical work and a sound recording of such musical work. (The composer is the author of the musical work. The performers and/or record producer are the authors of the sound recording). What form of notice, if any, must be placed upon a published phonorecord in order to protect the musical work recorded therein?

Under the Copyright Act of 1976, the notice required for copies of a work must be affixed "in such manner and location as to give reasonable notice of the claim of copyright."[8]

Question 5: How does this compare with the required placement of notice under the 1909 Act? See Sec. 20 (1909 Act).

Question 6: How does this compare with the required placement of notice on phonorecords under the 1976 Act? See Sec. 402(c).

What are the consequences of the omission of the required copyright notice from published copies or phonorecords? Under the 1909 Act it was clear that an unexcused omission injected the work into the public domain. That this is also true under the 1976 Act is indicated somewhat obliquely by Sec. 405(a), which provides: "The omission of the copyright notice * * * does not invalidate the copyright if" any one of certain excusing conditions is satisfied. The clear negative implication is that if none of these excusing conditions have been satisfied, then the omission of notice *does* invalidate the copyright.

3. As to what constitutes publication, see Chapter Two.
4. 17 U.S.C.A. §§ 401(a); 402(a).
5. 17 U.S.C.A. § 401(a).
6. 17 U.S.C.A. § 402(b).
7. 17 U.S.C.A. § 402(a).
8. 17 U.S.C.A. § 401(c).

What, then, are the conditions which excuse an omission of notice? Apart from one already discussed,[9] there are two such conditions. The first is that "the notice has been omitted from no more than a relatively small number of copies or phonorecords distributed to the public."[10]

Question 7: What constitutes a "relatively small number"? Would an omission of notice from 1,000 copies out of an edition of 100,000 constitute a "relatively small number"? What does "relatively" mean? Relative to what? Compare H.Rep., p. 147 with Reg.Supp.Rep., p. 106.

Question 8: How does this condition compare with the comparable provision in Section 21 of the 1909 Act? Is it more or less restrictive?

The other such condition, which alternatively will excuse an omission of notice, is satisfied if "registration for the work has been made before or is made within five years after the publication without notice, and a reasonable effort is made to add notice to all copies or phonorecords that are distributed to the public in the United States after the omission has been discovered".[11]

Question 9: Suppose the omission of notice is deliberate rather than unintentional, but registration is made within five years of such first publication. Will the omission be excused? The House Report states that "a work published without any copyright notice will still be subject to statutory protection for at least 5 years [within which time the registration requirement can be satisfied], whether the omission was * * * unintentional or deliberate."[12] Can this statement be reconciled with the "reasonable effort" requirement of Sec. 405(a)(2)? Compare Beacon Looms, Inc. v. S. Lichtenberg & Co., 552 F.Supp. 1305 (S.D.N.Y.1982) and O'Neill Developments, Inc. v. Galen Kilburn, Inc., 524 F.Supp. 710 (N.D.Ga.1981).

Question 10: Since the "reasonable effort" requirement applies only to copies and phonorecords published "in the United States", does this mean that, assuming registration within the required five year period, there may be a deliberate omission of notice from copies and phonorecords published outside of the United States? How does this affect the words "or elsewhere" as contained in Sections 401(a) and 402(a)?

Question 11: If an omission of notice is excused, what is the impact upon the liability of an innocent infringer who relied upon such omission? How do Secs. 405(b) and 406(a) differ in this regard?

Collateral Reference

Nimmer on Copyright, §§ 7.02, 7.03, 7.06, 7.08, 7.10, 7.12, 7.13, 7.14.

Note *

The Significance Under the Current Act of Notice
Requirements Under the 1909 Act

Although the notice requirements under the current Act, are largely the same as such requirements under the 1909 Act, there are some differences. In certain ways the 1909 notice requirements were more restrictive; in others

---

9. See the text at footnote 4 above.
10. 17 U.S.C.A. § 405(a)(1).
11. 17 U.S.C.A. § 405(a)(2).
12. H.Rep., p. 147.
* Nimmer on Copyright, § 7.04.

more liberal. Some of these differences are suggested in the preceding note, and others are indicated in the material following the next few cases. The notice requirements under the 1909 Act, to the extent that they vary from such requirements under the present Act, remain significant for several reasons. In the first place, with respect to publications occurring prior to January 1, 1978 (the effective date of the current Act), if a notice were used which was defective under the 1909 Act (even though it would have been proper under the current Act), this could inject such work into the public domain as of the time of such publication, in which case such work will not be entitled to copyright under the present Act.[1] There are also some forms of notice which would have been proper under the 1909 Act, but are improper under the notice provisions of the current Act. Publications prior to January 1, 1978, using such a form of notice obviously present no problem. But what of such publications occurring after the effective date of the current Act? As to works first published in 1978 or thereafter, if the affixed notices do not conform to the requirements of the current Act, this will trigger the consequences of defective notice. But a different rule is applicable to works first published prior to 1978. Subsequent publications of copies or phonorecords of such works occurring after January 1, 1978, may continue to bear the form of notice prescribed by the 1909 Act.[2] Alternatively, such subsequently published copies and phonorecords may bear a form of notice prescribed by the current Act.[3]

In this context, we turn now to some of the significant "notice" cases decided under the 1909 Act.

WRENCH v. UNIVERSAL PICTURES CO.

United States District Court, Southern District of New York, 1952.
104 F.Supp. 374.

Ryan, Judge. Plaintiff and both defendants have moved separately for summary judgment contending that as to their respective right to such relief there are no factual issues requiring trial. Rule 56, Fed.R. Civ.P., 28 U.S.C.A.

The claims asserted by plaintiff are for moneys she alleges are due her from defendant, Universal, under a written contract made on April 22, 1948.

By this contract plaintiff sold to Universal all motion picture rights for the entire world to three stories written by her (two of which had been published), and contracted to sell the rights to such additional story or stories and all adaptations and revisions which she might write and publish based upon the theme and idea of plaintiff's experiences as a lecturer. All of these stories were to be known and entitled collectively as It Gives Me Great Pleasure; and all were referred to in the contract as the "property." Universal was also given the right to use the title of the property or of any story as the title of any motion picture production based on the same theme. In the contract plaintiff agreed that she would protect and preserve the copyright on the property sold and to be sold from coming into the public domain so far

---

1. 17 U.S.C.A., Trans.Supp.Prov. § 103.
2. 17 U.S.C.A., Trans.Supp.Prov. § 108.
3. Id.

as might be legally possible, by affixing to each "copy or arrangement of said work or any part thereof published or offered for sale any notice necessary for copyright protection in the United States or necessary for like protection under the laws of other countries." Plaintiff undertook that as each story was published with proper copyright notice she would duly register the same "wheresoever its protection so requires." She also agreed to procure the execution and delivery of an instrument by any publisher to Universal assigning all rights sold to Universal, and contracted to specifically reserve Universal's rights in the conveyance and transfer of any rights in the property to another.

Upon execution of the contract it was further provided that plaintiff was to receive from Universal a down payment of $10,000., a further payment of $25,000. upon commencement of principal photography of the first photoplay, if any, based on the property sold or within one year from the contract date. Universal also agreed to pay plaintiff $.25 for each copy of the regular trade edition of a full-length compilation of the stories published in book form and sold in the United States and Canada within 18 months of the first publication, these payments, however, not to exceed the sum of $25,000.

The complaint admits receipt by plaintiff of the first payment of $10,000. and alleges as a breach of the contract Universal's failure to pay the balance allegedly due amounting to $50,000. Plaintiff asks judgment in that amount against Universal.

Universal by answer admits the making of the contract in suit, but denies any breach on its part. It affirmatively alleges that plaintiff did not duly perform in that she neglected and omitted, (1) to preserve the copyright on the property in the United States and throughout the world, (2) to specifically preserve and protect the rights of Universal when assigning rights in the property to others, (3) to procure the execution and delivery of assignments by publishers to Universal, and (4) to give Universal the legal and exclusive right to use the title to said property. Universal alleges that by reason of this failure of plaintiff to duly perform, the property became "unmarketable" and that title thereto was rendered "unmarketable, defective, clouded and doubtful."

As separate defenses Universal pleads its election to rescind the contract and alleges readiness to restore to plaintiff everything it received under the contract. As a further defense it alleges the failure of plaintiff to furnish statements of sales of the book, a "condition precedent" to Universal's obligation to pay the additional $25,000. which was to be calculated on the number of books sold. By counterclaim it seeks to recover the $10,000. it paid plaintiff on the signing of the contract.

Plaintiff has asserted an alternative claim against Dodd, Mead, the publisher of her book It Gives Me Great Pleasure. Dodd, Mead, on May 17, 1948, undertook by contract with plaintiff to copyright the property and "to take all the usual precautions to protect said copyright." Plaintiff's position is that if Universal's counterclaim is sustained, she is entitled to judgment against Dodd, Mead for the damage to her resulting from any of the alleged imperfections in the copyright on the property arising from the publication of the book. Plaintiff, however, "does not concede that any such imperfections exist."

Defendant Dodd, Mead's answer denies any breach of its contract with plaintiff, and asserts affirmatively failure on the part of plaintiff to furnish complete or necessary information and assignments on prior copyrights and publications. Dodd, Mead also alleges that any injury plaintiff has sustained arises solely from her own failure to duly perform her contract with Universal, and that in this Dodd, Mead did not participate.

From the pleadings, affidavits and documents submitted the following facts appear undisputed:

Plaintiff is well-known as a lecturer and author of several books and short stories. Many of her works have appeared in leading magazines and some have been made into successful motion pictures. Based on the theme of her experiences as a lecturer plaintiff wrote several short stories recounting numerous amusing anecdotes. The first, entitled "My Heart's In My Mouth", was published and copyrighted by the Atlantic Monthly in June, 1944; the second, a story entitled "Luggage For the South," was published and copyrighted in May, 1945 by the New Yorker magazine; the third story, entitled "Cincinnati and I," was not published until October, 1948. It was the picture rights to these three stories which were specifically sold to Universal by contract of April 22, 1948.

Following the making of the contract, plaintiff wrote nine additional stories. These plaintiff had contracted to sell Universal before they were written. Six of them were published and copyrighted in the New Yorker, prior to November; four were written but were not published in any magazine. In November, 1948, the book It Gives Me Great Pleasure was published by Dodd, Mead.

Deriving its title from the first story it contained the book collected as chapters under their original titles but with revisions, the eight stories previously published and copyrighted by the Atlantic Monthly and the New Yorker magazines, and the four unpublished stories. The book was based entirely on the theme and idea of plaintiff's experiences as a lecturer, each chapter relating a separate incident. The book as published represented the "property", the rights to which plaintiff had agreed to and did sell to Universal.

The copyright notice affixed to the reverse of the front or fly leaf of the book reads: "Copyright, 1945, 1948 by Emily Kimbrough." There appears beneath this a further notation that several of the chapters (named) "originally appeared in somewhat different form as stories in the New Yorker." Neither "1944," the year of the Atlantic Monthly copyright of the chapter entitled "My Heart's In My Mouth," nor the fact that it had once appeared in that magazine as a story is mentioned. That the chapter in the book and the story of the same name originally published and copyrighted by the Atlantic Monthly recount the same incidents is not disputed; that plaintiff is the sole author is not questioned.

At the time the book was published the record owner of title to the copyright on the story "My Heart's In My Mouth" was the Atlantic Monthly. Since it retained no interest in the story after its first publication in that magazine, the Atlantic Monthly readily reassigned the copyright to plaintiff upon her request. This, however, did not take place until December 10, 1948—after publication of the book—and was not recorded until January 6, 1949.

Early in 1949, in anticipation of its obligation to pay plaintiff on April 22, 1949, the $25,000. due under the contract, Universal had the title to the copyright searched. Upon examination of the results of this search, Universal questioned the sufficiency of the notice of copyright in the book. Acting on the advice of counsel on April 8, 1949, Universal sent a letter advising plaintiff that it elected to and did rescind the contract on the ground that the copyright was "incorrect and insufficient." Universal, at the time, offered to return to plaintiff "everything of value" received under the contract "on condition that plaintiff repay the $10,000. paid upon execution of the contract."

On April 22, 1949, plaintiff's attorneys wrote in reply refusing "to accept or accede to this purported rescission." Later when Universal advised that it was standing firm on its notice of rescission, plaintiff filed this suit.

We will first consider the motion of the defendant Universal for summary judgment. Here, we have presented the question whether the copyright on the book It Gives Me Great Pleasure published by defendant Dodd, Mead in 1948 is sufficient to protect the copyright on that part of it which consists of the story "My Heart's In My Mouth."

The book contains as a chapter the story originally published and copyrighted in the July, 1944 issue of the Atlantic Monthly magazine. It is the contention of Universal that this republication was without sufficient copyright notice, and it is urged that this story is now in the public domain.

The notice of copyright it is claimed is faulty and insufficient because (1) the year "1945" is claimed as the year of the prior copyright and that this is in fact a later year than the actual year of the copyright on the chapter "My Heart's In My Mouth," the correct year being "1944"; and (2) the existing copyright for this chapter was not owned by plaintiff as claimed, for in fact the Atlantic Monthly was the record owner.

In sum, then, the position of Universal is that a substantial portion of the property, the subject matter of the contract, has lost copyright protection and has fallen into the public domain, and even if this be not so, that the faulty notice of copyright had created a "cloud on the title" to the property and has rendered it "unmarketable." This, Universal urges affords justification in law for its non-performance of the terms of its written contract, for its failure to make the payments provided for in its undertaking, for the repudiation of its signed agreement and for its demand for the return of the $10,000. paid to plaintiff.

We conclude that the copyright on the property is valid and that no part of it has fallen into the public domain.

It is settled that the common law right in the property is lost by publication whether or not there be copyright notice, Holmes v. Hurst, 1899, 174 U.S. 82, 19 S.Ct. 606, 43 L.Ed. 904; Egner v. E.C. Schirmer Music Co., 1 Cir., 1943, 139 F.2d 398, and that statutory copyright is created only by proper copyright notice printed in the original publication, 17 U.S.C.A. § 10, and in each republication. DeJonge & Co. v. Breuker & Kessler, 1914, 235 U.S. 33, 36, 35 S.Ct. 6, 59 L.Ed. 113; Mifflin v. Dutton, 1903, 190 U.S. 265, 23 S.Ct. 771, 47 L.Ed. 1043.

If the story published and copyrighted in 1944 had been republished and copyrighted alone and without change in 1948 with no mention of the 1944 copyright, it would have fallen into the public domain. This would be so because "the substitution of the name of an assignee in a notice of copyright prior to the recordation of the assignment, results in an abandonment of the copyright", Group Publishers v. Winchell, D.C., 86 F.Supp. 573, 576, and the recital of a date later than the actual copyright date invalidates the copyright for the reason that it attempts to extend the copyright protection for longer than the statutory period. American Code Co. v. Bensinger, 2 Cir., 282 F. 829; Basevi v. Edward O'Toole, D.C., 26 F.Supp. 41, 48.

But we agree with plaintiff that here this was not the result, for it was not an instance of a republication of the same work at a later date. The revision of the original story "My Heart's In My Mouth" we find after comparison to be substantial and sufficient to constitute it a new work. Davies v. Columbia Pictures, D.C., 20 F.Supp. 809. In addition, it has been republished in chapter form as an integral part of a book which undisputably contains substantial new matter and which as a new work under Section 7 of the Copyright Law 17 U.S.C.A. § 7 is entitled to separate copyright. West Publishing Co. v. Edward Thompson Co., 2 Cir., 176 F. 833. And this would be so even if it were found that the chapter and the story "My Heart's In My Mouth", as first published, were similar. National Comics v. Fawcett Publications, 2 Cir., 1951, 191 F.2d 594. The publication of a new work with its own copyright notice dispenses with the necessity of listing any prior copyright in order to protect it. This is provided for by the wording of the statute that such publication "shall not affect the force and validity of any subsisting copyright upon the matter employed or any part thereof." To the same effect is the statement of Ball, Law of Copyright and Literary Property, that

> A second impression of the book with the addition of new matter * * * constitutes a second edition, and this may be the subject of a new and distinct copyright. Such copyright will protect all the matter in the second

edition in which copyright is already subsisting, as well as new matter therein, although it does not operate to extend the term or scope of the copyright previously secured for the first edition. (Sec. 76, pp. 172–74).

See also, National Comics v. Fawcett Publications, as to the sufficiency of the later copyright date.

That the plaintiff had the consent of the proprietor of the earlier copyright as required by the statute is evidenced by the letter of the Atlantic Monthly to plaintiff's agent dated June 15, 1944, as well as by the subsequent assignment of the copyright to her.

Since the only copyright date necessary to protect the property is 1948, the insertion of "1945" in the copyright notice in the book was superfluous. There is no merit to Universal's contention that this unnecessary notation of the 1945 copyright imposed a duty on plaintiff of also reciting the 1944 copyright, for where there has been sufficient compliance with the statute an erroneous belief that more is required cannot invalidate what has properly been done. Although the listing of prior copyrights is a practice of publishers "there is nothing in any act of congress to show that each successive edition must specify the date of the original copyright". Lawrence v. Dana, C.C.Mass.1869, 15 Fed.Cas. pp. 26, 52, No. 8.136.

Universal also urges that assuming the 1948 notice to be sufficient, the copyright of the book is defective because in plaintiff's application for her United States copyright she failed to state that the book was a new edition. But, irregularities in the copyright application standing alone do not affect the validity of the copyright, where, as here, there has been compliance with the statute. United States v. Backer, 2 Cir., 1943, 134 F.2d 533; Baron v. Leo Feist, Inc., D.C., 78 F.Supp. 686, 692, affirmed, 2 Cir., 1949, 173 F.2d 288. There is no claim by Universal that either it or anyone else was misled by this omission in the application; there is no evidence to indicate a purpose to deceive; the omission was innocuous.

Nor, do we find any substance to Universal's objection that the notice of copyright in the book was sufficiently defective to affect the "marketability of the title to said copyright," even though it be held that it did not render the copyright invalid. We assume for decision that the contract between plaintiff and Universal contained an implied warranty of marketability of title to the property even though we find none formally expressed. Universal's objection to the notice of copyright, it seems to us on analysis, if sustained would result not in defeating plaintiff's title to the copyright, but in the very destruction of the copyright property itself. If the objection were held to be of substance, the property would be lost by statutory abandonment; it would not survive that it might be claimed by another. The objection raises no issue as to ownership or title. While we take it as settled that a purchaser is not "bound to take a title which he can defend only by a resort to parol evidence, which time, death, or some other casualty may place beyond his reach", Moore v. Williams, 1889, 115 N.Y. 586, 591, 22

N.E. 233, 234, 5 L.R.A. 654, such a situation is not here presented by the undisputed facts. We regard Hollywood Plays v. Columbia Pictures Corp., 299 N.Y. 61, 85 N.E.2d 865, 10 A.L.R.2d 722, and like holdings as entirely inapposite.

The motion of Universal for summary judgment is denied, for we conclude that the United States copyright is valid. * * *

Questions

1. Does the Copyright Act of 1976 incorporate the rule of the *Wrench* case (followed in other 1909 Act cases) that the notice to be placed upon copies of a derivative work or compilation need only contain the year of first publication of such work, and not the earlier year of first publication of any pre-existing work contained therein? See Sec. 401(b)(2). Is this rule equally applicable to the notice to be placed upon phonorecords of sound recordings which constitute derivative works or compilations? If so, why the difference in wording as between Secs. 401(b)(2) and 402(b)(2)? Is *any* notice required on a phonorecord vis a vis pre-existing musical or literary works? What about pre-existing sound recordings? What is the effect of Section 404?

2. The *Wrench* opinion indicates that, apart from the special rule re derivative works and compilations mentioned above, a notice which contains a year later than the actual year of first publication will be considered an invalid notice. Other decisions under the 1909 Act modified this rule so that if the year in the notice is no more than one year later than the actual year of first publication, the notice will not be considered invalid. See e.g., Davis v. E.I. du Pont de Nemours & Co., 240 F.Supp. 612 (S.D.N.Y.1965). Has this rule been incorporated in the Act of 1976? See Sec. 406(b).

3. What is the effect under the current Copyright Act of a year stated in the copyright notice which is earlier than the year in which publication in fact first occurred? Section 406(b) provides that in such circumstances "any period computed from the year of first publication under Sec. 302 is to be computed from the year in the notice." This was the rule under the 1909 Act. See e.g., National Comics Publications, Inc. v. Fawcett Publications, Inc., 191 F.2d 594 (2d Cir.1951). Thus, under the 1909 Act the period for the first copyright term of 28 years (and the time when renewal for the second term must be claimed) was measured from the earlier year contained in the notice rather than, as would otherwise be the case, from the year of actual first publication. But under the Copyright Act of 1976 will this continue to be true as to works first copyrighted pre-1978, and therefore under Sec. 304 still subject to the renewal structure? If so, why the limiting reference in Sec. 406(b) to "Sec. 302", which does not relate to works subject to a renewal term? Since Section 302 in the main relates to works subject to a life of the author plus 50 year term rather than a "period computed from the year of first publication", does this provision of Sec. 406(b) insofar as it is limited to Sec. 302 works have any meaning?

4. Under the current Copyright Act how do the legal consequences differ depending upon whether the name contained in a copyright notice is not the true copyright owner, or alternatively, no name at all is contained in the purported notice? Compare Sec. 406(a) with Sec. 405(b).

5. Does the rule contained in Sec. 406(a) constitute a codification of the rule under the 1909 Act? See e.g., Klasmer v. Baltimore Football, Inc., 200 F.Supp. 255 (D.Md.1961), which holds that an incorrect name in a copyright

notice will constitute such notice defective even if the defendant is not thereby misled. But suppose the name in the notice on a derivative work contained the name of the copyright owner of such work, but not the name of the copyright owner of a pre-existing work contained therein. Under the 1909 Act was this a defective notice vis a vis the pre-existing work? Does the *Wrench* opinion speak to this situation? Would it have made a difference whether the pre-existing work had itself been the subject of common law rather than statutory copyright at the time of publication of the derivative work? See Goodis v. United Artists Television, Inc., infra.

Collateral Reference

Nimmer on Copyright, §§ 7.08[B][2], [C], 7.09[A], 7.12[C].

HEIM v. UNIVERSAL PICTURES CO.
Circuit Court of Appeals, Second Circuit, 1946.
154 F.2d 480.

Plaintiff sued defendants for infringement of his statutory copyright to his song, "Ma Este Meg Boldog Vagyok," asking an injunction and an accounting. The alleged infringement consists of the use of a portion of plaintiff's song in defendant's song, "Perhaps," which formed part of a motion-picture, "Nice Girl," produced by Universal Pictures Co. Inc., in which "Perhaps" was sung. Franchetti, composer of "Perhaps," was named as one of the defendants but was not served.

The plaintiff is a citizen of Hungary, resident in the United States since March 8, 1939. As he was inducted into the United States army in October, 1942, he was not available to testify in court, and his deposition was admitted in evidence at the trial. He is a successful composer who wrote the music for a well-known foreign produced motion-picture which brought the actress Hedy Lamar to the attention of American motion-picture producers. He wrote his song in Hungary between 1934 and 1935, and assigned his rights therein in 1935 to Rozsavolgyi & Co., a Hungarian publisher. The song was first published in Hungary on November 11, 1935. An American copyright was secured by the publisher on September 14, 1936, by a registration and the deposit of one copy of the best edition published in Hungary. The application and the registration certificate show the correct date of publication. The copy deposited bears the notice "Copyright 1936 by Rozsavolgyi & Co. Budapest." * * *

Before L. HAND, CLARK and FRANK, CIRCUIT JUDGES.

FRANK, CIRCUIT JUDGE.

1. The Hungarian publisher, the proprietor at the time of the copyright registration on September 14, 1936, was a citizen of a foreign country with which the United States has a treaty extending copyright protection to Hungarian citizens in accord with § [9](b). As publication in Hungary occurred on November 11, 1935, the registration followed publication, and therefore § [10], not § [12], applied. As on the date of publication the author was a citizen of Hungary, and the song had then

been published solely in a foreign state, there was compliance with § [13], as amended in 1914, by the deposit of one complete copy.[1] * * *

It follows that the mistake of date in the notice of copyright was not, on any theory, a violation of §§ [10] and [19]; for § [10] merely requires that the notice be affixed to each copy "published or offered for sale in the United States by authority of the copyright proprietor." We construe the statute, as to a publication in a foreign country by a foreign author (i.e., as to a publication described in the 1914 amendment), not to require, as a condition of obtaining or maintaining a valid American copyright, that any notice be affixed to any copies whatever published in such foreign country, regardless of whether publication first occurred in that country or here, or whether it occurred before or after registration here.[2]

It seems to be suggested by some text-writers [3] that, under the 1914 amendment, where publication abroad precedes publication here, the first copy published abroad must have affixed to it the notice described in § [19]. Such a requirement would achieve no practical purpose, for a notice given by a single copy would obviously give notice to virtually no one. There is no doubt textual difficulty in reconciling all the sections, as has been often observed; the most practicable and, as we think, the correct interpretation, is that publication abroad will be in all cases enough, provided that, under the laws of the country where it takes place, it does not result in putting the work into the public domain. Assuming, arguendo, that plaintiff's publication in Hungary did not do so, it could not affect the American copyright that copies of his song were at any time sold there without any notice of the kind required by our statute, and it would therefore be of no significance, in its effect on the American copyright, if copies sold in Hungary bore a notice containing the wrong publication date. On that assumption, there would be no

---

1. The 1914 amendment inserted the words "or if the work is by an author who is a citizen or subject of a foreign State or nation and has been published in a foreign country, one complete copy of the best edition then published in such foreign country."

2. In United Dictionary Co. v. G. & C. Merriam Co., 1908, 208 U.S. 260, 28 S.Ct. 290, 52 L.Ed. 478, it was held that if a work were copyrighted here, the omission of notice of the American copyright from an edition subsequently published in England did not invalidate the copyright.

We do not read the 1914 Amendment as a mere codification of the ruling in that case, i.e., as limited to cases where the foreign publication occurs after an American copyright has been obtained or after publication in this country.

Universal Film Mfg. Co. v. Copperman, D.C., 212 F. 301, 303, 304, related to a copyright which antedated the 1914 amendment to § 12. Basevi v. Edward O'Toole Co., D.C., 26 F.Supp. 41, 46, we think was wrongly decided on this point.

3. Ladas, The International Protection of Literary and Artistic Property (1938) 698, says, in speaking of the 1914 amendment to § 12: "It would seem difficult to give a safe interpretation of the Act in this respect. However, if the rule established in the first part of § 9 is to be given effect to, i.e., the rule that a person 'may secure copyright for his work by publication thereof with the notice of copyright required by the Act;' it would seem that no person is entitled to claim statutory copyright under the Act, unless, when first publishing the work abroad or in the United States, he has affixed the statutory notice. Thereafter, the notice need not appear on each copy of the work published outside the United States, since the second part of § 9 requires this only of 'each copy thereof published or offered for sale in the United States.'" See also 13 C.J. 1063, note 33.

need to consider whether, had the notice with the mistaken date been affixed to copies published or offered for sale in the United States by authority of the proprietor, that mistake would have invalidated the copyright, especially in the light of § [21]. We do not know whether the publication in Hungary was such as to amount to dedication in that country, but as we are affirming the dismissal of the complaint for other reasons, it is not necessary to decide that question. * * *

On the issue of copying, it was proper for the trial judge to avail himself of (although not to be bound by) expert testimony. He heard the experts of both sides. In effect, he found that plaintiff's method of dealing with the common trite note sequence did not possess enough originality, raising it above the level of the banal,[4] to preclude coincidence as an adequate explanation of the identity. We cannot say that the judge erred. Whether, had he reached a contrary conclusion, we would have affirmed, we do not consider.

Affirmed.

CLARK, CIRCUIT JUDGE (concurring in the result).

1. The opinion holds that American copyright is secured by publication abroad without the notice of copyright admittedly required for publication here. This novel conclusion, here suggested for the first time, seems to me impossible in the face of the statutory language that the person thereto entitled "may secure copyright for his work by publication thereof with the notice of copyright required by this title," § [10] of the Copyright Act, 17 U.S.C.A. § [10], and § [19] defining the "notice of copyright required by section [10] of this title," with the provision that as to a work of the character here involved "the notice shall include also the year in which the copyright was secured by publication." It is against the view of such expert copyright judges as Hough, J., in Italian Book Co. v. Cardilli, D.C.S.D.N.Y., 273 F. 619, and Universal Film Mfg. Co. v. Copperman, D.C.S.D.N.Y., 212 F. 301, affirmed 2 Cir., 218 F. 577, certiorari denied 235 U.S. 704, 35 S.Ct. 209, 59 L.Ed. 433, and Woolsey, J., in Basevi v. Edward O'Toole Co., D.C.S.D.N.Y., 26 F.Supp. 41, and apparently the universal assumption of text writers. See Howell, The Copyright Law, 1942, 73; Ladas, The International Protection of Literary and Artistic Property, 1938, 698; Ball, The Law of Copyright and Literary Property, 1944, 217; Copyright Protection in the Americas (Law & Treaty Series No. 16) 66; 18 C.J.S. Copyright and Literary Property, § 66, p. 190.

While the ground of the decision is not made clear, apparently it is based upon the second part of § [10], reading as follows: "and such notice shall be affixed to each copy thereof published or offered for sale

---

4. We do not mean that such originality is essential to the validity of a copyright. See Bleistein v. Donaldson Lithographing Co., 188 U.S. 239, 249, 250, 23 S.Ct. 298, 47 L.Ed. 460; Sheldon v. Metro-Goldwyn Pictures Corp., 2 Cir., 81 F.2d 49, 53, 54; Fred Fisher, Inc. v. Dillingham, D.C., 298 F. 145, 149; cf. Hein v. Harris, C.C., 175 F. 875.

As to the needed quantum of originality, see Chamberlin v. Uris Sales Corp., 2 Cir., 150 F.2d 512, 513; Shafter, loc. cit., 223, 224.

in the United States by authority of the copyright proprietor, except in the case of books seeking ad interim protection under section [22] of this title." But this deals with the preserving of the copyright after the original publication has secured it, Sieff v. Continental Auto Supply, Inc., D.C.Minn., 39 F.Supp. 683; Fleischer Studios v. Ralph A. Freundlich, Inc., 2 Cir., 73 F.2d 276, certiorari denied Ralph A. Freundlich, Inc. v. Fleischer Studios, 294 U.S. 717, 55 S.Ct. 516, 79 L.Ed. 1250; Basevi v. Edward O'Toole Co., supra; Record & Guide Co. v. Bromley, C.C.E.D. Pa., 175 F. 156; 18 C.J.S., Copyright and Literary Property, § 71, p. 193, and is indeed the only direct requirement for notice of the already acquired copyright. Other sections rest upon such a requirement, e.g., § [19] as to the form of notice, § [20] as to its location on the publication and § [21] dealing with the effect of accidental omission of notice from a copy or copies. The second part of § [10], therefore, does not destroy the effect of what is said in the first part of the same section.

There is nothing in § [13] to support the stated thesis. That section requires deposit of copies before an action of infringement is brought, but explicitly applies only "after copyright has been secured by publication of the work with the notice of copyright as provided in section [10] of this title." Hence its amendment in 1914, to require only one copy (instead of two) of a work by a citizen of a foreign state published abroad, while perhaps affording some additional evidence that § [10] was intended to include publication abroad, 18 C.J.S., Copyright and Literary Property, § 66, p. 191, contains nothing to suggest the exception here read into § [10]. Moreover, the reference in § [10] to books seeking ad interim protection under § [22] is significant; the latter section affords protection to a limited class of publications— books first published abroad in the English language—under a special procedure; all others must follow the general procedure and preserve their copyright in America by affixing the required notice to copies published or offered for sale. The provision does include, at least by implication, the rule settled by United Dictionary Co. v. G. & C. Merriam Co., 208 U.S. 260, 28 S.Ct. 290, 52 L.Ed. 478, that notice of copyright must be carried only on copies published or offered for sale here; but it does not suggest an exception, operating against American authors, in the process of originally securing the copyright by publication.[5]

The opinion seeks further support because the requirement would achieve "no practical purpose." There perhaps may be some doubt as

---

5. This view is also supported by the legislative history of § [10], showing that the words "in the United States" originally appeared in the first, or crucial, part of the statute. Howell, loc. cit. supra. In that earlier form, restricting the securing of copyright to publication in the United States, the requirement of publication with notice was unambiguous. But the broadening of the provision as to place of publication was not accompanied by any change at all as to the requirement of notice. Of course there does now arise the question, not yet settled, whether faulty publication abroad may be superseded by later correct publication here. Cf. Howell, loc. cit. supra; Ladas, op. cit. supra at 696; Shafter, Musical Copyright, 2d Ed.1939, 118; 18 C.J.S., Copyright and Literary Property, § 25, pp. 166, 167; Italian Book Co. v. Cardilli, D.C.S. D.N.Y., 273 F. 619.

to the utility of any notice; it is said not to be required in "most foreign countries." Howell, 73. But if Congress thought it a necessary requirement for the literary monopoly it granted, common fairness would seem to suggest that it apply also to publication abroad, or at least that foreign publication be not made notoriously easier and more profitable than domestic publication. And the required notice does furnish a certain amount of information and warning to competitors and possible infringers, perhaps enough to warn them away from infringement in many an obvious case. That more drastic requirements might have accomplished more does not justify elimination of those which were specifically retained.

Since, therefore, the record shows incorrect dating of the Hungarian publication, we must face the decision in Baker v. Taylor, C.C.S.D. N.Y., Fed.Cas. No. 782, that statement of a later than the actual date invalidates a copyright, and the general view that it still represents the law. See e.g., American Code Co. v. Bensinger, 2 Cir., 282 F. 829, 836; Howell, 66; Ladas, 746; Shafter, 98. True, in Baker v. Taylor, supra, there was more than a mistake, for the error was persisted in after it was discovered. But it is difficult to get away from the rationale suggested in the cases that stating a later date is a more serious mistake than stating an earlier date, for the former may be a wrong to the public as extending the term, while the latter at most only penalizes the copyright owner. Callaghan v. Myers, 128 U.S. 617, 654, 657, 9 S.Ct. 177, 32 L.Ed. 547. Sec. [21] of the Act does not help, for this is not the case of omission of the notice by accident or mistake "from a particular copy or copies," but a mistake in the publication by which the original copyright was secured. The liberalizing trend shown by the Act of 1909 does not appear to have extended to this requirement, and I fear that on the authorities we must hold the copyright invalid. On that ground alone, and with some hesitation, I would support the judgment below. * * *

Questions

1. What is the "textual difficulty" to which Judge Frank refers? Can you suggest a rationale that supports the Frank conclusion without such difficulty?

2. Do you agree with Judge Clark's thesis that the second clause in Sec. 10 of the 1909 Act deals only "with the preserving of the copyright after the original publication has secured it"? Does the text support this conclusion? In the first clause, what does the modifier "required by this title" mean?

3. If pre-1978 a work was first published within the United States, bearing a proper copyright notice, and thereafter (still pre-1978) it was published abroad with no copyright notice, was the work thereby injected into the public domain? Do Frank and Clark agree on the answer to this question?

4. If, on or after January 1, 1978, the first publication of a work occurs outside of the United States, must the copies or phonorecords thus published bear a copyright notice? If, on or after January 1, 1978, the first publication of a work occurs within the United States bearing a proper copyright notice, must

subsequent copies published abroad also bear such copyright notice? See Sections 401(a) and 402(a). Cf. Section 405(a)(2).

5. If pre-1978 a work was first published within the United States, bearing a proper copyright notice, must additional copies published abroad on or after January 1, 1978 also bear such a copyright notice? See 17 U.S.C.A., Trans. & Supp.Prov. § 108.

Collateral References

Katz, *Is Notice of Copyright Necessary in Works Published Abroad?—A Query and a Quandry*, (1953) Washington L.Q. 55.

Nimmer on Copyright, § 7.12[D].

B. REGISTRATION AND DEPOSIT

WASHINGTONIAN PUBLISHING CO. v. PEARSON

Supreme Court of the United States, 1939.
306 U.S. 30, 59 S.Ct. 397, 83 L.Ed. 470.

Mr. Justice McReynolds delivered the opinion of the Court.

By this suit, instituted in the District of Columbia, March 8, 1933, petitioner seeks an injunction, damages, etc., because of alleged unauthorized use of a magazine article copyrighted under Act March 4, 1909 (Ch. 320, 35 Stat. 1075; U.S.C.A., Title 17).

The trial court sustained petitioner's claim and directed ascertainment of profits, damages, etc. The Court of Appeals ruled that, as copies of the magazine had not been *promptly* deposited in the Copyright Office as directed by § [13], the action could not be maintained. It accordingly reversed the decree of the trial court and remanded the cause.

The record discloses—

December 10, 1931, petitioner published an issue of "The Washingtonian," a monthly magazine, and claimed copyright by printing thereon the required statutory notice. Fourteen months later, February 21, 1933, copies were first deposited in the Copyright Office and a certificate of registration secured. This suit followed, March 8, 1933.

In August, 1932, Liveright, Inc., published and offered for general sale a book written by two of the respondents and printed by another, which contained material substantially identical with an article contained in The Washingtonian of December, 1931. The usual notice claimed copyright of this book. August 26, 1932, copies were deposited in the Copyright Office and certificate of registration issued.

Respondents concede that petitioner secured upon publication a valid copyright of The Washingtonian. But they insist that although prompt deposit of copies is not prerequisite to copyright, no action can be maintained because of infringement prior in date to a tardy deposit. Counsel assert—"The very foundation of the right to maintain an action for infringement is deposit of copies and registration of the work.

Neither of these has the slightest bearing upon the creation of the copyright itself under Section [10]. That is obtained merely by publication with notice as required by the Act." Also, "If copies were not deposited promptly after publication the opportunity to comply with the requirement of promptness was gone forever as to that particular work."

Petitioner submits that under the statute *prompt* deposit of copies is not prerequisite to an action for infringement; and that under the facts here disclosed deposit before suit was enough.

The Act of 1909 is a complete revision of the copyright laws, different from the earlier Act both in scheme and language. It introduced many changes and was intended definitely to grant valuable, enforceable rights to authors, publishers, etc., without burdensome requirements; "to afford greater encouragement to the production of literary works of lasting benefit to the world." [1]

Under the old Act deposit of the work was essential to the existence of copyright. This requirement caused serious difficulties and unfortunate losses. (See H.R. Report, note 1, supra.) The present statute (§ [10]) declares—"Any person entitled thereto by this Act may secure copyright for his work by publication thereof with the notice of copyright required by this Act [§ [19]]; * * *" And respondents rightly say "It is no longer necessary to deposit anything to secure a copyright of a published work, but only to publish with the notice of copyright."

Section [11] declares—

---

1. Report of House Committee on Patents, February 22, 1909 (No. 2222). Among other things this says—

"Sections [13] and [14] deal with the deposit of copies, and should be considered together. They materially alter the existing law, which provides that in order to make the copyright valid there must be deposited two complete copies of the book or other article not later than the date of first publication. The failure of a shipping clerk to see that the copies go promptly forward to Washington may destroy a copyright of great value, and many copyrights have been lost because by some accident or mistake this requirement was not complied with. The committee felt that some modification of this drastic provision, under which the delay of a single day might destroy a copyright, might well be made. The bill reported by the committee provides that there shall be 'promptly' deposited in the copyright office, or in the mail addressed to the register of copyrights, two complete copies of the best edition then published, and that no action or proceeding shall be maintained for the infringement of copyright in any work until the provisions with respect to the deposit of copies and the registration of such work shall have been complied with.

"If the works are not promptly deposited, we provide that the register of copyrights may at any time after publication of the work, upon actual notice, require the proprietor of the copyright to deposit, and then in default of deposit of copies of the work within three months from any part of the United States, except an outlying territorial possession of the United States, or within six months from any outlying territorial possession of the United States, or from any foreign country, the proprietor of the copyright shall be liable to a fine of $100 and to pay to the Library of Congress twice the amount of the retail price of the best edition of the work, and the copyright shall become void. It was suggested that the forfeiture of the copyright for failure to deposit copies was too drastic a remedy, but your committee feel that in many cases it will be the only effective remedy: certainly the provision for compelling the deposit of copies by the imposition of a fine would be absolutely unavailing should the copyright proprietor be the citizen or subject of a foreign state."

That such person may obtain registration of his claim to copyright by complying with the provisions of this Act, including the deposit of copies, and upon such compliance the register of copyrights shall issue to him the certificate provided for in section fifty-five of this Act.

Section [13]—

That after copyright has been secured by publication of the work with the notice of copyright as provided in section [10] of this Act, there shall be promptly deposited in the copyright office or in the mail addressed to the register of copyrights, Washington, District of Columbia, two complete copies of the best edition thereof then published, * * * No action or proceeding shall be maintained for infringement of copyright in any work until the provisions of this Act with respect to the deposit of copies and registration of such work shall have been complied with.

Section [14]—

That should the copies called for by section [13] of this Act not be promptly deposited as herein provided, the register of copyrights may at any time after the publication of the work, upon actual notice, require the proprietor of the copyright to deposit them, and after the said demand shall have been made, in default of the deposit of copies of the work within three months from any part of the United States, * * * the proprietor of the copyright shall be liable to a fine of one hundred dollars and to pay to the Library of Congress twice the amount of the retail price of the best edition of the work, and the copyright shall become void.

Sections [213] and [214] were new legislation. They show clearly enough that deposit of copies is not required primarily in order to insure a complete, permanent collection of all copyrighted works open to the public. Deposited copies may be distributed or destroyed under the direction of the Librarian [2] and this is incompatible with the notion that copies are now required in order that the subject matter of protected works may always be available for information and to prevent unconscious infringement.

Although immediately upon publication of The Washingtonian for December, 1931, petitioner secured copyright of the articles therein, respondents maintain that through failure promptly to deposit copies in the Copyright Office the right to sue for infringement was lost. In effect, that the provision in § [13] relative to suits should be treated as though it contained the words "promptly," also "unless" instead of "until," and read—No action or proceeding shall be maintained for infringement of copyright in any work *unless* the provisions of this Act with respect to the deposit of copies *promptly* and registration of such work shall have been complied with.

Plausible arguments in support of this view were advanced by the Court of Appeals. We think, however, its adoption would not square with the words actually used in the statute, would cause conflict with

---

2. See Report Register Copyrights for 1938. During the year there were 166,248 registrations; 194,433 current articles deposited were transferred to the Library of Congress. Also 3,612 motion picture films, and 43,302 deposits from other classes were returned to the authors or proprietors.

its general purpose, and in practice produce unfortunate consequences. We cannot accept it.

Petitioner's claim of copyright came to fruition immediately upon publication. Without further notice it was good against all the world. Its value depended upon the possibility of enforcement.

The use of the word "until" in § [13] rather than "unless" indicates that mere delay in making deposit of copies was not enough to cause forfeiture of the right theretofore distinctly granted.

Section [13] provides "That after copyright has been secured by publication of the work with the notice of copyrights as provided in section [10] of this Act, there shall be promptly deposited in the copyright office" two copies, etc. The Act nowhere defines "promptly," and to make the continued existence of copyright depend upon promptness would lead to unfortunate uncertainty and confusion. The great number of copyrights annually obtained is indicated by note [2], supra. The difficulties consequent upon the former requirement of deposit before publication are pointed out in the Committee Report. These would be enlarged if whenever effort is made to vindicate a copyright it would become necessary to show deposits were made promptly after publication especially since there is no definition of "promptly."

Section [14] authorizes the register of copyrights to give notice if he finds undue delay and to require deposit of copies. Upon failure to comply within three months the proprietor shall be subject to a fine and the copyright shall become void. Evidently mere delay does not necessarily invalidate the copyright; its existence for three months after actual notice is recognized. Without right of vindication a copyright is valueless. It would be going too far to infer that tardiness alone destroys something valuable both to proprietor and the public.

Section [21] saves the copyright notwithstanding omission of notice; § [24] declares "That the copyright secured by this Act shall endure for twenty-eight years from the date of first publication, whether the copyrighted work bears the author's true name or is published anonymously or under an assumed name: * * *" Furthermore, proper publication gives notice to all the world that immediate copyright exists. One charged with such notice is not injured by mere failure to deposit copies. The duty not to infringe is unaffected thereby. A certificate of registration provided for by § [209] apparently may be obtained at any time and becomes evidence of the facts stated therein.

Sections * * * 24, which permit renewal of a copyright by application and registration within its last year although the deposited copyrighted publication may have been disposed of under §§ [213–214], give clear indication that the requirement for deposit is not for the purpose of a permanent record of copyrighted publications and that such record is not indispensable to the existence of the copyright.

The penalty for delay clearly specified in § [14] is adequate for punishment of delinquents and to enforce contributions of desirable books to the Library. To give § [13] a more drastic effect would tend to defeat the broad purpose of the enactment. The Report of the Congressional Committee points out that forfeiture after notice and three months' further delay was thought too severe by some. Nowhere does it suggest approval of the much more drastic result now insisted upon by respondents.

Read together as the Committee which reported the bill said they should be, §§ [13 and 14] show, we think, the Congress intended that prompt deposit when deemed necessary should be enforced through actual notice by the register; also that while no action can be maintained before copies are actually deposited, mere delay will not destroy the right to sue. Such forfeitures are never to be inferred from doubtful language.

This view is in accord with the interpretation of somewhat similar provisions of the English Copyright Act. Goubaud v. Wallace and Cate v. Devon Constitutional Newspaper Co., supra. Also with the conclusions reached in Lumiere v. Pathé Exchange and Mittenthal v. Berlin, supra.

The challenged decree must be reversed. The cause will be remanded to the District Court.

Reversed.

MR. JUSTICE BLACK, dissenting.

Questions

1. Does the *Washingtonian* case hold that the delay in registration was "reasonable" and hence that there was compliance with the "promptly" requirement? If the delay had been for 27 years rather than for 14 months would the result have been the same? What if it had been for 29 years?

2. Under the *Washingtonian* rule would the plaintiff be entitled to recover in a statutory infringement action if

   (a) the act of infringement occurred before either publication or registration?

   (b) the act of infringement occurred after publication but before registration?

   (c) filing of the action occurred after the act of infringement but before registration?

3. Under the 1909 Act, could Ernest Hemingway have obtained a statutory copyright on *For Whom the Bell Tolls* prior to its publication? Could Eugene O'Neil have obtained a statutory copyright on *Strange Interlude* prior to its publication? What types of unpublished works were eligible for statutory copyright under the 1909 Act? See Sec. 12 of the 1909 Act.

Collateral Reference

Nimmer on Copyright, 7.16[A][2].

Note and Questions

The Significance of Registration Under the Current Act

In a preceding Note we have seen that the current Copyright Act provides that registration may be an excuse for the omission of a copyright notice. See Sec. 405(a)(2). In what other ways is registration important under the current Act? As under the 1909 Act, the current Act provides that registration is a condition precedent to the filing of an infringement action. See Sec. 411(a).

Question 1: If the Copyright Office refuses to register a work, must the copyright claimant bring a mandamus action against the Register to obtain such registration before an infringement action may be filed? See Sec. 411(a). Compare the rule under the 1909 Act as stated in Vacheron Watches, Inc. v. Benrus Watch Co., 260 F.2d 637 (2d Cir.1958).

Question 2: Once registration occurs, may a copyright owner recover for infringing acts which occurred prior to registration? Are the remedies available in such circumstances limited in any manner? See Sec. 412. What is the significance in this regard as to whether a work had been published (although not registered) at the time of the infringing conduct?

The current Copyright Act further provides that in order for a registration certificate to constitute prima facie evidence of the validity of the copyright, and of the facts stated in the certificate, registration must have occurred within five years after first publication of the work. See Sec. 410(c). A comparable provision under the 1909 Act provided a prima facie effect for a registration certificate regardless of when registration occurred. See Sec. 209 (1909 Act).

Question 3: Is the five year cut off date under Sec. 410(c) applicable retroactively to works first published prior to January 1, 1978, the effective date of the current Copyright Act? To works first published prior to January 1, 1973?

Under certain circumstances the recordation of a transfer of copyright, or of other documents relating to a copyright in a work, will constitute constructive notice to all persons of the facts stated in the recorded document. See Sec. 205(c). One of the conditions to such constructive notice is that the work to which the document pertains be registered. See Sec. 205(c)(2). No such registration requirement existed in order to effectuate constructive notice of transfers under the recordation provisions of the 1909 Act. See Sec. 30 (1909 Act).

Question 4: Is the requirement of registration of a work as a condition to constructive notice of transfers of copyright in such work applicable retroactively to transfers recorded pre-1978?

Collateral Reference

Nimmer on Copyright, §§ 1.11, 7.16[B]–[E].

Note *

Deposit Distinguished From Registration

Deposit and registration under the Copyright Act are "separate though closely related."[1] The function of deposit is to provide the Library of Congress via the Copyright Office with copies and phonorecords of all works published within the United States.[2] The function of registration is to create a written record of the copyright ownership in a work. Registration necessarily requires an accompanying deposit.[3] Deposit, on the other hand, may be accomplished without an accompanying registration.[4] It may be argued that deposit has a copyright as well as an archival function in that in an infringement action it permits a determination of whether the work which the copyright owner claims to have been infringed is in fact the same work in which copyright was originally claimed. But this copyright function is attenuated by the fact that the Library of Congress need not add all deposited works to its collection,[5] it apparently is not required to preserve those works which it does add to its collection, and those which it does not so add, although retained by the Copyright Office, need only be preserved "for the longest period considered practicable and desirable by the Register of Copyrights and the Librarian of Congress."[6] However, copies and phonorecords of unpublished works may not be destroyed unless a facsimile reproduction of the deposit is preserved for the term of copyright in the work.[7]

While registration is a condition precedent to the filing of an infringement action, and certain other rights (as discussed in the preceding Note), registration per se is never mandatory. Deposit, on the other hand, may be mandatory.

Sec. 407(a) states in absolute terms that deposit is required "within three months after the date of * * * publication * * *."[8] But a failure to comply with this three month deadline is without legal consequences. Deposit becomes mandatory only if the Register of Copyrights makes a written demand for the deposit.[9] The recipient of such a written demand has three months after its receipt in which to comply with the deposit requirement. Sec. 407(d) provides that a failure to so comply within such three month period will subject the person upon whom demand was made to the following liability:

---

* Nimmer on Copyright, § 7.17.

1. H.Rep., p. 150.
2. 17 U.S.C.A. § 407(a). See also 17 U.S.C.A. § 704(b).
3. 17 U.S.C.A. § 408(b). Note that the deposit requirement as a part of the registration process applies to unpublished as well as published works. See 17 U.S.C.A. § 408(b)(1).
4. 17 U.S.C.A. § 407.
5. 17 U.S.C.A. § 704(b).
6. 17 U.S.C.A. § 704(d).
7. 17 U.S.C.A. § 704(d). Note also that other deposits made in connection with registration must be preserved for the full term of copyright if the person making the deposit so requests. 17 U.S.C.A. § 704(e). However, this does not constitute a safeguard as against one who is claiming protection for a work other than the work in which copyright was originally claimed, since he would not make such a request.
8. 17 U.S.C.A. § 407(a).
9. The question arises as to whether such written demand may be made as soon as the work is published, or not until the expiration of three months after publication. 17 U.S.C.A. § 407(d) provides that such written demand may be made "At any time after publication of a work." This suggests that such demand may be made immediately upon publication. However, such demand may only be made "of the persons obligated to make * * * deposit." Since, under Sec. 407(a), no person is "obligated" until the expiration of three months from publication, arguably the written demand may not be made until after such three month period.

"(1) to a fine of not more than $250 for each work; and

(2) to pay into a specifically designated fund in the Library of Congress the total retail price of the copies of phonorecords demanded, or, if no retail price has been fixed,[10] the reasonable cost of the Library of Congress of acquiring them; and

(3) to pay a fine of $2500, in addition to any fine or liability imposed under clauses (1) and (2), if such person willfully or repeatedly fails or refuses to comply with such a demand."

It should be noted that the penalties for the failure to comply with such a deposit demand do not include a forfeiture of copyright.[11] The copyright is preserved notwithstanding an unexcused refusal to comply with the deposit requirements. In this the current Act departs from the 1909 Act under which if the Register of Copyrights "by actual notice" demanded deposit, a failure to comply within three months (or within six months if the copyright proprietor was in an outlying territorial possession of the United States or in a foreign country) resulted in the copyright becoming void,[12] and in addition the copyright proprietor became liable to a fine of $100 and to pay to the Library of Congress twice the amount of the retail price of the best edition of the work. This provision of the 1909 Act remains applicable under the current Act with respect to any work which first obtained statutory copyright as a published work prior to January 1, 1978.[13] Thus, a failure to comply with a demand for deposit made by the Register of Copyrights, whether such demand is made before or after January 1, 1978, if it pertains to a work published and copyrighted before said date, will result in a loss of copyright.[14]

C. THE MANUFACTURING CLAUSE

1. *The Manufacturing Clause Under the Copyright Act of 1976*

Note

The Manufacturing Clause under the current Act (Section 601) in brief summary requires printing within the United States or Canada of all copies of works consisting preponderantly of nondramatic literary material that is in the English language. Compared with the Manufacturing Clause under the 1909 Act, considered below, it has been severely limited in its impact. It is applicable only to authors who are domiciliaries of the United States. Moreover, a violation of its terms will not result in an invalidation of the copyright. At

---

10. E.g., "where the copies or phonorecords are not available for sale through normal trade channels—as would be true of many motion picture films, video tapes, and computer tapes * * *." H.Rep., p. 152.

11. "Neither the deposit requirements of this subsection nor the acquisition provisions of subsection (e) are conditions of copyright protection." 17 U.S.C.A. § 407(a).

12. 17 U.S.C.A. § 14 (1909 Act); see Washingtonian Pub. Co. v. Pearson, 306 U.S. 30 (1939); King Features Syndicate Inc. v. Bouve, 48 U.S.P.Q. 237 (D.D.C.1940).

13. 17 U.S.C.A., Trans.Supp.Prov., Sec. 110. But note that U.C.C. claimants under the 1909 Act are exempt from mandatory deposit. See 17 U.S.C.A. § 9(c) (1909 Act).

14. See Reg.Supp.Rep., p. 163. Any work which entered the public domain prior to 1978 by reason of the failure to comply with a deposit demand is, of course, ineligible for copyright under the current Act.

most it will constitute a defense in an infringement action against one who has engaged in unlicensed reproduction or public distribution of the copyrighted work, and who has himself complied with the domestic manufacturing requirements. Moreover, such a defense will be unavailable with respect to infringements which began after registration of an authorized version of the work, copies of which have been domestically manufactured, even if initially copies of the work had been printed in violation of the Clause. Finally, for most purposes the Manufacturing Clause under the current Act will cease to be operative as of July 1, 1986. For an in-depth analysis of the current Manufacturing Clause the student should consult Nimmer on Copyright, § 7.22.

2. *The Manufacturing Clause Under the Copyright Act of 1909*

HOFFENBERG v. KAMINSTEIN

United States, Court of Appeals, District of Columbia Circuit, 1968.
396 F.2d 684.

Before WILBUR K. MILLER, SENIOR CIRCUIT JUDGE, and BURGER and WRIGHT, CIRCUIT JUDGES.

PER CURIAM. Appellant and Terry Southern, both American citizens, are co-authors of the novel "Candy" which was first printed and published in the English language in France in 1958 with the appropriate statutory copyright notice. See 17 U.S.C.A. §§ 19 and 20 (1964). On March 11, 1965, more than six years after first publication of the foreign edition in France, appellant submitted to appellee an application for registration of a claim to ad interim copyright in the foreign edition. On the same date he submitted an application for registration of a claimed copyright in an American edition of "Candy" which was substantially the same text as the French edition. On March 31, 1965, the Copyright Office refused to register either the claimed ad interim copyright for the French edition or the claim to copyright in the American edition, stating as its reason failure to comply with the provisions of Sections 16,[1] 22[2] and 23 of the Copyright Code, 17 U.S.C.A. §§ 16, 22, 23 (1964). On June 25, 1965, appellant filed the present action in the District Court to compel the Register of Copyrights to issue a certificate of registration covering only the 1964 American edition. On cross-motions for summary judgment, the District Court granted the Register's motion, denied appellant's motion, and dismissed the action.

Except when the ad interim provisions of Sections 22 and 23 are met, Section 16 of the Copyright Code allows copyright registration of English-language books by United States citizens only where the first publication is printed in the United States. Implementing these provisions of the Copyright Code pursuant to 17 U.S.C.A. § 207 (1964), in 1956 the Register of Copyrights promulgated the following regulation:

---

1. Section 16 requires generally that for an English-language book to be registered for copyright in the United States it must be printed in the United States.

2. Section 22 requires that the application for ad interim copyright of a foreign edition of an English-language book be made within six months after publication abroad.

Ad interim registrations. (1) An American edition of an English-language book or periodical identical in substance to that first published abroad will not be registered unless an ad interim registration is first made. 37 C.F.R. § 202.4(b) (1967).

Since the novel "Candy" was first published and printed [3] abroad in the English language and there is no ad interim registration of that edition, registration of the American edition was properly refused.

A regulation, of course, is presumptively valid and ordinarily should be upheld unless it is inconsistent with the statute. New York Foreign Freight Forwarders & Brokers Ass'n v. F.M.C., 2 Cir., 337 F.2d 289, 295 (1964), cert. denied, 380 U.S. 910, 914, 85 S.Ct. 893, 13 L.Ed.2d 797 (1965). The above regulation is not only not inconsistent with the pertinent sections of the Copyright Code, but in our judgment it accurately reflects the intention of Congress. *Compare* United States v. Zazove, 334 U.S. 602, 611, 68 S.Ct. 1284, 92 L.Ed. 1601 (1948). Even if there were some doubt, we would be required to resolve that doubt in favor of the Register's interpretation. Udall v. Tallman, 380 U.S. 1, 16, 85 S.Ct. 792, 13 L.Ed.2d 616 (1965).

Affirmed.

CIRCUIT JUDGE BURGER concurs in the result.

Questions

1. Does the *Hoffenberg* decision in effect hold that unless the ad interim provisions (Secs. 22 and 23 of the 1909 Act) had been observed, failure to comply with the Manufacturing Clause (Sec. 16 of the 1909 Act) injected the work into the public domain? Does the text of Sec. 16 justify such a conclusion? What bearing does Sec. 18 of the 1909 Act have on this question? If, as held in *Hoffenberg,* failure to comply with the 1909 Act Manufacturing Clause rendered the copyright in the work unenforcible, was this the equivalent of holding that the work had thereby entered the public domain? Why does this question remain significant under the current Copyright Act? See the current Transitional and Supplementary Provisions, Sec. 103.

2. If Hoffenberg and Southern had written "Candy" in French rather than in English does the court indicate the result would have been different? Is the court's reading of Sec. 16 of the 1909 Act correct in this regard? If the authors had been French citizens, but wrote "Candy" in English, would the result have been different?

3. If a work was first manufactured and published within the United States, might later editions of the same work be manufactured abroad without violating the 1909 Act Manufacturing Clause?

4. What justification, if any, is there for a manufacturing clause?

Collateral References

Rembar, *Xenophilia in Congress: Ad Interim Copyright and the Manufacturing Clause,* 69 Col.L.Rev. 770 (1969).

---

3. Appellee concedes that, where a foreign edition is printed in the United States, a subsequent American edition may be registered without compliance with the ad interim provisions of 17 U.S.C.A. §§ 22 and 23.

Nimmer on Copyright, § 7.23.

Grubb, *The Status of Works Published in Violation of the Manufacturing Requirements of the 1909 Copyright Law after the Effective Date of the 1976 Copyright Law,* 27 Bull. Copr. Soc'y 264 (1980).

Lyons, *Manufacturing Clause Report: Editor's Note. Introduction. Recapitulation and Conclusion. The Manufacturing Clause: A Legislative History,* 29 Bull. Copr. Soc'y 1 (1981).

Chapter Four

THE NATURE OF THE RIGHTS PROTECTED BY COPYRIGHT

Note *

The Copying Requirement and Other Limitations on the Rights
of the Copyright Owner

An examination of the rights accorded to an owner of literary property under the Copyright Act might begin with a delineation of certain fundamental limitations inherent in the nature of copyright. In the first place, copyright does not confer an absolute monopoly in the patent sense. As a corollary to the basic principle that copyright may be claimed in an original work even if the work lacks novelty, the rights of a copyright owner are not infringed if a subsequent work, although substantially similar, has been independently created without reference to the prior work. Thus absent copying there can be no infringement of copyright regardless of the extent of similarity.

The requirement of copying constitutes what might be termed an external limitation in that it confines the exercise of copyright to works which emanate directly or indirectly from the copyright proprietor. There is in addition what might be termed an internal limitation. That is, not every unauthorized use of a work, even assuming such work emanates from a copyrighted work is necessarily an infringement of copyright. A use of a copyrighted work is not an infringing act if such use does not fall within the scope of those rights expressly granted to the copyright proprietor. Thus privately reading a literary work, or privately performing a dramatic or musical work constitute uses of a copyrighted work which do not infringe the rights granted to the copyright owner. In this sense the rights of a copyright owner under the Copyright Act are rights of express enumeration. These rights are set forth in Sec. 106 of the Act, and will be considered in the remainder of this chapter. Such rights are cumulative, and those rights which the copyright owner elects to reserve to himself are not waived or lost by reason of his exercise or grant to another of certain other of such rights.

A. THE REPRODUCTION RIGHT

WHITE–SMITH MUSIC CO. v. APOLLO CO.

Supreme Court of the United States, 1908.
209 U.S. 1, 28 S.Ct. 319, 52 L.Ed. 655.

---

* Nimmer on Copyright, § 8.01[A].

Mr. Justice Day delivered the opinion of the court.

These cases may be considered together. They are appeals from the judgment of the Circuit Court of Appeals for the Second Circuit (147 Fed.Rep. 226), affirming the decree of the Circuit Court of the United States for the Southern District of New York, rendered August 4, 1905 (139 Fed.Rep. 427), dismissing the bills of the complainant (now appellant) for want of equity. Motions have been made to dismiss the appeals, and a petition for writ of certiorari has been filed by appellant. In view of the nature of the cases the writ of certiorari is granted, the record on the appeals to stand as a return to the writ. Montana Mining Co. v. St. Louis Mining Co., 204 U.S. 204.

The actions were brought to restrain infringement of the copyrights of two certain musical compositions, published in the form of sheet music, entitled, respectively, "Little Cotton Dolly" and "Kentucky Babe." The appellee, defendant below, is engaged in the sale of piano players and player pianos, known as the "Apollo," and of perforated rolls of music used in connection therewith. The appellant, as assignee of Adam Geibel, the composer, alleged compliance with the copyright act, and that a copyright was duly obtained by it on or about March 17, 1897. The answer was general in its nature, and upon the testimony adduced a decree was rendered, as stated, in favor of the Apollo Company, defendant below, appellee here. * * * The appellee is the manufacturer of certain musical instruments adapted to be used with perforated rolls. The testimony discloses that certain of these rolls, used in connection with such instruments, and being connected with the mechanism to which they apply, reproduce in sound the melody recorded in the two pieces of music copyrighted by the appellant. * * *

Without entering into a detailed discussion of the mechanical construction of such instruments and rolls, it is enough to say that they are what has become familiar to the public in the form of mechanical attachments to pianos, such as the pianola, and the musical rolls consist of perforated sheets, which are passed over ducts connected with the operating parts of the mechanism in such manner that the same are kept sealed until, by means of perforations in the rolls, air pressure is admitted to the ducts which operate the pneumatic devices to sound the notes. This is done with the aid of an operator, upon whose skill and experience the success of the rendition largely depends. As the roll is drawn over the tracker board the notes are sounded as the perforations admit the atmospheric pressure, the perforations having been so arranged that the effect is to produce the melody or tune for which the roll has been cut. * * *

[The Court then cited a number of lower court and foreign decisions holding that a perforated "piano" roll does not constitute a copy of the music which it reproduces.]

Since these cases were decided Congress has repeatedly had occasion to amend the copyright law. The * * * cases, * * * must have been well known to the members of Congress; and although the manufacture of mechanical musical instruments had not grown to the proportions which they have since attained they were well known, and the omission of Congress to specifically legislate concerning them might well be taken to be an acquiescence in the judicial construction given to the copyright laws. * * *

In the last analysis this case turns upon the construction of a statute, for it is perfectly well settled that the protection given to copyrights in this country is wholly statutory. Wheaton v. Peters, 8 Pet. 590; Banks v. Manchester, 128 U.S. 244, 253; Thompson v. Hubbard, 131 U.S. 123, 151; American Tobacco Company v. Werckmeister, 207 U.S. 284.

Musical compositions have been the subject of copyright protection since the statute of February 3, 1831, c. 16, 4 Stat. 436, and laws have been passed including them since that time. When we turn to the consideration of the act it seems evident that Congress has dealt with the tangible thing, a copy of which is required to be filed with the Librarian of Congress, and wherever the words are used (copy or copies) they seem to refer to the term in its ordinary sense of indicating reproduction or duplication of the original. Section 4956 (3 U.S.Comp. Stat. 3407) provides that two copies of a book, map, chart or musical composition, etc., shall be delivered at the office of the Librarian of Congress. Notice of copyright must be inserted in the several copies of every edition published, if a book, or if a musical composition, etc., upon some visible portion thereof. Section 4962, Copyright Act, 3 U.S.Comp. Stat. 3411. Section 4965 (3 U.S.Comp.Stat. 3414) provides in part that the infringer "shall forfeit every sheet thereof, and one dollar for every sheet of the same found in his possession," etc., evidently referring to musical compositions in sheets. Throughout the act it is apparent that Congress has dealt with the concrete and not with an abstract right of property in ideas or mental conceptions.

We cannot perceive that the amendment of § 4966 by the act of January 6, 1897, c. 4, 29 Stat. 481 (3 U.S.Comp.Stat. 3415), providing a penalty for any person publicly performing or representing any dramatic or musical composition for which a copyright has been obtained, can have the effect of enlarging the meaning of the previous sections of the act which were not changed by the amendment. The purpose of the amendment evidently was to put musical compositions on the footing of dramatic compositions so as to prohibit their public performance. There is no complaint in this case of the public performance of copyrighted music; nor is the question involved whether the manufacturers of such perforated music rolls when sold for use in public performance might be held as contributing infringers. This amendment was evidently passed for the specific purpose referred to, and is entitled to little consideration in construing the meaning of the terms of the act theretofore in force.

What is meant by a copy? We have already referred to the common understanding of it as a reproduction or duplication of a thing.

A definition was given by Bailey, J., in West v. Francis, 5 B. & A. 743, quoted with approval in Boosey v. Whight, supra. He said: "A copy is that which comes so near to the original as to give to every person seeing it the idea created by the original."

Various definitions have been given by the experts called in the case. The one which most commends itself to our judgment is perhaps as clear as can be made, and defines a copy of a musical composition to be "a written or printed record of it in intelligible notation." It may be true that in a broad sense a mechanical instrument which reproduces a tune copies it; but this is a strained and artificial meaning. When the combination of musical sounds is reproduced to the ear it is the original tune as conceived by the author which is heard. These musical tones are not a copy which appeals to the eye. In no sense can musical sounds which reach us through the sense of hearing be said to be copies as that term is generally understood, and as we believe it was intended to be understood in the statutes under consideration. A musical composition is an intellectual creation which first exists in the mind of the composer; he may play it for the first time upon an instrument. It is not susceptible of being copied until it has been put in a form which others can see and read. The statute has not provided for the protection of the intellectual conception apart from the thing produced, however meritorious such conception may be, but has provided for the making and filing of a tangible thing, against the publication and duplication of which it is the purpose of the statute to protect the composer.

Also it may be noted in this connection that if the broad construction of publishing and copying contended for by the appellants is to be given to this statute it would seem equally applicable to the cylinder of a music box, with its mechanical arrangement for the reproduction of melodious sounds, or the record of the graphophone, or to the pipe organ operated by devices similar to those in use in the pianola. All these instruments were well known when these various copyright acts were passed. Can it be that it was the intention of Congress to permit them to be held as infringements and suppressed by injunctions?

After all, what is the perforated roll? The fact is clearly established in the testimony in this case that even those skilled in the making of these rolls are unable to read them as musical compositions, as those in staff notation are read by the performer. It is true that there is some testimony to the effect that great skill and patience might enable the operator to read his record as he could a piece of music written in staff notation. But the weight of the testimony is emphatically the other way, and they are not intended to be read as an ordinary piece of sheet music, which to those skilled in the art conveys, by reading, in playing or singing, definite impressions of the melody.

These perforated rolls are parts of a machine which, when duly applied and properly operated in connection with the mechanism to which they are adapted, produce musical tones in harmonious combination. But we cannot think that they are copies within the meaning of the copyright act.

It may be true that the use of these perforated rolls, in the absence of statutory protection, enables the manufacturers thereof to enjoy the use of musical compositions for which they pay no value. But such considerations properly address themselves to the legislative and not to the judicial branch of the Government. As the act of Congress now stands we believe it does not include these records as copies or publications of the copyrighted music involved in these cases.

The decrees of the Circuit Court of Appeals are

Affirmed.

Mr. Justice Holmes, concurring specially.

In view of the facts and opinions in this country and abroad to which my brother Day has called attention I do not feel justified in dissenting from the judgment of the court, but the result is to give to copyright less scope than its rational significance and the ground on which it is granted seem to me to demand. Therefore I desire to add a few words to what he has said.

The notion of property starts, I suppose, from confirmed possession of a tangible object and consists in the right to exclude others from interference with the more or less free doing with it as one wills. But in copyright property has reached a more abstract expression. The right to exclude is not directed to an object in possession or owned, but is *in vacuo,* so to speak. It restrains the spontaneity of men where but for it there would be nothing of any kind to hinder their doing as they saw fit. It is a prohibition of conduct remote from the persons or tangibles of the party having the right. It may be infringed a thousand miles from the owner and without his ever becoming aware of the wrong. It is a right which could not be recognized or endured for more than a limited time, and therefore, I may remark in passing, it is one which hardly can be conceived except as a product of statute, as the authorities now agree.

The ground of this extraordinary right is that the person to whom it is given has invented some new collocation of visible or audible points,—of lines, colors, sounds, or words. The restraint is directed against reproducing this collocation, although but for the invention and the statute any one would be free to combine the contents of the dictionary, the elements of the spectrum, or the notes of the gamut in any way that he had the wit to devise. The restriction is confined to the specific form, to the collocation devised, of course, but one would expect that, if it was to be protected at all, that collocation would be protected according to what was its essence. One would expect the protection to be coextensive not only with the invention, which, though free to all, only one had the ability to achieve, but with the possibility of reproducing the result which gives to the invention its meaning and worth. A musical composition is a rational collocation of sounds apart from concepts, reduced to a tangible expression from which the collocation can be reproduced either with or without continuous human intervention. On principle anything that mechanically reproduces that collocation of sounds ought to be held a copy, or if the statute is too narrow ought to be made so by a further act, except so far as some extraneous consideration of policy may oppose. What license may be implied from a sale of the copyrighted article is a different and harder question, but I leave it untouched, as license is not relied upon as a ground for the judgment of the court.

Questions

1. Do you agree that to regard a music roll or a phonograph record as a copy of the music recorded is to give the word "copy" a "strained and artificial meaning"?

2. Was "the great dissenter", Mr. Justice Holmes, correct in his judgment that a dissent in this case would be unjustified "in view of the facts and opinions in this country and abroad to which my brother Day has called attention"?

3. Was the *White-Smith* definition of "copy" adopted under the 1909 Act? See Corcoran v. Montgomery Ward & Co., 121 F.2d 572 (9th Cir.1941); Walt Disney Productions v. Alaska Television Network, Inc., 310 F.Supp. 1073 (W.D.Wash.1969). Was the *White-Smith* definition of "copy" adopted under the current Copyright Act? See Section 101 (definition of "copies").

4. Is the Sec. 106(1) reproduction right under the current Copyright Act infringed by the unlicensed reproduction of a copyrighted work in phonorecord form? Was the right "to copy" under Section 1(a) of the 1909 Act infringed by such an unlicensed reproduction? Did an unlicensed phonorecord infringe any other right under the 1909 Act?

5. Is the unlicensed "in-put" of a copyrighted work into a computer an infringement of the reproduction right under the current Act? See Sec. 117.

6. Does the reproduction right prohibit the making of ephemeral copies? Is the picture that appears on a television screen a "copy"? See Sec. 101 (definition of "copies" and of "fixed"). Cf. Patterson v. Century Productions, 93 F.2d 489 (2d Cir.1937). See also Sec. 112. Are the recordings referred to as "ephemeral" in Sec. 112, ephemeral in the same sense as a picture which appears on a television or motion picture theater screen?

7. Suppose A creates an original work of which B thereafter makes an unauthorized copy. Subsequently C copies from B with B's permission. C does not know that B copied from A. Has C infringed A's reproduction right? Would your answer be different if B's copy had been authorized by A? If C's copy had not been authorized by B?

8. Is the reproduction right infringed if the copier neither sells nor publishes his unauthorized copy?

Collateral Reference

Nimmer on Copyright, §§ 8.01, 8.02.

GROSS v. SELIGMAN
Circuit Court of Appeals, Second Circuit, 1914.
212 F. 930.

This cause comes here upon appeal from an order of the District Court, Southern District of New York, enjoining defendant from publishing a photograph. The suit is brought under the provisions of the Copyright Act. One Rochlitz, an artist, posed a model in the nude, and therefrom produced a photograph, which he named the "Grace of Youth." A copyright was obtained therefor; all the artist's rights being sold and assigned to complainants. Two years later the same artist placed the same model in the identical pose, with the single exception that the young woman now wears a smile and holds a cherry stem between her teeth. He took a photograph of this pose, which he called "Cherry Ripe"; this second photograph is published by defendants, and has been enjoined as an infringement of complainant's copyright.

Before LACOMBE, COXE and WARD, CIRCUIT JUDGES.

LACOMBE, CIRCUIT JUDGE (after stating the facts as above). This is not simply the case of taking two separate photographs of the same young woman.

When the Grace of Youth was produced a distinctly artistic conception was formed, and was made permanent as a picture in the very method which the Supreme Court indicated in the Oscar Wilde Case (Burrow-Giles Company v. Sarony, 111 U.S. 53, 4 Sup.Ct. 279, 28 L.Ed. 349) would entitle the person producing such a picture to a copyright to protect it. It was there held that the artist who used the camera to produce his picture was entitled to copyright just as he would have been had he produced it with a brush on canvas. If the copyrighted picture were produced with colors on canvas, and were then copyrighted and sold by the artist, he would infringe the purchaser's rights if thereafter the same artist, using the same model, repainted the same picture with only trivial variations of detail and offered it for sale.

Of course when the first picture has been produced and copyrighted every other artist is entirely free to form his own conception of the Grace of Youth, or anything else, and to avail of the same young woman's services in making it permanent, whether he works with pigments or a camera. If, by chance, the pose, background, light, and shade, etc., of this new picture were strikingly similar, and if, by reason of the circumstance that the same young woman was the prominent feature in both compositions, it might be very difficult to distinguish the new picture from the old one, the new would still not be an infringement of the old because it is in no true sense a *copy* of the old. This is a risk which the original artist takes when he merely produces a likeness of an existing face and figure, instead of supplementing its features by the exercise of his own imagination.

It seems to us, however, that we have no such new photograph of the same model. The identity of the artist and the many close identi-

204 RIGHTS PROTECTED BY COPYRIGHT Ch. 4

Defendant's Cherry Ripe

Complainant's Grace of Youth

ties of pose, light, and shade, etc., indicates very strongly that the first picture was used to produce the second. Whether the model in the second case was posed, and light and shade, etc., arranged with a copy of the first photograph physically present before the artist's eyes, or whether his mental reproduction of the exact combination he had already once effected was so clear and vivid that he did not need the physical reproduction of it, seems to us immaterial. The one thing, viz., the exercise of artistic talent, which made the first photographic picture a subject of copyright, has been used not to produce another picture, but to duplicate the original.

The case is quite similar to those where indirect copying, through the use of living pictures, was held to be an infringement of copyright. Hanfstaengle v. Baines & Co. (L.R.1894) A.C. 20, 30; Turner v. Robinson, 10 Irish Chancery 121, 510.

The eye of an artist or a connoisseur will, no doubt, find differences between these two photographs. The backgrounds are not identical, the model in one case is sedate, in the other smiling; moreover the young woman was two years older when the later photograph was taken, and some slight changes in the contours of her figure are discoverable. But the identities are much greater than the differences, and it seems to us that the artist was careful to introduce only enough differences to argue about, while undertaking to make what would seem to be a copy to the ordinary purchaser who did not have both photographs before him at the same time. In this undertaking we think he succeeded.

The order is affirmed.

Question

Recall Justice Holmes' statement in Bleistein v. Donaldson Lithographing Co., supra: "Others are free to copy the original. They are not free to copy the copy." Wasn't the defendant here only copying "the original"? Was he copying only that which was original in nature, or also that which was original with the "artist" in making the first photograph?

Collateral Reference

Nimmer on Copyright, § 8.01[C].

Note * and Questions

The Phonorecord Compulsory License of Nondramatic Musical Works—A Limitation on the Reproduction Right

The reproduction right granted to a copyright owner inheres in all works of authorship. It is for the most part an exclusive right. Section 115 of the Copyright Act modifies the exclusivity of this right in that it is compulsory upon a copyright owner to grant a license under certain prescribed conditions. Such a compulsory license is, however, applicable only to nondramatic musical works. Thus, the Section 115 compulsory license has no application to any

---

* Nimmer on Copyright, § 8.04.

other works, including literary and dramatic works. Neither does it apply to sound recordings. Here, however, it is necessary to make a distinction between a nondramatic musical work *per se,* and a sound recording which may incorporate such a musical work. The compulsory license may apply to the musical work even though its only embodiment in a material object is in a phonorecord which constitutes a sound recording. If the conditions of the compulsory license are satisfied, a licensee thereunder may make and distribute phonorecords of the musical work. But the compulsory license does not authorize the licensee to duplicate and distribute a sound recording which contains the licensed musical work if such sound recording was not made by or for the compulsory licensee. If a sound recording is itself legally protected, the compulsory license does not vitiate such protection. Therefore a compulsory licensee who wishes to reproduce the licensed musical work in the form in which it is embodied in a protected sound recording, must first obtain a consensual license from the copyright owner or other holder of the rights [1] in such sound recording. Otherwise, he may exercise his rights under the compulsory license only by assembling his own musicians, singers, recording engineers and equipment, etc. for the purpose of recording anew the musical work which is the subject of the compulsory license.[2]

Question 1: Does the Sec. 115 compulsory license confer the right to make copies of a nondramatic musical work notwithstanding the exclusive right granted under Sec. 106(1)? Recall the distinction between "copies" and "phonorecords".

Question 2: Assuming the Sec. 115 compulsory license to be applicable, does it constitute a license of any rights other than the Sec. 106(1) reproduction right? Does it have any impact upon the performance right (Sec. 106(4))? The adaptation right (Sec. 106(2))? The distribution right (Sec. 106(3))?

Question 3: What act triggers application of the Sec. 115 compulsory license? Is it the same act which triggered the comparable compulsory license under Sec. 1(e) of the 1909 Act? Suppose a composer authorizes the recording of his musical work in the United States, and further authorizes the public distribution of phonorecords of such recording in Europe, which in fact occurs. Does this trigger the Sec. 115 compulsory license? Would it have triggered the old Sec. 1(e) compulsory license? Suppose a composer authorizes the recording of his musical work on the sound track of a motion picture, which is then distributed in the United States. Does this trigger the Sec. 115 compulsory license?

Question 4: Is the Sec. 115 compulsory license available to one who manufactures phonorecords intended primarily for sale to radio stations and to juke box operators? What if the phonorecord manufacturer's primary purpose is to sell phonorecords to the public for private use, but in fact most of his sales are made to radio stations and juke box operators?

---

1. Statutory copyright inheres only in sound recordings first fixed on or after February 15, 1972. See Sec. 301(c). However, there may be state law protection for sound recordings first fixed prior thereto. Id.

2. We discuss here only the non-applicability of the compulsory license to sound recordings. On the related but distinct issue of whether the compulsory license is applicable to a musical work embodied in a sound recording if such musical work is reproduced by the duplication of the sound recording, see Duchess Music Corp. v. Stern, infra, and the textual material which follows.

A Sec. 115 compulsory licensee is accorded a limited adaptation right in connection with his recording of the licensed musical work. He may make a musical arrangement of the work "to the extent necessary to conform it to the style or manner of interpretation of the performance involved, but the arrangement shall not change the basic melody or fundamental character of the work. * * *." [3] A limited adaptation right is clearly necessary if the compulsory license provision is to be implemented, since different performers require some variation in musical arrangements. Still, the variation may not be so great as to allow the music to be "perverted, distorted or travestied." [4]

Question 5: If the authorized recording which triggered the compulsory license was instrumental only, may the compulsory licensee include the composer's lyrics? May he add his own lyrics? If such authorized recording contained both music and lyrics, may a licensee produce a purely instrumental version?

Question 6: May a compulsory licensee claim copyright in the musical arrangement he makes pursuant to his limited adaptation right?

Any person who wishes to obtain a compulsory license under Section 115 of the current Act must serve a notice of his intention to do so on the copyright owner of the musical work as to which a license is sought. This notice must be served either before, or within thirty days after such person has made phonorecords of such musical work, and it must in any event be served before any distribution of such phonorecords. If such notice is served upon the copyright owner, it is unnecessary also to file such notice with the Copyright Office. If, however, the registration and other public records of the Copyright Office do not identify the copyright owner, and also include an address at which such notice can be served, it is sufficient to file such notice with the Copyright Office.

Question 7: What are the consequences of a failure to serve (or file) such a notice within the time periods above specified? Suppose that a given number of phonorecords are made and distributed prior to service of the required notice, the notice is then served, and thereafter additional phonorecords are made and distributed. Do the making and distribution of the earlier group of phonorecords constitute infringements? Is this true of the later group of phonorecords?

Assuming the copyright owner has authorized an act which triggers the Sec. 115 compulsory license, and that such a licensee has duly served a notice of intention to obtain a compulsory license, the copyright owner may not claim that the resulting manufacture and distribution of phonorecords embodying his musical work constitute copyright infringement. He is, however, entitled to be paid statutory royalties, as described below. But the copyright owner's right to be paid such royalties is conditioned upon his having theretofore identified himself in the Copyright Office by registration, or other recordation.[5] Failing such an identification, the compulsory licensee may make and distribute phonorecords royalty free. However, once such registration or other recordation occurs, the copyright owner is entitled to be paid the appropriate royalties for all phonorecords which are thereafter made and distributed.

---

3. 17 U.S.C.A. § 115(a)(2).
4. H.Rep., p. 109.
5. Since any "document pertaining to a copyright may be recorded in the Copyright Office * * *" (Section 205(a)), any such document which serves to identify the copyright owner will suffice. This is to be contrasted with a special notice of use required to be filed under Sec. 1(e) of the 1909 Act, which specifically indicated that the copyright owner had authorized the recording of his work, and had therefore triggered the Sec. 1(e) compulsory license.

Question 8: Suppose one who would claim the benefit of a compulsory license has failed to serve a notice of intention to obtain a compulsory license, and the copyright owner of the musical work assertedly subject to such license has also failed to file the required notification as to his identity. Does the putative licensee's failure render his making and distribution of phonorecords an infringement, or does the copyright owner's failure immunize from liability such phonorecord making and distribution? Would the answer have been the same under the Section 1(e) compulsory license of the 1909 Act, assuming the putative licensee failed to serve such a notice, and the copyright owner failed to file a notice of use? See Norbay Music, Inc. v. King Records, Inc., 290 F.2d 617 (2d Cir.1961).

Question 9: After January 1, 1978 composer A licensed record manufacturer B to make a sound recording of A's song. After the public distribution of B's sound recording, C "wrote" a song which was copied from, and was substantially similar to A's song, but differed in some respects. C then made his own sound recording of his song, without attempting to obtain a compulsory license from A, and without obtaining either A's or B's consent. C's sound recording further imitated the sound and style of B's sound recording to such extent as to render the two substantially similar. Has C infringed A's copyright in the song? Has C infringed B's copyright in the sound recording? See Sec. 114(b) of the Copyright Act.

The current compulsory license royalty rate for every phonorecord (containing the copyright owner's musical work) distributed on or after July 1, 1984 is either 4.5 cents, or .85 cent per minute of playing time or fraction thereof, whichever amount is larger.[6] Thus, if a single phonorecord contains more than one copyrighted musical work, a separate royalty payment is due for each such work contained on the same phonorecord.

Question 9: Is the royalty under Sec. 115 payable for each phonorecord "made" or for each phonorecord "made and distributed"? How does this compare with the basis for payment under Sec. 1(e) of the 1909 Act?

Collateral References

Henn, *The Compulsory License Provisions of the U.S. Copyright Law*, Studies in Copyright 877 (Fisher ed. 1963).

Nimmer on Copyright, § 8.04.

B. THE DISTRIBUTION RIGHT *

UNITED STATES v. ATHERTON
United States Court of Appeals, Ninth Circuit, 1977.
561 F.2d 747.

Before CHAMBERS, KOELSCH, and HUFSTEDLER, CIRCUIT JUDGES.

---

6. Effective January 1, 1986 the 4.5 cents rate goes to 5 cents, and the .85 cent per minute of playing time goes to .95 cent per minute of playing time. The prescribed royalty rate is subject to periodic readjustment by the Copyright Royalty Tribunal. 17 U.S.C.A. § 801(b)(1). This is to be contrasted with the royalty of 2 cents per phonorecord under the 1909 Act, which was not subject to administrative revision. See 17 U.S.C.A. § 1(e) (1909 Act).

* The adaptation right, or the right "to prepare derivative works based upon the copyrighted work" under Sec. 106(2) of the Copyright Act, is not here separately considered because it largely overlaps with the reproduction and performance rights. See

HUFSTEDLER, CIRCUIT JUDGE: Atherton appeals from his conviction upon five counts of an indictment charging him with copyright infringement in violation of 17 U.S.C.A. § 104 and one count charging him with interstate transportation of stolen property in violation of 18 U.S.C.A. § 2314. He challenges the constitutionality of 17 U.S.C.A. § 104, contends that the evidence was insufficient to sustain the conviction, and argues that the court improperly excluded evidence. We uphold the constitutionality of Section 104, following United States v. Wise (9th Cir.1977) 550 F.2d 1180, and reverse the conviction for insufficiency of the evidence.

Atherton bought, sold, collected prints of motion pictures. He advertised films for sale in catalogues. His customers were primarily motion picture collectors and dealers. The photoplays which are the subject of the copyright counts are "The Exorcist," "Airport," "The Way We Were," "Forty Carats," and "Young Winston." The copyrights were owned by Universal Studios ("Airport"), Columbia Pictures ("The Way We Were," "Young Winston," "Forty Carats"), and Warner Bros. ("The Exorcist"). Atherton had no license or any kind of permission from the copyright holders to use or sell the prints of these photoplays. He sold prints of the films at prices ranging from $135 ("Young Winston") to $500 ("The Exorcist").

Before United States v. Wise, supra, and United States v. Drebin (9th Cir.1977) 557 F.2d 1316 [filed July 21, 1977] which came down while this appeal was pending, many of the issues on this appeal were open in the Circuit. *Wise* resolves almost all of the issues raised in respect of the copyright counts. Thus, the identical attacks on the constitutionality of Section 104 were decided against Atherton's challenges in *Wise*. *Wise* also established the five elements that the Government must prove in a Section 104 prosecution: (1) Infringement of a copyright, (2) of a work that has not been the subject of a "first sale," (3) done wilfully, (4) with knowledge that the copyrighted work has not been the subject of a "first sale," and (5) for profit. The Government adequately proved infringement, wilfulness, and profit, but it failed to negate first sale or to prove Atherton's *scienter*. The interstate transportation count (18 U.S.C.A. § 2314) was not involved in *Wise*, but that count was considered in *Drebin*. We overturn that count because, unlike *Drebin*, the Government failed to prove that the value of the print ("The Exorcist") was at least $5,000, the minimum valuation necessary to bring the acts within the statute.

I

Section 104 provides, in pertinent part: "Any person who wilfully and for profit shall infringe any copyright secured by this title, or who shall knowingly and wilfully aid or abet such infringement, shall be deemed guilty of a misdemeanor, * * *." Although nothing in Section

Nimmer on Copyright, § 8.09[A]. However, a substantively significant application of the adaptation right is considered infra, in the chapter on moral rights.

104 specifically refers to "the first sale doctrine," that doctrine has been judicially read into the statute from a judicial gloss drawn on 17 U.S.C.A. § 27. As the *Wise* court explains: "[T]he first sale doctrine provides that where a copyright owner parts with title to a particular copy of his copyrighted work, he divests himself of his exclusive right to vend that particular copy. While the proprietor's other copyright rights (reprinting, copying, etc.) remain unimpaired, the exclusive right to vend the transferred copy rests with the vendee, who is not restricted by statute from further transfers of that copy, even though in breach of an agreement restricting its sale." (United States v. Wise, supra, 550 F.2d at 1187.) The "sale" embodied in the first sale concept is a term of art. The sale is not limited to voluntary sales of a copyrighted work for a sale price that takes into account both the value of the materials upon which the copyrightable idea is affixed together with the idea itself. In this context, the first sale doctrine includes involuntary transfers, and as we shall explain later, sales of the copyrighted work for salvage, or other purposes unrelated to the transfer of the intangible creation or idea which is the subject of the copyright.

The Government tried to prove that the prints that Atherton sold could never have been the subject of a first sale because, under the distribution systems of each of the proprietors of the copyrights involved, the prints were never sold. The Government did not try to prove the source from which Atherton acquired any of the films. Rather, its theory was that if it could prove that no prints were subject to any first sale, it would follow that the prints that Atherton sold could not have been subject to a first sale. The Government's theory was successful in respect of the film "The Exorcist." However, it failed to prove that there was no first sale with respect to the prints of the other films for which Atherton was prosecuted.

Here, as in *Wise*, employees of the motion picture studios who owned the copyrights testified, in substance, that the films were not sold, but rather licensed or used by licensees for limited purposes and for limited periods of time. Although none of the films in this case was subject to an outright sale, each of the films, other than "The Exorcist," had been the subject of transfers for television purposes that fall within the definition of first sale, as articulated and applied in *Wise*.

The first sale occurred in respect of "Airport" by reason of Universal's agreement with ABC Television Network. The transfer agreement provides "notwithstanding anything to the contrary contained in this subparagraph (e) or elsewhere in this Agreement, ABC may retain permanently, at ABC's election and cost, a print or recording of each Film for file, reference, and audition purposes." Here, as in *Wise*, this contractual provision clearly contemplates the sale of a film print to ABC at its election. No evidence was adduced at trial concerning whether ABC exercised its election, and in the absence of that proof, the Government failed to prove the absence of a first sale of the photoplay "Airport." The Columbia Pictures' contracts regarding "The Way We Were," "Young Winston," and "Forty Carats" contain a similar clause permitting ABC at its election and cost to retain a file-screening print. Consideration for the transfer of this library copy, the surrender of possession in respect of that copy, and Columbia's failure specifically to retain title together constitute a first sale.

The fact that Universal and Columbia made first sales of the prints that they transferred to ABC, of course, does not mean that any of the prints thus transferred were the source of Atherton's prints. The Government's proof failed because it made no effort to prove the source of Atherton's prints, relying entirely upon its theory that no first sales had occurred to anyone. That theory collapsed upon proof that first sales were made to ABC. The Government's deficiency in proof thus compels reversal of all counts except the copyright count involving "The Exorcist."

Atherton also contended below, and here contends, that first sales had occurred by reason of the sales of worn-out prints to film salvage companies. The general proceedings of film studios in selling films for scrap are adequately described in the *Wise* and *Drebin* cases. *Wise,* however, did not have to decide whether a sale for salvage could be deemed a first sale in a prosecution for violation of Section 104. In *Wise* no evidence was introduced to rebut the testimony that the films there in question could not have been pieced together to create a feature-length motion picture from the products sold to film salvage firms. In Atherton's case, he tried to introduce evidence that at least one full-length feature motion picture had been recovered and sold by one of the salvage companies whose services were used by the copyright holders in this case. The district court sustained an objection based upon relevancy. The district court also rejected an offer of proof. If sale to a salvage company can be a first sale, the proffered evidence was relevant. The evidence was not offered to prove that Atherton acquired the prints that he resold from a salvage company, but rather to prove that first sales had occurred, thus tending to impeach the testimony of the prosecution witnesses that the films were never "sold."

In a criminal prosecution, a sale for salvage purposes can be a first sale. (United States v. Drebin, supra.) We recognize that authorities are divided on the question whether a sale to a purchaser with restrictions that are subsequently breached constitutes a first sale for copyright purposes in civil cases. In Bobbs-Merrill Co. v. Straus (1908) 210 U.S. 339, 28 S.Ct. 722, 52 L.Ed. 1086, the defendant sold copies of a copyrighted work for less than one dollar, knowing that in doing so he had breached an agreement between the defendant's vendor and the copyright owner not to sell or to allow copies to be sold for less than one dollar. The Supreme Court held that any transfer of title is a first sale, and no copyright remedy is permissible to enforce the breach of contract involved. The same theory was followed in Harrison v. Maynard (2d Cir.1894) 61 F. 689, in which a copyright remedy was foreclosed when a scrap dealer to whom the copyright holder had sold fire damaged, unbound book sheets to a book dealer in violation of the scrap dealer's express agreement to use them for scrap use only. *Harrison* was followed by Independent News Company v. Williams (3d Cir.1961) 293 F.2d 510 (Comic books given to a salvage dealer for use as paper stock only were resold by the dealer in violation of the restricted use.). A different view was expressed, by way of *dictum,* in Platt & Munk Co. v. Republic Graphics (2d Cir.1963) 315 F.2d 847, which can be labeled "the just reward" variation on the first sale doctrine. The theory is that a transfer equals a first sale, whether or not the transfer is involuntary, if the copyright proprietor has received a just reward for the use of his article. The theory was applied in Lantern Press, Inc. v. American Publishers Co. (E.D.N.Y.1976) 419 F.Supp. 1267, a case in which the defendant purchased paperbound versions of plaintiff's books and rebound them in hardback for sales to schools and libraries. The end product yielded the copyright holder a lesser return than it would have earned from an original hard cover edition, but the court concluded that there was no violation of the copyright because the copyright holder had received a just reward for the transfer. We do not think that the just reward theory should be imported into the first sale doctrine as incorporated into Section 104, upon which this criminal prosecution is based. Rather, we follow the trail left by Bobbs-Merrill Co. v. Straus, supra, to reach the conclusions of *Harrison* and *Independent News* and United States v. Drebin, supra, that a transfer to a salvage company for a consideration is a first sale in a Section 104 prosecution. The copyright holder is thus remitted to his civil remedies without the potential deterrent force of a criminal prosecution against the vendee who has purchased copyrighted material sold to him by a vendor who violated restrictions on the transfer to him.

The Government successfully proved the absence of a first sale of "The Exorcist." The testimony was uncontroverted that "The Exorcist," at the time Atherton sold a copy of the print, had not been the subject of any television contracts, VIP contracts, armed service contracts, or airline contracts, and that no prints of the film had been sent to salvage companies. "The Exorcist" copyright count must nevertheless be reversed because the Government failed to prove that Atherton knew that no print of "The Exorcist" had been subject to first sale. The Government's failure to prove *scienter* in respect of each of these films is understandable because, until the decision in *Wise,* it was by no means clear that *scienter* was required. The Government did introduce evidence, strong enough to withstand an attack on appeal, that Atherton sold these prints intentionally and that he knew that sales in violation of the copyright law were illegal. But the evidence with respect to his knowledge of first sale, unlike the evidence in the *Wise* and *Drebin* cases, was slight. In view of the uncertain state of the law at the time this case was tried, no one can be faulted for the poor record. On retrial of this count, the Government should have an opportunity to cure the evidentiary deficiencies.

II

Atherton's conviction for transporting a print of "The Exorcist" in violation of 18 U.S.C.A. § 2314 raises some interesting, almost metaphysical, legal issues. The most intriguing question is whether the intangible idea protected by the copyright is sufficiently reified by being embodied on a film that the copyright becomes "goods, wares, or merchandise" within the meaning of Section 2314. That question has been resolved against Atherton in United States v. Drebin, supra. Here, however, unlike *Drebin,* the Government failed to prove that the property was worth $5,000.

* * *

If the Government is unable to produce proof of the source of Atherton's prints of "Airport," "Young Winston," "Forty Carats," and "The Way We Were," those counts will be subject to dismissal. Atherton is entitled to a new trial on the "Exorcist" count.

Reversed.

Questions

1. Under Sec. 104 of the 1909 Act any act of civil copyright infringement also constituted criminal copyright infringement if it was done "wilfully and for profit". Is this also true under the current Act? See Sec. 506(a), and Nimmer on Copyright, § 15.01.

2. Is the first sale doctrine recognized under the current Act? See Sec. 109(a). Does there have to be a "sale" under Sec. 109(a) in order to cut off the copyright owner's right to control distribution of a given copy? Suppose title in such copy passes by gift rather than by sale. Alternatively, suppose a manufacturer of copies under license from the copyright owner is the original owner of the copies he has made, so that title never "passes" to him either by sale or gift. In either of these cases is the Sec. 109(a) limitation on the Sec. 106(3) distribution right effective?

3. Does Sec. 109(a) by its terms cut off the distribution right as to copies which the copyright owner has rented, leased or loaned? Under *Atherton* when will a "loan" be regarded as the equivalent of a "first sale"? If there has not been a "first sale", may the copyright owner prevent one who is in lawful possession (but without ownership) of a copy from renting or lending such copy? May the copyright owner prevent a buyer of a copy from renting such copy?

4. If there has been a "first sale", are the copyright owner's rights—other than the distribution right—cut off or affected in any manner?

5. Where should the burden of proof lie—on the plaintiff to prove the absence of a "first sale", or on the defendant to prove that the copy in issue had been the subject of a "first sale"? Is the prima facie validity provision of Sec. 410(c) relevant to this question? Who is more likely to have within his knowledge evidence on the "first sale" issue? Should the imposition of the burden of proof on this issue vary depending upon whether the action is for civil or criminal copyright infringement? Compare United States v. Wise, 550 F.2d 1180 (9th Cir.1977) and American International Pictures, Inc. v. Foreman, 576 F.2d 661 (5th Cir.1978).

6. Is the court correct in concluding that shipment of an infringing film print constitutes the transportation of stolen "goods, wares, or merchandise" within the meaning of 18 U.S.C.A. § 2314? See Nimmer, "National Security Secrets v. Free Speech: The Issues Left Undecided in the Ellsberg Case", 26 Stan.L.Rev. 311 (1974).

7. Note that Sec. 109 has been amended so as to exclude from application of the first sale doctrine the rental of phonorecords. Should there be an amendment to likewise exclude the rental of video cassettes?

Collateral References

Nimmer on Copyright, §§ 8.11, 8.12, 12.11[E], 15.01.

Nolan, *All Rights Not Reserved After the First Sale*, 23 Bull.Cr.Soc. 76 (1975).

C. THE PERFORMANCE RIGHT

1. *The Requirement That the Performance Be Public*

Note *

Section 106(4) of the Copyright Act provides that in the case of literary, musical, dramatic, and choreographic works, pantomines, and motion pictures and other audiovisual works, the copyright owner thereof has the exclusive right to perform the work publicly. Thus, only those performances which occur "publicly" are included under the performance right.

It would, of course, be unthinkable for an infringement to arise every time someone for his own amusement, or that of his friends, were to read a book aloud, or sing a song.[1] Inevitably, however, by stipulating that a performance must occur "publicly" in order to infringe, difficult problems of degree and interpretation must arise. These are now to be considered.

[1]—The Composition of the Audience. A work is performed "publicly" if it is performed "at a place open to the public or at any place where a substantial number of persons outside of a normal circle of a family and its social acquaintances is gathered * * * ".[2] By this definition of "publicly" the current Act attempts to clarify what was sometimes a difficult issue under the 1909 Act. It was clear under the prior Act, and remains clear under the present Act that a performance limited to members of the family and invited guests is not a public performance. A more troublesome situation under the 1909 Act arose where the performance was not open to the public at large, but a substantial number of persons outside of a normal family circle and their social acquaintances was gathered. It was held, for example, that a performance in a club where only members and invited guests were present was not a public performance.[3] On the other hand, performances were held to be public where they occurred in clubs which catered primarily to their own members but did not place effective restrictions on attendance by uninvited members of the general public.[4] This line of cases, and particularly the *Wyatt* decision, suggested that under the 1909 Act a performance was never "public" as long as the audience was limited to a particular group rather than the general public, no matter how large the composition of such group. There were other cases

---

* Nimmer on Copyright, § 8.14[C].

1. "No license is required by the Copyright Act, for example, to sing a copyrighted lyric in the shower." Twentieth Century Music Corp. v. Aiken, 422 U.S. 151, 155 (1975).

2. 17 U.S.C.A. § 101.

3. Metro-Goldwyn-Mayer Distrib. Corp. v. Wyatt, 21 C.O.Bull. 203 (D.C.Md.1932).

4. Lerner v. Club Wander In, Inc., 174 F.Supp. 731 (D.C.Mass.1959); M. Witmark & Sons v. Tremont Social & Athletic Club, 188 F.Supp. 787 (D.C.Mass.1960).

under the 1909 Act which, to the contrary, indicated that a performance would be held to be "public" even if the composition of the audience were restricted in some manner if under such restriction a substantial segment of the public were enabled to attend.[5] This approach has been codified under the current Act, and the *Wyatt* line of cases has been expressly disavowed.[6] Thus, if "a substantial number of persons outside of a normal circle of a family and its social acquaintances is gathered"[7] the performance is rendered "publicly" even if some restrictions on who may attend are imposed. Moreover, the fact that only an insubstantial number of persons actually attend a performance will not derogate from its character as a public performance if under the restrictions imposed a substantial number of persons outside of a normal family circle, and its social acquaintances could have attended. Failure at the box office does not vitiate liability. On the other hand, if under the restrictions imposed a number of persons outside of the family circle and social acquaintances did or could attend, the performance is still not rendered "publicly" unless the number of such other persons who could attend is "substantial."

[2]—**Performances In Which the Audience is Dispersed.** If a substantial or unrestricted number of persons are enabled to view or hear a given performance, it is not necessary that such persons be physically assembled in order to constitute the performance "public." This is made explicit under the current Copyright Act by its provision that to "perform * * * a work 'publicly' means * * * (2) to transmit or otherwise communicate a performance * * * of the work to a place specified by clause (1)[8] or to the public, by any device or process, whether the members of the public capable of receiving the performance * * * receive it in the same place or in separate places * * * ".[9] Thus a television or radio broadcast received in the privacy of individual homes is nevertheless a "public" performance. Likewise, music transmitted by leased telephone wires to private customers who purchase the service constitutes a public performance. Similarly, a hotel transmission of a radio broadcast to its guests was held to be "public" even if such transmission was heard over loud-speakers which were placed only in the individual guest rooms and not in any public rooms where the guests congregated.[10]

Suppose there is no proof that a substantial number, or indeed, that any persons were in fact operating their respective receiving apparatus at the time of transmission of a given work. Does such transmission nevertheless constitute a *public* performance? The House Report states that it does, and that no such proof is necessary.[11] This confirms that a "public" performance merely requires that such performance be "open" to, that is, available to a substantial number of persons. It is not necessary that they in fact attend or receive the performance.

---

5. See Lerner v. Schectman, 228 F.Supp. 354 (D.C.Minn.1964); Broadcast Music, Inc. v. Walters, 181 U.S.P.Q. 327 (N.D.Okla. 1973); Gershwin Publishing Corp. v. Columbia Artists Management, Inc., 312 F.Supp. 581 (S.D.N.Y.1970), aff'd 443 F.2d 1159 (2d Cir.1971).

6. H.Rep., p. 64.

7. 17 U.S.C.A. § 101.

8. I.e., "any place where a substantial number of persons outside of a normal circle of a family and its social acquaintances is gathered * * *."

9. 17 U.S.C.A. § 101 (definition of "To perform or display a work 'publicly' ").

10. Buck v. Jewell-LaSalle Realty Co., 283 U.S. 191 (1931); Society of European Stage Authors & Composers v. New York Hotel Statler Co., 19 F.Supp. 1 (S.D.N.Y. 1937).

11. H.Rep., p. 65.

COLUMBIA PICTURES INDUSTRIES, INC. v. REDD HORNE INC.

District Court, Western District Pennsylvania, 1983.
568 F.Supp. 494.

MENCER, DISTRICT JUDGE.

* * *

This is an action for copyright infringement brought under Title 17 of the United States Code, entitled "Copyrights", 17 U.S.C. §§ 101–810 (1976). The plaintiffs, seven major motion picture producers and distributors, are either the owners or co-owners of copyrights in the motion pictures which are the subject matter of this lawsuit or are the exclusive licensees for distribution of these motion pictures or have by contract the right to enforce these copyrights. The alleged infringement we are concerned with here results from the defendants' use of video cassette copies of these copyrighted motion pictures in a video showcasing operation. The defendants operate retail outlets for home video equipment and accessories at two locations in Erie, Pennsylvania. These facilities, Maxwell's Video Showcase and Maxwell's Video Showcase East (collectively Maxwell's), sell and rent video cassette recorders and prerecorded video cassettes of copyrighted materials and also sell blank video cassettes. It is alleged that Maxwell's performs video cassettes of the plaintiffs' copyrighted motion pictures to customers at its facilities in violation of the plaintiffs' exclusive rights under the federal copyright laws.

* * *

The alleged performance of video cassettes at Maxwell's facilities is the sole basis for the plaintiffs' charge of copyright infringement in this particular lawsuit.[3] The plaintiffs base their claim of infringement on the argument that Maxwell's showcasing constitutes a "public performance" of the plaintiffs' copyrighted motion pictures, and is an infringement of the exclusive right to perform their copyrighted work publicly which is enjoyed by copyright owners. In order to place the discussion in the proper context, we find it necessary to set forth in some detail a description of the two Maxwell's facilities and the showcasing activities which allegedly result in infringement of the plaintiffs' copyrights before proceeding to an analysis of the applicable statutory provisions governing the issue.

The original Maxwell's Video Showcase opened on the west side of Erie on July 22, 1981. Maxwell's Video Showcase East opened some fifteen months later on October 29, 1982 following the success of the original Maxwell's and some area competitors. The west side store is approximately sixty feet wide by sixty feet long and consists of a small showroom area in the front of the store and the showcase area in the rear portion of the store. The showroom area contains the equipment

---

3. It is important to note here what is not at issue in this infringement action. The plaintiffs do not challenge either the possession of the video cassette copies by the defendants or the rental of the cassettes for private in-home use by Maxwell's patrons.

and materials which Maxwell's has available for sale or rent and a counter area which is attended by employees of Maxwell's. This showroom area also contains dispensing machines for popcorn and carbonated beverages. There is a wall about three feet behind the counter area. The showcase area, or viewing rooms, are located beyond this wall. These viewing rooms are essentially private booths with space for either two, three or four viewers. The west side facility initially contained twenty-one such rooms and was later expanded to contain forty-four viewing rooms. * * * At both facilities approximately twenty percent of the rooms hold up to four people and the remainder will accommodate only two.

The procedure to be followed by a patron wishing to utilize one of the viewing rooms is exactly the same at both facilities. Maxwell's terms the use of these rooms an in-store rental. The rental is initiated by the viewer selecting the motion picture he wishes to see from a catalogue of the film titles available at Maxwell's. This catalogue changes periodically with the addition of new titles to Maxwell's library of cassettes. The patron then reserves a room and is charged a fee for the use of the room and the video cassette copy of the chosen film if the cassette is available at that time.[4] The fee is based on the time of day and on the number of persons using the room. The patrons may then help themselves to popcorn and cold drinks before going to their assigned room. The cassette does not begin to run until the viewers have situated themselves in the room and closed the door. Closing the door to the viewing room activates an automatic signal in the counter area at the front of the store where an employee of Maxwell's starts the video cassette machine which contains the cassette selected by the viewer. The individual viewers may adjust the lighting in the rooms by use of a rheostat located in the room. They may also adjust the various volume, brightness and color levels on the television set, however, the video cassette machines are all located in one central area on the wall behind the counter in the front showroom and are operated only by employees of Maxwell's.

Access to a particular room is limited to the two, three or four individuals who rent it as a group. Strangers are not grouped in order to fill a particular room to capacity and no one can enter a room which is occupied. * * *

* * * On May 31 the defendants moved for summary judgment and the plaintiffs countered with their own motion for summary judgment on June 1. * * * The parties have stated, and the Court finds, that there are no issues of material fact which would preclude the entry of summary judgment in this action. We are, therefore, in a position to enter a ruling on all outstanding motions at this time.

* * *

The plaintiffs do not contend that the video cassette copies of plaintiffs' copyrighted movies which are used in the defendants' in-store

---

4. There is only one copy of each film available at each of the two locations at any given time, therefore, if two strangers wish to view the same video cassette at the same time in the same store one will be unable to do so.

rental, or showcasing, operation were obtained by any illegitimate means; and, in fact, the cassettes used by the defendants were obtained either by purchasing them from the plaintiffs or their authorized distributors. In other words, the plaintiffs do not allege that the defendants have no right to possess the particular video cassette copies they have purchased or that rental of such copies for in-home use infringes their copyrights. The complaint is based solely on the allegation that the defendants' showcasing operation is a public performance, as that term is defined by the federal copyright laws, and that the exclusive right to perform a work publicly is retained by the copyright owner despite the sale of a particular copy of the owner's copyrighted work.

* * * The plaintiffs' sales of video cassette copies of their copyrighted motion pictures to the defendants resulted only in a waiver of the exclusive distribution right held in those particular copies sold, 17 U.S.C. § 109(a) (1976), therefore, any other rights the plaintiffs held in the motion pictures remain with them in their capacity as copyright owners.

* * * Thus the plaintiffs retain the exclusive right to perform their motion pictures publicly despite the sale of video cassette copies to the defendants.

* * * The issue is thus reduced to a determination of whether Maxwell's showcasing of copyrighted pre-recorded video cassettes constitutes a public performance of the motion pictures embodied in those cassettes. If it does it is an infringement of the plaintiffs' copyrights.

The exclusive right of a copyright owner to perform his copyrighted work in public is found in clause (4) of section 106. We begin our analysis of section 106(4) with the definitions "perform" and "perform * * * a work 'publicly'" which are found in 17 U.S.C. § 101 (1976). "To perform a work means ... in the case of a motion picture or other audiovisual work, to show its images in any sequence or to make the sounds accompanying it audible." 17 U.S.C. § 101 (1976). The House of Representatives report accompanying the 1976 Act provides further explanation of what constitutes a performance of motion pictures.

> The definition of "perform" in relation to a "motion picture or other audio visual work" is "to show its images in any sequence or to make the sounds accompanying it audible." The showing of portions of a motion picture * * must therefore be sequential to constitute a "performance" rather than a "display", but no particular order need be maintained. The purely aural performance of a motion picture sound track, or of sound portions of an audiovisual work, would constitute a performance of the "motion picture or other audiovisual work"; but, where some of the sounds have been reproduced separately on phonorecords, a performance from the phonorecord would not constitute performance of the motion picture or audiovisual work.

H.R.Rep. No. 1476, 94th Cong., 2d Sess. 63–64, *reprinted in* 1976 U.S.Code Cong. & Ad.News 5659, 5677. There can be no doubt that the playing of a video cassette results in a sequential showing of its images and in making the sounds accompanying it audible. Video cassette showcasing, such as that done at Maxwell's, is a performance under the copyright laws. Our inquiry is thus further reduced to a determination of whether or not such performances are public and, therefore, an infringement of the plaintiffs' copyrights.

The applicable statutory definition states that:

> [t]o perform * * * it at a place open to the public or at any place where a substantial number of persons outside of a normal circle of a family and its social acquaintances is gathered * * *.

17 U.S.C. § 101 (1976). The plaintiffs contend that the definition found in clause (1) is written in the disjunctive form resulting in the creation of two separate categories of what is public, i.e., (1) at a place open to the public or (2) at any place where a substantial number of persons outside of a normal circle of a family and its social acquaintances is gathered. The defendants argue that the definition consists of two complementary phrases designed to express congressional concern with the composition of the group viewing a performance as opposed to the place where the viewing occurs. In support of this argument the defendants cite the legislative history accompanying this portion of the definition of public performance.

> Under clause (1) of the definition of "publicly" in section 101, a performance * * * is "public" if it takes place "at a place open to the public or at any place where a substantial number of persons outside of a normal circle of a family and its social acquaintances is gathered." One of the principal purposes of the definition was to make clear that, contrary to the decision in *Metro-Goldwyn-Mayer Distributing Corp. v. Wyatt*, 21 C.O.Bull. 203 (D.Md.1932), performances in "semi-public" places such as clubs, lodges, factories, summer camps, and schools are "public performances" subject to copyright control. The term "a family" in this context would include an individual living alone, so that a gathering confined to the individual's social acquaintances would normally be regarded as private. Routine meetings of businesses and governmental personnel would be excluded because they do not represent the gathering of a "substantial number of persons."

H.R.Rep. No. 1476, 94th Cong., 2d Sess. 64, *reprinted in* 1976 U.S.Code Cong. & Ad.News 5659, 5677–78. The parties' positions may create what amounts to a distinction without a difference; nevertheless, the language of the statute and its legislative history indicate that Congress' concern was with the composition of the audience. This conclusion does not emasculate the plaintiffs' contention that a public performance could occur in either a place open to the public in a general sense or in a place access to which is in some way restricted and which is therefore more in the nature of a semi-public place. Lerner v. Schectman, 228 F.Supp. 354 (D.Minn.1964), a case decided under the 1909 Act, holds that a performance may be found to be public even if the composition of the audience is restricted to some degree if, despite such restriction, a substantial portion of the public has the potential to attend the performance. See also 2 M. Nimmer, § 8.14[C][1], at 8–138–39. Maxwell's does not limit use of its viewing rooms in any manner other than a requirement that all viewers be either relatives or close social acquaintances. The defendants contend that this restriction on the use of the viewing rooms is enough to take Maxwell's showcasing outside the realm of a public performance. The plaintiffs argue that Maxwell's is clearly open to the public and that, at any rate, it is a place where a substantial number of persons "outside of a normal circle of a family and its social acquaintances is gathered."

We find that the composition of the audience at Maxwell's is of a public nature, and that showcasing the plaintiffs' copyrighted motion pictures results in repeated public performances which infringe the plaintiffs' copyrights. Our finding is based on the view that the viewing rooms at Maxwell's more closely resemble mini-movie theaters than living rooms away from home. At least as regards the composition of the audiences at Maxwell's, the showcasing operation is not distinguishable in any significant manner from the exhibition of films at a conventional movie theater. Both types of facilities are open to all members of the general public. Access to the actual viewing area of both theaters is limited to paying customers. Seating in both facilities is of a finite number and, at both facilities, the actual performance of the motion picture is handled by employees of the theater. We recognize that each performance at Maxwell's is limited in its potential audience size to a maximum of four viewers at any one time, however, we do not believe this limitation takes Maxwell's showcasing operation outside the ambit of the statutory definition of a public performance because the potential exists for a substantial portion of the public to attend such performances over a period of time.

Our conclusion that Maxwell's showcasing constitutes infringing public performances is bolstered by the second clause of the statutory definition of public performance. Under this clause, to perform a work publicly means:

> (2) to transmit or otherwise communicate a performance * * * of the work to a place specified by clause (1) or to the public, by means of any device or process, whether the members of the public capable of receiving the performance * * * receive it in the same place or in separate places and at the same time or at different times.

17 U.S.C. § 101 (1976). Professor Nimmer, in a remarkably prescient discussion of this portion of the definition, concluded that Congress intended that "*if the same copy* * * * of a given work is repeatedly played (i.e. 'performed') by different members of the public, albeit at different times, this constitutes a 'public' performance." 2 M. Nimmer, § 8.14[C][3], at 8–142. Nimmer cites as one example the peep show where, although no more than one person at a time can observe a given performance, repeated playing of the same copy of the material results in numerous performances seen by the public, Nimmer, foreseeing an operation similar to Maxwell's, goes on to state that:

> one may anticipate the possibility of theaters in which patrons occupy separate screening rooms, for greater privacy, and in order not to have to await a given hour for commencement of a given film. These too should

obviously be regarded as public performances within the underlying rationale of the Copyright Act.

Id. at 8–142. The two Maxwell's facilities each have only one copy of a given film title and, therefore, must perform the same copy of a given work repeatedly. We find that Congress intended that this portion of the definition also serve as protection for copyright owners from infringing performances such as those accomplished by Maxwell's showcasing.

* * *

Conclusion

The defendants' showcasing operations at Maxwell's Video Showcase and Maxwell's Video Showcase East constitute public performances of the plaintiffs' copyrighted works and are therefore infringements of that exclusive right. The plaintiffs' motion for summary judgment will be granted and, accordingly, the defendants' motion for summary judgment will be denied. * * *

Questions

1. Does the decision in this case turn upon the references to "at different times" in the Section 101 definition of "To perform or display a work 'publicly'," or would the same result be justified even without this phrase?

2. Does the performance of music on a commercial phonograph record in the privacy of one's home constitute a public performance because other members of the public in the privacy of their respective homes are playing duplicates of the same recorded performance "at different times"? Would such a construction effectively undermine the Section 115 compulsory license?

3. Do individual performances in private homes recorded on video cassettes constitute "public" performances? Should it make any difference if the video cassette has been rented rather than purchased from a video store? Should a rental rather than a purchase of a commercial phonograph record affect the answer to Question 2 above?

Collateral Reference

Nimmer on Copyright, § 8.14[C][3].

2. *The Requirement That the Performance Be for Profit*

Note *

Under Sections 1(c) and 1(e) of the 1909 Act, the unauthorized public performance of a musical or nondramatic literary work would infringe only if such performance were for profit. This was in contrast with an unauthorized public performance of a dramatic work, which infringed regardless of whether or not it was for profit. Why this distinction? It was reasoned that if a dramatic work was performed, even on a non-profit basis, those who viewed such performance were not likely thereafter to attend a performance for profit

---

* Nimmer on Copyright, § 8.15[A].

of the same work. Therefore any performance of a dramatic work was thought in some degree to diminish the potential revenue to be obtained from performances for profit. It was thought that this is not true of performances of musical compositions and nondramatic literary works. That is, so the argument went, one who attends a nonprofit performance of such a work rather than being sated with it, is more likely thereafter to wish to see a professional (for profit) performance of the same work.

This distinction appears to have had some merit in the case of musical compositions where the public interest is not exhausted by an initial performance regardless of whether or not it be for profit. It may well be questioned, however, whether this rationale is equally applicable to nondramatic literary works. A public reading of selections from Hemingway or Mark Twain even if not for profit is very likely to reduce the potential audience available for a subsequent for profit reading of the same work. The same would be true in some, but probably in a lesser degree with respect to the reading of poetry.

If the above rationale did not completely justify the imposition of a "for profit" limitation on musical and nondramatic literary work performing rights, there was at least one additional justification. It was thought that to prohibit unlicensed nonprofit performances of musical and nondramatic literary works in such public places as schools and churches would constitute an undue restriction on the benefits which should be available to the public. However, this objective was capable of achievement without immunizing all nonprofit performances of such works. This more selective approach has been adopted under the current Act. Instead of exempting all not-for-profit performances in the case of musical and nondramatic literary works, the Act first broadly includes all public performances within the rights of the copyright owner, and then carves out certain discrete exceptions. Two of the major exemptions, under Secs. 110(1) and 110(4), are subject to the condition that the performances are not for profit, but in each case this condition, although necessary, is not sufficient. We will first explore the pre-1978 case law on what constitutes a nonprofit performance, which for the purposes of these exemptions may still be applicable. We will then turn to certain of the other conditions which must be satisfied under the Secs. 110(1) and (4) exemptions.

HERBERT v. SHANLEY

Supreme Court of the United States, 1917.
242 U.S. 591, 37 S.Ct. 232, 61 L.Ed. 511.

Mr. Justice Holmes delivered the opinion of the court.

These two cases present the same question: whether the performance of a copyrighted musical composition in a restaurant or hotel without charge for admission to hear it infringes the exclusive right of the owner of the copyright to perform the work publicly for profit. Act of March 4, 1909, c. 320, § 1(e), 35 Stat. 1075. The last numbered case was decided before the other and may be stated first. The plaintiff owns the copyright of a lyric comedy in which is a march called "From Maine to Oregon." It took out a separate copyright for the march and published it separately. The defendant hotel company caused this march to be performed in the dining room of the Vanderbilt Hotel for the entertainment of guests during meal times, in the way now common, by an orchestra employed and paid by the company. It was held by the Circuit Court of Appeals, reversing the decision of the District Court, that this was not a performance for profit within the meaning of the act. 221 Fed.Rep. 229. 136 C.C.A. 639.

The other case is similar so far as the present discussion is concerned. The plaintiffs were the composers and owners of a comic opera entitled "Sweethearts," containing a song of the same title as a leading feature in the performance. There is a copyright for the opera and also one for the song which is published and sold separately. This the Shanley Company caused to be sung by professional singers, upon a stage in its restaurant on Broadway, accompanied by an orchestra. The District Court after holding that by the separate publication the plaintiffs' rights were limited to those conferred by the separate copyright, a matter that it will not be necessary to discuss, followed the

Plaintiff Victor Herbert, well-known composer, and founder of the American Society of Composers, Authors and Publishers (ASCAP).

decision in 221 Fed.Rep. 229, as to public performance for profit. 222 Fed.Rep. 344. The decree was affirmed by the Circuit Court of Appeals. 229 Fed.Rep. 340, 143 C.C.A. 460.

If the rights under the copyright are infringed only by a performance where money is taken at the door they are very imperfectly protected. Performances not different in kind from those of the defendants could be given that might compete with and even destroy the success of the monopoly that the law intends the plaintiffs to have. It is enough to say that there is no need to construe the statute so narrowly. The defendants' performances are not eleemosynary. They are part of a total for which the public pays, and the fact that the price of the whole is attributed to a particular item which those present are expected to order, is not important. It is true that the music is not the sole object, but neither is the food, which probably could be got cheaper elsewhere. The object is a repast in surroundings that to people having limited powers of conversation or disliking the rival noise give a luxurious pleasure not to be had from eating a silent meal. If music did not pay it would be given up. If it pays it pays out of the public's pocket. Whether it pays or not the purpose of employing it is profit and that is enough.

Decrees reversed.

Questions

1. In the Sec. 110(4) exemption under the current Copyright Act, what is the meaning of the phrase "without any purpose of direct or indirect commercial advantage"? The House Report states that this phrase "expressly adopts the principle established by the court decisions construing the 'for profit' limitation [under the 1909 Act]." H.Rep., p. 85. Why, then, did the drafters select this new phrase rather than simply requiring that the performance not be "for profit"? Consider this in connection with the next case.

2. Why is the Sec. 110(4) exemption limited to the performance of nondramatic literary and musical works? Why is there no such limitation under the Sec. 110(1) exemption?

3. In addition to the absence of a "commercial advantage", what other conditions must be satisfied in order to claim a Sec. 110(4) exemption? What if compensation is paid to the producer? Is the producer necessarily the "promoter" or the "organizer"? What if a performer receives compensation for certain services which include but are not limited to the performance in question? What "reasons" for objection must be stated by a copyright owner under Sec. 110(4)(B)(ii)? Is a copyright owner entitled to be informed of a contemplated performance sufficiently in advance so as to be able to serve a notice of objection within the required seven days before the date of performance?

4. In addition to the requirement of a "nonprofit" institution, what other conditions must be satisfied in order to claim a Sec. 110(1) exemption? What constitutes an "educational" institution? Are "face-to-face teaching activities" limited to in person (or "live") performances as distinguished from motion picture or other audiovisual performances? Since exempted performances are limited to those "by instructors or pupils", does this mean that a performance

by an invited guest will not qualify for the Sec. 110(1) exemption? What substantive limitation is involved in limiting the Sec. 110(1) exemption to performances "in the course of * * * teaching activities"? What constitutes a "similar place devoted to instruction"?

Collateral Reference

Nimmer on Copyright, §§ 8.15[B] and [E]. On the other Section 110 exemptions, see generally § 8.15.

Note *

The Rise and Fall of The Doctrine of Secondary Transmissions Under the 1909 Act

In *Buck v. Jewell-LaSalle Realty Co.*[1] the defendant, operator of the LaSalle Hotel in Kansas City, Mo., maintained in its hotel a master radio receiving set which was wired to each of the public and private rooms in the hotel. Individual loudspeakers were located in each room. The defendant had no contractual or other arrangement with any broadcasting stations. It simply picked up via its master receiving set programs broadcast over the air in the same manner any other listener with a radio might do. A copyrighted popular song owned by the plaintiffs was repeatedly broadcast without authority by a local radio station. Defendant received such broadcasts over its master radio receiving set, so that they were heard through the loudspeakers located throughout the hotel. Plaintiffs brought an action for copyright infringement against both Wilson Duncan, the operator of the radio station, and also against defendant. A decree *pro confesso* for failure to answer was entered against Duncan.[2] Ultimately the following question was certified to the Supreme Court:

> "Do the acts of a hotel proprietor, in making available to his guests through the instrumentality of a radio receiving set and loud speakers installed in his hotel and under his control and for the entertainment of his guests, the hearing of a copyrighted musical composition which has been broadcast from a radio transmitting station, constitute a performance of such a composition within the meaning of 17 U.S.C.A. sec. 1(e)?"

The Supreme Court answered the aforesaid question by holding that the specified acts by the defendant did indeed constitute a performance under Sec. 1(e) of the 1909 Act. In an opinion per Justice Brandeis, the Court reasoned that since radio waves are not in themselves audible, but must be rectified or converted into direct currents which actuate a loudspeaker in order to reproduce in the air sound waves of audible frequencies, this process was "essentially a reproduction" of the original rendition and as such a second performance, or what has later come to be called a secondary transmission.

Despite certain analytical inadequacies,[3] the *Jewell-LaSalle* doctrine went unchallenged for many years. But with the advent of cable television, also

---

* Nimmer on Copyright, § 8.18[A].

1. 283 U.S. 191, 51 S.Ct. 410, 75 L.Ed. 971 (1931).

2. See Buck v. Duncan, 32 F.2d 366 (W.D.Mo.1929).

3. See Nimmer on Copyright, § 8.18[A].

known as community antenna television, or CATV,[4] the question was raised as to whether the doctrine of secondary transmissions was applicable in this new medium. Cable television systems receive the signals of television broadcasting stations, amplify them, and then transmit such signals by cable or microwave, and ultimately send the signals by wire to their paying subscribers.[5] Originally, the primary function of cable television was to facilitate satisfactory reception of local television stations for persons living in localities which by reason of mountainous terrain, tall buildings, or other conditions could not receive a satisfactory signal through direct broadcast from such stations. Later, however, an equally or more important function of cable television became that of making available in a given community signals from distant television stations which by reason of the distance of the stations would not otherwise be available, even under conditions of clear reception. As of 1976 there were some 3500 cable television systems throughout the nation with approximately 10.8 million subscribers, and an annual revenue of about $770 million.[6] Since then it has increasingly become a primary form of television reception.

Most cable television programming does not consist of programs originated by the cable systems. It consists rather of the transmission, or more accurately the "secondary transmission"[7] of signals broadcast by others. The cable television operators took the position that they need not obtain licenses from the copyright owners of the material thus broadcast. The copyright owners, however, argued that the function of cable television was essentially the same as that of the LaSalle Hotel in the *Jewell-LaSalle* case, and that, therefore, under the doctrine of that case cable television systems were infringing their copyrights by "performing" without a license the material contained in the television broadcasts.

This issue was ultimately decided by the United States Supreme Court in *Fortnightly Corp. v. United Artists Television, Inc.,*[8] which held that the functions of a cable television system did not constitute a "performance" within the meaning of Sections 1(c) and 1(d) of the 1909 Act. The Court started from the premise that cable television systems do not "'perform' the respondent's copyrighted works in any conventional sense of that term, or in any manner envisaged by the Congress that enacted the law in 1909." Recognizing that the statutory language must be read "in the light of drastic technological change," it nevertheless concluded that such change could not transform the cable television function of enhancing the viewer's capacity to receive the broadcaster's signals into a "performance." The Court acknowledged that a performance in the copyright sense may be something less than the conventional performance rendered before an audience present at the place of performance. Thus a television station by the act of broadcasting is rendering a performance in a copyright sense notwithstanding the fact that viewers play an indispensable role in the process because, unlike an entirely passive audience present at the

---

4. This is the abbreviation for the commonly used designation "community antenna television." The district court in the *Fortnightly* case (discussed infra) referred to this designation as a misnomer since the "systems are not 'community' ventures. They are largescale commercial enterprises * * *." 255 F.Supp. at 180. The terms "cable television" and "cable systems" are increasingly used instead of CATV.

5. See United States v. Southwestern Cable Co., 392 U.S. 157, 88 S.Ct. 1994, 20 L.Ed.2d 1001 (1968).

6. H.Rep., p. 88.

7. "A 'secondary transmission' is the further transmitting of a primary transmission simultaneously with the primary transmission * * *." 17 U.S.C.A. Sec. 111(f).

8. 392 U.S. 390, 88 S.Ct. 2084, 20 L.Ed.2d 1176 (1968).

place of performance, television viewers must themselves supply sets and antenna in order to accomplish the broadcaster's performance. "Thus, while both broadcaster and viewer play crucial roles in the total television process, a line is drawn between them. One is treated as active performer; the other, as passive beneficiary." [9] Having posed this dichotomy, the Court concluded that cable television "falls on the viewer's side of the line," since it merely enhances the viewer's capacity to receive the signals.

Policy questions aside, the Court's reasoning was faultless but for the major obstacle of how to treat the precedent of the *Jewell-LaSalle* case, and the secondary transmission doctrine which it fostered. If that doctrine were still to be regarded as viable law, then the Court's analogy to the broadcaster's performance (upon which its conclusion was predicated) was in error. Under *Jewell-LaSalle*, although the broadcaster accomplished the primary performance, a television viewer by activating his set himself brought about a secondary or multiple performance.

The Supreme Court in *Fortnightly* implicitly discarded the secondary transmission doctrine, and explicitly dealt with the *Jewell-LaSalle* case by referring to it as "a questionable 35-year-old decision that in actual practice has not been applied outside its own factual context,[10] and which "must be understood as limited to its own facts." [11]

The *Fortnightly* decision left unanswered certain additional questions relating to the copyright status of cable television operations. Some of these questions were later answered by the Supreme Court in *Teleprompter Corp. v. Columbia Broadcasting Sys., Inc.*[12] The plaintiffs in *Teleprompter* had argued that the changes in the method of operation of cable television that had occurred since the time of the *Fortnightly* case warranted a determination that cable television falls on the broadcaster's "side of the line." The most significant of these changes was the fact that the cable systems in *Fortnightly* all involved local signals, while in *Teleprompter* a number of the defendant systems imported distant signals, i.e., they transmitted to their subscribers programs from television stations whose distance from the community serviced by the cable system was such that antennae, even of an advanced type such as that used by cable systems, located in or near such community could not have received the signal "off the air." The community could receive such distant signals only by reason of the cable televisions' use of antennae at a point distant from the ultimate community of reception, and its further use of transmitting equipment, such as microwave relays, to send the signals received over the air to the cable television community. The Court of Appeals held that "when a CATV system imports distant signals it is no longer within the ambit of the *Fortnightly* doctrine, and there is no reason to treat it differently from any other person who, without license, displays a copyrighted work to an audience who would not otherwise receive it. For this reason, we conclude that the CATV system is a 'performer' of whatever programs from these distant signals that it distributes to its subscribers." [13] But this holding was reversed by the Supreme Court, which held that "the reception and rechanneling of

9. 392 U.S. at 398–9.
10. 392 U.S. at 401, n. 30.
11. 392 U.S. at 397, n. 18, 88 S.Ct. at 2088, n. 18.
12. 415 U.S. 394, 94 S.Ct. 1129, 39 L.Ed.2d 415 (1974).
13. Columbia Broadcasting System, Inc. v. Teleprompter Corp., 476 F.2d 338 (2d Cir.1973), judgment affirmed in part reversed in part 415 U.S. 394, 94 S.Ct. 1129, 39 L.Ed.2d 415 (1974).

these signals for simultaneous viewing is essentially a viewer function, irrespective of the distance between the broadcasting station and the ultimate viewer."

Although the decisions in *Fortnightly* and *Teleprompter* effectively foreclosed application of the secondary transmission doctrine to cable television under the 1909 Act, this arguably left intact the *Jewell-LaSalle* holding in its original context, i.e., that of secondary transmissions of radio transmissions. The multiple performance doctrine came full circle when the remaining viability of *Jewell-LaSalle* in the radio context was squarely raised in *Twentieth Century Music Corp. v. Aiken*.[14] Aiken had a radio in his restaurant which he played throughout each day for the entertainment of his customers. The radio had outlets to four speakers, installed in the restaurant ceiling. ASCAP (representing Twentieth Century Music Corp. and other music publishers) demanded that Aiken obtain from it a performing rights license on the theory that he was engaging in secondary transmissions as in *Jewell-LaSalle*. Aiken refused. The District Court held for the plaintiff,[15] but the Court of Appeals for the Third Circuit reversed, holding that *Fortnightly* rather than *Jewell-LaSalle* controlled.[16] The Supreme Court affirmed the Court of Appeals, and in doing so all but sounded the death knell of the secondary transmission doctrine. Relying upon *Fortnightly,* the court in effect held that the act of picking up radio signals off the air and transmitting them through radio speakers simply did not constitute a "performance," and hence need not be licensed. What the defendant did fell on the "viewer's" (or, in this case, the listener's) side of the broadcaster-viewer line drawn in *Fortnightly.* Such reception was held not to constitute a performance separate from and in addition to the performance attributable to the broadcasting station.

Questions

1. Could the Supreme Court in *Fortnightly* have distinguished *Jewell-LaSalle* rather than limiting it to "its own facts"? What significance, if any, is there in the fact that in *Fortnightly* the CATV subscribers each operated his own television set while in *Jewell-LaSalle* the guests in their hotel rooms merely activated loudspeakers?

2. As a matter of policy, and not of statutory construction, should an unlicensed CATV operation constitute an act of copyright infringement? Would this result in a double payment to the copyright owner?

Collateral Reference

Nimmer on Copyright, § 8.18[A], [E][4][a].

Note

Secondary Transmissions under the Copyright Act of 1976

Among the many difficult issues debated in connection with the copyright

---

14. 422 U.S. 151, 95 S.Ct. 2040, 45 L.Ed.2d 84 (1975).

15. Twentieth Century Music Corp. v. Aiken, 356 F.Supp. 271 (W.D.Pa.1973). Judge Weis' opinion begins: "Whether this is a 'Jewell' of a case for the plaintiffs or a 'Fortnightly' event for the defendant is the question to be resolved * * *." The court concluded that it was a "Jewell" of a case.

16. Twentieth Century Music Corp. v. Aiken, 500 F.2d 127 (3d Cir.1974).

revision which resulted in the current Act, none was more intractible than that of whether and to what extent secondary transmissions of copyrighted works by cable television systems should be regarded as within the ambit of copyright control. As indicated in the preceding Note, by reason of the *Fortnightly* and *Teleprompter* decisions, under the 1909 Act cable television operators were free of copyright liability. After heated debate, Congress concluded "that cable systems are commercial enterprises whose basic retransmission operations are based on the carriage of copyrighted program material and that copyright royalties should be paid by cable operators to the creators of such programs."[1] At the same time, it was recognized "that it would be impractical and unduly burdensome to require every cable system to negotiate with every copyright owner whose work was retransmitted by a cable system."[2] The compromise solution was to adopt in Section 111 a compulsory license system whereby the cable operators are not required to obtain the consent of the copyright owners, nor to negotiate license fees, but copyright owners are entitled to be paid prescribed royalties for the secondary transmission of their works by cable television. The complex compulsory license system which emerged as a result of this compromise is analyzed in depth in Nimmer on Copyright, § 8.18[E].

Questions

1. If a case involving the facts of *Jewell-LaSalle* (see preceding Note) were to arise under the current Act, would the court reach the same result? See Sec. 111(a)(1). Did the secondary transmission by the LaSalle Hotel consist "entirely" of a relaying "to the private lodgings of guests * * *"?

2. If a case involving the facts of *Aiken* (see preceding Note) were to arise under the current Act, would the court reach the same result? See Sec. 110(5). Is the Sec. 110(5) exemption available to a restaurant operating "a single receiving apparatus of a kind commonly used in private homes" if a "cover charge" is imposed on all patrons regardless of whether and how much they order? If a "minimum charge" is imposed? If there are more than four loudspeakers attached to the receiving apparatus?

Collateral Reference

Nimmer on Copyright, § 8.18[C][1], [2].

3. Performing Rights Societies

Note *

The performance right as it relates to musical works is probably the most important of the performance rights, and surely the most difficult to police and enforce on an individual basis. The number of unauthorized performances of a dramatic work are rarely so numerous as to present any great problem of detection or collection. Musical works, however, by their very nature may be performed on such an extensive basis as to render it impossible for individual composers and publishers to enforce effectively their performance rights on an individual basis. This problem resulted in the founding in 1914 of the Ameri-

---

1. H.Rep., p. 89.
2. Id.

* Nimmer on Copyright, § 8.19.

can Society of Composers, Authors and Publishers, generally known as ASCAP. Under its auspices song writers and publishers collectively enforce their performance rights. The moving force in the founding of this first American performing rights society was Victor Herbert and his attorney, Nathan Burkan. ASCAP remains to date one of the most important of the performing rights societies. Another important such society currently in operation in the United States is Broadcast Music, Inc., known as B.M.I. There are in addition several small performing rights societies which are privately owned. The most important of these is SESAC, Inc., formerly known as the Society of European Stage Authors and Composers.

The manner in which performing rights societies operate is a most complex and voluminous subject raising problems primarily of an anti-trust rather than copyright nature. The subject is beyond the scope of this treatise,[1] and will be but briefly sketched here in terms of the ASCAP method of operation.

ASCAP as the transferee of its members, licenses the small or non-dramatic performing rights[2] in the musical works of its members. Therefore any person or business enterprise which wishes to perform any such work in a non-dramatic manner must look either to ASCAP, or under the consent decree first entered in 1941,[3] to the individual composer. ASCAP grants two types of licenses. One is a blanket license which permits the licensee to publicly perform for profit in a non-dramatic manner any of the songs in the ASCAP repertory in return for either a flat fee or a percentage of gross receipt fee. The other form of license provides for payment of a specified fee for each program in which any such music is so performed. Problems have arisen under the consent decree with respect to a licensee's right to obtain a license for a single selection.

The consent decree changed the practice with respect to granting performing licenses for music contained in motion pictures. Formerly theater exhibitors were required to obtain such licenses, but under the current practice licensing occurs at the source. That is, motion picture producers must obtain performing licenses, as well as synchronization licenses.[4] Performing rights and synchronization rights are generally jointly granted in a single instrument by music publishers via the Harry Fox Agency, Inc. However, such performing licenses currently do not include the right to perform the music on film in connection with television broadcasts of such film. Accordingly, television stations (and now cable systems, as well) must also be licensed in order to exhibit on television films containing such music.

The monies collected by ASCAP are pooled in a common fund, and thereafter divided equally between the publisher members and the writer

1. See Shemel and Krasilovsky, This Business of Music (Rev. ed. 1977), pp. 162–178.

2. As to the distinction between small (or non-dramatic) performing rights and grand (or dramatic) performing rights, see The Robert Stigwood Group Limited v. Sperber, infra.

3. United States v. ASCAP, 32 C.O.Bull. 601 (S.D.N.Y.1960), 37 C.O.Bull. 559 (S.D.N.Y.1969). See also the consent decree against B.M.I. in United States v. Broadcast Music, Inc., 35 C.O.Bull. 870 (S.D.N.Y.1966).

4. In the usage of the motion picture industry, a synchronization license is a license of the right to reproduce a musical work on a motion picture sound track. See M. Witmark and Sons v. Jensen, 80 F.Supp. 843 (D.C.Minn.1948); Paine v. Electrical Research Prods., Inc., 27 F.Supp. 780 (S.D.N.Y.1939); Encore Music Publishers, Inc. v. London Film Prods., Inc., 89 U.S.P.Q. 501 (S.D.N.Y.1951); Foreign & Domestic Music Corp. v. Licht, 196 F.2d 627 (2d Cir.1952).

members. The individual allocation within such two groups is made according to complex formulae set forth in the amended consent decree.

ASCAP has been subjected to much anti-trust litigation,[5] and has also encountered considerable difficulty with state laws intended to modify or eliminate ASCAP's functioning within their borders.[6]

THE ROBERT STIGWOOD GROUP LIMITED v. SPERBER

United States Court of Appeals, Second Circuit, 1972.
457 F.2d 50.

Before MURRAH, KAUFMAN and OAKES, CIRCUIT JUDGES.

IRVING R. KAUFMAN, CIRCUIT JUDGE:

The rock opera *Jesus Christ Superstar* and several of its individual musical compositions have enjoyed large commercial success as well as substantial critical acclaim. More than two million records and tape cartridges of the full opera have been sold, the authorized touring production grossed over one million dollars in its first four weeks, and tickets to the Broadway version have been among the more difficult to acquire. We can understand, therefore, the desire of promoters and producers throughout the country to capitalize on the success of *Jesus Christ Superstar*, and it is not surprising that one consequence of its explosive yet impermanent popularity is litigation. The role of the courts must be to prevent exploitation of the opera in a manner that infringes the rights of the creators of the work and their assignees.

I

Timothy Rice wrote the libretto for *Jesus Christ Superstar* and Andrew Lloyd Webber composed the score of the opera's overture and 22 songs which depict the last seven days in the life of Christ. Rice and Webber assigned the rights in the work (except "King Herod's Song") to Leeds Music Limited which duly obtained United States copyrights for the opera as a "dramatico-musical composition" pursuant to 17 U.S.C. § 5(d) and for several of the individual songs as "musical compositions" pursuant to 17 U.S.C. § 5(e). Leeds Music Limited assigned the United States copyrights to Leeds Music Corporation. The Robert Stigwood

---

5. Alden-Rochelle, Inc. v. ASCAP, 80 F.Supp. 888 (S.D.N.Y.1948); see M. Witmark & Sons v. Jensen, 80 F.Supp. 843 (D.C.Minn.1948); Buck v. Gallagher, 36 F.Supp. 405 (W.D.Wash.1940); Columbia Broadcasting Sys., Inc. v. ASCAP, 400 F.Supp. 737 (S.D.N.Y.1975); cf. Affiliated Music Enterprises, Inc. v. Sesac, Inc., 160 F.Supp. 865 (S.D.N.Y.1958); Schwartz v. Broadcast Music, Inc., 180 F.Supp. 322 (S.D.N.Y.1959); Sam Fox Publishing Co. v. United States, 366 U.S. 683 (1961); Columbia Broadcasting Sys., Inc. v. ASCAP, 337 F.Supp. 394 (S.D.N.Y.1972).

6. Watson v. Buck, 313 U.S. 387 (1941); Marsh v. Buck, 313 U.S. 406 (1941); see Buck v. Gallagher, 307 U.S. 95 (1939); Gibbs v. Buck, 307 U.S. 66 (1939); Taylor v. Washington, 29 Wash.2d 638, 188 P.2d 671 (1948); Remick Music Corp. v. Interstate Hotel Co., 58 F.Supp. 523 (D.C.Neb.1944) aff'd 157 F.2d 744 (8th Cir.1946); Woodman of the World Life Ins. Soc'y v. ASCAP, 146 Neb. 358, 19 N.W.2d 540 (1945); Buck v. Harton, 33 F.Supp. 1014 (M.D.Tenn.1940); Palm Tavern, Inc. v. ASCAP, 153 Fla. 544, 15 So.2d 191 (1943).

Group Limited ("Stigwood") acquired the rights for stage productions and dramatic presentations of the opera, and its rights are those allegedly infringed. Defendant Betty Sperber is a booking agent doing business as "The Original American Touring Company" ("OATC") and concerts presented by it are represented as being performed by The Original American Touring Company. The business details of the concerts are handled by Betty Sperber Management of which Sperber is President. Each OATC so-called concert consists of 20 of the 23 songs from *Jesus Christ Superstar,* sung sequentially with one exception, and three additional religious works. Sperber avers that other programs not involving *Jesus Christ Superstar* are planned by OATC.

Stigwood brought this suit, *inter alia,* to enjoin: one, OATC's performance of *Jesus Christ Superstar* or portions thereof; two, any references to *Jesus Christ Superstar* in advertisements for OATC performances; and three, use of the name The Original American Touring

A scene from the Universal film *Jesus Christ Superstar.*

Company. The district court's preliminary injunction, 332 F.Supp. 1206, issued pursuant to 17 U.S.C. § 112, barred only the references to *Jesus Christ Superstar* in OATC advertisements, and both parties appealed.

OATC's claim that its productions do not infringe Stigwood's rights is based upon the usual and customary agreement between the American Society of Composers, Authors and Publishers ("ASCAP") and Leeds Music Corporation, an ASCAP member. Although a complete description of the purpose of ASCAP and its methodology are unnecessary to our decision, some understanding of its function is vital to an examination of the agreements it makes with its members. The Copyright Act of 1909 granted several rights to the holders of copyrights in works including the exclusive right "to perform the copyrighted work publicly for profit if it be a musical composition." 17 U.S.C. § 1(e). Composers and publishers soon realized it was impractical for each copyright holder to attempt to enforce this right since he could not possibly police all public performances for profit of every musical composition throughout the United States. ASCAP was formed to meet this need. By obtaining licenses from its members, this organization, staffed for the purpose, could enforce the performing rights of its members. It was believed, however, that each copyright owner could appropriately police and license performances of musical comedies or operas because of the relative infrequency of such productions and the lengthy preparation and publicity which must precede these productions. See, Nimmer, "Copyright 1955," 43 Cal.L.Rev. 791, 798 (1955).

In any event, ASCAP is authorized by its members to license only nondramatic performing rights of compositions in its repertory. Consequently, pursuant to the standard ASCAP agreement utilized here, ASCAP was authorized by Leeds to give:

> 1. (b) The non-exclusive right of public performance of the separate numbers, songs, fragments or arrangements, melodies or selections forming part or parts of musical plays and dramatico-musical compositions, the Owner reserving and excepting from this grant the right of performance of musical plays and dramatico-musical compositions in their entirety, or any part of such plays or dramatico-musical compositions on the legitimate stage.

Thus, while ASCAP licensees[1] can perform the individual songs from *Jesus Christ Superstar,* whether copyrighted individually or merely as part of the opera as a whole, paragraph 3 of the standard license indicates that it does not extend to presentations of:

---

1. Stigwood also makes the claim that some of the promoters with whom Sperber has dealt and who are planning to present OATC performances have not obtained ASCAP licenses. Such performances, of course, would be improper. But, no such promoter is a defendant to this action, nor is a resolution of this claim essential to our ruling. In any event, OATC insists that it undertakes to ensure that the promoters of its shows obtain ASCAP licenses. Such licenses are, of course, non-exclusive and are readily obtainable. See United States v. American Society of Composers, Authors and Publishers, Civil Action No. 13–95 (1941), Amended Consent Decree, 1950.

(a) Oratorios, choral, operatic, or dramatico-musical works * * * in their entirety or songs or other excerpts from operas or musical plays accompanied either by word, pantomime, dance or visual representation of the work from which the music is taken; but fragments or instrumental selections from such works may be instrumentally rendered without words, dialogue, costume, accompanying dramatic action or scenic accessory and unaccompanied by any stage action or visual representation (by motion picture or otherwise) of the work of which such music forms a part.

Both parties and the court agree, therefore, that selections from *Jesus Christ Superstar* can be properly presented by ASCAP licensees if they are presented in "nondramatic" performances. See generally, M. Nimmer, Copyright § 125.6 (1971). Accordingly, we must decide if OATC's performances fall into the "dramatic" or "nondramatic" category.

The Copyright Act distinguishes between "musical" and "dramatico-musical" works.[2] The former are infringed only by public performances for profit whereas the latter are infringed by any public performance. *Compare* 17 U.S.C.A. § 1(d) *with* 17 U.S.C.A. § 1(e). In our effort to find some guidance in distinguishing between musical and dramatico-musical productions, we were soon to learn of the dearth of cases on the subject. We received some aid, however, from Judge Learned Hand's statement that a performance in "words and music alone may constitute a dramatic performance, and it did not matter that the performance was only of a scene or part of a scene." Herbert v. Shanley, 222 F. 344, 345 (S.D.N.Y.1915) (citations omitted), affirmed, 229 F. 340 (2d Cir.1916), reversed on other grounds, 242 U.S. 591, 37 S.Ct. 232, 61 L.Ed. 513 (1917). The Supreme Court's reversal of *Herbert*, however, nipped this line of cases in the bud by construing the "for profit" language so liberally that it obviated the need for further litigation over what was "dramatic" or "nondramatic." 242 U.S. at 594–595, 37 S.Ct. 232.

The only case cited to us which discusses the scope of the ASCAP license is April Productions, Inc. v. Strand Enterprises, Inc., 221 F.2d 292 (2d Cir.1955). In *April* the copyright owner of *The Student Prince* sued the proprietor of a cabaret, "The Harem," for infringement based upon performances there of a medley of songs from *The Student Prince*. The medley was a small part of one of ten scenes of the nightclub's show, and was not connected by a story line or otherwise. The Court stated:

> Even if The Harem put on a dramatic performance, [the entire show of ten scenes], the selections * * * were not part of it. The worst that could be said would be that they were sung in an intermission between the acts of a dramatic performance. Such a rendition is "nondramatic" within the meaning of the license.

---

2. Dramatico-musical works are considered dramas for the purpose of 17 U.S.C.A. § 1(d). See 37 C.F.R. § 202.7 (1972).

221 F.2d at 296. In the opinion, Judge Dimock (District Judge, sitting by designation), laboring without guidance or precedent, of course, was unable to cite us to a single authority.

In any event, Strand's use of several songs from *The Student Prince* pales by comparison with Sperber's use of almost the entire score from *Jesus Christ Superstar*. The twenty musical compositions from *Superstar* were almost the entire OATC performance rather than less than one-tenth as in "The Harem" club's show. Moreover, *April* has been severely criticized as inadequately protective of and virtually extinguishing dramatic performing rights with respect to musical compositions. As Professor Nimmer puts it:

> Under the rule of this case one could by simply obtaining an ASCAP license perform in a new musical play all of the music from "South Pacific" providing the "book" for the new production is not borrowed from "South Pacific." The ASCAP membership could hardly have intended to permit the performance of their musical compositions in Broadway musicals or similar productions in return for mere payment of the ASCAP fee.

M. Nimmer, Copyright § 125.6 (1971).

Where the defendant has not even supplied a *new* "book" in its performances, a determination that dramatic rights have been infringed would seem simple. But, OATC asserts that plaintiff's "book" is not used either and insists that there is no story line whatever to defendant's performances. Recently, in Rice v. American Program Bureau, 446 F.2d 685 (2d Cir.1971) a panel of this court in a 2–1 decision, favored this contention of defendants. *Rice* also dealt with performances of *Jesus Christ Superstar* allegedly executed pursuant to the ASCAP license. Because of the sparse record before it, the majority was unable to conclude that the performance was "dramatic." It did however, make clear that "presentation of all of the songs from the opera *Jesus Christ Superstar* without costumes, words, or scenery, but in sequence could arguably develop the overall plot of the opera, and * * * might possibly be 'dramatic'." Id. at 690. We have come to the conclusion that the fuller record before us establishes that a dramatic story is developed by defendant's productions, as Judge Smith in his dissenting opinion in *Rice* would have found and District Judge Motley did find even on the skimpier record there.

The facts before us vividly paint the dramatic nature of OATC's performance. Nowhere has Sperber disputed the accuracy of Stigwood's Exhibit 3 which is a program of one of OATC's concerts. A comparison between this exhibit and Exhibit 4, which is the list of songs incorporated in the recording of the opera,[3] establishes that 20 of 23 *Superstar* selections are performed in defendant's concert, all but one in identical sequence as in the copyrighted opera. The conclusion is inescapable that the story of the last seven days in the life of Christ

---

3. The copyrighted score and libretto contain music and lyrics for an overture and 22 songs without intervening dialogue. The authorized recorded version faithfully reproduces the work on two records with a total playing time of 87 minutes and 16 seconds.

is portrayed in the OATC performances substantially as in *Superstar.* One might appropriately ask why, if OATC did not intend that the same story be told, would it insist on preserving the sequence of the songs presented in *Jesus Christ Superstar,* which when performed in that fashion, tell the story even in the absence of intervening dialogue? As *Rice* instructed, the lack of scenery or costumes in the OATC production does not *ipso facto* prevent it from being dramatic.[4] See Shafter, Musical Copyright 57 (2d Ed.1939). Indeed, radio performances of operas are considered dramatic, because the story is told by the music and lyrics. See Finkelstein, "Public Performance Rights in Music and Performance Rights Societies," 7 Copyright Problems Analyzed 69, 77 (1952); see also "Radio Music," Music Lovers' Encyclopedia 809 (Rev.Ed.1954). There can be no question that the OATC concerts, in which singers enter and exit, maintain specific roles and occasionally make gestures, and in which the story line of the original play is preserved by the songs which are sung in almost perfect sequence using 78 of the 87 minutes of the original copyrighted score, is dramatic. And, the admitted desire of defendants to make reference to the opera in its advertisement provides further evidence that the performance is intended to come as close as possible to the original dramatico-musical. See M. Nimmer, Copyright § 34 (1971).

Once we have concluded as we do, that Stigwood will probably succeed at the trial in establishing that OATC's concerts infringe Stigwood's copyrights, we must modify the preliminary injunction below to prevent further infringing performances, if irreparable injury will result. Further, once a prima facie case of infringement has been made out, a preliminary injunction should issue, even in the absence of a detailed showing of irreparable injury where dramatico-musical works are concerned, since "a copyright holder in the ordinary case may be presumed to suffer irreparable harm when his right to the exclusive use of the copyrighted material is invaded." American Metropolitan Enterprises of New York v. Warner Bro. Records, Inc., 389 F.2d 903, 905 (2d Cir.1968). See *Rice,* supra, 446 F.2d at 688; Rushton v. Vitale, 218 F.2d 434 (2d Cir.1957); Chappell & Co. v. Fields, 210 F. 864 (2d Cir.1914).

Fashioning the injunctive provisions in the instant case presents complexities we should explicate. It would not be sufficient merely to enjoin further concerts which follow the format set forth in Exhibit 3. Simply making insignificant changes in sequence that would still not materially affect the performance we have described or interfere with the development of the story, would not be sufficient. Nor would a simple limitation on the number of selections which could be performed suffice. Even the presentation of five or six songs could under certain circumstances, develop an essential portion of the drama, for example,

---

4. Professor Nimmer states that "a performance of a musical composition is dramatic if it aids in telling a story; otherwise it is not." M. Nimmer, Copyright § 125.6 (1971). The presence or absence of scenery and costumes is not of paramount importance in making such a determination.

the last two days in the life of Christ, thus infringing on a part of the opera. The sequence of the songs seems to be the linchpin in this case. If the songs are not sung in sequence, i.e., no song follows another song in the OATC concert in the same order as the original opera, and there are no costumes, scenery, or intervening dialogue, we are confident that the resulting performance could not tell the story of *Jesus Christ Superstar*.

II

In view of our disposition of the primary issue in this case and the accompanying discussion, our resolution of the remaining issues may be of only academic interest. Nevertheless, we feel obliged to affirm the conclusion reached below and in *Rice* that defendants cannot make reference to *Jesus Christ Superstar* in its advertisements. Sperber argues that there can be no copyright in titles, and, for the first time on appeal, claims that no protection can be afforded on any other theory because of Supreme Court decisions in Sears, Roebuck & Co. v. Stiffel Co., 376 U.S. 225, 84 S.Ct. 784, 11 L.Ed.2d 661 (1964) and Compco Corp. v. Day-Brite Lighting, Inc., 376 U.S. 234, 84 S.Ct. 779, 11 L.Ed.2d 669 (1964). We disagree. *Sears* and *Compco* prevent protection outside of the copyright laws, of works which Congress could have protected but chose not to. It may be that titles are not "writings" in the constitutional sense and thus cannot be protected by copyright but can be protected under unfair competition doctrine. In any event, *Sears* and *Compco* carved out a specific exemption for trademarks and labels of products which can be protected to prevent deception of the public. That is precisely the situation we have here. Thus, while Sears could manufacture a pole lamp identical to Stiffel's, it could not call it a Stiffel pole lamp. Similarly, OATC may perform songs under the ASCAP license but may not indicate that they are from the opera. The Senate Judiciary Committee, in its proposed general revision of the Copyright Law, preserves the right to regulate deceptive trade practices outside of the copyright laws. S.543, § 301(b)(3), 91st Cong., 1st sess. (1969). Since the title *Jesus Christ Superstar* may well be associated with the opera as a whole and thus a "secondary meaning" has developed, we agree with the district court that defendants must be enjoined from directly or indirectly advertising or in any way representing any presentation as being from *Jesus Christ Superstar* or any song, instrumental selection or excerpt as taken therefrom in whole or in part. We also agree, however, that subject to the conditions we have set forth in Part I, the individual song titles can be listed.

III

Finally, although we do not doubt that the defendants chose the name "The Original American Touring Company" with the hope of misleading the public, we agree with the district court that there is insufficient evidence in the record to support an inference of likelihood of confusion strong enough to underpin a preliminary injunction to restrain the use of that name, provided the restrictions we have set forth are observed. See Remco Industries, Inc. v. Toyomenka, Inc., 286 F.Supp. 948 (S.D.N.Y.1967), affirmed 397 F.2d 977 (2d Cir.1968). The likelihood of confusion is especially slight in view of the inability of OATC to make reference to *Jesus Christ Superstar* in its promotional efforts.

The preliminary injunction is modified and it is ordered that defendants be enjoined from:

(1) performing any song in such a way as to follow another song in the same order as in the original *Jesus Christ Superstar* opera;

(2) performing any songs from the opera accompanied by dramatic action, scenic accessory or costumes; and

(3) advertising or in any way representing any presentations as being from *Jesus Christ Superstar* or any song, instrumental selection or excerpt as taken therefrom in whole or in part.

The preliminary injunction is modified as we have indicated. The mandate shall issue forthwith.

Question

Assume that the play "Pygmalion" by George Bernard Shaw is in the public domain, but that the musical play "My Fair Lady" by Alan Jay Lerner and Frederick Loewe (a derivative work based upon "Pygmalion") is protected by copyright, as are also all of the songs contained therein. Assume further that the "My Fair Lady" songs are a part of the ASCAP repertory. Suppose that the producer of a Broadway production of "Pygmalion" obtains an ASCAP license, but does not obtain a dramatic performing rights license to "My Fair Lady". May he have his actors sing the "My Fair Lady" songs at appropriate cues during the play's performance? May he have the actors sing such songs during the between-acts intermissions? Should it matter that the "Pygmalion"—"My Fair Lady" story (or "book") could not be derived merely from a sequential singing of the songs in the same way that the sequential singing of the "Jesus Christ Superstar" songs depicted the last seven days in the life of Christ? Should it matter if the "Pygmalion" story could be derived from such sequential singing, but no additional story contribution by Lerner and Loewe could be thus derived?

Collateral References

Nimmer on Copyright, § 10.10[E].

Perrone, "Small and Grand Performing Rights", 20 Bull.Cr.Soc. 19 (1972).

D. THE DISPLAY RIGHT

Note and Questions

Sec. 106(5) of the Copyright Act of 1976 for the first time conferred upon copyright owners an exclusive right to publicly display certain types of works. Specifically, such right may be claimed in literary, musical, dramatic, and choreographic works, and in pantomimes, pictorial, graphic, and sculptural works, and in the individual images of motion pictures, and other audiovisual works. By the Section 101 definition, "to 'display' a work means to show a copy of it, either directly or by means of a film, slide, television image, or any other device or process * * *." An unauthorized display will not constitute an infringement unless it is done "publicly." Note that the display right applies only to copies, not to phonorecords. It includes not only showing a copy directly, but also by projection of an image on a screen, or other surface by any method, and the transmission of an image by electronic or other means, as well as the showing of an image on a cathode ray tube, or similar apparatus in connection with computers or other devices.

Question 1: Since the projection of images from a motion picture may constitute either a "display" or a "performance", when will it be considered the former, and when the latter? In what circumstances will such a distinction be significant?

Question 2: Is the unauthorized transmission of text from the printed page of a book or journal so that it may be read by electronic means on cathode ray tubes or similar apparatus an infringement of the reproduction right? Of the performance right? Of the display right? See Sec. 117.

Question 3: Artist A sold the original of his painting to B, but reserved the copyright therein. Is B an infringer if, without A's consent, he exhibits the painting in his living room? In a museum? In an art gallery where he offers it for re-sale? In a motion picture which includes a full close-up of A's painting, provided the motion picture is exhibited only in the museum where the painting is hanging? If the motion picture is exhibited on television? If A leased rather than sold his painting to B, what is the answer to each of the above questions? See Sec. 109(b).

Collateral Reference

Nimmer on Copyright, § 8.20[A], [B].

Chapter Five

DURATION AND RENEWAL OF COPYRIGHT

A. DURATION

Note* and Questions

[A]—Duration of Copyright for Works Created on or After January 1, 1978

[1]—Life Plus Fifty as the Basic Term of Protection. Except for anonymous and pseudonymous works, and works made for hire, as to which a different term of protection is prescribed, if a work was created on or after January 1, 1978, the term of statutory copyright in such work begins upon its creation, and endures for the life of the author plus fifty years after his death.[1]

Question 1: When is a work "created" so as to begin the term of statutory copyright?

The termination of the statutory copyright term in a given work occurs fifty years after the occurrence of an unequivocal event, i.e. the death of the author of the work. Where the date of the author's death is generally known, the computation of the copyright term presents no problem. But what if such date is not known? The Copyright Act provides a means whereby members of the public may safely assume that a work has entered the public domain even though it is not possible to determine whether or when the author of such work has died. The Register of Copyrights is directed to maintain records relating to authors, indicating the date of an author's death,[2] or alternatively indicating that a given author was living on a particular date.[3] Such records are to be compiled from statements recorded in the Copyright Office by "any person having an interest in a copyright."

Question 2: Who may be said to have such an "interest"? Is it only persons who have some form of ownership in the copyright, i.e. a "right, title, and *interest*", or does it refer to anyone, including strangers, who may be "interested"?

---

* Nimmer on Copyright, § 9.01.
1. 17 U.S.C.A. § 302(a).
2. 17 U.S.C.A. § 302(d).
3. Id.

In addition, to the extent the Register considers practicable, such records may also be based on data contained in any of the files of the Copyright Office or in other reference sources.[4] The content of such records as compiled by the Copyright Office become legally significant once a given work has either been published for at least 75 years, or has been "created" for at least 100 years, whichever occurs sooner. At such time, the benefit of a presumption that the work has entered the public domain may be claimed by anyone who obtains from the Copyright Office a certified report indicating that its records disclose nothing to indicate that the author of such a work is living or has been dead for less than 50 years.

Question 3: Does such a certified report inject the work into the public domain, or does it merely constitute a defense in an infringement action for one who can produce such a report? What is the difference?

Question 4: If the recipient of such a certified report in fact knows that the author has not been dead for 50 years, may he nevertheless rely upon the certified report in an infringement action brought against him?

[2]—Life Plus Fifty As Applied to Joint Works. Sec. 302(b) of the Copyright Act provides: "In the case of a joint work prepared by two or more authors who did not work for hire, the copyright endures for a term consisting of the life of the last surviving author and fifty years after such last surviving author's death." Thus, in order to determine the duration of a joint work copyright, it is necessary to be aware of the identity of all of the joint authors, and of the dates of their respective deaths, in order to measure fifty years from the death of the last survivor. Where there are numerous joint authors of a given work, this may present some difficulty.

The fact that the term of protection for joint works is calculated from the death of the last surviving joint author makes it advantageous for an older author to choose a younger one as his joint author. Indeed, it even suggests that some works which would otherwise be written by a single author will become joint works solely in order to measure the term of protection upon the life of a younger "joint author." Of course, this result will not be achieved if it can be proven that the relationship of joint authorship was not bona fide.

Question 5: If all of the joint authors worked in a "for hire" relationship, what is the duration of protection for the work? See Para. 3, below.

Question 6: What is the duration of protection for a work written by three joint authors, if one of them worked for hire, and the other two did not? What if two of them worked for hire and the third did not?

[3]—The Term of Copyright For Works Made for Hire, and Anonymous and Pseudonymous Works, Created on or After January 1, 1978. The life of the author cannot very well serve as a measure of the duration of copyright in an anonymous or pseudonymous work, since by definition the identity of the author may not be known. Likewise, in the case of a work made for hire it is often difficult to identify any given individual as the author. Therefore, as to all such works, if they were created on or after January 1, 1978, instead of the life plus fifty term, copyright endures for a term of seventy-five years from the year of first publication of such a work, or a term of one hundred years from the year of its creation, whichever expires first.[5]

---

4. 17 U.S.C.A. § 302(e).

5. 17 U.S.C.A. § 302(c).

It was thought that on the average seventy-five years from publication is "roughly equivalent" to life plus fifty.[6] The alternate term of one hundred years from creation was thought necessary in order "to set a time limit on protection of unpublished material" in compliance with the "limited times" provision of the Constitution.[7] The Register of Copyrights has observed: "While it is true enough that proof of the precise time of an event such as 'creation,' usually private in nature, is likely to involve problems, it is important to remember that the question would arise only where a work has remained unpublished for more than 25 years after it was created. The primary importance of 'creation' would probably be to scholars who, upward of a century later, need to determine a work's copyright status; their task would not be to establish the exact date of creation, but simply to determine whether the work had been created more than 100 years earlier."[8] As to published works determining the date of creation presents no problem as long as it is known that the work has been published for at least seventy-five years. The copyright notice on a work indicates a date of publication which may safely be relied upon for this purpose, even though in some instances (as in the case of a derivative work) the actual date of first publication may be earlier.

In some instances it is advantageous to characterize a work as one made for hire in order to come within the special term for such works. This is particularly true where the author at the time of creation is of advanced years so that 50 years from his death will expire considerably before 75 years from publication or 100 years from creation. If the author is very young the advantage may cut the other way.

Question 7: To what extent is it within the discretion of the parties to characterize a work as one which is or is not made for hire in order to determine the term of protection for the work? See Secs. 101 and 201(b) (definition of "work made for hire").

The same relative advantages, depending upon the age of the author, exist with respect to anonymous and pseudonymous works. Here it is obviously within the power of the author to determine whether or not his work will qualify as either anonymous or pseudonymous. By simply withholding any identification of the author on copies or phonorecords of the work, it is by definition "anonymous." By identifying the author under a fictitious name on copies or phonorecords of the work, it is by definition "pseudonymous." But suppose that the true identity of the author is a matter of public knowledge even though the copies or phonorecords of his work fail to make such identification. This will not alter the characterization of the work as either anonymous or pseudonymous. However, if before the end of the copyright term for such work the true identity of the author, or if it is a joint work, the true identity of any one of the joint authors, is revealed by either a registration or recordation described below, then the applicable term of protection for such work will be the same as it would have been if the work had not been anonymous or pseudonymous.[9] Thus, if the work is by a single author, the term of copyright will then expire fifty years after the author's death. If there are joint authors, the term of copyright will expire fifty years after the death of the last surviving joint author. If the anonymous or pseudonymous work is one made for hire,

6. Reg.Supp.Rep., p. 92.
7. H.Rep., p. 137.
8. Reg.Supp.Rep., pp. 90–91.
9. 17 U.S.C.A. § 302(c).

then the term will remain one based upon 75 years from publication or 100 years from creation.

The registration referred to above which will serve to identify an author for the purpose of transmuting the copyright term is the registration with the Copyright Office provided by Sec. 408(a) of the Act, as well as Sec. 408(d) which permits corrections and amplifications of prior registration. The act of registration does not necessarily serve to identify an author since it is expressly provided by the Act that the name of the author need not be registered in the case of an anonymous or pseudonymous work.[10] However, if the copyright owner or the owner of any exclusive right in the work elects to identify the author by such registration, then such identification will trigger the transmutation of term provided by Sec. 302(c). What if neither the copyright owner nor the owner of any such exclusive right elects to make such identification by registration? No one else has standing to make such a registration.[11] There is, however, an alternate route by which others may cause the author of a work to be identified so as to transmute the copyright term. Sec. 302(c) provides:

> "Any person having an interest in the copyright in an anonymous or pseudonymous work may at any time record, in records to be maintained by the Copyright Office for that purpose, a statement identifying one or more authors of the work; the statement shall also identify the person filing it, the nature of that person's interest, the source of the information recorded, and the particular work affected * * *."

Question 8: What is the nature of the "interest" which must be possessed by a person seeking to identify an anonymous or pseudonymous author? Is it a property interest in the work?

Question 9: What if the recorded information purporting to identify the author of an anonymous or pseudonymous work is inaccurate? May the Copyright Office evaluate the reliability of the information sought to be recorded, and in its discretion refuse to record? What if the recorded information were in fact inaccurate? If the true author challenged its accuracy would he by making such challenge identify himself so as to lose his claim of anonymity or pseudonymity?

[B]—Duration of Copyright For Works Protected by Common Law Copyright Until January 1, 1978

Prior to January 1, 1978, the effective date of the current Copyright Act, a work was protected by common law copyright in perpetuity unless and until such work was either published, or had obtained a statutory copyright as an unpublished work. Upon January 1, 1978 the state law of common-law copyright was almost totally preempted by the federal copyright law. Thus, works which were unpublished as of January 1, 1978 (and, therefore, had neither achieved statutory copyright as published works, nor entered the public domain as of that date), and which further had not theretofore qualified for statutory copyright as unpublished works, became subject to statutory copyright by reason of the preemption provisions of the current Act. Sec. 303 of the present Act provides that the term of protection for any such work begins on January 1, 1978, and continues for the same term as would have been applicable for such a work if it had been created on or after January 1, 1978. Thus, for the most

---

10. 17 U.S.C.A. § 409(2).   11. 17 U.S.C.A. § 408(a).

part the term of protection for works the subject of common law copyright until the effective date of the current Act becomes the life of the author plus 50 years.

Question 10: Suppose that the author of an unpublished work had been dead for more than 50 years as of January 1, 1978. Was such work immediately injected into the public domain upon such date? See Sec. 303.

[C]—Duration of Copyright For Works Which Obtained Statutory Copyright Prior to January 1, 1978

The life plus fifty term of protection is not applicable to works which obtained statutory copyright prior to January 1, 1978, the effective date of the current Copyright Act. Under Sec. 304(a), all such works, if they did not enter the public domain prior to such date, are protected for an initial term of copyright of twenty eight years, commencing upon the date statutory copyright was originally secured. The term of statutory copyright may be extended for an additional or renewal period of 47 years provided a renewal copyright in the work has been obtained in accordance with the requirements discussed in the remainder of this chapter. The renewal period commences immediately upon expiration of the original term of copyright. Therefore, if a work is renewed the total duration of statutory copyright is 75 years from first publication or earlier registration. It should be clear that this renewal structure is applicable only to works which were in statutory copyright prior to January 1, 1978, and had not theretofore entered the public domain. As to works which were in their first 28 year term of copyright prior to January 1, 1978, the measure of the statutory original and renewal terms presents no great problem. The situation is somewhat more complex, however, with respect to works which were already in their renewal term on January 1, 1978, the effective date of the current Act. Under the 1909 Act the renewal term, like the first term, was for 28 years, or a total for both terms of 56 years. The current Act extended the renewal term (but not the first term) by an additional 19 years, so that the renewal term now is for 47 years rather than 28 years. Under Sec. 304(b), any work which as of January 1, 1978, had already begun its renewal term thus became entitled to an additional 19 years of copyright protection, or a total of 75 years from the time the first term copyright was originally secured.

Since under the 1909 Act the duration of statutory copyright, original and renewal terms, totaled 56 years, does this mean that any work as to which such 56 year period expired prior to January 1, 1978 entered the public domain? If so, such a work would be ineligible for further protection under the current Act notwithstanding the 19 year extension of the renewal term under the current Act.[12] In order to avoid this result, the Congress while considering adoption of the general revision of the copyright laws which ultimately resulted in the current Act, provided for a series of interim extensions of copyright.[13] By reason of these extensions, any work as to which the 28 year renewal term would otherwise have expired under the 1909 Act anytime between September 19, 1962, and December 31, 1976, was granted an extension of such renewal term until December 31, 1976. This means that the renewal term in all such works was extended so as to be subsisting on December 31, 1976. Section 304(b)

---

12. See 17 U.S.C.A., Trans.Supp.Prov. § 103.

13. See P.L. 87–668, P.L. 89–142, P.L. 90–141, P.L. 90–416, P.L. 91–147, P.L. 91–555, P.L. 92–170, P.L. 92–566, and P.L. 93–573.

of the current Act in turn provides: "The duration of any copyright, the renewal term of which is subsisting at any time between December 31, 1976, and December 31, 1977, inclusive * * * is extended to endure for a term of seventy-five years from the date copyright was originally secured." Thus the current Act confers upon those works which were the subject of the above described interim extensions (as well as those works not covered by the interim extensions, but whose 28 year renewal terms would have expired during the period of December 31, 1976, through December 31, 1977) the benefit of the 19 year extension of the renewal term. It was thought to be inequitable to deprive such works of the benefit of such extension simply because of the long delays in the legislative process while conferring it upon other works which were in statutory copyright but whose 28 year renewal term did not expire prior to the effective date of the current Act.

Question 11: Are the interim extensions constitutionally questionable? What of the constitutional validity of the 19 year extension of the renewal term under the current Act?

Question 12: In calculating whether a given work has entered the public domain by reason of the expiration of its renewal term, as to which works should you apply a measure of 56 years from first publication (or prior registration), and as to which should you apply a 75 year measure?

Collateral Reference

Nimmer on Copyright, § 9.01. See also Id., §§ 1.05[A] and 1.10[C][1].

B. RENEWAL OF COPYRIGHT

*Note**

The Rationale of the Renewal Concept

One may well wonder why a Congress which saw fit to do away with the complex and clumsy renewal structure in connection with works which had not secured statutory copyright before the effective date of the current Act,[1] should elect to retain that structure as to works which were already in statutory copyright upon such date. The Committee Reports explain this retention on the ground that the renewal expectancies created under the 1909 Act "are the subject of existing contracts, and it would be unfair and immensely confusing to cut off or alter these interests,"[2] as would be necessary if the duration of protection for such works were transmuted to a unitary term of life plus fifty.

But this in turn raises the question of the rationale of the Congress which adopted the renewal structure under the 1909 Act. They too were retaining rather than creating a renewal structure,[3] and to that extent their purpose may also have been, in some degree, to protect existing expectancies. But they also extended the renewal structure to works created after the effective date of the

---

* Nimmer on Copyright, § 9.02.

1. As to such works the reversion of rights principle was achieved, without renewal, under the termination of transfers provisions. See Ch. Six infra.

2. H.Rep., p. 139.

3. The pattern of two consecutive terms rather than a single term of copyright was first instituted in the Statute of Anne, 8 Anne, c. 19 (1709) and was contained in the first federal copyright law, Act of May 31, 1790, 1 Stat. 124, and in every subsequent federal copyright enactment.

1909 Act. Here something more than the protection of expectancies was involved. The House Report for the 1909 Act explained its purpose as follows: "It not infrequently happens that the author sells his copyright outright to a publisher for a comparatively small sum. If the work proves to be a great success and lives beyond the term of twenty-eight years, your committee felt that it should be the exclusive right of the author to take the renewal term, and the law should be framed as is the existing law, so that he could not be deprived of that right." [4]

In construing the renewal provision it has been judicially stated that "There are at least sentimental reasons for believing that Congress may have intended that the author, who according to tradition receives but little for his work, and afterwards sees large profits made out of it by publishers, should later in life be brought into his kingdom." [5] And by another court: "The second period is intended not as an incident of the first for the benefit of the then owner of the expiring copyright, but as a second recognition extended by the law to the author of the work that has proven permanently meritorious * * *." [6] In the leading decision of the Supreme Court on the renewal provision, Fred Fisher Music Co. v. M. Witmark & Sons,[7] a decision which did much to limit authors' renewal rights,[8] the "basic consideration of policy underlying the renewal provision" was said to be the right of "the author to sell his 'copyright' without losing his renewal interest."

It is, then, clear that the renewal provision was intended to benefit authors by enabling them or their families to have a second opportunity to market their works after an original sale of the copyright. But why should the property of authors be singled out for this paternalistic treatment when other property owners are presumed to know what they are about and are denied such a second chance? Is it, (as the Supreme Court rhetorically inquired) that "authors are congenitally irresponsible, [and] that frequently they are so sorely pressed for funds that they are willing to sell their work for a mere pittance"?[9] Whatever merit there may be to the foregoing proposition, it would seem to miss the most compelling reason justifying a renewal provision. That is, that the form of property designated copyright, unlike real property and other forms of personal property, is by its very nature incapable of accurate monetary evaluation prior to its exploitation.[10]

Whether a popular song, or novel or a play will strike the public fancy and prove an all time best seller or alternatively will meet the more common fate of complete oblivion poses a problem that the most knowledgeable experts admit is a matter of pure guesswork. In these circumstances an author (at least one without a reputation for past successes) must necessarily find himself in a poor bargaining position when he initially negotiates the sale of his copyright.[11] For this reason a "second chance" may well be warranted for authors at a time when the economic worth of his work has been proven. This reasoning is

---

4. H.R.Rep. No. 2222, 60th Cong.2d Sess. p. 14.

5. White-Smith Music Publishing Co. v. Goff, 187 F. 247, 251 (1st Cir.1911).

6. Harris v. Coca-Cola Co., 73 F.2d 370, 371 (5th Cir.1934).

7. 318 U.S. 643 (1943).

8. The *Fisher* opinion is contained in this chapter, infra.

9. Fisher Music Co. v. Witmark, 318 U.S. 643, 656 (1943).

10. Bartok v. Boosey & Hawkes, Inc., 523 F.2d 941, 944–945 (2d Cir.1975).

11. This rationale is suggested in Ringer, "Renewal of Copyright," Copyright Office Study No. 31, p. 125.

somewhat less persuasive when the original sale is on a percentage royalty basis so that the author automatically shares in whatever returns his work may bring. Even in such a case, however, the nature of the royalty formula (e.g., whether based on gross receipts, or "net profits" defined in such manner as to leave virtually nothing after deduction of "costs") and the numerical amount of the percentage may well vary depending upon the author's bargaining position.

Questions

1. Does the above rationale satisfy you as offering adequate grounds for offering authors a "second chance"?

2. Could such a second chance have been based upon a framework other than the clumsy renewal device? See the discussion of termination of transfers in Chapter Six, infra.

Collateral References

Bricker, *Renewal and Extension of Copyright,* 29 So.Cal.Law Rev. 23 (1955).

Ringer, *Renewal of Copyright,* Studies on Copyright 503 (Fisher ed. 1963) (Copyright Law Revision Study No. 31, 1960, U.S.Govt.Print.Off.1960).

1. Who Is Entitled to Claim Renewal?

DE SYLVA v. BALLENTINE, GUARDIAN

Supreme Court of the United States, 1956.
351 U.S. 570, 76 S.Ct. 974, 100 L.Ed. 1415.

Opinion of the Court by MR. JUSTICE HARLAN, announced by MR. JUSTICE BURTON.

The present Copyright Act provides for a second 28-year copyright after the expiration of the original 28-year term, if application for renewal is made within one year before the expiration of the original term. This right to renew the copyright appears in § 24 of the Act:

> *And provided further,* That in the case of any other copyrighted work, * * * the author of such work, if still living, or the widow, widower, or children of the author, if the author be not living, or if such author, widow, widower, or children be not living, then the author's executors, or in the absence of a will, his next of kin shall be entitled to a renewal and extension of the copyright in such work for a further term of twenty-eight years when application for such renewal and extension shall have been made to the copyright office and duly registered therein within one year prior to the expiration of the original term of copyright. * * *

In this case, an author who secured original copyrights on numerous musical compositions died before the time to apply for renewals arose. He was survived by his widow and one illegitimate child, who are both still living. The question this case presents is whether that child is entitled to share in the copyrights which come up for renewal during the widow's lifetime.

Respondent, the child's mother, brought this action on the child's behalf against the widow, who is the petitioner here, seeking a declaratory judgment that the child has an interest in the copyrights already renewed by the widow and those that will become renewable during her lifetime, and for an accounting of profits from such copyrights as have been already renewed. The District Court, holding that the child was within the meaning of the term "children" as used in the statute but that the renewal rights belonged *exclusively* to the widow, gave judgment for the widow. Agreeing with the District Court on the first point, the Court of Appeals reversed, holding that on the author's death *both* widow and child shared in the renewal copyrights. 226 F.2d 623. Because of the great importance of these questions in the administration of the Copyright Act, we granted certiorari, 350 U.S. 931.

The controversy centers around the words "or the widow, widower, or children of the author, if the author be not living." Two questions are involved: (1) do the widow and children take as a class, or in order of enumeration, and (2) if they take as a class, does "children" include an illegitimate child. Strangely enough, these questions have never before been decided, although the statutory provisions involved have been part of the Act in their present form since 1870.

I.

The widow first contends that, after the death of the author, she alone is entitled to renew copyrights during her lifetime, exclusive of any interest in "children" of the author. That is, she interprets the clause as providing for the passing of the renewal rights, on the death of the author, first to the widow, and then only after her death to the "children" of the author. If the word "or" which follows "widower" is to be read in its normal disjunctive sense, this is not an unreasonable interpretation of the statute, which might then well be read to mean that "children" are to renew only if there is no "widow" or "widower." The statute is hardly unambiguous, however, and presents problems of interpretation not solved by literal application of words as they are "normally" used. The statute must be read as a whole, and putting each word in its proper context we are unable to say, as the widow contends we should, that the clear purport of the clause in question is the same as if it read "or the widow, or widower, if the author be not living, or the children of the author, if the author, and widow or widower, be not living."

We start with the proposition that the word "or" is often used as a careless substitute for the word "and"; that is, it is often used in phrases where "and" would express the thought with greater clarity. That trouble with the word has been with us for a long time: see, *e.g.,* United States v. Fisk, 3 Wall. 445. In this instance, we need look no further than the very next clause in this same section of the Copyright Act for an example of this careless usage: " * * * or if such author, widow, widower *or* children be not living, then the author's executors. * * *" If the italicized "or" in that clause is read disjunctively, then the author's executors would be entitled to renew the copyright if any *one* of the persons named "be not living." It is clear, however, that the executors do not succeed to the renewal interest unless *all* of the named persons are dead, since from the preceding clause it is at least made explicit that the "widow, widower, or children of the author" all come before the executors, after the author's death. The clause would be more accurate, therefore, were it to read "author, widow or widower, *and* children." It is argued with some force, then, that if in the succeeding clause the "or" is to be read as meaning "and" in the same word grouping as is involved in the clause in question, it should be read that way in this clause as well. If this is done, it is then an easy step to read "widow" *and* "children" as succeeding to the renewal interest as a class, as the Court of Appeals held they did.

This Court has already traced the development of the renewal term in the several copyright statutes enacted in this country. See Fred Fisher Music Co. v. M. Witmark & Sons, 318 U.S. 643. * * * In 1831, however, a new Act was passed, which for the first time gave to the author's family the right to renew after his death. Act of February 3, 1831, 4 Stat. 436. * * *

It is significant that this statute, which instituted the present scheme of allowing a copyright to be renewed after the author's death, provided for the renewal interest in the "widow *and* child, or children," rather than in the widow or children separately. Petitioner concedes that under this statute the widow and children took as a class. This statute marked a major development in this phase of copyright legislation and created a system which, in its basic form, has been continued even to the present statute.

Section 88 of the Act of July 8, 1870, 16 Stat. 212, in consolidating the language of § 2 of the 1831 Act, made one important change in the language of the renewal section: the right of renewal was given to the author's widow *or* children, rather than to the widow *and* children. * *

This section became § 4954 of the Revised Statutes, and was amended in 1891, 26 Stat. 1107, by deleting the requirement that the author be a citizen or resident of the United States. The section was otherwise left intact. The present renewal provision appeared first as § 23 of the Copyright Act of March 4, 1909, 35 Stat. 1080, and was continued without change in 17 U.S.C.A. § 24.

Knowing, as we do, that "or" can be ambiguous when used in such a context as this, it is difficult to say that the change made in the 1870 Copyright Act had the effect of changing, as petitioner contends it did, the children's interest from an interest shared with the widow to one which became effective only after her death. There is no legislative history, either when the 1870 Act was passed or in the subsequent sessions of Congress, to indicate that Congress in fact intended to change in this respect the existing scheme of distribution of the renewal rights. Rather, what scant material there is indicates that no substantial changes in the Act were intended. It would not seem unlikely that the framers of the 1870 statute, interested in compressing the somewhat cumbersome phrasing of the prior Copyright Act, simply deleted the words "and child" with the thought that the remaining phrase "or children" expressed precisely the same result, leaving unaffected the rights of the author's children which had been the same for almost forty years.

We then come to the 1909 Copyright Act. By § 23 of that Act, now 17 U.S.C.A. § 24, there were added to those entitled to renewal rights after the author's death—the widow or children—the author's executors, or, in the absence of a will, his next of kin. Each of these named classes is separated in the statute by a condition precedent to the passing of the renewal rights, namely, that the persons named in the preceding class be deceased. As already noted, it is at least clear that, if the author and his widow have both died, survived by a child, that child is entitled to renew copyrights maturing during his lifetime. But if this interest were to take effect only *after* the death of the widow, it might be expected that the drafters of the Act would have separated "widow or widower" from "children" with the same condition precedent used in defining the succession of the other classes to the renewal rights, since it would in effect be placing the children in a class lower than that occupied by the widow or widower. Granting that the absence of this structure might simply have been due to carelessness in adding the new class to the prior renewal section, we think it may nevertheless be taken as some indication that the widow and children are to take the right to renew at the same time * * *

While the matter is far from clear, we think, on balance, the more likely meaning of the statute to be that adopted by the Court of Appeals, and we hold that, on the death of the author, the widow and children of the author succeed to the right of renewal as a class, and are each entitled to share in the renewal term of the copyright.

II.

We come, then, to the question of whether an illegitimate child is included within the term "children" as used in § 24. The scope of a federal right is, of course, a federal question, but that does not mean that its content is not to be determined by state, rather than federal law. Cf. Reconstruction Finance Corp. v. Beaver County, 328 U.S. 204; Board of County Commissioners v. United States, 308 U.S. 343, 351–352. This is especially true where a statute deals with a familial relationship; there is no federal law of domestic relations, which is primarily a matter of state concern.

If we look at the other persons who, under this section of the Copyright Act, are entitled to renew the copyright after the author's death, it is apparent that this is the general scheme of the statute. To decide who is the widow or widower of a deceased author, or who are his executors or next of kin, requires a reference to the law of the State which created those legal relationships. The word "children," although it to some extent describes a purely physical relationship, also describes a legal status not unlike the others. To determine whether a child has been legally adopted, for example, requires a reference to state law. We think it proper, therefore, to draw on the ready-made body of state law to define the word "children" in § 24. This does not mean that a State would be entitled to use the word "children" in a way entirely strange to those familiar with its ordinary usage, but at least to the extent that there are permissible variations in the ordinary concept of "children" we deem state law controlling. Cf. Seaboard Air Line Railway v. Kenney, 240 U.S. 489.

This raises two questions: first, to what State do we look, and second, given a particular State, what part of that State's law defines the relationship. The answer to the first question, in this case, is not difficult, since it appears from the record that the only State concerned is California, and both parties have argued the case on that assumption. The second question, however, is less clear. An illegitimate child who is acknowledged by his father, by a writing signed in the presence of a witness, is entitled under § 255 of the California Probate Code [1] to inherit his father's estate as well as his mother's. The District Court found that the child here was within the terms of that section. Under California law the child is not legitimate for all purposes, however; compliance with § 230 of the Civil Code [2] is necessary for full legitimation, and there are no allegations in the complaint sufficient to bring the child within that section. Hence, we may take it that the child is not "adopted" in the sense that he is to be regarded as a legitimate child of the author.

Considering the purposes of § 24 of the Copyright Act, we think it sufficient that the status of the child is that described by § 255 of the California Probate Code. The evident purpose of § 24 is to provide for the family of the author after his death. Since the author cannot assign his family's renewal rights, § 24 takes the form of a compulsory bequest of the copyright to the designated persons. This is really a question of the descent of property, and we think the controlling question under state law should be whether the child would be an heir of the author. It is clear that under § 255 the child is, at least to that extent, included within the term "children."

1. "Every illegitimate child is an heir of his mother, and also of the person who, in writing, signed in the presence of a competent witness, acknowledges himself to be the father, and inherits his or her estate, in whole or in part, as the case may be, in the same manner as if he had been born in lawful wedlock; but he does not represent his father by inheriting any part of the estate of the father's kindred, either lineal or collateral, unless, before his death, his parents shall have intermarried, and his father, after such marriage, acknowledges him as his child, or adopts him into his family; in which case such child is deemed legitimate for all purposes of succession. An illegitimate child may represent his mother and may inherit any part of the estate of the mother's kindred, either lineal or collateral."

2. "The father of an illegitimate child, by publicly acknowledging it as his own, receiving it as such, with the consent of his wife, if he is married, into his family, and otherwise treating it as if it were a legitimate child, thereby adopts it as such; and such child is thereupon deemed for all purposes legitimate from the time of its birth. The foregoing provisions of this Chapter do not apply to such an adoption."

Finally, there remains the question of what are the respective rights of the widow and child in the copyright renewals, once it is accepted that they both succeed to the renewals as members of the same class. Since the parties have not argued this point, and neither court below has passed on it, we think it should not be decided at this time.

For the foregoing reasons, the judgment of the Court of Appeals is

Affirmed.

MR. JUSTICE DOUGLAS, with whom MR. JUSTICE BLACK joins, concurring.

The meaning of the word "children" as used in § 24 of the Copyright Act is a federal question. Congress could of course give the word the meaning it has under the laws of the several States. See Hutchinson Investment Co. v. Caldwell, 152 U.S. 65, 68–69; Poff v. Pennsylvania R. Co., 327 U.S. 399, 401. But I would think the statutory policy of protecting dependents would be better served by uniformity, rather than by the diversity which would flow from incorporating into the Act the laws of forty-eight States. Cf. Clearfield Trust Co. v. United States, 318 U.S. 363, 367; National Metropolitan Bank v. United States, 323 U.S. 454, 456; Heiser v. Woodruff, 327 U.S. 726, 732; United States v. Standard Oil Co., 332 U.S. 301, 307.

An illegitimate child was given the benefits of the Federal Death Act by Middleton v. Luckenbach S.S. Co., 70 F.2d 326, 329–330 * * *

I would take the same approach here and, regardless of state law, hold that illegitimate children were "children" within the meaning of § 24 of the Copyright Act, whether or not state law would allow them dependency benefits.

With this exception, I join in the opinion of the Court.

Questions

1. Suppose that the author DeSylva obtained a renewal copyright in a given work, and three years later died, providing in his will that his widow, but not his child, should be entitled to exclusive ownership of the copyright during the balance of the renewal term. If the child were to challenge the widow's exclusive right, what result? How is such a case distinguishable from the instant case? Would the result be different if DeSylva died prior to the expiration of the 28th year of the original copyright term, but after he properly claimed a renewal by filing an appropriate form in the Copyright Office during such 28th year?

2. In construing an ambiguous statute, what weight should be given to the views of the persons directly affected, in this case the widows and children of authors? As to their actual practice pre-*DeSylva*, see Nimmer, Copyright 1956: Recent Trends in the Law of Artistic Property, 4 UCLA Law Rev. 323, 332–334 (1957).

3. If DeSylva had left more than one child, how should the renewal interest be divided between the widow and children?

4. Are the statutory definitions of "children", and of "widow" and "widower" as contained in Sec. 101 of the new Copyright Act applicable to Sec. 304(a), which incorporates the renewal provision (Sec. 24) of the 1909 Act almost verbatim? What reason is there to believe that they are not so applicable? If not, to what statutory provision would these definitions apply? Should the definition of "children" under Sec. 304(a) turn on state law? Does a state law definition which excludes illegitimate children violate the equal protection clause of the fourteenth amendment? See Levy v. Louisiana, 391 U.S. 68 (1968); Jerry Vogel Music Co. v. Edward B. Marks Music Corp., 425 F.2d 834 (2d Cir.1969). Suppose that state law provides that a woman ceases to be a "widow" after she re-marries. Should such a law control the meaning of "widow" under Sec. 304(a)? See Marks Music Corp. v. Borst Music Pub. Co., 110 F.Supp. 913 (D.C.N.J.1953).

5. As to what types of works does renewal vest in the "proprietor" rather than in the author, or his widow and children, etc.? What is the justification for these exceptions to the author's "second chance"? Is the "proprietor" entitled to claim renewal under Sec. 304(a), the proprietor as of the time the work was created, as of the time the original term copyright was obtained, or as of the time renewal is claimed? How does a "corporate body" as mentioned in Sec. 304(a) differ from "an employer for whom such work is made for hire"?

6. Suppose that pre-1978 the author of a work in common law copyright assigned all of his rights in the work. When the assignee thereafter obtains a statutory copyright in the work, is the author entitled to claim renewal rights if the original assignment made no mention of such rights?

Collateral Reference

Nimmer on Copyright, §§ 9.03–9.05.

2. Assignability of Renewal

FRED FISHER MUSIC CO. v. M. WITMARK & SONS

Supreme Court of the United States, 1943.
318 U.S. 643, 63 S.Ct. 773, 87 L.Ed. 1055.

Mr. Justice Frankfurter delivered the opinion of the Court.

This case presents a question never settled before, even though it concerns legislation having a history of more than two hundred years. The question itself can be stated very simply. Under § 23 of the Copyright Act of 1909, 35 Stat. 1075, as amended, [now Sec. 24] a copyright in a musical composition lasts for twenty-eight years from the date of its first publication, and the author can renew the copyright, if he is still living, for a further term of twenty-eight years by filing an application for renewal within a year before the expiration of the first twenty-eight year period. Section 42 [now Sec. 28] of the Act provides that a copyright "may be assigned * * * by an instrument in writing signed by the proprietor of the copyright * * * *" Concededly, the author can assign the original copyright and, after he has secured it, the renewal copyright as well. The question is—does the Act prevent the author from assigning his interest in the renewal copyright before he has secured it?

This litigation arises from a controversy over the renewal rights in the popular song "When Irish Eyes Are Smiling." It was written in 1912 by Ernest R. Ball, Chauncey Olcott, and George Graff, Jr., each of whom was under contract to a firm of music publishers, M. Witmark & Sons. Pursuant to the contracts, Witmark on August 12, 1912, applied for and obtained the copyright in the song. On May 19, 1917, Graff and Witmark made a further agreement, under which, for the sum of $1,600, Graff assigned to Witmark "all rights, title and interest" in a number of songs, including "When Irish Eyes Are Smiling." The contract provided for the conveyance of "all copyrights and renewals of copyrights and the right to secure all copyrights and renewals of copyrights in the [songs], and any and all rights therein that I [Graff] or my heirs, executors, administrators or next of kin may at any time be entitled to." To that end, Witmark was given an irrevocable power of attorney to execute in Graff's name all documents "necessary to secure to [Witmark] the renewals and extensions of the copyrights in said compositions and all rights therein for the terms of such renewals and extensions." In addition, Graff agreed that, "upon the expiration of the first term of any copyright," he would execute and deliver to Witmark "all papers necessary in order to secure to it the renewals and extensions of all copyrights in said compositions and all rights therein for the terms of such renewals and extensions." This agreement was duly recorded in the Copyright Office.

On August 12, 1939, the first day of the twenty-eighth year of the copyright in "When Irish Eyes Are Smiling," Witmark applied for and registered the renewal copyright in Graff's name.[1] On the same day, exercising its power of attorney under the agreement of May 19, 1917, Witmark also assigned to itself Graff's interest in the renewal. Eleven days later, Graff himself applied for and registered the renewal copyright in his own name; and on October 24, 1939, he assigned his renewal interest to another music publishing firm, Fred Fisher Music Co., Inc. Both Graff and Fisher knew of the prior registration of the renewal by Witmark and of the latter's assignment to itself. Relying upon the validity of the assignment made to it on October 24, 1939, and without obtaining permission from Witmark, Fisher published and sold copies of "When Irish Eyes Are Smiling," representing to the trade that it owned the renewal rights in the song. Witmark thereupon brought this suit to enjoin these activities. The District Court granted a preliminary injunction *pendente lite* solely upon the ground that there was no statutory bar against an author's assignment of his interest in the renewal before it was secured. 38 F.Supp. 72. The court considered no evidence and made no findings upon the question whether equitable relief should be denied on other grounds, such as inadequacy

---

1. Ball and Olcott were no longer living at the time, and under § 23 of the Act their interests in the renewal passed to their widows. Witmark is also the assignee of Mrs. Olcott's interest in the renewal copyright, and Mrs. Ball has assigned her interest to another music publisher. The validity of neither assignment is involved in this suit.

of consideration and the like.[2] Upon appeal to the Circuit Court of Appeals for the Second Circuit under § 129 of the Judicial Code, 28 U.S.C.A. § 227, permitting appeals from interlocutory decrees, the order was affirmed. 125 F.2d 949. The Circuit Court of Appeals limited itself, as did the parties before it, to the question of statutory construction, wholly apart from the particular circumstances of the case. The court expressly left open "other contentions which the parties may wish and be entitled to raise on the merits, including possibly claims of inadequacy of consideration." 125 F.2d at 954. The petition for certiorari in this Court stated that the "sole question is whether * * * an agreement to assign his renewal, made by an author in advance of the twenty-eighth year of the original term of copyright, is valid and enforceable." Because of the obvious importance of this question of the proper construction of the Copyright Act, we brought the case here. 317 U.S. 611.

Plainly, there is only one question before us—does the Copyright Act nullify an agreement by an author, made during the original copyright term, to assign his renewal? The explicit words of the statute give the author an unqualified right to renew the copyright. No limitations are placed upon the assignability of his interest in the renewal. If we look only to what the Act says, there can be no doubt as to the answer. But each of the parties finds support for its conclusion in the historical background of copyright legislation, and to that we must turn to discover whether Congress meant more than it said.

Anglo-American copyright legislation begins in 1709 with the Statute of 8 Anne, c. 19. That act gave the author and his assigns the exclusive copyright for fourteen years from publication, and after the expiration of such term, if the author was still living, the copyright could be renewed for another fourteen years. The statute did not expressly provide that the author could assign his renewal interest during the original copyright term. But the English courts held that the author's right of renewal, although contingent upon his surviving the original fourteen-year period, could be assigned, and that if he did survive the original term he was bound by the assignment. Carnan v. Bowles, 2 Bro.C.C. 80; Rundell v. Murray, Jac. 311; see Maugham, Law of Literary Property (1828) 73; Curtis on Copyright (1847) 235. Subsequent English legislation eliminated the problem by providing for one continuous term of copyright. In 1814 the statute was amended to provide that the author and his assigns should have the copyright for twenty-eight years, "and also, if the author shall be living at the end of that period, for the residue of his natural life." 54 Geo. III, c. 156. In 1842 the copyright term was extended to forty-two years or the life of the author and seven years, whichever should prove longer. 5 & 6 Vict., c. 45; see Macgillivray, Law of Copyright (1902) 56–57. The

---

2. In opposing the motion for a preliminary injunction, Graff submitted an affidavit stating he "was in desperate financial straits" when he entered into the agreement of May 19, 1917. The District Court made no findings upon and did not otherwise deal with the issue that this allegation may raise.

English law today, with minor qualifications not relevant here, gives the author and his assigns the exclusive copyright for the life of the author and fifty years after his death. Copyright Act of 1911, 1 & 2 Geo. V, c. 34; see Oldfield, Law of Copyright (1912) 60–66; Robertson, Law of Copyright (1912) 44–50; Copinger, Law of Copyright (7th ed. 1936) 78–86.

In this country, the copyright laws enacted by the original thirteen states prior to 1789 were based largely upon the Statute of Anne. In 1783 the Continental Congress passed a resolution calling upon the states to adopt copyright legislation for the protection of authors and publishers. The resolution recommended that copyright be given to authors and publishers "for a certain time, not less than fourteen years from the first publication; and to secure to the said authors, if they shall survive the term first mentioned, and to their executors, administrators and assigns, the copyright of such books for another term of time not less than fourteen years." Journals of the Continental Congress, 1774–1789 (1922), vol. XXIV, pp. 326–27. When the resolution was adopted, laws governing copyrights were on the statute-books of at least three states, Connecticut, Massachusetts, and Maryland. The Connecticut and Maryland statutes substantially followed the Statute of Anne: in both states copyright was granted for a term of fourteen years, renewable for another term of the same length if the author survived the original term. Connecticut, Acts & Laws (Green, 1783) 617–19; Maryland, Laws (Green, 1783) c. 34. The Maryland statute employed the phraseology of the Statute of Anne, providing simply that the privilege of renewal belonged to the author. The Connecticut statute, however, explicitly incorporated the construction made by the English courts, and conferred the right of renewal upon the author and "his heirs and assigns." The Massachusetts statute created a single copyright term of twenty-one years. Massachusetts, Acts & Laws (Edes, 1783) 236.

In response to the resolution of the Congress, nine of the ten other states enacted copyright legislation. Only Delaware did not adopt a copyright statute. Five states accepted the recommendation of the Congress and followed the Statute of Anne: two copyright terms of fourteen years, the second term contingent upon the author's surviving the first. New Jersey, Acts of the General Assembly (Collins, 1783) c. 21; Pennsylvania, Laws (Bradford, 1784) c. 125; South Carolina, Acts, Ordinances and Resolves (Miller, 1784) 49–51; Candler, Colonial Records of Georgia (1911), vol. XIX, part 2, pp. 485–89; Laws of New York, 1786, c. 54. Four of these, like the earlier Connecticut statute, explicitly provided that the right of renewal could be exercised by the author's heirs and assigns, namely, New Jersey, Pennsylvania, Georgia, and New York. The four remaining states enacted statutes providing for single terms of varying lengths, ranging from fourteen to twenty-one years. New Hampshire, Laws (Melcher, 1789) 161–62; Rhode Island, Acts and Resolves (Carter, 1783) 6–7; Virginia, Acts (Dunlap & Hayes, 1785) 8–9; North Carolina, Laws 1785, c. 24.

Exercising the power granted by Article 1, § 8 of the Constitution—"To promote the Progress of Science and useful Arts, by securing for limited Times to Authors and Inventors the exclusive Right to their respective Writings and Discoveries"—the first Congress enacted a copyright statute, the Act of May 31, 1790, 1 Stat. 124. As might have been expected, this Act reflected its historical antecedents. The author was given the copyright for fourteen years and "if, at the expiration of the said term, the author or authors, or any of them, be living, and a citizen or citizens of these United States, or resident therein, the same exclusive right shall be continued to him or them, his or their executors, administrators or assigns, for the further term of fourteen years." 1 Stat. 124. In view of the language and history of this provision, there can be no doubt that if the present case had arisen under the Act of 1790, there would be no statutory restriction upon the assignability of the author's renewal interest. The petitioners contend, however, that such a limitation was introduced by subsequent legislation, particularly the Copyright Acts of 1831 and 1909.

The Act of February 3, 1831, 4 Stat. 436, amended the 1790 Act in two important respects: the original term was increased from fourteen to twenty-eight years, and the renewal term, although still only fourteen years long, could pass to the author's widow or children if he did not survive the original term. The renewal provision, like the Statute of Anne, did not refer to the author's "assigns." The purpose of these changes, as stated in the report of the Committee on the Judiciary of the House of Representatives was "chiefly to enlarge the period for the enjoyment of copy-right, and thereby to place authors in this country more nearly upon an equality with authors in other countries * * * In the United States, by the existing laws, a copy-right is secured to the author, in the first instance, for fourteen years; and if, at the end of that period, he be living, then for fourteen years more; but, if he be not then living, the copy-right is determined, although, by the very event of the death of the author, his family stand in more need of the only means of subsistence ordinarily left to them." Register of Debates, vol. 7, appendix CXIX.

Plainly, therefore, the Copyright Act of 1831 merely enlarged the benefits of the copyright; it extended the length of the original term and gave the author's widow and children that which theretofore they did not possess, namely, the right of renewal to which the author would have been entitled if he had survived the original term. The petitioners attach much significance to a sentence appearing in the report of the committee: "The question is, whether the author or the bookseller should receive the reward." Ibid. The meaning of this sentence, read in its context, is quite clear. By providing that, if the author should not survive the original term, his renewal interest should, instead of falling into the public domain, pass to his widow and children, Congress was of course preferring the author to the bookseller. But neither expressly nor impliedly did the Act of 1831 impose any restraints upon the right of the author himself to assign his contingent interest in the renewal. That the Act contained no such limitation was accepted without question both by the courts, see Pierpont v. Fowle, 19 Fed.Cas. 652 (C.C.Mass.1846), and Paige v. Banks, 13 Wall. 608, with which compare White-Smith Music Pub. Co. v. Goff, 187 F. 247, 250–53, and by commentators, see Curtis on Copyright (1847) 235; 2 Morgan, Law of Literature (1875) 229–30; Spalding, Law of Copyright (1878) 111; Drone on Copyright (1879) 326–32; Bowker on Copyright (1886) 20, 34; 2 Kent's Commentaries (12th ed. 1873) 510; Solberg, Copyright Protection and Statutory Formalities (1904) 24. Representative Ellsworth,[3] who submitted the committee report on the bill that became the Copyright Act of 1831, himself stated unequivocally that an agreement to assign the renewal was binding upon the author. See Ellsworth, Copy-Right Manual (1862) 29.

We come, finally, to the Copyright Act of March 4, 1909, 35 Stat. 1075, which, except for some minor amendments not relevant here, is the statute in effect at the present time. In December, 1905, President Theodore Roosevelt urged the Congress to undertake a revision of the copyright laws. H.Doc. 1, 59th Cong., 1st Sess., p. LII. In response to this message the Librarian of Congress, under whose authority the Copyright Office functions, invited persons interested in copyright legislation to attend a conference for the purpose of devising a satisfactory measure. Several conferences were held in 1905 and 1906, resulting in a bill which was introduced in the House and Senate by the chairman of the Committee on Patents in each body. This bill (H.R. 19853 and S.6330, 59th Cong., 1st Sess.) provided, in the case of books and musical compositions, for a single copyright term lasting for the life of the author and for fifty years thereafter. Joint hearings by the House and Senate Committees were held on this bill, but no action was taken by the Fifty-ninth Congress. At the next session of Congress, this and other bills to revise the copyright laws were again introduced. Extensive public hearings were held. The result of this elaborate legislative consideration of the problem of copyright was a bill (H.R. 28192; S.9440) which became the Copyright Act of 1909. As stated in the report of the House committee, this bill "differs in many respects from any of the bills previously introduced. Your committee believes that in all its essential features it fairly meets and solves the difficult problems with which the committee had to deal * * * " H.Rep. 2222, 60th Cong., 2d Sess., p. 4. Under the bill, copyright was given for twenty-eight years, with a renewal period of the same duration. The report of the House committee indicates the reasons for this provision. This section of the report, to which much importance has been attached by the judges of the court below and by the parties, must be read in the light of the specific problem with which the Congress was presented: should there be one long term, as was provided for in the bill resulting from the conferences held by the Librarian of Congress, or should there

---

3. William Wolcott Ellsworth, the son of Oliver Ellsworth, third Chief Justice of the United States. See Biographical Directory of the American Congress, 1774–1927 (1928) 943.

be two shorter terms? The House and Senate committees chose the latter alternative. They were aware that an assignment by the author of his "copyright" in general terms did not include conveyance of his renewal interest. See Pierpont v. Fowle, 19 Fed.Cas. 652 (C.C.Mass. 1846); 2 Morgan, Law of Literature (1875) 229–30; Macgillivray, Law of Copyright (1902) 267. During the hearings of the Joint Committee, Representative Currier, the chairman of the House committee, referred to the difficulties encountered by Mark Twain:

> Mr. Clemens told me that he sold the copyright for Innocents Abroad for a very small sum, and he got very little out of the Innocents Abroad until the twenty-eight-year period expired, and then his contract did not cover the renewal period, and in the fourteen years of the renewal period he was able to get out of it all of the profits. (Hearings before the Committees on Patents of the Senate and House of Representatives on Pending Bills to Amend and Consolidate the Acts respecting Copyright, 60th Cong., 1st Sess., p. 20.)

By providing for two copyright terms, each of relatively short duration, Congress enabled the author to sell his "copyright" without losing his renewal interest. If the author's copyright extended over a single, longer term, his sale of the "copyright" would terminate his entire interest. That this is the basic consideration of policy underlying the renewal provision of the Copyright Act of 1909 clearly appears from the report of the House committee which submitted the legislation (the Senate committee adopted the report of the House committee, see Sen.Rep. 1108, 60th Cong., 2d Sess.):

> Section 23 deals with the term of the copyright. Under existing law the copyright term is twenty-eight years, with the right of renewal by the author, or by the author's widow or children if he be dead, for a further term of fourteen years. The act of 1790 provided for an original term of fourteen years, with the right of renewal for fourteen years. The act of 1831 extended the term to its present length. It was urged before the committee that it would be better to have a single term without any right of renewal, and a term of life and fifty years was suggested. Your committee, after full consideration, decided that it was distinctly to the advantage of the author to preserve the renewal period. It not infrequently happens that the author sells his copyright outright to a publisher for a comparatively small sum. If the work proves to be a great success and lives beyond the term of twenty-eight years, your committee felt that it should be the exclusive right of the author to take the renewal term, and the law should be framed *as is the existing law* [italics ours], so that he could not be deprived of that right.
>
> The present term of twenty-eight years, with the right of renewal for fourteen years, in many cases is insufficient. The terms, taken together, ought to be long enough to give the author the exclusive right to his work for such a period that there would be no probability of its being taken away from him in his old age, when, perhaps, he needs it the most. A very small percentage of the copyrights are ever renewed. All use of them ceases in most cases long before the expiration of twenty-eight years. In the comparatively few cases where the work survives the original term the author

ought to be given an adequate renewal term. In the exceptional case of a brilliant work of literature, art, or musical composition it continues to have a value for a long period, but this value is dependent upon the merit of the composition. Just in proportion as the composition is meritorious and deserving will it continue to be profitable, provided the copyright is extended so long; and it is believed that in all such cases where the merit is very high this term is certainly not too long.

Your committee do not favor and the bill does not provide for any extension of the original term of twenty-eight years, but it does provide for an extension of the renewal term from fourteen years to twenty-eight years; and it makes some change in existing law as to those who may apply for the renewal. Instead of confining the right of renewal to the author, if still living, or to the widow or children of the author, if he be dead, we provide that the author of such work, if still living, may apply for the renewal, or the widow, widower, or children of the author, if the author be not living, or if such author, widow, widower, or children be not living, then the author's executors, or, in the absence of a will, his next of kin. It was not the intention to permit the administrator to apply for the renewal, but to permit the author who had no wife or children to bequeath by will the right to apply for the renewal. (H.Rep. 2222, 60th Cong., 2d Sess., pp. 14–15.)

The report cannot be tortured, by reading it without regard to the circumstances in which it was written, into an expression of a legislative purpose to nullify agreements by authors to assign their renewal interests. If Congress, speaking through its responsible members, had any intention of altering what theretofore had not been questioned, namely, that there were no statutory restraints upon the assignment by authors of their renewal rights, it is almost certain that such purpose would have been manifested. The legislative materials reveal no such intention.

We agree with the court below, therefore, that neither the language nor the history of the Copyright Act of 1909 lend support to the conclusion that the "existing law" prior to 1909, under which authors were free to assign their renewal interests if they were so disposed, was intended to be altered. We agree, also, that there are no compelling considerations of policy which could justify reading into the Act a construction so at variance with its history. The policy of the copyright law, we are told, is to protect the author—if need be, from himself—and a construction under which the author is powerless to assign his renewal interest furthers this policy. We are asked to recognize that authors are congenitally irresponsible, that frequently they are so sorely pressed for funds that they are willing to sell their work for a mere pittance, and therefore assignments made by them should not be upheld. It is important that we distinguish between two problems implied in these situations: whether, despite the contrary direction given to this legislation by the momentum of history, we are to impute to Congress the enactment of an absolute statutory bar against assignments of authors' renewal interests, and secondly, whether, although there be no such statutory bar, a particular assignment should be denied enforcement by the courts because it was made under oppressive circumstances. The first question alone is presented here, and we make no intimations upon the other. It is one thing to hold that the courts should not make themselves instruments of injustice by lending their aid to the enforcement of an agreement where the author was under such coercion of circumstances that enforcement would be unconscionable. Cf. Union Pacific R. Co. v. Public Service Comm'n, 248 U.S. 67, 70; Lonergan v. Buford, 148 U.S. 581, 589–91; Snyder v. Rosenbaum, 215 U.S. 261, 265–66; Post v. Jones, 19 How. 150, 160; The Elfrida, 172 U.S. 186, 193–94. It is quite another matter to hold as we are asked in this case, that regardless of the circumstances surrounding a particular assignment, no agreements by authors to assign their renewal interests are binding.

It is not for courts to judge whether the interests of authors clearly lie upon one side of this question rather than the other. If an author cannot make an effective assignment of his renewal, it may be worthless to him when he is most in need. Nobody would pay an author for something he cannot sell. We cannot draw a principle of law from the familiar stories of garret-poverty of some men of literary genius. Even if we could do so, we cannot say that such men would regard with favor a rule of law preventing them from realizing on their assets when they are most in need of funds. Nor can we be unmindful of the fact that authors have themselves devised means of safeguarding their interests. We do not have such assured knowledge about authorship, and particularly about song writing, or the psychology of gifted writers and composers, as to justify us as judges in importing into Congressional legislation a denial to authors of the freedom to dispose of their property possessed by others. While authors may have habits making for intermittent want, they may have no less a spirit of independence which would resent treatment of them as wards under guardianship of the law.

We conclude, therefore, that the Copyright Act of 1909 does not nullify agreements by authors to assign their renewal interests. * *

Affirmed.

Questions

1. Justice Frankfurter found great significance in that portion of the House Committee Report on the renewal provision of the 1909 Act which stated that the law should be framed *as is the existing law* [italics by the Court], so that he [the author] could not be deprived of that right". What "right" was the House Committee referring to? Wasn't the Committee Report arguing that the author should not be "deprived" of the right to sell the work anew if it proves to have a value beyond the first 28 years of publication? Didn't the Committee Report further indicate that a unitary term of life plus fifty years was rejected precisely because under such a term an author might be "deprived" of such a right? Under the holding in the instant case is there any greater assurance that an author will not be "deprived" of such right under a renewal structure than there would be under a unitary term of life plus fifty years? In referring to "the existing law", is it possible that the Committee, lacking Justice Frank-

furter's erudition, was mistaken as to the assignability of renewals under then existing law? In determining legislative intent, which should be given greater weight, the Committee's reference to "existing law", or its stated desire that the author "not be deprived of that right"?

2. Under the holding in the instant case, of what value to an author is the renewal right? If there were a single term of 75 years rather than an original and a renewal term totalling 75 years, could an author with bargaining power still require a reversion of rights to him after the first 28 years? If an author lacks bargaining power, under the renewal structure can he resist assigning rights in the renewal term at the same time that he assigns rights in the original term if the buyer so insists? In each instance isn't it simply a matter of the author's bargaining power, with the renewal framework quite irrelevant?

3. What do you think of the Court's argument that if a renewal interest is not assignable in advance of its vesting, it may be worthless to an author "when he is in most need."? What is the commercial reality as to the market value of rights which may only be enjoyed some 28 years later? In any event, can the purchaser of an inchoate renewal interest ever be assured that he will in fact acquire the vested renewal? See Miller Music Corp. v. Daniels, 362 U.S. 373 (1960).

4. What should be the rule on an issue which the Court in the instant case said it was not deciding, i.e. whether "a particular assignment should be denied enforcement by the courts because it was made under oppressive circumstances."? Could inadequacy of consideration ever constitute such oppressive circumstances? See Rossiter v. Vogel, 148 F.2d 292 (2d Cir.1945). Cf. Rose v. Bourne, Inc., 279 F.2d 79 (2d Cir.1960).

5. If a prospective buyer demands as a condition to the purchase of rights in an original term that the author also assign renewal rights, does this constitute a violation of the "tying arrangements" provisions of the Sherman Act? See Karp, *Tying Acquisitions of Original and Renewal Copyright Interests,* 10 N.Y.L.F. 25 (1964).

6. Suppose an author during his lifetime assigns his renewal rights to X, and then dies before the renewal vests, leaving neither widow nor children, but with a will which leaves his renewal rights to Y. Who prevails as between X and Y? Should an author be able, in this manner, to cut off his inter vivos assignee? See Miller Music Corp. v. Charles N. Daniels, Inc., 362 U.S. 373 (1960).

7. If an author's wife and children join with him in an assignment of renewal rights, is such assignment binding upon the wife and children if the author does not survive until the renewal copyright vests? Is it necessary in order to bind the wife and children in such circumstances that they receive consideration separate from that which flowed to the author? Is the answer to the preceding question different if the wife and children consent to the assignment of renewal subsequent to the author's execution of a renewal assignment but prior to the author's death? What is the effect if some, but not all, of the children join in an assignment of renewal?

8. If at the time an author agrees to assign the renewal interest he has living a wife and children, is there any way that the assignee can be certain that he will acquire the renewal when it vests even if the author is not living at that time?

9. If an instrument purports to convey all of an author's "right, title and interest by way of copyrights or otherwise in and to" certain musical compositions, does the grantee obtain renewal rights? See Marks Music Corp. v. C.K. Harris Publishing Co., 255 F.2d 518 (2d Cir.1958), holding that renewal is not assigned in the absence of express language to this effect. Cf. Venus Music Corp. v. Mills Music Inc., 261 F.2d 577 (2d Cir.1958), holding that the word "forever" may impliedly include renewal rights.

10. If A grants to X "all rights throughout the world" in a certain work without mention of renewal rights, may A then grant to Y the renewal copyright within the United States? May A grant to Y the copyright outside the United States commencing with the beginning of the renewal term within the United States? Note that the copyright term in most other jurisdictions is unitary, not divided into an original and renewal period.

Collateral Reference

Nimmer on Copyright, § 9.06.

ROHAUER v. KILLIAM SHOWS, INC.

United States Court of Appeals, Second Circuit, 1977.
551 F.2d 484.

Before: WATERMAN, FRIENDLY and MULLIGAN, CIRCUIT JUDGES.

FRIENDLY, CIRCUIT JUDGE. This well briefed and argued appeal raises a question of copyright law of first impression.[1] The question is of considerable importance despite the small amount of money here at stake. The issue is this: When the author of a copyrighted story has assigned the motion picture rights and consented to the assignee's securing a copyright on motion picture versions, with the terms of the assignment demonstrating an intention that the rights of the purchaser shall extend through a renewal of the copyright on the story, does a purchaser which has made a film and obtained a derivative copyright and renewal copyright thereon infringe the copyright on the story if it authorizes the performance of the copyrighted film after the author has died and the copyright on the story has been renewed by a statutory successor under 17 U.S.C.A. § 24 who has made a new assignment of motion picture and television rights? As has been so often true in cases arising under the Copyright Act of 1909, neither an affirmative nor a negative answer is completely satisfactory. A court must grope to ascertain what would have been the thought of the 1909 Congress on an issue about which it almost certainly never thought at all. See Twentieth Century Music Corp. v. Aiken, 422 U.S. 151, 156 (1975). In returning an affirmative answer to the question posed, JUDGE BAUMAN recognized that the negative would not be illogical, see 379 F.Supp. at 727. While we recognize that an affirmative answer likewise is by no

---

1. Appellants loudly assert this to be so. Appellees concede we have a case of first impression but only "in the strictest possible sense." For reasons later developed, we think it is a case of first impression *simpliciter*.

means illogical, we believe a negative answer is more in keeping with the letter and purposes of the statute as best we can discern them.

There is no dispute about the facts. Sometime before May 15, 1925, Edith Maude Hull (Mrs. Hull), a British subject, wrote a novel entitled "The Sons of the Sheik." The novel was published in the United States about that time by Small, Maynard & Co., Inc., which obtained a United States copyright, assigned by it to Mrs. Hull in November 1925. By an instrument dated December 7, 1925, Mrs. Hull, as Seller, for a consideration of $21,000, granted, sold and assigned to Joseph H. Moskowitz, as Purchaser, all the motion picture rights to the story for the entire world, "together with the sole and exclusive right to make motion picture versions thereof," to secure copyright on the films, and to "vend, exhibit, exploit and otherwise dispose of the same." The Seller agreed "to renew or procure the renewal of the copyrights" in the story prior to their expiration and thereupon to assign to the Purchaser the motion picture rights for the renewal term.[2]

Pursuant to this agreement, a highly successful silent motion picture entitled "The Son of the Sheik," starring Rudolph Valentino, was produced and released for exhibition in the United States in 1926. On August 24, 1926, the picture was registered in the Copyright Office by and in the name of Feature Productions, Inc., an assignee of Moskowitz. This copyright was renewed on March 18, 1954, in the name of Artcinema Associates, Inc., the then proprietor of the copyright; the renewal copyright was sold in 1961 to Gregstan Enterprises, Inc., a corporation headed by Paul Killiam, and was assigned by Gregstan to the defendant Killiam Shows, Inc. (hereafter Killiam) in 1968.

Mrs. Hull died in 1943. On May 22, 1952, the United States copyright in the novel was renewed in the name of her daughter, Cecil Winstanley Hull (Miss Hull), a party plaintiff herein, the author's sole surviving child. On May 6, 1965, Miss Hull assigned to plaintiff Rohauer all of her "right, title and interest (if any) in and to the motion picture and television rights of every kind and character throughout the world and in all languages" to "Sons of the Sheik." Rohauer paid 446 pounds 10 shillings (then the equivalent of $1250) for this assignment.

On July 13, 1971, the motion picture was shown on television station WNET, owned by defendant Educational Broadcasting Corporation (hereafter Broadcasting) and operating on Channel 13 in the New York metropolitan area. The videotape required for this exhibition was made by Broadcasting from a print of the film made available to it

---

2. The appellants concede that because of Mrs. Hull's death before the accrual of the right to a renewal of the United States copyright in the novel, they could not obtain specific enforcement of this agreement in respect of such copyright; they rely on the clause as demonstrating an intention of the parties, which appellees do not dispute, that the Purchaser should be entitled to the motion picture rights both for the original and for any renewal term.

Rudolph Valentino and co-star in *Son of the Sheik*.

by Killiam. No license had been obtained from plaintiffs Rohauer or Miss Hull, although Rohauer's attorney had informed an officer of Killiam in 1966 of his assignment from Miss Hull and had advised that any showing of the picture would constitute an infringement. Similar notice was given by Rohauer's counsel to Broadcasting the day before the first television showing. After this action was commenced the film was shown twice more on Channel 13.

The plaintiffs claimed and the District Court held, 379 F.Supp. 723 (S.D.N.Y.1974), that upon the expiration of the original term of the copyright in the novel and Miss Hull's succession to the renewal term, all rights of defendants and their predecessors to authorize the exhibition of the motion picture terminated. Defendants-appellants contend that while after the expiration of the original term of the copyright in the novel and the daughter's succession, no new motion picture versions could lawfully be made on the basis of the 1925 grant from Mrs. Hull, their predecessors and they were entitled to renew the copyright on a film already made and copyrighted and to authorize its exhibition.

I

In endeavoring to answer the question here posed, we turn first to the words of the statute. Derivative copyright is provided for in 17 U.S.C. § 7, which states in pertinent part:

> Compilations or abridgments, adaptations, arrangements, dramatizations, translations, or other versions of works in the public domain or of copyrighted works when produced with the consent of the proprietor of the copyright in such works * * * shall be regarded as new works subject to copyright under the provisions of this title; but the publication of any such new works shall not affect the force or validity of any subsisting copyright upon the matter employed or any part thereof, or be construed to imply an exclusive right to such use of the original works, or to secure or extend copyright in such original works.

Section 24 of title 17 begins by stating that "[t]he copyright secured by this title shall endure for twenty-eight years from the date of first publication." An initial proviso states that in several cases there enumerated, including "any work copyrighted * * * by an employer for whom such work is made for hire," the proprietor of the copyright shall be entitled to renewal and extension for a further twenty-eight year term. The problem here arises from a second proviso, stating in pertinent part:

> That in the case of any other copyrighted work * * * the author of such work, if still living, or the widow, widower, or children of the author, if the author be not living, * * * shall be entitled to a renewal and extension of the copyright in such work for a further term of twenty-eight years when application for such renewal and extension shall have been made to the copyright office and duly registered therein within one year prior to the expiration of the original term of copyright * * *.

The thrust of the portion of § 7 down to the semicolon—and it is a strong thrust—is rather clear.[3] Doubtless aware, even in those simpler days, that new versions of copyrighted works might involve a degree of intellectual effort and expense quite as great as or considerably greater than the contribution of the author of the underlying work, Congress provided that derivative works "shall be regarded *as new works subject to copyright under the provisions of this title*" (emphasis supplied); plaintiffs-appellees do not dispute that the current proprietor of such a copyright, if the work was originally copyrighted as a work "made for

---

3. The 1909 Copyright Act was the first in this country to provide explicit protection for derivative works, although § 5 of the 1891 Act had provided that new "alterations, revisions, and additions" made to books of foreign authors could be copyrighted, 26 Stat. 1108; § 4 of the 1865 Act provided that the "books" subject to copyright under the 1831 Act included "any second or subsequent edition which shall be published with any additions," 13 Stat. 540; and the 1856 Act made explicit the copyright protection of dramatic compositions, 11 Stat. 138, although the right to dramatize an underlying work was not reserved to the author of the work until 1870, 16 Stat. 212. Protection for derivative works was further provided under case law, which considered compilations, digests, and translations as among the works subject to copyright, see Gray v. Russell, 10 Fed.Cas. 1035 (No. 5,728) (C.C.D.Mass.1839) (Story, J.); Banks v. McDivitt, 2 Fed.Cas. 759 (No. 961) (C.C.S.D.N.Y.1875); Shook v. Rankin, 21 Fed.Cas. 1335 (No. 12,804) (C.C.N.D.Ill. 1875).

hire", is entitled to effect a renewal of the derivative copyright under § 24. Shapiro, Bernstein & Co. v. Bryan, 123 F.2d 697 (2d Cir.1941); Picture Music, Inc. v. Bourne, Inc., 457 F.2d 1213 (2d Cir.), cert. denied, 409 U.S. 997 (1972).

When we look to the second half of the sentence, taking the subjects in reverse order, we find that defendants-appellants are not attempting "to secure or extend copyright" in Mrs. Hull's original work. Likewise they do not assert that Killiam's derivative copyright implies "an exclusive right to such use of the original works"; they concede that any such exclusive right would rest on the agreement of December 7, 1925 and at least implicitly that any such exclusivity, as distinguished from a right of continued use, terminated with the original term of the copyright on the novel. Likewise, they do not assert that the publication of the derivative work has any effect on the "validity" of any subsisting copyright. Plaintiffs say, however, that defendants' acts do affect the "force" of Miss Hull's renewal copyright on the novel, since the defendants are invading their exclusive right under § 1 of the Copyright Act to make copies of the work; to "make any other version thereof, if it be a literary work; to dramatize it if it be a nondramatic work"; to make any "transcription or record" of the underlying work from which it might be exhibited or produced in whole or part; and to perform the work in public for profit. Each exhibition of the Valentino film presumably thus constitutes a "dramatization" of the underlying story exclusively reserved to plaintiffs, see Kalem Company v. Harper Brothers, 222 U.S. 55, 61 (1911) (Holmes, J.), and an unauthorized "copying" of the underlying story, see Patterson v. Century Productions, Inc., 93 F.2d 489 (2d Cir.1937), cert. denied 303 U.S. 655 (1938). On a parity of reasoning creation of any new prints of the film presumably amounts to manufacturing a new "transcription or record" of the underlying novel, see Sheldon v. Metro-Goldwyn Pictures Corporation, 106 F.2d 45, 52 (2d Cir.), cert. denied 308 U.S. 617 (1939), aff'd 309 U.S. 390 (1940); Metro-Goldwyn-Mayer Distributing Corporation v. Bijou Theatre Co., 59 F.2d 70, 73 (1 Cir.1932). In addition, the Authors League of America, Inc. argues in its amicus brief that the "force" of the renewal copyright on an underlying work includes the proprietor's right to "refrain from vending or licensing" and "simply * * * to exclude others from using his property," Fox Film Corp. v. Doyal, 286 U.S. 123, 127 (1932), including preventing any public exhibition for profit of the derivative work.

Defendants answer that sufficient "force" is given to the renewal copyright on the novel if it is held to prevent any new or "second generation" derivative works, without going to the extent of holding that the owner of the derivative copyright may not "print, reprint, publish, copy, and vend the copyrighted work" represented by the derivative copyright, along with others whom the new owner of the underlying copyright may license to make derivative works not infringing the "new matter" added by the owner of the derivative copyright.

A legislative history of the 1909 Copyright Act edited and compiled by E. Fulton Brylawski and Abe Goldman which became available only late in 1976,[4] after this appeal had been argued, indicates to us that the "force or validity" clause of § 7 has no bearing on the problem here at issue. In the bills introduced on May 31, 1906, § 7 [then § 6] read as follows:

> Sec. 6. That additions to copyrighted works and alterations, revisions, abridgments, dramatizations, translations, compilations, arrangements, or other versions of works, whether copyrighted or in the public domain, shall be regarded as new works subject to copyright under the provisions of this Act; but no such copyright shall affect the force or validity of any subsisting copyright upon the matter employed or any part thereof, or be construed to grant an exclusive right to such use of the original works.

The clear import of the "but" clause was to protect an author of an original work against two risks thought to be possible as a result of the recognition of derivative copyright. Since the bills as they then stood did not contain the qualification "when produced with the consent of the proprietor of the copyright in such works", it was necessary to provide that derivative copyright should not "be construed to grant an exclusive right to such use of the original works"; such exclusive use would result only from contractual arrangements. The other objective was that nothing done by the proprietor of the derivative copyright should impair the underlying copyright.

Most of the discussion of the derivative copyright section focused on the concern that recognition of derivative copyright might extend the duration of the copyright in the original work. After some discussion whether this did not require a provision that derivative copyright should cease on the expiration of the underlying copyright,[5] the problem was ultimately met by the addition of the final words, "or to secure or extend copyright in such original works."[6]

The change in the language of the "force or validity" clause—from "no such copyright shall affect" to "the publication of any such new works shall not affect"—was due to a comment by Mr. W.B. Hale, representing the American Law Book Company at Joint Hearings before the House and Senate Committees on Patents on March 26, 1908 (Legislative History K78). Addressing himself to the Kittredge bill, see note 6, Mr. Hale testified as follows:

4. Legislative History of the 1909 Copyright Act (E. Brylawski & A. Goldman, eds.) (Fred B. Rothman & Co., 1976).

5. *See* Stenographic Report of the Proceedings of the Librarian of Congress' Conference on Copyright, 1st Session, June 1, 1905, reprinted in Legislative History, supra note 4, at C106–108.

6. The first Kittredge bill, S. 8190, introduced on January 29, 1907, included the phrase "when produced with the consent of the proprietor of the copyright in such works" and the final phrase "or to secure or extend," etc. However, the "force or validity" clause still began "but no such copyright." This pattern was followed by the second Kittredge bill, S. 2900, introduced December 18, 1907, and in the other bills introduced prior to March 1908 (H.R. 25133, Rep. Currier, January 29, 1907; H.R. 243, Rep. Currier, December 2, 1907; S. 2499, Sen. Smoot, December 16, 1907; R.H. 11794, Rep. Barchfeld, January 6, 1908).

Mr. Hale * * *.

There is another verbal criticism I should like to make in section 6 of the Kittredge bill, which also relates to compilations, abridgments, etc.

The Chairman [Senator Smoot]. I think it is the same in the other bills.

Mr. Hale. Yes; it is the same in all the bills. I heartily agree with and am in favor of that section; but in line 12, in lieu of the words "but no such copyright shall effect the force or validity," etc., I would prefer to substitute these words: "and the publication of any such new work shall not affect the copyright," etc.

That is to meet this situation. It is the publication of a book without copyright protection that forfeits the copyright, or the publication of a book without proper notice, or anything of that kind. Under the act, as it stands now, it says the copyright shall not affect it. I would like to meet the case of a new compiled work, within the meaning of this clause, that is not copyrighted, or where, by reason of some accident the copyright fails. That should not affect the original copyrights in the works that have entered into and formed a part of this new compiled work. It does not change the intent of the section in any way.

This makes clear,[7] as indeed a close reading of the language of what is now § 7 would do alone, that the "force or validity" clause has no bearing on the problem here before us, that is rather how far an author's consent under the first clause of § 7 continues to authorize publication of the copyrighted derivative work during a renewal term of the underlying copyright secured by a statutory successor under § 24.

II

Turning to the precedents, we do not find that any of the Supreme Court decisions discussed at length in the briefs, primarily Fox Film Corporation v. Knowles, 261 U.S. 326 (1923), Fred Fisher Music Co. v. M. Witmark & Sons, 318 U.S. 643 (1943), De Sylva v. Ballentine, 351 U.S. 570 (1956), and Miller Music Corp. v. Charles N. Daniels, Inc., 362 U.S. 373 (1960), has any real bearing on the issue here before us, either in holding or in opinion. All these cases were concerned with the relative rights of persons claiming full assignment or ownership of the renewal term of an underlying copyright. None involved the question here presented of effecting a proper reconciliation between the grant of derivative copyright in § 7 and the final proviso of § 24 with respect to renewals of underlying copyrights.

Appellees contend that even if this be so, the question here at issue has been settled in their favor by lower court decisions, notably Fitch v.

---

7. The House report accompanying the final version of the 1909 bill, H.R.Rep. No. 2222, 60th Cong., 2d Sess. 10 (accompanying H.R. 28192) noted simply—and incompletely:

Section 6 reenacts existing law and permits the copyrighting of abridgments and new versions of works, or works republished with new matter, but provides that such copyright shall give no exclusive right to the use of the original works or in any way extend the copyright on such original works.

Shubert, 20 F.Supp. 314 (S.D.N.Y.1937); G. Ricordi & Co. v. Paramount Pictures, Inc., 189 F.2d 469 (2d Cir.1951), cert. denied, 342 U.S. 849; and Sunset Securities Company v. Coward McCann, Inc., 297 P.2d 137 (Dist.Ct. of Appeal 2d Dist.1956), vacated 47 Cal.2d 907, 306 P.2d 777 (1957). Apart from the fact that none of these cases except *Ricordi* would bind us as a precedent, we do not find that any of them decided the question here at issue.

The *Fitch* case involved a dispute between the plaintiff Richard W. Fitch who, as next of kin of the author Clyde Fitch, had obtained a renewal copyright after Clyde Fitch's death on a play called "Barbara Frietchie, The Frederick Girl," and the defendants who had produced a musical version of the play, known as "My Maryland." Clyde Fitch had died intestate without widow or child in 1909, years before the expiration in 1928 of the original term of the copyright in the play. His interest in the initial term passed first to his mother and, after her death, by her bequest to the Actors' Fund of America. In 1925, contemplating the production of an operetta based on "Barbara Frietchie" the Shuberts negotiated a license agreement with the Actors' Fund; the operetta was first produced in 1927, and was leased by the Shuberts for amateur performances over many years thereafter. In 1927 Richard Fitch renewed the copyright on the play and, after the Shuberts had mounted another production, sued them in 1937 for infringement. Although the ultimate holding was that the defendants had acquired a license from the plaintiff by direct dealings with him in the renewal term, Judge Patterson did say, 20 F.Supp. at 315.

[I]t is clear that the plaintiff acquired a new and independent right in the copyright, free and clear of any rights, interests, or licenses attached to the copyright for the initial term * * *. It is evident therefore that all rights which the defendants acquired in 1925 to use the Fitch play as the basis of a musical operetta expired when the copyright for the original term expired in 1928 and when a new grantee appeared as owner of the Fitch play for the renewal term.

However, this was said in a case where without dispute the original license agreement was limited to the first term; not only did the license agreement make no reference to renewal rights, Epoch Producing Corporation v. Killiam Shows, Inc., 522 F.2d 737, 747 (2d Cir.1975), cert. denied, 424 U.S. 955 (1976), but no one could have meant it to do so. The Shuberts had not obtained the license agreement from an author who could contemplate renewal, but from a charitable grantee after the author's death, when the renewal rights had passed by statute to the next of kin surviving at the end of the original term.

Ricordi was a suit by G. Ricordi & Co. for a declaratory judgment against Paramount Pictures, Inc. The case involved the story, play and opera entitled "Madame Butterfly." The novel was written in 1897 by John Luther Long, published that year in Century Magazine and copyrighted by the Century Company. In 1900 David Belasco wrote a play with the consent of the copyright owner which, however, was not copyrighted until 1917. In 1901 Long and Belasco entered into a contract with Ricordi giving it the exclusive right to make a libretto for an opera of Belasco's dramatic version of Madame Butterfly. In 1904 Ricordi copyrighted the famous opera composed by Puccini and subsequently secured an assignment from Puccini's son of the renewal copyright therein. In 1925 Long obtained a renewal of the copyright on his novel and in 1932, subsequent to Long's death, his administrator granted the motion picture rights therein to Paramount. In the same year, with the Belasco play still in its first copyright term, Paramount obtained from the trustee of Belasco's will an assignment of the motion picture rights to the play; no renewal of the copyright in the play was ever effected. Ricordi sought a declaration that it was entitled to make a motion picture of the opera free from any interference by Paramount. This court, speaking through Judge Swan for a particularly distinguished bench including Judge Learned Hand and Judge Frank, held that Ricordi was not entitled to so broad a declaration. Ricordi's renewal copyright in the opera extended only to so much of the opera as was "a new work." Hence it was not entitled to make general use of the novel for a motion picture version of its opera but was restricted for that purpose to what was copyrightable as new matter in its operatic version.

Ricordi is not determinative here, however, for a fundamental reason: the original 1901 agreement between Long, Belasco, and Ricordi did not purport to run beyond the original term of Long's copyright on the novel. Ricordi neither sought nor obtained operatic rights in the renewal term of the novel in the 1901 agreement, or in any other negotiation.[8] To conclude that the renewal term of a copyright is a new estate free from previous licenses is one thing when, as in *Ricordi*, the parties have never bargained for renewal rights, and another when, as in the case of Mrs. Hull and Joseph Moskowitz, the assignment agreement explicitly included rights to the derivative work during the renewal term.

We find even less helpful to the plaintiffs the decisions previously cited in the California case of Sunset Securities Company v. Coward McCann, Inc. For whatever it may be worth, the opinion of the District Court of Appeal is favorable to the defendants and the reversal by the California Supreme Court was on the grounds of contract rather than of copyright law.

The short of the matter is that we have been cited to no case holding that the inability of an author to carry out his promise to effect a renewal of a copyright because of his death prior to the date for obtaining renewal terminates *as a matter of copyright law* the right of a

---

8. As the *Ricordi* court noted, the 1901 agreement "made no allusion to renewal of copyright." 189 F.2d at 471. It did not even contain more oblique language granting operatic rights "for all time." Though Belasco's play fell into the public domain in 1945 at the end of its first term, Long did renew the copyright on his novel, and Ricordi conceded it had never sought a new license for operatic rights from Long for the renewal term.

holder of a derivative copyright to continue to publish a derivative work copyrighted before the author's death on which the copyright was thereafter renewed. It is equally true that we have been cited no case upholding such a right.

With arguments based on the "force or validity" clause of § 7 eliminated by the legislative history, we do not believe, despite language in the cases to the effect that the proprietor of a derivative copyright is "protected" only as to the "new matter" conceived by him and that a statutory successor obtains a "new estate" in the underlying copyright, that the vesting of renewed copyright in the underlying work in a statutory successor deprives the proprietor of the derivative copyright of a right, stemming from the § 7 "consent" of the original proprietor of the underlying work, to use so much of the underlying copyrighted work as already has been embodied in the copyrighted derivative work, as a matter of copyright law. That view is only a slight extension of this court's decision in Edmonds v. Stern, 248 F. 897 (2d Cir.1918). There the purchaser of a song, having copyrighted it with the consent of the composer, prepared an operetta and copyrighted an orchestral medley based on the operetta which utilized, among other things, the notes of the song. Later the purchaser assigned the copyright in the song back to the composer. The court held, as an alternate ground of decision, that the reassignment would not deprive the proprietor of the copyright of the score of the right to sell copies of the medley since, as Judge Hough said, 248 F. at 898,

> The two things [the song and the orchestral score] were legally separate, and independent of each other; it makes no difference that such separate and independent existence might to a certain extent have grown out of plaintiff's consent to the incorporation of his melody in the orchestration. When that consent was given, a right of property sprang into existence, not at all affected by the conveyance of any other right.[9]

So here when the purchaser from Mrs. Hull embodied her story in a motion picture which was copyrighted under § 7, the vesting of the renewal right of the story in her daughter did not affect the property right in the copyrighted derivative work.

The District Court and appellees rely also on the views of the leading text writer, Professor Nimmer, and of commentators to the effect that in circumstances such as those here presented performance of the derivative copyrighted film after the expiration of the original term of the underlying copyright and renewal by a statutory successor constitutes an infringement. The only portion of Nimmer's text which deals specifically with this problem is § 118, entitled "The Effect of a Termination of Rights After the Original Term of Copyright Upon

---

9. It is true that in stating the facts the court noted that the orchestral arrangement "of course, contained no words." We think that in saying this, the court was simply following the usual and proper judicial practice of deciding only an easier case that is before it rather than a harder one that is not. To our minds the court's reasoning would cover the sale of a text and score of the operetta as well as of the purely orchestral medley.

Previously Created Copies." This discussion, which covers both book publishers and motion picture producers, makes no reference to the special problem of derivative copyright and statutory successors. Mr. Bricker's article, "Renewal and Extension of Copyright," 29 S.Cal.L. Rev. 23, 43 (1955), likewise discusses the instant problem only briefly and in a conclusory manner. Barbara A. Ringer, the present Register of Copyrights, in her 1960 study for the Senate Judiciary Committee entitled "Renewal of Copyright" (Study No. 31), reprinted in 1 Studies on Copyright 503 (Copyright Society of the U.S.A.1963), is quite tentative on the subject:

> It would seem, on the basis of judicial authority, legislative history, and the opinions of the commentators, that someone cannot avoid his obligations to the owner of a renewal copyright merely because he created and copyrighted a "new version" under a license or assignment which terminated at the end of the first term.

1 Studies on Copyright 565–66 (footnotes omitted), see also id. at 564. Ms. Ringer does not single out the problem of statutory succession and continued use in a case where, unlike *Fitch*, a derivative copyright owner has been promised rights to the renewal term by the deceased author.[10] Professor (now Mr. Justice) Benjamin Kaplan, in his Carpentier Lectures, An Unhurried View of Copyright 112 (1967), after characterizing the renewal provisions of § 24 as "a goulash," states that the distinction extrapolated from the *Fred Fisher* case, supra, 318 U.S. 643, as between authors who do or do not survive the original term "may operate in a peculiarly perverse way where on the faith of a transfer from the now-deceased author, the transferee has created a 'derivative work,' say a movie based on the original novel." One can hardly take this as an authoritative pronouncement that the transferee would not even be entitled to exhibit those copies he has already made, still less as meaning that Mr. Justice Kaplan would be opposed to a holding which avoided so "peculiarly perverse" a result. As against these comments, appellants cite an article by Professor Donald Engel, 12 Bulletin of the Copyright Society 83, 119–20 & n. 126 (1964), which concludes:

> The cases indicate that the proprietor of the copyright in an authorized new work who no longer has authorization to use the underlying work may continue to use the new work in substantially identical form but may not create a new version of the new work which also constitutes a new version of the underlying work.

and says of *Ricordi,* correctly in our judgment:

> the "Madame Butterfly" case did not hold that the proprietor of the copyright in the new work was precluded from making copies of or permitting public performances of the opera, but merely held that he could

---

10. Unlike Ms. Ringer, we do not see any significance for the purposes of this case in the references in the 1906–1908 hearings indicating that derivative copyright protected only so much of a new version as was "new matter." See, e.g., Hearings before the House and Senate Committees on Patents on S. 6330 and H.R. 19853, at 364–65 (December 1906). This was said to answer expressed fears that the grant of derivative copyright might extend the term of copyright in the underlying work. See the discussion in text, supra.

not make *general* use of the protected underlying material for the creation of a motion picture, itself a new work based upon the underlying copyright which he no longer had authorization to use.

See also Kupferman, "Renewal of Copyright—Section 23 of the Copyright Act of 1909," 44 Columbia L.Rev. 712, 724 (1944). We thus do not discern any such impressive record of unanimity among the commentators as influenced the Supreme Court in the *Fred Fisher* case, supra, 318 U.S. at 658–59 nn. 5–8. Likewise we find little force in the apparent practice of at least some holders of derivative copyrights to obtain consents from identifiable statutory successors. Plaintiffs offered no evidence how widespread the practice is, and when the consent can be obtained cheaply, it is obvious good sense to get it so long as the law remains unsettled.

To such extent as it may be permissible to consider policy considerations, the equities lie preponderantly in favor of the proprietor of the derivative copyright. In contrast to the situation where an assignee or licensee has done nothing more than print, publicize and distribute a copyrighted story or novel, a person who with the consent of the author has created an opera or a motion picture film will often have made contributions both literary, musical and economic as great as or greater than the original author. As pointed out in the Bricker article, supra, 29 S.Cal.L.Rev. at 33, the purchaser of derivative rights has no truly effective way to protect himself against the eventuality of the author's death before the renewal period since there is no way of telling who will be the surviving widow, children or next of kin or the executor until that date arrives. To be sure, this problem exists in equal degree with respect to assignments or licenses of underlying copyright, but in such cases there is not the countervailing consideration that large and independently copyrightable contributions will have been made by the transferee. As against this, the author can always protect his heirs by imposing a contractual limit upon the assignment. It is true that this might not be practicable from a business standpoint in cases where the assignment was made shortly before the expiration of the initial term, but those are the very cases where the inequity of terminating the transferee's rights with respect to so much of the underlying work as is embodied in the derivative work is the greatest.

We find recognition of these policy considerations in §§ 203(b)(1) and 304(c)(6)(A) of the recently enacted copyright revision bill, 90 Stat. 2541 (1976). In connection with a new plan whereby copyright in any work created on or after January 1, 1978 or created before that date but not then yet published or copyrighted shall, with certain exceptions, run for the life of the author, plus 50 years, with any grant of a transfer or license subject to a right of termination between the 35th and 40th year of the grant; and the renewal term of any existing copyright is extended for another 19 years subject to a right of termination of any transfer or license at the end of the 28th year of the renewal term over a like period of five years, Congress expressly provided:

A derivative work prepared under authority of the grant before its termination may continue to be utilized under the terms of the grant after its termination, but this privilege does not extend to the preparation after the termination of other derivative works based upon the copyrighted work covered by the terminated grant.

§§ 203(b)(1), 304(c)(6)(A). While it is true that this proviso was part of a package which extended the temporal rights of authors (but also of their assignees) and that the proviso thus does not deal with the precise situation here presented, we nevertheless regard it as evidence of a belief on the part of Congress of the need for special protection for derivative works.[11] We agree, of course, that provisions of the new Act cannot be read as varying clear provisions of the 1909 Act in cases to which the new Act does not apply. However, the present situation fits rather well under Judge Lumbard's language in Goodis v. United Artists Television, Inc., 425 F.2d 397, 403 (2d Cir.1970):

> Our decision today is that the result which the proposed legislation would compel is not precluded in any way by the decisions rendered under the present Copyright Act. As discussed earlier, the "problem" with which the proposed legislation deals is one which exists because of judicial dicta rendered in cases not apposite to the factual situation before us in this case.

For these reasons we hold that the licensing by Killiam of exhibition of the film already copyrighted and its exhibition by Broadcasting did not violate the renewal copyright.[12]

In view of this holding we have no occasion to pass on the various affirmative defenses raised by appellants and rejected by the District Court. There are two principal ones. Plaintiff Rohauer is alleged to come into court with unclean hands since he frequently exhibited the movie prior to 1965 without obtaining a license either from Miss Hull or from the proprietors of the motion picture copyright. The other is a defense of res judicata based upon a judgment of the District Court for

---

11. See S.Rep. No. 473, 94th Cong., 1st Sess. 111 (1975):

An important limitation on the rights of a copyright owner under a terminated grant is specified in section 203(b)(1). This clause provides that, notwithstanding a termination, a derivative work prepared earlier may "continue to be utilized" under the conditions of the terminated grant; the clause adds, however, that this privilege is not broad enough to permit the preparation of other derivative works. In other words, a film made from a play could continue to be licensed for performance after the motion picture contract had been terminated, but any remake rights covered by the contract would be cut off.

See also Second Supplementary Report of the Register of Copyrights on the General Revision of the U.S. Copyright Law: 1975 Revision Bill, October—December 1975, ch. XI, p. 10:

Section 203 is a compromise that attempts to balance the interests of individual authors and their transferees in a fairer way than the present renewal provision.

12. Plaintiffs-appellees contend that even assuming the general correctness of our conclusion, there would be an infringement here since the print licensed by Killiam was used by Broadcasting to create a new videotape for television transmission; plaintiffs contend that this amounts to a "new version" of the original film. Since it was stipulated that such a videotape was necessary for television transmission, we see no reason to consider this tape to be a new version of the film. As appellees admit, only a few new subtitles were used in the videotape; the newly incorporated music alone, which was certainly not within plaintiffs' copyright, is not sufficient to make it a new work.

the Southern District of Iowa in an action by Rohauer against another license of Killiam which the latter defended, where the court dismissed the complaint because of Rohauer's refusal to submit to discovery, Rohauer v. Eastin-Phelan Corporation, Civ. 72–25–D (S.D.Iowa, Feb. 7, 1974), aff'd 499 F.2d 120 (8th Cir.1974). If we were obliged to rule on these defenses, we would regard them as warranting somewhat more consideration than did the district judge.

The judgment is reversed with instructions to dismiss the complaint.

Questions

1. Does the *Rohauer* court assume that the copyright in a derivative work attaches to everything contained therein, including the underlying work as to which the derivative work copyright owner is only a licensee? Is this a correct assumption? Recall G. Ricordi & Co. v. Paramount Pictures, Inc., supra.

2. Does the *Rohauer* court hold that a purported grant of renewal rights, where such rights never vest in the grantor, is to be given the same effect as would be the case if such rights had vested? Is the grantee of such a purported grant entitled to produce a new derivative work during the renewal period? If the purported grant is invalid for this purpose, how can it nevertheless be held valid for the purpose of continuing to "utilize" during the renewal term a derivative work validly created during the original term of the underlying copyright? Do Secs. 203(b)(1) and 304(c)(6)(A) of the new Copyright Act justify this result? Does the fact that these sections apply to termination of transfers rather than to renewal copyright imply to the contrary that no such continued "utilization" right may be claimed where the rights in the underlying work cease by reason of a failure of the renewal to vest in the grantor rather than by reason of the grantor's termination of the transfer of rights in the underlying work?

3. Does the manner in which the *Rohauer* court distinguished *Ricordi* satisfy you? Should a purported grant of rights, if the grantor has no power to make such a grant because such rights never vest in him, be held to convey any rights? Suppose that the defendant's grantor in *Rohauer* had never owned either the original term or renewal copyrights in the work. If such grantor had "purported" to grant rights under the renewal term copyright, would a court give any effect to such a grant? If not, why should the result be different if the grantor did own the original term copyright, but still did not own the purportedly granted rights in the renewal term?

4. Should *Rohauer* be followed under the new Copyright Act? Is the second sentence of Sec. 103(b) contrary to the court's interpretation of the comparable Sec. 7 provision in the 1909 Act?

Collateral Reference

Nimmer on Copyright, §§ 3.07[A], 9.07.

Chapter Six

TRANSFERS OF COPYRIGHT

Note *

Employment for Hire—Constitutional Limitations

There would appear to be no constitutional objection to permitting the assignee of an author to claim copyright in the work assigned. The author's property right derived from the Constitutional authority is unquestionably assignable.

A more difficult issue is raised, however, by the related question as to whether an employer for hire merely by virtue of such status may claim to be the "author" of the work created by his employee. Section 201(b) of the Copyright Act provides: "In the case of a work made for hire, the employer or other person for whom the work was prepared is considered the author for purposes of this title * * *". Section 26 of the 1909 Act similarly provided that "the word 'author' shall include an employer in the case of works made for hire." The constitutional validity of the 1909 Act provision was never ruled upon, but Judge Friendly in a dissenting opinion (but not dissenting on this point), noted that the Constitution "authorized only the enactment of legislation securing 'authors' the exclusive right of their writings", and concluded: "It would thus be quite doubtful that Congress could grant employers the exclusive right to the writings of employees regardless of the circumstances."[1] This analysis is predicated upon the argument that an employer qua employer cannot by definition be regarded as an "author" and therefore in the absence of an assignment from his author-employee may not constitutionally be entitled to claim copyright. A constitutional defense of Sec. 201(b) of the current Act, and of Sec. 26 of the 1909 Act[2] merely on the basis that Congress has created a sort of legal fiction in regarding an employer as the author renders meaningless the Copyright Clause's use of the term. If Congress may "deem" an employer to be the author, is there any limit to the other classes of persons (besides the true author) who may be the recipient of Congressional beneficence in this manner?[3]

---

* Nimmer on Copyright, § 1.06[C].

1. Scherr v. Universal Match Corp., 417 F.2d 497, 502 (2d Cir.1969).

2. The validity of Sec. 26 of the 1909 Act remains relevant under the current Act since it determines who is the present copyright owner of works made prior to January 1, 1978, the effective date of the current Act.

3. "The power to create presumptions is not a means of escape from constitutional restrictions." Bailey v. Alabama, 219 U.S. 219, 239 (1911).

It would seem, however, that Sec. 201(b) passes constitutional muster by reason of its further provision that the parties may agree "otherwise" as to who "owns all rights comprised in the copyright." Congress has in effect created an implied assignment of rights from the employee-author to his employer—in the absence of an express agreement to the contrary. Thus the employer may be regarded as at least a "quasi-assignee" and as such entitled to the privileges of the author, even if he may not be regarded as the author himself. Section 26 of the 1909 Act did not expressly provide for the validity of such an agreement reserving to the employee rights which would otherwise belong to the employer, but the courts recognized that the Sec. 26 designation of the employer as "author" was based upon a rebuttable presumption of assignment rather than the mere fact of the employer status.

It was, therefore, clear even under the 1909 Act that the parties to an employment agreement might expressly agree that copyright ownership in the resulting work was reserved to the employee.[4]

Under Sec. 201(b) of the current Act the parties may agree that the employee rather than the employer "owns all rights comprised in the copyright," but the proviso that "the employer or other person for whom the work was prepared is considered the author for purposes of this title" is not subject to variation by agreement between the parties. Is it unconstitutional to thus confer authorship status upon the employer "regardless of the circumstances?"[5] Probably not, since the employer is not thereby favored over the employee regardless of the intent of the parties. They may agree that the "rights comprised in the copyright" are effectively owned by the employee. The other legal consequences of authorship status, which are not subject to contrary agreement by the parties, do not favor the employer over the employee. They go rather to the copyrightability of the work, and to the term of protection.[6] The same results could have been achieved even if the employee rather than the employer were deemed the "author." The fiction of the employer as author was employed for these purposes not in order to achieve substantive results that could not have been otherwise achieved, but rather because of the "convenience and simplicity" of this manner of achieving such results.[7]

A. INDIVISIBILITY

Note *

The Doctrine of Indivisibility Under the 1909 Act

As a preliminary to the discussion of transfers of copyright under the current Act, it is necessary first to understand the doctrine of indivisibility as it existed prior to 1978. This is required both because the impact of that doctrine on the copyright status of certain pre-1978 works continues in effect post-1978, and because the so-called divisibility of copyright under the current Act to some extent maintains indivisibility concepts.

---

4. See Scherr v. Universal Match Corp., 417 F.2d 497 (2d Cir.1969).

5. See Scherr v. Universal Match Corp., 417 F.2d 497, 502 (2d Cir.1969) (Friendly, J. dissenting).

6. See Nimmer on Copyright, §§ 5.05[C], 9.01[A][4], 11.02[A][2].

7. See Reg.Supp.Rep., p. 66.

* Nimmer on Copyright, § 10.01.

[A]—The Nature of Indivisibility and the Distinction Between an Assignment and a License

Since the 1909 Act spoke of a single "copyright" to which the author of a work was entitled, and referred in the singular to "the copyright proprietor," it was inferred that the bundle of rights which accrued to a copyright owner were "indivisible," that is, incapable of assignment in parts.[1] This notion, which found its historical roots in an early English copyright case [2] and an American patent case [3] when literally followed renders it impossible to "assign" anything less than the totality of rights commanded by copyright. A transfer of anything less than such a totality was said to be a "license" rather than an assignment.[4] The purpose of such indivisibility was to protect alleged infringers from the harassment of successive law suits.[5] This result was achieved since only the copyright proprietor (which would include an assignee but not a licensee) had standing to bring an infringement action. However, the necessity for such a procedural safeguard was rendered largely nugatory by later adopted rules whereby an exclusive licensee might bring an infringement action subject to the requirement of joining the copyright proprietor as a party plaintiff or defendant.

Whatever justification for indivisibility remained in terms of avoidance of multiplicity of actions was far outweighed by the impeding effect it had upon commerce in copyrighted works. When the doctrine of indivisibility was first enunciated the only effective manner in which copyrighted materials could be exploited was through the reproduction of copies. Hence no great hardship resulted from the doctrine which limited assignments to transfers of all rights under the copyright since there was little incentive to reserve rights other than the reproduction right. The subsequently developed media of communications completely altered this situation. Today the value of motion picture rights in a novel will often far exceed the value of the right to publish the work in book form. Moneys derived from performing and recording popular songs are greatly in excess of the value of "copying" such songs in sheet music form. In short, the development of motion pictures, television, phonograph records, and legitimate stage productions as well as the emergence of the performing rights societies have meant that as a matter of commercial reality "copyright" is now a label for a collection of diverse property rights each of which is separately

---

1. Goldwyn Pictures Corp. v. Howells Sales Co., 282 Fed. 9 (2d Cir.1922); M. Witmark & Sons v. Pastime Amusement Co., 298 Fed. 490 (E.D.S.C.1924); New Fiction Publishing Co. v. Star Co., 220 Fed. 994 (S.D.N.Y.1915); See Ed Brawley, Inc. v. Gaffney, 399 F.Supp. 115 (N.D.Cal.1975), Dam v. Kirke La Shelle Co., 166 Fed. 589 (C.C.N.Y.1908) aff'd 175 Fed. 902 (2d Cir. 1910); Commissioner v. Wodehouse, 337 U.S. 369 (1949).

2. Jeffreys v. Boosey, 4 H.L. (Clark) 184, 10 Eng.Rep. 681 (1854). But cf. Roberts v. Meyers, 20 Fed.Cas. 898, No. 11906 (C.C.Mass.1860).

3. Waterman v. Mackenzie, 138 U.S. 252 (1891).

4. Hirshon v. United Artists Corp., 243 F.2d 640 (D.C.Cir.1957). Goldwyn Pictures Corp. v. Howells Sales Co., 282 Fed. 9 (2d Cir.1922); Goldsmith v. Commissioner, 143 F.2d 466 (2d Cir.1944) (cf. concurring opinion; Rohmer v. Commissioner, 153 F.2d 61 (2d Cir.1946); Misbourne Pictures Ltd. v. Johnson, 90 F.Supp. 978 (S.D.N.Y.1950) aff'd 189 F.2d 774 (2d Cir.1951); Hiawatha Card Co. v. Colourpicture Publishers, Inc., 255 F.Supp. 1015 (E.D.Mich.1966); County of Ventura v. Blackburn, 362 F.2d 515 (9th Cir.1966); First Fin. Marketing Servs. Group, Inc. v. Field Promotions, Inc., 286 F.Supp. 295 (S.D.N.Y.1968).

5. For a most thorough and perceptive analysis of the procedural considerations underlying the doctrine of indivisibility, see the dissenting opinion by Mr. Justice Frankfurter in Commissioner v. Wodehouse, 337 U.S. 369, 401 (1949). See also Fields v. Commissioner, 14 T.C. 1202 (1950); New Fiction Publishing Co. v. Star Co., 220 Fed. 994 (S.D.N.Y.1915).

marketable. The doctrine of indivisibility did not prevent commercial dealings in such separate rights, but it greatly impeded such dealings, and produced technical pitfalls for both buyers and sellers.[6]

[B]—The Substantive Significance Under the 1909 Act of Whether a Grant Was an Assignment or a License [7]

[1]—**Standing to Sue.** Under the 1909 Act, only the proprietor of the copyright had standing to sue for infringement thereof.[8] Since a licensee, as distinguished from an assignee, did not acquire the proprietorship of the copyright, he could not bring an infringement action unless he joined the copyright proprietor in the action.[9] As to *exclusive* licensees this disability was not of great significance in view of procedural machinery available which permitted such a licensee to require that the copyright proprietor be joined in the action.[10] Still, as to a nonexclusive licensee this represented a genuine hardship since it meant that absent cooperation from the copyright proprietor he was unable to prevent competition from one who has not paid for the right to exploit the work. The fact that generally the copyright proprietor would himself wish to pursue such infringers did not assure that this would be true in all instances. Even exclusive licensees were in a somewhat disadvantageous position in this respect both because of the procedural necessity of joining the proprietor, and also because apparently the proprietor might himself bring an infringement action without joining the exclusive licensee even if the action involved the subject matter of the license.[11] The procedural necessity of joinder although not insuperable at the very least offered opportunity for procedural pitfalls in joining the wrong parties, and in incurring delays in joinder which might be most serious where injunctive relief was required.

[2]—**The Right to Claim Copyright.** Perhaps the most serious consequence of the doctrine of indivisibility occurred by reason of the rule that statutory copyright in a theretofore unregistered work was obtained by publication bearing a copyright notice in the name of the copyright owner. The problem thereby raised was felt most acutely and can best be illustrated in the field of magazine rights. If an author of an unpublished (and unregistered) manuscript granted to a magazine publisher the right to reproduce the work in magazine form, but reserved all other rights (e.g., motion picture and book publication rights) then for reasons indicated above the publisher would be merely a licensee, and not the proprietor of the work. Therefore, if, as was and

---

6. For pre-1978 judicial modification of the doctrine of indivisibility see Nimmer on Copyright, § 10.01[B], and Goodis v. United Artists Television, Inc., set forth below.

7. For certain additional areas of substantive significance in this regard see Nimmer on Copyright, § 10.01[C].

8. Nathan v. Monthly Review Press, Inc., 309 F.Supp. 130 (S.D.N.Y.1969) (Treatise cited); see Klauber Bros., Inc. v. Westchester Lace Works, Inc., 181 U.S.P.Q. 523 (S.D.N.Y.1974); Ed Brawley, Inc. v. Gaffney, 399 F.Supp. 115 (N.D.Cal.1975); Greenbie v. Noble, 151 F.Supp. 45 (S.D.N.Y.1957).

9. Ilyin v. Avon Publications, 144 F.Supp. 368 (S.D.N.Y.1956); Stephens v. Howells Sales Co., 16 F.2d 805 (S.D.N.Y. 1926); Public Ledger v. New York Times, 275 Fed. 562 (S.D.N.Y.1921) aff'd 279 Fed. 747 (2d Cir.1922); Goldwyn Pictures Corp. v. Howells Sales Co., 282 Fed. 9 (2d Cir. 1922); New Fiction Publishing Co. v. Star Co., 220 Fed. 994 (S.D.N.Y.1915); Field v. True Comics, Inc., 89 F.Supp. 611 (S.D.N.Y. 1950); Local Trademarks, Inc. v. Powers, 56 F.Supp. 751 (E.D.Pa.1944); First Fin. Marketing Servs. Group, Inc. v. Field Promotions, Inc., 286 F.Supp. 295 (S.D.N.Y.1968).

10. See First Fin. Marketing Servs. Group, Inc. v. Field Promotions, Inc., 286 F.Supp. 295 (S.D.N.Y.1968).

11. See Widenski v. Shapiro, Bernstein & Co., 147 F.2d 909 (1st Cir.1945).

is usually the case, the magazine carried a notice only in the name of the magazine publisher without a separate notice in the name of the contributing author, applying the doctrine of indivisibility the result was that the author's work was published without a valid notice in the name of the work's "proprietor" and it was consequently injected into the public domain.[12] We turn now to the *Goodis* case, in which the Court of Appeals for the Second Circuit modified the indivisibility doctrine under the 1909 Act.

Collateral References

Henn, "Magazine Rights—A Division of Indivisible Copyright," 40 Cornell L.Q. 411 (1955).

Kaminstein, *Divisibility of Copyrights,* Studies on Copyright 623 (1963).

GOODIS v. UNITED ARTISTS TELEVISION, INC.
United States Court of Appeals, Second Circuit, 1970.
425 F.2d 397.

Before LUMBARD, CHIEF JUDGE, WATERMAN and KAUFMAN, CIRCUIT JUDGES.

LUMBARD, CHIEF JUDGE. This appeal raises the important question whether a magazine publisher who acquires only the right to serialize a novel before it is published in book form has such an interest in the work that notice of copyright in the publisher's name will protect the copyright of the author of the novel. It also requires us to review the construction of a contract granting motion picture rights which defendants raise as a defense to this infringement action.

We all agree that the district court erred in concluding that copyright was not obtained by the publisher and that Goodis' work was thus thrown into the public domain without copyright protection. Moreover, since a majority of the panel, Judges Waterman and Kaufman, are of the view that interpretation of the contract involves factual determinations which should not have been made on a motion for summary judgment, we reverse the judgment of the district court and remand for further proceedings on those questions.

The plaintiffs are the executors of David Goodis, author of the novel "Dark Passage," a work which has proved both popular and adaptable to presentation in many of the entertainment media. When Goodis completed the novel in 1945, he made arrangements for the book to be printed in April, 1946. Later, on December 20, 1945, Goodis sold the exclusive motion picture rights in the novel to Warner Broth-

---

12. Letter Edged In Black Press, Inc. v. Public Bldg. Comm'n, 320 F.Supp. 1303 (N.D.Ill.1970). See Geisel v. Poynter Prods., Inc., 295 F.Supp. 331 (S.D.N.Y. 1968); Dam v. Kirke La Shelle Co., 175 Fed. 902 (2d Cir.1910); Leigh v. Barnhart, 96 F.Supp. 194 (D.C.N.J.1951); Kaplan v. Fox Film Corp., 19 F.Supp. 780 (S.D.N.Y.1937); Mail & Express Co. v. Life Publishing Co., 192 Fed. 899 (2d Cir.1912); Mifflin v. R.H. White Co., 190 U.S. 260 (1903); cf. Leigh v. Gerber, 86 F.Supp. 320 (S.D.N.Y.1949); Ford v. Charles E. Blaney Amusement Co., 148 Fed. 642 (C.C.N.Y.1906).

For a discussion of a trust theory, constructed by some courts in order to avoid such a harsh result, see Nimmer on Copyright, § 10.01[C][2].

ers for $25,000. The contract was Warner Brothers' standard form for acquiring movie rights, but, as we state below, it contained additional specially negotiated clauses to cover radio and television broadcast rights.

Before the book was published, Goodis also received $12,000 from Curtis Publishing Co. for the right to serialize the novel in "The Saturday Evening Post," one of Curtis' publications. The book publisher agreed to postpone distribution of the book until October, 1946, and "Dark Passage" was first published in eight installments of "The Saturday Evening Post" running from July 20 to September 7, 1946. Each issue contained a single copyright notice in the magazine's name as provided by the Copyright Act. There was no notice in Goodis' own name.

In due course, Warner Brothers produced a motion picture, also titled "Dark Passage," based on the novel. After the film was exhibited in theaters and shown on television, Warner Brothers in 1956 assigned its contract rights to defendant United Artists. United Artists produced a television film series, "The Fugitive," which was broadcast in weekly installments by defendant American Broadcasting Co. The series enjoyed considerable popularity on television, and early in 1965 Goodis instituted this action claiming $500,000 damages for copyright infringement. The defendants answered that the television series was covered by the contract which had been assigned to them by Warner Brothers.

In 1966, the defendants took Goodis' deposition and learned of his serialization agreement with Curtis. At this point, they conceived the theory that the work had fallen into the public domain because Curtis, a "mere licensee," had taken out copyright in its own name only. By stipulation the defendants amended their answer to include this affirmative defense.

The district court granted defendants' motion for summary judgment and dismissed the complaint on the grounds (1) that "Dark Passage" had fallen into the public domain, and (2) that the contract between Goodis and Warner Brothers clearly conveyed the right to produce a film series like "The Fugitive."

I. The Copyright

We unanimously conclude that where a magazine has purchased the right of first publication under circumstances which show that the author has no intention to donate his work to the public, copyright notice in the magazine's name is sufficient to obtain a valid copyright on behalf of the beneficial owner, the author or proprietor.

In the district court, defendants argued that the single copyright notice in the magazine's name was not sufficient to preserve Goodis' rights in "Dark Passage"; thus, the novel, not being protected upon first publication, was thrown into the public domain as it appeared, installment by installment, in the "Saturday Evening Post." While it is clear that a periodical under some circumstances may obtain copyright for itself on the contents of an issue by a single copyright notice containing its own name, 17 U.S.C.A. § 3; Kaplan v. Fox Film Corp., 19 F.Supp. 780 (S.D.N.Y.1937), defendants urged that Curtis could only obtain copyright on behalf of the beneficial owner for those installments of which it was a "proprietor" or "assignee," rather than a mere "licensee." 17 U.S.C.A. §§ 3, 9; Morse v. Fields, 127 F.Supp. 63 (S.D.N.Y.1954). Relying on Morse v. Fields and cases with similar language, the district court concluded as a matter of law that Curtis could not have been an assignee because it had been granted only a license for a one-time serialization of the novel.

Such a determination rests on the doctrine of "indivisibility of copyright," which rejects partial assignments of copyrights and requires a proprietor or assignee of a copyright to hold nothing less than all the rights in a copyrighted work. It is true that Curtis did not own all the rights in "Dark Passage" at the time it was first published; in fact, at that time Goodis and Warner Brothers had already contracted for the exclusive motion picture rights.

We are convinced, however, that the doctrine of indivisibility of copyright is a judge-made rule which relates primarily to the requisite interest needed to bring an infringement action. See generally, H. Warner, Radio and Television Rights § 53 (1953). The most frequently cited policy for applying the indivisibility rule is to avoid multiple infringement actions, each brought by the holder of a particular right in a literary work without joining as co-plaintiff the author or proprietor of the copyrighted work. New Fiction Pub. Co. v. Star Co., 220 F. 994 (S.D.N.Y.1915). Even after the Copyright Act underwent substantial revision and liberalization in 1909, the courts in this circuit indicated support for the doctrine. See Goldwyn Pictures Corp. v. Howells Sales Co., 282 F. 9 (2d Cir.1922); New Fiction Pub. Co. v. Star Co., supra; but cf. Photo-Drama Motion Picture Co., Inc. v. Social Uplift Film Corp., 213 F. 374 (S.D.N.Y.1914), aff'd, 220 F. 448 (2d Cir.1915). The doctrine was seriously questioned in subsequent years, Houghton Mifflin Co. v. Stackpole Sons, Inc., 104 F.2d 306, 311–2 (2d Cir.1939), but has not been overruled.

But, regardless of the vitality of the indivisibility theory as it applies to the question of standing to sue, we do not think that it is determinative as to the requisite interest of a party who may act to obtain copyright. In the cases relied upon by the district court, it was found either that a complete assignment had been made, Mail & Express Co. v. Life Pub. Co., 192 F. 899 (2d Cir.1912); Morse v. Fields, supra, or that the plaintiff claiming infringement was not the author or proprietor of the work, Egner v. E.C. Schirmer Music Co., 139 F.2d 398 (1st Cir.), cert. denied, 322 U.S. 730 (1943); Kaplan v. Fox Film Corp., supra. We find nothing in the established cases which requires us to extend the logic of those precedents to a case where an author is plaintiff. We are loath to bring about the unnecessarily harsh result of thrusting the author's product into the public domain when, as here, everyone interested in "Dark Passage" could see Curtis' copyright notice and could not have believed there was any intention by Goodis to surrender the fruits of his labor.

Courts have been understandably reluctant to invoke the doctrine of indivisibility where the author or proprietor of the work is the plaintiff and the result would be to deprive the plaintiff of the fruits of his creative effort. In Bisel v. Ladner, 1 F.2d 436 (3rd Cir.1924), a publisher who had taken out copyright in his own name was deemed to hold legal title to the copyright for the "beneficial owner," the author-plaintiff, although it was clear the publisher had not acquired all rights in the work. See also, Maurel v. Smith, 271 F. 211 (2d Cir.1921); Harms v. Stern, 229 F. 42 (2d Cir.1916); Quinn Brown Pub. Co. v. Chilton Co., 15 F.Supp. 213 (S.D.N.Y.1936); Harper & Bros. v. M.A. Donohue & Co., 144 F. 491 (N.D.Ill.1905).

The holdings in New Fiction Pub. Co. v. Star Co., supra, and Goldwyn Pictures Corp. v. Howells Sales Co., supra, do not present any barrier to our conclusions. In *New Fiction,* an author named Goodman had obtained copyright on his work and had sold serial rights to the plaintiff company, which sued when the defendant infringed the serial rights. The district court found Goodman had not divested himself of all interest in the work and, following the indivisibility theory, it dismissed plaintiff's action. Judge Mayer, after discussing the policy supporting the doctrine, concluded his opinion by noting: "It will be understood that I am not passing on the question which would be presented if Goodman were a party plaintiff." Supra, at 997. A similar question was resolved against the plaintiff in *Goldwyn,* the court specially pointing out that "[w]e express no opinion in respect of what the legal status of plaintiff would be if Mrs. Gunther [the authoress-proprietor] were joined as party plaintiff." Supra, at 12. Likewise in the instant case, although we hold Curtis had sufficient interest to obtain copyright in behalf of Goodis, we express no opinion on whether a publisher in Curtis' position could maintain an infringement action without joining the author.

We believe a distinction between applying the indivisibility doctrine to cases where the issue is standing to sue for infringement and cases where the issue is protection of the author's interest is supported by the Copyright Act and by common sense. Under the Copyright Act of 1831,[1] an author or proprietor obtained copyright, before publication, by depositing a copy of the title of his work in the district court in the district of his domicile. Thus, had Goodis completed his novel before 1909 and made the required deposit, he would have obtained copyright in his own name before publication and would have been free to market

---

1. Section 1 of the 1831 Act provides: "the author or authors of any book * * * not printed and published, * * * shall have the sole right and liberty of printing * * * " Section 4 provides: "no person shall be entitled to the benefit of this act, unless he shall, before publication, deposit a printed copy of the title of such book * * * in the clerk's office of the District Court of the district wherein the author or proprietor shall reside."

his work to his best advantage, selling serial rights, dramatic rights, etc. at his pleasure, without jeopardizing his copyright. In several cases before 1909 harsh forfeitures resulted from technical failures to comply with the statute, even though there was little chance that the public might have been misled by the errors. Mifflin v. R.H. White Co., 190 U.S. 265 (1903); Mifflin v. Dutton, 190 U.S. 260 (1903).

In 1909 the Copyright Act was amended and the method of obtaining copyright simplified. Under the revised Act, an author or proprietor could secure statutory protection by actual publication of the work with notice in conformity with the Act.[2] Although appellees characterize this change as irrelevant, we think it is critical. Suddenly the author who might previously have obtained copyright before publication had to guard against any legal infirmity surrounding first publication which might throw his work into the public domain.[3] One can understand the requirement that only an author or proprietor perfect copyright under the 1831 statute, since copyright had to be obtained before publication and the author or proprietor was expected to have exclusive control over the work. After 1909, however, it was to be expected that first publication of the work, whether in magazine or book form, would be the means of obtaining copyright. To require full proprietorship by the initial publisher would too often provide a trap for the unwary author who had assumed the publisher would attend to copyrighting the work in his behalf.

In considering the 1909 amendments and the liberalizing spirit in which they were enacted, we note that the proposed general revision of the copyright law, introduced in the 90th Congress and referred to the House and Senate Judiciary Committees,[4] would make the result reached by the district court in the present case impossible. S. 597, 90th Cong., 1st Sess. §§ 201(c), 403(a), 403(b), 405(a) (1967). In summary, these proposed provisions[5] make it clear that: (1) the author of a

2. Section 10 of the 1909 Act provides: "Any person entitled thereto * * * may secure copyright for his work by publication thereof with the notice of copyright required by this title * * *."

3. Section 2 of the Copyright Act of 1909 expressly recognizes the author's common law copyright in an unpublished work. Furthermore, under section 12 of the Act, authors of certain types of work, of which copies are not reproduced for sale, may obtain a pre-publication statutory copyright by depositing a copy of a work or a part of the work with claim of copyright. However, an author will lose his section 2 or section 12 copyright in a work if he publishes it without complying with the notice provisions of section 10.

4. The proposed legislation to which we refer is thorough and complete. It is the product of a great deal of work by the Register of Copyrights, his staff, a panel of consultants drawn from the copyright bar, 22 days of hearings in 1965 (at which over 150 witnesses testified), and numerous executive sessions of a subcommittee of the House Committee on the Judiciary H.R.Rep. No. 863, 90th Cong., 1st Sess., at 2–3 (1967). The House Report just cited contains excellent descriptions of the proposed provisions coupled with accurate summaries of the existing law in areas where the new statute would work a change. (See e.g., H.R.Rep. No. 83, supra, at 96–100, discussing the federal preemption section of the proposed act.) As such, the Report constitutes a valuable reference tool to be used in cases arising under the present Copyright Act.

5. As under the present Act, copyright is secured by publication with notice. § 401(a) Proposed Act.

Section 201(c) provides:

(c) Contributions to Collective Works.—Copyright in each separate contribution to a literary work which is published for the first time in a "collective work" such as a periodical holds a copyright distinct from that in the collective work as a whole, § 201(c); (2) that first publication in a collective work under a general copyright notice in the name of the periodical publisher is sufficient to secure the author's copyright in the work, § 403(a); and (3), that where the person named in the copyright notice applicable to a collective work is not the owner of the copyright in a separate contribution which appears in the collective work without its own notice, the case is treated simply as one with an error in the name in the notice, such error not affecting the validity or ownership of the copyright. §§ 403(b), 405(a).[6]

The report of the House Committee on the Judiciary states that these proposed provisions deal "with a troublesome problem under the present law: the notice requirements applicable to contributions published in periodicals and other collective works." H.R.Rep. No. 83, 90th Cong., 1st Sess. 113 (1967). Our decision today is that the result which the proposed legislation would compel is not precluded in any way by the decisions rendered under the present Copyright Act. As discussed

collective work is distinct from copyright in the collective work as a whole, and vests initially in the author of the contribution. In the absence of an express transfer of copyright or of any rights under it, the owner of copyright in the collective work is presumed to have acquired only the privilege of reproducing and distributing the contribution as part of that particular collective work, any revision of that collective work, and any later collective work in the same series.

Section 403(a) [now Sec. 404(a)] provides:

(a) A separate contribution to a collective work may bear its own notice of copyright, as provided by sections 401 and 402 [401 through 403]. However, a single notice applicable to the collective work as a whole is sufficient to satisfy the requirements of sections 401 and 402 [401 through 403] with respect to the separate contributions it contains (not including advertisements inserted on behalf of persons other than the owner of copyright in the collective work), regardless of the ownership of copyright in the contributions and whether or not they have been previously published.

Section 403(b) [now Sec. 404(b)] provides:

(b) Where the person named in a single notice applicable to a collective work as a whole is not the owner of copyright in a separate contribution that does not bear its own notice, the case is governed by the provisions of section 405(a) [now Sec. 406(a)].

Section 405(a) [now Sec. 406(a)] provides:

(a) Error in Name.—Where the person named in the copyright notice on copies or phonorecords publicly distributed by authority of the copyright owner is not the owner of copyright, the validity and ownership of the copyright are not affected. In such a case, however, any person who innocently begins an undertaking that infringes the copyright has a complete defense to any action for such infringement if he proves that he was misled by the notice and began the undertaking in good faith under a purported transfer or license from the person named therein, unless before the undertaking was begun:

(1) registration for the work had been made in the name of the owner of copyright; or

(2) a document executed by the person named in the notice and showing the ownership of the copyright had been recorded.

The person named in the notice is liable to account to the copyright owner for all receipts from purported transfers or licenses made by him under the copyright.

6. Section 405(a) [now Sec. 406(a)] does give a limited defense to one who infringes in a case where there is an error in the name in the notice "if he proves that he was misled by the notice and began the [infringing] undertaking in good faith under a purported transfer or license from the person named [in the erroneous notice]. * * *" See note 5, supra. As we note infra, the present case does not present such a problem, and we express no opinion on such a case.

earlier, the "problem" with which the proposed legislation deals is one which exists because of judicial dicta rendered in cases not apposite to the factual situation before us in this case. We believe that it is time to settle the disquieting implications of these dicta in cases where the author sues for infringement.

In reaching this result, we also take account of modern business practices. Today many magazines market new writings in serial form. It should be expected that serialization will often be the "first publication" of a work, since much of the value of such an arrangement to the periodical lies in reaching magazine readers before the complete book has been released.

The harsh results before the 1909 amendments should be avoided if possible, particularly as here where the magazine's own notice of copyright is more than adequate to apprise any innocent party that he might be infringing another's copyright. As both *amicus curiae* briefs point out, the principal purpose of the statutory notice provisions is to inform the public that copyright is claimed.[7] Appellees do not dispute that the Curtis notice was perfectly adequate for this purpose. Although placing a special notice in the author's own name on each installment appearing in the magazine would be a more careful practice than we find here, we do not think that failure to do so, by itself, should cause an author to suffer forfeiture.

That such an arrangement between Curtis and Goodis is in the nature of a "partial assignment" is no reason to require a different result. This circuit 30 years ago understood the desirability of recognizing partial assignments. Houghton Mifflin Co. v. Stackpole Sons, Inc., supra. Where the question is the interest needed to obtain copyright, we reiterate that the important considerations are the intention of the parties to obtain copyright and the adequacy of notice to the public; the characterization of the publisher as assignee or licensee is secondary. * * *

Reversed and remanded.[a]

Questions

1. Suppose that "Dark Passage" had not been published in either magazine or book form at the time that Warner Brothers released their motion picture based upon the Goodis work. If the only copyright notice on the motion picture film was in Warner Brothers' name, what effect would this have had on the copyright in the underlying Goodis work? Would this depend on whether the view of indivisibility adopted in the instant case was followed?

2. Suppose that "Dark Passage" had first been published in book form with a copyright notice in the author's name, followed by the publication in

---

[7]. To avoid accidental forfeiture, courts have liberally construed what constitutes adequate notice. See, e.g., Peter Pan Fabrics, Inc. v. Martin Weiner Corp., 274 F.2d 487 (2d Cir.1960); National Comics Publications Inc. v. Fawcett Publications, Inc., 191 F.2d 594 (2d Cir.1951).

[a]. That part of the court's opinion dealing with the contractual aspects of the case is set forth infra.

"The Saturday Evening Post" bearing only the notice in the name of the magazine. Would the indivisibility issue posed in the instant case have been presented in such circumstances? What was the pre-1978 rule on notice for derivative works where the underlying work was the subject of statutory copyright?

3. What impact does the pre-1978 doctrine of indivisibility (either with or without the *Goodis* modification of that doctrine) continue to have on the current protection of works created pre-1978?

Collateral Reference

Nimmer on Copyright, § 10.01[C], [D].

Note *

The Abolition of Indivisibility Under the Current Act

A "transfer of copyright ownership" under the current Act is defined as "an assignment, mortgage, exclusive license, or any other conveyance, alienation, or hypothecation of a copyright or of any of the exclusive rights comprised in a copyright, whether or not it is limited in time or place of effect, but not including a nonexclusive license."[1] It will be seen that the above definition employs terminology that distinguishes between an "assignment" and a "license." Such terminology emerged from the 1909 Act case law which applied the doctrine of indivisibility. But the consequences of whether a given conveyance is an assignment or a license are largely altered. An exclusive license, even if it is "limited in time or place of effect," is equated with an assignment, and each is considered to be a "transfer" of copyright ownership. Nonexclusive licenses, however, do not constitute "transfers," and some residue of the impact of indivisibility with respect to licenses under the 1909 Act remains under the current Act vis à vis nonexclusive licenses.

Section 201(d)(2) of the Copyright Act is said to constitute an "explicit statutory recognition of the principle of divisibility of copyright."[2] It provides:

"Any of the exclusive rights comprised in a copyright, including any subdivision of any of the rights specified in section 106, may be transferred * * * and owned separately. The owner of any particular exclusive right is entitled, to the extent of that right, to all of the protection and remedies accorded to the copyright owner by this title."

Thus, indivisibility is abolished as regards exclusive licensees, who are regarded as the copyright owners of the rights which they have been licensed.[3]

Questions

1. Since Sec. 201(d)(2) provides for divisibility only with respect to "any of the exclusive rights comprised in a copyright, including any subdivision of the rights specified in Sec. 106", what of an exclusive license of rights which encompass only a part of a given Sec. 106 subdivision? May there be a

---

* Nimmer on Copyright, § 10.02.

1. 17 U.S.C.A. § 101.

2. H.Rep., p. 123.

3. " 'Copyright owner', with respect to any one of the exclusive rights comprised in a copyright, refers to the owner of that particular right." 17 U.S.C.A. § 101.

"transfer" of hard-cover book rights, reserving paper-back rights? May there be a "transfer" of rights limited to a particular geographic area, or to a particular time period? See H.Rep., p. 123. Since most nonexclusive licenses are capable of being couched in the language of exclusivity, if limited to the particular time and place in which the licensee intends to operate without interfering with similar operations by other "exclusive" licensees, at some point does the distinction between an exclusive and nonexclusive license break down?

2. Does divisibility under the current Copyright Act mean that an exclusive licensee becomes the owner of a new and entirely separate copyright? What are the implications of this question with regard to publication, registration, and copyright notice? Suppose that prior to publication or registration, A, the author, grants an exclusive license of paperback rights to B, and an exclusive license of hard-cover rights to C. Suppose further that A is a foreign author who would not qualify for copyright once his work is published, but may claim copyright in his unpublished work. Compare Secs. 104(a) and 104(b). If thereafter B publishes a paper-back edition of the work, but C has not yet published a hard-cover edition, may C's "work" be the subject of an enforceable copyright under Sec. 104(a), or is it a "work" excluded from copyright by reason of Sec. 104(b)? Alternatively, suppose that the work which is the subject of A's exclusive licenses to B and C is a work which has been made "for hire", and is therefore subject to a copyright term of 75 years from publication (or 100 years from creation if that is sooner). See Sec. 302(c). Is the term of C's "copyright" to be measured from B's earlier publication, or from C's later publication? Consider the new statutory provision whereby in general there is no right to recover statutory damages or attorney's fees for infringements which occur prior to registration. See Sec. 412. If in the above hypothetical B registers his claim of copyright but C fails to register his claim before such time as C's rights are infringed, is C precluded from recovering statutory damages and attorney's fees for such infringement? Suppose that B fails to place a copyright notice on the paper-back copies which he publishes, and further fails to register the work within five years of first publication, so that his work thereafter enters the public domain. See Sec. 405(a), and particularly Sec. 405(a)(2). What effect will this failure by B have upon C's rights? If C has published his hard-cover copies all with a proper notice, will he thereby avoid injection of his rights into the public domain notwithstanding B's failure?

Collateral Reference

Nimmer on Copyright, §§ 10.02[A], 10.02[C].

B. RECORDATION

VIDOR v. SERLIN

Court of Appeals of New York, 1960.
7 N.Y.2d 502, 166 N.E.2d 680, 199 N.Y.S.2d 669.

DESMOND, CHIEF JUDGE. In 1954 Charles Vidor, a producer of motion pictures, made a written agreement with defendant Romola Nijinsky whereby Mrs. Nijinsky purported to sell to Vidor the exclusive motion-picture, television, radio and allied rights in two books written by Mrs. Nijinsky, of both of which she held the recorded copyright, and which described the life and works of her late husband, the famous ballet dancer Vaslav Nijinsky. Concurrently with that agreement, Mrs. Nijinsky gave Vidor a separate instrument of assignment of the same rights. The assignment was recorded in the United States Copyright Office (see U.S.Code, tit. 17, § 30) a few days later.

This suit was brought by Vidor (his executrix is now plaintiff) for a declaratory judgment: first, that plaintiff is the sole owner of the motion-picture and allied rights in the literary works above referred to; and, second, that neither defendant Basil N. Bass (his executor is now substituted as defendant) nor defendant Oscar Serlin has any such rights in the two books. Bass and Serlin by answer set up alleged rights of theirs as based on an agreement made in March, 1940 between Bass and Mrs. Nijinsky (assigned by Bass to Serlin in November, 1940). Also, they served on Mrs. Nijinsky a cross complaint in which they asked for damages against her because she had twice sold the rights in question and had thus cast a cloud on their rights and caused them damage and put them to expense.

It is conceded that the Nijinsky-Bass agreement was not recorded in the Copyright Office until long after Vidor's assignment was so recorded pursuant to the applicable Federal statute (U.S.Code, tit. 17, § 30, supra). Defendants Harlow (executor of the Bass will) and Serlin argue, however, that the former instrument was not an "assignment of copyright" but a mere license as to the motion-picture and allied rights (coupled with an agreement making Bass the booking agent of Mrs. Nijinsky for a proposed American lecture tour) and that, as such, it could be, but was not required to be, recorded under the statute (U.S.Code, tit. 17, § 30, supra). They assert that the lack of recording did not invalidate the license and that it effectively transferred all the rights of Mrs. Nijinsky. Furthermore, say Serlin and Bass' executor, Vidor took his assignment with knowledge or notice of the prior equities of Serlin as assignee of Bass, and Vidor's failure to use due diligence in inquiring as to Serlin's position is fatal to Vidor's (or his estate's) claim. Mrs. Nijinsky's answer argued that her contract with Bass was an instrument capable of statutory recordation and should have been recorded so as to give notice, that Vidor as a bona fide purchaser without notice became sole owner of the motion-picture rights and that Serlin and the Bass estate, because of their alleged breaches of their agreement with her and because of their concealments of the relationship between Bass and Serlin, etc., can have no relief against her.

There was a trial (Justice Greenberg without a jury) which ended in findings as follows: that the Bass-Nijinsky contract was an instrument capable of being recorded as was the Bass-Serlin assignment thereof, that neither was recorded until more than six months after Vidor's recording and that Vidor had neither actual notice thereof nor notice implied by law, that the Vidor-Nijinsky agreement and assignment were duly recorded in the Copyright Office, that plaintiff owns all the disputed rights and that neither the Bass estate nor Serlin has any motion-picture or similar rights in the two literary works. The Trial Judge did not pass on the Bass-Nijinsky agreement issues but found that Mrs. Nijinsky never knew of the relationship between Bass and Serlin or consented to the assignment by the former to the latter. The judgment subsequently entered was to the effect that the assignment from Bass to Serlin was ineffective, that plaintiff owns the motion-picture and allied rights and that defendants Serlin and Bass' executor have no such rights.

On appeal, the Appellate Division affirmed except that it added to the judgment, by modification, a dismissal of the cross complaint against Mrs. Nijinsky, explaining in a memorandum that the Bass-Serlin assignment was ineffective because the dramatic rights given by Mrs. Nijinsky to Bass were not separately assignable without her consent which was never given and that, in any event, "whatever rights Serlin or his assignor might have acquired were lost as the result of the breach of Bass' managerial obligations under the purported agreement". [184 N.Y.S. 483.]

No one doubts that Vidor's assignment was recordable and properly recorded. Appellants, nevertheless, say that the recording act did not give Vidor priority over Bass, since, so they argue, the Nijinsky-Bass document was at most a license, not an "assignment" of the sort described in section 30 of title 17 of the United States Code. Their submission is that such a non-recordable license loses nothing by the statute and that its priority in time gives it priority in rank. The first answer is in the Nijinsky-Bass contract itself since in terms it "assigns" to Bass "any and all rights" of Mrs. Nijinsky. A more complete answer is in the controlling case of Photo-Drama Motion Picture Co. v. Social Uplift Film Corp., 2 Cir., 220 F. 448, 449, 450, which says that a separate conveyance of motion-picture rights "must be recorded to avail of the constructive notice which the section contemplates."

It is, therefore, clear enough that, since Vidor did record his assignment, his rights thereunder are prior to any rights of the Bass estate or Serlin, unless Vidor had knowledge or notice of the Nijinsky-Bass and Bass-Serlin documents—that is, of Serlin's claims. We will assume that if Vidor had knowledge of facts putting him on inquiry, he would not be a bona fide purchaser, regardless of recording. But the trial court here made findings, affirmed by the Appellate Division, that Vidor had no knowledge or actual or implied notice of Serlin's claims. Those findings have support in the record. Vidor denied ever having had notice. Before signing with Mrs. Nijinsky he had retained attorneys to clear the title and was told by the attorneys that it was "clear". One of the reports from an attorney included newspaper and theatrical trade paper items to the effect that Serlin owned performing rights to the book "Nijinsky" but, as Vidor testified, these "publicity releases" did not necessarily have any significance as to actual truth. When Vidor learned that the original copyright was held by a book publisher, he arranged to get from the publisher an assignment containing no exceptions. Mrs. Nijinsky in her assignment to Vidor warranted that she had not granted the rights to anyone else. There is testimony of an "invariable custom" whereby one who acquires motion-picture rights files an assignment in the Copyright Office. On the whole record it cannot be said that Vidor had knowledge of Serlin's rights or claims or such notice as required him to make other inquiries. The findings, therefore, that Vidor was a bona fide purchaser for value are well based and sufficient to give Vidor clear priority over Serlin as to ownership of the motion-picture rights.

As between Serlin and Mrs. Nijinsky also, there is support for the judgment in favor of the latter. The trial court held that no consent to or ratification of the Bass-Serlin assignment ever came from Mrs. Nijinsky. Clearly, there was evidentiary basis for the latter holding. As to the necessity for consent, the document which says nothing about assignment seems to be an entire contract, providing not only for the transfer to Bass of some rights to the books but calling also for the performance by Bass of services as booking agent for an American lecture tour.

The Appellate Division, as we have seen, went farther than the trial court and made a new fact finding (see Bernardine v. City of New York, 294 N.Y. 361, 366, 62 N.E.2d 604, 605, 161 A.L.R. 364) that Bass had breached his "managerial obligations". There is ample proof that he did little or nothing in that direction and that he got no lecture engagements at all. This brings us to another ground for holding that Bass-Serlin could not have priority rights as against Vidor. Since it has been established in this very lawsuit that neither Bass nor his attempted assignee Serlin ever performed their agreement with Mrs. Nijinsky at all, that adjudication is available not only to Mrs. Nijinsky but to Vidor, too (see Israel v. Wood Dolson Co., 1 N.Y.2d 116, 151 N.Y.S.2d 1, 134 N.E.2d 97). It is, therefore, still another reason for defeating the Bass-Serlin claim to priority over Vidor.

The judgment should be affirmed, with costs to respondents against appellants.

DYE, FULD, FROESSEL, VAN VOORHIS, BURKE and FOSTER, JJ., concur.

Judgment affirmed.

Questions

1. In what respects do the recordation provisions of Sec. 205(e) under the current Copyright Act differ from the comparable provisions of Sec. 30 under the 1909 Act?

2. Suppose that an author transfers "exclusive motion picture rights" in his work to X on January 15, 1979, and thereafter transfers the same rights to Y on February 1, 1979. Who will prevail as between X and Y if:

   (a) Y records his transfer on February 4, 1979, and X records his transfer on February 14, 1979?

   (b) X records his transfer on February 20, 1979, and Y records his transfer on February 22, 1979?

   (c) Y records his transfer on February 10, 1979, and X records his transfer on August 15, 1979? What additional facts must you know in order to answer this question? Would your answer be any different if Y recorded his transfer on August 10, 1979? On August 20, 1979?

3. Suppose that an author transfers "exclusive motion picture rights" in his work to X on January 15, 1979, and thereafter executes a written grant of "nonexclusive motion picture rights" to Y on February 1, 1979. Who will prevail as between X and Y if (a) X records his transfer on February 2, 1979, and (b) Y first learns of the transfer to X on February 5, 1979, and (c) Y records his license on March 1, 1979 and (d) Y is not required to pay any consideration for his license? See Sec. 205(f).

Collateral References

Miller, A., *Problems in the Transfer of Interests in a Copyright,* ASCAP Copyright Law Symposium No. Ten 131 (1959).

Nimmer on Copyright, § 10.07.

Rothenberg, *Oral Copyright Contracts and the Statute of Frauds,* 25 Bull. Cr.Soc. 159 (1977).

Kaplan, *Literary and Artistic Property (Including Copyright) as Security: Problems Facing the Lender,* 19 Law and Contemporary Problems 254 (1954).

Concoff, *Motion Picture Secured Transactions Under the Uniform Commercial Code: Problems in Perfection,* 13 UCLA Law Rev. 1214 (1966).

GROUP PUBLISHERS v. WINCHELL

United States District Court, Southern District of New York, 1949.
86 F.Supp. 573.

S.H. KAUFMAN, DISTRICT JUDGE. Plaintiff, Group Publishers, Inc., sues Walter Winchell and The Hearst Corporation for alleged infringement of copyright, and both plaintiff and defendants move for summary judgment.

The complaint alleges that on January 7, 1947 Natamsa Publishing Company, Inc. secured a copyright on an original book entitled "The Romance of Money"; that by an instrument in writing, Natamsa assigned all its interest in said material and the copyright thereof to plaintiff; that since December 30, 1946 said book has been published by plaintiff in accordance with the copyright statute; that plaintiff is sole proprietor of all rights in the copyright and that after January 7, 1947 defendants infringed the copyright by the publication in Winchell's column in the New York Daily Mirror, a newspaper published by defendant The Hearst Corporation, and by publications elsewhere, of material copied largely from "The Romance of Money".

Copies of plaintiff's book and of the alleged infringing article in the Mirror are annexed to the complaint. From these it appears that plaintiff's publication is a printed booklet of 16 pages containing approximately 60 separate insets purporting to describe interesting episodes in the historical evolution of money as a medium of exchange, from the use of bricks of pressed tea by the early Mongolians to the present use of coins and paper. The various steps, or comments thereon, or in reference thereto, are described in very brief narrative, each in a separate inset and each accompanied by an illustration depicting the occasion described or some attending circumstance. The alleged infringing article in the Winchell column of the Mirror consisted of a column of 26 short paragraphs, none of which is illustrated. Of these 26 paragraphs, all except one or two state the same fact as appears in one or more of the insets in plaintiff's publication, though at times slightly paraphrased or coupled with brief additional comment.

Defendants' answer admits the publication and puts in issue the other material allegations of the complaint.

On defendants' motion, Eagle-Lion Films, Inc. was brought in as third-party defendant, but it is unnecessary to describe the claim alleged in the third-party plaintiffs' complaint or the third-party defendant's answer thereto inasmuch as the motions now before the court relate only to the cause of action alleged by plaintiff against defendants Winchell and The Hearst Corporation, to which the third-party defendant has not been made a party. Malkin v. Arundel Corporation, D.C., 36 F.Supp. 948, 951; Crim v. Lumbermens Mut. Casualty Co., D.C., 26 F.Supp. 715, 720; Thompson v. Cranston, D.C., 2 F.R.D. 270; see 3 Moore's Federal Practice (2d ed.), p. 495.

The answer of the third-party defendant to the complaint of the plaintiff, after putting in issue all material allegations of the complaint except the allegation of publication pleads as a defense that before the alleged infringement by defendants plaintiff had published its books bearing a copyright notice stating that plaintiff was the copyright proprietor, without first recording the alleged assignment to it from Natamsa; that such publication violated the copyright laws and by reason thereof plaintiff abandoned its alleged copyright and dedicated the material in the book to the public.

The affidavit of Winchell, submitted in opposition to plaintiff's motion describes the circumstances in which the column was written and sets forth that defendants' publication was without knowledge of plaintiff's publication and in good faith.

In opposition to plaintiff's motion, the third-party defendant submits a photostat of the assignment from Natamsa to plaintiff, the accuracy and completeness of which are not disputed. This is dated May 18, 1948 and by it the assignor "hereby assigns" to plaintiff all its right, title and interest in the copyright of "The Romance of Money". A photostatic copy of the certificate of the Register of Copyrights, attesting that the assignment was received in the Copyright Office on May 20, 1948, and that a search did not disclose the recordation of any other assignment referring to said work, was also submitted and its accuracy and completeness are likewise not disputed. From these documents, it would appear that plaintiff did not acquire the copyright by assignment from Natamsa until upwards of four months after the alleged infringing publication. The assignment does not in terms confer any rights against prior infringers.

To meet this, plaintiff states, by affidavit of its president, that although the assignment recorded on May 20, 1948 was executed by Natamsa on May 18, 1948, that assignment was merely a "confirmatory" assignment, the "actual" assignment having taken place on September 11, 1947 pursuant to an agreement dated July 17, 1947 between Natamsa and plaintiff's president individually. A photostatic copy of the agreement of July 17, 1947, referred to in the affidavit, is attached thereto. * * *

The question presented by the motion is whether or not a triable issue is shown to exist with respect to (a) the copyrightability of the material in plaintiff's book; (b) whether the copyright has been infringed; (c) whether or not plaintiff was the owner of the copyright at the time of the alleged infringement; and (d) the effect of plaintiff's publication bearing a copyright notice stating that plaintiff was the copyright proprietor, prior to the recording of the assignment from Natamsa to plaintiff.

The copyrightability of plaintiff's work is clear. * * * However, since a determination of the last two questions presented is dispositive of this motion, only those need be discussed.

We come then to the question whether or not plaintiff owned the copyright at the time of the infringement.

The infringement occurred on or about January 2, 1948.

The assignment by Natamsa directly to plaintiff was executed on May 18, 1948, upwards of four months later.

Prior thereto, and on September 11, 1947, Marquand had delivered to Group the bill of sale dated July 17, 1947. This bill of sale, however, was not to be immediately effective, and did not become effective until its delivery to Mr. Group on September 11, 1947. It purported to convey to Mr. Group an assignment by Natamsa to Group Publishers, Inc. of the copyright of "The Romance of Money". Group Publishers, Inc. was not in existence on July 17, 1947, when the bill of sale was executed, but its existence was contemplated, as the agreement shows, and it did come into existence prior to the delivery of the bill of sale. The agreement pursuant to which the bill of sale was executed and delivered provides that on notice to Natamsa of the organization of the corporation it should be deemed the purchaser, with the same force and effect as if named in the agreement. When notice of the incorporation of Group Publishers, Inc. was given to Natamsa does not appear, but that seems immaterial. Though Schedule "B" annexed to the bill of sale to Mr. Group, in its description of the property to be conveyed, includes an "assignment of copyright" to plaintiff, there is no claim that any such assignment was executed prior to the one of May 18, 1948, and until such assignment was put in writing there was no valid assignment of the copyright to plaintiff. Public Ledger Co. v. Post

Printing & Publishing Co., 8 Cir., 294 F. 430; Davenport Quigley Expedition v. Century Products, D.C., 18 F.Supp. 974; § 28, Tit. 17 U.S.C.A.

Further, the assignment, as written and executed, does not purport to grant the assignee any right to sue for infringements antedating the assignment, and without such authorization in the assignment, no such right is conferred. Kriger v. MacFadden Publications, Inc., D.C., 43 F.Supp. 170; cf. United States v. Loughrey, 172 U.S. 206, 19 S.Ct. 153, 43 L.Ed. 420; Moore v. Marsh, 7 Wall. 515, 74 U.S. 515, 19 L.Ed. 37; see Ball, Law of Copyright and Literary Property (1944), pp. 543–4.

Defendants are also entitled to prevail, as a matter of law, on the ground that the substitution of the name of an assignee in a notice of copyright prior to the recordation of the assignment, results in an abandonment of the copyright and a dedication of the work to the public.

Section 19 of Title 17 U.S.C.A., prescribes the manner and form of notice required to secure the rights accorded by the statute. It declares that notice shall consist of "the word 'Copyright' or the abbreviation 'Copr.', accompanied by the name of the copyright proprietor, and if the work be a printed literary, musical, or dramatic work, the notice shall include also the year in which the copyright was secured by publication * * *".

Section 32 of Title 17 U.S.C.A., deals specifically with the substitution of the name of the assignee for that of the assignor in the prescribed notice and declares: "When an assignment of the copyright in a specified book or other work has been recorded the assignee may substitute his name for that of the assignor in the statutory notice of copyright prescribed by this title."

Strict compliance with the statutory requirements is essential to the perfection of the copyright itself and failure fully to conform to the form of notice prescribed by the act results in abandonment of the right and a dedication of one's work to the public. See Krafft v. Cohen, 3 Cir., 117 F.2d 579; Fleischer Studios v. Ralph A. Freundlich, Inc., 2 Cir., 73 F.2d 276, 277, certiorari denied 294 U.S. 717, 55 S.Ct. 516, 79 L.Ed. 1250; Universal Film Mfg. Co. v. Copperman, D.C., 212 F. 301, 302, affirmed 2 Cir., 218 F. 577, certiorari denied 235 U.S. 704, 35 S.Ct. 209, 59 L.Ed. 433; Wildman v. New York Times Co., D.C., 42 F.Supp. 412; Sieff v. Continental Auto Supply, D.C., 39 F.Supp. 683; Smith v. Bartlett, D.C., 18 F.Supp. 35.

The Congressional policy reflected in the statute is that the notice of copyright shall contain, as proprietor, the name of the holder of record; for indiscriminate substitution could result in considerable confusion and would not "sufficiently aid in tracing * * * title if need be." Fleischer Studios v. Ralph A. Freundlich, Inc., supra, 73 F.2d at page 277.

Plaintiff claims that the words of Section 32 are merely permissive or hortatory and do not prohibit an assignee, absent recordation, from freely substituting his name in the notice of copyright for that of the assignor. But to put this interpretation on the language of that section completely emasculates the provision and renders its inclusion within the act meaningless; for the section would serve no purpose if the assignee could, with equal force, substitute his name for that of the assignor prior to recordation.

The interpretation just given has been the considered construction of Section 32 given by authorities in the field of copyright law [1] and seems the only consistent interpretation which will give meaning to the language of the provision. Having substituted the name "Group Publishers, Inc." in the copyright notice before recordation of the assignment of the copyright to it, plaintiff may no longer assert rights under the copyright and defendants' motion for summary judgment must be granted. See Thompson v. Hubbard, 131 U.S. 123, 9 S.Ct. 710, 33 L.Ed. 76; Record & Guide Co. v. Bromley, C.C., 175 F. 156; Amdur, Copyright Law and Practice (1936), p. 490.

Settle order on notice.

Questions

1. Was the so-called *Winchell* doctrine carried over to the current Copyright Act? If not, what relevance does it continue to have under the current Act?

2. Suppose at the time of the assignment from Natamsa to Group the work "The Romance of Money" was protected by common law copyright, and that the assignment was never recorded in the Copyright Office. If upon publication of the work by Group a copyright notice in Group's name was affixed to the work, would this have injected the work into the public domain?

3. Suppose that pre-1978 A, the proprietor of the statutory copyright in a book, published 5000 copies of the book with a copyright notice in A's name. Thereafter A assigned the copyright to B, and the assignment was duly recorded. If, following such recordation, copies of the book bearing a copyright notice in A's name were published (pre-1978), did this inject the work into the public domain? Would it have made any difference whether the copies in question were manufactured prior to the execution or recordation of the assignment?

Collateral References

Latman, *The Recordation of Copyright Assignments and Licenses*, Studies on Copyright 761 (Fisher ed. 1963).

Nimmer on Copyright, § 10.07[D].

---

[1]. See Ladas, The International Protection of Literary and Artistic Property (1938), Vol. II, p. 745; Weil, American Copyright Law (1917), p. 564; Bowker, Copyright, Its History and Its Law (1912), pp. 135–136.

C. COPYRIGHT DISTINCT FROM THE TANGIBLE OBJECT
PUSHMAN v. NEW YORK GRAPHIC SOCIETY

Court of Appeals of New York, 1942.
287 N.Y. 302, 39 N.E.2d 249.

DESMOND, JUDGE. Plaintiff, who is an artist, brought this suit in 1940 for an injunction to enjoin the defendants from making reproductions of a painting executed by plaintiff and which he had sold outright to the University of Illinois in 1930, for $3,600. This painting was not copyrighted under the copyright laws of the United States. Special Term denied the injunction and dismissed the complaint on the merits, writing an opinion and decision, 25 N.Y.S.2d 32, in which it is said that the only question in the case is as to whether an artist after giving an absolute and unconditional bill of sale of his painting, still retains such a common law copyright in it as to be able to prevent commercial reproduction. Appellate Division, First Department, one of the justices dissenting, affirmed without opinion. 262 App.Div. 729, 28 N.Y.S.2d 711.

Plaintiff, Pushman, has an international reputation as an artist, for his execution of still life subjects in color. He has been painting for fifty years; his original works command substantial prices and many of them are held by museums and collectors. In 1930 he completed the painting, entitled "When Autumn is Here," which is the subject of this action. He turned the painting over for sale to Grand Central Art Galleries which seems to be a mutual organization of artists for sale of their works, as agent for them. All the evidence is that the plaintiff did not state that he was seeking to reserve reproduction rights in his painting and that he made no such reservation at any time up to and including the sale to the University. There is evidence here of a general practice of this gallery whereby whenever it sold a painting to a purchaser who was in the reproduction business, which of course would not include the University, the Gallery negotiated a separate written agreement between the artist and the purchaser covering reproduction rights. Pushman never expressly authorized the Gallery to sell the rights to reproduce this painting, nor did he forbid it. Shortly after this painting was sent to the Gallery for sale, the manager of the Gallery took it and a number of others to the University of Illinois where he exhibited them publicly for sale. The University chose seven of these paintings, including the one by plaintiff here in suit. The University would not pay plaintiff's asking price of $5,000 and so the Gallery sold it to the University for $3,600. All this took place in 1930. The painting remained at the University until 1940 when the University sold to the defendant, New York Graphic Society, Inc., the right to make reproductions. The trial proofs had been made by defendants and the reproductions were about to be put on the market when plaintiff learned of the project and brought this suit.

Both parties bear down hard on the leading case of Parton v. Prang, 18 Fed.Cas. No. 10,784, page 1273. That suit, very similar to this, was decided on the pleadings. The artist plaintiff Parton who was seeking, like plaintiff here, to enjoin the reproduction of one of his paintings by a defendant who had bought the painting from a dealer, lost the suit. True, it was argued in that case that the artist had lost his rights to object because of certain negotiations with the defendant, but the court, leaving that question undecided, held positively that "if the sale was an absolute and unconditional one, and the article was absolutely and unconditionally delivered to the purchaser, the whole property in the manuscript or picture passes to the purchaser, including the right of publication, unless the same is protected by copyright, in which case the rule is different." 18 Fed.Cas. No. 10,784, at page 1278. In Parton v. Prang there was cited Turner v. Robertson, 10 Irish Chancery Rep. 121, 143, which case is considered authoritative and wherein it is said: "it would be a waste of time to add more than that the copyright is incident to the ownership and passes, at the common law, with a transfer of the work of art." In Weil on Copyright Law, at page 116, the author cites the Prang case for the proposition that prima facie a transfer of a work of art "will be deemed to be intended to carry the common law copyright with it unless a contrary intention be manifested." In Drone on Copyrights it is said at page 106 that the "unconditional sale of a painting is a transfer of the entire property in it." In Dam v. Kirk La Shelle Co., 2 Cir., 175 F. 902, 904, 41 L.R.A., N.S., 1002, 20 Ann.Cas. 1173, in this circuit (not in point on the facts) it is said that "a sale or assignment without reservation would seem necessarily to carry all the rights incidental to ownership."

The most recent case called to our attention is Yardley v. Houghton Mifflin Co., 2 Cir., 108 F.2d 28, certiorari denied 309 U.S. 686, 60 S.Ct. 891, 84 L.Ed. 1029. That case concerns a painting copyrighted by the artist. In building a public school in New York City, the contractor was obligated to furnish a mural painting for the wall of one of the rooms. The artist was selected by the city but paid by the contractor. Nothing was said in the contract as to who was to own the copyright but when the painting was actually installed it had already been copyrighted by the artist. The court held that in the absence of any reservation, the copyright passed to the city and that the city owned and could sell the right to reproduce. I do not believe that this case is distinguishable because that painting was commissioned by the purchaser, or because the purchaser was a municipal corporation.

We are, of course, concerned here with the so-called common law copyright, not statutory copyright. This common law copyright is sometimes called the right of first publication. There is no question but that it is a different and independent right from the usual right of ownership of an article of personal property. Stephens v. Cady, 14 How. 528, 530, 14 L.Ed. 528. The Stephens case quotes Lord Mansfield as saying it is "a property in notion, and has no corporeal tangible substance." There is no doubt that in New York State the separate common law copyright or control of the right to reproduce belongs to the artist or author until disposed of by him and will be protected by the courts. Oertel v. Wood, 40 How.Prac. 10; Howitt v. Street & Smith Publications, Inc., 276 N.Y. 345, 350, 12 N.E.2d 435. Such is the holding of the case of Werckmeister v. Springer Lithographing Co., C.C.,

63 F. 808, at page 811, which says that the painting itself may be transferred without a transfer of the common law rights of publishing or restricting publication, and that the ownership of the painting itself does not necessarily carry with it the common law copyright. The same thing is held in Caliga v. Inter-Ocean Newspaper Co., 7 Cir., 157 F. 186, 188, affirmed 215 U.S. 182, 30 S.Ct. 38, 54 L.Ed. 150. Palmer v. DeWitt, 47 N.Y. 532, 7 Am.Rep. 480, is not direct authority either way on the case before us.

We are not helped here by the cases which say that an artist's separate common law copyright does not necessarily pass with the sale of the painting. The question is whether it did pass with the sale of this painting. We think it follows from the authorities above cited that it did so pass and that an artist must, if he wishes to retain or protect the reproduction right, make some reservation of that right when he sells the painting. The Parton case above cited has always been considered as so holding. There are seemingly contrary expressions in same cases, such as the dictum in Stephens v. Cady, 14 How. at page 531, 14 L.Ed. 528, that the right to reproduce "will not pass with the manuscript unless included by express words in the transfer." Appellant cites also other authorities which say that the sale of a work of art does not carry with it the right of reproduction "unless such was the evident intent of the parties." But this begs the question. What was the intent of the parties? The whole tenor of the Prang case, as we read it, is that an ordinary, straight out bill of sale shows an intention to convey the artist's whole property in his picture. Here there is no substantial proof of a contrary intent.

We are not entering into a separate discussion as to whether by this sale and the public exhibition the artist is to be held to have "published" the work so that his common law right is lost. Special Term so held. See Keene v. Kimball, 16 Gray, Mass., 545, 77 Am.Dec. 426; Baker v. Taylor, Fed.Cas. No. 782. Nor need we examine into the equities, as did Special Term. Our conclusion is that under the cases and the texts, this unconditional sale carried with it the transfer of the common law copyright and right to reproduce. Plaintiff took no steps to withhold or control that right. "The courts cannot read words of limitation into a transfer which the parties do not choose to use." Dam v. Kirk La Shelle Co., 2 Cir., 175 F. 902, 904, 41 L.R.A., N.S., 1002, 20 Ann.Cas. 1173.

The judgment of the Appellate Division should be affirmed, with costs.

LEHMAN, C.J., and LOUGHRAN, FINCH, RIPPEY, LEWIS, and CONWAY, JJ., concur.

Judgment affirmed.

NEW YORK
General Business Law
BOOK 19
Article 12-E

Reproduction Rights—Works of Fine Art

§ 223. Definition.

For the purpose of this article, the term "fine art" shall mean a painting, sculpture, drawing or work of graphic art, and the term "artist" shall mean the creator of a work of fine art.

§ 224. Right to reproduce works of fine art.

Whenever a work of fine art is sold or otherwise transferred by or on behalf of the artist who created it, or his heirs or personal representatives, the right of reproduction thereof is reserved to the grantor until it passes into the public domain by act or operation of law unless such right is sooner expressly transferred by an instrument, note or memorandum in writing signed by the owner of the rights conveyed or his duly authorized agent. Nothing herein contained, however, shall be construed to prohibit the fair use of such work of art.

History: Add, L.1966, ch. 668, eff. Sept. 1, 1966.

Laws 1966, ch. 668, § 1, provides as follows:

Section 1. It is hereby found that advances in color printing and other means of graphic reproduction, combined with technological processes for reproducing three-dimensional objects, have created a whole new dimension in the field of the fine arts. The traditional concept of a work of fine art as a unique one-of-a-kind creation has been replaced by important new property rights of substantial monetary value based on the reproduction of works of fine art. The creation of these new property rights has generated confusion and controversy as to who has title thereto and may authorize and realize proceeds from the reproduction of works of fine art. It is therefore declared to be the policy of this state to establish clear guideposts for all parties concerning legal ownership of the right of reproduction of works of fine art. In establishing such guideposts, it is declared to be the intent of this legislation that the right of reproduction, at the present state of commerce and technology, shall be interpreted as including: reproduction of works of fine art as prints suitable for framing; facsimile casts of sculpture; reproductions used for greeting cards; reproductions in general books and magazines not devoted primarily to art, and in newspapers in other than art or news sections (when such reproductions in books, magazines and newspapers are used for purposes similar to those of material for which the publishers customarily pay); art films; television (except from stations operated for educational purposes or on programs for educational purposes from all stations); and reproductions used in any form of advertising, including magazines, calendars, newspapers, posters, billboards, films, or television.

It is further the intent of this legislation that such right of reproduction shall not be interpreted as including: reproductions published by museums in the form of exhibition catalogues, books, slides, photographs, postcards, and small prints not suitable for framing; reproductions in art magazines, art books, and art sections and news sections of newspapers; reproductions in general books and magazines not primarily devoted to art but of an educational, historical or critical nature (providing that such reproductions are not used for purposes similar to those of material for which the publishers customarily pay); slides and film strips not intended for a mass audience; and television from stations operated for educational purposes or on programs for educational purposes from all stations.

[Note that California has enacted a similar law (West's Ann.Cal. Civil Code, § 982(c)), which differs in certain respects from its New York counterpart. See Nimmer on Copyright, § 10.09[B].]

Questions

1. Since common law copyright with respect to most works (including works of art), ceased to exist on January 1, 1978 due to federal preemption (see Sec. 301(a)), does the *Pushman* doctrine retain any significance in view of Secs. 202 and 204(a) of the current Copyright Act? May *Pushman* still be significant in determining the current copyright owner of a work of art first sold pre-1978? In view of the New York and California statutes mentioned in the preceding note, does *Pushman* retain any significance in those states?

2. Should it be presumed that an artist intends to assign copyright together with the transfer of the tangible object absent an expressed intent to reserve copyright, or should it be presumed that copyright in such circumstances is reserved absent an expressed intent to assign the copyright? Which presumption is more likely to comport with the expectation of the parties?

3. If an artist in New York after September 1, 1966 but before January 1, 1978, sold a painting and expressly reserved "all reproduction rights", might the buyer thereafter publish an art book including a reproduction of the artist's painting? Are "art books" excluded from the presumption of the reservation of the right of reproduction, or are they excluded from the right of reproduction itself under New York common law copyright?

Collateral References

Cohen, *An Artist Sells a Painting: The Courts Go Astray,* 5 UCLA Law Rev. 235 (1958).

Nimmer on Copyright, § 10.09.

D. DETERMINATION OF MEDIA TO WHICH LICENSES APPLY

BARTSCH v. METRO–GOLDWYN–MAYER, INC.

United States Court of Appeals, Second Circuit, 1968.
391 F.2d 150.

FRIENDLY, CIRCUIT JUDGE. This appeal from a judgment of the District Court for the Southern District of New York raises the question whether, on the facts here appearing, an assignee of motion picture rights to a musical play is entitled to authorize the telecasting of its copyrighted film. Although the issue seems considerably closer to us than it did to Judge Bryan, we affirm the judgment dismissing the complaint of the copyright owner.

In January 1930, the authors, composers, and publishers of and owners of certain other interests in a German musical play "Wie Einst in Mai," which had been produced in this country as "Maytime" with a changed libretto and score, assigned to Hans Bartsch

> the motion picture rights and all our right, title and interest in and in connection with such motion picture rights of the said operetta or musical play, throughout the world, together with the sole and exclusive rights to use, adapt, translate, add to and change the said operetta or musical play and the title thereof in the making of motion picture photoplays, and to project, transmit and otherwise reproduce the said work or any adaptation or version thereof, visually or audibly by the art of cinematography or any process analogous thereto, and to copyright, vend, license and exhibit such motion picture photoplays throughout the world; together with the further sole and exclusive rights by mechanical and/or electrical means to record, reproduce and transmit sound, including spoken words, dialogue, songs and music, and to change such dialogue, if extracted from said works, and to interpolate or use other dialogue, songs and music in or in connection with or as part of said motion picture photoplays, and the exhibition, reproduction and transmission thereof, and to make, use, license, import and vend any and all records or other devices required or desired for any such purposes.

> In May of that year Bartsch assigned to Warner Bros. Pictures, Inc. the motion picture rights throughout the world, in and to a certain musical play entitled "WIE EINST IN MAI," libretto and lyrics by Rudolph Schanzer and Rudolph Bernauer, music by Walter Kollo and Willy Bredschneider, for the full period of all copyrights and any renewed and extended terms thereof, together with the sole and exclusive right to use, adapt, translate, add to, subtract from, interpolate in and change said musical play, and the title thereof (subject so far as the right to use said title is concerned to Paragraph 7 hereof), in the making of motion picture photoplays and to project, transmit and otherwise reproduce the said musical play or any adaptation or version thereof visually or audibly by the art of cinematography or any process analogous thereto, and to copyright, vend, license and exhibit such motion picture photoplays throughout the world, together with the further sole and exclusive right by mechanical and/or electrical means to record, reproduce and transmit sound, including spoken words, dialogue, songs and music, and to change such dialogue, if extracted from said musical play, and at its own expense and responsibility to interpolate and use other dialogue, songs and music in or in connection with or as part of said motion picture photoplays, and the exhibition, reproduction and transmission thereof, and to make, use, license, import, vend and copyright any and all records or other devices made or required or desired for any such purposes.

By another clause Bartsch reserved the right to exercise for himself the rights generally granted to Warner Brothers insofar as these concerned

German language motion pictures in certain countries and subject to specified restrictions:

> but it is expressly understood and agreed that nothing herein contained shall in any way limit or restrict the absolute right of Purchaser to produce, release, distribute and/or exhibit the photoplay or photoplays produced hereunder based in whole or in part on "Wie Einst in Mai" and/or "Maytime," in all countries of the world, including the territory mentioned in this paragraph, at any time, and regardless of the right herein reserved to the Owner.

A further clause recited

> The rights which the Purchaser obtains from the Owner in "Wie Einst in Mai" and/or "Maytime" are specifically limited to those granted herein. All other rights now in existence or which may hereafter come into existence shall always be reserved to the Owner and for his sole benefit, but nothing herein contained shall in any way limit or restrict the rights which Purchaser has acquired or shall hereafter acquire from any other person, firm or corporation in and to "Wie Einst in Mai" and/or "Maytime."

Warner Brothers transferred its rights to defendant Metro-Goldwyn-Mayer, Inc. early in 1935, which made, distributed and exhibited a highly successful motion picture "Maytime." The co-authors of the German libretto, one in 1935 and the other in 1938, transferred all their copyright interests and renewal rights to Bartsch, whose rights in turn have devolved to the plaintiff, his widow. The controversy stems from MGM's licensing its motion picture for television, beginning in 1958.

Although the district judge upheld MGM's contention that the 1930 assignment from Bartsch to Warner Brothers included the right to permit telecasting of the motion picture to be made from the musical play, he thought there was "a further reason why plaintiff cannot prevail in this action," namely, that Bartsch had granted all that he had. This does not do justice to plaintiff's argument. Her position is that in 1930 Bartsch not only did not but could not grant the right to televise the motion picture since, under the similar language of the assignment to him, it was not his to grant; her claim of infringement is based not on the 1930 assignment to Bartsch of the motion picture rights but on the authors' later assignments of the full copyright.

The district court, appearing to consider that defendant's rights turned on the authorization "to project, transmit and otherwise reproduce the said musical play or any adaptation or version thereof visually and audibly by the art of cinematography *or any process analogous thereto*," concluded that television came within the phrase we have italicized. We have grave doubt on that score. We freely grant that "analogous" is a broader word than "similar," and also that the first step in a telecast of a film, namely, the projection of the motion picture to an electronic pickup, is "analogous" to throwing the picture on a theatre screen. But to characterize the to us nigh miraculous processes whereby these images actuate airwaves so as to cause electronic changes in sets in millions of homes which are then "unscrambled" or "descanned" and thus produce pictures on television screens—along with the simultaneous electronic transmission of sound—as "analogous" to cinematography pushes the analogy beyond the breaking point. This is particularly so since the district court's construction would seem to lead to the conclusion that the assignment would entitle the assignee to "project, transmit and otherwise reproduce" the musical play by a live telecast—a right which pretty clearly was not granted and indeed has not been claimed.

As we read the instruments, defendant's rights do not turn on the language we have been discussing but rather on the broad grant, in the assignments to and from Bartsch, of "the motion picture rights throughout the world," which were spelled out to include the right "to copyright, vend, license and exhibit such motion picture photoplays throughout the world." The "to project, transmit and otherwise reproduce" language appears rather to have been directed at how the musical play was to be made into a photoplay. This may well have seemed a more vexing problem in 1930, due to uncertainties as to the best method for linking visual and audible reproduction, cf. Paramount Publix Corp. v. American Tri-Ergon Corp., 294 U.S. 464, 55 S.Ct. 449, 79 L.Ed. 997 (1935), and whether a grant of motion picture rights to a play or novel included the right to sound reproduction, see L.C. Page & Co. v. Fox Film Corp., 83 F.2d 196 (2 Cir.1936), than today. Being unclear whether sound reproduction would require alterations in previous methods of converting a play into a photoplay, Warner Brothers sought and obtained a considerable degree of freedom in that regard. On this view the clause whose meaning has been so hotly debated is irrelevant to the point here at issue, and decision turns rather on whether a broad assignment of the right "to copyright, vend, license and exhibit such motion picture photoplays throughout the world" includes the right to "license" a broadcaster to "exhibit" the copyrighted motion picture by a telecast without a further grant by the copyright owner.

A threshold issue—which the pre-*Erie L.C. Page* decision was not required to take into account—is whether this question should be determined under state or federal law. The seventeenth paragraph of Bartsch's assignment says, somewhat unhelpfully, that "Each and every term of this agreement shall be construed in accordance with the laws of the United States of America *and* of the State of New York." [Emphasis supplied.] We hold that New York law governs. The development of a "federal common law" of contracts is justified only when required by a distinctive national policy and, as we found in T.B. Harms v. Eliscu, 339 F.2d 823, 828 (2 Cir.1964), citing many cases, "the general interest that copyrights, like all other forms of property, should be enjoyed by their true owner is not enough to meet this * * * test." Contrast Murphy v. Colonial Savings and Loan Ass'n, 388 F.2d 609 (2 Cir.1967), and Ivy Broadcasting Company, Inc. v. American Telephone & Telegraph Co., 391 F.2d 486 (2 Cir.1968), with McFaddin Express, Inc. v. Adley Corp., 363 F.2d 546 (2 Cir.), cert. denied, 385 U.S. 900, 87 S.Ct.

206, 17 L.Ed.2d 132 (1966). The fact that plaintiff is seeking a remedy granted by Congress to copyright owners removes any problem of federal jurisdiction but does not mean that federal principles must govern the disposition of every aspect of her claim. Cf. DeSylva v. Ballentine, 351 U.S. 570, 76 S.Ct. 974, 100 L.Ed. 1415 (1956).

Unfortunately, when we turn to state law, we find that it offers little assistance. Two other situations must be distinguished. This is not a case like Manners v. Morosco, 252 U.S. 317, 40 S.Ct. 335, 64 L.Ed. 590 (1920), cited with approval, Underhill v. Schenck, 238 N.Y. 7, 143 N.E. 773, 33 A.L.R. 303 (1924), in which an all encompassing grant found in one provision must be limited by the context created by other terms of the agreement indicating that the use of the copyrighted material in only one medium was contemplated. The words of Bartsch's assignment, as we have shown, were well designed to give the assignee the broadest rights with respect to *its* copyrighted property, to wit, the photoplay. "Exhibit" means to "display" or to "show" by any method, and nothing in the rest of the grant sufficiently reveals a contrary intention.[1] Nor is this case like Kirke La Shelle Co. v. Paul Armstrong Co., 263 N.Y. 79, 188 N.E. 163 (1938), in which the new medium was completely unknown at the time when the contract was written. Rather, the trial court correctly found that, "During 1930 the future possibilities of television were recognized by knowledgeable people in the entertainment and motion picture industries," though surely not in the scope it has attained. While Kirke La Shelle teaches that New York will not charge a grantor with the duty of expressly saving television rights when he could not know of the invention's existence, we have found no case holding that an experienced businessman like Bartsch is not bound by the natural implications of the language he accepted when he had reason to know of the new medium's potential.[2]

Plaintiff, naturally enough, would not frame the issue in precisely this way. Instead, she argues that even in 1930 Warner Brothers often attempted to obtain an express grant of television rights and that its failure to succeed in Bartsch's case should persuade us that, despite the broad language, only established forms of exhibition were contemplated. She buttresses this argument by producing a number of 1930 assignments to Warner Brothers, some of which specifically granted the

---

1. The plaintiff points to paragraph 13 of the agreement, reproduced in the text, as indicating an intention to exclude television rights. The provision limits the rights of the assignee to those "specifically * * * granted herein," and save to Bartsch "all other rights now in existence or which may hereafter come into existence." We cannot read this as standing for more than the truism that whatever Bartsch had not granted, he had retained.

2. In Ettore v. Philco Television Broadcasting Corp., 229 F.2d 481, cert. denied, 351 U.S. 926, 76 S.Ct. 783, 100 L.Ed. 1456 (1956), the Third Circuit, applying Pennsylvania law, held that a 1955 contract granting moving picture rights did not permit the grantee to televise the film. However, unlike Bartsch, the grantor, Ettore, was not an experienced businessman but a prize fighter, and the Court relied heavily on his lack of sophistication in determining whether it was fair to charge him with knowledge of the new medium. Id. at 491, n. 14.

right to televise motion pictures and others of which granted full television rights, and by adducing testimony of the Warner Brothers lawyer who had approved the assignment from Bartsch that on many occasions Warner Brothers attempted to secure an express grant of such rights but did not always succeed.

However, this is not enough to show that the Bartsch assignments were a case of that sort. For all that appears Warner Brothers may have decided that, in dealing with Bartsch, it would be better tactics to rely on general words that were sufficiently broad rather than seek an express inclusion and perhaps end up with the opposite, or may have used a form regular in the industry without thinking very precisely about television, or—perhaps most likely—may simply have parroted the language in the grant from Bartsch's assignors to him on the theory it would thus be getting all he had, whatever that might be. Indeed, it is really the assignment to Bartsch rather than the one from him that must control.[3] While plaintiff suggests that Warner Brothers may have furnished Bartsch the forms to be used with his assignors, this is sheer speculation. There is no showing that the form was unique to Warner Brothers; indeed the contrary appears.

With Bartsch dead, his grantors apparently so, and the Warner Brothers lawyer understandably having no recollection of the negotiation, any effort to reconstruct what the parties actually intended nearly forty years ago is doomed to failure. In the end, decision must turn, as Professor Nimmer has suggested, The Law of Copyright § 125.3 (1964), on a choice between two basic approaches more than on an attempt to distill decisive meaning out of language that very likely had none. As between an approach that "a license of rights in a given medium (e.g., 'motion picture rights') includes only such uses as fall within the unambiguous core meaning of the term (e.g., exhibition of motion picture film in motion picture theaters) and exclude any uses which lie within the ambiguous penumbra (e.g., exhibition of motion picture film on television)" and another whereby "the licensee may properly pursue any uses which may reasonably be said to fall within the medium as described in the license," he prefers the latter. So do we. But see Warner, Radio and Television Rights § 52 (1953). If the words are broad enough to cover the new use, it seems fairer that the burden of framing and negotiating an exception should fall on the grantor; if Bartsch or his assignors had desired to limit "exhibition" of the motion

---

3. From all that appears, it would seem that this first assignment was negotiated in Germany and that German law would apply in its interpretation. Since neither party has suggested that German law differs from New York law in any relevant respect, we have not embarked on an independent investigation of the matter. El Hoss Engineering & Transportation Co. v. American Independent Oil Co., 183 F.Supp. 394, 399 (S.D.N.Y.1960), rev'd on other grounds, 289 F.2d 346 (2 Cir.), cert. denied, 368 U.S. 837, 82 S.Ct. 51, 7 L.Ed.2d 38 (1961). Though new Rule 44.1 establishes that courts may, in their discretion, examine foreign legal sources independently, it does not require them to do so in the absence of any suggestion that such a course will be fruitful or any help from the parties. Miller, Federal Rule 44.1 and the "Fact" Approach to Determining Foreign Law: Death Knell for a Die Hard Doctrine, 65 Mich.L.Rev. 615, 692–702 (1967).

picture to the conventional method where light is carried from a projector to a screen directly beheld by the viewer, they could have said so. A further reason favoring the broader view in a case like this is that it provides a single person who can make the copyrighted work available to the public over the penumbral medium, whereas the narrower one involves the risk that a deadlock between the grantor and the grantee might prevent the work's being shown over the new medium at all. Quite apart from the probable impracticality, the assignments are broad enough even on plaintiff's view to prevent the copyright owners from licensing anyone else to make a photoplay for telecasting. The risk that some May might find the nation's television screens bereft of the annual display of "Maytime," interlarded with the usual liberal diet of commercials, is not one a court can take lightly.

Affirmed.

Questions

1. Suppose the medium of television had been completely unknown at the time of Bartsch's assignment to Warner Brothers. Would the *Bartsch* court have decided the case in favor of the copyright owner? Would such a decision have been justified?

2. Do you agree with the court's determination in the instant case that the words "by the art of cinematography *or any process analogous thereto*" are not broad enough to include television? Suppose, as is often the case in motion picture assignments, that the above quoted language is applicable not (as in the instant case) to the underlying work but only to the exhibition of any motion picture film based upon the underlying work. Should it still be concluded that exhibition of motion picture film by television is not "analogous" to the exhibition of the film "by the art of cinematography"?

Collateral References

Cohn, *Old Licenses and New Uses,* 19 Law and Contemporary Problems 184 (1954).

Colton, *Contracts in the Entertainment and Literary Fields,* 1953 Copyright Problems Analyzed 139 (CCH 1953).

Nimmer on Copyright, § 10.10[B].

GOODIS v. UNITED ARTISTS TELEVISION, INC.

United States Court of Appeals, Second Circuit, 1970.
425 F.2d 397.

[The first portion of this opinion is set forth at p. 281 supra.]

Having concluded that the copyright was validly obtained in behalf of Goodis and that he may maintain an action for infringement, I turn to the contract for motion picture rights on which defendants rely. The views of the majority on this issue are set forth in Judge Waterman's opinion. My own view is that the district court properly decided this question on a motion for summary judgment.

The relevant provisions of the contract are carefully set forth and discussed in the district judge's memorandum opinion, 278 F.Supp. 122 (S.D.N.Y.1968). The critical clause in paragraph 19(c) of the contract conveys " * * * the right to broadcast and transmit *any photograph produced hereunder* by the process of television * * * " [emphasis added]. Although my brothers discuss "springboards" and "sequels," the only question which the district court had to decide was whether this particular television series could be produced under this particular contract.

This is not a case where the question is the right to broadcast a movie on television, cf. Bartsch v. Metro-Goldwyn-Mayer, Inc., 270 F.Supp. 896 (S.D.N.Y.1967), aff'd, 391 F.2d 150 (2d Cir.), cert. denied 393 U.S. 826 (1968). The contract clearly provided for the presentation of the movie "Dark Passage" on television and appellant concedes the propriety of such broadcasts. Appellant claims, however, that "any photoplay produced hereunder" does not encompass "The Fugitive," a film series produced directly for television without any intention to show it in motion picture theaters. I think a fair interpretation of the contract indicates that the grant of motion picture rights was sufficiently broad to include this use.

Under paragraph 17, defendants purchased the "absolute and unlimited right * * * to make such changes, *variations*, modifications, *alterations, adaptations, arrangements, additions in* and/or eliminations and omissions from *said Writings and/or the characters, plot,* dialogue, *scenes, incidents, situations, action,* language and theme thereof * * * " [emphasis added]. Under paragraph 19(c), Goodis retained "[t]he right to broadcast said Writings by television from the performances given by living actors."

Had Goodis sold specific, limited rights in 1945 and retained for his future use or disposition the general reservoir of broadcast rights, I might be persuaded that a question of fact existed. But Goodis retained only the specific right to "broadcast said Writings by television from performances by living actors," and I find it difficult to imagine a broader transfer of rights than that which these parties drafted. It seems clear to me the district judge properly decided on summary judgment that defendants could produce and televise films in any manner they might choose other than from the performances of live actors.

The majority claims that my construction may affect the interpretation of many similar contracts which do not explicitly mention the right to make "sequels" using the original characters. I do not share this concern.

First, unlike most of the contract, which was Warner Brothers' standard form, the paragraph describing television broadcast rights was specially drafted by the parties. It is unlikely any other contracts drafted circa 1945 will be affected by our determination of these parties' intentions as expressed in these specially negotiated terms.

Second, although the majority shows great concern for the use of "sequels," the question of sequels was not, in my opinion, before the district court. In paragraph 16 of the complaint, Goodis took particular care to show an exact parallel between "Dark Passage" and "The Fugitive." The content of "The Fugitive" was not raised by Goodis as a factual issue in his opposition to the summary judgment motion. For all that appears in the record, the "sequel" argument was raised for the first time on appeal in an effort to overturn the grant of summary judgment.

The majority implies in a footnote that this view reflects a return to "dangerously technical methods of pleading." Apparently they are assuming that a litigant in Goodis' position would have to walk a narrow line between pleading sufficient identity for infringement on the one hand and sufficient difference for a "sequel" claim on the other. Whether or not this might be a real problem in the ordinary infringement action, it is certainly not crucial in a case where a defendant has a contractual right to use a work and the only question is whether he has exceeded his rights.

Although I agree that there was no forfeiture of "Dark Passage" into the public domain because of the procedure used to secure copyright, I would affirm the grant of summary judgment by the district court as the contractual rights of the parties were clearly defined.

Reversed and remanded.

WATERMAN, CIRCUIT JUDGE, with whom KAUFMAN, CIRCUIT JUDGE, joins (concurring partially with CHIEF JUDGE LUMBARD).

My brother Kaufman and I concur in that part of Chief Judge Lumbard's opinion which holds that Goodis did not surrender his copyright in Dark Passage because of the Saturday Evening Post publication. We do not agree with his view that the defendant below is entitled to summary judgment on the issue of whether the contract between Goodis and Warner Brothers conveyed the right to make and broadcast a television series such as The Fugitive. Accordingly, on this branch of the case our holding is that of the majority.

The party to whom summary judgment is awarded must have shown "that there is no genuine issue as to any material fact and that the moving party is entitled to a judgment as a matter of law." Fed.R.Civ.P. 56(c). The question presented here is whether the contract language demonstrates unambiguously that Goodis meant to convey to Warner Brothers the right to create a television series such as The Fugitive or whether a genuine issue of material fact exists as to what the parties intended by the language they used.

The rights which the contract conveyed to Warner Brothers "in said writings" included "the exclusive, complete and entire motion picture rights," and "the right to broadcast and transmit any photoplay produced hereunder by the process of television * * * provided that such broadcasts and transmissions are given from the film of such photoplay and not directly from the performances of living actors." The judge below held that the term "any photoplay produced hereunder" unambiguously included a television series of photoplays such as The Fugitive. Accordingly, he awarded summary judgment to the defendants.

We disagree. It is our holding that the contract language does not so clearly permit production of The Fugitive as to entitle the defendant to the grant of a summary judgment.

The language of the contract clearly conveys to Warner Brothers the right to make a movie of Dark Passage and to show that movie on television. Moreover, Paragraph 17 of the contract conveys the right to vary the plot and characters of Dark Passage in making that movie. The question before us, however, is whether the contract unambiguously fails to put any limits on the degree to which Warner Brothers could change or modify the original story while using the story's characters.

In an appeal from summary judgment we must resolve all disputed questions of fact in favor of the appellant. Therefore, we accept appellant's factual representations in the complaint and assume that The Fugitive television series took the characters in Dark Passage and, using the novel's plot as a springboard, placed the characters the author created in a whole series of new plot situations developed by the motion picture company. It seems to us that the right to make "additions in * * * said writings" and in the characters and plot of Dark Passage does not necessarily go so far as to show that there is no genuine issue as to whether the characters of Dark Passage may be depicted in photoplay adventures which bear little relationship to the "said writings" of Dark Passage. Viewed in the context of the entire contract, the "additions" and "alterations" clauses of Paragraph 17 could be read in a more restrictive manner to permit only those alterations necessary to adapt a written story to the medium of film. Similarly, use of the word "unlimited" with respect to the rights to alter and supplement could have been intended only to prevent Goodis from protesting that his story had been distorted or mutilated.

Among the reasons that have caused us to conclude that this case should not be decided without a full inquiry into the intent of the parties is that our disposition of this appeal may affect the interpretation of other contracts which convey some of the divisible rights in a given story but do not explicitly mention among the conveyed rights the right to make subsequent stories employing the same characters, i.e., "sequels" as such stories are called in the publishing industry. Too, a proper decision as to what the parties intended in this case may largely depend upon the general custom and expectations of authors and of members of the publishing, broadcasting, and film vocations. Because this case reaches us after a grant of summary judgment we have before us no evidence as to these customs and expectations. Many authors have used characters they created in one novel in a whole series of subsequent works; surely it would be rash of us to hold on summary judgment that the sale of rights in one of an author's works ends, without specific mention that it ends, the author's exclusive ownership of the valuable characters he created in that one work, when he may well desire to create sequels of his own using these same characters. Accord, Warner Bros. Pictures, Inc. v. Columbia Broadcasting System, 216 F.2d 945 (9 Cir.1954), cert. denied 348 U.S. 971 (1955).[1]

We further note, contrary to our brother Lumbard's view, that the issue of the right of defendants to use the characters from Dark Passage in new plot situations was properly raised by appellant before the district court. The court below was not misled into thinking that The Fugitive contained no plot material beyond that of Dark Passage. Judge Mansfield noted in his opinion that the plaintiff asserted that the contract limited Warner Brothers' rights to a photoplay made from the original story, so it is obvious that the judge understood plaintiff's contention that The Fugitive was not identical to Dark Passage although it built upon that story's theme and used the author's characters.[2] Moreover, common sense indicates that the material used in a television series which was broadcast for one hour a week for more than one season could not possibly be confined to the limited material found in a single movie or in a short novel. The arguments made to this court were therefore properly raised below. Once plaintiff's assertion was understood below, namely that Goodis had retained certain rights in the characters of Dark Passage, and that The Fugitive used these characters, it is certainly not crucial whether the complaint used the term of art "sequel" in referring to the television series.

---

1. In that case the original owners of the copyright to The Maltese Falcon had sold Warner Brothers the right to use that story in moving pictures, radio, and television. When the original owners subsequently used the characters developed in The Maltese Falcon in a new radio series, The Adventures of Sam Spade, Warner Brothers contended that the contract gave it the exclusive right to the use of the characters as well as the exclusive right to the use of the original story in the specified media. The court, however, held that the assignment of copyright in the Falcon did not convey rights to the characters so that the rights in the characters remained in the author, citing, Nichols v. Universal Pictures Corp., 45 F.2d 119 (2 Cir.1930), cert. denied, 282 U.S. 902 (1931), and Warner Brothers Pictures, Inc. v. Majestic Pictures Corp., 70 F.2d 310 (2 Cir.1934). Although the Ninth Circuit did not reach the question whether Warner Brothers [sic? Did Judge Waterman mean C.B.S. rather than Warner Brothers?] could have used the characters of the Falcon in a new series even without an exclusive copyright—by asserting, in effect, that now the Falcon's characters were in the public domain—we think such a conclusion would be clearly untenable from the standpoint of public policy, for it would effectively permit the unrestrained pilfering of characters.

2. Paragraph 16 of the complaint alleges that "defendant * * * had no rights in and to the broadcast of said writings or any part thereof by television except use of the original motion picture" which Warner Brothers had previously made from the novel, and Paragraph 17 alleges that United Artists, Warner Brothers' successor in interest, made a television series entitled The Fugitive in breach of the contract. Paragraph 18 et seq. go on to allege and describe similarities between The Fugitive and Dark Passage in order to establish infringement. Judge Lumbard appears to assert that Goodis, in order thus to establish infringement, alleged such a substantial identity between The Fugitive series and Dark Passage that he conceded The Fugitive series to be a photoplay made from Dark Passage within the meaning of the contract. We disagree, for to trap a plaintiff in such a well-concealed pitfall would mark a return to dangerously technical methods of pleading.

Reversed and remanded for further proceedings below.

Questions

1. Did Goodis contend that he had reserved the right to produce a photoplay based upon his work if such photoplay is intended exclusively (or primarily?) for television exhibition, or did he contend that he had reserved the right to produce a photoplay (regardless of the manner of exhibition) which constitutes a "sequel" to his work in that it portrays the leading character taken from his work in a story or stories which are not taken from his work? As to which contention did a majority of the court find a genuine issue of material fact?

2. Is Judge Waterman's statement of the holding in Warner Bros. v. Columbia Broadcasting System, supra, misleading? Is the instant case inconsistent with the Ninth Circuit view (as expressed in *Warner Bros.*) as to the protectibility of characters? Can the two cases be reconciled on contract grounds?

3. Is a copyright owner who claims infringement of "sequel rights" forced "to walk a narrow line between pleading sufficient identity for infringement on the one hand and sufficient difference for a 'sequel' claim on the other"? Isn't the identity as to one component (the character) and the difference as to another (the story line in the plaintiff's work)? If the copyright owner fails to prove a difference in story line doesn't he still have a cause of action for infringement of his work? Does this depend upon whether he has granted "remake rights"? See Edgar Rice Burroughs, Inc. v. Metro-Goldwyn-Mayer, Inc., supra.

Note and Questions

Termination of Transfers and Nonexclusive Licenses

The renewal provisions incorporated in the 1909 Act, and continued under the present Act with respect to works in statutory copyright prior to January 1, 1978, were intended to grant to authors and their families a second opportunity to market their works after an original transfer of copyright. The rationale for this second chance is discussed in a prior chapter. The Congress which enacted the present Copyright Act recognized as justification for a reversion of rights the necessity of "safeguarding authors against unremunerative transfers * * * needed because of the unequal bargaining position of authors, resulting in part from the impossibility of determining a work's prior value until it has been exploited."[1] But the renewal structure was found to be an unsatisfactory means of achieving reversion for authors. It is procedurally clumsy and difficult. The fact that reversion under the renewal system is tied to the term of copyright creates a real possibility that works will be injected into the public domain by reason of an inadvertent failure to renew. Finally, the objective of a second chance for authors was largely frustrated by the Supreme Court decision in Fisher v. Witmark, supra, recognizing the validity of assignments of renewal rights prior to their vesting.

The termination provisions of the current Act constitute an attempt to avoid the difficulties encountered under the renewal concept, while at the same

---

1. H.Rep., p. 124.

time achieving a reversion of rights. There is but a single term of copyright for works which did not acquire statutory copyright prior to the effective date of the current Act, thus avoiding unintended injection of works into the public domain by failure to renew. Reversion occurs through the termination of transfers and nonexclusive licenses rather than by the termination of an original copyright term and the creation of a second term.

The student should study carefully the complex provisions of Secs. 203 and 304(c), and then be prepared to answer the following questions:

1. To what types of grants do the termination provisions apply? Do they apply to nonexclusive licenses as well as to "transfers"? Do they apply to all, some or no pre-1978 grants of common law copyright? Do they apply to transfers of copyright under a "for hire" relationship? Do they apply to grants by will? By intestacy?

2. Do the termination provisions apply only to those grants as to which the author (rather than a successor) is the grantor? Is a distinction in this regard made as between pre- and post-1978 grants? If after January 1, 1978 an author grants his copyright to X, who in turn grants such copyright to Y, is Y's grant subject to termination?

3. What rights are subject to termination? Does the grant of the right to use the title of a work terminate when the rights in the work per se terminate? Do foreign rights terminate when domestic rights terminate?

4. What are the rights of the copyright owner of a derivative work when his grant from the owner of the underlying work terminates? May the grantee of motion picture rights in a novel continue to publicly perform a motion picture made prior to such termination? May he make new film prints of the same motion picture after the effective date of termination? May he produce a new motion picture based upon the same underlying work after such termination? Are the answers to any of the above different if the derivative work consists of a musical arrangement of an (underlying) song rather than of a motion picture version of an (underlying) novel?

5. Who is entitled to terminate if the author-grantor does not survive until termination vesting? In what proportion do the author's surviving spouse, children and grandchildren participate? Who is entitled to terminate a pre-1978 grant of renewal rights?

6. When do termination rights vest? Does this date differ from the date when such rights revert?

7. During what five year period may termination be effected as to grants executed on or after January 1, 1978? As to grants executed pre-1978? What is the significance in this regard as to whether book publication rights have been granted?

8. How is termination effected? What is the earliest date when a termination notice may be served? What is the latest date? What must be stated in the notice? Upon whom must the notice be served? Must the termination notice be recorded in the Copyright Office? When?

9. Is an agreement waiving the right to terminate legally valid? Is an agreement to grant anew the rights subject to termination valid if executed before the notice of termination has been served? If executed before the rights have terminated?

10. What devices, if any, are open to a grantee to assure in advance of termination the continued enjoyment of the rights subject to termination?

11. What is the effect of a failure to serve a notice of termination within the required time period?

Collateral References

Cohen, "*Derivative Works*" *under the Termination Provisions in the 1976 Copyright Act,* 28 Bull. Copr. Soc'y 380 (1981).

Curtis, *"Protecting Authors In Copyright Transfers: Revision Bill § 203 and the Alternatives",* 72 Colum.L.Rev. 799 (1972).

Stein, *"Termination of Transfers and Licenses Under the New Copyright Act: Thorny Problems For the Copyright Bar,"* 24 UCLA L.Rev. 1141 (1977).

Nimmer on Copyright, §§ 11.01–11.09.

Chapter Seven

INFRINGEMENT ACTIONS

A. JURISDICTION

T.B. HARMS COMPANY v. ELISCU

United States Court of Appeals, Second Circuit, 1964.
339 F.2d 823.

Before FRIENDLY, KAUFMAN and ANDERSON, CIRCUIT JUDGES.

FRIENDLY, CIRCUIT JUDGE. A layman would doubtless be surprised to learn that an action wherein the purported sole owner of a copyright alleged that persons claiming partial ownership had recorded their claim in the Copyright Office and had warned his licensees against disregarding their interests was not one "arising under any Act of Congress relating to * * * copyrights" over which 28 U.S.C.A. § 1338 gives the federal courts exclusive jurisdiction. Yet precedents going back for more than a century teach that lesson and lead us to affirm Judge Weinfeld's dismissal of the complaint.

The litigation concerns four copyrighted songs; we shall state the nub of the matter as alleged in the complaint without going into details irrelevant to the jurisdictional issue. The music for the songs was composed by Vincent Youmans for use in a motion picture, "Flying Down to Rio," pursuant to a contract made in 1933 with RKO Studios, Inc. He agreed to assign to RKO the recordation and certain other rights relating to the picture during the existence of the copyrights and any renewals. RKO was to employ a writer of the lyrics and to procure the publishing rights in these for Youmans, who was "to pay said lyric writer the usual and customary royalties on sheet music and mechanical records." Subject to this, Youmans could assign the publication and small performing rights to the music and lyrics as he saw fit. In fact RKO employed two lyric writers, Gus Kahn and the defendant Edward Eliscu, who agreed to assign to RKO certain rights described in a contract dated as of May 25, 1933. Max Dreyfus, principal stockholder of the plaintiff Harms, which has succeeded to his rights, acquired Youmans' reserved rights to the music and was his designee for the assignment with respect to the lyrics. Allegedly—and his denial of this is a prime subject of dispute—Eliscu then entered into an agreement dated June 30, 1933, assigning his rights to the existing and renewal copyrights to Dreyfus in return for certain royalties.

When the copyrights were about to expire, proper renewal applications were made by the children of Youmans, by the widow and children of Kahn, and by Eliscu. The two former groups executed assignments of their rights in the renewal copyrights to Harms. But Eliscu, by an instrument dated February 19, 1962, recorded in the Copyright Office, assigned his rights in the renewal copyrights to defendant Ross Jungnickel, Inc., subject to a judicial determination of his ownership. Thereafter Eliscu's lawyer advised ASCAP and one Harry Fox—respectively the agents for the small performing rights and the mechanical recording license fees—that Eliscu had become vested with a half interest in the renewal copyrights and that any future payments which failed to reflect his interest would be made at their own risk; at the same time he demanded an accounting from Harms. Finally, Eliscu brought an action in the New York Supreme Court for a declaration that he owned a one-third interest in the renewal copyrights and for an accounting.

Harms then began the instant action in the District Court for the Southern District of New York for equitable and declaratory relief against Eliscu and Jungnickel. Jurisdiction was predicated on 28 U.S.C. § 1338; plaintiff alleged its own New York incorporation and did not allege the citizenship of the defendants, which concededly is in New York. Defendants moved to dismiss the complaint for failure to state a claim on which relief can be granted and for lack of federal jurisdiction; voluminous affidavits were submitted. The district court dismissed the complaint for want of federal jurisdiction, 226 F.Supp. 337 (1964).

In line with what apparently were the arguments of the parties, Judge Weinfeld treated the jurisdictional issue as turning solely on whether the complaint alleged any act or threat of copyright infringement. He was right in concluding it did not. Infringement, as used in copyright law, does not include everything that may impair the value of the copyright; it is doing one or more of those things which § 1 of the Act, 17 U.S.C. § 1, reserves exclusively to the copyright owner. See Nimmer, Copyright §§ 100, 141 (1963). The case did not even raise what has been the problem presented when a defendant licensed to use a copyright or a patent on certain terms is alleged to have forfeited the grant; in such cases federal jurisdiction is held to exist if the plaintiff has directed his pleading against the offending use, referring to the license only by way of anticipatory replication, but not if he has sued to set the license aside, seeking recovery for unauthorized use only incidentally or not at all. See Chief Justice Taft's review of the cases in Luckett v. Delpark, 270 U.S. 496, 46 S.Ct. 397, 70 L.Ed. 703 (1926); and Hart & Wechsler, The Federal Courts and the Federal System, 754–58 (1953). Here neither Eliscu nor Jungnickel had used or threatened to use the copyrighted material; their various acts, as the district judge noted, sought to establish their ownership of the copyrights by judicial and administrative action, including notice to the parties concerned.

However, the jurisdictional statute does not speak in terms of infringement, and the undoubted truth that a claim for infringement "arises under" the Copyright Act does not establish that nothing else can. Simply as a matter of language, the statutory phrasing would not compel the conclusion that an action to determine who owns a copyright does not arise under the Copyright Act, which creates the federal copyright with an implied right to license and an explicit right to assign. But the gloss afforded by history and good sense leads to that conclusion as to the complaint in this case.

Although Chief Justice Marshall, construing the "arising under" language in the context of Article III of the Constitution, indicated in Osborn v. Bank of the United States, 9 Wheat. 738, 22 U.S. 738, 822–827, 6 L.Ed. 204 (1824), that the grant extended to every case in which federal law furnished a necessary ingredient of the claim even though this was antecedent and uncontested, the Supreme Court has long given a narrower meaning to the "arising under" language in statutes defining the jurisdiction of the lower federal courts. Romero v. International Terminal Operating Co., 358 U.S. 354, 379 n. 51, 79 S.Ct. 468, 3 L.Ed.2d 368 (1959); Mishkin, The Federal "Question" in the District Courts, 53 Colum.L.Rev. 157, 160–63 (1953). If the ingredient theory of Article III had been carried over to the general grant of federal question jurisdiction now contained in 28 U.S.C. § 1331, there would have been no basis—to take a well-known example—why federal courts should not have jurisdiction as to all disputes over the many western land titles originating in a federal patent, even though the controverted questions normally are of fact or of local land law. Quite sensibly, such extensive jurisdiction has been denied. Shoshone Mining Co. v. Rutter, 177 U.S. 505, 20 S.Ct. 726, 44 L.Ed. 864 (1900).

The cases dealing with statutory jurisdiction over patents and copyrights have taken the same conservative line. The problem apparently first reached the Supreme Court in Wilson v. Sanford, 10 How. 99, 51 U.S. 99, 13 L.Ed. 344 (1850), under the Act of July 4, 1836, § 17, 5 Stat. 17, which allowed appeal to the Court, irrespective of the amount, in actions "arising under" the patent laws. The suit aimed to prevent use of a patented invention by a licensee who allegedly had failed to comply with the terms of the license and thus had forfeited its rights. Chief Justice Taney, dismissing the appeal, held the statute inapplicable to a dispute as to license or contract rights which "depended altogether upon the rules and principles of equity, and in no degree whatever upon any act of Congress concerning patent rights." The same principle was applied, and sometimes stated less cautiously, in decisions construing later legislation granting the federal courts exclusive jurisdiction of all suits "arising under" the patent or copyright laws of the United States. Act of July 8, 1870, §§ 55, 106, 16 Stat. 206, 215; Rev.Stat. §§ 629 Ninth and 711 Fifth (1875); Judicial Code of 1911, §§ 24 Seventh, 256 Fifth, 36 Stat. 1092, 1161. To take one of many examples, the Court said in New Marshall Engine Co. v. Marshall Engine Co., 223 U.S. 473, 478, 32 S.Ct. 238, 239, 56 L.Ed. 513 (1912):

> The Federal courts have exclusive jurisdiction of all cases arising under the patent laws, but not of all questions in which a patent may be the subject-matter of the controversy. For courts of a state may try questions of title, and may construe and enforce contracts relating to patents. Wade v. Lawder, 165 U.S. 624, 627, 41 L.Ed. 852, 17 Sup.Ct.Rep. 425.

Just as with western land titles, the federal grant of a patent or copyright has not been thought to infuse with any national interest a dispute as to ownership or contractual enforcement turning on the facts or on ordinary principles of contract law. Indeed, the case for an unexpansive reading of the provision conferring exclusive jurisdiction with respect to patents and copyrights has been especially strong since expansion would entail depriving the state courts of any jurisdiction over matters having so little federal significance.

In an endeavor to explain precisely what suits arose under the patent and copyright laws, Mr. Justice Holmes stated that "[a] suit arises under the law that creates the cause of action"; in the case *sub judice,* injury to a business involving slander of a patent, he said, "whether it is a wrong or not depends upon the law of the State where the act is done" so that the suit did not arise under the patent laws. American Well Works Co. v. Layne & Bowler Co., 241 U.S. 257, 260, 36 S.Ct. 585, 586, 60 L.Ed. 987 (1916). The Holmes "creation" test explains the taking of federal jurisdiction in a great many cases, notably copyright and patent infringement actions, both clearly authorized by the respective federal acts, 17 U.S.C.A. § 101; 35 U.S.C.A. § 281, and thus unquestionably within the scope of 28 U.S.C.A. § 1338; indeed, in the many infringement suits that depend only on some point of fact and require no construction of federal law, no other explanation may exist.

Harms' claim is not within Holmes' definition. The relevant statutes create no explicit right of action to enforce or rescind assignments of copyrights, nor does any copyright statute specify a cause of action to fix the locus of ownership. To be sure, not every federal cause of action springs from an express mandate of Congress; federal civil claims have been "inferred" from federal statutes making behavior criminal or otherwise regulating it. See, e.g., Tunstall v. Brotherhood of Locomotive Firemen, 323 U.S. 210, 65 S.Ct. 235, 89 L.Ed. 187 (1944); Reitmeister v. Reitmeister, 162 F.2d 691 (2 Cir.1947); Note, Implying Civil Remedies From Federal Regulatory Statutes, 77 Harv.L.Rev. 285 (1963). Such statutes invariably impose a federal duty and usually create some express remedy as well, while the relevant copyright provision merely authorizes an assignment by written instrument, 17 U.S.C. § 28. It is true that although this difference carries the present case outside the classic doctrine of implied remedies, see Restatement, Torts § 286 (1934), expansion may not be foreclosed where appropriate, cf. Wheeldin v. Wheeler, 373 U.S. 647, 661–663, 83 S.Ct. 1441, 10 L.Ed.2d 605 (1963) (Brennan, J., dissenting); we would not be understood, for example, as necessarily agreeing with the implication of Republic Pictures Corp. v. Security-First National Bank, 197 F.2d 767, 770 (9 Cir.1952), that federal jurisdiction would not exist if a complaint alleged that a state declined to enforce assignments of copyright valid under federal law. But no such case is here presented.

It has come to be realized that Mr. Justice Holmes' formula is more useful for inclusion than for the exclusion for which it was intended. Even though the claim is created by state law, a case may "arise under" a law of the United States if the complaint discloses a need for determining the meaning or application of such a law. The path-breaking opinion to this effect was Smith v. Kansas City Title & Trust Co., 255 U.S. 180, 41 S.Ct. 243, 65 L.Ed. 577 (1921), pointedly rendered over a dissent by Mr. Justice Holmes, 255 U.S. at 213–215, 41 S.Ct. 243. A recent application of this principle to 28 U.S.C. § 1338 is De Sylva v. Ballentine, 351 U.S. 570, 76 S.Ct. 974, 100 L.Ed. 1415 (1956), where the Supreme Court decided on the merits a claim to partial ownership of copyright renewal terms. Since there was no diversity of citizenship and no infringement, the only, and a sufficient, explanation for the taking of jurisdiction was the existence of two major questions of construction of the Copyright Act.[1] But Harms likewise does not meet this test. The crucial issue is whether or not Eliscu executed the assignment to Dreyfus; possibly the interpretation of the initial May, 1933, contract is also relevant, but if any aspect of the suit requires an interpretation of the Copyright Act, the complaint does not reveal it.[2]

Having thus found that appropriate pleading of a pivotal question of federal law may suffice to give federal jurisdiction even for a "state-created" claim, we cannot halt at questions hinging only on the language of the Copyright Act. For a new and dynamic doctrine, taking its name from Clearfield Trust Co. v. United States, 318 U.S. 363, 63 S.Ct. 573, 87 L.Ed. 838 (1943), instructs us that even in the absence of express statute, federal law may govern what might seem an issue of local law because the federal interest is dominant. Sola Elec. Co. v. Jefferson Elec. Co., 317 U.S. 173, 175–176, 63 S.Ct. 172, 87 L.Ed. 165 (1942), is relevant here, not only for its holding that the radiations of the anti-trust laws governed an estoppel question in a patent license case but also for the Court's unwillingness to say whether the estoppel rule would have been "local" or "federal" even if the antitrust laws had not been invoked—a question which Scott Paper Co. v. Marcalus Mfg. Co., 326 U.S. 249, 255, 66 S.Ct. 101, 90 L.Ed. 47 (1945), apparently settled in favor of federal principles. If this "federal common law"

---

[1] Although the parties did not question federal jurisdiction and the Court did not mention it, the issue had been sharply raised by a dissent in the Court of Appeals, see 226 F.2d 623, 634 (9 Cir.1955), and can hardly have passed unnoticed.

[2] Harms likewise does not bring itself within the test by reliance on the provision of § 24 of the Copyright Act that in the case of any work copyrighted "by an employer for whom such work is made for hire the proprietor of the copyright shall be entitled" to the renewal rights. The allocation of rights under the May, 1933, contract is governed by the contract itself, and the complaint suggests no manner in which the construction of § 24 of the Copyright Act might be relevant.

governed some disputed aspect of a claim to ownership of a copyright or for the enforcement of a license, federal jurisdiction might follow—though one would wish to consider whether this might be founded on 28 U.S.C.A. § 1331 rather than on § 1338 and thus be concurrent and require a jurisdictional amount. But there is not the slightest reason to think that any legal question presented by Harms' complaint falls in the shadow of a federal interest suggested by the Copyright Act or any other source.

Mindful of the hazards of formulation in this treacherous area, we think that an action "arises under" the Copyright Act if and only if the complaint is for a remedy expressly granted by the Act, e.g., a suit for infringement or for the statutory royalties for record reproduction, 17 U.S.C.A. § 101, cf. Joy Music, Inc. v. Seeco Records, Inc., 166 F.Supp. 549 (S.D.N.Y.1958), or asserts a claim requiring construction of the Act, as in De Sylva, or, at the very least and perhaps more doubtfully, presents a case where a distinctive policy of the Act requires that federal principles control the disposition of the claim. The general interest that copyrights, like all other forms of property, should be enjoyed by their true owner is not enough to meet this last test.

Something should be said as to cases in this circuit deciding on the merits copyright claims apparently not involving infringement. There has been discussion whether the assumption of jurisdiction in Rossiter v. Vogel, 134 F.2d 908 (2 Cir.1943), was properly rested on a basis similar to that suggested in this opinion with respect to De Sylva, see Cresci v. Music Publishers Holding Corp., 210 F.Supp. 253, 258–259 (S.D.N.Y.1962); Nimmer, Copyright § 131.12 at 570–571 (1963). But a glance at the complaint in that case, which relied on diverse citizenship as well as on what is now 28 U.S.C. § 1338, shows that the problem of federal jurisdiction was hardly troublesome and indicates why it went unmentioned. The equally undiscussed assumption of jurisdiction in Venus Music Corp. v. Mills Music, Inc., 261 F.2d 577 (2 Cir.1958), cannot be thus explained, since there was no diversity, see 156 F.Supp. 753 (S.D.N.Y.1957). But the jurisdictional problem was doubtless obscured by the insistence of both parties that this action was for copyright infringement, see 156 F.Supp. at 753, and by the surface similarity with Rossiter v. Vogel, supra, as that case stands in the reports. Whether or not the complaint in Venus presented questions of copyright law sufficient to meet the criteria we have outlined—an issue on which we express no opinion—the complaint here does not.

One more question remains. Bell v. Hood, 327 U.S. 678, 66 S.Ct. 773, 90 L.Ed. 939 (1946), is often taken as indicating that if a complaint comes close enough to presenting a federal claim that the court has trouble in deciding that it doesn't, dismissal of that claim should be for "failure to state a claim upon which relief can be granted" rather than for lack of jurisdiction. Even if we were to assume that the district judge should have adopted the former ground in dismissing the claims allegedly created by federal law, his disposition ought nevertheless be affirmed. Montana-Dakota Util. Co. v. Northwestern Pub. Serv. Co.,

341 U.S. 246, 249–250, 71 S.Ct. 692, 95 L.Ed. 912 (1951). The only apparent consequence of Bell v. Hood as applied to this case is that if the complaint is close enough to the line to give "jurisdiction," the court may have power to adjudicate a "pendent" or "ancillary" state claim. See 327 U.S. at 686, 71 S.Ct. at 778 (dissenting opinion of Chief Justice Stone). But a federal court need not try such a state claim when the non-existence of the federal claim has been determined on motion prior to trial on the merits, see Hart & Wechsler, supra, at 808 and decisions there cited—and the case against its doing so is particularly strong when as here, a prior suit for the same relief is pending in a state court.

Affirmed.

Questions

1. Suppose A and B enter into a contract whereby A agrees to assign his copyright to B in return for B's promise to pay to A $50,000 thirty days after the copyright is assigned. If after assignment, B fails to make the required payment and A sues for rescission, does jurisdiction lie in the state or federal court? If in the state court, may it upon ordering rescission, enjoin B from further use of A's work?

2. Should an action for declaratory relief to determine ownership of a copyright lie in the federal courts? Is it relevant whether the party against whom relief is sought threatens to use the work in a manner which will constitute copyright infringement if such person is found not to be the copyright owner?

3. If the parties enter into a consensual license in place of the compulsory license under Sec. 115, and such license varies only slightly the terms which would be applicable under the compulsory license, does federal or state jurisdiction apply in an action for non-payment of royalties under such license? Compare Shapiro, Bernstein & Co., Inc. v. Gabor, 266 F.Supp. 613 (S.D.N.Y. 1966) with Golden West Melodies, Inc. v. Capitol Records, Inc., 274 Cal.App.2d 713, 79 Cal.Rptr. 442 (1969).

Collateral Reference

Nimmer on Copyright, § 12.01.

B. COPYING

1. Access

SELLE v. GIBB

United States Court of Appeals, Seventh Circuit, 1984.
741 F.2d 896.

Before WOOD and CUDAHY, CIRCUIT JUDGES, and NICHOLS, SENIOR CIRCUIT JUDGE.

CUDAHY, CIRCUIT JUDGE.

The plaintiff, Ronald H. Selle, brought a suit against three brothers, Maurice, Robin and Barry Gibb, known collectively as the popular singing group, the Bee Gees, alleging that the Bee Gees, in their hit tune, "How Deep Is Your Love," had infringed the copyright of his song, "Let It End." The jury returned a verdict in plaintiff's favor on the issue of liability in a bifurcated trial. The district court, Judge George N. Leighton, granted the defendants' motion for judgment notwithstanding the verdict and, in the alternative, for a new trial. Selle v. Gibb, 567 F.Supp. 1173 (N.D.Ill.1983). We affirm the grant of the motion for judgment notwithstanding the verdict.

* * *

Selle composed his song, "Let It End," in one day in the fall of 1975 and obtained a copyright for it on November 17, 1975. He played his song with his small band two or three times in the Chicago area and sent a tape and lead sheet of the music to eleven music recording and publishing companies. Eight of the companies returned the materials to Selle; three did not respond. This was the extent of the public dissemination of Selle's song. Selle first became aware of the Bee Gees' song, "How Deep Is Your Love," in May 1978 and thought that he recognized the music as his own, although the lyrics were different. He also saw the movie, "Saturday Night Fever," the sound track of which features the song "How Deep Is Your Love," and again recognized the music. He subsequently sued the three Gibb brothers; Paramount

The Bee Gees.

Pictures Corporation, which made and distributed the movie; and Phonodisc, Inc., now known as Polygram Distribution, Inc., which made and distributed the cassette tape of "How Deep Is Your Love."

The Bee Gees are internationally known performers and creators of popular music. They have composed more than 160 songs; their sheet music, records and tapes have been distributed worldwide, some of the albums selling more than 30 million copies. The Bee Gees, however, do not themselves read or write music. In composing a song, their practice was to tape a tune, which members of their staff would later transcribe and reduce to a form suitable for copyrighting, sale and performance by both the Bee Gees and others.

In addition to their own testimony at trial, the Bee Gees presented testimony by their manager, Dick Ashby, and two musicians, Albhy Galuten and Blue Weaver, who were on the Bee Gees' staff at the time "How Deep Is Your Love" was composed. These witnesses described in detail how, in January 1977, the Bee Gees and several members of their staff went to a recording studio in the Chateau d'Herouville about 25 miles northwest of Paris. There the group composed at least six new songs and mixed a live album. Barry Gibb's testimony included a detailed explanation of a work tape which was introduced into evidence and played in court. This tape preserves the actual process of creation during which the brothers, and particularly Barry, created the tune of the accused song while Weaver, a keyboard player, played the tune which was hummed or sung by the brothers. Although the tape does not seem to preserve the very beginning of the process of creation, it does depict the process by which ideas, notes, lyrics and bits of the tune were gradually put together.

Following completion of this work tape, a demo tape was made. The work tape, demo tape and a vocal-piano version taken from the demo tape are all in the key of E flat. Lead sheet music, dated March 6, 1977, is in the key of E. On March 7, 1977, a lead sheet of "How Deep Is Your Love" was filed for issuance of a United States copyright, and in November 1977, a piano-vocal arrangement was filed in the Copyright Office.

The only expert witness to testify at trial was Arrand Parsons, a professor of music at Northwestern University who has had extensive professional experience primarily in classical music. He has been a program annotator for the Chicago Symphony Orchestra and the New Orleans Symphony Orchestra and has authored works about musical theory. Prior to this case, however, he had never made a comparative analysis of two popular songs. Dr. Parsons testified on the basis of several charts comparing the musical notes of each song and a comparative recording prepared under his direction.

According to Dr. Parsons' testimony, the first eight bars of each song (Theme A) have twenty-four of thirty-four notes in plaintiff's composition and twenty-four of forty notes in defendants' composition which are identical in pitch and symmetrical position. Of thirty-five rhythmic impulses in plaintiff's composition and forty in defendants', thirty are identical. In the last four bars of both songs (Theme B), fourteen notes in each are identical in pitch, and eleven of the fourteen rhythmic impulses are identical. Both Theme A and Theme B appear in the same position in each song but with different intervening material.

Dr. Parsons testified that, in his opinion, "the two songs had such striking similarities that they could not have been written independent of one another." Tr. 202. He also testified that he did not know of two songs by different composers "that contain as many striking similarities" as do the two songs at issue here. However, on several occasions, he declined to say that the similarities could only have resulted from copying.

Following presentation of the case, the jury returned a verdict for the plaintiff on the issue of liability, the only question presented to the jury. Judge Leighton, however, granted the defendants' motion for judgment notwithstanding the verdict and, in the alternative, for a new trial. He relied primarily on the plaintiff's inability to demonstrate that the defendants had access to the plaintiff's song, without which a claim of copyright infringement could not prevail regardless how similar the two compositions are. Further, the plaintiff failed to contradict or refute the testimony of the defendants and their witnesses describing the independent creation process of "How Deep Is Your Love." Finally, Judge Leighton concluded that "the inferences on which plaintiff relies is not a logical, permissible deduction from proof of 'striking similarity' or substantial similarity; it is 'at war with the undisputed facts,' and it is inconsistent with the proof of nonaccess to plaintiff's song by the Bee Gees at the time in question." 567 F.Supp. at 1183 (citations omitted).

* * *

Selle's primary contention on this appeal is that the district court misunderstood the theory of proof of copyright infringement on which he based his claim. Under this theory, copyright infringement can be demonstrated when, even in the absence of any direct evidence of access, the two pieces in question are so strikingly similar that access can be inferred from such similarity alone. Selle argues that the testimony of his expert witness, Dr. Parsons, was sufficient evidence of such striking similarity that it was permissible for the jury, even in the absence of any other evidence concerning access, to infer that the Bee Gees had access to plaintiff's song and indeed copied it.

In establishing a claim of copyright infringement of a musical composition, the plaintiff must prove (1) ownership of the copyright in the complaining work; (2) originality of the work; (3) copying of the work by the defendant, and (4) a substantial degree of similarity between the two works. See Sherman, *Musical Copyright Infringement: The Requirement of Substantial Similarity.* Copyright Law Symposium, Number 92, American Society of Composers, Authors and Publishers 81–82. Columbia University Press (1977) [hereinafter "Sherman, *Musical Copyright Infringement*"]. The only element which is at issue in this appeal is proof of copying; the first two elements are essentially conceded, while the fourth (substantial similarity) is, at least in these circumstances, closely related to the third element under plaintiff's theory of the case.

Proof of copying is crucial to any claim of copyright infringement because no matter how similar the two works may be (even to the point of identity), if the defendant did not copy the accused work, there is no infringement. Arnstein v. Edward B. Marks Music Corp., 82 F.2d 275 (2d Cir.), *motion to set aside decree denied,* 86 F.2d 715 (2d Cir.1936). However, because direct evidence of copying is rarely available, the plaintiff can rely upon circumstantial evidence to prove this essential element, and the most important component of this sort of circumstantial evidence is proof of access. See generally 3 Nimmer, *Copyright* § 13.02 at 13–9 (1983) [hereinafter "Nimmer, *Copyright* "]. The plaintiff may be able to introduce direct evidence of access when, for example, the work was sent directly to the defendant (whether a musician or a publishing company) or a close associate of the defendant. On the other hand, the plaintiff may be able to establish a reasonable possibility of access when, for example, the complaining work has been widely disseminated to the public. See, e.g., Abkco Music, Inc. v. Harrisongs Music, Ltd., 722 F.2d 988, 998 (2d Cir.1983) (finding of access based on wide dissemination); Sherman, *Musical Copyright Infringement,* at 82.

If, however, the plaintiff does not have direct evidence of access, then an inference of access may still be established circumstantially by proof of similarity which is so striking that the possibilities of independent creation, coincidence and prior common source are, as a practical matter, precluded. If the plaintiff presents evidence of striking similarity sufficient to raise an inference of access, then copying is presumably proved simultaneously, although the fourth element (substantial similarity) still requires proof that the defendant copied a substantial amount of the complaining work. The theory which Selle attempts to apply to this case is based on proof of copying by circumstantial proof of access established by striking similarity between the two works.

One difficulty with plaintiff's theory is that no matter how great the similarity between the two works, it is not their similarity per se which establishes access; rather, their similarity tends to prove access in light of the nature of the works, the particular musical genre involved and other circumstantial evidence of access. In other words, striking similarity is just one piece of circumstantial evidence tending to show access and must not be considered in isolation; it must be considered together with other types of circumstantial evidence relating to access.

As a threshold matter, therefore, it would appear that there must be at least some other evidence which would establish a reasonable possibility that the complaining work was *available* to the alleged infringer. As noted, two works may be identical in every detail, but, if the alleged infringer created the accused work independently or both works were copied from a common source in the public domain, then there is no infringement. Therefore, if the plaintiff admits to having kept his or her creation under lock and key, it would seem logically impossible to infer access through striking similarity. Thus, although it has frequently been written that striking similarity *alone* can establish access, the decided cases suggest that this circumstance would be most unusual. The plaintiff must always present sufficient evidence to support a reasonable possibility of access because the jury cannot draw an inference of access based upon speculation and conjecture alone.

* * *

The greatest difficulty perhaps arises when the plaintiff cannot demonstrate any direct link between the complaining work and the defendant but the work has been so widely disseminated that it is not unreasonable to infer that the defendant might have had access to it.

* * *

* * * It is not necessary for us, given the facts of this case, to determine the number of copies which must be publicly distributed to raise a reasonable inference of access. Nevertheless, in this case, the availability of Selle's song, as shown by the evidence, was virtually *de minimis*.

In granting the defendants' motion for judgment notwithstanding the verdict, Judge Leighton relied primarily on the plaintiff's failure to adduce any evidence of access and stated that an inference of access may not be based on mere conjecture, speculation or a bare possibility of access. 567 F.Supp. at 1181. Thus, in Testa v. Janssen, 492 F.Supp. 198, 202–03 (W.D.Pa.1980), the court stated that "[t]o support a finding of access, plaintiffs' evidence must extend beyond mere speculation or conjecture. And, while circumstantial evidence is sufficient to establish access, a defendant's opportunity to view the copyrighted work must exist by a reasonable possibility—not a bare possibility" (citation omitted). * * *

* * * Judge Leighton's conclusions that there was no more than a bare possibility that the defendants could have had access to Selle's song and that this was an insufficient basis from which the jury could have reasonably inferred the existence of access seem correct. The plaintiff has failed to meet even the minimum threshold of proof of the possibility of access and, as Judge Leighton has stated, an inference of access would thus seem to be "at war with the undisputed facts." 567 F.Supp. at 1183.

* * *

The grant of the motion for judgment notwithstanding the verdict might, if we were so minded, be affirmed on the basis of the preceding analysis of the plaintiff's inability to establish a reasonable inference of access. This decision is also supported by a more traditional analysis of proof of access based only on the proof of "striking similarity" between the two compositions. The plaintiff relies almost exclusively on the testimony of his expert witness, Dr. Parsons, that the two pieces were, in fact, "strikingly similar." [3] Yet formulating a meaningful definition of "striking similarity" is no simple task, and the term is often used in a conclusory or circular fashion.

Sherman defines "striking similarity" as a term of art signifying "that degree of similarity as will permit an inference of copying even in the absence of proof of access * * *." Sherman, *Musical Copyright Infringement,* at 84 n. 15. Nimmer states that, absent proof of access, "the similarities must be so striking as to preclude the possibility that the defendant independently arrived at the same result." Nimmer, *Copyright,* at 13–14.

"Striking similarity" is not merely a function of the number of identical notes that appear in both compositions, * * * An important factor in analyzing the degree of similarity of two compositions is the uniqueness of the sections which are asserted to be similar.

If the complaining work contains an unexpected departure from the normal metric structure or if the complaining work includes what appears to be an error and the accused work repeats the unexpected element or the error, then it is more likely that there is some connection between the pieces. See, e.g., Nordstrom v. Radio Corporation of America, 251 F.Supp. 41, 42 (D.Colo.1965). If the similar sections are particularly intricate, then again it would seem more likely that the compositions are related. Finally, some dissimilarities may be particularly suspicious. See, e.g., Meier Co. v. Albany Novelty Manufacturing Co., 236 F.2d 144, 146 (2d Cir.1956) (inversion and substitution of certain words in a catalogue in a "crude effort to give the appearance of dissimilarity" are themselves evidence of copying); Blume v. Spear, 30 F. 629, 631 (S.D.N.Y.1887) (variations in infringing song were placed so as to indicate deliberate copying); Sherman, *Musical Copyright Infringement,* at 84–88. While some of these concepts are borrowed from literary copyright analysis, they would seem equally applicable to an analysis of music.

The judicially formulated definition of "striking similarity" states that "plaintiffs must demonstrate that 'such similarities are of a kind that can only be explained by copying, rather than by coincidence, independent creation, or prior common source.'" Testa v. Janssen, 492 F.Supp. 198, 203 (W.D.Pa.1980) (quoting Stratchborneo v. Arc Music Corp., 357 F.Supp. 1393, 1403 (S.D.N.Y.1973)). See also Scott v. WKJG, Inc., 376 F.2d 467, 469 (7th Cir.1967) (the similarities must be "so striking and of such nature as to preclude the possibility of coincidence, accident or independent creation."); Arnstein v. Porter, 154 F.2d 464, 468 (2d Cir.1946) (same); Scott v. Paramount Pictures Corp., 449 F.Supp. 518, 520 (D.D.C.1978) (same). Sherman adds:

---

3. Plaintiff also relies on the fact that both songs were played on numerous occasions in open court for the jury to hear and on the deposition testimony of one of the Bee Gees, Maurice, who incorrectly identified Theme B of Selle's song as the Bee Gees' composition, "How Deep Is Your Love."

> To prove that certain similarities are "striking," plaintiff must show that they are the sort of similarities that cannot satisfactorily be accounted for by a theory of coincidence, independent creation, prior common source, or any theory other than that of copying. Striking similarity is an extremely technical issue—one with which, understandably, experts are best equipped to deal.

Sherman, *Musical Copyright Infringement,* at 96.

Finally, the similarities should appear in a sufficiently unique or complex context as to make it unlikely that both pieces were copied from a prior common source, Sheldon v. Metro-Goldwyn Pictures Corp., 81 F.2d 49, 54 (2d Cir.), cert. denied, 298 U.S. 669, 56 S.Ct. 835, 80 L.Ed. 1392 (1936), or that the defendant was able to compose the accused work as a matter of independent creation, Nichols v. Universal Pictures Corp., 45 F.2d 119, 122 (2d Cir.1930), cert. denied, 282 U.S. 902, 51 S.Ct. 216, 75 L.Ed. 795 (1931). See also Darrell v. Joe Morris Music Co., 113 F.2d 80 (2d Cir.1940) ("simple, trite themes * * * are likely to recur spontaneously * * * and [only few] * * * suit the infantile demands of the popular ear"); Arnstein v. Edward B. Marks Music Corp., 82 F.2d 275, 277 (2d Cir.1936). Cf. Abkco Music, Inc. v. Harrisongs Music, Ltd., 722 F.2d 988, 998 (2d Cir.1983) (finding of a "highly unique pattern" makes copying more likely). With these principles in mind, we turn now to an analysis of the evidence of "striking similarity" presented by the plaintiff.

As noted, the plaintiff relies almost entirely on the testimony of his expert witness, Dr. Arrand Parsons. The defendants did not introduce any expert testimony, apparently because they did not think Parsons' testimony needed to be refuted. Defendants are perhaps to some degree correct in asserting that Parsons, although eminently qualified in the field of classical music theory, was not equally qualified to analyze popular music tunes. More significantly, however, although Parsons used the magic formula, "striking similarity," he only ruled out the possibility of independent creation; he did not state that the similarities could only be the result of copying. In order for proof of "striking similarity" to establish a reasonable inference of access, especially in a case such as this one in which the direct proof of access is so minimal, the plaintiff must show that the similarity is of a type which will preclude any explanation other than that of copying.

In addition, to bolster the expert's conclusion that independent creation was not possible, there should be some testimony or other evidence of the relative complexity or uniqueness of the two compositions. Dr. Parsons' testimony did not refer to this aspect of the compositions and, in a field such as that of popular music in which all songs are relatively short and tend to build on or repeat a basic theme, such testimony would seem to be particularly necessary. * * *

* * *

The plaintiff's expert witness does not seem to have addressed any issues relating to the possibility of prior common source in both widely disseminated popular songs and the defendants' own compositions. At oral argument, plaintiff's attorney stated that the burden of proving common source should be on the defendant; however, the burden of proving "striking similarity," which, by definition, includes taking steps to minimize the possibility of common source, is on the plaintiff. In essence, the plaintiff failed to prove to the requisite degree that the similarities identified by the expert witness—although perhaps "striking" in a non-legal sense—were of a type which would eliminate any explanation of coincidence, independent creation or common source, including, in this case, the possibility of common source in earlier compositions created by the Bee Gees themselves or by others. In sum, the evidence of striking similarity is not sufficiently compelling to make the case when the proof of access must otherwise depend largely upon speculation and conjecture.

Therefore, because the plaintiff failed both to establish a basis from which the jury could reasonably infer that the Bee Gees had access to his song and to meet his burden of proving "striking similarity" between the two compositions, the grant by the district court of the defendants' motion for judgment notwithstanding the verdict is affirmed. * * *

Questions

1. Does the fact that a work has been widely disseminated in itself constitute proof of access? Does this constitute "double circumstantial evidence"? See Morse v. Fields, 127 F.Supp. 63 (S.D.N.Y.1954). What if a book has had only a modest sale but is in the public library in the city in which defendant's writer resides? What if plaintiff's manuscript is simply located in the same city in which defendant's writer resides? See Columbia Pictures Corp. v. Krasna, 65 N.Y.S.2d 67 (Sup.Ct.1946).

2. If the similarity between plaintiff's and defendant's works is sufficiently striking, should that excuse the plaintiff from the necessity of proving access? See Heim v. Universal Pictures Co., 154 F.2d 480 (2d Cir.1946). In such circumstances, must the similarity be so great as to preclude the possibility that defendant independently arrived at the same result? See Jones v. Supreme Music Corp., 101 F.Supp. 989 (S.D.N.Y.1951).

3. If the plaintiff offers evidence of both access and substantial similarity, does this *require* a finding of copying? Isn't it still possible that the similarity was coincidental and the result of independent efforts by the defendant? Yet, how can the plaintiff be expected to prove more than access and substantial similarity? In such circumstances what should happen to the burden of proof?

4. In finding that the plaintiff failed to offer at least "the minimum threshold of proof of the possibility of access" does the *Selle* court effectively reject "striking similarity" as a substitute for such proof? Is the court correct in its conclusion that striking similarity "must not be considered in isolation; it must be considered together with other types of circumstantial evidence relating to access"? If "striking similarity" is to be defined, as the *Selle* court suggests, as that similarity "which is so striking that the possibilities of independent creation, coincidence and prior common source are, as a practical matter, precluded," why should it be necessary in addition to offer "other types of circumstantial evidence relating to access"? Does the decision in *Selle* at bottom rest upon the court's rejection of the expert witness' opinion as to the

presence of striking similarity? Is striking similarity more difficult to establish in the case of musical notations as compared with literary texts?

5. If, upon plaintiff's having presented proof of access and substantial similarity, the burden then shifts to the defendant to prove independent creation or copying from a common source, should such burden also shift to the defendant where the plaintiff proves striking similarity in lieu of proof of access? Who should have the burden on this issue, which is peculiarly within defendants' knowledge? If the jury in *Selle* had rendered a verdict for the defendants, would the trial court have been correct in denying a motion by plaintiff for judgment notwithstanding the verdict? Given the fact that the jury rendered a verdict for plaintiff, was the trial court in *Selle* correct in granting defendants' motion for judgment notwithstanding the verdict?

Collateral Reference

Nimmer on Copyright, §§ 12.11[D], 13.02.

2. Similarity

NICHOLS v. UNIVERSAL PICTURES CORPORATION

Circuit Court of Appeals, Second Circuit, 1930.
45 F.2d 119.

Before L. HAND, SWAN, and AUGUSTUS N. HAND, CIRCUIT JUDGES.

L. HAND, CIRCUIT JUDGE. The plaintiff is the author of a play, "Abie's Irish Rose," which it may be assumed was properly copyrighted under section five, subdivision (d), of the Copyright Act, 17 U.S.C.A. § 5(d). The defendant produced publicly a motion picture play, "The Cohens and The Kellys," which the plaintiff alleges was taken from it. As we think the defendant's play too unlike the plaintiff's to be an infringement, we may assume, arguendo, that in some details the defendant used the plaintiff's play, as will subsequently appear, though we do not so decide. It therefore becomes necessary to give an outline of the two plays.

"Abie's Irish Rose" presents a Jewish family living in prosperous circumstances in New York. The father, a widower, is in business as a merchant, in which his son and only child helps him. The boy has philandered with young women, who to his father's great disgust have always been Gentiles, for he is obsessed with a passion that his daughter-in-law shall be an orthodox Jewess. When the play opens the son, who has been courting a young Irish Catholic girl, has already married her secretly before a Protestant minister, and is concerned to soften the blow for his father, by securing a favorable impression of his bride, while concealing her faith and race. To accomplish this he introduces her to his father at his home as a Jewess, and lets it appear that he is interested in her, though he conceals the marriage. The girl somewhat reluctantly falls in with the plan; the father takes the bait, becomes infatuated with the girl, concludes that they must marry, and assumes that of course they will, if he so decides. He calls in a rabbi, and prepares for the wedding according to the Jewish rite.

A scene from the defendant's motion picture, *The Cohens and The Kellys*.

Meanwhile the girl's father, also a widower, who lives in California, and is as intense in his own religious antagonism as the Jew, has been called to New York, supposing that his daughter is to marry an Irishman and a Catholic. Accompanied by a priest, he arrives at the house at the moment when the marriage is being celebrated, but too late to prevent it, and the two fathers, each infuriated by the proposed union of his child to a heretic, fall into unseemly and grotesque antics. The priest and the rabbi become friendly, exchange trite sentiments about religion, and agree that the match is good. Apparently out of abundant caution, the priest celebrates the marriage for a third time, while the girl's father is inveigled away. The second act closes with each father, still outraged, seeking to find some way by which the union, thus trebly insured, may be dissolved.

The last act takes place about a year later, the young couple having meanwhile been abjured by each father, and left to their own resources.

They have had twins, a boy and a girl, but their fathers know no more than that a child has been born. At Christmas each, led by his craving to see his grandchild, goes separately to the young folks' home, where they encounter each other, each laden with gifts, one for a boy, the other for a girl. After some slapstick comedy, depending upon the insistence of each that he is right about the sex of the grandchild, they become reconciled when they learn the truth, and that each child is to bear the given name of a grandparent. The curtain falls as the fathers are exchanging amenities, and the Jew giving evidence of an abatement in the strictness of his orthodoxy.

"The Cohens and The Kellys" presents two families, Jewish and Irish, living side by side in the poorer quarters of New York in a state of perpetual enmity. The wives in both cases are still living, and share in the mutual animosity, as do two small sons, and even the respective dogs. The Jews have a daughter, the Irish a son; the Jewish father is in the clothing business; the Irishman is a policeman. The children are in love with each other, and secretly marry, apparently after the play opens. The Jew, being in great financial straits, learns from a lawyer that he has fallen heir to a large fortune from a great-aunt, and moves into a great house, fitted luxuriously. Here he and his family live in vulgar ostentation, and here the Irish boy seeks out his Jewish bride, and is chased away by the angry father. The Jew then abuses the Irishman over the telephone, and both become hysterically excited. The extremity of his feelings makes the Jew sick, so that he must go to Florida for a rest, just before which the daughter discloses her marriage to her mother.

On his return the Jew finds that his daughter has borne a child; at first he suspects the lawyer, but eventually learns the truth and is overcome with anger at such a low alliance. Meanwhile, the Irish family who have been forbidden to see the grandchild, go to the Jew's house, and after a violent scene between the two fathers in which the Jew disowns his daughter, who decides to go back with her husband, the Irishman takes her back with her baby to his own poor lodgings. The lawyer, who had hoped to marry the Jew's daughter, seeing his plan foiled, tells the Jew that his fortune really belongs to the Irishman, who was also related to the dead woman, but offers to conceal his knowledge, if the Jew will share the loot. This the Jew repudiates, and leaving the astonished lawyer walks through the rain to his enemy's house to surrender the property. He arrives in great dejection, tells the truth, and abjectly turns to leave. A reconciliation ensues, the Irishman agreeing to share with him equally. The Jew shows some interest in his grandchild, though this is at most a minor motive in the reconciliation, and the curtain falls while the two are in their cups, the Jew insisting that in the firm name for the business, which they are to carry on jointly, his name shall stand first.

It is of course essential to any protection of literary property, whether at common-law or under the statute, that the right cannot be limited literally to the text, else a plagiarist would escape by immaterial variations. That has never been the law, but, as soon as literal appropriation ceases to be the test, the whole matter is necessarily at large, so that, as was recently well said by a distinguished judge, the decisions cannot help much in a new case. Fendler v. Morosco, 253 N.Y. 281, 292, 171 N.E. 56. When plays are concerned, the plagiarist may excise a separate scene [Daly v. Webster, 56 F. 483 (C.C.A.2); Chappell v. Fields, 210 F. 864 (C.C.A.2); Chatterton v. Cave, L.R. 3 App.Cas. 483]; or he may appropriate part of the dialogue (Warne v. Seebohm, L.R. 39 Ch.D. 73). Then the question is whether the part so taken is "substantial," and therefore not a "fair use" of the copyrighted work; it is the same question as arises in the case of any other copyrighted work. Marks v. Feist, 290 F. 959 (C.C.A.2); Emerson v. Davies, Fed.Cas. No. 4436, 3 Story, 768, 795–797. But when the plagiarist does not take out a block in situ, but an abstract of the whole, decision is more troublesome. Upon any work, and especially upon a play, a great number of patterns, of increasing generality will fit equally well, as more and more of the incident is left out. The last may perhaps be no more than the most general statement of what the play is about, and at times might consist only of its title; but there is a point in this series of abstractions where they are no longer protected, since otherwise the playwright could prevent the use of his "ideas," to which, apart from their expression, his property is never extended. Holmes v. Hurst, 174 U.S. 82, 86, 19 S.Ct. 606, 43 L.Ed. 904; Guthrie v. Curlett, 36 F.2d 694 (C.C.A.2). Nobody has ever been able to fix that boundary, and nobody ever can. In some cases the question has been treated as though it were analogous to lifting a portion out of the copyrighted work (Rees v. Melville, MacGillivray's Copyright Cases [1911–1916], 168); but the analogy is not a good one, because, though the skeleton is a part of the body, it pervades and supports the whole. In such cases we are rather concerned with the line between expression and what is expressed. As respects plays, the controversy chiefly centers upon the characters and sequence of incident, these being the substance.

We did not in Dymow v. Bolton, 11 F.(2d) 690, hold that a plagiarist was never liable for stealing a plot; that would have been flatly against our rulings in Dam v. Kirk La Shelle Co., 175 F. 902, 41 L.R.A. (N.S.) 1002, 20 Ann.Cas. 1173, and Stodart v. Mutual Film Co., 249 F. 513, affirming my decision in (D.C.) 249 F. 507; neither of which we meant to overrule. We found the plot of the second play was too different to infringe, because the most detailed pattern, common to both, eliminated so much from each that its content went into the public domain; and for this reason we said, "this mere subsection of a plot was not susceptible of copyright." But we do not doubt that two plays may correspond in plot closely enough for infringement. How far that correspondence must go is another matter. Nor need we hold that the same may not be true as to the characters, quite independently of the "plot" proper, though, as far as we know, such a case has never arisen. * * * [See deleted passage Chapter One, Par. C.4. supra.]

In the two plays at bar we think both as to incident and character, the defendant took no more—assuming that it took anything at all—than the law allowed. The stories are quite different. One is of a religious zealot who insists upon his child's marrying no one outside his faith; opposed by another who is in this respect just like him, and is his foil. Their difference in race is merely an obbligato to the main theme, religion. They sink their differences through grandparental pride and affection. In the other, zealotry is wholly absent; religion does not even appear. It is true that the parents are hostile to each other in part because they differ in race; but the marriage of their son to a Jew does not apparently offend the Irish family at all, and it exacerbates the existing animosity of the Jew, principally because he has become rich, when he learns it. They are reconciled through the honesty of the Jew and the generosity of the Irishman; the grandchild has nothing whatever to do with it. The only matter common to the two is a quarrel between a Jewish and an Irish father, the marriage of their children, the birth of grandchildren and a reconciliation.

If the defendant took so much from the plaintiff, it may well have been because her amazing success seemed to prove that this was a subject of enduring popularity. Even so, granting that the plaintiff's play was wholly original, and assuming that novelty is not essential to a copyright, there is no monopoly in such a background. Though the plaintiff discovered the vein, she could not keep it to herself; so defined, the theme was too generalized an abstraction from what she wrote. It was only a part of her "ideas."

Nor does she fare better as to her characters. It is indeed scarcely credible that she should not have been aware of those stock figures, the low comedy Jew and Irishman. The defendant has not taken from her more than their prototypes have contained for many decades. If so, obviously so to generalize her copyright, would allow her to cover what was not original with her. But we need not hold this as matter of fact, much as we might be justified. Even though we take it that she devised her figures out of her brain de novo, still the defendant was within its rights.

There are but four characters common to both plays, the lovers and the fathers. The lovers are so faintly indicated as to be no more than stage properties. They are loving and fertile; that is really all that can be said of them, and anyone else is quite within his rights if he puts loving and fertile lovers in a play of his own, wherever he gets the cue. The plaintiff's Jew is quite unlike the defendant's. His obsession is his religion, on which depends such racial animosity as he has. He is affectionate, warm and patriarchal. None of these fit the defendant's Jew, who shows affection for his daughter only once, and who has none but the most superficial interest in his grandchild. He is tricky, ostentatious and vulgar, only by misfortune redeemed into honesty. Both are grotesque, extravagant and quarrelsome; both are fond of display; but these common qualities make up only a small part of their simple pictures, no more than any one might lift if he chose. The Irish fathers are even more unlike; the plaintiff's a mere symbol for religious fanaticism and patriarchal pride, scarcely a character at all. Neither quality appears in the defendant's, for while he goes to get his grandchild, it is rather out of a truculent determination not to be forbidden, than from pride in his progeny. For the rest he is only a grotesque hobbledehoy, used for low comedy of the most conventional sort, which any one might borrow, if he chanced not to know the exemplar.

The defendant argues that the case is controlled by my decision in Fisher v. Dillingham (D.C.) 298 F. 145. Neither my brothers nor I wish to throw doubt upon the doctrine of that case, but it is not applicable here. We assume that the plaintiff's play is altogether original, even to an extent that in fact it is hard to believe. We assume further that, so far as it has been anticipated by earlier plays of which she knew nothing, that fact is immaterial. Still, as we have already said, her copyright did not cover everything that might be drawn from her play; its content went to some extent into the public domain. We have to decide how much, and while we are as aware as any one that the line, wherever it is drawn, will seem arbitrary, that is no excuse for not drawing it; it is a question such as courts must answer in nearly all cases. Whatever may be the difficulties a priori, we have no question on which side of the line this case falls. A comedy based upon conflicts between Irish and Jews, into which the marriage of their children enters, is no more susceptible of copyright than the outline of Romeo and Juliet.

The plaintiff has prepared an elaborate analysis of the two plays, showing a "quadrangle" of the common characters, in which each is represented by the emotions which he discovers. She presents the resulting parallelism as proof of infringement, but the adjectives employed are so general as to be quite useless. Taken for example the attribute of "love" ascribed to both Jews. The plaintiff has depicted her father as deeply attached to his son, who is his hope and joy; not so, the defendant, whose father's conduct is throughout not actuated by any affection for his daughter, and who is merely once overcome for the moment by her distress when he has violently dismissed her lover. "Anger" covers emotions aroused by quite different occasions in each case; so do "anxiety," "despondency" and "disgust." It is unnecessary to go through the catalogue for emotions are too much colored by their causes to be a test when used so broadly. This is not the proper approach to a solution; it must be more ingenuous, more like that of a spectator, who would rely upon the complex of his impressions of each character.

We cannot approve the length of the record, which was due chiefly to the use of expert witnesses. Argument is argument whether in the box or at the bar, and its proper place is the last. The testimony of an expert upon such issues, especially his cross-examination, greatly extends the trial and contributes nothing which cannot be better heard after the evidence is all submitted. It ought not to be allowed at all;

and while its admission is not a ground for reversal, it cumbers the case and tends to confusion, for the more the court is led into the intricacies of dramatic craftsmanship, the less likely it is to stand upon the firmer, if more naive, ground of its considered impressions upon its own perusal. We hope that in this class of cases such evidence may in the future be entirely excluded, and the case confined to the actual issues; that is, whether the copyrighted work was original, and whether the defendant copied it, so far as the supposed infringement is identical. * *

Decree affirmed.

Questions

1. Judge Hand points out that " 'ideas' * * * apart from their expression" are not protected by copyright, but that copyright is not "limited literally to the text". It follows, then, that copyright may be claimed in something more abstract then the literal text, but less abstract than the "idea" of the text. How does one draw the line that separates the non-protectible "idea" from the protectible "expression"? Consider Professor Chafee's response: "No doubt the line does lie somewhere between the author's idea and the precise form in which he wrote it down. I like to say that the protection covers the 'pattern' of the work * * * the sequence of events, and the development of the interplay of characters." Chafee, Reflections on the Law of Copyright, 45 Col.Law Rev. 503, 513 (1945).

2. Do you agree that the similarities between "Abie's Irish Rose" and "The Cohens and The Kellys" lie on the idea side of the idea-expression dichotomy? Are the two works based upon the same "idea" (at the most abstract level) as Romeo and Juliet"? What is that abstract idea? Is the musical play "Westside Story" based upon the same abstract idea? On which side of the idea-expression dichotomy do the similarities between "Romeo and Juliet" and "Westside Story" lie? (If you are not familiar with "Westside Story" it would be a worthwhile exercise to read it (Arthur Laurents, *Westside Story* (Random House 1958)) and then read or re-read "Romeo and Juliet", after which you should enumerate the similarities in these superficially dissimilar works. Copyright lawyers are often required to make this sort of comparative study. After you have completed your list of similarities compare the list in Nimmer on Copyright, § 13.03[A][1].

3. Why aren't ideas, as distinguished from the "expression of ideas" protected by copyright? Would such protection promote or discourage "the progress of science and useful arts"? Would there be any First Amendment problems if ideas per se were protected by copyright?

Collateral References

Sorenson and Sorenson, *Re-Examining the Traditional Legal Test of Literary Similarity: A Proposal for Content Analysis*, 37 Cornell L.Q. 638 (1952).

Nimmer, *Does Copyright Abridge the First Amendment Guarantees of Free Speech and Press?* 17 UCLA Law Rev. 1180, 1189 (1970).

SHELDON v. METRO–GOLDWYN PICTURES CORP.

Circuit Court of Appeals, Second Circuit, 1936.
81 F.2d 49.

Before L. HAND, SWAN, and CHASE, CIRCUIT JUDGES.

L. HAND, CIRCUIT JUDGE. The suit is to enjoin the performance of the picture play, "Letty Lynton," as an infringement of the plaintiffs' copyrighted play, "Dishonored Lady." The plaintiffs' title is conceded, so too the validity of the copyright; the only issue is infringement. The defendants say that they did not use the play in any way to produce the picture; the plaintiffs discredit this denial because of the negotiations between the parties for the purchase of rights in the play, and because the similarities between the two are too specific and detailed to have resulted from chance. The judge thought that, so far as the defendants had used the play, they had taken only what the law allowed, that is, those general themes, motives, or ideas in which there could be no copyright. Therefore he dismissed the bill.

An understanding of the issue involves some description of what was in the public demesne, as well as of the play and the picture. In 1857 a Scotch girl, named Madeleine Smith, living in Glasgow, was brought to trial upon an indictment in three counts; two for attempts to poison her lover, a third for poisoning him. The jury acquitted her on the first count, and brought in a verdict of "Not Proven" on the second and third. The circumstances of the prosecution aroused much interest at the time not only in Scotland but in England; so much indeed that it became a cause célèbre, and that as late as 1927 the whole proceedings were published in book form. An outline of the story so published, which became the original of the play here in suit, is as follows: The Smiths were a respectable middle-class family, able to send their daughter to a "young ladies' boarding school"; they supposed her protected not only from any waywardness of her own, but from the wiles of seducers. In both they were mistaken, for when at the age of twenty-one she met a young Jerseyman of French blood, Emile L'Angelier, ten years older, and already the hero of many amorous adventures, she quickly succumbed and poured out her feelings in letters of the utmost ardor and indiscretion, and at times of a candor beyond the standards then, and even yet, permissible for well-nurtured young women. They wrote each other as though already married, he assuming to dictate her conduct and even her feelings; both expected to marry, she on any terms, he with the approval of her family. Nevertheless she soon tired of him and engaged herself to a man some twenty years older who was a better match, but for whom she had no more than a friendly complaisance. L'Angelier was not, however, to be fobbed off so easily; he threatened to expose her to her father by showing her letters. She at first tried to dissuade him by appeals to their tender memories, but finding this useless and thinking herself otherwise undone, she affected a return of her former passion and invited him to visit her again. Whether he did was the turning point of the trial; the evidence, though it really left the issue in no doubt, was too indirect to satisfy the jury, perhaps in part because of her advocate's argument that to kill him only insured the discovery of her letters. It was shown that she had several times bought or tried to buy poison,—prussic acid and arsenic,—and that twice before his death L'Angelier became violently ill, the second time on the day after her purchase. He died of arsenical poison, which the prosecution charged

Joan Crawford and co-star in defendant's *Letty Lynton*.

that she had given him in a cup of chocolate. At her trial, Madeleine being incompetent as a witness, her advocate proved an alibi by the testimony of her younger sister that early on the night of the murder as laid in the indictment, she had gone to bed with Madeleine, who had slept with her throughout the night. As to one of the attempts her betrothed swore that she had been with him at the theatre.

This was the story which the plaintiffs used to build their play. As will appear they took from it but the merest skeleton, the acquittal of a wanton young woman, who to extricate herself from an amour that stood in the way of a respectable marriage, poisoned her lover. The incidents, the characters, the mis en scène, the sequence of events, were all changed; nobody disputes that the plaintiffs were entitled to their copyright. All that they took from the story they might probably have taken, had it even been copyrighted. Their heroine is named Madeleine Cary; she lives in New York, brought up in affluence, if not in luxury; she is intelligent, voluptuous, ardent and corrupt; but, though she has had a succession of amours, she is capable of genuine affection. Her lover and victim is an Argentinian, named Moreno, who makes his living as a dancer in night-clubs. Madeleine has met him once in Europe before the play opens, has danced with him, has excited his concupiscence; he presses presents upon her. The play opens in his rooms, he and his dancing partner who is also his mistress, are together; Madeleine on the telephone recalls herself to him and says she wishes to visit him, though it is already past midnight. He disposes of his mistress by a device which does not deceive her and receives Madeleine; at once he falls to wooing her, luring her among other devices by singing a Gaucho song. He finds her facile and the curtain falls in season.

The second act is in her home, and introduces her father, a bibulous dotard, who has shot his wife's lover in the long past; Laurence Brennan, a self-made man in the fifties, untutored, self-reliant and reliable, who has had with Madeleine a relation, half paternal, half-amorous since she grew up; and Denis Farnborough, a young British labor peer, a mannekin to delight the heart of well ordered young women. Madeleine loves him; he loves Madeleine; she will give him no chance to declare himself, remembering her mottled past and his supposedly immaculate standards. She confides to Brennan, who makes clear to her the imbecility of her self-denial; she accepts this enlightenment and engages herself to her high-minded paragon after confessing vaguely her evil life and being assured that to post-war generations all such lapses are peccadillo.

In the next act Moreno, who has got wind of the engagement, comes to her house. Disposing of Farnborough, who chances to be there, she admits Moreno, acknowledges that she is to marry Farnborough, and asks him to accept the situation as the normal outcome of their intrigue. He refuses to be cast off, high words pass, he threatens to expose their relations, she raves at him, until finally he knocks her down and commands her to go to his apartment that morning as before.

After he leaves full of swagger, her eye lights on a bottle of strychnine which her father uses as a drug; her fingers slowly close upon it; the audience understands that she will kill Moreno. Farnborough is at the telephone; this apparently stiffens her resolve, showing her the heights she may reach by its execution.

The scene then shifts again to Moreno's apartment; his mistress must again be put out, most unwillingly for she is aware of the situation; Madeleine comes in; she pretends once more to feel warmly, she must wheedle him for he is out of sorts after the quarrel. Meanwhile she prepares to poison him by putting the strychnine in coffee, which she asks him to make ready. But in the course of these preparations during which he sings her again his Gaucho song, what with their proximity, and this and that, her animal ardors are once more aroused and drag her, unwillingly and protesting, from her purpose. The play must therefore wait for an hour or more until, relieved of her passion, she appears from his bedroom and while breakfasting puts the strychnine in his coffee. He soon discovers what has happened and tries to telephone for help. He does succeed in getting a few words through, but she tears away the wire and fills his dying ears with her hatred and disgust. She then carefully wipes away all traces of her finger prints and manages to get away while the door is being pounded in by those who have come at his call.

The next act is again at her home on the following evening. Things are going well with her and Farnborough and her father, when a district attorney comes in, a familiar of the household, now in stern mood; Moreno's mistress and a waiter have incriminated Madeleine, and a cross has been found in Moreno's pocket, which he superstitiously took off her neck the night before. The district attorney cross-questions her, during which Farnborough several times fatuously intervenes; she is driven from point to point almost to an avowal when as a desperate plunge she says she spent the night with Brennan. Brennan is brought to the house and, catching the situation after a moment's delay, bears her out. This puts off the district attorney until seeing strychnine brought to relieve the father, his suspicions spring up again and he arrests Madeleine. The rest of the play is of no consequence here, except that it appears in the last scene that at the trial where she is acquitted, her father on the witness stand accounts for the absence of the bottle of strychnine which had been used to poison Moreno.

At about the time that this play was being written an English woman named Lowndes wrote a book called Letty Lynton, also founded on the story of Madeleine Smith. Letty Lynton lives in England; she is eighteen years old, beautiful, well-reared and intelligent, but wayward. She has had a more or less equivocal love affair with a young Scot, named McLean, who worked in her father's chemical factory, but has discarded him, apparently before their love-making had gone very far. Then she chances upon a young Swede—half English—named Ekebon, and their acquaintance quickly becomes a standardized amour, kept secret from her parents, especially her mother, who is an uncompromising moralist, and somewhat estranged from Letty anyway. She and her lover use an old barn as their place of assignation; it had been fitted up as a play house for Letty when she was a child. Like Madeleine Smith she had written her lover a series of indiscreet letters which he has kept, for though he is on pleasure bent Ekebon has a frugal mind, and means to marry his sweetheart and set himself up for life. They are betrothed and he keeps pressing her to declare it to her parents, which she means never to do. While he is away in Sweden Letty meets an unmarried peer considerably older than she, poor, but intelligent and charming; he falls in love with her and she accepts him, more because it is a good match than for any other reason, though she likes him well enough, and will make him suppose that she loves him.

Thereupon Ekebon reappears, learns of Letty's new betrothal, and threatens to disclose his own to her father, backing up his story with her letters. She must at once disown her peer and resume her engagement with him. His motive, like L'Angelier's, is ambition rather than love, though conquest is a flattery and Letty a charming morsel. His threats naturally throw Letty into dismay; she has come to loathe him and at any cost must get free, but she has no one to turn to. In her plight she thinks of her old suitor, McLean, and goes to the factory only to find him gone. He has taught her how to get access to poisons in his office and has told of their effect on human beings. At first she thinks of jumping out the window, and when she winces at that, of poisoning herself; that would be easier. So she selects arsenic which is less painful and goes away with it; it is only when she gets home that she thinks of poisoning Ekebon. Her mind is soon made up, however, and she makes an appointment with him at the barn; he has told her father, she writes, and Ekebon is to see him on Monday, but meanwhile on Sunday they will meet secretly once more. She has prepared to go on a week-end party and conceals her car near the barn. He comes; she welcomes him with a pretence of her former ardors, and tries to get back her letters. Unsuccessful in this she persuades him to drink a cup of chocolate into which she puts the arsenic. After carefully washing the pans and cups, she leaves with him, dropping him from her car near his home; he being still unaffected. On her way to her party she pretends to have broken down and by asking the help of a passing cyclist establishes an alibi. Ekebon dies at his home attended by his mistress; the letters are discovered and Letty is brought before the coroner's inquest and acquitted chiefly through the alibi, for things look very bad for her until the cyclist appears.

The defendants, who are engaged in producing speaking films on a very large scale in Hollywood, California, had seen the play and wished to get the rights. They found, however, an obstacle in an association of motion picture producers presided over by Mr. Will Hays, who thought the play obscene; not being able to overcome his objections, they returned the copy of the manuscript which they had had. That was in the spring of 1930, but in the autumn they induced the plaintiffs to get up a scenario, which they hoped might pass moral muster. Although this did not suit them after the plaintiffs prepared it, they must still have thought in the spring of 1931 that they could satisfy Mr. Hays, for they then procured an offer from the plaintiffs to sell their rights for $30,000. These negotiations also proved abortive because the play continued to be objectionable, and eventually they cried off on the bargain. Mrs. Lowndes' novel was suggested to Thalberg, one of the vice-presidents of the Metro-Goldwyn Company, in July, 1931; and again in the following November, and he bought the rights to it in December. At once he assigned the preparation of a play to Stromberg, who had read the novel in January, and thought it would make a suitable play for an actress named, Crawford, just then not employed. Stromberg chose Meehan, Tuchock and Brown to help him, the first two with the scenario, the third with the dramatic production. All these four were examined by deposition; all denied that they had used the play in any way whatever; all agreed that they had based the picture on the story of Madeleine Smith and on the novel, "Letty Lynton." All had seen the play, and Tuchock had read the manuscript, as had Thalberg, but Stromberg, Meehan and Brown swore that they had not; Stromberg's denial being however worthless, for he had originally sworn the contrary in an affidavit. They all say that work began late in November or early in December, 1931, and the picture was finished by the end of March. To meet these denials, the plaintiffs appeal to the substantial identity between passages in the picture and those parts of the play which are original with them.

The picture opens in Montevideo where Letty Lynton is recovering from her fondness for Emile Renaul. She is rich, luxurious and fatherless, her father having been killed by his mistress's husband; her mother is seared, hard, selfish, unmotherly; and Letty has left home to escape her, wandering about in search of excitement. Apparently for the good part of a year she has been carrying on a love affair with Renaul; twice before she has tried to shake loose, has gone once to Rio where she lit another flame, but each time she has weakened and been drawn back. Though not fully declared as an amour, there can be no real question as to the character of her attachment. She at length determines really to break loose, but once again her senses are too much for her and it is indicated, if not declared, that she spends the night with Renaul. Though he is left a vague figure only indistinctly associated with South America somewhere or other, the part was cast for an action with a marked foreign accent, and it is plain that he was meant to be understood, in origin anyway, as South American, like Moreno in the play. He is violent, possessive and sensual; his power over Letty lies in his strong animal attractions. However, she escapes in the morning while he is asleep, whether from his bed or not is perhaps uncertain; and with a wax figure in the form of a loyal maid—Letty in the novel had one—boards a steamer for New York. On board she meets Darrow, a young American, the son of a rich rubber manufacturer, who is coming back from a trip to Africa. They fall in love upon the faintest provocation and become betrothed before the ship docks, three weeks after she left Montevideo. At the pier she finds Renaul who has flown up to reclaim her. She must in some way keep her two suitors apart, and she manages to dismiss Darrow and then to escape Renaul by asking him to pay her customs duties, which he does. Arrived home her mother gives her a cold welcome and refuses to concern herself with the girl's betrothal. Renaul is announced; he has read of the betrothal in the papers and is furious. He tries again to stir her sensuality by the familiar gambit, but this time he fails; she slaps his face and declares that she hates him. He commands her to come to his apartment that evening; she begs him to part with her and let her have her life; he insists on renewing their affair. She threatens to call the police; he rejoins that if so her letters will be published, and then he leaves. Desperate, she chances on a bottle of strychnine, which we are to suppose is an accoutrement of every affluent household, and seizes it; the implication is of intended suicide, not murder. Then she calls Darrow, tells him that she will not leave with him that night for his parents' place in the Adirondacks as they had planned; she renews to him the pledge of her love, without him she cannot live, an intimation to the audience of her purpose to kill herself.

That evening she goes to Renaul's apartment in a hotel armed with her strychnine bottle, for use on the spot; she finds him cooling champagne, but in bad temper. His caresses which he bestows plentifully enough, again stir her disgust not her passions, but he does not believe it and assumes that she will spend the night with him. Finding that he will not return the letters, she believes herself lost and empties the strychnine into a wine glass. Again he embraces her; she vilifies him; he knocks her down; she vilifies him again. Ignorant of the poison he grasps her glass, and she, perceiving it, lets him drink. He woos her again, this time with more apparent success, for she is terrified; he sings a Gaucho song to her, the same one that has been heard at Montevideo. The poison begins to work and, at length supposing that she has meant to murder him, he reaches for the telephone; she forestalls him, but she does not tear out the wire. As he slowly dies, she stands over him and vituperates him. A waiter enters; she steps behind a curtain; he leaves thinking Renaul drunk; she comes out, wipes off all traces of her fingerprints and goes out, leaving however her rubbers which Renaul had taken from her when she entered.

Next she and Darrow are found at his parents' in the Adirondacks; while there a detective appears, arrests Letty and takes her to New York; she is charged with the murder of Renaul; Darrow goes back to New York with her. The finish is at the district attorney's office; Letty and Darrow, Letty's mother, the wax serving maid are all there. The letters appear incriminating to an elderly rather benevolent district attorney; also the customs slip and the rubbers. Letty begins to break down; she admits that she went to Renaul's room, not to kill him but to get him to release her. Darrow sees that that story will not pass, and volunteers that she came to his room at a hotel and spent the night with him. Letty confirms this and mother, till then silent, backs up their story; she had traced them to the hotel and saw the lights go out, having ineffectually tried to dissuade them. The maid still further confirms them and the district attorney, not sorry to be discomfited, though unbelieving, discharges Letty.

We are to remember that it makes no difference how far the play was anticipated by works in the public demesne which the plaintiffs did not use. The defendants appear not to recognize this, for they have filled the record with earlier instances of the same dramatic incidents and devices, as though, like a patent, a copyrighted work must be not only original, but new. That is not however the law as is obvious in the case of maps or compendia, where later works will necessarily be anticipated. At times, in discussing how much of the substance of a play the copyright protects, courts have indeed used language which seems to give countenance to the notion that, if a plot were old, it could not be copyrighted. London v. Biography Co. (C.C.A.) 231 F. 696; Eichel v. Marcin (D.C.) 241 F. 404. But we understand by this no more than that in its broader outline a plot is never copyrightable, for it is plain beyond peradventure that anticipation as such cannot invalidate a copyright. Borrowed the work must indeed not be, for a plagiarist is not himself pro tanto an "author"; but if by some magic a man who had never known it were to compose anew Keats's Ode on a Grecian Urn, he would be an "author," and, if he copyrighted it, others might not copy that poem, though they might of course copy Keats's. Bleistein v. Donaldson Lithographing Co., 188 U.S. 239, 249, 23 S.Ct. 298, 47 L.Ed. 460; Gerlach-Barklow Co. v. Morris & Bendien, Inc., 23 F.(2d) 159, 161 (C.C.A.2); Weil, Copyright Law, p. 234. But though a copyright is for this reason less vulnerable than a patent, the owner's protection is more limited, for just as he is no less an "author" because others have preceded him, so another who follows him, is not a tort-feasor unless he pirates his work. Jewelers' Circular Publishing Co. v. Keystone Co., 281 F. 83, 92, 26 A.L.R. 571 (C.C.A.2); General Drafting Co. v. Andrews, 37 F.(2d) 54, 56 (C.C.A.2); Williams v. Smythe (C.C.) 110 F. 961; American, etc., Directory Co. v. Gehring Pub. Co. (D.C.) 4 F.(2d) 415; New Jersey, etc., Co. v. Barton Business Service (D.C.) 57 F.(2d) 353. If the copyrighted work is therefore original, the public demesne is important only on the issue of infringement; that is, so far as it may break the force of the inference to be drawn from likenesses between the work and the putative piracy. If the defendant has had access to other material which would have served him as well, his disclaimer becomes more plausible.

In the case at bar there are then two questions: First, whether the defendants actually used the play; second, if so, whether theirs was a "fair use." The judge did not make any finding upon the first question, as we said at the outset, because he thought the defendants were in any case justified; in this following our decision in Nichols v. Universal Pictures Corporation, 45 F.(2d) 119. The plaintiffs challenge that opinion because we said that "copying" might at times be a "fair use"; but it is convenient to define such a use by saying that others may "copy" the "theme," or "ideas," or the like, of a work, though not its "expression." At any rate so long as it is clear what is meant, no harm is done. In the case at bar the distinction is not so important as usual, because so much of the play was borrowed from the story of Madeleine Smith, and the plaintiffs' originality is necessarily limited to the variants they introduced. Nevertheless, it is still true that their whole contribution may not be protected; for the defendants were entitled to use, not only all that had gone before, but even the plaintiffs' contribution itself, if they drew from it only the more general patterns; that is, if they kept clear of its "expression." We must therefore state in detail those similarities which seem to us to pass the limits of "fair use." Finally, in concluding as we do that the defendants used the play pro tanto, we need not charge their witnesses with perjury. With so many sources before them they might quite honestly forget what they took; nobody knows the origin of his inventions; memory and fancy merge even in adults. Yet unconscious plagiarism is actionable quite as much as deliberate. Buck v. Jewell-La Salle Realty Co., 283 U.S. 191, 198, 51 S.Ct. 410, 75 L.Ed. 971, 76 A.L.R. 1266; Harold Lloyd Corporation v. Witwer, 65 F.(2d) 1, 16 (C.C.A.9); Fred Fisher, Inc., v. Dillingham (D.C.) 298 F. 145.

The defendants took for their mis en scène the same city and the same social class; and they chose a South American villain. The heroines had indeed to be wanton, but Letty Lynton "tracked" Madeleine Cary more closely than that. She is overcome by passion in the first part of the picture and yields after announcing that she hates Renaul and has made up her mind to leave him. This is the same weakness as in the murder scene of the play, though transposed. Each heroine's waywardness is suggested as an inherited disposition; each has had an arrant parent involved in scandal; one killed, the other becoming an outcast. Each is redeemed by a higher love. Madeleine Cary must not be misread; it is true that her lust overcomes her at the critical moment, but it does not extinguish her love for Farnborough; her body, not her soul, consents to her lapse. Moreover, her later avowal, which she knew would finally lose her her lover, is meant to show the basic rectitude of her nature. Though it does not need Darrow to cure Letty of her wanton ways, she too is redeemed by a nobler love. Neither Madeleine Smith, nor the Letty of the novel, were at all like that; they wished to shake off a clandestine intrigue to set themselves up in the world; their love as distinct from their lust, was pallid. So much for the similarity in character.

Coming to the parallelism of incident, the threat scene is carried out with almost exactly the same sequence of event and actuation; it has no prototype in either story or novel. Neither Ekebon nor L'Angelier went to his fatal interview to break up the new betrothal; he was beguiled by the pretence of a renewed affection. Moreno and Renaul each goes to his sweetheart's home to detach her from her new love;

when he is there, she appeals to his better side, unsuccessfully; she abuses him, he returns the abuse and commands her to come to his rooms; she pretends to agree, expecting to finish with him one way or another. True, the assault is deferred in the picture from this scene to the next, but it is the same dramatic trick. Again, the poison in each case is found at home, and the girl talks with her betrothed just after the villain has left and again pledges him her faith. Surely the sequence of these details is pro tanto the very web of the authors' dramatic expression; and copying them is not "fair use."

The death scene follows the play even more closely; the girl goes to the villain's room as he directs; from the outset he is plainly to be poisoned while they are together. (The defendants deny that this is apparent in the picture, but we cannot agree. It would have been an impossible dénoument on the screen for the heroine, just plighted to the hero, to kill herself in desperation, because the villain has successfully enmeshed her in their mutual past; yet the poison is surely to be used on some one.) Moreno and Renaul each tries to arouse the girl by the memory of their former love, using among other aphrodisiacs the Gaucho song; each dies while she is there, incidentally of strychnine not arsenic. In extremis each makes for the telephone and is thwarted by the girl; as he dies, she pours upon him her rage and loathing. When he is dead, she follows the same ritual to eradicate all traces of her presence, but forgets telltale bits of property. Again these details in the same sequence embody more than the "ideas" of the play; they are its very raiment.

Finally in both play and picture in place of a trial, as in the story and novel, there is substituted an examination by a district attorney, and this examination is again in parallel almost step by step. A parent is present; so is the lover; the girl yields progressively as the evidence accumulates; in the picture, the customs slip, the rubbers and the letters; in the play, the cross and the witnesses, brought in to confront her. She is at the breaking point when she is saved by substantially the same most unexpected alibi; a man declares that she has spent the night with him. That alibi there introduced is the turning point in each drama and alone prevents its ending in accordance with the classic canon of tragedy; i.e., fate as an inevitable consequence of past conduct, itself not evil enough to quench pity. It is the essence of the authors' expression, the very voice with which they speak.

We have often decided that a play may be pirated without using the dialogue. Daly v. Palmer, Fed.Cas. No. 3,552, 6 Blatch. 256; Daly v. Webster, 56 F. 483, 486, 487; Dam v. Kirk La Shelle Co., 175 F. 902, 907, 41 L.R.A.(N.S.) 1002, 20 Ann.Cas. 1173; Chappell & Co. v. Fields, 210 F. 864. Dymow v. Bolton, 11 F.(2d) 690; and Nichols v. Universal Pictures Corporation, supra, 45 F.(2d) 119, do not suggest otherwise. Were it not so, there could be no piracy of a pantomime, where there cannot be any dialogue; yet nobody would deny to pantomime the name of drama. Speech is only a small part of a dramatist's means of expression; he draws on all the arts and compounds his play from words and gestures and scenery and costume and from the very looks of the actors themselves. Again and again a play may lapse into pantomime at its most poignant and significant moments; a nod, a movement of the hand, a pause, may tell the audience more than words could tell. To be sure, not all this is always copyrighted, though there is no reason why it may not be, for those decisions do not forbid which hold that mere scenic tricks will not be protected. Serrana v. Jefferson (C.C.) 33 F. 347; Barnes v. Miner (C.C.) 122 F. 480; Bloom et al. v. Nixon (C.C.) 125 F. 977. The play is the sequence of the confluents of all these means, bound together in an inseparable unity; it may often be most effectively pirated by leaving out the speech, for which a substitute can be found, which keeps the whole dramatic meaning. That as it appears to us is exactly what the defendants have done here; the dramatic significance of the scenes we have recited is the same, almost to the letter. True, much of the picture owes nothing to the play; some of it is plainly drawn from the novel; but that is entirely immaterial; it is enough that substantial parts were lifted; no plagiarist can excuse the wrong by showing how much of his work he did not pirate. We cannot avoid the conviction that, if the picture was not an infringement of the play, there can be none short of taking the dialogue.

The decree will be reversed and an injunction will go against the picture together with a decree for damages and an accounting. The plaintiffs will be awarded an attorney's fee in this court and in the court below, both to be fixed by the District Court upon the final decree.

Decree reversed.

Questions

1. What does the term "fair use" mean as employed by Judge Hand in the instant case? Is there an alternative meaning?

2. Suppose the only elements common between plaintiff's and defendant's works were also contained in the actual facts of Madeleine Smith's life. If the trier of fact concluded that defendant had copied from plaintiff, would this constitute copyright infringement?

SID & MARTY KROFFT TELEVISION PRODUCTIONS, INC. v. McDONALD'S CORP.

United States Court of Appeals, Ninth Circuit, 1977.
562 F.2d 1157.

Before CARTER, GOODWIN, and SNEED, CIRCUIT JUDGES.

JAMES M. CARTER, CIRCUIT JUDGE:

This is a copyright infringement action. Plaintiffs Sid and Marty Krofft Television Productions, Inc., and Sid and Marty Krofft Productions, Inc. were awarded $50,000.00 in their action against defendants McDonald's Corporation and Needham, Harper & Steers, Inc. Defendants were found to have infringed plaintiffs' "H.R. Pufnstuf" children's television show by the production of their "McDonaldland" television commercials.

Plaintiffs argue on appeal that the district court erred in awarding damages pursuant to 17 U.S.C. § 101(b). They contend that the court should have ordered an accounting of profits by defendants or, alternatively, should have awarded statutory "in lieu" damages.

Defendants cross-appeal. They contend that their television commercials did not infringe upon plaintiffs' television series as a matter of law. To find infringement, they suggest, would abridge their first amendment rights. They also refute plaintiffs' contentions as to damages.

We believe that the district court's finding of infringement was not clearly erroneous, and see no merit to defendants' first amendment claims. We find, however, that the district court was in error in awarding damages. We therefore affirm in part, reverse in part, and remand for further proceedings.

Facts

In 1968, Sid and Marty Krofft were approached by the NBC television network to create a children's television program for exhibition on Saturday morning.[1] The Kroffts spent the next year creating the H.R. Pufnstuf television show, which was introduced on NBC in September 1969. The series included several fanciful costumed characters, as well as a boy named Jimmy, who lived in a fantasyland called "Living Island," which was inhabited by moving trees and talking books. The television series became extremely popular and generated a line of H.R. Pufnstuf products and endorsements.

In early 1970, Marty Krofft, the President of both Krofft Television and Krofft Productions and producer of the show, was contacted by an executive from Needham, Harper & Steers, Inc., an advertising agency. He was told that Needham was attempting to get the advertising account of McDonald's hamburger restaurant chain and wanted to base a proposed campaign to McDonald's on the H.R. Pufnstuf characters. The executive wanted to know whether the Kroffts would be interested in working with Needham on a project of this type.

Needham and the Kroffts were in contact by telephone six or seven more times. By a letter dated August 31, 1970, Needham stated it was going forward with the idea of a McDonaldland advertising campaign based on the H.R. Pufnstuf series. It acknowledged the need to pay the Kroffts a fee for preparing artistic designs and engineering plans.

---

1. The Kroffts are fifth generation puppeteers who have been in the entertainment industry in this country over 40 years. The evidence showed that they enjoyed years of success with their puppet shows in cities around the country—most notably the Le Puppet de Paris adult puppet show. The Kroffts created the characters for "The Banana Splits," a popular children's television series produced by Hanna Barbera, before being asked to create their own show.

Shortly thereafter, Marty Krofft telephoned Needham only to be told that the advertising campaign had been cancelled.

In fact, Needham had already been awarded McDonald's advertising account and was proceeding with the McDonaldland project.[2] Former employees of the Kroffts were hired to design and construct the costumes and sets for McDonaldland. Needham also hired the same voice expert who supplied all of the voices for the Pufnstuf characters to supply some of the voices for the McDonaldland characters. In January 1971, the first of the McDonaldland commercials was broadcast on network television. They continue to be broadcast.

Prior to the advent of the McDonaldland advertising campaign plaintiffs had licensed the use of the H.R. Pufnstuf characters and elements to the manufacturers of toys, games, lunch boxes, and comic books. In addition, the H.R. Pufnstuf characters were featured in Kellogg's cereal commercials and used by the Ice Capades. After the McDonaldland campaign, which included the distribution of toys and games, plaintiffs were unable to obtain new licensing arrangements or extend existing ones.[3] In the case of the Ice Capades, the H.R. Pufnstuf characters were actually replaced by the McDonaldland characters.

Plaintiffs filed suit in September 1971. The complaint alleged, *inter alia*, that the McDonaldland advertising campaign infringed the copyrighted H.R. Pufnstuf television episodes as well as various copyrighted articles of Pufnstuf merchandise.[4]

* * *

A verdict in favor of plaintiffs was returned and damages of $50,000.00 assessed. After the verdict, the parties briefed the question of whether plaintiffs were entitled to additional monetary recovery in the form of profits or statutory "in lieu" damages. The district court denied plaintiffs' claim for such relief. The court found that these matters were properly for the jury to consider so that it would not exercise its discretion in hearing further evidence. These appeals followed.

I. INFRINGEMENT

PROOF OF INFRINGEMENT

It has often been said that in order to establish copyright infringement a plaintiff must prove ownership of the copyright and "copying"

---

2. On June 24, 1970, Needham made a presentation of a McDonaldland advertising campaign to McDonald's. Needham was awarded the account by a contract dated June 29, 1970. In July, three representatives of Needham came to the Kroffts' offices in Los Angeles to discuss the design and engineering work that would be required to produce the McDonaldland commercials. It is evident, therefore, that Needham was deceiving the Kroffts in their contacts after the June 29 contract.

3. The evidence reveals that certain persons with whom plaintiffs dealt for licensing believed that the H.R. Pufnstuf characters were being licensed to McDonald's for use in their McDonaldland campaign. Accordingly, they did not pursue licensing arrangements for the characters themselves.

4. The complaint also contained claims for relief in unfair competition, tortious interference, quasi-contract, and contract. The judgment and this appeal are based solely on the copyright claim.

by the defendant. See, e.g., Reyher v. Children's Television Workshop, 533 F.2d 87, 90 (2 Cir.1976); Universal Athletic Sales Co. v. Salkeld, 511 F.2d 904, 907 (3 Cir.1975); 2 M. Nimmer on Copyright § 141 at 610–11 (1976) (hereinafter "Nimmer"). "Copying," in turn, is said to be shown by circumstantial evidence of access to the copyrighted work and substantial similarity between the copyrighted work and defendant's work. Reyher v. Children's Television Workshop, supra, 533 F.2d at 90; 2 Nimmer § 141.2 at 613. But an analysis of the cases suggests that these statements frequently serve merely as boilerplate to copyright opinions.

Under such statements, infringement would be established upon proof of ownership, access, and substantial similarity. Application of this rule, however, would produce some untenable results. For example, a copyright could be obtained over a cheaply manufactured plaster statue of a nude. Since ownership of a copyright is established, subsequent manufacturers of statues of nudes would face the grave risk of being found to be infringers if their statues were substantially similar and access were shown. The burden of proof on the plaintiff would be minimal, since most statues of nudes would in all probability be substantially similar to the cheaply manufactured plaster one.

Clearly the scope of copyright protection does not go this far. A limiting principle is needed. This is provided by the classic distinction between an "idea" and the "expression" of that idea. It is an axiom of copyright law that the protection granted to a copyrighted work extends only to the particular expression of the idea and never to the idea itself. Mazer v. Stein, 347 U.S. 201, 217–18, 74 S.Ct. 460, 98 L.Ed. 630 (1954); Baker v. Selden, 101 U.S. 99, 102–03, 25 L.Ed. 841 (1879). This principle attempts to reconcile two competing social interests: rewarding an individual's creativity and effort while at the same time permitting the nation to enjoy the benefits and progress from use of the same subject matter.

The real task in a copyright infringement action, then, is to determine whether there has been copying of the expression of an idea rather than just the idea itself. "[N]o one infringes, unless he descends so far into what is concrete [in a work] as to invade * * * [its] expression." National Comics Publications v. Fawcett Publications, 191 F.2d 594, 600 (2 Cir.1951). Only this expression may be protected and only it may be infringed.[6]

---

[6]. The idea-expression dichotomy has been criticized by some commentators as outmoded because it was developed under older, narrower statutes which have since been considerably broadened. See, e.g., Collins, Some Obsolescent Doctrines of the Law of Copyright, 1 S.Cal.L.Rev. 127 (1928); Umbreit, A Consideration of Copyright, 87 U.Pa.L.Rev. 932 (1939); Note, Copyright Protection for Mass-Produced Commercial Products: A Review of the Developments Following Mazer v. Stein, 38 U.Chi.L.Rev. 807 (1971). Yet the distinction accurately conceptualizes the fundamental elements in an artistic creation and balances the competing interests inherent in the copyright law. We have surveyed the literature and have found that no better formulation has been devised. Moreover, most of these criticisms are directed at the fact that the courts tend to pay only lipservice to the idea-expression distinction without it being fairly descriptive of the results of modern

The difficulty comes in attempting to distill the unprotected idea from the protected expression. No court or commentator in making this search has been able to improve upon Judge Learned Hand's famous "abstractions test" articulated in Nichols v. Universal Pictures Corporation, 45 F.2d 119 (2 Cir.1930), cert. denied, 282 U.S. 902, 51 S.Ct. 216, 75 L.Ed. 795 (1931):

> Upon any work, and especially upon a play, a great number of patterns of increasing generality will fit equally well, as more and more of the incident is left out. The last may perhaps be no more than the most general statement of what the play is about, and at times might consist of only its title; but there is a point in this series of abstractions where they are no longer protected, since otherwise the playwright could prevent the use of his "ideas," to which, apart from their expression, his property is never extended. 45 F.2d at 121.

See also Chafee, Reflections on the Law of Copyright, 45 Colum.L.Rev. 503 (1945); Esezobar, Concepts in Copyright Protection, 23 Bull.Cprt. Soc. 258 (1976); Note, "Expression" and "Originality" in Copyright Law, 11 Washburn L.J. 400 (1972).

The test for infringement therefore has been given a new dimension. There must be ownership of the copyright and access to the copyrighted work. But there also must be substantial similarity not only of the general ideas but of the expressions of those ideas as well. Thus two steps in the analytic process are implied by the requirement of substantial similarity.

The determination of whether there is substantial similarity in ideas may often be a simple one. Returning to the example of the nude statue, the idea there embodied is a simple one—a plaster recreation of a nude human figure. A statue of a horse or a painting of a nude would not embody this idea and therefore could not infringe. The test for similarity of ideas is still a factual one, to be decided by the trier of fact. See International Luggage Registry v. Avery Products Corp., 541 F.2d 830, 831 (9 Cir.1976); Williams v. Kaag Manufacturers, Inc., 338 F.2d 949, 951 (9 Cir.1964).

We shall call this the "extrinsic test." It is extrinsic because it depends not on the responses of the trier of fact, but on specific criteria which can be listed and analyzed. Such criteria include the type of artwork involved, the materials used, the subject matter, and the setting for the subject. Since it is an extrinsic test, analytic dissection and expert testimony are appropriate. Moreover, this question may often be decided as a matter of law.

The determination of when there is substantial similarity between the forms of expression is necessarily more subtle and complex. As Judge Hand candidly observed, "Obviously, no principle can be stated as to when an imitator has gone beyond copying the 'idea,' and has

---

cases. This is a criticism more of the application of the distinction than of the distinction itself, and can be alleviated by the courts being more deliberate in their consideration of this issue.

borrowed its 'expression.' Decisions must therefore inevitably be ad hoc." Peter Pan Fabrics, Inc. v. Martin Weiner Corp., 274 F.2d 487, 489 (2 Cir.1960). If there is substantial similarity in ideas, then the trier of fact must decide whether there is substantial similarity in the expressions of the ideas so as to constitute infringement.

The test to be applied in determining whether there is substantial similarity in expressions shall be labeled an intrinsic one—depending on the response of the ordinary reasonable person. See International Luggage Registry v. Avery Products Corp., supra, 541 F.2d at 831; Harold Lloyd Corp. v. Witwer, 65 F.2d 1, 18–19 (9 Cir.1933). See generally Nimmer § 143.5. It is intrinsic because it does not depend on the type of external criteria and analysis which marks the extrinsic test. As this court stated in Twentieth Century-Fox Film Corp. v. Stonesifer, 140 F.2d 579, 582 (9 Cir.1944):

> "The two works involved in this appeal should be considered and tested, not hypercritically or with meticulous scrutiny, but by the observations and impressions of the average reasonable reader and spectator."

Because this is an intrinsic test, analytic dissection and expert testimony are not appropriate.

This same type of bifurcated test was announced in Arnstein v. Porter, 154 F.2d 464, 468–69 (2 Cir.1946), cert. denied, 330 U.S. 851, 67 S.Ct. 1096, 91 L.Ed. 1294 (1947). The court there identified two separate elements essential to a plaintiff's suit for infringement: copying and unlawful appropriation. Under the *Arnstein* doctrine, the distinction is significant because of the different tests involved.

> "[T]he trier of fact must determine whether the similarities are sufficient to prove copying. On this issue, analysis ('dissection') is relevant, and the testimony of experts may be received to aid the trier of facts. * * * If copying is established, then only does there arise the second issue, that of illicit copying (unlawful appropriation). On that issue * * * the test is the response of the ordinary lay hearer; accordingly, on that issue, 'dissection' and expert testimony are irrelevant." 154 F.2d at 468 (footnotes omitted).

We believe that the court in *Arnstein* was alluding to the idea-expression dichotomy which we make explicit today. When the court in *Arnstein* refers to "copying" which is not itself an infringement, it must be suggesting copying merely of the work's idea, which is not protected by the copyright. To constitute an infringement, the copying must reach the point of "unlawful appropriation," or the copying of the protected expression itself. We analyze this distinction in terms both of the elements involved—idea and expression—and of the tests to be used—extrinsic and intrinsic—in an effort to clarify the issues involved.

The Tests Applied

In the context of this case, the distinction between these tests is important. Defendants do not dispute the fact that they copied the idea of plaintiffs' Pufnstuf television series—basically a fantasyland filled with diverse and fanciful characters in action. They argue, however, that the expressions of this idea are too dissimilar for there to be an infringement. They come to this conclusion by dissecting the constituent parts of the Pufnstuf series—characters, setting, and plot—and pointing out the dissimilarities between these parts and those of the McDonaldland commercials.

This approach ignores the idea-expression dichotomy alluded to in *Arnstein* and analyzed today. Defendants attempt to apply an extrinsic test by the listing of dissimilarities in determining whether the expression they used was substantially similar to the expression used by plaintiffs. That extrinsic test is inappropriate; an intrinsic test must here be used. As the court in *Arnstein* stated:

> "Whether (if he copied) defendant unlawfully appropriated presents, too, an issue of fact. The proper criterion on that issue is not an analytic or other comparison of the respective * * * compositions * * *. The plaintiff's legally protected interest in the potential financial return from his compositions which derive from the lay public's approbation of his efforts. The question, therefore, is whether defendant took from plaintiff's works so much of what is pleasing to the [eyes and] ears of lay [persons], who comprise the audience for whom such popular [works are] composed, that defendant wrongfully appropriated something which belongs to the plaintiff. Surely, then, we have an issue of fact which a jury is peculiarly fitted to determine." 154 F.2d at 472–73 (footnotes omitted).

Analytic dissection, as defendants have done, is therefore improper.

Defendants contest the continued viability of *Arnstein*. It is true that *Arnstein's* alternative holding that summary judgment may not be granted when there is the slightest doubt as to the facts has been disapproved. See, e.g., First National Bank of Arizona v. Cities Service Co., 391 U.S. 253, 288–90, 88 S.Ct. 1575, 20 L.Ed.2d 569 (1968); Beal v. Lindsay, 468 F.2d 287, 291 (2 Cir.1972); Janis v. Wilson, 385 F.Supp. 1143, 1147 (D.S.D.1974); Keller v. California Liquid Gas Corp., 363 F.Supp. 123, 126 (D.Wyo.1973). But the case's tests for infringement have consistently been approved by this court. See, e.g., Goodson-Todman Enterprises, Inc. v. Kellogg Co., 513 F.2d 913, 914 (9 Cir.1975); Overman v. Loesser, 205 F.2d 521, 523 (9 Cir.1953). They have also been accepted by other courts. See, e.g., Universal Athletic Sales Co. v. Salkeld, supra, 511 F.2d at 907; Scott v. WKJG, Inc., 376 F.2d 467, 469 (7 Cir.1967).[7] We believe *Arnstein* is still good law.

Since the intrinsic test for expression is uniquely suited for determination by the trier of fact, this court must be reluctant to reverse it.

* * *

---

7. The two-step approach of *Arnstein* does have its detractors. Judge Moore in a Second Circuit case described this approach as "merely an alternative way of formulating the issue of substantial certainty." Ideal Toy Corp. v. Fab-Lu Ltd., 360 F.2d 1021, 1023 n. 2 (2 Cir.1966). But the approach certainly tends to decrease the importance of the trier of fact in the first step and increase this importance in the second step. See 2 Nimmer § 143.53 at 641–43. In this it represents a significant modification of the older audience test. Id. We do not resurrect the *Arnstein* approach today. Rather, we formulate an extrinsic-intrinsic test for infringement based on the idea-expression dichotomy. We believe that the *Arnstein* court was doing nearly the same thing. But the fact that it may not have been does not subtract from our analysis.

The present case demands an even more intrinsic determination because both plaintiffs' and defendants' works are directed to an audience of children. This raises the particular factual issue of the impact of the respective works upon the minds and imaginations of young people. * * *

The H.R. Pufnstuf series became the most popular children's show on Saturday morning television. This success led several manufacturers of children's goods to use the Pufnstuf characters. It is not surprising, then, that McDonald's hoped to duplicate this peculiar appeal to children in its commercials.[8] It was in recognition of the subjective and unpredictable nature of children's responses that defendants opted to recreate the H.R. Pufnstuf format rather than use an original and unproven approach.

Defendants would have this court ignore that intrinsic quality which they recognized to embark on an extrinsic analysis of the two works. For example, in discussing the principal characters—Pufnstuf and Mayor McCheese—defendants point out:

> "Pufnstuf" wears what can only be described as a yellow and green dragon suit with a blue cummerbund from which hangs a medal which says "mayor". "McCheese" wears a version of pink formal dress—"tails"—with knicker trousers. He has a typical diplomat's sash on which is written "mayor", the "M" consisting of the McDonald's trademark of an "M" made of golden arches.

So not only do defendants remove the characters from the setting, but dissect further to analyze the clothing, colors, features, and mannerisms of each character. We do not believe that the ordinary reasonable person, let alone a child, viewing these works will even notice that Pufnstuf is wearing a cummerbund while Mayor McCheese is wearing a diplomat's sash.

Duplication or near identity is not necessary to establish infringement. Runge v. Lee, 441 F.2d 579, 582 (9 Cir.1971); Williams v. Kaag Manufacturers, Inc., supra, 338 F.2d at 951. As this court stated in Universal Pictures Co., Inc. v. Harold Lloyd Corp., infra, 162 F.2d 354, at 360:

> [A]n infringement is not confined to literal and exact repetition or reproduction; it includes also the various modes in which the matter of any work may be adopted, imitated, transferred, or reproduced, with more or less colorable alterations to disguise the piracy.

And, as Judge Learned Hand put it, copyright "cannot be limited literally to the text, else a plagiarist would escape by immaterial variations." Nichols v. Universal Pictures Corp., 45 F.2d 119, 121 (2 Cir.1930).

---

8. McDonald's advertising campaign was divided into two distinct parts: its general audience advertising and its children advertising. The McDonaldland commercials were used exclusively on children's programming. The apparent success of this format is suggested by the fact that the McDonaldland commercials are still appearing on television over six years after their introduction.

We have viewed representative samples of both the H.R. Pufnstuf show and McDonaldland commercials. It is clear to us that defendants' works are substantially similar to plaintiffs'.[9] They have captured the "total concept and feel" of the Pufnstuf show. Roth Greeting Cards v. United Card Co., 429 F.2d 1106, 1110 (9 Cir.1970). We would so conclude even if we were sitting as the triers of fact. There is no doubt that the findings of the jury in this case are not clearly erroneous.

Unity of Idea and Expression

Defendants argue that dissection is proper and that duplication or near identity is necessary because the competing works are *things,* rather than dramatic works. They cite numerous cases in which infringement was found because the defendants' works were nearly identical to those of the plaintiffs. See, e.g., Bleistein v. Donaldson Lithographing Co., 188 U.S. 239, 250, 23 S.Ct. 298, 47 L.Ed. 460 (1903) (circus posters); Sunset House Distributing Corp. v. Doran, 304 F.2d 251, 252 (9 Cir.1962) (plastic Santa Claus); King Features Syndicate v. Fleischer, 299 F. 533, 534 (2 Cir.1924) (doll). Defendants fail to perceive, however, that near identity may be required in some cases not because the works are things, but because the expression of those works and the idea of those works are indistinguishable.

Herbert Rosenthal Jewelry Corp. v. Kalpakian, 446 F.2d 738 (9 Cir.1971), upon which defendants rely, is illustrative of this point. In that case, plaintiff sued for infringement of its jeweled bee pin, claiming it should be protected against the manufacture of any substantially similar object. This court responded:

> What is basically at stake is the extent of the copyright owner's monopoly—from how large an area of activity did Congress intend to allow the copyright owner to exclude others? We think the production of jeweled bee pins is a larger private preserve than Congress intended to be set aside in the public market without a patent. A jeweled bee pin is therefore an idea that defendants were free to copy. Plaintiff seems to agree, for it disavows any claim that defendants cannot manufacture and sell jeweled bee pins and concedes that only plaintiffs' particular design or expression of the jeweled bee pin idea is protected under its copyright. The difficulty, as we have noted, is that on this record the idea and its expression appear to be indistinguishable. There is no greater similarity between the pins of

---

9. Even a dissection of the two works reveals their similarities. The "Living Island" locale of Pufnstuf and "McDonaldland" are both imaginary worlds inhabited by anthromorphic [sic] plants and animals and other fanciful creatures. The dominant topographical features of the locales are the same: trees, caves, a pond, a road, and a castle. Both works feature a forest with talking trees that have human faces and characteristics.

The characters are also similiar. Both lands are governed by mayors who have disproportionately large round heads dominated by long wide mouths. They are assisted by "Keystone cop" characters. Both lands feature strikingly similar crazy scientists and a multi-armed evil creature.

It seems clear that such similarities go beyond merely that of the idea into the area of expression. The use of the basic idea of the works does not inevitably result in such similarities. Certainly a jury applying an intrinsic test could find such similarities of expression substantial.

plaintiff and defendants than is inevitable from the use of jewel-encrusted bee forms in both.

When the idea and its expression are thus inseparable, copying the expression will not be barred, since protecting the expression in such circumstances would confer a monopoly of the idea upon the copyright owner free of the conditions and limitations imposed by the patent law. Id. at 742.

See also Herbert Rosenthal Jewelry Corp. v. Honora Jewelry Co., Inc., 509 F.2d 64, 65 (2 Cir.1974).

The idea and the expression will coincide when the expression provides nothing new or additional over the idea. Thus, the expression of a jeweled bee pin contains nothing new over the idea of a jeweled bee pin. Returning to our own example, the idea of a plaster statue of a nude will probably coincide with the expression of that idea when an inexpensive manufacturing process is used. There will be no separately distinguishable features in the statue's expression over the idea of a plaster nude statue.[10]

The complexity and artistry of the expression of an idea will separate it from even the most banal idea. Michaelangelo's David is, as an idea, no more than a statue of a nude male. But no one would question the proposition that if a copyrighted work it would deserve protection even against the poorest of imitations. This is because so much more was added in the expression over the idea.

When idea and expression coincide, there will be protection against nothing other than identical copying of the work. When other defendants made jeweled bees from the same molds as plaintiffs, they were held liable. See Herbert Rosenthal Jewelry Corp. v. Grossbardt, 436 F.2d 315 (2 Cir.1970). Therefore, the scope of copyright protection increases with the extent expression differs from the idea.

* * *

No standard more demanding than that of substantial similarity should be imposed here. This is not a case where the idea is indistinguishable as a matter of law from the expression of that idea. See Goodson-Todman Enterprises, Inc. v. Kellogg Co., supra, 513 F.2d at 914. The expression inherent in the H.R. Pufnstuf series differs markedly from its relatively simple idea. The characters each have developed personalities and particular ways of interacting with one another and their environment. The physical setting also has several unique features.

Lest we fall prey to defendants' invitation to dissect the works, however, we should remember that it is the *combination* of many different elements which may command copyright protection because of its particular subjective quality. Reyher v. Children's Television Workshop, Inc., supra, 533 F.2d at 91–92; Ideal Toy Corp. v. Sayco Doll Corp.,

---

10. A description of the "what" and the "how" of a work serves as a useful tool in determining whether the expression of an idea differs from the idea itself. If, in describing how a work is expressed, the description differs little from a simple description of what the work is, then idea and expression coincide.

302 F.2d 623, 624 (2 Cir.1962). As the court said in Malkin v. Dubinsky, 146 F.Supp. 111, 114 (S.D.N.Y.1956): "While any one similarity taken by itself seems trivial, I cannot say at this time that it would be improper for a jury to find that the over-all impact and effect indicate substantial appropriation." The same is true here.

* * *

Access

In addition to substantial similarity, a plaintiff must show access in order to prove infringement. Reyher v. Children's Television Workshop, supra, 533 F.2d at 90; 2 Nimmer § 141.2 at 613. Access is proven when the plaintiff shows that the defendant had an opportunity to view or to copy plaintiff's work. Arrow Novelty Co. v. Enco National Corp., 393 F.Supp. 157, 160 (S.D.N.Y.), aff'd, 515 F.2d 504 (2 Cir.1975); Universal Athletic Sales Co. v. Salkeld, 340 F.Supp. 899, 901 (W.D.Pa.1972). In this case, there is no dispute as to defendants' access to plaintiffs' work. Indeed, defendants were engaged in negotiations with plaintiffs for licensing of the works even while preparing the McDonaldland commercials.

No amount of proof of access will suffice to show copying if there are no similarities. Williams v. Kaag Manufacturers, Inc., supra, 338 F.2d at 951; Arnstein v. Porter, supra, 154 F.2d at 468. This is not to say, however, that where clear and convincing evidence of access is presented, the quantum of proof required to show substantial similarity may not be lower than when access is shown merely by a preponderance of the evidence. As Professor Nimmer has observed:

> [C]lear and convincing evidence of access will not avoid the necessity of also proving substantial similarity since access without similarity cannot create an inference of copying. However, this so-called "Inverse Ratio Rule" * * * would seem to have some limited validity. That is, since a very high degree of similarity is required in order to dispense with proof of access, it must logically follow that where proof of access is offered, the required degree of similarity may be somewhat less than would be necessary in the absence of such proof. 2 Nimmer § 143.4 at 634.

Accord, Fink v. Goodson-Todman Enterprises, Ltd., 9 Cal.App.3d 996, 1013, 88 Cal.Rptr. 679 (1970). We agree. But see Arc Music Corp. v. Lee, 296 F.2d 186 (2 Cir.1961).

In this case, representatives of Needham actually visited the Kroffts' headquarters in Los Angeles to discuss the engineering and design work necessary to produce the McDonaldland commercials. They did this *after* they had been awarded the contract by McDonald's and apparently with no intention to work with the Kroffts. We believe that this degree of access justifies a lower standard of proof to show substantial similarity. Since the subjective test applies, it is impossible to quantify this standard. But there is no question it is met here.

* * *

III. Conclusion

In view of the holdings set forth in both portions of this opinion the judgment of the district court finding infringement is affirmed. The district court's denial of plaintiffs' motion for an accounting is reversed. The case is remanded for an accounting, after which the district court may, in its discretion, award statutory "in lieu" damages.

Affirmed in part and Reversed in part.

[That portion of the court's opinion dealing with the asserted First Amendment defense is set forth at p. 426 infra.]

Questions

1. Do you agree with the court's conclusion that a painting of a nude would not necessarily embody the "idea" contained in a statue of a nude? Does the medium in which a work is first executed constitute all, or even a part, of its "idea"? Should "the type of artwork involved", or "the materials used" be considered relevant in determining similarity as between plaintiff's and defendant's works for copyright purposes?

2. Under the *Krofft* "extrinsic" and "intrinsic" tests, once a court determines that there is similarity of "idea", when if ever is it proper for the court to determine as a matter of law (notwithstanding an actual or potential jury verdict to the contrary) that the similarity is not one of "expression"? If in Nichols v. Universal Pictures Corporation, supra, the trier of fact had found for the plaintiff, under the *Krofft* test would it be improper for the appellate court to reverse the finding of substantial similarity since there was at the least a similarity of "idea"?

Collateral References

Carman, *The Function of the Judge and Jury in the "Literary Property" Lawsuit,* 42 Cal.Law Rev. 52 (1954).

Karp, *Copyright Litigation,* 7 Copyright Problems Analyzed 143 (CCH 1952).

Nimmer on Copyright, § 13.03.

MUSTO v. MEYER

United States District Court, Southern District of New York, 1977.
434 F.Supp. 32.

BONSAL, DISTRICT JUDGE. As the late Sir Arthur Conan Doyle wrote in The Yellow-Face, which appears in The Memoirs of Sherlock Holmes published by Penguin Books, "[s]ave for the occasional use of cocaine he [Holmes] had no vices, and he only turned to the drug as a protest against the monotony of existence when cases were scanty and the papers uninteresting." This passage provides a backdrop for this lawsuit.

Plaintiff, David F. Musto ("Musto"), author of an article entitled "A Study in Cocaine: Sherlock Holmes and Sigmund Freud" which appeared in the April 1, 1968 edition of the Journal of the American Medical Association (volume 204, No. 1) (the "article") is suing the defendants for damages alleging that the defendants infringed upon his copyright by publishing, distributing and selling in 1974 a hardcover and paperback edition of a book entitled The Seven Per Cent Solution (the "book"), and by making and producing a feature length film of the book known by the same name. The defendants include the editor of the book, Nicholas Meyer; the publisher of the hardcover edition, E.P. Dutton & Co., Inc.; the publisher of the paperback edition, Ballantine Books; and the makers of the film, Universal Pictures. Musto alleges that a substantial portion of the book and film is copied from his article and that the writing and publishing of the book and the subsequent making of the motion picture infringes upon his copyright and is therefore actionable at law.

The defendants deny the allegations in the complaint and move pursuant to Rule 12(c) of the Federal Rules of Civil Procedure for an order dismissing the complaint for failure to state a cause of action upon which relief may be granted.

General Background

Musto's article is a brief but interesting history of the use of cocaine in Europe and America in the 19th century. The article is highlighted by Musto's speculation, somewhat tongue-in-cheek on the use of cocaine by the fictional character Sherlock Holmes and by the famous psychiatrist Sigmund Freud. Musto suggests that Holmes may have been a heavy user of the drug and that his addiction led him to believe that Professor Moriarty, the alleged master criminal, was after him. Musto hypothesizes that Holmes' mysterious disappearance between 1891 and 1894, described in Sir Arthur Conan Doyle's The Final Problem, may have been for the reason that Holmes was being treated for his chronic overuse of cocaine, possibly by Freud. Musto concludes with an exposition of Freud's apparent fascination with and study of the effects of cocaine, and the use of cocaine in America.

The book purports to be an edited version of a recently discovered manuscript written in 1939 by the late John H. Watson, M.D. the alleged biographer and friend of Holmes. The book opens with a scene in which Watson learns that his friend, Holmes, is suffering from overuse of the drug cocaine. In an effort to rid Holmes of his habit, Watson engages the services of Holmes' brother, Mycroft, to trick Holmes into pursuing the notorious Professor Moriarty to Vienna, Austria where Sigmund Freud can hopefully cure Holmes of his addiction. Once in Vienna, Freud cures Holmes of the habit by use of hypnosis and the two then embark upon a Holmesian adventure involving political intrigue that culminates in a high-speed train chase across the Bavarian countryside. At the end of the book, we are told that Holmes' antipathy for Professor Moriarty stems from the fact that Moriarty, as Holmes' mathematics tutor, carried the sad news to Holmes that Holmes' father had killed his mother because of an illicit love affair. The book has become a bestseller and is the subject of a motion picture.

Musto contends that Meyer, and by implication the other defendants, copied both literal and non-literal portions of his article and thus violated his copyright. After oral argument on defendants' motion for judgment on the pleadings, the Court directed Musto's attorney to submit a memorandum outlining in detail the alleged copying and granted defendants' attorneys time to respond. Both parties have complied with the Court's directions. Since the parties have had ample opportunity to address themselves to the issues at hand and since the Court has been supplied with a copy of the article and the alleged infringing book, the Court, in its discretion, will consider defendants' motion for judgment on the pleadings as a motion for summary judgment pursuant to Rule 56. See Fed.R.Civ.P. 12(c).

Dr. Watson (Robert Duvall), Sherlock Holmes (Nicol Williamson) and Dr. Freud (Alan Arkin) in a scene from the Universal motion picture *The Seven-Per-Cent Solution*.

The Copyright Claims

In a copyright infringement action the plaintiff must first prove ownership of the copyright and then copying by the defendant. See Nimmer, The Law of Copyright § 141 (1976). Generally speaking, a copyright registration certificate constitutes prima facie evidence of ownership. 17 U.S.C. § 209; Edward B. Marks Music Corp. v. Wonnell, 61 F.Supp. 722 (S.D.N.Y.1945). Here, there does not appear to be any dispute between the parties that Musto is the owner of the copyright on the article.

Copying is generally established by proof of access by the defendant and substantial similarity between the works. Access is ordinarily defined as the opportunity to copy, Detective Comics, Inc. v. Bruns Publications, Inc., 28 F.Supp. 399 (S.D.N.Y.1939), modified, 111 F.2d 432 (2d Cir.1940) and, here again, there does not appear to be any dispute that Meyer had access to the article. In the book's acknowledgments, Meyer states that "[p]sychiatrist Dr. David F. Musto, in a brilliant essay published in Journal of the American Medical Association plausibly connected Holmes with Dr. Sigmund Freud through the all-important link of cocaine." Meyer also acknowledges that he incorporated into the book's plot the imaginative theories of other writers who have analyzed the works of Sir Arthur Conan Doyle and the exploits of his imaginary figure, Sherlock Holmes.

Substantial similarity, on the other hand, is a more difficult concept to define. See Nimmer, supra at § 143.1. Here, the parties vigorously contest the existence of substantial similarity between the two works.

Substantial Similarity

The Copyright Act does not protect against the borrowing of the ideas contained in a copyrighted work but only against the copying of the "expression of the idea" contained in such works. 17 U.S.C. § 1; see Holmes v. Hurst, 174 U.S. 82, 19 S.Ct. 606, 43 L.Ed. 904 (1899); Mazer v. Stein, 347 U.S. 201, 217, 74 S.Ct. 460, 98 L.Ed. 630 (1954); Dymow v. Bolton, 11 F.2d 690 (2d Cir.1926); MacDonald v. Du Maurier, 144 F.2d 696 (2d Cir.1944); Peter Pan Fabrics, Inc. v. Martin Weiner Corp., 274 F.2d 487 (2d Cir.1960); Fuld v. National Broadcasting Company, 390 F.Supp. 877 (S.D.N.Y.1975). While the distinction between an "idea" and "expression of an idea" is necessarily vague, Peter Pan Fabrics, Inc. v. Martin Weiner Corp., supra, 274 F.2d at 489, the courts over the years have developed approaches to the problem that have been commonly referred to as the "abstractions test," Nichols v. Universal Pictures Corp., 45 F.2d 119, 121 (2d Cir.), cert. denied, 282 U.S. 902, 51 S.Ct. 216, 75 L.Ed. 795 (1930); Burnett v. Lambino, 204 F.Supp. 327 (S.D.N.Y.1962), and the so-called "pattern" test. See Nimmer, supra at § 143.11; see also Sorenson and Sorenson, Re-examining the Traditional Legal Test of Literary Similarity: A Proposal for Content Analysis, 37 Corn.L.Q. 638 (1952).

Here, Musto appears to rely on the "pattern" test in alleging that Meyer copied original and non-historical elements from his article. For instance, Musto contends that the following elements in his article reappear in the book: (1) the reading public had been misled by Sir Arthur Conan Doyle in The Final Problem as to what really happened to Holmes during his three-year absence in Central Europe; (2) Watson diagnosed Holmes in The Final Problem as suffering from cocaine induced paranoia; (3) Watson does not believe Holmes' "fantastic" talk about Moriarty but instead is "pained" by it; (4) Watson writes a letter to Sigmund Freud in the magazine *Lancet* in an effort to secure help for Holmes; (5) Freud has withdrawn his initial advocacy of cocaine and is now treating victims of the drug; (6) Holmes' trip to Europe was not to follow Moriarty but to receive medical attention from Freud; (7) Freud successfully treated Holmes for cocaine addiction; and (8) in return for this help Holmes revealed to Freud his style of reasoning. While certain of these elements in the article do appear in the book, the similarity between the two appears to end there.

For instance, in the article, Musto attempts to connect episodes in Holmes' earlier career to the theory that Holmes was addicted to cocaine. Musto refers freely to Doyle's earlier writings, especially the opening scenes from The Final Problem, to support the theory that Holmes was suffering " * * * from the side effect of chronic cocaine use which often induces an extremely suspicious cast of mind and leads the sufferer to weave elaborate schemes to explain facts of whose significance only he is aware." (Article at 29). Musto then refers to the possibility that Holmes received treatment for his addiction from Freud before beginning a discussion of Freud's association with the drug. On the whole, it appears that the article is directed primarily to a discussion of the use and effects of cocaine in the 19th century with the added dimension of a connection between Freud and Holmes through the link of cocaine.

The book, on the other hand, attempts to set straight the record as to what really happened to Holmes during his alleged wanderings through Central Europe. While borrowing heavily at the beginning and at times copying *verbatim* from Doyle's The Final Problem, Meyer links Holmes to cocaine to introduce the setting of another Holmesian adventure, only this time with Sigmund Freud in Central Europe. The adventure starts out with Holmes following Professor Moriarty from London to Vienna with the aid of Toby, the remarkable bloodhound, who picks up an enduring trail of vanilla extract. The trail leads Holmes to the home of Sigmund Freud where Holmes realizes that he has been tricked by his friend, Watson. After a somewhat testy exchange of mental prowess with Freud, Holmes finally succumbs to Freud's arduous and painful cure of cocaine addiction. Holmes remains in a depressed state of mind following the cure until Freud encroaches upon him to come to the aid of Nancy Osborn Slater Von Leinsdorf, the American wife of Baron Von Leinsdorf. The mystery is rather elementary by Holmesian standards, but it provides a challenge to Freud's deductive reasoning and stimulates Holmes sufficiently so that he soon returns to his normal self.

Musto contends that the literal similarities between the book and his article are such that it appears that Meyer copied passages *verbatim*, including the following:

Musto	Meyer
"It struck me, records Watson that he (Holmes) was looking paler and thinner than usual." (Musto p. 29, col. 1, par. 1)	"He (Holmes) seemed thinner and paler than usual * * *" (Meyer p. 28, line 9)
"You have probably never heard of Professor Moriarty, said he. Never. Aye, there's the genius and the wonder of the thing! he cried. The man pervades London and no one has heard of him." (Musto, p. 29, col. 1, par. 4)	"Have you ever heard of Professor Moriarty?, he asked. * * * Never. Aye, there's the genius and the wonder of the thing! * * * The man pervades London * * * and no one has heard of him." (Meyer, p. 29–30)

Musto concedes, however, that he borrowed the above quotations for his article from Sir Arthur Conan Doyle's The Final Problem which is in the public domain. Nevertheless, he contends that he is protected by his copyright as against an infringer who copies primary material from a secondary source, and that in any event the Court must presume against the defendants, not only access but copying of all common material, including public domain matter. See MacDonald v. Du Maurier, supra.

The protection afforded by a copyright extends generally only to those elements of a work which are original. See 17 U.S.C. § 1; Chamberlin v. Uris Sales Corp., 150 F.2d 512 (2d Cir.1945). If a copyrighted work is derivative in the sense that it is based in whole or part upon a prior or underlying work, the copyright on the derivative work will not necessarily protect the underlying work. If, for instance, the underlying work is in the public domain, as is Sir Arthur Conan Doyle's The Final Problem, the copyright on the derivative work will not protect the underlying work. See Nimmer, supra at § 41; American Code Co. v. Bensinger, 282 F. 829 (2d Cir.1922).

Assuming there was direct copying by Meyer of portions of Musto's article, see Dellar v. Samuel Goldwyn, Inc., 104 F.2d 661, 662 (2d Cir.1939); Collins v. Metro-Goldwyn Pictures Corp., 106 F.2d 83 (1939), it does not appear that the book contains anything similar other than the "idea" that Holmes was addicted to cocaine and that his addiction was cured by Sigmund Freud.[1] Certainly there is no similarity between the article and the book as to the objective or type of reader appeal, the fashioning of a plot, the delineation of characters, or the literary skill employed to reach the final objective. See MacDonald v. Du Maurier, supra, 144 F.2d at 702 (dissenting opinion). Musto's article, although

---

1. Holmes' use of cocaine was described by Sir Arthur Conan Doyle in The Yellow Face.

somewhat tongue-in-cheek, was written for a professional journal with a bent toward informing his readership of the uses of cocaine in the 19th century. Meyer's book, meanwhile, was written as a revised version of an earlier Doyle story on the adventures of Sherlock Holmes with a view toward capturing the imagination of Holmes' followers. Since ideas and basic plots, or even isolated incidents are not protected by the copyright laws, 17 U.S.C. § 1; Holmes v. Hurst, supra; Dymow v. Bolton, supra; Nichols v. Universal Pictures Corp., supra; Shipman v. R.K.O. Radio Pictures, 100 F.2d 533 (2d Cir.1938), it would appear that Musto's claim must fail.

The Instant Motion

Motions for judgment on the pleadings or summary judgment in copyright infringement cases have been generally frowned upon in this Circuit, Dellar v. Samuel Goldwyn, Inc., supra; MacDonald v. Du Maurier, supra; Arnstein v. Porter, 154 F.2d 464 (2d Cir.1946). However, such motions may be granted for the defendant if, after assuming copying, the Court finds that any similarity between the works is insubstantial or that undisputed facts raise a complete defense as a matter of law. Nimmer, supra at § 138; See, Fuld v. National Broadcasting Co., supra; Buckler v. Paramount Pictures, Inc., 133 F.Supp. 223 (S.D.N.Y.1955); see also, Meeropol v. Nizer, 417 F.Supp. 1201 (S.D.N.Y.1976).

Here, the similarity between the article and the book is limited to the idea that Sir Arthur Conan Doyle misled the reading public in The Final Problem as to the real activities of Sherlock Holmes in Central Europe, that Holmes was really addicted to cocaine at the time, and that Holmes' friend, Watson, tricked Holmes into following Professor Moriarty to Vienna so that he could be cured of his habit by Sigmund Freud. Even assuming the "idea" of Holmes' cocaine addiction was copied by Meyer from Musto's article without any reference to Sir Arthur Conan Doyle's earlier works, the Court finds as a matter of law that the copying involved only an "idea" and not an "expression of an idea" and therefore is not actionable under the copyright laws. See Mazer v. Stein, supra; Baker v. Selden, 101 U.S. 99 (1879); Reyher v. Children's Television Workshop, 533 F.2d 87 (2d Cir.1976); Fuld v. National Broadcasting Co., supra.

Since the defendants have a complete defense as a matter of law with respect to Musto's claim of infringement by the publication of the book, defendants' motion for judgment on the pleadings will be granted as to the first claim contained in Musto's complaint.

The second claim relates to the motion picture film which has not been furnished to the Court. Accordingly, defendants' motion for judgment on the pleadings as to the second claim is denied without prejudice.

Settle judgment on notice.

Questions

1. Do you agree that the similarity between Musto's and Meyer's respective works is only of "idea" and not of "expression"? Is there any contradiction between the court's description of the "idea" which the two works have in common (as contained near the end of the opinion) and the earlier listed eight "elements" which the court appears to acknowledge may be found in both works? Do those eight elements, when taken together, constitute "expression" rather than "idea"?

2. Does there appear to be greater or less similarity in this case as compared with the degree of similarity in the *Krofft* case? If *Musto* and *Krofft* are irreconcilable, which better applies the idea-expression dichotomy?

C. THE DEFENSE OF FAIR USE

Note *

In determining whether given conduct constitutes copyright infringement, the courts have long recognized that certain acts of copying are defensible as "fair use". Section 107 of the Copyright Act of 1976 for the first time accorded express statutory recognition of this judge-made rule of reason. However, this codification was "intended to restate the present [i.e., pre-1978] judicial doctrine of fair use, not to change, narrow, or enlarge it in any way."[1] Therefore, in determining the scope and limits of fair use, reference must be made to pre- as well as post-1978 cases. Still, some clarification of this most obscure doctrine, which has been called "the most troublesome in the whole law of copyright,"[2] may be derived from the text of Section 107 in the current Copyright Act.

Before turning to this statutory gloss, certain preliminary matters should be considered. It is sometimes suggested that fair use is predicated on the implied or tacit consent of the author. This is manifestly a fiction since a restrictive legend on a work prohibiting copying in whole or in part gives no greater protection than the copyright notice standing alone. Moreover, the fact that a copier acknowledges the source of the copied material does not make a fair use of what is otherwise a substantial taking. Fair use is said to constitute an issue of fact,[3] but what facts will be sufficient to raise this defense in any given case is not easily answered. A part of the difficulty in comprehending the limits of fair use would appear to lie in the broad and to some extent contradictory manner in which the courts defined the concept prior to codification in the current Act. It has been said that an insubstantial similarity was not actionable and was therefore a "fair use."[4] Under this formulation fair use is simply the opposite of substantial similarity, so that any similarity which

---

* Nimmer on Copyright, § 13.05.

1. H.Rep., p. 66.

2. Dellar v. Samuel Goldwyn, Inc., 104 F.2d 661 (2d Cir.1939).

3. Eisenschiml v. Fawcett Publications, Inc., 246 F.2d 598 (7th Cir.1957); see New York Tribune, Inc. v. Otis & Co., 39 F.Supp. 67 (S.D.N.Y.1941); Holdredge v. Knight Publishing Corp., 214 F.Supp. 921 (S.D.Cal. 1963). But cf. Time, Inc. v. Bernard Geis Assocs., 293 F.Supp. 130 (S.D.N.Y.1968).

4. See Twentieth Century-Fox Film Corp. v. Stonesifer, 140 F.2d 579 (9th Cir. 1944); Mathews Conveyor Co. v. Palmer-Bee Co., 135 F.2d 73 (6th Cir.1943); Meredith Corp. v. Harper & Row, Publishers, Inc., 378 F.Supp. 686 (S.D.N.Y.1974) aff'd 500 F.2d 1221 (2d Cir.1974).

is not substantial by definition is a fair use. Other courts suggested that fair use arises when there is copying of the theme or ideas, but not of the expression of ideas.[5] This too equates fair use with the absence of substantial similarity, but in the narrower context of the idea-expression dichotomy. At least prior to 1978, it was certainly possible, as did the foregoing definitions in whole or in part, to employ the term fair use as a label for similarity which is not

"What is 'fair use'?"

Bion Smalley

[5]. See Sheldon v. Metro-Goldwyn Pictures Corp., 81 F.2d 49 (2d Cir.1936); Shipman v. RKO, 100 F.2d 533 (2d Cir.1938); Holdredge v. Knight Publishing Corp., 214 F.Supp. 921 (S.D.Cal.1963).

substantial. It was possible, but not very helpful since this approach merely restated the problem of determining substantial similarity, and ignores what may be regarded as the crucial problem of fair use. That problem arises where it is established by admission or by the preponderance of the evidence that the defendant has copied sufficiently from the plaintiff so as to cross the line of substantial similarity. The result must necessarily constitute an infringement unless the defendant is rendered immune from liability because the particular use which he has made of plaintiff's material is a "fair use." In this more meaningful sense fair use is a defense not because of the absence of substantial similarity but rather despite the fact that the similarity is substantial. It is in this sense that the term "fair use" was usually employed in the pre-1978 cases, and it is in this sense that the term is used in Sec. 107 of the current Act.

Strictly speaking, Sec. 107 does not attempt to define "fair use." Rather, it lists "the factors to be considered" for the purpose of "determining whether the use made of a work in any particular case is a fair use." It does not, and does not purport, to provide a rule which may automatically be applied in deciding whether any particular use is "fair." This is so for several reasons. First, the factors contained in Sec. 107 are merely by way of example, and are not necessarily an exhaustive enumeration. This means that factors other than those enumerated may prove to have a bearing upon the determination of fair use.[6] In addition, Sec. 107 gives no guidance as to the relative weight to be ascribed to each of the listed factors. Finally, each of these factors taken alone is defined in only the most general terms, so that the courts are left with almost complete discretion in determining whether any given factor is present in any particular case. Nevertheless, the Sec. 107 factors do offer some guidelines in the determination of fair use, and must therefore be considered. They consist of:

"(1) the purpose and character of the use, including whether such use is of a commercial nature or is for nonprofit educational purposes;

(2) the nature of the copyrighted work;

(3) the amount and substantiality of the portion used in relation to the copyrighted work as a whole; and

(4) the effect of the use upon the potential market for or value of the copyrighted work."

In studying the cases which follow the student should determine whether and to what extent each of the above factors was instrumental in determining the result.

Collateral Reference

Seltzer, *Exemptions and Fair Use In Copyright*, (1978).

BENNY v. LOEW'S INCORPORATED

United States Court of Appeals, Ninth Circuit, 1956.
239 F.2d 532.

Before BONE, MCALLISTER, and CHAMBERS, CIRCUIT JUDGES.

---

6. For other useful lists of fair use factors see Cohen, "Fair Use in the Law of Copyright," ASCAP Copyright Law Symposium No. 6, 43 (1955); Latman, "Fair Use of Copyrighted Works," Copyright Office Study No. 14; Schulman, "Fair Use and the Revision of the Copyright Act," 53 Iowa L.Rev. 832, 833 (1968), quoted with approval in Tennessee Fabricating Co. v. Moultrie Mfg. Co., 421 F.2d 279, 283 (5th Cir.1970).

MCALLISTER, CIRCUIT JUDGE. Patrick Hamilton, an English author and a British subject, some time prior to December, 1938, conceived and wrote an original play entitled, "Gas Light." It was published and protected by copyright in February, 1939. Shortly thereafter, it was publicly performed in England, first, in Richmond, and later, in London. On December 5, 1941, it was produced as a play in New York under the name, "Angel Street," and had a successful run of 1,295 consecutive performances, extending over a period of more than 37 months.

On October 7, 1942, the exclusive motion picture rights for "Gas Light" were acquired by Loew's, Inc., better known under its trade name of Metro-Goldwyn-Mayer.

Loew's spent $2,458,000 in the production and distribution of the motion picture photoplay of "Gas Light." The actual making of the film extended over a period of more than two and a half years.

In producing the motion picture, Loew's acquired the services of three great artists in the cinema field, Charles Boyer, Ingrid Bergman, and Joseph Cotton.

The photoplay, "Gas Light," was exhibited in the United States and fifty-six foreign countries. Approximately fifty-two million persons paid admission to see it. The gross receipts in rentals for the play amounted to $4,857,000.

There is no question of the right of the dramatic work to protection under the copyright laws of both Great Britain and the United States.

On October 14, 1945, Jack Benny, a successful performer in the field of comedy, after securing Loew's consent to present a parody of "Gas Light" on radio, caused to be written, produced, performed, and broadcast over a national radio network a fifteen-minute burlesque of the play. In preparing the program, the radio writers for Benny had access to the acting script of the motion picture, "Gas Light."

More than six years later, on January 27, 1952, the Columbia Broadcasting System caused to be written and produced a half-hour-long television show burlesquing "Gas Light," with Jack Benny in the leading role. It was broadcast over the Columbia Broadcasting System network and was "sponsored" by the American Tobacco Company. Neither Mr. Benny nor the Columbia Broadcasting System nor the American Tobacco Company secured consent from Loew's or Mr. Hamilton to publish and broadcast the television burlesque, or, as it is sometimes called, the parody.

Immediately after the presentation of the television show, Loew's dispatched a telegram to the Columbia Broadcasting System, notifying that company that Loew's was the owner of the exclusive rights of production and recording of the play, "Gas Light," and adaptations thereof by means of talking films, sound tracks, and television; that Columbia had used substantial portions of the play in its television

Charles Boyer and Ingrid Bergman in plaintiff's *Gas Light*.

program; and that Loew's intended to enforce its rights against infringement. A short time thereafter, counsel for Columbia replied to the above telegram, informing Loew's that its burlesque appropriation of the play, "Gas Light," was a "fair use" of the dramatic work, and that Columbia had the right to parody it as it did in the television show. Loew's, in turn, informed Columbia that the burlesque television show constituted an infringement of the copyright of "Gas Light"; and when Columbia prepared for a similar presentation over several television channels, Loew's filed this action, and secured a temporary restraining order.

Upon a trial of the issues, the district court found that the Benny television play was copied in substantial part from Loew's motion picture photoplay, "Gas Light"; that the portion so copied was a substantial part of the copyrighted material in such photoplay; and that the Benny television presentation was an infringement of the copyrighted photoplay, "Gas Light." The court, accordingly, granted injunctive relief, restraining the showing of the television play, all of which appears in the able and comprehensive opinion by Judge James M. Carter, reported in 131 F.Supp. 165.

On review, the chief contention advanced by appellants is that the burlesque presentation of "Gas Light" was a "fair use" of appellees' photoplay; that, although the play was copyrighted, and neither Benny, Columbia, nor the American Tobacco Company had received any consent on the part of the copyright owners to adapt the play in the way they did, nevertheless, they had the right to adapt the original copyrighted dramatic work of the author of the play and of the photoplay version as a burlesque, and to present, vend, and appropriate it thus, for their own profit.

Appellees submit that the Copyright Act insures to the copyright owners the exclusive right to any lawful use of their property, whereby they may get a profit out of it. They further submit that there is no doctrine of fair use which justifies the appropriation of substantial copyrighted material of a dramatic work without the consent of the copyright owner, whether such appropriation is made for the purpose of pirating the work openly, or under the guise of a burlesque or a parody.

In considering the law and its application to this case, the facts themselves are most important. The play is a remarkable dramatic production. As outlined by appellees and somewhat supplemented by the record, the play tells the story of a man who sets out upon a deliberate plan to drive his wife insane. He is motivated in this endeavor by the need of having access to a house which was inherited by his wife and in which they live. Some years prior, he had murdered the aunt of his wife for the sake of some valuable jewels which he had intended to steal, but in which he had been frustrated. His method of achieving his objective of finding the jewels without the wife's knowledge, and, at the same time, avoiding her suspicion, is to keep her attention diverted by inducing in her the belief that she is having hallucinations, suffering great lapses of memory, and gradually losing her mind. He does this by abstracting, without her knowledge, articles which he had entrusted to his wife, and by removing a portrait from the wall, making her believe that she had been responsible for the misplacement of the articles and the removal of the picture, of which she had lost all recollection. He fosters such a belief in her, in part, by causing the servants to bear witness that they did not remove the portrait. The suspense aroused by the picture is focused upon whether he will succeed in his scheme of finding the jewels and driving his wife insane. He fails, because of the intervention of a detective from Scotland Yard who, suspicious of the husband's conduct, has become interested in, and then obviously enamoured, of the heroine. The detective apprehends the husband at the climax of the plot, binds him to a chair in his own home to secure his arrest, and then reveals the truth, which he has learned, to the wife. At her request, she is given an opportunity to talk to the husband, who attempts once again, through his personal charm, to subdue her to his will. She, however, resists. In this scene, at her husband's request, she procures a knife, which he has kept nearby. The suspense is heightened by the question whether she will use the knife to cut her husband's bonds, as he has asked her to do, or whether she has come to a determination to kill him. She does neither, but contents herself with denouncing him, and turning him over to the police.

A comparison of appellees' "Gas Light" and the Columbia television show discloses the following: * * * If the material taken by appellants from "Gas Light" is eliminated, there are left only a few gags, and some disconnected and incoherent dialogue. If the television play were presented without appellants' contribution, there would be left the plot, story, principal incidents, and same sequence of events as in the photoplay.

A review of the record, a comparison of the scripts of appellees' photoplay and appellants' television play, and a viewing of the motion picture photoplay and the television play, as projected upon the screen—all convince us that the findings of fact of the district court that appellants copied the photoplay in substantial part, and that the part so copied was a substantial part of the television play and of the material in appellees' photoplay, are clearly supported by the evidence.

Appellants' chief defense is that the use which they made of appellees' photoplay in their television play was a fair use, by reason of the fact that the material which they appropriated from the motion picture, "Gas Light," was used in the creation of a burlesque, and that by reason of such circumstance, they are not guilty of infringement.

The so-called doctrine of fair use of copyrighted material appears in cases in federal courts having to do with compilations, listings, digests, and the like, and is concerned with the use made of prior compilations, listings, and digests. In certain of these cases, it is held that a writer may be guided by earlier copyrighted works, may consult original authorities, and may use those which he considers applicable in support of his own original text; but even in such cases, it is generally held that if he appropriate the fruits of another's labors, without alteration, and without independent research, he violates the rights of the copyright owner. In these instances, as has been said, there are certain to be considerable resemblances, "just as there must be between the work of two persons compiling a directory, or a dictionary, or a guide for railroad trains, or for automobile trips. In such cases the question is whether the writer has availed himself of the earlier writer's work without doing any independent work himself." Chautauqua School of Nursing v. National School of Nursing, 2 Cir., 238 F. 151, 153. See also cases digested in 18 F.Dig., Copyrights, Section 55. But up to the time of the present controversy, no federal court, in any adjudication, has supposed that there was a doctrine of fair use applicable to copying the substance of a dramatic work, and presenting it, with few variations, as a burlesque. The fact that a serious dramatic work is copied practically verbatim, and then presented with actors walking on their hands or with other grotesqueries, does not avoid infringement of the copyright. "Counsel have not disclosed a single authority, nor have we been able to find one, which lends any support to the proposition that wholesale copying and publication of copyrighted material can *ever* be fair use." Leon v. Pacific Telephone & Telegraph Co., 9 Cir., 91 F.2d 484, 486. (Emphasis supplied.) Whether the audience is gripped with tense emotion in viewing the original drama, or, on the other hand, laughs at the burlesque, does not absolve the copier. Otherwise, any individual or corporation could appropriate, in its entirety, a serious and famous dramatic work, protected by copyright, merely by introducing comic devices of clownish garb, or movement, or facial distortion of the actors, and presenting it as burlesque. One person has the sole right to do this—the copyright owner, inasmuch as, under Title 17 U.S.C.A. § 1, he has the exclusive right to make any other version of the work that he desires. He can have it read or sung or danced or pantomimed or burlesqued, because, in the language of the statute, he has the sole right to "exhibit, perform, represent, produce, or reproduce it in any manner or by any method whatsoever."

The fact that it has been Mr. Benny's custom to present from time to time, his, or the Columbia Broadcasting System's "version" of various dramatic works during the past twenty-five years, is no defense to this action for infringement of copyright. Appellants cannot copy and present another's dramatic work as they have in the instance before us, unless they receive the consent of the copyright owner.

An apparently alternative contention that the presentation of the burlesque was, in effect, literary or dramatic criticism and, therefore, not subject to an action for infringement of copyright, would seem to be a parody upon the meaning of criticism.

The record in this case includes a beguiling dissertation on the history of the drama, of English literature, of parody, and of burlesque, by Dr. Frank C. Baxter, a widely recognized and eminent authority in this field of study. Briefs of appellants' counsel, too, disclose a wealth of literary appreciation. However, there is only a single decisive point in the case: One cannot copy the substance of another's work without infringing his copyright. A burlesque presentation of such a copy is no defense to an action for infringement of copyright. As was said by the district judge, a "parodized or burlesque taking is to be treated no differently from any other appropriation; that, as in all other cases of alleged taking, the issue becomes first one of fact, i.e., what was taken and how substantial was the taking; and if it is determined that there was a substantial taking, infringement exists." 131 F.Supp. 183.

The finding of the district court that appellants had copied a substantial part of appellees' photoplay is clearly supported by the evidence. The judgment is affirmed upon the findings of fact and conclusions of law of the district court and for the reasons set forth in the opinion of Judge James M. Carter.[a]

WALT DISNEY PRODUCTIONS v. THE AIR PIRATES

United States Court of Appeals, Ninth Circuit, 1978.
581 F.2d 751.

[The facts, and earlier portion of this opinion are set forth at p. 80 supra in the section on character protection.]

B. Infringement and Fair Use

Defendants do not contend that their admitted copying was not substantial enough to constitute an infringement, and it is plain that copying a comic book character's graphic image constitutes copying to an extent sufficient to justify a finding of infringement. See 2 Nimmer on Copyright § 143.12; see generally Sid & Marty Krofft Television Productions, Inc. v. McDonald's Corp., 562 F.2d 1157 (9th Cir.1977); Henry Holt & Co. Inc. v. Liggett & Myers Tobacco Co., 23 F.Supp. 302 (E.D.Pa.1938). Defendants instead claim that this infringement should be excused through the application of the fair use defense, since it purportedly is a parody of Disney's cartoons.

At least since this Court's controversial ruling in Benny v. Loew's Inc., 239 F.2d 532 (9th Cir.1956), affirmed by an equally divided Court, 356 U.S. 43, the standards for applying the fair use defense in parody cases, like the standards for applying fair use in other contexts, have been a source of considerable attention and dispute. See 2 Nimmer on Copyright § 145. As a general matter, while some commentators have urged that the fair use defense depends only on whether the infringing work fills the demand for the original (see, e.g., Note, Piracy or Parody: Never the Twain, 38 U.Colo.L.Rev. 550 (1966); see generally 2 Nimmer on Copyright § 145), this Court and others have also consistently focused on the substantiality of the taking. See e.g., Benny v. Loew's Inc., 239 F.2d 532 (9th Cir.1956), affirmed by an equally divided Court, 356 U.S. 43; Rosemont Enterprises, Inc. v. Random House, Inc., 366 F.2d 303 (2d Cir.1966), certiorari denied, 385 U.S. 1009; 17 U.S.C.A. § 107(3) (codifying old law). But cf. Williams & Wilkins Co. v. United States, 487 F.2d 1345 (Ct.Cl.1973), affirmed by an equally divided Court, 420 U.S. 376.

In inquiring into the substantiality of the taking, the district court read our *Benny* opinion to hold that any substantial copying by a

---

[a.] On writ of certiorari, the U.S. Supreme Court affirmed by an equally divided court, with Mr. Justice Douglas not participating. 356 U.S. 43 (1958).

defendant, combined with the fact that the portion copied constituted a substantial part of the defendant's work, automatically precluded the fair use defense. That such a strict reading of *Benny* was unjustified is indicated first by the fact that it would essentially make any fair use defense fruitless. If the substantiality of the taking necessary to satisfy the first half of that test is no different from the substantiality necessary to constitute an infringement, then the *Benny* test would be reduced to an absurdity, covering any infringement except those falling within the much-criticized and abandoned exception for cases in which the part copied was not a substantial part of the defendant's work. Compare Rosemont Enterprises, Inc. v. Random House, Inc., 256 F.Supp. 55 (S.D.N.Y.1966), reversed on other grounds, 366 F.2d 303 (2d Cir.1966), certiorari denied, 385 U.S. 1009; see 2 Nimmer on Copyright § 143.2.

The language in *Benny* concerning the substantiality of copying can be given a reading much more in keeping with the context of that case and the established principles at the time of that case if the opinion is understood as setting a threshold that eliminates from the fair use defense copying that is virtually complete or almost verbatim. Accord 2 Nimmer on Copyright § 145. It was an established principle at the time of *Benny* that such verbatim copying precluded resort to the fair use defense. See, e.g., Leon v. Pacific Telephone & Telegraph Co., 91 F.2d 484 (9th Cir.1937).[12] Moreover, the *Benny* facts presented a particularly appropriate instance to apply that settled principle. As the *Benny* district court found, Benny's "Autolight" tracked the parodied "Gas Light" in almost every respect: the locale and period, the setting, characters, story points, incidents, climax and much of the dialogue all were found to be identical. 131 F.Supp. 165, 171. In this context, *Benny* should not be read as taking the drastic step of virtually turning the test for fair use into the test for infringement. See Columbia Pictures Corp. v. National Broadcasting Co., 137 F.Supp. 348 (S.D.Cal.1955). To do otherwise would be to eliminate fair use as a defense except perhaps for those infringers who added an extra act at the end of their parody.

Thus *Benny* should stand only as a threshold test that eliminates near-verbatim copying. In the absence of near-verbatim copying, other courts have analyzed the substantiality of copying by a parodist by asking whether the parodist has appropriated a greater amount of the original work than is necessary to "recall or conjure up" the object of his satire. Berlin v. E.C. Publications, Inc., 329 F.2d 541 (2d Cir.1964), certiorari denied, 379 U.S. 822; see Columbia Pictures Corp. v. National Broadcasting Co., 137 F.Supp. 348 (S.D.Cal.1955).[13]

In order to facilitate application of either the *Benny* threshold test or the *Berlin* test, it is important to determine what are the relevant

---

12. In fact, *Leon* was cited favorably in *Benny*. 239 F.2d at 536.

13. In so construing *Benny*, we necessarily disagree with its dictum that a parody is treated no differently than any other taking. See Berlin v. E.C. Publications, Inc., 329 F.2d 541 (2d Cir.1964), certiorari denied, 379 U.S. 822.

The Air Pirates' version of Mickey and Minnie.

parts of each work that are compared in analyzing similarity. Plaintiff assumes in its brief that the graphic depiction, or pictorial illustration, is separately copyrightable as a component part, so that a verbatim copy of the depiction alone would satisfy the *Benny* test. Defendants proceed on the assumption that comparing their characters with plaintiff's involves a comparison not only of the physical image but also of the character's personality, pattern of speech, abilities, and other traits. Apparently this issue has not been addressed previously, and neither position is without merit. On the one hand, since an illustration in a book or catalogue can be copyrighted separately (see, e.g., Lin-Brook Builders Hardware v. Gertler, 352 F.2d 298 (9th Cir.1965)), it might follow that an illustration in a comic strip is entitled to the same protection by virtue of Section 3 of the former Copyright Act (note 7 supra). On the other hand, to a different extent than in other illustrations, a cartoon character's image is intertwined with its personality and other traits, so that the "total concept and feel" (Roth Greeting Cards v. United Card Co., 429 F.2d 1106, 1110 (9th Cir.1970)) of even the component part cannot be limited to the image itself.[14]

14. While not explicitly noting these competing arguments or focusing on whether an image is a protectable component part, most of the cases dealing with cartoon characters have considered the character's personality and other traits in addition to its image. See, e.g., Detective Comics, Inc. v. Bruns Publications, Inc., 111 F.2d 432 (2d Cir.1940); Warner Brothers Inc. v. Film Ventures International, 403 F.Supp. 522, 525 (C.D.Cal.1975). See also Sid & Marty Krofft Television v. McDonald's Corp., 562 F.2d 1157, 1169 (9th Cir.1977); 1 Nimmer on Copyright § 30; Note, The Protection Afforded Literary and Cartoon Characters Through Trademark, Unfair Competition and Copyright, 68 Harv.L.Rev. 349 (1954). In what appears to be the only two cases that have viewed a character only as an image (King Features Syndicate v. Fleischer, 299 F. 533 (2d Cir.1924); Fleischer v. Freundlich, 73 F.2d 276 (2d Cir.1936)), the alleged copying was of a doll, which could have only an image and no conceptual character traits; therefore the issue of whether the comic character's depiction included a personality was not raised.

We need not decide which of these views is correct, or whether this copying was so substantial to satisfy the *Benny* test, because it is our view that defendants took more than is allowed even under the *Berlin* test as applied to both the conceptual and physical aspects of the characters. In evaluating how much of a taking was necessary to recall or conjure up the original, it is first important to recognize that given the widespread public recognition of the major characters involved here, such as Mickey Mouse and Donald Duck, in comparison with other characters very little would have been necessary to place Mickey Mouse and his image in the minds of the readers. Second, when the medium involved is a comic book, a recognizable caricature is not difficult to draw, so that an alternative that involves less copying is more likely to be available than if a speech, for instance, is parodied. Also significant is the fact that the essence of this parody did not focus on how the characters looked, but rather parodied their personalities, their wholesomeness and their innocence.[15] Thus arguably defendants' copying could have been justified as necessary more easily if they had paralleled closely (with a few significant twists) Disney characters and their actions in a manner that conjured up the particular elements of the innocence of the characters that were to be satirized. While greater license may be necessary under those circumstances, here the copying of the graphic image appears to have no other purpose than to track Disney's work as a whole as closely as possible.

Defendants' assertion that they copied no more than necessary appears to be based on an affidavit, which stated that "the humorous effect of parody is best achieved when at first glance the material appears convincingly to be the original, and upon closer examination is discovered to be quite something else" (Br. 20–21). The short answer to this assertion, which would also justify substantially verbatim copying, is that when persons are parodying a copyrighted work, the constraints of the existing precedent do not permit them to take as much of a component part as they need to make the "best parody." Instead, their desire to make the "best parody" is balanced against the rights of the copyright owner in his original expressions. That balance has been struck at giving the parodist what is necessary to conjure up the original, and in the absence of a special need for accuracy (compare Meeropol v. Nizer, 560 F.2d 1061, 1071 (2d Cir.1977)), certiorari denied, 434 U.S. 1013, that standard was exceeded here. By copying the images in their entirety, defendants took more than was necessary to place firmly in the reader's mind the parodied work and those specific attributes that are to be satirized. See Netterville, Parody, Mimicry and Humorous Commentary, 35 So.Cal.L.Rev. 225, 238 (1962).

---

15. In making this distinction, we do not regard it as fatal, as some courts have done (see, e.g., Walt Disney Productions v. Mature Pictures Corp., 389 F.Supp. 1397 (S.D. N.Y.1975)), that the "Air Pirates" were parodying life and society in addition to parodying the Disney characters. Such an effect is almost an inherent aspect of any parody. To the extent that the Disney characters are not also an object of the parody, however, the need to conjure them up would be reduced if not eliminated.

Because the amount of defendant's copying exceeded permissible levels, summary judgment was proper. See Berlin v. E.C. Publications, 329 F.2d 541 (2d Cir.1964), certiorari denied, 379 U.S. 822. While other factors in the fair use calculus may not be sufficient by themselves to preclude the fair use defense, this and other courts have accepted the traditional American rule that excessive copying precludes fair use. See e.g., Benny v. Loew's Inc., 239 F.2d 532 (9th Cir.1956), affirmed by an equally divided Court, 356 U.S. 43; Walt Disney Productions v. Mature Pictures Corp., 389 F.Supp. 1397 (S.D.N.Y.1975); see generally Berlin v. E.C. Publications, 329 F.2d 541 (2d Cir.1964), certiorari denied, 379 U.S. 822.[16]

[On the First Amendment defense, the court acknowledged that there is "some tension between the First Amendment and the Copyright Act", but held the defense to be inapplicable "in light of our recent decision in Sid & Marty Krofft Television Productions, Inc. v. McDonald's Corp., 562 F.2d 1157, 1170 (9th Cir.1977)." The *Krofft* opinion is set forth infra.]

Judgment affirmed as to copyright infringement * * *.

Questions

1. Does the "recall or conjure up" test mean that as long as the copying is less than "near-verbatim", the degree of similarity that may be permissible under the doctrine of fair use is greater where the copier is engaged in a satire of the plaintiff's work? Why should a greater amount of copying be permitted where the defendant's work is satirical? Is it because satire is a socially useful art which should be encouraged? But if there are many non-satirical works of equal or greater social utility, why should satirical works be favored in this manner? Is it because it is more difficult to obtain a consensual license from an author where the licensee intends to parody or satirize the author's work?

2. What criteria should a court apply in determining in any particular case how much copying a satirist need engage in in order to "recall or conjure up" the plaintiff's work? Is this a workable standard?

3. Is the court of the view that copying of "comic book" characters may more likely constitute fair use if the character traits as well as appearance are copied? Do you agree? Should this be true if, but only if, the copying is for purposes of satire?

ELSMERE MUSIC, INC. v. NATIONAL BROADCASTING CO.

482 F.Supp. 741.
District Court, Southern District of New York, 1980.

---

16. This exclusion of other factors is not a drastic step, since the level of permissible copying selected in *Benny* was set with a recognition of and as a compromise with other concerns such as the nature and character of the use.

Sec. C   THE DEFENSE OF FAIR USE   379

GOETTEL, DISTRICT JUDGE:

In the dark days of 1977, when the City of New York teetered on the brink of bankruptcy and its name had become synonymous with sin, there came forth upon the land a message of hope. On the television screens of America there appeared the image of a top-hatted Broadway showgirl, backed by an advancing phalanx of dancers, chanting:

"I-I-I-I-I-I Love New Yo-o-o-o-o-o-rk!"

Repeated again and again (to musical accompaniment), with increasing intensity throughout the commercial, this slogan was to become the theme for an extensive series of advertisements that were to bring the nation assurances from the stars of Broadway, ranging from Dracula to the Cowardly Lion, that all was well, and that they too *loved* New York.

As an ad campaign for an ailing city, it was an unparalleled success. Crucial to the campaign was the brief but exhilarating musical theme written by Steve Karmen who had previously authored a number of highly successful commercial jingles, including "You Can Take Salem Out of the Country" and "Weekends Were Made for Michelob." While the "I Love New York" song was written for the New York State Department of Commerce, its initial use and identity focused on New York City.

The success of this campaign did not go unnoticed in the entertainment world. On May 20, 1978, the popular weekly variety program "Saturday Night Live" ("SNL") performed a comedy sketch over defendant National Broadcasting Company's network. In this sketch the cast of SNL, portraying the mayor and the members of the Chamber of Commerce of the biblical city of Sodom, are seen discussing Sodom's poor public image with out of towners, and the effect this was having on the tourist trade. In an attempt to recast the City's image in a more positive light, a new advertising campaign emphasizing the less sensational aspects of Sodom nightlife is unveiled. As the highlight of this campaign the song "I Love Sodom" is sung *a cappella* by a chorus line of three SNL regulars to the tune of "I Love New York," with the words "I Love Sodom" repeated three times.

The plaintiff, Elsmere Music, Inc., the copyright proprietor of "I Love New York," did not see the humor of the sketch. It sued for copyright infringement.

The parties have now, pursuant to Fed.R.Civ.P. 56(b), cross moved for summary judgment. As no dispute exists as to the facts giving rise to this action, but only as to the legal consequences, the Court believes this case to be appropriate for summary disposition. See SEC v. Research Automation Corp., 585 F.2d 31 (2d Cir.1978).

The defendant admits that its sketch and song were intended to resemble the original "I Love New York" advertising campaign and jingle. It claims, however, that the use made of the plaintiff's melody was no more than was necessary to create an effective parody, and that as such was, at worst, a *de minimis* infringement. Alternatively, the defendant asserts that, even if the infringement was more than *de minimis*, it still did not constitute an actionable copyright violation since such use was permitted as a fair use under section 101 of the 1976 Copyright Act, 17 U.S.C. § 107.

The plaintiff contests these assertions. It contends that the use made was not *de minimis*, and in fact was far more extensive than was necessary to conjure up the original. In addition, it claims that the singing of "I Love Sodom" did not constitute a fair use since it was part of a sketch that parodied New York City and the problems it was having, rather than one parodying New York State, its advertising campaign, or the song "I Love New York" itself.

In its entirety, the original song "I Love New York" is composed of a 45 word lyric and 100 measures. Of this only four notes, D C D E (in that sequence), and the words "I Love" were taken and used in the SNL sketch (although they were repeated 3 or 4 times). As a result, the defendant now argues that the use it made was insufficient to constitute copyright infringement.

This Court does not agree. Although it is clear that, on its face, the taking involved in this action is relatively slight, on closer examination it becomes apparent that this portion of the piece, the musical phrase that the lyrics "I Love New York" accompany, is the heart of the composition.[6] Use of such a significant (albeit less than extensive) portion of the composition is far more than merely a *de minimis* taking. See Sheldon v. Metro-Goldwyn Pictures Corp., 81 F.2d 49 (2d Cir.), cert. denied, 298 U.S. 669, 56 S.Ct. 835, 80 L.Ed. 1392 (1936); Life Music, Inc. v. Wonderland Music Co., 241 F.Supp. 653 (S.D.N.Y.1965). The tune of "I Love Sodom" is easily recognizable as "having been appropriated from the copyrighted work," Ideal Toy Corp. v. Fab-Lu Ltd., 360 F.2d 1021, 1022 (2d Cir.1966); Fleischer Studios, Inc. v. Ralph A. Freundlich Inc., 73 F.2d 276, 278 (2d Cir.1934), and is a taking of a substantial nature. See H.C. Wainwright & Co. v. Wall Street Transcript Corp., 418 F.Supp. 620 (S.D.N.Y.1976). Accordingly, such taking is capable of rising to the level of a copyright infringement.

Having so determined, the Court must next address the question of whether the defendant's copying of the plaintiff's jingle constituted a fair use which would exempt it from liability under the Copyright Act. Fair use has been defined as "a privilege in others than the owner of the copyright to use the copyrighted material in a reasonable manner without his consent, notwithstanding the monopoly granted to the owner of the copyright." H. Ball, The Law of Copyright and Literary Property 260 (1944). See Meeropol v. Nizer, 560 F.2d 1061, 1068 (2d Cir.1977), cert. denied, 434 U.S. 1013, 98 S.Ct. 727, 54 L.Ed.2d 756

---

6. It is this musical phrase, for example, that is constantly repeated during the course of most of the "I Love New York" campaign's television commercials and serves as the musical theme for such commercials.

(1978); Rosemont Enterprises, Inc. v. Random House, Inc., 366 F.2d 303, 306 (2d Cir.1966), cert. denied, 385 U.S. 1009, 87 S.Ct. 714, 17 L.Ed.2d 546 (1967). The determination of whether a use constitutes a fair use or is a copyright infringement requires an examination of the facts in each case. Meeropol v. Nizer, supra, 560 F.2d at 1068. To assist in making this determination, section 101 of the 1976 Copyright Act, 17 U.S.C. § 107, sets forth several criteria to be considered: "(1) the purpose and character of the use * * *; (2) the nature of the copyrighted work; (3) the amount and substantiality of the portion used in relation to the copyrighted work as a whole; and (4) the effect of the use upon the potential market for or value of the copyrighted work." [8]

The defendant asserts that the purpose and nature of its copying of "I Love New York" was parody, and that its copying was thus a fair use of the song. It has been held that an author is entitled to more extensive use of another's copyrighted work in creating a parody than in creating other fictional or dramatic works, Columbia Pictures Corp. v. National Broadcasting Co., 137 F.Supp. 348, 354 (S.D.Cal.1955), since "short of * * * [a] complete identity of content, the disparity of functions between a serious work, and a satire based upon it, may justify the defense of fair use even where substantial similarity exists." 3 M. Nimmer, *Nimmer on Copyright* § 13.05[C], at 13–60–61 (1979).

In the leading case of Berlin v. E.C. Publications, Inc., 329 F.2d 541 (2d Cir.1964), the court was faced with deciding whether certain parody lyrics printed in *Mad Magazine*, intended to comment humorously upon the "idiotic" world of that time, and designed to be sung to the tunes of various popular songs, infringed upon the copyrights of those songs.[9] Noting that "as a general proposition, * * * parody and satire are deserving of substantial freedom," the court held that, as the defendants had taken no more of the original songs than was necessary to "recall or 'conjure up' the object of his satire," and as the parody had "neither the intent nor the effect of fulfilling the demand for the original," no infringement had taken place. Id. at 545. See Columbia Pictures Corp. v. National Broadcasting Co., supra. See generally Light, *Parody, Burlesque, and the Economic Rationale for Copyright*, 11 Conn.L.Rev. 615 (1979).

The song "I Love Sodom," as well as the sketch of which it was a part, was clearly an attempt by the writers and cast of SNL to satirize the way in which New York City has attempted to improve its somewhat tarnished image through the use of a slick advertising campaign. As such, the defendant's copying of the song "I Love New York" seems to come within the definition of parody. The plaintiff, however, relying

---

8. These criteria, and the statutory fair use exception in general, were intended by Congress to codify, and not supplant, the common law doctrine of fair use. See H.R. Rep. No. 1476, 94th Cong., 2d Sess. 66, *reprinted in* [1976] U.S.Code Cong. & Admin.News, pp. 5659, 5680.

9. Among the songs that were the subjects of this parody were, "The Last Time I Saw Paris," which was reproduced as "The First Time I Saw [Roger] Maris," and "A Pretty Girl is Like a Melody," which was transformed into "Louella Schwartz Describes Her Malady."

upon MCA, Inc. v. Wilson, 425 F.Supp. 443 (S.D.N.Y.1976), and Walt Disney Productions v. Mature Pictures Corp., 389 F.Supp. 1397 (S.D.N.Y.1975), contends that, while the sketch may have parodied New York City and its problems, it had nothing to do with, and did not parody, either New York State and its "I Love New York" advertising campaign or the song "I Love New York" itself. As a result, the plaintiff asserts that the copying of its song constituted an infringement upon it and not a fair use.

In MCA, Inc. v. Wilson, supra, the court was presented with the question of whether the song "Cunnilingus Champion of Company C" as used in the play "Let My People Come—A Sexual Musical" infringed upon the copyright of the song "Boogie Woogie Bugle Boy of Company B." Finding that the defendant's song, although it "may have sought to parody life, or more particularly sexual mores and taboos," did not attempt to parody or "comment ludicrously upon Bugle Boy" itself, the court held that there had been no fair use and that as a result the plaintiff's copyright had been infringed. Id. at 453–54. Similarly, in Walt Disney Productions v. Mature Pictures Corp., supra, 389 F.Supp. at 1398, the court held that, while the defendants may have been seeking in their display of bestiality to parody life, they did not parody the Mickey Mouse March but sought only to improperly use the copyrighted material. In neither of these cases did the infringed upon musical piece relate, in any respect, to the subject that was being parodied.

The plaintiff asserts that, as the defendants did not attempt to parody the song "I Love New York" itself, the singing of "I Love Sodom" did not, under *MCA* or *Walt Disney*, constitute a fair use. We cannot agree. The song "I Love Sodom" in the sketch was intended to symbolize a catchy, upbeat tune that would divert a potential tourist's attention from the town's reputation for gambling, gluttony, idol worshipping, and, of course, sodomy. The song was as much a parody of the song "I Love New York,"—a catchy, upbeat tune intended to alter a potential tourist's perceptions of New York—as it was of the overall "I Love New York" advertising campaign.

In addition, even if it were found that "I Love Sodom" did not parody the plaintiff's song itself, that finding would not preclude a finding of fair use. Under the holding of Berlin v. E.C. Publications, Inc., supra, and the criteria set down in section 101 of the 1976 Copyright Act, 17 U.S.C. § 107, the issue to be resolved by a court is whether the use in question is a valid satire or parody, and not whether it is a parody of the copied song itself. To the extent that either *MCA* or *Walt Disney* can be read to require that there be an identity between the song copied and the subject of the parody, this Court disagrees.

Similarly, the Court does not accept the plaintiff's contention that, because "I Love Sodom" and the sketch of which it was a part related to the city and not the state of New York, they did not constitute a valid parody of the "I Love New York" advertising campaign. Although "I

Love New York" may originally have been commissioned by the state, and may continue to be utilized as the theme for the state advertising campaign, the manner in which the song has been used has also served to create a strong identification between the song and the City of New York. The extensive use of the "I Love New York" jingle and theme in connection with many advertisements (in both the print and electronic media) relating exclusively to New York City, has made the song as much the anthem of the city as of the state. As a result, the Court believes that this campaign and song, which have been used, at least in substantial part, to sell the city, are an appropriate target of parody with regard to the City of New York. See Rosemont Enterprises, Inc. v. Random House, Inc., 366 F.2d 303, 309 (2d Cir.1966); Time Inc. v. Bernard Geis Associates, 293 F.Supp. 130 (S.D.N.Y.1968).

Having found that the SNL sketch and song validly parodied the plaintiff's jingle and the "I Love New York" advertising campaign in general, the Court next turns to the important question of whether such use has tended to interfere with the marketability of the copyrighted work. See Meeropol v. Nizer, supra, 560 F.2d at 1070; Mura v. Columbia Broadcasting System, Inc., 245 F.Supp. 587, 590 (S.D.N.Y. 1965). In this regard, it is clear to the Court that the defendant's playing of the song "I Love Sodom" has not so interfered. The song has not affected the value of the copyrighted work. Neither has it had—nor could it have—the "effect of fulfilling the demand for the original." Berlin v. E.C. Publications, Inc., supra, 329 F.2d at 545. Just as imitation may be the sincerest form of flattery, parody is an acknowledgment of the importance of the thing parodied. In short, the defendant's version of the jingle has not in the least competed with or detracted from plaintiff's work.

We turn finally to the extent of the use. The plaintiff argues that, as a result of the multiple repetition of the phrase "I Love Sodom" at the end of the SNL sketch, the defendant has appropriated more of the plaintiff's work than was necessary to "conjure up" the original. The Court does not agree. In the "I Love New York" television advertisements, and particularly in the "show tour" commercials, which relate specifically to the city, the phrase "I Love New York" is repeated to musical accompaniment continuously throughout. Thus, while a single recital of "I Love Sodom" might have alerted a viewer of the sketch as to the target of the parody, the repetition of the phrase served not only to insure that its viewers were so alerted, but also to parody the form of these frequently broadcast advertisements themselves. As a result, the repetition furthered the overall satirical effect. In addition, the Court believes that the repetition of the phrase, sung *a capella* and lasting for only eighteen seconds, cannot be said to be clearly more than was necessary to "conjure up" the original. Nor was it so substantial a taking as to preclude this use from being a fair one.

Basing its decision on undisputed facts presented by the parties, as well as on a videotaped viewing of the television sketch containing the alleged infringement, the Court finds that the defendant's use of the plaintiff's jingle in the SNL sketch was a fair use, and that as a result no copyright violation occurred. Accordingly, the plaintiff's motion for summary judgment is denied, and the defendant's motion for summary judgment is granted. This action is hereby dismissed.

So Ordered.

Questions

1. Is the *Elsmere* court correct in concluding that a parody fair use defense would lie even if the plaintiff's song per se were not the subject of parody? Does such a conclusion conflict with the underlying rationale for regarding parody as fair use?

2. Suppose A's novel is published and meets with only slight commercial success. Thereafter, B produces a motion picture based upon A's novel, and using the same title. A does not consent to the making of the motion picture, and receives no payment from B. However, the distribution of B's motion picture results in greatly increasing A's book sales. In an infringement action by A against B, can B claim the defense of fair use? Is this hypothetical case distinguishable from *Elsmere*? See Marvin Worth Productions v. Superior Films Corp., 319 F.Supp. 1269 (S.D.N.Y.1970).

Note

The Court of Appeals affirmed the decision by the *Elsmere* district court. 623 F.2d 252 (2d Cir.1980). In its opinion the Court of Appeals stated:

> The District Court concluded, among other things, that the parody did not make more extensive use of appellant's song than was necessary to "conjure up" the original. 482 F.Supp. at 747. While we agree with this conclusion, we note that the concept of "conjuring up" an original came into the copyright law not as a limitation on how much of an original may be used, but as a recognition that a parody frequently needs to be more than a fleeting evocation of an original in order to make its humorous point. Columbia Pictures Corp. v. National Broadcasting Co., 137 F.Supp. 348, 354 (S.D.Cal.1955). A parody is entitled at least to "conjure up" the original. Even more extensive use would still be fair use, provided the parody builds upon the original, using the original as a known element of modern culture and contributing something new for humorous effect or commentary.

Question

Does the above passage from the *Elsmere* court of appeals opinion constitute a green light to copy an unlimited amount from a copyrighted work as long as "something new for humorous effect or commentary" is added? Cf. Warner Brothers, Inc. v. American Broadcasting Cos., 654 F.2d 204 (2d Cir.1981).

Collateral References

Note. The Parody Defense to Copyright Infringement: Productive Use After *Betamax*, 97 Harv. L.R. 1395 (1984).

Rosett, *Burlesque as Copyright Infringement,* ASCAP Copyright Law Symposium No. Nine 1 (1956).

Selvin, *Parody and Burlesque of Copyrighted Works as Infringement,* 6 Bull.Cr.Soc. 53 (1958).

Yankwich, *Parody and Burlesque in the Law of Copyright,* 33 Canadian Bar Review 1130 (1955).

Nimmer on Copyright, § 13.05[C].

WIHTOL v. CROW

United States Court of Appeals, Eighth Circuit, 1962.
309 F.2d 777.

Before SANDBORN and BLACKMUN, CIRCUIT JUDGES, and REGISTER, DISTRICT JUDGE.

SANDBORN, CIRCUIT JUDGE. The appellants were the plaintiffs in an action for injunctive relief and damages against the defendants (appellees) for the alleged infringement of copyrights covering a musical composition consisting of a song or hymn entitled "My God and I." From a judgment dismissing the complaint and awarding the defendants costs and attorneys' fees (199 F.Supp. 682), the plaintiffs have appealed.

The song in suit was composed by Austris A. Wihtol, who, under his trade name, obtained a copyright for the song ("English text and choral arrangement"). It was first published in the United States August 15, 1935, and duly registered in the United States Copyright Office on September 11, 1935. Wihtol later produced a version of the song "arranged for solo voice with new piano score, with new text added * * *." This version was first published March 1, 1944, and registered in the Copyright Office on September 30, 1944, by Wihtol and his wife, doing business as The Kama Co.

According to the plaintiff Wihtol's evidence, the song has achieved a worldwide distribution, and has produced some $25,000 annually from royalties. It has been performed largely in churches and schools. Wihtol depends upon the income from the song for his support. Part of the income is derived from granting licenses for the making of special arrangements of the song.

The defendant Nelson E. Crow was the head of the Vocal Department of the Junior College and High School of the Clarinda, Iowa, School District, during the school year 1958–59. He has a Degree of Master of Music Education. He was employed by the School District and was paid a salary for his services in supervising its choral music activities. He selected what was to be sung by the choral groups of the School and supplied the members of such groups with printed copies of the music to be sung. Crow, during this same period, was also the Choir Director of the First Methodist Church of Clarinda, and its organist. He received compensation from it for his services. His duties as Director included the selecting of choral music for the choir and the furnishing of printed copies of the music to its members.

In November of 1958, Crow, without the permission of the plaintiffs, copied the song "My God and I," incorporating it in a new arrangement made by him. He had found the copyrighted version of the song as published and sold by the plaintiffs—of which the School had acquired some 25 copies—unsuitable for choir use. About 48 copies of his new arrangement, adapted for such use, were produced by him upon one of the School's duplicating machines. The new arrangement of the song was performed once by the High School choir of 84 voices at one of the regular monthly School chapel services, and was performed at church services on one Sunday by the much smaller choir of the First Methodist Church. Crow had furnished the choirs with copies of his new arrangement. The copies contained the words "arranged Nelson E. Crow," and made no reference to Wihtol.

In June of 1959, Crow wrote The Kama Co., advising of the new arrangement he had made of the song, and stating that he had "adlibbed a choral humming introduction of four measures" but otherwise had left the score in its original context and had omitted no part of the solo version. In his letter he suggested that The Kama Co. might be interested in his arrangement, and said: " * * * I will attempt to get the score ready for your perusal next fall—if you are interested." In response to his letter, The Kama Co. requested that copies of his arrangement of the song be forwarded for inspection. Receiving no reply to this request, Wihtol went to Clarinda, Iowa. Crow was not there. Wihtol discussed the matter of infringement with Mrs. Crow. Wihtol gathered the impression that there was to be no peaceful solution of the controversy, and returned to Los Angeles.

Under date of July 28, 1959, The Kama Co. wrote Crow as follows:

Dear Mr. Crowe:

We regret that you did not comply with our request of sending immediately a copy of your score for inspection. Not hearing from you, it was necessary to make investigation, thereby involving expense which could have been avoided and which also impairs the friendly and co-operative atmosphere that should exist between publishers and music users. The plain fact is that you are guilty of Copyright infringement and subject to assessments and penalties that the law imposes on infringers.

For the preservation of good will for the sake of any future dealings that may come about, we will ask you to comply with the easiest terms possible.

The copyright law permits us to ask a Statutory Fee, of not more than 5,000 dollars and not less than 250 dollars. For the present, we will be satisfied with the minimum of 250 dollars and will allow you 90 days from this date, for compliance.

For the present, we will not institute a criminal complaint for Willful Infringement (maximum penalty—one year in jail and 1,000 dollar fine) because we wish to let you off as easily as possible.

For the sake of a peaceful and pleasant settlement, please have all of the copies you made delivered to our office in California immediately. The copies are so made that other people can be involved too and very seriously.

If this matter is amicably settled, in all likelihood, we may have an interesting offer for you for the future.

> Very truly yours,
> THE KAMA CO.,
> P.O. Box 301,
> Glendale, Calif.,
> /s/ L. ENGELHART.

On September 1, 1959, Crow forwarded to The Kama Co. 44 copies of the arrangement he had made of the copyrighted song, which were all the copies he had. The instant action was brought on January 15, 1960.

The defendants, in their separate answers to the complaint of the plaintiffs, denied any infringement of the copyrights in suit. The School District denied that Crow, in doing what he had done with the copyrighted song, was its agent and was acting within the scope of his authority as alleged in the complaint. It asserted that, if he was such an agent, the District was not liable for damages, since he was acting in a governmental capacity. The Church, in its answer, denied that the acts of Crow, complained of, were done as its agent.

The District Court, in disposing of this troublesome case growing out of the unfortunate but unintentional and seemingly harmless mistake of Nelson E. Crow, determined: (1) that there had been no infringement, but only a "fair use" by him of the copyrighted song; * *; (4) that, because of the offensive intimation contained in the letter of July 28, 1959, from The Kama Co. to Crow that he was, or might be, subject to criminal prosecution, the defendants should each be awarded an attorney's fee of $500 against the plaintiffs. This Court is now called upon to review these rulings. * * *

Obviously the plaintiffs had the exclusive right to copy their copyrighted song, and obviously Nelson E. Crow had no right whatever to copy it. The fact that his copying was done without intent to infringe would be of no help to him,[1] as the trial court recognized, if the copying constituted an infringement.

The trial court, however, was of the opinion that innocent intent had a bearing on the question of fair use, and ruled that Crow did nothing more than make a fair, noninfringing use of the copyrighted song in suit.

Whatever may be the breadth of the doctrine of "fair use," it is not conceivable to us that the copying of all, or substantially all, of a copyrighted song can be held to be a "fair use" merely because the infringer had no intent to infringe. In Bradbury v. Columbia Broad-

---

1. Johns & Johns Printing Co. v. Paull-Pioneer Music Corporation, 8 Cir., 102 F.2d 282, 283; Sheldon v. Metro-Goldwyn Pictures Corporation, 2 Cir., 81 F.2d 49, 54, certiorari denied, 298 U.S. 669, 56 S.Ct. 835, 80 L.Ed. 1392; Khan v. Leo Feist, Inc., D.C.S.D.N.Y., 70 F.Supp. 450, 459, affirmed C.C.A. 2, 165 F.2d 188; Advertisers Exchange, Inc. v. Hinkley, W.D.Mo., 101 F.Supp. 801, 805, affirmed C.A. 8, 199 F.2d 313.

casting System, Inc., 9 Cir., 287 F.2d 478, the court, in considering the doctrine of "fair use" of a copyrighted production, said (page 485):

> To constitute an invasion of copyright it is not necessary that the whole of a work should be copied, nor even a large portion of it in form or substance, but that, if so much is taken that the value of the original is sensibly diminished, or the labors of the original author are substantially, to an injurious extent, appropriated by another, that is sufficient to constitute an infringement. The test of infringement is whether the work is recognizable by an ordinary observer as having been taken from the copyrighted source. Slight differences and variations will not serve as a defense. The means of expressing an idea is subject to copyright protection and where one uses his own method or way of expressing his idea,' as Bradbury has done, such adornment constitutes a protectible work. Universal Pictures Co. v. Harold Lloyd Corporation, 9 Cir., 162 F.2d 354, 361, 363.

Compare Benny v. Loew's Incorporated, 9 Cir., 239 F.2d 532, 536; and note what the Seventh Circuit Court of Appeals held to be an infringement of Wihtol's song, in Wihtol v. Wells, 231 F.2d 550. It must be kept in mind that the applicable law is purely statutory and that the Copyright Act has little elasticity or flexibility.

The copying of the plaintiffs' song by Crow was, in our opinion, an infringement of the plaintiffs' copyrights in suit. * * *

On behalf of the First Methodist Church, it is argued that it cannot be held liable for the acts of Nelson E. Crow in copying the song in suit; that: "Although not proven either way it appears most probable that the Defendant Crow was an independent contractor. He was paid for his services periodically but furnished most of his own tools and materials." It seems to us that the only inference that reasonably can be drawn from the evidence is that in selecting and arranging the song in suit for use by the Church choir, Crow was engaged in the course and scope of his employment by the Church.

The allowance of $500 attorney's fees to each defendant was not justified, and of course would not have been made if the trial court had found infringement, since, under 17 U.S.C.A. § 116, attorney's fees may be allowed, in the discretion of the court, only to the prevailing party. The objectionable paragraph in the letter of The Kama Co. to Crow with respect to criminal prosecution for infringement, and the testimony of Wihtol, in his direct examination at the trial, relative to the circumstances under which his song was composed, which testimony the defendants assail as perjury, would not justify the judgment against the plaintiffs or the allowance of attorneys' fees to the defendants. The testimony was not perjury since it related to an immaterial matter, as the trial judge stated in his findings. Whatever may be thought of Wihtol, the song in suit is a copyrighted production, which the plaintiffs can protect and defend against all infringements, intentional or otherwise. * * *

The judgment appealed from is reversed, and the case is remanded to the District Court for further proceedings not inconsistent with this opinion.

Questions

1. Is the decision in the instant case unfair to Mr. Crow? What would happen to the market for the song "My God and I" if every school teacher in every school throughout the nation were permitted to make copies of the song each for his own students?

2. Suppose that each of Mr. Crow's 48 students had made his own single copy of *Wihtol's* song. Should each such student be able to claim the defense of fair use? Should it make any difference whether a single copy made by an individual for his own non-commercial use is copied by hand, or reproduced by Xerox or some other form of reprography?

3. The instant case raises the question whether innocent intent should ever constitute a defense in an infringement action. Three different types of innocence may be distinguished. There is the infringer who, like Crow, believes in good faith that his conduct does not constitute infringement although he knows very well that he is copying from the plaintiff's work. Then there is the unconscious copier, who has forgotten that he is drawing upon the material of another. See Sheldon v. Metro-Goldwyn Pictures Corp., supra. Finally, there is the copier who believes that he is authorized to copy from the work of a third party, but does not know that the third party's work is in turn an infringement of the plaintiff's work. Should any distinction be made in legal liability as between each of these types of innocent copying?

Note

Teacher Photocopying Guidelines

A set of guidelines stating the minimum, but not necessarily the maximum, reach of fair use in connection with teacher photocopying was agreed upon by representatives of author-publisher and educational organizations,[1] and was endorsed by the House Report as "a reasonable interpretation of the minimum standards of fair use."[2]

These guidelines[3] are as follows:

---

1. However, representatives of the American Association of University Professors and the Association of American Law Schools withheld their support from the guidelines because they were regarded as "too restrictive with respect to classroom situations at the university and graduate level." H.Rep., p. 72.

2. H.Rep., p. 72. These guidelines were also accepted by the Senate in the subsequent Conference Report. Conf.Rep., p. 70.

3. Note that a separate set of guidelines was adopted by the interested organizations and approved by the House and Senate in connection with educational uses of music. H.Rep., p. 70. How would the facts of the Wihtol v. Crow, supra, have been decided under such guidelines? Under the music guidelines copying "for the purpose of performance" is prohibited except for "emergency copying to replace purchased copies which for any reason are not available for an imminent performance provided purchased replacement copies shall be substituted in due course." Even in such circumstances would the making and reproduction of a musical arrangement be permissible?

"Guidelines

I. *Single Copying for Teachers*

A single copy may be made of any of the following by or for a teacher at his or her individual request for his or her scholarly research or use in teaching or preparation to teach a class:

    A. A chapter from a book;

    B. An article from a periodical or newspaper;

    C. A short story, short essay or short poem, whether or not from a collective work.

    D. A chart, graph, diagram, drawing, cartoon or picture from a book, periodical, or newspaper;

II. *Multiple Copies for Classroom Use*

Multiple copies (not to exceed in any event more than one copy per pupil in a course) may be made by or for the teacher giving the course for classroom use or discussion; *provided that:*

    A. The copying meets the tests of brevity and spontaneity as defined below; *and,*

    B. Meets the cumulative effect test as defined below; *and,*

    C. Each copy includes a notice of copyright.

Definitions

    Brevity

(*i*) Poetry: (a) A complete poem if less than 250 words and if printed on not more than two pages or, (b) from a longer poem, an excerpt of not more than 250 words.

(*ii*) Prose: (a) Either a complete article, story or essay of less than 2,500 words, or (b) an excerpt from any prose work of not more than 1,000 words or 10% of the work, whichever is less, but in any event a minimum of 500 words.

[Each of the numerical limits stated in "i" and "ii" above may be expanded to permit the completion of an unfinished line of a poem or of an unfinished prose paragraph.]

(*iii*) Illustration: One chart, graph, diagram, drawing, cartoon or picture per book or per periodical issue.

(*iv*) "Special" works: Certain works in poetry, prose or in "poetic prose" which often combine language with illustrations and which are intended sometimes for children and at other times for a more general audience fall short of 2,500 words in their entirety. Paragraph "ii" above notwithstanding such "special works" may not be reproduced in their entirety; however, an excerpt comprising not more than two of the published pages of such special work and containing not more than 10% of the words found in the text thereof, may be reproduced.

    Spontaneity

(*i*) The copying is at the instance and inspiration of the individual teacher, and

(*ii*) The inspiration and decision to use the work and the moment of its use for maximum teaching effectiveness are so close in time that it would be unreasonable to expect a timely reply to a request for permission.

Cumulative Effect

(*i*) The copying of the material is for only one course in the school in which the copies are made.

(*ii*) Not more than one short poem, article, story, essay or two excerpts may be copied from the same author, nor more than three from the same collective work or periodical volume during one class term.

(*iii*) There shall not be more than nine instances of such multiple copying for one course during one class term.

[The limitations stated in "ii" and "iii" above shall not apply to current news periodicals and newspapers and current news sections of other periodicals.]

III. *Prohibitions as to I and II Above*

Notwithstanding any of the above, the following shall be prohibited:

(A) Copying shall not be used to create or to replace or substitute for anthologies, compilations or collective works. Such replacement or substitution may occur whether copies of various works or excerpts therefrom are accumulated or reproduced and used separately.

(B) There shall be no copying of or from works intended to be "consumable" in the course of study or of teaching. These include workbooks, exercises, standardized tests and test booklets and answer sheets and like consumable material.

(C) Copying shall not:

(a) substitute for the purchase of books, publishers' reprints or periodicals.

(b) be directed by higher authority.

(c) be repeated with respect to the same item by the same teacher from term to term.

(D) No charge shall be made to the student beyond the actual cost of the photocopying."

Questions

1. Although it remains open to the courts to determine that given acts of teacher photocopying which go beyond the limits of the guidelines nevertheless constitute fair use (the House Report describes the guidelines as stating "*minimum* standards of fair use" H.Rep., p. 72, emphasis added), is the converse proposition also true? Is it open to the courts to determine that given acts of teacher photocopying which clearly fall within the permissible limits of the guidelines, nevertheless do not constitute fair use? What is the impact of the following passage in the House Report: "Section 107 is intended to restate the present [pre-1978] judicial doctrine of fair use, not to change, narrow, *or enlarge it* in any way"? H.Rep., p. 66 (emphasis added).

2. With respect to a reproduction for classroom use, if the work consists of 2499 words may it be reproduced in its entirety? What if it consists of 2500 words?

3. What constitutes a "special" work within the meaning of Par. (iv) of the "Brevity" guideline? May it be "special" although it does not "combine language with illustrations"? Although it is not "intended" for children?

4. Does the "Spontaneity" requirement encourage the lack of advance preparation of course materials?

Collateral Reference

Nimmer on Copyright, § 13.05[E][3].

THE WILLIAMS & WILKINS CO. v. THE UNITED STATES

United States Court of Claims, 1973.
487 F.2d 1345.

Before COWEN, CHIEF JUDGE, and DAVIS, SKELTON, NICHOLS, KASHIWA, KUNZIG and BENNETT, JUDGES.

DAVIS, JUDGE. We confront a ground-breaking copyright infringement action under 28 U.S.C. § 1498(b), the statute consenting to infringement suits against the United States. Plaintiff Williams & Wilkins Company, a medical publisher, charges that the Department of Health, Education, and Welfare, through the National Institutes of Health (NIH) and the National Library of Medicine (NLM), has infringed plaintiff's copyrights in certain of its medical journals by making unauthorized photocopies of articles from those periodicals. Modern photocopying in its relation to copyright spins off troublesome problems, which have been much discussed. Those issues have never before been mooted or determined by a court. In this case, an extensive trial was held before former Trial Judge James F. Davis who decided that the Government was liable for infringement. On review, helped by the briefs and agreements of the parties and the amici curiae, we take the other position and hold the United States free of liability in the particular situation presented by this record.

I

Plaintiff, though a relatively small company, is a major publisher of medical journals and books. It publishes 37 journals, dealing with various medical specialties. The four journals in suit are *Medicine, Journal of Immunology, Gastroenterology,* and *Pharmacological Reviews. Medicine* is published by plaintiff for profit and for its own benefit. The other three journals are published in conjunction with specialty medical societies which, by contract, share the journals' profits with plaintiff. The articles published in the journals stem from manuscripts submitted to plaintiff (or one of the medical societies) by physicians or other scientists engaged in medical research. The journals are widely disseminated throughout the United States (and the world) in libraries, schools, physicians' offices, and the like. Annual subscription prices range from about $12 to $44; and, due to the esoteric nature of the journals' subject matter, the number of annual subscriptions is relatively small, ranging from about 3,100 (*Pharmacological Reviews*) to about 7,000 (*Gastroenterology*). Most of the revenue derived from the journals comes from subscription sales, though a small part comes from advertising. * * *

NIH, the Government's principal medical research organization, is a conglomerate of institutes located on a multiacre campus at Bethesda, Maryland. Each institute is concerned with a particular medical specialty, and the institutes conduct their activities by way of both intramural research and grants-in-aid to private individuals and organizations. * * * To assist its intramural programs, NIH maintains a technical library. The library houses about 150,000 volumes, of which about 30,000 are books and the balance scientific (principally medical) journals. The library is open to the public, but is used mostly by NIH in-house research personnel. The library's budget for 1970 was $1.1 million; of this about $85,000 was for the purchase of journal materials.

The NIH library subscribes to about 3,000 different journal titles, four of which are the journals in suit. The library subscribes to two copies of each of the journals involved. As a general rule, one copy stays in the library reading room and the other copy circulates among interested NIH personnel. Demand by NIH research workers for access to plaintiff's journals (as well as other journals to which the library subscribes) is usually not met by in-house subscription copies.

Bion Smalley
[D2428]

Consequently, as an integral part of its operation, the library runs a photocopy service for the benefit of its research staff. On request, a researcher can obtain a photocopy of an article from any of the journals in the library's collection. Usually, researchers request photocopies of articles to assist them in their on-going projects; sometimes photocopies are requested simply for background reading. The library does not monitor the reason for requests or the use to which the photocopies are put. The photocopies are not returned to the library; and the record shows that, in most instances, researchers keep them in their private files for future reference.

The library's policy is that, as a rule, only a single copy of a journal article will be made per request and each request is limited to about 40 to 50 pages, though exceptions may be, and have been, made in the case of long articles, upon approval of the Assistant Chief of the library branch. Also, as a general rule, requests for photocopying are limited to only a single article from a journal issue. Exceptions to this rule are routinely made, so long as substantially less than an entire journal is photocopied, i.e., less than about half of the journal. Coworkers can, and frequently do, request single copies of the same article and such requests are honored.

Four regularly assigned employees operate the NIH photocopy equipment. The equipment consists of microfilm cameras and Xerox copying machines. In 1970, the library photocopy budget was $86,000 and the library filled 85,744 requests for photocopies of journal articles (including plaintiff's journals), constituting about 930,000 pages. On the average, a journal article is 10 pages long, so that, in 1970, the library made about 93,000 photocopies of articles.

NLM, located on the Bethesda campus of NIH, was formerly the Armed Forces Medical Library * * *. NLM is a repository of much of the world's medical literature, in essence a "librarians' library." As part of its operation, NLM cooperates with other libraries and like research-and-education-oriented institutions (both public and private) in a so-called "interlibrary loan" program. Upon request, NLM will loan to such institutions, for a limited time, books and other materials in its collection. In the case of journals, the "loans" usually take the form of photocopies of journal articles which are supplied by NLM free of charge and on a no-return basis. NLM's "loan" policies are fashioned after the General Interlibrary Loan Code, which is a statement of self-imposed regulations to be followed by all libraries which cooperate in interlibrary loaning. The Code provides that each library, upon request for a loan of materials, shall decide whether to loan the original or provide a photoduplicate. The Code notes that photoduplication of copyrighted materials may raise copyright infringement problems, particularly with regard to "photographing *whole issues* of periodicals or books with *current copyrights,* or in making *multiple copies* of a publication." [Emphasis in original text.] NLM, therefore, will provide only one photocopy of a particular article, per request, and will not photocopy on any given request an entire journal issue. Each photocopy reproduced by NLM contains a statement in the margin, "This is a single photostatic copy made by the National Library of Medicine for purposes of study or research in lieu of lending the original." * * *

Generally, requests for more than 50 pages of material will not be honored, though exceptions are sometimes made, particularly for Government institutions. Requests for more than one copy of a journal article are rejected, without exception. If NLM receives a request for more than one copy, a single copy will be furnished and the requester advised that it is NLM's policy to furnish only one copy.

In 1968, a representative year, NLM received about 127,000 requests for interlibrary loans. Requests were received, for the most part, from other libraries or Government agencies. However, about 12 percent of the requests came from private or commercial organizations, particularly drug companies. Some requests were for books, in which event the book itself was loaned. Most requests were for journals or journal articles; and about 120,000 of the requests were filled by photocopying single articles from journals, including plaintiff's journals. Usually, the library seeking an interlibrary loan from NLM did so at the request of one of its patrons. If the "loan" was made by photocopy, the photocopy was given to the patron who was free to dispose of it as he wished. NLM made no effort to find out the ultimate use to which the photocopies were put; and there is no evidence that borrowing libraries kept the "loan" photocopies in their permanent collections for use by other patrons.

Defendant concedes that, within the pertinent accounting period, NLM and the NIH library made at least one photocopy of each of eight articles (designated by plaintiff as the Count I-to-Count VIII articles) from one or more of the four journals in suit. These requests, as shown at the trial, were made by NIH researchers and an Army medical officer (stationed in Japan) in connection with their professional work and were used solely for those purposes. In seven of the eight counts in the petition, the article requested was more than two years old; in the eighth instance it was 21 or 22 months old.

II

Perhaps the main reason why determination of the [infringement] question is so difficult is that the text of the Copyright Act of 1909, which governs the case, does not supply, by itself, a clear or satisfactory answer. Section 1 of the Act, 17 U.S.C. § 1, declares that the copyright owner "shall have the exclusive right: (a) To print, reprint, publish, copy, and vend the copyrighted work; * * *." Read with blinders, this language might seem on its surface to be all-comprehensive—especially the term "copy"—but we are convinced, for several reasons, that "copy" is not to be taken in its full literal sweep. In this instance, as in so many others in copyright, "[T]he statute is hardly unambiguous * * * and presents problems of interpretation not solved by literal application of words as they are 'normally' used * * *." DeSylva v. Ballentine, 351

U.S. 570, 573, 76 S.Ct. 974, 100 L.Ed. 1415 (1956). See, also, Fortnightly Corp. v. United Artists Television, Inc., 392 U.S. 390, 395–396, 88 S.Ct. 2084, 20 L.Ed.2d 1176 (1968).

The court-created doctrine of "fair use" (discussed in Part III, infra) is alone enough to demonstrate that Section 1 does not cover all copying (in the literal sense). Some forms of copying, at the very least of portions of a work, are universally deemed immune from liability, although the very words are reproduced in more than *de minimis* quantity. Furthermore, it is almost unanimously accepted that a scholar can make a handwritten copy of an entire copyrighted article for his own use, and in the era before photoduplication it was not uncommon (and not seriously questioned) that he could have his secretary make a typed copy for his personal use and files. These customary facts of copy-right-life are among our givens. The issue we now have is the complex one of whether photocopying, in the form done by NIH and NLM, should be accorded the same treatment—not the ministerial lexicographic task of deciding that photoduplication necessarily involves "copying" (as of course it does in dictionary terms).

* * *

III

In the fifty-odd years since the 1909 Act, the major tool for probing what physical copying amounts to unlawful "copying" (as well as what is unlawful "printing," "reprinting" and "publishing") has been the gloss of "fair use" which the courts have put upon the words of the statute.

* * *

In addition, the development of "fair use" has been influenced by some tension between the direct aim of the copyright privilege to grant the owner a right from which he can reap financial benefit and the more fundamental purpose of the protection "To promote the Progress of Science and the useful Arts." U.S.Const., art. 1, § 8. * * *

It has sometimes been suggested that the copying of an entire copyrighted work, any such work, cannot ever be "fair use," but this is an overbroad generalization, unsupported by the decisions [12] and rejected by years of accepted practice. The handwritten or typed copy of an article, for personal use, is one illustration, let alone the thousands of

---

12. Leon v. Pacific Telephone & Telegraph Co., 91 F.2d 484, 486 (C.A. 9, 1937) and Public Affairs Associates, Inc. v. Rickover, 109 U.S.App.D.C. 128, 284 F.2d 262, 272 (C.A.D.C.1960), vacated and remanded, 369 U.S. 111, 82 S.Ct. 580, 7 L.Ed.2d 604 (1962), which are often cited in this connection, both involved actual publication and distribution of many copies, not the simple making of a copy for individual personal or restricted use. In Wihtol v. Crow, 309 F.2d 777 (C.A. 8, 1962), 48 copies of the copyrighted song were made and distributed, and there were a number of public performances using these copies. It was as if the defendant had purchased one copy of sheet music and then duplicated it for an entire chorus.

On the other hand, New York Tribune, Inc. v. Otis & Co., 39 F.Supp. 67 (S.D.N.Y. 1941), shows that copying of an entire copyrighted item is not enough, in itself, to preclude application of "fair use." Although it was already plain that an entire copyrighted item (a newspaper editorial) had been reproduced, the court ordered further proceedings to take account of other factors.

copies of poems, songs, or such items which have long been made by individuals, and sometimes given to lovers and others. Trial Judge James F. Davis, who considered the use now in dispute not to be "fair," nevertheless agreed that a library could supply single photocopies of entire copyrighted works to attorneys or courts for use in litigation. It is, of course, common for courts to be given photocopies of recent decisions, with the publishing company's headnotes and arrangement, and sometimes its annotations. There are other examples from everyday legal and personal life. * * *

The majority of the court has concluded that, on this record, the challenged use should be designated "fair," not "unfair." In the rest of this part of our opinion, we discuss *seriatim* the various considerations which merge to that conclusion. But we can help focus on what is probably the core of our evaluation by stating summarily, in advance, three propositions we shall consider at greater length: First, plaintiff has not in our view shown, and there is inadequate reason to believe, that it is being or will be harmed substantially by these specific practices of NIH and NLM; second, we are convinced that medicine and medical research will be injured by holding these particular practices to be an infringement; and, third, since the problem of accommodating the interests of science with those of the publishers (and authors) calls fundamentally for legislative solution or guidance, which has not yet been given, we should not, during the period before congressional action is forthcoming, place such a risk of harm upon science and medicine.

1. We start by emphasizing that (a) NIH and NLM are non-profit institutions, devoted solely to the advancement and dissemination of medical knowledge which they seek to further by the challenged practices, and are not attempting to profit or gain financially by the photocopying; (b) the medical researchers who have asked these libraries for the photocopies are in this particular case (and ordinarily) scientific researchers and practitioners who need the articles for personal use in their scientific work and have no purpose to reduplicate them for sale or other general distribution; and (c) the copied articles are scientific studies useful to the requesters in their work. On both sides—library and requester—scientific progress, untainted by any commercial gain from the reproduction, is the hallmark of the whole enterprise of duplication. There has been no attempt to misappropriate the work of earlier scientific writers for forbidden ends, but rather an effort to gain easier access to the material for study and research.
* * *

2. Both libraries have declared and enforced reasonably strict limitations which, to our mind, keep the duplication within appropriate confines. The details are set forth in Part I supra, and in our findings.
* * *

[P]laintiff points to the very large number, in absolute terms, of the copies made each year by the two libraries. We do not think this decisive.[15] In view of the large numbers of scientific personnel served and the great size of the libraries—NIH has over 100,000 volumes of journal materials alone, and NLM is currently binding over 18,000 journals each year—the amount of copying does not seem to us to have been excessive or disproportionate. The important factor is not the absolute amount, but the twin elements of (i) the existence and purpose of the system of limitations imposed and enforced, and (ii) the effectiveness of that system to confine the duplication for the personal use of scientific personnel who need the material for their work, with the minimum of potential abuse or harm to the copyright owner. The practices of NIH and NLM, as shown by the record, pass both of these tests, despite the large number of copies annually sent out. * * *

3. We also think it significant, in assessing the recent and current practices of the two libraries, that library photocopying, though not of course to the extent of the modern development, has been going on ever since the 1909 Act was adopted. * * *

4. There is no doubt in our minds that medical science would be seriously hurt if such library photocopying were stopped. We do not spend time and space demonstrating this proposition. It is admitted by plaintiff and conceded on all sides. * * * It is, moreover, wholly unrealistic to expect scientific personnel to subscribe regularly to large numbers of journals which would only occasionally contain articles of interest to them. Nor will libraries purchase extensive numbers of whole subscriptions to all medical journals on the chance that an indeterminate number of articles in an indeterminate number of issues will be requested at indeterminate times. The result of a flat proscription on library photocopying would be, we feel sure, that medical and scientific personnel would simply do without, and have to do without, many of the articles they now desire, need, and use in their work.[18]

5. Plaintiff insists that it has been financially hurt by the photocopying practices of NLM and NIH, and of other libraries. The trial judge thought that it was reasonable to infer that the extensive photocopying has resulted in some loss of revenue to plaintiff and that plaintiff has lost, or failed to get, "some undetermined and indeterminable number of journal subscriptions (perhaps small)" by virtue of the photocopying. He thought that the persons requesting photocopies constituted plaintiff's market and that each photocopy user is a potential subscriber "or at least a potential source of royalty income for licensed copying."[19] Studies rejecting as "fair use" the kind of photo-

---

15. In 1970, NIH copied 85,744 and NLM 93,746 articles.

18. We think the alternative of compulsory licensing is not open to us under the present copyright statute. * * *

19. It is wrong to measure the detriment to plaintiff by loss of presumed royalty income—a standard which necessarily assumes that plaintiff had a right to issue licenses. That would be true, of course, only if it were first decided that the defendant's practices did not constitute "fair use." In determining whether the company has been sufficiently hurt to cause these practices to become "unfair," one cannot assume at the start the merit of the plaintiff's position, i.e., that plaintiff had the right to license. That conclusion results only if it is

copying involved here have also assumed, without real proof, that the journal publishers have been and will be injured. See, e.g., Project—New Technology and the Law of Copyright: Reprography and Computers, 15 U.C.L.A.L.Rev. 931 (1968); Sophor & Heilprin, "The Determination of Legal Facts and Economic Guideposts with Respect to the Dissemination of Scientific and Educational Information as It Is Affected by Copyright—A Status Report" (1967).

The record made in this case does not sustain that assumption. Defendant made a thorough effort to try to ascertain, so far as possible, the effect of photoduplication on plaintiff's business, including the presentation of an expert witness. The unrefuted evidence shows that (a) between 1958 and 1969 annual subscriptions to the four medical journals involved increased substantially (for three of them, very much so), annual subscription sales likewise increased substantially, and total annual income also grew; (b) between 1959 and 1966, plaintiff's annual taxable income increased from $272,000 to $726,000, fell to $589,000 in 1967, and in 1968 to $451,000; (c) but the four journals in suit account for a relatively small percentage of plaintiff's total business and over the years each has been profitable (though 3 of them show losses in particular years and in all years the profits have not been large, varying from less than $1,000 to about $15,000, some of which has been shared with the sponsoring medical societies);[20] and (d) plaintiff's business appears to have been growing faster than the gross national product or of the rate of growth of manpower working in the field of science. Defendant's expert concluded that the photocopying shown here had not damaged plaintiff, and may actually have helped it. The record is also barren of solid evidence that photocopying has caused economic harm to any other publisher of medical journals. * * *

If photocopying were forbidden, the researchers, instead of subscribing to more journals or trying to obtain or buy back-issues or reprints (usually unavailable), might expend extra time in note-taking or waiting their turn for the library's copies of the original issues—or they might very well cut down their reading and do without much of the information they now get through NLM's and NIH's copying system. The record shows that each of the individual requesters in this case already subscribed, personally, * * *

To us it is very important that plaintiff has failed to prove its assumption of economic detriment, in the past or potentially for the future. One of the factors always considered with respect to "fair use," see supra, is the effect of the use on the owner's potential market for the work. This record simply does not show a serious adverse impact, either on plaintiff or on medical publishers generally, from the photocopying practices of the type of NIH and NLM. In the face of this

first determined that the photocopying is "unfair."

20. Defendant explains the loss years and the fall-off in some subscriptions in some years as due to particular circumstances (which are spelled out) other than photocopying.

record, we cannot mechanically assume such an effect, or hold that the amount of photoduplication proved here "must" lead to financial or economic harm. This is a matter of proof and plaintiff has not transformed its hypothetical assumption, by evidence, into a proven fact. * * *

6. * * *

While, as we have said, this record fails to show that plaintiff (or any other medical publisher) has been substantially harmed by the photocopying practices of NIH and NLM, it does show affirmatively that medical science will be hurt if such photocopying is stopped. Thus, the balance of risks is definitely on defendant's side—until Congress acts more specifically, the burden on medical science of a holding that the photocopying is an infringement would appear to be much greater than the present or foreseeable burden on plaintiff and other medical publishers of a ruling that these practices fall within "fair use."

Plaintiff's answer is that it is willing to license the libraries, on payment of a reasonable royalty, to continue photocopying as they have. Our difficulty with that response—in addition to the absence of proof that plaintiff has yet been hurt, and the twin doubts whether plaintiff has a viable license system and whether any satisfactory program can be created without legislation [24]—is that the 1909 Act does not provide for compulsory licensing in this field. All that a court can do is to determine the photocopying an infringement, leaving it to the owner to decide whether to license or to prohibit the practice. Plaintiff and other publishers cannot enjoin governmental libraries (because 28 U.S.C. § 1498, supra note 1, is the sole remedy), but if photocopying of this type is an infringement the owners are free under the law to seek to enjoin any and all nongovernmental libraries. A licensing system would be purely voluntary with the copyright proprietor. We consider it entirely beyond judicial power, under the 1909 Act,[25] to order an owner to institute such a system if he does not wish to. We think it equally outside a court's present competence to turn the determination of "fair use" on the owner's willingness to license—to hold that photo-

---

24. Defendant and its amici strongly attack plaintiff's so-called licensing plan as nothing more than a shell. The American Library Association points out, for instance, that the Williams & Wilkins license would apparently not apply to inter-library loans or to requests from persons not physically present in the library building.

There is also debate over whether a feasible ASCAP-type or clearinghouse system can be developed without legislation, and if so whether it would be desirable. *See, e.g.,* Note, Education and Copyright Law: An Analysis of the Amended Copyright Revision Bill and Proposals for Statutory Licensing and a Clearinghouse System, 56 Va.L.Rev. 664 (1970); also published as MacLean, Education and Copyright Law: An Analysis of the Amended Copyright Revision Bill and Proposals for Statutory Licensing and a Clearinghouse System, in ASCAP, "Copyright Law Symposium, Number Twenty," 1 (1972); Breyer, The Uneasy Case for Copyright: A Study of Copyright in Books, Photocopies and Computer Programs, 84 Harv.L.Rev. 281, 330ff. (1970); Note: New Technology and the Law of Copyright; Reprography and Computers, 15 UCLA L.Rev. 939, 961ff. (1968).

25. A court's powers under the antitrust legislation is another matter.

copying (without royalty payments) is not "fair use" if the owner is willing to license at reasonable rates but becomes a "fair use" if the owner is adamant and refuses all permission (or seeks to charge excessive fees).

The truth is that this is now preeminently a problem for Congress: to decide the extent photocopying should be allowed, the questions of a compulsory license and the payments (if any) to the copyright owners, the system for collecting those payments (lump-sum, clearinghouse, etc.), the special status (if any) of scientific and educational needs. Obviously there is much to be said on all sides. The choices involve economic, social, and policy factors which are far better sifted by a legislature. The possible intermediate solutions are also of the pragmatic kind legislatures, not courts, can and should fashion. But Congress does not appear to have put its mind directly to this problem in 1909, undoubtedly because the issue was not considered pressing at that time. That statute is, unfortunately, the one we must apply, and under it we have the choice only of thumb's up or thumb's down, for the photocopying practice involved in this litigation, without any real Congressional guidance. Intermediate or compromise solutions are not within our authority.[26] The theme of this subpart 6 of Part III of the opinion is that, on balance and on this record, thumb's up seems to us less dangerous to the varying interests at stake during the period which remains before Congress definitely takes hold of the subject. * * *

IV

Fusing these elements together, we conclude, that plaintiff has failed to show that the defendant's use of the copyrighted material has been "unfair," and conversely we find that these practices have up to now been "fair." There has been no infringement. As Professor (now Mr. Justice) Kaplan observed, it is "fundamental that 'use' is not the same as 'infringement' [and] that use short of infringement is to be encouraged * * *." Kaplan, An Unhurried View of Copyright 57 (1967); see Fortnightly Corp. v. United Artists Television, Inc., 392 U.S. 390, 393–395, 88 S.Ct. 2084, 20 L.Ed.2d 1176 (1968).

So as not to be misunderstood, we reemphasize four interrelated aspects of our holding. The first is that the conclusion that defendant's particular use of plaintiff's copyrighted material has been "fair" rests upon all of the elements discussed in Part III, supra, and not upon any one, or any combination less than all. We do not have to, and do not, say that any particular component would be enough, either by itself or together with some of the others. Conversely, we do not have to, and do not, say that all the elements we mention are essential to a finding of "fair use." They all happen to be present here, and it is enough for this case to rule, as we do, that at least when all coexist in combination a "fair use" is made out.

26. It has been suggested, however, that publishers now have the power to adopt the intermediate solution of charging more for subscriptions sold to libraries or other entities which engage regularly in photocopying.

Connected with this point is the second one that our holding is restricted to the type and context of use by NIH and NLM, as shown by this record. That is all we have before us, and we do not pass on dissimilar systems or uses of copyrighted materials by other institutions or enterprises, or in other fields, or as applied to items other than journal articles, or with other significant variables. We have nothing to say, in particular, about the possibilities of computer print-outs or other such products of the newer technology now being born. Especially since we believe, as stressed infra, that the problem of photo and mechanical reproduction calls for legislative guidance and legislative treatment, we feel a strong need to obey the canon of judicial parsimony, being stingy rather than expansive in the reach of our holding.

The third facet articulates the same general premise—our holding rests upon this record which fails to show a significant detriment to plaintiff but does demonstrate injury to medical and scientific research if photocopying of this kind is held unlawful. We leave untouched, because we do not have to reach them, the situations where the copyright owner is shown to be hurt or the recipients (or their interests) would not be significantly injured if the reproductions were ruled to infringe.

Finally, but not at all least, we underline again the need for Congressional treatment of the problems of photocopying. The 1909 Act gives almost nothing by way of directives, the judicial doctrine of "fair use" is amorphous and open-ended, and the courts are now precluded, both by the Act and by the nature of the judicial process, from contriving pragmatic or compromise solutions which would reflect the legislature's choices of policy and its mediation among the competing interests. * * * Hopefully, the result in the present case will be but a "holding operation" in the interim period before Congress enacts its preferred solution.

On this record and for these reasons, we hold the plaintiff not entitled to recover and dismiss the petition.[a]

Cowen, Chief Judge (dissenting).

It is my opinion that our former Trial Judge James F. Davis fully and correctly resolved the difficult and perplexing issues presented by this case in his scholarly and well-reasoned opinion [172 U.S.P.Q. 670]. I would therefore adopt his opinion, findings of fact, and recommended conclusions of law as a basis for a judgment by the court in favor of the plaintiff. * * *

Although the court states that it rejects the trial determinations as to both actual and potential damage to plaintiff, I think the opinion shows that the court's conclusion is based primarily on its finding that plaintiff failed to prove actual damages. In so doing, the majority

---

[a.] This decision by the Court of Claims was affirmed in the Supreme Court by an equally divided court (Mr. Justice Blackmun not participating in the decision), 420 U.S. 376 (1975).

relies heavily on evidence that the plaintiff's profits have grown faster than the gross national product and that plaintiff's annual taxable income has increased. This evidence is irrelevant to the economic effects of photocopying the journals in this case, because these periodicals account for a relatively small percent of plaintiff's total business. Moreover, the extent of plaintiff's taxable income for the years mentioned does not reflect the effect of defendant's photocopying of plaintiff's journals, and particularly the effect it will have on the prospects for continued publication in the future.

By the very nature of an action for infringement, the copyright proprietor often has a difficult burden of proving the degree of injury. It is well established, however, that proof of actual damages is not required, and the defense of fair use may be overcome where potential injury is shown. See, e.g., Henry Holt & Co., Inc. v. Liggett & Myers Tobacco Co., 23 F.Supp. 302, 304 (E.D.Pa.1938). As Professor Nimmer has stated, the courts look to see whether defendant's work "tends to diminish or prejudice the potential sale of the plaintiff's work." M. Nimmer, Nimmer on Copyright § 145 at 646 (1973 ed.). * * *

* * *

Beginning about 1960, photocopying changed character. The introduction to the marketplace of the office copying machine made photocopying rapid, cheap and readily available. The legitimate interests of copyright owners must, accordingly, be measured against the changed realities of technology. Professor Nimmer in his treatise Copyright capsules the point at 653:

> Both classroom and library reproduction of copyrighted materials command a certain sympathy since they involve no commercial exploitation and more particularly in view of their socially useful objectives. *What this overlooks is the tremendous reduction in the value of copyrighted works which must result from a consistent and pervasive application of this practice.* One who creates a work for educational purposes may not suffer greatly by an occasional unauthorized reproduction. But if every school room or library may by purchasing a single copy supply a demand for numerous copies through photocopying, mimeographing or similar devices, the market for copyrighted educational materials would be almost completely obliterated. This could well discourage authors from creating works of a scientific or educational nature. If the 'progress of science and useful arts' is promoted by granting copyright protection to authors, such progress may well be impeded if copyright protection is largely undercut in the name of fair use. [Emphasis supplied.] * * *

Defendant also contends that traditionally, scholars have made handwritten copies of copyrighted works for use in research or other scholarly pursuits; that it is in the public interest that they do so because any harm to copyright owners is minimal compared to the public benefits derived therefrom; and that the photocopying here in suit is essentially a substitute for handcopying by the scholars themselves. That argument is not persuasive. In the first place, defendant concedes that its libraries photocopy substantially more material than scholars can or do copy by hand. Implicit in such concession is a recognition that laborious handcopying and rapid machine photocopying are totally different in their impact on the interests of copyright owners. Furthermore, there is no case law to support defendant's proposition that the making of a handcopy by scholars or researchers of an *entire* copyrighted work is permitted by the copyright laws. Certainly the statute does not expressly permit it; and no doubt the issue has never been litigated because, as a practical matter, such copying is *de minimis* and causes no real threat to the copyright owner's legitimate right to control duplication and dissemination of copyrighted works. The photocopying done by NLM and the NIH library, on the other hand, poses a real and substantial threat to copyright owners' legitimate interests. Professor Nimmer discusses the point succinctly, at § 13.05[E][4][a] p. 13–101 of his treatise, and his language can hardly be improved upon:

> It may be argued that library reproduction is merely a more modern and efficient version of the time-honored practice of scholars in making handwritten copies of copyrighted works, for their own private use. In evaluating this argument several factors must be considered. In the first place, the drudgery of making handwritten copies probably means that such copies in most instances are not of the complete work, and the quantitative insignificance of the selected passages are such as generally not to amount to a *substantial* similarity. Secondly, there would appear to be a qualitative difference between each individual scholar performing the task of reproduction for himself, and a library or other institution performing the task on a wholesale basis for all scholars. If the latter is fair use, then must not the same be said for a non-profit publishing house that distributes to scholars unauthorized copies of scientific and educational works on a national or international basis? Finally, it is by no means clear that the underlying premise of the above argument is valid.
>
> There is no reported case on the question of whether a single handwritten copy of all or substantially all of a protected work made for the copier's own private use is an infringement or fair use. If such a case were to arise the force of custom might impel a court to rule for the defendant on the ground of fair use. Such a result, however, could not be reconciled with the rationale for fair use suggested above since the handwritten copy would serve the same function as the protected work, and would tend to reduce the exploitation value of such work. Moreover, if such conduct is defensible then is it not equally a fair use for the copier to use his own photocopying or other duplicating device to achieve the same result? Once this is acknowledged to be fair use, the day may not be far off when no one need purchase books since by merely borrowing a copy from a library any individual will be able to make his own copy through photocopying or other reproduction devices which technological advances may soon make easily and economically available.

* * *

KUNZIG, JUDGE, joins in the foregoing dissenting opinion.

NICHOLS, JUDGE (dissenting).

I have difficulty regarding a use as fair, when a user benefits as extensively from the copyrighted material as this one does, yet adamantly refuses to make any contribution to defray the publisher's cost, or compensate for the author's effort and expertise, except the nominal subscription price of two copies of each periodical. Defendant's libraries, and others, have attempted to exercise a measure of self-restraint hitherto, but there is nothing in the majority decision to induce them to continue, that is not more than counterbalanced by other material that will encourage unrestricted piracy. However, hedged, the decision will be read, that a copyright holder has no rights a library is bound to respect. We are making the Dred Scott decision of copyright law. * *

Questions

1. Did the court in *Williams & Wilkins* confuse the issues of damages and liability? Does the fact that the plaintiff is unable to prove the amount of its damages justify invoking the defense of fair use? Is not the fact that damages are notoriously difficult to prove in copyright actions the reason why a plaintiff has the right to recover statutory damages instead of actual damages? See Sec. 504(a) and (c) of the current Copyright Act. In determining "the effect of the use upon the potential market for or value of the copyrighted work" (Sec. 107(4)) should not a court look to the effect of such a "use" by all potential defendants, and without limitation as to the number of reproductions, and volume of users, and find the "use" to be "fair" only when the totality of such use would not appreciably affect the potential market for or value of the plaintiff's work?

2. When the motion picture medium was first developed, would a court have been justified in concluding that a motion picture dramatization of a copyrighted novel was fair use on the ground that the copyright owner of the novel could prove no injury since if the copyright in the novel could preclude motion picture dramatizations the producers of films would simply avoid using copyrighted novels as the basis of their productions? Is this analogous to the *Williams & Wilkins'* justification of the fair use defense on the ground that "if photocopying were forbidden, the researchers, instead of subscribing to more journals or trying to obtain or buy back-issues * * * might expend extra time in notetaking or waiting their turn for the library's copies of the original issues— or they might very well cut down their reading and do without much of the information they now get through NLM's and NIH's copying system"?

3. Is there some distortion in the court's balancing the injury to the plaintiff due to "these specific practices of NIH and NLM" as against the interests of "medicine and medical research" in general? Is this like balancing the interest of a particular author in his novel against the public's interest in literature generally?

4. If *Williams & Wilkins* had been decided under the current Copyright Act, would the defendant's conduct have been immunized from liability under the special exemption for libraries contained in Section 108? See generally Nimmer on Copyright, § 8.03.

5. Outside the special ambit of Sec. 108 (dealing with nonprofit library photocopying) most photocopying is defensible only if it is found to constitute fair use under Sec. 107. Does Williams & Wilkins remain a guiding precedent on this issue? Since Mr. Justice Blackmun did not participate in the Supreme Court decision, there was an evenly divided court which, therefore, affirmed the Court of Claims. See Williams & Wilkins Co. v. United States, 420 U.S. 376 (1975). How is Justice Blackmun likely to vote in any new photocopying case? Does Wihtol v. Crow, supra, give any clue to the answer to that question? Does

Sony Corp. of America v. Universal City Studios, Inc., infra? Are *Wihtol* and *Williams & Wilkins* in conflict? If so, which decision is more likely to be followed in future copyright litigation?

Collateral Reference

Nimmer on Copyright, § 13.05[E][4].

TIME, INC. v. BERNARD GEIS ASSOCIATES

United States District Court, Southern District of New York, 1968.
293 F.Supp. 130.

[The first portions of this opinion, including the facts, are set forth at p. 41 supra.]

* * *

In determining the issue of fair use, the balance seems to be in favor of defendants.

There is a public interest in having the fullest information available on the murder of President Kennedy. Thompson did serious work on the subject and has a theory entitled to public consideration. While doubtless the theory could be explained with sketches of the type used at page 87 of the Book and in The Saturday Evening Post, the explanation actually made in the Book with copies is easier to understand. The Book is not bought because it contained the Zapruder pictures; the Book is bought because of the theory of Thompson and its explanation, supported by Zapruder pictures.

There seems little, if any, injury to plaintiff, the copyright owner. There is no competition between plaintiff and defendants. Plaintiff does not sell the Zapruder pictures as such and no market for the copyrighted work appears to be affected. Defendants do not publish a magazine. There are projects for use by plaintiff of the film in the future as a motion picture or in books, but the effect of the use of certain frames in the Book on such projects is speculative. It seems more reasonable to speculate that the Book would, if anything, enhance the value of the copyrighted work; it is difficult to see any decrease in its value. * * *

The motion of plaintiff is denied.

The Clerk is directed to enter judgment in favor of defendants.

So ordered.

Question

Is the court correct in looking only to actual and not potential competition between the parties? Is Time's market for a book using frames from the Zapruder film affected by the Geis book?

Sec. C   THE DEFENSE OF FAIR USE   407

SONY CORPORATION OF AMERICA v. UNIVERSAL CITY STUDIOS, INC.

Supreme Court of the United States, 1984.
464 U.S. 417, 104 S.Ct. 774, 78 L.Ed.2d 574.

JUSTICE STEVENS delivered the opinion of the Court.

Petitioners manufacture and sell home video tape recorders. Respondents own the copyrights on some of the television programs that are broadcast on the public airwaves. Some members of the general public use video tape recorders sold by petitioners to record some of these broadcasts, as well as a large number of other broadcasts. The question presented is whether the sale of petitioners' copying equipment to the general public violates any of the rights conferred upon respondents by the Copyright Act.

Respondents commenced this copyright infringement action against petitioners in the United States District Court for the Central District of California in 1976. Respondents alleged that some individuals had used Betamax video tape recorders (VTR's) to record some of respondents' copyrighted works which had been exhibited on commercially sponsored television and contended that these individuals had thereby infringed respondents' copyrights. Respondents further maintained that petitioners were liable for the copyright infringement allegedly committed by Betamax consumers because of petitioners'

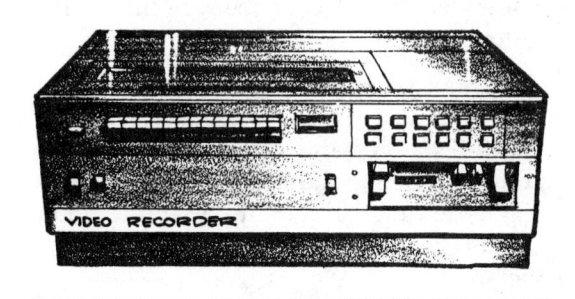

A commentary on the contributory infringement issue in *Sony* published after the Court of Appeals decision, and before the Supreme Court reversal.

marketing of the Betamax VTR's. Respondents sought no relief against any Betamax consumer. Instead, they sought money damages and an equitable accounting of profits from petitioners, as well as an injunction against the manufacture and marketing of Betamax VTR's.

After a lengthy trial, the District Court denied respondents all the relief they sought and entered judgment for petitioners. 480 F.Supp. 429 (1979). The United States Court of Appeals for the Ninth Circuit reversed the District Court's judgment on respondent's copyright claim, holding petitioners liable for contributory infringement and ordering the District Court to fashion appropriate relief. 659 F.2d 963 (1981). * * *

An explanation of our rejection of respondents' unprecedented attempt to impose copyright liability upon the distributors of copying equipment requires a quite detailed recitation of the findings of the District Court. In summary, those findings reveal that the average member of the public uses a VTR principally to record a program he cannot view as it is being televised and then to watch it once at a later time. This practice, known as "time-shifting," enlarges the television viewing audience. For that reason, a significant amount of television programming may be used in this manner without objection from the owners of the copyrights on the programs. For the same reason, even the two respondents in this case, who do assert objections to time-shifting in this litigation, were unable to prove that the practice has impaired the commercial value of their copyrights or has created any likelihood of future harm. * * *

* * * Sony's Betamax VTR is a mechanism consisting of three basic components: (1) a tuner, which receives electromagnetic signals transmitted over the television band of the public airwaves and separates them into audio and visual signals; (2) a recorder, which records such signals on a magnetic tape; and (3) an adapter, which converts the audio and visual signals on the tape into a composite signal that can be received by a television set.

* * *

The respondents and Sony both conducted surveys of the way the Betamax machine was used by several hundred owners during a sample period in 1978. Although there were some differences in the surveys, they both showed that the primary use of the machine for most owners was "time-shifting,"—the practice of recording a program to view it once at a later time, and thereafter erasing it. Time-shifting enables viewers to see programs they otherwise would miss because they are not at home, are occupied with other tasks, or are viewing a program on another station at the time of a broadcast that they desire to watch. Both surveys also showed, however, that a substantial number of interviewees had accumulated libraries of tapes. Sony's survey indicated that over 80% of the interviewees watched at least as much regular television as they had before owning a Betamax. Respondents offered no evidence of decreased television viewing by Betamax owners.

Sony introduced considerable evidence describing television programs that could be copied without objection from any copyright holder, with special emphasis on sports, religious, and educational programming. For example, their survey indicated that 7.3% of all Betamax use is to record sports events, and representatives of professional baseball, football, basketball, and hockey testified that they had no objection to the recording of their televised events for home use.

* * *

The District Court assumed that Sony had constructive knowledge of the probability that the Betamax machine would be used to record copyrighted programs, but found that Sony merely sold a "product capable of a variety of uses, some of them allegedly infringing." 480 F.Supp. at 461. It reasoned:

> Selling a staple article of commerce *e.g.*, a typewriter, a recorder, a camera, a photocopying machine technically contributes to any infringing use subsequently made thereof, but this kind of 'contribution,' if deemed sufficient as a basis for liability, would expand the theory beyond precedent and arguably beyond judicial management.
>
> Commerce would indeed be hampered if manufacturers of staple items were held liable as contributory infringers whenever they 'constructively' knew that some purchasers on some occasions would use their product for a purpose which a court later deemed, as a matter of first impression, to be an infringement. *Ibid.*

* * *

The Court of Appeals reversed the District Court's judgment on respondents' copyright claim. It did not set aside any of the District Court's findings of fact. Rather, it concluded as a matter of law that the home use of a VTR was not a fair use because it was not a "productive use."[9] It therefore held that it was unnecessary for plaintiffs to prove any harm to the potential market for the copyrighted works, but then observed that it seemed clear that the cumulative effect of mass reproduction made possible by VTR's would tend to diminish the potential market for respondents' works. 659 F.2d, at 974.

On the issue of contributory infringement, the Court of Appeals first rejected the analogy to staple articles of commerce such as tape recorders or photocopying machines. It noted that such machines "may have substantial benefit for some purposes" and do not "even remotely raise copyright problems." Id., at 975. VTR's, however, are sold "for the primary purpose of reproducing television programming" and "virtually all" such programming is copyrighted material. Ibid. The Court of Appeals concluded, therefore, that VTR's were not suitable for any substantial noninfringing use even if some copyright owners elect not to enforce their rights.

* * *

On the matter of relief, the Court of Appeals concluded that "statutory damages may be appropriate," that the District Court should

---

9. "Without a 'productive use', i.e. when copyrighted material is reproduced for its intrinsic use, the mass copying of the sort involved in this case precludes an application of fair use." 659 F.2d, at 971–972.

reconsider its determination that an injunction would not be an appropriate remedy; and, referring to "the analogous photocopying area," suggested that a continuing royalty pursuant to a judicially created compulsory license may very well be an acceptable resolution of the relief issue. 659 F.2d, at 976.

* * *

If vicarious liability is to be imposed on petitioners in this case, it must rest on the fact that they have sold equipment with constructive knowledge of the fact that their customers may use that equipment to make unauthorized copies of copyrighted material. There is no precedent in the law of copyright for the imposition of vicarious liability on such a theory. The closest analogy is provided by the patent law cases to which it is appropriate to refer because of the historic kinship between patent law and copyright law.

In the Patent Code both the concept of infringement and the concept of contributory infringement are expressly defined by statute. The prohibition against contributory infringement is confined to the knowing sale of a component especially made for use in connection with a particular patent. There is no suggestion in the statute that one patentee may object to the sale of a product that might be used in connection with other patents. Moreover, the Act expressly provides that the sale of a "staple article or commodity of commerce suitable for substantial noninfringing use" is not contributory infringement.

When a charge of contributory infringement is predicated entirely on the sale of an article of commerce that is used by the purchaser to infringe a patent, the public interest in access to that article of commerce is necessarily implicated. A finding of contributory infringement does not, of course, remove the article from the market altogether; it does, however, give the patentee effective control over the sale of that item. Indeed, a finding of contributory infringement is normally the functional equivalent of holding that the disputed article is within the monopoly granted to the patentee.[21]

For that reason, in contributory infringement cases arising under the patent laws the Court has always recognized the critical importance of not allowing the patentee to extend his monopoly beyond the limits of his specific grant. These cases deny the patentee any right to control the distribution of unpatented articles unless they are "unsuited for any commercial noninfringing use." Dawson Chemical Co. v. Rohm & Hass Co., 448 U.S. 176, 198, 100 S.Ct. 2601, 2614, 65 L.Ed.2d 696 (1980). Unless a commodity "has no use except through practice of the patented method," ibid, the patentee has no right to claim that its distribution constitutes contributory infringement. "To form the basis

---

21. It seems extraordinary to suggest that the Copyright Act confers upon all copyright owners collectively, much less the two respondents in this case, the exclusive right to distribute VTR's simply because they may be used to infringe copyrights. That, however, is the logical implication of their claim. The request for an injunction below indicates that respondents seek, in effect, to declare VTR's contraband. Their suggestion in this Court that a continuing royalty pursuant to a judicially created compulsory license would be an acceptable remedy merely indicates that respondents, for their part, would be willing to license their claimed monopoly interest in VTR's to petitioners in return for a royalty.

for contributory infringement the item must almost be uniquely suited as a component of the patented invention." P. Rosenberg, Patent Law Fundamentals § 17.02[2] (1982). "[A] sale of an article which though adapted to an infringing use is also adapted to other and lawful uses, is not enough to make the seller a contributory infringer. Such a rule would block the wheels of commerce." Henry v. A.B. Dick Co., 224 U.S. 1, 48, 32 S.Ct. 364, 379, 56 L.Ed. 645 (1912), overruled on other grounds, Motion Picture Patents Co. v. Universal Film Mfg. Co., 243 U.S. 502, 517, 37 S.Ct. 416, 421, 61 L.Ed. 871 (1917).

We recognize there are substantial differences between the patent and copyright laws. But in both areas the contributory infringement doctrine is grounded on the recognition that adequate protection of a monopoly may require the courts to look beyond actual duplication of a device or publication to the products or activities that make such duplication possible. The staple article of commerce doctrine must strike a balance between a copyright holder's legitimate demand for effective—not merely symbolic—protection of the statutory monopoly, and the rights of others freely to engage in substantially unrelated areas of commerce. Accordingly, the sale of copying equipment, like the sale of other articles of commerce, does not constitute contributory infringement if the product is widely used for legitimate, unobjectionable purposes. Indeed, it need merely be capable of substantial noninfringing uses.

* * *

The question is thus whether the Betamax is capable of commercially significant noninfringing uses. In order to resolve that question, we need not explore *all* the different potential uses of the machine and determine whether or not they would constitute infringement. Rather, we need only consider whether on the basis of the facts as found by the district court a significant number of them would be non-infringing. Moreover, in order to resolve this case we need not give precise content to the question of how much use is commercially significant. For one potential use of the Betamax plainly satisfies this standard, however it is understood: private, noncommercial time-shifting in the home. It does so both (A) because respondents have no right to prevent other copyright holders from authorizing it for their programs, and (B) because the District Court's factual findings reveal that even the unauthorized home time-shifting of respondents' programs is legitimate fair use.

A. Authorized Time Shifting

Each of the respondents owns a large inventory of valuable copyrights, but in the total spectrum of television programming their combined market share is small. The exact percentage is not specified, but it is well below 10%. If they were to prevail, the outcome of this litigation would have a significant impact on both the producers and the viewers of the remaining 90% of the programming in the Nation. No doubt, many other producers share respondents' concern about the possible consequences of unrestricted copying. Nevertheless the findings of the District Court make it clear that time-shifting may enlarge the total viewing audience and that many producers are willing to allow private time-shifting to continue, at least for an experimental time period.[23]

* * *

Of course, the fact that other copyright holders may welcome the practice of time-shifting does not mean that respondents should be deemed to have granted a license to copy their programs. Third party conduct would be wholly irrelevant in an action for direct infringement of respondents' copyrights. But in an action for contributory infringement against the seller of copying equipment, the copyright holder may not prevail unless the relief that he seeks affects only his programs, or unless he speaks for virtually all copyright holders with an interest in the outcome. In this case, the record makes it perfectly clear that there are many important producers of national and local television programs who find nothing objectionable about the enlargement in the size of the television audience that results from the practice of time-shifting for private home use.[28] The seller of the equipment that expands those producers' audiences cannot be a contributory infringer if, as is true in this case, it has had no direct involvement with any infringing activity.

B. Unauthorized Time-Shifting

Even unauthorized uses of a copyrighted work are not necessarily infringing. An unlicensed use of the copyright is not an infringement unless it conflicts with one of the specific exclusive rights conferred by the copyright statute. Twentieth Century Music Corp. v. Aiken, 422 U.S. 151, 154–155, 95 S.Ct. 2040, 2043, 45 L.Ed.2d 84. Moreover, the definition of exclusive rights in § 106 of the present Act is prefaced by the words "subject to sections 107 through 118." Those sections describe a variety of uses of copyrighted material that "are not infringements of copyright notwithstanding the provisions of § 106." The most pertinent in this case is § 107, the legislative endorsement of the doctrine of "fair use."

---

23. The District Court did not make any explicit findings with regard to how much broadcasting is wholly uncopyrighted. The record does include testimony that at least one movie—My Man Godfrey—falls within that category, Tr. 2300–2301, and certain broadcasts produced by the federal government are also uncopyrighted. See 17 U.S.C. § 105. Cf. Schnapper v. Foley, 667 F.2d 102 (CADC 1981) (explaining distinction between work produced by the government and work commissioned by the government). To the extent such broadcasting is now significant, it further bolsters our conclusion. Moreover, since copyright protection is not perpetual, the number of audiovisual works in the public domain necessarily increases each year.

28. It may be rare for large numbers of copyright owners to authorize duplication of their works without demanding a fee from the copier. In the context of public broadcasting, however, the user of the copyrighted work is not required to pay a fee for access to the underlying work. The traditional method by which copyright owners capitalize upon the television medium—commercially sponsored free public broadcast over the public airwaves—is predicated upon the assumption that compensation for the value of displaying the works will be received in the form of advertising revenues. * * *

That section identifies various factors that enable a Court to apply an "equitable rule of reason" analysis to particular claims of infringement. Although not conclusive, the first factor requires that "the commercial or nonprofit character of an activity" be weighed in any fair use decision. If the Betamax were used to make copies for a commercial or profit-making purpose, such use would presumptively be unfair. The contrary presumption is appropriate here, however, because the District Court's findings plainly establish that time-shifting for private home use must be characterized as a noncommercial, nonprofit activity. Moreover, when one considers the nature of a televised copyrighted audiovisual work, see 17 U.S.C. § 107(2), and that timeshifting merely enables a viewer to see such a work which he had been invited to witness in its entirety free of charge, the fact that the entire work is reproduced, see id., at § 107(3), does not have its ordinary effect of militating against a finding of fair use.[33]

This is not, however, the end of the inquiry because Congress has also directed us to consider "the effect of the use upon the potential market for or value of the copyrighted work." Id., at § 107(4). The purpose of copyright is to create incentives for creative effort. Even copying for noncommercial purposes may impair the copyright holder's ability to obtain the rewards that Congress intended him to have. But a use that has no demonstrable effect upon the potential market for, or the value of, the copyrighted work need not be prohibited in order to protect the author's incentive to create. The prohibition of such noncommercial uses would merely inhibit access to ideas without any countervailing benefit.[34]

---

33. It has been suggested that "consumptive uses of copyrights by home VTR users are commercial even if the consumer does not sell the homemade tape because the consumer will not buy tapes separately sold by the copyright-holder." Home Recording of Copyrighted Works: Hearing before Subcommittee on Courts, Civil Liberties and the Administration of Justice of the House Committee on the Judiciary, 97th Congress, 2d Session, pt. 2, p. 1250 (1982) (memorandum of Prof. Laurence H. Tribe). Furthermore, "[t]he error in excusing such theft as noncommercial," we are told, "can be seen by simple analogy: jewel theft is not converted into a noncommercial veniality if stolen jewels are simply worn rather than sold." Ibid. The premise and the analogy are indeed simple, but they add nothing to the argument. The use to which stolen jewelry is put is quite irrelevant in determining whether depriving its true owner of his present possessory interest in it is venial; because of the nature of the item and the true owner's interests in physical possession of it, the law finds the taking objectionable even if the thief does not use the item at all. Theft of a particular item of personal property of course may have commercial significance, for the thief deprives the owner of his right to sell that particular item to any individual. Timeshifting does not even remotely entail comparable consequences to the copyright owner. Moreover, the timeshifter no more steals the program by watching it once than does the live viewer, and the live viewer is no more likely to buy pre-recorded videotapes than is the timeshifter. Indeed, no live viewer would buy a pre-recorded videotape if he did not have access to a VTR.

34. Cf. Latman, Fair Use of Copyrighted Works (1958), reprinted as Study No. 14 in Senate Judiciary Committee, Copyright Law Revision, Studies Prepared for the Subcommittee on Patents, Trademarks, and Copyrights, 86th Cong., 2d Sess., p. 30 (1960): "In certain situations, the copyright owner suffers no substantial harm from the use of the work * * *. Here again, is the partial marriage between the doctrine of fair use and the legal maxim *de minimis non curat lex.*"

Thus, although every commercial use of copyrighted material is presumptively an unfair exploitation of the monopoly privilege that belongs to the owner of the copyright, noncommercial uses are a different matter. A challenge to a noncommercial use of a copyrighted work requires proof either that the particular use is harmful, or that if it should become widespread, it would adversely affect the potential market for the copyrighted work. Actual present harm need not be shown; such a requirement would leave the copyright holder with no defense against predictable damage. Nor is it necessary to show with certainty that future harm will result. What is necessary is a showing by a preponderance of the evidence that *some* meaningful likelihood of future harm exists. If the intended use is for commercial gain, that likelihood may be presumed. But if it is for a noncommercial purpose, the likelihood must be demonstrated.

In this case, respondents failed to carry their burden with regard to home time-shifting. * * *

* * *

On the question of potential future harm from time-shifting, the District Court offered a more detailed analysis of the evidence. It rejected respondents' "fear that persons 'watching' the original telecast of a program will not be measured in the live audience and the ratings and revenues will decrease," by observing that current measurement technology allows the Betamax audience to be reflected. Id., at 466.[36] It rejected respondents' prediction "that live television or movie audiences will decrease as more people watch Betamax tapes as an alternative," with the observation that "[t]here is no factual basis for [the underlying] assumption." *Ibid.* It rejected respondents' "fear that time-shifting will reduce audiences for telecast reruns," and concluded instead that "given current market practices, this should aid plaintiffs rather than harm them." *Ibid.* And it declared that respondents' suggestion "that theater or film rental exhibition of a program will suffer because of time-shift recording of that program" "lacks merit." 480 F.Supp., at 467.

* * *

When these factors are all weighed in the "equitable rule of reason" balance, we must conclude that this record amply supports the

---

36. "There was testimony at trial, however, that Nielsen Ratings has already developed the ability to measure when a Betamax in a sample home is recording the program. Thus, the Betamax will be measured as a part of the live audience. The later diary can augment that measurement with information about subsequent viewing." 480 F.Supp., at 466.

In a separate section, the District Court rejected plaintiffs' suggestion that the commercial attractiveness of television broadcasts would be diminished because Betamax owners would use the pause button or fast-forward control to avoid viewing advertisements:

"It must be remembered, however, that to omit commercials, Betamax owners must view the program, including the commercials, while recording. To avoid commercials during playback, the viewer must fast-forward and, for the most part, guess as to when the commercial has passed. For most recordings, either practice may be too tedious. As defendants' survey showed, 92% of the programs were recorded with commercials and only 25% of the owners fast-forward through them. Advertisers will have to make the same kinds of judgments they do now about whether persons viewing televised programs actually watch the advertisements which interrupt them." *Id.,* at 468.

District Court's conclusion that home time-shifting is fair use. In light of the findings of the District Court regarding the state of the empirical data, it is clear that the Court of Appeals erred in holding that the statute as presently written bars such conduct.[40]

In summary, the record and findings of the District Court lead us to two conclusions. First, Sony demonstrated a significant likelihood that substantial numbers of copyright holders who license their works for broadcast on free television would not object to having their broadcasts time-shifted by private viewers. And second, respondents failed to demonstrate that time-shifting would cause any likelihood of nonminimal harm to the potential market for, or the value of, their copyrighted works. The Betamax is, therefore, capable of substantial noninfringing uses. Sony's sale of such equipment to the general public does not constitute contributory infringement of respondent's copyrights.

* * *

It may well be that Congress will take a fresh look at this new technology, just as it so often has examined other innovations in the past. But it is not our job to apply laws that have not yet been written. Applying the copyright statute, as it now reads, to the facts as they have been developed in this case, the judgment of the Court of Appeals must be reversed.

It is so ordered.

---

40. The Court of Appeals chose not to engage in any "equitable rule of reason" analysis in this case. Instead, it assumed that the category of "fair use" is rigidly circumscribed by a requirement that every such use must be "productive." It therefore concluded that copying a television program merely to enable the viewer to receive information or entertainment that he would otherwise miss because of a personal scheduling conflict could never be fair use. That understanding of "fair use" was erroneous.

Congress has plainly instructed us that fair use analysis calls for a sensitive balancing of interests. The distinction between "productive" and "unproductive" uses may be helpful in calibrating the balance, but it cannot be wholly determinative. Although copying to promote a scholarly endeavor certainly has a stronger claim to fair use than copying to avoid interrupting a poker game, the question is not simply two-dimensional. For one thing, it is not true that all copyrights are fungible. Some copyrights govern material with broad potential secondary markets. Such material may well have a broader claim to protection because of the greater potential for commercial harm. Copying a news broadcast may have a stronger claim to fair use than copying a motion picture. And, of course, not all uses are fungible. Copying for commercial gain has a much weaker claim to fair use than copying for personal enrichment. But the notion of social "productivity" cannot be a complete answer to this analysis. A teacher who copies to prepare lecture notes is clearly productive. But so is a teacher who copies for the sake of broadening his personal understanding of his specialty. Or a legislator who copies for the sake of broadening her understanding of what her constituents are watching; or a constituent who copies a news program to help make a decision on how to vote.

Making a copy of a copyrighted work for the convenience of a blind person is expressly identified by the House Committee Report as an example of fair use, with no suggestion that anything more than a purpose to entertain or to inform need motivate the copying. In a hospital setting, using a VTR to enable a patient to see programs he would otherwise miss has no productive purpose other than contributing to the psychological well-being of the patient. Virtually any time-shifting that increases viewer access to television programming may result in a comparable benefit. The statutory language does not identify any dichotomy between productive and nonproductive time-shifting, but does require consideration of the economic consequences of copying.

JUSTICE BLACKMUN, with whom JUSTICE MARSHALL, JUSTICE POWELL, and JUSTICE REHNQUIST join, dissenting.

* * *

The Betamax, like other VTRs, presently is capable of recording television broadcasts off the air on videotape cassettes, and playing them back at a later time.[1] Two kinds of Betamax usage are at issue here.[2] The first is "time-shifting," whereby the user records a program in order to watch it at a later time, and then records over it, and thereby erases the program, after a single viewing. The second is "library-building," in which the user records a program in order to keep it for repeated viewing over a longer term. Sony's advertisements, at various times, have suggested that Betamax users "record favorite shows" or "build a library." Sony's Betamax advertising has never contained warnings about copyright infringement, although a warning does appear in the Betamax operating instructions.

* * *

Although the word "copies" is in the plural in § 106(1), there can be no question that under the Act the making of even a single unauthorized copy is prohibited. The Senate and House Reports explain: "The references to 'copies or phonorecords,' although in the plural, are intended here and throughout the bill to include the singular (1 U.S.C. § 1)."[10] S.Rep. No. 94–473, p. 58 (1975) (1975 Senate Report); H.R.Rep. No. 94–1476, p. 61 (1976) (1976 House Report), U.S.Code Cong. & Admin.News 1976, p. 5675. * * *

* * *

Indeed, it appears that Congress considered and rejected the very possibility of a special private use exemption. The issue was raised early in the revision process, in one of the studies prepared for Congress under the supervision of the Copyright Office. Latman, Fair Use of Copyrighted Works (1958), reprinted in Senate Committee on the Judiciary, Copyright Law Revision, Studies Prepared for the Subcommittee on Patents, Trademarks, and Copyrights, 86th Cong., 2d Sess., 1 (1960) (Latman Fair Use Study). This study found no reported case support-

---

1. The Betamax has three primary components: a tuner that receives television ("RF") signals broadcast over the airwaves; an adapter that converts the RF signals into audio-video signals; and a recorder that places the audio-video signals on magnetic tape. Sony also manufactures VTRs without built-in tuners; these are capable of playing back prerecorded tapes and recording home movies on videotape, but cannot record off the air. Since the Betamax has its own tuner, it can be used to record off one channel while another channel is being watched.

The Betamax is available with auxiliary features, including a timer, a pause control, and a fast-forward control; these allow Betamax owners to record programs without being present, to avoid (if they are present) recording commercial messages, and to skip over commercials while playing back the recording. Videotape is reusable; the user erases its record by recording over it.

2. This case involves only the home recording for home use of television programs broadcast free over the airwaves. No issue is raised concerning cable or pay television, or the sharing or trading of tapes.

10. 1 U.S.C. § 1 provides in relevant part:

"In determining the meaning of any Act of Congress, unless the context indicates otherwise * * * words importing the plural include the singular * * *."

ing the existence of an exemption for private use, although it noted that "the purpose and nature of a private use, and in some cases the small amount taken, might lead a court to apply the general principles of fair use in such a way as to deny liability." Id., at 12. * * *

* * * I can conclude only that Congress, like the Register, intended to rely on the fair use doctrine, and not on a per se exemption for private use, to separate permissible copying from the impermissible.[16]

* * *

The doctrine of fair use has been called, with some justification, "the most troublesome in the whole law of copyright." Dellar v. Samuel Goldwyn, Inc., 104 F.2d 661, 662 (CA2 1939); see Triangle Publications, Inc. v. Knight-Ridder Newspapers, Inc., 626 F.2d 1171, 1174 (CA5 1980); Meeropol v. Nizer, 560 F.2d 1061, 1068 (CA2 1977), cert. denied, 434 U.S. 1013, 98 S.Ct. 727, 54 L.Ed.2d 756 (1978). Although courts have constructed lists of factors to be considered in determining whether a particular use is fair, no fixed criteria have emerged by which that determination can be made. This Court thus far has provided no guidance; although fair use issues have come here twice, on each occasion the Court was equally divided and no opinion was forthcoming. Williams & Wilkins Co. v. United States, 203 Ct.Cl. 74, 487 F.2d 1345 (1973), aff'd, 420 U.S. 376, 95 S.Ct. 1344, 43 L.Ed.2d 264 (1975); Benny v. Loew's, Inc., 239 F.2d 532 (CA9 1956), aff'd sub nom. CBS, Inc. v. Loew's Inc., 356 U.S. 43, 78 S.Ct. 667, 2 L.Ed.2d 583 (1958).

---

16. In Williams & Wilkins Co. v. United States, 203 Ct.Cl. 74, 487 F.2d 1345 (1973), aff'd by an equally divided Court, 420 U.S. 376, 95 S.Ct. 1344, 43 L.Ed.2d 264 (1975), decided during the process of the revision of the copyright statutes, the Court of Claims suggested that copying for personal use might be outside the scope of copyright protection under the 1909 Act. The court reasoned that because "hand copying" for personal use has always been regarded as permissible, and because the practice of making personal copies continued after typewriters and photostat machines were developed, the making of personal copies by means other than hand copying should be permissible as well. Id., at 84–88, 487 F.2d, at 1350–1352.

There appear to me to be several flaws in this reasoning. First, it is by no means clear that the making of a "hand copy" of an entire work is permissible; the most that can be said is that there is no reported case on the subject, possibly because no copyright owner ever thought it worthwhile to sue. See Latman Fair Use Study 11–12; 3 M. Nimmer, Copyright § 13.05[E][4][a] (1982). At least one early treatise asserted that infringement would result "if an individual made copies for his personal use, even in his own handwriting, as there is no rule of law excepting manuscript copies from the law of infringement." A. Weil, American Copyright Law § 1066 (1917). Second, hand copying or even copying by typewriter is self-limiting. The drudgery involved in making hand copies ordinarily ensures that only necessary and fairly small portions of a work are taken; it is unlikely that any user would make a hand copy as a substitute for one that could be purchased. The harm to the copyright owner from hand copying thus is minimal. The recent advent of inexpensive and readily available copying machines, however, has changed the dimensions of the problem. See Register's Second Supplementary Report ch. III, p. 3; Hearings on H.R. 2223 before the Subcommittee on Courts, Civil Liberties, and the Administration of Justice of the House Judiciary Committee, 94th Cong., 1st Sess., 194 (1975) (1975 House Hearings) (remarks of Rep. Danielson); id., at 234 (statement of Robert W. Cairns); id., at 250 (remarks of Rep. Danielson); id., at 354 (testimony of Irwin Karp); id., at 467 (testimony of Rondo Cameron); id ., at 1795 (testimony of Barbara Ringer, Register of Copyrights). Thus, "[t]he supposition that there is no tort involved in a scholar copying a copyrighted text by hand does not much advance the question of machine copying." B. Kaplan, An Unhurried View of Copyright 101–102 (1967).

Nor did Congress provide definitive rules when it codified the fair use doctrine in the 1976 Act; it simply incorporated a list of factors "to be considered": the "purpose and character of the use," the "nature of the copyrighted work," the "amount and substantiality of the portion used," and, perhaps the most important, the "effect of the use upon the *potential* market for or value of the copyrighted work" (emphasis supplied). § 107. No particular weight, however, was assigned to any of these, and the list was not intended to be exclusive. The House and Senate Reports explain that § 107 does no more than give "statutory recognition" to the fair use doctrine; it was intended "to restate the present judicial doctrine of fair use, not to change, narrow, or enlarge it in any way." 1976 House Report 66, U.S.Code Cong. & Admin.News 1976, p. 5680. See 1975 Senate Report 62; S.Rep. No. 93–983, p. 116 (1974); H.R.Rep. No. 83, 90th Cong., 1st Sess., 32 (1967); H.R.Rep. No. 2237, 89th Cong., 2d Sess., 61 (1966).

* * *

There are situations, nevertheless, in which strict enforcement of this monopoly would inhibit the very "Progress of Science and useful Arts" that copyright is intended to promote. An obvious example is the researcher or scholar whose own work depends on the ability to refer to and to quote the work of prior scholars. Obviously, no author could create a new work if he were first required to repeat the research of every author who had gone before him. The scholar, like the ordinary user, of course could be left to bargain with each copyright owner for permission to quote from or refer to prior works. But there is a crucial difference between the scholar and the ordinary user. When the ordinary user decides that the owner's price is too high, and forgoes use of the work, only the individual is the loser. When the scholar forgoes the use of a prior work, not only does his own work suffer, but the public is deprived of his contribution to knowledge. The scholar's work, in other words, produces external benefits from which everyone profits. In such a case, the fair use doctrine acts as a form of subsidy—albeit at the first author's expense—to permit the second author to make limited use of the first author's work for the public good. See Latman Fair Use Study 31; Gordon, Fair Use as Market Failure: A Structural Analysis of the *Betamax* Case and its Predecessors, 82 Colum.L.Rev. 1600, 1630 (1982).

A similar subsidy may be appropriate in a range of areas other than pure scholarship. The situations in which fair use is most commonly recognized are listed in § 107 itself; fair use may be found when a work is used "for purposes such as criticism, comment, news reporting, teaching, * * * scholarship, or research." The House and Senate Reports expand on this list somewhat, and other examples may be found in the case law. Each of these uses, however, reflects a common theme: each is a *productive* use, resulting in some added benefit to the public beyond that produced by the first author's work.[31]

---

31. Professor Seltzer has characterized these lists of uses as "reflect[ing] what in fact the subject matter of fair use has in the history of its adjudication consisted in:

The fair use doctrine, in other words, permits works to be used for "socially laudable purposes." See Copyright Office, Briefing Papers on Current Issues, reprinted in 1975 House Hearings 2051, 2055. I am aware of no case in which the reproduction of a copyrighted work for the sole benefit of the user has been held to be fair use.[32]

I do not suggest, of course, that every productive use is a fair use. A finding of fair use still must depend on the facts of the individual case, and on whether, under the circumstances, it is reasonable to expect the user to bargain with the copyright owner for use of the work. * * *

The making of a videotape recording for home viewing is an ordinary rather than a productive use of the Studios' copyrighted works. * * *

It may be tempting, as, in my view, the Court today is tempted, to stretch the doctrine of fair use so as to permit unfettered use of this new technology in order to increase access to television programming. But such an extension risks eroding the very basis of copyright law, by depriving authors of control over their works and consequently of their incentive to create. * * *

* * *

I recognize, nevertheless, that there are situations where permitting even an unproductive use would have no effect on the author's incentive to create, that is, where the use would not affect the value of, or the market for, the author's work. Photocopying an old newspaper clipping to send to a friend may be an example; pinning a quotation on one's bulletin board may be another. In each of these cases, the effect on the author is truly *de minimis*. Thus, even though these uses provide no benefit to the public at large, no purpose is served by preserving the author's monopoly, and the use may be regarded as fair.

Courts should move with caution, however, in depriving authors of protection from unproductive "ordinary" uses. * * *

I therefore conclude that, at least when the proposed use is an unproductive one, a copyright owner need prove only a *potential* for harm to the market for or the value of the copyrighted work. See 3 M. Nimmer, Copyright § 13.05[E][4][c], p. 13–84 (1982). Proof of actual

it has always had to do with the use by a second author of a first author's work." L. Seltzer, Exemptions and Fair Use in Copyright 24 (1978) (emphasis removed). He distinguishes "the mere reproduction of a work in order to use it for its intrinsic purpose—to make what might be called the 'ordinary' use of it." When copies are made for "ordinary" use of the work, "ordinary *infringement* has customarily been triggered, not notions of fair use" (emphasis in original). Ibid. See also M. Nimmer, Copyright § 13.05[A][1] (1982) ("Use of a work in each of the foregoing contexts either necessarily or usually involves its use in a derivative work").

32. Williams & Wilkins Co. v. United States, 203 Ct.Cl. 74, 487 F.2d 1345 (1973), aff'd by an equally divided Court, 420 U.S. 376, 95 S.Ct. 1344, 43 L.Ed.2d 264 (1975), involved the photocopying of scientific journal articles; the Court of Claims stressed that the libraries performing the copying were "devoted solely to the advancement and dissemination of medical knowledge," 203 Ct.Cl., at 91, 487 F.2d, at 1354, and that "medical science would be seriously hurt if such library photocopying were stopped." Id., at 95, 487 F.2d, at 1356.

* * *

harm, or even probable harm, may be impossible in an area where the effect of a new technology is speculative, and requiring such proof would present the "real danger * * * of confining the scope of an author's rights on the basis of the present technology so that, as the years go by, his copyright loses much of its value because of unforeseen technical advances." Register's Supplementary Report 14. Infringement thus would be found if the copyright owner demonstrates a reasonable possibility that harm will result from the proposed use. When the use is one that creates no benefit to the public at large, copyright protection should not be denied on the basis that a new technology that may result in harm has not yet done so.

The Studios have identified a number of ways in which VTR recording could damage their copyrights. VTR recording could reduce their ability to market their works in movie theaters and through the rental or sale of pre-recorded videotapes or videodiscs; it also could reduce their rerun audience, and consequently the license fees available to them for repeated showings. Moreover, advertisers may be willing to pay for only "live" viewing audiences, if they believe VTR viewers will delete commercials or if rating services are unable to measure VTR use; if this is the case, VTR recording could reduce the license fees the Studios are able to charge even for first-run showings. Library-building may raise the potential for each of the types of harm identified by the Studios, and time-shifting may raise the potential for substantial harm as well.[35]

Although the District Court found no likelihood of harm from VTR use, 480 F.Supp., at 468, I conclude that it applied an incorrect substantive standard and misallocated the burden of proof. * * *

The District Court's reluctance to engage in prediction in this area is understandable, but, in my view, the court was mistaken in concluding that the Studios should bear the risk created by this uncertainty. The Studios have demonstrated a potential for harm, which has not been, and could not be, refuted at this early stage of technological development.

---

35. A VTR owner who has taped a favorite movie for repeated viewing will be less likely to rent or buy a tape containing the same movie, watch a televised rerun, or pay to see the movie at a theater. Although time-shifting may not replace theater or rerun viewing or the purchase of prerecorded tapes or discs, it may well replace rental usage; a VTR user who has recorded a first-run movie for later viewing will have no need to rent a copy when he wants to see it. Both library-builders and time-shifters may avoid commercials; the library builder may use the pause control to record without them, and all users may fast-forward through commercials on playback.

The Studios introduced expert testimony that both time-shifting and librarying would tend to decrease their revenue from copyrighted works. See 480 F.Supp., at 440. The District Court's findings also show substantial library-building and avoidance of commercials. Both sides submitted surveys showing that the average Betamax user owns between 25 and 32 tapes. The Studios' survey showed that at least 40% of users had more than 10 tapes in a "library"; Sony's survey showed that more than 40% of users planned to view their tapes more than once; and both sides' surveys showed that commercials were avoided at least 25% of the time. *Id.*, at 438–439.

The District Court's analysis of harm, moreover, failed to consider the effect of VTR recording on "the *potential* market for or the value of the copyrighted work," as required by § 107(4). The requirement that a putatively infringing use of a copyrighted work, to be "fair," must not impair a "potential" market for the work has two implications. First, an infringer cannot prevail merely by demonstrating that the copyright holder suffered no net harm from the infringer's action. Indeed, even a showing that the infringement has resulted in a net benefit to the copyright holder will not suffice. Rather, the infringer must demonstrate that he had not impaired the copyright holder's ability to demand compensation from (or to deny access to) any group who would otherwise be willing to pay to see or hear the copyrighted work. Second, the fact that a given market for a copyrighted work would not be available to the copyright holder were it not for the infringer's activities does not permit the infringer to exploit that market without compensating the copyright holder. See Iowa State University Research Foundation, Inc. v. American Broadcasting Cos., 621 F.2d 57 (CA2 1980).

In this case, the Studios and their *amici* demonstrate that the advent of the VTR technology created a potential market for their copyrighted programs. That market consists of those persons who find it impossible or inconvenient to watch the programs at the time they are broadcast, and who wish to watch them at other times. These persons are willing to pay for the privilege of watching copyrighted work at their convenience, as is evidenced by the fact that they are willing to pay for VTRs and tapes; undoubtedly, most also would be willing to pay some kind of royalty to copyright holders. The Studios correctly argue that they have been deprived of the ability to exploit this sizable market.

It is thus apparent from the record and from the findings of the District Court that time-shifting does have a substantial adverse effect upon the "potential market for" the Studios' copyrighted works. Accordingly, even under the formulation of the fair use doctrine advanced by Sony, time-shifting cannot be deemed a fair use.

* * *

Contributory Infringement

From the Studios' perspective, the consequences of home VTR recording are the same as if a business had taped the Studios' works off the air, duplicated the tapes, and sold or rented them to members of the public for home viewing. The distinction is that home VTR users do not record for commercial advantage; the commercial benefit accrues to the manufacturer and distributors of the Betamax. I thus must proceed to discuss whether the manufacturer and distributors can be held contributorily liable if the product they sell is used to infringe.

* * * Although the liability provision of the 1976 Act provides simply that "[a]nyone who violates any of the exclusive rights of the copyright owner * * * is an infringer of the copyright," 17 U.S.C.

§ 501(a), the House and Senate Reports demonstrate that Congress intended to retain judicial doctrines of contributory infringement. * *

The doctrine of contributory copyright infringement, however, is not well-defined. One of the few attempts at definition appears in Gershwin Publishing Corp. v. Columbia Artists Management, Inc., 443 F.2d 1159 (CA2 1971). In that case the Second Circuit stated that "one who, with knowledge of the infringing activity, induces, causes or materially contributes to the infringing conduct of another, may be held liable as a 'contributory' infringer." Id., at 1162 (footnote omitted). While I have no quarrel with this general statement, it does not easily resolve the present case * * *.

* * *

Sony argues that the manufacturer or seller of a product used to infringe is absolved from liability whenever the product can be put to any substantial noninfringing use. Brief for Petitioners 41-42. The District Court so held, borrowing the "staple article of commerce" doctrine governing liability for contributory infringement of patents. See 35 U.S.C. § 271. This Court today is much less positive. See ante, at 788. I do not agree that this technical judge-made doctrine of patent law, based in part on considerations irrelevant to the field of copyright * * * should be imported wholesale into copyright law. * * *

I recognize, however, that many of the concerns underlying the "staple article of commerce" doctrine are present in copyright law as well. As the District Court noted, if liability for contributory infringement were imposed on the manufacturer or seller of every product used to infringe—a typewriter, a camera, a photocopying machine—the "wheels of commerce" would be blocked. 480 F.Supp., at 461; see also Kalem Co. v. Harper Brothers, 222 U.S., at 62, 32 S.Ct., at 21.

I therefore conclude that if a *significant* portion of the product's use is *noninfringing*, the manufacturers and sellers cannot be held contributorily liable for the product's infringing uses. See ante, at 788. If virtually all of the product's use, however, is to infringe, contributory liability may be imposed; if no one would buy the product for noninfringing purposes alone, it is clear that the manufacturer is purposely profiting from the infringement, and that liability is appropriately imposed. In such a case, the copyright owner's monopoly would not be extended beyond its proper bounds; the manufacturer of such a product contributes to the infringing activities of others and profits directly thereby, while providing no benefit to the public sufficient to justify the infringement.

The Court of Appeals concluded that Sony should be held liable for contributory infringement, reasoning that "[v]ideotape recorders are manufactured, advertised, and sold for the primary purpose of reproducing television programming," and "[v]irtually all television programming is copyrighted material." 659 F.2d, at 975. While I agree with the first of these propositions,[42] the second, for me, is problematic. The key question is not the amount of television programming that is copyrighted, but rather the amount of VTR usage that is infringing.[43] Moreover, the parties and their *amici* have argued vigorously about both the amount of television programming that is covered by copyright and the amount for which permission to copy has been given. The proportion of VTR recording that is infringing is ultimately a question of fact, and the District Court specifically declined to make findings on the "percentage of legal versus illegal home-use recording." 480 F.Supp., at 468. In light of my view of the law, resolution of this factual question is essential. I therefore would remand the case for further consideration of this by the District Court.

* * *

The Court's disposition of the case turns on its conclusion that time-shifting is a fair use. Because both parties agree that time-shifting is the primary use of VTRs, that conclusion, if correct, would settle the issue of Sony's liability under almost any definition of contributory infringement. The Court concludes that time-shifting is fair use for two reasons. Each is seriously flawed.

The Court's first reason for concluding that time-shifting is fair use is its claim that many copyright holders have no objection to time-shifting, and that "respondents have no right to prevent other copyright holders from authorizing it for their programs." *Ante*, at 789. The Court explains that a finding of contributory infringement would "inevitably frustrate the interests of broadcasters in reaching the portion of their audience that is available only through time-shifting." *Ante*, at 790. Such reasoning, however, simply confuses the question of liability with the difficulty of fashioning an appropriate remedy. It may be that an injunction prohibiting the sale of VTRs would harm the interests of copyright holders who have no objection to others making copies of their programs. But such concerns should and would be taken into account in fashioning an appropriate remedy once liability has been found. Remedies may well be available that would not interfere with authorized time-shifting at all. The Court of Appeals mentioned the possibility of a royalty payment that would allow VTR sales and time-shifting to continue unabated, and the parties may be able to devise other narrowly tailored remedies. Sony may be able, for example, to build a VTR that enables broadcasters to scramble the signal of individual programs and "jam" the unauthorized recording of them.

42. Although VTRs also may be used to watch prerecorded video cassettes and to make home motion pictures, these uses do not require a tuner such as the Betamax contains. See n. 1, supra. The Studios do not object to Sony's sale of VTRs without tuners. Brief for Respondents 5, n. 9. In considering the noninfringing uses of the Betamax, therefore, those uses that would remain possible without the Betamax's built-in tuner should not be taken into account.

43. Noninfringing uses would include, for example, recording works that are not protected by copyright, recording works that have entered the public domain, recording with permission of the copyright owner, and, of course, any recording that qualifies as fair use. See, e.g., Bruzzone v. Miller Brewing Co., 202 U.S.P.Q. 809 (N.D.Cal. 1979) (use of home VTR for market research studies).

Even were an appropriate remedy not available at this time, the Court should not misconstrue copyright holders' rights in a manner that prevents enforcement of them when, through development of better techniques, an appropriate remedy becomes available.

The Court's second stated reason for finding that Sony is not liable for contributory infringement is its conclusion that even unauthorized time-shifting is fair use. Ante, at 791. This conclusion is even more troubling. * * * It is true that the legislative history states repeatedly that the doctrine must be applied flexibly on a case-by-case basis, but those references were only in the context of productive uses. Such a limitation on fair use comports with its purpose, which is to facilitate the creation of new works. * * *

Having bypassed the initial hurdle for establishing that a use is fair, the Court then purports to apply to time-shifting the four factors explicitly stated in the statute. The first is "the purpose and character of the use, including whether such use is of a commercial nature or is for nonprofit educational purposes." § 107(1). The Court confidently describes time-shifting as a noncommercial, nonprofit activity. * * * Purely consumptive uses are certainly not what the fair use doctrine was designed to protect, and the awkwardness of applying the statutory language to time-shifting only makes clearer that fair use was designed to protect only uses that are productive.

The next two statutory factors are all but ignored by the Court—though certainly not because they have no applicability. The second factor—"the nature of the copyrighted work"—strongly supports the view that time-shifting is an infringing use. The rationale guiding application of this factor is that certain types of works, typically those involving "more of diligence than of originality or inventiveness," New York Times Co. v. Roxbury Data Interface, Inc., 434 F.Supp. 217, 221 (NJ 1977), require less copyright protection than other original works. Thus, for example, informational works, such as news reports, that readily lend themselves to productive use by others, are less protected than creative works of entertainment. Sony's own surveys indicate that entertainment shows account for more than 80 percent of the programs recorded by Betamax owners.

The third statutory factor—"the amount and substantiality of the portion used"—is even more devastating to the Court's interpretation. It is undisputed that virtually all VTR owners record entire works, see 480 F.Supp., at 454, thereby creating an exact substitute for the copyrighted original. Fair use is intended to allow individuals engaged in productive uses to copy small portions of original works that will facilitate their own productive endeavors. Time-shifting bears no resemblance to such activity, and the complete duplication that it involves might alone be sufficient to preclude a finding of fair use. It is little wonder that the Court has chosen to ignore this statutory factor.

The fourth factor requires an evaluation of "the effect of the use upon the potential market for or value of the copyrighted work." This is the factor upon which the Court focuses, but once again, the Court has misread the statute. As mentioned above, the statute requires a court to consider the effect of the use on the *potential* market for the copyrighted work. The Court has struggled mightily to show that VTR use has not reduced the value of the Studios' copyrighted works in their present markets. Even if true, that showing only begins the proper inquiry. The development of the VTR has created a new market for the works produced by the Studios. That market consists of those persons who desire to view television programs at times other than when they are broadcast, and who therefore purchase VTR recorders to enable them to time-shift. Because time-shifting of the Studios' copyrighted works involves the copying of them, however, the Studios are entitled to share in the benefits of that new market. Those benefits currently go to Sony through Betamax sales. Respondents therefore can show harm from VTR use simply by showing that the value of their copyrights would *increase* if they were compensated for the copies that are used in the new market. The existence of this effect is self-evident.

The Court of Appeals, having found Sony liable, remanded for the District Court to consider the propriety of injunctive or other relief. Because of my conclusion as to the issue of liability, I, too, would not decide here what remedy would be appropriate if liability were found. I concur, however, in the Court of Appeals' suggestion that an award of damages, or continuing royalties, or even some form of limited injunction, may well be an appropriate means of balancing the equities in this case.[51] Although I express no view on the merits of any particular proposal, I am certain that, if Sony were found liable in this case, the District Court would be able to fashion appropriate relief. The District Court might conclude, of course, that a continuing royalty or other equitable relief is not feasible. The Studios then would be relegated to statutory damages for proved instances of infringement. But the difficulty of fashioning relief, and the possibility that complete relief may be unavailable, should not affect our interpretation of the statute.

* * *

Questions

1. Are there a significant number of public domain works currently broadcast on television? Do the facts alluded to in the Court's footnote 23 support the contention that there are such a significant number?

---

51. Other Nations have imposed royalties on the manufacturers of products used to infringe copyright. See, e.g., Copyright Laws and Treaties of the World (UNESCO/BNA 1982) (English translation), reprinting Federal Act on Copyright in Works of Literature and Art and on Related Rights (Austria), § 42(5)–(7), and An Act dealing with Copyright and Related Rights (Federal Republic of Germany), Art. 53(5). A study produced for the Commission of European Communities has recommended that these requirements "serve as a pattern" for the European community. A. Dietz, Copyright Law in the European Community 135 (1978). While these royalty systems ordinarily depend on the existence of authors' collecting societies, see id., at 119, 136, such collecting societies are a familiar part of our copyright law. See generally Broadcast Music, Inc. v. Columbia Broadcasting System, Inc., 441 U.S. 1, 4–5, 99 S.Ct. 1551, 1554, 60 L.Ed.2d 1 (1979). Fashioning relief of this sort, of course, might require bringing other copyright owners into court through certification of a class or otherwise.

2. Do you agree that unauthorized time shifting should be regarded as fair use? Is such a conclusion based upon a double-payment argument, i.e., that television sponsors will pay broadcasters an additional sum by reason of a larger audience for their commercials even if such larger audience views the commercials via time-shifting, and that copyright owners benefit from such increased sponsor payments, and therefore should not be paid a second time under an infringement claim? Does this argument, in turn, depend upon the conclusion (see footnote 36 in *Sony*) that viewers will not "fast-forward" the commercials? If that conclusion was valid at the time of trial in 1979, is it equally valid under current technology?

3. If by reason of current fast-forward technology sponsors will not be willing to pay to broadcasters an additional sum because of an additional time shifting audience, does this also bear upon the continuing viability of the Court's conclusion as to the extent of authorized time-shifting?

4. If in some future case a court were to find liability and contributory infringement by the manufacturer, would the court be justified in imposing a continuing royalty in lieu of an injunction?

5. Is the decision in *Sony* applicable to audio home taping as well as video home taping? Is audio home taping primarily for library-building purposes rather than for time-shifting purposes? Is the double-payment argument equally applicable to audio home taping?

Collateral References

Gordon, *Fair Use as Market Failure: A Structural and Economic Analysis of the Betamax Case and Its Predecessors*, 82 Colum.L.Rev. 1600 (1982).

Patry, *In Praise of the Betamax Decision: An Examination of the Universal City Studios Inc. v. Sony Corp. of America Case*, 22 S.Tex.L.J. 211 (1982).

Nimmer on Copyright, § 13.05[F][5][b].

Note: The last fair use case to be considered in this section is *Harper & Row, Publishers, Inc. v. Nation Enterprises*, which may be found in Appendix E.

D. THE DEFENSE OF THE FIRST AMENDMENT

SID & MARTY KROFFT TELEVISION PRODUCTIONS, INC. v. McDONALD'S CORP.

United States Court of Appeals, Ninth Circuit, 1977.
562 F.2d 1157.

[The facts and other parts of this opinion are set forth at p. 348 supra in the section on similarity.]

Copyright and the First Amendment

Defendants argue that the first amendment operates in this case to limit the protection for plaintiffs' works. They seem to suggest that a more demanding standard than that of substantial similarity should be imposed, and that the threshold question about copying becomes one of "constitutional fact" to be reviewed de novo on appeal. Defendants attempt to analogize the copyright area to those of obscenity and defamation in suggesting that prior law must be modified to accommodate expanding first amendment rights.

The constitutionality of the copyright law was settled long ago by the Supreme Court. In Kalem Co. v. Harper Brothers, 222 U.S. 55, 32 S.Ct. 20, 56 L.Ed. 92 (1911), the defendant argued that the copyright law could not grant an author an exclusive right to dramatize his works. In rejecting this contention, the Court stated:

> It is argued that the law, construed as we have construed it, goes beyond the power conferred upon Congress by the Constitution, to secure to authors for a limited time the exclusive right to their writings. Art. I, § 8, cl. 8. It is suggested that to extend the copyright to a case like this is to extend it to the ideas, as distinguished from the words in which the ideas are clothed. But there is no attempt to make a monopoly of the ideas expressed. The law confines itself to a particular, cognate, and well-known form of reproduction. If to that extent a grant of monopoly is thought a proper way to secure the right to the writings, this court cannot say that Congress was wrong. Id. at 63, 32 S.Ct. at 22.

The Court recognized that the protection of the copyright laws is necessary to provide an incentive for artistic creation which ultimately advances the public good. See Twentieth Century Music Corp. v. Aiken, 422 U.S. 151, 156, 95 S.Ct. 2040, 45 L.Ed.2d 84 (1975).

But the impact, if any, of the first amendment on copyright has not been discussed by the Court.[15] We believe this silence stems not from neglect but from the fact that the idea-expression dichotomy already serves to accommodate the competing interests of copyright and the first amendment. The "marketplace of ideas" is not limited by copyright because copyright is limited to protection of expression. As one commentator has stated:

> [T]he idea-expression line represents an acceptable definitional balance as between copyright and free speech interests. In some degree it encroaches upon freedom of speech in that it abridges the right to reproduce the "expression" of others, but this is justified by the greater public good in the copyright encouragement of creative works. In some degree it encroaches upon the author's right to control his work in that it renders his "ideas" per se unprotectible, but this is justified by the greater public need for free access to ideas as part of the democratic dialogue.

Nimmer, Does Copyright Abridge the First Amendment Guarantees of Free Speech and Press?, 17 U.C.L.A.L.Rev. 1180, 1192–93 (1970). Cf. Lee v. Runge, 404 U.S. 887, 892–93, 92 S.Ct. 197, 30 L.Ed.2d 169 (1971) (Douglas, J., dissenting).

Ideas which may be of public interest are not subject to copyright; the specific form of expression of these ideas are. Thus, the political

---

15. In Sears, Roebuck & Co. v. Stiffel Co., 376 U.S. 225, 84 S.Ct. 784, 11 L.Ed.2d 661 (1964), and Compco Corp. v. Day-Brite Lighting, Inc., 376 U.S. 234, 84 S.Ct. 779, 11 L.Ed.2d 669 (1964), the court reasoned that in an economy based on free competition, the constitutionality authorized monopolies of patent and copyright must be strictly construed. It therefore found invalid state doctrines of unfair competition which expanded these monopolies. The court's concern was with monopolies as commercial, not political, impediments, and thus it did not reach first amendment considerations. See also Lee v. Runge, 404 U.S. 887, 892–93, 92 S.Ct. 197, 30 L.Ed.2d 169 (1971) (Douglas, J. dissenting).

views of Dr. Martin Luther King may be widely disseminated. But the precise expression of these views in a speech may be protected. King v. Mister Maestro, Inc., 224 F.Supp. 101 (S.D.N.Y.1963). See also Public Affairs Associates, Inc. v. Rickover, 177 F.Supp. 601 (D.D.C.1960), rev'd, 109 U.S.App.D.C. 128, 284 F.2d 262 (1960), rev'd, 369 U.S. 111, 82 S.Ct. 580, 7 L.Ed.2d 604 (1962), on remand, 268 F.Supp. 444 (D.D.C.1967); Atlantic Monthly Co. v. Post Pub. Co., 27 F.2d 556 (D.Mass.1928). Similarly, the facts about a historical figure are available to all to use. But if the expression of those facts in a biography is substantially copied infringement will be found. See, e.g., Toksvig v. Bruce Publishing Co., 181 F.2d 664 (7 Cir.1950); Marvin Worth Productions v. Superior Films Corp., 319 F.Supp. 1269 (S.D.N.Y.1970); Holdredge v. Knight Publishing Corp., 214 F.Supp. 921 (C.D.Cal.1963).

With the law of copyright permitting the free use of ideas, it is not surprising that the few courts addressing the issue have not permitted defendants who copy a work's expression to hide behind the first amendment. See, e.g., Duchess Music Corp. v. Stern, 458 F.2d 1305, 1310–11 (9 Cir.1972); United States v. Bodin, 375 F.Supp. 1265, 1267–68 (W.D.Okl.1974); McGraw Hill, Inc. v. Worth Publishers, Inc., 335 F.Supp. 415, 422 (S.D.N.Y.1971). In Walt Disney Productions v. Air Pirates, 345 F.Supp. 108 (N.D.Cal.1972), plaintiff sued for infringement of several of its famous cartoon characters by defendants, who used them for purposes of literary criticism. Defendants claimed that the first amendment limited the scope of plaintiff's copyright protection. The court responded:

> However defendants would have it, the hard fact remains that both parties are dealing in cartoon series, comic books or strips, and that the mode which the defendants have chosen for the expression of their concepts amounts to a substantial taking of plaintiff's expression of its concepts, even assuming vast difference in the content of those concepts. It can scarcely be maintained that there is no other means available to defendants to convey the message they have, nor is it even clear that other means are not available within the chosen genre of comics and cartoons. To paraphrase, it is true that it would be easier to copy substantial portions of the expression as distinguished from the idea itself to the Disney works, but the value of such labor-saving utility is far outweighed by the copyright interest in encouraging creation by protecting expression. Id. at 115 (footnotes omitted).

The district court in *Disney* recognized that the expression inherent in plaintiff's works differs from the mere idea of those works. The "idea" of Mickey Mouse is, after all, no more than a mouse. Yet the particular expression of that mouse has phenomenal commercial value and is recognized worldwide. Defendants there could have chosen any number of ways to express their idea of a mouse, but chose to copy Disney's. So too the defendants in this case had many ways to express the idea of a fantasyland with characters, but chose to copy the expression of plaintiffs'. The first amendment will not protect such imitation.

There may be certain rare instances when first amendment considerations will operate to limit copyright protection for graphic expressions of newsworthy events.[16] For example, in Time, Inc. v. Bernard Geis Associates, 293 F.Supp. 130 (S.D.N.Y.1968), Life magazine sued a historian for copying frames of the Zapruder films of the assassination of John F. Kennedy. Although the court did not expressly invoke the first amendment, it did justify the defendant's right to copy frames of the film on the ground of the "public interest in having the fullest information available on the murder of President Kennedy." Id. at 146. Plaintiffs' work in this case is neither a graphic expression nor concerning newsworthy events. Therefore, no first amendment considerations operate.[17]

Questions

1. Should the First Amendment ever constitute a defense for one who under the Copyright Act is an infringer? Does the Copyright Clause of the Constitution (Art. I, Sec. 8, Cl. 8) by conferring a copyright power upon Congress render such power immune from the thrust of the First Amendment? If constitutional grants of power were not subject to the First Amendment (and the other articles of the Bill of Rights) would this not render the Bill of Rights a meaningless recital since absent a grant of power the federal government may not act even without the limitation of the Bill of Rights?

2. Recalling that the First Amendment provides that "Congress shall make no law * * * abridging the freedom of speech * * * ", is not the Copyright Act precisely a law made by Congress which abridges the freedom of speech of those who would repeat the copyrighted "speech" of others. Does anything in the text of the First Amendment limit the free speech guarantee to speech which is original with the speaker? If not, is the Copyright Act itself unconstitutional?

---

16. This exception to the rule that first amendment considerations do not operate to limit copyright protection was suggested by Professor Nimmer. Nimmer, Does Copyright Abridge the First Amendment Guarantees of Free Speech and Press?, 17 U.C.L. A.L.Rev. 1180, 1199 (1970). He suggests a system of compulsory licensing for "news photographs," which he defines as all products of the photographic and analogous processes (including motion pictures and video tape but excluding paintings, sculpture, and the like) depicting an event which was the subject of news stories appearing in the press. He gives the photographs of the My Lai massacre as an example.

17. In Rosemont Enterprises, Inc. v. Random House, Inc., 366 F.2d 303 (2 Cir. 1966), Howard Hughes attempted to enjoin Random House from publishing a biography of Hughes. The biography was based on information contained in a series of articles appearing in Look magazine over which Hughes (via Rosemont) held a copyright. Had the biography merely attempted to use the information in the articles we would agree with the Second Circuit's refusal to enjoin because such information represents the "idea" of a biography on Hughes. But the Random House biography copied verbatim almost 27% of one of the Look articles and 14% of all of the articles. Rosemont Enterprises, Inc. v. Random House, Inc., 256 F.Supp. 55, 61 (S.D.N.Y.1966). We believe this represents an unjustifiable appropriation of the expression of the idea, and hence disapprove of the result in Rosemont. Because there are available alternatives in the form of expressing any verbal ideas, first amendment considerations should not limit copyright protection in this area. We need not reach this precise issue today, however, since it is clear that neither the H.R. Pufnstuf series nor McDonaldland commercials are newsworthy.

3. Is the *Krofft* court correct in concluding that the respective interests served by copyright and the First Amendment may be reconciled by a "definitional balance" which incorporates the idea-expression dichotomy?

4. Are there some instances when the demands of the First Amendment must be held to permit the copying of expression as well as idea? Is the Zapruder film in Time, Inc. v. Bernard Geis Associates, supra, such a case? What about the photographs of the My Lai massacre? What about "news photographs"? What constitutes a "news photograph"?

Collateral Reference

Nimmer on Copyright, § 1.10.

Nimmer on Freedom of Speech, § 2.05[C][2].

Chapter Eight

COPYRIGHT REMEDIES

Note *

The Relationship Between Actual Damages, Defendant's Profits, and Statutory Damages

[A]—The Right to Both Actual Damages and Defendant's Profits

Section 504(b) of the current Copyright Act removes an ambiguity that existed under the 1909 Act by explicitly specifying that the copyright owner who prevails in an infringement action "is entitled to recover the actual damages suffered by him or her as a result of the infringement, *and* any profits of the infringer that are attributable to the infringement * * *."[1] That this was intended to permit a recovery of actual damages "plus" the infringer's profits is further confirmed in the House Report.[2] Prima facie it would appear that this merely continues the rule of Sec. 101(b) of the 1909 Act which provided for a recovery of actual damages "as well as all the profits which the infringer shall have made from such infringement * * *." However, the Committee Report on the 1909 Act stated: "The provision that the copyright proprietor may have such damages as well as the profits which the infringer shall have made is substantially the same provision found in § 4921 of the Revised Statutes relating to remedies for the infringement of patents. The courts have usually construed that to mean that the owner of the patent might have one or the other, whichever was the greater. As such a provision was found both in the trade mark and patent laws, the committee felt that it might be properly included in the copyright laws."[3] This contradiction between the language of the 1909 Act and the legislative intent resulted in a confused state of the law wherein some courts awarded damages or profits in the alternative, while others awarded both cumulatively.

Although under the current Act a prevailing plaintiff is clearly entitled to recover both actual damages and the infringer's profits, the latter measure is recoverable only if and to the extent that such profits have not already been "taken into account in computing the actual damages".[4] It may be wondered how the defendant's profits could ever be taken into account in computing the plaintiff's actual damages in view of "the different purposes served by awards

---

* Nimmer on Copyright, § 14.01.
1. 17 U.S.C.A. § 504(b) (Emphasis added.) See also 17 U.S.C.A. § 504(a)(1).
2. H.Rep., p. 161.
3. H.R.Rep. No. 2222, 60th Cong., 2d Sess. (1909), p. 15.
4. 17 U.S.C.A. § 504(b).

of damages and profits. Damages are awarded to compensate the copyright owner for losses from the infringement, and profits are awarded to prevent the infringer from unfairly benefiting from a wrongful act."[5] The House Report goes on to state: "Where the defendant's profits are nothing more than a measure of the damages suffered by the copyright owner, it would be inappropriate to award damages and profits cumulatively, since in effect they amount to the same thing."[6] But how could the defendant's profits ever constitute "nothing more than a measure of the damages suffered by the copyright owner" since by definition the defendant's profits are something other than the losses suffered by the plaintiff from the infringement? Apparently what is here intended is that to the extent the actual damages consist of the plaintiff's lost profits they will be deducted from the measure of the defendant's profits in making an award of the latter.[7]

[B]—The Right to Statutory Damages

One of the most obscure issues under the 1909 Act was the question of when statutory damages (sometimes called "in lieu" damages[8]) might properly be awarded. Under the current Act it is now clear that it is the copyright owner who may at his discretion elect to recover statutory damages instead of actual damages and profits.[9] Such election may be made at any time before final judgment is rendered.[10] Contrary to some decisions under the 1909 Act, it is further clear under the current Act that an election to recover statutory damages precludes not only a recovery of actual damages, but also a recovery of the defendant's profits.[11]

A. DEFENDANT'S PROFITS *

SHELDON v. METRO–GOLDWYN CORP.

Supreme Court of the United States, 1940.
309 U.S. 390, 60 S.Ct. 681, 84 L.Ed. 825.

Mr. Chief Justice Hughes delivered the opinion of the Court.

The questions presented are whether, in computing an award of profits against an infringer of a copyright, there may be an apportionment so as to give to the owner of the copyright only that part of the profits found to be attributable to the use of the copyrighted material as distinguished from what the infringer himself has supplied, and, if so, whether the evidence affords a proper basis for the apportionment decreed in this case.

---

5. H.Rep., p. 161.

6. Id.

7. The plaintiff's lost profits might be equal to, less than, or greater than the defendant's actual profits. See Nimmer on Copyright, § 14.02.

8. The 1909 Act provided for an award "in lieu of actual damages and profits, such damages as to the court shall appear to be just * * *." 17 U.S.C.A. § 101(b) (1909 Act), with a prescribed minimum and maximum award.

9. 17 U.S.C.A. § 504(c)(1). See also 17 U.S.C.A. § 504(a). "[T]he plaintiff in an infringement suit is not obliged to submit proof of damages and profits and may choose to rely on the provision for minimum statutory damages." H.Rep., p. 161.

10. 17 U.S.C.A. § 504(c)(1).

11. Statutory damages are awarded "instead of actual damages *and* profits * * *." 17 U.S.C.A. § 504(c)(1). (Emphasis added.)

* For a discussion of the computation of the plaintiff's actual damages, see Nimmer on Copyright, § 14.02.

Petitioners' complaint charged infringement of their play "Dishonored Lady" by respondents' motion picture "Letty Lynton," and sought an injunction and an accounting of profits. The Circuit Court of Appeals, reversing the District Court, found and enjoined the infringement and directed an accounting. 81 F.2d 49. Thereupon the District Court confirmed with slight modifications the report of a special master which awarded to petitioners all the net profits made by respondents from their exhibitions of the motion picture, amounting to $587,604.37. 26 F.Supp. 134, 136. The Circuit Court of Appeals reversed, holding that there should be an apportionment and fixing petitioners' share of the net profits at one-fifth. 106 F.2d 45, 51. In view of the importance of the question, which appears to be one of first impression in the application of the copyright law, we granted certiorari. December 4, 1939.

Petitioners' play "Dishonored Lady" was based upon the trial in Scotland, in 1857, of Madeleine Smith for the murder of her lover,—a *cause célèbre* included in the series of "Notable British Trials" which was published in 1927. The play was copyrighted as an unpublished work in 1930, and was produced here and abroad. Respondents took the title of their motion picture "Letty Lynton" from a novel of that name written by an English author, Mrs. Belloc Lowndes, and published in 1930. That novel was also based upon the story of Madeleine Smith and the motion picture rights were bought by respondents. There had been negotiations for the motion picture rights in petitioners' play, and the price had been fixed at $30,000, but these negotiations fell through. * * *

Respondents contend that the material taken by infringement contributed in but a small measure to the production and success of the motion picture. They say that they themselves contributed the main factors in producing the large net profits; that is, the popular actors, the scenery, and the expert producers and directors. Both courts below have sustained this contention.

The District Court thought it "punitive and unjust" to award all the net profits to petitioners. The court said that, if that were done, petitioners would receive the profits that the "motion picture stars" had made for the picture "by their dramatic talent and the drawing power of their reputations." "The directors who supervised the production of the picture and the experts who filmed it also contributed in piling up these tremendous net profits." The court thought an allowance to petitioners of 25 per cent. of these profits "could be justly fixed as a limit beyond which complainants would be receiving profits in no way attributable to the use of their play in the production of the picture." But, though holding these views, the District Court awarded all the net profits to petitioners, feeling bound by the decision of the Court of Appeals in Dam v. Kirk La Shelle Co., 175 F. 902, 903, a decision which the Court of Appeals has now overruled.

The Court of Appeals was satisfied that but a small part of the net profits was attributable to the infringement, and, fully recognizing the difficulty in finding a satisfactory standard, the court decided that there should be an apportionment and that it could fairly be made. The court was resolved "to avoid the one certainly unjust course of giving the plaintiffs everything, because the defendants cannot with certainty compute their own share." The court would not deny "the one fact that stands undoubted," and, making the best estimate it could, it fixed petitioners' share at one-fifth of the net profits, considering that to be a figure "which will favor the plaintiffs in every reasonable chance of error."

First. Petitioners insist fundamentally that there can be no apportionment of profits in a suit for a copyright infringement; that it is forbidden both by the statute and the decisions of this Court. We find this basic argument to be untenable.

The Copyright Act in § 25(b) [now § 101(b)] provides that an infringer shall be liable—

> (b) To pay to the copyright proprietor such damages as the copyright proprietor may have suffered due to the infringement, as well as all the profits which the infringer shall have made from such infringement, * * * or in lieu of actual damages and profits, such damages as to the court shall appear to be just, * * *

We agree with petitioners that the "in lieu" clause is not applicable here, as the profits have been proved and the only question is as to their apportionment.

Petitioners stress the provision for recovery of "all" the profits, but this is plainly qualified by the words "which the infringer shall have made from such infringement." This provision in purpose is cognate to that for the recovery of "such damages as the copyright proprietor may have suffered due to the infringement." The purpose is thus to provide just compensation for the wrong, not to impose a penalty by giving to the copyright proprietor profits which are not attributable to the infringement.

Prior to the Copyright Act of 1909, there had been no statutory provision for the recovery of profits, but that recovery had been allowed in equity both in copyright and patent cases as appropriate equitable relief incident to a decree for an injunction. Stevens v. Gladding, 17 How. 447, 455. That relief had been given in accordance with the principles governing equity jurisdiction, not to inflict punishment but to prevent an unjust enrichment by allowing injured complainants to claim "that which, *ex aequo et bono,* is theirs, and nothing beyond this." Livingston v. Woodworth, 15 How. 546, 560. See Root v. Railway Co., 105 U.S. 189, 194, 195. Statutory provision for the recovery of profits in patent cases was enacted in 1870.[1] The principle which was applied

---

1. Act of July 8, 1870, § 55, 16 Stat. 198, 206; R.S. 4921.

both prior to this statute and later was thus stated in the leading case of Tilghman v. Proctor, 125 U.S. 136, 146:

> The infringer is liable for actual, not for possible gains. The profits, therefore, which he must account for, are not those which he might reasonably have made, but those which he did make, by the use of the plaintiff's invention; or, in other words, the fruits of the advantage which he derived from the use of that invention, over what he would have had in using other means then open to the public and adequate to enable him to obtain an equally beneficial result. If there was no such advantage in his use of the plaintiff's invention, there can be no decree for profits, and the plaintiff's only remedy is by an action at law for damages.

In passing the Copyright Act, the apparent intention of Congress was to assimilate the remedy with respect to the recovery of profits to that already recognized in patent cases. Not only is there no suggestion that Congress intended that the award of profits should be governed by a different principle in copyright cases but the contrary is clearly indicated by the committee reports on the bill. As to § 25(b) the House Committee said: [2]

> Section 25 deals with the matter of civil remedies for infringement of a copyright. * * * The provision that the copyright proprietor may have such damages as well as the profits which the infringer shall have made is substantially the same provision found in section 4921 of the Revised Statutes relating to remedies for the infringement of patents. The courts have usually construed that to mean that the owner of the patent might have one or the other, whichever was the greater. As such a provision was found both in the trademark and patent laws, the committee felt that it might be properly included in the copyright laws.

We shall presently consider the doctrine which has been established upon equitable principles with respect to the apportionment of profits in cases of patent infringement. We now observe that there is nothing in the Copyright Act which precludes the application of a similar doctrine based upon the same equitable principles in cases of copyright infringement.

Nor do the decisions of this Court preclude that course. Petitioners invoke the cases of Callaghan v. Myers, 128 U.S. 617, and Belford v. Scribner, 144 U.S. 488. In the Callaghan case, the copyright of a reporter of judicial decisions was sustained with respect to the portions of the books of which he was the author, although he had no exclusive right in the judicial opinions. On an accounting for the profits made by an infringer, the Court allowed the deduction from the selling price of the actual and legitimate manufacturing cost. With reference to the published matter to which the copyright did not extend, the Court found it impossible to separate the profits on that from the profits on the other. And in view of that impossibility, the defendant, being responsible for the blending of the lawful with the unlawful, had to

---

2. House Report No. 2222, 60th Cong., 2d sess., p. 15. See, also, Senate Report No. 1108, 60th Cong., 2d sess., p. 15.

abide the consequences, as in the case of one who has wrongfully produced a confusion of goods. A similar impossibility was encountered in Belford v. Scribner, a case of a copyright of a book containing recipes for the household. The infringing books were largely compilations of these recipes, "the matter and language" being "the same as the complainant's in every substantial sense," but so distributed through the defendants' books that it was "almost impossible to separate the one from the other." The Court ruled that when the copyrighted portions are so intermingled with the rest of the piratical work "that they cannot well be distinguished from it," the entire profits realized by the defendants will be given to the plaintiff.

We agree with the court below that these cases do not decide that no apportionment of profits can be had where it is clear that all the profits are not due to the use of the copyrighted material, and the evidence is sufficient to provide a fair basis of division so as to give to the copyright proprietor all the profits that can be deemed to have resulted from the use of what belonged to him. Both the Copyright Act and our decisions leave the matter to the appropriate exercise of the equity jurisdiction upon an accounting to determine the profits "which the infringer shall have made from such infringement."

Second. The analogy found in cases of patent infringement is persuasive. There are many cases in which the plaintiff's patent covers only a part of a machine and creates only a part of the profits. The patented invention may have been used in combination with additions or valuable improvements made by the infringer and each may have contributed to the profits. In Elizabeth v. Pavement Co., 97 U.S. 126, 142, cited in the *Callaghan* and *Belford* cases, supra, it had been recognized that if a separation of distinct profit derived from such additions or improvements was shown, an apportionment might be had. See Garretson v. Clark, 111 U.S. 120, 121. The subject was elaborately discussed in the case of Westinghouse Co. v. Wagner Co., 225 U.S. 604, where it was distinctly ruled that "if plaintiff's patent only created a part of the profits, he is only entitled to recover that part of the net gains." There, the Court was concerned with the question of burden of proof. It was said that the plaintiff suing for profits was under the burden of showing that they had been made. The defendant had submitted evidence tending to show that it had added non-infringing and valuable improvements which had contributed to the making of profits; and the plaintiff in reply had insisted that these additions had made no such contribution. But assuming, as had been found, that the additions were non-infringing and valuable improvements, and a *prima facie* case of contribution to profits thus appearing, the burden of apportionment would rest upon the plaintiff. But in that relation it had still to be considered that the act of the defendant had made it "not merely difficult but impossible to carry the burden of apportionment" and in such case, as the "inseparable profit must be given to the patentee or infringer," the law placed the loss on the wrongdoer.

The question of burden of proof does not arise in the instant case, as here the defendants voluntarily assumed that burden and the court below has held that it has been sustained. What is apposite, however, is the ruling in the *Westinghouse* case as to apportionment and the sort of evidence admissible upon that question. The Court pointed to the difficulties of working out an account of profits and thought that the problem was analogous to that presented where it is necessary to separate interstate from intrastate earnings and expenses in order to determine whether an intrastate rate is confiscatory. The Court observed that "while recognizing the impossibility of reaching a conclusion that is mathematically exact," there has been received, in addition to other relevant evidence, "the testimony of experts as to the relative cost of doing a local and through business." Chicago, M. & St. P. Ry. Co. v. Tompkins, 176 U.S. 167, 178. The Court thought that "What is permissible in an effort to separate costs may also be done in a patent case where it is necessary to separate profits."

The principle as to apportionment of profits was clearly stated in the case of Dowagiac Co. v. Minnesota Co., 235 U.S. 641,—a case which received great consideration. The Court there said:

> We think the evidence, although, showing that the invention was meritorious and materially contributed to the value of the infringing drills as marketable machines, made it clear that their value was not entirely attributable to the invention, but was due in a substantial degree to the unpatented parts or features. The masters and the courts below so found and we should hesitate to disturb their concurring conclusions upon this question of fact, even had the evidence been less clear than it was.
>
> In so far as the profits from the infringing sales were attributable to the patented improvements they belonged to the plaintiff, and in so far as they were due to other parts or features they belonged to the defendants. But as the drills were sold in completed and operative form the profits resulting from the several parts were necessarily commingled. It was essential therefore that they be separated or apportioned between what was covered by the patent and what was not covered by it, for, as was said in Westinghouse Co. v. Wagner Co., supra (225 U.S. 615): "In such case, if plaintiff's patent only created a part of the profits, he is only entitled to recover that part of the net gains." Id., 646.

In the *Dowagiac* case, we again referred to the difficulty of making an exact apportionment and again observed that mathematical exactness was not possible. What was required was only "reasonable approximation" which usually may be attained "through the testimony of experts and persons informed by observation and experience." Testimony of this character was said to be "generally helpful and at times indispensable in the solution of such problems." The result to be accomplished "is a rational separation of the net profits so that neither party may have what rightfully belongs to the other." Id., p. 647.

We see no reason why these principles should not be applied in copyright cases. Petitioners cite our decision in the trade-mark case of Hamilton-Brown Shoe Co. v. Wolf Bros. Co., 240 U.S. 251, but the Court there, recognizing the rulings in the *Westinghouse* and *Dowagiac* cases, found on the facts that an apportionment of profits was "inherently impossible." The burden cast upon the defendant had not been sustained.

In 1922, some years after the *Dowagiac* decision, and in harmony with it, Congress amended § 70 of the patent law [3] so as to provide expressly that if "damages or profits are not susceptible of calculation and determination with reasonable certainty, the court may, on evidence tending to establish the same, in its discretion, receive opinion or expert testimony, which is hereby declared to be competent and admissible, subject to the general rules of evidence applicable to this character of testimony." The amendment, so far as it relates to the reception of expert testimony, recognized and cannot be deemed to enlarge the rules already applied in courts of equity, and the fact that the copyright law was not similarly amended cannot be considered to detract from the jurisdiction of the court to receive similar evidence in copyright cases whenever it is found to be competent.

Petitioners stress the point that respondents have been found guilty of deliberate plagiarism, but we perceive no ground for saying that in awarding profits to the copyright proprietor as a means of compensation, the court may make an award of profits which have been shown not to be due to the infringement. That would be not to do equity but to inflict an unauthorized penalty. To call the infringer a trustee *ex maleficio* merely indicates "a mode of approach and an imperfect analogy by which the wrongdoer will be made to hand over the proceeds of his wrong." Larson Co. v. Wrigley Co., 277 U.S. 97, 99, 100. He is in the position of one who has confused his own gains with those which belong to another. Westinghouse Co. v. Wagner Co., supra, p. 618. He "must yield the gains begotten of his wrong." Duplate Corp. v. Triplex Co., 298 U.S. 448, 457. Where there is a commingling of gains, he must abide the consequences, unless he can make a separation of the profits so as to assure to the injured party all that justly belongs to him. When such an apportionment has been fairly made, the copyright proprietor receives all the profits which have been gained through the use of the infringing material and that is all that the statute authorizes and equity sanctions.

Both courts below have held in this case that but a small part of the profits were due to the infringement, and, accepting that fact and the principle that an apportionment may be had if the evidence justifies it, we pass to the consideration of the basis of the actual apportionment which has been allowed.

Third. The controlling fact in the determination of the apportionment was that the profits had been derived, not from the mere performance of a copyrighted play, but from the exhibition of a motion picture which had its distinctive profit-making features, apart from the use of

---

3. Act of February 18, 1922, § 8, 42 Stat. 392, amending R.S. 4921, 35 U.S.C.A. 70.

any infringing material, by reason of the expert and creative operations involved in its production and direction. In that aspect the case has a certain resemblance to that of a patent infringement, where the infringer has created profits by the addition of noninfringing and valuable improvements. And, in this instance, it plainly appeared that what respondents had contributed accounted for by far the larger part of their gains.

Respondents had stressed the fact that, although the negotiations had not ripened into a purchase, the price which had been set for the motion picture rights in "Dishonored Lady" had been but $30,000. And respondents' witnesses cited numerous instances where the value, according to sales, of motion picture rights had been put at relatively small sums. But the court below rejected as a criterion the price put upon the motion picture rights, as a bargain had not been concluded and the inferences were too doubtful. The court also ruled that respondents could not count the effect of "their standing and reputation in the industry." The court permitted respondents to be credited "only with such factors as they bought and paid for; the actors, the scenery, the producers, the directors and the general overhead."

The testimony showed quite clearly that in the creation of profits from the exhibition of a motion picture, the talent and popularity of the "motion picture stars" generally constitutes the main drawing power of the picture, and that this is especially true where the title of the picture is not identified with any well-known play or novel. Here, it appeared that the picture did not bear the title of the copyrighted play and that it was not presented or advertised as having any connection whatever with the play. It was also shown that the picture had been "sold," that is, licensed to almost all the exhibitors as identified simply with the name of a popular motion picture actress before even the title "Letty Lynton" was used. In addition to the drawing power of the "motion picture stars," other factors in creating the profits were found in the artistic conceptions and in the expert supervision and direction of the various processes which made possible the composite result with its attractiveness to the public.

Upon these various considerations, with elaboration of detail, respondents' expert witnesses gave their views as to the extent to which the use of the copyrighted material had contributed to the profits in question. The underlying facts as to the factors in successful production and exhibition of motion pictures were abundantly proved, but, as the court below recognized, the ultimate estimates of the expert witnesses were only the expression "of their very decided opinions." These witnesses were in complete agreement that the portion of the profits attributable to the use of the copyrighted play in the circumstances here disclosed was very small. Their estimates given in percentages of receipts ran from five to twelve per cent; the estimate apparently most favored was ten per cent as the limit. One finally expressed the view that the play contributed nothing. There was no rebuttal. But the court below was not willing to accept the experts' testimony "at its face value." The court felt that it must make an award "which by no possibility shall be too small." Desiring to give petitioners the benefit of every doubt, the court allowed for the contribution of the play twenty per cent. of the net profits.

Petitioners are not in a position to complain that the amount thus allowed by the court was greater than the expert evidence warranted. Nor is there any basis for attack, and we do not understand that any attack is made, upon the qualifications of the experts. By virtue of an extensive experience, they had an intimate knowledge of all pertinent facts relating to the production and exhibition of motion pictures. Nor can we say that the testimony afforded no basis for a finding. What we said in the *Dowagiac* case is equally true here,—that what is required is not mathematical exactness but only a reasonable approximation. That, after all, is a matter of judgment; and the testimony of those who are informed by observation and experience may be not only helpful but, as we have said, may be indispensable. Equity is concerned with making a fair apportionment so that neither party will have what justly belongs to the other. Confronted with the manifest injustice of giving to petitioners all the profits made by the motion picture, the court in making an apportionment was entitled to avail itself of the experience of those best qualified to form a judgment in the particular field of inquiry and come to its conclusion aided by their testimony. We see no greater difficulty in the admission and use of expert testimony in such a case than in the countless cases involving values of property rights in which such testimony often forms the sole basis for decision.

Petitioners also complain of deductions allowed in the computation of the net profits. These contentions involve questions of fact which have been determined below upon the evidence and we find no ground for disturbing the court's conclusions.

The judgment of the Circuit Court of Appeals is

Affirmed.

Questions

1. Is the apportionment of profits principle, articulated in *Sheldon*, incorporated in the current Copyright Act? See Sec. 504(b).

2. Does the *Sheldon* opinion indicate that the plaintiff will be entitled to 100% of defendant's profits where the defendant fails to offer evidence "sufficient to provide a fair basis of division" as between profits attributable to the infringing elements in defendant's work and those attributable to the non-infringing elements? Compare Alfred Bell & Co. v. Catalda Fine Arts, 86 F.Supp. 399 (S.D.N.Y.1949) mod. 191 F.2d 99 (2d Cir.1951) (plaintiff awarded 100% of defendant's profits where court concluded that defendant failed to establish a basis of apportionment) with Orgel v. Clark Boardman Co., Ltd., 301 F.2d 119 (2d Cir.1962) (plaintiff limited to 50% of defendant's profits despite defendant's failure to offer evidence as to a fair basis of apportionment). Under the current Act, who has the burden of proving either the presence or absence of "elements

of profit attributable to factors other than the copyrighted work"? See Sec. 504(b).

3. What elements of cost may properly be deducted in computing the defendant's profits? What about the cost of infringing copies which were not "sold"? What about overhead? See Alfred Bell & Co. Ltd. v. Catalda Fine Arts Inc., supra.

Collateral Reference

Nimmer on Copyright, § 14.03.

B. STATUTORY DAMAGES

F.W. WOOLWORTH CO. v. CONTEMPORARY ARTS, INC.

Supreme Court of the United States, 1952.
344 U.S. 228, 73 S.Ct. 222, 97 L.Ed. 276.

Mr. Justice Jackson delivered the opinion of the Court.

Respondent brought this action under the Copyright Act to recover for infringement of copyright on a work of art entitled "Cocker Spaniel in Show Position." The District Court found the copyright, of which respondent was assignee, valid and infringed and awarded statutory damages of $5,000, with a $2,000 attorney's fee. The Court of Appeals affirmed. We granted certiorari, limiting the issues to the measure of the recovery, as to which conflict appears among lower courts.[1]

Respondent made small sculptures and figurines, among which were statues of the cocker spaniel, and marketed them chiefly through gift and art shops. Petitioner, from a different source, bought 127 dozen cocker spaniel statuettes and distributed them through thirty-four Woolworth stores. Unbeknown to Woolworth, these dogs had been copied from respondent's and by marketing them it became an infringer.

By the Act an infringer becomes liable—

> To pay to the copyright proprietor such damages as the copyright proprietor may have suffered due to the infringement, as well as all the profits which the infringer shall have made from such infringement, and in proving profits the plaintiff shall be required to prove sales only, and the defendant shall be required to prove every element of cost which he claims, or in lieu of actual damages and profits, such damages as to the court shall appear to be just, and in assessing such damages the court may, in its discretion, allow the amounts as hereinafter stated * * * and such damages shall in no other case exceed the sum of $5,000 nor be less than the sum of $250, and shall not be regarded as a penalty. * * * 17 U.S.C.A. § 101(b).

Profits made by the petitioner from the infringement were sufficiently proved to enable assessment of that element of liability. Petitioner itself showed, without contradiction, that the 127 dozen dogs

---

1. F.W. Woolworth Co. v. Contemporary Arts, 193 F.2d 162, 167–169; Sammons v. Colonial Press, 126 F.2d 341, 350; Davilla v. Brunswick-Balke Collender Co., 94 F.2d 567; Malsed v. Marshall Field & Co., 96 F.Supp. 372, 376–377.

were bought at 60 cents apiece and sold for $1.19 each, yielding a gross profit of $899.16. The infringer did not assume the burden, which the statute casts upon it, of proving any other costs that might be deductible, so the gross figure is left to stand as the profit factor of the infringer's total liability.

As to the other ingredient in computing liability, damages suffered by the copyright proprietor, the record is inadequate to establish an actually sustained amount. Enough appears to indicate that real and substantial injury was inflicted. Respondent had gross annual income of about $35,000 and engaged only eight employees, indicating its small production. Its statuettes were of three media and prices: red plaster retailed at $4, red porcelain at $9, while a black and white porcelain brought $15. There was evidence that the cheaper infringing statuette was inferior in quality. Respondent proved loss of some customers and offered, but was not allowed, to show complaints from sales outlets about the Woolworth competition, decline in respondent's sales, and eventual abandonment of the line with an unsalable stock on hand. The trial judge excluded or struck most of this testimony on the ground that authority to allow statutory damages rendered proof of actual damage unnecessary. It might have been better practice to have received the evidence, even if it fell short of establishing the measure of liability; for when recovery may be awarded without any proof of injury, it cannot hurt and may aid the exercise of discretion to hear any evidence on the subject that has probative value. However, petitioner cannot complain of this exclusion, which was in response to its objections. At length, the court said: "If you establish this was an infringement of copyright, it is inescapably clear there is enough evidence in this case upon which to predicate damage up to $5000. I don't think Mr. Barnes [counsel for defendant] disagrees with that, do you?" Mr. Barnes: "No, your Honor."

The court, having found infringement, accordingly allowed recovery of "statutory damages in the amount of Five Thousand Dollars ($5,000.) as provided by the Copyright Laws of the United States," with an injunction and attorney's fee.

Petitioner's contention here is that the statute was misapplied because its own gross profit of $899.16 supplied an actual figure which became the exclusive measure of its liability. It argues that an infringing defendant, by coming forward with an undisputed admission of its own profit from the infringement, can tie the hands of the court and limit recovery to that amount. We cannot agree.

In Douglas v. Cunningham, 294 U.S. 207, 209, we said:

> The phraseology of the section was adopted to avoid the strictness of construction incident to a law imposing penalties, and to give the owner of a copyright some recompense for injury done him, in a case where the rules of law render difficult or impossible proof of damages or discovery of profits.

To fulfill that purpose, the statute has been interpreted to vest in the trial court broad discretion to determine whether it is more just to allow a recovery based on calculation of actual damages and profits, as found from evidence, or one based on a necessarily somewhat arbitrary estimate within the limits permitted by the Act.

> In other words, the court's conception of what is just in the particular case, considering the nature of the copyright, the circumstances of the infringement and the like, is made the measure of the damages to be paid, but with the express qualification that in every case the assessment must be within the prescribed limitations, that is to say, neither more than the maximum nor less than the minimum. Within these limitations the court's discretion and sense of justice are controlling, but it has no discretion when proceeding under this provision to go outside of them. L.A. Westermann Co. v. Dispatch Printing Co., 249 U.S. 100, 106–107.

Few bodies of law would be more difficult to reduce to a short and simple formula than that which determines the measure of damage recoverable for actionable wrongs. The necessary flexibility to do justice in the variety of situations which copyright cases present can be achieved only by exercise of the wide judicial discretion within limited amounts conferred by this statute. It is plain that the court's choice between a computed measure of damage and that imputed by statute cannot be controlled by the infringer's admission of his profits which might be greatly exceeded by the damage inflicted. Indeed sales at a small margin might cause more damage to the copyright proprietor than sales of the infringing article at a higher price.

Whether discretionary resort to estimation of statutory damages is just should be determined by taking into account both components and the difficulties in the way of proof of either. In this case the profits realized were established by uncontradicted evidence, but the court was within the bounds of its discretion in concluding that the amount of damages suffered was not computable from the testimony. Lack of adequate proof on either element would warrant resort to the statute in the discretion of the court, subject always to the statutory limitations.

The case before us illustrates what capricious results would follow from the practice for which petitioner contends. It has admitted gross profits, which make no deduction for sales costs, overheads or taxes and, hence, may appear substantial on this particular record. But gross profits is not what a copyright owner is entitled to recover, but only such profits as remain after the defendant reduces them, as it may, by proof of allowable elements of cost. If we sustain petitioner's contention that profits may be the sole measure of liability as matter of law, such profits could be diminished even to the vanishing point.

Net profits realized by a far-flung distributing enterprise like Woolworth's upon sales of a given item in a few of its many stores can be calculated only by a process of allocating overheads, sales expenses, taxes, and a host of items. A plaintiff in the position of the present one could hardly verify or contest such apportionments unless it should audit the whole Woolworth business.

Moreover, a rule of liability which merely takes away the profits from an infringement would offer little discouragement to infringers. It would fall short of an effective sanction for enforcement of the copyright policy. The statutory rule, formulated after long experience, not merely compels restitution of profit and reparation for injury but also is designed to discourage wrongful conduct. The discretion of the court is wide enough to permit a resort to statutory damages for such purposes. Even for uninjurious and unprofitable invasions of copyright the court may, if it deems it just, impose a liability within statutory limits to sanction and vindicate the statutory policy.

Petitioner cites Sheldon v. Metro-Goldwyn Pictures Corp., 309 U.S. 390, 399, where this Court said that the "in lieu" clause "is not applicable here, as the profits have been proved and the only question is as to their apportionment," a statement on which petitioner leans almost its whole weight. There net profits from exhibition of an infringing picture were found to be $587,604.37. The copyright owner could show no such value to himself of his copyright; indeed, he had negotiated its sale at $30,000. The Court of Appeals cut the award of these actual profits to one-fifth thereof, upon the ground that success of the picture had been largely due to factors not contributed by the infringement. The propriety of this reduction was the sole issue before this Court. Petitioner copyright owner asserted that in such circumstances the "in lieu" clause "is not involved here." This Court agreed that under those facts resort to the statute was not appropriate. That case did not present the question now here. Nor does anything in Jewell-LaSalle Realty Co. v. Buck, 283 U.S. 202, in the light of its facts, support petitioner. It holds use of the "in lieu" clause permissible, "there being no proof of actual damages," but it does not hold that partial or unacceptable proof on that subject will preclude resort to the "in lieu" clause.

We think that the statute empowers the trial court in its sound exercise of judicial discretion to determine whether on all the facts a recovery upon proven profits and damages or one estimated within the statutory limits is more just. We find no abuse of that discretion.

The judgment below is

Affirmed.

Mr. Justice Black, with whom Mr. Justice Frankfurter concurs, dissenting [opinion omitted].

Questions

1. Does the current Copyright Act alter the rule, enunciated in the instant case, as to who may determine whether statutory damages shall be awarded instead of actual damages and/or defendant's profits? See Sec. 504(c)(1).

2. In whom lies the discretion to determine (within the applicable minimum and maximum limits) the actual amount of statutory damages, the

plaintiff, the judge, or the jury? See Sid & Marty Krofft Television Productions, Inc. v. McDonald's Corp., 562 F.2d 1157 (9th Cir.1977).

3. In what circumstances is the $250 statutory damages minimum reduced to $100? In what circumstances must such minimum be remitted entirely? In what circumstances is the $10,000 statutory damages maximum increased to a $50,000 maximum? See Sec. 504(c)(2).

4. If a work has not been registered in the Copyright Office prior to commencement of the infringement, is the plaintiff entitled to recover statutory damages? See Sec. 412.

5. If the defendant's infringing work copies from three different copyrighted works owned by the plaintiff, is the plaintiff entitled to a minimum statutory damages award of 3 × $250? Suppose the defendant has copied from a derivative work owned by the plaintiff, which work contains two preexisting works, also owned by the plaintiff, and the defendant's infringing work has copied from such derivative work material originally contained in each of such preexisting works, and has also copied material originally contained in the derivative work. In these circumstances is the statutory minimum $250 or 3 × $250? See Sec. 504(c)(1).

6. Suppose that A is the copyright owner of a novel, and B, as an exclusive licensee from A, is the copyright owner of a motion picture based upon A's novel. Suppose further that C writes and produces a play which copies from B's motion picture both material which was original with B, and also material which was original with A, but was incorporated in B's film, and that A and B in a single action sue C for infringement of their respective copyrights. Are A and B together limited to a minimum statutory damages award of $250, or are they each entitled to a separate $250 minimum? Does the last sentence of Sec. 504(c)(1) speak to this situation?

7. Does the Sec. 504(c)(1) reference to "all infringements involved in the action" mean that in an action for infringement of a single copyrighted work the applicable statutory damages minimum is $250 regardless of how many different infringing acts the defendant has committed? If so, is it open to a plaintiff to avoid this limitation by simply suing the same infringer in a number of separate actions, each for a different act of infringement, and thereby recover at least a $250 minimum in each such action? Would the doctrine of res judicata bar more than one such action?

Collateral Reference

Nimmer on Copyright, § 14.04.

C. ATTORNEY'S FEE

CLOTH v. HYMAN

United States District Court, Southern District of New York, 1956.
146 F.Supp. 185.

HERLANDS, DISTRICT JUDGE. Plaintiffs having consented to an adverse summary judgment in this literary copyright infringement action, the Court is required to decide two questions: (1) whether the Court, in its discretion, should award reasonable attorneys' fees to the victorious defendants; and (2) if so, what amount would be reasonable in the circumstances of this case.

In opposing any award of attorneys' fees, plaintiffs assert that this action was brought in the sincere belief that their copyrighted story had been pirated by defendants.

In support of defendants' request for substantial fees, defendants charge that plaintiffs' cry of plagiarism is knowingly false, and that this is a "strike" suit. * * *

It is clear that defendants' novel and play are not plaintiffs' offspring. Plaintiffs' story and the latrine inspection episode in defendants' writings are literary siblings sired by the same army anecdote. This conclusion coupled with the previous finding that the latrine inspection episode contained in "Bucking for Section 8" was not original with plaintiff Cloth, leads to the Court's definitive judgment that plaintiffs did not act in good faith when they instituted this action.

In joining this litigation as co-plaintiff, the corporate plaintiff [Gleason Publications, Inc.] acted with a degree of casualness that amounted to sheer recklessness. In his pre-trial deposition, the president and majority stockholder of the corporate plaintiff testified that he had been unable to find or otherwise obtain a single copy of the very magazine of which he claims to be the copyright proprietor (Transcript, 92, 93). He admitted that he had no actual knowledge as to whether plaintiff Cloth's writing had ever been printed in his magazine (Transcript, 110). He had never bothered to check whether, in fact, there were any similarities between Cloth's writing and "No Time for Sergeants" (Transcript, 107, 108). He was unable to produce any of the three assignments, referred to in the complaint, which form the basis of his claim to proprietorship of the writing here involved (Transcript, 81, 83, 86, 87, 90). The offhand manner in which the corporate plaintiff brought this action as the "copyright proprietor" after Cloth visited Gleason's office is depicted in the following testimony by Gleason (Transcript, 109):

> He (Cloth) said that in Readers' Scope, in which he published the material, that there was an article, or articles, I have forgotten which now, which he considered had been infringed upon, and why didn't I call up Mr. Feinman; and I said—I looked at my spindle, I hadn't been in the office for some time, so I called up Mr. Feinman, and he called this to my attention, and I said "go ahead".

To charge an author with wilfully infringing a copyright by plagiarism is to charge him with a crime. 17 U.S.C.A. § 104. Dr. Samuel Johnson once said that the charge of plagiarism was " 'one of the most reproachful * * * of literary crimes' ". Quoted in Lewys v. O'Neill, D.C.S.D.N.Y.1931, 49 F.2d 603, 606.

Plaintiffs' unreliability in this litigation is further illustrated by their resort to a weathervane argument that shifts with the winds of necessity. The complaint (paragraphs 11 and 12) charges that defendants' book and the play were "copied largely" from Cloth's story. Plaintiffs abandoned this assertion after the argument when—in order to devaluate the services of defendants' attorneys—plaintiffs minimize the alleged infringement: "From the very inception there was no question that the claimed infringement was a relatively small part of the book and play." (Plaintiffs' memorandum, p. 10)

The applicable statute, 17 U.S.C.A. § 116,[1] makes it mandatory for the Court to allow "full costs" to the prevailing party, but it is discretionary with the Court to award "a reasonable attorney's fee" as part of the costs.

In exercising judicial discretion, it is well to keep in mind Chief Justice Marshall's classic dictum:

> When they (the courts) are said to exercise a discretion, it is a mere legal discretion, a discretion to be exercised in discerning the course prescribed by law; and, when that is discerned, it is the duty of the court to follow it. Osborn v. President, etc., of Bank of United States, 1824, 9 Wheat. 738, 865, 22 U.S. 738, 865, 6 L.Ed. 204.

In the present case, the statute does not exposit the public policy [2] to be effectuated by the Court's exercise of its discretion in awarding "a reasonable attorney's fee" to the prevailing party. Nor does the statute suggest a formula or standard of evaluation.

The statute has, however, received extensive judicial exposition. Upon the basis of that authority, these general principles may be formulated:

(1) An attorney's fee is properly awarded when the infringement action has been commenced in bad faith, as where the evidence establishes that the plaintiff's real motive is to vex and harass the defendant or where plaintiff's claim is so lacking in merit as to present no arguable question of law or genuine issue of fact. Nichols v. Universal Pictures Corporation, 2 Cir., 1930, 45 F.2d 119; Rush v. Oursler, D.C.S.D.N.Y.1930, 39 F.2d 468; Lowenfels v. Nathan, D.C.S.D.N.Y.1932, 2 F.Supp. 73; Lewys v. O'Neill, D.C.S.D.N.Y.1931, 49 F.2d 603; Rose v. Connelly, D.C.S.D.N.Y.1941, 38 F.Supp. 54.

(2) Where the claim of infringement is not synthetic, capricious or otherwise unreasonable, such fees have not been allowed. Edward B.

---

1. "In all actions, suits, or proceedings under this title, * * * full costs shall be allowed, and the court may award to the prevailing party a reasonable attorney's fee as part of the costs."

2. The public policies to be subserved by the sanction of awarding counsel fees may vary from field to field. Unless cognate policies are to be enforced, the decisions in one field would not be valid analogies in another. While, therefore, the cases cannot be reduced to a common denominator of policy or rationale, they are suggestive of a methodology of judicial analysis. Cf. Academy Award Products, Inc., v. Bulova Watch Company, Inc., 2 Cir., 1956, 233 F.2d 449; Colgate-Palmolive Company v. Carter Products, Inc., 4 Cir., 1956, 230 F.2d 855, 866; Lampert v. Hollis Music, Inc., D.C.E.D.N.Y.1956, 138 F.Supp. 505, 510; Lucien Lelong, Inc. v. Dana Perfumes, Inc., D.C.N.D.Ill.1955, 138 F.Supp. 575, 583; John Hancock Mutual Life Insurance Company v. Doran, D.C.S.D.N.Y.1956, 138 F.Supp. 47, 50, note 2; Sunbeam Corporation v. Quint, D.C.D.Mass.1956, 139 F.Supp. 804; United States of America v. 44.00 Acres of Land, etc., 2 Cir., 1956, 234 F.2d 410. Study of the subject of counsel fees in even one particular area of the law, e.g., derivative and other class litigation, may give rise to a veritable literature. Cf. the penetrating article by Professor George D. Hornstein, Legal Therapeutics: The "Salvage" Factor in Counsel Fee Awards, 69 Harv.L.Rev. 658 (1956).

Marks Music Corp. v. Continental Record Co., 2 Cir., 1955, 222 F.2d 488; Morse v. Fields, D.C.S.D.N.Y.1954, 127 F.Supp. 63.

(3) "Generally speaking," it is "more consonant with the authorization in 17 U.S.C.A. § 40 [now section 116] of 'a reasonable attorney's fee'" to award "only a fair fee fairly earned * * * rather than a punitive award". Chief Judge Clark (then Circuit Judge sitting as District Judge) in Rose v. Connelly, supra, 38 F.Supp. at page 56.

(4) In determining [3] what is a reasonable attorney's fee, the Court should take into account the following elements, among others: the amount of work necessary; the amount of work done; the skill employed; the monetary amount involved; [4] and the result achieved.

The foregoing principles and criteria have been applied to the evidence in this case in deciding to award reasonable attorneys' fees to the defendants herein and in fixing the amount of such fees.

Accordingly, the Court hereby awards severally to the defendants the following attorneys' fees: to Evans and Rogers, the sum of $1,250; to Hyman, the sum of $1,250; and to Random House, Inc., the sum of $500.

These allowances are to be recoverable against the plaintiffs and are to be included, in accordance with the provisions of 17 U.S.C.A. § 116, as part of the costs to be taxed severally to the defendants in the judgment dismissing the complaint herein.

Settle order and judgment on notice.

Questions

1. Note that a discretionary award of an attorney's fee may be made, under Sec. 505 "to the prevailing party". Who is the prevailing party if the plaintiff:

- (a) alleges several causes of action, only one of which is for copyright infringement, and prevails on the copyright count but loses on the other counts? Compare B. & B. Auto Supply Co. v. Plesser, 205 F.Supp. 36 (S.D.N.Y.1962) with Gelles-Widmer Co. v. Milton Bradley Co., 132 U.S.P.Q. 30 (N.D.Ill.1961).

- (b) alleges copyright infringement of two separate works, and prevails as to one but not as to the other? See M. Witmark and Sons v. Standard Music Roll, 221 F. 376 (3d Cir.1915).

- (c) prevails as against certain defendants but not as against certain others? See H.M. Kolbe Co., Inc. v. Armgus Textile Co., Inc., 315 F.2d 70 (2d Cir.1963).

---

3. Referring to the statute, 17 U.S.C.A. § 116, District Judge Woolsey said in Lewys v. O'Neill, D.C.S.D.N.Y.1931, 49 F.2d 603, 618:

"Fortunately in copyright cases Congress has seen fit to leave the courts free to adopt the wise English practice of throwing a large part of the expense of litigation on the unsuccessful party."

4. Plaintiffs' action involved the probable life or death of a most valuable stage and literary production. Over a million copies of the Hyman novel have been sold. The Levin play has been and is a complete "sellout," grossing already over a million dollars. It is expected to run continuously for possibly three or four years.

(d) prevails in a copyright infringement action, while the defendant prevails in a counterclaim, also for copyright infringement? See Official Aviation Guide Co. v. American Aviation Associates, Inc., 162 F.2d 541 (7th Cir.1947).

2. Should an attorney's fee be awarded only if there is some element of moral blame against the losing party? Should such moral blame attach if the losing party had predicated his legal position on a ground squarely contrary to that adopted in an applicable precedent by the U.S. Supreme Court? See Rose v. Bourne, Inc., 176 F.Supp. 605 (S.D.N.Y.1959). What if the losing party's attorney believes the precedent to be wrong, and that there is a reasonable possibility that the precedent will be overruled? When is a legal position not only wrong, but so untenable as to indicate bad faith in pursuing it? See Shapiro, Bernstein & Co. v. 4636 So. Vermont Ave., Inc., 367 F.2d 236 (9th Cir.1966). Should the prevailing party ever be denied an attorney's fee because of his moral blame in pursuing the action? See Leo Feist, Inc. v. Apollo Records, N.Y.Corp., 300 F.Supp. 32 (S.D.N.Y.1969).

3. If a work has not been registered in the Copyright Office prior to commencement of the infringement, is the plaintiff eligible for an award of attorney's fees? See Sec. 412.

Collateral Reference

Nimmer on Copyright, § 14.10.

Note *

The Copyright Royalty Tribunal

The current Copyright Act contains four different compulsory license provisions. With respect to phonorecord duplication and distribution of nondramatic musical works, Sec. 115 continues (with some changes) the Sec. 1(e) compulsory license which existed under the 1909 Act. In addition, compulsory licenses of varying types have been instituted under Sec. 116 with respect to juke box performances of nondramatic musical works, under Sec. 111 with respect to cable television, and under Sec. 118 with respect to certain performances and displays by noncommercial educational broadcast stations. The royalty rates payable under each of these compulsory licenses, other than that pertaining to noncommercial educational broadcast stations, are prescribed in the statutory text.[1] In order to permit periodic adjustments of such royalty rates in the light of future developments, without burdening Congress with "controversial piece-meal amendments to the copyright law",[2] the current Copyright Act created a Copyright Royalty Tribunal,[3] with rate adjusting authority as to each of these compulsory licenses. In addition, the royalty rate with respect to the compulsory licensing of noncommercial educational broadcast stations is in the first instance (assuming failure of a consensual agreement by the interested parties) to be determined by the Copyright Royalty Tribunal.[4] Such an initial rate is also subject to readjustment by the Tribunal in light of future developments.

* Nimmer on Copyright, § 14.11.
1. See 17 U.S.C.A. §§ 115(c)(2); 116(b)(1)(A); 111(d)(2).
2. Sen.Rep., p. 156.
3. 17 U.S.C.A. § 801(a).
4. 17 U.S.C.A. § 118(b)(3).

The times when each such readjustment of royalty rates may occur are set forth in the Act. Proceedings for the readjustment of the phonorecord, juke box, and cable television compulsory license rates may each occur in 1980.[5] Thereafter, proceedings for further readjustment of the cable television compulsory license rates may occur in 1985, and in each subsequent fifth calendar year.[6] Additional proceedings for further readjustment of the phonorecord compulsory license rates may occur in 1987, and in each subsequent tenth calendar year.[7] Additional proceedings for further readjustment of the juke box compulsory license rates may occur in 1990, and in each subsequent tenth calendar year.[8] Additional proceedings for further readjustment of the educational broadcasting compulsory license rates may occur in 1982, and at five year intervals thereafter.[9]

In addition to its rate making authority, the Copyright Royalty Tribunal is also charged with the duty of distributing the cable television and juke box royalty fees [10] to the appropriate copyright owners whose works have been subject to such compulsory licenses.[11] It does not have this responsibility in the case of the phonorecord and educational broadcasting compulsory licenses, where direct payment between the licensees, and the copyright owners (or one or more societies representing the owners) was contemplated. In the event of a dispute as to who are the copyright owners entitled to be paid either the cable television or juke box royalty fees, or as to the amount to which any particular claimant is entitled, the Copyright Royalty Tribunal is authorized to resolve such dispute after conducting an appropriate proceeding.[12]

The decisions of the Tribunal both with respect to rate adjustments and as regards the distribution of royalties are subject to appeal to the United States Court of Appeals under Chapter 7 of the Administrative Procedure Act.[13] There are a number of complex questions having to do with the standards to be applied by the Tribunal in making rate adjustments, and with the Tribunal's authority in resolving royalty distribution disputes, which pose problems of administrative law, and as such are beyond the scope of this work.[14]

5. 17 U.S.C.A. § 804(a)(1).

6. 17 U.S.C.A. § 804(a)(2)(A).

7. 17 U.S.C.A. § 804(a)(2)(B).

8. 17 U.S.C.A. § 804(a)(2)(C).

9. 17 U.S.C.A. §§ 118(c) and 804(c).

10. Such royalty fees must be paid by the compulsory licensees to the Register of Copyrights (17 U.S.C.A. §§ 111(2), and 116(b)(1)(A)) who in turn is to deposit such funds (after reasonable deduction of costs) with the Treasury of the United States (17 U.S.C.A. §§ 111(d)(3), and 116(c)(1)), where they are available for distribution by the Copyright Royalty Tribunal.

11. 17 U.S.C.A. §§ 111(d)(4), (5) and 116(c)(2)–(5).

12. 17 U.S.C.A. §§ 111(d)(5)(B) and 116(c)(3).

13. 17 U.S.C.A. § 810. See H.Rep., p. 179.

14. See the excellent discussion of these issues in Brylawski, "The Copyright Royalty Tribunal," 24 UCLA Law Rev. 1265 (1977).

Chapter Nine

FEDERAL PREEMPTION OF STATE LAW

Introductory Note

The law of copyright constitutes the subject of all of the preceding chapters. The chapters which follow deal with other aspects of law pertaining to literary, musical and artistic works. This means that for the most part the preceding chapters are concerned with federal law, while the chapters which follow are, in the main, concerned with state law. Since both sets of laws deal with the same subject matter—works of authorship—there is a threshold question which must be explored before dealing with the substantive content of the various strands of state law which follow. That is the issue of the extent to which the federal copyright law has preempted state law relating to the same subject matter. This topic has already been touched upon in Chapter One, as it relates to the law of common law copyright. It remains to be explored in depth, however, vis a vis other areas of state law.

A. PREEMPTION PRE-1978

SEARS, ROEBUCK & CO. v. STIFFEL CO.

Supreme Court of the United States, 1964.
376 U.S. 225, 84 S.Ct. 784, 11 L.Ed.2d 661.

Mr. Justice Black delivered the opinion of the Court.

The question in this case is whether a State's unfair competition law can, consistently with the federal patent laws, impose liability for or prohibit the copying of an article which is protected by neither a federal patent nor a copyright. The respondent, Stiffel Company, secured design and mechanical patents on a "pole lamp"—a vertical tube having lamp fixtures along the outside, the tube being made so that it will stand upright between the floor and ceiling of a room. Pole lamps proved a decided commercial success, and soon after Stiffel brought them on the market Sears, Roebuck & Company put on the market a substantially identical lamp, which it sold more cheaply, Sears' retail price being about the same as Stiffel's wholesale price. Stiffel then brought this action against Sears in the United States District Court for the Northern District of Illinois, claiming in its first count that by copying its design Sears had infringed Stiffel's patents and in its second count that by selling copies of Stiffel's lamp Sears had caused confusion in the trade as to the source of the lamps and had thereby engaged in unfair competition under Illinois law. There was evidence that identifying tags were not attached to the Sears lamps although labels appeared on the cartons in which they were delivered to customers, that customers had asked Stiffel whether its lamps differed from Sears', and that in two cases customers who had bought Stiffel lamps had complained to Stiffel on learning that Sears was selling substantially identical lamps at a much lower price.

The District Court, after holding the patents invalid for want of invention, went on to find as a fact that Sears' lamp was "a substantially exact copy" of Stiffel's and that the two lamps were so much alike, both in appearance and in functional details, "that confusion between them is likely, and some confusion has already occurred." On these findings the court held Sears guilty of unfair competition, enjoined Sears "from unfairly competing with [Stiffel] by selling or attempting to sell pole lamps identical to or confusingly similar to" Stiffel's lamp, and ordered an accounting to fix profits and damages resulting from Sears' "unfair competition."

The Court of Appeals affirmed.[1] 313 F.2d 115. That court held that, to make out a case of unfair competition under Illinois law, there was no need to show that Sears had been "palming off" its lamps as Stiffel lamps; Stiffel had only to prove that there was a "likelihood of confusion as to the source of the products"—that the two articles were sufficiently identical that customers could not tell who had made a particular one. Impressed by the "remarkable sameness of appearance" of the lamps, the Court of Appeals upheld the trial court's findings of likelihood of confusion and some actual confusion, findings which the appellate court construed to mean confusion "as to the source of the lamps." The Court of Appeals thought this enough under Illinois law to sustain the trial court's holding of unfair competition, and thus held Sears liable under Illinois law for doing no more than copying and marketing an unpatented article.[2] We granted certiorari

---

1. No review is sought here of the ruling affirming the District Court's holding that the patent is invalid.

2. 313 F.2d, at 118 and nn. 6, 7. At least one Illinois case has held in an exhaustive opinion that unfair competition under the law of Illinois is not proved unless the defendant is shown to have "palmed off" the article which he sells as that of another seller; the court there said that "[t]he courts in this State do not treat the 'palming off' doctrine as merely the designation of a typical class of cases of unfair competition, but they announce it as the rule of law itself—the test by which it is determined whether a given state of facts constitutes unfair competition as a matter of law. * * The 'palming off' rule is expressed in a positive, concrete form which will not admit of 'broadening' or 'widening' by any proper judicial process." Stevens-Davis Co. v. Mather & Co., 230 Ill.App. 45, 65–66 (1923). In spite of this the Court of Appeals in its opinions both in this case and in Day-Brite Lighting, Inc. v. Compco Corp., 311 F.2d 26, rev'd, post, p. 234, relied upon one of its previous decisions in a trade-name case, Independent Nail & Packing Co. v. Stronghold Screw Products, 205 F.2d 921 (C.A. 7th Cir. 1953), which concluded that as to use of trade names the *Stevens-Davis* rule had been overruled by two subsequent Illinois decisions. Those two cases, however, discussed only misleading use of trade names,

to consider whether this use of a State's law of unfair competition is compatible with the federal patent law. 374 U.S. 826.

Before the Constitution was adopted, some States had granted patents either by special act or by general statute,[3] but when the Constitution was adopted provision for a federal patent law was made one of the enumerated powers of Congress because, as Madison put it in *The Federalist* No. 43, the States "cannot separately make effectual provision" for either patents or copyrights.[4] That constitutional provision is Art. I, § 8, cl. 8, which empowers Congress "To promote the Progress of Science and useful Arts, by securing for limited Times to Authors and Inventors the exclusive Right to their respective Writings and Discoveries." Pursuant to this constitutional authority, Congress in 1790 enacted the first federal patent and copyright law, 1 Stat. 109, and ever since that time has fixed the conditions upon which patents and copyrights shall be granted, see 17 U.S.C.A. §§ 1–216; 35 U.S.C.A. §§ 1–293. These laws, like other laws of the United States enacted pursuant to constitutional authority, are the supreme law of the land. See Sperry v. Florida, 373 U.S. 379 (1963). When state law touches upon the area of these federal statutes, it is "familiar doctrine" that the federal policy "may not be set at naught, or its benefits denied" by the state law. Sola Elec. Co. v. Jefferson Elec. Co., 317 U.S. 173, 176 (1942). This is true, of course, even if the state law is enacted in the exercise of otherwise undoubted state power.

The grant of a patent is the grant of a statutory monopoly;[5] indeed, the grant of patents in England was an explicit exception to the statute of James I prohibiting monopolies.[6] Patents are not given as favors, as was the case of monopolies given by the Tudor monarchs, see

not copying of articles of trade. One prohibited the use of a name so similar to that of another seller as to deceive or confuse customers, even though the defendant company did not sell the same products as the plaintiff and so in one sense could not be said to have palmed off its goods as those of a competitor, since the plaintiff was not a competitor. Lady Esther, Limited v. Lady Esther Corset Shoppe, Inc., 317 Ill.App. 451, 46 N.E.2d 165 (1943). The other Illinois case on which the Court of Appeals relied was a mandamus action which held that under an Illinois statute a corporation was properly denied registration in the State when its name was "deceptively similar" to that of a corporation already registered. Investors Syndicate of America, Inc. v. Hughes, 378 Ill. 413, 38 N.E.2d 754 (1941). The Court of Appeals, by holding that because Illinois forbids misleading use of trade names it also forbids as unfair competition the mere copying of an article of trade without any palming off, thus appears to have extended greatly the scope of the Illinois law of unfair competition beyond the limits indicated in the Illinois cases and beyond any previous decisions of the Seventh Circuit itself. Because of our disposition of these cases we need not decide whether it was correct in doing so.

3. See I Walker, Patents (Deller ed. 1937), § 7.

4. The Federalist (Cooke ed. 1961) 288.

5. Patent rights exist only by virtue of statute. Wheaton v. Peters, 8 Pet. 591, 658 (1834).

6. The Statute of Monopolies, 21 Jac. I, c. 3 (1623), declared all monopolies "contrary to the Laws of this Realm" and "utterly void and of none Effect." Section VI, however, excepted patents of 14 years to "the true and first Inventor and Inventors" of "new Manufactures" so long as they were "not contrary to the Law, nor mischievous to the State, by raising Prices of Commodities at home, or Hurt of Trade, or generally inconvenient. * * *" Much American patent law derives from English patent law. See Pennock v. Dialogue, 2 Pet. 1, 18 (1829).

The Case of Monopolies (Darcy v. Allein), 11 Co.Rep. 84 b., 77 Eng.Rep. 1260 (K.B. 1602), but are meant to encourage invention by rewarding the inventor with the right, limited to a term of years fixed by the patent, to exclude others from the use of his invention. During that period of time no one may make, use, or sell the patented product without the patentee's authority. 35 U.S.C. § 271. But in rewarding useful invention, the "rights and welfare of the community must be fairly dealt with and effectually guarded." Kendall v. Winsor, 21 How. 322, 329 (1859). To that end the prerequisites to obtaining a patent are strictly observed, and when the patent has issued the limitations on its exercise are equally strictly enforced. To begin with, a genuine "invention" or "discovery" must be demonstrated "lest in the constant demand for new appliances the heavy hand of tribute be laid on each slight technological advance in an art." Cuno Engineering Corp. v. Automatic Devices Corp., 314 U.S. 84, 92 (1941); see Great Atlantic & Pacific Tea Co. v. Supermarket Equipment Corp., 340 U.S. 147, 152–153 (1950); Atlantic Works v. Brady, 107 U.S. 192, 199–200 (1883). Once the patent issues, it is strictly construed, United States v. Masonite Corp., 316 U.S. 265, 280 (1942), it cannot be used to secure any monopoly beyond that contained in the patent, Morton Salt Co. v. G.S. Suppiger Co., 314 U.S. 488, 492 (1942), the patentee's control over the product when it leaves his hands is sharply limited, see United States v. Univis Lens Co., 316 U.S. 241, 250–252 (1942), and the patent monopoly may not be used in disregard of the antitrust laws, see International Business Machines Corp. v. United States, 298 U.S. 131 (1936); United Shoe Machinery Corp. v. United States, 258 U.S. 451, 463–464 (1922). Finally, and especially relevant here, when the patent expires the monopoly created by it expires, too, and the right to make the article— including the right to make it in precisely the shape it carried when patented—passes to the public. Kellogg Co. v. National Biscuit Co., 305 U.S. 111, 120–122 (1938); Singer Mfg. Co. v. June Mfg. Co., 163 U.S. 169, 185 (1896).

Thus the patent system is one in which uniform federal standards are carefully used to promote invention while at the same time preserving free competition.[7] Obviously a State could not, consistently with the Supremacy Clause of the Constitution,[8] extend the life of a patent beyond its expiration date or give a patent on an article which lacked the level of invention required for federal patents. To do either would run counter to the policy of Congress of granting patents only to true inventions, and then only for a limited time. Just as a State cannot encroach upon the federal patent laws directly, it cannot, under some other law, such as that forbidding unfair competition, give protection of a kind that clashes with the objectives of the federal patent laws.

---

7. The purpose of Congress to have national uniformity in patent and copyright laws can be inferred from such statutes as that which vests exclusive jurisdiction to hear patent and copyright cases in federal courts, 28 U.S.C.A. § 1338(a), and that section of the Copyright Act which expressly saves state protection of unpublished writings but does not include published writings, 17 U.S.C.A. § 2.

8. U.S. Const., Art. VI.

In the present case the "pole lamp" sold by Stiffel has been held not to be entitled to the protection of either a mechanical or a design patent. An unpatentable article, like an article on which the patent has expired, is in the public domain and may be made and sold by whoever chooses to do so. What Sears did was to copy Stiffel's design and to sell lamps almost identical to those sold by Stiffel. This it had every right to do under the federal patent laws. That Stiffel originated the pole lamp and made it popular is immaterial. "Sharing in the goodwill of an article unprotected by patent or trade-mark is the exercise of a right possessed by all—and in the free exercise of which the consuming public is deeply interested." Kellogg Co. v. National Biscuit Co., supra, 305 U.S., at 122. To allow a State by use of its law of unfair competition to prevent the copying of an article which represents too slight an advance to be patented would be to permit the State to block off from the public something which federal law has said belongs to the public. The result would be that while federal law grants only 14 or 17 years' protection to genuine inventions, see 35 U.S.C.A. §§ 154, 173, States could allow perpetual protection to articles too lacking in novelty to merit any patent at all under federal constitutional standards. This would be too great an encroachment on the federal patent system to be tolerated.

Sears has been held liable here for unfair competition because of a finding of likelihood of confusion based only on the fact that Sears' lamp was copied from Stiffel's unpatented lamp and that consequently the two looked exactly alike. Of course there could be "confusion" as to who had manufactured these nearly identical articles. But mere inability of the public to tell two identical articles apart is not enough to support an injunction against copying or an award of damages for copying that which the federal patent laws permit to be copied. Doubtless a State may, in appropriate circumstances, require that goods, whether patented or unpatented, be labeled or that other precautionary steps be taken to prevent customers from being misled as to the source, just as it may protect businesses in the use of their trademarks, labels, or distinctive dress in the packaging of goods so as to prevent others, by imitating such markings, from misleading purchasers as to the source of the goods.[9] But because of the federal patent laws a State may not, when the article is unpatented and uncopyrighted, prohibit the copying of the article itself or award damages for such copying. Cf. G. Ricordi & Co. v. Haendler, 194 F.2d 914, 916 (C.A.2d Cir.1952). The judgment below did both and in so doing gave Stiffel the equivalent of a patent monopoly on its unpatented lamp. That was error, and Sears is entitled to a judgment in its favor.

Reversed.

---

9. It seems apparent that Illinois has not seen fit to impose liability on sellers who do not label their goods. Neither the discussions in the opinions below nor the briefs before us cite any Illinois statute or decision requiring labeling.

COMPCO CORP. v. DAY–BRITE LIGHTING, INC.
Supreme Court of the United States, 1964.
376 U.S. 234, 84 S.Ct. 779, 11 L.Ed.2d 669.

Mr. Justice Black delivered the opinion of the Court.

As in Sears, Roebuck & Co. v. Stiffel Co., ante, p. 225, the question here is whether the use of a state unfair competition law to give relief against the copying of an unpatented industrial design conflicts with the federal patent laws. Both Compco and Day-Brite are manufacturers of fluorescent lighting fixtures of a kind widely used in offices and stores. Day-Brite in 1955 secured from the Patent Office a design patent on a reflector having cross-ribs claimed to give both strength and attractiveness to the fixture. Day-Brite also sought, but was refused, a mechanical patent on the same device. After Day-Brite had begun selling its fixture, Compco's predecessor began making and selling fixtures very similar to Day-Brite's. This action was then brought by Day-Brite. One count alleged that Compco had infringed Day-Brite's design patent; a second count charged that the public and the trade had come to associate this particular design with Day-Brite, that Compco had copied Day-Brite's distinctive design so as to confuse and deceive purchasers into thinking Compco's fixtures were actually Day-Brite's and that by doing this Compco had unfairly competed with Day-Brite. The complaint prayed for both an accounting and an injunction.

The District Court held the design patent invalid; but as to the second count, while the court did not find that Compco had engaged in any deceptive or fraudulent practices, it did hold that Compco had been guilty of unfair competition under Illinois law. The court found that the overall appearance of Compco's fixture was "the same, to the eye of the ordinary observer, as the overall appearance" of Day-Brite's reflector, which embodied the design of the invalidated patent; that the appearance of Day-Brite's design had "the capacity to identify [Day-Brite] in the trade and does in fact so identify [it] to the trade"; that the concurrent sale of the two products was "likely to cause confusion in the trade"; and that "[a]ctual confusion has occurred." On these findings the court adjudged Compco guilty of unfair competition in the sale of its fixtures, ordered Compco to account to Day-Brite for damages, and enjoined Compco "from unfairly competing with plaintiff by the sale or attempted sale of reflectors identical to, or confusingly similar to" those made by Day-Brite. The Court of Appeals held there was substantial evidence in the record to support the District Court's finding of likely confusion and that this finding was sufficient to support a holding of unfair competition under Illinois law.[1] 311 F.2d 26. Although the District Court had not made such a finding, the appellate court observed that "several choices of ribbing were apparently available to meet the functional needs of the product," yet Compco "chose precisely the same design used by the plaintiff and followed it so

---

1. The Court of Appeals also affirmed the holding that the design patent was invalid. No review of this ruling is sought here.

closely as to make confusion likely." 311 F.2d, at 30. A design which identifies its maker to the trade, the Court of Appeals held, is a "protectable" right under Illinois law, even though the design is unpatentable.[2] We granted certiorari. 374 U.S. 825.

To support its findings of likelihood of confusion and actual confusion, the trial court was able to refer to only one circumstance in the record. A plant manager who had installed some of Compco's fixtures later asked Day-Brite to service the fixtures, thinking they had been made by Day-Brite. There was no testimony given by a purchaser or by anyone else that any customer had ever been misled, deceived, or "confused," that is, that anyone had ever bought a Compco fixture thinking it was a Day-Brite fixture. All the record shows, as to the one instance cited by the trial court, is that both Compco and Day-Brite fixtures had been installed in the same plant, that three years later some repairs were needed, and that the manager viewing the Compco fixtures—hung at least 15 feet above the floor and arranged end to end in a continuous line so that identifying marks were hidden—thought they were Day-Brite fixtures and asked Day-Brite to service them.[3] Not only is this incident suggestive only of confusion *after* a purchase had been made, but also there is considerable evidence of the care taken by Compco to prevent customer confusion, including clearly labeling both the fixtures and the containers in which they were shipped and not selling through manufacturers' representatives who handled competing lines.

Notwithstanding the thinness of the evidence to support findings of likely and actual confusion among purchasers, we do not find it necessary in this case to determine whether there is "clear error" in these findings. They, like those in Sears, Roebuck & Co. v. Stiffel Co., supra, were based wholly on the fact that selling an article which is an exact copy of another unpatented article is likely to produce and did in this case produce confusion as to the source of the article. Even accepting the findings, we hold that the order for an accounting for damages and the injunction are in conflict with the federal patent laws. Today we have held in Sears, Roebuck & Co. v. Stiffel Co., supra, that when an article is unprotected by a patent or a copyright, state law may not forbid others to copy that article. To forbid copying would interfere with the federal policy, found in Art. I, § 8, cl. 8, of the Constitution and in the implementing federal statutes, of allowing free access to copy whatever the federal patent and copyright laws leave in the public domain. Here Day-Brite's fixture has been held not to be entitled to a design or mechanical patent. Under the federal patent laws it is, therefore, in the public domain and can be copied in every detail by whoever pleases. It is true that the trial court found that the configu-

---

2. As stated in Sears, Roebuck & Co. v. Stiffel Co., ante, at p. [448], n. 2, we do not here decide whether the Court of Appeals was correct in its statement of Illinois law.

3. The only testimony about this incident was given by a sales representative of Day-Brite, who said that the plant manager had climbed up on a forklift truck to look at the fixtures. The manager was not called as a witness.

ration of Day-Brite's fixture identified Day-Brite to the trade because the arrangement of the ribbing had, like a trademark, acquired a "secondary meaning" by which that particular design was associated with Day-Brite. But if the design is not entitled to a design patent or other federal statutory protection, then it can be copied at will.

As we have said in *Sears,* while the federal patent laws prevent a State from prohibiting the copying and selling of unpatented articles, they do not stand in the way of state law, statutory or decisional, which requires those who make and sell copies to take precautions to identify their products as their own. A State of course has power to impose liability upon those who, knowing that the public is relying upon an original manufacturer's reputation for quality and integrity, deceive the public by palming off their copies as the original. That an article copied from an unpatented article could be made in some other way, that the design is "nonfunctional" and not essential to the use of either article, that the configuration of the article copied may have a "secondary meaning" which identifies the maker to the trade, or that there may be "confusion" among purchasers as to which article is which or as to who is the maker, may be relevant evidence in applying a State's law requiring such precautions as labeling; however, and regardless of the copier's motives, neither these facts nor any others can furnish a basis for imposing liability for or prohibiting the actual acts of copying and selling. Cf. Kellogg Co. v. National Biscuit Co., 305 U.S. 111, 120 (1938). And of course a State cannot hold a copier accountable in damages for failure to label or otherwise to identify his goods unless his failure is in violation of valid state statutory or decisional law requiring the copier to label or take other precautions to prevent confusion of customers as to the source of the goods.[4]

Since the judgment below forbids the sale of a copy of an unpatented article and orders an accounting for damages for such copying, it cannot stand.

Reversed.

Questions

1. Does the Supreme Court acknowledge any area of copyright to which the *Sears-Compco* federal preemption doctrine does not apply? Note Sec. 2 of the 1909 Act.

2. Does the *Sears-Compco* doctrine apply to:

(a) Works as to which Congress lacks constitutional power to accord copyright protection because they are not "writings"?

(b) Types of works which might properly be the subject of federal copyright protection but as to which Congress has failed to accord such protection (as distinguished from individual works which fall within a type that is protected by copyright, but which individually fail of such

---

[4]. As we pointed out in Sears, Roebuck & Co. v. Stiffel Co., ante, p. [451], n. 9, there is no showing that Illinois has any such law.

protection because of lack of originality, failure to observe formalities, etc.)?

(c) Works which are protected by copyright (i.e. in such circumstances is there federal preemption so as to preclude a concurrent state law remedy)?

3. If a defendant markets a work which he knows to have acquired a "secondary meaning" relating to the plaintiff's products, does this in itself constitute "palming off" by the defendant? If so, doesn't the *Compco* opinion indicate that a state "has power to impose liability" in such circumstances? Can this be reconciled with the decision in *Compco?*

Collateral References

Bricker, *Thirty Months After Sears and Compco,* 14 Bull.Cr.Soc. 293 (1967).

Goldstein, *Federal System Ordering of the Copyright Interest,* 69 Col.Law Rev. 49 (1969).

Kalodner and Vance, *The Relation Between Federal and State Protection of Literary and Artistic Property,* 72 Harv.Law Rev. 1079 (1959).

Price, *The Moral Judge and the Copyright Statute: The Problem of Stiffel and Compco,* ASCAP Copyright Law Symposium No. Fourteen 90 (1966).

GOLDSTEIN v. CALIFORNIA

Supreme Court of the United States, 1973.
412 U.S. 546, 93 S.Ct. 2303, 37 L.Ed.2d 163.

MR. CHIEF JUSTICE BURGER delivered the opinion of the Court.

We granted certiorari to review petitioners' conviction under a California statute making it a criminal offense to "pirate" recordings produced by others.

In 1971, an information was filed by the State of California, charging petitioners in 140 counts with violating § 653h of the California Penal Code. The information charged that, between April 1970, and March 1971, petitioners had copied several musical performances from commercially sold recordings without the permission of the owner of the master record or tape.[1] Petitioners moved to dismiss the com-

---

1. In pertinent part, the California statute provides:

"(a) Every person is guilty of a misdemeanor who:

"(1) knowingly and willfully transfers or causes to be transferred any sounds recorded on a phonograph record, * * * tape, * * * or other article on which sounds are recorded, with intent to sell or cause to be sold, * * * such article on which such sounds are so transferred, without the consent of the owner.

"(2) * * *

"(b) As used in this section, 'person' means any individual, partnership, corporation or association; and 'owner' means the person who owns the master phonograph record, * * * master tape, * * * or other device used for reproducing recorded sounds on phonograph records, * * * tapes, * * * or other articles on which sound is recorded, and from which the transferred recorded sounds are directly or indirectly derived."

Specifically, each count of the information alleged that, in regard to a particular recording, petitioners had, "at and in the City of Los Angeles, in the County of Los

plaint on the grounds that § 653h was in conflict with Art. I, § 8, cl. 8, of the Constitution, the "Copyright Clause," and the federal statutes enacted thereunder. Upon denial of their motion, petitioners entered pleas of *nolo contendere* to 10 of the 140 counts; the remaining counts were dismissed. On appeal, the Appellate Department of the Superior Court sustained the validity of the statute. After exhausting other state appellate remedies, petitioners sought review in this Court.

I

Petitioners were engaged in what has commonly been called "record" or "tape piracy"—the unauthorized duplication of recordings of performance by major musical artists.[3] Petitioners would purchase from a retail distributor a single tape or phonograph recording of the popular performances they wished to duplicate. The original recordings were produced and marketed by recording companies with whom petitioners had no contractual relationship. At petitioners' plant, the recording was reproduced on blank tapes, which could in turn be used to replay the music on a tape player. The tape was then wound on a cartridge. A label was attached, stating the title of the recorded performance—the same title as had appeared on the original recording, and the name of the performing artists.[4] After final packaging, the tapes were distributed to retail outlets for sale to the public, in competition with those petitioners had copied.

Petitioners made no payments to the artists whose performances they reproduced and sold, nor to the various trust funds established for their benefit; no payments were made to the producer, technicians, or other staff personnel responsible for producing the original recording and paying the large expenses incurred in production.[5] No payments were made for the use of the artists' names or the album title.

The challenged California statute forbids petitioners from transferring any performance fixed on a tape or record onto other records or

---

Angeles, State of California * * * wilfully, unlawfully and knowingly transferred and caused to be transferred sounds recorded on a tape with the intent to sell and cause to be sold, such tape on which such sounds [were] so transferred. * * *"

3. Since petitioners did not proceed to trial, the factual record before the Court is sparse. However, both parties indicate that a complete description of petitioner's method of operation may be found in the record of Tape Industries Asso. of America v. Younger, 316 F.Supp. 340 (CD Cal.1970), appeal dismissed for lack of jurisdiction, 401 U.S. 902, 91 S.Ct. 880, 27 L.Ed.2d 801 (1971)., appeal pending United States Court of Appeals, CA 9, No. 26,628.

4. An additional label was attached to each cartridge by petitioners, stating that no relationship existed between petitioners and the producer of the original recording or the individuals whose performances had been recorded. Consequently, no claim is made that petitioners misrepresented the source of the original recordings or the manufacturer of the tapes.

5. The costs of producing a single original long playing record of a musical performance may exceed $50,000 or $100,000. Tape Industries Asso. of America v. Younger, 316 F.Supp. at 344 (1970); Hearings on S. 646 and H.R. 6927 before Subcommittee No. 3 of the Committee on the Judiciary, House of Representatives, 92d Cong., 1st Sess., at 27–28 (1971). For the performance recorded on this record, petitioners would pay only the retail cost of a single long playing record or a single tape.

tapes with the intention of selling the duplicates, unless they have first received permission from those who, under state law, are the owners of the master recording. Although the protection afforded to each master recording is substantial, lasting for an unlimited time, the scope of the proscribed activities is narrow. No limitation is placed on the use of the music, lyrics or arrangement employed in making the master recording. Petitioners are not precluded from hiring their own musicians and artists and recording in exact imitation of the performance embodied on the master recording. Petitioners are even free to hire the same artists who made the initial recording in order to duplicate the performance. In essence, the statute thus provides copyright protection solely for the specific expressions which comprise the master record or tape.

Petitioners' attack on the constitutionality of § 653h has many facets. First, they contend that the statute establishes a state copyright of unlimited duration, and thus conflicts with Art. I, § 8, cl. 8, of the Constitution. Second, petitioners claim that the state statute interferes with the implementation of federal policies, inherent in the federal copyright statutes. 17 U.S.C. § 1 et seq. According to petitioners, it was the intention of Congress, as interpreted by this Court in Sears, Roebuck and Co. v. Stiffel Co., 376 U.S. 225, 84 S.Ct. 784, 11 L.Ed.2d 661 (1964), and Compco Corp. v. Day-Brite Lighting, 376 U.S. 234, 84 S.Ct. 779, 11 L.Ed.2d 669 (1964), to establish a uniform law throughout the United States to protect original writings. As part of the federal scheme, it is urged that Congress intended to allow individuals to copy any work which was not protected by a federal copyright. Since § 653h effectively prohibits the copying of works which are not entitled to federal protection, petitioners contend that it conflicts directly with congressional policy and must fall under the Supremacy Clause of the Constitution. Finally, petitioners argue that 17 U.S.C. § 2, which allows States to protect unpublished writings, does not authorize the challenged state provision; since the records which petitioners copied had previously been released to the public, petitioners contend that they had, under federal law, been published.

We note at the outset that the federal copyright statutes to which petitioners refer were amended by Congress while their case was pending in the state courts. In 1971, Pub.L. 92–140 was passed to allow federal copyright protection of recordings. However, § 3 of the amendment specifically provides that such protection is to be available only to sound recordings "fixed, published and copyrighted" on and after February 15, 1972, and before January 1, 1975, and that nothing in Title 17, as amended is to "be applied retroactively or [to] be construed as affecting in any way any rights with respect to sound recordings fixed before" February 15, 1972. The recordings which petitioners copied were all "fixed" prior to February 15, 1972. Since, according to the language of § 3 of the amendment, Congress did not intend to alter the legal relationships which govern these recordings, the amendments have no application in petitioners' case.[7]

II

Petitioners' first argument rests on the premise that the state statute under which they were convicted lies beyond the powers which the States reserved in our federal system. If this is correct, petitioners must prevail, since the States cannot exercise a sovereign power which, under the Constitution, they have relinquished to the Federal Government for its exclusive exercise.

A

The principles which the Court has followed in construing state power were stated by Alexander Hamilton in Number 32 of The Federalist:

> An entire consolidation of the States into one complete national sovereignty would imply an entire subordination of the parts; and whatever powers might remain in them, would be altogether dependent on the general will. But as the plan of the [Constitutional] convention aims only at a partial union or consolidation, the State governments would clearly retain all the rights of sovereignty which they before had, and which were not, by this act, *exclusively* delegated to the United States. This exclusive delegation, or rather this alienation, of State sovereignty would only exist in three cases: where the Constitution in express terms granted an exclusive authority to the Union; where it granted in one instance an authority to the Union, and in another prohibited the States from exercising the like authority; and where it granted an authority to the Union, to which a similar authority in the States would be absolutely and totally *contradictory* and *repugnant.*[8]"

The first two instances mentioned present no barrier to a State's enactment of copyright statutes. The clause of the Constitution granting to Congress the power to issue copyrights does not provide that such power shall vest exclusively in the Federal Government. Nor does the Constitution expressly provide that such power shall not be exercised by the States.

In applying the third phase of the test, we must examine the manner in which the power to grant copyrights may operate in our federal system. The objectives of our inquiry were recognized in Cooley v. Board of Wardens, 12 How. (53 U.S.) 299, 13 L.Ed. 996 (1851), when, in determining whether the power granted to Congress to regulate commerce [9] was "compatible with the existence of a similar power in the States," the Court noted:

---

7. No question is raised in the present case as to the power of the States to protect recordings fixed after February 15, 1972.

8. A. Hamilton, J. Madison, J. Jay, The Federalist, B.F. Wright, ed. (Cambridge, Mass., 1961) (hereafter "The Federalist")

241; see Cooley v. Board of Wardens, 12 How. (53 U.S.) 299, 318–319, 13 L.Ed. 996 (1851).

9. Article I, § 8, cl. 3.

> Whatever subjects of this power are in their nature national, or admit of only one uniform system, or plan of regulation, may justly be said to be of such a nature as to require exclusive legislation by Congress. 12 How. (53 U.S.), at 319.

The Court's determination that Congress alone may legislate over matters which are *necessarily* national in import reflects the basic principle of federalism. "The genius and character of the [federal] government," CHIEF JUSTICE MARSHALL said,

> seem to be, that its action is to be applied to all external concerns of the nation, and to those internal concerns which affect the States generally; but not to those which are completely within a particular State, which do not affect other States, and with which it is not necessary to interfere, for the purpose of executing some of the general powers of government. Gibbons v. Ogden, 9 Wheat. (22 U.S.) 1, 195, 6 L.Ed. 23 (1824).

The question whether exclusive federal power must be inferred is not a simple one, for the powers recognized in the Constitution are broad and the nature of their application varied. The warning sounded by the Court in *Cooley* may equally be applicable to the Copyright Clause:

> Either absolutely to affirm, or deny that the nature of [the federal power over commerce] requires exclusive legislation by Congress is to lose sight of the nature of the subjects of this power, and to assert concerning all of them, what is really applicable but to a part. 12 How. (53 U.S.), at 319.

We must also be careful to distinguish those situations in which the concurrent exercise of a power by the Federal Government and the States or by the States alone *may possibly* lead to conflicts and those situations where conflicts *will necessarily* arise. "It is not * * * a mere possibility of inconvenience in the exercise of powers, but an immediate constitutional repugnancy that can by implication alienate and extinguish a preexisting right of [state] sovereignty." The Federalist, No. 32, at 243.

Article I, § 8, cl. 8, of the Constitution gives to Congress the power—

> To promote the Progress of Science and useful Arts, by securing for limited Times to Authors and Inventors the exclusive Right to their respective Writings and Discoveries * * *.

The clause thus describes both the objective which Congress may seek and the means to achieve it. The objective is to promote the progress of science and the arts. As employed, the terms "to promote" are synonymous with the words "to stimulate," "to encourage," or "to induce." [10] To accomplish its purpose, Congress may grant to authors the exclusive right to the fruits of their respective works. An author who possesses an unlimited copyright may preclude others from copying his creation for commercial purposes without permission. In other

---

10. See Kendall v. Winsor, 21 How. (62 U.S.) 322, 328, 16 L.Ed. 165 (1858); Mitchell v. Tilghman, 19 Wall. (86 U.S.) 287, 418, 22 L.Ed. 125 (1873); Bauer & Cie v. O'Donnell, 229 U.S. 1, 10, 33 S.Ct. 616, 617, 57 L.Ed. 1041 (1913).

words, to encourage people to devote themselves to intellectual and artistic creation, Congress may guarantee to authors and inventors a reward in the form of control over the sale or commercial use of copies of their works.

The objective of the Copyright Clause was clearly to facilitate the granting of rights national in scope. While the debates on the clause at the Constitutional Convention were extremely limited, its purpose was described by James Madison in No. 43 of the Federalist Papers:

> The utility of this power will scarcely be questioned. The copyright of authors has been solemnly adjudged, in Great Britain, to be a right of common law. The right to useful inventions seems with equal reason to belong to the inventors. The public good fully coincides in both cases with the claims of individuals. The States cannot separately make effectual provision for either of the cases, and most of them have anticipated the decision of this point, by laws passed at the instance of Congress.[11]

The difficulty noted by Madison relates to the burden placed on an author or inventor who wishes to achieve protection in all States when no federal system of protection is available. To do so, a separate application is required to each state government; the right which in turn may be granted has effect only within the granting State's borders.[12] The national system which Madison supported eliminates the need for multiple applications and the expense and difficulty involved. In effect, it allows Congress to provide a reward greater in scope than any particular State may grant to promote progress in those fields which Congress determines worthy of national action.

Although the copyright clause thus recognizes the potential benefits of a national system, it does not indicate that all writings are of national interest or that state legislation is, in all cases, unnecessary or precluded. The patents granted by the States in the 18th century show, to the contrary, a willingness on the part of the States to promote those portions of science and the arts which were of local importance. Whatever the diversity of people's backgrounds, origins and interests and whatever the variety of business and industry in the 13 colonies, the range of diversity is obviously far greater today in a country of 210 million people in 50 States. In view of that enormous diversity, it is unlikely that all citizens in all parts of the country place the same importance on works relating to all subjects. Since the subject matter to which the copyright clause is addressed may thus be of purely local importance and not worthy of national attention or protection, we

---

11. The Federalist, at 309.

12. Numerous examples may be found in our early history of the difficulties which the creators of items of national import had in securing protection of their creations in all States. For example, Noah Webster, in his effort to obtain protection for his book, A Grammatical Institute of the English Language, brought his claim before the legislatures of at least six States, and perhaps as many as 12. See B. Bugbee, The Genesis of American Patent and Copyright Law (Wash., D.C., 1967) 108–110, 120–124; H.R. Rep. No. 2222, 60th Cong., 2d Sess., at 2 (1909). Similar difficulties were experienced by John Fitch and other inventors who desired to protect their efforts to perfect a steamboat. See Federico, State Patents, 13 J. of the Patent Office Society 166, 170–176 (1931).

cannot discern such an unyielding national interest as to require an inference that state power to grant copyrights has been relinquished to *exclusive* federal control.

The question to which we next turn is whether, in actual operation, the exercise of the power to grant copyrights by some States will prejudice the interests of other States. As we have noted, a copyright granted by a particular State has effect only within its boundaries. If one State grants such protection, the interests of States which do not are not prejudiced since their citizens remain free to copy within their borders those works which may be protected elsewhere. The interests of a State which grants copyright protection may, however, be adversely affected by other States that do not; individuals who wish to purchase a copy of a work protected in their own State will be able to buy unauthorized copies in other States where no protection exists. However, this conflict is neither so inevitable nor so severe as to compel the conclusion, that state power has been relinquished to the exclusive jurisdiction of the Congress. Obviously when some States do not grant copyright protection—and most do not—that circumstance reduces the economic value of a state copyright, but it will hardly render the copyright worthless. The situation is no different from that which may arise in regard to other state monopolies, such as a food concession in a limited enclosure, such as a state park, or a state lottery; in each case, citizens may escape the effect of one State's monopoly by making purchases in another area or another State. Similarly, in the case of state copyrights, except as to individuals willing to travel across state lines in order to purchase records or other writings protected in their own State, each State's copyrights will still serve to induce new artistic creations within that State—the very objective of the grant of protection. We do not see here the type of prejudicial conflicts which would arise, for example, if each State exercised a sovereign power to impose imposts and tariffs; nor can we discern a need for uniformity such as that which may apply to the regulation of interstate shipments.

Similarly, it is difficult to see how the concurrent exercise of the power to grant copyrights by Congress and the States will necessarily and inevitably lead to difficulty. At any time Congress determines that a particular category of "writing" is worthy of national protection and the incidental expenses of federal administration, federal copyright protection may be authorized. Where the need for free and unrestricted distribution of a writing is thought to be required by the national interest, the Copyright Clause and the Commerce Clause would allow Congress to eschew all protection. In such cases, a conflict would develop if a State attempted to protect that which Congress intended to be free from restraint or to free that which Congress had protected. However, where Congress determines that neither federal protection nor freedom from restraint is required by the national interest, it is at liberty to stay its hand entirely.[16] Since state protection would not

16. For example, Congress has provided that writings which may eventually be the subject of a federal copyright, may be protected under state law prior to publication. 17 U.S.C. § 2.

then conflict with federal action, total relinquishment of the States' power to grant copyright protection cannot be inferred.

As we have seen, the language of the Constitution neither explicitly precludes the States from granting copyrights nor grants such authority exclusively to the Federal Government. The subject matter to which the copyright clause is addressed may at times be of purely local concern. No conflict will necessarily arise from a lack of uniform state regulation, nor will the interest of one State be significantly prejudiced by the actions of another. No reason exists why Congress must take affirmative action either to authorize protection of all categories of writings or to free them from all restraint. We therefor conclude that, under the Constitution, the States have not relinquished all power to grant to authors "the exclusive Right to their respective Writings."

B

Petitioners base an additional argument on the language of the Constitution. The California statute forbids individuals from appropriating recordings at any time after release. From this, petitioners argue that the State has created a copyright of *unlimited* duration, in violation of that portion of Art. I, § 8, cl. 8, which provides that copyrights may only be granted "for limited Times." Read literally, the text of Art. I does not support petitioners' position. Section 8 enumerates those powers which have been granted *to Congress*; Whatever limitations have been appended to such powers can only be understood as a limit on congressional, and not state, action. Moreover, it is not clear that the dangers to which this limitation was addressed apply with equal force to both the Federal Government and the States. When Congress grants an exclusive right or monopoly, its effects are pervasive; no citizen or State may escape its reach. As we have noted, however, the exclusive right granted by a State is confined to its borders. Consequently, even when the right is unlimited in duration, any tendency to inhibit further progress in science or the arts is narrowly circumscribed. The challenged statute cannot be voided for lack of a durational limitation.

III

Our conclusion that California did not surrender its power to issue copyrights does not end the inquiry. We must proceed to determine whether the challenged state statute is void under the Supremacy Clause. No simple formula can capture the complexities of this determination; the conflicts which may develop between state and federal action are as varied as the fields to which congressional action may apply. "Our primary function is to determine whether, under the circumstances of this particular case, [the state] law stands as an obstacle to the accomplishment and execution of the full purposes and objectives of Congress." Hines v. Davidowitz, 312 U.S. 52, 67, 61 S.Ct. 399, 404, 85 L.Ed. 581 (1941). We turn then to federal copyright law to determine what objectives Congress intended to fulfill.

By Art. I, § 8, cl. 8, of the Constitution, the States granted to Congress the power to protect the "Writings" of "Authors." These terms have not been construed in their narrow literal sense but, rather, with the reach necessary to reflect the broad scope of constitutional principles. While an "author" may be viewed as an individual who writes an original composition, the term, in its constitutional sense, has been construed to mean an "originator," "he to whom anything owes its origin." Burrow-Giles Lithographic Co. v. Sarony, 111 U.S. 53, 58, 4 S.Ct. 279, 281, 28 L.Ed. 349 (1884). Similarly, although the word "writings" might be limited to script or printed material, it may be interpreted to include any physical rendering of the fruits of creative intellectual or aesthetic labor. Id., Trade Mark Cases, 100 U.S. 82, 94, 25 L.Ed. 550 (1879). Thus, recordings of artistic performances may be within the reach of Clause 8.

While the area in which Congress *may* act is broad, the enabling provision of Clause 8 does not require that Congress act in regard to all categories of materials which meet the constitutional definitions. Rather, whether any specific category of "Writings" is to be brought within the purview of the federal statutory scheme is left to the discretion of the Congress. The history of federal copyright statutes indicates that the congressional determination to consider specific classes of writings is dependent not only on the character of the writing, but also on the commercial importance of the product to the national economy. As our technology has expanded the means available for creative activity and has provided economical means for reproducing manifestations of such activity, new areas of federal protection have been initiated.[17]

---

17. The first congressional copyright statute, passed in 1790, governed only maps, charts, and books. Act of May 31, 1790, c. 15, 1 Stat. 124. In 1802, the Act was amended in order to grant protection to any person "who shall invent and design, engrave, etch or work * * * any historical or other print or prints. * * *" Act of April 29, 1802, c. 36, 2 Stat. 171. Protection was extended to musical compositions when the copyright laws were revised in 1831. Act of Feb. 3, 1831, c. 16, 4 Stat. 436. In 1865, at the time when Mathew Brady's pictures of the Civil War were attaining notoriety, photographs and photographic negatives were expressly added to the list of protected works. Act of Mar. 3, 1865, c. 123, 13 Stat. 540. Again in 1870, the list was augmented to cover paintings, drawings, chromos, statuettes, statuary, and models or designs of fine art. Act of July 8, 1870, c. 230, 16 Stat. 198.

In 1909, Congress agreed to a major consolidation and amendment of all federal copyright statutes. A list of 11 categories of protected work was provided. The relevant sections of the Act are discussed in the text of our opinion. The House Report on the proposed bill specifically noted that amendment was required because "the reproduction of various things which are the subject of copyright has enormously increased," and that the President has specifically recommended revision, among other reasons, because the prior laws "omit[ted] protection for many articles which, under modern reproductive processes, are entitled to protection." H.R.Rep. No. 2222, supra, n. 12, at 1 (quoting Samuel J. Elder and President Theodore Roosevelt).

Since 1909, two additional amendments have been added. In 1912, the list of categories in § 5 was expanded specifically to

Petitioners contend that the actions taken by Congress in establishing federal copyright protection preclude the States from granting similar protection to recordings of musical performances. According to petitioners, Congress addressed the question of whether recordings of performances should be granted protection in 1909; Congress determined that any individual who was entitled to a copyright on an original musical composition should have the right to control to a limited extent the use of that composition on recordings, but that the record itself, and the performance which it was capable of reproducing were not worthy of such protection.[18] In support of their claim, petitioners cite the House Report on the 1909 Act, which states:

> It is not the intention of the committee to extend the right of copyright to the mechanical reproductions themselves, but only to give the composer or copyright proprietor the control, in accordance with the provisions of the bill, of the manufacture and use of such devices. H.R.Rep. No. 2222, 60th Cong., 2d Sess., 9 (1909).

To interpret accurately Congress' intended purpose in passing the 1909 Act and the meaning of the House Report petitioners cite, we must remember that our modern technology differs greatly from that which existed in 1909. The Act and the report should not be read as if they were written today, for to do so would inevitably distort their intended meaning; rather, we must read them against the background of 1909 in which they were written.

In 1831, Congress first extended federal copyright protection to original musical compositions. An individual who possessed such a copyright had the exclusive authority to sell copies of the musical score; individuals who purchased such a copy did so for the most part to play the composition at home on piano or other instrument. Between 1831 and 1909, numerous machines were invented which allowed the composition to be reproduced mechanically. For example, one had only to insert a piano roll or disc with perforations in appropriate places into a player piano to achieve almost the same results which previously required someone capable of playing the instrument. The mounting sales of such devices detracted from the value of the copyright granted for the musical composition. Individuals who had use of a piano roll and an appropriate instrument had little if any need for a copy of the

---

include motion pictures. The House Report on the amendment noted:

"The occasion for this proposed amendment is the fact that the production of motion-picture photoplays and motion pictures other than photoplays has become a business of vast proportions. The money invested therein is so great and the property rights so valuable that the committee is of the opinion that the copyright laws ought to be so amended as to give to them distinct and definite recognition and protection." H.R.Rep. No. 756, 62d Cong., 2d Sess., at 1 (1912).

Finally, in 1971, § 5 was amended to include "sound recordings." Congress was spurred to action by the growth of record piracy, which was in turn due partly to technological advances. See Hearings on S. 646 and H.R. 6927, supra, n. 5, at 4–5, 11 (1971). It must be remembered that the "record piracy" charged against petitioners related to recordings fixed by the original producer prior to Feb. 15, 1972, the effective date of the 1971 Act. See p. 5, supra.

18. 17 U.S.C. § 1(e).

sheet music. The problems which arose eventually reached this Court in 1908 in the case of White-Smith Music Publishing Co. v. Apollo Co., 209 U.S. 1, 28 S.Ct. 319, 52 L.Ed. 655 (1908). There, the Apollo Company had manufactured piano rolls capable of reproducing mechanically compositions covered by a copyright owned by appellant. Appellant contended that the piano rolls constituted "copies" of the copyrighted composition and that their sale, without permission, constituted an infringement of the copyright. The Court held that piano rolls, as well as records, were not "copies" of the copyrighted composition, in terms of the federal copyright statutes, but were merely component parts of a machine which executed the composition. Despite the fact that the piano rolls employed the creative work of the composer, all protection was denied.

It is against this background that Congress passed the 1909 statute. After pointedly waiting for the Court's decision in *White-Smith Music Publishing Company,* Congress determined that the copyright statutes should be amended to insure that *composers of original musical works* received adequate protection to encourage further artistic and creative effort. Henceforth, under § 1(e), records and piano rolls were to be considered as "copies" of the original composition they were capable of reproducing, and could not be manufactured unless payment was made to the *proprietor of the composition copyright.* The section of the House Report cited by petitioners was intended only to establish the limits of *the composer's* right; composers were to have no control over the recordings themselves. Nowhere does the report indicate that Congress considered records as anything but a component part of a machine, capable of reproducing an original composition or that Congress intended records, as *renderings of original artistic performance* to be free from state control.[23]

Petitioners' argument does not rest entirely on the belief that Congress intended specifically to exempt recordings of performances from state control. Assuming that no such intention may be found, they argue that Congress so occupied the field of copyright protection as

---

23. Petitioners do not argue that § 653h conflicts with that portion of 17 U.S.C. § 1(e) which provides:

"[W]henever the owner of a musical copyright has used or permitted or knowingly acquiesced in the use of the copyrighted work upon the parts of instruments serving to reproduce mechanically the musical work, any other person may make similar use of the copyrighted work upon the payment to the copyright proprietor of a royalty of 2 cents on each such part manufactured. * * *"

Assuming *arguendo* that petitioners' use of the composition they duplicated constitutes a "similar use," the challenged state statute might be claimed to diminish the return which is due the composer by lessening the number of copies produced, and thus to conflict with § 1(e). However, as we have noted above, the means presently available for reproducing recordings were not in existence in 1909 when 17 U.S.C. § 1(e) was passed. We see no indication that the challenged state statute detracts from royalties which Congress intended the composer to receive. Furthermore, many state statutes may diminish the number of copies produced. Taxing statutes, for example, may raise the cost of producing or selling records and thereby lessen the number of records which may be sold or inhibit new companies from entering this field of commerce. We do not see in these statutes the direct conflict necessary to render a state statute invalid.

to pre-empt all comparable state action. Rice v. Santa Fe Elevator Corporation, 331 U.S. 218, 67 S.Ct. 1146, 91 L.Ed. 1447 (1947). This assertion is based on the language of 17 U.S.C. §§ 4 and 5, and on this Court's opinions in Sears, Roebuck and Co. v. Stiffel Co., 376 U.S. 225, 84 S.Ct. 784, 11 L.Ed.2d 661 (1964), and Compco Corp. v. Day-Brite Lighting, 376 U.S. 234, 84 S.Ct. 779, 11 L.Ed.2d 669 (1964).

Section 4 of the federal copyright laws provides:

[T]he works for which copyright may be secured under this [Act] shall include all writings of an author.

Section 5, which lists specific categories of protected works, adds:

[T]he above specifications shall not be held to limit the subject-matter of copyright as defined in section 4 of this [Act]. * * *

Since § 4 employs the constitutional term "writings," it may be argued that Congress intended to exercise its authority over all works to which the constitutional provision might apply. However, in the more than 60 years which have transpired since enactment of this provision, neither the Copyright Office, the courts, nor the Congress has so interpreted it. The Register of Copyrights, who is charged with administration of the statute, has consistently ruled that "claims to exclusive rights in mechanical recordings * * *, or in the performances they reproduce" are not entitled to protection under § 4. 37 CFR § 202.8(b) (1972).[25] With one early exception,[26] American courts have agreed with this interpretation;[27] and in 1971, prior to passage of the statute which extended federal protection to recordings fixed on or after Feb. 15, 1972, Congress acknowledged the validity of that interpretation. Both the House and Senate Reports on the proposed legislation recognized that recordings qualified as "writings" within the meaning of the Constitution, but had not previously been protected under the federal copyright statute. H.R.Rep. No. 92–487, 92d Cong., 1st Sess. (1971), at 2, 5; S.Rep. No. 92–72, 92d Cong., 1st Sess. (1971), at 4, U.S.Code Cong. & Admin.News p. 1566. In light of this consistent interpretation by the courts, the agency empowered to administer the copyright statutes, and Congress itself, we cannot agree that §§ 4 and 5 have the broad scope petitioners claim.

---

25. The registration of records under the provisions of the 1909 Act would give rise to numerous administrative difficulties. It is difficult to discern how an individual who wished to copyright a record could comply with the notice and deposit provisions of the statute. 17 U.S.C. §§ 12, 13, 19, 20. Nor is it clear to whom the copyright could rightfully be issued or what constituted publication. Finally, the administrative and economic burden of classifying and maintaining copies of records would have been considerable. See Chafee, Reflections on the Law of Copyright II, 45 Col.L.Rev. 719, 735 (1945); Ringer, The Unauthorized Duplication of Sound Recordings, Studies Prepared for the Subcommittee on Patents, Trade-marks, and Copyrights of the Committee on the Judiciary, United States Senate, 86th Cong., 2d Sess., at 2 (1961); Hearings on S. 646 and H.R. 6927, supra, n. 5, at 11, 14.

26. Fonotopia Limited v. Bradley, 171 F. 951, 963 (EDNY 1909).

27. Aeolian Co. v. Royal Music Roll Co., 196 F. 926, 927 (WDNY 1912); Waring v. WDAS Broadcasting Station, 327 Pa. 433, 437–438, 194 A. 631 (1937); Capitol Records v. Mercury Records Corp., 221 F.2d 657, 661–662 (CA2 1955); Jerome v. Twentieth Century Fox-Film Corp., 67 F.Supp. 736, 742 (SDNY 1946).

Sears and *Compco,* on which petitioners rely, do not support their position. In those cases, the question was whether a State could, under principles of state unfair competition law, preclude the copying of mechanical configurations which did not possess the qualities required for the granting of a federal design or mechanical patent. The Court stated:

> [T]he patent system is one in which uniform standards are carefully used to promote invention while at the same time preserving free competition. Obviously a State could not, consistently with the Supremacy Clause of the Constitution, extend the life of a patent beyond its expiration date or give a patent on an article which lacked the level of invention required for federal patents. To do either would run counter to the policy of Congress of granting patents only to true inventions, and then only for a limited time. Just as a State cannot encroach upon the federal patent laws directly, it cannot, under some other law, such as that forbidding unfair competition, give protection of a kind that clashes with the objectives of the federal patent laws. Sears, Roebuck and Co. v. Stiffel Co., 376 U.S., at 230–231, 84 S.Ct., at 788 (1964) (footnotes omitted).

In regard to mechanical configurations, Congress had balanced the need to encourage innovation and originality of invention against the need to insure competition in the sale of identical or substantially identical products. The standards established for granting federal patent protection to machines thus indicated not only which articles in this particular category Congress wished to protect, but which configurations it wished to remain free. The application of state law in these cases to prevent the copying of articles which did not meet the requirements for federal protection disturbed the careful balance which Congress had drawn and thereby necessarily gave way under the Supremacy Clause of the Constitution. No comparable conflict between state law and federal law arises in the case of recordings of musical performances. In regard to this category of "Writings," Congress has drawn no balance; rather, they have left the area unattended, and no reason exists why the State should not be free to act.[28]

IV

More than 50 years ago, Justice Brandeis observed in dissent in International News Service v. Associated Press:

> The general rule of law is, that the noblest of human productions—knowledge, truths ascertained, conceptions, and ideas—become, after voluntary communications to others free as the air to common use. 248 U.S. 215, 250, 39 S.Ct. 68, 76, 63 L.Ed. 211 (1918).

But there is no fixed, immutable line to tell us which "human productions" are private property and which are so general as to

---

28. Petitioners place great stress on their belief that the records or tapes which they copied had been "published." We have no need to determine whether, *under state law,* these recordings had been published or what legal consequences such publication might have. *For purposes of federal law,* "publication" serves only as a term of the art which defines the legal relationships which Congress has adopted under the federal copyright statutes. As to categories of writings which Congress has not brought within the scope of the federal statute, the term has no application.

become "free as the air." In earlier times, a performing artist's work was largely restricted to the stage; once performed, it remained "recorded" only in the memory of those who had seen or heard it. Today, we can record that performance in precise detail and reproduce it again and again with utmost fidelity. The California statutory scheme evidences a legislative policy to prohibit "tape" and "record piracy," conduct that may adversely affect the continued production of new recordings, a large industry in California. Accordingly, the State has, by statute, given to recordings the attributes of property. No restraint has been placed on the use of an idea or concept; rather, petitioners and other individuals remain free to record the same compositions in precisely the same manner and with the same personnel as appeared on the original recording.

In sum, we have shown that § 653h does not conflict with the federal copyright statute enacted by Congress in 1909. Similarly, no conflict exists between the federal copyright statute passed in 1971 and the present application of § 653h, since California charged petitioners only with copying recordings fixed prior to February 15, 1972. Finally, we have concluded that our decisions in *Sears* and *Compco,* which we reaffirm today, have no application in the present case, since Congress has indicated neither that it wishes to protect, nor to free from protection, recordings of musical performances fixed prior to February 15, 1972.

We conclude that the State of California has exercised a power which it retained under the Constitution, and that the challenged statute, as applied in this case, does not intrude into an area which Congress has, up to now, preempted. Until and unless Congress takes further action with respect to recordings fixed prior to February 15, 1972, the California statute may be enforced against acts of piracy such as those which occurred in the present case.

Affirmed.

Mr. Justice Douglas, with whom Mr. Justice Brennan and Mr. Justice Blackmun concur, dissenting. * * *

Prior to February 25, 1972, copyright protection was not extended to sound recordings. *Sears* and *Compco* make clear that the federal policy expressed in Art. I, § 8, cl. 8, is to have "national uniformity in patent and copyright laws," 376 U.S., at 231, 84 S.Ct. at 788 n. 7, a policy bolstered by Acts of Congress "which vests exclusive jurisdiction to hear patent and copyright cases in federal courts * * * and that section of the Copyright Act which expressly saves state protection of unpublished writings but does not include published writings." Ibid.

Prior to February 15, 1972, sound recordings had no copyright protection. And even under that Act the copyright would be effective "only to sound recordings fixed, published, and copyrighted on and after the effective date of this Act (February 15, 1972) and before January 1, 1975."

California promotes in her law monopoly; the federal policy promotes monopoly only when a copyright is issued, and it fosters competition in all other instances. Moreover, federal law limits its monopoly to 28 years plus a like renewal period, while California extends her monopoly into perpetuity.

Cases like *Sears* were surcharged with "unfair competition" and the present one with "pirated recordings." But free access to products on the market is the consumer interest protected by the failure of Congress to extend patents or copyrights into various areas. * * *

I would reverse the judgment below.

MR. JUSTICE MARSHALL, with whom MR. JUSTICE BRENNAN and MR. JUSTICE BLACKMUN, join, dissenting. * * *

In my view, Congress has demonstrated its desire to exercise the full grant of constitutional power. Title 17, U.S.C. § 4, states: "The works for which copyright may be secured under this title shall include *all the writings of an author*" (emphasis added). The use of the constitutional terms "writings" and "author" rather strongly suggests that Congress intended to follow the constitutional grant. It could exercise the power given it by the Constitution in two ways: either by protecting all writings, or by protecting all writings within designated classes and leaving open to competition all writings in other classes. Section 5 shows that the latter course was chosen, for it enumerates various classes of works that may be registered.[2] Ordinarily, the failure to enumerate "sound recordings" in § 5 would not be taken as an expression of Congress' desire to let free competition reign in the reproduction of such recordings, for, because of the realities of the legislative process, it is generally difficult to infer from a failure to act any affirmative conclusions. Cf. Cleveland v. United States, 329 U.S. 14, 22, 67 S.Ct. 13, 17, 91 L.Ed. 12 (1946) (Rutledge, J., concurring). But in *Sears* and its companion case, Compco Corp. v. Day-Brite Lighting, Inc., 376 U.S. 234, 84 S.Ct. 779, 11 L.Ed.2d 669 (1964), the Court determined that with respect to patents and copyrights, the ordinary practice was not to prevail. In view of the importance of not imposing unnecessary restraints on competition, the Court adopted in those cases a rule of construction that, unless the failure to provide patent or copyright protection for some class of works could clearly be shown to reflect a judgment that state regulation was permitted, the silence of Congress would be taken to reflect a judgment that free competition should prevail. I do not find in *Sears* and *Compco* a limitation on that rule of construction to general classes that Congress has enumerated although of course on the facts of those cases only items in such classes

---

2. From the language of § 4 and the proviso of § 5, it could be rather strongly argued that Congress had intended to afford protection to every writing. I agree with the Court, however, that the consistent administrative interpretation of those sections, in conjunction with the practical difficulty of applying to novel cases certain statutory requirements, like that requiring placement of the notice of copyright on every copy, 17 U.S.C.A. § 10, precludes such an argument.

were involved; rather, the broadest language was used in those cases.[3] Nor can I find in the course of legislation sufficient evidence to convince me that Congress determined to permit state regulation of the reproduction of sound recordings. For whenever technological advances made extension of copyright protection seem wise, Congress has acted promptly. See *ante,* n. 17.[4] This seems to me to reflect the same judgment that the Court found in *Sears* and *Compco:* Congress has decided that free competition should be the general rule, until it is convinced that the failure to provide copyright or patent protection is hindering "the Progress of Science and useful Arts."

The business of record piracy is not an attractive one; persons in the business capitalize on the talents of others without needing to assess independently the prospect of public acceptance of a performance. But the same might be said of persons who copy "mechanical configurations." Such people do provide low-cost reproductions that may well benefit the public. In light of the presumption of *Sears* and *Compco* that congressional silence betokens a determination that the benefits of competition outweigh the impediments placed on creativity by the lack of copyright protection, and in the absence of a congressional determination that the opposite is true, we should not let our distaste for "pirates" interfere with our interpretation of the copyright laws. I would therefore hold that, as to sound recordings fixed before February 15, 1972, the States may not enforce laws limiting reproduction.

Questions

1. Do you agree with the Supreme Court's reason for concluding that the Copyright Clause of the Constitution is not an "exclusive" grant of federal power? Does the "enormous diversity" in the population justify the conclusion that "the subject matter to which the copyright clause is addressed may * * * be of purely local importance and not worthy of national attention or protection * * * "? Is there sufficient national uniformity in lists of the best selling books, the motion pictures with the greatest "box-office" grosses, the highest rated television programs, the most frequently performed music, and the sales

---

3. It bears noting that in Sears, Roebuck & Co. v. Stiffel Co., 376 U.S. 225, 84 S.Ct. 784, 11 L.Ed.2d 661 (1964), repeatedly referred to the patent and copyright statutes as if the same rules of interpretation applied to both. See, e.g., 396 U.S., at 228, 231 n. 7; Compco Corp. v. Day-Brite Lighting Inc., 376 U.S. 234, 237, 84 S.Ct. 779, 781, 11 L.Ed.2d 669 (1964).

4. Between 1909 and 1951, Congress' attention was repeatedly drawn to problems of copyrighting sound recordings. Many bills to provide copyright protection for such recordings were introduced, but none were enacted. See Ringer, The Unauthorized Duplication of Sound Recordings 21–37 (Study No. 26 of Studies Prepared for the Subcommittee on Patents, Trademarks, and Copyrights of the Committee on the Judiciary, United States Senate, 86th Cong., 2d Sess.) (1961). Respondent argues that Congress failed to enact these bills primarily out of uncertainty about the relationship between federal law and international copyright conventions, and was comforted in the knowledge that protection was available under state law. See Brief for Respondent, 28–32. However, it is enough that Congress was aware of the problem, and could have acted, as it did when other technological innovations presented new problems, rather expeditiously. The problems that Congress confronted in 1971 did not spring up in 1970, but had existed, and Congress had not acted, for many years before.

of sound recordings so as to indicate that such "enormous diversity" relates to factors other than state or regional differences? What would have been the pre-1978 impact of a ruling that the Copyright Clause precludes concurrent state power to enact copyright laws?

2. What is the distinction between preemption under the Copyright Clause and preemption under the Supremacy Clause of the Constitution?

3. Does the *Goldstein* opinion adequately distinguish *Sears* and *Compco*? If *Sears* and *Compco* stand for the proposition that an absence of federal protection implies a congressional policy to permit copying which may not be countered by state law, why does it not follow that the absence of federal copyright protection for pre-1972 sound recordings negates state law protection for such recordings? Is the *Goldstein* court being disingenuous when it concludes that the principle stated in *Sears* and *Compco* was limited to the patent sphere, and had no application to copyright?

4. Could the *Goldstein* opinion have distinguished *Sears* and *Compco* in a more satisfactory manner? Could it have been said that *Sears* and *Compco* spoke only to the situation where there was a failure of a given invention (or writing) to meet the required statutory standards of novelty (or originality), while *Goldstein* deals with the markedly different problem where Congress has simply elected not to afford federal protection to a given "category" of work? May it be said that federal preemption is implied in the former, while not in the latter situation?

Collateral Reference

Nimmer on Copyright, § 1.01[A].

B. PREEMPTION UNDER THE CURRENT COPYRIGHT ACT

Note

The Legislative History of Section 301(b)(3)

Section 301 of the current Copyright Act deals with the issue of preemption. In order to understand its full implications some knowledge of the legislative history of Sec. 301(b)(3) is helpful. As originally drafted (Sec. 301(b)(3), H.R. 4347, 89th Cong., 2d Sess. (1966)) it read:

"(b) Nothing in this title annuls or limits any rights or remedies under the common law or statutes of any State with respect to— * * *

(3) activities violating rights that are not equivalent to any of the exclusive rights within the general scope of copyright as specified by Sec. 106, including breaches of contract, breaches of trust, invasion of privacy, defamation, and deceptive trade practices such as passing off and false representation."

As finally sent to the floor of the House of Representatives for enactment, Sec. 301(b)(3) of the bill which became the Copyright Act of 1976 had been amended so as to add several additional state created rights which were said to be immune from federal preemption. Thus, Sec. 301(b)(3) as reported out by the Committee and sent to the House read as follows:

"(b) Nothing in this title annuls or limits any rights or remedies under the common law or statutes of any State with respect to— * * *

(3) activities violating *legal or equitable* rights that are not equivalent to any of the exclusive rights within the general scope of copyright as specified by section 106, including *rights against misappropriation not equivalent to any of such exclusive rights,* breaches of contract, breaches of trust, *trespass, conversion,* invasion of privacy, defamation, and deceptive trade practices such as passing off and false representation."

It will be seen that the italicized words in the above quoted passage had been added to the original Sec. 301(b)(3). The Department of Justice, among others, had objected to the open-ended reference to "misappropriation" in Sec. 301(b)(3), as amended.

In a letter dated July 27, 1976 addressed to Chairman Robert Kastenmeier of the House Sub-Committee, the Justice Department stated: "The 'misappropriation' theory is vague and uncertain * * *. This apparently would permit states to prohibit the reproduction of the literary expression itself under a 'misappropriation' theory * * *. [It] is almost certain to nullify preemption * * *". Concluding that "'Misappropriation' is not necessarily synonymous with copyright infringement * * *"[1] the House Committee declined to follow the Justice Department's suggested deletion.

But when the bill was debated on the floor of the House, Congressman Seiberling of Ohio rose to address the House as follows:

"Mr. SEIBERLING. Mr. Chairman, I offer an amendment * * *. [The Seiberling amendment proposed deletion of all of the latter part of Sec. 301(b)(3) beginning with the word "including," followed by the examples of non-preempted state created rights.] Mr. Chairman, my amendment is intended to save the 'Federal preemption' of State law section which is Sec. 301 of the bill, from being inadvertently nullified because of the inclusion of certain examples in the exemptions from preemption. This amendment would simply strike the examples listed in Sec. 301(b)(3). The amendment is strongly supported by the Justice Department, which believes that it would be a serious mistake to cite as an exemption from preemption the doctrine of 'misappropriation.' The doctrine was created by the Supreme Court in 1922,[2] and it has generally been ignored by the Supreme Court itself and the lower courts ever since. Inclusion of a reference to the misappropriation doctrine in this bill, however, could easily be construed by the courts as authorizing the States to pass misappropriation laws. We should not approve such enabling legislation, because a misappropriation law could be so broad as to render the preemption section meaningless."[3]

Based upon the above remarks, the purpose of the Seiberling amendment was entirely clear. But that purpose became ambiguous by reason of the ensuing colloquy between Congressman Railsback of Illinois (the ranking Republican member of the House sub-committee which reported out the bill) and Congressman Seiberling:

"Mr. RAILSBACK. Mr. Chairman, may I ask the gentleman from Ohio, for the purpose of clarifying the amendment that by striking the word 'misappropriation,' the gentleman in no way is attempting to change the

---

1. H.Rep., p. 132.
2. Congressman Seiberling obviously was referring to International News Service v. Associated Press, infra, which was decided in 1918, not 1922.
3. 122 Cong.Rec. p. H 10910 (September 22, 1976).

existing state of the law, that is as it may exist in certain States that have recognized the right of recovery relating to 'misappropriation'; is that correct?

Mr. SEIBERLING. That is correct. All I am trying to do is prevent the citing of them as examples in the statute. We are, in effect, adopting a rather amorphous body of State law and codifying it, in effect. Rather I am trying to have this bill leave the State law alone and make it clear we are merely dealing with copyright laws, laws applicable to copyrights.

Mr. RAILSBACK. Mr. Chairman, I personally have no objection to the gentleman's amendment in view of that clarification and I know of no objections from this side." [4]

By reason of the above exchange, what was clear in Congressman Seiberling's original statement became most obscure. Mr. Seiberling apparently did not understand the full implications of his original statement. To "save the 'Federal preemption' of State law," his professed original purpose, was precisely *not* to "leave the State law alone," as he later concluded. This confusion was further compounded by Chairman Kastenmeier's remarks which immediately followed:

"Mr. KASTENMEIER. Mr. Chairman, I too have examined the gentleman's amendment and was familiar with the position of the Department of Justice. Unfortunately, the Justice Department did not make its position known to the committee until the last day of the markup * * *. However, Mr. Chairman, I think that the amendment the gentleman is offering is consistent with the position of the Justice Department and accept it on this side as well." [5]

With approval of the amendment expressed by both the chairman of the House sub-committee which reported out the bill, and the minority leader of the sub-committee, the amendment passed without objection.[6] But the respective interpretations of the amendment voiced by these two gentlemen were diametrically opposed. Mr. Railsback assumed that it did not affect state law, while Mr. Kastenmeier assumed that it did.[7] The maker of the amendment, Mr. Seiberling, expressed both views.

Questions

1. In view of the foregoing ambiguous legislative history, how should the courts treat the state law of misappropriation? Does misappropriation constitute a right that is "equivalent to any of the exclusive rights within the general scope of copyright as specified by Sec. 106"? Is it the equivalent of the right of reproduction under Sec. 106(1)? Cf. Capitol Records, Inc. v. Erickson, 2 Cal. App.3d 526, 82 Cal.Rptr. 798 (1969).

2. Is it necessary that a state created right be exactly coextensive with a federally created right under Sec. 106 in order for such a state right in a work of authorship to be preempted? Would a state created right which required the

---

4. Id.
5. Id.
6. Id.
7. Mr. Kastenmeier's reliance upon the Justice Department's position can only be interpreted as an intent to tighten the preemptive effect of Sec. 301, which, as indicated above, was the reason the Justice Department in its letter to Mr. Kastenmeier suggested the amendment which Mr. Seiberling later offered.

author's consent for private as well as public performances be immune from preemption as not being "equivalent" to the Sec. 106(4) right which only extends to public performances? Would a state created right which extended only to private performances be the subject of a Sec. 301 preemption? See H.Rep., p. 131.

3. Is a state created right "equivalent" to a Sec. 106 right and hence (insofar as it is applicable to "works of authorship") the subject of preemption if the act which constitutes a violation of such right consists merely of reproduction, performance, distribution or display, regardless of whether some such acts would violate the state created right but not the comparable Sec. 106 right, or vice versa? Is misappropriation an example? Suppose the state created right is not violated unless there is not only reproduction, performance, distribution, or display of a work of authorship, but also some other element, not required for infringement of a Sec. 106 right? For example, what of an action for breach of contract for failure to pay royalties under a book publication agreement? What element is required in addition to the acts of reproduction and/or distribution?

4. What works of authorship are not subject to preemption even if the state created right is "equivalent" to a Sec. 106 right? What of a sound recording fixed prior to February 15, 1972? Any others?

Collateral References

Brown, "*Unification: A Cheerful Requiem For Common Law Copyright,*" 24 UCLA L.Rev. 1070 (1977).

Goldstein, "*Preempted State Doctrines, Involuntary Transfers and Compulsory Licenses: Testing the Limits of Copyright,*" 24 UCLA L.Rev. 1107 (1977).

Gorman, "*An Overview of the Copyright Act of 1976,*" 126 U.Pa.L.Rev. 856 (1978).

Nimmer on Copyright, § 1.01[B].

Chapter Ten

AUTHORS' MORAL RIGHTS

Note *

The Scope of Moral Rights

Certain European countries,[1] and other Berne Union members [2] have long recognized rights which are personal to authors, and as such viable separate and apart from copyright. These rights are known as *droit moral* or moral rights. They may be generally summarized as including the following author's rights: to be known as the author of his work; to prevent others from being named as the author of his work; to prevent others from falsely attributing to him the authorship of work which he has not in fact written; to prevent others from making deforming changes in his work; to withdraw a published work from distribution if it no longer represents the views of the author; and to prevent others from using the work or the author's name in such a way as to reflect on his professional standing.

The Copyright Act accords no express recognition of moral rights. Moreover, in a number of both federal and state decisions the statement has been made that moral rights are not recognized in the United States.[3] Nevertheless, the time honored judicial practice of distilling new wine in old bottles has resulted in an increasing accretion of case law which in some degree accords the substance of moral rights generally under more conventional and respectable labels such as unfair competition, defamation, invasion of privacy and breach of contract. It may not be said that this development has brought to American authors moral rights protection in the full bloom of the European counterpart. Moreover, such rights are not usually regarded as rights of "copyright." Still, the American development of these rights, under whatever label, is sufficiently advanced as to require some consideration of their substance.

---

* Nimmer on Copyright, § 8.21[A], [B].

1. Moral rights appear to be of greatest importance in France (Law No. 57–296, March 11, 1957, Art. 6), German Federal Republic (Law of Sept. 9, 1965, Arts. 12–14), and Italy (Law No. 633, April 22, 1941, Arts. 20–24).

2. See Art. 6 bis, Berne Convention (Brussels and Paris texts).

3. Gilliam v. American Broadcasting Companies, Inc., 538 F.2d 14 (2d Cir.1976); Vargas v. Esquire, Inc., 164 F.2d 522 (7th Cir.1947); Crimi v. Rutgers Presbyterian Church, 194 Misc. 570, 89 N.Y.S.2d 813 (1949). See Granz v. Harris, p. 240 infra, and Shostakovich v. Twentieth Century-Fox Film Corp., p. 251 infra.

Collateral References

Merryman, *"The Refrigerator of Bernard Buffet,"* 27 Hastings L.J. 1023 (1976).

Treece, *"American Law Analogues of the Author's 'Moral Right',"* 16 Am.J.Comp.Law 487 (1968).

Sarraute, *"Current Theory on the Moral Right of Authors and Artists Under French Law,"* 16 Am.J.Comp.Law 465 (1968).

A. DISTORTION

GRANZ v. HARRIS

United States Court of Appeals, Second Circuit, 1952.
198 F.2d 585.

Before SWAN, CHIEF JUDGE, and AUGUSTUS N. HAND and FRANK, CIRCUIT JUDGES.

SWAN, CHIEF JUDGE. This is an appeal by the plaintiff from a judgment dismissing his complaint on the merits after trial to the court without a jury. The complaint sought rescission of a contract of sale of master phonographic recordings of portions of a jazz concert presented by the plaintiff, damages for breach of the contract, an accounting of profits, a permanent injunction, and attorney's fees in the amount of $3,000. Federal jurisdiction rests on diversity of citizenship. The district judge rendered an opinion, reported in 98 F.Supp. 906, and made detailed findings of fact and conclusions of law in conformity with his opinion. Only two of the findings of fact are attacked by the appellant. They will be discussed hereinafter.

Norman Granz is a well-known promoter and producer of jazz concerts under the designation "Jazz At The Philharmonic." One such concert he caused to be recorded in its entirety on a sixteen-inch master disc from which he re-recorded on six twelve-inch master discs that part of the concert constituting the rendition of two musical compositions entitled "How High the Moon" and "Lady Be Good." These master discs, three for each composition, revolved at 78 revolutions per minute, and were usable in manufacturing commercial phonograph records of the same size and playable at the same speed as the master discs. Granz sold the master discs to the defendant pursuant to a contract dated August 15, 1945. The contract required that in the sale of phonograph records manufactured from the purchased masters the defendant should use the credit-line "Presented by Norman Granz" and explanatory notes which Granz had prepared. Some time in 1948 the defendant re-recorded the musical content of the purchased masters on ten-inch 78 rpm masters from which he manufactured phonograph records of the same size and speed. Such records he sold both in an album and separately. Concededly, at first the album cover did not conform to the contract in that, although it bore the designation "Jazz At The Philharmonic" it did not contain the credit-line or the explanatory notes, but the court found that the cover was later corrected upon the plaintiff's demand. He found also that there was no deletion of music in the ten-inch 78 rpm records. In 1950 the defendant re-recorded the entire contents of the purchased masters on a ten-inch 33⅓ rpm master and from this manufactured records of the same size and speed for retail sale.

The questions presented by the appeal are whether any right of the plaintiff was violated by the defendant: (1) by manufacturing and selling ten-inch 33⅓ rpm records; or (2) by manufacturing and selling ten-inch 78 rpm records; or (3) by selling records singly instead of as part of an album containing both "How High the Moon" and "Lady Be Good."

On the authority of RCA Mfg. Co. v. Whiteman, 2 Cir., 114 F.2d 86, certiorari denied 311 U.S. 712, 61 S.Ct. 393, 85 L.Ed. 463, and a finding that the contract was one of sale rather than license, the district court answered the first question in the negative, 98 F.Supp. 906, 910. We agree with this conclusion and see no need to add to his opinion.

He also gave a negative answer to the third question, 98 F.Supp. 910–911. We adopt his reasoning and conclusion on this point also.

Determination of the second question turns upon findings of fact. Obviously a ten-inch record revolving at 78 revolutions a minute has a shorter playing time and a smaller content than a twelve-inch record revolving at the same speed. Findings 25 and 26 state that all that was deleted in the smaller record was audience reaction consisting of whistles, cheers and screams;[1] that there was no deletion of music, and the plaintiff's contribution to the original musical production was not changed or affected in any way; and, "Accordingly, when the defendant, at the plaintiff's insistence, corrected the album covers of the ten-inch 78 rpm records to conform to the agreement, he was not, as claimed, attributing to the plaintiff the work of some one else." The court based his finding that there was no deletion of music on his own listening to the records (exhibits 4 and 14 played in the court room) and on the testimony of Mr. Hammond, a musical expert called by the plaintiff. A perusal of this expert's testimony discloses statements patently at odds with the judge's finding. Nor can we understand, after ourselves listening to the records, the judge's finding that nothing but audience reaction was omitted from the ten-inch records. Fully eight minutes of music appear to us to have been omitted, including saxophone, guitar, piano and trumpet solos. In our opinion the trial judge's finding that there was no substantial musical deletions is erroneous.

We are therefore faced with the question whether the manufacture and sale by the defendant of the abbreviated ten-inch records violated any right of the plaintiff. Disregarding for the moment the terms of the contract, we think that the purchaser of the master discs could

---

1. It is not claimed, nor could it be successfully, that the reaction of the audience was the product of the plaintiff's skill or talent, or that he had any property right to it or to the reproduction of it.

lawfully use them to produce the abbreviated record and could lawfully sell the same provided he did not describe it as a recording of music presented by the plaintiff. If he did so describe it, he would commit the tort of unfair competition. But the contract required the defendant to use the legend "Presented by Norman Granz," that is, to attribute to him the musical content of the records offered for sale. This contractual duty carries by implication, without the necessity of an express prohibition, the duty not to sell records which make the required legend a false representation. In our opinion, therefore, sale of the ten-inch abbreviated records was a breach of the contract. No specific damages were shown to have resulted. As such damages are difficult to prove and the harm to the plaintiff's reputation as an expert in the presentation of jazz concerts is irreparable, injunctive relief is appropriate. Hence we think the plaintiff was entitled to an injunction against having the abbreviated ten-inch records attributed to him unless he waived his right. As already noted the district court found that the album cover of the shortened record was corrected "at the plaintiff's insistence," and consequently the defendant was not "attributing to the plaintiff the work of some one else." The only evidence we can discover to support the theory of waiver is the following bit of testimony by the defendant who was called as a witness by the plaintiff:

> As soon as I have received the letter from his [Granz's] attorney, probably about a couple of weeks later or month later, I called in my attorney and he said, What is Norman Granz's complaint, and he said he wanted to see his attorney, and he said he did not like the arrangement, and that was the question discussed, change the cover.

What this testimony means is far from clear. Even if Granz's attorney requested that the cover be corrected immediately and without waiting for the case to come to trial, we are not satisfied that this would necessarily operate as a waiver of Granz's right to an injunction, if sale of the abbreviated records under the legend "Presented by Norman Granz" constituted a breach of contract or the tort of unfair competition, as we have found it did. Whether he intended to waive all claims or whether that result would follow regardless of his intention depends upon what was said and done in the negotiations regarding correction of the cover. We think the case must be remanded for additional evidence on this point and a finding as to what, if anything, Granz did consent.

Dismissal of the complaint is affirmed with respect to sales of the ten-inch 33⅓ rpm records and with respect to selling records singly. With respect to the sale of ten-inch 78 rpm records and the claim of attorney's fees the cause is remanded for further proceedings in conformity with the opinion. One-half costs of appeal are awarded the appellant.

FRANK, CIRCUIT JUDGE, (concurring).

1. I agree, of course, that, whether by way of contract or tort, plaintiff (absent his consent to the contrary) is entitled to prevention of the publication, as his, of a garbled version of his uncopyrighted

product. This is not novel doctrine: Byron obtained an injunction from an English court restraining the publication of a book purporting to contain his poems only, but which included some not of his authorship.[2] American courts, too, have enforced such a right.[3] Those courts have also enjoined the use by another of the characteristics of an author of repute in such manner as to deceive buyers into erroneously believing that they were buying a work of that author.[4] Those courts, moreover, have granted injunctive relief in these circumstances: An artist sells one of his works to the defendant who substantially changes it and then represents the altered matter to the public as that artist's product. Whether the work is copyrighted or not, the established rule is that, even if the contract with the artist expressly authorizes reasonable modifications (e.g., where a novel or stage play is sold for adaptation as a movie), it is an actionable wrong to hold out the artist as author of a version which substantially departs from the original.[5] Under the authorities, the defendant's conduct here, as my colleagues say, may also be considered a kind of "unfair competition" or "passing off." [6] The irreparable harm, justifying an injunction, becomes apparent when one thinks what would be the result if the collected speeches of Stalin were published under the name of Senator Robert Taft, or the poems of Ella Wheeler Wilcox as those of T.S. Eliot.

2. If, on the remand, the evidence should favor the plaintiff, I think we should grant him further relief, i.e., an injunction against publication by the defendant of any truncated version of his work, even if it does not bear plaintiff's name. I would rest the grant of that relief on an interpretation of the contract.

Plaintiff, in asking for such relief, relied in part not on the contract but on the doctrine of artists' "moral right," a compendious label of a

---

2. Byron v. Johnston, 2 Mer. 28, 35 Eng. Rep. 851. See also Ridge v. English Illustrated Magazine, 29 T.L.R. 592.

3. See Clemens v. Belford, Clark & Co., D.C.N.D.Ill., 14 F. 728, 730–731; D'Altomonte v. New York Herald, 154 App.Div. 453, 139 N.Y.S. 200, modified 208 N.Y. 695, 102 N.E. 1101; Ben Oliel v. Press Publishing Co., 251 N.Y. 250, 167 N.E. 432.

4. Estes v. Williams, D.C.S.D.N.Y., 21 F. 189; Fisher v. Star Co., 231 N.Y. 414, 132 N.E. 133, 19 A.L.R. 937; See also Prouty v. National Broadcasting Co., D.C.Mass., 26 F.Supp. 265; cf. Gardella v. Log Cabin Products Co., 2 Cir., 89 F.2d 891, 895. Cf. Hogg v. Kirby, 32 Eng.Rep. 336.

5. Packard v. Fox Film Corp., 207 App. Div. 311, 202 N.Y.S. 164; see also Curwood v. Affiliated Distributors, Inc., D.C.S.D. N.Y., 283 F. 219, 222; Drummond v. Altemus, C.C.E.D.Pa., 60 F. 338; cf. Archbold v. Sweet, 172 Eng.Rep. 947; Royle v. Dillingham, 53 Misc. 383, 384, 104 N.Y.S. 783; Lee v. Gibbings, 67 L.T.R. 263; Cox v. Cox, 68 Eng.Rep. 1211, 1214; Annot. Unfair Competition—Art—Literature, 19 A.L.R. 949.

6. See, e.g., Uproar Co. v. National Broadcasting Co., D.C.Mass., 8 F.Supp. 358; Fisher v. Star Co., 231 N.Y. 414, 132 N.E. 133, 19 A.L.R. 937; Estes v. Williams, C.C. S.D.N.Y., 21 F. 189; Royle v. Dillingham, 53 Misc. 383, 104 N.Y.S. 783; cf. Packard v. Fox Film Co., supra.

The unfair competition doctrine has yielded some judge-made monopolies of doubtful value to the public. See, e.g., Standard Brands v. Smidler, 2 Cir., 151 F.2d 34, 38–43; General Time Instrument Corp. v. U.S. Time Corporation, 2 Cir., 165 F.2d 853, 855, dissenting opinion; Triangle Publications v. Rohrlich, 2 Cir., 167 F.2d 969, 980, dissenting opinion; cf. Chafee, Unfair Competition, 53 Harv.L.Rev. (1940) 1289, 1318–19. But the application of that doctrine here is obviously in the public interest.

"bundle of rights"[7] enforced in many "civil law" countries.[8] Able legal thinkers,[9] pointing out that American courts have already recognized a considerable number of the rights in that "bundle," have urged that our courts use the "moral right" symbol. Those thinkers note that the label "right of privacy" served to bring to the attention of our courts a common center of perspectives previously separated in the decisions,[10] and that the use of that label induced further novel and valuable judicial perspectives.

To this suggestion there are these objections: (a) "Moral right" seems to indicate to some persons something not legal, something meta-legal. (b) The "moral right" doctrine, as applied in some countries, includes very extensive rights which courts in some American jurisdictions are not yet prepared to acknowledge;[11] as a result, the phrase "moral right" seems to have frightened some of those courts to such an extent that they have unduly narrowed artists' rights.[12] (c) Finally, it is not always an unmitigated boon to devise and employ such a common name.[a] As we have said elsewhere:[13] "A new name, a novel label expressive of a new generalization, can have immense consequences. Emerson said, 'Generalization is always a new influx of the divinity into the mind. Hence the thrill that attends it.' Confronted with disturbing variety, we often feel a tension from which a generalization, an abstraction, relieves us. It serves as a de-problemizer, aiding us to pass from an unstable, problematical, situation to a more stable one. It satisfies a craving, meets what Emerson called 'the insatiable demand of harmony in man,' a demand which translates itself into the so-called 'law' of 'the least effort.' But the solution of a problem through the invention of a new generalization is no final solution: The new generalization breeds new problems. Stressing a newly perceived likeness between many particular happenings which had theretofore seemed unlike, it may blind us to continuing unlikenesses. Hypnotized by a label which emphasizes identities, we may be led to ignore differences. * * * For, with its stress on uniformity, an abstraction or generalization tends to become totalitarian in its attitude towards uniqueness."

---

7. See Rohmer v. Commissioner, 2 Cir., 153 F.2d 61, 63; Standard Oil Co. v. Clark, 2 Cir., 163 F.2d 917, 930–939.

8. See Roeder, Doctrine of Moral Right, 53 Harv.L.Rev. 554, 565–572; Ladas, International Protection of Literary and Artistic Property, Vol. I, 575 et seq.; Katz, Doctrine of Moral Right, 24 So.Cal.L.Rev. 375 (1951).

9. See citations in preceding footnote.

10. Warren and Brandeis, The Law of Privacy, 4 Harv.L.Rev. (1890) 193.

11. See, e.g., Katz, The Doctrine of Moral Right, 24 So.Cal.L.Rev. (1951) 374, 390, 394, 395, 396 and especially 399; Roeder, Moral Right, 53 Harv.L.Rev. (1940) 554, 561, 565.

12. See, e.g., Vargas v. Esquire, 7 Cir., 164 F.2d 522, 526; Crimi v. Rutgers Presbyterian Church, 194 Misc. 570, 89 N.Y.S.2d 813 (right of a mural painter to enjoin destruction by church of his mural; court held that his was an interest in real estate and distinguishable from interests in literary property); Shostakovich v. Twentieth Century Fox Film Corp., 196 Misc. 67, 80 N.Y. S.2d 575.

a. Judge Frank apparently felt differently one year later when he coined the label "right of publicity" in Haelan Laboratories v. Topps Chewing Gum, p. 749 infra.

13. Guiseppi v. Walling, 2 Cir., 144 F.2d 608, 618–619, 155 A.L.R. 761.

Without rejecting the doctrine of "moral right," I think that, in the light of the foregoing, we should not rest decision on that doctrine where, as here, it is not necessary to do so.

Questions

1. Did the court conclude that sale of the ten-inch 78 rpm records might constitute unfair competition, or breach of contract, or both? If, absent a contract between the parties, such sale would be unfair competition, does it cease to be unfair competition by reason of the contract? What does a contract theory add to the plaintiff's rights?

2. Do you agree with the court that the contractual duty to give Granz a credit line "carries by implication, without the necessity of an express prohibition, the duty not to sell records which make the required legend a false representation"? What about an alternative implication: i.e. that the duty to give such credit is subject to an implied condition that the content of the records are such as to make the credit line a true statement? Is Judge Frank, in his concurring opinion, assuming the possibility of such a construction when he refers to the possibility of a truncated version that "does not bear plaintiff's name"? In such circumstances, Judge Frank indicates that he would grant relief "on an interpretation of the contract". What interpretation?

GILLIAM v. AMERICAN BROADCASTING COMPANIES, INC.

United States Court of Appeals, Second Circuit, 1976.
538 F.2d 14.

Before LUMBARD, HAYS and GURFEIN, CIRCUIT JUDGES.

LUMBARD, CIRCUIT JUDGE. Plaintiffs, a group of British writers and performers known as "Monty Python," appeal from a denial by Judge Lasker in the Southern District of a preliminary injunction to restrain the American Broadcasting Company (ABC) from broadcasting edited versions of three separate programs originally written and performed by Monty Python for broadcast by the British Broadcasting Corporation (BBC). We agree with Judge Lasker that the appellants have demonstrated that the excising done for ABC impairs the integrity of the original work. We further find that the countervailing injuries that Judge Lasker found might have accrued to ABC as a result of an injunction at a prior date no longer exist. We therefore direct the issuance of a preliminary injunction by the district court.

Since its formation in 1969, the Monty Python group has gained popularity primarily through its thirty-minute television programs created for BBC as part of a comedy series entitled "Monty Python's Flying Circus." In accordance with an agreement between Monty Python and BBC, the group writes and delivers to BBC scripts for use in the television series. This scriptwriters' agreement recites in great detail the procedure to be followed when any alterations are to be made in the script prior to recording of the program. The essence of this section of the agreement is that, while BBC retains final authority to make changes, appellants or their representatives exercise optimum control over the scripts consistent with BBC's authority and only minor changes may be made without prior consultation with the writers. Nothing in the scriptwriters' agreement entitles BBC to alter a program once it has been recorded. The agreement further provides that, subject to the terms therein, the group retains all rights in the script.

Under the agreement, BBC may license the transmission of recordings of the television programs in any overseas territory. The series has been broadcast in this country primarily on non-commercial public broadcasting television stations, although several of the programs have been broadcast on commercial stations in Texas and Nevada. In each instance, the thirty-minute programs have been broadcast as originally recorded and broadcast in England in their entirety and without commercial interruption.

In October 1973, Time-Life Films acquired the right to distribute in the United States certain BBC television programs, including the Monty Python series. Time-Life was permitted to edit the programs only "for insertion of commercials, applicable censorship or governmental * * * rules and regulations, and National Association of Broadcasters and time segment requirements." No similar clause was included in the scriptwriters' agreement between appellants and BBC. Prior to this time, ABC had sought to acquire the right to broadcast excerpts from various Monty Python programs in the spring of 1975, but the group rejected the proposal for such a disjoined format. Thereafter, in July 1975, ABC agreed with Time-Life to broadcast two ninety-minute specials each comprising three thirty-minute Monty Python programs that had not previously been shown in this country.

Correspondence between representatives of BBC and Monty Python reveals that these parties assumed that ABC would broadcast each of the Monty Python programs "in its entirety." On September 5, 1975, however, the group's British representative inquired of BBC how ABC planned to show the programs in their entirety if approximately 24 minutes of each 90 minute program were to be devoted to commercials. BBC replied on September 12, "we can only reassure you that ABC have decided to run the programmes 'back to back,' and that there is a firm undertaking not to segment them."

ABC broadcast the first of the specials on October 3, 1975. Appellants did not see a tape of the program until late November and were allegedly "appalled" at the discontinuity and "mutilation" that had resulted from the editing done by Time-Life for ABC. Twenty-four minutes of the original 90 minutes of recording had been omitted. Some of the editing had been done in order to make time for commercials; other material had been edited, according to ABC, because the original programs contained offensive or obscene matter.

In early December, Monty Python learned that ABC planned to broadcast the second special on December 26, 1975. The parties began negotiations concerning editing of that program and a delay of the broadcast until Monty Python could view it. These negotiations were futile, however, and on December 15 the group filed this action to enjoin the broadcast and for damages. Following an evidentiary hearing, Judge Lasker found that "the plaintiffs have established an impairment of the integrity of their work" which "caused the film or program * * * to lose its iconoclastic verve." According to Judge Lasker, "the damage that has been caused to the plaintiffs is irreparable by its nature." Nevertheless, the judge denied the motion for the preliminary injunction on the grounds that it was unclear who owned the copyright in the programs produced by BBC from the scripts written by Monty Python; that there was a question of whether Time-Life and BBC were indispensable parties to the litigation; that ABC would suffer significant financial loss if it were enjoined a week before the scheduled broadcast; and that Monty Python had displayed a "somewhat disturbing casualness" in their pursuance of the matter.

Judge Lasker granted Monty Python's request for more limited relief by requiring ABC to broadcast a disclaimer during the December 26 special to the effect that the group dissociated itself from the program because of the editing. A panel of this court, however, granted a stay of that order until this appeal could be heard and permitted ABC to broadcast, at the beginning of the special, only the legend that the program had been edited by ABC. We heard argument on April 13 and, at that time, enjoined ABC from any further broadcast of edited Monty Python programs pending the decision of the court.

I

In determining the availability of injunctive relief at this early stage of the proceedings, Judge Lasker properly considered the harm that would inure to the plaintiffs if the injunction were denied, the harm that defendant would suffer if the injunction were granted, and the likelihood that plaintiffs would ultimately succeed on the merits. See Hamilton Watch Co. v. Benrus Watch Co., 206 F.2d 738 (2d Cir.1953). We direct the issuance of a preliminary injunction because we find that all these factors weigh in favor of appellants.

* * *

We then reach the question whether there is a likelihood that appellants will succeed on the merits. In concluding that there is a likelihood of infringement here, we rely especially on the fact that the editing was substantial, i.e., approximately 27 per cent of the original program was omitted, and the editing contravened contractual provisions that limited the right to edit Monty Python material. It should be emphasized that our discussion of these matters refers only to such facts as have been developed upon the hearing for a preliminary injunction. Modified or contrary findings may become appropriate after a plenary trial.

Judge Lasker denied the preliminary injunction in part because he was unsure of the ownership of the copyright in the recorded program. Appellants first contend that the question of ownership is irrelevant because the recorded program was merely a derivative work taken from the script in which they hold the uncontested copyright. Thus, even if BBC owned the copyright in the recorded program, its use of that work would be limited by the license granted to BBC by Monty Python for use of the underlying script. We agree.

Section 7 of the Copyright Law, 17 U.S.C. § 7, provides in part that "adaptations, arrangements, dramatizations * * * or other versions of * * * copyrighted works when produced with the consent of the proprietor of the copyright in such works * * * shall be regarded as new works subject to copyright * * *." Manifestly, the recorded program falls into this category as a dramatization of the script,[3] and thus the program was itself entitled to copyright protection. However, section 7 limits the copyright protection of the derivative work, as works adapted from previously existing scripts have become known, to the novel additions made to the underlying work. Reyher v. Children's Television Workshop, 533 F.2d 87 (2d Cir.1976), and the derivative work does not affect the "force or validity" of the copyright in the matter from which it is derived. See Grove Press, Inc. v. Greenleaf Publishing Co., 247 F.Supp. 518 (S.D.N.Y.1965). Thus, any ownership by BBC of the copyright in the recorded program would not affect the scope or ownership of the copyright in the underlying script.

Since the copyright in the underlying script survives intact despite the incorporation of that work into a derivative work, one who uses the script, even with the permission of the proprietor of the derivative work, may infringe the underlying copyright. See Davis v. E.I. DuPont deNemours & Co., 240 F.Supp. 612 (S.D.N.Y.1965) (defendants held to have infringed when they obtained permission to use a screenplay in preparing a television script but did not obtain permission of the author of the play upon which the screenplay was based.)

---

3. ABC has not argued that the principles of section 7 do not apply because Monty Python's copyright in its unpublished script is a common law copyright rather than a statutory copyright, which can exist only after publication. In any event, we find that the same principles discussed below with respect to derivative works adapted from material in which there is a statutory copyright also apply to material in which there is a common law copyright. See RCA Manufacturing Co. v. Whiteman, 114 F.2d 86, 88 (2d Cir.), cert. denied 311 U.S. 712, 61 S.Ct. 393, 85 L.Ed. 463 (1940); 17 U.S.C.A. § 2.

The law is apparently unsettled with respect to whether a broadcast of a recorded program constitutes publication of that program and the underlying script so as to divest the proprietor of the script of his common law copyright. See 1 M. Nimmer, Copyright §§ 56.3, 57. Arguably, once the scriptwriter obtains the economic benefit of the recording and the broadcast, he has obtained all that his common law copyright was intended to secure for him; thus it would not be unfair to find that publication of the derivative work divested the script of its common law protection. On the other hand, several types of performances from scripts have been held not to constitute divestive publication, see e.g., Uproar Co. v. NBC, 81 F.2d 373 (1st Cir.1936), and it is unclear whether a broadcast of the recording in itself constitutes publication. See M. Nimmer, supra, § 56.3. Since ABC has not objected to Monty Python's assertion of common law copyright in an unpublished script, we need not entertain the question on this appeal from denial of a preliminary injunction. We leave initial determination of this perplexing question to the district court in its determination of all the issues on the merits. This disposition is especially proper in view of the fact that, apart from the copyright claims, there will be a trial of the unfair competition claim.

If the proprietor of the derivative work is licensed by the proprietor of the copyright in the underlying work to vend or distribute the derivative work to third parties, those parties will, of course, suffer no liability for their use of the underlying work consistent with the license to the proprietor of the derivative work. Obviously, it was just this type of arrangement that was contemplated in this instance. The scriptwriters' agreement between Monty Python and BBC specifically permitted the latter to license the transmission of the recordings made by BBC to distributors such as Time-Life for broadcast in overseas territories.

One who obtains permission to use a copyrighted script in the production of a derivative work, however, may not exceed the specific purpose for which permission was granted. Most of the decisions that have reached this conclusion have dealt with the improper extension of the underlying work into media or time, i.e., duration of the license, not covered by the grant of permission to the derivative work proprietor.[4] See Bartsch v. Metro-Goldwyn-Mayer, Inc., 391 F.2d 150 (2d Cir.), cert. denied 393 U.S. 826, 89 S.Ct. 86, 21 L.Ed.2d 96 (1968); G. Ricordi & Co. v. Paramount Pictures Inc., 189 F.2d 469 (2d Cir.), cert. denied 342 U.S. 849, 72 S.Ct. 77, 96 L.Ed. 641 (1951). Cf. Rice v. American Program Bureau, 446 F.2d 685 (2d Cir.1971). Appellants herein do not claim that the broadcast by ABC violated media or time restrictions contained in the license of the script to BBC. Rather, they claim that revisions in the script, and ultimately in the program, could be made only after consultation with Monty Python, and that ABC's broadcast of a program edited after recording and without consultation with Monty Python exceeded the scope of any license that BBC was entitled to grant.

The rationale for finding infringement when a licensee exceeds time or media restrictions on his license—the need to allow the proprietor of the underlying copyright to control the method in which his work is presented to the public—applies equally to the situation in which a licensee makes an unauthorized use of the underlying work by publishing it in a truncated version. Whether intended to allow greater economic exploitation of the work, as in the media and time cases, or to ensure that the copyright proprietor retains a veto power over revisions desired for the derivative work, the ability of the copyright holder to control his work remains paramount in our copyright law. We find, therefore, that unauthorized editing of the underlying work, if proven, would constitute an infringement of the copyright in that work similar to any other use of a work that exceeded the license granted by the proprietor of the copyright.

---

4. Thus, a leading commentator on the subject concludes:

If the copyright owner of an underlying work limits his consent for its use in a derivative work to a given medium (e.g. opera), the copyright owner of the derivative work may not exploit such derivative work in a different medium (e.g. motion pictures) to the extent the derivative work incorporates protectible material from the underlying work.

1 M. Nimmer, Copyright § 45.3.

If the broadcast of an edited version of the Monty Python program infringed the group's copyright in the script, ABC may obtain no solace from the fact that editing was permitted in the agreements between BBC and Time-Life or Time-Life and ABC. BBC was not entitled to make unilateral changes in the script and was not specifically empowered to alter the recordings once made; Monty Python, moreover, had reserved to itself any rights not granted to BBC. Since a grantor may not convey greater rights than it owns, BBC's permission to allow Time-Life, and hence ABC, to edit appears to have been a nullity. See Hampton v. Paramount Pictures Corp., 279 F.2d 100 (9th Cir.), cert. denied, 364 U.S. 882, 81 S.Ct. 170, 5 L.Ed.2d 103 (1970); Ilyin v. Avon Publications, 144 F.Supp. 368, 372 (S.D.N.Y.1956).

ABC answers appellants' infringement argument with a series of contentions, none of which seems meritorious at this stage of the litigation. The network asserts that Monty Python's British representative, Jill Foster, knew that ABC planned to exclude much of the original BBC program in the October 3 broadcast. ABC thus contends that by not previously objecting to this procedure, Monty Python ratified BBC's authority to license others to edit the underlying script.

* * * On the present record, it cannot be said that there was any ratification of BBC's grant of editing rights. ABC, of course, is entitled to attempt to prove otherwise during the trial on the merits.

ABC next argues that under the "joint work" theory adopted in Shapiro, Bernstein & Co. v. Jerry Vogel Music, Inc., 221 F.2d 569 (2d Cir.1955), the script produced by Monty Python and the program recorded by BBC are symbiotic elements of a single production. Therefore, according to ABC, each contributor possesses an undivided ownership of all copyrightable elements in the final work and BBC could thus have licensed use of the script, including editing, written by appellants.

The joint work theory as extended in *Shapiro* has been criticized as inequitable unless "at the time of creation by the first author, the second author's contribution [is envisaged] as an integrated part of a single work," and the first author intends that the final product be a joint work. See 1 M. Nimmer, Copyright §§ 67–73. Furthermore, this court appears to have receded from a broad application of the joint work doctrine where the contract which leads to collaboration between authors indicates that one will retain a superior interest. See Szekely v. Eagle Lion Films, Inc., 242 F.2d 266 (2d Cir.), cert. denied, 354 U.S. 922, 77 S.Ct. 1382, 1 L.Ed.2d 1437 (1957). In the present case, the screenwriters' agreement between Monty Python and BBC provides that the group is to retain all rights in the script not granted in the agreement and that at some future point the group may license the scripts for use on television to parties other than BBC. These provisions suggest that the parties did not consider themselves joint authors of a single work. This matter is subject to further exploration at the trial, but in the present state of the record, it presents no bar to issuance of a preliminary injunction.

Aside from the question of who owns the relevant copyrights, ABC asserts that the contracts between appellants and BBC permit editing of the programs for commercial television in the United States. ABC argues that the scriptwriters' agreement allows appellants the right to participate in revisions of the script only *prior* to the recording of the programs, and thus infers that BBC had unrestricted authority to revise after that point. This argument, however, proves too much. A reading of the contract seems to indicate that Monty Python obtained control over editing the script only to ensure control over the program recorded from that script.[6] Since the scriptwriters' agreement explicitly retains for the group all rights not granted by the contract, omission of any terms concerning alterations in the program after recording must be read as reserving to appellants exclusive authority for such revisions.[7]

Finally, ABC contends that appellants must have expected that deletions would be made in the recordings to conform them for use on commercial television in the United States. ABC argues that licensing in the United States implicitly grants a license to insert commercials in a program and to remove offensive or obscene material prior to broadcast. According to the network, appellants should have anticipated that most of the excised material contained scatological references inappropriate for American television and that these scenes would be replaced with commercials, which presumably are more palatable to the American public.

The proof adduced up to this point, however, provides no basis for finding any implied consent to edit. Prior to the ABC broadcasts, Monty Python programs had been broadcast on a regular basis by both

---

6. The scriptwriters' agreement, of course, concerns the recorded program as well as the script. BBC's rights under the agreement involve primarily the licensing of the recorded program, not the script itself. Thus, the scriptwriters' agreement would have been the proper and expected place to find any intended authorization for editing of the recorded program.

7. McGuire v. United Artists Television Productions, Inc., 254 F.Supp. 270 (S.D.Cal. 1966), cited by appellee for the proposition that failure of a writer explicitly to reserve control over a recording of his script automatically forfeits that control, is inapposite. That case involved the question of whether a writer who had been granted an undetermined measure of "creative control" over the script could prevent editing of the film for insertion of commercials. The court found only that the parties had reached no agreement on the scope of the writer's "creative control." Here, however, that scope is clearly delineated by the agreement that retains for appellants those rights not granted to BBC, and hence, to BBC's licensees.

In a performer's agreement between Monty Python and BBC, the group warranted that any manuscript that it provided to BBC for performance would be either "original material of (its) own which (it) is fully at liberty to use for all purposes of this Agreement * * * or original material which (it) is fully at liberty to use for all purposes of this Agreement by reason of (its) holding all necessary licenses or permissions." ABC contends that somehow this clause provides an implicit right to edit for commercial television because that act would be consistent with the warranty that the parties are "fully at liberty" to use the scripts for any purpose. Judge Lasker found that the performer's agreement was wholly irrelevant to the issue of a preliminary injunction. While we need not express any opinion on that ruling at this time, it is obvious from a reading of the contract that the sole purpose of the clause relied upon by ABC is to hold BBC harmless from a claim by any party that the Monty Python scripts infringe upon another work.

commercial and public television stations in this country without interruption or deletion. Indeed, there is no evidence of any prior broadcast of edited Monty Python material in the United States. These facts, combined with the persistent requests for assurances by the group and its representatives that the programs would be shown intact belie the argument that the group knew or should have known that deletions and commercial interruptions were inevitable.

Several of the deletions made for ABC, such as elimination of the words "hell" and "damn," seem inexplicable given today's standard television fare.[8] If, however, ABC honestly determined that the programs were obscene in substantial part, it could have decided not to broadcast the specials at all, or it could have attempted to reconcile its differences with appellants. The network could not, however, free from a claim of infringement, broadcast in a substantially altered form a program incorporating the script over which the group had retained control.

Our resolution of these technical arguments serves to reinforce our initial inclination that the copyright law should be used to recognize the important role of the artist in our society and the need to encourage production and dissemination of artistic works by providing adequate legal protection for one who submits his work to the public. See Mazer v. Stein, 347 U.S. 201, 74 S.Ct. 460, 98 L.Ed. 630 (1954). We therefore conclude that there is a substantial likelihood that, after a full trial, appellants will succeed in proving infringement of their copyright by ABC's broadcast of edited versions of Monty Python programs. In reaching this conclusion, however, we need not accept appellants' assertion that any editing whatsoever would constitute infringement. Courts have recognized that licensees are entitled to some small degree of latitude in arranging the licensed work for presentation to the public in a manner consistent with the licensee's style or standards.[9] See Stratchborneo v. Arc. Music Corp., 357 F.Supp. 1393, 1405 (S.D.N.Y. 1973); Preminger v. Columbia Pictures Corp., 49 Misc.2d 363, 267 N.Y.S.2d 594 (Sup.Ct.), aff'd 25 A.D.2d 830, 269 N.Y.S.2d 913 (1st Dept.), aff'd 18 N.Y.2d 659, 273 N.Y.S.2d 80, 219 N.E.2d 431 (1966). That privilege, however, does not extend to the degree of editing that occurred here especially in light of contractual provisions that limited the right to edit Monty Python material.

II

It also seems likely that appellants will succeed on the theory that, regardless of the right ABC had to broadcast an edited program, the cuts made constituted an actionable mutilation of Monty Python's work. This cause of action, which seeks redress for deformation of an artist's work, finds its roots in the continental concept of droit moral, or

---

8. We also note that broadcast of the Monty Python specials was scheduled by ABC for an 11:30 p.m. to 1:00 a.m. time slot.

9. Indeed, the scriptwriters' agreement permitted BBC to make "minor" changes without consulting Monty Python. * * *

moral right, which may generally be summarized as including the right of the artist to have his work attributed to him in the form in which he created it. See 1 M. Nimmer, supra, at § 110.1.

American copyright law, as presently written, does not recognize moral rights or provide a cause of action for their violation, since the law seeks to vindicate the economic, rather than the personal, rights of authors. Nevertheless, the economic incentive for artistic and intellectual creation that serves as the foundation for American copyright law, Goldstein v. California, 412 U.S. 546, 93 S.Ct. 2303, 37 L.Ed.2d 163 (1973); Mazer v. Stein, 347 U.S. 201, 74 S.Ct. 460, 98 L.Ed. 630 (1954), cannot be reconciled with the inability of artists to obtain relief for mutilation or misrepresentation of their work to the public on which the artists are financially dependent. Thus courts have long granted relief for misrepresentation of an artist's work by relying on theories outside the statutory law of copyright, such as contract law, Granz v. Harris, 198 F.2d 585 (2d Cir.1952) (substantial cutting of original work constitutes misrepresentation), or the tort of unfair competition, Prouty v. National Broadcasting Co., 26 F.Supp. 265 (D.Mass.1939). See Strauss, The Moral Right of the Author 128–138, in Studies on Copyright (1963). Although such decisions are clothed in terms of proprietary right in one's creation, they also properly vindicate the author's personal right to prevent the presentation of his work to the public in a distorted form. See Gardella v. Log Cabin Products Co., 89 F.2d 891, 895–96 (2d Cir.1937); Roeder, The Doctrine of Moral Right, 53 Harv.L. Rev. 554, 568 (1940).

Here, the appellants claim that the editing done for ABC mutilated the original work and that consequently the broadcast of those programs as the creation of Monty Python violated the Lanham Act § 43(a), 15 U.S.C. § 1125(a).[10] This statute, the federal counterpart to state unfair competition laws, has been invoked to prevent misrepresentations that may injure plaintiff's business or personal reputation, even where no registered trademark is concerned. See Mortellito v. Nina of California, 335 F.Supp. 1288, 1294 (S.D.N.Y.1972). It is sufficient to violate the Act that a representation of a product, although technically true, creates a false impression of the product's origin. See Rich v. RCA Corp., 390 F.Supp. 530 (S.D.N.Y.1975) (recent picture of plaintiff on cover of album containing songs recorded in distant past held to be a false representation that the songs were new); Geisel v. Poynter Products, Inc., 283 F.Supp. 261, 267 (S.D.N.Y.1968).

These cases cannot be distinguished from the situation in which a television network broadcasts a program properly designated as having been written and performed by a group, but which has been edited,

---

10. That statute provides in part:

Any person who shall affix, apply, or annex, or use in connection with any goods or services, * * * a false designation of origin, or any false description or representation * * * and shall cause such goods or services to enter into commerce * * * shall be liable to a civil action by any person * * who believes that he is or is likely to be damaged by the use of any such false description or representation.

without the writer's consent, into a form that departs substantially from the original work. "To deform his work is to present him to the public as the creator of a work not his own, and thus makes him subject to criticism for work he has not done." Roeder, supra, at 569. In such a case, it is the writer or performer, rather than the network, who suffers the consequences of the mutilation, for the public will have only the final product by which to evaluate the work.[11] Thus, an allegation that a defendant has presented to the public a "garbled," Granz v. Harris, supra (Frank, J., concurring), distorted version of plaintiff's work seeks to redress the very rights sought to be protected by the Lanham Act, 15 U.S.C. § 1125(a), and should be recognized as stating a cause of action under that statute. See Autry v. Republic Productions, Inc., 213 F.2d 667 (9th Cir.1954); Jaeger v. American Int'l Pictures, Inc., 330 F.Supp. 274 (S.D.N.Y.1971), which suggest the violation of such a right if mutilation could be proven.

During the hearing on the preliminary injunction, Judge Lasker viewed the edited version of the Monty Python program broadcast on December 26 and the original, unedited version. After hearing argument of this appeal, this panel also viewed and compared the two versions. We find that the truncated version at times omitted the climax of the skits to which appellants' rare brand of humor was leading and at other times deleted essential elements in the schematic development of a story line.[12] We therefore agree with Judge Lasker's conclusion that the edited version broadcast by ABC impaired the integrity of appellants' work and represented to the public as the product of appellants what was actually a mere caricature of their talents. We believe that a valid cause of action for such distortion exists and that therefore a preliminary injunction may issue to prevent repetition of the broadcast prior to final determination of the issues.[13]

11. This result is not changed by the fact that the network, as here, takes public responsibility for editing. See Rich v. RCA Corp., supra.

12. A single example will illustrate the extent of distortion engendered by the editing. In one skit, an upper class English family is engaged in a discussion of the tonal quality of certain words as "woody" or "tinny." The father soon begins to suggest certain words with sexual connotations as either "woody" or "tinny," whereupon the mother fetches a bucket of water and pours it over his head. The skit continues from this point. The ABC edit eliminates this middle sequence so that the father is comfortably dressed at one moment and, in the next moment, is shown in a soaked condition without any explanation for the change in his appearance.

13. Judge Gurfein's concurring opinion suggests that since the gravamen of a complaint under the Lanham Act is that the origin of goods has been falsely described, a legend disclaiming Monty Python's approval of the edited version would preclude violation of that Act. We are doubtful that a few words could erase the indelible impression that is made by a television broadcast, especially since the viewer has no means of comparing the truncated version with the complete work in order to determine for himself the talents of plaintiffs. Furthermore, a disclaimer such as the one originally suggested by Judge Lasker in the exigencies of an impending broadcast last December would go unnoticed by viewers who tuned in to the broadcast a few minutes after it began.

We therefore conclude that Judge Gurfein's proposal that the district court could find some form of disclaimer would be sufficient might not provide appropriate relief.

For these reasons we direct that the district court issue the preliminary injunction sought by the appellants.

* * *

GURFEIN, CIRCUIT JUDGE (concurring).

I concur in my brother Lumbard's scholarly opinion, but I wish to comment on the application of Section 43(a) of the Lanham Act, 15 U.S.C. § 1125(a).

I believe that this is the first case in which a federal appellate court has held that there may be a violation of Section 43(a) of the Lanham Act with respect to a common-law copyright. The Lanham Act is a trademark statute, not a copyright statute. Nevertheless, we must recognize that the language of Section 43(a) is broad. It speaks of the affixation or use of false designations of origin or false descriptions or representations, but proscribes such use "in connection with any goods or services." It is easy enough to incorporate trade names as well as trademarks into Section 43(a) and the statute specifically applies to common law trademarks, as well as registered trademarks. Lanham Act § 45, 15 U.S.C. § 1127.

In the present case, we are holding that the deletion of portions of the recorded tape constitutes a breach of contract, as well as an infringement of a common-law copyright of the original work. There is literally no need to discuss whether plaintiffs also have a claim for relief under the Lanham Act or for unfair competition under New York law. I agree with Judge Lumbard, however, that it may be an exercise of judicial economy to express our view on the Lanham Act claim, and I do not dissent therefrom. I simply wish to leave it open for the District Court to fashion the remedy.

The Copyright Act provides no recognition of the so-called *droit moral,* or moral right of authors. Nor are such rights recognized in the field of copyright law in the United States. See 1 Nimmer on Copyright, § 110.2 (1975 ed.). If a distortion or truncation in connection with a use constitutes an infringement of copyright, there is no need for an additional cause of action beyond copyright infringement. *Id.* at § 110.3. An obligation to mention the name of the author carries the implied duty, however, as a matter of contract, not to make such changes in the work as would render the credit line a false attribution of authorship, Granz v. Harris, 198 F.2d 585 (2d Cir.1952).

So far as the Lanham Act is concerned, it is not a substitute for *droit moral* which authors in Europe enjoy. If the licensee may, by contract, distort the recorded work, the Lanham Act does not come into play. If the licensee has no such right by contract, there will be a violation in breach of contract. The Lanham Act can hardly apply literally when the credit line correctly states the work to be that of the plaintiffs which, indeed it is, so far as it goes. The vice complained of is that the truncated version is not what the plaintiffs wrote. But the Lanham Act does not deal with artistic integrity. It only goes to misdescription of origin and the like. See Societe Comptoir De L'Industrie Cotonniere Etablissements Boussac v. Alexander's Dept. Stores, Inc., 299 F.2d 33, 36 (2d Cir.1962).

The misdescription of origin can be dealt with, as Judge Lasker did below, by devising an appropriate legend to indicate that the plaintiffs had not approved the editing of the ABC version.[1] With such a legend, there is no conceivable violation of the Lanham Act. If plaintiffs complain that their artistic integrity is still compromised by the distorted version, their claim does not lie under the Lanham Act, which does not protect the copyrighted work itself but protects only against the misdescription or mislabelling.

So long as it is made clear that the ABC version is not approved by the Monty Python group, there is no misdescription of origin. So far as the content of the broadcast itself is concerned, that is not within the proscription of the Lanham Act when there is no misdescription of the authorship.

I add this brief explanation because I do not believe that the Lanham Act claim necessarily requires the drastic remedy of permanent injunction. That form of ultimate relief must be found in some other fountainhead of equity jurisprudence.

Questions

1. Would the decision in the instant case have been different if Monty Python had not "reserved to itself any rights not granted to BBC"? Is such a reservation implied even if not expressed? See Warner Bros. Pictures, Inc. v. Columbia Broadcasting Sys., Inc. (the "Sam Spade" case), supra.

2. What right under the Copyright Act which Monty Python "reserved" did the *Gilliam* court find to have been infringed? Did the court conclude that Monty Python's reproduction and distribution rights had been infringed? If so, does the court's conclusion rely upon a tacit finding that the licensed reproduction and distribution rights were subject to an implied condition in the license whereby such rights could be exercised only if no material changes were made in the work? Is such an implied condition reasonably to be inferred from the facts given? Is there any other right under the Copyright Act which the court might have found to have been infringed without requiring an arguably strained construction of the license agreement? What about Sec. 106(2)?

3. Would the copyright cause of action upheld in *Gilliam* be applicable in any circumstances where there would not also exist a cause of action under Sec. 43(a) of the Lanham Act?

Collateral Reference

Nimmer on Copyright, § 8.21[C].

---

[1]. I do not imply that the appropriate legend be shown only at the beginning of the broadcast. That is a matter for the District Court.

Note *

Artists' Moral Rights in California and New York

The California Art Preservation Act. Effective January 1, 1980, California adopted a form of moral rights law known as the California Art Preservation Act.[1] It provides, inter alia, that "No person except an artist who owns and possesses a work of fine art which the artist has created, shall intentionally commit, or authorize the intentional commission of, any physical defacement, mutilation, alteration, or destruction of a work of fine art." It will be seen that the foregoing prohibition against defacement, mutilation, alteration, or destruction is applicable only to works of fine art. The Art Preservation Act, moreover, does not apply to a work of fine art which has been "prepared under contract for commercial use by its purchaser." Furthermore, the provision above quoted may be invoked only if the act of defacement, mutilation, alteration or destruction was done "intentionally." However, such acts even if not intentional will give rise to a cause of action if they are the result of "gross negligence," and if done by a "person who frames, conserves, or restores a work of fine art" or who authorizes the commission of any such act. An artist's rights under the Art Preservation Act may be waived, but only by "an instrument in writing expressly so providing which is signed by the artist." Rights under the Art Preservation Act may be asserted as to any act of defacement, mutilation, alteration or destruction occurring after January 1, 1980, regardless of when the affected work of fine art was created. There is, however, a three-year statute of limitations, and the artist's rights, which upon his death pass to his heirs, legatees or personal representatives, terminate fifty years after the artist's death. The remedies afforded under the Art Preservation Act include injunctive relief, actual damages, punitive damages, reasonable attorneys' and expert witness fees, and any other relief which the court deems proper.

Is the California Art Preservation Act invalid by reason of federal preemption arising from the Copyright Act? It has been noted earlier that in order for such preemption to occur the following two elements must coalesce: (1) the rights created under state law must be "equivalent" to one or more of the rights contained in the Copyright Act; and (2) such rights under state law must be applicable to works which constitute "works of authorship" within the subject matter of the Copyright Act. This second element is clearly applicable to the California Art Preservation Act since any "work of fine art" within the meaning of such Act is also a "pictorial, graphic or sculptural work" under the Copyright Act. But are the rights created under the Art Preservation Act "equivalent" to rights created under the Copyright Act? Nothing in the Copyright Act goes to the right to prevent "physical defacement, mutilation, * * * or destruction of a work of fine art" as provided in the Art Preservation Act. It would appear, then, that there is no federal preemption as to such rights. However, the additional right under the Art Preservation Act giving the artist the right to prevent "alteration" of his work would seem to be precisely "equivalent" to the right under the Copyright Act "to prepare derivative works based upon the copyrighted work." Therefore, the right to prevent an "alteration" which does not amount to a "defacement" or "mutilation"

---

* Nimmer on Copyright, § 8.21[C][2], [3].

1. California Civil Code, Section 987 (amended in 1982).

would appear to be subject to federal preemption, and is, therefore, invalid under state law. It may further be argued that since whether an alteration constitutes a defacement or mutilation is a matter of subjective aesthetic judgment, it follows that these rights are also preempted. It is to be hoped that courts will save these rights from preemption by constructing objective standards as to what constitutes defacement or mutilation.

The New York Artists' Authorship Rights Act. Effective January 1, 1984 New York adopted a form of moral rights law known as the Artists' Authorship Rights Act.[2] It is similar to the California Art Preservation Act, but differs in a number of respects. It prohibits the unauthorized public display, publication or reproduction of a work of fine art "in an altered, defaced, mutilated or modified form," but only "if the work is displayed, published or reproduced as being the work of the artist, or under circumstances under which it would reasonably be regarded as being the work of the artist, and damage to the artist's reputation is reasonably likely to result therefrom." It might, then, be concluded that despite unauthorized alteration, defacement, mutilation or modification, liability may be avoided by not identifying the artist by name. When the artist would be likely to be identified with the work even without mention of the artist's name, liability might be avoided by an appropriate disclaimer, indicating that changes in the work were made by someone other than the artist. But failure to identify the artist by name might result in liability under another provision of the Artists' Authorship Rights Act, whereby "the artist shall retain at all times the right to claim authorship." Even including the artist's name, but with a disclaimer of the type described above, unless carefully worded, might be held to constitute a violation of this right to be identified as the author of one's artistic work. It is only a public display, publication or reproduction where there is knowledge by the defendant that such alteration, defacement, mutilation or modification has occurred that will produce liability. Moreover, there is no liability if such changes occur "from the passage of time, or the inherent nature of the materials," or by reason of "an ordinary result" from a change in the medium of reproduction. Changes as a result of conservation will not create liability "unless the conservation work can be shown to be negligent." Finally, the Act does not apply "to work prepared under contract for advertising or trade unless the contract so provided." This apparently excludes from application of the Act works of art produced in either a "for hire" relationship, or made on commission even if not "for hire." The New York Artists' Authorship Rights Act would seem to be subject to the same arguments for federal preemption as are available in connection with the California Art Preservation Act.

Collateral Reference

Damich, *The New York Artists' Authorship Rights Act: A Comparative Critique*, 84 Colum.L.R. 1733 (1984).

EDGAR RICE BURROUGHS, INC. v. METRO–GOLDWYN–MAYER, INC.

District Court of Appeals, Second District, Division 1, California, 1962.
205 Cal.App.2d 441, 23 Cal.Rptr. 14.

LILLIE, JUSTICE. In April 1931, plaintiff executed a contract granting MGM the right to create and write an original story using the

---

2. Article 12–J, New York General Business Law, Secs. 228 m–q.

character, Tarzan, and to produce a photoplay based thereon. Thereafter, it wrote an original story and produced a photoplay known as the 1932 version of "Tarzan, the Ape Man" (hereinafter referred to as the first photoplay). Under Paragraph 14 of the contract, MGM had the "right to reissue said first photoplay, and likewise to remake said first photoplay and also to produce additional photoplays based on said story. Metro agrees, however, that all remakes of the first photoplay produced by it hereunder, as well as all other photoplays produced by it hereunder subsequent to the making of said first photoplay, shall be based substantially upon the same story as that used by Metro in connection with said first photoplay and that in such subsequent remake and/or additional photoplay there will be no material changes or material departures from the story used in connection with said first photoplay." In 1959 MGM produced a remake of the first photoplay under the same title, "Tarzan, the Ape Man" (hereinafter referred to as the second photoplay).

Thereafter plaintiff filed suit against MGM for breach of contract alleging mainly a violation of Paragraph 14, in that the remake was not "based substantially upon the same story" as the first photoplay, and that it contained "material changes" and "material departures." A demurrer on the ground the complaint failed to state facts sufficient to constitute a cause of action, in that plaintiff did not attach copies of the photoplays thereto, was sustained with leave to amend. Plaintiff then filed its first amended complaint incorporating the two photoplays—the scripts were attached thereto as "A" and "B", and the two films were pleaded by reference. A general demurrer thereto was sustained without leave to amend; at the hearing thereon the lower court viewed the photoplays, determined as a matter of law they were not dissimilar within the meaning of the language of the contract, and concluded the pleading failed to state facts sufficient to constitute a cause of action. Thereupon, plaintiff moved the lower court to reconsider its ruling; the motion was granted. Upon a second hearing the demurrer was again sustained, but with leave to file a second amended complaint upon plaintiff's representation that it would contain all ultimate facts which plaintiff was able to plead. A general demurrer to the second amended complaint was interposed. Upon considering the contract and finding it to be clear and unambiguous, and after viewing the two productions incorporated in the second amended complaint and finding that they are "based substantially upon the same story" and that the second photoplay contains no "material changes or material departures," the lower court concluded that there is a substantial similarity between the two productions as a matter of law within the meaning of the contract, and sustained the demurrer without leave to amend. It is from the judgment dismissing the second amended complaint on the order sustaining the demurrer plaintiff appeals.

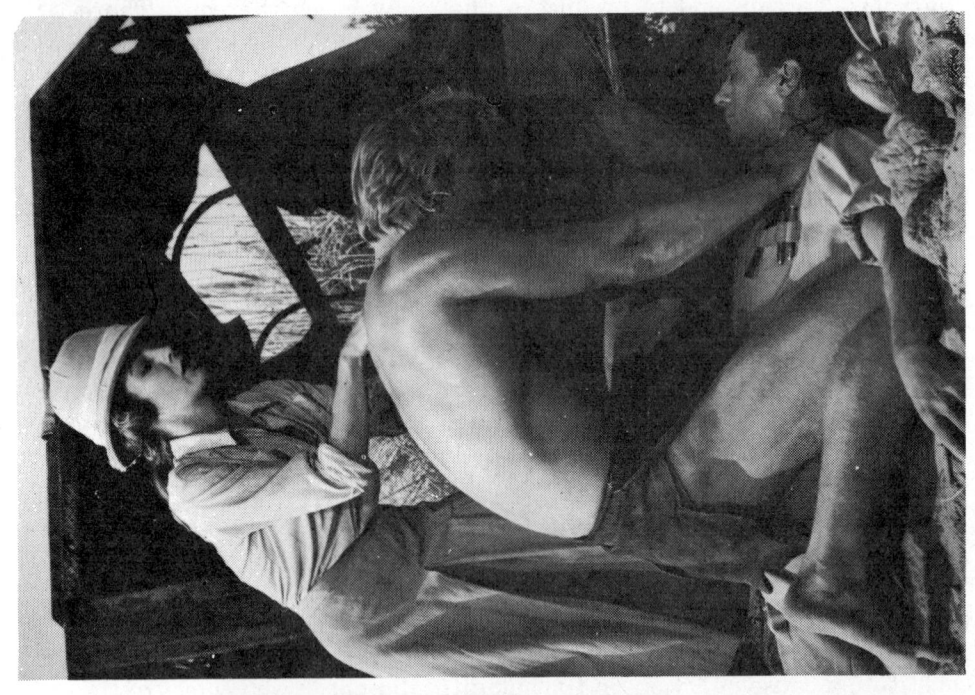

Tarzan, The Ape Man, the 1932 version (left) and the 1959 version (right).

* * *

Appellant contends that there is nothing in the contract giving MGM the right to update, modernize and adapt the story to current times and conditions, and any effort to do so was inconsistent with the express prohibition against "material changes" or "material departures"; and that the language of Paragraph 14—"based substantially upon the same story" and "material changes or material departures"—renders the contract so ambiguous as to require evidence of the intent of the parties at the time the contract was executed and the custom and practice in the industry. The lower court concluded in connection with MGM's "remake" rights under the contract that "inherent (therein) * * there must be and is the right to update and modernize clothes, customs, dialogue, mood and tempo; to use current, modern techniques of color and camera; to adapt the story to the way people live and look at life in this and future generations, rather than in the generation in which the original photoplay was made." (Memorandum Decision, p. 4.)

Paragraph 14 of the contract gives MGM, subject to certain limitations contained therein, the following separate and distinct rights—to *make* a photoplay based on the original story, to *reissue* the first photoplay, to *remake* the first photoplay, and to *produce additional* photoplays based on the original story—"for the full duration of the copyright period of any photoplay or photoplays produced by it hereunder, including any renewals thereof, and to the full extent thereof, and forever, as long as any rights in such story and/or photoplay and/or 'remakes' and/or further photoplays are recognized in law or in equity." Therefore, under the contract MGM is given the right of unlimited remakes of the first photoplay for virtually an unlimited period of time in the future. Thus, if there is not inherent therein the right to update, modernize and adapt the story to life in today's generation and employ current methods and techniques, the right of unlimited remakes of the first photoplay (as distinguished from the right to rephotograph the same) to be exercised for the time expressly provided in the contract, is without value. That the right to update and modernize was in fact contemplated by the parties is reflected in another portion of the contract, giving MGM "all rights, both present and future and whether or not the same be now known or recognized, which may be necessary to produce, exhibit and/or transmit photoplays based on said story * * " (Paragraph 5).

Further, the use of the word "material" in describing the changes or departures prohibited and the word "substantially" in permitting remakes—(Paragraph 14), clearly allows changes and departures from the original story; and under the terms of the contract these permitted variations could reasonably relate to nothing other than those resulting from updating, modernizing and adapting the original story natural and inherent in, and concomitant with, the right to remake the first photoplay and the right to produce additional photoplays based on the original story. And such changes are not material or substantial in nature as long as the locus of the play, the order of sequence, the development of the plot, and the theme, thought and main action of the story are preserved. Our attention has been called to Manners v. Famous Players-Lasky Corporation, 262 F. 811 (D.C.N.Y.), wherein language far more restrictive than "material changes or material departures" was interpreted. The contract provided: "No alterations, eliminations, or additions to be made in the play without the approval of the author"; and in discussing defendant's right to produce a motion picture based on the story "Peg O' My Heart" under this language, the court said at page 815: "If these substantial features ('locus of the play or the order of sequence or development of the plot') are retained, then such pictures as may be necessary to explain the action of the play, and as may be necessary in substitution for dialogue, may be entirely proper, and not in violation of the (contract) * * *." Also on the issue of similarity between plaintiff's story and defendant's photoplay in Curwood v. Affiliated Distributors, Inc. et al., 283 F. 219 (D.C.N.Y.), the court held that as long as appropriate expression to the theme, thought and main action of the original story is retained "scenery, action, and characters may be added to the original story, and even supplant subordinate portions thereof, * * *." (p. 222.)

* * *

Finding that the contract is clear and unambiguous in its terms, and, after viewing and comparing the two photoplays, finding that the second is based substantially upon the same story as the first and that there are no material changes or material departures in the second photoplay, we conclude, as did the lower court, that there is substantial similarity between the two productions as a matter of law within the meaning of the contract; and the case was properly determined upon demurrer.

The judgment is affirmed.

WOOD, P.J., and FOURT, J., concur.

Questions

1. What is a "remake" right? How does it differ from a "sequel" right?

2. Should a remake right always be held to imply a right to "update and modernize"? Should it depend on whether the setting of the original version of the film was a contemporaneous one? Should it depend on the importance to the story of the original setting?

3. Suppose that the contract between Burroughs and M.G.M. said nothing, one way or the other, about M.G.M.'s right to make changes, and that in fact M.G.M. made extensive changes. Would Burroughs have any legal grounds to complain? Suppose the ape man is no longer called "Tarzan", Burroughs' name is not mentioned in the "credits", and the story line is substantially changed. Would there be a breach of contract? Would there be unfair competition? Would there be copyright infringement?

4. Suppose that in the contract between Burroughs and M.G.M., the right to make changes in the work is expressly (or impliedly) reserved to Burroughs, but M.G.M. does not expressly promise not to make any such changes. If

M.G.M. in fact makes extensive changes is this a breach of contract (recalling the distinction between conditions and covenants)? Is it copyright infringement? What about Sec. 106(2)? When is a work sufficiently different to constitute a derivative work, but still sufficiently similar to fall within the orbit of the original version copyright?

B. THE RIGHT TO PREVENT USE OF AN AUTHOR'S NAME

1. Truthful Attribution

WILLIAMS v. WEISSER
Court of Appeal, Second District, Division 5, 1969.
78 Cal.Rptr. 542.

KAUS, PRESIDING JUSTICE. Defendant Weisser, who does business under the fictitious name of Class Notes, appeals from a judgment which enjoins him from copying, publishing and selling notes of lectures delivered by plaintiff in his capacity as an Assistant Professor of Anthropology at the University of California at Los Angeles ("UCLA"). The judgment also awards plaintiff $1,000.00 in compensatory and $500.00 in exemplary damages.

A joint pretrial restatement described the nature of the case as follows: "Plaintiff is Assistant Professor at UCLA in the Anthropology Department. Defendant does business in Westwood, California as Class Notes selling outlines for various courses given at UCLA. In 1965, defendant paid Karen Allen, a UCLA student, to attend plaintiff's class in Anthropology 1 to take notes from the lectures, and to type up the notes. Allen delivered the typed notes to defendant and defendant placed a copyright notice thereon in defendant's name, reproduced the typed notes, and sold and offered them for sale. Plaintiff objected. Defendant did not cease these activities until served with summons, complaint and temporary restraining order. Plaintiff seeks a permanent injunction, general damages, and punitive damages."

At the pretrial it was agreed that: "Defendant has used plaintiff's name in selling the publications here in question."

The judgment in plaintiff's favor was based on two grounds: 1. defendant infringed plaintiff's common law copyright in his lectures; and 2. defendant invaded plaintiff's privacy by the use of plaintiff's name. (Fairfield v. American Photocopy, etc., Co., 138 Cal.App.2d 82, 291 P.2d 194.)

[The court affirmed the judgment of common law copyright infringement, holding that the plaintiff's lectures were properly the subject of common law copyright, that the plaintiff rather than UCLA was the owner of the common law copyright, and that no divestive publication had occurred. The court then turned to the issue of the use of plaintiff's name.]

PRIVACY

Although defendant speaks of "fair use," the context of his argument shows that he is not relying on the defense of fair use as known in the law of copyright. (Nimmer on Copyright § 145.) Rather he claims a defense to the alternative basis on which the court found in plaintiff's favor, that is to say, invasion of privacy.

Liability on that theory was predicated on defendant's use of plaintiff's name in connection with the publication, distribution and sale of the notes. It is defendant's position that, copyright aside, he was privileged to publish the notes and to use plaintiff's name in connection with such publication because "[p]laintiff intentionally placed himself in the public eye when he undertook his employment as an instructor * * *." In other words defendant seeks to apply the doctrine of such cases as Werner v. Times-Mirror Co., 193 Cal.App.2d 111, 14 Cal.Rptr. 208; Smith v. National Broadcasting Co., 138 Cal. App.2d 807, 812, 292 P.2d 600; Cohen v. Marx, 94 Cal.App.2d 704, 211 P.2d 320 and Metter v. Los Angeles Examiner, 35 Cal.App.2d 304, 312, 95 P.2d 491.

Leaving aside the extent to which a person thrusts himself upon the public eye by giving a course at UCLA, defendant forgets to mention certain aspects of this particular case which bring it into the field of actionable privacy.

An author who owns the common law copyright to his work can determine whether he wants to publish it and, if so, under what circumstances. Plaintiff had prepared his notes for a specific purpose—as an outline to lectures to be delivered to a class of students. Though he apparently considered them adequate for that purpose, he did not desire a commercial distribution with which his name was associated. Right or wrong, he felt that his professional standing could be jeopardized. There is evidence that other teachers at UCLA did not object to representatives of Class Notes being in the classroom, indeed some cooperated with defendant in revising the product of the note takers. Plaintiff considered the Anthropology 1 notes sold by defendant as defective in several respects, chiefly because of certain omissions. Any person aware of the cooperation given by other faculty members could reasonably believe that plaintiff had assisted in the final product. We think that these considerations easily bring the case within the ambit of Fairfield v. American Photocopy, etc., Co., 138 Cal.App.2d 82, 291 P.2d 194. There the defendant used the plaintiff's name in advertising a certain product. He was said to be one of the many satisfied users of the product. He had been a user, but had returned the product to the defendant. The court held that defendant's conduct was "an unauthorized and unwarranted appropriation of plaintiff's personality as a lawyer for pecuniary gain and profit." (138 Cal.App.2d at 87, 291 P.2d at 197.) We think that the *Fairfield* case is indistinguishable from the one at bar. * * *

Questions

1. Suppose that UCLA rather than Professor Williams owned the copyright in the Williams lectures. Would Williams nevertheless have a cause of action for invasion of privacy by reason of the use of his name on defendant's outlines? Should Weisser's liability to Williams in such circumstances turn on whether or not UCLA has licensed Weisser to reproduce the outlines? Isn't the "privacy" injury to Williams with which the court is concerned the same in either event?

2. Is the court's rationale applicable only in the case of unpublished works? Suppose Williams published a work on anthropology, and then some years later decided that the theories he advanced in that work were totally wrong. Should he be able to object to the continued use of his name as the author of that work? Should the answer turn on whether or not in the contract with his publisher he had consented to the use of his name as the author of the work? Is such a consent always implied in publishing contracts in the absence of an express reservation? What if there is no effective publishing contract because the work has entered the public domain?

SHOSTAKOVICH et al. v. TWENTIETH CENTURY–FOX FILM CORP.

Supreme Court, Special Term, New York County, Part III, 1948.
80 N.Y.S.2d 575.

KOCH, JUSTICE. Plaintiffs are composers of international renown. They are citizens and residents of the Union of Socialist Soviet Republics. Defendant, a domestic corporation has produced a picture known as "The Iron Curtain" which is now being exhibited in theatres throughout this country. In the public mind, this title has come to indicate the boundary between that part of Europe which is under the sovereignty of, occupied by or under the influence of the U.S.S.R., as distinguished from the rest of the continent. The picture depicts recent disclosures of espionage in Canada attributed to representatives of the U.S.S.R. There is shown, preliminarily, but not as part of the picture proper, as is customary in the showing of motion pictures, the names of the players, the producer, the cameramen, and similar informative data. Included is this statement: "Music—From The Selected Works of the Soviet Composers—Dmitry Shostakovich, Serge Prokofieff, Aram Khachaturian, Nicholai Miashovsky—Conducted by Alfred Newman". Such practice in the theatrical, advertising and kindred businesses is known as giving a "credit line". During the picture, music of the several plaintiffs is reproduced, from time to time, for a total period of approximately 45 minutes. The entire running time of the film is 87 minutes. The use of the music can best be described as incidental, background matter. Aside from the use of their music neither the plot nor the theme of the play, in any manner, concerns plaintiffs. In addition to the use of their names on the "credit lines" the name of one plaintiff is used when one of the characters in the play is shown placing a recording of this particular plaintiff's music on a phonograph. Again this is incidental, the name is mentioned in an appreciative, familiar fashion, the impression given being that the character has come upon a record of a composition which he recognizes and appreciates hearing. All the music, it is conceded, for the purposes of this motion, is in the public domain and enjoys no copyright protection whatever.

Plaintiffs seek to enjoin pendente lite and permanently the use of their names and music in the picture and in any advertising or publicity matter relating to it. Only one cause of action is set forth in the complaint. Primarily, libel and violation of the Civil Rights Law

Plaintiff Dmitry Shostakovich

are charged. It may also be that the allegations can be construed to spell out causes for (a) the deliberate infliction of an injury without just cause and (b) a violation of plaintiffs' moral rights as composers. In addition to the injunctive relief a money judgment is asked.

On this motion plaintiffs base their rights to relief on these grounds: (1) the provision for injunctive relief contained in § 51 of the Civil Rights Law; (2) the injunctive power of this court to restrain publication of defamatory matter (Koussevitzky v. Allen, Towne & Heath, 272 App.Div. 759, 69 N.Y.S.2d 432); (3) the deliberate infliction of an injury without just cause (Advance Music Corporation v. American Tobacco Co., 296 N.Y. 79, 70 N.E.2d 401); and (4) the violation of plaintiffs' moral rights as composers. The Doctrine of Moral Right, etc., 53 Harvard Law Review, 554.

The application must be denied insofar as relief is sought under § 51 of the Civil Rights Law. In Jaccard v. R.H. Macy & Co. Inc., 265 App.Div. 15, 37 N.Y.S.2d 570, it was held that the use of a designer's name in advertising the sale of a dress copied without her consent from her original, uncopyrighted design was not an invasion of the right of privacy protected by §§ 50 and 51 of the Civil Rights Law. While the analogy between a dress design and plaintiffs' music might be considered unfortunate by some, the legal principle is the same. Plaintiffs' compositions are similarly unprotected and the use of their names in conjunction therewith is, therefore not subject to restraint under the Civil Rights Law. The lack of copyright protection has long been held to permit others to use the names of authors in copying, publishing or compiling their works. Clemens v. Belford, Clark & Co., C.C., 14 F. 728.

Passing to the right to injunctive relief restraining the publication of alleged libelous matter, it is first noted that under the ancient doctrine of this state there was no right to enjoin the publication of defamatory matter. Koussevitzky v. Allen, Towne & Heath, 188 Misc. 479, 68 N.Y.S.2d 779. In affirming the denial of injunctive relief in that case however, the Appellate Division, 272 App.Div. 759, 69 N.Y. S.2d 432, 433, in this department said, in a per curiam opinion: "Our affirmance * * * should not be construed as a determination by this court that injunctive relief may not be had to restrain the publication of defamatory statements in a proper case". Two questions are, therefore, presented for consideration: (1) have plaintiffs been libeled; (2) if so, is this a proper case in which to grant injunctive relief. The gravamen of plaintiffs' charge is that by the portrayal of the espionage activities of the representatives of the U.S.S.R. in Canada and by the depicted disowning of these activities by one of these representatives a picture with an anti-Soviet theme has been published. The use of plaintiffs' music in such a picture, it is argued, indicates their "approval", "endorsement" and "participation" therein thereby casting upon them "the false imputation of being disloyal to their country". The court in the presence of and with the consent of counsel for both sides has seen the picture. There is no ground for any contention that plaintiffs have participated in its production or given their approval or endorsement thereto. It is urged that the use of plaintiffs' names and music "necessarily implies" their consent, approval or collaboration in the production and distribution of the picture because "the public at large knows that living composers receive payment for the use of their names and creations in films". The error in this reasoning is in the necessary implication. No such implication exists, necessarily or otherwise, where the work of the composer is in the public domain and may be freely published, copied or compiled by others. Jaccard v. Macy & Co. Inc., supra; Clemens v. Belford, Clark & Co., supra. In the absence of such implication the existence of libel is not shown and the drastic relief asked cannot be granted. Such is likewise the ruling if plaintiffs' contention is that they are being used, unwillingly, as a means to disseminate libelous matter. In such a case the pre-requisite of exercising the injunctive power would again be a clear showing of the existence of libel.

The third and fourth grounds will be considered together. There is no longer any doubt that the deliberate infliction of a wilful injury without just cause is actionable. Advance Music Corporation v. American Tobacco Co., supra. The wrong which is alleged here is the use of plaintiffs' music in a moving picture whose theme is objectionable to them in that it is unsympathetic to their political ideology. The logical development of this theory leads inescapably to the Doctrine of Moral Right (53 Harvard Law Review). There is no charge of distortion of the compositions nor any claim that they have not been faithfully reproduced. Conceivably, under the doctrine of Moral Right the court could in a proper case, prevent the use of a composition or work, in the public domain, in such a manner as would be violative of the author's rights. The application of the doctrine presents much difficulty however. With reference to that which is in the public domain there arises a conflict between the moral right and the well established rights of others to use such works. Clemens v. Belford Clark & Co., supra. So, too, there arises the question of the norm by which the use of such work is to be tested to determine whether or not the author's moral right as an author has been violated. Is the standard to be good taste, artistic worth, political beliefs, moral concepts or what is it to be? In the present state of our law the very existence of the right is not clear, the relative position of the rights thereunder with reference to the rights of others is not defined nor has the nature of the proper remedy been determined. Quite obviously therefore, in the absence of any clear showing of the infliction of a wilful injury or of any invasion of a moral right, this court should not consider granting the drastic relief asked on either theory. The motion is accordingly denied in all respects.

Questions

1. Why didn't the plaintiffs sue for copyright infringement? All works first published in the Soviet Union prior to May 27, 1973 (the date of the Soviet accession to the Universal Copyright Convention) were and are in the public domain in the United States. At the time of this case was the public domain

status of Soviet works generally known to the American public? Is that question relevant to the issue in this case?

2. Is the decision in the instant case consistent with the rationale in Williams v. Weisser, supra? Are the cases distinguishable because the New York court was applying its own statutory version of the right of privacy, while the California court was applying the common law right of privacy?

Collateral Reference

Nimmer on Copyright, § 8.21[D][1].

2. False Attribution

CLEVENGER v. BAKER, VOORHIS & CO.
Court of Appeals of New York, 1960.
8 N.Y.2d 187, 168 N.E.2d 643, 203 N.Y.S.2d 812.

FROESSEL, JUDGE. The sole issue before us on this appeal is whether the complaint states facts sufficient to constitute any cause of action. Under familiar rules, we must accord the complaint a liberal construction (Civil Practice Act, § 275), and if it states, in some recognizable form, any cause of action known to our law, then it was improperly dismissed below (Dulberg v. Mock, 1 N.Y.2d 54, 56, 150 N.Y.S.2d 180, 181; Al Raschid v. News Syndicate Co., 265 N.Y. 1, 3, 191 N.E. 713).

According to the complaint, plaintiff has been a member of the Bar since 1912, "is the author of 86 Law Books of approved merit", and "has edited 500 Practice Annuals". In 1922 he wrote and published "Clevenger's Annual Practice of New York", and the following year sold this work, together with copyright, to defendants. From 1923 to 1956 he edited the annual editions of the work, and "by careful and competent annual Revision * * * achieved state-wide reputation of being a reliable Editor of reliable guide to New York Practice". In 1956 he "terminated his editorship" and "revoked his consent to use of his name as Editor of any later Edition thereof".

Notwithstanding that termination and revocation, the published 1957 edition of the work stated on the title page, below the words "Annually Revised", that it had been edited and annotated by plaintiff. In November, 1957 defendants issued a "Title Page Correction" in the form of a gummed sheet reading:

1922–1956 Revisions by JOS. R. CLEVENGER, A.B., LL.B.

1957 Revision by PUBLISHER'S EDITORIAL STAFF,

and instructed its subscribers to paste this sheet over the words reading: "Edited and Annotated by JOS. R. CLEVENGER, A.B., LL.B. of the New York City Bar". According to the complaint, the format of this title page correction was in accord with defendants' publishing practice and we judicially notice the fact that the title pages of the latest annual supplements to such leading works as Gilbert-Bliss and Cahill-Parsons (published by defendants herein), Carmody-Wait (copublished by one of the defendants herein), Nichols-Cahill, Williston on Contracts and Wigmore on Evidence, among others, all state that the annual supplement was edited or prepared by the publisher's editorial staff, or by a named individual or individuals.

In 1959, "without plaintiff's consent or approval", the work was published with a title page that read, in pertinent part, as follows:

CLEVENGER'S ANNUAL PRACTICE OF NEW YORK

* * *

1959

ANNUALLY REVISED

The 1959 edition was in fact revised by defendants' editorial staff, not by plaintiff, and it is alleged that "defendants purposely excluded from title page of 1959 Edition all names except plaintiff's name of 'Clevenger's' in order to mislead Lawyers to believe erroneously that plaintiff edited said 1959 Edition because they could see only the name 'Clevenger's' ".

The complaint further alleges that there were "over 200 misleading Errors of omission and commission in Texts of Practice Acts and Court Rules" in the 1959 edition, which are specifically alleged by section and rule number, and which allegedly consisted of omitting parts of amended sections and rules, omitting names of counties authorized to collect fees, misdescribing amendments, omitting or misstating effective dates of sections added or amended, omitting many current citations, and misstating, misclassifying and misapplying annotations. By virtue of the misleading format of the title page, "many Lawyers and Law Librarians" attributed these errors to plaintiff, causing him to feel disgraced, dishonored and humiliated, and irreparably impairing his "reputation as Lawyer and Law Writer, laboriously built up by careful and competent work over a period of fifty years", with the result that he "has lost all employment, for first time in his lifetime, and can no longer obtain employment". The complaint seeks compensatory and exemplary damages in the sum of $200,000.

We agree with the dissenting Justices in the Appellate Division that the complaint states a cause of action in libel. The gravamen of the wrong pleaded is that the numerous errors of omission and commission in the 1959 edition of the work, impliedly attributed to plaintiff by the misleading format of the title page, have "irreparably impaired" his otherwise excellent reputation as a reliable legal writer and lawyer. Since a jury could reasonably find that the wording and arrangement of the title page in question would mislead the reader to believe that the revision work had been done by plaintiff, the facts pleaded amount to actionable defamation. As this court noted in Ben-Oliel v. Press Pub. Co., 251 N.Y. 250, 256, 167 N.E. 432, 434: "To publish in the name of a well-known author any literary work, the authorship of which would tend to injure an author holding his position in the world of letters, has been held to be a libel. Lee v. Gibbings (1892), 67 Law T. (N.S.) 263; Newell, Slander & Libel (4th Ed.), p. 39, note, p. 42." See, also, D'Altomonte v. New York Herald Co., 154 App.Div. 453, 139 N.Y.S. 200, modified and affirmed 208 N.Y. 596, 102 N.E. 1101; Locke v. Benton & Bowles, 253 App.Div. 369, 2 N.Y.S.2d 150.

The doctrine enunciated in the Ben-Oliel case (supra) has deep roots in the common law, and the case of Archbold v. Sweet (5 Car. & P. 219, 172 Eng.Rep. 947; 1 Moo. & Rob. 162, 174 Eng.Rep. 55), decided by an English court in 1832, is practically on all fours with the present case. See, also, Lee v. Gibbings, 67 L.T. 263, 264–265. Archbold, a well-known legal writer of the time, was the author of a text on criminal pleading and evidence. After editing two editions of the work, he sold the copyright to the defendant who published a third edition thereof, *not* edited by Archbold, with the following title page: "A Summary of the Law relative to Pleading and Evidence in Criminal Cases, with Precedents of Indictments, &c., and the Evidence necessary to support them. By J.F. Archbold, Esq., Barrister at Law. Third Edition, with very considerable Additions, including Lord Lansdowne's Act, &c."

This third edition contained many inaccuracies, and Archbold brought an action for damages, claiming that many members of the legal profession had attributed the editorship of the third edition to him, and that he was thereby "greatly injured in his reputation" as a barrister and a legal author. Defendant moved for a nonsuit, arguing, in much the same vein as defendants here, that, having purchased the copyright, he had a perfect right to publish the third edition, and that the mere failure to indicate the name of the actual editor of the third edition was not actionable. In refusing to nonsuit plaintiff, the court noted (5 Car. & P., supra, pp. 224–225): "Taking up this title page and reading it, I should certainly feel satisfied that the third edition was by Mr. Archbold." The case was submitted to the jury, who were instructed, in pertinent part, as follows (5 Car. & P., p. 227): "The question of fact is this, whether the third edition would be understood by those who bought it to be the work of the plaintiff; for, if so, I think the errors are such as would be injurious to the plaintiff's reputation."

The crux of the Archbold decision was that the title page was so worded and arranged as to convey to the reader the erroneous impression that the latest edition was the sole work of Mr. Archbold, since his was the only name that appeared thereon as author. That is precisely the claim advanced by the plaintiff here. The fact that Clevenger's name preceded, rather than followed, the title of the work is hardly a controlling distinction, since the nub of the claimed defamatory misrepresentation in the present case, as in the Archbold case, is that the only person identified on the title page as having anything to do with the writing of the work is the plaintiff. Defendants herein, like the defendant in the Archbold case, had a perfect right to state that plaintiff was the *author* of the original text, but the purchase of the copyright did not carry with it a license to defame by impliedly misrepresenting plaintiff as *reviser* of an *annual edition* that contained many inaccuracies and with which he had nothing to do.

As to the theories other than defamation mentioned in the briefs and in the opinions below, we do not think the pleaded facts properly support any of them.

The judgment appealed from should be reversed, and the order of Special Term denying defendants' motion to dismiss the complaint reinstated, with costs in this court and in the Appellate Division.

DESMOND, C.J., and DYE, FULD, VAN VOORHIS, BURKE and FOSTER, JJ., concur.

Judgment reversed, etc.

Question

Suppose that the defendant's work did not contain "numerous errors of omission and commission"? Same result? Could plaintiff nevertheless recover on an alternative theory? Would the false use of plaintiff's name constitute unfair competition? Cf. the dicta in Clemens v. Belford, Clark & Co., 14 Fed. 728 (C.C.N.D.Ill.1883). Could plaintiff claim invasion of privacy? Recall Williams v. Weisser, supra. Is the *Williams* case distinguishable? To what extent is the decision in this case affected by New York Times v. Sullivan, infra?

Note

What Constitutes False Attribution?

Theodor Seuss Geisel, under the *nom de plume* "Dr. Seuss", is well-known as the creator of bizarre animals beloved by many children. In 1932 he entered into an agreement with Liberty Magazine whereby he created a number of cartoons depicting such animals. Liberty became the copyright owner of the cartoons. Many years later Poynter Products, Inc. acquired from an assignee of Liberty the right to make three-dimensional animal dolls based upon the cartoon animals. Dr. Seuss had no part in the design or manufacture of the dolls but the designer did refer to the Liberty cartoons. The dolls were marketed bearing such statements as "From the Original Illustrations of Dr. Seuss", "From the Wonderful World of Dr. Seuss", and "from Dr. Seuss' Merry Menagerie". Geisel brought an action claiming, inter alia, violation of Sec. 43(a) of the Lanham Act (15 U.S.C.A. § 1125(a)) (prohibiting the affixation of "a false designation of origin, or any false description or representation * * * "). Upon motion for preliminary injunction (Geisel v. Poynter Products, Inc., 283 F.Supp. 261 (S.D.N.Y.1968)), the court found that the dolls "deviate substantially and materially from the 1932 illustrations", and that the defendants were "falsely representing these dolls as the product of Dr. Seuss, which they are not, or as having been approved by Dr. Seuss, when they were not." The preliminary injunction was granted based upon a "reasonable probability" of violation of Sec. 43(a). Thereafter, prior to trial but after April 9, 1968, the defendants marketed the same dolls with the following altered legend: "Toys Created, Designed & Produced Exclusively by Don Poynter MERRY MENAGERIES Based on Liberty Magazine Illustrations by Dr. Seuss." At trial the court concluded (Geisel v. Poynter Products, Inc., 295 F.Supp. 331, 353 (S.D.N.Y. 1968)):

"While defendants' prior activities created a false impression that the dolls were designed, manufactured or authorized by plaintiff, no such impression was intended to be, is, or can be, created by defendants' 'use' of the name 'Dr. Seuss' *after* April 9th.

No actual deception or confusion of, or tendency to deceive, the public is possible. Defendants have, in fact, satisfied the criteria of full and meticulously truthful disclosure. The phrase 'based on' or the word 'based,' as used by defendants after April 9th, like the phrases 'derived from,' 'suggested by,' or 'inspired by,' accurately characterizes the genetic link between the cartoons and the dolls. Differences between the two are readily discerned. The dolls are not exact reproductions or replicas of the cartoons. But these morphological differences are within the accepted limits in the licensed toy trade.

A comparison of other cartoon characters with the dolls or toys based on or derived from them discloses that some deviations between them, as between the cartoons and the dolls herein, are the inevitable result of the transmutation from two-dimensional drawings or cartoons to three-dimensional figures, manufacturing difficulties (including choice of material or medium), cost considerations, and aesthetic objectives (such as making the toy doll figures more 'doll-like' or 'huggable')."

Collateral Reference

Nimmer on Copyright, § 8.21[D][2].

C. THE RIGHT TO REQUIRE USE OF AN AUTHOR'S NAME

SMITH v. MONTORO

United States Court of Appeals, Ninth Circuit, 1981.
648 F.2d 602.

Before PECK, ANDERSON, and PREGERSON, CIRCUIT JUDGES.

PREGERSON, CIRCUIT JUDGE:

This is an appeal from a judgment granting defendant's motion to dismiss under Fed.R.Civ.P. 12(b)(6) for failure to state a federal claim. The district court held that the complaint did not allege facts sufficient to constitute a violation of section 43(a) of the Lanham Act, 15 U.S.C. § 1125(a). Appellant argues that the district court erred since the acts alleged in the complaint are the economic equivalent of "palming off," or misuse of a trade name, thus meeting the district court's standard for stating a claim under section 43(a). For the reasons stated below, we reverse.

BACKGROUND

Paul Smith contracted to star in a film to be produced by Producioni Atlas Cinematografica ("PAC"), an Italian film company. The contract allegedly provided that Smith would receive star billing in the screen credits and advertising for the film and that PAC would so provide in any subsequent contracts with distributors of the film. PAC then licensed defendants Edward Montoro and Film Venture International, Inc. ("FVI") to distribute the film in this country under the name "Convoy Buddies." Plaintiff complains, however, that Montoro and FVI removed Smith's name and substituted the name of another actor, "Bob Spencer," in place of Smith's name in both the film credits

514 AUTHORS' MORAL RIGHTS Ch. 10

One of defendant's advertisements.

and advertising material. Plaintiff alleges that, as a result of defendants' substitution, plaintiff has been damaged in his reputation as an actor, and has lost specific employment opportunities.

The complaint sought damages under several theories, including breach of contract, "false light publicity," violation of section 43(a) of the Lanham Act, and violation of Cal.Civ.Code § 3344 regarding commercial appropriation of a person's likeness. There being no diversity of citizenship, federal subject matter jurisdiction was based solely on plaintiff's Lanham Act claim. Plaintiff asserted that the district court had jurisdiction of the state law claims as a matter of pendent jurisdiction.

In proceedings held on May 1, 1978, the district judge explained his "tentative view" that defendants' motion should be granted and the complaint dismissed as "not stating a valid cause of action under the Lanham Act." While noting "there are many diverging interpretations of the Lanham Act" and that "some courts give a broad construction to it regarding it as a remedial kind of statute," the judge stated that "[i]t is my view * * * that the Lanham Act is limited in its scope and intent to merchandising practices in the nature of, or *economically equivalent* to, palming off one's goods as those of a competitor, and/or misuse of trademarks and trade names." (Emphasis added.) According to the district court, the acts alleged in the complaint

> are not the economic equivalent of palming off or misuse of a trademark or trade names. The acts are more in the nature of breaches of contract or tort which are properly the subject of state law. There is certainly in this case no intent to divert a competitor's business by misleading consumers. Plaintiff's claim is not that his name was misused, but that it wasn't used at all. Therefore, the nature of the misrepresentation alleged in this case, in my view, is not within the intended scope of the statute.

As an "alternative ground" for dismissal of the Lanham Act claim, the district court indicated that "there is an issue additionally of the plaintiff's standing to bring this suit under the Lanham Act since the plaintiff is not in any sort of competition with the defendants." Shortly after the hearing, the court issued a minute order stating that defendants' motion to dismiss was granted. Judgment was entered on May 5, 1978. The remaining state law claims were dismissed for lack of jurisdiction.

Discussion

I. Federal Claim

A. Elements of a Claim under Section 43(a)

Section 43(a) of the Lanham Act, 15 U.S.C. § 1125(a), forbids the use of false designations of origin and false descriptions or representations in the advertising and sale of goods and services. See New West Corp. v. NYM Co. of Cal., Inc., 595 F.2d 1194, 1198 (9th Cir.1979). The statute provides in pertinent part as follows:

> Any person who shall affix, apply, or annex, or use in connection with any goods or services * * * a false designation of origin, or any false designa-

tion or representation * * * and shall cause such goods or services to enter into commerce * * * shall be liable to a civil action * * * by any person who believes that he is or is likely to be damaged by the use of any such false designation or representation.

Appellant argues that defendants violated section 43(a) by affixing or using "a false designation or representation," i.e., another actor's name in place of appellant's, in connection with the movie's advertising and credits. Appellant claims standing under section 43(a) as a person "who believes that he is or is likely to be damaged" by the use of another actor's name in place of his. Thus, appellant's claim, although one of first impression, appears to fall within the express language of section 43(a).

The district court appears to have rejected appellant's argument on the ground that, to state a claim under section 43(a), a complaint must allege merchandising practices "in the nature of, or economically equivalent to, palming off * * * and/or misuse of trademarks and trade names."

"Palming off" or "passing off" is the selling of a good or service of one's own creation under the name or mark of another. See 2 J. McCarthy, *Trademarks and Unfair Competition* § 25.1 (1973); 1 R. Callman, *Unfair Competition, Trademarks and Monopolies*, § 18.2(b)(1), at 294 (1980 Supp. to 3d ed.). Passing off may be either "express" or "implied." Express passing off occurs when an enterprise labels goods or services with a mark identical to that of another enterprise, or otherwise expressly misrepresents that the goods originated with another enterprise. Implied passing off occurs when an enterprise uses a competitor's advertising material, or a sample or photograph of the competitor's product, to impliedly represent that the product it is selling was produced by the competitor. 1 R. Callman, supra. Such practices have consistently been held to violate both the common law of unfair competition and section 43(a) of the Lanham Act. See id. 2 J. McCarthy, supra, § 25.1; and cases cited infra.

To the extent that the district court's standard for section 43(a) claims could be read as limiting such claims to cases of palming off, such a narrow rule would be contrary to established case law. As one commentator has explained, the law of unfair competition and trademarks "has progressed far beyond the old concept of fraudulent passing off, to encompass any form of competition or selling which contravenes society's current concepts of 'fairness' * * *." 2 J. McCarthy, supra, § 25:1. See also, e.g., L & L White Metal Casting Corp. v. Joseph, 387 F.Supp. 1349, 1356 (E.D.N.Y.1975) ("The purpose of [section 43(a)] was to create a new federal cause of action for false representation of goods in commerce in order to protect persons engaged in commerce from, among other things, unfair competition, fraud and deception which had theretofore only been protected by the common law. While this section is broad enough to cover situations involving the common law 'palming off' of the defendants' products by the use of the plaintiff's photographs, it is also comprehensive enough to include other forms of misrepresentation and unfair competition not involving 'palming off.'") (citations omitted).

The district court's ruling was entirely consistent with the vast majority of section 43(a) cases, however, to the extent that it indicated that a section 43(a) claim may be based on economic practices or conduct "economically equivalent" to palming off. Such practices would include "reverse passing off," which occurs when a person removes or obliterates the original trademark, without authorization, before reselling goods produced by someone else. See Borchard, *Reverse Passing Off—Commercial Robbery or Permissible Competition?*, 67 Trademark Rep. 1 (1977). Reverse passing off is accomplished "expressly" when the wrongdoer removes the name or trademark on another party's product and sells that product under a name chosen by the wrongdoer. See 1 R. Callman, supra, § 18.2(b)(1). "Implied" reverse passing off occurs when the wrongdoer simply removes or otherwise obliterates the name of the manufacturer or source and sells the product in an unbranded state. Id.

In the instant case, appellant argues that the defendants' alleged conduct constitutes reverse passing off and that appellant's complaint therefore stated a section 43(a) claim even under the district court's own standard. Appellees argue, however, that the protection afforded by the Lanham Act is limited to "sales of goods" and does not extend to claims that a motion picture shown to the public might contain false information as to origin.

The short answer to appellees' argument is that the Lanham Act explicitly condemns false designations or representations in connection with "*any* goods or *services*." The prohibitions of this section have been applied to motion picture representations. See, e.g., Dallas Cowboys Cheerleaders, Inc. v. Pussycat Cinema Ltd., 467 F.Supp. 366 (S.D.N.Y.), aff'd, 604 F.2d 200 (2d Cir.1979). Moreover, the names of movie actors and other performers may, under certain circumstances, be registered under the Lanham Act as service marks[2] for entertainment services. See, e.g., Re Carson, 197 U.S.P.Q. (BNA) 554 (Trademark Trial & App.Bd.1977); Re Ames, 160 U.S.P.Q. (BNA) 214 (Trademark Trial & App.Bd.1966). Although appellant has not alleged that his name is registered as a service mark, registration of a trademark or service mark is not a prerequisite for recovery under section 43(a). See New West Corp. v. NYM Co. of California, Inc., 595 F.2d 1194, 1198 (9th Cir.1979) ("To recover for a violation of this section it is not necessary that a mark or trade-mark be registered. The dispositive question is whether the party has a reasonable interest to be protected against false advertising.") (citations omitted).

2. The term "service mark" is defined in section 45 of the Lanham Act:

"[S]ervice mark" means a mark used in the sale or advertising of services to identify the services of one person and distinguish them from the services of others.

As to registration of a person's name as a service mark, see also sections 2(e)(3) and (f) of the Lanham Act, 15 U.S.C. §§ 1052(e)(3) and (f).

* * *

According to appellant's complaint, defendants not only removed appellant's name from all credits and advertising, they also substituted a name of their own choosing. Appellees' alleged conduct therefore amounts to *express* reverse passing off. As a matter of policy, such conduct, like traditional palming off, is wrongful because it involves an attempt to misappropriate or profit from another's talents and workmanship. Moreover, in reverse palming off cases, the originator of the misidentified product is involuntarily deprived of the advertising value of its name and of the goodwill that otherwise would stem from public knowledge of the true source of the satisfactory product. See *Borchard,* supra, at 4; 1 J. McCarthy, supra, § 3:5; F. Schechter, *The Rational Basis of Trademark Protection,* 22 Trademark Bull. 139, 144–45 (1927), reprinted in 60 Trademark Rep. 334, 337 (1970). The ultimate purchaser (or viewer) is also deprived of knowing the true source of the product and may even be deceived into believing that it comes from a different source. *Borchard,* supra, at 4–5.

In the film industry, a particular actor's performance, which may have received an award or other critical acclaim, may be the primary attraction for movie-goers. Some actors are said to have such drawing power at the box office that the appearance of their names on the theater marquee can almost guarantee financial success. Such big box office names are built, in part, through being prominently featured in popular films and by receiving appropriate recognition in film credits and advertising. Since actors' fees for pictures, and indeed, their ability to get any work at all, is often based on the drawing power their name may be expected to have at the box office, being accurately credited for films in which they have played would seem to be of critical importance in enabling actors to sell their "services," i.e., their performances. We therefore find that appellant has stated a valid claim for relief under section 43(a) of the Lanham Act.[6]

B. STANDING UNDER THE LANHAM ACT

As an alternative ground for dismissal, the district court raised the issue of the plaintiff's standing to sue, on the ground that appellant was "not in any sort of competition" with the defendants. On this appeal, appellees contend that appellant has no standing to sue under the Lanham Act since appellant is not a member of a "purely commercial class." We reject this argument and hold that appellant is entitled to press his claim for "false representation" in federal court under section 43(a).

---

6. In a case involving very similar facts, the district court denied a motion to dismiss and ruled orally that a cause of action for unfair competition under section 43(a) had been stated. See Perin Film Enterprises v. TWG Productions, 400 P.T.C. Journ. (10–19–78) A–13 (S.D.N.Y.1978). The plaintiff had served as executive producer of the television series "For You * * * Black Woman." During the second year of production, after having served as executive producer of the first 22 shows, plaintiff was dismissed and received no credit for his services. Instead, the name of [an] employee of the show's underwriter was substituted as the "executive in charge of production." The parties entered into settlement negotiations shortly after the court's ruling, and the ruling was never subsequently embodied in published opinion.

On its face, section 43(a) gives standing to sue to "any person who believes that he is or is likely to be damaged." See L'Aiglon Apparel Co. v. Lana Lobell, Inc., 214 F.2d 649, 651 (3d Cir.1954) ("It seems to us that Congress has defined a statutory civil wrong of false representation of goods in commerce and has given a broad class of suitors injured or likely to be injured by such wrong the right to relief in the federal courts."). The word "person" in section 43(a) includes "juristic persons" (e.g., firms, corporations, unions, and associations) as well as "natural persons." 15 U.S.C. § 1127. Moreover, the plaintiff under section 43(a) need not be in actual competition with the alleged wrongdoer. See Fleischmann Distilling Corp. v. Maier Brewing Co., 314 F.2d 149, 151 (9th Cir.), cert. denied, 374 U.S. 830, 83 S.Ct. 1870, 10 L.Ed.2d 1053 (1963); F.E.L. Publications, Ltd. v. National Conference of Catholic Bishops, 466 F.Supp. 1034, 1044 (N.D.Ill.1978); Mortellito v. Nina of California, Inc., 335 F.Supp. 1288, 1294 (S.D.N.Y.1972).

The Second Circuit has ruled that section 43(a) does not give standing to consumers. Colligan v. Activities Club of New York, Ltd., 442 F.2d 686 (2d Cir.), cert. denied, 404 U.S. 1004, 92 S.Ct. 559, 30 L.Ed.2d 557 (1971). This reading of section 43(a) has been sharply criticized. See, e.g., 2 J. McCarthy, supra, § 27:5. At any rate, however, it is clear that appellant, as one in the business of providing his talents for use in the creation of an entertainment product, is uniquely situated to complain of injury resulting from a film distributor's misidentification of appellant's contribution to the product. According to one commentator, the "dispositive question" as to a party's standing to maintain an action under section 43(a) is whether the party "has a reasonable interest to be protected against false advertising." 1 R. Callman, supra, § 18.2(b), at 625 (3d ed. 1967). See also New West Corp. v. NYM Co. of Calif., Inc., 595 F.2d 1194, 1198 (9th Cir.1979). The vital interest of actors in receiving accurate credit for their work has already been described. Accordingly, we hold that appellant has standing to sue in federal court based on defendants' alleged violation of section 43(a).

II. STATE LAW CLAIMS

In addition to the claim under section 43(a), appellant's complaint alleged claims under state law for breach of contract, "false light publicity," and commercial appropriation of a person's likeness under Cal.Civ.Code § 3344. Since we are reversing the dismissal of appellant's Lanham Act claim, the dismissal for lack of jurisdiction of appellant's state law claims is also reversed. "One important benefit of section 43(a) is that it grants federal question jurisdiction totally apart from federal diversity jurisdiction." 2 J. McCarthy, supra, § 27:6.A. Thus, once in federal court under section 43(a), a plaintiff can allege related claims of unfair competition under common law and any available state statutory provisions.

CONCLUSION

As the district court stated, a section 43(a) claim may be based on practices or conduct "economically equivalent" to palming off. We find that appellant did state such a claim by alleging that defendants engaged in conduct amounting to "express reverse palming off." Since appellant also has standing to sue under section 43(a), the district court's dismissal of the complaint for failure to state a federal claim is reversed. The dismissal of the pendent state law claims is also reversed. Reversed and remanded.

Questions

1. Is the principle upon which the *Montoro* decision is based equally applicable if the plaintiff is an author rather than an actor?

2. Is there a cause of action under Section 43(a) of the Lanham Act whenever a copyright infringer attributes the infringing work to an author other than the author of the infringed work? Should it make a difference for these purposes as to whether the infringing work is a verbatim, or close to verbatim copy, or whether on the other hand the defendant's author (who is credited by defendant) has made many changes in plaintiff's work, but has nevertheless copied so much of plaintiff's work as to constitute copyright infringement?

Collateral References

Berman and Rosenthal, *Screen Credit and the Law,* 9 UCLA Law Rev. 156 (1962).

Strauss, *The Moral Right of the Author,* Studies on Copyright 963 (Fisher ed. 1963) (Copyright Law Revision Study No. 4, 1959, U.S. Gov't.Print. Off.1960).

Nimmer on Copyright, § 8.21[E].

D. DROIT DE SUITE

Note *

[A]—The Nature of the Droit de Suite

In addition to, but distinguishable from moral rights, or the droit moral, the copyright laws of France, Italy and Germany have also recognized a droit de suite, which roughly translated, is the right of an artist to "follow" or participate in the proceeds realized from the resale of the tangible embodiment of his work.[1] The droit de suite was conceived of as an attempt to equalize the copyright status of artists with that of authors. Not that copyright in its conventional form is not as available to painters as it is to writers. The problem arises from the fact that conventional copyright protection though

---

* Nimmer on Copyright, § 8.22[A].

1. See Plaisant, "The French Law on Proceeds Right—Analysis and Critique;" De Sanctis and Fabiani, "The Right on the Increase in Value of the Works of Fine Arts in the Italian Copyright Law," and Ulmer (Max-Planck-Institut), "The Droit de Suite in German Law," all first published in Legal Protection For The Artist (Nimmer ed., 1968).

meaningful to writers, may be irrelevant to painters and other creators in the graphic arts. The prime (though not the only) protection afforded by copyright is the right to control reproductions of a given work. Since economic exploitation of the written word is mainly realized through reproduction, the right to control the making of copies constitutes the writer's key to the economic fruits of his creative efforts. Not so with the artist. Reproductions of works of art have not in the past, and probably still do not to any great extent, represent a meaningful source of income for most artists. His prime source of income derives from the sale of the original tangible embodiment of his artistic efforts. The money an artist receives upon the sale of a painting (even if he has reserved reproduction rights) probably represents the only income which he will receive from that particular work. It is this disparity in meaningful copyright protection between the writer and the graphic artist that the droit de suite is intended to correct. Under it, each time the tangible embodiment of an artist's work (e.g., a painting) is re-sold, the artist is entitled to be paid a royalty, based upon a portion of the proceeds from the re-sale.

Whether or not this European doctrine should be imported into American copyright law was for many years the subject of some considerable debate.[2] Neither the 1909 Act, nor the current Copyright Act adopts the droit de suite principle.

[B]—The California Resale Royalties Act

The State of California has enacted a Resale Royalties Act,[3] which constitutes the first, and thus far only, American recognition of the droit de suite. Its text is set forth below:

"Sec. 986. Work of fine art; sale; payment of percentage to artist or deposit for Arts Council; failure to pay; action for damages; exemptions

"(a) Whenever a work of fine art is sold and the seller resides in California or the sale takes place in California, the seller or his agent shall pay to the artist of such work of fine art or to such artist's agent 5 percent of the amount of such sale. The right of the artist to receive an amount equal to 5 percent of the amount of such sale is not transferable and may be waived only by a contract in writing providing for an amount in excess of 5 percent of the amount of such sale.

"(1) When a work of art is sold at an auction or by a gallery, dealer, broker, museum, or other person acting as the agent for the seller the agent shall withhold 5 percent of the amount of the sale, locate the artist and pay the artist.

"(2) If the seller or the agent is unable to locate and pay the artist within 90 days, an amount equal to 5 percent of the amount of the sale shall be transferred to the Arts Council.

"(3) If a seller or his agent fails to pay an artist the amount equal to 5 percent of the sale of a work of fine art by the artist or fails to transfer

---

2. See Price, "Government Policy and Economic Security for Artists: The Case of the Droit de Suite," 77 Yale L.J. 1333 (1968). See also Hauser, "The French Droit de Suite: The Problem of Protection for the Underprivileged Artist under the Copyright Law," 11 ASCAP Symposium 1 (1962); Schulder, "Art Proceeds Act: A Study of the Droit de Suite and a Proposed Enactment for the United States," 61 N.W.U.L. Rev. 19 (1966).

3. West's Ann.Cal.Civil Code, § 986.

such amount to the Arts Council, the artist may bring an action for damages within three years after the date of sale or one year after the discovery of the sale, whichever is longer.

"(4) Moneys received by the council pursuant to this section shall be deposited in an account in the Special Deposit Fund in the State Treasury.

"(5) The Arts Council shall attempt to locate any artist for whom money is received pursuant to this section. If the council is unable to locate the artist and the artist does not file a written claim for the money received by the council within seven years of the date of sale of the work of fine art, the right of the artist terminates and such money shall be transferred to the operating fund of the council as reimbursement to fund programs of the council.

"(6) Any amounts of money held by any seller or agent for the payment of artists pursuant to this section shall be exempt from attachment or execution of judgment by the creditors of such seller or agent.

"(b) Subdivision (a) shall not apply to any of the following:

"(1) To the initial sale of a work of fine art where legal title to such work at the time of such initial sale is vested in the artist thereof.

"(2) To the resale of a work of fine art for a gross sales price of less than one thousand dollars ($1,000).

"(3) To a resale after the death of such artist.

"(4) To the resale of the work of fine art for a gross sales price less than the purchase price paid by the seller.

"(5) To a transfer of a work of fine art which is exchanged for one or more works of fine art or for a combination of cash, other property, and one or more works of fine art where the fair market value of the property exchanged is less than one thousand dollars ($1,000).

"(c) For purposes of this section, the following terms have the following meanings:

"(1) 'Artist' means the person who creates a work of fine art.

"(2) 'Fine art' means an original painting, sculpture, or drawing.

"(d) This section shall become operative on January 1, 1977, and shall apply to works of fine art created before and after its operative date.

"(e) If any provision of this section or the application thereof to any person or circumstance is held invalid for any reason, such invalidity shall not affect any other provisions or applications of this section which can be effected, without the invalid provision or application, and to this end the provisions of this section are severable."

Question

Is the California Resale Royalties Act preempted by Section 301(a) of the Copyright Act? Does the state law apply to works which "come within the subject matter of copyright as specified by sections 102 and 103"? Does it create rights which are "equivalent to any of the exclusive rights within the general scope of copyright as specified by section 106"? Does the state law conflict with the federal policy reflected in Section 109(a), which permits uninhibited resale of works of art following their initial sale? See Morseburg v. Balyon, 621 F.2d 972 (9th Cir.1980).

Collateral References

Camp, *Art Resale and the Art Resale Market: An Empirical Study*, 28 Bull. Copr. Soc'y 146 (1980).

Price and Sandison, *A Guide to the California Resale Royalties Act* (1976).

Nimmer on Copyright, § 8.22[B].

Chapter Eleven

UNFAIR COMPETITION

A. NEWS

INTERNATIONAL NEWS SERVICE v. ASSOCIATED PRESS

Supreme Court of the United States, 1918.
248 U.S. 215, 39 S.Ct. 68, 63 L.Ed. 211.

MR. JUSTICE PITNEY delivered the opinion of the court.

The parties are competitors in the gathering and distribution of news and its publication for profit in newspapers throughout the United States. The Associated Press, which was complainant in the District Court, is a coöperative organization, incorporated under the Membership Corporations Law of the State of New York, its members being individuals who are either proprietors or representatives of about 950 daily newspapers published in all parts of the United States. That a corporation may be organized under that act for the purpose of gathering news for the use and benefit of its members and for publication in newspapers owned or represented by them, is recognized by an amendment enacted in 1901 (Laws N.Y.1901, c. 436). Complainant gathers in all parts of the world, by means of various instrumentalities of its own, by exchange with its members, and by other appropriate means, news and intelligence of current and recent events of interest to newspaper readers and distributes it daily to its members for publication in their newspapers. The cost of the service, amounting approximately to $3,500,000 per annum, is assessed upon the members and becomes a part of their costs of operation, to be recouped, presumably with profit, through the publication of their several newspapers. Under complainant's by-laws each member agrees upon assuming membership that news received through complainant's service is received exclusively for publication in a particular newspaper, language, and place specified in the certificate of membership, that no other use of it shall be permitted, and that no member shall furnish or permit anyone in his employ or connected with his newspaper to furnish any of complainant's news in advance of publication to any person not a member. And each member is required to gather the local news of his district and supply it to the Associated Press and to no one else.

Defendant is a corporation organized under the laws of the State of New Jersey, whose business is the gathering and selling of news to its customers and clients, consisting of newspapers published throughout the United States, under contracts by which they pay certain amounts at stated times for defendant's service. It has widespread newsgathering agencies; the cost of its operations amounts, it is said, to more than $2,000,000 per annum; and it serves about 400 newspapers located in the various cities of the United States and abroad, a few of which are represented, also, in the membership of the Associated Press.

The parties are in the keenest competition between themselves in the distribution of news throughout the United States; and so, as a rule, are the newspapers that they serve, in their several districts.

Complainant in its bill, defendant in its answer, have set forth in almost identical terms the rather obvious circumstances and conditions under which their business is conducted. The value of the service, and of the news furnished, depends upon the promptness of transmission, as well as upon the accuracy and impartiality of the news; it being essential that the news be transmitted to members or subscribers as early or earlier than similar information can be furnished to competing newspapers by other news services, and that the news furnished by each agency shall not be furnished to newspapers which do not contribute to the expense of gathering it. And further, to quote from the answer: "Prompt knowledge and publication of world-wide news is essential to the conduct of a modern newspaper, and by reason of the enormous expense incident to the gathering and distribution of such news, the only practical way in which a proprietor of a newspaper can obtain the same is, either through coöperation with a considerable number of other newspaper proprietors in the work of collecting and distributing such news, and the equitable division with them of the expenses thereof, or by the purchase of such news from some existing agency engaged in that business."

The bill was filed to restrain the pirating of complainant's news by defendant in three ways: First, by bribing employees of newspapers published by complainant's members to furnish Associated Press news to defendant before publication, for transmission by telegraph and telephone to defendant's clients for publication by them; Second, by inducing Associated Press members to violate its by-laws and permit defendant to obtain news before publication; and Third, by copying news from bulletin boards and from early editions of complainant's newspapers and selling this, either bodily or after rewriting it, to defendant's customers.

The District Court, upon consideration of the bill and answer, with voluminous affidavits on both sides, granted a preliminary injunction under the first and second heads; but refused at that stage to restrain the systematic practice admittedly pursued by defendant, of taking news bodily from the bulletin boards and early editions of complainant's newspapers and selling it as its own. The court expressed itself as satisfied that this practice amounted to unfair trade, but as the legal question was one of first impression it considered that the allowance of an injunction should await the outcome of an appeal. 240 Fed.Rep. 983, 996. Both parties having appealed, the Circuit Court of Appeals sustained the injunction order so far as it went, and upon complainant's appeal modified it and remanded the cause with directions to issue an injunction also against any bodily taking of the words or substance of complainant's news until its commercial value as news had passed away. 245 Fed.Rep. 244, 253. The present writ of certiorari was then allowed. 245 U.S. 644.

The only matter that has been argued before us is whether defendant may lawfully be restrained from appropriating news taken from bulletins issued by complainant or any of its members, or from newspapers published by them, for the purpose of selling it to defendant's clients. Complainant asserts that defendant's admitted course of conduct in this regard both violates complainant's property right in the news and constitutes unfair competition in business. And notwithstanding the case has proceeded only to the stage of a preliminary injunction, we have deemed it proper to consider the underlying questions, since they go to the very merits of the action and are presented upon facts that are not in dispute. As presented in argument, these questions are: 1. Whether there is any property in news; 2. Whether, if there be property in news collected for the purpose of being published, it survives the instant of its publication in the first newspaper to which it is communicated by the news-gatherer; and 3. Whether defendant's admitted course of conduct in appropriating for commercial use matter taken from bulletins or early editions of Associated Press publications constitutes unfair competition in trade.

The federal jurisdiction was invoked because of diversity of citizenship, not upon the ground that the suit arose under the copyright or other laws of the United States. Complainant's news matter is not copyrighted. It is said that it could not, in practice, be copyrighted, because of the large number of dispatches that are sent daily; and, according to complainant's contention, news is not within the operation of the copyright act. Defendant, while apparently conceding this, nevertheless invokes the analogies of the law of literary property and copyright, insisting as its principal contention that, assuming complainant has a right of property in its news, it can be maintained (unless the copyright act be complied with) only by being kept secret and confidential, and that upon the publication with complainant's consent of uncopyrighted news by any of complainant's members in a newspaper or upon a bulletin board, the right of property is lost, and the subsequent use of the news by the public or by defendant for any purpose whatever becomes lawful. * * *

In considering the general question of property in news matter, it is necessary to recognize its dual character, distinguishing between the substance of the information and the particular form or collocation of words in which the writer has communicated it.

No doubt news articles often possess a literary quality, and are the subject of literary property at the common law; nor do we question that such an article, as a literary production, is the subject of copyright by the terms of the act as it now stands. In an early case at the circuit Mr. Justice Thompson held in effect that a newspaper was not within the protection of the copyright acts of 1790 and 1802 (Clayton v. Stone, 2 Paine, 382; 5 Fed.Cas. No. 2872). But the present act is broader; it provides that the works for which copyright may be secured shall include "all the writings of an author," and specifically mentions "periodicals, including newspapers." Act of March 4, 1909, c. 320, §§ 4 and 5, 35 Stat. 1075, 1076. Evidently this admits to copyright a contribution to a newspaper, notwithstanding it also may convey news; and such is the practice of the copyright office, as the newspapers of the day bear witness. See Copyright Office Bulletin No. 15 (1917), pp. 7, 14, 16–17.

But the news element—the information respecting current events contained in the literary production—is not the creation of the writer, but is a report of matters that ordinarily are *publici juris;* it is the history of the day. It is not to be supposed that the framers of the Constitution, when they empowered Congress "to promote the progress of science and useful arts, by securing for limited times to authors and inventors the exclusive right to their respective writings and discoveries" (Const., Art. I, § 8, par. 8), intended to confer upon one who might happen to be the first to report a historic event the exclusive right for any period to spread the knowledge of it.

We need spend no time, however, upon the general question of property in news matter at common law, or the application of the copyright act, since it seems to us the case must turn upon the question of unfair competition in business. And, in our opinion, this does not depend upon any general right of property analogous to the common-law right of the proprietor of an unpublished work to prevent its publication without his consent; nor is it foreclosed by showing that the benefits of the copyright act have been waived. We are dealing here not with restrictions upon publication but with the very facilities and processes of publication. The peculiar value of news is in the spreading of it while it is fresh; and it is evident that a valuable property interest in the news, as news, cannot be maintained by keeping it secret. Besides, except for matters improperly disclosed, or published in breach of trust or confidence, or in violation of law, none of which is involved in this branch of the case, the news of current events may be regarded as common property. What we are concerned with is the business of making it known to the world, in which both parties to the present suit are engaged. That business consists in maintaining a prompt, sure, steady, and reliable service designed to place the daily events of the world at the breakfast table of the millions at a price that, while of trifling moment to each reader, is sufficient in the aggregate to afford compensation for the cost of gathering and distributing it, with the added profit so necessary as an incentive to effective action in the commercial world. The service thus performed for newspaper readers is not only innocent but extremely useful in itself, and indubitably constitutes a legitimate business. The parties are competitors in this field; and, on fundamental principles, applicable here as elsewhere, when the rights or privileges of the one are liable to conflict with those of the other, each party is under a duty so to conduct its own business as not unnecessarily or unfairly to injure that of the other. Hitchman Coal & Coke Co. v. Mitchell, 245 U.S. 229, 254.

Obviously, the question of what is unfair competition in business must be determined with particular reference to the character and circumstances of the business. The question here is not so much the rights of either party as against the public but their rights as between themselves. See Morison v. Moat, 9 Hare, 241, 258. And although we may and do assume that neither party has any remaining property interest as against the public in uncopyrighted news matter after the moment of its first publication, it by no means follows that there is no remaining property interest in it as between themselves. For, to both of them alike, news matter, however little susceptible of ownership or dominion in the absolute sense, is stock in trade, to be gathered at the cost of enterprise, organization, skill, labor, and money, and to be distributed and sold to those who will pay money for it, as for any other merchandise. Regarding the news, therefore, as but the material out of which both parties are seeking to make profits at the same time and in the same field, we hardly can fail to recognize that for this purpose, and as between them, it must be regarded as quasi property, irrespective of the rights of either as against the public.

In order to sustain the jurisdiction of equity over the controversy, we need not affirm any general and absolute property in the news as such. The rule that a court of equity concerns itself only in the protection of property rights treats any civil right of a pecuniary nature as a property right (In re Sawyer, 124 U.S. 200, 210; In re Debs, 158 U.S. 564, 593); and the right to acquire property by honest labor or the conduct of a lawful business is as much entitled to protection as the right to guard property already acquired. Truax v. Raich, 239 U.S. 33, 37–38; Brennan v. United Hatters, 73 N.J.L. 729, 742; Barr v. Essex Trades Council, 53 N.J.Eq. 101. It is this right that furnishes the basis of the jurisdiction in the ordinary case of unfair competition.

The question, whether one who has gathered general information or news at pains and expense for the purpose of subsequent publication through the press has such an interest in its publication as may be protected from interference, has been raised many times, although never, perhaps, in the precise form in which it is now presented.

Board of Trade v. Christie Grain & Stock Co., 198 U.S. 236, 250, related to the distribution of quotations of prices on dealings upon a board of trade, which were collected by plaintiff and communicated on confidential terms to numerous persons under a contract not to make them public. This court held that, apart from certain special objections that were overruled, plaintiff's collection of quotations was entitled to the protection of the law; that, like a trade secret, plaintiff might keep to itself the work done at its expense, and did not lose its right by communicating the result to persons, even if many, in confidential relations to itself, under a contract not to make it public; and that strangers should be restrained from getting at the knowledge by inducing a breach of trust.

In National Tel. News Co. v. Western Union Tel. Co., 119 Fed.Rep. 294, the Circuit Court of Appeals for the Seventh Circuit dealt with news matter gathered and transmitted by a telegraph company, and consisting merely of a notation of current events having but a transient value due to quick transmission and distribution; and, while declaring that this was not copyrightable although printed on a tape by tickers in the offices of the recipients, and that it was a commercial not a literary product, nevertheless held that the business of gathering and communicating the news—the service of purveying it—was a legitimate business, meeting a distinctive commercial want and adding to the facilities of the business world, and partaking of the nature of property in a sense that entitled it to the protection of a court of equity against piracy.

Other cases are cited, but none that we deem it necessary to mention.

Not only do the acquisition and transmission of news require elaborate organization and a large expenditure of money, skill, and effort; not only has it an exchange value to the gatherer, dependent chiefly upon its novelty and freshness, the regularity of the service, its reputed reliability and thoroughness, and its adaptability to the public needs; but also, as is evident, the news has an exchange value to one who can misappropriate it.

The peculiar features of the case arise from the fact that, while novelty and freshness form so important an element in the success of the business, the very processes of distribution and publication necessarily occupy a good deal of time. Complainant's service, as well as defendant's, is a daily service to daily newspapers; most of the foreign news reaches this country at the Atlantic seaboard, principally at the City of New York, and because of this, and of time differentials due to the earth's rotation, the distribution of news matter throughout the country is principally from east to west; and, since in speed the telegraph and telephone easily outstrip the rotation of the earth, it is a simple matter for defendant to take complainant's news from bulletins or early editions of complainant's members in the eastern cities and at the mere cost of telegraphic transmission cause it to be published in western papers issued at least as early as those served by complainant. Besides this, and irrespective of time differentials, irregularities in telegraphic transmission on different lines, and the normal consumption of time in printing and distributing the newspaper, result in permitting pirated news to be placed in the hands of defendant's readers sometimes simultaneously with the service of competing Associated Press papers, occasionally even earlier.

Defendant insists that when, with the sanction and approval of complainant, and as the result of the use of its news for the very purpose for which it is distributed, a portion of complainant's members communicate it to the general public by posting it upon bulletin boards so that all may read, or by issuing it to newspapers and distributing it indiscriminately, complainant no longer has the right to control the use to be made of it; that when it thus reaches the light of day it becomes the common possession of all to whom it is accessible; and that any purchaser of a newspaper has the right to communicate the intelligence which it contains to anybody and for any purpose, even for the purpose of selling it for profit to newspapers published for profit in competition with complainant's members.

The fault in the reasoning lies in applying as a test the right of the complainant as against the public, instead of considering the rights of complainant and defendant, competitors in business, as between themselves. The right of the purchaser of a single newspaper to spread knowledge of its contents gratuitously, for any legitimate purpose not unreasonably interfering with complainant's right to make merchandise of it, may be admitted; but to transmit that news for commercial use, in competition with complainant—which is what defendant has done and seeks to justify—is a very different matter. In doing this defendant, by its very act, admits that it is taking material that has been acquired by complainant as the result of organization and the expenditure of labor, skill, and money, and which is salable by complainant for money, and that defendant in appropriating it and selling it as its own is endeavoring to reap where it has not sown, and by disposing of it to newspapers that are competitors of complainant's members is appropriating to itself the harvest of those who have sown. Stripped of all disguises, the process amounts to an unauthorized interference with the normal operation of complainant's legitimate business precisely at the point where the profit is to be reaped, in order to divert a material portion of the profit from those who have earned it to those who have not; with special advantage to defendant in the competition because of the fact that it is not burdened with any part of the expense of gathering the news. The transaction speaks for itself, and a court of equity ought not to hesitate long in characterizing it as unfair competition in business.

The underlying principle is much the same as that which lies at the base of the equitable theory of consideration in the law of trusts—that he who has fairly paid the price should have the beneficial use of the property. Pom.Eq.Jur., § 981. * * *

The contention that the news is abandoned to the public for all purposes when published in the first newspaper is untenable. Abandonment is a question of intent, and the entire organization of the

Associated Press negatives such a purpose. The cost of the service would be prohibitive if the reward were to be so limited. No single newspaper, no small group of newspapers, could sustain the expenditure. Indeed, it is one of the most obvious results of defendant's theory that, by permitting indiscriminate publication by anybody and everybody for purposes of profit in competition with the news-gatherer, it would render publication profitless, or so little profitable as in effect to cut off the service by rendering the cost prohibitive in comparison with the return. The practical needs and requirements of the business are reflected in complainant's by-laws which have been referred to. Their effect is that publication by each member must be deemed not by any means an abandonment of the news to the world for any and all purposes, but a publication for limited purposes; for the benefit of the readers of the bulletin or the newspaper as such; not for the purpose of making merchandise of it as news, with the result of depriving complainant's other members of their reasonable opportunity to obtain just returns for their expenditures.

It is to be observed that the view we adopt does not result in giving to complainant the right to monopolize either the gathering or the distribution of the news, or, without complying with the copyright act, to prevent the reproduction of its news articles; but only postpones participation by complainant's competitor in the processes of distribution and reproduction of news that it has not gathered, and only to the extent necessary to prevent that competitor from reaping the fruits of complainant's efforts and expenditure, to the partial exclusion of complainant, and in violation of the principle that underlies the maxim *sic utere tuo*, etc.

It is said that the elements of unfair competition are lacking because there is no attempt by defendant to palm off its goods as those of the complainant, characteristic of the most familiar, if not the most typical, cases of unfair competition. Howe Scale Co. v. Wyckoff, Seamans & Benedict, 198 U.S. 118, 140. But we cannot concede that the right to equitable relief is confined to that class of cases. In the present case the fraud upon complainant's rights is more direct and obvious. Regarding news matter as the mere material from which these two competing parties are endeavoring to make money, and treating it, therefore, as *quasi* property for the purposes of their business because they are both selling it as such, defendant's conduct differs from the ordinary case of unfair competition in trade principally in this that, instead of selling its own goods as those of complainant, it substitutes misappropriation in the place of misrepresentation, and sells complainant's goods as its own.

Besides the misappropriation, there are elements of imitation, of false pretense, in defendant's practices. The device of rewriting complainant's news articles, frequently resorted to, carries its own comment. The habitual failure to give credit to complainant for that which is taken is significant. Indeed, the entire system of appropriating complainant's news and transmitting it as a commercial product to defendant's clients and patrons amounts to a false representation to them and to their newspaper readers that the news transmitted is the result of defendant's own investigation in the field. But these elements, although accentuating the wrong, are not the essence of it. It is something more than the advantage of celebrity of which complainant is being deprived.

The doctrine of unclean hands is invoked as a bar to relief; it being insisted that defendant's practices against which complainant seeks an injunction are not different from the practice attributed to complainant, of utilizing defendant's news published by its subscribers. At this point it becomes necessary to consider a distinction that is drawn by complainant, and, as we understand it, was recognized by defendant also in the submission of proofs in the District Court, between two kinds of use that may be made by one news agency of news taken from the bulletins and newspapers of the other. The first is the bodily appropriation of a statement of fact or a news article, with or without rewriting, but without independent investigation or other expense. This form of pirating was found by both courts to have been pursued by defendant systematically with respect to complainant's news, and against it the Circuit Court of Appeals granted an injunction. This practice complainant denies having pursued, and the denial was sustained by the finding of the District Court. It is not contended by defendant that the finding can be set aside, upon the proofs as they now stand. The other use is to take the news of a rival agency as a "tip" to be investigated, and if verified by independent investigation the news thus gathered is sold. This practice complainant admits that it has pursued and still is willing that defendant shall employ.

Both courts held that complainant could not be debarred on the ground of unclean hands upon the score of pirating defendant's news, because not shown to be guilty of sanctioning this practice.

As to securing "tips" from a competing news agency, the District Court (240 Fed.Rep. 991, 995), while not sanctioning the practice, found that both parties had adopted it in accordance with common business usage, in the belief that their conduct was technically lawful, and hence did not find in it any sufficient ground for attributing unclean hands to complainant. The Circuit Court of Appeals (245 Fed.Rep. 247) found that the tip habit, though discouraged by complainant, was "incurably journalistic," and that there was "no difficulty in discriminating between the utilization of 'tips' and the bodily appropriation of another's labor in accumulating and stating information."

We are inclined to think a distinction may be drawn between the utilization of tips and the bodily appropriation of news matter, either in its original form or after rewriting and without independent investigation and verification; whatever may appear at the final hearing, the proofs as they now stand recognize such a distinction; both parties avowedly recognize the practice of taking tips, and neither party alleges it to be unlawful or to amount to unfair competition in business. In a line of English cases a somewhat analogous practice has been held not to amount to an infringement of the copyright of a directory or other book containing compiled information. In Kelly v. Morris, L.R. 1 Eq. 697, 701, 702, Vice Chancellor Sir William Page Wood (afterwards Lord Hatherly), dealing with such a case, said that defendant was "not entitled to take one word of the information previously published without independently working out the matter for himself, so as to arrive at the same result from the same common sources of information, and the only use that he can legitimately make of a previous publication is to verify his own calculations and results when obtained." This was followed by Vice Chancellor Giffard in Morris v. Ashbee, L.R. 7 Eq. 34, where he said: "In a case such as this no one has a right to take the results of the labour and expense incurred by another for the purposes of a rival publication, and thereby save himself the expense and labour of working out and arriving at these results by some independent road." A similar view was adopted by Lord Chancellor Hatherly and the former Vice Chancellor, then Giffard, L.J., in Pike v. Nicholas, L.R. 5 Ch.App.Cas. 251, and shortly afterwards by the latter judge in Morris v. Wright, L.R. 5 Ch.App.Cas. 279, 287, where he said, commenting upon Pike v. Nicholas: "It was a perfectly legitimate course for the defendant to refer to the plaintiff's book, and if, taking that book as his guide, he went to the original authorities and compiled his book from them, he made no unfair or improper use of the plaintiff's book; and so here, if the fact be that Mr. Wright used the plaintiff's book in order to guide himself to the persons on whom it would be worth his while to call, and for no other purpose, he made a perfectly legitimate use of the plaintiff's book."

A like distinction was recognized by the Circuit Court of Appeals for the Second Circuit in Edward Thompson Co. v. American Law Book Co., 122 Fed.Rep. 922, and in West Publishing Co. v. Edward Thompson Co., 176 Fed.Rep. 833, 838.

In the case before us, in the present state of the pleadings and proofs, we need go no further than to hold, as we do, that the admitted pursuit by complainant of the practice of taking news items published by defendant's subscribers as tips to be investigated, and, if verified, the result of the investigation to be sold—the practice having been followed by defendant also, and by news agencies generally—is not shown to be such as to constitute an unconscientious or inequitable attitude towards its adversary so as to fix upon complainant the taint of unclean hands, and debar it on this ground from the relief to which it is otherwise entitled.

There is some criticism of the injunction that was directed by the District Court upon the going down of the mandate from the Circuit Court of Appeals. In brief, it restrains any taking or gainfully using of the complainant's news, either bodily or in substance, from bulletins issued by the complainant or any of its members, or from editions of their newspapers, *"until its commercial value as news to the complainant and all of its members has passed away."* The part complained of is the clause we have italicized; but if this be indefinite, it is no more so than the criticism. Perhaps it would be better that the terms of the injunction be made specific, and so framed as to confine the restraint to an extent consistent with the reasonable protection of complainant's newspapers, each in its own area and for a specified time after its publication, against the competitive use of pirated news by defendant's customers. But the case presents practical difficulties; and we have not the materials, either in the way of a definite suggestion of amendment, or in the way of proofs, upon which to frame a specific injunction; hence, while not expressing approval of the form adopted by the District Court, we decline to modify it at this preliminary stage of the case, and will leave that court to deal with the matter upon appropriate application made to it for the purpose.

The decree of the Circuit Court of Appeals will be

Affirmed.

Mr. Justice Clarke took no part in the consideration or decision of this case.

Mr. Justice Holmes. When an uncopyrighted combination of words is published there is no general right to forbid other people repeating them—in other words there is no property in the combination or in the thoughts or facts that the words express. Property, a creation of law, does not arise from value, although exchangeable—a matter of fact. Many exchangeable values may be destroyed intentionally without compensation. Property depends upon exclusion by law from interference, and a person is not excluded from using any combination of words merely because someone has used it before, even if it took labor and genius to make it. If a given person is to be prohibited from making the use of words that his neighbors are free to make some other ground must be found. One such ground is vaguely expressed in the phrase unfair trade. This means that the words are repeated by a competitor in business in such a way as to convey a misrepresentation that materially injures the person who first used them, by appropriating credit of some kind which the first user has earned. The ordinary case is a representation by device, appearance, or other indirection that the defendant's goods come from the plaintiff. But the only reason why it is actionable to make such a representation is that it tends to give the defendant an advantage in his competition with the plaintiff and that it is thought undesirable that an advantage should be gained in that way. Apart from that the defendant may use such unpatented devices and uncopyrighted combinations of words as he likes. The ordinary case, I say, is palming off the defendant's product as the plaintiff's, but the same evil may follow from the opposite falsehood—from saying, whether in words or by implication, that the plaintiff's product is the defendant's, and that, it seems to me, is what has happened here.

Fresh news is got only by enterprise and expense. To produce such news as it is produced by the defendant represents by implication that it has been acquired by the defendant's enterprise and at its expense.

When it comes from one of the great news-collecting agencies like the Associated Press, the source generally is indicated, plainly importing that credit; and that such a representation is implied may be inferred with some confidence from the unwillingness of the defendant to give the credit and tell the truth. If the plaintiff produces the news at the same time that the defendant does, the defendant's presentation impliedly denies to the plaintiff the credit of collecting the facts and assumes that credit to the defendant. If the plaintiff is later in western cities it naturally will be supposed to have obtained its information from the defendant. The falsehood is a little more subtle, the injury a little more indirect, than in ordinary cases of unfair trade, but I think that the principle that condemns the one condemns the other. It is a question of how strong an infusion of fraud is necessary to turn a flavor into a poison. The dose seems to me strong enough here to need a remedy from the law. But as, in my view, the only ground of complaint that can be recognized without legislation is the implied misstatement, it can be corrected by stating the truth; and a suitable acknowledgment of the source is all that the plaintiff can require. I think that within the limits recognized by the decision of the Court the defendant should be enjoined from publishing news obtained from the Associated Press for hours after publication by the plaintiff unless it gives express credit to the Associated Press; the number of hours and the form of acknowledgment to be settled by the District Court.

Mr. Justice McKenna concurs in this opinion.

Mr. Justice Brandeis dissenting.

There are published in the United States about 2,500 daily papers. More than 800 of them are supplied with domestic and foreign news of general interest by the Associated Press—a corporation without capital stock which does not sell news or earn or seek to earn profits, but serves merely as an instrumentality by means of which these papers supply themselves at joint expense with such news. Papers not members of the Associated Press depend for their news of general interest largely upon agencies organized for profit. Among these agencies is the International News Service which supplies news to about 400 subscribing papers. It has, like the Associated Press, bureaus and correspondents in this and foreign countries; and its annual expenditure in gathering and distributing news is about $2,000,000. Ever since its organization in 1909, it has included among the sources from which it gathers news copies (purchased in the open market) of early editions of some papers published by members of the Associated Press and the bulletins publicly posted by them. These items, which constitute but a small part of the news transmitted to its subscribers, are generally verified by the International News Service before transmission; but frequently items are transmitted without verification; and occasionally even without being re-written. In no case is the fact disclosed that such item was suggested by or taken from a paper or bulletin published by an Associated Press member.

No question of statutory copyright is involved. The sole question for our consideration is this: Was the International News Service properly enjoined from using, or causing to be used gainfully, news of which it acquired knowledge by lawful means (namely, by reading publicly posted bulletins or papers purchased by it in the open market) merely because the news had been originally gathered by the Associated Press and continued to be of value to some of its members, or because it did not reveal the source from which it was acquired?

The "ticker" cases, the cases concerning literary and artistic compositions, and cases of unfair competition were relied upon in support of the injunction. But it is admitted that none of those cases affords a complete analogy with that before us. The question presented for decision is new; and it is important.

News is a report of recent occurrences. The business of the news agency is to gather systematically knowledge of such occurrences of interest and to distribute reports thereof. The Associated Press contended that knowledge so acquired is property, because it costs money and labor to produce and because it has value for which those who have it not are ready to pay; that it remains property and is entitled to protection as long as it has commercial value as news; and that to protect it effectively the defendant must be enjoined from making, or causing to be made, any gainful use of it while it retains such value. An essential element of individual property is the legal right to exclude others from enjoying it. If the property is private, the right of exclusion may be absolute; if the property is affected with a public interest, the right of exclusion is qualified. (But the fact that a product of the mind has cost its producer money and labor, and has a value for which others are willing to pay, is not sufficient to ensure to it this legal attribute of property. The general rule of law is, that the noblest of human productions—knowledge, truths ascertained, conceptions, and ideas—become, after voluntary communication to others, free as the air to common use. Upon these incorporeal productions the attribute of property is continued after such communication only in certain classes of cases where public policy has seemed to demand it.) These exceptions are confined to productions which, in some degree, involve creation, invention, or discovery. But by no means all such are endowed with this attribute of property. The creations which are recognized as property by the common law are literary, dramatic, musical, and other artistic creations; and these have also protection under the copyright statutes. The inventions and discoveries upon which this attribute of property is conferred only by statute, are the few comprised within the patent law. There are also many other cases in which courts interfere to prevent curtailment of plaintiff's enjoyment of incorporeal productions; and in which the right to relief is often called a property right, but is such only in a special sense. In those cases, the plaintiff has no absolute right to the protection of his production; he has merely the qualified right to be protected as against the defendant's acts, because of the special relation in which the latter stands or the wrongful method or means employed in acquiring the knowledge or the manner in which it is used. Protection of this character is afforded where the suit is based upon breach of contract or of trust or upon unfair competition.

The knowledge for which protection is sought in the case at bar is not of a kind upon which the law has heretofore conferred the attributes of property; nor is the manner of its acquisition or use nor the purpose to which it is applied, such as has heretofore been recognized as entitling a plaintiff to relief.

First: Plaintiff's principal reliance was upon the "ticker" cases; but they do not support its contention. The leading cases on this subject rest the grant of relief, not upon the existence of a general property right in news, but upon the breach of a contract or trust concerning the use of news communicated; and that element is lacking here.

* * *

If the news involved in the case at bar had been posted in violation of any agreement between the Associated Press and its members, questions similar to those in the "ticker" cases might have arisen. But the plaintiff does not contend that the posting was wrongful or that any papers were wrongfully issued by its subscribers. On the contrary it is conceded that both the bulletins and the papers were issued in accordance with the regulations of the plaintiff. Under such circumstances, for a reader of the papers purchased in the open market, or a reader of the bulletins publicly posted, to procure and use gainfully, information therein contained, does not involve inducing anyone to commit a breach either of contract or of trust, or committing or in any way abetting a breach of confidence.

Second: Plaintiff also relied upon the cases which hold that the common-law right of the producer to prohibit copying is not lost by the private circulation of a literary composition, the delivery of a lecture, the exhibition of a painting, or the performance of a dramatic or musical composition. These cases rest upon the ground that the common law recognizes such productions as property which, despite restricted communication, continues until there is a dedication to the public under the copyright statutes or otherwise. But they are inapplicable for two reasons. (1) At common law, as under the copyright acts, intellectual productions are entitled to such protection only if there is underneath something evincing the mind of a creator or originator, however modest the requirement. The mere record of isolated happenings, whether in words or by photographs not involving artistic skill, are denied such protection. (2) At common law, as under the copyright acts, the element in intellectual productions which secures such protection is not the knowledge, truths, ideas, or emotions which the composition expresses, but the form or sequence in which they are expressed; that is, "some new collocation of visible or audible points,—of lines, colors, sounds, or words." See White-Smith Music Co. v. Apollo Co., 209 U.S. 1, 19; Kalem Co. v. Harper Brothers, 222 U.S. 55, 63. An author's theories, suggestions, and speculations, or the systems, plans, methods, and arrangements of an originator, derive no such protection from the statutory copyright of the book in which they are set forth; and they are likewise denied such protection at common law. * * *

Third: If news be treated as possessing the characteristics not of a trade secret, but of literary property, then the earliest issue of a paper of general circulation or the earliest public posting of a bulletin which embodies such news would, under the established rules governing literary property, operate as a publication, and all property in the news would then cease. Resisting this conclusion, plaintiff relied upon the cases which hold that uncopyrighted intellectual and artistic property survives private circulation or a restricted publication; and it contended that in each issue of each paper, a restriction is to be implied that the news shall not be used gainfully in competition with the Associated Press or any of its members. There is no basis for such an implication. But it is also well settled that where the publication is in fact a general one, even express words of restriction upon use are inoperative. In other words, a general publication is effective to dedicate literary property to the public, regardless of the actual intent of its owner. * *

Fourth: Plaintiff further contended that defendant's practice constitutes unfair competition, because there is "appropriation without cost to itself of values created by" the plaintiff; and it is upon this ground that the decision of this court appears to be based. "To appropriate and use for profit, knowledge and ideas produced by other men, without making compensation or even acknowledgment, may be inconsistent with a finer sense of propriety; but, with the exceptions indicated above, the law" has heretofore sanctioned the practice. Thus it was held that one may ordinarily make and sell anything in any form, may copy with exactness that which another has produced, or may otherwise use his ideas without his consent and without the payment of compensation, and yet not inflict a legal injury; and that ordinarily one is at perfect liberty to find out, if he can by lawful means, trade secrets of another, however valuable, and then use the knowledge so acquired gainfully, although it cost the original owner much in effort and in money to collect or produce.

Such taking and gainful use of a product of another which, for reasons of public policy, the law has refused to endow with the attributes of property, does not become unlawful because the product happens to have been taken from a rival and is used in competition with him. The unfairness in competition which hitherto has been recognized by the law as a basis for relief, lay in the manner or means of conducting the business; and the manner or means held legally unfair, involves either fraud or force or the doing of acts otherwise prohibited by law. In the "passing off" cases (the typical and most common case of unfair competition), the wrong consists in fraudulently representing by word or act that defendant's goods are those of plaintiff. See Hanover Milling Co. v. Metcalf, 240 U.S. 403, 412–413. In the other cases, the diversion of trade was effected through physical or moral coercion, or by inducing breaches of contract or of trust or by enticing away employees. In some others, called cases of simulated competition, relief was granted because defendant's purpose was unlawful; namely, not competition but deliberate and wanton destruction of plaintiff's business.

That competition is not unfair in a legal sense, merely because the profits gained are unearned, even if made at the expense of a rival, is shown by many cases besides those referred to above. He who follows the pioneer into a new market, or who engages in the manufacture of an article newly introduced by another, seeks profits due largely to the labor and expense of the first adventurer; but the law sanctions, indeed encourages, the pursuit. * * *

The means by which the International News Service obtains news gathered by the Associated Press is also clearly unobjectionable. It is taken from papers bought in the open market or from bulletins publicly posted. No breach of contract such as the court considered to exist in Hitchman Coal & Coke Co. v. Mitchell, 245 U.S. 229, 254; or of trust such as was present in Morison v. Moat, 9 Hare, 241; and neither fraud nor force, is involved. The manner of use is likewise unobjectionable. No reference is made by word or by act to the Associated Press, either in transmitting the news to subscribers or by them in publishing it in their papers. Neither the International News Service nor its subscribers is gaining or seeking to gain in its business a benefit from the reputation of the Associated Press. They are merely using its product without making compensation. See Bamforth v. Douglass Post Card & Machine Co., 158 Fed.Rep. 355; Tribune Co. of Chicago v. Associated Press, 116 Fed.Rep. 126. That, they have a legal right to do; because the product is not property, and they do not stand in any relation to the Associated Press, either of contract or of trust, which otherwise precludes such use. The argument is not advanced by characterizing such taking and use a misappropriation.

It is also suggested, that the fact that defendant does not refer to the Associated Press as the source of the news may furnish a basis for the relief. But the defendant and its subscribers, unlike members of the Associated Press, were under no contractual obligation to disclose the source of the news; and there is no rule of law requiring acknowledgment to be made where uncopyrighted matter is reproduced. The International News Service is said to mislead its subscribers into believing that the news transmitted was originally gathered by it and that they in turn mislead their readers. There is, in fact, no representation by either of any kind. Sources of information are sometimes given because required by contract; sometimes because naming the source gives authority to an otherwise incredible statement; and sometimes the source is named because the agency does not wish to take the responsibility itself of giving currency to the news. But no representation can properly be implied from omission to mention the source of information except that the International News Service is transmitting news which it believes to be credible. * * *

Fifth: The great development of agencies now furnishing country-wide distribution of news, the vastness of our territory, and improvements in the means of transmitting intelligence, have made it possible for a news agency or newspapers to obtain, without paying compensation, the fruit of another's efforts and to use news so obtained gainfully in competition with the original collector. The injustice of such action is obvious. But to give relief against it would involve more than the application of existing rules of law to new facts. It would require the making of a new rule in analogy to existing ones. The unwritten law possesses capacity for growth; and has often satisfied new demands for justice by invoking analogies or by expanding a rule or principle. This process has been in the main wisely applied and should not be discontinued. Where the problem is relatively simple, as it is apt to be when private interests only are involved, it generally proves adequate. But with the increasing complexity of society, the public interest tends to become omnipresent; and the problems presented by new demands for justice cease to be simple. Then the creation or recognition by courts of a new private right may work serious injury to the general public, unless the boundaries of the right are definitely established and wisely guarded. In order to reconcile the new private right with the public interest, it may be necessary to prescribe limitations and rules for its enjoyment; and also to provide administrative machinery for enforcing the rules. It is largely for this reason that, in the effort to meet the many new demands for justice incident to a rapidly changing civilization, resort to legislation has latterly been had with increasing frequency.

The rule for which the plaintiff contends would effect an important extension of property rights and a corresponding curtailment of the free use of knowledge and of ideas; and the facts of this case admonish us of the danger involved in recognizing such a property right in news, without imposing upon news-gatherers corresponding obligations. * *

A legislature, urged to enact a law by which one news agency or newspaper may prevent appropriation of the fruits of its labors by another * * * might conclude that it was impossible to put an end to the obvious injustice involved in such appropriation of news, without opening the door to other evils, greater than that sought to be remedied. Such appears to have been the opinion of our Senate which reported unfavorably a bill to give news a few hours' protection;[1] and

---

1. Senate Bill No. 1728, 48th Cong., 1st sess. The bill provides:

"That any daily or weekly newspaper, or any association of daily or weekly newspapers, published in the United States or any of the Territories thereof, shall have the sole right to print, issue, and sell, for the term of eight hours, dating from the hour of going to press, the contents of said daily or weekly newspaper, or the collected news of said newspaper association, exceeding one hundred words.

which ratified, on February 15, 1911, the convention adopted at the Fourth International American Conference;[2] and such was evidently the view also of the signatories to the International Copyright Union of November 13, 1908;[3] as both these conventions expressly exclude news from copyright protection. * * *

Courts are ill-equipped to make the investigations which should precede a determination of the limitations which should be set upon any property right in news or of the circumstances under which news gathered by a private agency should be deemed affected with a public interest. Courts would be powerless to prescribe the detailed regulations essential to full enjoyment of the rights conferred or to introduce the machinery required for enforcement of such regulations. Considerations such as these should lead us to decline to establish a new rule of law in the effort to redress a newly-disclosed wrong, although the propriety of some remedy appears to be clear.

Questions

1. Justice Holmes found that there was a kind of reverse palming off, a representation "that the plaintiff's product is the defendant's". Do you agree that in fact such a representation was implied by the defendant's conduct? Is there always, sometimes, or never such a representation merely by reason of the defendant's marketing a product which is copied from the plaintiff's? Does the Pitney opinion for the Court view "misappropriation" as necessarily containing such a representation? Does it regard "misappropriation" as a form of unfair competition even without such a representation? Is "misappropriation" synonymous with copying?

2. Since the instant case applied federal common law, it ceased to be a binding precedent even in the federal courts after Erie R.R. v. Tompkins, 304

"Sec. 2. That for any infringement of the copyright granted by the first section of this act the party injured may sue in any court of competent jurisdiction and recover in any proper action the damages sustained by him from the person making such infringement, together with the costs of suit."

It was reported on April 18, 1884, by the Committee on the Library, without amendment, and that it ought not to pass. Journal of the Senate, 48th Cong., 1st sess., p. 548. No further action was apparently taken on the bill.

When the copyright legislation of 1909, finally enacted as Act of March 4, 1909, c. 320, 35 Stat. 1075, was under consideration, there was apparently no attempt to include news among the subjects of copyright. Arguments before the Committees on Patents of the Senate and House of Representatives on Senate Bill No. 6330 and H.R.Bill No. 19853, 59th Cong., 1st sess., June 6, 7, 8, and 9, and December 7, 8, 10, and 11, 1906; Hearings on Pending Bills to Amend and Consolidate Acts Respecting Copyright, March 26, 27 and 28, 1908.

2. 38 Stat. 1785, 1789, Article 11.

3. Bowker, Copyright: Its History and its Law, pp. 330, 612, 613. See the similar provisions in the Berne Convention (1886) and the Paris Convention (1896). Id., pp. 612, 613.

In 1898 Lord Herschell introduced in Parliament a bill, § 11 of which provides: "Copyright in respect of a newspaper shall apply only to such parts of the newspaper as are compositions of an original literary character, to original illustrations therein, *and to such news and information as have been specially and independently obtained.*" (Italics ours.) House of Lords, Sessional Papers, 1898, vol. 3, Bill No. 21. Birrell, Copyright in Books, p. 210. But the bill was not enacted, and in the English law as it now stands there is no provision giving even a limited copyright in news as such. Act of December 16, 1911, 1 and 2 Geo. V, c. 46.

U.S. 64 (1938). State courts have nevertheless continued to apply the misappropriation doctrine of this case, at least in the area of news protection. Is unfair competition of the misappropriation variety preempted under Sec. 301 of the Copyright Act? Recall the Congressional debate on this issue, set out in Chapter Nine. In determining the applicability of preemption to the *INS* misappropriation doctrine, what is the relevance of the passage in the *INS* opinion referring to the status of news under the copyright clause of the Constitution? Can Congress preempt a field which it lacks the constitutional power to enter?

3. Is Justice Brandeis' warning that "the creation or recognition by courts of a new private right may work serious injury to the general public * * *" consistent with the position he took in the landmark article *The Right to Privacy,* discussed in a later chapter?

Collateral Reference

Baird, *Common Law Intellectual Property and the Legacy of International News Service v. Associated Press,* 50 U.Chi.L.Rev. 411 (1983).

B. TITLES

JACKSON v. UNIVERSAL INTERNATIONAL PICTURES

Supreme Court of California in Bank, 1950.
36 Cal.2d 116, 222 P.2d 433.

EDMONDS, JUSTICE. Frederick Jackson, the author of a play which was not a theatrical success, sued to recover damages assertedly resulting from the unauthorized use of its title. The principal ground relied upon as requiring a reversal of the judgment in his favor is that the evidence shows no acquisition by the title of a secondary meaning.

The first count of the complaint alleged that Jackson is the author of a play which he entitled "Slightly Scandalous." The play was rehearsed in Los Angeles and produced in Philadelphia and New York with publicity announcing the times of performance. The title thereby acquired a secondary meaning. Later, Universal produced a motion picture under the same title. Universal's distribution, advertising and showing of its picture misled the public and infringed upon Jackson's right in the title of his play. The second count of the complaint alleged that Universal had made a "deliberate, wrongful and unfair misappropriation and use of plaintiff's name and title" in connection with the motion picture. Universal denied these allegations generally.

The evidence presented upon trial may be summarized as follows:

Jackson is a writer with about 40 years of experience. He has written plays which were produced in New York and London and sold the motion picture rights to several of them. In 1943, he wrote "Slightly Scandalous." In the following year, while the play was being rehearsed in Los Angeles prior to production, a press agent was employed to publicize it. During the next two months about 40 stories concerning it were prepared and distributed to 550 metropolitan and suburban newspapers.

Only a small percentage of this material was published. A one-inch item appeared in the Hollywood Reporter, a trade journal. It stated that the play would open in Philadelphia and be presented in New York two weeks later with Janet Beecher in the leading role. The Los Angeles Evening Herald-Express, with a daily circulation of 325,000, reported that the author was adding final directorial touches to "Slightly Scandalous" before its initial production in Philadelphia.

Variety, a theatrical magazine having a circulation of 600,000 and sold at newsstands in the principal cities, included reference to the play in a section entitled "Shows in Rehearsal." The Los Angeles Times, which has a daily circulation in excess of 280,000, mentioned in a story concerning another play that the title of the one in which Janet Beecher was to be starred had been changed to "Slightly Scandalous." Rehearsal would commence in Hollywood immediately, it was said, preparatory to a New York appearance.

The play opened in Philadelphia as scheduled. It was advertised in newspapers there prior to and during its two weeks run, in space ranging from 10 to 60 lines. The producer also placed 20,000 "heralds" in hotels and restaurants and used outdoor advertising with "24-sheets" on 50 poster boards.

The play ran for almost two weeks in Philadelphia. The drama critics were uncomplimentary, and although the theater was nearly filled to its capacity of 1,500 persons at one performance, attendance at all of the others averaged about 200. The total of the audiences at the 15 performances did not exceed 3,000.

The New York opening followed, but the play closed after seven performances. Advertising was carried by 10 newspapers there in space varying from 12 to 50 lines. But, as in Philadelphia, the newspaper comments were critical and the public showed little interest. In a theater which seated 1,000 there was an average attendance of about 100 at each performance. The play has not since been presented.

A witness for Jackson, after qualifying as an expert, testified that "Some of the most successful pictures have been made of plays that have been flops." Examples were cited. This testimony was corroborated by other witnesses.

To establish a secondary meaning to the title of his play, Jackson presented the testimony of five witnesses. Three of them told the jury that they had seen reviews or advertisements of the play and thought that the picture was based upon it. The testimony of the other two was substantially to the same effect.

Other testimony showed that Jackson's agent requested Universal Pictures to "cover" the eastern production of the play after it had been submitted to that company's West Coast story editor during the period of rehearsal in Los Angeles. A report concerning the play and its reception on Broadway was sent to the company's executive offices.

About two years later, Universal released and distributed throughout the country a motion picture by the same name. It was stipulated that three months before this picture was released, Universal knew of Jackson's play and referred to their attorneys the question as to whether the title "Slightly Scandalous" should be selected for their production. The picture originally carried the title, "Oh Say Can You Sing." The attorneys for Universal were notified by Jackson's attorney that his client would sue for damages if the title to his play were used.

Jackson does not claim that there is any similarity whatever between the picture and the play. He bases his cause of action entirely upon the use of the title.

The evidence offered by Universal generally is to the effect that the public did not connect the motion picture with Jackson's play and only a handful of people had previously heard of the title. In the company's defense, its witnesses stressed the unsuccessful presentations in Philadelphia and New York.

As grounds for the reversal of the judgment, Universal asserts that the evidence is not sufficient to justify the conclusion that "Slightly Scandalous" had acquired and retained a secondary meaning with relation to Jackson's play. The company also challenges an instruction as incorrect and prejudicially erroneous. Instructions offered by it were erroneously refused, it is asserted, and Jackson's damages in the amount of $17,500 are excessive. It is also claimed that the title was abandoned by Jackson's two year non-use of it. Finally, the appellant charges, Jackson's attorney was guilty of prejudicial conduct.

The position of Jackson is that the question as to whether a secondary meaning has attached to a literary or dramatic title is a question of fact. As substantial evidence sufficient to justify the jury's verdict, he refers to the testimony concerning prior use, advertising, and the general impression of the public in New York, Philadelphia and Los Angeles. He also relies upon the statements of his five witnesses that because of the title they associated the play with the motion picture. Nation-wide knowledge of a title is not essential to the acquisition of a secondary meaning, he declares, nor is success of the play a requirement. The correct test, as he analyzes the question, is whether an effect or reaction is created upon the public mind. He also contends that deliberate and unauthorized appropriation of a prior user's name, title or trademark is actionable.

As to the claimed procedural errors, the conduct of counsel was not prejudicial, he asserts, because it was promptly cured by an instruction to the jury. Moreover, the denial of the motion for a new trial was a determination that it did not influence the jury.

The points presented by *amici curiae* for Jackson are broader in scope. It is claimed that secondary meaning is established when the title is identified by the general public and it does not depend upon popularity. Although a play is unpopular or "panned" by the critics, unfavorable comments, or any discussion of the play, fixes the title in the mind of the general public as the product of a particular playwright. Moreover, widespread publicity and advertising renders a title valuable and subject to protection entirely apart from rights derived from secondary meaning. The "general public," they say, need only be a substantial number of people not necessarily residing throughout the nation.

An author of a play has no inherent right in the title to his production. Paramore v. Mack Sennett, Inc., D.C., 9 F.2d 66, 67; Martenet v. United Artists Corp., D.C., 56 F.Supp. 639, 640. Only when the title has acquired a secondary meaning identifying it in the public mind with the play is he entitled to its exclusive use. Warner Bros. Pictures v. Majectic Pictures Corp., 2 Cir., 70 F.2d 310, 311; Amusement S. Corp. v. Academy Pictures D. Corp., 162 Misc. 608, 294 N.Y.S. 279; see Nims, Unfair Competition and Trade Marks [4th Ed.1947], Sec. 274–a. Therefore, regardless of any deliberate use by Universal of "Slightly Scandalous" with knowledge of Jackson's prior use, he is not entitled to damages unless his literary product had acquired a secondary meaning.

There is no initial property right in household semantics or words which are merely descriptive, fanciful or geographic in nature. G. & C. Merriam Co. v. Saalfield, 6 Cir., 198 F. 369, 373. However, if words have been used by an author or manufacturer in such a manner that the public has learned to associate them with the product, book or play, they acquire a "secondary meaning". This principle, which was first applied in trademark cases, renders the words or symbols protectible and transferable because of that association. A play may become known to the public by its title, which thereby acquires a secondary meaning and attains a protectible status. Manners v. Triangle Film Corp., 2 Cir., 247 F. 301; Hemingway v. Film Alliance of the United States, Inc., 174 Misc. 725, 21 N.Y.S.2d 827.

In Johnston v. Twentieth Century-Fox Film Corp., 82 Cal.App.2d 796, 813, 187 P.2d 474, 484, the court stated, "The question whether a title has acquired a secondary meaning is one of fact." Other decisions to the same effect are International Film Service Co., Inc. v. Associated Producers, Inc., D.C., 273 F. 585; Bayer Co. v. United Drug Co., D.C., 272 F. 505, 509; Saland v. Monogram Pictures Corp., Sup., 67 N.Y.S.2d 436; Hemingway v. Film Alliance of the United States, Inc., 174 Misc. 725, 21 N.Y.S.2d 827. The Restatement of the Law of Torts, in stating this rule, adds: "No particular period of use is required." (Sec. 716b.)

There is substantial evidence in the record to support the implied finding of the jury that "Slightly Scandalous" had acquired a secondary meaning. Jackson's play was publicized in three of the largest cities in this country. The rehearsal and production of the play were announced in dramatic and motion picture journals in Hollywood and New York. Although only about 3,750 persons attended performances of the play, there is no basis for a holding, as a matter of law, that they and the undetermined number who saw the advertising are not sufficient in number to provide a basis for secondary meaning. The precise size of this segment of the public is important in connection with the amount of damages which should be awarded, but it does not determine whether the title has acquired a secondary meaning.

This court, in speaking of the word "public", has said that it " ' * * * does not mean all the people, nor most of the people, nor very many of the people of a place, but so many of them as contradistinguishes them from a few.' " Mary Pickford Co. v. Bayly Bros., Inc., 12 Cal.2d 501, 514, 86 P.2d 102, 108. The title of a play produced only in New York may acquire a secondary meaning which entitles it to protection throughout the United States. Aronson v. Fleckenstein, C.C., 28 F. 75; Hemingway v. Film Alliance of the United States, Inc., 174 Misc. 725, 21 N.Y.S.2d 827; Frohman v. Payton, 34 Misc. 275, 68 N.Y.S. 849. And the writer of a play recovered damages for the unauthorized use of its title although it was never produced in any city in the United States but had run for some weeks in Paris, France. Frohman v. Wm. Morris, 68 Misc. 461, 123 N.Y.S. 1090.

Popularity is not a requirement for secondary meaning because notoriety and adverse discussion may bring about wide-spread identification of the play by its title and may pique the public interest. Likewise, advertising, even of an unpopular play, may cause the public to identify it as one which has been a "Broadway production".

Although some decisions indicate that the word or phrase constituting the title must have been used " * * * long and * * * exclusively by one producer with reference to his article * * * ", G. & C. Meriam Co. v. Saalfield, 6 Cir., 198 F. 369, 373, and, in some cases, the length of the use may be persuasive, the essence of the acquisition of secondary meaning is the impact upon the public mind. "The duration of user required to create a secondary meaning can be measured by no accurate test. In the Yorkshire Relish case the time was twenty-five years, * * * in the Anatolia Licorice case, six weeks. From these instances it will be seen that there is no rule as to the length of time required." Nims, Unfair Competition and Trade Marks [4th Ed.1947], vol. 1, sec. 38a, p. 162.

Judge Learned Hand has said in relation to trademarks that " * * * it is the priority of user alone that controls, even though, when the defendant comes into the field, it may not be fully established, or may not even be enough established to have become associated largely in the public mind with the plaintiff's make. * * * Were it not so, it would be of extreme difficulty to show at just what point in time the mark became associated with the maker in enough of his customers' minds to justify the inference that the defendant's use might have become confusing. Therefore, once his use begins, the rest of the public must avoid his fanciful mark." Waldes v. International Manufacturers' Agency, Inc., D.C., 237 F. 502, 505.

Universal claims that, in order to gain secondary meaning, the title must be associated specifically with the author of the play rather than with the play. The contention is unrealistic and contrary to authority. "Secondary meaning may exist between a name and the manufacturer or seller whose identity is not known to the buyer * * *. He [the buyer] does not know its [the manufacturer's] name, or its location, or whether it is a corporation or an individual." Nims, Unfair Competition and Trade Marks [4th Ed.1947], vol. 1, sec. 42, pp. 169, 170.

In all probability only a very small percentage of persons who know something about plays can remember or identify the names of the authors. Usually, advertising and publicity are concentrated upon the title and the actors rather than the name of the playwright. There is no logical basis for holding that a public well acquainted with the title and the play could not confer secondary meaning upon that title merely because of unfamiliarity with the author's name.

The question of abandonment falls within the same category; it is one of fact to be determined by the jury upon substantial evidence. International Film Service, Inc. v. Associated Producers, Inc., D.C., 273 F. 585; Goldman v. R.K.O. Radio Pictures, Inc., 149 Misc. 226, 267 N.Y.S. 28. In Goldman v. R.K.O. Radio Pictures, Inc., supra, 267 N.Y.S. at page 29, the court stated: " * * * a lapse of thirteen years in the use of a title, under the circumstances of this case, raises a question of fact as to whether the title ['The Public Defender'] still retains a secondary significance * * *."

In the present case, there is evidence that several plays written by Jackson had been sold to motion picture producers, from two to ten years after they were produced in New York. It is also significant that in the United States, copyrights protect literary and dramatic properties for an initial period of 28 years with the right of renewal. The evidence, that Jackson had not produced his play for two years after it had closed in New York, does not compel a holding, as a matter of law, that he had abandoned his rights.

The instruction given at the request of Jackson and attacked as prejudicially erroneous refers to exhibits showing the extent of the advertising in the eastern cities at a total cost of $3,300. It is argued that although the court correctly directed the jury not to allow compensation for this expense, the cost of the advertising charges should not have been allowed in evidence. But the instruction directed the jury to limit its consideration to " * * * the value of the title in question and whether it had acquired a secondary meaning as hereinbefore defined, as a result of volume or extent of advertising." Considering the instruction as a whole, it correctly presented the applicable rule of law.

The rejected instructions concerned the principle that there is no property right implicit in the name or title of a literary work until a secondary meaning has attached to it. But in at least five different instructions, one of which was requested by Universal, the jury was told that the burden of proving a secondary meaning to the title of his play rested upon Jackson. Read together, they adequately covered the subject.

Considering the issue of damages, the sum of $17,500 does not appear to be excessive. The record includes testimony to the effect that other titles to unsuccessful plays have been sold for larger amounts. The value of property wrongfully taken is a matter for the determination of the jury and the evidence as a whole supports the award in Jackson's favor.

The conduct of counsel attacked as prejudicial was the cross-examination of an expert witness of Universal. He was asked whether he was prejudiced because his employer "was just held for $25,000 damages in an action [of the same kind]." The objection of Universal was sustained, and the jury directed to disregard the whole incident. Another occurrence, cited as misconduct, involved a quarrel between counsel as to which of them submitted a certain document.

There is no showing that the reference to other litigation was untrue. Considering the record as a whole and the ruling upon the motion for a new trial, it cannot be said that the misconduct was prejudicial.

The judgment is affirmed.

GIBSON, C.J., and SHENK, CARTER, TRAYNOR, SCHAUER and SPENCE, JJ., concur.

Questions

1. Are you satisfied with the court's definition of the "public" in determining secondary meaning? Can you suggest a better definition?

2. Was the use of the title "Slightly Scandalous" in connection with the Jackson play sufficient, in your view, to go to the jury on the issue of secondary meaning? How extensive a use should be required in order to create an issue of fact for the jury? Suppose the title of the Jackson play had been mentioned in several publicity announcements in trade newspapers (such as Daily Variety or The Hollywood Reporter), but the play itself had never been publicly performed—would this be enough to go to the jury? See Willpat Productions, Inc. v. Sigma III Corp., 227 F.Supp. 354 (S.D.N.Y.1964). What advice would you give a client who asks you how he might most effectively protect a title for an unpublished work?

3. Should the testimony of five witnesses, as in the instant case, be sufficient to establish that the "public" in fact identifies the title with the plaintiff's work? If more witnesses should be required, how many more? How can a defendant effectively rebut the plaintiff's evidence of secondary meaning? Is it enough to offer a number of witnesses who testify that they were not in fact misled by the defendant's use of the same title as that used for plaintiff's work? Should evidence based upon public opinion polling techniques be admissible? See Caughey, The Use of Public Polls, Surveys and Sampling, 44 Cal.L.Rev. 539 (1956); 76 A.L.R.2d 619 (1961).

4. After the copyright in a work expires, so that the work itself enters the public domain, may the author, or anyone claiming through him, prohibit use of the title of the work (assuming the title has acquired a secondary meaning) by persons reproducing and selling copies of the public domain work? Would such title protection subvert the copyright principle that works must enter the

public domain after protection for "limited times"? See G. & C. Merriam Co. v. Syndicate Pub. Co., 237 U.S. 618 (1915). After a work has entered the public domain may anyone freely use the title of the work (again assuming that it has achieved a secondary meaning) in connection with a new and different work? See Litwin v. Maddux, 7 Misc.2d 750, 164 N.Y.S.2d 489 (1957).

Collateral References

Netterville and Hirsch, *Piracy and Privilege in Literary Titles*, 32 So. Cal.Law Rev. 101 (1959).

Callmann, *Unfair Competition in Ideas and Titles*, 42 Cal.Law Rev. 77 (1954).

Nimmer on Copyright, § 2.16.

KIRKLAND v. NATIONAL BROADCASTING CO., INC.

United States District Court, Eastern District of Pennsylvania, 1976.
425 F.Supp. 1111.

DITTER, DISTRICT JUDGE. The question presented in this case is whether plaintiff has any proprietary rights in a name used by defendant as the title for a TV series. * * * I must grant defendant's motion for summary judgment.

I. FACTUAL AND PROCEDURAL BACKGROUND

In 1933, plaintiff originated and authored a story entitled "Land of the Lost," which eventually became a radio program broadcast on various networks from 1943 to 1948.[1] During this period, children who listened to the program formed "Land of the Lost" clubs, but these clubs apparently ceased functioning prior to January, 1954. Other commercial uses of plaintiff's concept included comic books, a record album, a book entitled "The Land of the Lost," and three cartoons, produced by Paramount Pictures, Inc., following an assignment by plaintiff to Paramount of a portion of her copyright interest.[3]

The present controversy stems from a children's television program entitled "Land of the Lost," which commenced broadcast on the NBC television network in September, 1974, and which continues to appear

---

1. The first broadcast was over the Blue Network on September 5, 1943. Thereafter, it was broadcast over the American Broadcasting Co., Inc. (October, 1943—September 15, 1945), the Mutual Broadcasting Network (October 14, 1945—June 29, 1946) and, once again, the ABC Network (October 11, 1947—July 3, 1948).

The basic theme of plaintiff's program involved two children in a rowboat on a lake who encountered a red fish named Red Lantern, who guided the children through the Land of the Lost, where "everything that is lost since the beginning of time goes there and comes to life, lives in its own place * * *" (Deposition of Mrs. Kirkland at page 14). In each succeeding show, the group would travel to new places, such as Kitchenville, and new characters developed from lost objects would be introduced.

3. All of these ventures apparently took place between the years 1945 and 1951, although Mrs. Kirkland did receive royalties on the comic books and album until 1955, and for the books for a few years thereafter.

each Saturday morning.[4] The theme of this story involves two teenagers and their father who travel through a "time vortex" into a prehistoric world. In mid-1974, NBC began issuing press releases detailing its plans for the show. Counsel for Mrs. Kirkland contacted RCA, NBC's parent company, and there was later correspondence between Mrs. Kirkland and NBC (Defendant's Exhibits L through P). However, no compromise could be reached and on February 26, 1975, plaintiff commenced this suit, alleging the common law action of unfair competition for use of the title. Following discovery, defendant moved for summary judgment.

In order for a summary judgment motion to be granted, the movant must show two things: (1) there is no genuine issue as to any material fact and (2) he is entitled to judgment as a matter of law. Fed.R.Civ. Proc. 56(c); see generally 6 Moore's Federal Practice § 56.09–56.23 (1974). It is clear that plaintiff may not rely on the conclusory allegations of her complaint when faced with this motion, Gittlemacker v. Prasse, 428 F.2d 1, 6 (3d Cir.1970); Brown v. Cliff, 341 F.Supp. 177, 179 (E.D.Pa.1972), but must "show by some admissible evidence that there is a genuine issue as to a material fact." Berry Brothers Buick, Inc. v. General Motors Corp., 257 F.Supp. 542, 545 (E.D.Pa.1966), aff'd 377 F.2d 552 (3d Cir.1967). I find no factually disputed issues which are material and accordingly resolve the instant motion solely on the questions of law.

II. THE CLAIM OF UNFAIR COMPETITION

Although nothing in the Copyright Clause of the Constitution [5] nor in the new Copyright Act itself [6] expressly precludes protection for titles under the copyright laws, it has been well-established that a copyright in literary material does not secure any right in the title itself. Duff v. The Kansas City Star Co., 299 F.2d 320, 323 (8th Cir.1962); Warner Bros. Pictures, Inc. v. Majestic Pictures Corp., 70 F.2d 310 (2d Cir.1934); Harms, Inc. v. Tops Music Enterprises, Inc. of Cal., 160 F.Supp. 77, 81 (S.D.Cal.1958); 1 Nimmer on Copyright, § 34, p. 140 (1976).[7] This protection has, in certain limited circumstances, been afforded under the trademark theory, National Lampoon, Inc. v. American Broadcasting Cos., Inc., 376 F.Supp. 733 (S.D.N.Y.), aff'd 497 F.2d 1343 (2d Cir.1974) (title as trade name); In re Cooper, 254 F.2d 611, 45

---

4. NBC does not own this program, but only licenses the right to broadcast it. In turn, NBC pays a fee to those who produce the show, Sid & Marty Krofft, a practice common in television programming.

5. Article I, § 8, cl. 8, provides that Congress shall have the power

"To promote the Progress of Science and useful Arts, by securing for limited Times to Authors and Inventors the exclusive Right to their respective Writings and Discoveries."

6. This revision, P.L. 94–553, 94th Congress, 2d Session, printed at 45 U.S.L.W. 145 (December 7, 1976), replaces in entirety Title 17 of the United States Code, originally enacted and codified on July 30, 1947.

7. See also 2 Nims, Unfair Competition and Trademarks, § 272, p. 889 (4th ed. 1947), wherein it is stated that "[t]he right secured by the copyright laws is the right to use a literary composition—the product of the mind and genius of the author—not the name or title given to it."

CCPA 923 (1938) (title for series of books), but generally, a title will be safeguarded only under a theory of unfair competition. 1 Nimmer, supra at 141; see generally, Netterville and Hirsch, Piracy and Privilege in Literary Titles, 32 S.Cal.L.Rev. 101 (1959).

Unfair competition is an equitable concept, resting on general principles of fairness in business practices. American Heritage Life Ins. Co. v. Heritage Life Ins. Co., 494 F.2d 3, 14 (5th Cir.1974). The unfair competition concept is to be distinguished from trademark or copyright infringement in that it does not involve the violation of an exclusive right to use a work, mark, or symbol, but rather involves conduct which is contrary to honest industrial and commercial practice. House of Westmore v. Denney, 151 F.2d 261, 265 (3d Cir.1945); Surgical Supply Service, Inc. v. Adler, 206 F.Supp. 564, 570 (E.D.Pa.1962). Although specific guidelines are wanting, there are at least two essentials which must be established before unfair competition can be found: secondary meaning and likelihood of confusion. I shall consider them separately.

A. Secondary Meaning

First, in order to protect a literary title from appropriation on the ground of unfair competition, the title must have attained a secondary significance or "secondary meaning." Becker v. Loew's, Inc., 133 F.2d 889, 893 (7th Cir.), cert. denied, 319 U.S. 772, 63 S.Ct. 1438, 87 L.Ed. 1720 (1943). "To establish secondary meaning, the article itself must be so clearly identified with its source that its supply from any other source is clearly calculated to deceive the public and lead it to purchase the goods of one for that of another." Zangerle & Peterson Co. v. Venice Furniture Novelty Mfg. Co., 133 F.2d 266, 270 (7th Cir.1943); Field Enterprises Educational Corp. v. Grosset & Dunlap, Inc., 256 F.Supp. 382, 388 (S.D.N.Y.1966). The plaintiff must show that the primary significance of the title in the minds of the consuming public is not in the title but the producer. Alfred Dunhill, etc. v. Kasser Dist. Prod. Corp., 350 F.Supp. 1341, 1359 (E.D.Pa.1972) aff'd 480 F.2d 917 (3d Cir.1973). Its existence is usually determined by reference to the following criteria: (1) the length of time the name or title has been used, (2) nature and extent of popularizing and advertising the name and (3) the efforts made in promoting the consciousness of the public in connecting the name or title with a particular product or literary work. Dunhill v. Kasser, supra, 350 F.Supp. at 1359; 3 Callmann, Unfair Competition, Trademarks and Monopolies, § 77.3, p. 349 (3d ed. 1969).

Having considered those factors, I conclude that "Land of the Lost" does not now have a secondary meaning. It is entirely possible that this title did have such significance between 1943 and 1950, but that significance has been lost for one simple reason: by the time this suit was filed, 24 years had elapsed since the last commercial use of the title by Mrs. Kirkland. The name is no longer primarily associated by the public with the plaintiff—not even by that portion of the public which was alive at the time of her radio show. Despite plaintiff's contention that some parents of the children now exposed to the TV show possibly possess subconscious recognition of plaintiff and her radio show, she has failed to introduce any evidence or material fact to sustain such a claim.

B. Likelihood of Confusion

Were I to find that secondary meaning did exist, plaintiff must still clear a second hurdle, i.e., defendant's use of the title has or will result in confusion of the public as to the source of the work. Dunhill v. Kasser, supra, 350 F.Supp. at 1360. It is not necessary that there be actual confusion by the public, but the mere possibility that a consumer may be misled is not enough; there must just be a likelihood of confusion. Surgical Supply Service, Inc. v. Adler, 321 F.2d 536, 539 (3d Cir.1963).

The Restatement of Torts § 729 lists the following factors as those which courts generally use to determine whether a likelihood of confusion exists:

> (a) the degree of similarity between the designation and the trade-mark or trade name in
>
>> (i) appearance;
>>
>> (ii) pronunciation of the words used;
>>
>> (iii) verbal translation of the pictures or designs involved;
>>
>> (iv) suggestion; [8]
>
> (b) the intent of the actor in adopting the designation;
>
> (c) the relation in use and manner of marketing between the goods or services marketed by the actor and those marketed by the other;
>
> (d) the degree of care likely to be exercised by purchasers.

These criteria have been adopted by the Third Circuit. Sears, Roebuck & Co. v. Johnson, 219 F.2d 590, 592 (3d Cir.1955); Robert Bruce, Inc. v. Sears, Roebuck & Co., 343 F.Supp. 1333, 1345 (E.D.Pa.1972). Having reviewed them, I conclude that there is no likelihood of confusion in this case.

First, an analysis of the relative markets utilized by both parties demonstrates that their uses are anything but competing. Of course, competition between the names or titles is not always necessary, but the uses must be more than unrelated, noncompeting and dissimilar. Dunhill v. Kasser, supra, 350 F.Supp. at 1362–63. The uncontestable fact is that plaintiff has not used this title commercially for 25 years,[9] and the market exposed to her use has changed considerably. Those

---

8. There can be no dispute that there is a one hundred percent similarity between plaintiff's title and defendant's title, and for this reason, discussion on this subsection is not necessary.

9. Although plaintiff contends to the contrary, her alleged uses do not satisfy the requirement of commercial use. See discussion infra.

children who listened to the radio show, participated in clubs, and read the comic books are now at least thirty years of age. They are not likely to be exposed to defendant's television show, since the program is designed to reach children between the ages of six and 13. Moreover, the Nielson Television Index, taken for the period September, 1974 to February, 1975, indicated that less than two percent of the United States population watching an average episode of defendant's show were even alive in 1950, the last year of commercial use by the plaintiff and two years after the last year of the radio program. Realistically speaking, it is not very likely that those young children watching the television show are doing so because they equate that show with the comic books and radio show of Mrs. Kirkland. Once again, I reject plaintiff's argument concerning the possible subconscious recollections of the parents of these children, and hold that insufficient facts have been presented to create any issue as to possible confusion on this basis.

Second, whether the prospective purchasers mentioned in section 729(d) of the Restatement are the television networks and advertisers, as asserted by defendant, or is the public, as contended by plaintiff, both agree that the key question is one of harm, and whether such purchasers need protection. Should I agree with plaintiff and hold that the public is the proper area to protect, there is no question that the possibility of harm to the public does not now exist. If television watchers tune into defendant's program because they remember plaintiff's program and discover upon viewing that the program is different, they may, as defendant suggests, simply turn off the set. They have not been harmed, unless one construes the minutes lost as damaging. Because of the facts in this case, this factor is unimportant in determining a likelihood of confusion.[12]

Finally, an examination of the actor's intent must be made. As Judge Becker noted in Robert Bruce, Inc. v. Sears, Roebuck & Co., supra, 343 F.Supp. at 1349, intent should not be viewed in the abstract, but must be balanced with the other factors of the case. He also held, however, that if the mark or name is adopted in good faith, in reliance upon the advice of counsel, and with no intent to deceive the public and cause confusion, the defendant will be relieved from liability. 343 F.Supp. at 1342.

The facts here permit no reasonable inference but that NBC's use of this title was an act of good faith. First, it must be remembered that the name of the show was picked by the producers, with minimal participation by NBC officials, and with the advice by counsel that the title was in the public domain and available for use. Second, plaintiff's contention that the one NBC official who did participate in the titled

---

12. Of course, this situation could change. For instance, if NBC or the Kroffts began marketing products for children, such as T-shirts, games, etc., based on their show, then more of an argument could be made that the potential for harm existed. However, because I find that there could be no confusion due to the vastly dissimilar markets exposed to each party's use and because of the evidence of abandonment discussed infra, such a possibility of additional products resulting from defendant's television show could still be considered unimportant.

discussions had knowledge of plaintiff's past use is unsupported by any factual allegation.[14] Finally, NBC prepared a licensing agreement for the program only after the title search had been completed by the producers.

Based upon the facts, the depositions and affidavits presented in this case, I have found no evidence of a likelihood of confusion and no intent to deceive the public or cause confusion. Accordingly, defendant's motion for summary judgment must be granted on this ground.

* * *

IV. Conclusion

Plaintiff has not established that there is a genuine factual dispute at issue with regard to the existence of a secondary meaning or the likelihood of confusion by the public. * * * Accordingly, summary judgment must be entered against her.

Questions

1. Does the lapse of 24 years between the plaintiff's last commercial use of the title, and the year when suit was filed necessarily mean that the title "is no longer primarily associated by the public with the plaintiff"? If a famous old motion picture film has not been in commercial distribution for more than 24 years, should anyone be able to appropriate the title of such film for a new work? Doesn't some significant segment of the public continue to associate the title with the original film, even if a new generation of film-goers does not? Are the facts of the above hypothetical distinguishable from the facts of the *Kirkland* case?

2. Do you agree with the court that the relative markets utilized by both parties demonstrates a lack of competition? Is not television precisely the potential market which plaintiff would naturally seek for a children's program that had been marketed through the radio medium during the 1940s before the advent of television?

3. Does the court's finding of an absence of "harm" because any misled viewer upon tuning in and discovering that the defendant's program is not that of the plaintiff, may "simply turn off the set" justify a judgment for the defendant? Would that rationale justify the producer of a new television series

---

14. Plaintiff, in 1969, attempted to sell her program to NBC by contacting George Barimo. She contends that because George Barimo knew Joe Taritero, the NBC official who participated with the Krofft's in selecting the title, there is a factual issue as to whether Barimo told Taritero of Mrs. Kirkland's program. However, she has not presented anything else to substantiate this claim and Mr. Taritero has denied that he was aware of plaintiff's use until after the title was selected (Deposition of Joseph Taritero, pp. 47–48).

Plaintiff's other argument, that references to her program were made on KYW, NBC's affiliate in Philadelphia, on two separate occasions, and thus made NBC aware of the existence of her use, must be rejected on similar grounds. Plaintiff has advanced neither authority nor facts from which I can find that the content of broadcasts from one affiliated TV station can be imputed to the knowledge of NBC, let alone the one official participating in the selection. KYW airs certain network programs offered by NBC, but the local programs produced by KYW are created without the knowledge or approval of NBC. (See Affidavit of J. Marshall Wellborn, dated December 23, 1975). Mr. Taritero has denied knowledge of the existence of Mrs. Kirkland or her program prior to selection of the title and plaintiff has not attempted to refute this.

in using the title "All In The Family" on the ground that any misled viewers would soon enough discover that the new series was not about Archie Bunker and his family, at which point they could "simply turn off the set"?

4. If factors (a), (c), and (d) of Restatement of Torts § 729 all indicate a likelihood of confusion, should a court nevertheless hold for the defendant if it further finds under factor (b) that there was no intent in adopting the designation to produce a likelihood of confusion?

5. In order to qualify as a so-called technical trademark, the words may not be merely descriptive of the goods to which they are affixed. See Restatement, Torts, Sec. 715(c); Lanham Act, Sec. 2(e)(1) (15 U.S.C.A. § 1052(e)(1)). Does a title fail to qualify because it is in this sense descriptive of the book or other work to which it is affixed? See In re Cooper, 254 F.2d 611 (CCPA 1958) (title held to be descriptive). However, words which because they are descriptive fail to qualify as technical trademarks, may acquire substantially the same protection as trade names once they have acquired a "secondary meaning". See Restatement, Torts, Sec. 716(b); Lanham Act, Sec. 2(f) (15 U.S.C.A. § 1052(f)) (the Lanham Act, however, does not use the designation "trade name" for this purpose). This, essentially, is the rationale of protection in Jackson v. Universal International Pictures, supra. Would the title of a series of books (e.g. The Hardy Boys) qualify for registration as a technical trademark? What about the title of a television series (as distinguished from the title of a particular episode)? See Lanham Act, Sec. 45 (15 U.S.C.A. § 1127): " * * * Titles, character names and other distinctive features of radio or television programs may be registered as service marks notwithstanding that they, or the programs, may advertise the goods of the sponsor." Does this permit registration of a single program?

CAPITAL FILMS CORPORATION v. CHARLES FRIES PRODUCTIONS, INC.

United States Court of Appeals, Fifth Circuit, 1980.
628 F.2d 387.

Before GOLDBERG, GARZA and REAVLEY, CIRCUIT JUDGES.

GARZA, CIRCUIT JUDGE:

I

In 1962 Falcon International Corporation (Falcon) organized for the purpose of producing and distributing motion picture films. In 1964, following the assassination of President Kennedy, Falcon produced a film entitled "The Trial of Lee Harvey Oswald" based upon the legal proceedings which might have occurred had Oswald not been murdered. The film was publicized in cities throughout the nation and advertised in the entertainment sections of several large newspapers including the New York Times and Daily Variety. The world premiere was held on April 22, 1964 at Milwaukee, Wisconsin where some 6,000 persons viewed the film. In the following weeks several thousand others viewed the film. The film was not a commercial success and was indefinitely withdrawn from distribution.

In April, 1976, in the midst of a renewed public interest in the assassination, Falcon learned that Charles Fries Productions (Appellee-

Fries), a movie production company, and the American Broadcasting Company (Appellee-ABC) planned on producing and televising a movie by the title of "The Trial of Lee Harvey Oswald". Although the Fries-ABC film presented its story in a somewhat different format than the Falcon film, it basically depicted the murder trial of Lee Harvey Oswald. Falcon contacted ABC and informed it that Falcon had produced a similar movie in 1964, bearing the same exact title and that Falcon intended to re-release the film.

A short time later, Falcon sold the film to Capital Films (Appellant-Capital). Capital undertook to distribute the movie and engaged several test showings of the film. After it became clear that ABC planned on televising its version bearing the same title, Capital filed suit for injunctive relief which was denied. The Fries-ABC film was televised in two parts in September and October of 1977.

II

Capital filed this action in Texas state district court. On July 21, 1977, the case was removed to the United States District Court under 28 U.S.C. § 1441 on the basis of diversity of citizenship under 28 U.S.C. § 1332.

Capital's initial complaint alleged unfair competition in that the title and concepts had been plagiarized from its film. On August 26, 1977, Appellees filed their motion for summary judgment in response to the claim of unfair competition. * * *

* * * the District Court granted Appellee's motion for summary judgment.

In a memorandum opinion, the District Court set out what it considered to be the two essential issues of fact of unfair competition which Capital must have created in order to withstand summary judgment. The Court held that (1) the title "The Trial of Lee Harvey Oswald" of the 1964 Falcon film must have acquired a secondary meaning and (2) that the use of the same title in the Fries-ABC movie had the likelihood of confusing the public such that it would watch the Fries-ABC movie believing it to be the 1964 movie. Regarding the first issue, the Court found that Capital has produced sufficient evidence to create a genuine issue of fact of whether the 1964 Falcon film had acquired a secondary meaning. Our review of Capital's summary judgment proof in opposition leads us to the same conclusion.

Regarding the "likelihood of confusion" issue, the Court found that Capital had failed to create a genuine issue of fact as to the likelihood of confusion in the public mind concerning the source of the Fries-ABC movie. Relying exclusively on Kirkland v. National Broadcasting Co. Inc., 425 F.Supp. 1111 (E.D.Pa.1976), aff'd 565 F.2d 152 (3rd Cir.1977), the Court reasoned that any public confusion would only be "momentary" since a television viewer familiar with and expecting to see the 1964 Falcon movie would quickly realize that the two movies by the same title were not the same. The Court found that a reasonable jury could not "conclude that ABC intended to pass off its movie as Capital's movie". This holding and its underlying legal principles will be discussed below in part IV of this opinion.

* * *

IV

We have held that a remand has become necessary for procedural reasons and now turn to the issues of substantive law which should govern the case. As noted earlier, the District Court correctly held that a genuine issue of material fact existed concerning "secondary meaning". However, regarding the other element of unfair competition, the Court found that it would be impossible for a "jury to conclude that ABC intended to pass off its movie as plaintiff's movie" and, therefore, concluded there was no fact issue concerning "likelihood of confusion." Capital contends that the Court erred on the confusion issue by applying an inaccurate standard of law.[2] Capital contends that the law of unfair competition does not require that Capital show the public would be confused into believing that ABC televised the 1964 Falcon film. Instead, Capital argues that it is sufficient to show that the subsequent use by Fries-ABC of the identical title confused the public as to the source of the 1964 Falcon movie. Capital relies on the landmark case of Big O Tire Dealers, Inc. v. Goodyear Tire and Rubber Co., 408 F.Supp. 1219, 189 U.S.P.Q. 17 (D.Colo.1976), *modified on other grounds*, 561 F.2d 1365, 195 U.S.P.Q. 417 (10th Cir.1977), cert. dismissed, 434 U.S. 1052, 98 S.Ct. 905, 54 L.Ed.2d 805 (1978). The *Big O* case concerned a relatively small tire company (Big O Tire Dealers, Inc.) which introduced two lines of tires as "Big O Big Foot 60" and "Big O Big Foot 70" in the Fall of 1973. Almost a year later, Goodyear decided to use the term "Bigfoot" in a nationwide advertising campaign to promote the sale of its new polysteel radial tire. Big O Tire Dealers brought suit against Goodyear for unfair competition. The District Court charged the jury that likelihood of confusion occurs when a later user uses a tradename in a manner which is likely to cause confusion among ordinarily prudent purchasers or prospective purchasers as to the source of a product. The effect of this instruction was to permit the jury to base liability on any kind of public confusion. Big O did not claim or present any evidence showing that Goodyear intended to trade on or palm off Goodyear products as being those of Big O. Instead, Big O contended Goodyear's use of Big O's trademark created a likelihood of confusion concerning the source of Big O's "Big Foot" tires. 561 F.2d at 1371. Goodyear argued that liability could not be imposed without a showing that Goodyear intended to trade on the goodwill of Big O or to palm off Goodyear products as being those of Big O. 561 F.2d at 1372. The Tenth Circuit posed the issue quite well:

---

2. The District Court also held that "likelihood of confusion" is a separate element of unfair competition to be proven from scratch. Capital argues that "likelihood of confusion" is an inevitable result of "secondary meaning" in cases of identical movie titles. However, application of the doctrine of Reverse Confusion to this case makes it unnecessary for us to address this issue.

The facts of this case are different from the usual trademark infringement case. As the trial judge stated, the usual trademark infringement case involves a claim by a plaintiff with a substantial investment in a well established trademark. The plaintiff would seek recovery for the loss of income resulting from a second user attempting to trade on the goodwill associated with that established mark by suggesting to the consuming public that his product comes from the same origin as the plaintiff's product. The instant case, however, involves reverse confusion wherein the infringer's use of plaintiff's mark results in confusion as to the origin of plaintiff's product. 561 F.2d at 1371.

In affirming the District Court, the Tenth Circuit adopted the rationale and language of Judge Matsch's response to Goodyear's argument:

The logical consequence of accepting Goodyear's position would be the immunization from unfair competition liability of a company with a well established trade name and with the economic power to advertise extensively for a product name taken from a competitor. If the law is to limit recovery to passing off, anyone with adequate size and resources can adopt any trademark and develop a new meaning for that trademark as identification of the second user's products. The activities of Goodyear in this case are unquestionably unfair competition through an improper use of a trademark and that must be actionable. 408 F.Supp. at 1236.

* * * Reverse Confusion has now become a recognized doctrine within the scope of unfair competition, and we see no reason why it should not be applied in this case unless the law of Texas—the forum of this case—would prevent its application.

* * *

We * * * conclude that nothing in the jurisprudence of Texas prohibits the application of the doctrine of Reverse Confusion and upon remand of this case, the District Court should apply it in this case.

* * *

Questions

1. In order for the first user of a title to assert a "reverse confusion" theory as against a second user, is it necessary that the first user prove secondary meaning? Should such secondary meaning relate to the plaintiff's work or to the defendant's work?

2. Does the "reverse confusion" theory amount to protection against "misappropriation" of a title? Is it the equivalent of investing the first user of a title with a property right in such title? Is such a misappropriation or property right created by state law subject to federal preemption under Sec. 301 of the Copyright Act? Is a title a "work of authorship" within the meaning of Sec. 301(a)? Is it part of such a work?

3. In 1957 Paramount and Cecil B. De Mille produced and released a multi-million dollar motion picture based upon the story of Moses, and entitled "The Ten Commandments". The motion picture was widely publicized, and the public undoubtedly associated the title with the De Mille motion picture. Just after this film was released a "low budget" motion picture with a biblical setting was also released under the title "The Ten Commandments". Could the producer of the low budget film have defended an unfair competition action on the ground that the secondary meaning of the title "The Ten Commandments"

did not refer *exclusively* to the Paramount motion picture, in that it also refers to the Bible? See Gordon v. Warner Bros. Pictures Inc., 269 Cal.App.2d 31, 74 Cal.Rptr. 499 (1969). Similarly, if Walt Disney Productions could establish a secondary meaning for its motion picture "Alice in Wonderland", could anyone else nevertheless make a motion picture using the same title on the ground that the Disney secondary meaning is not exclusive since the title also bears a secondary meaning to the public domain Lewis Carroll story upon which both films are based? See Walt Disney Productions, Inc. v. Souvaine Selective Pictures, 192 F.2d 856 (2d Cir.1951). Is the "Alice in Wonderland" situation distinguishable from "The Ten Commandments" incident?

C. CHARACTERS

WARNER BROTHERS PICTURES, INC. v. COLUMBIA BROADCASTING SYSTEM, INC.

United States Court of Appeals, Ninth Circuit, 1954.
216 F.2d 945.

STEPHENS, CIRCUIT JUDGE.

[The first portion of this opinion is set forth at p. 74 supra.]

Warner claims the radio broadcasts, "The Adventures of Sam Spade" and the "Suspense" broadcast of "The Kandy Tooth", and others, wherein the characters of the Falcon were used by name and their peculiarities, constituted unfair use and competition. The trial court found against such contention and we think the conclusion does not constitute clear error.

It is patent that the characters of The Maltese Falcon could not fairly be used in such a manner as to cause the Falcon to be materially lessened in its commercial worth by degrading or cheapening them so that the public would not be interested in their capers.[1] They could not be used in such a manner as to deceive the public or to "palm off" to the public the idea that they were really witnessing The Maltese Falcon when they viewed showings of the other stories.[2] We think there was no reversible error in the court's conclusions on these points.

* * *

Question

Is an unfair competition action a useful device for the protection of characters under the limitations imposed in the instant case? Is one who wishes to take another's character and use it in his own "sequel" likely to intentionally "degrade" or "cheapen" the characters as used in his own vehicle? Is one who wishes to produce such a "sequel" likely to wish the public to believe that they are seeing the original work in which the characters first appeared, rather than a sequel?

1. Manners v. Morosco, 1919, 252 U.S. 317, 40 S.Ct. 335, 64 L.Ed. 590; Harper Brothers v. Klaw, D.C.1916, 232 F. 609.

2. Stork Restaurant v. Sahati, 9 Cir., 166 F.2d 348; Lone Ranger v. Cox, 4 Cir., 124 F.2d 650.

560 UNFAIR COMPETITION Ch. 11

Collateral Reference

Note, *The Protection Afforded Literary and Cartoon Characters Through Trademark, Unfair Competition, and Copyright,* 68 Harv.Law Rev. 349 (1954).

DALLAS COWBOY CHEERLEADERS, INC. v. PUSSYCAT CINEMA, LIMITED

United States Court of Appeals, Second Circuit, 1979.
604 F.2d 200.

Before MULLIGAN, TIMBERS and VAN GRAAFEILAND, CIRCUIT JUDGES.

VAN GRAAFEILAND, CIRCUIT JUDGE:

This is an appeal from orders of the United States District Court for the Southern District of New York granting plaintiff's motions for a preliminary injunction prohibiting Pussycat Cinema, Ltd., and Michael Zaffarano from distributing or exhibiting the motion picture "Debbie Does Dallas." On March 14 this Court granted defendants' motion to stay the injunction and ordered an expedited appeal. The case was argued before us on April 6, following which we dissolved the stay and reinstated the preliminary injunction. We now affirm the orders of the district court.

Plaintiff in this trademark infringement action is Dallas Cowboys Cheerleaders, Inc., a wholly owned subsidiary of the Dallas Cowboys

Football Club, Inc. Plaintiff employs thirty-six women who perform dance and cheerleading routines at Dallas Cowboys football games. The cheerleaders have appeared frequently on television programs and make commercial appearances at such public events as sporting goods shows and shopping center openings. In addition, plaintiff licenses others to manufacture and distribute posters, calendars, T-shirts, and the like depicting Dallas Cowboys Cheerleaders in their uniforms. These products have enjoyed nationwide commercial success, due largely to the national exposure the Dallas Cowboys Cheerleaders have received through the news and entertainment media. Moreover, plaintiff has expended large amounts of money to acquaint the public with its uniformed cheerleaders and earns substantial revenue from their commercial appearances.

At all the football games and public events where plaintiff's cheerleaders appear and on all commercial items depicting the cheerleaders, the women are clad in plaintiff's distinctive uniform. The familiar outfit consists of white vinyl boots, white shorts, a white belt decorated with blue stars, a blue bolero blouse, and a white vest decorated with three blue stars on each side of the front and a white fringe around the bottom. In this action plaintiff asserts that it has a trademark in its uniform and that defendants have infringed and diluted that trademark in advertising and exhibiting "Debbie Does Dallas."

Pussycat Cinema, Ltd., is a New York corporation which owns a movie theatre in New York City; Zaffarano is the corporation's sole stockholder. In November 1978 the Pussycat Cinema began to show "Debbie Does Dallas," a gross and revolting sex film whose plot, to the extent that there is one, involves a cheerleader at a fictional high school, Debbie, who has been selected to become a "Texas Cowgirl."[1] In order to raise enough money to send Debbie, and eventually the entire squad, to Dallas, the cheerleaders perform sexual services for a fee. The movie consists largely of a series of scenes graphically depicting the sexual escapades of the "actors". In the movie's final scene Debbie dons a uniform strikingly similar to that worn by the Dallas Cowboys Cheerleaders and for approximately twelve minutes of film footage engages in various sex acts while clad or partially clad in the uniform. Defendants advertised the movie with marquee posters depicting Debbie in the allegedly infringing uniform and containing such captions as "Starring Ex Dallas Cowgirl Cheerleader Bambi Woods" and "You'll do more than cheer for this X Dallas Cheerleader."[2] Similar advertisements appeared in the newspapers.

Plaintiff brought this action alleging trademark infringement under section 43(a) of the Lanham Act (15 U.S.C. § 1125(a)), unfair

---

1. The official appellation of plaintiff's cheerleaders is "Dallas Cowboys Cheerleaders", but the district court found that plaintiff also has a trademark in the names "Dallas Cowgirls" and "Texas Cowgirls" which have been made popular by the media.

2. Bambi Woods, the woman who played the role of Debbie, is not now and never has been a Dallas Cowboys Cheerleader.

competition, and dilution of trademark in violation of section 368–d of the New York General Business Law. The district court, in its oral opinion of February 13, 1979, found that "plaintiff ha[d] succeeded in proving by overwhelming evidence the merits of each one of its contentions." Defendants challenge the validity of all three claims.

A preliminary issue raised by defendants is whether plaintiff has a valid trademark in its cheerleader uniform.[3] Defendants argue that the uniform is a purely functional item necessary for the performance of cheerleading routines and that it therefore is not capable of becoming a trademark. We do not quarrel with defendants' assertion that a purely functional item may not become a trademark. See In re Honeywell, Inc., 532 F.2d 180, 182–83 (C.C.P.A.1976). However, we do not agree that all of the characteristics of plaintiff's uniform serve only a functional purpose or that, because an item is in part incidentally functional, it is necessarily precluded from being designated as a trademark. Plaintiff does not claim a trademark in all clothing designed and fitted to allow free movement while performing cheerleading routines, but claims a trademark in the particular combination of colors and collocation of decorations that distinguish plaintiff's uniform from those of other squads.[4] Cf. Socony Vacuum Oil Co. v. Rosen, 108 F.2d 632, 636 (6th Cir.1940); John Wright, Inc. v. Casper Corp., 419 F.Supp. 292, 317 (E.D.Pa.1976). It is well established that, if the design of an item is nonfunctional and has acquired secondary meaning,[5] that design may become a trademark even if the item itself is functional. Ives Laboratories, Inc. v. Darby Drug Co., 601 F.2d 631, 642 (2d Cir.1979); Truck Equipment Service Co. v. Fruehauf Corp., 536 F.2d 1210, 1215 (8th Cir.), cert. denied, 429 U.S. 861, 97 S.Ct. 164, 50 L.Ed.2d 139 (1976). Moreover, when a feature of the construction of the item is arbitrary, the feature may become a trademark even though it serves a useful purpose. In re Deister Concentrator Co., 289 F.2d 496, 506, 48 C.C.P.A. 952 (1961); Fotomat Corp. v. Cochran, 437 F.Supp. 1231 (D.Kan.1977). Thus, the fact that an item serves or performs a function does not mean that it may not at the same time be capable of indicating sponsorship or origin, particularly where the decorative aspects of the item are nonfunctional. See In re Penthouse International Ltd., 565

---

3. At present plaintiff does not have a registered trademark or service mark in its uniform. However, plaintiff still may prevail if it establishes that it has a common law trademark or service mark. See Boston Professional Hockey Association v. Dallas Cap & Emblem Manufacturing, Inc., 510 F.2d 1004, 1010 (5th Cir.), cert. denied, 423 U.S. 991, 96 S.Ct. 408, 46 L.Ed.2d 312 (1975); New York General Business Law § 368–d. Whether plaintiff's uniform is considered as a trademark or a service mark, the standards for determining infringement are the same. West & Co. v. Arica Institute, Inc., 557 F.2d 338, 340 n. 1 (2d Cir.1977).

4. Plaintiff's design imparts a western flavor appropriate for a Texas cheerleading squad. The design is in no way essential to the performance of cheerleading routines and to that extent is not a functional aspect of the uniform.

5. Secondary meaning is "[t]he power of a name or other configuration to symbolize a particular business, product or company * * *." Ideal Toy Corp. v. Kenner Products Division of General Mills Fun Group, Inc., 443 F.Supp. 291, 305 n. 14 (S.D.N.Y. 1977). There is no dispute in this case that plaintiff's uniform is universally recognized as the symbol of the Dallas Cowboys Cheerleaders.

F.2d 679, 681 (Cust. & Pat.App.1977). See also In re World's Finest Chocolate, Inc., 474 F.2d 1012 (Cust. & Pat.App.1973). In the instant case the combination of the white boots, white shorts, blue blouse, and white star-studded vest and belt is an arbitrary design which makes the otherwise functional uniform trademarkable.[6]

* * *

Having found that plaintiff has a trademark in its uniform, we must determine whether the depiction of the uniform in "Debbie Does Dallas" violates that trademark. The district court found that the uniform worn in the movie and shown on the marquee closely resembled plaintiff's uniform and that the public was likely to identify it as plaintiff's uniform. Our own comparison of the two uniforms convinces us that the district court was correct, and defendants do not seriously contend that the uniform shown in the movie is not almost identical with plaintiff's. Defendant's contention is that, despite the striking similarity of the two uniforms, the public is unlikely to be confused within the meaning of section 43(a) of the Lanham Act.

Defendants assert that the Lanham Act requires confusion as to the origin of the film, and they contend that no reasonable person would believe that the film originated with plaintiff. Appellants read the confusion requirement too narrowly. In order to be confused, a consumer need not believe that the owner of the mark actually produced the item and placed it on the market. See Syntex Laboratories, Inc. v. Norwich Pharmacal Co., 437 F.2d 566, 568 (2d Cir.1971); Boston Professional Hockey Association v. Dallas Cap & Emblem Mfg., Inc., 510 F.2d 1004, 1012 (5th Cir.), cert. denied, 423 U.S. 868, 96 S.Ct. 132, 46 L.Ed.2d 98 (1975). The public's belief that the mark's owner sponsored or otherwise approved the use of the trademark satisfies the confusion requirement. In the instant case, the uniform depicted in "Debbie Does Dallas" unquestionably brings to mind the Dallas Cowboys Cheerleaders. Indeed, it is hard to believe that anyone who had seen defendants' sexually depraved film could ever thereafter disassociate it from plaintiff's cheerleaders. This association results in confusion which has "a tendency to impugn [plaintiff's services] and injure plaintiff's business reputation * * *."

Plaintiff expects to establish on trial that the public may associate it with defendants' movie and be confused into believing that plaintiff sponsored the movie, provided some of the actors, licensed defendants to use the uniform, or was in some other way connected with the production. The trademark laws are designed not only to prevent consumer confusion but also to protect "the synonymous right of a trademark owner to control his product's reputation." James Burrough Ltd. v. Sign of the Beefeater, Inc., 540 F.2d 266, 274 (7th Cir.1976) (Markey, C.J.). The district court did not err in holding that plaintiff had established a likelihood of confusion within the meaning of the Lanham Act sufficient to entitle it to a preliminary injunction and that

---

6. Although color alone is not capable of becoming a trademark, a combination of colors together with a distinctive arbitrary design may serve as a trademark. Quabaug Rubber Co. v. Fabiano Shoe Co., 567 F.2d 154, 161 (1st Cir.1977).

plaintiff had a right to preliminary relief on its claims of unfair competition and dilution. * * *

* * *

Accordingly, we affirm the orders of the district court.

* * *

Questions

1. Would the court have reached the same conclusion if defendants' motion picture had not included sexually explicit matter? Is such matter relevant to plaintiff's cause of action?

2. When the court expressed the doubt that "anyone who had seen defendants' sexually depraved film could thereafter disassociate it from plaintiff's cheerleaders," was the court merely stating that after such viewing anyone seeing plaintiff's cheerleaders would be reminded of defendants' film, or was it further stating that such viewers would believe that plaintiff was somehow associated with defendants' film? If it is the former meaning, is that sufficient to constitute a cause of action?

3. Does this case constitute authority for the protection of dress designs on an unfair competition theory?

4. When will the use of a character in a medium different from that employed by the plaintiff constitute unfair competition? See Tomlin v. Walt Disney Productions, 18 Cal.App.3d 226, 96 Cal.Rptr. 118 (1971).

EDGAR RICE BURROUGHS, INC. v. CHARLTON PUBLICATIONS, INC.

United States District Court, Southern District of New York, 1965.
243 F.Supp. 731.

[Plaintiff, the copyright owner of the "Tarzan" stories by Edgar Rice Burroughs, brought this action, claiming in its fourth count unfair competition by reason of defendants' unauthorized use of the "Tarzan" character. Defendants moved to dismiss the fourth count.]

SUGARMAN, DISTRICT JUDGE. Sears, Roebuck & Co. v. Stiffel Co., 376 U.S. 225, 84 S.Ct. 784, 11 L.Ed.2d 661 and Compco Corp. v. Day-Brite Lighting, Inc., 376 U.S. 234, 84 S.Ct. 779, 11 L.Ed.2d 669, upon which movants rely on this motion to dismiss the fourth count of the complaint, recognize that a state may, in appropriate circumstances require that precautionary steps be taken to prevent customers from being misled or confused as to the source of the goods.

The fourth count *inter alia* charges that defendants' publications were "calculated to and did represent, suggest and imply falsely and fraudulently (a) that the character and characterization of "TARZAN" and the stories in which said character appeared were, or included, the literary efforts of Edgar Rice Burroughs or (b) plaintiffs' association, sponsorship or connection with defendants' said publications * * * " thereby "deceiving, misleading and confusing the public".

A motion to dismiss for failure to state a claim should not be granted unless it appears to a certainty that the plaintiff would be entitled to no relief under any state of facts which could be proved in support of his claim. If, within the framework of the complaint, evidence may be introduced which will sustain a grant of relief to the plaintiff, the complaint is sufficient.

The motion is denied.

It is so ordered. No further order is necessary.

Question

Does the copying of a well-known character always involve the false implications alleged? If not, under what circumstances may such implications arise? Does the presence of such implications serve to avoid federal preemption under *Sears-Compco?* Under Sec. 301 of the current Copyright Act? See DC Comics, Inc. v. Filmation Associates, 486 F.Supp. 1273 (S.D.N.Y.1980) (Lanham Act protection available with respect to names and nicknames of "entertainment characters" as well as their physical appearance and costumes, but not as to their physical abilities or personal traits).

Chapter Twelve

THE PROTECTION OF IDEAS BY EXPRESS OR IMPLIED CONTRACT

DONAHUE v. ZIV TELEVISION PROGRAMS, INC.
District Court of Appeal, Second District, Division 3, California, 1966.
245 Cal.App.2d 593, 54 Cal.Rptr. 130.

KAUS, JUSTICE. After a jury had awarded plaintiffs a verdict in the sum of $250,000, the exact amount of their prayer, the trial court granted defendants' motions for a judgment notwithstanding the verdict and for a new trial. The latter order was based on the insufficiency of the evidence. Plaintiffs appealed from the judgment and the order. Defendants cross-appealed. (Calif. Rules of Court 3(a).)

The theory of plaintiffs' case was this: before and during the year 1955 they conceived an idea for a television format which they entitled "The Underwater Legion."[1] Sometime in 1955 they submitted the format in written form, together with twelve story outlines, one screenplay and a proposed budget to defendant Ziv Television Programs, Inc. It was expressly and impliedly agreed between the plaintiffs and Ziv that if Ziv used the plaintiffs' format, it would pay for it. At that time defendant Tors was a producer, employed by Ziv and shooting segments of a series called "Science Fiction Theatre." In 1956 and 1957 defendants Ziv and Tors started to produce a television program entitled "Sea Hunt" which "used, exploited and utilized" plaintiffs' format and story outlines. The show was first shown to the public in 1958. Plaintiffs never received any compensation.

Defendants denied many of the details concerning the submission, but as will presently appear, we are not concerned with that conflict in the evidence. In the main, defendants put on a fairly impressive case to the effect that the idea for "Sea Hunt" was independently conceived by Tors. On appeal they urge that their evidence to that effect is so

---

1. Actually plaintiff Donahue had the basic idea, plaintiff Ross later joined forces with him "refining" it, and plaintiff Webb had helped Donahue create the "presentation." Webb sold his interest to Donahue and Ross in 1957 for $1,100, apparently before defendants' television series went on the air and became a success.

strong that the judgment notwithstanding the verdict must be upheld on the authority of Teich v. General Mills, Inc., 170 Cal.App.2d 791, 339 P.2d 627. They also argue that there is no similarity between any "protectible" portion of plaintiffs' material and "Sea Hunt," that there is no evidence of any express contract between Ziv and plaintiffs, no evidence of any contract express or implied between Tors and plaintiffs and none that plaintiffs' format and story outlines had any market value.

The issues presented by the cross-appeal will be discussed later.

Both parties, very sensibly, make certain concessions. Plaintiffs, though not abandoning their appeal from the order granting a new trial, recognize that, there being substantial evidence in support of defendants' case, any attempt to urge error in making that order would be futile. (Gunn v. President Tank Lines, Inc., 163 Cal.App.2d 615, 617–618, 329 P.2d 1003.) Defendants admit that for the purpose of testing the correctness of the judgment n.o.v. certain conflicts in the evidence must be disregarded. Thus, defendants state in their brief and we agree: "We must accept as a basic premise that sometime in 1955 one or more of the plaintiffs had meetings with Gordon, a Ziv vice president, and submitted to him the material testified to by plaintiffs; namely, Exhibits 1 and 2 (being numerous story outlines, budget and a script of 'Rendezvous at Point Charlie') * * *." [2]

If we could agree with defendants that Teich v. General Mills, Inc., supra, 170 Cal.App.2d 791, 339 P.2d 627, compels a finding that "Sea Hunt" was independently conceived by Tors, we could avoid the other issues, but we cannot so agree. In *Teich* the plaintiff submitted a scheme to include a kit for making sun pictures as a premium with defendant's product. Defendant later distributed its product with a very similar kit. After analyzing the evidence concerning the submission the court said: "We must recognize therefore the existence of an inference of copying and use of plaintiff's idea." A judgment notwithstanding the verdict was nevertheless affirmed, the court holding that defendant's evidence to the effect that it did not use plaintiff's idea, but a similar one submitted by an advertising agency, was "clear, positive, uncontradicted and of such a nature that it cannot rationally be disbelieved * * *." (Ibid. p. 799, 339 P.2d p. 632.) (See Leonard v. Watsonville Community Hospital, 47 Cal.2d 509, 515, 305 P.2d 36.)

Just where testimony becomes "clear, positive, uncontradicted and of such a nature that it cannot rationally be disbelieved" is, of course, a matter of judgment. In *Teich* it appeared to the Court that the nature of defendant's testimony, coming in large part from third parties, had the requisite qualities. There was correspondence, stipulated to be genuine, which clearly indicated that General Mills got the idea for the kit from the advertising agency. In the present case the defense is not nearly as compelling. Without in any way intimating our own evalua-

---

2. Exhibit 3 is also entitled "Rendezvous at Point Charlie" but is a rather different version of the script submitted. Exhibit 3 formed the basis of plaintiffs' pilot film.

tion of the evidence—we have already indicated that the defense had an impressive case—it simply does not measure up to the quality of the evidence in *Teich*. To a very large extent Tors' recital of his interest in underwater backgrounds was uncorroborated. Some of the written material he produced to prove this interest could have been gathered after the event. His testimony differed sharply on certain points with that of plaintiffs' witnesses, whom the jury evidently believed. There is no need to further detail the vulnerability of the defense. We are quite satisfied that the judgment cannot be affirmed on the basis that independent conception was conclusively proven.

We therefore must meet the issue of whether there was substantial evidence that defendants used plaintiffs' material.

Two slightly different versions of the suggested format were before the jury. The differences are so trifling that it will suffice to copy only one:

"PRESENTATION * * *

UNDERWATER LEGION

Underwater Legion is a world organization of hand picked men who have dedicated their lives to the sea. Divers all, each one a specialist in a chosen field. They live and fight to keep the seas clean.

Johnny Neptune is the head of the International Organization of the Underwater Legion. On all jobs he takes on personally, Bomber—a big ex-frogman and the strong man of the outfit—is Johnny's right hand man. And together with Mike—a young protype of Johnny—they make an unbeatable trio.

Their home is the flagship 'Courageous', a large seagoing vessel which is equipped with every modern aid for traveling on or beneath the surface of the sea. The 'Courageous' has aqua-lungs and heavy diving suits, 3 stage and single stage compressors, radio homing devices and compasses, and underwater radio.

The 'Courageous' also has a little sister ship, the 'Dolphin', a fast two engine cruiser that works with it. The 'Dolphin' can outrun any ship afloat.

The 'Courageous' and 'Dolphin' usually lie at anchor in the harbor at San Pedro and a constant radio and sonar watch is kept on the bridge. The Underwater Legion is always in touch with the central council of the United Nations, and all local law enforcement agencies in the world. This makes the background for our stories worldwide." [3]

---

3. Strangely, neither the complaint nor plaintiffs' contentions incorporated in the pre-trial order specifically claim that the format just copied was part of the submission; rather they refer to the twelve outlines, the budget and the script. It is true, however, that an almost identical format is part of the script. Defendants at no point objected to the variance between the pleading and the proof, nor do they raise any such issue on appeal. They obviously are not prejudiced. (Desny v. Wilder, 46 Cal.2d 715, 750–751, 299 P.2d 257; Gudelj v. Gudelj, 41 Cal.2d 202, 211–212, 259 P.2d 656; Chelini v. Nieri, 32 Cal.2d 480, 486, 196 P.2d 915.)

No comparable format of "Sea Hunt" was before the jury and it therefore has to be reconstructed from various episodes of the series which are in evidence.

It appears to us that a jury could easily find that the format of "Sea Hunt" is quite similar. The list of differences is shorter than that of the similarities. The differences are: Mike Nelson, the hero, is not the head of an organization, but operates alone. However, he cooperates with other organizations, and in one episode we viewed, he trains a Florida police department to become an effective underwater police force. There are no counterparts to "Bomber" and "Mike." Nelson operates from a single boat, rather than two, and it lies at anchor at Marineland, rather than San Pedro.

The strongest similarity between "The Underwater Legion" and "Sea Hunt" lies in the "gadgetry," the use of various types of equipment for operating under water, which in turn necessitates the extensive use of underwater photography. Although underwater photography was by no means novel in 1955, the idea of a television series featuring such photography, together with use of diving equipment in an adventure series could be found to have been original.

Before 1955 skin diving had become a popular sport. It was the idea of plaintiffs that a television series which would capitalize on the increased interest in underwater life and activities could be a success. An idea which can be the subject matter of a contract need not be novel or concrete. (Chandler v. Roach, 156 Cal.App.2d 435, 319 P.2d 776.) It may be valuable to the person to whom it is disclosed simply because the disclosure takes place at the right time. The success of "Sea Hunt" tends to prove that somebody, whether it be plaintiffs or Tors, submitted a valuable idea to Ziv. Whether Ziv used plaintiffs' format or Tors' is another question, but certain evidence of similarities between some "Sea Hunt" episodes and parts of the twelve outlines and the screenplay submitted by plaintiffs may have suggested to the jury that "Sea Hunt" was based on plaintiffs' format.

Only length, but little else, would be added to this opinion were we to set down in detail what these similarities are. Those concerned know what we refer to.

We do not imply that the outlines were protectible literary property or that there was any copying as to form or manner of expression. It is just that there are enough similarities in basic plot ideas, themes, sequences and dramatic "gimmicks" that a jury might well have thought that plaintiffs' format and outlines had been submitted to Ziv as asserted by them and that it was their format which was the inspiration for "Sea Hunt," rather than Tors' alleged original idea.

Defendants' argument that "there is no substantial evidence that defendants kept or used any protectible portion of plaintiffs' material" ignores that plaintiffs' do not now claim that their material is protectible, in the sense that they can claim a common law copyright thereto. Their suit rests entirely on an express or implied promise to pay the reasonable value of the material, in other words, on a contract. The difference between these theories was noted in the dissent of then Associate Justice Traynor in Stanley v. Columbia Broadcasting System, Inc., 35 Cal.2d 653, 674, 221 P.2d 73, 85, 23 A.L.R.2d 216 ("The policy that precludes protection of an abstract idea by copyright does not prevent its protection by contract. Even though an idea is not property subject to exclusive ownership, its disclosure may be of substantial benefit to the person to whom it is disclosed. That disclosure may therefore be consideration for a promise to pay"), developed in Weitzenkorn v. Lesser, 40 Cal.2d 778, 791, 792, 256 P.2d 947 and explained at length in Desny v. Wilder, 46 Cal.2d 715, 734, 740, 299 P.2d 257. It is therefore useless to cite, as defendants do, such cases as Burtis v. Universal Pictures Co., 40 Cal.2d 823, 256 P.2d 933; Jacobs v. Medford, 210 Cal.App.2d 164, 26 Cal.Rptr. 591, and others which were not contract actions. Here, plaintiffs suggested to Ziv that it would be profitable to produce an adventure television series based on the extensive use of diving equipment and underwater photography, with a male hero whose base of operations is a boat anchored in Southern California, but whose assignments take him into many different waters. To illustrate this idea they submitted twelve story outlines and one complete script. Defendants' television series follows the format in most of its important facets and some of their episodes contained situations which a jury might have difficulty in finding as being original with them. The evidence of use of plaintiffs' idea is ample.

It is argued that there was no evidence of any express contract as to Ziv and no evidence of any contract, express or implied, as to Tors. Thus, it is implicitly conceded that there is evidence of an implied contract with respect to Ziv. However, since there seems to be so much confusion between "implied in fact" contracts and those "implied in law" and further confusion between "express contracts" and "express promises" we will set forth the evidence as to each defendant.

Plaintiff Donahue testified to a series of meetings between himself and one Gordon, a vice president of Ziv in charge of talent, whose office was in Los Angeles. Ziv's home office was in New York as was its president, a Mr. John Sinn. Asked whether during those meetings there was any discussion concerning compensation, Donahue said that "no definite figures were mentioned, except that a deal would be worked out * * *." Further: "Well, Mr. Gordon, at a meeting when Mr. Ross wasn't present, made an offer of 5% for Mr. Webb and myself and a job, 5% of the series that was to be done plus we'd both function under the Ziv Banner as employees." This offer was refused because it took no account of the plaintiff Ross.

Ross testified that at one of the meetings, when Gordon said that as far as he was concerned the series would definitely be done, subject to final approval from Mr. Sinn, Gordon said that the compensation would be "under a regular package deal that Ziv made with independent producers * * *." No figures were mentioned.

Gordon testified that the initial meeting between himself, Donahue and Webb was arranged by Bill Shiffrin, an agent.[4] He further testified as follows concerning that meeting: "A And I told them, 'There are several types of deals. There is a royalty deal, royalty payment deal.' Q What was that now—royalty payment deal? A Yes. A percentage of profit deal, a personal service deal to be determined to what extent they could contribute to the project. Q Let me get these slowly. A Profit participation. Q And the next deal? A A personal service deal depending on what they could contribute to the project, and an outright buy-out deal which in many instances constitutes a capital gains [sic]. Q You told them that? A Yes, I did. I further told them that I had no authority to make a deal and I only could make a deal if New York authorized it. Q All this was said at the first meeting? A Yes. Q There is no question in your mind about that? A To the best of my knowledge." There is also evidence that Gordon forwarded what he received from plaintiffs to Sinn in New York "as a possibility for a series." Sinn returned the covering letter with a penciled memorandum on it: "Need more info! *How much?*"[5] (Our emphasis.)

As to Tors the following evidence is significant: Ross testified that after his last conversation with Gordon he met Tors on the Ziv lot. Tors said that he had heard about "Underwater Legion" and asked him a lot of questions about it. This was in 1955. Tors thought it was one of the freshest ideas to come along "and he wanted to get in on it." He asked whether he could become a partner. A few days later Ross again met Tors on the Ziv lot. Approval from Sinn in New York was still expected. Tors told him that "New York had made him wait for months to get an okay and they would just keep him on the string this way." Tors then asked him whether any of his stories were conceivably suitable for the show which he was then producing for Ziv, "Science

---

4. There is in evidence the office copy of a letter from Gordon to Shiffrin, dated March 28, 1955, in which Gordon purports to return to Shiffrin the "prospectus" on "Underwater Legion." It contains the following paragraph: "Before our company can express further interest, I think we should sit down and talk about costs, etc. We would not be interested in just a distribution deal." From this letter the jury could have drawn several inferences favorable to plaintiffs: 1. that Gordon considered the meeting to have been one where plaintiffs had offered something valuable, although no agreement had been reached; and, 2. that plaintiffs, rather than Gordon, were telling the truth concerning the nature of the material submitted. Gordon's testimony was to the effect that all he had received from plaintiffs was a single sheet of paper containing three fragmentary story outlines with the words "Johnny Neptune" penciled across the top of the page; there was no format, no budget, no twelve outlines and no screenplay. Plaintiffs' format was entitled "Underwater Legion"; although Gordon explained that that title was used orally during the meeting, this explanation did not have to be believed and it may have struck the jury as curious that the letter should refer to the title written on a submission which Gordon says he never received. The jurors may also have felt that to dignify the piece of paper which Gordon says he did receive with the word "prospectus" was not in line with his further testimony that a prospectus is a "plan or format or outline of a proposed television series."

5. If it was plaintiffs' submission which was sent to Sinn by Gordon, which submission contained a complete budget for the show, Sinn's query, "How much?" could be inferred to relate to the compensation for those who had submitted the idea.

Fiction Theatre." It was then agreed that Tors would produce a free pilot film for "Underwater Legion" if Ross prepared a script for "Science Fiction Theatre." The script was furnished, but Tors called him two weeks later and said he did not like it. He never produced the pilot film for plaintiffs.

A pilot film was produced by plaintiffs themselves in the spring of 1956. A few months thereafter, according to the plaintiff Donahue, he and Tors first met on the ocean off Avalon.[6] In the course of that conversation Tors said that he had seen the plaintiffs' pilot film, thought it was a very good idea and that he would like to produce the series. Donahue said that he was associated with Ross as a producer. Tors replied that they could forego Ross' participating and work with Tors and that he would then see that Ziv bought the property because he, Tors, was a known functioning producer. Donahue declined. During that meeting Tors also confirmed that he had already talked to Ross. After this conversation Donahue demonstrated various types of underwater equipment including a submarine which he had along.

Tors confirmed meeting Ross on the Ziv lot. Ross told him that he had an idea for an underwater television pilot film. Tors said: "This is very close to my heart because I have been working for many years on underwater research * * *." He engaged Ross to do an underwater script for "Science Fiction Theatre," with the idea that if it was good, a new underwater series could be developed from that one episode. He never received such a script.

Tors became the producer of "Sea Hunt." His compensation was "5% of the gross" plus a salary in connection with the production of each episode.

Desny v. Wilder, 46 Cal.2d 715, 299 P.2d 257, lays down several rules:

1. Recovery for the use of an idea must be based on a true contract which the court, were it not for precedent (ibid. p. 735, 299 P.2d 257), would prefer to call an express contract, which may be proved by either express promises or by "circumstantial evidence."[7] (Ibid. p. 738, fn. 9, 299 P.2d 257.) The court recognizes, however, that usage and the Civil Code (§ 1621) have established the term "implied-in-fact" for express contracts proved by circumstantial evidence.

2. These contracts are to be distinguished from "implied-in-law" contracts or quasi-contracts which are imposed by the law for the

---

6. This is corroborated by Tors as far as the fact of the meeting is concerned. The conversation is, however, denied. Donahue later testified that he had shown the pilot film to Gordon at Ziv and left a copy there.

7. In Weitzenkorn v. Lesser, 40 Cal.2d 778, 794, 256 P.2d 947, 959, the court said: "The only distinction between an implied-in-fact contract and an express contract is that, in the former, the promise is not expressed in words but is implied from the promisor's *conduct*." (Emphasis ours.) To speak of "conduct" rather than "circumstantial evidence" is probably more precise since the distinction between express and implied-in-fact contracts does not lie in the method of proof but the manner in which the terms of the contract are manifested. (Civ.Code §§ 1620, 1621.)

purpose of bringing about justice without reference to the intention of the parties. (Ibid. p. 735, 299 P.2d 257.)

3. There are, however, certain situations where the law will recognize a true contract, although the transaction is not consensual. Examples are given on page 736, 299 P.2d on page 268 of the opinion, such as Professor Williston's buyer who goes into a store, is told the price of an article, takes it and says: "I decline to pay the price you ask, but will take it at its fair value." Such a buyer is held liable for the price asked.[8]

4. Recovery for the use of an idea must be based either on an express or an implied in fact contract. (Ibid. pp. 732–734, 299 P.2d 257.) This had already been established in Weitzenkorn v. Lesser, 40 Cal.2d 778, 789, 791–792, 256 P.2d 947. The law will not imply a promise, never made expressly or impliedly, to pay for something which defendant can have for the taking.

5. An express promise to pay for the conveyance of an idea which the promisor finds valuable, will be enforced although the promise is made after the conveyance, and strictly speaking the consideration for such a promise is "past," the promise being supported by moral consideration. (Desny v. Wilder, supra, 46 Cal.2d at 738, 299 P.2d 257; Civ.Code § 1606.)

6. If the discloser of the idea must rely on circumstances to prove a promise, the mere fact "that the idea has been conveyed, is valuable, and has been used for profit," is insufficient. (Ibid. p. 739, 299 P.2d p. 270.) The circumstances preceding and attending disclosure, together with the conduct of the offeree acting with knowledge of the circumstances must furnish the evidence of a promise implied in fact. " * * * if the idea purveyor has clearly conditioned his offer to convey the idea upon an obligation to pay for it if it is used by the offeree and the offeree, knowing the condition before he knows the idea, voluntarily accepts its disclosure (necessarily on the specified basis) and finds it valuable and uses it, the law will either apply the objective test * * * and hold that the parties have made an express (sometimes called implied-in-fact) contract, or under those circumstances, as some writers view it, the law itself, to prevent fraud and unjust enrichment, will imply a promise to compensate." (Ibid. p. 739, 299 P.2d p. 270.)[9]

---

8. If we accept the modern theory that contracts are formed not because there is a "meeting of the minds," but because the parties' objective words and acts are themselves the basis of contractual liability, rather than evidence of the required state of mind, it is evident that such contracts are not in a separate category at all. Indeed the two articles referred to by the Supreme Court in Desny v. Wilder-Williston, Mutual Assent in the Formation of Contracts, 14 Ill.L.Rev. 25, and Costigan, Implied-in-Fact Contracts and Mutual Assent, 33 Harv.L. Rev. 376—agree that these "no-meeting-of-the-minds express contracts" are true contracts. Since California does accept the objective theory of contract formation—King v. Stanley, 32 Cal.2d 584, 591, 197 P.2d 321—we believe that the formulation of the difference between express and implied in fact contracts of *Weitzenkorn* is more accurate than that of *Desny*.

9. We believe the last portion of the above quotation has caused at least one writer (Kaplan, Further Remarks on Compensation For Ideas in California, 46 Cal.L. Rev. 699, 711, fn. 48) to "confess to a linger-

7. Although the purveyor of the idea conditions his offer to disclose on an obligation to pay for it, he to whom it is disclosed must have an opportunity to reject disclosure on the terms offered. "The idea man who blurts out his idea without having first made his bargain has no one but himself to blame for the loss of his bargaining power." (Ibid. p. 739, 299 P.2d p. 270.)

It seems clear to us that "the circumstances preceding and attending disclosure" support the implied finding of the jury that there was a contract as to Ziv. Admittedly, the first contact between Gordon and plaintiffs was through an appointment set up by Shiffrin, an agent. This fact alone must have indicated to Gordon that the persons whom the agent brought together with him were not social callers. The many instances where compensation was discussed between Gordon and the plaintiffs are strong evidence that Gordon realized all along that plaintiffs expected to be paid for their idea. Otherwise we would have to assume that although their undisclosed hope of being compensated came as a surprise to him and he was under no legal obligation to pay, he nevertheless, without demur, talked money.

With respect to Tors the situation is radically different. Although plaintiffs might have proceeded against him on various theories, such as breach of a confidential relationship (Thompson v. California Brewing Co., 150 Cal.App.2d 469, 474, 310 P.2d 436) or inducing a breach of contract (Imperial Ice Co. v. Rossier, 18 Cal.2d 33, 112 P.2d 631), they chose to proceed only on a breach of contract theory.[10] Construing the evidence most favorably, there is a submission to Ziv, an implied promise by Ziv to pay if the idea was used, and a later employment of Tors under circumstances which indicate that at the time of the employment Tors was aware of Ziv's obligation to plaintiffs. There is no evidence that he was a partner of or joint venturer with Ziv. He worked for Ziv on a salary plus a participation in the "gross." There is nothing to indicate that he was to share in the losses and no evidence that through his contract of employment he came to own any part of the protectible property rights which Ziv acquired in "Sea Hunt." While, if plaintiffs' evidence is believed in toto, Tors' conduct may appear morally reprehensible, we see no legal way of holding him liable for the debt of Ziv. One is perhaps bedazzled by the fact that Tors not only was an employee who agreed to produce the show knowing of Ziv's obligation, but that in addition he claimed—and the jury found the claim to be false—that the format was his own creation. Yet, to hold

---

ing doubt" if in *Desny* the court is not blurring the boundary between implied-in-fact and implied-in-law contracts which had been so clearly drawn in *Weitzenkorn.* We do not share this doubt. The language clearly refers to the type of true contract of which Professor Williston's buyer is an example.

10. The complaint pleads that plaintiffs' submission was "confidential material." It is quite clear, however, that plaintiffs did not pursue Tors on any theory but express or implied contract. The only reference to a confidential relationship is a contention in plaintiffs' pre-trial statement that "a confidential relationship existed between the plaintiffs and defendants [*sic*] Ziv Television Programs, Inc." No instructions on any theory other than contract were given or requested by plaintiffs.

him liable because of that fact would be to punish him rather than to compensate plaintiffs on a theory put in issue. If the fact that Tors claims to have created the format is put aside, we can see no difference—at least on a contract theory—between him and, say, a cameraman who was hired on the same terms and who knew at the time of hiring that Ziv did not intend to keep its contract with plaintiffs. Nor can it make any difference that Tors already was an employee at the time plaintiffs negotiated with Gordon. It was not he who before or at the time of the submission impliedly promised to pay and certainly he, at no time, made any express promise; but even if we could torture his statements to Donahue and Ross into evidence of some kind of a promise made at a time when to his knowledge the idea was still in the process of being submitted in confidence, it is plain that it was Ziv and not he who used it. The truth is that throughout this litigation plaintiffs never really developed a theory of liability as to Tors and that his status as the producer of "Sea Hunt" for Ziv and as its principal witness at the trial, in some undisclosed fashion persuaded everybody that his liability, in contract, was coextensive with that of his employer.

As we say, there may be theories on which Tors could have been pursued. Since we must reverse the judgment notwithstanding the verdict with respect to Ziv, it is very tempting to reach the same result with respect to Tors and suggest to plaintiffs that they move to amend their complaint. This we cannot do. If Tors were the only defendant, it could surely not be suggested that a correct judgment notwithstanding the verdict should be reversed to give plaintiffs a chance to try it all over again on a different theory.

Defendants claim that no contract could have been created because it was at all times made clear to plaintiffs that the decision whether or not to base a show on their idea was Sinn's, and that any deal would have to be authorized by him. To go along with that suggestion as justifying the judgment notwithstanding the verdict would be to hold that Gordon, a vice president, had less authority to bind Ziv than Billy Wilder's secretary had to bind Wilder and Paramount. (See Desny v. Wilder, supra, 46 Cal.2d p. 745, 299 P.2d 257.) In any event there is evidence that Sinn made the decision to go ahead with "Sea Hunt."[11] Although defendants' evidence is that he did so when Tors revealed his idea to him, the jury did not have to accept that part. As far as the evidence to the effect that Sinn was the only person authorized to negotiate the exact terms is concerned, that is quite irrelevant in the present posture, as the law determines them. (Cook v. Thomson, 230 Cal.App.2d 866, 868, 41 Cal.Rptr. 323; Civ.Code § 1611.) The only way Sinn's asserted sole authority to deal with plaintiffs could be relevant would be by evidence that before disclosure of the idea to Gordon, it had been brought home to plaintiffs that Gordon's conduct "preceding and attending disclosure" was not what it appeared to be and that in making the disclosure they were taking a risk. If it is unfair, in an

---

11. Sinn did not testify at the trial. We do not believe that there is anything in the record to show whether he was then living and, if so, where.

idea case, to bind the defendant to a contract without giving him an opportunity to reject the proffered disclosure, it is equally unfair to let the idea man make his disclosure under circumstances which reek of authority without giving him an opportunity to refuse disclosure to someone who has no actual power to deal.

The precise point in plaintiffs' dealings with Gordon when Gordon's asserted lack of authority was mentioned to plaintiffs is by no means clear from the record. We cannot, therefore, uphold the judgment notwithstanding the verdict on the basis suggested.

It is claimed that there was no substantial evidence that plaintiffs' material had any market value. Plaintiff Ross had been in the entertainment industry for 20 years at the time of the trial. He had made many films, although he had never produced or financed a television show. He gave his reasons for his opinion which put the value of the submission at $1,000,000.

Although ideas are not property, we see no reason why the person who conceives an idea which may be the subject of contract, should not be competent to testify to its value or, perhaps more accurately, to the value of his services in disclosing it. The rule which permits an owner to testify to the value of his property (Long Beach City H. S. Dist. of Los Angeles County v. Stewart, 30 Cal.2d 763, 772–773, 185 P.2d 585, 173 A.L.R. 249) and also permits a party to testify to the value of his own services (Coogan Finance Corp. v. Beatcher, 120 Cal.App. 278, 280–281, 7 P.2d 695) is ample justification for holding Ross to have been a competent witness to the value of the submission. It has been persuasively argued that the rule of law which permits the conveyance of ideas which are "as free as air" nevertheless to be the consideration for a promise to pay for them, can be justified on the theory that what is really bargained for are the services of conveying the idea. (Nimmer on Copyright, § 169.1.) In Desny v. Wilder, 46 Cal.2d 715, 733, 299 P.2d 257, 266, the Supreme Court said: "The lawyer or doctor who applies specialized knowledge to a state of facts and gives advice for a fee is selling and conveying an idea. In doing that he is rendering a service. The lawyer and doctor have no property rights in their ideas, as such, but they do not ordinarily convey them without solicitation by client or patient."

We cannot say that there was no evidence to support a judgment for plaintiffs in some amount. In any event, there would be little justice in affirming a judgment notwithstanding the verdict on the basis that the only evidence as to damages, admitted over objection, was incompetent after all. If the trial court made a mistake in admitting Ross' testimony as to value—and we do not say that it did—it should not be able to turn around and grant a judgment notwithstanding the verdict on the basis that damages were not proven by legally competent evidence. Plaintiffs had a right to rely on the court's ruling. The proper remedy would be a new trial, which Ziv will, of course, have.

In closing this portion of our opinion, we note that we have tried to be very careful to state that the various issues discussed represented questions for the jury under the applicable principles of law. If at any point we have given the impression that plaintiffs are entitled to prevail on any issue as a matter of law, it was inadvertent.

In their cross appeal defendants make several points. We will only discuss those which are likely to be problems at the next trial.

It is claimed that the trial court abused its discretion in refusing to allow an amendment to the answer which would have pleaded the bar of the two year statute of limitations of section 339, subdivision 1 of the Code of Civil Procedure. It is further claimed that the uncontradicted evidence shows that the action would have been barred had the statute been pleaded.

Defendants filed their answer on July 18, 1960. The case was pre-tried on October 13, 1961, at which time it was set for trial for March 21, 1962. The trial date was thereafter continued from time to time. Defendants filed their notice of motion for an order allowing the filing of an amendment to the answer on July 8, 1963, at which time the case had been set for trial on July 30, 1963. The declaration of defendants' counsel which accompanied the notice of motion is set forth in full in the footnote.[12] Thompson v. California Brewing Co., 191 Cal.App.2d 506, 12 Cal.Rptr. 783, referred to in the declaration, had been decided on April 25, 1961, more than two years before the attempt to amend.

Under these circumstances we can not possibly say that the trial court abused its discretion in not allowing the amendment when defendants' first application was made or in similar rulings made at the beginning of and during the trial. While the facts of the present case are perhaps not quite as strong as those in Moss Estate Co. v. Adler, 41 Cal.2d 581, 261 P.2d 732, the language of the Supreme Court is in point. "The trial court was thus presented with a situation wherein defendant sought to file an amended answer alleging a new defense based on different facts on the eve of the trial more than a year after the original answer was filed and more than two months after she had notice of the date set for trial. Defendant was aware of the facts at the time the original answer was filed, but she gave no excuse for her delay. The original answer gave no inkling of the facts alleged in the proposed amended answer, and a continuance would have been required had leave to file been granted. Under these circumstances we cannot say

---

12. "I am one of the attorneys for the defendants in the within matter. In the course of my preparation for trial, and upon reviewing the pleadings, it appeared to me that the causes of action in the Second Amended Complaint might be barred by the provisions of Cal.Code Civ.Proc. § 339(1), as that section was applied in Thompson v. California Brewing Company, 191 Cal. App.2d 506, 12 Cal.Rptr. 783 (1961). I therefore believe that in order to allow a full trial on the merits of the matter, defendants should be allowed to amend their Answer to raise this issue." Another declaration set forth that on June 19, 1963 counsel for plaintiffs had been requested to consent to the amendment. The request was refused on June 28, 1963.

that the trial court abused its discretion in denying defendant leave to file her proposed amended answer." (Ibid. p. 586, 261 P.2d p. 735.)

The statute of limitations would have injected an entirely new issue into the case. While it is true that the evidence in the present record is uncontradicted to the effect that Ziv and Tors made the first pilot film for "Sea Hunt" in November 1956, and the second pilot in January of 1957—the complaint was filed in June 1959—that may be due to the fact that the statute of limitations not being in issue, plaintiffs produced no evidence to the contrary.

Moreover, an entirely new legal issue would have arisen. We are not nearly as certain as defendants seem to be, that the making of two pilot films is the "use" for which defendants impliedly promised to pay. What if after making the pilot films Ziv had decided that the idea was not so good after all and shelved the project? In Thompson v. California Brewing Co., supra, the "use" which was held to start the running of the statute of limitations was a test advertising campaign along the lines suggested by the plaintiff, directed to the public, a campaign which the appellate court characterized as rather extensive. (Ibid. p. 509, 12 Cal.Rptr. 783.) The first comparable use of "Sea Hunt" was the syndication of the program in January 1958, well within the statutory period.

We do not decide the legal question posed by the attempted plea. We merely point to it as justifying the trial court in exercising its discretion.

Nothing we have said is intended to preclude the trial court from entertaining another motion to amend the answer and ruling on it in accordance with established legal principles in the light of the facts as they may then be made to appear.

Defendants make various contentions with respect to certain of their instructions which were refused and some of plaintiffs' which were given. Some of the problems they raise are not likely to recur at the next trial and some are disposed of by our discussion up to this point. We will limit ourselves to the remainder.

Several of the instructions discussed by defendants refer to the significance of the alleged use by defendants of certain ideas in the script which Ross testified he gave to Tors, but which Tors said he never received. This script, in turn, was supposedly based on one of the twelve story outlines initially submitted by plaintiffs. In connection with this matter, defendants' proposed instructions and their criticism of the one that was given rest on two misconceptions: 1. the thought that because Ross testified that he gave the story to Tors, that fact is conclusively established against plaintiffs. The jury was entitled to disbelieve Ross and to believe Tors on that point.[13] (Trembley v.

---

13. If Tors did not get the story from him, it could be inferred that he saw it in Ziv's hands as part of the submission.

Benedetti, 134 Cal.App.2d 553, 555–556, 286 P.2d 426; 9 Wigmore on Evidence, § 259a; McCormick on Evidence, § 243.) 2. the theory that Tors became the "owner" of the script, if Ross' version is true. It will be recalled that Tors supposedly had promised to make a free pilot film for "Underwater Legion" in return for the script, but that he said he did not like it when he saw it. If he nevertheless used it without furnishing the promised consideration—the pilot—it is by no means clear to us that he was free to do so.

Defendants requested an instruction to the effect that defendants were liable only if they used "novel" portions of plaintiffs' submission. That such an instruction is erroneous was established in Chandler v. Roach, 156 Cal.App.2d 435, 441–442, 319 P.2d 776. As Professor Nimmer says in his great work: "Where there is an express contract for an idea which does not by its terms require that the idea in question be 'novel' there would seem to be no justification for a court to imply such a requirement. A person may well contract to pay for the disclosure of a non-novel idea, and even if the contract does not expressly negate the requirement of novelty, it is not reasonable to assume that the purchaser necessarily sought or expected novelty. The fact that subsequent to disclosure the defendant *used* the idea in itself should indicate that he sought the idea regardless of its novelty." (Nimmer on Copyright, § 173.2.)

Defendants requested an instruction to the general effect that in determining the value of plaintiffs' submission the jury was not entitled to include therein "any value of the finished product which was achieved solely as the consequence of efforts expended by Ziv * * * the plaintiffs cannot recover for the enhanced value which their material acquired as a consequence of independent efforts and expenditures * * by the defendants * * * " During the trial defendants had successfully prevented the jury from learning how much money Tors had made getting his percentage of the gross of "Sea Hunt." Plaintiffs' evidence as to value was not based on the value of "Sea Hunt." Telling juries what they may *not* do is dangerous business and we do not question the wisdom of the trial court in refusing to instruct the jury that they could not include in their award something concerning which there was no evidence, but the value of which they might attempt to guess.

Finally, defendants complain of the refusal of the court to give the instruction quoted in the footnote.[14] This instruction is a paraphrase of the language of the Supreme Court in Burtis v. Universal Pictures Co., 40 Cal.2d 823, 832–833, 256 P.2d 933, a common law copyright case. In *Burtis,* the court was concerned with a comparison "as to form and manner of expression". It only found similarities "between parts of the

---

14. "In determining whether similarity exists between the 'Sea Hunt' teleplay and plaintiffs' story or story outlines, you are not to apply the technique of dissection or expert analysis in an endeavor to locate isolated instances of similarity but you should examine the entire story in each instance to see whether one is similar to the other, and when the only similarities which appear are as the result of the dissection of the basic elements in each, there is no similarity of use which the law recognizes."

basic dramatic core of each story". That being the case, no cause of action for plagiarism was proved. We are dealing with a contract to pay for the idea for a format, if used. An instruction which directed the jury to examine a "story" would have been entirely misleading. Plaintiffs' claim does not rest on similarities between stories and such similarities as we have mentioned were used by us merely to show that there was evidence that defendants received the format in the form testified to by plaintiffs and that Ziv used it.

The judgment notwithstanding the verdict is reversed as to Ziv and affirmed as to Tors. The order granting a new trial to Ziv is affirmed. The judgment notwithstanding the verdict as to Tors having been affirmed, the order granting a new trial as to him is not effective. (Code Civ.Proc., § 629.) The appeal from the order granting him a new trial is therefore dismissed as moot. The appeal by defendants from the judgment is also dismissed. (Brignoli v. Seaboard Transportation Co., 29 Cal.2d 782, 792, 178 P.2d 445.)

SHINN, P.J., and FORD, J., concur.

Questions

1. Should ideas be regarded as "property", protectible on a copyright, or other property theory? Would such protection "promote the progress of science and useful arts", or would it stifle such progress? Is an idea, reduced to written form, a "writing" constitutionally capable of copyright protection? Would copyright protection for ideas violate the First Amendment guarantee of freedom of speech and freedom of press? See Nimmer, Does Copyright Abridge the First Amendment Guarantees of Free Speech and Free Press? 17 U.C.L.A. Law Rev. 1180 (1970).

2. With respect to contractual protection for an unprotectible idea, how do the rules differ as between an implied-in-fact promise and an express promise? Under the court's view will one who "blurts out his idea without having first made his bargain" be entitled to recover under a contract theory if after the blurting out, the idea recipient *expressly* promises to pay for the idea? What is the consideration which would support such an express promise? What are the usual limits of "moral obligation" as consideration under the law of contracts? Does the use of "moral obligation" as consideration in this context exceed those limits?

3. State the elements necessary under Desny v. Wilder, as interpreted in *Donahue,* in order for the trier of fact to be justified in finding an implied-in-fact contract obligating the recipient of an unprotectible idea to pay for its disclosure. May an idea discloser "clearly condition * * * his offer to convey the idea upon an obligation to pay for it" by conduct rather than by words? If the idea recipient "knowing the condition before he knows the idea, voluntarily accepts its disclosure", does such voluntary acceptance constitute conduct which may imply a promise to pay for the idea if it is used? What constitutes such a voluntary acceptance? Suppose A sends an unsolicited letter to B stating: "Enclosed herewith in a sealed envelope is an idea which if used by you will make us both a great deal of money". If B, after reading the letter, opens the envelope and reads the idea, and thereafter uses it, will he be contractually obligated to A?

4. Under the *Desny-Donahue* theory of implied-in-fact contract, when is the contract created, when the idea is disclosed or when it is used by the idea recipient? When does the idea recipient's duty to pay arise? Is the idea discloser the offeror or the offeree? Is the contract of a bilateral or unilateral nature? See Restatement, Contracts, Secs. 12 and 55. What practical consequences may flow from the answers to the foregoing questions? Consider the statute of limitations, and the "contracts not to be performed within one year" section of the statute of frauds. See Blaustein v. Burton, 9 Cal.App.3d 161, 88 Cal.Rptr. 319 (1970).

5. If Ziv had offered persuasive evidence that it had received a submission of a substantially similar idea from another source, would this have constituted a defense? Should it make a difference whether the other submission had been made before or after the plaintiffs' submission? See Minniear v. Tors, 266 Cal.App.2d 495, 72 Cal.Rptr. 287 (1968) in which a different plaintiff claimed to have submitted the idea of making an underwater adventure series to Ziv and Tors, and in which the court reversed the trial court's judgment of nonsuit on plaintiff's contract count. See also Mann v. Columbia Pictures, Inc., 126 Cal.App.3d 57, 178 Cal.Rptr. 500 (1981), opinion vacated 128 Cal.App.3d 628, 180 Cal.Rptr. 522 (1982).

6. Does the *Donahue* court, in rejecting the proposed instruction set forth at footnote 14, in effect hold that the copyright requirement of substantial similarity is inapplicable to an implied-in-fact contract action? Do you agree with such a conclusion? Compare Henreid v. Four Star Television, 266 Cal. App.2d 435, 72 Cal.Rptr. 223 (1968) in which the court affirmed the sustaining of defendant's demurrer to plaintiff's implied-in-fact contract action on the ground that the only similarity between the plaintiff's submission and the defendant's television series "Burke's Law" was that "both heroes travel in chauffeur-driven Rolls Royces". This the court concluded did not constitute "substantial or material similarity". If substantial similarity were a necessary element in implied-in-fact contract actions would this not render such actions meaningless since if such element can be shown would not the plaintiff prefer to rely on a copyright infringement theory? Should an idea recipient be presumed to promise to pay only if there is substantial similarity in the copyright sense?

7. Do you agree that the courts should not inject a requirement of "novelty" in an implied-in-fact contract action? The traditional view is that an idea may not be the subject of an implied-in-fact contract unless it is novel. See Masline v. New York, N.H. & H.R. Co., 95 Conn. 702, 112 Atl. 639 (1921). As *Donahue* indicates, this is no longer the view in California. In New York apparently the requirement of novelty will not be injected by the courts (if the parties have not done so) in an express contract action (Krisel v. Duran, 258 F.Supp. 845 (S.D.N.Y.1966), though the principle is less clear in implied-in-fact contract actions. Compare Fredrick Chusid & Co. v. Marshall Leeman & Co., 279 F.Supp. 913 (S.D.N.Y.1968) and Krisel v. Duran, 303 F.Supp. 573 (S.D.N.Y. 1969). Must the idea at least be "novel" to the idea recipient? Isn't this but another way of requiring that the defendant have copied the idea from the plaintiff in order to trigger contractual liability? Are some ideas so banal as not to be capable of implied-in-fact contract protection even if the idea recipient had not prior to submission considered the idea? Or should the fact that the idea recipient uses the idea (always a necessary condition to implied-in-fact contract liability) in itself render its banality irrelevant, or conclusively prove that in fact it is not banal?

8. Do you agree with Justice Kaus that Professor Williston's buyer is analogous to an idea recipient who expressly declines to pay for a submitted idea but nevertheless uses it? Is it significant that an idea is not "property"? What is the status in California of a quasi-contract action for the use of an idea in view of *Weitzenkorn, Desny,* and *Donahue?*

9. If Donahue had sued Tors for breach of a confidential relationship would he have recovered? See Nimmer on Copyright, § 16.06 (1978).

10. Does Sec. 301 of the current Copyright Act preempt the state law of contracts insofar as such law protects the submission of "ideas" for "works of authorship"? See Lear, Inc. v. Adkins, 395 U.S. 653 (1969).

Collateral References

Kaplan, *Implied Contract and the Law of Literary Property,* 42 Cal.Law Rev. 28 (1954).

Kaplan, *Further Remarks on Compensation for Ideas in California,* 46 Cal.Law Rev. 699 (1958).

Havighurst, *The Right to Compensation for an Idea,* 49 Northwestern Law Rev. 295 (1954).

Olsson, *Dreams for Sale,* 23 Law and Contemporary Problems 34 (1958).

Libott, *Round the Prickly Pear: The Idea-Expression Fallacy in a Mass Communications World,* 14 UCLA Law Rev. 735 (1967).

Nimmer on Copyright, §§ 16.04, 16.05.

BLAUSTEIN v. BURTON

District Court of Appeal, Second District Division 5, California, 1970.
9 Cal.App.3d 161, 88 Cal.Rptr. 319.

STATEMENT OF FACTS

Appellant [Julian Blaustein], in his deposition testified that he had been in the motion picture business since 1935. After serving as a reader, a story editor, the head of a story department, and an editorial supervisor, he became a producer of motion picture films in 1949. The films he has produced include Broken Arrow; Mr. 880; Half Angel; Just One More Chance; Take Care of My Little Girl; The Day the Earth Stood Still; The Outcasts of Poker Flat; Don't Bother to Knock; Desiree; The Racers; Storm Center; Cowboy; Bell, Book and Candle; The Wreck of the Mary Deare; Two Loves; The Four Horsemen of the Apocalypse, and Khartoum. * * *

During 1964, appellant conceived an idea consisting of a number of constituent elements including the following: (a) the idea of producing a motion picture based upon William Shakespeare's play, The Taming of the Shrew; (b) the idea of casting respondents Richard Burton and Elizabeth Taylor Burton as the stars of this motion picture; (c) the idea of using as the director of the motion picture Franco Zeffirelli, a stage director who at that time had never directed a motion picture and who was relatively unknown in the United States; (d) the idea of eliminating from the film version of the play the so-called "frame" i.e., the play within a play device which Shakespeare employed, and beginning the film with the main body of the story; (e) the idea of including in the film version the two key scenes (i.e., the wedding scene and the wedding night scene) which in Shakespeare's play occur offstage and are merely described by a character on stage; (f) the idea of filming the picture in Italy, in the actual Italian settings described by Shakespeare.

On April 6, 1964, appellant met with Hugh French, an established motion picture agent who was then, and was at the time of the taking of the deposition (March 20, 1968), the agent for respondent Richard Burton. Prior to such meeting, appellant knew that Mr. French was Mr. Burton's agent and Mr. French knew that appellant was a motion picture producer, as appellant and Mr. French had been involved in business dealings together in the past. At such meeting, appellant first

© 1966 Columbia Pictures Courtesy of Columbia Pictures

Defendants Elizabeth Taylor (Mrs. Burton) and Richard Burton
in *The Taming of the Shrew.*

asked Mr. French "if he could tell me anything about the availability of Mr. and Mrs. Burton." Mr. French replied: "Well, they have many commitments; but, as you know, they are always interested in good ideas or good scripts or good projects." Appellant then replied: "Well, I have a thought about a picture for the Burtons, but it makes no sense to discuss it unless you would be interested in it or unless you tell me that they would be available to consider a production beyond their current commitments." Mr. French responded: "No, indeed, I would like to hear what you have in mind." Appellant then said that he thought there would be something uniquely attractive at that time to do a film based on Shakespeare's Taming of the Shrew with respondents as the stars of the picture. Mr. French's reaction was "instantaneous and affirmative." Appellant then asked Mr. French if the idea had ever been previously discussed, and Mr. French replied no, that to his knowledge it had not been. Mr. French further stated that he would discuss appellant's idea with Mr. Burton, and would try to arrange a meeting in New York between appellant and the Burtons.

* * *

[A]ppellant met with Martin Gang on June 25, 1964. Mr. Gang at that time was appellant's lawyer. Mr. Gang's firm was also the attorneys for respondents Richard Burton and Elizabeth Taylor Burton. Aaron Frosch, a New York lawyer, acted as general counsel for Mr. and Mrs. Burton. At the meeting between appellant and Mr. Gang, appellant disclosed his above described idea, and related his dealings up to that point with Mr. French. Appellant told Mr. Gang that "Mr. French has so far been unable to arrange a meeting" with Mr. and Mrs. Burton. Mr. Gang offered to attempt to arrange such a meeting. Mr. Gang thereupon phoned Aaron Frosch and informed him of appellant's desire to meet with Mr. and Mrs. Burton and of the reasons for such a meeting. Mr. Frosch stated that he believed that he could arrange such a meeting, suggesting that appellant phone him upon appellant's arrival in New York.

Upon his arrival in New York, appellant phoned Mr. Frosch's secretary on June 29, 1964, and was told to contact Richard Hanley, appointments secretary for Mr. and Mrs. Burton. Appellant did phone Mr. Hanley, who recognized him and stated "It looks fine. Richard and Elizabeth know you are here and we will get it set up as quickly as we can." On the afternoon of June 30, 1964, Mr. Hanley phoned appellant and said: "Can you come up to see them?" Appellant proceeded to Mr. and Mrs. Burton's hotel suite, was introduced to Mr. Burton by Mr. Hanley, and then met for a period alone with Mr. Burton. Later, Mrs. Burton joined them. At the beginning of the conversation between appellant and Mr. Burton regarding The Taming of the Shrew, Mr. Burton commented upon what a good idea it was for Mrs. Burton and him to make such a motion picture, adding, "I don't know how come we hadn't thought of it."

After Mrs. Burton joined them, appellant explained in full his ideas regarding the proposed project. This included the use of Mr. Zeffirelli as the director. Mr. Burton said of Zeffirelli "I think he is a marvelous idea. The idea of who directs this picture is naturally very important, and I just think you have made a very good choice. And you have met with him?", to which appellant replied in the affirmative. They then discussed the cost of the film, and of appellant's prior discussion with Mr. Zeffirelli relative to the cost area. Mr. Burton stated "Well, certainly with you as an experienced producer, you can contribute that part of it to him." * * *

Toward the end of the meeting, Mr. Burton stated, "Well, let's plan to go ahead now. Elizabeth and I would like to do this. We think Zeffirelli is a good idea. We will accept him. You tell me you have worked out a potential deal with him." * * *

The meeting ended with a mutual expression of looking forward to working together.

After the above meeting, and before appellant left the United States, he called Martin Gang in California from New York City. In this telephone conversation, he told Mr. Gang "Look, you do whatever you think is right about structuring a deal with Aaron Frosch, and you know I am not going to be difficult about my end of this because this is a very important picture to me and I don't want you to feel that we have got to fight with anybody, whatever might come up, about any fees and my participation and so forth. It's a picture I want very badly to do, and please keep me in touch." Mr. Gang replied, "Congratulations. I will get onto it right away and keep you informed." * * *

On December 30, 1964, appellant met with Mr. Gang and Mr. Rudin in Mr. Gang's office in Los Angeles. At this meeting appellant learned that his position in the project was in jeopardy. * * *

In March 1965, a meeting was held in Dublin, Ireland, where Mr. Burton was filming another motion picture, attended by Mickey Rudin, among others. The meeting concerned The Taming of the Shrew project, including appellant's participation in connection therewith. Following this meeting, Mr. Rudin stopped off in London, en route back to Los Angeles, and on March 18, 1965, phoned appellant. In that phone conversation, Mr. Rudin stated to appellant that "[he] might not be the producer if the picture is ever made." Mr. Rudin further stated, "under any conditions, however, there would be a reward for your contribution to the project." On March 20, 1965, appellant addressed a letter to Messrs. Rudin and Gang in which he said in part: "There's no point rehashing the various elements involved; nor is there any point attempting to 'try the case', particularly with my own attorney. I realize I must simply accept whatever Aaron Frosch and you agree is proper 'reward' for my contribution. But it's important to me, Mickey, that you understand I can never consider any such payment to be a satisfactory substitute for the function that has been denied me on a project I initiated." * * *

Mr. Gang wrote to appellant on April 27, 1965, stating that Mr. Rudin had reported to him that "there is no question in anybody's mind that this was your idea, of 'Taming of the Shrew' and bringing Zeffirelli in was your idea, and this is so recognized by all the principals, including Mr. Burton and Mr. Zeffirelli."

In December 1965, appellant heard rumors of a "deal" being made for the production of The Taming of the Shrew involving the respondents and was informed by Mr. Gang that discussions to this effect were then taking place with Columbia Pictures Corporation. In a letter to Mr. Gang dated January 3, 1965, but, in fact, written and sent on January 3, 1966, appellant suggested the possibility of informing Columbia of his participation in the project, noting that "Burton has acknowledged the obligation involved," and stating, "I should imagine Columbia wouldn't hesitate to acknowledge Burton's (and Zeffirelli's) obligation to me as an obligation of the production—provided it's discussed at the proper time, which is during the negotiations of the entire deal." Mr. Gang's response to this suggestion was to advise appellant against contacting Columbia since by doing so "he might upset the possibility of any deal being made because Columbia wouldn't want to get involved in litigation, and that if he wanted to get any rewards out of it for any reason, without giving any legal opinions, that it would be best not to upset that apple cart." Appellant did not communicate with Columbia.

Thereafter, a motion picture based upon William Shakespeare's play The Taming of the Shrew was produced and exhibited commencing in or about March 1967. The motion picture stars respondents Richard Burton and Elizabeth Taylor Burton, and is directed by Franco Zeffirelli. The motion picture was financed and distributed by Columbia Pictures Corporation [although at the time of taking Mr. Gang's deposition (March 26, 1968), the formal contract between Columbia and the respondents remained to be completed.] Mr. Rudin has represented Mr. and Mrs. Burton in the negotiations with Columbia. The motion picture as completed utilizes the following ideas disclosed by appellant to respondents: (1) It is based upon the Shakespearean play The Taming of the Shrew; (2) it stars Elizabeth Taylor Burton and Richard Burton in the roles of Katherine and Petruchio, respectively; (3) the director is Franco Zeffirelli; (4) it eliminates the "frame", i.e., the play within a play device found in the original Shakespearean play, and begins with the main body of the story; and (5) it includes an enactment of the two key scenes previously referred to by appellant which in Shakespeare's play occur off-stage.

In addition, the film was photographed in Italy, although not the actual locales in Italy described by Shakespeare.

Respondents have paid no monies to appellant, nor have they accorded him any screen or advertising credit.

Respondents, while not challenging the foregoing statement of facts, except to say that they do not acquiesce in the claimed "characterizations" and "conclusions" contained therein, urge that critical facts have been omitted therefrom. These critical facts, according to respondents, as revealed by the record, are as follows: In connection with appellant's meeting on April 6, 1964, with Hugh French, motion picture agent for respondent Richard Burton, appellant, was, according to his own testimony, familiar with the function of an agent for an established star in the motion picture industry. Appellant was aware of the role usually played by an agent for an established star, which was to screen projects submitted to the star, in turn submitting them to the star for a determination of interest. If there is interest, the agent usually pursues it further on the star's behalf.

Appellant was aware that an agent for a major star cannot commit the star without the star's approval. This is the practice in very close to one hundred percent of the cases and in that sense differs from other agencies. The "few cases" in which the star permits his agent to make commitments on his behalf "are very rare."

Appellant testified in his deposition that there is nothing unique about doing Shakespeare on the screen. It has been done many times. It has been done by leading stars of the calibre of Laurence Olivier. Respondent Richard Burton has himself previously appeared in a motion picture made of Shakespeare's Hamlet. Shakespearean productions in motion picture form have been made in the United States, with leading stars, and also in England, the Soviet Union and other countries of the world.

Appellant testified that there is nothing unique about the idea of making a motion picture entitled "The Taming of the Shrew," based on Shakespeare's play of that title. Such has been done in the United States before the making of the film here in issue, and the earlier film featured in its leading roles (Petruchio and Katherine) stars who were then married to each other and who were perhaps the leading idols of the screen at the time, Mary Pickford and Douglas Fairbanks. The Pickford-Fairbanks film "The Taming of the Shrew" was done in the 1930's. The declaration of Norman B. Rudman filed in support of the motion disclosed that the earlier version of the film also (1) eliminated the "frame" (the play within a play device utilized by Shakespeare), and (2) depicted on screen the wedding night scenes which in the Shakespearean original occurs offstage and are merely described by narration. * * *

When Mr. Gang, at appellant's request, telephoned Aaron Frosch on June 25, 1964, to assist appellant in obtaining an audience with the Burtons, Mr. Frosch had already known about the proposal of the Burtons doing a film The Taming of the Shrew because of appellant's approach to Mr. Zeffirelli, who was also a client of Mr. Frosch's office. * * *

[Blaustein sued the Burtons for breach of express and implied-in-fact contracts. The trial court granted defendants' motion for summary judgment. The appellate court's discussion of the law, and its holding are omitted so that, in the problem which follows, the student can test his knowledge of the law as applied to the above stated facts.]

Problem

Applying the law expounded in Donahue v. Ziv Television Programs, Inc., supra, may it be concluded under the above Statement of Facts that Julian Blaustein entered into either an express or an implied-in-fact contract with Richard Burton and Elizabeth Taylor? If so, what was the nature of the contract? Did a contract arise out of the meeting between Blaustein and Burton's agent, Hugh French, on April 6, 1964? Did a contract arise out of the meeting between Blaustein and Burton and Taylor on June 30, 1964? Did a contract arise out of the conversation between Rudin and Blaustein on March 18, 1965? With respect to each of these transactions consider whether *all* of the following elements were present:

(1) The idea discloser informed the idea recipient in advance of disclosure that he intended to disclose an idea. (Recall that "the idea man who blurts out his idea without having first made his bargain has no one but himself to blame for the loss of his bargaining power" Desny v. Wilder, as quoted in *Donahue*).

(2) The idea discloser did not intend the disclosure as a gratuity, but rather expected to be paid in the event the idea recipient used the idea thus disclosed.

(3) In advance of disclosure the idea recipient reasonably understood that the idea discloser expected such payment if the idea were used.

(4) The idea recipient voluntarily permitted the disclosure of the idea to occur.

(5) The idea discloser in fact disclosed the idea to the idea recipient.

(6) The idea disclosed was one that had not in fact previously been considered by the idea recipient.

(7) The idea recipient in fact used the idea thus disclosed.

If all of the above elements were not present in connection with the Rudin-Blaustein conversation of March 18, 1965, is there any other basis for concluding that a binding *express* contract had been thereby created? Was Blaustein's idea "novel"? If not, does that preclude his recovery? Suppose Blaustein had suggested to Burton and Taylor the "idea" to star in all of the Shakespeare plays, not just "Taming of the Shrew", all other facts being the same. Would that have justified a different result?

YADKOE v. FIELDS

District Court of Appeal, Second District, Division 1, California, 1944.
66 Cal.App.2d 150, 151 P.2d 906.

DORAN, JUSTICE. Defendant has appealed from a judgment for $8,000 in favor of respondent, upon the verdict of a jury rendered in the court below. Plaintiff's first amended complaint, which forms the basis of this action against appellant, is stated in two counts. The pertinent allegations are as follows:

> That prior to the matters hereinafter alleged plaintiff composed, prepared and was the original author of certain literary material, consisting of a so-called "snake story" and certain other comic gags and material suitable for use in motion picture productions and in radio broadcasts; that said literary material was submitted by plaintiff to the defendant W.C. Fields for use by him, upon payment of the reasonable value thereof, in his

work as a motion picture actor and radio entertainer; that on or about September 10, 1938, said defendant acknowledged receipt by him of a portion of plaintiff's said literary material; within two (2) years last past said W.C. Fields * * * used and embodied said material in the motion picture "You Can't Cheat an Honest Man", featuring said W.C. Fields as an actor, and also used and embodied the same in certain radio programs or broadcasts featuring said W.C. Fields as the principal star and entertainer. That prior to the submission of said literary material to the defendant W.C. Fields, as above set forth, plaintiff had at no time transferred said material to any person, firm or corporation or granted permission for the use thereof, and plaintiff is now and at all times in this complaint referred to was the owner of said literary material and entitled to the sole use thereof.

That the reasonable value of the literary material above referred to was $20,000; that said material was used by defendants without any

W. C. Fields in *You Can't Cheat an Honest Man.*

payment therefor to plaintiff; that since use by defendants of said material no compensation of any kind has been paid by defendants or any of them to plaintiff; that there is now due, owing and unpaid to plaintiff from defendants and each of them the said sum of $20,000; that plaintiff has demanded said sum from said defendants, and each of them, but that said defendants have failed and refused and still fail and refuse to pay said sum or any part thereof.

There is incorporated in the second cause of action the allegations contained in the first two paragraphs of the first count, which include all the allegations above quoted, with the exception of the paragraph last above quoted. To these incorporated allegations there is added the following: "That no compensation for use of said literary material has been paid by defendants, or any of them, to plaintiff; that at no time did defendants, or any of them, obtain from plaintiff the right to make use of said literary material without compensation; that by reason of the matters herein alleged plaintiff has been damaged by defendants, and each of them, in the sum of $20,000."

Appellant's demurrer to respondent's first amended complaint was overruled; and appellant's motion for a non-suit was denied. During a discussion at the beginning of the trial, between the trial judge and counsel for both parties, as to the exact nature of the causes of action as stated in the complaint, the trial judge expressed the opinion that the entire complaint was one based upon an implied contract to pay for the reasonable value of the use of the material involved; and plaintiff's counsel agreed that that was the correct interpretation.

Respondent first communicated with appellant through a letter dated August 8, 1938, in evidence, which reads as follows:

>   43 Bock Ave Aug 8th 1938
>   Newark NJ Newark NJ

Mr. W.C. Fields:

Dear Bill:

    Enclosed find a radio script which I think suits your inimitable style of super-comedy

    To say that I rate you as the greatest of comedians is putting it mildly you old rascal you.

    There isn't a greater master of mimicry, buffoonery, or what have you on the stage, radio, or screen

    When you open up your hocus pocus, hipper dipper, strong men weep and pay their income tax.

    When I read in a daily paper that a medico tried to limit your liquid refreshment I knew the millenium was here.

    Bill without his nourishment.

    Egad! What next? Is there no Justice? Gazooks! Must an old Indian fighter turn squaw.

    When Goofus, Gufus, Hoofus and Affadufus are allegedly doing comedy on the "air," your very absence and silence is "funny."

You "Old Reprobate."

When are you coming back to us over the "ether" without an operation except on our funny bone.

What's that? "Bill" Cody "Fields" has retired from the "Fields" of comedy

Preposterous! Idiotic! Fantastic! Whatever you think the enclosed radio script is worth is O.K. with me "Bill."

Pardon a young mans brashness in addressing you so familiarly, but I know you'll understand

With sincerest best wishes to you for a long life and happy days I remain

>Sincerely yours
>Harry Yadkoe
>43 Bock Ave.
>Newark N.J.

To the foregoing letter appellant made the following reply:

>"September 9, 1938.

Mr. Harry Yadkoe

43 Bock Ave.

Newark, N.J.

Dear Harry Yadkoe:

I liked your wheezes and your treatment, which follows along the line I have been giving our dear customers. Thanks for your gay compliments and thanks for the snake story. I shall use it in conjunction with one I have either on the radio or in a picture. I am about to embark on a new radio series and if you would like to submit a couple of scripts gratis and I am able to use them, who knows, both parties being willing, we might enter into a contract. My reason for injecting the vile word "gratis" is that we get so many letters from folks who if we even answer in the negative, immediately begin suit for plagiarism. Whilst we have never had to pay off, they sometimes become irritating no end.

>Very truly yours,
>W.C. Fields (signed)
>W.C. Fields
>c/o Beyer & MacArthur Agents
>Taft Bldg.,
>Cor. Hollywood Blvd. & Vine
>Sts., Hollywood Calif.

Under date of September 23, 1938, respondent wrote appellant the following letter:

Mr. W.C. Fields

Dear Bill:

Enclosed find two scripts as per your request.

A word of advice Bill when wrestling "Hisspo" the python. He don't understand "double talk," being a little shy on grey matter, but watch him closely when he is using the double "scissors."

All kidding aside "Bill" give the folks both barrels this fall.

There's only one man belongs at the top in "radio" and "screen" and that's "Bill Fields."

Sincerely yours
Harry Yadkoe

P.S. Your letter to me was dated Sept. 9th, the envelope was postmarked Sept. 16th, I received it Sept. 21st.

Respondent wrote a third letter to appellant, as follows:

October 4, 1938

Mr. W.C. Fields

Dear Bill:

Enclosed find some scenes and dialogue for your next picture "You Can't Cheat an Honest Man."

It is perfectly suited to your manificent (sic) talent for "comedy and satire."

With best wishes,
Sincerely yours,
Harry Yadkoe

P.S. Get that contract ready, Bill.

Appellant contends that: "A careful examination of the record discloses that from the mass of material, both written and oral, which plaintiff claimed to have submitted to defendant, only four items were used by defendant." The mention of "oral material" obviously refers to the oral testimony given by respondent as to certain of the material claimed to have been submitted to appellant, and which was not produced in court by appellant. It does not appear to be contended by appellant that any of the material was submitted in other than written form. The items as listed by appellant are:

Item 1. In one script submitted, respondent referred to "Death Valley on the Mojave" and to the "borax mines." Appellant in a later radio broadcast used Death Valley as a locale to which appellant made a trip which he described in the broadcast, making references to "borax" as the basis for certain gags. However, it appears from the record that respondent made no claim that this constituted a use of respondent's material.

Item 2. In the same script, which has reference to a course of training in preparation for a wrestling bout with a python, respondent employed the following language: "Then a jog to the 'Blue Pacific' followed by the 'sheriff' (an old pal), a few pick-me-ups on the way and a swim to Catalina with a porpoise on my back (What? No Ham?) Back again and stomach exercise (with a good meal). While running back my pants caught fire from friction so I just put on an extra burst of speed and blew it out. (No, no fire department.)" In connection with this material respondent complained of the use by appellant in a subsequent radio broadcast of an episode in which appellant was swimming to Catalina Island and his bathing suit started to smoke, and in which appellant encountered an exhausted seal on the way over which appellant threw on his back and that the seal helped paddle every once in a while.

Item 3. Respondent complained of the use in the motion picture "You Can't Cheat an Honest Man," in which picture appellant played one of the principal characters, of an episode wherein a woman fainted each time that appellant mentioned snakes and on each such occasion whiskey was called for, ostensibly to be used in treating the lady, but actually for the purpose of being drunk by the character being played by appellant. In this connection, respondent testified at the trial:

A. I sent him this snake story, here, this part here—

Q. By Mr. Moore: That is Plaintiff's Exhibit 12 that you are referring to? A. Exhibit 12, yes, sir. And in addition to that I sent him some "Snake-isms" and sequences and in the sequences I have him coming home and as he comes home he starts telling, boasting how he conquered the snake, how he beat it wrestling and as he does so this woman hears the mention of snakes and faints; as she faints he gives her a drink of liquor and takes a drink of liquor himself and goes right on talking about snakes and the same thing happens and he takes another drink, and as he finishes he tries to get out and his wife goes to him and they just embrace—he sees the commotion he caused. The sequence also tells the rules how to hunt big game, never to use high-powered rifles on lions, just look them in the eye and sort of hypnotize him, that is all—crocodiles are not worthy of a big game hunter's attention, just ignore them.

Item 4. Respondent also complained of the scene in the aforesaid motion picture in which a character named Blacamon, an animal trainer, hypnotized animals, and actually ignored crocodiles. In the synopsis of the "Snake Story" which respondent testified he had sent to appellant, appears the following: "I am the big game hun*d*er of old. For many days and many nights we travel, sighting only lions, tigers and crocodiles, or crocodilly, as we of the big game say. Hunting lions is child's play. You don't shoot them, 'yes, indeedy'. You just use nature's own weapons. You look them in the eye, and Leo the Lion is yours. Aren't you 'Bwana Simba' the lion master? Tigers the same. Crocodiles, chockadillies, sissy stuff. You just ignore them, trample them underfoot, pay no attention to em."

The appeal from the judgment herein is based upon the following grounds: 1. That the trial court committed reversible error in denying defendant's motion for a non-suit. 2. That the material submitted by plaintiff was not protectible since it was not property subject to exclusive ownership and a judgment against defendant for its alleged use is against law. 3. That there is no evidence in the record of the value of the use of such material even if it were original, literary and protectible, and for that reason the judgment is against law. Appellant argues as follows: "Plaintiff's theory as stated by his counsel in open court was that plaintiff was the original author and owner of certain literary material which was used by defendant without permission and that plaintiff was entitled to the reasonable value of the use of plaintiff's material. Implicit in plaintiff's theory are the following points: a. That plaintiff's literary material was a product of the mind. b. That as such it was entitled to protection under the law. c. That defendant used a substantial part of plaintiff's literary material. d. That the use made by defendant of plaintiff's original literary material was not a 'fair use.'"

Appellant, in thus outlining the "theory," misconstrues the nature of respondent's action. The basis of the action as framed by the allegations of the complaint, and as demonstrated by the evidence, is that of an implied contract to pay for the use of respondent's material. In fact, the evidence, as shown by the correspondence above quoted, wherein appellant has expressly accepted the material submitted by respondent with his first letter, and has invited respondent to submit further material, would, to such extent, indicate an express contract, from which a promise to pay respondent for such material, if used by appellant, could reasonably be implied. The only item of agreement left unexpressed is the amount or rate of compensation to be paid respondent. The basis of the action here involved distinguishes it from the ordinary case of appropriation or misappropriation of the literary material of an author. * * *

Sufficient evidence was presented on behalf of respondent for consideration by the jury of the issues raised by the pleadings; the evidence sustains the judgment and the judgment is in accord with the law applicable to the particular facts of the case. The judgment is affirmed.

YORK, P.J., and WHITE, J., concur.

Question

Why doesn't Fields use of "the vile word 'gratis'" preclude any contractual obligation on his part? It is now rather common for motion picture and television companies, as well as other commercial recipients of ideas, to require persons wishing to submit to first sign a "release form" which customarily expressly negates any contractual relationship between the idea discloser and the idea recipient. For examples of such forms see Olsson, Dreams For Sale, 23 Law and Contemporary Problems 34, 56–58 (1958). Are there any valid grounds for the courts to refuse to enforce such release forms? Should it make a difference whether the form purports to release the recipient from copyright as well as contractual liability? See generally Nimmer on Copyright, § 16.-05[D], fn. 30.

Chapter Thirteen

DEFAMATION

Note

Aspects of Defamation Not Directly Related to Literary
and Artistic Works

In this chapter we deal with the law of defamation insofar as it arises in connection with the depiction of or reference to actual persons in literary and artistic works. For the most part, literary works in this connection refer to works of fiction or fictionalized works based upon fact, and not to purely factual works, though, of course, for copyright purposes literary works do include such factual works.

The law of defamation raises many complex issues which need not be treated here in any depth. Since we are concerned only with defamation arising out of the dissemination of literary and artistic works, we need do no more than note a number of issues that arise usually in other contexts. There is, for example, the distinction between libel and slander. This is significant because in general there may be no recovery in a slander action absent a showing of special damages except where the slander carries an imputation falling within one of the following four categories: 1. a criminal offense; 2. a loathsome disease; 3. a matter incompatible with the proper exercise of the plaintiff's business, trade, profession or office; or 4. unchastity (if the plaintiff is a woman). See Restatement of Torts, § 570 and Restatement (Second) of Torts, § 569 (Tent.Draft No. 12, 1966). On the other hand, there may be a recovery for libel without any showing of special damages regardless of whether or not the libel falls within one of the foregoing four categories. (There is, however, a lively debate as to whether special damages must be proven in order to recover in a libel action where the defamatory meaning is not apparent on the face of the publication, but must be made out by proof of extrinsic facts. This particular form of libel is known as libel "per quod". See Eldredge, The Spurious Rule of Libel Per Quod, 79 Harv.L.Rev. 733 (1966), and the reply, Prosser, More Libel Per Quod, 79 Harv.L.Rev. 1629 (1966).)

Generally the distinction between libel and slander does not become an issue in connection with the dissemination of literary and artistic works. "Libel consists of the publication of defamatory matter by written or printed words, [or] by its embodiment in physical form * * * " (Restatement of Torts, § 568(1)), while "slander consists of the publication of defamatory matter by spoken words, transitory gestures * * * " (Restatement of Torts, § 568(2).) Since, for the most part, literary and artistic works are disseminated in written or other physical form, it is libel rather than slander that usually concerns lawyers dealing with such works. The question does arise sometimes, however, within the context of radio and television broadcasts. The courts have divided on this question. Some take the view that a defamatory broadcast constitutes libel. Sorenson v. Wood, 123 Neb. 348, 243 N.W. 82 (1932); Coffey v. Midland Broadcasting Co., 8 F.Supp. 889 (D.C.Mo.1934). The New York rule apparently regards a defamatory broadcast based upon a script as libel, and other broadcasts as slander. Hartmann v. Winchell, 296 N.Y. 296, 73 N.E.2d 30 (1947), but cf. Shor v. Billingsley, 4 Misc.2d 857, 158 N.Y.S.2d 476 (1956) (broadcast without script treated as libel). Since most television broadcasts are now based upon either a motion picture film or a video tape, the rationale of the script rule (the broadcasting company's opportunity to inspect in advance and censor) would suggest that all such broadcasts fall on the libel side. California by statute (Civil Code, Sec. 46) treats all defamatory radio and television broadcasts as slander rather than libel. The American Law Institute has proposed the rule that the broadcasting of defamatory matter over radio or television be treated as libel regardless of whether or not such broadcasting is read from a manuscript. Restatement (Second) of Torts, § 568A (Tent.Draft No. 11, 1965).

The defense of truth is, of course, as applicable to defamation actions involving literary and artistic works, as it is to defamation in other contexts. (See Restatement of Torts, § 582). However, the absolute and conditional privileges which may sometimes be invoked in defamation actions usually have no application in this area. These include an absolute privilege for judicial officers, attorneys, parties, witnesses, and jurors in connection with judicial proceedings, legislators in the performance of the legislative function, governmental officers in the exercise of an executive function, and husbands and wives as to their respective spouses. (See Restatement of Torts, §§ 585–592). Similarly, the recognized conditional privileges (usually conditioned upon the publisher's actual and reasonable belief in the truth of the defamatory statement) for the most part have no application to the dissemination of literary and artistic works. Such conditional privileges attach to statements affecting an important interest of the person making the statement, or of the recipient or a third person, or possibly involving the well being of the immediate family of the person making the statement. The foregoing is a bare, and somewhat over-simplified, outline of such privileges. For their further exploration the student should consult Harper and James, The Law of Torts (Little Brown 1956), Secs. 5.21–5.27 and Restatement of Torts, §§ 593–605. In addition, there is the general doctrine of "fair comment" (Harper and James, supra, Sec. 5.28) which can on occasion arise in connection with the dissemination of literary and artistic works, and related to this is the constitutional impact of the First Amendment (see New York Times v. Sullivan, infra). Finally, note should be taken of the impact of the "equal-time" requirements of the Federal Communication Acts in connection with speeches by political candidates. Since under the Act a station may not censor the speeches of candidates, the Supreme Court has held that this results in a federal immunity for such stations from defamation liability. Farmers Education and Coop. Union of America v. WDAY, Inc., 360 U.S. 525, 3 L.Ed.2d 1407, 79 S.Ct. 1302 (1959).

Collateral References

L.H. Eldredge, *The Law of Defamation* (1978).

R.D. Sack, *Libel, Slander, and Related Problems* (1980).

A. THE NATURE OF THE INJURY

Restatement of Torts

§ 559. Defamatory Communication Defined.

A communication is defamatory if it tends so to harm the reputation of another as to lower him in the estimation of the community or to deter third persons from associating or dealing with him.

Comment:

a. The word "communication" is used to denote the fact that one person has brought an idea to the perception of another. As to the distinction between a "communication" and a "publication," see § 577.

b. Types of disparagement. Communications are often defamatory because they tend to expose another to hatred, ridicule or contempt. A defamatory communication may tend to disparage another by reflecting unfavorably upon his personal morality or integrity or it may consist of imputations which, while not affecting another's personal reputation, tend to discredit his financial standing in the community, and this is so whether or not the other is engaged in business or industry.

c. Social aversion. A communication may be defamatory of another although it has no tendency to affect adversely the other's personal or financial reputation. Thus, the imputation of certain physical and mental attributes such as disease or insanity are defamatory because they tend to deter third persons from associating with the person so characterized. Although such imputations reflect upon neither the personal nor business character of the other, they are nevertheless defamatory under the rule stated in this Section.

d. Actual harm to reputation not necessary. To be defamatory, it is not necessary that the communication actually cause harm to another's reputation or deter third persons from associating or dealing with him. Its character depends upon its general tendency to have such an effect. In a particular case it may not do so either because the other's reputation is so hopelessly bad or so unassailable that no words can affect it harmfully, or because of the lack of credibility of the defamer.

e. Standard by which defamation is determined. A communication to be defamatory need not tend to prejudice the other in the eyes of everyone in the community or of all of his associates nor even in the eyes of a majority of them. It is enough that the communication tend to prejudice him in the eyes of a substantial and respectable minority of them and that it be made to them or in a manner which makes it proper to assume that it will reach them. On the other hand it is not enough that the communication be derogatory in the view of a single individual or a very small group of persons, if the group is not large enough to constitute a substantial minority. If the communication be defamatory only in the eyes of a minority group, it must be shown that it has reached persons of that group although if it is published in a newspaper it will be presumed, unless the contrary is shown, that it was read by such persons. While defamation is not a question of majority opinion, neither is it a question of the existence of some individual or individuals with views sufficiently peculiar to regard as derogatory what the vast majority of persons regard as innocent. The fact that a communication tends to prejudice another in the eyes of even a substantial group is not enough if the group is one whose standards are so anti-social that it is not proper for the courts to recognize them. If the communication is obviously defamatory in the eyes of the community generally, the fact that the particular recipient of it does not regard it as discreditable is not controlling.

PECK v. TRIBUNE CO.

Supreme Court of the United States, 1909.
214 U.S. 185, 29 S.Ct. 554, 53 L.Ed. 960.

Mr. Justice Holmes delivered the opinion of the court:

This is an action on the case for a libel. The libel alleged is found in an advertisement printed in the defendant's newspaper, The Chicago Sunday Tribune, and, so far as is material, is as follows: "Nurse and Patients Praise Duffy's. Mrs. A. Schuman, One of Chicago's Most Capable and Experienced Nurses, Pays an Eloquent Tribute to the Great Invigorating, Life-Giving, and Curative Properties of Duffy's Pure Malt Whisky." Then followed a portrait of the plaintiff, with the words, "Mrs. A. Schuman," under it. Then, in quotation marks, "After years of constant use of your Pure Malt Whisky, both by myself and as given to patients in my capacity as nurse, I have no hesitation in recommending it as the very best tonic and stimulant for all weak and run-down conditions," etc., etc., with the words, "Mrs. A. Schuman, 1576 Mozart St., Chicago, Ill.," at the end, not in quotation marks, but conveying the notion of a signature, or at least that the words were hers. The declaration alleged that the plaintiff was not Mrs. Schuman, was not a nurse, and was a total abstainer from whisky and all spirituous liquors. There was also a count for publishing the plaintiff's likeness without leave. The defendant pleaded not guilty. At the trial, subject to exceptions, the judge excluded the plaintiff's testimony in support of her allegations just stated, and directed a verdict for the defendant. His action was sustained by the circuit court of appeals, 83 C.C.A. 202, 154 Fed. 330.

Of course, the insertion of the plaintiff's picture in the place and with the concomitants that we have described imported that she was the nurse and made the statements set forth, as rightly was decided in Wandt v. Hearst's Chicago American, 129 Wis. 419, 421, 6 L.R.A. (N.S.) 919, 116 Am.St.Rep. 959, 109 N.W. 70, 9 A. & E.Ann.Cas. 864; Morrison v. Smith, 177 N.Y. 366, 69 N.E. 725. Therefore the publication was of and concerning the plaintiff notwithstanding the presence of another fact, the name of the real signer of the certificate, if that was Mrs. Schuman, that was inconsistent, when all the facts were known, with the plaintiff's having signed or adopted it. Many might recognize the plaintiff's face without knowing her name, and those who did know it might be led to infer that she had sanctioned the publication under an alias. There was some suggestion that the defendant published the portrait by mistake, and without knowledge that it was the plaintiff's portrait, or was not what it purported to be. But the fact, if it was one, was no excuse. If the publication was libelous, the defendant took the risk. As was said of such matters by Lord Mansfield, "Whenever a man publishes, he publishes at his peril." R. v. Woodfall, Lofft, 776, 781. See further, Hearne v. Stowell, 12 Ad. & El. 719, 726; Shepheard v. Whitaker, L.R. 10 C.P. 502; Clarke v. North American Co., 203 Pa. 346, 351, 352, 53 Atl. 237. The reason is plain. A libel is harmful on its face. If a man sees fit to publish manifestly hurtful statements concerning an individual, without other justification than exists for an advertisement or a piece of news, the usual principles of tort will make him liable if the statements are false, or are true only of someone else. See Morasse v. Brochu, 151 Mass. 567, 575, 8 L.R.A. 524, 21 Am.St.Rep. 474, 25 N.E. 74.

The question, then, is whether the publication was a libel. It was held by the circuit court of appeals not to be, or, at most, to entitle the plaintiff only to nominal damages, no special damage being alleged. It was pointed out that there was no general consensus of opinion that to drink whisky is wrong, or that to be a nurse is discreditable. It might have been added that very possibly giving a certificate and the use of one's portrait in aid of an advertisement would be regarded with irony, or a stronger feeling, only by a few. But it appears to us that such inquiries are beside the point. It may be that the action for libel is of little use, but, while it is maintained, it should be governed by the general principles of tort. If the advertisement obviously would hurt the plaintiff in the estimation of an important and respectable part of the community, liability is not a question of a majority vote.

We know of no decision in which this matter is discussed upon principle. But obviously an unprivileged falsehood need not entail universal hatred to constitute a cause of action. No falsehood is thought about or even known by all the world. No conduct is hated by all. That it will be known by a large number, and will lead an appreciable fraction of that number to regard the plaintiff with contempt, is enough to do her practical harm. Thus, if a doctor were represented as advertising, the fact that it would affect his standing with others of his profession might make the representation actionable, although advertising is not reputed dishonest, and even seems to be regarded by many with pride. See Martin v. The Picayune (Martin v. Nicholson Pub. Co.) 115 La. 979, 4 L.R.A. (N.S.) 861, 40 So. 376. It seems to us impossible to say that the obvious tendency of what is imputed to the plaintiff by this advertisement is not seriously to hurt her standing with a considerable and respectable class in the community. Therefore it was the plaintiff's right to prove her case and go to the jury, and the defendant would have got all that it could ask if it had been permitted to persuade them, if it could, to take a contrary view.

Culmer v. Canby, 41 C.C.A. 302, 101 Fed. 195, 197; Twombly v. Monroe, 136 Mass. 464, 469. See Gates v. New York Recorder Co., 155 N.Y. 228, 49 N.E. 769.

It is unnecessary to consider the question whether the publication of the plaintiff's likeness was a tort *per se*. It is enough for the present case that the law should at least be prompt to recognize the injuries that may arise from an unauthorized use in connection with other facts, even if more subtilty is needed to state the wrong than is needed here. In this instance we feel no doubt.

Judgment reversed.

Questions

1. If the advertisement had falsely represented that the plaintiff smoked cigarettes rather than that she drank whiskey, would this have been libelous? Would the answer be any different today than it was in 1909?

2. If the plaintiff were falsely represented as being a Democrat when in fact she was a Republican, would this be libelous because it "hurt the plaintiff in the estimation of an important and respectable part of the community", i.e. the Republicans?

3. Would cigarette smoking, in Question 1., or being a Democrat, in Question 2., meet the Restatement standard of so harming the plaintiff's reputation "as to lower him in the estimation of the community"? Would it "deter third persons from associating or dealing with" plaintiff?

KELLY v. LOEW'S INC.

United States District Court, District of Massachusetts, 1948.
76 F.Supp. 473.

WYZANSKI, DISTRICT JUDGE. This is an action of libel brought by a commander of the United States Navy against the producer of the motion picture, They Were Expendable. The parties have waived a jury trial. The complaint refers first to the publication of the script of the cinema, and second to its exhibition at two Boston theatres, Loew's Orpheum and Loew's State, neither of which is owned by defendant. The gist of the three counts is that the portrayal of plaintiff, thinly disguised as the motion picture character, "Rusty Ryan," held him up to ridicule because it showed him engaging in conduct unbecoming an officer and gentleman. Particularly the script and the cinema are said to have shown him, in relation to naval officers and men, as headstrong, undisciplined, aggressive, resistant to orders and self-seeking, and in relation to a United States Army nurse, as unduly amorous. These portrayals are claimed to have damaged him by affecting his professional reputation and thus causing him embarrassment and mental discomfort.

Lt. Ryan (John Wayne), Lt. Davis (Donna Reed), and Lt. Brickley (Robert Montgomery) in defendant's motion picture *They Were Expendable*.

Defendant's answer raises among other points that (1) the script was never published to any one, (2) defendant is not responsible for the showing of the motion picture in the Boston theatres; (3) there is no evidence that any one who saw the picture in Boston did identify Rusty Ryan with plaintiff; (4) neither the script nor the picture holds plaintiff up to ridicule in the eyes of any respectable part of the general public or even of the narrow circle of his own profession; and (5) plaintiff has given defendant a license to portray him as he was shown in the script and in the movie.

* * * In December 1941, having attained the rank of lieutenant in the United States Navy, [plaintiff] was stationed at the United States Naval Base at Cavite in the Philippines. At the time he was unmarried. He was the executive officer to Lieutenant Bulkeley commanding Motor Torpedo Boat Squadron Three, popularly referred to as PT boats. The relationship between plaintiff and Bulkeley was respectful and cordial but not intimate—first names never being used between them. PT boats of the type they commanded had by 1941 been used in active warfare by the British, Italian and other foreign navies, but our Navy had no occasion to use them in actual combat prior to the day of Pearl Harbor. There is, however, no reason for finding that in 1941 the United States Navy was skeptical about the usefulness of PT boats or that the persons, including plaintiff, who were assigned to duty aboard such ships regarded or had any occasion to regard the assignment either as unworthy of an able man or likely to limit his opportunities to serve his country or participate in engagements that tested a man's mettle, proficiency and courage.

In the weeks immediately preceding the attack on Pearl Harbor the PT boats in the Philippines, having received indirectly from the Commander-In-Chief warnings that war was imminent, were constantly on patrol. The night before the attack, after having performed his duties, plaintiff went to the Army and Navy Club for a hearty steak dinner, topped off with brandy and a cigar. Then he retired to his bachelor quarters to sleep. Between 2:30 and 4:30 a.m. he was awakened by news of the Japanese raid on Hawaii. Immediately he reported to duty and in the next few days was under fire from Japanese planes which attacked the Philippines. In these engagements he was not wounded. However, before hostilities had been declared his finger had swollen from the bite of a tropical insect, and after the war was under way plaintiff snagged his finger on some metal, probably on the ladder of one of the boats. He first showed his finger to his bowling companion who was a doctor. Then his commanding officer learned of the injury. After Pearl Harbor day, plaintiff was ordered by Lt. Bulkeley to the Army hospital at Corregidor where he was kept as a patient for about a month and to which during a second and a third month he was required to report as an out-patient two or three times a week.

At the Army hospital there was an Army nurse, holding the rank of second lieutenant, named Peggy. She was one of about 14 nurses assigned to Corregidor where there were approximately eleven thousand men. She was a girl in her twenties of moderate girth and height who wore glasses and who while perhaps not accurately described as "cute" was undeniably attractive to the men at Corregidor.

When plaintiff entered the hospital he fell under the care of Peggy, whose authority or rank he never challenged. From time to time thereafter she ministered to his medical needs. Plaintiff and Peggy became friendly but there is no evidence that there was any romantic attachment or any amorous intimacy. * * *

After plaintiff was discharged from the hospital he participated in naval engagements of historic importance. The squadron of which Lt. Bulkeley was commander and plaintiff executive officer was assigned tasks of major significance, and never was limited to messenger duty or like routine tasks. In view of the small size of the boats and the limited availability of torpedoes, fuel oil and like supplies, the PT boats performed incredible feats of warfare.

In March 1942, the PT boats were given a mission that became world famous. Lt. Bulkeley, plaintiff and others carried from Cavite to Mindanao General MacArthur, his wife, their son, Admiral Rockwell and other high military and naval personnel. Plaintiff commanded the PT boat which transported Admiral Rockwell. The skill and bravery with which this mission was performed earned each of the PT officers and men the Silver Star.

After arriving at Mindanao the Motor Torpedo Boats continued their superb work of slowing and diminishing the effectiveness of the Japanese advance. It is possible that one of the exploits of Lt. Kelly's boat was the sinking of a Japanese cruiser of the Kuma class. Eyewitnesses ashore believed they saw the cruiser sink, but later reports of naval engagements involving the particular cruiser thought to have been sunk cast some doubt upon the reports of the eyewitnesses. Whatever may be the truth with respect to this particular incident, there is no room for controversy regarding the over-all naval success of the squadron, the danger which the officers and men faced, the casualties they bore and the heroism with which they responded in the nation's most critical hour.

Plaintiff could well testify—though unlike Aeneas he would never volunteer the statement—"Quaeque ipse miserrima vidi, Et quorum para magna fui." (II Aeneid 5). Indeed if one were to select for special notice any particular event in the history of the squadron, the selection made by defendant's attorney could hardly be bettered. Returning from a battle plaintiff's boat became fouled with some coral heads. It was attacked by four Japanese seaplanes. The planes killed or injured all except plaintiff and three other members of the crew. Plaintiff helped ashore his wounded companions, but the Japanese planes continued strafing the survivors. Acting with incredible presence of mind, dispatch and gallantry plaintiff beached his boat and saved some of his wounded companions. Those who had been lost in the battle were buried in an Anglo-American cemetery after a funeral service performed by a priest but unattended by plaintiff who had other duties to fulfill.

In the spring of 1942 the United States Navy, desiring that its officers and men in the United States should have training in the use of motor torpedo boats by officers familiar with their value in active combat, ordered Lt. Bulkeley, plaintiff and others to the naval training station at Melville, Rhode Island. The transportation from Mindanao was by airplane, and there was no time at which plaintiff offered or thought of offering to disregard his orders and surrender to another the airplane seat which he had been directed to occupy * * *.

Hardly had he reached [Rhode Island] when plaintiff was requested by an official of the United States Navy to allow himself to be interviewed by William L. White—a reputable and widely known reporter then on the staff of the periodical, Reader's Digest. Plaintiff understood that he and his fellow survivors of the PT boats were to tell their stories so that Mr. White could write a factual account for the magazine. For three and one-half days for six or seven hours a day Mr. White asked plaintiff questions. And at the end Mr. White left the station without showing his manuscript or even his notes to plaintiff.

In September or October 1942 plaintiff received an advance copy of a book called They Were Expendable written by William L. White and published by Harcourt, Brace & Co. The book begins with a foreword stating that the author was told the story "largely in the officers' quarters of the Motor Torpedo Boat Station at Melville, Rhode Island, by four young officers"; "because the navy was then keeping him [Lt. Bulkeley] so busy fulfilling his obligations as a national hero, Bulkeley had to delegate to Lieutenant Robert Bolling Kelly a major part of the task of rounding out the narrative. I think the reader will agree that the choice was wise, for Lieutenant Kelly, in addition to being a brave and competent naval officer, has a sense of narrative and a keen eye for significant detail, two attributes which may never help him in battle but which were of great value to this book." And at the end of the book there is a three page table of the real names of the "officers and enlisted personnel attached to motor torpedo boat squadron three". Thus the book purports to be and in fact is a substantially accurate report of "historical events"—as that phrase is used in the letter of December 21, 1942 to which reference is made later in this opinion. However, there is in the book some mild profanity which I attribute not to plaintiff but to Mr. White's sense of fitness.

The White book describes with historical fidelity [the events above described] * * *

Two aspects of the White account require special attention—the author's portrayal of plaintiff's relations to Peggy and of plaintiff's character as an officer.

Mr. White shows the lieutenant and nurse as friendly in a perfectly proper way, and yet with an affectionate concern for one another. Lt. Kelly's first impression of Peggy was that she had "a cute way of telling you very firmly what you had to do". They became companions and they had dates, went together to a party or two and at least once sat at the mouth of Corregidor's tunnel where "every five minutes an army truck would barge tactlessly around the curve". Before he left with the MacArthur party she called him over the signal-corps phone and though he couldn't tell her his mission, he said "I guess it's good-bye, Peggy". Often after they separated his mind went back to her, her plight at Bataan and memories of her gifts of food and drugs for an emergency. As he boarded the airplane to go to Australia he "remembered the last thing she said to me—her voice was just as clear as if it had been two seconds ago, instead of many weeks, over that signal-corps telephone in the army hut on Bataan after I had told her this was good-bye. 'Well,' she said, 'it's been awfully nice, hasn't it'".

Mr. White shows plaintiff as a man of magnificent courage and deep feeling but at no time out of control of himself. This self-restraint is indeed almost a salient characteristic. * * * In short, Mr. White's impression—like the one I myself gathered from plaintiff's appearance in court—is that he has unusual steadiness of temper.

Since the true names of the plaintiff and the others were set forth in the foreword and in the body of Mr. White's book, I find that their names and identities became widely known in book-reading communities, such as Boston and its suburbs.

Recognizing the dramatic value of the book, a score of representatives of motion picture producers approached plaintiff, who was still on duty in the continental United States, to secure his permission to portray his character and exploits on the screen. Plaintiff repeatedly refused. I find that his primary reason was his natural reserve and distaste for self-advertisement; his secondary and distinctly minor reason was that the publicity might operate to prejudice his professional career. To meet the second objection, Honorable Frank Knox, a former newspaper publisher, then Secretary of the Navy, on December 15, 1942 wrote a letter directly to plaintiff stating that the proposed motion picture "seems to be for the best interests of the Navy Department. A copy of this letter has been forwarded to the Bureau of Personnel for inclusion in your official record." Reading between the lines of that letter, plaintiff understood and I conclude that a reasonable person would have understood that the letter was the equivalent not of a command but of a peremptory preference carrying overtones of possible consequences if the writer's pleasure or displeasure were awakened by the recipient's reaction.

Even after receiving Secretary Knox's letter, plaintiff desired to limit the license which he would give defendant as the producer of the motion picture, They Were Expendable. He rejected various drafts of a proposed license which were submitted to him. Finally, on December 21, 1942 he signed a letter which he did not write and which was submitted to him by the Office of Public Relations of the United States Navy which in this instance was, I find, acting on behalf of the motion picture producer which was the intended beneficiary of the license. The text of the letter is as follows:

(Undated)

Loew's Incorporated
1540 Broadway
New York, N.Y.
Dear Sirs:—

    I am one of the Navy officers of whom Mr. White wrote in his book "They Were Expendable." You are proposing to produce this book, or your version of it, in motion pictures and television and radio performances, but the law in some of the states is that before you impersonate me or use a character that would correspond to me, you need my approval. I now waive, as to you and your assigns and licensees, all personal rights and objections to any use to be made of me or my personality which has the approval of the United States Navy. If the Navy approves, then so far as I am concerned I can be depicted or a character used that may correspond to me, in pictures, radio and television performances and their publicity, with such action, depiction, dialogue and story (fictional or actual), as passes Navy approval. As to name, any name except my exact name can be used for this character that meets Navy approval, even if it is similar to my real name.

This release is granted by me subject to your agreement that the romance shall not be elaborated beyond the portrayal of it in the book and, if possible, shall be played down; and that the historical events in the picture shall be portrayed as accurately as possible in such a screen dramatization.

Yours very truly,
s/ Robert B. Kelly

Some time passed and plaintiff's mind was on matters far removed from the motion picture world. On May 28, 1944 plaintiff married Miss Hazel Babcock Watts, who was living with her parents in their home in Malden, Massachusetts. He secured a short leave and he and his bride spent part of their honeymoon, perhaps a fortnight, in her parents' home. He met then, as he had met previously when he was courting his future wife, her family and friends who were living in the Greater Boston area.

Afterwards plaintiff and his wife went to Florida where he was officially stationed. In that Florida neighborhood defendant happened to be taking some of the "shots" for the film, They Were Expendable. Plaintiff's recollection being refreshed by hearing of that enterprise, he determined to call upon defendant's officers at Culver City, California, when, a few weeks later, he and his wife were in San Diego preparatory to plaintiff's departing for the Far East to participate in the Okinawa campaign and occupation.

On arriving in California in February 1945, plaintiff conferred with Messrs. Wead and Reed, employees of defendant. Wead was a former commander in the United States Navy who, after having been crippled in service, retired to become an employee of defendant in producing motion pictures concerned with naval subjects. Wead and Reed sent for the script of They Were Expendable. Both of them examined it. One of them, probably Reed, handed the script to the other, probably Wead, who in turn handed it to plaintiff. Wead expressed confidence that plaintiff would be satisfied with the script and suggested that plaintiff should notify him if he had any comments.

On returning to his hotel, plaintiff hastily leaved through the pages of the script. He read perhaps a third or a quarter of it, and up to them found nothing that gave him pain. In the confusion of departure, the script was put in Mrs. Kelly's bag, not in plaintiff's. Later Mrs. Kelly sent the script to her husband but he did not read it until June, 1945, after the Okinawa campaign. At once he wrote a letter of protest to defendant. Defendant's representative replied that the picture had reached the cutting stage and that it was too late to alter it, but that the representative was confident that plaintiff would be satisfied.

In January 1946, the motion picture, They Were Expendable, as produced by defendant, was exhibited in Loew's State and Loew's

Orpheum in Boston and was seen by large crowds—though there is no evidence as to any particular person or class of persons who attended the performances. Following the showing plaintiff was in the Greater Boston area and at social and like gatherings he often felt embarrassment, uneasiness and self-consciousness in seeing such acquaintances and meeting such new persons as had seen the portrayal of him in the movie. * * *

The picture, They Were Expendable, opens with the statements that it is based upon the book, They Were Expendable, by William L. White, and that it was produced under the direction of Commander John Ford, U.S.N., and with the cooperation and assistance of the United States Navy. It concludes with a list of the characters, of which in the order given by defendant, the first is "Lt. Brickley" played by Robert Montgomery and the second is "Lt. 'Rusty' Ryan" played by John Wayne. And there is the customary legend that "The events, characters, and firms depicted in this photoplay are fictitious. Any similarity to actual persons, living or dead, or to actual firms is purely coincidental."

Between the start and the end of the film the story is given in the following form. The PT boats were a new venture in 1941. Regular naval officers looked upon them with skepticism. But Brickley had great faith in them and had induced his intimate friend, Ryan, to stake his career on their future. When first reviewed by high officers in the Philippines, the squadron received such a cold reception that Ryan decided that Brickley was overenthusiastic and that the PT boats would never be recognized for their value. Immediately he went to a bar to write out his request for transfer from PT duty to destroyer duty. He was about to present the request when the announcement came in the bar that Pearl Harbor had been attacked. Ryan at once changed his mind and tore up the request for a change of assignment. They both reported to the admiral in charge of Cavite. He then gave the PT boats only messenger and ferry service. Ryan was put out; kicked a can in disgust; and showed general displeasure. However, he remained with the squadron. And shortly afterwards while dining with his fellows, he and they heard a Japanese air attack coming. All hurried to the PT boats, put them out to sea, and at once were bombed by Japanese planes. In this engagement Ryan got shrapnel in his arm.

At first Ryan ignored the arm wound. One day he and Brickley were summoned by the admiral to discuss an important combat task. Both received assignments. Ryan proposed to ignore his wound. Brickley, however, became aware of its importance and sent him to the Corregidor hospital. An attractive, slim nurse, holding the rank of second lieutenant and named " 'Sandy' Davis", ordered him to lie down and put on a blanket. At first Ryan objected and inquired as to her rank. She reminded him of her authority as a nurse. He obeyed, lay down and covered himself with a blanket. She and an orderly pulled off his trousers in a perfectly proper way. There seemed to be no sympathy between the nurse and Ryan. Another patient who was an onlooker said that every man in the hospital was fond of Sandy.

Some days later there was a dance to give the nurses some recreation. Initially Ryan, when asked by Sandy, said he didn't dance and wouldn't go to the dance. After strains of music reached him, Ryan strolled over to the dance hall. Sandy asked him if he really didn't dance. He said he did. They danced and then they went out on a porch and sat down. In the picture she nestled close to him. In the tradition of the third chapter of Genesis, the female took the lead. But so far as defendant's film shows, Ryan did no more than offer a comforting arm and hand.

The film then showed plaintiff returning to PT duty. His boat as well as others participated in stirring naval engagements, including the battle with the Japanese cruiser and the later bombardment and destruction of Ryan's PT boat by Japanese planes. In one of these scenes Ryan acts heroically saving his wounded companion from strafing by Japanese seaplanes. After that attack has concluded there is a funeral for those of Ryan's crew who died. No priest is available. So the survivors assemble in a Catholic church where Ryan as senior officer conducts the service by saying a few words and reciting a moving poem. An enlisted man, after requesting Ryan's permission, plays "Taps" on his harmonica. Overcome with emotion, Ryan leaves during the final notes of "Taps" and rushes to a neighboring bar. The proprietor is about to close for the day. Ryan seizes a bottle of liquor from the proprietor's basket, makes him re-open the bar, sits down at a table and pours out two drinks for himself. Others of the crew drink at the main bar.

In one of the intervals between the battles comes the assignment of Brickley and Ryan to carry from the Philippines dignitaries whose identity is not at first disclosed. As they are about to leave Cavite, Ryan tries to get Sandy on the telephone to say good-bye. They start talking but the connection is interrupted by the wires being torn down by army officers or men. Ryan goes to his boat. One of his juniors has the helm. When Ryan sees who the dignitaries are, he shoves his junior aside and takes the wheel. The boats safely transport the principal personages, General MacArthur and his family and an Admiral called "Blackwell".

Finally there is an order from Washington directing Brickley, Ryan and two others to return to the United States to discuss with high naval officials the value of PT boats and their performance. Brickley and Ryan are reluctant to leave their associates who have not been similarly removed from danger. But they nonetheless bid their companions farewell in a moving scene in which the Chief Boatswain's Mate who is left behind wounded says "The book doesn't mean much out here so I'm going to say: So long Brick. You've been a swell guy." Brickley replies: "So long, Irish." The Chief Boatswain's Mate Mulcahey says "So long Rusty". Ryan answers: "So long, you big Mick".

Arrived at the airport, Brickley and Ryan are given seats 27 and 28 in a plane with space for 30. At first the men who should receive spaces 29 and 30 do not appear. Two substitutes are seated. Then, as the plane is about to take off, the men originally assigned for seats 29 and 30 arrive. One of the substitutes as he leaves gives Ryan a message for home. Ryan impulsively offers the substitute his seat and says he, Ryan "has business" still to do in the Philippines—by which the audience might infer either that Ryan wants to continue fighting or that Ryan has to see Sandy. Brickley intervenes sharply asking Ryan "Who're you working for—yourself." The picture comes to an end. * *

Looked at in the broadest way, both the film and the script depict Ryan as a gallant officer, zealous to serve the nation, respectful of his superiors, companionable with his equals, considerate of his men, responsive—but not too responsive—to the charms of women. He has the striking virtues of his race—kindliness, generosity, humor, love of his fellow men, impetuous eagerness for action, exuberance of spirit. He is the sort of man that crowds like because they admire his virtues and condone his faults. They see the brave heart of the hero, the sportsmanship of the open fighter, the quick emotion of the sensitive man. And if they also see hastiness, occasional intemperance, minor infractions of rules, impatience at official blindness, they regard those as being not faults at all or the sort of faults which are the mark of the man of courageous action, the man of large heart, the man who lives by the spirit and not by the letter.

But Ryan appears somewhat differently if he is looked at in the tradition of the professional class of naval officers. He then appears an undisciplined man. Discontented with a PT boat assignment which seems to lead neither to glory nor the grave, he impatiently prepares a request for transfer. He gives vent to his feelings by kicking around cans. He reprimands men in public. He resents and at first resists the authority which an army nurse has over a patient in any army hospital. He shoves a man away from the helm of his boat. He loses his composure when conducting ceremonies for the dead. He seeks consolation for his grief not merely by going to a bar, but by requiring the bar-keep to remain open and by seizing from his possession a bottle of liquor. He fraternizes with his commanding officer and with his men. He is, until reminded of his duty, prepared to ignore the order that he return to the United States merely so that he can attend to his own personal business with a girl. Viewed from the professional aspect Ryan may be a hard fighter of noble character, but he does not measure up to the, shall I say, "regulation" model of a good officer.

On the facts as I have just stated them, these are my conclusions of law.

1. This case is properly removed into the United States District Court on the basis of diversity of citizenship. I find that plaintiff is a citizen of Massachusetts and defendant a Delaware corporation, and

there is at stake a controversy involving, exclusive of costs and interest, more than $3,000.

2. In this proceeding I am required to follow the principles of conflict of laws which prevail in the state courts of Massachusetts. Klaxon Co. v. Stentor Co., 313 U.S. 487, 61 S.Ct. 1020, 85 L.Ed. 1477; Hartmann v. Time, Inc., 3 Cir., 166 F.2d 127. The ordinary rule of conflicts invoked by Massachusetts in tort cases is to apply the law of the place of the wrong. Murphy v. Smith, 307 Mass. 64, 29 N.E.2d 726; National Fruit Product Co. v. Dwinell-Wright Co., D.C.Mass., 47 F.Supp. 499, 504.

There is no difficulty in applying that ordinary rule to count 1. That related solely to the script; and at the trial the only evidence offered of a showing of the script was evidence of a showing in California. Thus California law would be applied by Massachusetts to that transaction. Murphy v. Smith, supra.

Greater complexity arises in connection with counts 2 and 3. Complaint was made in those counts and evidence was received on those counts with respect to showings of the film itself solely in two Massachusetts theatres during specified weeks. * * *

The foregoing authorities seem to me to justify my concluding that the Massachusetts rule is that where a person who is domiciled in Massachusetts and whose chief reputation is not shown to have any particular locus complains in Massachusetts of only the circulation within Massachusetts of an alleged defamatory statement, the court applies Massachusetts law. * * *

3. With respect to the script the first serious issue is whether there was any publication at all. * * *

4. [T]he script was published only to persons in the motion picture industry. Even Wead was an employee only of defendant, not of the Navy. And a central question is, if we assume that they identified plaintiff with the character Ryan, was their opinion of him or his reputation lowered or likely to be lowered in any way by reading the script? We are in this aspect of the case concerned with what would be the opinion not of the general public nor of naval officers, nor of plaintiff himself, but of persons in the motion picture industry. There is no reason to believe that persons in that industry are peculiarly sensitive to standards of naval discipline, official propriety and etiquette. Nor is there ground for supposing that they hold cool detachment in higher esteem than warmth of heart, vigor of expression and display of intensity of feeling. Hence to that audience the publication of the script—including love scenes somewhat more torrid than those that finally appeared on the screen—was not the publication of anything that held plaintiff up to contempt, hatred or ridicule in their eyes or that lowered their estimate of plaintiff's reputation. To that audience it was not a defamatory statement. Cf. Restatement, Torts, § 559, comment (e), p. 142, lines 3–9; § 569, comment (d); § 614(2).

5. Nor on this record can it be successfully contended that regardless of the views of persons in the motion picture industry, the script was defamatory per se because it depicted plaintiff as engaged in unlawful conduct. It is conceivable that Rusty Ryan by action, gesture or word, may have violated a regulation adopted by the Navy pursuant to statute, and may thus have committed an offense punishable by court-martial. But the pleadings and the testimony at bar point to no such violation. It is not the task of the Court to search out every naval regulation, to consider whether any part of Ryan's conduct offends that regulation and then to decide whether the insinuation of such offence is for purposes of a libel suit to be regarded as the charge of a crime of the type which if oral makes a statement defamatory per se. Bander v. Metropolitan Life Ins. Co., 313 Mass. 337, 341, 47 N.E.2d 595. Cf. Restatement, Torts, § 571, comment on clause (a), p. 173.

6. Now I turn from the script to the motion picture itself. Defendant first contends that it is not accountable for the showing of the picture at the two Boston theatres referred to in the complaint. If I understand counsel's argument, it is that one who produces an allegedly defamatory motion picture for exhibition and who distributes it to an exhibitor, is not liable for the injury inflicted by that particular exhibitor's showing. This argument is so preposterous as hardly to require answer and certainly not citation of extensive rebutting authority. The producer intended the very exhibition that occurred. It was not a performance independent of its will but the ultimate end toward which the whole production was directed. That the final exhibitor was technically an independent contractor not an agent of the producer is irrelevant. Merchants' Ins. Co. of Newark, N.J. v. Buckner, 6 Cir., 98 F. 222, 230, 231; Restatement, Torts, § 577, comment (f).

7. If counsel means to imply that defendant is not accountable at bar because plaintiff has embraced in his suit only the injury suffered from the showing in two theatres in Boston and has not embraced other injuries suffered from other showings, also caused by defendant directly, or through agents, or through independent contractors, the answer is equally plain. There is no obligation to complain of all the damages caused by defendant. However, if because of the doctrine of "composite torts" the damages not claimed are part of the same cause of action as the damages that were claimed, then of course a new action will not lie for the unclaimed damages. * * *

10. I now turn to what is to my mind the most difficult problem in this case—did the motion picture of They Were Expendable shown at the Boston theatres cause the audiences in those theatres to have a lower opinion of Commander Kelly—did it affect his reputation by causing him to be held up to contempt, hatred or ridicule?

The romantic incidents of Ryan's career certainly could not bring Commander Kelly into even a Puritan's ridicule or disesteem. Ryan's conduct toward ladies would have been becoming to anyone, sailor or civilian, officer or man. His conduct on duty, however, raises more subtle issues. And in resolving them it is important to emphasize one consideration of law and another of fact.

In deciding whether a statement is defamatory, the rule is to determine what its effect is upon any respectable, substantial part of the community to which the statement was addressed. Thus if the community or audience includes a professional group to which the subject of the statement belongs, the question is the effect of the statement upon that group with its special professional standards. Mr. Justice Holmes gave an apt illustration in Peck v. Tribune Co., 214 U.S. 185, where he said at page 190, 29 S.Ct. 554, at page 556, 53 L.Ed. 960, 16 Ann.Cas. 1075, "If a doctor were represented as advertising, the fact that it would effect his standing with others of his profession might make the representation actionable, although advertising is not reputed dishonest and even seems to be regarded by many with pride". See accord Restatement, Torts § 559(e).

And in applying that rule of law to the case at bar, we are to remember that the showing complained of was in January, 1946—a mere four months after hostilities had ceased and at a period when this Court takes judicial notice that the Port of Boston was crowded with permanent officers of the United States Navy, some of whom it may reasonably be inferred went to a motion picture in the production of which the Navy cooperated.

Thus the issue narrowly stated is whether to permanent officers of the United States Navy the portrayal of plaintiff as resembling Ryan would tend to lower his reputation. In the light of the lack of evidence that Annapolis men were in the audience it would not seem proper to confine the professional group whose opinion we are testing to the narrow circle of those who had graduated from the Naval Academy. And obviously it would be improper to use plaintiff's personal reaction except so far as it is typical of any naval officer's reaction as the test whether the portrayal held him up to contempt, hatred or ridicule.

The testimony warrants this Court in finding and the Court finds that as a group naval officers like other professional groups, such as doctors, lawyers or judges have a standard of judgment of their colleagues which is peculiar to their profession and which differs sharply from the appraisal of the uninitiated. As plaintiff's counsel suggested at the bar, this difference can be shown by analogy. Suppose a motion picture showed Mr. Justice Holmes on the bench deciding cases in a way that laymen would regard as eminently just and fair, but in a way that lawyers would say showed an unprofessional disregard of statutes, precedents, traditions and canons of judicial conduct. Would not Mr. Justice Holmes, were he alive, have a good cause of action for defamation? To be sure, all professional men have to stomach a certain amount of lay misrepresentation of their virtues. [Cf. Holmes-Pollock Letters: vol. I, p. 106, letter from Holmes to Pollock, Sept. 23, 1902; vol. I, p. 107, letter from Pollock to Holmes, Oct. 3, 1902.] Yet there comes a point when what the layman regards as a statement of virtuous conduct, a professional regards as portrayal of a vice—and not necessarily, from the professional approach, a venial vice. And the law recognizes that the professional man's interest in not having added to his career imaginary facts that tend to lessen his colleagues' opinion of him, rises superior to the motion picture producer's interest in embellishing a true story with colorful episodes not plainly stamped as imaginary but designed to increase the popularity of the motion picture.

Yet it is said by defendant's counsel that the motion picture will pass through even this needle's eye. He says that the profession would—and the Court therefore should—look at the picture as a whole; that it would regard the main theme as the account of a motorboat torpedo squadron as a unit in the Philippines; that it would not suppose that every single trait of Lt. Kelly (as he then was) was accurately pictured in the character of Ryan; and that even a professional officer would come away with a sense of what a hero and what a credit to the Navy Lt. Kelly, alias Ryan, was.

I concur that it would be unsound to isolate each single episode, action and utterance of Ryan and ask whether an audience of professional Navy men would say that that single item was unbecoming an officer and gentleman. But I do not agree that an audience of professionals would say They Were Expendable was purely a picture of corporate accomplishment by a squadron and that the individuals had more or less fictitious attributes. I am of the view that like the general public, the officer group would identify Lieutenants Bulkeley and Kelly with the characters Brickley and Ryan. And I think they would go away from that showing of the movie with a clear picture of the difference in professional standards of the two naval officers represented by the two principal characters on the screen. They would conclude that each had a brave heart but that Lt. Bulkeley was a self-controlled responsible officer, but his executive officer had a temperamental streak which occasionally carried him just out of bounds. I am not led to a contrary conclusion by defendant's argument that letters from high naval officers showed approval of the picture. The fact that the picture was liked by a certain number of naval officers seems to me irrelevant—they were considering the picture as a whole and its treatment of the service as an entity, not approving of the professional conduct of each character. Moreover, some of those naval officers were no doubt more mindful of the virtues of publicity for the Navy than of the rights of each separate individual to be fairly portrayed.

Indeed so far as I can tell, the difference in treatment of Lt. Bulkeley and plaintiff may be the real clue to why this action was brought. There were so many truthful elements in the picture of the two men that the average naval officer might suppose that the contrast in adherence to professional canons also tended to be true. Thus the representation was an example of the maxim, "the greater the truth, the greater the libel".

This explanation is indeed the only one that is consistent with the type of man Commander Kelly revealed himself to be not only on the PT boats in the Pacific but also in his attempts to avoid publicity by the Navy and in his behavior in the courtroom in Boston. Here he showed candor, modesty, courage, simplicity and presence of mind such as one rarely sees on the witness stand. * * *

11. But defendant says that even if the picture did hold plaintiff up to ridicule or otherwise defamed him, plaintiff gave defendant a license to show just that picture.

Plaintiff did, after repeated requests including one from the Secretary of the Navy, execute the letter of December 21, 1942. I cannot find that as a matter of law he was coerced to execute the document. However, in view of the fact that it was drafted by others to serve the interests of others, and that plaintiff was a most reluctant signatory, I conclude that the instrument should be construed as favorably to plaintiff as possible. The opening sentences of the letter make it evident that what plaintiff was waiving was only his right to privacy in those states in which such a right was recognized. That is, he was giving a license which would prevent him from making the particular type of claim which Mr. Brandeis and Mr. Warren in their famous paper, The Right To Privacy, 4 Harv.L.Rev. 193, had proposed to have recognized and which was urged (unsuccessfully) before the New York Courts by a person who thought he was depicted in A Bell for Adano. Toscani v. Hersey, 271 App.Div. 445, 65 N.Y.S.2d 814. Plaintiff was not giving up any claim he might have on account of the common law of libel (such as is covered in Restatement, Torts, Bk. III, c. 24–27) not to mention the common law of intentional infliction of mental distress (such as is covered in the amendments proposed to Restatment, Torts, § 46). Thus plaintiff was not making a surrender, waiver or license adequate to excuse defendant from liability for the defamation alleged in the case at bar.

Moreover, in my view the provisions of the license limited defendant to depicting plaintiff or a character that corresponded to him. I find as a fact that in essential elements of professional fitness Rusty Ryan does not correspond to plaintiff. Therefore, one of the terms of the license was not met. I need not consider in detail whether defendant met other terms of the license (1) by securing approval of the United States Navy; (2) by not elaborating the romance beyond the portrayal of it in Mr. White's book; and (3) by portraying as accurately as possible historical events. It will be sufficient for me to say that I find a failure of defendant to meet the third and last of those terms.

12. There remains the final question as to what damages plaintiff may recover on account of the showing of the motion picture at the Boston theatres. There is no evidence that those showings lowered his reputation in the eyes of anyone who had the power to promote his naval career. And no actual injury to his career has been shown. Indeed, the award of decorations, the making permanent of his rank of

Sec. A   THE NATURE OF THE INJURY   615

Commander and the assignment to teach at Annapolis all suggest that plaintiff suffered no appreciable damage in his profession.

He testified that he did suffer social embarrassment in gatherings in Boston where there were guests who had actually seen or probably seen the movie. It is elementary that in Massachusetts as in most other jurisdictions plaintiff's mental anguish or suffering is an element of damage recoverable in a libel suit. Finger v. Pollack, 188 Mass. 208, 74 N.E. 317; Restatement, Torts, § 623; Magruder, Mental Disturbance in Torts, 49 Harv.L.Rev. 1033, 1055, 1056. But it has been said that "the injury to feelings which the law of defamation recognizes is not the suffering from the making of the charge, but is the suffering which is caused by other people's conduct towards him in consequence of it." Wigmore Evidence, Rev.Ed., 1940, vol. I, § 209, p. 704. If that were the law, then Commander Kelly could not recover because he has not shown that his injured feelings were the result of the conduct of persons in his profession who alone are the audience which I have found might have a lower opinion of him. But Professor Wigmore's statement does not state the law of Massachusetts. Marble v. Chapin, 132 Mass. 225; Curley v. Curtis Pub. Co., D.C.Mass., 48 F.Supp. 27. The most dramatic proof is Marble's case. Chapin falsely told Mary Cummings that "Mr. Marble has had intercourse with you". Miss Cummings knew it was not so; could not have had her estimate of Mr. Marble lowered by the defamation; and never repeated the statement. Yet Mr. Marble was allowed to keep a verdict for his mental suffering. In short, in Massachusetts let there be a finding that defendant published a libel and it follows that the trier of fact can award plaintiff compensation for the injury to his feelings, dependent upon the trier's estimate of plaintiff's sensitivity. Curley v. Curtis Pub. Co., D.C.Mass., 48 F.Supp. 27.

And as the trier of fact I find that plaintiff while possessed of an exterior that is calm, cool and collected has an inner spirit of fineness and distinction. Such persons suffer more than readily appears to those who customarily measure by the gross proportions of the motion picture world.

There is only one factor which in any way suggests that plaintiff is not of the fiber that I have pictured; and not entitled to have his suffering measured on that basis. That was his admission that he had applied for and been granted the Purple Heart as a recognition of a wound which, while it may have been service-inflicted, was certainly not the result of unusual risks peculiar to war. Defendant's counsel hammered hard on this point, and I believe with some justification. But I am not persuaded that plaintiff lapsed more than momentarily from his customary attitude of depreciating all types of self-advertisement.

Doubt as to plaintiff's sensitivity cannot be premised on his willingness to bring this libel suit. To be sure, many men of dignity, particularly professional men, are accustomed to face with a stiff upper lip public minor misunderstanding of their work. But men of the finest grain may feel that when calumniators have circulated false and mischievous canards about their official accomplishments or private lives a libel suit is justifiable principally to secure judicial declarations of the truth rather than substantial monetary damages. [Compare Theodore Roosevelt v. Newett, reported in H.P. Pringle, Theodore Roosevelt. A Biography (1931), pp. 573, 574]. Moreover, a man of the highest character and sensitivity may on the advice of counsel come into court and ask a large recovery for libel on the ground among others that that is the best way to attract public attention as prominently to plaintiff's ultimate vindication as public attention was originally attracted to defendant's misrepresentation.

Since the only elements of damage proved relate to (1) loss of reputation among naval officers who attended performances in two Boston theatres and to (2) mental disturbance, the recovery cannot be of large proportions. Commander Kelly may, however, take some justified pride in a judicial finding that despite quite as gruelling a cross-examination as any witness is apt to face in court he stands out as a man of exemplary physical and mental courage, of self-restraint and self-discipline, remarkably indifferent to self-advertisement but understandably disturbed by widespread depiction of him as deserting the ideals of his profession and adopting the patterns of culture favored by the movie-going public. At the request of the Secretary of the Navy, Commander Kelly, agreed to sacrifice his reputation as a "chevalier sans peur et sans reproche".

On the first count, judgment for defendant without costs.

On the second and third counts, judgment for plaintiff for $3,000 with costs.

Questions

1. If in fact Kelly had been married at the time of the war-time incidents depicted in the motion picture, would the portrayal of Ryan's relationship with the nurse Sandy Davis have been libelous?

2. Do you agree with Judge Wyzanski's conclusion in connection with his hypothetical motion picture about Justice Holmes? Wouldn't lawyers seeing such a film assume the depicted departure from professional standards to be literary license and not a reflection on the real Justice Holmes? Would a similar conclusion be reached by Navy men viewing the motion picture here in issue? Is Judge Wyzanski's conclusion as to the nature of the professional Navy reaction to the manner in which Ryan was portrayed based upon evidence or upon judicial notice? Is this a proper subject for judicial notice?

3. Do you agree with the Wigmore rule which limits defamation damages for mental suffering to that "caused by other people's conduct"? Is there any inconsistency in requiring evidence affecting reputation in order to establish liability in a defamation action, but permitting recovery of damages for mental suffering not necessarily accruing from loss of reputation?

4. Do you agree with the court's construction of the letter of consent addressed to Loew's Inc. signed by Kelly? What argument could you make that the consent went to defamation as well as invasion of privacy?

Sec. A   THE NATURE OF THE INJURY   617

5. Is there any way in which the "customary legend" to the effect that the events, characters, etc. are "fictitious" could have been re-worded so as to give the defendant an effective defense in this action?

On the choice of law problem alluded to in the instant case, see Note, The Choice of Law in Multistate Defamation—A Functional Approach, 77 Harv.Law Rev. 1463 (1964); Restatement (Second) of Torts, § 577A; Restatement (Second), of Conflict of Laws, § 379e (Tent.Draft No. 9, 1964).

BURTON v. CROWELL PUBLISHING CO.
Circuit Court of Appeals, Second Circuit, 1936.
82 F.2d 154.

Before L. HAND, SWAN, and CHASE, CIRCUIT JUDGES.

L. HAND, CIRCUIT JUDGE. This appeal arises upon a judgment dismissing a complaint for libel upon the pleadings. The complaint alleged that the defendant had published an advertisement—annexed and incorporated by reference—made up of text and photographs; that one of the photographs was "susceptible of being regarded as representing plaintiff as guilty of indecent exposure and as being a person physically deformed and mentally perverted"; that some of the text, read with the offending photograph, was "susceptible of being regarded as falsely representing plaintiff as an utterer of salacious and obscene language"; and finally that "by reason of the premises plaintiff has been subjected to frequent and conspicuous ridicule, scandal, reproach, scorn, and indignity." The advertisement was of "Camel" cigarettes; the plaintiff was a widely known gentleman steeple-chaser, and the text quoted him as declaring that "Camel" cigarettes "restored" him after "a crowded business day." Two photographs were inserted; the larger, a picture of the plaintiff in riding shirt and breeches, seated apparently outside a paddock with a cigarette in one hand and a cap and whip in the other. This contained the legend, "Get a lift with a Camel"; neither it, nor the photograph, is charged as part of the libel, except as the legend may be read upon the other and offending photograph. That represented him coming from a race to be weighed in; he is carrying his saddle in front of him with his right hand under the pommel and his left under the cantle; the line of the seat is about twelve inches below his waist. Over the pommel hangs a stirrup; over the seat at his middle a white girth falls loosely in such a way that it seems to be attached to the plaintiff and not to the saddle. So regarded, the photograph becomes grotesque, monstrous, and obscene; and the legends, which without undue violence can be made to match, reinforce the ribald interpretation. That is the libel. The answer alleged that the plaintiff had posed for the photographs and been paid for their use as an advertisement; a reply, that they had never been shown to the plaintiff after they were taken. On this showing the judge held that the advertisement did not hold the plaintiff up to the hatred, ridicule, or contempt of fair-minded people, and that in any event he consented to its use and might not complain.

We dismiss at once so much of the complaint as alleged that the advertisement might be read to say that the plaintiff was deformed, or that he had indecently exposed himself, or was making obscene jokes by means of the legends. Nobody could be fatuous enough to believe any

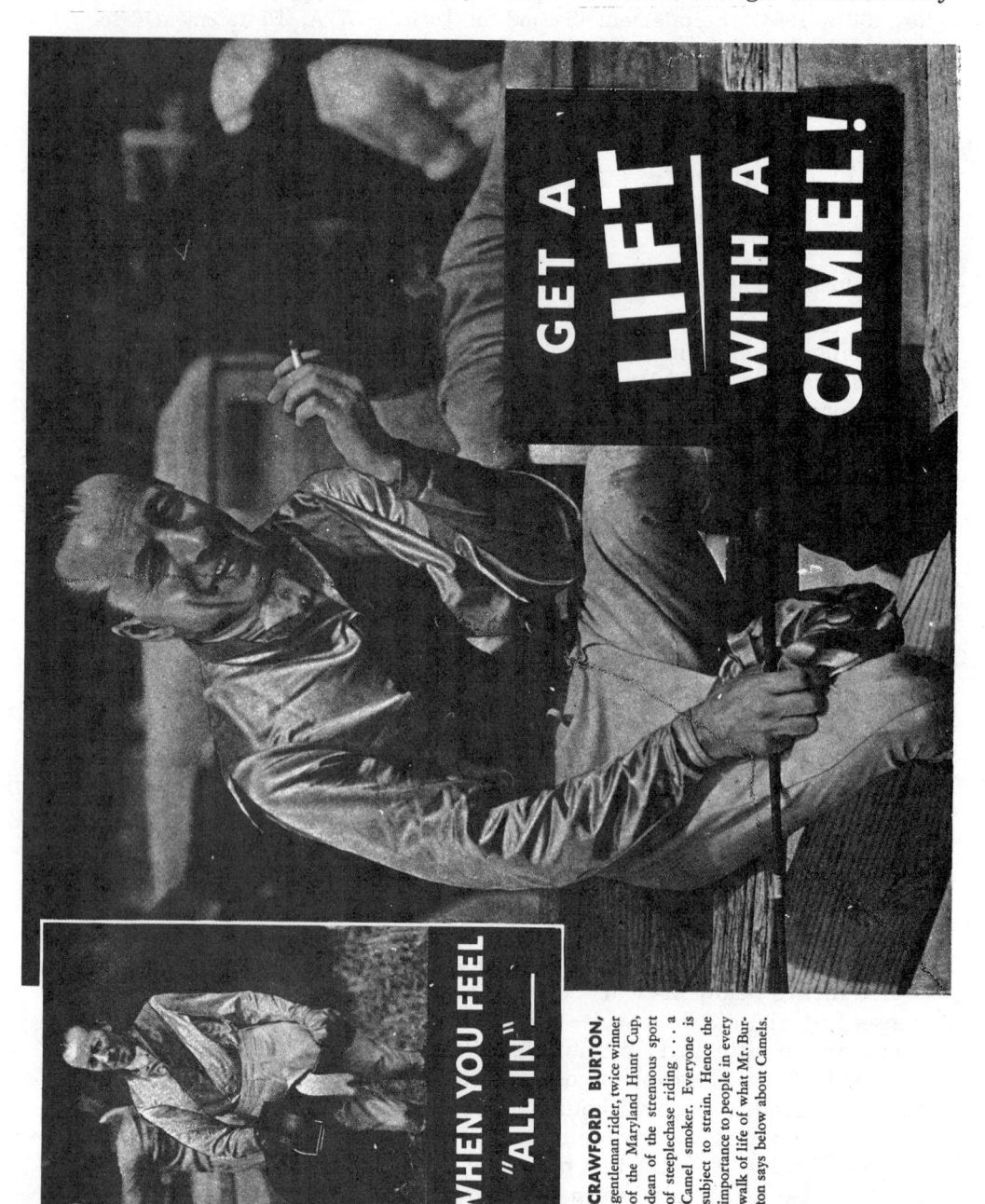

The plaintiff as shown in the advertisement in defendant's magazine.

of these things; everybody would at once see that it was the camera, and the camera alone, that had made the unfortunate mistake. If the advertisement is a libel, it is such in spite of the fact that it asserts nothing whatever about the plaintiff, even by the remotest implications. It does not profess to depict him as he is; it does not exaggerate any part of his person so as to suggest that he is deformed; it is patently an optical illusion, and carries its correction on its face as much as though it were a verbal utterance which expressly declared that it was false. It would be hard for words so guarded to carry any sting, but the same is not true of caricatures, and this is an example; for, notwithstanding all we have just said, it exposed the plaintiff to overwhelming ridicule. The contrast between the drawn and serious face and the accompanying fantastic and lewd deformity was so extravagant that, though utterly unfair, it in fact made of the plaintiff a preposterously ridiculous spectacle; and the obvious mistake only added to the amusement. Had such a picture been deliberately produced, surely every right-minded person would agree that he would have had a genuine grievance; and the effect is the same whether it is deliberate or not. Such a caricature affects a man's reputation, if by that is meant his position in the minds of others; the association so established may be beyond repair; he may become known indefinitely as the absurd victim of this unhappy mischance. Literally, therefore, the injury falls within the accepted rubric; it exposes the sufferer to "ridicule" and "contempt." Nevertheless, we have not been able to find very much in the books that is in point, for although it has long been recognized that pictures may be libels, and in some cases they have been caricatures, in nearly all they have impugned the plaintiff at least by implication, directly or indirectly uttering some falsehood about him. 5 Coke, 125 a & b; Cropp v. Tilney, 11 Mod. 99 (semble); DuBost v. Beresford, 2 Camp. 511; Austin v. Culpepper, 2 Shower, 313; Ellis v. Kimball, 16 Pick. (33 Mass.) 132; Brown v. Harrington, 208 Mass. 600, 95 N.E. 655; Merle v. Sociological, etc., Co., 166 App.Div. 376, 152 N.Y.S. 829.

The defendant answers that every libel must affect the plaintiff's character; but if by "character" is meant those moral qualities which the word ordinarily includes, the statement is certainly untrue, for there are many libels which do not affect the reputation of the victim in any such way. Thus, it is a libel to say that a man is insane (Totten v. Sun Printing & Pub. Co. [C.C.] 109 F. 289; Southwick v. Stevens, 10 Johns. [N.Y.] 443; Belknap v. Ball, 83 Mich. 583, 47 N.W. 674, 11 L.R.A. 72, 21 Am.St.Rep. 622); or that he has negro blood if he professes to be white (Stultz v. Cousins [C.C.A.6] 242 F. 794); or is too educated to earn his living (Martin v. Press Pub. Co., 93 App.Div. 531, 87 N.Y.S. 859); or is desperately poor (Moffatt v. Cauldwell, 3 Hun [N.Y.] 26); or that he is a eunuch (Eckert v. Van Pelt, 69 Kan. 357, 76 P. 909, 66 L.R.A. 266); or that he has an infectious disease, even though not venereal (Villers v. Monsley, 2 Wils. 403; Simpson v. Press Pub. Co., 33 Misc. 228, 67 N.Y.S. 401); or that he is illegitimate (Shelby v. Sun P. & P. Ass'n, 38 Hun

[N.Y.] 474, affirmed on opinion below, 109 N.Y. 611, 15 N.E. 895); or that his near relatives have committed a crime (Van Wiginton v. Pulitzer Pub. Co., 218 F. 795 [C.C.A.8]; Merrill v. Post Pub. Co., 197 Mass. 185, 83 N.E. 419); or that he was mistaken for Jack Ketch (Cook v. Ward, 6 Bing. 409); or that a woman was served with process in her bathtub (Snyder v. New York Press Co., 137 App.Div. 291, 121 N.Y.S. 944). It is indeed not true that all ridicule (Lamberti v. Sun P. & P. Ass'n, 111 App.Div. 437, 97 N.Y.S. 694), or all disagreeable comment (Kimmerle v. New York Evening Journal, Inc., 262 N.Y. 99, 186 N.E. 217; Cohen v. New York Times Co., 153 App.Div. 242, 138 N.Y.S. 206), is actionable; a man must not be too thin-skinned or a self-important prig; but this advertisement was more than what only a morbid person would not laugh off; the mortification, however ill-deserved, was a very substantial grievance.

A more plausible challenge is that a libel must be something that can be true or false, since truth is always a defense. It would follow that if, as we agree, the picture was a mistake on its face and declared nothing about the plaintiff, it was not a libel. We have been able to find very little on the point. In Dunlop v. Dunlop Rubber Co. (1920) 1 Irish Ch. & Ld.Com. 280, 290–292, the picture represented the plaintiff in foppish clothes, and the opinion seems to rely merely upon the contempt which that alone might have aroused, but those who saw it might have taken it to imply that the plaintiff was in fact a fop. In Zbyszko v. New York American, 228 App.Div. 277, 239 N.Y.S. 411, however, though the decision certainly went far, nobody could possibly have read the picture as asserting anything which was in fact untrue; it was the mere association of the plaintiff with a gorilla that was thought to lower him in others' esteem. Nevertheless, although the question is almost tabula rasa, it seems to us that in principle there should be no doubt. The gravamen of the wrong in defamation is not so much the injury to reputation, measured by the opinions of others, as the feelings, that is, the repulsion or the light esteem, which those opinions engender. We are sensitive to the charge of murder only because our fellows deprecate it in most forms; but a head-hunter, or an aboriginal American Indian, or a gangster, would regard such an accusation as a distinction, and during the Great War an "ace," a man who had killed five others, was held in high regard. Usually it is difficult to arouse feelings without expressing an opinion, or asserting a fact; and the common law has so much regard for truth that it excuses the utterance of anything that is true. But it is a non sequitur to argue that whenever truth is not a defense, there can be no libel; that would invert the proper approach to the whole subject. In all wrongs we must first ascertain whether the interest invaded is one which the law will protect at all; that is indeed especially important in defamation, for the common law did not recognize all injuries to reputation, especially when the utterance was oral. But the interest here is by hypothesis one which the law does protect; the plaintiff has been substantially enough ridiculed to be in a position to complain. The defendant must therefore find some excuse, and truth would be an excuse if it could be pleaded. The only reason why the law makes truth a defense is not because a libel must be false, but because the utterance of truth is in all circumstances an interest paramount to reputation; it is like a privileged communication, which is privileged only because the law prefers it conditionally to reputation. When there is no such countervailing interest, there is no excuse; and that is the situation here. In conclusion therefore we hold that because the picture taken with the legends was calculated to expose the plaintiff to more than trivial ridicule, it was prima facie actionable; that the fact that it did not assume to state a fact or an opinion is irrelevant; and that in consequence the publication is actionable.

Finally, the plaintiff's consent to the use of the photographs for which he posed as an advertisement was not a consent to the use of the offending photograph; he had no reason to anticipate that the lens would so distort his appearance. If the defendant wished to fix him with responsibility for whatever the camera might turn out, the result should have been shown him before publication. Possibly any one who chooses to stir such a controversy in a court cannot have been very sensitive originally, but that is a consideration for the jury, which, if ever justified, is justified in actions for defamation.

Judgment reversed; cause remanded for trial.

Questions

1. Did the photograph of the plaintiff tend to "lower him in the estimation of the community or * * * deter third persons from associating or dealing with him"? (See Restatement of Torts, § 559, supra). By reason of the Burton case, and some similar cases, the Reporter for the Restatement (Second) of Torts suggested a new section:

"A defamatory communication may consist of words or other matter which ridicule another." (Restatement (Second) of Torts, § 567A (Tent. Draft No. 11, 1965)).

This was not adopted in the final draft. But see Restatement (Second) of Torts, § 566, Comment d.

2. Bear this case in mind when you consider the "false light" variety of the right of privacy infra. Do the facts of this case more properly come within that branch of the law of privacy? Does it make any difference which theory (defamation or privacy) is said to be applicable? Does the fact that "truth" is irrelevant in the instant case bear upon such a difference? Consider this further in connection with the discussion infra of the impact of the First Amendment on defamation and privacy.

B. IDENTIFICATION

KELLY v. LOEW'S INC.
United States District Court, District of Massachusetts, 1948.
76 F.Supp. 473.

[Earlier and later portions of this opinion are set forth supra.]

8. Defendant next makes the point that plaintiff failed to bear the burden of showing that the audiences in the Boston theatre identified him with the character Rusty Ryan. Physically they did not look alike, as the Court could see by comparing the motion picture with the plaintiff when he was on the stand. Emotionally they did not resemble one another—plaintiff being a man of far greater reserve, composure and dignity. Nominally they were distinguishable—Ryan does not sound like Kelly. But all these distinctions are beside the point. The motion picture recited that it was based on William L. White's book, They Were Expendable; and that book throughout uses Kelly's true name and the author in the foreword and elsewhere makes it plain that Kelly is a living officer identical with plaintiff in this suit. Thus by giving the key—if key were needed—to unlock the mysteries of the picture defendant plainly asked the audience to believe—and I conclude that many of them did believe—that Ryan in the movie was substantially like Kelly in life. The disingenuous legend that the persons and events shown in the picture were fictitious and that any similarity to actual persons living or dead was purely coincidental would not have been treated by the average person or naval officer as any more than a tongue-in-the-cheek disclaimer in view of the express reference by the movie to Mr. White's book, in view of the statement of Navy cooperation and in view of the unmistakable portrayal of General MacArthur, his family and other historic personages, including both Lt. Bulkeley and plaintiff.

9. Related to the last point, defendant seems to suggest that there is no showing that anyone in the Boston audiences personally knew Commander Kelly in 1946. If this is the suggestion, it is without merit. The question is not whether the audience knew Commander Kelly personally, but whether they knew his reputation. That his reputation was known in Boston is demonstrable in two alternative ways: first, his exploits had been reported in Mr. White's best-selling non-fiction book; and second, his exploits had been reported over the radio (Ex. 2, p. 198) and were well known in large cities. Thus in New York City, where he had not lived at least since infancy and which had therefore no reason to have a greater knowledge than Boston would have of him, he was the feature attraction of a parade and two banquets intended to promote the sale of government bonds. Moreover, one would have to be peculiarly blind to the racial and religious composition of Greater Boston, to the understandable pride that every group takes in heroes drawn from backgrounds like its own, and to the conspicuous record which plaintiff had made in the Navy to suppose that Commander Kelly was entirely

unknown to the audiences at the State and Orpheum theatres in Boston.

Questions

1. Is the existence of a "key", i.e. a book or other extrinsic material which uses the plaintiff's true name, and identifies him as the person portrayed in defendant's work, necessary in order to identify a plaintiff where his true name is not used in defendant's work?

2. Suppose that the defendant's motion picture had not indicated that it was based upon the William L. White book, but in fact it was so based. Different result?

3. Suppose that the plaintiff's true name appears in a book, but is changed in the motion picture based upon the book, and suppose further that the book jacket refers to the motion picture, but the motion picture does not refer to the book. In such circumstances should the book be regarded as a "key" so as to constitute the motion picture an invasion of privacy? See University of Notre Dame v. Twentieth Century-Fox Film Corp., 22 App.Div.2d 452, 256 N.Y.S.2d 301 (1965), aff'd 15 N.Y.2d 940, 259 N.Y.S.2d 832 (1965).

YOUSSOUPOFF v. METRO–GOLDWYN–MAYER PICTURES, LIMITED

English Court of Appeal, 1934.
50 Times L.R. 581, 99 A.L.R. 864.

This was an appeal by Metro-Goldwyn-Mayer Pictures, Limited, cinematograph film producers and distributors, of Upper St. Martin's Lane, W.C.I., from the verdict and judgment at the trial before Mr. Justice Avory and a special jury of the action in which Princess Irina Alexandrovna, of Russia, the wife of Prince Youssoupoff, of Rue Guttenberg, Boulogne-sur-Seine, Paris, was awarded * * * £25,000 against Metro-Goldwyn-Mayer Pictures, Limited.

The Princess claimed damages for an alleged libel which she said was contained in a sound film entitled Rasputin, the Mad Monk, alleging that the defendants had published in the film pictures and words which were understood to mean that she, therein called "Princess Natasha," had been seduced by Rasputin.

The defendants denied that the film was defamatory, and further said that it did not refer to the Princess.

The jury returned a verdict in favor of Princess Youssoupoff and awarded her £25,000 damages, and Mr. Justice Avory entered judgment for her for that amount, with costs.

The grounds of the appeal were that there was no reasonable evidence identifying Princess Youssoupoff with the character of Princess Natasha in the film, and no evidence that Princess Natasha had been seduced by or become the mistress of Rasputin. If, it was contended, the film indicated any relations between Rasputin and Natasha, it indicated a rape of Natasha and not a seduction, and the spoken words complained of constituted, if anything, a slander not actionable without proof of special damage. It was further contended that an allegation that a married woman has been the victim of a rape may not be actionable by her, that the amount of damages awarded to Princess Youssoupoff was unreasonable and excessive, and that Mr. Justice Avory misdirected the jury in various respects.

The following judgments were delivered:

Lord Justice Scrutton. An English company called Metro-Goldwyn-Mayer Pictures, Limited, which produces films circulated to the cinemas in this country, and which, according to its solicitor and chairman, is controlled by a firm of similar name in America, produced in this country a film which dealt with the alleged circumstances in which the influence of a man called Rasputin, an alleged monk, on the Czar and Czarina brought about the destruction of Russia. The film

Princess Natasha (Diana Wynyard), the Czarina (Ethel Barrymore) and Rasputin (Lionel Barrymore) in defendant's motion picture *Rasputin, the Mad Monk*.

also dealt with the undoubted fact that Rasputin was ultimately murdered by persons who conceived him to be the evil genius of Russia.

In the course of that film a lady who had relations of affection with the person represented as the murderer was represented as having also had relations, which might be either relations of seduction or relations of rape, with the man Rasputin, a man of the worst possible character. When the film was produced in this country the plaintiff alleged that reasonable people would understand that she was the woman who was represented as having had these illicit relations. The plaintiff is a member of the Russian Royal House, Princess Irina Alexandrovna of Russia, and she was married after the incidents in question to a man who undoubtedly was one of the persons concerned in the killing of Rasputin. She issued a writ for libel against the English company. The English company declined to stop presenting the film. The action for libel proceeded. It was tried before one of the most experienced Judges on the Bench and a special jury, the constitutional tribunal for trying actions of libel, and, after several days' hearing, and after the jury had twice gone to see the film itself, they returned a verdict for the plaintiff with £25,000 damages.

The defendants now appeal from that verdict, and, as I understand the argument put before us by Sir William Jowitt and Mr. Wallington, for the defendants, it falls under three heads. First of all, they say that there was no evidence on which a jury, properly directed, could find that reasonable people would understand the Princess Natasha of the film to be Princess Irina, the plaintiff. That was the first point—the question of identification. Secondly, they say that if we are to take the Princess Natasha of the film to be identified with the Princess Irina, the plaintiff, there was no evidence on which a jury, reasonably directed, could find the film to be defamatory of the plaintiff. Thirdly, they say: "Assuming both of those points are decided against us, the damages were excessive. They were such as no jury, properly directed, could give in the circumstances of the case."

I deal with each of those three points in turn. First of all, there is the question of identification. Now, if this case had been heard before 1910 there would undoubtedly have been scope for very elaborate arguments, and this Court would probably have had to reserve judgment to consider the numerous authorities which would have been cited. But since the decision in 1910 in a case which is always identified with the name of Mr. Artemus Jones, and since a subsequent decision of this Court in which somewhat similar principles were applied in a case which is identified with the name of General Corrigan, of the Mexican Army, there is, fortunately, no difficulty about the law. In Hulton and Co., Limited v. Jones (26 Times L.R. 128; [1910] A.C. 20) a Manchester paper published by Messrs. Hulton published what was supposed to be an amusing article about a gentleman named Artemus Jones, who, on one side of his life, was a blameless churchwarden at Peckham and, on the other side of his life, indulged in wild careers unfitted for such a churchwarden at Le Touquet. A Mr. Artemus Jones—there may be several—conceived that that article was a libel upon him, and he brought an action for libel. The editor and proprietors of the paper said, rightly or wrongly, that they had never heard of Mr. Artemus Jones as an existing being, and that they had not the slightest intention of libelling him. There was some unfortunate doubt whether the gentleman who wrote the article had not a personal grudge against the real Mr. Artemus Jones, but, at any rate, the proprietors and publishers of the paper said: "We are innocent of any intention to injure Mr. Artemus Jones, of whom we never heard."

The case resulted in this way. In spite of a very careful judgment by Lord Justice Moulton in the Court of Appeal, counterbalanced by an equally learned and convincing judgment of Lord Justice Farwell in the Court of Appeal, the House of Lords unanimously came to the conclusion which is expressed in the first lines of the headnote in this way: "In an action for libel it is no defence to show that the defendant did not intend to defame the plaintiff, if reasonable people would think the language to be defamatory of the plaintiff;" and the Lord Chancellor quoted in his judgment this passage from the summing-up: "The real point upon which your verdict must turn is, ought or ought not sensible and reasonable people reading this article to think that it was a mere imaginary person such as I have said—Tom Jones, Mr. Pecksniff as a humbug, Mr. Stiggins, or any of that sort of names that one reads of in literature used as types? If you think any reasonable person would think that"—that is to say, that it was mere type and did not mean anybody—"it is not actionable at all. If, on the other hand, you do not think that, but think that people would suppose it to mean some real person—those who did not know the plaintiff of course would not know who the real person was, but those who did know of the existence of the plaintiff would think that it was the plaintiff—then the action is maintainable."

A somewhat similar point was raised in the case where General Corrigan got damages—Cassidy v. Daily Mirror Newspapers, Limited, 45 Times L.R. 485, [1929] 2 K.B. 331, 69 A.L.R. 720. General Corrigan, who sometimes called himself Cassidy, being at a race meeting, conceived the idea of being photographed with a young lady to whom he said he was engaged. This photograph was sent up as an object of interest to a daily paper, which at once inserted it. Now, it so happened that the General was in fact married to a lady who lived in a London suburb, and was visited by the suburban ladies in the vicinity, who had hitherto considered that she was an honest married woman. When they took in the daily paper and saw that the gentleman describing himself as the husband of the lady was representing himself as being engaged to somebody else they very naturally, as respectable women, conceived evil ideas of the lady whom they had hitherto thought to be an honest woman and whom they now suspected of being a kept woman. Thereupon the lady brought an action against the paper, and the paper said what before 1910 would have been the sort of thing you would expect them to say: "Why, good gracious, madam, we never heard of you. We had no intention of libelling you. We did not know you existed, and all we have done is to publish an interesting photograph, stating that the gentleman in the photograph says he is engaged to the lady in the photograph." Just as Hulton and Co., Limited v. Jones, supra, had caused a difference of opinion with a very excellent judgment by Lord Justice Moulton, so again the case of the General did cause a difference of opinion with again, if I may say so, a very excellent judgment of my brother Greer, but, unfortunately, the majority of the Court, myself and Lord Russell, took another view, and this Court is now bound by the view laid down by the Lord Chancellor in the Hulton case, supra, and by the case of General Corrigan, and we follow the law that though the person who writes and publishes the libel may not intend to libel a particular person and, indeed, has never heard of that particular person, the plaintiff, yet, if evidence is produced that reasonable people knowing some of the circumstances, not necessarily all, would take the libel complained of to relate to the plaintiff, an action for libel will lie.

That, therefore, was the class of evidence put before the jury in this case. On the one side, various people, some of them representatives of England in Russia at the time of these occurrences, some of them people who had been merely reading books about Russia and thought they knew something about it, were called to say that they saw the film, and they understood it to relate to the present plaintiff, the Princess Irina. On the other side, other people who knew something about Russia, or who did not know anything about Russia, were called to say that they saw the film, that they did not think it related to the plaintiff, and they gave their views as to whom they did think the characters in the film related.

There was evidence each side. I think counsel for the defendants agree that it would have been impossible for the judge to have stopped the case because the film was not capable of a defamatory meaning, and the jury, who are a tribunal particularly suited to try an action for libel, for the reason that I am going to allude to under the second head, came to the view that reasonable people would take the film to relate to the plaintiff in the action. It is not my business to express an opinion on the matter. It was the jury's business, and the only question for me is whether there was evidence on which the jury might come to the conclusion to which they have come. That being my position, I can quite see that there is a great deal of evidence on which the jury might take the view that the plaintiff was identified reasonably with the Princess Natasha.

The Princess Natasha plays a comparatively subordinate part in the film, but that subordinate part is brought in because she was on terms of affection which were likely to culminate in marriage with a man in the film who was one of the murderers of Rasputin. The question, then, was not only "Who is Princess Natasha in the film?" but "Who is Prince Chegodieff in the film?" he being the man who in the film is represented as having a great deal to do with the killing of Rasputin. So far as Prince Chegodieff is concerned, a certain Prince Youssoupoff had written a book setting out his part in the murder, and that book had had a very wide circulation. The Prince Chegodieff depicted in the film until you get near the killing has circumstances connected with him which might or might not refer to another person, a Prince of the Royal House, Prince Dmitri, although some of the characteristics of the Prince Chegodieff in the film do not fit in with the description given of Prince Dmitri in certain letters. But there was ground for the jury thinking that many people would naturally, in view of the book published by Prince Youssoupoff, take the view that the Prince Chegodieff in the film was intended to be and would reasonably be understood to be the Prince Youssoupoff, who was one of the murderers.

The murder took place in a palace on the Moika River, which was undoubtedly the property of the Youssoupoff family, and as the first step of identification there was evidence from which it was quite possible and quite reasonable for the jury to take the view that Prince Chegodieff in the film is Prince Youssoupoff of real fact, the man who in the book has published his account of how he murdered Rasputin. Then, who is Princess Natasha in the film? She is a member of the Royal Family. She is addressed in the film as "Your Royal Highness." She is on terms of great intimacy, which apparently will result in marriage, with the Prince Chegodieff, whom we have identified with Prince Youssoupoff. There is obviously evidence, in my opinion, on which the jury might come to the conclusion that the Princess Natasha in the film is the Princess Irina Youssoupoff of the Royal Family who is now married to Prince Youssoupoff and was at the time of the incident betrothed to him either publicly or privately.

Therefore, on the first point, I come to the conclusion that we cannot possibly interfere with the verdict of the jury, who are the constitutional tribunal, when they think, as they obviously have thought, that reasonable people, not all reasonable people but many reasonable people, would take the film representing Princess Natasha as also representing and referring to the plaintiff in the action, the Princess Irina. They would undoubtedly be helped to that by the defendants' own description of the film: "This concerns the destruction of an Empire brought about by the mad ambition of one man," obviously Rasputin. There is a list of eight principal characters given: "A few of the characters are still alive; the rest met death by violence." Of the eight characters mentioned above the Czar, Czarina, Rasputin, the Czarevitch, and the Grand Duke Igor did meet death by violence. The rest are "still alive." The rest are Prince Chegodieff, Princess Natasha, and Dr. Remezov. Part of the defence in the action seems really to be: "It is quite true that the defendants said that this is a story of fact, but it is really all a fiction. We ought to have used, if we described it properly, the formula which is now put at the beginning of most novels: 'All circumstances in this novel are imaginary, and none of the characters are in real life.'" Of course, that would not have fitted in with a representation that it was really a representation of the relations of the Royal Family with Rasputin and the people who killed Rasputin. But the film is so far from the real facts in some cases that one regrets that it was represented at all as being any genuine representation of the facts which had happened. However that may be, on the first point, whether there was evidence on which the jury could reasonably find that a considerable number of reasonable people who saw the film would identify the Princess Natasha of the film with the Princess Irina of Russia, I think that there was such evidence.

Now the second point is this, and it takes some courage to argue it, I think: suppose that the jury are right in treating Princess Irina, the plaintiff, as the Princess Natasha in real life, the film does not contain anything defamatory of her. There have been several formulae for describing what is defamation. The learned Judge at the trial uses the stock formula "calculated to bring into hatred, ridicule, or contempt," and because it has been clearly established some time ago that that is not exhaustive because there may be things which are defamatory which have nothing to do with hatred, ridicule, or contempt, he adds the words "or causes them to be shunned or avoided." I, myself, have always preferred the language which Mr. Justice Cave used in Scott v. Sampson, L.R. 8 Q.B.Div. 491, a false statement about a man to his discredit. I think that satisfactorily expresses what has to be found. It has long been established that, with one modification, libel or no libel is for the jury, and the Court very rarely interferes with a finding by the jury that a particular statement is a libel or is no libel. The only exception is that it has been established with somewhat unfortunate results that a Judge may say: "No reasonable jury could possibly think this a libel, and consequently I will not ask the jury the question whether it is a libel or not." In a case in which that was conclusively established the law and the facts got so far from each other that the majority of the Judges—there was a great difference of opinion—held that a certain circular issued by a firm of brewers to their customers saying that they would not take the cheques of a particular bank was not capable of a defamatory meaning, though, in fact, it resulted in a run of a quarter of a million on the bank immediately it was issued.

Fortunately, however, in this case we have not to deal with that exception because it is not suggested that the Judge in this case could have withdrawn the question of this libel from the jury on the point that it was not capable of a defamatory meaning. When you get the matter going to the jury it is extremely rare that the Court interferes with the finding of the jury whether a thing is libel or no libel. That has resulted from the action of Parliament in Mr. Fox's Libel Act in settling a dispute between Lord Mansfield and another eminent Judge as to the powers of the Judge in dealing with questions of libel. Lord Mansfield was of opinion that if a libel came before the Courts the Judge was to say whether it was a libel, and it was only for the jury to assess damages or to find guilty or not guilty on the direction. That was considered so contrary to the constitution with regard to juries that Parliament intervened and passed an Act, known as Mr. Fox's Libel Act, by which the matter was left to the jury. I am not going further with it than that because I myself have, in a case of Broome v. Agar, 44 Times L.R. 339, given a long judgment setting out the history of the matter and quoting with approval a passage in a then leading textbook: "The proper course is for the Judge to define what is a libel in point of law and to leave it to the jury to say whether the publication in question falls within that definition. And this is a question pre-eminently for the jury; whichever way they find, the Court will rarely, if ever, disturb the verdict, if the question was properly left to them." I have the more confidence in overcoming my natural modesty in citing my own judgment because in the House of Lords in Lockhart v. Harrison, 44 Times L.R. 794, a very similar case, Lord Buckmaster, giving an important judgment, said that my judgment contained, in his opinion, a most accurate statement of the true position.

If libel alone is for the jury on those lines, why is it said that the jury in this case have come to a wrong decision? I desire to approach this argument seriously if I can, because I have great difficulty in approaching it seriously. I understand the principal thing argued by the defendants is this: "This procedure, as it contains some spoken words, is slander and not libel. Slanders are not as a rule actionable unless you prove special damage. No special damage was proved in this case. Consequently, the plaintiff must get within the exceptions in which slander is actionable without proof of special damage." One of those exceptions is the exception which is amplified in the Slander of Women Act, 1891—namely, if the slander imports unchastity or adultery to a woman—and this is the argument as I understand it: "To say of a woman that she is raped does not impute unchastity." From that we get to this, which was solemnly put forward, that to say of a woman of good character that she had been ravished by a man of the worst possible character is not defamatory. That argument was solemnly presented to the jury, and I only wish the jury could have expressed, and that we could know, what they thought of it, because it seems to me to be one of the most legal arguments that were ever addressed to, I will not say a business body, but a sensible body.

That, really, as I understand it, is the argument upon which is based the contention that no reasonable jury could come to the conclusion that to say of a woman that she had been ravished by a man of very bad character when as a matter of fact she never saw the man at all and was never near him is not defamatory of the woman.

I really have no language to express my opinion of that argument. I therefore come, on the second point, to the view that there is no ground for interfering with the verdict of the jury (assuming the identification to stand, as I have assumed), that the words and the pictures in the film are defamatory of the lady whom they have found to be Princess Irina.

Then one comes to the third point, and that is the amount of damages. It is the law that in libel, though not in slander, you need not prove any particular damage in order to recover a verdict. What, then, is the position, the jury being the tribunal in libel or no libel, and, following from that, the tribunal as to the damages caused by libel, whose verdict is very rarely interfered with by the Court of Appeal? What have the jury to do? They have to give a verdict of amount without having any proof of actual damage. They need not have any proof of actual damage. They have to consider the nature of the libel as they understand it, the circumstances in which it was published, and the circumstances relating to the person who publishes it, right down to the time when they give their verdict, whether the defence made is true, and, if so, whether that defence has ever been withdrawn—the whole circumstances of the case. It is not the Judge who has to decide the amount. The constitution has thought, and I think there is great advantage in it, that the damages to be paid by a person who says false things about his neighbour are best decided by a jury representing the public, who may state the view of the public as to the action of the man who makes false statements about his neighbour, the plaintiff.

It is for that reason that it is extremely rare for the Court of Appeal to interfere with the verdict of the jury as to the amount of damages when the libel is established. It is very often the case that the individual Judges of the Court of Appeal, if they had been asked their verdict on the amount of damages, would have given a smaller sum. Sometimes they would have given a larger sum, but the question is not what amount the Judges would have given. The question is what amount the jury, as representing the public, the community, have fixed, and it is extremely rare to have that amount interfered with by the Court. A test has been formulated, and it is this, as has been correctly stated several times: the Courts will interfere only if the amount of damages is such that in all the circumstances no twelve reasonable men could have given it. If the Court comes to that view, it will interfere with the verdict, but even then it cannot fix the amount itself, but must send the case back to another jury who may very easily repeat the first verdict, and the Court cannot go on sending the case back to a jury until at last they get a verdict with which the Judges agree. Those are the reasons which justify the relation of the Court of Appeal to the amount of damages found by juries.

Applying that test to this case, I will say a word about the summing-up in a minute, I find it quite impossible to say that the amount of damages here is such that no reasonable jury could have given it. There is the position of the plaintiff, a high position, although the Royal Family of Russia have fallen from their high position. There is the amount of publicity given by circulating the film through a large circle of cinemas to be seen at cheap prices by an enormous number of people. Apparently in this case there were performances for a week in more than 16, possibly 20, cinemas. Looking at all those matters, I come to the conclusion that, if the jury were properly directed, this

Court cannot possibly interfere with the amount of the damages, even if any individual member of it, or all three members, had thought that if they had been on the jury they might have given a smaller sum.

Now, as to the summing-up. I have read the summing-up very carefully. I have listened to the comments on it and the objections which have been made to it. I am acquainted with the rule that insufficient, small, trivial deviations from accuracy in a summing-up should not affect the result unless the Court thinks that they have had a serious influence on it. Taking all these matters into consideration, I see no ground for disturbing this verdict on the ground of the summing-up of the very experienced Judge who delivered it.

For these reasons, in my opinion, this appeal should be dismissed, with costs.

LORD JUSTICE GREER:

After hearing the arguments on both sides in this case I have come to the same conclusion.

So far as the case raises questions of liability, the questions raised in this appeal are quite simple and very easy to deal with. If anyone printed and published the following words, "The lady who was engaged to Prince Youssoupoff had had sexual relations with the mad monk Rasputin," nobody could suggest that that was not a libel which ought to meet with serious consequences. The question as to the liability of the defendants in this case was: Did they say it? I do not think myself that this case has any similarity to cases like Cassidy v. Daily Mirror Newspapers, Limited, 45 Times L.R. 485, [1929] 2 K.B. 331, 69 A.L.R. 720, and Hulton and Co., Limited v. Jones, 26 Times L.R. 128, [1910] A.C. 20, 16 Ann.Cas. 166, because here, if the jury are right in their identification, although the defendants did not use the name of the plaintiff, they used a description of her that could apply to no one but the plaintiff. If anyone says, for example, that the Prime Minister of Ruritania is a fraudulent thief and there is evidence that the plaintiff is the Prime Minister of Ruritania, that is quite clearly a case in which he can recover, though his name has never been mentioned. If the jury come, as they may, to the conclusion that what has been said in the course of this film by means that amount to libel rather than slander is that the lady who was at one time betrothed to Prince Youssoupoff is a lady who had sexual relations with Rasputin, there is no answer, and there could be no real answer, to a claim for damages for libel brought by her. * * *

LORD JUSTICE SLESSER. * * *

I, for myself, cannot see that from the plaintiff's point of view it matters in the least whether this libel suggests that she has been seduced or ravished. The question whether she is or is not the more or the less moral seems to me immaterial in considering this question whether she has been defamed, and for this reason, that, as has been frequently pointed out in libel, not only is the matter defamatory, if it brings the plaintiff into hatred, ridicule, or contempt by reason of some moral discredit on her part, but also if it tends to make the plaintiff be shunned and avoided and that without any moral discredit on her part. It is for that reason that persons who have been alleged to have been insane, or to be suffering from certain diseases, and other cases where no direct moral responsibility could be placed upon them, have been held to be entitled to bring an action to protect their reputation and their honour.

One may, I think, take judicial notice of the fact that a lady of whom it has been said that she has been ravished, albeit against her will, has suffered in social reputation and in opportunities of receiving respectful consideration from the world. It is to shut one's eyes to realities to make these nice distinctions, but in this case I see no reason to suppose that this jury did come to a conclusion on this film that the imaginary lady depicted in the film, the Princess Natasha, was ravished and not seduced. I have looked at the pictures carefully, I have read the language, and it seems to me perfectly consistent with either view, and to assume at the outset that this film does represent a ravishment and not a seduction seems to me itself to assume that which the jury might have refused to assume at all. More particularly am I disinclined to take any view on this subject, because I have not seen the film and the jury have, and, as Sir Patrick Hastings has told us, they have seen it more than once. If it be the case that the jury may have thought the lady was seduced, of course the whole of this argument falls to the ground for want of any foundation of fact. * * * For these reasons I agree that this appeal fails.

Questions

1. Did the publication of Prince Youssoupoff's book constitute an essential "key" without which the court would have held for the defendant on the issue of identification? Even without reference to such book, were there not some persons who knew the facts disclosed in the book, and would therefore have been able to identify the plaintiff as Princess Natasha? Does the fact that many more persons were able to make the identification by reason of the book go to the issue of liability, or measure of damages, or is it of any significance?

2. Would the court that decided Kelly v. Loew's Inc., supra, have held for the defendant in the instant case on the ground that here, unlike *Kelly*, the defendant did not refer in its motion picture or advertising to the extrinsic "key"? Should it make any difference whether the defendant is the one who discloses the "key" which permits a substantial number of persons to make the identification?

3. Do you agree with the court that the distinction between an alleged seduction and an alleged rape is without significance under the law of defamation? Is it arguable that although there may have been no significant distinction between the two allegations in England of the 1930s, there is a meaningful distinction in contemporary United States?

BINDRIM v. MITCHELL

District Court of Appeal, Second District, Division 4, California, 1979.
92 Cal.App.3d 61, 155 Cal.Rptr. 29.

KINGSLEY, J.—This is an appeal taken by Doubleday and Gwen Davis Mitchell from a judgment for damages in favor of plaintiff-respondent Paul Bindrim, Ph.D. The jury returned verdicts on the libel counts against Doubleday and Mitchell and on the contract count against Mitchell.

The court denied defendants' motion for judgment NOV and granted a new trial subject to the condition that new trial would be denied if plaintiff would consent to (1) a reduction of the libel verdict against Mitchell from $38,000 to $25,000; (2) a striking of the $25,000 punitive damage award against Doubleday on the libel count; and (3) a striking of the $12,000 damage award on the contract count against Mitchell.

Plaintiff consented without prejudice on these issues in any appeal to be taken from the judgment. Defendants appealed and plaintiff cross-appealed from the judgment reducing the original jury verdict.

Plaintiff is a licensed clinical psychologist and defendant is an author. Plaintiff used the so-called "Nude Marathon" in group therapy as a means of helping people to shed their psychological inhibitions with the removal of their clothes.

Defendant Mitchell had written a successful best seller in 1969 and had set out to write a novel about women of the leisure class. Mitchell attempted to register in plaintiff's nude therapy but he told her he would not permit her to do so if she was going to write about it in a novel. Plaintiff said she was attending the marathon solely for therapeutic reasons and had no intention of writing about the nude marathon. Plaintiff brought to Mitchell's attention paragraph B of the written contract which reads as follows: "The participant agrees that he will not take photographs, write articles, or in any manner disclose who has attended the workshop or what has transpired. If he fails to do so he releases all parties from this contract, but remains legally liable for damages sustained by the leaders and participants."

Mitchell reassured plaintiff again she would not write about the session, she paid her money and the next day she executed the agreement and attended the nude marathon.

Mitchell entered into a contract with Doubleday two months later and was to receive $150,000 advance royalties for her novel.

Mitchell met Eleanor Hoover for lunch and said she was worried because she had signed a contract and painted a devastating portrait of Bindrim.

Mitchell told Doubleday executive McCormick that she had attended a marathon session and it was quite a psychological jolt. The novel was published under the name "Touching" and it depicted a nude encounter session in Southern California led by "Dr. Simon Herford."

Plaintiff first saw the book after its publication and his attorneys sent letters to Doubleday and Mitchell. Nine months later the New American Library published the book in paperback.

The parallel between the actual nude marathon sessions and the sessions in the book "Touching" was shown to the jury by means of the tape recordings Bindrim had taken of the actual sessions. Plaintiff complains in particular about a portrayed session in which he tried to encourage a minister to get his wife to attend the nude marathon. Plaintiff alleges he was libeled by the passage below:

Excerpts from "Touching"

Page 126–27

The minister was telling us how the experience had gotten him further back to God.

And all the time he was getting closer to God, he was being moved further away from his wife, who didn't understand, she didn't understand at all. She didn't realize what was coming out of the sensitivity training sessions he was conducting in the church.

he felt, he, more than felt, he knew, that if she didn't begin coming to the nude marathons and try to grasp what it was all about, the marriage would be over.

"You better bring her to the next marathon," Simon said.

"I've been trying," said the minister. "I only pray she comes."

"You better do better than pray," said Simon. "You better grab her by the cunt and drag her here."

"I can only try."

"You can do more than try. You can grab her by the cunt,

"A man with that kind of power, whether it comes from God or from his own manly strength, strength he doesn't know he has, can drag his wife here by the fucking cunt.

"I know," Alex said softly. "I know."

Transcript of Actual Session

"I've come a little way,"

"I'd like to know about your wife. She hasn't been to a marathon?"

"No."

"Isn't interested? Has no need?"

"I don't—she did finally say that she would like to go to a standard sensitivity training session somewhere. She would be—I can't imagine her in a nude marathon. She can't imagine it."

"Why?"

"Neither could I when I first came.

"Yeh. She might. I don't know."

"It certainly would be a good idea for two reasons: one, the minor one is that you are involved here, and if she were in the same thing, and you could come to some of the couple ones, it would be helpful to you. But more than that, almost a definite recipe for breaking up a marriage is for one person to go into growth groups and sense change and grow ..."

"I know that."

"Boy they sure don't want that, and once they're clear they don't need that mate anymore, and they are not very patient."

"But it is true, the more I get open the more the walls are built between us. And it's becoming a fairly intelligent place, a fairly open place, doing moderate sensitivity eyeballing stuff with the kids. I use some of these techniques teaching out class work."

"Becoming more involved?"

"Yeh, involved at the same time that I am more separated from. It's a paradox again, isn't it?"

"Mmm."

Plaintiff asserts that he was libeled by the suggestion that he used obscene language which he did not in fact use. Plaintiff also alleges various other libels due to Mitchell's inaccurate portrayal of what actually happened at the marathon. Plaintiff alleges that he was injured in his profession and expert testimony was introduced showing that Mitchell's portrayal of plaintiff was injurious and that plaintiff was identified by certain colleagues as the character in the book, Simon Herford.

* * *

Appellants claim that, even if there are untrue statements, there is no showing that plaintiff was identified as the character, Simon Herford, in the novel "Touching."

Appellants allege that plaintiff failed to show he was identifiable as Simon Herford, relying on the fact that the character in "Touching" was described in the book as a "fat Santa Claus type with long white hair, white sideburns, a cherubic rosy face and rosy forearms" and that Bindrim was clean shaven and had short hair. * * * In the case at bar, the only differences between plaintiff and the Herford character in "Touching" were physical appearance and that Herford was a psychiatrist rather than psychologist. Otherwise, the character Simon Herford was very similar to the actual plaintiff. We cannot say * * * that no one who knew plaintiff Bindrim could reasonably identify him with the fictional character. Plaintiff was identified as Herford by several witnesses and plaintiff's own tape recordings of the marathon sessions show that the novel was based substantially on plaintiff's conduct in the nude marathon.

* * *

There is overwhelming evidence that plaintiff and "Herford" were one.

* * *

However, * * * even though there was support for finding that plaintiff is identified as the character in Mitchell's novel, there still can be no recovery by plaintiff if the statements in "Touching" were not libelous. There can be no libel predicated on an opinion. The publication must contain a false statement of fact. (*Gregory v. McDonnell Douglas Corp.* (1976) 17 Cal.3d 596 [131 Cal.Rptr. 641, 552 P.2d 425].)

Plaintiff alleges that the book as a whole was libelous and that the book contained several false statements of fact. Plaintiff relies in part on the above quoted conversation between plaintiff and the minister as one libelous statement of fact. Plaintiff also argues that a particular incident in the book is libelous. That incident depicts an encounter group patient as so distressed upon leaving from the weekend therapy that she is killed when her car crashes. Plaintiff also complains of an incident in the book where he is depicted as "pressing," "clutching," and "ripping" a patient's cheeks and "stabbing against a pubic bone." Plaintiff complains, too, of being depicted as having said to a female patient, "Drop it, bitch." * * *

Our inquiry then, is directed to whether or not any of these incidents can be considered false statements of fact. It is clear from the transcript of the actual encounter weekend proceeding that some of the incidents portrayed by Mitchell are false: i.e., substantially inaccurate description of what actually happened. It is also clear that some of these portrayals cast plaintiff in a disparaging light since they portray his language and conduct as crude, aggressive, and unprofessional.

* * *

* * * Defendants contend that the fact that the book was labeled as being a "novel" bars any claim that the writer or publisher could be found to have implied that the characters in the book were factual representations not of the fictional characters but of an actual nonfictional person. That contention, thus broadly stated, is unsupported by the cases. The test is whether a reasonable person, reading the book, would understand that the fictional character therein pictured was, in actual fact, the plaintiff acting as described. * * * Whether a reader, identifying plaintiff with the "Dr. Herford" of the book, would regard the passages herein complained of as mere fictional embroidering or as reporting actual language and conduct, was for the jury. Its verdict adverse to the defendants cannot be overturned by this court.

V

Defendants raise the question of whether there is "publication" for libel where the communication is to only one person or a small group of persons rather than to the public at large. Publication for purposes of defamation is sufficient when the publication is to only one person other than the person defamed. (*Brauer v. Globe Newspaper Co.* (1966) 351 Mass. 53 [217 N.E.2d 736, 739].) Therefore, it is irrelevant whether all readers realized plaintiff and Herford were identical.

* * *

THE CROSS-APPEAL

Bindrim contends that the trial court erred in striking the damage award on the contract count. We are aware of no authority that a professional person can, by contract or otherwise, prevent one of his patients from reporting the treatment that patient received. Since the whole theory of plaintiff's therapy was that of group encounter, what Mitchell saw done to and by other members of the group was part of her own treatment. She was free to report what went on. The limits to her right to report were those involved in the libel counts. Plaintiff has no separate cause of action for the mere reporting.

* * *

Cross-respondents argue that the compensatory damages should be reduced to a total of $25,000 against both defendants. Judge Wells entered a judgment in the sum of $50,000, by charging each defendant $25,000. The jury's verdict should be reconciled when possible. (*Maheu v. Hughes Tool Co.* (1977) *supra*, 569 F.2d 459.) Insofar as the defendants are jointly and severally liable as joint or successive tortfeasors, we enter a $50,000 compensatory damage verdict against both defendants, for which they are jointly or severally liable.

Plaintiff's cross-appeal on the issue of punitive damages is well taken and the $25,000 award of punitive damages by the jury against Doubleday should stand. The jury had discretion not to award punitive damages against one of the defendants, since as we have said before, the greater wealth of one defendant is relevant.

* * *

Otherwise the judgment is affirmed. Neither party shall recover costs on appeal.

* * *

FILES, P.J., Dissenting.—* * *

* * *

IDENTIFICATION

Whether or not an allegedly defamatory communication was made "of and concerning the plaintiff" is an issue involving constitutional rights. (*New York Times v. Sullivan* (1964) 376 U.S. 254, 288 [11 L.Ed.2d 686, 711, 84 S.Ct. 710, 95 A.L.R. 1412]; see Rest.2d Torts, § 580A com. (g).) Criticism of an institution, profession or technique is protected by the First Amendment; and such criticism may not be suppressed merely because it may reflect adversely upon someone who cherishes the institution or is a part of it.

Defendants' novel describes a fictitious therapist who is conspicuously different from plaintiff in name, physical appearance, age, personality and profession.

Indeed the fictitious Dr. Herford has none of the characteristics of plaintiff except that Dr. Herford practices nude encounter therapy. Only three witnesses, other than plaintiff himself, testified that they "recognized" plaintiff as the fictitious Dr. Herford. All three of those witnesses had participated in or observed one of plaintiff's nude marathons. The only characteristic mentioned by any of the three witnesses as identifying plaintiff was the therapy practiced.

* * *

Plaintiff has no monopoly upon the encounter therapy which he calls "nude marathon." Witnesses testified without contradiction that other professionals use something of this kind. There does not appear to be any reason why anyone could not conduct a "marathon" using the style if not the full substance of plaintiff's practices.

Plaintiff's brief discusses the therapeutic practices of the fictitious Dr. Herford in two categories: Those practices which are similar to plaintiff's technique are classified as identifying. Those which are unlike plaintiff's are called libelous because they are false. Plaintiff has thus resurrected the spurious logic which Professor Kalven found in the position of the plaintiff in *New York Times v. Sullivan, supra,* 376 U.S. 254. Kalven wrote: "There is revealed here a new technique by which defamation might be endlessly manufactured. First, it is argued that, contrary to all appearances, a statement referred to the plaintiff; then, that it falsely ascribed to the plaintiff something that he did not do, which should be rather easy to prove about a statement that did not refer to plaintiff in the first place. * * *" Kalven, *The New York Times Case: A Note on "The Central Meaning of the First Amendment,"* 1964 Sup.Ct.Rev. 191, 199.

* * *

The only instruction given the jury on the issue of identification stated that plaintiff had the burden of proving "That a third person read the statement and reasonably understood the defamatory meaning and that the statement applied to plaintiff."

That instruction was erroneous and prejudicial in that it only required proof that one "third person" understood the defamatory meaning.

The word "applied" was most unfortunate in the context of this instruction. The novel was about nude encounter therapy. Plaintiff practiced nude encounter therapy. Of course the novel "applied to plaintiff," particularly insofar as it exposed what may result from such therapy. This instruction invited the jury to find that plaintiff was libeled by criticism of the kind of therapy he practiced. The effect is to mulct the defendants for the exercise of their First Amendment right to comment on the nude marathon.

* * *

From an analytical standpoint, the chief vice of the majority opinion is that it brands a novel as libelous because it is "false," i.e., fiction; and infers "actual malice" from the fact that the author and publisher knew it was not a true representation of plaintiff. From a constitutional standpoint the vice is the chilling effect upon the publisher of any novel critical of any occupational practice, inviting litigation on the theory "when you criticize my occupation, you libel me."

I would reverse the judgment.

* * *

Questions

1. If the only resemblance between plaintiff and the fictional character "Simon Herford" were that both conducted nude marathon group therapy sessions, should this be held sufficient to permit the trier of fact to find that plaintiff was identified in defendants' work? On this issue is it significant whether plaintiff was the only practitioner of nude therapy? one of a small number? one of many? Were there other elements of resemblance between plaintiff and "Herford"? Were they sufficient to justify a finding of identification? Does it matter if the only persons who might make such an identification were those who were enrolled in plaintiff's therapy sessions?

2. Is the court correct in its conclusion that a doctor may not by contract "prevent one of his patients from reporting the treatment that patient received"? What is the basis for the court's conclusion that the law of contracts does not operate in this context? Is there any such basis?

Collateral Reference

Wilson, *The Law of Libel and the Art of Fiction*, 44 Law & Contemp.Probs. 27 (Autumn 1981).

C. FIRST AMENDMENT DEFENSE

NEW YORK TIMES CO. v. SULLIVAN

Supreme Court of the United States, 1964.
376 U.S. 254, 84 S.Ct. 710, 11 L.Ed.2d 686.

MR. JUSTICE BRENNAN delivered the opinion of the Court.

We are required in this case to determine for the first time the extent to which the constitutional protections for speech and press limit a State's power to award damages in a libel action brought by a public official against critics of his official conduct.

Respondent L.B. Sullivan is one of the three elected Commissioners of the City of Montgomery, Alabama. He testified that he was "Commissioner of Public Affairs and the duties are supervision of the Police Department, Fire Department, Department of Cemetery and Department of Scales." He brought this civil libel action against the four individual petitioners, who are Negroes and Alabama clergymen, and against petitioner the New York Times Company, a New York corporation which publishes the New York Times, a daily newspaper. A jury in the Circuit Court of Montgomery County awarded him damages of $500,000, the full amount claimed, against all the petitioners, and the Supreme Court of Alabama affirmed. 273 Ala. 656, 144 So.2d 25.

Respondent's complaint alleged that he had been libeled by statements in a full-page advertisement that was carried in the New York Times on March 29, 1960. Entitled "Heed Their Rising Voices," the advertisement began by stating that "As the whole world knows by now, thousands of Southern Negro students are engaged in widespread non-violent demonstrations in positive affirmation of the right to live in human dignity as guaranteed by the U.S. Constitution and the Bill of Rights." It went on to charge that "in their efforts to uphold these guarantees, they are being met by an unprecedented wave of terror by those who would deny and negate that document which the whole world looks upon as setting the pattern for modern freedom. * * * " Succeeding paragraphs purported to illustrate the "wave of terror" by describing certain alleged events. The text concluded with an appeal for funds for three purposes: support of the student movement, "the struggle for the right-to-vote," and the legal defense of Dr. Martin Luther King, Jr., leader of the movement, against a perjury indictment then pending in Montgomery. * * *

Of the 10 paragraphs of text in the advertisement, the third and a portion of the sixth were the basis of respondent's claim of libel. They read as follows:

Third paragraph:

> In Montgomery, Alabama, after students sang "My Country, 'Tis of Thee" on the State Capitol steps, their leaders were expelled from school, and truckloads of police armed with shotguns and tear-gas ringed the Alabama State College Campus. When the entire student body protested

Sec. C FIRST AMENDMENT DEFENSE 641

THE NEW YORK TIMES, TUESDAY, MARCH 29, 1960. L 25

Heed Their Rising Voices

"The growing movement of peaceful mass demonstrations by Negroes is something new in the South, something understandable.... Let Congress heed their rising voices, for they will be heard."

—New York Times editorial
Saturday, March 19, 1960

As the whole world knows by now, thousands of Southern Negro students are engaged in widespread non-violent demonstrations in positive affirmation of the right to live in human dignity as guaranteed by the U. S. Constitution and the Bill of Rights. In their efforts to uphold these guarantees, they are being met by an unprecedented wave of terror by those who would deny and negate that document which the whole world looks upon as setting the pattern for modern freedom....

In Orangeburg, South Carolina, when 400 students peacefully sought to buy doughnuts and coffee at lunch counters in the business district, they were forcibly ejected, tear-gassed, soaked to the skin in freezing weather with fire hoses, arrested en masse and herded into an open barbed-wire stockade to stand for hours in the bitter cold.

In Montgomery, Alabama, after students sang "My Country, 'Tis of Thee" on the State Capitol steps, their leaders were expelled from school, and truckloads of police armed with shotguns and tear-gas ringed the Alabama State College Campus. When the entire student body protested to state authorities by refusing to re-register, their dining hall was padlocked in an attempt to starve them into submission.

In Tallahassee, Atlanta, Nashville, Savannah, Greensboro, Memphis, Richmond, Charlotte, and a host of other cities in the South, young American teen-agers, in face of the entire weight of official state apparatus and police power, have boldly stepped forth as protagonists of democracy. Their courage and amazing restraint have inspired millions and given a new dignity to the cause of freedom.

Small wonder that the Southern violators of the Constitution fear this new, non-violent brand of freedom fighter ... even as they fear the upswelling right-to-vote movement. Small wonder that they are determined to destroy the one man who, more than any other, symbolizes the new spirit now sweeping the South—the Rev. Dr. Martin Luther King, Jr., world-famous leader of the Montgomery Bus Protest. For it is his doctrine of non-violence which has inspired and guided the students in their widening wave of sit-ins; and it this same Dr. King who founded and is president of the Southern Christian Leadership Conference—the organization which is spearheading the surging right-to-vote movement. Under Dr. King's direction the Leadership Conference conducts Student Workshops and Seminars in the philosophy and technique of non-violent resistance.

Again and again the Southern violators have answered Dr. King's peaceful protests with intimidation and violence. They have bombed his home almost killing his wife and child. They have assaulted his person. They have arrested him seven times—for "speeding," "loitering" and similar "offenses." And now they have charged him with "perjury"—a felony under which they could imprison him for ten years. Obviously, their real purpose is to remove him physically as the leader to whom the students and millions of others—look for guidance and support, and thereby to intimidate *all* leaders who may rise in the South. Their strategy is to behead this affirmative movement, and thus to demoralize Negro Americans and weaken their will to struggle. The defense of Martin Luther King, spiritual leader of the student sit-in movement, clearly, therefore, is an integral part of the total struggle for freedom in the South.

Decent-minded Americans cannot help but applaud the creative daring of the students and the quiet heroism of Dr. King. But this is one of those moments in the stormy history of Freedom when men and women of good will must do more than applaud the rising-to-glory of others. The America whose good name hangs in the balance before a watchful world, the America whose heritage of Liberty these Southern Upholders of the Constitution are defending, is *our* America as well as theirs ...

We must heed their rising voices—yes—but we must add our own.

We must extend ourselves above and beyond moral support and render the material help so urgently needed by those who are taking the risks, facing jail, and even death in a glorious re-affirmation of our Constitution and its Bill of Rights.

We urge you to join hands with our fellow Americans in the South by supporting, with your dollars, this Combined Appeal for all three needs—the defense of Martin Luther King—the support of the embattled students—and the struggle for the right-to-vote.

Your Help Is Urgently Needed ... NOW!!

Stella Adler
Raymond Pace Alexander
Harry Van Arsdale
Harry Belafonte
Julie Belafonte
Dr. Algernon Black
Marc Blitzstein
William Branch
Marlon Brando
Mrs. Ralph Bunche
Diahann Carroll

Dr. Alan Knight Chalmers
Richard Coe
Nat King Cole
Cheryl Crawford
Dorothy Dandridge
Ossie Davis
Sammy Davis, Jr.
Ruby Dee
Dr. Philip Elliott
Dr. Harry Emerson Fosdick

Anthony Franciosa
Lorraine Hansbury
Rev. Donald Harrington
Nat Hentoff
James Hicks
Mary Hinkson
Van Heflin
Langston Hughes
Morris Iushewitz
Mahalia Jackson
Mordecai Johnson

John Killens
Eartha Kitt
Rabbi Edward Klein
Hope Lange
John Lewis
Viveca Lindfors
Carl Murphy
Don Murray
John Murray
A. J. Muste
Frederick O'Neal

L. Joseph Overton
Clarence Pickett
Shad Polier
Sidney Poitier
A. Philip Randolph
John Raitt
Elmer Rice
Jackie Robinson
Mrs. Eleanor Roosevelt
Bayard Rustin
Robert Ryan

Maureen Stapleton
Frank Silvera
Hope Stevens
George Tabori
Rev. Gardner C. Taylor
Norman Thomas
Kenneth Tynan
Charles White
Shelley Winters
Max Youngstein

We in the south who are struggling daily for dignity and freedom warmly endorse this appeal

Rev. Ralph D. Abernathy (Montgomery, Ala.)
Rev. Fred L. Shuttlesworth (Birmingham, Ala.)
Rev. Kelley Miller Smith (Nashville, Tenn.)
Rev. W. A. Dennis (Chattanooga, Tenn.)
Rev. C. K. Steele (Tallahassee, Fla.)

Rev. Matthew D. McCollom (Orangeburg, S. C.)
Rev. William Holmes Borders (Atlanta, Ga.)
Rev. Douglas Moore (Durham, N. C.)
Rev. Wyatt Tee Walker (Petersburg, Va.)

Rev. Walter L. Hamilton (Norfolk, Va.)
I. S. Levy (Columbia, S. C.)
Rev. Martin Luther King, Sr. (Atlanta, Ga.)
Rev. Henry C. Bunton (Memphis, Tenn.)
Rev. S. S. Seay, Sr. (Montgomery, Ala.)
Rev. Samuel W. Williams (Atlanta, Ga.)

Rev. A. L. Davis (New Orleans, La.)
Mrs. Katie E. Whickham (New Orleans, La.)
Rev. W. H. Hall (Hattiesburg, Miss.)
Rev. J. E. Lowery (Mobile, Ala.)
Rev. T. J. Jemison (Baton Rouge, La.)

Please mail this coupon TODAY!

Committee To Defend Martin Luther King
and
The Struggle For Freedom In The South
312 West 125th Street, New York 27, N. Y.
UNiversity 6-1700

I am enclosing my contribution of $_____
for the work of the Committee.

Name_____ (PLEASE PRINT)
Address_____
City_____ Zone_____ State_____

☐ I want to help   ☐ Please send further information

Please make checks payable to:
Committee To Defend Martin Luther King

COMMITTEE TO DEFEND MARTIN LUTHER KING AND THE STRUGGLE FOR FREEDOM IN THE SOUTH
312 West 125th Street, New York 27, N. Y. UNiversity 6-1700

Chairmen: A. Philip Randolph, Dr. Gardner C. Taylor; *Chairmen of Cultural Division*: Harry Belafonte, Sidney Poitier; *Treasurer*: Nat King Cole; *Executive Director*: Bayard Rustin; *Chairmen of Church Division*: Father George B. Ford, Rev. Harry Emerson Fosdick, Rev. Thomas Kilgore, Jr., Rabbi Edward E. Klein; *Chairman of Labor Division*: Morris Iushewitz

The offending advertisement.

[D2429]

to state authorities by refusing to re-register, their dining hall was pad locked in an attempt

Sixth paragraph:

> Again and again the Southern violators have answered Dr. King's peaceful protests with intimidation and violence. They have bombed his home almost killing his wife and child. They have assaulted his person. They have arrested him seven times—for "speeding," "loitering" and similar "offenses." And now they have charged him with "perjury"—a *felony* under which they could imprison him for *ten years*. * * *

Although neither of these statements mentions respondent by name, he contended that the word "police" in the third paragraph referred to him as the Montgomery Commissioner who supervised the Police Department, so that he was being accused of "ringing" the campus with police. He further claimed that the paragraph would be read as imputing to the police, and hence to him, the padlocking of the dining hall in order to starve the students into submission. As to the sixth paragraph, he contended that since arrests are ordinarily made by the police, the statement "They have arrested [Dr. King] seven times" would be read as referring to him; he further contended that the "They" who did the arresting would be equated with the "They" who committed the other described acts and with the "Southern violators." Thus, he argued, the paragraph would be read as accusing the Montgomery police, and hence him, of answering Dr. King's protests with "intimidation and violence," bombing his home, assaulting his person, and charging him with perjury. Respondent and six other Montgomery residents testified that they read some or all of the statements as referring to him in his capacity as Commissioner.

It is uncontroverted that some of the statements contained in the two paragraphs were not accurate descriptions of events which occurred in Montgomery. [Examples of inaccuracies omitted].

* * *

We reverse the judgment. We hold that the rule of law applied by the Alabama courts is constitutionally deficient for failure to provide the safeguards for freedom of speech and of the press that are required by the First and Fourteenth Amendments in a libel action brought by a public official against critics of his official conduct. We further hold that under the proper safeguards the evidence presented in this case is constitutionally insufficient to support the judgment for respondent.

I.

We may dispose at the outset of two grounds asserted to insulate the judgment of the Alabama courts from constitutional scrutiny. The first is the proposition relied on by the State Supreme Court—that "The Fourteenth Amendment is directed against State action and not private action." That proposition has no application to this case. Although this is a civil lawsuit between private parties, the Alabama courts have applied a state rule of law which petitioners claim to impose invalid restrictions on their constitutional freedoms of speech and press.

* * *

The second contention is that the constitutional guarantees of freedom of speech and of the press are inapplicable here, at least so far as the Times is concerned, because the allegedly libelous statements were published as part of a paid, "commercial" advertisement.

* * * That the Times was paid for publishing the advertisement is as immaterial in this connection as is the fact that newspapers and books are sold. Smith v. California, 361 U.S. 147, 150; cf. Bantam Books, Inc., v. Sullivan, 372 U.S. 58, 64, n. 6. Any other conclusion would discourage newspapers from carrying "editorial advertisements" of this type, and so might shut off an important outlet for the promulgation of information and ideas by persons who do not themselves have access to publishing facilities—who wish to exercise their freedom of speech even though they are not members of the press. * * * To avoid placing such a handicap upon the freedoms of expression, we hold that if the allegedly libelous statements would otherwise be constitutionally protected from the present judgment, they do not forfeit that protection because they were published in the form of a paid advertisement.

II.

Under Alabama law as applied in this case, a publication is "libelous per se" if the words "tend to injure a person * * * in his reputation" or to "bring [him] into public contempt"; the trial court stated that the standard was met if the words are such as to "injure him in his public office, or impute misconduct to him in his office, or want of official integrity, or want of fidelity to a public trust. * * * *" The jury must find that the words were published "of and concerning" the plaintiff, but where the plaintiff is a public official his place in the governmental hierarchy is sufficient evidence to support a finding that his reputation has been affected by statements that reflect upon the agency of which he is in charge. Once "libel per se" has been established, the defendant has no defense as to stated facts unless he can persuade the jury that they were true in all their particulars. His privilege of "fair comment" for expressions of opinion depends on the truth of the facts upon which the comment is based. Unless he can discharge the burden of proving truth, general damages are presumed, and may be awarded without proof of pecuniary injury. A showing of actual malice is apparently a prerequisite to recovery of punitive damages, and the defendant may in any event forestall a punitive award by a retraction meeting the statutory requirements. Good motives and belief in truth do not negate an inference of malice, but are relevant only in mitigation of punitive damages if the jury chooses to accord them weight.

The question before us is whether this rule of liability, as applied to an action brought by a public official against critics of his official conduct, abridges the freedom of speech and of the press that is guaranteed by the First and Fourteenth Amendments.

Respondent relies heavily, as did the Alabama courts, on statements of this Court to the effect that the Constitution does not protect libelous publications. Those statements do not foreclose our inquiry here. None of the cases sustained the use of libel laws to impose sanctions upon expression critical of the official conduct of public officials. * * * Like insurrection, contempt, advocacy of unlawful acts, breach of the peace, obscenity, solicitation of legal business, and the various other formulae for the repression of expression that have been challenged in this Court, libel can claim no talismanic immunity from constitutional limitations. It must be measured by standards that satisfy the First Amendment. * * *

Thus we consider this case against the background of a profound national commitment to the principle that debate on public issues should be uninhibited, robust, and wide-open, and that it may well include vehement, caustic, and sometimes unpleasantly sharp attacks on government and public officials. See Terminiello v. Chicago, 337 U.S. 1, 4; De Jonge v. Oregon, 299 U.S. 353.

The present advertisement, as an expression of grievance and protest on one of the major public issues of our time, would seem clearly to qualify for the constitutional protection. The question is whether it forfeits that protection by the falsity of some of its factual statements and by its alleged defamation of respondent.

Authoritative interpretations of the First Amendment guarantees have consistently refused to recognize an exception for any test of truth—whether administered by judges, juries, or administrative officials—and especially one that puts the burden of proving truth on the speaker. * * * That erroneous statement is inevitable in free debate, and that it must be protected if the freedoms of expression are to have the "breathing space" that they "need * * * to survive," * * *

Injury to official reputation affords no more warrant for repressing speech that would otherwise be free than does factual error. Where judicial officers are involved, this Court has held that concern for the dignity and reputation of the courts does not justify the punishment as criminal contempt of criticism of the judge or his decision. Bridges v. California, 314 U.S. 252. This is true even though the utterance contains "half-truths" and "misinformation." Pennekamp v. Florida, 328 U.S. 331, 342, 343, n. 5, 345. Such repression can be justified, if at all, only by a clear and present danger of the obstruction of justice. See also Craig v. Harney, 331 U.S. 367; Wood v. Georgia, 370 U.S. 375. If judges are to be treated as "men of fortitude, able to thrive in a hardy climate," Craig v. Harney, supra, 331 U.S., at 376, surely the same must be true of other government officials, such as elected city commissioners. Criticism of their official conduct does not lose its constitutional protection merely because it is effective criticism and hence diminishes their official reputations.

If neither factual error nor defamatory content suffices to remove the constitutional shield from criticism of official conduct, the combination of the two elements is no less inadequate. This is the lesson to be drawn from the great controversy over the Sedition Act of 1798, 1 Stat.

596, which first crystallized a national awareness of the central meaning of the First Amendment. * * *

Although the Sedition Act was never tested in this Court, the attack upon its validity has carried the day in the court of history. Fines levied in its prosecution were repaid by Act of Congress on the ground that it was unconstitutional. * * *

What a State may not constitutionally bring about by means of a criminal statute is likewise beyond the reach of its civil law of libel. The fear of damage awards under a rule such as that invoked by the Alabama courts here may be markedly more inhibiting than the fear of prosecution under a criminal statute. * * *

The judgment awarded in this case—without the need for any proof of actual pecuniary loss—was one thousand times greater than the maximum fine provided by the Alabama criminal statute, and one hundred times greater than that provided by the Sedition Act. And since there is no double-jeopardy limitation applicable to civil lawsuits, this is not the only judgment that may be awarded against petitioners for the same publication. Whether or not a newspaper can survive a succession of such judgments, the pall of fear and timidity imposed upon those who would give voice to public criticism is an atmosphere in which the First Amendment freedoms cannot survive. Plainly the Alabama law of civil libel is "a form of regulation that creates hazards to protected freedoms markedly greater than those that attend reliance upon the criminal law." Bantam Books, Inc., v. Sullivan, 372 U.S. 58, 70.

The state rule of law is not saved by its allowance of the defense of truth. A defense for erroneous statements honestly made is no less essential here than was the requirement of proof of guilty knowledge which, in Smith v. California, 361 U.S. 147, we held indispensable to a valid conviction of a bookseller for possessing obscene writings for sale. * * *

A rule compelling the critic of official conduct to guarantee the truth of all his factual assertions—and to do so on pain of libel judgments virtually unlimited in amount—leads to a comparable "self-censorship." Allowance of the defense of truth, with the burden of proving it on the defendant, does not mean that only false speech will be deterred.[1] * * * Under such a rule, would-be critics of official conduct may be deterred from voicing their criticism, even though it is believed to be true and even though it is in fact true, because of doubt whether it can be proved in court or fear of the expense of having to do so. They tend to make only statements which "steer far wider of the unlawful zone." Speiser v. Randall, supra, 357 U.S., at 526. The rule

---

1. Even a false statement may be deemed to make a valuable contribution to public debate, since it brings about "the clearer perception and livelier impression of truth, produced by its collision with error." Mill, On Liberty (Oxford: Blackwell, 1947), at 15; see also Milton, Areopagitica, in Prose Works (Yale, 1959), Vol. II, at 561.

thus dampens the vigor and limits the variety of public debate. It is inconsistent with the First and Fourteenth Amendments.

The constitutional guarantees require, we think, a federal rule that prohibits a public official from recovering damages for a defamatory falsehood relating to his official conduct unless he proves that the statement was made with "actual malice"—that is, with knowledge that it was false or with reckless disregard of whether it was false or not. * * *

Such a privilege for criticism of official conduct [2] is appropriately analogous to the protection accorded a public official when *he* is sued for libel by a private citizen. [Barr v. Matteo, 360 U.S. 564, 575] * * * It would give public servants an unjustified preference over the public they serve, if critics of official conduct did not have a fair equivalent of the immunity granted to the officials themselves.

We conclude that such a privilege is required by the First and Fourteenth Amendments.

III.

We hold today that the Constitution delimits a State's power to award damages for libel in actions brought by public officials against critics of their official conduct. Since this is such an action,[3] the rule requiring proof of actual malice is applicable. While Alabama law apparently requires proof of actual malice for an award of punitive damages, where general damages are concerned malice is "presumed." Such a presumption is inconsistent with the federal rule. * * * Since the trial judge did not instruct the jury to differentiate between general and punitive damages, it may be that the verdict was wholly an award of one or the other. But it is impossible to know, in view of the general verdict returned. Because of this uncertainty, the judgment must be reversed and the case remanded.

---

2. The privilege immunizing honest misstatements of fact is often referred to as a "conditional" privilege to distinguish it from the "absolute" privilege recognized in judicial, legislative, administrative and executive proceedings. See, e.g., Prosser, Torts (2d ed., 1955), § 95.

3. We have no occasion here to determine how far down into the lower ranks of government employees the "public official" designation would extend for purposes of this rule, or otherwise to specify categories of persons who would or would not be included. Cf. Barr v. Matteo, 360 U.S. 564, 573–575. Nor need we here determine the boundaries of the "official conduct" concept. It is enough for the present case that respondent's position as an elected city commissioner clearly made him a public official, and that the allegations in the advertisement concerned what was allegedly his official conduct as Commissioner in charge of the Police Department. As to the statements alleging the assaulting of Dr. King and the bombing of his home, it is immaterial that they might not be considered to involve respondent's official conduct if he himself had been accused of perpetrating the assault and the bombing. Respondent does not claim that the statements charged him personally with these acts; his contention is that the advertisement connects him with them only in his official capacity as the Commissioner supervising the police, on the theory that the police might be equated with the "They" who did the bombing and assaulting. Thus, if these allegations can be read as referring to respondent at all, they must be read as describing his performance of his official duties.

* * *

Since respondent may seek a new trial, we deem that considerations of effective judicial administration require us to review the evidence in the present record to determine whether it could constitutionally support a judgment for respondent. This Court's duty is not limited to the elaboration of constitutional principles; we must also in proper cases review the evidence to make certain that those principles have been constitutionally applied.

* * *

Applying these standards, we consider that the proof presented to show actual malice lacks the convincing clarity which the constitutional standard demands, and hence that it would not constitutionally sustain the judgment for respondent under the proper rule of law.

* * *

We think the evidence against the Times supports at most a finding of negligence in failing to discover the misstatements, and is constitutionally insufficient to show the recklessness that is required for a finding of actual malice. * * *

We also think the evidence was constitutionally defective in another respect: it was incapable of supporting the jury's finding that the allegedly libelous statements were made "of and concerning" respondent. * * *

The judgment of the Supreme Court of Alabama is reversed and the case is remanded to that court for further proceedings not inconsistent with this opinion.

Reversed and remanded.

MR. JUSTICE BLACK, with whom MR. JUSTICE DOUGLAS joins, concurring. * * *

I base my vote to reverse on the belief that the First and Fourteenth Amendments not merely "delimit" a State's power to award damages to "public officials against critics of their official conduct" but completely prohibit a State from exercising such a power. The Court goes on to hold that a State can subject such critics to damages if "actual malice" can be proved against them. "Malice," even as defined by the Court, is an elusive, abstract concept, hard to prove and hard to disprove. The requirement that malice be proved provides at best an evanescent protection for the right critically to discuss public affairs and certainly does not measure up to the sturdy safeguard embodied in the First Amendment. Unlike the Court, therefore, I vote to reverse exclusively on the ground that the Times and the individual defendants had an absolute, unconditional constitutional right to publish in the Times advertisement their criticisms of the Montgomery agencies and officials. * * *

MR. JUSTICE GOLDBERG, with whom MR. JUSTICE DOUGLAS joins, concurring in the result.

* * *

In my view, the First and Fourteenth Amendments to the Constitution afford to the citizen and to the press an absolute, unconditional privilege to criticize official conduct despite the harm which may flow from excesses and abuses. The prized American right "to speak one's mind," cf. Bridges v. California, 314 U.S. 252, 270, about public officials and affairs needs "breathing space to survive," N.A.A.C.P. v. Button, 371 U.S. 415, 433. The right should not depend upon a probing by the jury of the motivation of the citizen or press. * * *

This is not to say that the Constitution protects defamatory statements directed against the private conduct of a public official or private citizen. Freedom of press and of speech insures that government will respond to the will of the people and that changes may be obtained by peaceful means. Purely private defamation has little to do with the political ends of a self-governing society. The imposition of liability for private defamation does not abridge the freedom of public speech or any other freedom protected by the First Amendment.[4] * * *

Questions

1. Does the *Times* decision constitute an implicit balancing of the antithetical interests in freedom of speech and the protection of reputations? Did the Court strike a proper balance as between these two interests? See Note, immediately infra.

2. Is the First Amendment defense to defamation enunciated in *Times* and its progeny significant with respect to novels and dramatic productions? Does the *Times* rule apply to publications other than newspapers? Does intentional fictionalization or dramatization necessarily mean that the work is either knowingly false or that at least there is a reckless disregard as to whether or not it is false? If it were applicable, would the *Times* rule have helped the defendant in Youssoupoff v. Metro-Goldwyn-Mayer, supra? Would it have affected the result in Kelly v. Loew's Inc., supra?

Collateral References

Kalven, *The New York Times Case: A Note on "The Central Meaning of the First Amendment,"* 1964 Sup.Ct.Rev. 191.

Brennan, *The Supreme Court and the Meiklejohn Interpretation of the First Amendment,* 79 Harv.Law Rev. 1 (1965).

Wright, *Defamation, Privacy and the Publics' Right to Know: A National Problem and a New Approach,* 46 Tex.Law Rev. 630 (1968).

Green, *Continuing the Privacy Discussion: A Response to Judge Wright and President Bloustein,* 46 Tex.Law Rev. 750 (1968).

---

4. In most cases, as in the case at bar, there will be little difficulty in distinguishing defamatory speech relating to private conduct from that relating to official conduct. I recognize, of course, that there will be a gray area. The difficulties of applying a public-private standard are, however, certainly of a different genre from those attending the differentiation between a malicious and nonmalicious state of mind. If the constitutional standard is to be shaped by a concept of malice, the speaker takes the risk not only that the jury will inaccurately determine his state of mind but also that the jury will fail properly to apply the

Note *

The Balancing of Interests in New York Times Co. v. Sullivan

The Supreme Court in the *New York Times* case might have gone along with the Black and Douglas concurrence, holding that all defamatory statements are protected by the first amendment. This is the absolutist position, and while I have argued above that no one can or should take the position that all speech under all circumstances is immunized, it is certainly tenable to take the absolutist position with respect to abridgments based on the defamatory content of speech. At the other extreme, the Court might have taken the position, suggested in the dicta of earlier cases, that defamation is entirely outside the protection of the first amendment. Instead the Court held that all defamatory speech directed at public officials is within the orbit of first amendment protection except that speech which is knowingly false or which is made with reckless disregard of its truth or falsity. Why did the Court strike this particular balance? Since the *Times* decision was not explicitly based upon a balancing of interest, the Court's opinion is not very helpful in articulating the precise basis for the balance reached. But from portions of the opinion in *Times*, as well as the opinions in later cases applying the doctrine,[1] enough can be gleaned to permit an extrapolation of the Court's rationale. Such a rationale does, I submit, justify the definitional balance adopted by the Court.

In weighing the competing interests of speech and reputation, it is well to recall first some of the reasons why freedom of speech is important. Mr. Justice Brandeis in his concurring opinion in Whitney v. California[2] suggested three separate reasons: First, free speech is a necessary concomitant of a democratic society. We cannot intelligently make the decisions required of a self-governing people unless we are permitted to hear all possible views bearing upon such decisions. Second, quite apart from its utility in the democratic process, freedom of expression is an end in itself. Self-expression is a part of self-fulfillment, or as Justice Brandeis suggested, liberty is "the secret of happiness." Third, freedom of speech is a necessary safety valve. Those who are not permitted to express themselves in words are more likely to seek expression in violent deeds. There may be other justifications for freedom of expression, but these are sufficient for our purposes.

Competing with these speech values is society's interest in protecting reputations from injury by false statements. Though it is intangible, this injury can be no less real than the injury from physical attack. The evil of defamation is self-evident, and tort protection here requires no greater theoretical justification than does tort protection against assault and battery, and other attacks upon the person.[3]

---

constitutional standard set by the elusive concept of malice.

* This is an extract from Nimmer, The Right to Speak From *Times* to *Time:* First Amendment Theory Applied to Libel and Misapplied to Privacy, 56 Cal.Law Rev. 935 (1968).

1. Garrison v. Louisiana, 379 U.S. 64 (1964); Rosenblatt v. Baer, 383 U.S. 75 (1966); Curtis Publishing Co. v. Butts, 388 U.S. 130 (1967).

2. 274 U.S. 357, 372–80 (1927).

3. "The right of a man to the protection of his own reputation from unjustified invasion and wrongful hurt reflects no more than our basic concept of the essential dignity and worth of every human being—a concept at the root of any decent system of ordered liberty." Mr. Justice Stewart, concurring in Rosenblatt v. Baer, 383 U.S. 75, 92 (1966).

With these two competing interests in view, the threshold question must be whether the speech values justify the Court in sweeping away most of the law of defamation where the statement is made against a public figure. The injury to reputation which results from defamation is no less by reason of the speaker's belief in the truth of the false statements uttered. Yet, *Times* holds that defamatory statements are protected speech notwithstanding the resulting injury. I submit that the Court was correct in according greater weight to the interest in protecting good faith but erroneous speech than it did to the interest in protecting reputations.

The particular balancing can be defended on several grounds: First, the content of the public dialogue on issues vital to the democratic process should not be limited by what a jury decides is true. Ordinarily we are content to rely upon a jury's findings of fact for the purpose of determining rights as between immediate litigants. But when the "fact" to be determined relates to the truth or falsity of speech, it is not only the immediate litigants that are concerned. All of society has an interest in hearing and evaluating the speech. What twelve men believe to be false, millions of others may believe to be true, and they should not be precluded by the twelve from making their own independent evaluation of truth. Second, speech which society may vitally need to hear may be deterred by the fear that a jury will find it to be false even though in fact the fear may be ungrounded and the jury, if given the opportunity, would find it to be true. Third, assuming that the statement is objectively false, if the speaker in good faith believes it to be true, then at least two of the three speech values suggested above nevertheless remain applicable. These are the interest in self-expression and the safety valve factor. Fourth, the cure for good faith reputation injury, like the cure for other evils arising from erroneous speech, should be found not in repressing the speech, but in answering it. As Mr. Justice Brandeis concluded in *Whitney:* "[T]he remedy to be applied is more speech, not enforced silence."[4] It is true that the refutation of infamy at times may not have the same impact as the charge of infamy, but isn't that merely a special application of the general risk we are willing to assume when we put our faith in the free and unfettered exchange of ideas? Is it less true here than elsewhere that "the best test of truth is the power of the thought to get itself accepted in the competition of the market?"[5] This is not to say that a real injury to reputation may not occur, but only that the evil, serious as it may be, is less than the injury to society generally from the suppression of good faith speech.

But if this reasoning is acceptable, it may be argued that no defamatory utterance should be held outside the protection of the first amendment. The Court in *Times* did not go this far. It found the balance of interests to weigh in favor of reputation and against speech when the speech is knowingly false, or made with reckless disregard of truth. Can this further balancing in the opposite direction also be defended? I believe that it can. In striking this new balance consider first the evil of injury to reputation. That evil at least remains constant; it is no less serious when balanced against speech which is held to be knowingly false than it is when balanced against speech held to have been made in good faith. But does the other side of the balance, the interest in free speech, continue to have a greater weight? It seems clear that the speech values suggested above are inapplicable to speech which the speaker knows to

---

4. Whitney v. California, 274 U.S. 357, 377 (1927) (concurring opinion).

5. Abrams v. United States, 250 U.S. 616, 630 (1919) (dissenting opinion of Holmes, J.).

be false. A knowing lie hardly contributes to the democratic dialogue.[6] Quite the contrary, it distorts the collective search for truth. It is also hard to regard it as a necessary function of self-fulfillment. When I express ideas which I do not believe to be true, I am not in any real sense expressing my *self*, and abridgment of such expression is not an abridgment of self-fulfillment. Finally, the safety valve which is necessary for honestly believed, even though erroneous doctrine, is hardly necessary for that which is not truly believed. Men are not likely to resort to violence because they cannot express that which they do not believe.

But this does not answer the crucial objection made by the dissenters to the Court's exclusion of first amendment protection for the knowing and recklessly false. Their fear is that even if one speaks with a good faith belief in the truth of his speech, a jury may find that the statement was made with knowledge of its falsity or with reckless disregard of its truth or falsity, and more importantly, that many persons will be deterred from expressing themselves in good faith from the fear that a jury *might* make such a finding.

These are cogent objections which certainly bear weight, but, I would suggest, considerably lesser weight than the same concerns in connection with our original ad hoc balancing of speech against reputation. It is certainly possible that a jury will incorrectly find that a statement was made without belief in its truth, or in reckless disregard of truth when in fact the speaker acted in a good faith belief. But the issue before the jury will not be the broad question of the truth or falsity of the defamatory statement, but rather the narrow question of the speaker's good faith. A jury will probably not go wrong on this narrow question of fact in view of the Court's statement in *Times* that the Constitution demands a standard of "convincing clarity"[7] in the proof of knowing or reckless falsity. Moreover, the burden of proof on this narrow issue makes it increasingly likely that an appellate court will reverse jury determinations against the speaker when the standard of convincing clarity has not been met. Such appellate reversal will be far easier to obtain than if the only question were whether there was evidence by which the jury might have reasonably concluded that the statement itself was false. Finally, the deterrent effect of the risk that a jury might find that the speaker acted without an honest belief in what he said is probably not great. Remember that the issue is not whether the speaker had a reasonable belief, but only whether he had an honest, good faith belief. It seems likely that most people who do in good faith believe what they say would be willing to risk the possibility of an adverse court determination on the narrow issue of their good faith even if they would not be willing to risk a legal determination of the truth of their statement. Confirmation of this may be found in other related fields. In copyright, for example, it is my experience that one who believes that another has infringed his copyright does not hesitate to openly accuse the other of infringement even though there is some risk of liability for slander of title or disparagement if the

---

6. "For the use of the known lie as a tool is at once at odds with the premises of democratic government and with the orderly manner in which economic, social, or political change is to be effected." Garrison v. Louisiana, 379 U.S. 64, 75 (1964). But see New York Times Co. v. Sullivan, 376 U.S. 254, 279 n. 19 (1964), where the Court quotes John Stuart Mill: "Even a false statement may be deemed to make a valuable contribution to public debate, since it brings about 'the clear perception and livelier impression of truth'; produced by its collision with error," J. Mill, On Liberty 15 (Oxford ed. 1947).

7. 376 U.S. at 285–86.

court finds both that there was no infringement *and* that the accusation of infringement was made in bad faith.[8]

The foregoing considerations suggest that the injury to the interest in freedom of speech is measurably reduced when there is abridgment only of defamatory speech which is knowingly false or recklessly made rather than abridgment of all defamatory speech.

For me the conclusive demonstration that in this more limited context the interest in reputation outweighs the interest in speech is the weakness of the alternative. It is true that some impairment of speech values remains even if we abridge only knowingly false or reckless defamation. But consider the consequences of adopting the Black-Douglas view[9] that all defamation is protected under the first amendment. Under such a rule it is obvious that the interest in reputation would suffer greatly, if not be completely obliterated. But would we at least have a concomitant increase in the protection of speech values? Is it not clear that the contrary would be the case? Not only would the interest in reputation suffer, but the interest in speech itself would also suffer grave impairment. Remember that one of the chief reasons we value free speech is because of its central position in maintaining a democratic dialogue so necessary to an enlightened electorate.[10] Under a rule which immunized *all* defamation, reputation assassins could make with impunity and with utter disregard of the consequences completely irresponsible and monstrous accusations against anyone unfortunate enough to cross their path. Apart from the havoc this would wreak to reputations, what would it do to the democratic dialogue, one of the prime reasons for maintaining free speech? If there were no limits as to what might be said against a candidate for office, if accusations no matter how reckless and unfounded could be made with impunity, could we hope to preserve any rationality in our electoral processes? We might still hope that speech would answer speech; but if the basic values of free speech are inapplicable at this point, as indicated above, was not the Court wise to draw the line to save us from a blood bath of character assassination?

A final aspect of the Court's balancing in *Times* that must be considered is the limitation of first amendment immunity to defamatory statements concerning "public officials." Recently, in Curtis Publishing Company v. Butts,[11] the Court has gone further and extended such immunity to statements concerning "public figures" regardless of whether such persons are governmental officials.[12] Although admittedly something of a departure from the rationale

---

8. See Nimmer on Copyright, § 8.21[F].

9. See New York Times Co. v. Sullivan, 376 U.S. 254, 293 (1964) (concurring opinion).

10. For general discussion of the purpose of the first amendment see A. Meiklejohn, Political Freedom: The Constitutional Powers of the People (1960); Emerson, Toward a General Theory of the First Amendment, 72 Yale L.J. 877, 878–86 (1963); Kalven, The New York Times Case: A Note on "The Central Meaning of the First Amendment," 1964 Supreme Court Rev. 191 (1964).

11. 388 U.S. 130 (1967). This opinion combined the decisions in Curtis and in Associated Press v. Walker.

12. Four members of the Court (Justices Harlan, Clark, Stewart, and Fortas) would have applied a different rule as to a public figure who is not a public official, under which such persons could recover in a libel action only upon a showing that the defendant had engaged in "highly unreasonable conduct constituting an extreme departure from the standards of investigation and reporting ordinarily adhered to by responsible publishers." Id. at 155. Chief Justice Warren in a concurring opinion applied the *Times* standard without modification to public figures who are not public officials, expressing doubt that the standard suggested by Justice Harlan, "based on such an unusual and uncertain formulation could either guide a jury of laymen or afford

relied upon the Court in *Times*,[13] the *Curtis* extension to persons who are public figures but not public officials is certainly consonant with the fundamental objectives of the first amendment. Those objectives require full and free discussion of public issues. Since discussion of public issues cannot be meaningful without reference to the men involved on both sides of such issues, and since such men will not necessarily be public officials,[14] one cannot but agree that the Court was right in *Curtis* to extend the *Times* rule to all public figures. Here again the Court has engaged in implicit balancing.

It may be argued that the Court did not go far enough in that apparently it would not invoke the first amendment to immunize defamatory statements concerning nonpublic figures in the context of a discussion of issues of legitimate public interest.[15] If the touchstone of first amendment rights is the promotion of uninhibited discussion of public issues, then shouldn't such discussion be protected even if the persons involved are in no sense public figures?[16] I would suggest that the Court was correct in implying that at this point the reputation interest outweighs the speech interest. To take a rigidly libertarian position and fault the Court for not extending defamation immunity to all discussion of public issues would be to overlook a fundamental ingredient of first amendment theory. The Brandeis prescription for meeting error with "more speech," and Justice Holmes "best test of truth" are grounded upon the presupposition of a free market place of ideas. If and to the extent speech cannot be answered with speech, the theory breaks down. Because "'public figures' have as ready access as 'public officials' to mass media of communica-

---

protection for speech and debate. * * * *" Id. at 163. Justices Brennan and White joined in this portion of the Warren opinion, and Justices Black and Douglas concurred in the "grounds and reason stated" in this portion of the Chief's opinion, but only "in order for the Court to be able at this time to agree on [an opinion]. * * * " Id. at 170. This appears to mean that five of the Justices would, insofar as they would apply the *Times* standard at all, apply it without distinction between public officials and public figures who are not public officials. [See Gertz v. Robert Welch, Inc., infra.]

13. The *Times* opinion rested at least in part upon an analogy to the doctrine in Barr v. Matteo, 360 U.S. 564, 575 (1959), where statements of a federal official were found to be absolutely privileged if made "within the outer perimeter of his duties." See New York Times Co. v. Sullivan, 376 U.S. at 282 (1964). This rationale was also used in Washington Post Co. v. Keogh, 365 F.2d 965, 968 (D.C.Cir.1966).

14. See Curtis Publishing Co. v. Butts, 388 U.S. 130, 164 (1967) (concurring opinion of Warren, C.J.): " * * * many who do not hold public office at the moment are nevertheless intimately involved in the resolution of important public questions or, by reason of their fame, shape events in areas of concern to society at large."

15. As to the converse situation, i.e., a defamatory statement directed against the private conduct of a public official, Mr. Justice Douglas would apparently part company from Mr. Justice Black, and hold the first amendment does not prohibit liability in a libel action in such circumstances. See the concurring opinion of Mr. Justice Goldberg joined by Mr. Justice Douglas in *Times*, 376 U.S. at 301. The *Times* decision has been so understood by lower courts. See, e.g., People v. Mager, 25 App.Div.2d 363, 269 N.Y.S.2d 848 (1966). It is possible that the Supreme Court might not go this far in limiting first amendment protection since it was deemed appropriate in Garrison v. Louisiana, 379 U.S. 64, 72 n. 8 (1964) to state that as to "purely private libels" involving presumably both private issues and nonpublic figures, "nothing we say today is to be taken as intimating any views as to the impact of the constitutional guarantees. * * * *" But see authority cited note 56 infra.

16. "Yet if free discussion of public issues is the guide, I see no way to draw lines that exclude * * * anyone on the public payroll. * * * And [how about] industrialists who raise the price of a basic commodity? * * * And the labor leader who combines trade unionism with bribery and racketeering? * * * The question is whether a public *issue,* not a public official is involved." Rosenblatt v. Baer, 383 U.S. 89, 91 (1966) (concurring opinion of Douglas, J.).

tion, both to influence policy and to counter criticism of their views and activities" [17] the Court was justified in extending first amendment immunity to all public figures. But persons who have not achieved the celebrity of a public figure may not have access to the mass media to answer defamatory statements made against them. For this reason the speech interest at this point bears a lesser weight and may properly be subordinated to the reputation interest.[18]

It is important, however, not to use this reasoning to prove too much. Some would argue that in the present semimonopolistic posture of the news and information media, the presupposition of a free market place of ideas has become totally obsolete. One can agree that only if the monopolistic controls presently extant in newspapers and broadcasting are countered by devices for insuring the dissemination of minority views will the full values which underlie the first amendment be realized,[19] but this does not justify the withdrawal of first amendment immunity from public discussion because such devices are absent. Nevertheless, where the absence of the ability to mount an effective reply coincides with a strong antispeech interest such as the interest in reputation, the resulting balance of interests may properly be weighed against the right to speak. It is to be hoped that the *Curtis* extension of *Times* will not be followed by a further extension of first amendment immunity to defamatory statements concerning "private" persons involved in public issues.

Collateral References

Hill, *Defamation and Privacy Under the First Amendment*, 76 Columbia L.Rev. 1205 (1976).

Silver, *Libel, the "Higher Truths" of Art, and the First Amendment*, 126 U.Pa.L.Rev. 1065 (1978).

Nimmer on Freedom of Speech, § 2.05[C][1].

GERTZ v. ROBERT WELCH, INC.

Supreme Court of the United States, 1974.
418 U.S. 323, 94 S.Ct. 2997, 41 L.Ed.2d 789.

Mr. Justice Powell delivered the opinion of the Court.

This Court has struggled for nearly a decade to define the proper accommodation between the law of defamation and the freedoms of

---

17. Curtis Publishing Co. v. Butts, 388 U.S. 130, 164 (1967) (concurring opinion of Warren, C.J.).

18. In Rosenblatt v. Baer, 383 U.S. 75, 86 n. 13 (1966), the Court denied that the *Times* rule would be applicable to a night watchman accused of stealing state secrets since this "would virtually disregard society's interest in protecting reputation. The employee's position must be one which would invite public scrutiny and discussion of the person holding it, entirely apart from the scrutiny and discussion occasioned by the particular charges in controversy." Can this statement be reconciled with the immediately preceding footnote where the Court stated: "We intimate no view whatever whether there are other bases for applying the *New York Times* standards—for example, that in a particular case the interests in reputation are relatively insubstantial, because the subject of discussion has thrust himself into the vortex of the discussion of a question of pressing public concern"? Id. at 86 n. 12. Did the hypothetical night watchman "thrust himself into the vortex" by being present at a time when state secrets were stolen?

19. See Barron, Access to the Press—A New First Amendment Right, 80 Harv.L. Rev. 1641 (1967).

speech and press protected by the First Amendment. With this decision we return to that effort. We granted certiorari to reconsider the extent of a publisher's constitutional privilege against liability for defamation of a private citizen. 410 U.S. 925 (1973).

I

In 1968 a Chicago policeman named Nuccio shot and killed a youth named Nelson. The state authorities prosecuted Nuccio for the homicide and ultimately obtained a conviction for murder in the second degree. The Nelson family retained petitioner Elmer Gertz, a reputable attorney, to represent them in civil litigation against Nuccio.

Respondent publishes American Opinion, a monthly outlet for the views of the John Birch Society. Early in the 1960's the magazine began to warn of a nationwide conspiracy to discredit local law enforcement agencies and create in their stead a national police force capable of supporting a communist dictatorship. As part of the continuing effort to alert the public to this assumed danger, the managing editor of American Opinion commissioned an article on the murder trial of officer Nuccio. For this purpose he engaged a regular contributor to the magazine. In March of 1969 respondent published the resulting article under the title "FRAME–UP: Richard Nuccio And The War On Police." The article purports to demonstrate that the testimony against Nuccio at his criminal trial was false and that his prosecution was part of the communist campaign against the police.

In his capacity as counsel for the Nelson family in the civil litigation, petitioner attended the coroner's inquest into the boy's death and initiated actions for damages, but he neither discussed officer Nuccio with the press nor played any part in the criminal proceeding. Notwithstanding petitioner's remote connection with the prosecution of Nuccio, respondent's magazine portrayed him as an architect of the "frame-up." According to the article, the police file on petitioner took "a big, Irish cop to lift." The article stated that petitioner had been an official of the "Marxist League for Industrial Democracy, originally known as the Intercollegiate Socialist Society, which has advocated the violent seizure of our government." It labelled Gertz a "Leninist" and a "Communist-fronter." It also stated that Gertz had been an officer of the National Lawyers Guild, described as a communist organization that "probably did more than any other outfit to plan the Communist attack on the Chicago police during the 1968 Democratic convention."

These statements contained serious inaccuracies. The implication that petitioner had a criminal record was false. Petitioner had been a member and officer of the National Lawyers Guild some 15 years earlier, but there was no evidence that he or that organization had taken any part in planning the 1968 demonstrations in Chicago. There was also no basis for the charge that petitioner was a "Leninist" or a "Communist-fronter." And he had never been a member of the "Marxist League for Industrial Democracy" or the "Intercollegiate Socialist Society."

The managing editor of American Opinion made no effort to verify or substantiate the charges against petitioner. Instead, he appended an editorial introduction stating that the author had "concluded extensive research into the Richard Nuccio case." And he included in the article a photograph of petitioner and wrote the caption that appeared under it: "Elmer Gertz of the Red Guild harasses Nuccio." Respondent placed the issue of American Opinion containing the article on sale at newsstands throughout the country and distributed reprints of the article on the streets of Chicago.

Petitioner filed a diversity action for libel in the United States District Court for the Northern District of Illinois. He claimed that the falsehoods published by respondent injured his reputation as a lawyer and a citizen. Before filing an answer, respondent moved to dismiss the complaint for failure to state a claim upon which relief could be granted, apparently on the ground that petitioner failed to allege special damages. But the court ruled that statements contained in the article constituted libel *per se* under Illinois law and that consequently petitioner need not plead special damages. 306 F.Supp. 310 (N.D.Ill. 1969).

After answering the complaint, respondent filed a pre-trial motion for summary judgment, claiming a constitutional privilege against liability for defamation. It asserted that petitioner was a public official or a public figure and that the article concerned an issue of public interest and concern. For these reasons, respondent argued, it was entitled to invoke the privilege enunciated in New York Times Co. v. Sullivan, 376 U.S. 254 (1964). Under this rule respondent would escape liability unless petitioner could prove publication of defamatory falsehood "with 'actual malice'—that is, in the knowledge that it was false or with reckless disregard for whether it was true or not." *Id.*, at 279–280. Respondent claimed that petitioner could not make such a showing and submitted a supporting affidavit by the magazine's managing editor. The editor denied any knowledge of the falsity of the statements concerning petitioner and stated that he had relied on the author's reputation and on his prior experience with the accuracy and authenticity of his contributions to American Opinion.

The District Court denied respondent's motion for summary judgment in a memorandum opinion of Sept. 16, 1970. The court did not dispute respondent's claim to the protection of the *New York Times* standard. Rather, it concluded that petitioner might overcome the constitutional privilege by making a factual showing sufficient to prove publication of defamatory falsehood in reckless disregard of the truth. During the course of the trial, however, it became clear that the trial court had not accepted all of respondent's asserted grounds for applying the *New York Times* rule to this case. It thought that respondent's claim to the protection of the constitutional privilege depended on the contention that petitioner was either a public official under the *New York Times* decision or a public figure under Curtis Publishing Co. v. Butts, 388 U.S. 130 (1967), apparently discounting the argument that a privilege would arise from the presence of a public issue. After all the evidence had been presented but before submission of the case to the jury, the court ruled in effect that petitioner was neither a public official nor a public figure. It added that, if he were, the resulting application of the *New York Times* standard would require a directed verdict for respondent. Because some statements in the article constituted libel *per se* under Illinois law, the court submitted the case to the jury under instructions that withdrew from its consideration all issues save the measure of damages. The jury awarded $50,000 to petitioner.

Following the jury verdict and on further reflection, the District Court concluded that the *New York Times* standard should govern this case even though petitioner was not a public official or public figure. It accepted respondent's contention that that privilege protected discussion of any public issue without regard to the status of a person defamed therein. Accordingly, the court entered judgment for respondent notwithstanding the jury's verdict. This conclusion anticipated the reasoning of a plurality of this Court in Rosenbloom v. Metromedia, 403 U.S. 29 (1971).

Petitioner appealed to contest the applicability of the *New York Times* standard to this case. Although the Court of Appeals for the Seventh Circuit doubted the correctness of the District Court's determination that petitioner was not a public figure, it did not overturn that finding.[3] It agreed with the District Court that respondent could assert the constitutional privilege because the article concerned a matter of public interest, citing this Court's intervening decision in Rosenbloom v. Metromedia, Inc., supra. The Court of Appeals read Rosenbloom to require application of the New York Times standard to any publication or broadcast about an issue of significant public interest, without regard to the position, fame, or anonymity of the person defamed, and it concluded that respondent's statements concerned such an issue.[4]

---

3. The court stated:
"[Petitioner's] considerable stature as a lawyer, author, lecturer, and participant in matters of public import undermine the validity of the assumption that he is not a 'public figure' as that term has been used by the progeny of *New York Times*. Nevertheless, for purposes of decision we make that assumption and test the availability of the claim of privilege by the subject matter of the article." 471 F.2d, at 805.

4. In the Court of Appeals petitioner made an ingenious but unavailing attempt to show that respondent's defamatory charge against him concerned no issue of public or general interest. He asserted that the subject matter of the article was the murder trial of Officer Nuccio and that he did not participate in that proceeding. Therefore, he argued, even if the subject matter of the article generally were protected by the *New York Times* privilege, under the opinion of the *Rosenbloom* plurality, the defamatory statements about him were not. The Court of Appeals rejected this argument. It noted that the accusations against petitioner played an integral part in respondent's general thesis of a nationwide conspiracy to harass the police:

"[W]e may also assume that the article's basic thesis is false. Nevertheless, under the reasons of New York Times v. Sullivan, even a false statement made in support of a false thesis is protected unless made with knowledge of its falsity or with reckless disregard of its truth or falsity. It would undermine the rule of that case to permit the actual falsity of a statement to determine whether or not its publisher is entitled to the benefit of the rule.

"If, therefore, we put to one side the false character of the article and treat it as though its contents were entirely true, it

After reviewing the record, the Court of Appeals endorsed the District Court's conclusion that petitioner had failed to show by clear and convincing evidence that respondent had acted with "actual malice" as defined by *New York Times*. There was no evidence that the managing editor of American Opinion knew of the falsity of the accusations made in the article. In fact, he knew nothing about petitioner except what he learned from the article. The court correctly noted that mere proof of failure to investigate, without more, cannot establish reckless disregard for the truth. Rather, the publisher must act with a "high degree of awareness * * * of probable falsity." St. Amant v. Thompson, 390 U.S. 727, 731 (1968). Accord: Beckley Newspaper Corp. v. Hanks, 389 U.S. 81, 84–85 (1967); Garrison v. Louisiana, 379 U.S. 67, 75–76 (1964). The evidence in this case did not reveal that respondent had cause for such an awareness. The Court of Appeals therefore affirmed 471 F.2d 801 (1972). For the reasons stated below, we reverse.

II

The principal issue in this case is whether a newspaper or broadcaster that publishes defamatory falsehoods about an individual who is neither a public official nor a public figure may claim a constitutional privilege against liability for the injury inflicted by those statements. The Court considered this question on the rather different set of facts presented in Rosenbloom v. Metromedia, Inc., 403 U.S. 29 (1971). Rosenbloom, a distributor of nudist magazines, was arrested for selling allegedly obscene material while making a delivery to a retail dealer. The police obtained a warrant and seized his entire inventory of 3,000 books and magazines. He sought and obtained an injunction prohibiting further police interference with his business. He then sued a local radio station for failing to note in two of its newscasts that the 3,000 items seized were only "reportedly" or "allegedly" obscene and for broadcasting references to "the smut literature racket" and to "girlie-book peddlers" in its coverage of the court proceeding for injunctive relief. He obtained a judgment against the radio station, but the Court

---

cannot be denied that the comments about [petitioner] were integral to its thesis. They must be tested under the *New York Times* standard." 471 F.2d, at 806.

We think that the Court of Appeals correctly rejected petitioner's argument. Its acceptance might lead to arbitrary imposition of liability on the basis of an unwise differentiation among kinds of factual misstatements. The present case illustrates the point. Respondent falsely portrayed petitioner as an architect of the criminal prosecution against Nuccio. On its face this inaccuracy does not appear defamatory. Respondent also falsely labelled petitioner a "Leninist" and a "Communist-fronter." These accusations are generally considered defamatory. Under petitioner's interpretation of the "public or general interest" test, respondent would have enjoyed a constitutional privilege to publish defamatory falsehoods if petitioner had in fact been associated with the criminal prosecution. But this would mean that the seemingly innocuous mistake of confusing petitioner's role in the litigation against officer Nuccio would destroy the privilege otherwise available for calling petitioner a communist-fronter. Thus respondent's privilege to publish statements whose content should have alerted it to the danger of injury to reputation would hinge on the accuracy of statements that carried with them no such warning. Assuming that none of these statements was published with knowledge of falsity or with reckless disregard for the truth, we see no reason to distinguish among the inaccuracies.

Sec. C   **FIRST AMENDMENT DEFENSE**   659

of Appeals for the Third Circuit held the *New York Times* privilege applicable to the broadcast and reversed. 415 F.2d 892 (1969).

This Court affirmed the decision below, but no majority could agree on a controlling rationale. The eight Justices [5] who participated in *Rosenbloom* announced their views in five separate opinions, none of which commanded more than three votes. The several statements not only reveal disagreement about the appropriate result in that case; they also reflect divergent traditions of thought about the general problem of reconciling the law of defamation with the First Amendment. One approach has been to extend the *New York Times* test to an expanding variety of situations. Another has been to vary the level of constitutional privilege for defamatory falsehood with the status of the person defamed. And a third view would grant to the press and broadcast media absolute immunity from liability for defamation. To place our holding in the proper context, we preface our discussion of this case with a review of the several *Rosenbloom* opinions and their antecedents.

In affirming the trial court's judgment in the instant case, the Court of Appeals relied on Mr. Justice Brennan's conclusion for the *Rosenbloom* plurality that "all discussion and communication involving matters of public or general concern" warrant the protection from liability for defamation accorded by the rule originally enunciated in New York Times Co. v. Sullivan, 376 U.S. 254 (1964). There this Court defined a constitutional privilege intended to free criticism of public officials from the restraints imposed by the common law of defamation. The Times ran a political advertisement endorsing civil rights demonstrations by black students in Alabama and impliedly condemning the performance of local law enforcement officials. A police commissioner established in state court that certain misstatements in the advertisement referred to him and that they constituted libel *per se* under Alabama law. This showing left the Times with the single defense of truth, for under Alabama law neither good faith nor reasonable care would protect the newspaper from liability. This Court concluded that a "rule compelling the critic of official conduct to guarantee the truth of all his factual assertions" would deter protected speech, id., at 279, and announced the constitutional privilege designed to counter that effect:

> The constitutional guarantees require, we think, a federal rule that prohibits a public official from recovery of damages for a defamatory falsehood relating to his official conduct unless he proves that the statement was made with "actual malice"—that is, in the knowledge that it was false or with reckless disregard of whether it was true or not. *Id.*, at 279–280.[6]

---

5. Mr. Justice Douglas did not participate in the consideration or decision of *Rosenbloom*.

6. *New York Times* and later cases explicated the meaning of the new standard.

In *New York Times* the Court held that under the circumstances the newspaper's failure to check the accuracy of the advertisement against news stories in its own files did not establish reckless disregard for

Three years after *New York Times*, a majority of the Court agreed to extend the constitutional privilege to defamatory criticism of "public figures." This extension was announced in Curtis Publishing Co. v. Butts and its companion Associated Press v. Walker, 388 U.S. 130, 162 (1967). The first case involved the Saturday Evening Post's charge that Coach Wall Butts of the University of Georgia had conspired with Coach Bear Bryant of the University of Alabama to fix a football game between their respective schools. *Walker* involved an erroneous Associated Press account of Brigadier General Edwin Walker's participation in a University of Mississippi campus riot. Because Butts was paid by a private alumni association and Walker had retired from the Army, neither could be classified as a "public official" under *New York Times*. Although Mr. Justice Harlan announced the result in both cases, a majority of the Court agreed with Mr. Chief Justice Warren's conclusion that the *New York Times* test should apply to criticism of "public figures" as well as "public officials." [7] The Court extended the constitu-

---

the truth. 376 U.S., at 287–288. In St. Amant v. Thompson, 390 U.S. 727, 731 (1968), the Court equated reckless disregard of the truth with subjective awareness of probable falsity: "There must be sufficient evidence to permit the conclusion that the defendant in fact entertained serious doubts as to the truth of his publication." In Beckley Newspapers Corp. v. Hanks, 389 U.S. 81 (1967), the Court emphasized the distinction between the *New York Times* test of knowledge of falsity or reckless disregard of the truth and "actual malice" in the traditional sense of ill-will. Garrison v. Louisiana, 379 U.S. 64 (1964), made plain that the new standard applied to criminal libel laws as well as to civil actions and that it governed criticism directed at "anything which might touch on an official's fitness for office." Id. at 77. Finally, in Rosenblatt v. Baer, 383 U.S. 75, 85 (1966), the Court stated that "the 'public official' designation applies at the very least to those among the hierarchy of government employees who have, or appear to the public to have, substantial responsibility for or control over the conduct of government affairs."

In Time, Inc. v. Hill, 385 U.S. 374 (1967), the Court applied the *New York Times* standard to actions under an unusual state statute. The statute did not create a cause of action for libel. Rather, it provided a remedy for unwanted publicity. Although the law allowed recovery of damages for harm caused by exposure to public attention rather than by factual inaccuracies, it recognized truth as a complete defense. Thus, nondefamatory factual errors could render a publisher liable for something akin to invasion of privacy. The Court ruled that the defendant in such an action could invoke the *New York Times* privilege regardless of the fame or anonymity of the plaintiff. Speaking for the Court, Mr. Justice Brennan declared that this holding was not an extension of *New York Times* but rather a parallel line of reasoning applying that standard to this discrete context:

"This is neither a libel action by a private individual nor a statutory action by a public official. Therefore, although the First Amendment principles announced in *New York Times* guide our conclusion, we reach that conclusion only by applying these principles in this discrete context. It therefore serves no purpose to distinguish the facts here from those in *New York Times*. Were this a libel action, the distinction which has been suggested between the relative opportunities of the public official and the private individual to rebut defamatory charges might be germane. And the additional state interest in the protection of the individual against damages to his reputation would be involved. Cf. Rosenblatt v. Baer, 383 U.S. 75, 91 (Stewart, J., concurring)." Id., at 390–391.

7. Professor Kalven once introduced a discussion of these cases with the apt heading, "You Can't Tell the Players Without a Score Card." H. Kalven, The Reasonable Man and the First Amendment, 1967 Sup. Ct.Rev. 267, 275 (1967). Only three other Justices joined Mr. Justice Harlan's analysis of the issues involved. In his concurring opinion, Mr. Chief Justice Warren stated the principle for which these cases stand— that the *New York Times* test reaches both public figures and public officials. Mr. Justice Brennan and Mr. Justice White agreed with the Chief Justice on that question. Mr. Justice Black and Mr. Justice Douglas reiterated their view that publishers should

tional privilege announced in that case to protect defamatory criticism of nonpublic officials who "are nevertheless intimately involved in the resolution of important public questions, or, by reason of their fame, shape events in areas of concern to society at large." Id., at 164.

In his opinion for the plurality in Rosenbloom v. Metromedia, Inc., 403 U.S. 29 (1971), Mr. Justice Brennan took the *New York Times* privilege one step further. He concluded that its protection should extend to defamatory falsehoods relating to private persons if the statements concerned matters of general or public interest. He abjured the suggested distinction between public officials and public figures on the one hand and private individuals on the other. He focused instead on society's interest in learning about certain issues: "If a matter is a subject of public or general interest, it cannot suddenly become less so merely because a private individual is involved or because in some sense the individual did not choose to become involved." 403 U.S., at 43. Thus, under the plurality opinion, a private citizen involuntarily associated with a matter of general interest has no recourse for injury to his reputation unless he can satisfy the demanding requirements of the *New York Times* test.

Two members of the Court concurred in the result in *Rosenbloom* but departed from the reasoning of the plurality. Mr. Justice Black restated his view, long shared by Mr. Justice Douglas, that the First Amendment cloaks the news media with an absolute and indefeasible immunity from liability for defamation. Id., at 57. Mr. Justice White concurred on a narrower ground. Ibid. He concluded that "the First Amendment gives the press and the broadcast media a privilege to report and comment upon the official actions of public servants in full detail, with no requirement that the reputation or privacy of an individual involved in or affected by the official action be spared from public view." Id., at 62. He therefore declined to reach the broader questions addressed by the other Justices.

Mr. Justice Harlan dissented. Although he had joined the opinion of the Court in *New York Times*, in *Curtis Publishing Co.* he had contested the extension of the privilege to public figures. There he had argued that a public figure who held no governmental office should be allowed to recover damages for defamation "on a showing of highly unreasonable conduct constituting an extreme departure from the standards of investigation and reporting ordinarily adhered to by responsible publishers." 388 U.S., at 155. In his *Curtis Publishing Co.* opinion Mr. Justice Harlan had distinguished *New York Times* primarily on the ground that defamation actions by public officials "lay close to seditious libel. * * * " Id., at 133. Recovery of damages by one who held no public office, however, could not "be viewed as a vindication of governmental policy." Id., at 154. Additionally, he had intimated that, because most public officials enjoyed absolute immunity from

have an absolute immunity from liability for defamation, but they acquiesced in the Chief Justice's reasoning in order to enable a majority of the Justices to agree on the question of the appropriate constitutional privilege for defamation of public figures.

liability for their own defamatory utterances under Barr v. Matteo, 360 U.S. 564 (1959), they lacked a strong claim to the protection of the courts.

In *Rosenbloom*, Mr. Justice Harlan modified these views. He acquiesced in the application of the privilege to defamation of public figures but argued that a different rule should obtain where defamatory falsehood harmed a private individual. He noted that a private person has less likelihood "of securing access to the channels of communication sufficient to rebut falsehoods concerning him" than do public officials and public figures, id., at 70, and has not voluntarily placed himself in the public spotlight. Mr. Justice Harlan concluded that the States could constitutionally allow private individuals to recover damages for defamation on the basis of any standard of care except liability without fault.

Mr. Justice Marshall dissented in *Rosenbloom* in an opinion joined by Mr. Justice Stewart. Id., at 78. He thought that the plurality's "public or general interest" test for determining the applicability of the *New York Times* privilege would involve the courts in the dangerous business of deciding "what information is relevant to self-government." Id., at 79. He also contended that the plurality's position inadequately served "society's interest in protecting private individuals from being thrust into the public eye by the distorting light of defamation." Ibid. Mr. Justice Marshall therefore reached the conclusion, also reached by Mr. Justice Harlan, that the States should be "essentially free to continue the evaluation of the common law of defamation and to articulate whatever fault standards best suits the State's need," so long as the States did not impose liability without fault. Id., at 86. The principal point of disagreement among the three dissenters concerned punitive charges. Whereas Mr. Justice Harlan thought that the States could allow punitive damages in amounts bearing "a reasonable and purposeful relationship to the actual harm done * * *," id., at 75, Mr. Justice Marshall concluded that the size and unpredictability of jury awards of exemplary damages unnecessarily exacerbated the problems of media self-censorship and that such damages should therefore be forbidden.

III

We begin with the common ground. Under the First Amendment there is no such thing as a false idea. However pernicious an opinion may seem, we depend for its correction not on the conscience of judges and juries but on the competition of other ideas.[8] But there is no constitutional value in false statements of fact. Neither the intentional lie nor the careless error materially advances society's interest in "uninhibited, robust, and wide-open" debate on public issues. New

---

8. As Thomas Jefferson made the point in his first Inaugural Address: "If there be any among us who wish to dissolve this union or change its republican form of government, let them stand undisturbed as monuments of the safety with which error of opinion may be tolerated where reason is left free to combat it."

York Times Co. v. Sullivan, 376 U.S., at 270. They belong to that category of utterances which "are no essential part of any exposition of ideas, and are of such slight social value as a step to truth that any benefit that may be derived from them is clearly outweighed by the social interest in order and morality." Chaplinsky v. New Hampshire, 315 U.S. 568, 572 (1942).

Although the erroneous statement of fact is not worthy of constitutional protection, it is nevertheless inevitable in free debate. As James Madison pointed out in the Report on the Virginia Resolutions of 1798, "Some degree of abuse is inseparable from the proper use of everything; and in no instance is this more true than that of the press." 4 Elliot's Debates (1876), p. 571. And punishment of error runs the risk of inducing a cautious and restrictive exercise of the constitutionally guaranteed freedoms of speech and press. Our decisions recognize that a rule of strict liability that compels a publisher or broadcaster to guarantee the accuracy of his factual assertions may lead to intolerable self-censorship. Allowing the media to avoid liability only by proving the truth of all injurious statements does not accord adequate protection to First Amendment liberties. As the Court stated in New York Times Co. v. Sullivan, supra, 376 U.S., at 279, "Allowance of the defense of truth, with the burden of proving it on the defendant, does not mean that only false speech will be deterred." The First Amendment requires that we protect some falsehood in order to protect speech that matters.

The need to avoid self-censorship by the news media is, however, not the only societal value at issue. If it were, this Court would have embraced long ago the view that publishers and broadcasters enjoy an unconditional and indefeasible immunity from liability for defamation. See New York Times Co. v. Sullivan, 376 U.S. 254, 293 (1964) (opinion of Black, J.); Garrison v. Louisiana, 379 U.S. 64, 80 (1964) (opinion of Douglas, J.); Curtis Publishing Co. v. Butts, 388 U.S. 130, 170 (1967) (opinion of Black, J.). Such a rule would indeed obviate the fear that the prospect of civil liability for injurious falsehood might dissuade a timorous press from the effective exercise of First Amendment freedoms. Yet absolute protection for the communications media requires a total sacrifice of the competing value served by the law of defamation.

The legitimate state interest underlying the law of libel is the compensation of individuals for the harm inflicted on them by defamatory falsehoods. We would not lightly require the State to abandon this purpose, for, as Mr. Justice Stewart has reminded us, the individual's right to the protection of his own good name

> reflects no more than our basic concept of the essential dignity and worth of every human being—a concept at the root of any decent system of ordered liberty. The protection of private personality, like the protection of life itself, is left primarily to the individual states under the Ninth and Tenth Amendments. But this does not mean that the right is entitled to any less recognition by this Court as a basic of our constitutional system. Rosenblatt v. Baer, 383 U.S. 75, 92–93 (1963) (opinion of Stewart, J.).

Some tension necessarily exists between the need for a vigorous and uninhibited press and the legitimate interest in redressing wrongful injury. As Mr. Justice Harlan stated, "some antithesis between freedom of speech and press and libel actions persists, for libel remains premised on the content of speech and limits the freedom of the publisher to express certain sentiments, at least without guaranteeing legal proof of their substantial accuracy." Curtis Publishing Co. v. Butts, 388 U.S., at 152. In our continuing effort to define the proper accommodation between these competing concerns, we have been especially anxious to assure to the freedoms of speech and press that "breathing space" essential to their fruitful exercise. NAACP v. Button, 371 U.S. 415, 433 (1963). To that end this Court has extended a measure of strategic protection to defamatory falsehood.

The *New York Times* standard defines the level of constitutional protection appropriate to the context of defamation of a public person. Those who, by reason of the notoriety of their achievements or the vigor and success with which they seek the public's attention, are properly classed as public figures and those who hold governmental office may recover for injury to reputation only on clear and convincing proof that the defamatory falsehood was made with knowledge of its falsity or with reckless disregard for the truth. This standard administers an extremely powerful antidote to the inducement to media self-censorship of the common law rule of strict liability for libel and slander. And it exacts a correspondingly high price from the victims of defamatory falsehood. Plainly many deserving plaintiffs, including some intentionally subjected to injury, will be unable to surmount the barrier of the *New York Times* test. Despite this substantial abridgement of the state law right to compensation for wrongful hurt to one's reputation, the Court has concluded that the protection of the *New York Times* privilege should be available to publishers and broadcasters of defamatory falsehoods concerning public officials and public figures. New York Times Co. v. Sullivan, 376 U.S. 254 (1964); Curtis Publishing Co. v. Butts, 388 U.S. 130 (1967). We think that these decisions are correct, but we do not find their holdings justified solely by reference to the interest of the press and broadcast media in immunity from liability. Rather, we believe that the *New York Times* rule states an accommodation between this concern and the limited state interest present in the context of libel actions brought by public persons. For the reasons stated below, we conclude that the state interest in compensating injury to the reputation of private individuals requires that a different rule should obtain with respect to them.

Theoretically, of course, the balance between the needs of the press and the individual's claim to compensation for wrongful injury might be struck on a case-by-case basis. As Mr. Justice Harlan hypothesized, "it might seem, purely as an abstract matter, that the most utilitarian approach would be to scrutinize carefully every jury verdict in every libel case, in order to ascertain whether the final judgment leaves fully protected whatever First Amendment values transcend the legitimate state interest in protecting the particular plaintiff who prevailed." Rosenbloom v. Metromedia, Inc., 403 U.S. 29, 63 (1971) (footnote omitted). But this approach would lead to unpredictable results and uncertain expectations, and it could render our duty to supervise the lower courts unmanageable. Because an *ad hoc* resolution of the competing interests at stake in each particular case is not feasible, we must lay down broad rules of general application. Such rules necessarily treat alike various cases involving differences as well as similarities. Thus it is often true that not all of the considerations which justify adoption of a given rule will obtain in each particular case decided under its authority.

With that caveat we have no difficulty in distinguishing among defamation plaintiffs. The first remedy of any victim of defamation is self-help—using available opportunities to contradict the lie or correct the error and thereby to minimize its adverse impact on reputation. Public officials and public figures usually enjoy significantly greater access to the channels of effective communication and hence have a more realistic opportunity to counteract false statements than private individuals normally enjoy.[9] Private individuals are therefore more vulnerable to injury, and the state interest in protecting them is correspondingly greater.

More important than the likelihood that private individuals will lack effective opportunities for rebuttal, there is a compelling normative consideration underlying the distinction between public and private defamation plaintiffs. An individual who decides to seek governmental office must accept certain necessary consequences of that involvement in public affairs. He runs the risk of closer public scrutiny than might otherwise be the case. And society's interest in the officers of government is not strictly limited to the formal discharge of official duties. As the Court pointed out in Garrison v. Louisiana, 379 U.S. 64, 77 (1964), the public's interest extends to "anything that might touch on an official's fitness for office * * *. Few personal attributes are more germane to fitness for office than dishonesty, malfeasance, or improper motivation, even though these characteristics may also affect the official's private character."

Those classed as public figures stand in a similar position. Hypothetically, it may be possible for someone to become a public figure through no purposeful action of his own, but the instances of truly involuntary public figures must be exceedingly rare. For the most part those who attain this status have assumed roles of especial prominence in the affairs of society. Some occupy positions of such persuasive power and influence that they are deemed public figures for all purposes. More commonly, those classed as public figures have thrust

---

9. Of course, an opportunity for rebuttal seldom suffices to undo harm of defamatory falsehood. Indeed, the law of defamation is rooted in our experience that the truth rarely catches up with a lie. But the fact that the self-help remedy of rebuttal, standing alone, is inadequate to its task does not mean that it is irrelevant to our inquiry.

themselves to the forefront of particular public controversies in order to influence the resolution of the issues involved. In either event, they invite attention and comment.

Even if the foregoing generalities do not obtain in every instance, the communications media are entitled to act on the assumption that public officials and public figures have voluntarily exposed themselves to increased risk of injury from defamatory falsehoods concerning them. No such assumption is justified with respect to a private individual. He has not accepted public office nor assumed an "influential role in ordering society." Curtis Publishing Co. v. Butts, supra, 388 U.S., at 164 (opinion of Warren, C.J.). He has relinquished no part of his interest in the protection of his own good name, and consequently he has a more compelling call on the courts for redress of injury inflicted by defamatory falsehood. Thus, private individuals are not only more vulnerable to injury than public officials and public figures; they are also more deserving of recovery.

For these reasons we conclude that the States should retain substantial latitude in their efforts to enforce a legal remedy for defamatory falsehood injurious to the reputation of a private individual. The extension of the *New York Times* test proposed by the *Rosenbloom* plurality would abridge this legitimate state interest to a degree that we find unacceptable. And it would occasion the additional difficulty of forcing state and federal judges to decide on an *ad hoc* basis which publications address issues of "general or public interest" and which do not—to determine, in the words of Mr. Justice Marshall, "what information is relevant to self-government." Rosenbloom v. Metromedia, Inc., 403 U.S., at 79. We doubt the wisdom of committing this task to the conscience of judges. Nor does the Constitution require us to draw so thin a line between the drastic alternatives of the *New York Times* privilege and the common law of strict liability for defamatory error. The "public or general interest" test for determining the applicability of the *New York Times* standard to private defamation actions inadequately serves both of the competing values at stake. On the one hand, a private individual whose reputation is injured by defamatory falsehood that does concern an issue of public or general interest has no recourse unless he can meet the rigorous requirements of *New York Times*. This is true despite the factors that distinguish the state interest in compensating private individuals from the analogous interest involved in the context of public persons. On the other hand, a publisher or broadcaster of a defamatory error which a court deems unrelated to an issue of public or general interest may be held liable in damages even if it took every reasonable precaution to ensure the accuracy of its assertions. And liability may far exceed compensation for any actual injury to the plaintiff, for the jury may be permitted to presume damages without proof of loss and even to award punitive damages.

We hold that, so long as they do not impose liability without fault, the States may define for themselves the appropriate standard of liability for a publisher or broadcaster of defamatory falsehood injurious to a private individual.[10] This approach provides a more equitable boundary between the competing concerns involved here. It recognizes the strength of the legitimate state interest in compensating private individuals for wrongful injury to reputation, yet shields the press and broadcast media from the rigors of strict liability for defamation. At least this conclusion obtains where, as here, the substance of the defamatory statement "makes substantial danger to reputation apparent."[11] This phrase places in perspective the conclusion we announce today. Our inquiry would involve considerations somewhat different from those discussed above if a State purported to condition civil liability on a factual misstatement whose content did not warn a reasonably prudent editor or broadcaster of its defamatory potential. Cf. Time, Inc. v. Hill, 385 U.S. 374 (1967). Such a case is not now before us, and we intimate no view as to its proper resolution.

IV

Our accommodation of the competing values at stake in defamation suits by private individuals allows the States to impose liability on the publisher or broadcaster of defamatory falsehoods on a less demanding showing than that required by *New York Times*. This conclusion is not based on a belief that the considerations which prompted the adoption

---

10. Our caveat against strict liability is the prime target of Mr. Justice White's dissent. He would hold that a publisher or broadcaster may be required to prove the truth of a defamatory statement concerning a private individual and, failing such proof, that the publisher or broadcaster may be held liable for defamation even though he took every conceivable precaution to ensure the accuracy of the offending statement prior to its dissemination. Post, at 3031–3033 (slip op., at 20–24). In Mr. Justice White's view, one who publishes a statement that later turns out to be inaccurate can never be "without fault" in any meaningful sense, for "[i]t is he who circulated a falsehood *that he was not required to publish.*" Id. at 3033 (slip op., at 23) (emphasis added).

Mr. Justice White characterizes New York Times Co. v. Sullivan, supra, as simply a case of seditious libel. Post, at 3030 (slip op., at 18). But that rationale is certainly inapplicable to Curtis Publishing Co. v. Butts, supra, where Mr. Justice White joined four other Members of the Court to extend the knowing-or-reckless-falsity standard to media defamation of persons identified as public figures but not connected with the Government. Mr. Justice White now suggests that he would abide by that vote, id. at 3036 (slip op., at 30), but the full thrust of his dissent—as we read it—contradicts that suggestion. Finally, in Rosenbloom v. Metromedia, Inc., supra, Mr. Justice White voted to apply the *New York Times* privilege to media defamation of an individual who was neither a public official nor a public figure. His opinion states that the knowing-or-reckless-falsity standard should apply to media "comment upon the official actions of public servants," 403 U.S., at 62, including defamatory falsehoods about a person arrested by the police. If adopted by the Court, this conclusion would significantly extend the *New York Times* privilege.

Mr. Justice White asserts that our decision today "trivializes and denigrates the interest in reputation," Miami Herald Publishing Co. v. Tornillo, 418 U.S. 241, 262, (slip op., at 4) (White, J., concurring), that it "scuttle[s] the libel laws of the States in * * * wholesale fashion" and renders ordinary citizens "powerless to protect themselves." Post, at 3022 (slip op., at 2). In light of the progressive extension of the knowing-or-reckless-falsity requirement detailed in the preceding paragraph, one might have viewed today's decision allowing recovery under any standard save strict liability as a more generous accommodation of the state interest in comprehensive reputational injury to private individuals than the law presently affords.

11. Curtis Publishing Co. v. Butts, 388 U.S. 130, 155 (1967).

of the *New York Times* privilege for defamation of public officials and its extension to public figures are wholly inapplicable to the context of private individuals. Rather, we endorse this approach in recognition of the strong and legitimate state interest in compensating private individuals for injury to reputation. But this countervailing state interest extends no further than compensation for actual injury. For the reasons stated below, we hold that the States may not permit recovery of presumed or punitive damages, at least when liability is not based on a showing of knowledge of falsity or reckless disregard for the truth.

The common law of defamation is an oddity of tort law, for it allows recovery of purportedly compensatory damages without evidence of actual loss. Under the traditional rules pertaining to actions for libel, the existence of injury is presumed from the fact of publication. Juries may award substantial sums as compensation for supposed damage to reputation without any proof that such harm actually occurred. The largely uncontrolled discretion of juries to award damages where there is no loss unnecessarily compounds the potential of any system of liability for defamatory falsehood to inhibit the vigorous exercise of First Amendment freedoms. Additionally, the doctrine of presumed damages invites juries to punish unpopular opinion rather than to compensate individuals for injury sustained by the publication of a false fact. More to the point, the States have no substantial interest in securing for plaintiffs such as this petitioner gratuitous awards of money damages far in excess of any actual injury.

We would not, of course, invalidate state law simply because we doubt its wisdom, but here we are attempting to reconcile state law with a competing interest grounded in the constitutional command of the First Amendment. It is therefore appropriate to require that state remedies for defamatory falsehood reach no farther than is necessary to protect the legitimate interest involved. It is necessary to restrict defamation plaintiffs who do not prove knowledge of falsity or reckless disregard for the truth to compensation for actual injury. We need not define "actual injury," as trial courts have wide experience in framing appropriate jury instructions in tort action. Suffice it to say that actual injury is not limited to out-of-pocket loss. Indeed, the more customary types of actual harm inflicted by defamatory falsehood include impairment of reputation and standing in the community, personal humiliation, and mental anguish and suffering. Of course, juries must be limited by appropriate instructions, and all awards must be supported by competent evidence concerning the injury, although there need be no evidence which assigns an actual dollar value to the injury.

We also find no justification for allowing awards of punitive damages against publishers and broadcasters held liable under state-defined standards of liability for defamation. In most jurisdictions jury discretion over the amounts awarded is limited only by the gentle rule that they not be excessive. Consequently, juries assess punitive damages in wholly unpredictable amounts bearing no necessary relation to the actual harm caused. And they remain free to use their discretion selectively to punish expressions of unpopular views. Like the doctrine of presumed damages, jury discretion to award punitive damages unnecessarily exacerbates the danger of media self-censorship, but, unlike the former rule, punitive damages are wholly irrelevant to the state interest that justifies a negligence standard for private defamation actions. They are not compensation for injury. Instead, they are private fines levied by civil juries to punish reprehensible conduct and to deter its future occurrence. In short, the private defamation plaintiff who establishes liability under a less demanding standard than that stated by *New York Times* may recover only such damages as are sufficient to compensate him for actual injury.

V

Notwithstanding our refusal to extend the *New York Times* privilege to defamation of private individuals, respondent contends that we should affirm the judgment below on the ground that petitioner is either a public official or a public figure. There is little basis for the former assertion. Several years prior to the present incident, petitioner had served briefly on housing committees appointed by the mayor of Chicago, but at the time of publication he had never held any remunerative governmental position. Respondent admits this but argues that petitioner's appearance at the coroner's inquest rendered him a "de facto public official." Our cases recognize no such concept. Respondent's suggestion would sweep all lawyers under the *New York Times* rule as officers of the court and distort the plain meaning of the "public official" category beyond all recognition. We decline to follow it.

Respondent's characterization of petitioner as a public figure raises a different question. That designation may rest on either of two alternative bases. In some instances an individual may achieve such pervasive fame or notoriety that he becomes a public figure for all purposes and in all contexts. More commonly, an individual voluntarily injects himself or is drawn into a particular public controversy and thereby becomes a public figure for a limited range of issues. In either case such persons assume special prominence in the resolution of public questions.

Petitioner has long been active in community and professional affairs. He has served as an officer of local civil groups and of various professional organizations, and he has published several books and articles on legal subjects. Although petitioner was consequently well-known in some circles, he had achieved no general fame or notoriety in the community. None of the prospective jurors called at the trial had ever heard of petitioner prior to this litigation, and respondent offered no proof that this response was atypical of the local population. We would not lightly assume that a citizen's participation in community and professional affairs rendered him a public figure for all purposes. Absent clear evidence of general fame or notoriety in the community, and pervasive involvement in the affairs of society, an individual should not be deemed a public personality for all aspects of his life. It is preferable to reduce the public figure question to a more meaningful context by looking to the nature and extent of an individual's participation in the particular controversy giving rise to the defamation.

In this context it is plain that petitioner was not a public figure. * * * We therefore conclude that the *New York Times* standard is inapplicable to this case and that the trial court erred in entering judgment for the respondent. Because the jury was allowed to impose liability without fault and was permitted to presume damages without proof of injury, a new trial is necessary. We reverse and remand for further proceedings in accord with this opinion.

It is so ordered.

Questions

1. The *Gertz* court acknowledges that, at least occasionally, there may be "instances of truly involuntary public figures", but concludes that "the communications media are entitled to act on the assumption that public officials and public figures have voluntarily exposed themselves to increased risk of injury from defamatory falsehoods concerning them." Is such an assumption justified?

2. Under the *Gertz* formulation, does the *New York Times* standard apply to a defamatory statement made about a public official or public figure as to matters which are not "of public or general concern"? What would be an example of such a matter if it were about a public official of the first importance, such as the President of the United States?

3. Are there any First Amendment limitations on the state law of defamation if the statement is about a private figure? Does the answer to that question vary depending upon whether the matter discussed in the defamatory statement is "of public or general concern"? What are the First Amendment limitations on liability as to private figures? What are the First Amendment limitations on damages as to private figures? Will such limitations vary depending upon whether the defamatory statement was, on the one hand, negligently made, or on the other, knowingly false or made with reckless disregard of the truth?

4. Does the *Gertz* exclusion of punitive and presumed damages apply if the plaintiff is a public figure, and if the statement is knowingly false or made with reckless disregard of the truth? See Maheu v. Hughes Tool Co., infra.

TIME, INC. v. FIRESTONE

Supreme Court of the United States, 1976.
424 U.S. 448, 96 S.Ct. 958, 47 L.Ed.2d 154.

MR. JUSTICE REHNQUIST delivered the opinion of the Court.

Petitioner is the publisher of Time, a weekly news magazine. The Supreme Court of Florida affirmed a $100,000 libel judgment against petitioner which was based on an item appearing in Time that purported to describe the result of domestic relations litigation between respondent and her husband. We granted certiorari 421 U.S. 909, 95 S.Ct.

1557, 43 L.Ed.2d 773 (1975), to review petitioner's claim that the judgment violates its rights under the First and Fourteenth Amendments to the United States Constitution.

I

Respondent, Mary Alice Firestone, married Russell Firestone, the scion of one of America's wealthier industrial families, in 1961. In 1964, they separated, and respondent filed a complaint for separate maintenance in the Circuit Court of Palm Beach County, Fla. Her husband counterclaimed for divorce on grounds of extreme cruelty and adultery. After a lengthy trial the Circuit Court issued a judgment granting the divorce requested by respondent's husband. In relevant part the court's final judgment read:

> This cause came on for final hearing before the court upon the plaintiff wife's second amended complaint for separate maintenance (alimony unconnected with the causes of divorce), the defendant husband's answer and counterclaim for divorce on grounds of extreme cruelty and adultery, and the wife's answer thereto setting up certain affirmative defenses. * * *
>
> * * *
>
> According to certain testimony in behalf of the defendant, extramarital escapades of the plaintiff were bizarre and of an amatory nature which would have made Dr. Freud's hair curl. Other testimony, in plaintiff's behalf, would indicate that defendant was guilty of bounding from one bedpartner to another with the erotic zest of a satyr. The court is inclined to discount much of this testimony as unreliable. Nevertheless, it is the conclusion and finding of the court that neither party is domesticated, within the meaning of that term as used by the Supreme Court of Florida.
> * * *
>
> * * *
>
> In the present case, it is abundantly clear from the evidence of marital discord that neither of the parties has shown the least susceptibility to domestication, and that the marriage should be dissolved.
>
> * * *
>
> The premises considered, it is thereupon
>
> ORDERED AND ADJUDGED as follows:
>
> 1. That the equities in this cause are with the defendant; that defendant's counterclaim for divorce be and the same is hereby granted, and the bonds of matrimony which have heretofore existed between the parties are hereby forever dissolved.
>
> * * *
>
> 4. That the defendant shall pay unto the plaintiff the sum of $3,000 per month as alimony beginning January 1, 1968, and a like sum on the first day of each and every month thereafter until the death or remarriage of the plaintiff. * * *

Time's editorial staff, headquartered in New York, was alerted to the fact that a judgment had been rendered in the Firestone divorce proceeding by a wire service report and an account in a New York newspaper. The staff subsequently received further information regarding the Florida decision from Time's Miami bureau chief and from a "stringer" working on a special assignment basis in the Palm Beach area. On the basis of these four sources, Time's staff composed the following item, which appeared in the magazine's "Milestones" section the following week:

> DIVORCED. By Russell A. Firestone, Jr., 41, heir to the tire fortune: Mary Alice Sullivan Firestone, 32, his third wife; a onetime Palm Beach schoolteacher; on grounds of extreme cruelty and adultery; after six years of marriage, one son; in West Palm Beach, Fla. The 17-month intermittent trial produced enough testimony of extramarital adventures on both sides, said the judge, "to make Dr. Freud's hair curl."

Within a few weeks of the publication of this article respondent demanded in writing a retraction from petitioner, alleging that a portion of the article was "false, malicious and defamatory." Petitioner declined to issue the requested retraction.[1]

Respondent then filed this libel action against petitioner in the Florida Circuit Court. Based on a jury verdict for respondent, that court entered judgment against petitioner for $100,000, and after review in both the Florida District Court of Appeal, 279 So.2d 389 and the Supreme Court of Florida, 305 So.2d 172 the judgment was ultimately affirmed. Petitioner advances several contentions as to why the judgment is contrary to decisions of this Court holding that the First and Fourteenth Amendments of the United States Constitution limit the authority of state courts to impose liability for damages based on defamation.

II

Petitioner initially contends that it cannot be liable for publishing any falsehood defaming respondent unless it is established that the publication was made "with actual malice," as that term is defined in New York Times Co. v. Sullivan, 376 U.S. 254, 84 S.Ct. 710, 11 L.Ed.2d 686 (1964).[2] Petitioner advances two arguments in support of this contention: that respondent is a "public figure" within this Court's decisions extending *New York Times* to defamation suits brought by such individuals. See e.g., Curtis Publishing Co. v. Butts, 388 U.S. 130, 87 S.Ct. 1975, 18 L.Ed.2d 1094 (1967); and that the Time item constituted a report of a judicial proceeding, a class of subject matter which petitioner claims deserves the protection of the "actual malice" standard even if the story is proven to be defamatorily false or inaccurate. We reject both arguments.

In Gertz v. Robert Welch, Inc., 418 U.S. 323, 94 S.Ct. 2997, 41 L.Ed.2d 789 (1974), we have recently further defined the meaning of "public figure" for the purposes of the First and Fourteenth Amendments:

---

1. Under Florida law the demand for retraction was a prerequisite for filing a libel action, and permits defendants to limit their potential liability to actual damages by complying with the demand. Fla.Stat.Ann. §§ 770.01–770.02 (1963).

2. The "actual malice" test requires that a plaintiff prove that the defamatory statement was made "with knowledge that it was false or with reckless disregard of whether it was false or not." New York Times Co. v. Sullivan, 376 U.S. 254, 279–280, 84 S.Ct. 710, 726, 11 L.Ed.2d 686 (1964).

For the most part those who attain this status have assumed roles of especial prominence in the affairs of society. Some occupy positions of such persuasive power and influence that they are deemed public figures for all purposes. More commonly, those classed as public figures have thrust themselves to the forefront of particular public controversies in order to influence the resolution of the issues involved.

Respondent did not assume any role of especial prominence in the affairs of society, other than perhaps Palm Beach society, and she did not thrust herself to the forefront of any particular public controversy in order to influence the resolution of the issues involved in it.

Petitioner contends that because the Firestone divorce was characterized by the Florida Supreme Court as a "cause célèbre," it must have been a public controversy and respondent must be considered a public figure. But in so doing petitioner seeks to equate "public controversy" with all controversies of interest to the public. Were we to accept this reasoning, we would reinstate the doctrine advanced in the plurality opinion in Rosenbloom v. Metromedia, Inc., 403 U.S. 29, 91 S.Ct. 1811, 29 L.Ed.2d 296 (1971), which concluded that the *New York Times* privilege should be extended to falsehoods defamatory of private persons whenever the statements concern matters of general or public interest. In *Gertz,* however, the Court repudiated this position, stating that "extension of the *New York Times* test proposed by the *Rosenbloom* plurality would abridge [a] legitimate state interest to a degree that we find unacceptable." 418 U.S., at 346, 94 S.Ct., at 3010.

Dissolution of a marriage through judicial proceedings is not the sort of "public controversy" referred to in *Gertz,* even though the marital difficulties of extremely wealthy individuals may be of interest to some portion of the reading public. Nor did respondent freely choose to publicize issues as to the propriety of her married life. She was compelled to go to court by the State in order to obtain legal release from the bonds of matrimony. We have said that in such an instance "[r]esort to the judicial process * * * is no more voluntary in a realistic sense than that of the defendant called upon to defend his interests in court." Boddie v. Connecticut, 401 U.S. 371, 376, 91 S.Ct. 780, 785, 28 L.Ed.2d 113 (1971). Her actions, both in instituting the litigation and in its conduct, were quite different from those of General Walker in Curtis Publishing Co., supra.[3] She assumed no "special prominence in the resolution of public questions." *Gertz,* 418 U.S., at 351, 94 S.Ct. at 3013. We hold respondent was not a "public figure" for the purpose of

---

3. Nor do we think the fact that respondent may have held a few press conferences during the divorce proceedings in an attempt to satisfy inquiring reporters converts her into a "public figure." Such interviews should have had no effect upon the merits of the legal dispute between respondent and her husband or the outcome of that trial, and we do not think it can be assumed that any such purpose was intended. Moreover, there is no indication that she sought to use the press conferences as a vehicle by which to thrust herself to the forefront of some unrelated controversy in order to influence its resolution. See Gertz v. Robert Welch, Inc., 418 U.S. 323, 345, 94 S.Ct. 2997, 3009, 41 L.Ed.2d 789 (1974).

determining the constitutional protection afforded petitioner's report of the factual and legal basis for her divorce.

For similar reasons we likewise reject petitioner's claim for automatic extension of the *New York Times* privilege to all reports of judicial proceedings. It is argued that information concerning proceedings in our Nation's courts may have such importance to all citizens as to justify extending special First Amendment protection to the press when reporting on such events. We have recently accepted a significantly more confined version of this argument by holding that the Constitution precludes States from imposing civil liability based upon the publication of truthful information contained in official court records open to public inspection. Cox Broadcasting Corp. v. Cohn, 420 U.S. 469, 95 S.Ct. 1029, 43 L.Ed.2d 328 (1975).

Petitioner would have us extend the reasoning of *Cox Broadcasting* to safeguard even inaccurate and false statements, at least where "actual malice" has not been established. But its argument proves too much. It may be that all reports of judicial proceedings contain some informational value implicating the First Amendment, but recognizing this is little different from labeling all judicial proceedings matters of "public or general interest," as that phrase was used by the plurality in *Rosenbloom*. Whatever their general validity, use of such subject matter classifications to determine the extent of constitutional protection afforded defamatory falsehoods may too often result in an improper balance between the competing interests in this area. It was our recognition and rejection of this weakness in the *Rosenbloom* test which led us in *Gertz* to eschew a subject matter test for one focusing upon the character of the defamation plaintiff. See 418 U.S., at 344–346, 94 S.Ct., at 3009–3010. By confining inquiry to whether a plaintiff is a public officer or a public figure who might be assumed to "have voluntarily exposed themselves to increased risk of injury from defamatory falsehoods," we sought a more appropriate accommodation between the public's interest in an uninhibited press and its equally compelling need for judicial redress of libelous utterances. Cf. Chaplinsky v. New Hampshire, 315 U.S. 568, 62 S.Ct. 766, 86 L.Ed. 1031 (1942).

Presumptively erecting the *New York Times* barrier against all plaintiffs seeking to recover for injuries from defamatory falsehoods published in what are alleged to be reports of judicial proceedings would effect substantial depreciation of the individual's interest in protection from such harm, without any convincing assurance that such a sacrifice is required under the First Amendment. And in some instances such an undiscriminating approach might achieve results directly at odds with the constitutional balance intended. Indeed, the article upon which the *Gertz* libel action was based purported to be a report on the murder trial of a Chicago police officer. See 418 U.S., at 325–326, 94 S.Ct., at 3000. Our decision in that case should make it clear that no such blanket privilege for reports of judicial proceedings is to be found in the Constitution.

It may be argued that there is still room for application of the *New York Times* protections to more narrowly focused reports of what actually transpires in the courtroom. But even so narrowed, the suggested privilege is simply too broad. Imposing upon the law of private defamation the rather drastic limitations worked by *New York Times* cannot be justified by generalized references to the public interest in reports of judicial proceedings. The details of many, if not most, courtroom battles would add almost nothing towards advancing the uninhibited debate on public issues thought to provide principal support for the decision in *New York Times*. See 376 U.S., at 270, 84 S.Ct., at 720; cf. Rosenblatt v. Baer, 383 U.S. 75, 86, 86 S.Ct. 669, 676, 15 L.Ed.2d 597 (1966). And while participants in some litigation may be legitimate "public figures," either generally or for the limited purpose of that litigation, the majority will more likely resemble respondent, drawn into a public forum largely against their will in order to attempt to obtain the only redress available to them or to defend themselves against actions brought by the State or by others. There appears little reason why these individuals should substantially forfeit that degree of protection which the law of defamation would otherwise afford them simply by virtue of their being drawn into a courtroom. The public interest in accurate reports of judicial proceedings is substantially protected by *Cox Broadcasting Co.,* supra. As to inaccurate and defamatory reports of facts, matters deserving no First Amendment protection, see 418 U.S., at 340, 94 S.Ct., at 3007; we think *Gertz* provides an adequate safeguard for the constitutionally protected interests of the press and affords it a tolerable margin for error by requiring some type of fault.

III

Petitioner has urged throughout this litigation that it could not be held liable for publication of the "Milestones" item because its report of respondent's divorce was factually correct. In its view the Time article faithfully reproduced the precise meaning of the divorce judgment. But this issue was submitted to the jury under an instruction intended to implement Florida's limited privilege for accurate reports of judicial proceedings, App. 509; see 305 So.2d, at 177. By returning a verdict for respondent the jury necessarily found that the identity of meaning which petitioner claims does not exist even for laymen. The Supreme Court of Florida upheld this finding on appeal, rejecting petitioner's contention that its report was accurate as a matter of law. Because demonstration that an article was true would seem to preclude finding the publisher at fault, see *Cox Broadcasting Co.,* 420 U.S., at 498–500, 95 S.Ct., at 1047 (Powell, J., concurring), we have examined the predicate for petitioner's contention. We believe the Florida courts properly could have found the "Milestones" item to be false.

For petitioner's report to have been accurate, the divorce granted Russell Firestone must have been based on a finding by the divorce court that his wife had committed extreme cruelty towards him *and* that she had been guilty of adultery. This is indisputably what petitioner reported in its "Milestones" item, but it is equally indisputable that these were not the facts. Russell Firestone alleged in his counterclaim that respondent had been guilty of adultery, but the divorce court never made any such finding. Its judgment provided that Russell Firestone's "counterclaim for divorce be and the same is hereby granted," but did not specify that the basis for the judgment was either of the two grounds alleged in the counterclaim. The Supreme Court of Florida on appeal concluded that the ground actually relied upon by the divorce court was "lack of domestication of the parties," a ground not theretofore recognized by Florida law. The Supreme Court nonetheless affirmed the judgment dissolving the bonds of matrimony because the record contained sufficient evidence to establish the ground of extreme cruelty. 263 So.2d 223, 225 (1972).

Petitioner may well argue that the meaning of the trial court's decree was unclear,[4] but this does not license it to choose from among several conceivable interpretations the one most damaging to respondent. Having chosen to follow this tack,[5] petitioner must be able to establish not merely that the item reported was a conceivable or plausible interpretation of the decree, but that the item was factually correct. We believe there is ample support for the jury's conclusion, affirmed by the Supreme Court of Florida, that this was not the case. There was, therefore, sufficient basis for imposing liability upon petitioner if the constitutional limitations we announced in *Gertz* have been satisfied. These are a prohibition against imposing liability without fault, 418 U.S., at 347, 94 S.Ct., at 3010, and the requirement that compensatory awards "be supported by competent evidence concerning the injury." Id., at 350, 94 S.Ct., at 3012.

As to the latter requirement little difficulty appears. Petitioner has argued that because respondent withdrew her claim for damages to reputation on the eve of trial, there could be no recovery consistent with *Gertz*. Petitioner's theory seems to be that the only compensable injury in a defamation action is that which may be done to one's reputation, and that claims not predicated upon such injury are by definition not actions for defamation. But Florida has obviously decided to permit recovery for other injuries without regard to measuring the effect the falsehood may have had upon a plaintiff's reputation.

---

4. Petitioner is incorrect in arguing that a rational interpretation of an ambiguous document is constitutionally protected under our decision in Time, Inc. v. Pape, 401 U.S. 279, 91 S.Ct. 633, 28 L.Ed.2d 45 (1971). There we were applying the *New York Times* standard to test whether the defendant had acted in reckless disregard of the truth. Id., at 292, 91 S.Ct., at 640. But as we have concluded that the publication in this case need not be tested against the "actual malice" standard, *Pape* is of no assistance to petitioner.

5. In fact, it appears that none of petitioner's employees actually saw the decree prior to publication of the "Milestones" article. But we do not think this can affect the extent of constitutional protection afforded the statement. Moreover, petitioner has maintained throughout that it would have published an identical statement if its editorial staff had had an opportunity to peruse the judgment prior to their publication deadline, and has consistently contended that its article was true when compared to the words of that judgment.

This does not transform the action into something other than an action for defamation as that term is meant in *Gertz*. In that opinion we made it clear that States could base awards on elements other than injury to reputation, specifically listing "personal humiliation, and mental anguish and suffering" as examples of injuries which might be compensated consistently with the Constitution upon a showing of fault. Because respondent has decided to forgo recovery for injury to her reputation, she is not prevented from obtaining compensation for such other damages that a defamatory falsehood may have caused her.

The trial court charged, consistently with *Gertz*, that the jury should award respondent compensatory damages in "an amount of money that will fairly and adequately compensate her for such damages," and further cautioned that "It is only damages which are a direct and natural result of the alleged libel which may be recovered." App. 509. There was competent evidence introduced to permit the jury to assess the amount of injury. Several witnesses [6] testified to the extent of respondent's anxiety and concern over Time inaccurately reporting that she had been found guilty of adultery, and she herself took the stand to elaborate on her fears that her young son would be adversely affected by this falsehood when he grew older. The jury decided these injuries should be compensated by an award of $100,000. We have no warrant for re-examining this determination. Cf. Lincoln v. Power, 151 U.S. 436, 14 S.Ct. 387, 38 L.Ed. 224 (1894).

IV

Gertz established, however, that not only must there be evidence to support an award of compensatory damages, there must also be evidence of some fault on the part of a defendant charged with publishing defamatory material. No question of fault was submitted to the jury in this case, because under Florida law the only findings required for determination of liability were whether the article was defamatory, whether it was true, and whether the defamation, if any, caused respondent harm.

The failure to submit the question of fault to the jury does not, of itself establish noncompliance with the constitutional requirements established in *Gertz*, however. Nothing in the Constitution requires that assessment of fault in a civil case tried in a state court be made by a jury, nor is there any prohibition against such a finding being made in the first instance by an appellate, rather than a trial, court. The First and Fourteenth Amendments do not impose upon the States any limitations as to how, within their own judicial systems, fact-finding tasks shall be allocated. If we were satisfied that one of the Florida courts which considered this case had supportably ascertained petitioner was at fault, we would be required to affirm the judgment below.

---

6. These included respondent's minister, her attorney in the divorce proceedings, plus several friends and neighbors, one of whom was a physician and testified to having to administer a sedative to respondent in an attempt to reduce discomfort wrought by her worrying about the article.

But the only alternative source of such a finding, given that the issue was not submitted to the jury, is the opinion of the Supreme Court of Florida. That opinion appears to proceed generally on the assumption that a showing of fault was not required,[7] but then in the penultimate paragraph it recites:

> Furthermore, this erroneous reporting is clear and convincing evidence of the negligence in certain segments of the news media in gathering the news. Gertz v. Welch, Inc., supra. Pursuant to Florida law in effect at the time of the divorce judgment (Section 61.08, Florida Statutes), a wife found guilty of adultery could not be awarded alimony. Since petitioner had been awarded alimony, she had not been found guilty of adultery nor had the divorce been granted on the ground of adultery. A careful examination of the final decree prior to publication would have clearly demonstrated that the divorce had been granted on the grounds of extreme cruelty, and thus the wife would have been saved the humiliation of being accused of adultery in a nationwide magazine. This is a flagrant example of "journalistic negligence." 305 So.2d, at 178.

It may be argued this is sufficient indication the court found petitioner at fault within the meaning of *Gertz*. Nothing in that decision or in the First or Fourteenth Amendments requires that in a libel action an appellate court treat in detail by written opinion all contentions of the parties, and if the jury or trial judge had found fault in fact, we would be quite willing to read the quoted passage as affirming that conclusion. But without some finding of fault by the judge or jury in the Circuit Court, we would have to attribute to the Supreme Court of Florida from the quoted language not merely an intention to affirm the finding of the lower court, but an intention to find such a fact in the first instance.

Even where a question of fact may have constitutional significance, we normally accord findings of state courts deference in reviewing constitutional claims here. See, e.g. Lyons v. Oklahoma, 322 U.S. 596, 602–603, 64 S.Ct. 1208, 1212–1213, 88 L.Ed. 1481 (1944), Gallegos v. Nebraska, 342 U.S. 55, 60–61, 72 S.Ct. 141, 144–145, 96 L.Ed. 86 (1951) (opinion of Reed, J.). But that deference is predicated on our belief that at some point in the state proceedings some factfinder has made a

---

7. After reiterating its conclusion that the article was false, the Florida court noted that falsely accusing a woman of adultery is libelous *per se* and normally actionable without proof of damages. The court then recognized that our opinion in *Gertz* necessarily displaced this presumption of damages but ruled that the trial court's instruction was consistent with *Gertz* and that there was evidence to support the jury's verdict—conclusions with which we have agreed. The court went on to reject a claim of privilege under state law, pointing out that the privilege shielded only "fair and accurate" reports and the jury had resolved these issues against petitioner. The court appears to have concluded its analysis of petitioner's legal claims with this statement, which immediately precedes the paragraph set out in the text:

> "Careful examination and consideration of the record discloses that the judgment of the trial court is correct and should have been affirmed on appeal to the District Court." 305 So.2d, at 177–178.

There is nothing in the court's opinion which appears to make any reference to the relevance of some concept of fault in determining petitioner's liability.

conscious determination of the existence or nonexistence of the critical fact. Here the record before us affords no basis for such a conclusion.

It may well be that petitioner's account in its "Milestones" section was the product of some fault on its part, and that the libel judgment against it was, therefore, entirely consistent with *Gertz*. But in the absence of a finding in some element of the state court system that there was fault, we are not inclined to canvass the record to make such a determination in the first instance. Cf. Rosenblatt v. Baer, 383 U.S. 75, 87–88, 86 S.Ct. 669, 676–677, 15 L.Ed.2d 597 (1966). Accordingly, the judgment of the Supreme Court of Florida is vacated and the case remanded for further proceedings not inconsistent with this opinion.

So ordered.

MR. JUSTICE STEVENS took no part in the consideration or decision of this case.

MR. JUSTICE POWELL, with whom MR. JUSTICE STEWART joins, concurring.

A clear majority of the Court adheres to the principles of Gertz v. Robert Welch, Inc., 418 U.S. 323, 94 S.Ct. 997, 41 L.Ed.2d 789 (1974). But it is evident from the variety of views expressed that perceptions differ as to the proper application of such principles to this bizarre case. In order to avoid the appearance of fragmentation of the Court on the basic principles involved, I join the opinion of the Court. I add this concurrence to state my reaction to the record presented for our review.

* * *

There was substantial evidence, much of it uncontradicted, that the editors of Time exercised considerable care in checking the accuracy of the story prior to its publication. The Milestones item appeared in the December 22, 1967, issue of Time. This issue went to press on Saturday, December 16, the day after the Circuit Court rendered its decision at about 4:30 in the afternoon. The evening of the 15th the Time editorial staff in New York received an Associated Press dispatch stating that Russell A. Firestone, Jr., had been granted a divorce from his third wife, whom "he had accused of adultery and extreme cruelty." Later that same evening, Time received the New York Daily News edition for December 16, which carried a special bulletin substantially to the same effect as the AP dispatch.

On the morning of December 16, in response to an inquiry sent to its Miami Bureau, Time's New York office received a dispatch from the head of that Bureau quoting excerpts from the Circuit Court's opinion that strongly suggested adultery on the part of both parties.[4] Later that day the editorial staff received a message from Time's Palm Beach stringer that read, in part: "The technical grounds for divorce accord-

---

4. The excerpts included: "'According to certain testimony in behalf of the defendant [husband], extra marital escapades of the plaintiff [wife] were bizarre and of an amatory nature which would have made Dr. Freud's hair curl. Other testimony, in the plaintiff's behalf, would indicate that the defendant was guilty of bounding from one bed partner to another with the erotic zest of a satyr.'" (App. 544).

ing to Joseph Farrish, Jr., attorney for Mary Alice Firestone, were given as extreme cruelty and adultry [sic]." App. 532. The stringer's dispatch also included several quotations from the Circuit Court opinion.[5] At trial the senior editor testified that although no member of the New York editorial staff had read the Circuit Court's opinion, he had believed that both the stringer and the chief of Time's Miami Bureau had read it.

The opaqueness of the Circuit Court's decree is also a factor to be considered in assessing whether Time was guilty of actionable fault under the *Gertz* standard. Although it appears that neither the head of the Miami Bureau nor the stringer personally read the opinion or order, the stringer testified at trial that respondent's attorney Farrish and others read him portions of the decree over the telephone before he filed his dispatch with Time.[6] The record does not reveal whether the limited portions of the decree that shed light on the grounds for the granting of the divorce were read to the stringer.[7] But the ambiguity of the divorce decree may well have contributed to the stringer's view, and hence the Time editorial staff's conclusion, that a ground for the divorce was adultery by respondent. * * *

As I join the opinion of the Court remanding this case, it is unnecessary to decide whether the foregoing establishes as a matter of law that Time exercised the requisite care under the circumstances. Nor have I undertaken to identify all of the evidence that may be relevant or to point out conflicts that arguably have been resolved against Time by the jury. My point in writing is to emphasize that, against the background of a notorious divorce case, see Curtis Publishing Co., 388 U.S., at 158–159, 87 S.Ct., at 1993–1994,[8] and a decree that

---

5. Based on these news items and dispatches, the Time editorial team, consisting of a researcher, writer, and senior editor in charge of the Milestones section of the magazine, wrote, edited, and checked the article for accuracy. At trial they testified as to their complete belief in the truth of the news item at the time of publication.

6. Several hours after filing his dispatch, the stringer spoke with the divorce judge by telephone. According to testimony of the stringer at trial the divorce judge read him portions of the decree, and none of this information was inconsistent with that contained in his dispatch to Time; otherwise, he would have alerted Time's New York office immediately.

7. Time did not consider the stringer to be an employee. He worked for Time part-time and was compensated at an hourly rate, although he was guaranteed a minimum amount of work each year. In this case, he was contacted by the chief of the Miami Bureau and requested to investigate the Firestone divorce decree. There is thus a question whether the fault, if any, of the stringer in not personally reading the entire opinion and order, is even a factor that may be considered in assessing whether there was actionable fault by Time under *Gertz*. Cf. Cantrell v. Forest City Publishing Co., 419 U.S. 245, 253–254, 95 S.Ct. 465, 470–471, 42 L.Ed.2d 419 (1974).

8. In its first opinion remanding the case to the District Court of Appeal, after referring to the general prominence of the Firestones, the Supreme Court of Florida indicated that "their marital difficulties were equally well known; and the charges and countercharges of meretriciousness, flowing from both sides of the controversy, made their divorce action a veritable *cause celebre* in social circles across the country." 271 So.2d 745, 751 (1972). The District Court of Appeal similarly observed that in part due to the sensational and colorful testimony the 17-month divorce trial had been the object of national news coverage. 254 So.2d 386, 389 (1971). The reports Time received that the decree was granted on the ground of adultery therefore were consistent with the well-publicized trial revelations.

invited misunderstanding, there was substantial evidence supportive of Time's defense that it was not guilty of actionable negligence. At the very least the jury or court assessing liability in this case should have weighed these factors and this evidence before reaching a judgment.[9] There is no indication in the record before us that this was done in accordance with *Gertz*.[10]

Mr. Justice Brennan, dissenting. [opinion omitted]

Mr. Justice White, dissenting.

I would affirm the judgment of the Florida Supreme Court because First Amendment values will not be furthered in any way by application to this case of the fault standards newly drafted and imposed by Gertz v. Robert Welch, Inc., 418 U.S. 323, 94 S.Ct. 2997, 41 L.Ed.2d 789, upon which my Brother Rehnquist relies, or the fault standards required by Rosenbloom v. Metromedia, Inc., 403 U.S. 29, 91 S.Ct. 1811, 29 L.Ed.2d 296, upon which my Brother Brennan relies; and because, in any event, any requisite fault was properly found below.

The jury found on ample evidence that the article published by petitioner Time, Inc., about respondent Firestone was false and defamatory. This Court has held, and no one seriously disputes, that, regardless of fault, "there is no constitutional value in false statements of fact." "They belong to that category of utterances which ' * * * are of such slight social value as'" to be worthy of no First Amendment protection. Gertz v. Robert Welch, Inc., 418 U.S., at 340, 94 S.Ct., at 3007, quoting Chaplinsky v. New Hampshire, 315 U.S. 568, 572, 62 S.Ct. 766, 769, 86 L.Ed. 1031. This Court's decisions from New York Times Co. v. Sullivan, 376 U.S. 254, 84 S.Ct. 710, 11 L.Ed.2d 686, through Gertz v. Robert Welch, Inc., supra, holding that the Constitution requires a finding of some degree of fault as a precondition to a defamation award, have done so for one reason and one reason alone: unless innocent falsehood is allowed as a defense, some true speech will also be deterred. Thus "[t]he First Amendment requires that we protect some falsehood *in order to protect speech that matters*," Gertz v. Robert Welch, Inc., supra, 418 U.S. at 341, 94 S.Ct. at 3007 (emphasis supplied), e.g., true fact statements. In light of these decisions, the threshold question in the instant case should be whether requiring proof of fault on the part of Time, Inc., as a precondition to recovery in this case—and thereby possibly interfering with the State's desire to compensate respondent Firestone—will contribute in any way to the goal of protecting "speech that matters." I think it would not.

---

9. Indeed, I agree with the view expressed by Mr. Justice Marshall in his dissenting opinion: unless there exists some basis for a finding of fault other than that given by the Supreme Court of Florida there can be no liability.

10. The Florida District Court of Appeal, on the second appeal to it, reversed a judgment for respondent. In doing so, it applied the *New York Times* "actual malice" standard, but added: "Nowhere was there proof Time was even negligent, much less intentionally false or in reckless disregard of the truth." 254 So.2d, at 390. A problem infecting the various decisions in the Florida courts is the understandable uncertainty as to exactly what standard should be applied. This case was in litigation several years before *Gertz* was decided.

At the time of the defamatory publication in this case—December 1967—the law clearly authorized liability without fault in defamation cases of the sort involved here. Whatever the chilling effect of that rule of law on publication of "speech that matters" in 1967 might have been, it has already occurred and is now irremediable. The goal of protecting "speech that matters" by announcing rules, as this Court did in Gertz v. Welch, supra, and Rosenbloom v. Metromedia, Inc., 403 U.S. 29, 91 S.Ct. 1811, 29 L.Ed.2d 296 (1971), requiring fault as a precondition to a defamation recovery under circumstances such as are involved here, is *fully* achieved so long as fault is required for cases in which the publication occurred *after* the dates of those decisions. This is not such a case.

Therefore, to require proof of fault in this case—or in any other case predating *Gertz* and *Rosenbloom* in which a private figure is defamed—is to interfere with the State's otherwise legitimate policy of compensating defamation victims without furthering First Amendment goals *in any way at all*. In other areas in which the Court has developed a rule designed not to achieve justice in the case before it but designed to induce socially desirable conduct by some group in the future, the Court has declined to apply the rule to fact situations predating its announcement, e.g., Williams v. United States, 401 U.S. 646, 653, 91 S.Ct. 1148, 1152, 28 L.Ed.2d 388. The Court should follow a similar path here.

In any event, the judgment of the court below should be affirmed. My Brother Rehnquist concludes that negligence is sufficient fault, under Gertz v. Robert Welch, Inc., supra, to justify the judgment below, and that a finding of negligence may constitutionally be supplied by the Florida Supreme Court. I agree. Furthermore, the state court referred to Gertz v. Robert Welch, Inc., by name; noted the "convincing evidence of * * * negligence" in the case; pointed out that a careful examination of the divorce decree would have "clearly demonstrated" that the divorce was not grounded on adultery, as reported by Time, Inc.; and stated flatly "this is a flagrant example of 'journalistic negligence.'" It appears to me that the Florida Supreme Court has made a sufficiently "conscious determination," ante, p. —, of the fact of negligence. If it is *Gertz* that controls this case and if that decision is to be applied retroactively, I would affirm the judgment.

Mr. Justice Marshall, dissenting.

The Court agrees with the Supreme Court of Florida that the "actual malice" standard of New York Times Co. v. Sullivan, 376 U.S. 254, 84 S.Ct. 710, 11 L.Ed.2d 686 (1964), does not apply to this case. Because I consider the respondent, Mary Alice Firestone, to be a "public figure" within the meaning of our prior decisions, Gertz v. Robert Welch, Inc., 418 U.S. 323, 94 S.Ct. 2997, 41 L.Ed.2d 789 (1974); Curtis Publishing Co. v. Butts, 388 U.S. 130, 87 S.Ct. 1975, 18 L.Ed.2d 1094 (1967), I respectfully dissent.

I

Mary Alice Firestone was not a person "first brought to public attention by the defamation that is the subject of the lawsuit." Rosenbloom v. Metromedia, Inc., 403 U.S. 29, 78, 86, 91 S.Ct. 1811, 1841, 29 L.Ed.2d 296 (1971) (Marshall, J., dissenting). On the contrary, she was "prominent among the '400' of Palm Beach Society," and an "active [member] of the sporting set," Firestone v. Time, Inc., 271 So.2d 745, 751 (Fla.1972), whose activities predictably attracted the attention of a sizeable portion of the public. Indeed, Mrs. Firestone's appearances in the printed press were evidently frequent enough to warrant her subscribing to a press clipping service.

Mrs. Firestone brought suit for separate maintenance, with reason to know of the likely public interest in the proceedings. As the Supreme Court of Florida noted, Mr. and Mrs. Firestone's "marital difficulties were * * * well-known," and the lawsuit became "a veritable *cause celebre* in social circles across the country." Ibid. The 17-month trial and related events attracted national news coverage, and elicited no fewer than 43 articles in the Miami Herald and 45 articles in the Palm Beach Post and Palm Beach Times. Far from shunning the publicity, Mrs. Firestone held several press conferences in the course of the proceedings.

These facts are sufficient to warrant the conclusion that Mary Alice Firestone was a "public figure" for purposes of reports on the judicial proceedings she initiated. In Gertz v. Robert Welch, Inc., supra, 418 U.S., at 352, 94 S.Ct., at 1013, we noted that an individual can be a public figure for some purposes and a private figure for others. And we found two distinguishing features between public figures and private figures. First, we recognized that public figures have less need for judicial protection because of their greater ability to resort to self-help: "public figures usually enjoy significantly greater access to the channels of effective communication and hence have a more realistic opportunity to counteract false statements than private individuals normally enjoy." Id., at 344, 94 S.Ct., at 3009.

As the above recital of the facts makes clear, Mrs. Firestone is hardly in a position to suggest that she lacked access to the media for purposes relating to her lawsuit. It may well be that she would have had greater difficulty countering alleged falsehoods in the national press than in the Miami and Palm Beach papers that covered the proceedings so thoroughly. But presumably the audience Mrs. Firestone would have been most interested in reaching could have been reached through the local media. In any event, difficulty in reaching all those who may have read the alleged falsehood surely ought not preclude a finding that Mrs. Firestone was a public figure under *Gertz*. *Gertz* set no absolute requirement that an individual be able fully to counter falsehoods through self-help in order to be a public figure. We viewed the availability of the self-help remedy as a relative matter in

Gertz, and set it forth as a minor consideration in determining whether an individual is a public figure.

The second, "more important," consideration in *Gertz* was a normative notion that public figures are less deserving of protection than private figures: that although "it may be possible for someone to become a public figure through no purposeful action of his own," generally those classed as public figures have "thrust themselves to the forefront of particular public controversies" and thereby "invite[d] attention and comment." Id., at 344–345, 94 S.Ct., at 3009. And even if they have not, "the communications media are entitled to act on the assumption that * * * public figures have voluntarily exposed themselves to increased risk of injury from defamatory falsehood concerning them." Id., at 345, 94 S.Ct. at 3010.

We must assume that it was by choice that Mrs. Firestone became an active member of the "sporting set"—a social group with "especial prominence in the affairs of society," ibid., whose lives receive constant media attention. Certainly there is nothing in the record to indicate otherwise, and Mrs. Firestone's subscription to a press clipping service suggests that she was not altogether uninterested in the publicity she received. Having placed herself in a position in which her activities were of interest to a significant segment of the public, Mrs. Firestone chose to initiate a lawsuit for separate maintenance, and most significantly, held several press conferences in the course of that lawsuit. If these actions for some reason fail to establish as a certainty that Mrs. Firestone "voluntarily exposed [herself] to increased risk of injury from defamatory falsehood," surely they are sufficient to entitle the press to act on the assumption that she did. Accordingly Mrs. Firestone would appear to be a public figure under *Gertz.*

The Court resists this result by concluding that the subject matter of the alleged defamation was not a "public controversy" as that term was used in *Gertz.* In part, the Court's conclusion rests on what I view as an understatement of the degree to which Mrs. Firestone can be said to have voluntarily acted in a manner that invited public attention. But more fundamentally its conclusion rests on a reading of *Gertz* that differs from mine. The meaning that the Court attributes to the term "public controversy" used in *Gertz* resurrects the precise difficulties that I thought *Gertz* was designed to avoid.

It is not enough for the Court that, because of Mrs. Firestone's acquired prominence within a segment of society, her lawsuit had already attracted significant public attention and comment when the Time report was published. According to the Court, the controversy, already of interest to the public, was "not the sort of 'public controversy' referred to in *Gertz.*" Ante, at 965. The only explanation I can discern from the Court's opinion is that the controversy was not of the sort deemed relevant to the "affairs of society," ante, at 965, and the public's interest not of the sort deemed "legitimate" or worthy of judicial recognition.

If there is one thing that is clear from *Gertz*, it is that we explicitly rejected the position of the plurality in Rosenbloom v. Metromedia, Inc., 403 U.S. 29, 91 S.Ct. 1811, 29 L.Ed.2d 296 (1971), that the applicability of the *New York Times* standard depends upon whether the subject matter of a report is a matter of "public or general concern." We explained in *Gertz* that the test advanced by the *Rosenbloom* plurality

> would occasion the * * * difficulty of forcing state and federal judges to decide on an *ad hoc* basis which publications address issues of "general or public interest" and which do not—to determine, in the words of Mr. Justice Marshall, "what information is relevant to self-government." Rosenbloom v. Metromedia, Inc., 403 U.S., at 79, 91 S.Ct., at 1837. We doubt the wisdom of committing this task to the conscience of judges. 418 U.S., at 347, 94 S.Ct., at 3010.

Having thus rejected the appropriateness of judicial inquiry into "the legitimacy of interest in a particular event or subject," *Rosenbloom*, supra, 403 U.S., at 79, 91 S.Ct., at 1837 (Marshall, J., dissenting), *Gertz* obviously did not intend to sanction any such inquiry by its use of the term "public controversy." Yet that is precisely how I understand the Court's opinion to interpret *Gertz*.[1]

If *Gertz* is to have any meaning at all, the focus of analysis must be on the actions of the individual, and the degree of public attention that had already developed, or that could have been anticipated, before the report in question. Under this approach, the class of public figures must include an individual like Mrs. Firestone, who acquired a social prominence that could be expected to attract public attention, initiated a lawsuit that predictably attracted more public attention, and held press conferences in the course of and in regard to the lawsuit.[2] I

---

1. The Supreme Court of Florida's explanation of why the *New York Times* standard is inapplicable is equally inconsistent with *Gertz*. After referring to Mrs. Firestone's prominence in Palm Beach Society, the widespread attention her lawsuit received, and her granting of interviews to the news media, the Court reasoned as follows:

"That the public was curious, titillated or intrigued with the scandal in the Firestone divorce is beyond doubt. But we again emphasize the distinction we make between that genre of public interest and real public or general concern.

* * *

" * * * [W]e cannot find here any aspect of real public concern, and none has been shown to us, which would be furthered or enhanced by 'free discussion' and 'robust debate' about the divorce of Russell and Mary Alice Firestone.

"Nor did [Mrs. Firestone's] quoted interviews with the press raise the untidy affair to the dignity of true public concern. Unlike an actress who might grant interviews relating to the opening of her new play, [Mrs. Firestone] was not seeking public patronage. Publicity, or sympathy, perhaps, but not patronage. Irrespective of her subjective motives, objectively she was merely satiating the appetites of a curious press.

"In sum, the Firestone divorce action was unquestionably newsworthy, but reports thereof were not constitutionally protected as being matters of real public or general concern." 271 So.2d at 752.

This language is from an opinion that issued before *Gertz* was decided, but the reasoning was reaffirmed in the Supreme Court of Florida's final opinion in the case, Firestone v. Time, Inc., 305 So.2d 172, 174–175 (1974), which issued after our decision in *Gertz*.

2. The Court places heavy emphasis on the degree to which Mrs. Firestone attempted to "influence the resolution of" a particular controversy. In response to the observation that Mrs. Firestone held press con-

would hold that, for purposes of this case, Mrs. Firestone is a public figure, who must demonstrate that the report in question was published with "actual malice"—that is, with knowledge that it was false or with reckless disregard of whether it was false or not.

II

While the foregoing discussion is sufficient to dispose of the case under my reading of the law, two other aspects of the Court's opinion warrant comment. First, the Court appears to reject the contention that a rational interpretation of an ambiguous document is always entitled to some constitutional protection. The Court reads Time, Inc. v. Pape, 401 U.S. 279, 91 S.Ct. 633, 28 L.Ed.2d 45 (1971), as providing such protection only under the rubric of the *New York Times* "actual malice" standard. Ante, at 967 n. 4. I disagree. While the precise holding in *Pape* was that the choice of one of several rational interpretations of an ambiguous document is not enough to create a jury issue of "actual malice," the Court's reasoning suggests that its holding ought not be so confined. In introducing its discussion, the Court noted:

> [A] vast amount of what is published in the daily and periodical press purports to be descriptive of what somebody *said* rather than of what anybody *did*. Indeed, perhaps the largest share of news concerning the doings of government appears in the form of accounts of reports, speeches, press conferences, and the like. The question of the "truth" of such an indirect newspaper report presents rather complicated problems. 401 U.S., at 285-286, 91 S.Ct., at 637 (emphasis in original).

And in discussing the need for some protection for the publisher attempting to report the gist of a lengthy government document, the Court observed:

> Where the document reported on is so ambiguous as this one was, it is hard to imagine a test of "truth" that would not put the publisher virtually at the mercy of the unguided discretion of a jury. 401 U.S., at 291, 91 S.Ct., at 640.

Surely the Court's evident concern that publishers be accorded the leeway to offer rational interpretations of ambiguous documents was not restricted to cases in which the *New York Times* standard is applicable. That concern requires that protection for rational interpretations be accorded under the fault standard contemplated in *Gertz*. Thus my Brothers Powell and Stewart, while joining the opinion of the Court, recognize that the rationality of an interpretation of an ambigu-

---

ferences, for example, the Court notes that those conferences were not intended to influence the outcome of the trial or any other controversy. Ante, at 965-966 n. 3. *Gertz* did, of course, refer to the fact that persons often become public figures by attempting to influence the resolution of public questions. 418 U.S., at 345, 94 S.Ct., at 3009.

But the reference must be viewed as but an example of how one becomes a public figure. Surely *Gertz* did not intend to establish a requirement that an individual attempt to influence the resolution of a particular controversy before he can be termed a public figure. If that were the rule, Athletic Director Butts in Curtis Publishing Co. v. Butts, supra, would not be a public figure. We held that Butts was a public figure, and in *Gertz* we specifically noted that that decision was "correct." 418 U.S., at 343, 94 S.Ct., at 3008.

ous document must figure as a crucial element in any assessment of fault under *Gertz*. Ante, at 971–972 (Powell, J., concurring). I agree. The choice of one of several rational interpretations of an ambiguous document, without more, is insufficient to support a finding of fault under *Gertz*.

Finally, assuming that the Court is correct in its assessment of the law in this case, I find the Court's disposition baffling. The Court quotes that portion of the Supreme Court of Florida's opinion which, citing *Gertz,* states in no uncertain terms that Time's report was a "flagrant example of 'journalistic negligence.' " Firestone v. Time, Inc., 305 So.2d 172, 178 (1974). But the Court is unwilling to read that statement as a "conscious determination" of fault, and accordingly the Court remands the case for an assessment of fault.

Surely the Court cannot be suggesting that the quoted portion of the Supreme Court of Florida's opinion, which contained a citation to *Gertz,* had no meaning at all. And if it did have meaning, it must have reflected either an intention to find fault or an intention to affirm a finding of fault. It is quite clear that the opinion was not intended to affirm any finding of fault, for as the Court observes there was no finding of fault to affirm. The question of fault had not been submitted to the jury, and the District Court of Appeal had explicitly noted the absence of any proof that Time had been negligent. Time, Inc. v. Firestone, 254 So.2d 386, 390 (1971). The absence of any prior finding of fault only reinforces what the Supreme Court of Florida's language itself makes clear—that the Court was not simply affirming a finding of fault, but making such a finding in the first instance.

I therefore agree with my Brother White that the Supreme Court of Florida made a conscious determination of fault. I would add, however, that it is a determination that is wholly unsupportable. The sole basis for that Court's determination of fault was that under Florida law a wife found guilty of adultery cannot be, as Mrs. Firestone was, awarded alimony. Time, the Court reasoned, should have realized that a divorce decree containing an award of alimony could not, consistent with Florida law, have been based on adultery. But that reasoning assumes that judicial decisions can always be squared with the prior state of the law. * * * Unless there is some basis for a finding of fault other than that given by the Supreme Court of Florida, I think it clear that there can be no liability.

Questions

1. *Firestone* quotes *Gertz* for the proposition that "public figures" include those who "have thrust themselves to the forefront of particular public controversies in order to influence the resolution of the issues involved". Why was not Mary Alice Firestone precisely such a public figure vis a vis her widely publicized divorce? Is it because, as the *Firestone* court observes, one cannot equate " 'public controversy' with all controversies of interest to the public"? What, then, constitutes a "public controversy"? The *Firestone* court explains

that this involves "the resolution of public questions", but this, in turn, requires a definition of a "public question". The *Firestone* court does not attempt to define this term, but by its rejection of the *Rosenbloom* plurality must it be concluded that a "public question" is not to be equated with a matter "of public or general concern"? What, then, is a "public question"?

2. Can the ambiguous state in which the *Firestone* opinion leaves the definition of a public figure be clarified by focusing on that passage from *Gertz,* quoted in *Firestone,* which speaks of those who "occupy positions of such persuasive [does the court mean 'pervasive'?] power and influence that they are deemed public figures for all purposes." Does this suggest that a "public figure" for this purpose is one who exercises great power and influence in the resolution of "public questions"? Might the same be said as to one who is a "public figure" vis a vis a particular "public question"? If there must be a finding of such "power and influence" by the plaintiff in order to apply the *New York Times* standard, might one then conclude that a "public question" may be defined as a "matter of public or general concern" without thereby reviving *Rosenbloom,* which rejected the public figure requirement?

STREET v. NATIONAL BROADCASTING CO.

United States Court of Appeals, Sixth Circuit, 1981.
645 F.2d 1227.

Before MERRITT and BOYCE F. MARTIN, JR., CIRCUIT JUDGES, and PECK, SENIOR CIRCUIT JUDGE.

MERRITT, CIRCUIT JUDGE.

This is a Tennessee diversity case against the National Broadcasting Company for libel and invasion of privacy. The plaintiff-appellant, Victoria Price Street, was the prosecutrix and main witness in the famous rape trials of the Scottsboro boys, which occurred in Alabama more than forty years ago. NBC televised a play or historical drama entitled "Judge Horton and the Scottsboro Boys," dramatizing the role of the local presiding judge in one of those trials.

The movie portrays Judge Horton as a courageous and tragic figure struggling to bring justice in a tense community gripped by racial prejudice and intent on vengeance against nine blacks accused of raping two white women. In the movie Judge Horton sets aside a jury verdict of guilty because he believes that the evidence shows that the prosecutrix—plaintiff in this action—falsely accused the Scottsboro defendants. The play portrays the plaintiff in the derogatory light that Judge Horton apparently viewed her: as a woman attempting to send nine innocent blacks to the electric chair for a rape they did not commit.

This case presents the question of what tort and First Amendment principles apply to an historical drama that allegedly defames a living person who participated in the historical events portrayed. The plaintiff's case is based on principles of libel law and "false light" invasion of privacy arising from the derogatory portrayal. NBC raises alternative claims and defenses: (1) the claim that the published material is not defamatory; (2) the claim of truth; (3) the common law privilege of fair comment; (4) the common law privilege of fair report on a judicial proceeding; (5) the First Amendment claim that because the plaintiff is a public figure recovery must be based on a showing of malice; and (6) even if the malice standard is inapplicable, the claim that recovery must be based on a showing of negligence.

At the end of all the proof, District Judge Neese directed a verdict for defendant on the ground that even though plaintiff was not a public figure at the time of publication the defamatory matter was not negligently published. We affirm for the reason that the historical events and persons portrayed are "public" as distinguished from "private." A malice standard applies to public figures under the First Amendment, and there is no evidence that the play was published with malice.

The Scottsboro defendants together with the sheriff (extreme left) and their attorney Samuel Leibowitz. Inset: Victoria Price Street as she appeared in 1933 at the second Scottsboro trial.

WIDE WORLD PHOTOS

I. Statement of Facts

A. Historical Context

In April 1931, nine black youths were accused of raping two young white women while riding a freight train between Chattanooga, Tennessee, and Huntsville, Alabama. The case was widely discussed in the local, national, and foreign press. The youths were quickly tried in

Scottsboro, Alabama, and all were found guilty and sentenced to death. The Alabama Supreme Court affirmed the convictions. Weems v. State, 141 So. 215, 224 Ala. 524 (1932); Patterson v. State, 141 So. 195, 224 Ala. 531 (1932); Powell v. State, 141 So. 201, 224 Ala. 540 (1932). The United States Supreme Court reversed all convictions on the ground that the defendants were denied the right to counsel guaranteed by the Sixth Amendment. Powell v. Alabama, 287 U.S. 45, 53 S.Ct. 55, 77 L.Ed. 158 (1932). The defendants were retried separately after a change of venue from Scottsboro to Decatur, Alabama. Patterson was the first defendant retried, and this trial was the subject of the NBC production. In a jury trial before Judge Horton, he was tried, convicted, and sentenced to death. Judge Horton set the verdict aside on the ground that the evidence was insufficient. Patterson and one other defendant, Norris, were then tried before another judge on essentially the same evidence, convicted, and sentenced to death. The judge let the verdicts stand, and the convictions were affirmed by the Alabama Supreme Court. Patterson v. State, 156 So. 567, 229 Ala. 270 (1934), and Norris v. State, 156 So. 556, 229 Ala. 226 (1934). The United States Supreme Court again reversed, this time because blacks were systematically excluded from grand and petit juries. Norris v. Alabama, 294 U.S. 587, 55 S.Ct. 579, 79 L.Ed. 1074 (1935), and Patterson v. Alabama, 294 U.S. 600, 55 S.Ct. 575, 79 L.Ed. 1082 (1935). At his fourth retrial, Patterson was convicted and sentenced to seventy-five years in prison. Patterson v. State, 175 So. 371, 234 Ala. 342, cert. denied, 302 U.S. 733, 58 S.Ct. 121, 82 L.Ed. 567 (1937). Defendants Weems and Andrew Wright were also convicted on retrial and sentenced to a term of years. Defendant Norris was convicted and his death sentence was commuted to life imprisonment by the Alabama governor. Defendants Montgomery, Roberson, Williams, and Leroy Wright were released without retrial. Powell pled guilty to assault allegedly committed during an attempted escape. The last Scottsboro defendant was paroled in 1950.

The Scottsboro case aroused strong passions and conflicting opinions in the 1930s throughout the nation. Several all white juries convicted the Scottsboro defendants of rape. Two trial judges and the Alabama Supreme Court, at times by divided vote, let these verdicts stand. Judge Horton was the sole trial judge to find the facts in favor of the defendants. Liberal opinion supported Judge Horton's conclusions that the Scottsboro defendants had been falsely accused.

During the lengthy course of the Scottsboro trials, newspapers frequently wrote about Victoria Price. She gave some interviews to the press. Thereafter, she disappeared from public view. The Scottsboro trials and her role in them continued to be the subject of public discussion, but there is no evidence that Mrs. Street sought publicity. NBC incorrectly stated in the movie that she was no longer living. After the first showing of "Judge Horton and the Scottsboro Boys," plaintiff notified NBC that she was living, and shortly thereafter she filed suit. Soon after plaintiff filed suit, NBC rebroadcast the dramatization omitting the statement that plaintiff was no longer living.

B. The Dramatization

The script for "Judge Horton and the Scottsboro Boys" was based on one chapter of a book by Dr. Daniel Carter, an historian, entitled *Scottsboro: A Tragedy of the American South* (Louisiana State University Press, 1969). The movie is based almost entirely on the information in Dr. Carter's book, which, in turn, was based on Judge Horton's findings at the 1933 trial, the transcript of the trial, contemporaneous newspaper reports of the trial, and interviews with Judge Horton and others. NBC purchased the movie from an independent producer.

Plaintiff's major libel and invasion of privacy claims are based on nine scenes in the movie in which she is portrayed in a derogatory light. The essential facts concerning these claims are as follows:

1. After an opening prologue, black and white youths are shown fighting on a train. The train is halted, and the blacks are arrested. The next scene shows plaintiff standing next to Ruby Bates at the tracks. Plaintiff claims that this scene, in effect, makes her a perjurer because she testified at the 1933 trial and in this case that she fainted while alighting from the train and did not regain consciousness until she was taken to a local grocery store. Judge Horton, in his opinion sustaining the motion for a new trial, found that the observations of other witnesses and the testimony of the examining doctor contradicted her testimony in this respect. Horton concluded that it was unlikely that Victoria Price had fainted.

2. As plaintiff and Ruby Bates are led away from the tracks by the sheriff and his men, the sheriff in the play calls the two women a "couple of bums." There is no indication in Judge Horton's opinion, in the 1933 trial transcript, or in Dr. Carter's book that this comment was actually made.

3. In a pretrial conversation between two lawyers representing the defendant, the play portrays one of them as advising restraint in the cross-examination of plaintiff Price. He says to the other defense lawyer: "The Scottsboro transcripts are really clear * * *. The defense at the last trial made one thing very clear, Victoria was a *whore*, and they got it in the neck for it * * *." (Emphasis added.) There is no evidence that this specific conversation between the two defense lawyers actually occurred. Dr. Carter does state in his book that one of the purposes of the defense in cross-examining plaintiff was to discredit her testimony by introducing evidence that she was a common prostitute. *Scottsboro* at 206.

4. Plaintiff in this action contends that the movie falsely portrays her as defensive and evasive during her direct and cross-examination. Judge Horton found in his 1933 opinion granting a new trial that plaintiff was not a cooperative witness: "Her manner of testifying and her demeanor on the stand militate against her. Her testimony was contradictory, often evasive, and time and again she refused to answer pertinent questions."

5. Plaintiff claims that the last question put to her on cross-examination in the play is inaccurate. In the movie the defense attorney asks: "One more question: have you ever heard of a white woman being arrested for perjury when she was the complaining witness against Negroes in the entire history of the state of Alabama?" According to the 1933 trial transcript, the actual question was, "I want to ask you if you have ever heard of any single white woman ever being locked up in jail when she is the complaining witness against Negroes in the history of the state of Alabama?" Plaintiff objects to the insertion of the word "perjury" in the play.

6. In the play, Dr. Marvin Lynch, one of the doctors who examined plaintiff after she alighted from the train, approaches Judge Horton outside the courtroom and confides that he does not believe that the two women were raped by the Scottsboro boys. Dr. Lynch refuses to go on the witness stand and so testify, however. Plaintiff argues that this scene is improper because it is not supported in the 1933 trial record. This is true. Neither the 1933 trial transcript nor Judge Horton's opinion make reference to this incident. The Carter book does state, however, that Judge Horton told the author in a later interview that this incident occurred. *Scottsboro* at 214–15.

7. The play portrays events leading up to plaintiff's trip to Chattanooga with her friend, Ruby Bates. It was on the return trip to Alabama that the rape alleged occurred. Lester Carter, a defense witness in the play, testifies that he had intercourse with Ruby Bates on the night before the trip to Chattanooga and that plaintiff had intercourse with Jack Tiller. During the testimony there is a flashback that shows an exchange in a boxcar in which Ruby Bates suggests that they all go to Chattanooga and plaintiff says, "[m]aybe Ruby and me could hustle there while you two [Carter and Tiller] got some kind of fill-in work. What do you say?" This is an accurate abridgement of the substance of the actual testimony of Lester Carter at the 1933 trial, although Price denied, both at the 1933 trial and in the defamation trial below, that she had had intercourse with Tiller. Judge Horton specifically found that she did not tell the truth. The dramatization quoted or closely paraphrased substantial portions of Judge Horton's 1933 opinion. Judge Horton concluded that the testimony of Victoria Price "is not only uncorroborated, but is contradicted by other evidence," evidence that "greatly preponderates in favor of the defendant":

> When we consider, as the facts hereafter detailed will show, that this woman had slept side by side with a man the night before [the alleged rape] in Chattanooga, and had intercourse at Huntsville with Tiller on the night before she went to Chattanooga * * * the conclusion becomes clearer and clearer that this woman was not forced into intercourse with all of these Negroes upon the train, but that her condition [the presence of dead sperm in her vagina] was clearly due to the intercourse that she had on the nights previous to this time.

8. Lester Carter also testifies in the play that plaintiff urged him to say that he had seen her raped. The 1933 trial transcript reveals that Carter actually testified that he overheard plaintiff tell another white youth that "if you don't testify according to what I testify I will see that you are took off the witness stand * * *." Judge Horton in his opinion observed that there was evidence presented at the trial showing that Price encouraged others to support her version of what had happened.

9. Another witness in the play, Dallas Ramsey, testifies that he saw plaintiff and Ruby Bates in a "hobo jungle" near the train tracks in Chattanooga the night before the train trip back to Alabama. Ramsey testifies that plaintiff stated that she and her husband were looking for work and that "her old man" was uptown scrounging for food. The play dramatizes Ramsey's testimony while he is on the stand by a flashback to the scene at the "hobo jungle." The flashback gives the impression that plaintiff is perhaps inviting sexual advances from Ramsey, although the words used do not state this specifically. The substance of Ramsey's testimony, as portrayed in the play, is found in the 1933 trial transcript. The record provides no basis for the suggestive flashback.

The facts recited above illustrate that the play does cast plaintiff in an extremely derogatory light. She is portrayed as a perjurer, a woman of bad character, a woman who falsely accused the Scottsboro boys of rape knowing that the result would likely be the electric chair. The play is a gripping and effective portrayal of its point of view about her, the Scottsboro boys, and Judge Horton. As an effective dramatic production, the play has won many awards, including the George Foster Peabody Award for playwriting and awards from the Screenwriters' Guild and the American Bar Association.

II. Common Law Claims and Defenses

A. Defamatory Nature of the Published Material

Taken as a whole, the play conveys a defamatory image of the plaintiff. Although the words "bum" and "hustle" may be considered rhetorical hyperbole and therefore not necessarily defamatory, Letter Carriers v. Austin, 418 U.S. 264, 284–86, 94 S.Ct. 2770, 2781–82, 41 L.Ed.2d 745 (1974), the reference to plaintiff as a "whore" and her portrayal as a perjurer and a suborner of perjury is obviously defamatory. The suggestive flashbacks showing her inviting sexual advances of Ramsey and Tiller reinforce the defamation. The effect of the drama as a whole is to create a character, Victoria Price. She is portrayed as a loose woman who falsely accuses the Scottsboro boys of raping her. This image of her character is created throughout the play by her own words and actions in the flashbacks and in the witness chair and by what others say about her.

B. The Privilege of Fair Comment

The portrayal of Victoria Price in this way is not expressed in the play as a matter of opinion. The characterization is expressed as concrete fact. The common law privilege of fair comment, adopted in Tennessee and explained in Venn v. Tennessean Newspapers, Inc., 201 F.Supp. 47, 52 (M.D.Tenn.1962), aff'd, 313 F.2d 639 (6th Cir.), cert. denied, 374 U.S. 830, 82 S.Ct. 1872, 10 L.Ed.2d 1053 (1963), is now protected as opinion under the First Amendment, Gertz v. Robert Welch, Inc., 418 U.S. 323, 339–40, 94 S.Ct. 2997, 41 L.Ed.2d 789 (1974). But this play does not say to the viewer that this is NBC's opinion about the character and actions of Victoria Price. It shows her inviting sexual intercourse and swearing falsely. We do not believe this characterization fits within the traditional fair comment privilege protecting opinion. See Cianci v. New York Times Publishing Co., 639 F.2d 54 (2nd Cir.1980, as amended Oct. 27, 1980) (magazine article interpreting evidence of rape not expression of opinion).

C. The Defense of Truth and the Privilege of Fair Report of a Judicial Proceeding

In his opinion setting aside the verdict, Judge Horton found, in effect, that NBC's characterization of Victoria Price was true. The movie characterizes her as Judge Horton found the facts in his opinion. This does not mean, however, that the case should be withdrawn from the jury on the basis of the defense of truth or the privilege of fair report of a judicial proceeding.

Neither Judge Horton's findings nor the final convictions based on the testimony of Victoria Price and affirmed on appeal settle the question of truth. That still remains an open question. Technical doctrines of res judicata and collateral estoppel do not apply in this context. Neither Victoria Price nor NBC were parties in the 1930s trials. In addition, citizens obviously have a right to attack the fairness of a trial. Judicial proceedings resolve disputes, but they do not establish the truth for all time. In libel cases the question of truth is normally one for the jury in a defamation action.

Many of the scenes actually quote or paraphrase the trial transcript, but the movie is not a completely accurate report of the trial. Witnesses who corroborate Victoria Price's version of the facts are omitted. The portions of the original trial that show her as a perjurer and a promiscuous woman are emphasized. The flashbacks consistently show plaintiff's conduct in a derogatory light. The flashbacks entirely accept the theory of the case presented by Judge Horton and the defense and reject the theory of the case presented by the state and the plaintiff. Under such circumstances the common law privilege permitting publication of defamatory material as a part of a fair and accurate report on judicial proceedings is not satisfied. The element of balance and neutrality is missing. See Langford v. Vanderbilt University, 44 Tenn.App. 694, 318 S.W.2d 568 (1958).

III. The First Amendment Defenses

A. Plaintiff was a Public Figure During the Scottsboro Trials

Since common law defenses do not support the directed verdict for NBC, we must reach the constitutional issues, particularly the question whether plaintiff should be characterized as a "public figure." In *Gertz,* the Supreme Court held that one characterized as a "public figure," as distinguished from a private individual, "may recover for injury to reputation *only on clear and convincing proof* that the defamatory falsehood was made *with knowledge of its falsity or with reckless disregard for the truth.*" 418 U.S. at 342, 94 S.Ct. at 3008 (emphasis added). In balancing the need to protect "private personality" and reputation against the need "to assure to the freedoms of speech and press that 'breathing space' essential to their free exercise," the Supreme Court has developed a general test to determine public figure status.

Gertz establishes a two-step analysis to determine if an individual is a public figure. First, does a "public controversy" exist? Second, what is "the nature and extent of [the] individual's participation" in that public controversy? 418 U.S. at 352, 94 S.Ct. at 3013. Three factors determine the "nature and extent" of an individual's involvement: the extent to which participation in the controversy is voluntary, the extent to which there is access to channels of effective communication in order to counteract false statements, and the prominence of the role played in the public controversy. 418 U.S. at 344–45, 94 S.Ct. at 3009.

The Supreme Court has not clearly defined the elements of a "public controversy." It is evident that it is not simply any controversy of general or public interest. Not all judicial proceedings are public controversies. For example, "dissolution of a marriage through judicial proceedings is not the sort of 'public controversy' referred to in *Gertz.*" Time, Inc. v. Firestone, 424 U.S. 448, 455, 96 S.Ct. 958, 965, 47 L.Ed.2d 154 (1976). Several factors, however, lead to the conclusion that the Scottsboro case is the kind of public controversy referred to in *Gertz.* The Scottsboro trials were the focus of major public debate over the ability of our courts to render even-handed justice. It generated widespread press and attracted public attention for several years. It was also a contributing factor in changing public attitudes about the right of black citizens to equal treatment under law and in changing constitutional principles governing the right to counsel and the exclusion of blacks from the jury.

The first factor in determining the nature and extent of plaintiff's participation is the prominence of her role in the public controversy. She was the only alleged victim, and she was the major witness for the State in the prosecution of the nine black youths. Ruby Bates, the other young woman who earlier had testified against the defendants, later recanted her incriminating testimony. Plaintiff was left as the sole prosecutrix. Therefore, she played a prominent role in the public controversy.

The second part of the test of public figure status is also met. Plaintiff had "access to the channels of effective communication and hence * * * a * * * realistic opportunity to counteract false statements." *Gertz*, 418 U.S. at 344, 94 S.Ct. at 3009. The evidence indicates that plaintiff recognized her importance to the criminal trials and the interest of the public in her as a personality. The press clamored to interview her. She clearly had access to the media and was able to broadcast her view of the events.

The most troublesome issue is whether plaintiff "voluntarily" "thrust" herself to the forefront of this public controversy. It cannot be said that a rape victim "voluntarily" injects herself into a criminal prosecution for rape. See Time, Inc. v. Firestone, 424 U.S. 448, 457, 96 S.Ct. 958, 966, 47 L.Ed.2d 154 (1976). In such an instance, voluntariness in the legal sense is closely bound to the issue of truth. If she was raped, her participation in the initial legal proceedings was involuntary for the purpose of determining her public figure status; if she falsely accused the defendants, her participation in this controversy was "voluntary." But legal standards in libel cases should not be drawn so that either the courts or the press must first determine the issue of truth before they can determine whether an individual should be treated as a public or a private figure. The principle of libel law should not be drawn in such a way that it forces the press, in an uncertain public controversy, to guess correctly about a woman's chastity.

When the issue of truth and the issue of voluntariness are the same, it is necessary to determine the public figure status of the individual without regard to whether she "voluntarily" thrust herself in the forefront of the public controversy. If there were no evidence of voluntariness other than that turning on the issue of truth, we would not consider the fact of voluntariness. In such a case, the other factors—prominence and access to media—alone would determine public figure status. But in this case, there is evidence of voluntariness not bound up with the issue of truth. Plaintiff gave press interviews and aggressively promoted her version of the case outside of her actual courtroom testimony. In the context of a widely-reported, intense public controversy concerning the fairness of our criminal justice system, plaintiff was a public figure under *Gertz* because she played a major role, had effective access to the media and encouraged public interest in herself.

B. Plaintiff Remains a Public Figure for Purposes of Later Discussion of the Scottsboro Case

The Supreme Court has explicitly reserved the question of "whether or when an individual who was once a public figure may lose that status by the passage of time." Wolston v. Reader's Digest Ass'n, Inc., 443 U.S. 157, 166 n. 7, 99 S.Ct. 2701, 2707, n. 7, 61 L.Ed.2d 450 (1979). In *Wolston* the District of Columbia Circuit found that plaintiff was a public figure and retained that status for the purpose of later discussion of the espionage case in which he was called as a witness. The Supreme Court found that the plaintiff's role in the original public controversy was so minor that he was not a public figure. It therefore reserved the question of whether a person retains his public figure status.

Plaintiff argues that even if she was a public figure at the time of the 1930s trial, she lost her public figure status over the intervening forty years. We reject this argument and hold that once a person becomes a public figure in connection with a particular controversy, that person remains a public figure thereafter for purposes of later commentary or treatment of *that controversy*. This rule finds support in both case law and analysis of the constitutional malice standard.

* * *

Our analytical view of the matter is based on the fact that the Supreme Court developed the public figure doctrine in order that the press might have sufficient breathing room to compose the first rough draft of history. It is no less important to allow the historian the same leeway when he writes the second or the third draft.

Our nation depends on "robust debate" to determine the best answer to public controversies of this sort. The public figure doctrine makes it possible for publishers to provide information on such issues to the debating public, undeterred by the threat of liability except in cases of actual malice. Developed in the context of contemporaneous reporting, the doctrine promotes a forceful exchange of views.

Considerations that underlie the public figure doctrine in the context of contemporaneous reporting also apply to later historical or dramatic treatment of the same events. Past public figures who now live in obscurity do not lose their access to channels of communication if they choose to comment on their role in the past public controversy. And although the publisher of history does not operate under journalistic deadlines it generally makes little difference in terms of accuracy and verifiability that the events on which a publisher is reporting occurred decades ago. Although information may come to light over the course of time, the distance of years does not necessarily make more data available to a reporter: memories fade; witnesses forget; sources disappear.

There is no reason for the debate to be any less vigorous when events that are the subject of current discussion occurred several years earlier. The mere passage of time does not automatically diminish the significance of events or the public's need for information. A nation that prizes its heritage need have no illusions about its past. It is no more fitting for the Court to constrain the analysis of past events than to stem the tide of current news. From Alfred Dreyfus to Alger Hiss, famous cases have been debated and reinterpreted by commentators and historians. A contrary rule would tend to restrain efforts to shed new light on historical events and reconsideration of past errors.

The plaintiff was the pivotal character in the most famous rape case of the twentieth century. It became a political controversy as well as a legal dispute. As the white prosecutrix of nine black youths during an era of racial prejudice in the South, she aroused the attention of the nation. The prosecutions were among the first to focus the conscience of the nation on the question of the ability of our system of justice to provide fair trials to blacks in the South. The question persists today. As long as the question remains, the Scottsboro boys case will not be relegated to the dusty pages of the scholarly treatise. It will remain a living controversy.

C. Evidence Insufficient to Support Malice [6]

A plaintiff may not recover under the malice standard unless there is "clear and convincing proof" that the defamation was published "with knowledge of its falsity or with reckless disregard for the truth." *Gertz*, 418 U.S. at 342, 94 S.Ct. at 3008. There is no evidence that NBC had knowledge that its portrayal of Victoria Price was false or that NBC recklessly disregarded the truth. The derogatory portrayal of Price in the movie is based in all material respects on the detailed findings of Judge Horton at the trial and Dr. Carter in his book. When the truth is uncertain and seems undiscoverable through further investigation, reliance on these two sources is not unreasonable.

We gain perspective on this question when we put to ourselves another case. Dr. Carter, in his book, persuasively argues, based on the evidence, that the Communist Party financed and controlled the defense of the Scottsboro boys. A different playwright might choose to portray Judge Horton as some Southern newspapers portrayed him at the time—as an evil judge who associated himself with a Communist cause and gave his approval to interracial rape in order to curry favor with the eastern press. The problem would be similar had Judge Horton—for many years before his death an obscure private citizen—sued the publisher for libel.

Some controversial historical events like the Scottsboro trials become symbolic and take on an overlay of political meaning. Speech about such events becomes in part political speech. The hypothetical case and the actual case before us illustrate that an individual's social philosophy and political leanings color his historical perspective. His political opinions cause him to draw different lessons from history and to see historical events and facts in a different light. He believes the historical evidence he wants to believe and casts aside other evidence to the contrary. So long as there is no evidence of bad faith or conscious or extreme disregard of the truth, the speaker in such a situation does not violate the malice standard. His version of history may be wrong, but the law does not punish him for being a bad historian.

The malice standard is flexible and encourages diverse political opinions and robust debate about social issues. It tolerates silly arguments and strange ways of yoking facts together in unusual patterns.

---

6. The District Court found that even if plaintiff was a public figure forty years ago, she no longer was a public figure at the time of publication. The court then directed a verdict for NBC on grounds that there was no evidence of negligence. The evidence indicates, however, that there is arguably some proof of negligence by NBC. NBC was notified between the first and second showings of the film that not only was plaintiff alive but that she objected to her characterization in the movie. NBC made no attempt to verify the factual presentation in the movie thereafter. This arguably presents a jury-submissible case of negligence, as Judge Peck's dissent points out.

But it is not infinitely expandable. It does not abolish all the common law of libel even in the political context. It still protects us against the "big political lie," the conscious or reckless falsehood. We do not have that in this case.

Accordingly, the judgment of the District Court is affirmed.

* * *

JOHN W. PECK, SENIOR CIRCUIT JUDGE, dissenting.

The majority offers no convincing reasons in law or policy for extending to NBC the protection of the *New York Times* privilege of freedom from liability for defamatory statements made without "malice." Forty years after the events that made Mrs. Street famous (or infamous), the purposes behind the *legal* distinction (not the everyday distinction) between public figures and private individuals are served only by ranking Mrs. Street among the latter.

The majority exalts "robust debate on social issues." So do we all. If that were the only interest of weight in defamation and privacy cases, there would be no need to distinguish between public figures and private persons in our law. It would be much better to apply the *New York Times* "malice" test in all cases; yet it is no mystery why this is not our rule of law.

The Constitution does not protect damaging misstatements of fact because of their intrinsic worth. "[T]here is no constitutional value in false statements of fact." Gertz v. Robert Welch, Inc., 418 U.S. 323, 340, 94 S.Ct. 2997, 3007, 41 L.Ed.2d 789 (1974). False reports are protected because they are "inevitable in free debate." Id. The inevitability of *demonstrable* error lessens with the passage of time. Accordingly, when the pressures of contemporaneous reporting subside, the need for the protection of the "malice" standard disappears. A negligence[1] standard is enough. I would follow the reasoning of Justices Blackmun and Marshall, and hold that the passage of time can extinguish public figure status. See Wolston v. Reader's Digest Ass'n, Inc., 443 U.S. 157, 169–72, 99 S.Ct. 2701, 2708–10, 61 L.Ed.2d 450 (1979) (concurring opinion).

The majority adopts the rule, not that public figure status is eternal, but that it persists as long as the public controversy that gave rise to it. For my brethren, Scottsboro persists as a public controversy because the trials have taken on "an overlay of political meaning." In short, Mrs. Street is a public figure today because the majority thinks the Scottsboro affair merits public attention. This reasoning resurrects the "newsworthiness" test for applying the "malice" standard in defamation cases—a test proposed by a plurality of the Supreme Court in Rosenbloom v. Metromedia, Inc., 403 U.S. 29 (1971), and rejected by a majority of the Court in *Gertz*. It is not the business of judges to decide "what information is relevant to self-government." *Gertz*, supra, 418

---

1. Under *Gertz*, states may, in actions brought by private persons, set their own standards of liability for defamation, "so long as they do not impose liability without fault * * *." 418 U.S. at 347, 94 S.Ct. at 3010. Tennessee applies a negligence standard. Memphis Pub. Co. v. Nichols, 569 S.W.2d 412, 418 (Tenn.1978).

U.S. at 346, 94 S.Ct. at 3010 (quoting Justice Marshall's dissent in *Rosenbloom*).

Gertz put an end to the binary system where defamatory publications either enjoyed the protection of the "malice" standard or suffered the strict liability imposed by the common law. The majority ignores the distinctions drawn in *Gertz* and casts the issues of this case in terms of speech versus suppression of speech. This perception also overlooks the basic distinction in tort law between compensation and punishment. Although under *Gertz* and current Tennessee law Mrs. Street could recover actual damages upon showing falsity,[2] negligence, causation and injury, she could not receive punitive damages without proving "malice." See, e.g., Gertz at 418 U.S. 349, 94 S.Ct. at 3011; Maheu v. Hughes Tool Co., 569 F.2d 459 (9th Cir.1977); Davis v. Schuchat, 510 F.2d 731 (D.C.Cir.1975). Thus Mrs. Street's status as a public or private person determines only what she must prove to show a prima facie entitlement to compensatory damages. It does not determine whether the law may "punish" historians for error, or prohibit them from committing error.

By making a plaintiff's status hinge on its determination of the significance of a defendant's speech, the majority pushes the Court into a quagmire where the law of defamation is standardless, easily manipulated, and no more speech-protective than the judges who happen to be applying it. The better approach is to take the distinction between public and private figures back to its roots, and examine the present status of the plaintiff in light of the reasons behind the distinction, as did Justices Blackmun and Marshall in *Wolston*. See 443 U.S. at 170–72, 99 S.Ct. at 2709–2710 (concurring opinion).

The First Amendment affords less protection to the reputations of public figures not because news of them is deemed significant but because they can more easily rebut falsehoods in public media, and because they have as a rule assumed the risk of public commentary. In short, the law encourages and expects those labeled public figures to be uninhibited, robust debaters. See Wolston, supra, 443 U.S. at 164, 99

---

2. In *Nichols*, supra note 1, the Tennessee Supreme Court stated that there is a presumption of the falsity of an alleged defamatory utterance—a presumption which "the defendant may rebut by proving truth as a defense." 569 S.W.2d at 420. This correctly states the common law, but such a presumption cannot be reconciled with *Gertz's* command that states not impose liability without fault. See Herbert v. Lando, 441 U.S. 153, 159, 170, 175–76, 99 S.Ct. 1635, 1639, 1646, 1648–49, 60 L.Ed.2d 115 (1979); Cianci v. New Times Pub. Co., 639 F.2d 54 at 60 (2d Cir.1980, as amended Oct. 27, 1980) (per Friendly, J.). *Cianci* speaks only of cases within the ambit of *Sullivan*. I would go farther and hold that *Gertz* requires plaintiffs to prove falsity in all defamation cases. The majority adopts neither approach, but rather treats truth as a defense, although noting that public figure plaintiffs must show "malice" by clear and convincing evidence.

Under Tennessee law, *substantial* truth or falsity is at issue in defamation cases. *Nichols*, supra, 569 S.W.2d at 420–21. *Nichols* held that a literally true article could convey a defamatory meaning by the omission of essential, unobvious facts. I believe the logical extension of this is that a trivially inaccurate report could convey a substantially true meaning. This of all theories would best support the directed verdicts in this case, although I nonetheless believe the question of truth was improperly taken from the jury.

S.Ct. at 2706; *Gertz,* supra, 418 U.S. at 344, 94 S.Ct. at 3009. This is too much to expect of the plaintiff today.

Over forty years ago, the prominence Mrs. Street gained through the Scottsboro trials allowed her to speak through public media. She was unquestionably a public figure in the current legal sense. Today her voice cannot rebut network "docudramas," which literally reach the entire nation in "gripping" displays. Few people assume the risk that the most personal aspects of their lives will be presented to the nation as dramatic entertainments. The majority hold that Mrs. Street assumed that risk by her involvement in an unspecified number of interviews over forty years ago.

When NBC broadcast "Judge Horton," Mrs. Street was not only not a public figure, she was a nonentity. Dr. Carter, historian and author of the book on which "Judge Horton" was loosely based, had been unable to trace Mrs. Street, and had described her death in some detail.[3] The majority offers no convincing reason why those who would write of her today should not be liable for damages caused by their failure to make reasonable efforts to get their facts straight.

Gertz and its progeny compel the conclusion that public figure status is determined by looking at a plaintiff's media power or public involvement at the time of the alleged defamation. I know of no case holding a person as presently obscure as Mrs. Street a public figure. * *

II

NBC broadcast "Judge Horton" not once but twice. Nothing in the record shows that the network was even negligent in the first broadcast: the best available information from the leading scholar on the Scottsboro incident was that Victoria Price Street was dead.

After the first broadcast, Mrs. Street brought a defamation action against NBC and sought an injunction against republication of the program. The district court wisely refused to issue such an injunction. Mrs. Street's complaint vaguely alleged that NBC's program presented a false, sensationalized picture of her, but gave no examples of false statements in the program. Nothing in the record allows the inference that agents of NBC's did in fact seriously doubt the truth of any specific factual presentation in "Judge Horton." I therefore fully agree with the majority's conclusion that no jury question of "malice" existed under the subjective *New York Times* standard.

Yet under the objective, "ordinarily prudent person" standard that the courts of Tennessee apply in defamation actions brought by private

---

3. Wrote Bancroft Award winner Carter: "Like the Scottsboro boys, Victoria Price and Ruby Bates were also soon forgotten.

* * *

* * * In 1961, thirty miles apart from each other, Ruby Bates and Victoria Price died." D. Carter, Scottsboro: A Tragedy of the American South 415–16 (1969) (footnote omitted).

Even Homer nods.

persons, a jury could readily conclude that NBC was negligent in its second broadcast of "Judge Horton." NBC's counsel admitted at trial that no one at NBC compared the transcripts of the 1933 Patterson trial with the parts of the movie purporting to reenact that trial. Dr. Carter and the screenwriter of "Judge Horton" testified that no one at NBC discussed Mrs. Street's charges of falsity with them. NBC might have chosen to rely on the conclusions in Dr. Carter's historical work, but a jury would be permitted to determine whether this reliance was unreasonable in light of Dr. Carter's testimony that parts of "Judge Horton" find no support whatsoever in Dr. Carter's history.

My fundamental disagreement with the majority concerns the constitutionality of permitting states to impose liability for negligence in defamation cases where the pressures of contemporaneous reporting are totally absent. The majority argues that different pressures work on historians, since "the distance of years does not necessarily make more data available to a reporter: memories fade; witnesses forget; sources disappear." Obviously, a negligence standard does not expect a writer to discover what is forever lost. When truth is unknowable, falsity, and hence defamation, cannot be proven.

III

The majority's unstated assumption is that application of the *New York Times* "malice" standard necessarily creates "breathing space" for uninhibited speech.

> Yet a publisher's decision to print or broadcast a libelous story is only partly influenced by the probability of winning or losing a lawsuit. While the publication decision involves a complex calculus, the salient cost factors are likely to be the probability that the publisher will be sued, and the cost of defending if suit is brought. Rules affecting the publisher's ultimate liability are thus likely to be marginal considerations in the decision to publish.

L. Tribe, *American Constitutional Law* § 12–13 at 643 (1978). Since no evidentiary privilege protects the editorial process, Herbert v. Lando, 441 U.S. 153, 159–67, 99 S.Ct. 1635, 1639–44, 60 L.Ed.2d 115 (1979), litigation costs are not likely to vary with the application of *New York Times* "malice" or *Gertz* "fault" rules. In the present case, the district court did not decide the question of Mrs. Street's status until the close of all proof. Had this action been brought after *Lando,* and had the trial judge (contrary to his actual ruling) early in the trial held Mrs. Street a public figure, the evidence (and outcome) in the trial might have been different, but it is incredible that either the hypothetical or the actual outcomes would significantly influence future publishing decisions. Invocation of New York Times v. Sullivan does not exorcise what to the majority is the demon of self-censorship. Only abolition of the torts of defamation and invasion of privacy can do that, and that abolition is a price measured in individual dignity that our Constitution does not exact.

A living person is not a means to an end. Events may be symbolic, but individuals are not mere symbols.[9] The dramatic effect of "Judge Horton," and the merit of its historical interpretation, however important they may be to the majority, are not matters before us, nor were they before any jury. The substantial truth of factual assertions in the work, and the liability of the network for any material errors in them, were questions for the jury to decide.[a]

Questions

1. In view of the fact that *Street* was settled before the Supreme Court ruled on it, we shall probably never know why at least four of the Justices voted to grant a writ of certiorari. Was it because of a disagreement with the Court of Appeals' holding that Victoria Street was a "public figure" at the time of the NBC broadcasts? Do you agree with the Court of Appeals in this regard? Should the issue of the plaintiff's "access to channels of effective communication in order to counteract false statements" be determined as of the time the "public controversy" arose or as of the time the allegedly libelous statement concerning such controversy was made?

2. Was the Court of Appeals correct in denying NBC the privilege of a fair report of a judicial proceeding. Does this mean that a docu-drama producer may incur defamation liability if the production states as a fact that a given person has committed a crime even if that person, although claiming innocence, has been convicted of that crime, unless the production exhibits "balance and neutrality" by also stating the defendant's version of the facts? Is the same true of a newspaper?

3. Given the greater time frame in which preparation is possible in connection with a dramatic production as compared with a newspaper report, should the *New York Times-Gertz* First Amendment limitations on defamation liability be applied to dramatic productions based upon factual material?

Collateral References

Smolla, *Let the Author Beware: The Rejuvination of the American Law of Libel,* 132 U.Pa.L.Rev. 1 (1983).

Lewis, *New York Times Co. v. Sullivan Reconsidered: Time to Return to "the Central Meaning of the First Amendment,"* 83 Colum.L.Rev. 603 (1983).

---

9. The Supreme Court has repeatedly refused to find individuals public figures because they were involved in events of symbolic or exemplary import. See *Wolston,* supra, 443 U.S. at 166–68, 99 S.Ct. at 2707–2708 (failure to comply with subpoena of grand jury investigating Soviet espionage in United States did not result in public figure status); Time, Inc. v. Firestone, 424 U.S. 448, 454, 96 S.Ct. 958, 965, 47 L.Ed.2d 154 (1976) (society divorce is not a "public controversy" triggering application of malice standard in defamation action).

Firestone is vulnerable to the same criticisms as is *Rosenbloom's* "newsworthiness" test for first amendment privileges. See L. Tribe, supra, § 12–13 at 644. Yet one clear lesson of *Wolston* and *Firestone* is that the term "public controversy" is read narrowly, not broadly. With imagination, any human activity acquires "symbolic" importance.

a. The U.S. Supreme Court granted cert. in this case (454 U.S. 815 (1981)), but prior to decision the case was settled and the case dismissed (454 U.S. 1095 (1981)).

Chapter Fourteen

RIGHT OF PRIVACY—PUBLIC DISCLOSURE OF PRIVATE FACTS

A. THE NATURE OF THE INJURY

RESTATEMENT OF TORTS, § 867

"Interference with Privacy

A person who unreasonably and seriously interferes with another's interest in not having his affairs known to others or his likeness exhibited to the public is liable to the other."

RESTATEMENT (SECOND) OF TORTS, § 652D

"Publicity Given to Private Life

One who gives publicity to a matter concerning the private life of another is subject to liability to the other for invasion of his privacy, if the matter publicized is of a kind that

(a) would be highly offensive to a reasonable person, and

(b) is not of legitimate concern to the public."

Question

What, if any, substantive difference is there between the language of Restatement § 867 and Restatement (Second) § 652D?

Collateral References

Prosser, *Privacy*, 48 Cal.Law Rev. 383 (1960).

Bloustein, *Privacy as An Aspect of Human Dignity: An Answer to Dean Prosser*, 39 N.Y.U.Law Rev. 962 (1964).

MELVIN v. REID

District Court of Appeal, Fourth District, California, 1931.
112 Cal.App. 285, 297 P. 91.

MARKS, J. Appellant filed her complaint in the court below seeking judgment against defendants for money. The complaint contains four causes of action separately stated. The first is based upon the violation of what has become known as the "right of privacy." The other three causes of action are based upon a supposed property right in incidents of her life and her maiden name. Respondents filed general and special demurrers to each count of the complaint which were sustained. Appellant refused to amend, and appealed from the judgment entered after the right to amend had expired. Respondents made no point on their special demurrers, and the sole question to be decided upon this appeal is whether or not causes of action are stated.

It is alleged that appellant's maiden name was Gabrielle Darley; that a number of years ago she was a prostitute and was tried for murder, the trial resulting in her acquittal; that during the year 1918, and after her acquittal, she abandoned her life of shame and became entirely rehabilitated; that during the year 1919 she married Bernard Melvin and commenced the duties of caring for their home, and thereafter at all times lived an exemplary, virtuous, honorable, and righteous life; that she assumed a place in respectable society, and made many friends who were not aware of the incidents of her earlier life; that during the month of July, 1925, the defendants, without her permission, knowledge, or consent, made, photographed, produced, and released a moving picture film entitled "The Red Kimono," and thereafter exhibited it in moving picture houses in California, Arizona, and throughout many other states; that this moving picture was based upon the true story of the past life of appellant, and that her maiden name, Gabrielle Darley, was used therein; that defendants featured and advertised that the plot of the film was the true story of the unsavory incidents in the life of appellant; that Gabrielle Darley was the true name of the principal character; and that Gabrielle Darley was appellant; that by the production and showing of the picture, friends of appellant learned for the first time of the unsavory incidents of her early life. This caused them to scorn and abandon her, and exposed her to obloquy, contempt, and ridicule, causing her grievous mental and physical suffering to her damage in the sum of $50,000. These allegations were set forth in the first cause of action. It will not be necessary to detail the other three causes of action which are based upon an invasion of a supposed property right.

The law of privacy is of recent origin. It was first discussed in an essay published in a law journal in 1860. It did not gain prominence or notice of the bench or bar until an article appeared in 4 Harvard Law Review, p. 193, written by the Honorable Louis D. Brandeis in collaboration with Samuel D. Warren. Since the publication of this article, a number of cases have arisen in various states involving the so-called doctrine of the right of privacy. It is recognized in some jurisdictions, while others have refused to put it into effect.

A reading of most of the decisions in jurisdictions recognizing this right leaves the mind impressed with the lack of uniformity in the reasoning employed by the various jurists supporting it. Most of the cases turn upon questions of breaches of contracts, either express or implied, such as the breach of an implied contract on the part of a photographer to print only such pictures as may be ordered by his subject, and not to print others and use them for purposes of advertising. Others are based upon the breach of a trust or confidence which one placed in or gave to another. Others recognize a property right in private letters and private writings which will not permit their publication without consent. In others, the publication is so nearly akin to a libel that the final conclusions could be supported under the law of libel

A scene from *The Red Kimono*.

without invoking the doctrine of the right of privacy. In practically all jurisdictions in which this right is not recognized, the decisions are based upon the lack of a statute giving the plaintiff the right to protect a likeness or an incident of life, since the ancient common law did not recognize any such right. In the leading case of Roberson v. Rochester Folding-Box Co., 171 N.Y. 538, 64 N.E. 442, 59 L.R.A. 478, 89 Am.St. Rep. 828, the decision was based upon the lack of any statutory enactment giving a cause of action to protect such a right and the failure of the common law to recognize it. Shortly after this decision was handed down the Legislature of New York enacted a law prohibiting the publication of a person's likeness, or the story of, or incidents in, his life, without his consent, for purposes of advertisement or gain. Since 1903, when this legislation was enacted, practically all of the New York cases are based upon it, and are therefore of little assistance to us here.

The question is a new one in California. The only case to which we have been cited which even remotely relates to it is that of Crane v. Heine, 35 Cal.App. 466, 170 P. 433. This case, however, furnishes us with no authority for adopting in this state the doctrine of the right of privacy as it is known in other jurisdictions. * * *

The right of privacy as recognized in a number of states has been defined as follows: "The right of privacy may be defined as the right to live one's life in seclusion, without being subjected to unwarranted and undesired publicity. In short, it is the right to be let alone. 21 R.C.L. 1197, 1198. There are times, however, when one, whether willingly or not, becomes an actor in an occurrence of public or general interest. When this takes place, he emerges from his seclusion, and it is not an invasion of his right of privacy to publish his photograph with an account of such occurrence." Jones v. Herald Post Co., supra.

A few general principles, founded on authority or reason, seem to run through most of the better considered decisions from the jurisdictions which recognize the doctrine as well as those which do not. We may summarize them as follows:

(1) The right of privacy was unknown to the ancient common law.

(2) It is an incident of the persons and not of property—a tort for which a right of recovery is given in some jurisdictions.

(3) It is a purely personal action, and does not survive, but dies with the person.

(4) It does not exist where the person has published the matter complained of, or consented thereto.

(5) It does not exist where a person has become so prominent that by his very prominence he had dedicated his life to the public, and thereby waived his right to privacy. There can be no privacy in that which is already public.

(6) It does not exist in the dissemination of news and news events, nor in the discussion of events of the life of a person in whom the public

has a rightful interest, nor where the information would be of public benefit, as in the case of a candidate for public office.

(7) The right of privacy can only be violated by printings, writings, pictures, or other permanent publications or reproductions, and not by word of mouth.

(8) The right of action accrues when the publication is made for gain or profit. (This, however, is questioned in some cases.)

From the foregoing it follows as a natural consequence that the use of the incidents from the life of appellant in the moving picture is in itself not actionable. These incidents appeared in the records of her trial for murder, which is a public record, open to the perusal of all. The very fact that they were contained in a public record is sufficient to negative the idea that their publication was a violation of a right of privacy. When the incidents of a life are so public as to be spread upon a public record, they come within the knowledge and into the possession of the public and cease to be private. Had respondents, in the story of "The Red Kimono," stopped with the use of those incidents from the life of appellant which were spread upon the record of her trial, no right of action would have accrued. They went further, and in the formation of the plot used the true maiden name of appellant. If any right of action exists, it arises from the use of this true name in connection with the true incidents from her life together with their advertisements in which they stated that the story of the picture was taken from true incidents in the life of Gabrielle Darley, who was Gabrielle Darley Melvin.

In the absence of any provision of law, we would be loath to conclude that the right of privacy as the foundation for an action in tort, in the form known and recognized in other jurisdictions, exists in California. We find, however, that the fundamental law of our state contains provisions which, we believe, permit us to recognize the right to pursue and obtain safety and happiness without improper infringements thereon by others.

Section 1 of article 1 of the Constitution of California provides as follows: "All men are by nature free and independent, and have certain inalienable rights, among which are those of enjoying and defending life and liberty; acquiring, possessing, and protecting property; and pursuing and obtaining safety and happiness."

The right to pursue and obtain happiness is guaranteed to all by the fundamental law of our state. This right by its very nature includes the right to live free from the unwarranted attack of others upon one's liberty, property, and reputation. Any person living a life of rectitude has that right to happiness which includes a freedom from unnecessary attacks on his character, social standing, or reputation.

The use of appellant's true name in connection with the incidents of her former life in the plot and advertisements was unnecessary and indelicate, and a willful and wanton disregard of that charity which should actuate us in our social intercourse, and which should keep us from unnecessarily holding another up to the scorn and contempt of upright members of society.

Upon demurrer, the allegations of the complaint must be taken as true. We must therefore conclude that eight years before the production of "The Red Kimono" appellant had abandoned her life of shame, had rehabilitated herself, and had taken her place as a respected and honored member of society. This change having occurred in her life, she should have been permitted to continue its course without having her reputation and social standing destroyed by the publication of the story of her former depravity with no other excuse than the expectation of private gain by the publishers.

One of the major objectives of society as it is now constituted, and of the administration of our penal system, is the rehabilitation of the fallen and the reformation of the criminal. Under these theories of sociology, it is our object to lift up and sustain the unfortunate rather than tear him down. Where a person has by his own efforts rehabilitated himself, we, as right-thinking members of society, should permit him to continue in the path of rectitude rather than throw him back into a life of shame or crime. Even the thief on the cross was permitted to repent during the hours of his final agony.

We believe that the publication by respondents of the unsavory incidents in the past life of appellant after she had reformed, coupled with her true name, was not justified by any standard of morals or ethics known to us, and was a direct invasion of her inalienable right guaranteed to her by our Constitution, to pursue and obtain happiness. Whether we call this a right of privacy or give it any other name is immaterial, because it is a right guaranteed by our Constitution that must not be ruthlessly and needlessly invaded by others. We are of the opinion that the first cause of action of appellant's complaint states facts sufficient to constitute a cause of action against respondents. * *

The judgment is reversed, with instructions to the trial court to overrule respondents' demurrers to the first cause of action of the complaint and permit them to answer should they be so advised.

We concur: BARNARD, P.J.; JENNINGS, J.

Questions

1. Suppose that the motion picture had not used Gabrielle Darley's true name, but by reason of its inclusion of facts that had previously been of public record, she were identifiable by a considerable number of persons as the prostitute depicted in the film. Would this have constituted an invasion of privacy as the *Melvin* opinion defines the tort? Are facts once of public record, no matter in what form they are repeated, forever immune from a claim of privacy invasion?

2. Suppose the facts of Question 1., but in addition the film contained certain true and intimate facts of plaintiff's life that had not previously been a

matter of public record. Would the *Melvin* court have regarded this as an invasion of privacy? Does the *Melvin* opinion stand for the proposition that there may not be an invasion of privacy absent the use of the plaintiff's true name?

3. If the person depicted is no longer living, should his heirs have a right of action for invasion of privacy by reason of such depiction? In most jurisdictions it is held that the right is personal to the person depicted, and dies with him. See James v. Screen Gems, Inc., 174 Cal.App.2d 650, 344 P.2d 799 (1959) (action by widow of Jesse James, Jr. based upon her late husband's depiction in film shown on television); Young v. That Was The Week That Was, 312 F.Supp. 1337 (N.D.Ohio 1969) (derogatory reference to recently deceased mother, grandmother and greatgrandmother of plaintiffs); Maritote v. Desilu Productions, Inc., 345 F.2d 418, 18 A.L.R.3d 863 (7th Cir.1965) (action by widow and child of Al Capone, based upon his depiction in television series).

BERNSTEIN v. NATIONAL BROADCASTING CO.
United States District Court, District of Columbia, 1955.
129 F.Supp. 817.

KEECH, DISTRICT JUDGE. This case is before the court on the defendant's motion for summary judgment in two consolidated actions for invasion of privacy.

Both actions arise from the same undisputed facts. In 1919 plaintiff, Charles S. Bernstein, was convicted of bank robbery in Minnesota and sentenced to imprisonment for forty years. After serving nine years, he was paroled and pardoned. In 1933 in the District of Columbia, plaintiff, under the name of Charles Harris, was tried and convicted of first-degree murder and sentenced to death by electrocution. In 1934 the conviction was affirmed, Harris v. U.S., 63 App.D.C. 232, 71 F.2d 532, and a petition for certiorari denied by the Supreme Court, 293 U.S. 581, 55 S.Ct. 94, 79 L.Ed. 678. Through the efforts of a number of interested persons and committees working in plaintiff's behalf, and partly as the result of the work of Martha Strayer, a reporter on the Washington Daily News, in 1935 the death sentence was commuted to life imprisonment. In 1940, after plaintiff had served five years at various federal institutions, he received a conditional release from his life sentence, and in 1945 a Presidential pardon.

Plaintiff alleges that, "Commencing in 1940, and thereafter, * * [he] was no longer in the public eye; * * * lived an exemplary, virtuous, honorable, righteous, quiet and private life, free from the prying curiosity which accompanies either fame or notoriety; * * * shunned and avoided notoriety and publicity; * * * never exhibited or sought to exploit his name, personality or the incidents of his past life for money, profit, or commercial gain; * * * assumed a place in society, knew many people and made many friends who were not aware of the incidents of his earlier life."

Plaintiff's deposition shows that from the time of the trial until 1940, when plaintiff secured conditional release, his story was given much publicity by the newspapers and others working on his behalf.

Subsequent to his release in 1940, he obtained government employment in the District of Columbia, holding various positions and attaining Civil Service Grade CAF-11. In 1945, this employment ended, and thereafter, from 1945 to 1951, he lived in Front Royal, Virginia, operating a "resort lodge." In February, 1953, some time after the filing of these actions, plaintiff again secured government employment in the District, rooming in Washington but still maintaining his family home in Front Royal, Virginia.

In 1936 or 1937 a detective story magazine carried an article on plaintiff's case. In 1948 a radio program told plaintiff's story, using Martha Strayer's name, in a fictionalized version, but so similar to the facts that plaintiff and several others identified the story as his.

On January 18, 1952, the defendant NBC telecast "live" over 39 stations in its network a television program prepared by Prockter Television Enterprises, Inc., sponsored by American Cigarette & Cigar Company and advertising Pall Mall cigarettes, entitled "The Big Story." This program, classified by the Federal Communications Commission as a network commercial entertainment program, was a fictionalized dramatization based on the plaintiff's conviction and pardon, and lauding the efforts of Miss Strayer, the Daily News reporter, toward securing commutation of plaintiff's sentence. The same program was telecast over twelve other NBC network stations by means of a kineoscope recording on January 29, 31, February 1, 2, 3, and 8, 1952. The only true names used were those of Martha Strayer, the Washington Daily News, the President of the United States, and the District of Columbia. Over forty-three of the NBC stations telecasting "The Big Story," it was announced a week prior to the telecast here involved, that the following week's program would tell the true story of how Martha Strayer fought to save the life of an innocent man convicted of murder. On January 7, 1952, NBC issued a press release concerning the program.[1] Neither the television announcement nor press release mentioned plaintiff's name.

Plaintiff alleges that, although his true name was not used in the telecast, the actor who portrayed him resembled him physically and plaintiff's words and actions were reproduced both visually and aurally, creating a portrayal of plaintiff recognizable to him and to his friends and acquaintances, and clearly identifying plaintiff in the public mind.

1.

"January 7, 1952

"Women (sic) Reporter Frees an Innocent Man and Gets a 'Big Story'

"A women (sic) reporter's experience in uncovering evidence that saved an innocent man from the electric chair will be dramatized on NBC's authentic Big Story television program Friday, Jan. 18 (9:00 p.m., EST). TV actress Margaret Stewart will portray the reporter, Martha Strayer of the Washington (D.C.) Daily News.

"Sent to the death cell to interview a man awaiting execution, Miss Strayer heard a tragic story and was convinced of his innocence. Racing against time, Miss Strayer uncovered new evidence and was able to deliver a last-minute pardon to the condemned man.

"NBC—New York"

Prior to the telecast, Prockter Productions, Inc., obtained a release or waiver of the right of privacy from Martha Strayer to use her name and to portray her in connection with "The Big Story," but no such waiver or release was obtained from plaintiff.

About five days before January 18, 1952, plaintiff learned through his wife's cousin that NBC would carry a television program based upon his past life. He thereupon called the National Broadcasting Company in Washington and on January 17 and 18, 1952, wrote letters to the Company and its manager in Washington, requesting defendant not to broadcast the program. The program was telecast as scheduled.

Plaintiff alleges that the telecast of this program constituted "a willful and malicious invasion of * * * [his] right of privacy as recognized by the laws of New York, Ohio, Illinois, California, Connecticut, Massachusetts, Rhode Island, Pennsylvania, Delaware, Maryland, Virginia, Wisconsin, Alabama, Tennessee, Iowa, Minnesota, Washington, Texas, Michigan, Missouri, Florida, Utah, Georgia, West Virginia, Kentucky, Nebraska, New Jersey, and Indiana," and the District of Columbia, and that by reason of the telecasts "plaintiff's personality has been violated by being exposed, exhibited, and sold to the public; plaintiff has been subjected to the inquisitive notice of the general public to the injury of his personality, to the outrage of the finer sentiments of his nature and to the humiliation of his self-respect; and plaintiff, a private personality and having an individual personality, has thus been made notorious and conspicuous to the public and has been singled out for and identified to the public notice and attention, which is utterly obnoxious to plaintiff; and plaintiff has been caused and has suffered great mental pain and personal injury," for which he asks $250,000 actual damages. Plaintiff further alleges that the acts of defendant NBC were "willful, wanton, malicious, and intentional, and perpetrated with a reckless disregard of the rights of plaintiff and without his knowledge, consent and acquiescence," entitling him to punitive damages of $500,000.

The complaint in Civil Action 3517–52 is drafted on a single tort theory, alleging the telecast on January 18, 1952, over Station WNBW, Washington, D.C. Civil Action 5663–52 is drafted on a multiple tort theory, claiming a separate tort in each of twenty-eight states in which the program was telecast by relay of the "live" broadcast in New York or by re-broadcast by means of kineoscope recording, and asks varying amounts of actual and punitive damages for the telecast in each state.

Defendant in its motion for summary judgment contends that neither of the complaints states a cause of action upon which relief may be granted. * * *

The telecast here involved was one of a series of similar dramatizations, commending the accomplishments of newspaper reporters in bringing criminals to justice or in securing the release of innocent persons convicted of crime. In each of the programs the actual name of the reporter and his paper were used, but the names of other persons portrayed were changed, and the incidents were fictionalized for dramatic effect.

On this particular program, the man convicted of crime was called Dave Crouch and the murdered man Woody Benson. Benson, a gambler running a game in Alexandria, was shot as he walked along the sidewalk in the District of Columbia, by a man riding in a car. Crouch was arrested while asleep on a bench in a bus terminal in Washington. He was inadequately defended at his trial by a Mr. Kendall, an inexperienced court-assigned counsel, who did not call as an alibi witness Crouch's "common-law wife," Helen Slezak, with whom Crouch had spent the day of the murder in New York. Mr. Kendall showed lack of confidence in the success of the defense, in view of Crouch's previous conviction in Minnesota of which he was innocent and for which he had been pardoned. At the trial, the court admitted a detective's statement as to Crouch's Minnesota conviction, omitting any reference to the pardon. Kendall did not call Helen as a witness, on the ground that the "blue ribbon jury," "all respectable property owners," might be prejudiced against a common-law wife, although Dave explained to him that they were not legally married because Helen's husband would not give her a divorce. Crouch was convicted on the testimony of a Mrs. Hedlund, a garrulous middle-aged woman, who positively identified him as the murderer whom she had seen, as he fired the shot, when she looked from the window of her upstairs apartment. After conviction, Crouch was pictured as desperately playing solitaire in his cell and checking off on a calendar the days leading up to his execution, whenever Miss Strayer called upon him there.

Martha Strayer was portrayed as interesting a Mr. Burbage, an attorney of thirty-five years' experience in the Department of Justice, in attempting to have Crouch's sentence commuted, and herself discovering that Mrs. Hedlund could not have seen the murderer from her window, which would have been obscured at the time of the crime by leafed-out branches of a tree. Miss Strayer's newspaper stories were credited with bringing into her office a Mrs. Watson, a theretofore unknown eyewitness, who had clearly seen the crime and testified that the murderer was not Dave Crouch. The program represented Miss Strayer as the person whose faith in the innocence of Crouch and investigations and newspaper articles arousing public opinion resulted in saving Crouch the very day before the execution. In the final scene of the program, Crouch was shown with Mr. Burbage thanking Miss Strayer in her office, following his release from "Lewisburg Prison."

The record in the actual criminal case and the pleadings and deposition of plaintiff in this case, reveal: The plaintiff, as Charles Harris, was convicted of first-degree murder in connection with the shooting of Milton White Henry, a Washington gambler, on April 21, 1932, in the District of Columbia. About 6 a.m., while Henry, in his car, was stopped behind a milk wagon in the narrow street in front of his apartment, he was killed by a man who alighted from a Hudson automobile, shot him, and then jumped on the running board of the

Hudson which sped away. Harris was arrested in Philadelphia, while looking in a store window accompanied by his "wife". At the trial, he was identified as the murderer by a Mr. Rhodes, an attorney with the Federal Trade Commission, who testified that he had seen Harris at the time of the shooting from the window of his apartment and heard Harris tell the driver of the Hudson to "keep moving" and "step on it." Mr. Rhodes testified that the trees in front of his apartment were in bud at the time and "might have been forming leaves," but that he had an unobstructed view of the shooting. The driver of a laundry truck testified that on the day before the crime he had passed by the scene of the murder on three different delivery trips and, five different times, had seen the same car, identified as that driven by the men who committed the murder, with the same two men in it, and that the defendant was one of them.

At the trial Harris was represented by two attorneys of his own selection, one of whom had eight years' experience in the District of Columbia and a largely criminal practice. Plaintiff did not take the stand in his own behalf, but defense witnesses testified that he was in New York at the crucial time. The woman with whom Harris was living in New York was not called as a witness because counsel "didn't want to besmirch her character." Harris and the woman were not legally married because he had a living wife, and the woman's name did not in any way resemble "Helen Slezak." On appeal, Harris was represented by different counsel, one of whom, Mr. Burkinshaw, had had about two or three years' experience with the Department of Justice.

After affirmance of the conviction, new evidence was submitted to the Department of Justice in the form of affidavits from the Department of Agriculture and the Weather Bureau that the trees in front of Mr. Rhodes' apartment would have been fully leafed out at the time of the crime and the testimony of an eyewitness who came forward after the trial, a lady who, after viewing Harris at the Jail, stated he was not the man who did the shooting. Miss Strayer did interview Harris at the Jail on a number of occasions and discussed his case with him, but always in the Superintendent's office or in the "rotunda," not in Harris' cell. Harris did not play solitaire in his cell, as prisoners were not permitted to have cards. He spent a great deal of time reading history, philosophy, and psychology. He did not cross the days off a calendar prior to the execution date, which was postponed eight times by the court. The death sentence was stayed by warrant of reprieve signed by the President four days before the date fixed for electrocution. During the two years he was confined in the "death row" at the District Jail awaiting execution, plaintiff did undergo great mental and emotional strain. The plaintiff, after his release from Leavenworth, went to see Miss Strayer in her office to thank her for her part in securing his release, but he is not sure whether his attorney accompanied him.

Plaintiff alleges that the actor who portrayed Dave Crouch resembled him physically, as he appeared at the time of his trial. For the purpose of this motion, the court will assume that this resemblance exists.

Thus, the points of similarity between the plaintiff's life and the television story of Dave Crouch are reduced to: a conviction in the District of Columbia of first-degree murder in connection with the shooting of a gambler in Washington; failure to call a "common-law wife" as an alibi witness; Miss Strayer's effective interest in proving the defendant's innocence; securing of other counsel after the trial; emotional turmoil of the convicted man while awaiting execution; additional evidence as to the leaves in front of an eyewitness' apartment window; another eyewitness coming forward, after affirmance of the conviction, to state that defendant was not the murderer; thanking of Miss Strayer by the defendant after his release; and a physical resemblance between the actor and the plaintiff as he was twenty years ago.

Plaintiff concedes that there was nothing defamatory of him in the telecast and bases his entire complaint on the alleged invasion of his privacy. He concedes that his name was never mentioned, but contends that the physical resemblance of the actor who portrayed Dave Crouch to himself as he was twenty years before the telecast, and the similarities between the story of Dave Crouch with the facts of his own life, were such that his friends readily identified him as the person whose story was being portrayed.

Counsel further concedes that plaintiff's conviction and commutation of sentence, when they occurred, were matters in the public domain, and that a dramatization at that time based on the facts and containing nothing defamatory, similar to the program in question would not have been an invasion of plaintiff's privacy. It is contended, however, that by reason of the lapse of time since plaintiff's release in 1940 and the non-public character of his activities since that date, his life has regained its private character, and he was in 1952 entitled to protection from any invasion of his privacy by revival of the story of his conviction and the subsequent proceedings, with consequent emotional distress to him and interference with his social and employment relations. Plaintiff argues that his past history has lost its news interest and is of no educational value, and that the prime purpose of the telecast of "The Big Story" was to sell Pall Mall cigarettes by exploitation of his personal history.

Many points have been briefed and argued by counsel for the respective parties, but the case reduces itself to a few legal questions:

First, the law of what jurisdiction or jurisdictions is to be applied in resolving the other legal questions?

Second, can a public personage—to be specific, a person involved in a criminal trial—by virtue of the passage of time spent out of the public gaze, regain a private status so as to make his past legally protectible against invasion of privacy?

Third, do the facts alleged in plaintiff's complaints state a cause of action?

Fourth, is there any issue of material fact in this case which makes summary judgment inappropriate?

I

The confusion as to choice of law in actions for defamation and invasion of privacy arising from interstate publication is ably described by Dean Prosser at 51 Michigan Law Review 959.[2] He there discusses as possible choices: (1) the law of each place of "impact;" (2) the law of the first place of impact; (3) the law of the place of predominant impact; (4) the law of the place of defendant's act; (5) the law of defendant's principal place of business; (6) the law of the state of defendant's incorporation; (7) the law of the place of plaintiff's domicil; (8) the law of plaintiff's principal place of business; (9) "piecemeal law," or application of the law of different jurisdictions to different aspects of the case, such as liability, damages, effect of retraction, and so on; and (10) the law of the forum. The article cites cases illustrative of the various alternatives and points out the difficulties involved in applying each of them.

It is apparent to this court that the lumping of invasion of privacy with defamation leads to error in choice of law, since determination of the law applicable to an action for invasion of privacy by interstate publication must depend upon a consideration of the nature of the tort itself, which differs materially from slander or libel.

As well stated in Reed v. Real Detective Publishing Co., 1945, 63 Ariz. 294, 295, 305–306, 162 P.2d 133, 139:

> The gravamen of the action * * * is the injury to the feelings of the plaintiff, the mental anguish and distress caused by the publication. * * * Unlike libel and slander, the gist of the cause is not injury to the character or reputation which appertains to the standing of a person in the eyes of others and are attributes in law separate from the "person". * * *
>
> Since, under the law, recovery may be had for an invasion of the right of privacy for injured feelings alone, the wrongs redressed must be considered as a direct rather than an indirect injury and one that is wholly personal in character, not depending on any effect which the publication may have on the standing of the individual in the community. It seems to us that the mind of an individual, his feelings and mental processes, are as much a part of his person as his observable physical members. An injury, therefore, which affects the sensibilities is equally an injury to the person as an injury to the body would be. In that respect a cause of action for the violation of the right of privacy, causing mental suffering to the plaintiff, is

---

2. See also "The Choice of Law in Multistate Defamation and Invasion of Privacy; An Unsolved Problem," 60 Harv.L.Rev. 941 (1947), and " 'Peace of Mind' in 48 Pieces v. Uniform Right of Privacy," by Frederick J. Ludwig, 32 Minn.L.Rev. 734 (1948). A reading of these articles raises the question of the desirability of enactment of a federal statute as incident to regulation of interstate radio and television broadcasts, or adoption of a uniform law by the states.

an injury to the person. Wyatt v. Hall's Portrait Studio, 71 Misc. 199, 128 N.Y.S. 247. * * * [3]

The tort of invasion of privacy being a personal injury, the question whether plaintiff has a cause of action on the facts stated by him should be determined by the law of the jurisdiction where he sustained the injury,[4] or, as expressed in § 377 of the Restatement, Conflict of Laws (1934), "the state where the last event necessary to make an actor liable for an alleged tort takes place." The injury in these cases is the humiliation and outrage to plaintiff's feelings, resulting from the telecast. The last event necessary to make the defendant liable was not the final act in publication of the telecast, as plaintiff argues, but the reaction of the telecast on his own sensibilities.[5]

Thus, in Civil Action 3517–52, although the publication was set in motion in New York with the acting of the story and the transmission was completed in the District of Columbia by WNBW, the harm did not occur until the impact of the telecast upon plaintiff, in whatever jurisdiction he may be considered to have had his situs. Similarly, in Civil Action 5663–52, although the program was broadcast "live" simultaneously in a number of different states on January 18, 1952, and by kineoscope recording on subsequent dates in other jurisdictions, the impact of all the broadcasts occurred in one place, the jurisdiction where plaintiff was when his feelings were wounded.

Whether the telecasts on the different dates constituted separate torts or whether each was a part of one alleged invasion of plaintiff's privacy, and whether plaintiff's privacy, once shattered on January 18, 1952, was susceptible of further invasion by the subsequent telecasts of the kineoscope recording, are academic questions. The impact on plaintiff's sensibilities on all of these occasions would have occurred in one and the same jurisdiction, since during the entire period of the original telecast and rebroadcasts plaintiff was domiciled and had his major contacts in the same places. If a tortious invasion of privacy be held to have occurred, damages for the injury to plaintiff's feelings

---

3. Warren and Brandeis, in their classic article, The Right to Privacy, 4 Harv.L.Rev. 192, 197, wrote: "Owing to the nature of the instruments by which privacy is invaded, the injury inflicted bears a superficial resemblance to the wrongs dealt with by the law of slander and of libel, while a legal remedy for such injury seems to involve the treatment of mere wounded feelings, as a substantive cause of action. The principal on which the law of defamation rests, covers, however, a radically different class of effects. * * * It deals only with damage to reputation with the injury done to the individual in his external relations to the community, by lowering him in the estimation of his fellows * * * the effect of the publication upon his estimate of himself and upon his own feelings not forming an essential element in the cause of action. * * *"

4. Eastern Air Lines, Inc., v. Union Trust Co., D.C.Cir., 1955, 221 F.2d 62.

5. The Restatement, § 377, does not include in its illustrations an example of the place of infliction of mental suffering. The personal injury to the feelings of plaintiff, in Virginia or in the District of Columbia, inflicted by a telecast by defendant in New York or any of the other jurisdictions relaying the program, is analogous to physical injury to B in state Y, from a bullet fired by A in state X (place of wrong is Y), rather than akin to slander of the reputation of B, residing in state Y but known in state Z, by a broadcast by A in state X, heard by persons in Z conversant with B's good repute (place of the wrong is Z).

would be assessed under the law of the one jurisdiction which is determined to have been his situs, but he could recover there for the whole amount of harm inflicted on his feelings, considering, among other factors, the extent of the publication or publications in that and other jurisdictions.

Plaintiff may be considered to have suffered humiliation either at the place of his domicil, which would be his normal situs, or, if at the time of the tort he was spending most of his time elsewhere, at the place of the most of his contacts. It has been admitted that plaintiff's domicil at the time of the telecast was Virginia, where he maintained his family home, resided with his wife, paid taxes, and voted. Plaintiff argues that the greater number of his contacts were in the District of Columbia. Conceding, for the purpose of this motion, that most of plaintiff's contacts were in the District and that this is the jurisdiction where he suffered the greatest impact on his feelings as the result of the telecast, and therefore the law of the District should be applied, it would make no difference in the court's disposition of the motion for summary judgment, as shown by the discussion under point III.

II

As to the second question, whether a public person may, by the passage of time in private life, re-acquire a right of privacy as to his past life, there is a divergence of opinion.

The Restatement of the Law of Torts, § 867, summarizes the right of privacy very generally, stating:

> A person who unreasonably and seriously interferes with another's interest in not having his affairs known to others or his likeness exhibited to the public is liable to the other.

The Restatement then notes that the protection accorded one's privacy is relative to the custom of the time and place and to the habits and occupation of the plaintiff, and that one must expect the ordinary incidents of community life of which he is a part. It points out that public figures must pay the price of unwelcome publicity and that those who unwillingly come into the public eye in connection with a criminal prosecution, innocent or guilty, are objects of legitimate public interest during a period of time after their conduct or misfortune has brought them to the public attention, and that "until they have reverted to the lawful and unexciting life led by the great bulk of the community, they are subject to the privilege which publishers have to satisfy the curiosity of the public as to their leaders, heroes, villains and victims."

Several cases have been cited to the court which have dealt with the question whether time brings protection to a former public figure. Two in particular, which reach opposite conclusions, are relevant to the problem. In Sidis v. F.R. Pub. Corp., 2 Cir., 113 F.2d 806, 809, 138 A.L.R. 15, certiorari denied, 1940, 311 U.S. 711, 61 S.Ct. 393, 85 L.Ed. 462, a former child prodigy, who had sought oblivion for many years, loathing public attention, claimed an invasion of his right of privacy by an unvarnished factual account in The New Yorker magazine of his life (using his name), including the many years which he had lived out of the public eye and touching on many personal details. It was there held by the federal court sitting in New York (a jurisdiction which has rejected the right of privacy as unrecognized at common law and has strictly interpreted its statute affording limited protection) that although the plaintiff had dropped out of sight after 1910, "his subsequent history, containing as it did the answer to the question of whether or not he had fulfilled his early promise, was still a matter of public concern", and that the New Yorker sketch of the life of such an unusual personality possessed considerable popular news interest. The court there stated, 113 F.2d at page 809:

> * * * we would permit limited scrutiny of the "private" life of any person who has achieved, or has had thrust upon him, the questionable and indefinable status of a "public figure." * * *

> * * * Regrettably or not, the misfortunes and frailties of neighbors and "public figures" are subjects of considerable interest and discussion to the rest of the population. And when such are the mores of the community, it would be unwise for a court to bar their expression in the newspapers, books, and magazines of the day.

In Melvin v. Reid, 1931, 112 Cal.App. 285, 297 P. 91, 93 * * *, the court said: * * *

> We believe that the publication by respondents of the unsavory incidents in the past life of appellant after she had reformed, *coupled with her true name,* was not justified by any standard of morals or ethics known to us, and was a direct invasion of her inalienable right guaranteed to her by our [California] Constitution, to pursue and obtain happiness. (Emphasis supplied.)

In a third case, Mau v. Rio Grande Oil, Inc., D.C.Cal., 1939, 28 F.Supp. 845, the complaint was held to state a cause of action where it alleged that defendant had broadcast an advertising program dramatizing a holdup and shooting in which plaintiff had been the victim, a year after the incident and using plaintiff's name without his consent, and that hearing the broadcast had caused plaintiff mental anguish, aggravated by telephone calls from sympathetic friends who also heard it and were desirous of rehashing the near-tragedy which plaintiff wished to forget.

It should be noted that in each of these cases the complainant was identified by name in the publication by defendant, as the plaintiff in this case was not in the telecast.

This court agrees that we are not so uncivilized that the law permits, in the name of public interest, the unlimited and unwarranted revival by publication of a rehabilitated wrongdoer's past mistakes in such a manner as to identify him in his private setting with the old crime and hold him up to public scorn.[6] Persons formerly public,

---

6. Plaintiff has submitted the affidavits of a number of persons interested and experienced in criminology who state, in substance, that no greater harm can be done to

however, cannot be protected against disclosure and re-disclosure of known facts through the reading of old newspaper accounts and other publications, oral repetition of facts by those familiar with them, or reprinting of known facts of general interest, in a reasonable manner and for a legitimate purpose. The advocates of recognition of the right of privacy would not so extend it.[7] Public interest must be balanced against the individual's rights. Though fairness and decency dictate that some boundary be fixed beyond which persons may not go in pointing the finger of shame at those who have erred and repented, reasonable freedom of speech and press must be accorded and the fact of social intercourse must be recognized. Public identification of the present person with past facts, however, would constitute a new disclosure and, if unwarranted, would infringe upon an existing privacy. Thus, it would appear that the protection which time may bring to a formerly public figure is not against repetition of the facts which are already public property, but against unreasonable public identification of him in his present setting with the earlier incident.[8]

Determination of this question is not, however, essential to disposition of the present motion. Assuming *arguendo* that at the time of the telecast plaintiff had regained a private status carrying with it legal protection from republication of the facts of his past life, the complaints, as supplemented by plaintiff's deposition and the various admissions, stipulations, and answers to interrogatories by the respective parties, do not state a valid cause of action.

III

As concluded under point I, the two jurisdictions which might be

---

a man who has become rehabilitated after having been convicted of a criminal offense and demonstrated over a substantial period that he is fully rehabilitated, than to reveal his past criminal record in such a way as to bring it to the attention of his employer, fellow employees, neighbors, citizens of the community in which he lives and works, and the general public. With this general statement the court cannot disagree, but it is irrelevant to this case on the facts conceded by plaintiff.

7. "The right to privacy does not prohibit the communication of any matter which is of public or general interest. * * * It is the unwarranted invasion of individual privacy which is reprehended, and to be, so far as possible, prevented. * * * The general object in view is to protect the privacy of private life, and *to whatever degree and in whatever connection a man's life has ceased to be private, before the publication under consideration has been made, to that extent the protection is to be withdrawn.* * * * " Warren and Brandeis, The Right to Privacy, 4 Harv.L.Rev. 193, 214, 215. (Emphasis supplied.)

8. To hold otherwise leads to absurd results. For example, on the recent 75th Anniversary of one of Washington's large department stores, the window displays, containing costumes of various years since the store's establishment, featured reprints of front pages from Washington newspapers of each year. If one of these chanced to contain a report of an old crime, giving the names of the criminal and his victim, should it be said that the publication constitutes an actionable invasion of their privacy? Similarly, should any person whose name appears in one of the reproductions of old newspaper mats which permanently decorate the National Press Club walls, be permitted, after an interval of private life, to complain that maintenance of that wall decoration constitutes an invasion of his privacy? Should old newspaper files be withheld from the public after a certain period of time, lest persons not aware of past public facts learn of them in the future? Should reprints of old legal decisions omit names after a number of years have passed? To state these questions is to make the answer obvious.

deemed the place of plaintiff's injury and therefore held to govern his right of action, are Virginia and the District of Columbia.

The Virginia Code, 1950 ed., Vol. 2, provides:

§ 8–650. UNAUTHORIZED USE OF THE NAME OR PICTURE OF ANY PERSON. A person, firm, or corporation that knowingly uses for advertising purposes, or for the purposes of trade, the name, portrait, or picture of any person resident in the State, without having first obtained the written consent of such person, or if dead, of his surviving consort, or if none, his next of kin, or, if a minor, of his or her parent or guardian, as well as that of such minor, shall be deemed guilty of a misdemeanor and be fined not less than fifty nor more than one thousand dollars. Any person whose name, portrait, or picture is used within this State for advertising purposes or for the purposes of trade, without such written consent first obtained or the surviving consort or next of kin, as the case may be, may maintain a suit in equity against the person, firm, or corporation so using such person's name, portrait, or picture to prevent and restrain the use thereof; and may also sue and recover damages for any injuries sustained by reason of such use. And if the defendant shall have knowingly used such person's name, portrait, or picture in such manner as is forbidden or declared to be unlawful by this chapter, the jury, in its discretion, may award exemplary damages. (Code 1919, § 5782.)

No reported Virginia cases interpreting this statute have been cited to the court, nor has the court found any. It is apparent from a reading of § 8–650 that the right of action accorded is limited. The statute is modeled on the New York law,[9] discussed fully in the opinions in Gautier v. Pro-Football, Inc., 278 App.Div. 431, 106 N.Y.S.2d 553, affirmed 304 N.Y. 354, 107 N.E.2d 485, which cite many cases interpreting the law in connection with various phases of the right of privacy. Suffice it to say, the New York statute has been given a strict construction. Publication of "biographical narratives of a man's life when it is of legitimate public interest, and 'travel stories, stories of distant places, tales of historic personages and events, the reproduction of items of past news, and surveys of social conditions'" are generally considered beyond the purview of the statute. This principle has been extended to the newsreel, the radio, and television.[10]

It is patent that the television program here involved does not fall within the language or purpose of § 8–650 of the Virginia Code.

Whether a right of action for invasion of privacy exists in the District of Columbia has not been authoritatively determined. The history of the right of privacy in other jurisdictions is set forth in Judge Holtzoff's opinion in Peay v. Curtis Publishing Company, D.C.D.C.1948, 78 F.Supp. 305. * * *

Whether the right to protection of one's privacy be viewed as stemming from natural law, as a constitutional right, or as a right

---

9. Chaplin v. National Broadcasting Co., D.C.N.Y.1953, 15 F.R.D. 134, 138.

10. Gautier v. Pro-Football, Inc., 106 N.Y.S.2d 553, at 558, citing Lahiri v. Daily Mirror, Inc., 162 Misc. 776, 782, 295 N.Y.S. 382, 388, and Jeffries v. New York Evening Journal Publishing Co., 67 Misc. 570, 124 N.Y.S. 780.

which was afforded protection under the common law, though not by name, § 49–301 of the District Code does not preclude recognition in the District of Columbia of a common-law action for invasion of privacy.

What are the elements of such a common law action? Invasion of privacy has been summarized in the exhaustive annotation appearing at 138 A.L.R. 22, at 25 (supplemented at 168 A.L.R. 446 and 14 A.L.R.2d 750) as:

> The *unwarranted* appropriation or exploitation of one's personality, the publicising of one's private affairs with which the public has no *legitimate* concern, or the *wrongful* intrusion into one's private activities, in such manner as to outrage or cause mental suffering, shame, or humiliation to a person of ordinary sensibilities. (Emphasis supplied.)

Under this definition, which embodies the minimum requirements of the many cases there noted, the essential elements of an action for invasion of privacy would be: (1) private affairs in which the public has no legitimate concern; (2) publication of such affairs; (3) unwarranted publication, that is, absence of any waiver or privilege authorizing it; and (4) publication such as would cause mental suffering, shame, or humiliation to a person of ordinary sensibilities. As to the first element, the "private" affairs should be at least currently unknown to the public; and as to the second element, publication would necessarily include identification of the facts disclosed with the complainant. The third element, a mixed question of fact and law, and the fourth element, a fact question for the jury, need not be reached if either of the first two elements is not present.

On the undisputed facts disclosed by the various pleadings and admissions before the court on this motion, it is clear that the first two essential elements of a cause of action are lacking in the case at bar.

(1) The plaintiff's affairs were not private and were known to the public. His case had been given considerable publicity from the time of his trial in 1932 until his conditional release from imprisonment in 1940. Newspaper files at all times contained the story of his conviction and the subsequent proceedings, including plaintiff's past record and the failure to call his "common-law wife" as a witness at the trial. The Court of Appeals' decision affirming the conviction, printed in both the Reports of Cases Adjudged in the United States Court of Appeals for the District of Columbia and in the Federal Reporter, Second Series, reveals that the man who gave his name as Charles Harris at the time of his arrest subsequently gave the name Charles Bernstein to a detective and in his motion for a new trial. These volumes have been on many library shelves and available to all since 1934. About 1936 or 1937 a detective story magazine article on plaintiff's case was published. In 1948, a radio play, a fictionalized version of the case, using the name of Martha Strayer, was broadcast. * * *

(3) Plaintiff argues that privilege as to one publication or consent to disclosure for one purpose does not constitute privilege or waiver of

privacy as to all publications, citing a number of cases,[11] and therefore the fact that the public records were privileged or that plaintiff may have approved the newspaper campaign on his behalf from 1934 to 1940 and not objected to the magazine article of 1936 or 1937 or the radio program of 1948, did not authorize the telecast. Plaintiff further argues that prior wrongful publications cannot make a further wrongful publication legal.

Both general statements are correct. Quoting again from Warren and Brandeis, at page 217 of their article:

> * * * The right to privacy ceases upon the publication of the facts by the individual, or with his consent.
>
> This is but another application of the rule which has become familiar in the law of literary and artistic property. The cases there decided establish also what should be deemed a publication,—the important principle in this connection being that a private communication or circulation for a restricted purpose is not a publication within the meaning of the law.

Privilege or waiver as to a prior disclosure is relevant, therefore, insofar as it relates to the issue whether there was a limited disclosure for a particular purpose or whether the facts became public property. The same is true of any prior disclosure which was not consented to and not privileged. Certain affairs of the individual are inherently private, and wrongful publication of them could not authorize subsequent publicity.[12] In the final analysis, whether disclosed facts are to be held public property depends upon a weighing of all the factors in favor of the free circulation of information against the individual's desire to avoid notoriety.

Plaintiff, having conceded that the story of his conviction and pardon were public property at the time they occurred, argues that since the matter had lain dormant from 1940 until 1952, a period of twelve years, it had become "stale news." In view of the radio publication in 1948, plaintiff's affairs had, on his own admission, been out of the public eye only since 1948 or for four years preceding the defendant's telecast. Plaintiff's counsel did not attempt to draw a line as to when matters of current interest become "stale news." Although news value is one of the bases for the privilege to publish, this court prefers the broader test of "public or general interest," advocated by Warren and Brandeis, supra, at 214. This court holds, as a matter of law, that a criminal proceeding widely publicized for a period of at least eight years and containing elements of decided popular appeal does not lose its general public interest in a period of four years or even twelve years;[13] hence, republication in a reasonable manner was privileged.

---

11. Those relevant to the issue are: Melvin v. Reid, supra; Mau v. Rio Grande Oil Co., supra; Leverton v. Curtis Publishing Co., 3 Cir., 1951, 192 F.2d 974.

12. For example, the facts of the romance of a private person, disclosure of which was alleged in the Walcher case, supra, would not become public property through a wrongful disclosure.

13. This is obvious to anyone familiar with popular compendiums of old crimes, detective stories based on fact, and the more lurid Sunday newspaper supplements.

(4) Since it has been concluded that the facts of plaintiff's past life were not private affairs and that there was no invasion of plaintiff's privacy by defendant, it is not necessary to disposition of the motion to determine whether the publication was in such manner as to outrage or cause mental suffering, shame, or humiliation to a person of ordinary sensibilities, which plaintiff urges as an unresolved material issue of fact on which reasonable men might differ. Otherwise, despite the affidavits in support of plaintiff's opposition to the motion stating the reaction of third persons to defendant's telecast, this court would be inclined to rule, as a matter of law, that the telecast was not offensive to one of ordinary sensibilities in plaintiff's position.[14]

The program of January 18, 1952, although sponsored commercially,[15] was one of general interest. It did not single out plaintiff to expose him to public scorn, but was one of a series of television plays devoted to retelling in fictionalized form the stories of newspaper reporters who had done excellent work in promoting justice. As the New Yorker sketch in the Sidis case, supra, might be of current public value in pointing out to parents the unhappy results of forcing a child prodigy into public notoriety, "The Big Story" program was of current public value in demonstrating how an alert reporter, who has an interest in seeing the right prevail, may help an innocent man escape the unhappy consequences of a wrongful conviction, and perhaps might inspire some other reporter to greater efforts or some young person to embrace a newspaper career. There was a careful and honest attempt to conceal the identity of all persons save the reporter, and the facts of the case were sufficiently changed to avoid duplication of the actual proceeding. That the concealment of plaintiff's identity was accomplished is attested by plaintiff's own allegations showing that only those who knew the story recognized it. The convicted man was shown as an entirely sympathetic character, innocent, wrongfully accused, inadequately defended, convicted on flimsy evidence, and saved from a gross miscarriage of justice in the nick of time. The picture painted was more favorable than the facts of record.[16] If plaintiff had wished to publicize his innocence to those who knew of his conviction but had never heard

---

14. Plaintiff's counsel in his argument of the motion argued that disclosure of the so-called common-law marital relationship was an invasion of plaintiff's right of privacy for two reasons: "(1) It could be clearly offensive to a substantial segment of the population to know that there was a common-law marital relationship that one time existed. (2) It is important also because the disclosure of that fact caused mental distress, and so forth, to my client." It is to be emphasized that the reaction of third persons is not pertinent. It is the outrage, mental suffering, shame, or humiliation of a normal person in plaintiff's position which governs.

15. Plaintiff's counsel conceded in his argument that the right to be let alone does not depend upon whether there is commercial use of the publication or not. Garner v. Triangle Publications, Inc., D.C.N.Y.1951, 97 F.Supp. 546.

16. For example, only one prior difficulty with the law was mentioned, the offense for which Crouch received a pardon in Minnesota. Helen Slezak was referred to as Crouch's "common-law wife" although there could be no valid common-law relationship under the facts of the story or of plaintiff's liaison.

of his pardon, he could have chosen no more effective means than a popular nationwide television network program.

If anyone's sensibilities should have been wounded by the play, it was the judge, the detectives, and the trial counsel, whose parts were given such unsympathetic treatment as to be defamatory, had there been identification. The whole atmosphere of the trial, as portrayed in the telecast, was not such as to inspire viewers with confidence in the administration of justice in the District of Columbia. * * *

For the foregoing reasons, the court will grant defendant's motion for summary judgment. * * *

Questions

1. Was the fact that the plaintiff's name was not used in the defendant's broadcast mentioned by the court as simply a "make-weight", or was it crucial to the granting of defendant's motion for summary judgment? That portion of the *Bernstein* opinion which discusses the issue of identification, is set forth infra.

2. Had the plaintiff "reverted to the lawful and unexciting life led by the great bulk of the community" within the meaning of the Restatement, as quoted by the court? Was the court's decision in conformity with the Restatement? Cf. the somewhat broader privilege notwithstanding the lapse of time recognized in Restatement (Second) of Torts, § 652F, Comment i (Tent.Draft No. 13, 1967).

3. Referring to footnote 8, is there no meaningful distinction between the exhibition of an old newspaper article referring to activities of the plaintiff, and the broadcasting of a newly created television program depicting the plaintiff in the course of such activities?

4. Is the court correct in its interpretation of the status of "biographical narratives" under the New York statute? Consider Binns v. Vitagraph Co. of America, 210 N.Y. 51, 103 N.E. 1108 (1913) and Spahn v. Julian Messner, Inc., infra.

5. Does the "public or general interest" in recalling the facts of a widely publicized criminal proceeding of many years ago justify a dramatization in such manner as to identify the prime actor among his present contemporaries? (Whether or not there was such identification in *Bernstein* is discussed infra). Does it justify a dramatization which recalls the facts of the depicted incident to those who at the time knew of the plaintiff's participation in the depicted events? Should it make any difference whether the facts are recalled on the one hand by a non-fiction book or a documentary broadcast, or on the other by a novel or dramatization based upon fact?

6. Do you agree with the court "that the telecast was not offensive to one of ordinary sensibilities in plaintiff's position"? Under the "ordinary sensibilities" test should matter be regarded as "offensive" only if, assuming it were false, it would be defamatory? Only if it is injurious to the plaintiff's reputation?

GILL v. HEARST PUBLISHING CO.

Supreme Court of California, in Bank, 1953.
40 Cal.2d 224, 253 P.2d 441.

Plaintiffs, husband and wife, sought damages for an alleged invasion of their right of privacy, this by reason of the publication in the Ladies Home Journal, with defendant's consent, of an unauthorized photograph of plaintiffs, seated in an affectionate pose at their place of business, a confectionery and ice cream concession, in the Farmer's Market in Los Angeles. In a related case, Gill v. Curtis Publishing Co., 38 Cal.2d 273, 239 P.2d 630 (1952), the same plaintiff's claimed invasion of privacy by reason of the same publication. The California Supreme Court in *Curtis* reversed the lower court's grant of a judgment on the pleadings for the defendants, finding that by reason of the context in which the photograph appeared, "it may be at least inferred therefrom that [plaintiffs'] feelings were hurt and they suffered mental anguish." The photograph was published in connection with an article entitled "Love". The article was a somewhat philosophical and sociological discussion of love and its relation to divorce. One of the types of "love" discussed was love at first sight, which was said to be based solely upon sex attraction, a kind of love which the article concluded was "wrong", and which would be followed by divorce. Plaintiffs' photograph appeared as an illustration of this type of love. In the instant action against Hearst Publishing Co. the plaintiffs alleged that the photograph which had been published by Curtis had been taken without their authorization by an employee of Hearst, and that the Hearst Co. had consented to its publication by Curtis. Defendants demurred on the ground that although the complaint alleged that the photograph had been published by Curtis with Hearst's consent, it did not allege that Hearst had consented to the publication in connection with the article "Love". The lower court sustained defendants' demurrer without leave to amend. A judgment for defendants was entered pursuant thereto, from which judgment the plaintiffs appealed.

SPENCE, JUSTICE.

* * * As indicated in Gill v. Curtis Publishing Co., supra, 38 Cal.2d 273, 279, 239 P.2d 630, defendants would be liable in the event of their consent to publication of the photograph in connection with the article in the Ladies' Home Journal. Plaintiffs therefore maintain that any defect in the recitals of the amended complaint with reference to defendants' connection with the publication of the article as well as the photograph could be easily corrected by amendment. The incorporation of the article as an exhibit constitutes some basis for an inference that it may have been intended as an inseparable part of the photograph in presenting the extent of plaintiffs' complaint. Moreover, the allegation of consent is broad and it cannot be said that it necessarily negates a consent to publishing the article. The objection to plaintiffs' pleading thus goes to the matter of effecting a clarification of an

The disputed photograph of the Gills

uncertainty or an ambiguity. Manifestly, such defect is capable of being cured by amendment. Wennerholm v. Stanford University School of Medicine, 20 Cal.2d 713, 719, 128 P.2d 522, 141 A.L.R. 1358; Washer v. Bank of America Nat. Trust & Savings Ass'n, 21 Cal.2d 822, 833, 136 P.2d 297, 155 A.L.R. 1338. Under these circumstances, the trial court abused its discretion in sustaining defendants' demurrer without leave to amend. Wilk v. Vencill, 30 Cal.2d 104, 109, 180 P.2d 351.

The recognition of plaintiffs' right to proceed in the event of proper clarification involves the further observation that mere publication of the photograph standing alone does not constitute an actionable invasion of plaintiffs' right of privacy. The right "to be let alone" and to be protected from undesired publicity is not absolute but must be balanced against the public interest in the dissemination of news and information consistent with the democratic processes under the constitutional guarantees of freedom of speech and of the press. U.S. Const. Amends. I, XIV; Cal. Const. art. I, sec. 9; 41 Am.Jur., Privacy, sec. 9, pp. 931–933; Nizer, The Right of Privacy, 39 Michigan Law Rev. 526, 528–529; Gill v. Curtis Publishing Co., supra, 38 Cal.2d 273, 277–278, 239 P.2d 630. The right of privacy may not be extended to prohibit *any* publication of matter which may be of public or general interest, but rather the "general object in view is to protect the privacy of private life, and to whatever degree and in whatever connection a man's life has ceased to be private, before the publication under consideration has been made, to that extent the protection is to be withdrawn." Brandeis-Warren Essay, 4 Harvard Law Rev., 193, 215; Metter v. Los Angeles Examiner, 35 Cal.App.2d 304, 312, 95 P.2d 491. Moreover, the right of privacy is determined by the norm of the ordinary man; that is to say, the alleged objectionable publication must appear offensive in the light of "ordinary sensibilities." 41 Am.Jur., Privacy, sec. 12, p. 934. As has been said: " * * * liability exists only if the defendant's conduct was such that he should have realized that it would be offensive to persons of ordinary sensibilities. It is only where the intrusion has gone beyond the limits of decency that liability accrues. * * * It is only when the defendant should know that the plaintiff would be justified in feeling seriously hurt by the conduct that a cause of action exists." Rest., Torts, Vol. 4, sec. 867, comment d, pp. 400–401; see, also, cases collected: Annos. 138 A.L.R. 22, 46; 168 A.L.R. 446, 452; 14 A.L.R.2d 750, 752. Whether there has been such an offensive invasion of privacy is "to some extent one of law." 41 Am.Jur., Privacy, sec. 12, p. 935; Schuyler v. Curtis, 147 N.Y. 434, 42 N.E. 22, 26, 31 L.R.A. 286; Reed v. Real Detective Pub. Co., 63 Ariz. 294, 162 P.2d 133, 139; Cason v. Baskin, 155 Fla. 198, 20 So.2d 243, 251, 168 A.L.R. 430.

The picture allegedly was taken at plaintiffs' "place of business," a confectionery and ice cream concession in the Farmers' Market, Los Angeles. It shows plaintiffs, a young man and young woman, seated at a counter near a cash register, the young woman apparently in intent thought, with a notebook and pencil in her hands, which rest on the counter. Plaintiffs are dressed informally and are in a romantic pose, the young man having one arm about the young woman. There are at least five other persons plainly visible in the photograph in positions in close proximity to plaintiffs as the central figures. Apparently the picture has no particular news value but is designed to serve the function of entertainment as a matter of legitimate public interest. Rest., Torts, Vol. 4, sec. 867, comments c and d, pp. 399–401. However, the constitutional guaranties of freedom of expression apply with equal force to the publication whether it be a news report or an entertainment feature, Lovell v. City of Griffin, 303 U.S. 444, 452, 58 S.Ct. 666, 82 L.Ed. 949; Winters v. New York, 333 U.S. 507, 510, 68 S.Ct. 665, 92 L.Ed. 840; United States v. Paramount Pictures, Inc., 334 U.S. 131, 166, 68 S.Ct. 915, 92 L.Ed. 1260, and defendants' liability accrues only in the event that it can be said that there has been a wrongful invasion of plaintiffs' right of privacy. Cf. Gill v. Curtis Publishing Co., supra, 38 Cal.2d 273, 280, 239 P.2d 630.

In considering the nature of the picture in question, it is significant that it was not surreptitiously snapped on private grounds, but rather was taken of plaintiffs in a pose voluntarily assumed in a public market place. So distinguishable are cases such as Barber v. Time, Inc., 348 Mo. 1199, 159 S.W.2d 291, where the picture showed plaintiff in her bed at a hospital, which circumstance was held to constitute an infringement of the right of privacy. Here plaintiffs, photographed at their concession allegedly "well known to persons and travelers throughout the world" as conducted for "many years" in the "worldfamed" Farmers' Market, had voluntarily exposed themselves to public gaze in a pose open to the view of any persons who might then be at or near their place of business. By their own voluntary action plaintiffs waived their right of privacy so far as this particular public pose was assumed, 41 Am.Jur., Privacy, sec. 17 p. 937, for "There can be no privacy in that which is already public." Melvin v. Reid, 112 Cal.App. 285, 290, 297 P. 91, 93. The photograph of plaintiffs merely permitted other members of the public, who were not at plaintiffs' place of business at the time it was taken, to see them as they had voluntarily exhibited themselves. Consistent with their own voluntary assumption of this particular pose in a public place, plaintiffs' right to privacy as to this photographed incident ceased and it in effect became a part of the public domain, Brandeis-Warren Essay, 4 Harvard Law Rev. 193, 218; Melvin v. Reid, supra, 112 Cal.App. 285, 290–291, 297 P. 91, as to which they could not later rescind their waiver in an attempt to assert a right of privacy. Cohen v. Marx, 94 Cal.App.2d 704, 705, 211 P.2d 320. In short, the photograph did not disclose anything which until then had been private, but rather only extended knowledge of the particular incident to a somewhat larger public than had actually witnessed it at the time of occurrence.

Nor does there appear to be anything "uncomplimentary" or discreditable in the photograph itself, so that its publication might be objectionable as going "beyond the limits of decency" and reasonably indicate defendants' conduct to be such that they "should have realized it would be offensive to persons of ordinary sensibilities." Rest., Torts, vol. 4, sec. 867, comment d, pp. 400–401. Here the picture of plaintiffs, sitting romantically close to one another, the man with his arm around the woman, depicts no more than a portrayal of an incident which may be seen almost daily in ordinary life—couples in a sentimental mood on public park benches, in railroad depots or hotel lobbies, at public games, the beaches, the theatres. Such situation is readily distinguishable from cases where the right of privacy has been enforced with regard to the publication of a picture which was shocking, revolting or indecent in its portrayal of the human body. See Douglas v. Stokes, 149 Ky. 506, 149 S.W. 849, 42 L.R.A.,N.S., 386; Bazemore v. Savannah Hospital, 171 Ga. 257, 155 S.E. 194. In fact, here the photograph may very well be said to be complimentary and pleasing in its pictorial representation of plaintiffs.

Plaintiffs have failed to cite, and independent research has failed to reveal, any case where the publication of a mere photograph under the circumstances here prevailing—a picture (1) taken in a pose voluntarily assumed in a public place and (2) portraying nothing to shock the ordinary sense of decency or propriety—has been held an actionable invasion of the right of privacy. To so hold would mean that plaintiffs "under all conceivable circumstances had an absolute legal right to [prevent publication of] any photograph of them taken without their permission. If every person has such a right, no [periodical] could lawfully publish a photograph of a parade or a street scene. We are not prepared to sustain the assertion of such a right." Themo v. New England Newspaper Pub. Co., 306 Mass. 54, 27 N.E.2d 753, 755; see Rest., Torts, vol. 4, sec. 867, comment c, pp. 399–400. In so concluding, it must be remembered that there is no contention here that the publication of plaintiffs' photograph was for advertising or trade purposes. 41 Am.Jur., Privacy, sec. 22, p. 941; e.g. Pavesich v. New England Life Ins. Co., 122 Ga. 190, 50 S.E. 68, 69 L.R.A. 101; Kunz v. Allen, 102 Kan. 883, 172 P. 532, L.R.A.1918D, 1151 also 26 Southern Cal.Law Rev. 102, 103.

As heretofore indicated, however, we conclude that plaintiffs should have been accorded the right to amend their complaint, and that the trial court abused its discretion in sustaining defendants' demurrer without leave to amend.

The judgment is reversed.

GIBSON, C.J., and SHENK, EDMONDS, TRAYNOR and SCHAUER, JJ., concur.

CARTER, JUSTICE. I concur in that part of the majority decision which reverses the judgment for refusal of the trial court to allow plaintiffs to amend. I dissent, however, from the holding that the publication of the photograph alone did not violate plaintiffs' right of privacy.

It is difficult to ascertain upon what ground the majority opinion rests as will hereafter appear. As outlined in Gill v. Curtis Publishing Co., 38 Cal.2d 273, 239 P.2d 630, and authorities there cited, there are two main questions involved in right of privacy cases: (1) Is the publication of a character which would offend the feelings and sensibilities of the ordinary person; and (2) if it does so offend, is there such a public interest in the subject matter of the publication with reference to its news or educational significance that it may be published with impunity. In the first instance the question is whether there has been any tort (violation of the right of privacy) committed, and in the second, having found the tort, is it privileged.

Referring to the second question, first, it should be quite obvious that there is no news or educational value whatsoever in the photograph alone. It depicts two persons (plaintiffs) in an amorous pose. There is nothing to show whether they are or are not married. While some remote news significance might be attached to persons in such a pose on the theory that the public likes and is entitled to see persons in such a pose, there is no reason why the publisher need invade the privacy of John and Jane Doe for his purpose. He can employ models for that purpose and the portion of the public interested will never know the difference but its maudlin curiosity will be appeased.

For the same reasons the discussion in the majority opinion to the effect that plaintiffs consented to the publication because they assumed the pose in a public place is fallacious. But in addition, such a theory is completely at odds with the violation of the right of privacy. By plaintiffs doing what they did in view of a tiny fraction of the public, does not mean that they consented to observation by the millions of readers of the defendant's magazine. In effect, the majority holding means that anything anyone does outside of his own home is with consent to the publication thereof, because, under those circumstances he waives his right of privacy even though there is no news value in the event. If such were the case, the blameless exposure of a portion of the naked body of a man or woman in a public place as the result of inefficient buttons, hooks or other clothes-holding devices could be freely photographed and widely published with complete immunity. The majority opinion confuses the situation, as have some of the other cases, with the question of newsworthiness. It has been said that when a person is involved in either a public or private event, voluntarily or involuntarily, of news value, that he has waived his right of privacy. Plainly such is not the case where the event is involuntary such as the victim of a holdup. As we said in Gill v. Curtis Publishing Co., supra, 38 Cal.2d 273, 281, 239 P.2d 630, 635: "It should be observed, that referring to the use of a person's likeness for a legitimate public interest as not actionable because it indicates a waiver by the person of his right, is of doubtful validity, for it has been applied whether the publication having news value arose out of an incident of his own making or involuntarily and without his fault thrust upon him." There is no basis for the conclusion that the second a person leaves the portals of his home he consents to have his photograph taken under all circumstances thereafter. There being no legitimate public interest, there is no excuse for the publication.

The first ground, that the picture would not offend the senses of an ordinary person, is equally untenable. It is alleged in plaintiffs' complaint, and admitted by the demurrer that it so offended them. It is then a matter of proof at the trial. Certainly reasonable men could view the picture as showing plaintiffs in a sultry or sensual pose. For this Court to say as a matter of law that such portrayal would not seriously offend the feelings of an ordinary man is to take an extreme view to say the least. The question is one for the trier of fact. Gill v. Curtis Publishing Co., supra, 38 Cal.2d 273, 280, 239 P.2d 630. If it is in part a question of law it is so only to the extent that the right does not extend to "supersensitiveness or agoraphobia." 41 Am.Jur., Privacy, § 12. An examination of the photograph shows that it would offend the feelings of persons other than oversensitive ones.

Finally, adding to the confusion of the precise ground upon which it rests, the majority opinion makes point of the fact that the picture was not used for advertising purposes, and that if it did not hold as it does, there would be liability for a person's picture appearing among others in a parade. Obviously the first has no bearing upon whether an ordinary man would be offended. The offense would exist or not exist regardless of whether it was used for advertising. The second adds nothing because the parade and those engaging in it are matters of public interest and the persons engaging therein are intentionally placing themselves on public display—parade.

In announcing a rule of law defining the right of a private citizen to be left alone, and not have his photograph published to the four winds, especially when he is depicted in an uncomplimentary pose, courts should consider the effect of such publication upon the sensibility of the ordinary private citizen, and not upon the sensibility of those persons who seek and enjoy publicity and notoriety and seeing their pictures on public display, or those who are in the "public eye" such as public officials, clergymen, lecturers, actors and others whose professional career brings them in constant contact with the public and in whom the public or some segment thereof is interested. Obviously anything the latter group may do or say has news or educational value—such cannot be said of the persons engaged in private business or employment who constitute more than 90% of our population. These private citizens, who desire to be left alone, should have and enjoy a right of privacy so long as they do nothing which can reasonably be said to have news value. Certainly this right is entitled to protection. It seems to me that the law should be so molded as to protect the right of the 90% who do not desire publicity or notoriety and who may be offended by publications such as that here involved. And, when the right of privacy of such a person is violated, and redress is sought in the courts for the indignity suffered, the courts should apply the general rules applicable to the redress of wrongs and submit the issues of fact to a jury when demanded. But the majority of this Court, following its present trend, has again seen fit to deny plaintiffs their constitutional right to a jury trial on the issues of fact here presented by arrogating to itself both the fact finding and law making power. To this holding I most emphatically dissent.

Questions

1. Should the fact that plaintiff's pose was seen by a small segment of the public in the Farmers' Market in itself constitute a defense to the publication of the pose to a much greater segment of the public on the ground that the publication did not disclose anything that was "private"? Is the *Hearst* opinion in this regard inconsistent with the same court's decision in the *Curtis* case? Or is the *Curtis* decision distinguishable because it, unlike *Hearst,* is a "false light" type of privacy invasion? See the discussion of false light privacy in the next chapter. Should it make any difference whether the original disclosure to the smaller audience was voluntary? Cf. Daily Times Democrat v. Graham, 276 Ala. 380, 162 So.2d 474 (1964). If the consent to the disclosure of private facts is by its terms limited to a given audience, should a disclosure to a greater or different audience constitute an invasion of privacy? Even if there is a violation of the terms of the consent, and possibly therefore a breach of contract, can it be said that the further disclosure invades *privacy*? Compare Canessa v. J.I. Kislak, Inc., 97 N.J.Super. 327, 235 A.2d 62 (1967) (consent to publication of photograph in The Jersey Journal held not to constitute a waiver of right of privacy in connection with republication in a commercial pamphlet) and Gautier v. Pro-Football, 304 N.Y. 354, 107 N.E.2d 485 (1952) (professional appearance before a live audience waives right of privacy with respect to unconsented televising of such performance).

2. Does the *Hearst* opinion hold that a publication must be "'uncomplimentary' or discreditable" in order to be offensive to a person of ordinary sensibilities, and therefore to constitute an invasion of privacy? Is this a proper view? In Samuel v. Curtis Pub. Co., 122 F.Supp. 327, 329 (N.D.Cal.1954) the court cited the *Hearst* case for the following rule of law: "Where the photograph portrays nothing to shock the ordinary sense of decency or propriety, where there is nothing uncomplimentary or discreditable in the photograph itself, and where the caption and article add nothing that makes the photograph uncomplimentary or discreditable no actionable invasion of privacy occurs." Does this accurately reflect the *Hearst* opinion? Does it suggest a broader standard? Compare the *Samuel* interpretation of *Hearst* with that of another federal court in Strickler v. National Broadcasting Co., p. 787 infra.

MAU v. RIO GRANDE OIL, INC.

United States District Court, Northern District of California, S.D., 1939.
28 F.Supp. 845.

St. Sure, District Judge. This is an action in tort invoking the right to privacy, or what Judge Cooley called the right "to be let alone."

Plaintiff, employed as a chauffeur, was, on March 22, 1937, held up by a robber and shot, suffering serious injury. His nerves received a severe shock, and as a result of the encounter he became "mentally ill, nervous and distraught." Mere mention of the shooting caused acute nervous attacks. On and prior to August 4, 1938, defendant Rio Grande Oil, Inc., a corporation, was engaged in producing through the radio facilities of defendant Columbia Broadcasting System, Inc., a corporation, an advertising program entitled "Calling All Cars." On the last mentioned date, Rio Grande caused to be broadcast in San Francisco over the Columbia network a dramatization of the holdup and shooting, using plaintiff's name without his consent. When plaintiff heard the broadcast he suffered mental anguish, aggravated by telephone calls from sympathetic friends who also heard the broadcast and were desirous of rehashing the near-tragedy which plaintiff wished to forget. On the day following the broadcast, and as a direct result thereof, plaintiff's physical and mental condition were such that he was unable to drive an automobile with safety, and he was promptly discharged by his employer. He asks for special and general damages. The above facts are from the complaint, jurisdiction appearing through diversity of citizenship and sufficient amount in controversy. The case is before the court on motion to dismiss. * * *

It is settled that in tort cases in which the jurisdiction of the Federal courts rests upon diversity of citizenship, they will follow the law of the place where the tort was committed. Applying the holding in Melvin v. Reid to the facts here, it follows that plaintiff's right to be let alone, has been violated, and, upon proof of his case, he may recover damages. The motion to dismiss will be denied.

Questions

1. Should a publication of private facts which does not injure the subject's reputation ever be considered "offensive" so as to constitute an invasion of privacy? Should embarrassing but non-reputation injuring facts be considered "offensive" in this sense? Consider Daily Times Democrat v. Graham, 276 Ala. 380, 162 So.2d 474 (1964) wherein plaintiff, a 44 year old woman, while attending a "Fun House" was subjected to a hidden device that blew jets of air up from the exit platform. As plaintiff "was leaving her dress was blown up by the air jets and her body was exposed from the waist down, with the exception of that portion covered by her 'panties'. At that moment [defendant's] photographer snapped a picture of the [plaintiff] in this situation." Upon plaintiff's action for invasion of privacy, what result?

2. Was the depiction of the plaintiff in *Mau* reputation-injuring? Was it embarrassing? If it was neither, should it nevertheless be regarded as "offensive" for the purpose of stating a privacy cause of action? How would you characterize the mental distress that Mau may have suffered from the broadcast?

JOHNSON v. EVENING STAR NEWSPAPER CO.
United States Court of Appeals, District of Columbia Circuit, 1965.
344 F.2d 507, 120 U.S.App.D.C. 122.

Before FAHY, WASHINGTON and BURGER, CIRCUIT JUDGES.

Per Curiam. Appellant was the innocent victim of a mistaken identification as the person who committed two serious crimes in the

District of Columbia. He was arrested, charged with the crimes and spent some time in jail before being released when the mistake was discovered. Appellees in their newspapers of wide circulation published accounts of his clearance, giving his name, address and other identifying information, with some details of the resumption of his family life after his ordeal. He sued appellees for damages, claiming that such publications invaded his right of privacy. Appellees' motions to dismiss were granted and the complaint was dismissed.

We think the facts as set forth in the complaint, admitted for purposes of the motion to dismiss, failed to state a cause of action. We therefore affirm.

The publications contain no criticism whatever of appellant. There was not the slightest adverse reflection upon him or suggestion of defamation or ridicule of him. His identification as the victim of the mistake, by including his name and otherwise placing him in his environment did not give rise to a recoverable wrong. The principal events were already in the public domain, and were of news interest. The identifying details were incidental to the story and were not an enlargement which carried the publications beyond legitimate bounds. Elmhurst v. Pearson, 80 U.S.App.D.C. 372, 153 F.2d 467 (1946).

Affirmed.

Questions

1. Is *Mau*, supra, distinguishable from *Johnson?* For the purpose of a privacy claim is it meaningfully different to be depicted as the victim of a crime, or as one wrongfully accused of a crime? Does a dramatization of fact as in *Mau* significantly differ from a news report as in *Johnson?*

2. Under the *Johnson* view, would any publication that is not reputation-injuring constitute an invasion of privacy?

Collateral References

Kalven, *Privacy in Tort Law—Were Warren and Brandeis Wrong?*, 31 Law and Contemporary Problems 326 (1966).

Wade, *Defamation and the Right of Privacy,* 15 Vand.Law Rev. 1093 (1962).

DeSALVO v. TWENTIETH CENTURY–FOX FILM CORP.

United States District Court, District of Massachusetts, 1969.
300 F.Supp. 742.

GARRITY, DISTRICT JUDGE. Plaintiff filed this suit in the Massachusetts Superior Court for Suffolk County on September 29, 1968, to restrain and enjoin the release and showing of the defendant Twentieth Century-Fox Film Corporation's (hereinafter Fox) motion picture "The Boston Strangler", and for damages. Defendant removed the case to this court on October 1, and plaintiff's petition for a temporary restraining order was denied on that date after hearing. On October 7 the Walter Reade Organization, Inc. (hereinafter Reade), which had scheduled to open a six-week engagement of the motion picture in New York on October 16, 1968, was allowed to intervene as an additional party defendant.

After a hearing at which extensive testimony, including that of plaintiff, was received and at which the court viewed the motion picture, the motion for a preliminary injunction was denied on October 11. Trial commenced on December 20 and, after various short continuances, was concluded on December 30. In accordance with orders of the court the parties have filed requests for findings of fact and conclusions of law.

Findings of Fact

1. The relevant facts begin over four years ago after the end of the wave of murders commonly attributed to the so-called "Boston Strangler." In November, 1964 plaintiff was arrested and charged by the Commonwealth of Massachusetts with ten separate indictments of robbery, assault, and other related non-capital crimes, and was committed by the Superior Court for Middlesex County to the Bridgewater State Hospital for pretrial psychiatric examination. After the examination, on February 4, 1965, the Middlesex County Superior Court committed him to the Bridgewater State Hospital indefinitely upon a finding that he was not mentally competent to stand trial. At some time during this period, plaintiff's name became connected in some fashion with the so-called "Boston Strangler."

2. Plaintiff retained Attorney F. Lee Bailey, Jr., of Boston to represent him in late February or early March, 1965. One of the reasons for which Attorney Bailey was originally retained was to give plaintiff an opinion as to whether or not plaintiff's life story was saleable. At that time Attorney Bailey told plaintiff that in his opinion it would not be in plaintiff's interest for plaintiff himself to write a book about his life, but that there were a number of books upon the so-called "Boston Strangler" in the process of being written and that it might be possible for plaintiff to receive some compensation in return for an agreement not to sue the author and publisher. Plaintiff asked Attorney Bailey to explore the latter possibility and Bailey did so over the next year.

3. On May 6, 1965, on a petition filed in the Probate Court for Middlesex County, temporary guardians of the estate and of the person were appointed for plaintiff. Plaintiff's brother Joseph DeSalvo was appointed guardian of his estate, and on May 11 bond was approved appointing George F. McGrath of Boston, an attorney and Commissioner of Corrections for the Commonwealth of Massachusetts, guardian of plaintiff's person. From that time until April 26, 1966, when the guardianship petition was dismissed and the guardianships terminated, Attorney McGrath was responsible for the management of plaintiff's affairs.

4. During the period of the temporary guardianship, Attorney McGrath helped plaintiff manage his finances and discussed his financial situation with him. In addition, plaintiff and Attorney McGrath discussed the possibility of plaintiff's receiving compensation for sale of the rights to his life history, particularly with regard to the ethical implications of plaintiff's accepting money from the sale of his rights to stories of crimes in which he had participated. During the period of the temporary guardianship, as a result of his discussion with and observations of plaintiff, Attorney McGrath came to the conclusion that plaintiff was capable of handling his own business and financial affairs and he so informed the Probate Court at the hearing on April 26, 1966.

5. Dr. Robert R. Mezer, a psychiatrist licensed by the Commonwealth of Massachusetts, examined plaintiff on February 11, 1966, pursuant to the request of plaintiff's then counsel, Attorney Bailey. The purpose of the examination was to enable Dr. Mezer to give an expert opinion as to whether plaintiff should be released from his temporary guardianship. At the completion of the examination Dr. Mezer concluded that plaintiff was a chronic, undifferentiated schizophrenic but that he understood the import of guardianship, had a functional understanding of his financial affairs and condition, and was competent to handle his own financial and business affairs. Dr. Mezer testified to that effect at the hearing in the Probate Court on April 26, 1966.

6. Dr. Ames Robey, a psychiatrist licensed by the Commonwealth of Massachusetts and the State of Michigan, was Medical Director of the Bridgewater State Hospital from 1963 through July 21, 1966. In that capacity Dr. Robey visited plaintiff almost daily during plaintiff's stay at Bridgewater, conducted full psychiatric examinations on at least 23 occasions, and reported to various courts at various times as to plaintiff's mental condition. Dr. Robey also concluded from his examinations and observations that plaintiff was a chronic, undifferentiated schizophrenic; and testified at the hearing on April 26, 1966 that plaintiff required guardianship to conduct his business affairs.

7. Shortly after the Probate Court dismissed the petition for appointment of a guardian for plaintiff, Attorney McGrath left Massachusetts to assume his present position as Commissioner of Correction for the City of New York, New York. Attorney McGrath has kept in contact with plaintiff since that time and has advised him in regard to some business affairs.

8. In the spring of 1966, Attorney Bailey advised plaintiff that Gerold Frank was planning to publish a book entitled "The Boston Strangler" in which plaintiff would be named as the so-called "Boston Strangler." Attorney Bailey advised plaintiff that it was his opinion that Mr. Frank was going to publish his book whether or not he received a release from plaintiff and that if plaintiff wished to make an agreement with Mr. Frank it would be a good idea because there was a question as to whether or not plaintiff had anything to sell. Plaintiff

told Attorney Bailey to see what could be done, and Attorney Bailey conducted further discussions with Mr. Frank and with his publisher and agent. At the conclusion of the discussions Attorney Bailey reported to plaintiff the substance of a proposed agreement, and plaintiff agreed to it. Mr. Frank's literary agent, the William Morris Agency of New York City, thereupon drew up a written agreement.

9. Although he was no longer serving as plaintiff's guardian, Attorney McGrath reviewed the proposed agreement between plaintiff and Mr. Frank and discussed it with plaintiff. Attorney Bailey took the written agreement to plaintiff at Bridgewater on June 17, 1966, and explained the import and substance of the written agreement to plaintiff in detail. Plaintiff thereupon signed the agreement on June 17, 1966, in the presence of Attorney McGrath and Attorney Bailey, and both witnessed his signature. Both witnesses were of the opinion that plaintiff knew and understood the import of the agreement that he was signing and that he was signing it of his own volition.

10. Plaintiff testified that Attorney Bailey did not explain the contents of the agreement to him but rather that he simply placed the agreement before him and demanded that he sign it. This detailed testimony is utterly inconsistent with plaintiff's earlier testimony that he did not remember signing the agreement and that he did not even know who he was. The court expressly rejected plaintiff's account of these events on the basis of the recurrent inconsistencies in plaintiff's testimony, plaintiff's selective recall which allowed him to testify to what he appeared to feel was advantageous to his case but almost completely precluded any meaningful cross-examination, and plaintiff's general demeanor on the witness stand.

11. The agreement signed by plaintiff on June 17, 1966 provides that plaintiff thereby released to Mr. Gerold Frank all rights that plaintiff may have had or might thereafter obtain to all literary and biographical material concerning plaintiff's life. The agreement specifically released to Mr. Frank plaintiff's rights to any published account of his life and to any motion picture or other dramatic representation, version, or portrayal of plaintiff. The agreement provided that Mr. Frank could assign any and all rights that he received under the written agreement to any third party or parties. In addition, plaintiff agreed not to sue Mr. Frank or any assignee of Mr. Frank for libel, violation of a right of privacy, or "anything else" which might result for any work portraying plaintiff. In consideration for the release of the above rights plaintiff was to receive payments of money according to a specified schedule.

12. On June 27, 1966, Dr. Mezer again examined plaintiff. The examination was conducted to enable Dr. Mezer to testify at a hearing scheduled for June 30, 1966 on the issue of whether plaintiff was mentally competent to stand trial on the criminal charges which were still pending against him in the Middlesex Superior Court. Dr. Mezer

found plaintiff to be alert and, after Attorney Bailey had reviewed the charges with plaintiff, very much aware of his situation.

13. Dr. Robey examined plaintiff a number of times during June, 1966 in an attempt to reach a conclusion as to plaintiff's mental competency to stand trial on the criminal charges pending against him. Dr. Robey concluded from these examinations that plaintiff understood the criminal charges, that he understood the possible consequences of those charges, and that he was able to understand and follow Attorney Bailey's instructions not to cooperate with Dr. Robey. Because of plaintiff's refusal to cooperate in a mental examination, Dr. Robey was not able to reach a definite conclusion as to plaintiff's mental competency to stand trial but, lacking evidence to the contrary, he continued to hold his previous opinion that plaintiff was not mentally competent to stand criminal trial.

14. On June 30, 1966, the Middlesex Superior Court held a hearing to determine whether plaintiff was mentally competent to stand trial. At this hearing both the Commonwealth and plaintiff took the position that plaintiff was mentally competent to stand trial. At the completion of the hearing the court found plaintiff mentally competent to stand trial and remanded him to custody to await trial.

15. Both Dr. Robey and Dr. Mezer qualified in the instant case as experts in psychiatry and testified to plaintiff's capacity to enter into a valid contract in June 1966. Dr. Mezer was of the opinion that, notwithstanding plaintiff's chronic, undifferentiated schizophrenia, plaintiff had the ability to understand his financial situation and the import and terms of the agreement with Gerold Frank; Dr. Robey was of the opinion that plaintiff lacked such understanding in June 1966 and that he continues to lack such capacity to this day. The court rejects Dr. Robey's opinion on the grounds of (a) his stated difficulties in interviewing plaintiff in June 1966, (b) the previous rejections of his opinions on related issues of plaintiff's mental capacity before the Probate Court in April 1966 and before the Superior Court in June 1966, and (c) the court's own observations of plaintiff on the witness stand. The court accepts and adopts Dr. Mezer's testimony and finds that in June 1966 plaintiff was aware of and understood his financial situation and understood the substantial import and terms of the agreement with Gerold Frank.

16. On July 4, 1966 plaintiff signed a letter to Mr. Frank informing him that plaintiff had appointed Attorney McGrath his agent and fiduciary in regard to plaintiff's agreement with Mr. Frank, directing that all payments to be made to plaintiff under the agreement should be delivered to Attorney McGrath payable to "Robert McKay", and that Attorney McGrath had authority to endorse and cash those checks. This letter was witnessed by Attorney Bailey. Attorney Bailey testified that plaintiff understood the import of the letter and voluntarily signed it. No evidence was offered that this letter or the authorization given by it has ever been revoked.

17. After receipt of the July 4, 1966 letter the William Morris Agency, as agent for Mr. Frank, sent a check for $15,000 to Attorney McGrath to meet the advance provided for in the June 17, 1966 agreement. Attorney McGrath endorsed the check and delivered it to Attorney Bailey who cashed the check and deposited the proceeds in his office account. To date a total of $18,443.52 (including the $15,000 advance) has been deposited in Attorney Bailey's account.[1]

18. Gerold Frank's book, "The Boston Strangler", was published in October 1966 and a paperback edition was released in 1967. The book has had substantial sales.[2] The book specifically names plaintiff as the "Boston Strangler" and deals very extensively and in detail with events which plaintiff is stated to have participated in as the "Strangler." The book makes no apparent substantial attempt to deal with plaintiff or his involvement as the "Strangler" in a sympathetic or complimentary light. It does not appear, however, that plaintiff has at any time protested publication or sale of the book or attempted to stop its sale, although plaintiff read the book in early 1967.

19. At the trial for the criminal assaults in the Middlesex County Superior Court, on January 13, 1967, Attorney Bailey made an opening for the defense in which he stated that DeSalvo was insane and had committed 13 acts of homicide within a period of 18 months. These assertions in court were made by Attorney Bailey as a result of lengthy discussions between him and the plaintiff.

20. By agreements dated May 10, 1967 and November 2, 1967, Fox purchased from Gerold Frank the portions of the agreement which plaintiff had made with Mr. Frank on June 17, 1966 which related to the motion picture and related rights.

21. In January 1968 defendant began filming its motion picture "The Boston Strangler" in Boston. The filming was attended by much publicity, particularly in the newspapers in the Boston area, and was the subject of considerable public interest. Plaintiff was aware of the filming and familiar with many details of the movie. He corresponded with the director of the motion picture and with consultants working on it. During the filming and subsequent preparation of the motion picture, plaintiff made no attempts to stop filming or preparation of the motion picture.

22. While the motion picture "The Boston Strangler" deals specifically with the series of murders committed in the Boston metropolitan

---

1. These moneys have been used to pay expenses but not legal fees incurred in connection with the criminal defense and appeal of plaintiff, to disburse $3000 to one of plaintiff's brothers at plaintiff's request to pay off a financing agreement on the brother's automobile, and a deposit remains to cover a possible judgment that may be returned against Attorney Bailey for a reward offered for the non-fatal capture and return of plaintiff to custody after an escape from Bridgewater.

2. The affidavit of Ezra M. Eisen, Secretary and Treasurer of the publisher, The New American Library, submitted at the hearing on the motion for a temporary injunction, indicates that total sales of the book through August 1968 exceeded 860,000 copies.

area, it depicts generally typical problems confronted by any large city in protecting itself against sexual deviates unable to control their own conduct. In its portrayal of plaintiff, the motion picture is concerned largely with a struggle within himself to confess to crimes of which he considered himself guilty. At the very least, the portrayal of plaintiff in the motion picture is no more condemnatory of him than is the book.

23. Although plaintiff was aware that defendant was preparing to release the motion picture "The Boston Strangler" at least as early as the fall of 1967, the first indication to defendant Fox that plaintiff had any criticism of the film or would make any attempt to prohibit exhibition of the motion picture was in a letter from plaintiff's present trial counsel to defendant on September 18, 1968. This suit was brought eighteen days prior to the scheduled public release of the motion picture by defendant Fox. No explanation for the delay in protesting and seeking to prevent exhibition of the motion picture has been offered, other than a suggestion that plaintiff was confused.

Conclusions of Law

1. Plaintiff executed an agreement on June 17, 1966 in favor of Gerold Frank releasing for valuable consideration all rights that he might have to the use of his name in, but not limited to, literary works and motion pictures in connection with incidents commonly known as "The Boston Strangler." At the time that plaintiff executed the agreement of June 17, 1966 in favor of Gerold Frank, plaintiff was aware of and understood the import, purpose and terms of the agreement. Plaintiff's mental condition at the time of his signing the June 17, 1966 agreement, therefore, was not such as to render it void or voidable. See Meserve v. Jordan Marsh Co., 1960, 340 Mass. 660, 165 N.E.2d 905.

2. Plaintiff has received the consideration as it has become due as provided in the June 17, 1966 agreement. The rights released by plaintiff in the June 17, 1966 agreement involving the production of a motion picture portraying plaintiff as the "Boston Strangler" have been duly assigned to defendant Fox for valuable consideration. The June 17, 1966 agreement, as assigned to defendant, therefore bars recovery by plaintiff for an alleged defamation or invasion of privacy of plaintiff by a motion picture owned by defendant which portrays plaintiff as "The Boston Strangler." Sharman v. C. Schmidt & Sons, Inc., E.D.Pa., 1963, 216 F.Supp. 401.

3. Due to the exceptional public interest in the so-called "Boston Strangler" incidents and the extensive publicity surrounding plaintiff as a possible "Boston Strangler," particularly pending and during his criminal trial on the criminal charges on which he was convicted and is presently confined, the public interest in the "Boston Strangler" and in plaintiff as possible "Boston Strangler" preclude maintenance of an action by plaintiff for defamation or invasion of privacy unless plaintiff proves publication that is knowingly false or falsely made with reckless disregard for the truth. Time, Inc. v. Hill, 1967, 385 U.S. 374, 87 S.Ct.

534, 17 L.Ed.2d 456. Plaintiff has not met the burden of proving that the portrayal of plaintiff as the "Boston Strangler" in defendant's film of that name was knowingly false or was falsely made with a reckless disregard for the truth; the vast preponderance of the evidence establishes the contrary.

4. Plaintiff unreasonably delayed without justifiable excuse the commencement of this action. Maintenance of this action is therefore barred under the equitable doctrine of laches.

On the basis of the forgoing findings of fact and conclusions of law, judgment is ordered for the defendant and the defendant-intervenor.

Question

If the court in *DeSalvo* had found either that the plaintiff had not consented to his portrayal in defendant's motion picture, or that he was incapable of giving such consent, would the result have been different? What is the answer to Attorney Bailey's query as to whether plaintiff "had anything to sell"? Does the court hold, in paragraph 3. of its Conclusions of Law, that regardless of consent, plaintiff could not assert invasion of privacy because of the public interest in him as the "Boston Strangler"? Should it make any difference in this regard that defendant's motion picture dramatized, even though it did not falsify, the events depicted? Can there be dramatization without falsification?

B. IDENTIFICATION

LEVEY v. WARNER BROTHERS PICTURES

District Court, Southern District of New York, 1944.
57 F.Supp. 40.

BONDY, DISTRICT JUDGE. The plaintiff, Ethel Levey, claiming that her right of privacy has been violated by the production and exhibition of the motion picture "Yankee Doodle Dandy" by the defendant, Warner Bros. Pictures, Inc., brought this action under the Civil Rights Law of the State of New York, Consol. Laws, c. 6, to recover damages and to enjoin the further distribution and exhibition of the picture in this state in its present form.

The action was removed to this court from the Supreme Court of this state, on the ground of diversity of citizenship of the parties.

Section 51 of the Civil Rights Law of the State of New York provides that any person whose name, portrait or picture is used within the State of New York for advertising purposes or for the purposes of trade without his written consent first obtained, may maintain an equitable action against the person, firm or corporation so using his name, portrait or picture to prevent the use thereof, and may also sue to recover damages for injuries sustained by reason of such use.

To establish that her picture or portrait was used in the motion picture, the plaintiff told the story of her life. She described theatrical performances in which she took part with George M. Cohan and also the following events of her life, which she claims were featured in the picture:

She testified that in 1898, when she was seventeen years of age and had met with some success as an actress and singer in vaudeville, she was invited to join others in a room in a hotel in Chicago. There she met George M. Cohan for the first time. He was then about twenty years of age and appearing in another vaudeville with his father, mother and sister. Cohan proposed to her the first time they met. He gave her two songs which he had composed and which she sang the following Monday at the opening of the show in which she took a part. She became Cohan's sweetheart and continued to sing songs which he composed. In July, 1899, they were married and thereafter she took a leading part in the plays which he wrote and produced. She also testified that it was largely through her efforts that in 1904 Sam H. Harris, a producer, was induced to finance the production and exhibition of the play "Little Johnny Jones," which was one of the outstanding Cohan successes. In 1905 at the opening in Chicago of the musical play "Forty-Five Minutes From Broadway," written by her husband Cohan, she was in a box with him and his parents and heard the popular song "Mary" sung by Fay Templeton, a well-known actress. In December, 1906, the plaintiff and Cohan separated and in June, 1907, she obtained a divorce. In the same year Cohan married a girl with whom he lived until his death November 9, 1942.

After her divorce and until recently, the plaintiff spent most of her time abroad, where she married again in 1916.

In 1941 the defendant obtained the consent of George M. Cohan in writing, to produce and exhibit a motion picture based on his life and experiences and the right to use therein plays, songs and music written and composed by him.

In 1942, thirty-five years after the divorce, the defendant produced and exhibited in the State of New York the motion picture "Yankee Doodle Dandy" which was, as the plaintiff in her complaint characterizes it, "a dramatic and fictional biographic presentation of the life of one George M. Cohan, one of the foremost and successful actors, playwrights, composers, directors and theatrical producers of the early twentieth century and for many years thereafter."

The picture shows the life of George M. Cohan, more or less fictional, from the time of his birth, July 4, 1878, to 1940, when the President of the United States presented the Congressional Medal of Honor to him. In the picture Cohan is impersonated by James Cagney and a fictitious character "Mary" by Joan Leslie. At the beginning it shows Mary and Cohan, when advanced in years and towards the end of the theatrical career of Cohan, as husband and wife and at a time when the picture of Mary could not have any reference to the plaintiff. It does not disclose that Cohan ever was divorced and it gives the impression that Mary was the only woman he ever married. In the picture, which reverts to an earlier period of Cohan's life, Mary when about seventeen years of age, stage struck and ambitious for a theatrical career, after having seen Cohan perform on the stage, goes uninvited into his dressing room. He is still in his disguise of an old man with a beard. They dance for one another. When his disguise is removed, Mary is terrorized to discover that Cohan is a young man about twenty years of age. Cohan at once becomes interested in Mary and writes songs for her. Mary and Cohan meet Harris and together they succeed in obtaining financial aid for the production of "Little Johnny Jones" but in a manner entirely different from that in which plaintiff described, it was obtained. In the picture Mary is seen in a box with Cohan and Sam Harris at the first production of "Forty-Five Minutes From Broadway" in New York City in 1905. Fay Templeton, impersonated by Irene Manning, sings the song "Mary" which the picture reveals had been written for Mary and with the intention that it was to be sung by Mary. On this occasion Mary is seen wearing a wedding ring indicating for the first time that she and Cohan were married.

The picture features music and reproduces scenes from musical plays written and produced by Cohan not only during the comparatively few years during which he was married to the plaintiff, but also from innumerable other musical plays which he wrote and produced during his long and successful career as an actor, composer, author, playwright and producer. No use is made in the picture of the name Mrs. George M. Cohan or Ethel Levey, the stage name by which the plaintiff generally has been known. In the picture there is not reenacted by Joan Leslie any character played by the plaintiff. With one exception Mary never sings alone any song which was sung alone by plaintiff. Mary does not take a leading or conspicuous part in the picture. In it she is a member of the chorus and sings and dances as a member of the chorus. Joan Leslie, who impersonates Mary, does not look nor act like plaintiff. Similarities, if any, between the events of plaintiff's life and the episodes shown in the picture are too insignificant to characterize the plaintiff and are merely incidental to the theme of the picture. It may be that persons who knew the plaintiff or saw her act in plays from which scenes were reproduced in the picture may have been reminded that the plaintiff took part therein but neither the plaintiff herself nor any one who knew her or saw her act or heard her sing would reasonably be led to believe that Joan Leslie portrayed the plaintiff. The reproduction in the picture of songs plaintiff sang and of scenes in which she took part and the introduction of fictional characters and a largely fictional treatment of Cohan's life may hurt plaintiff's feelings but they do not violate her right of privacy.

The right of privacy in this state exists only to the extent that it has been granted by statute, the enactment of which followed the decision by the Court of Appeals of this state in Roberson v. Rochester Folding Box Co., 171 N.Y. 538, 64 N.E. 442, 59 L.R.A. 478, 89 Am.St. Rep. 828, holding that under the laws of this state as theretofore existing a person whose actual portrait has been used for advertising without his consent did not have any redress. "The statute is in part, at least, penal, and should be construed accordingly," Binns v. Vitagraph Co., 210 N.Y. 51, 55, 103 N.E. 1108, 1110, L.R.A.1915C, 839, Ann.Cas.1915B, 1024, and it accordingly has been strictly construed in this state. See Humiston v. Universal Film Manufacturing Co., 189 App.Div. 467, 476, 178 N.Y.S. 752; Pfaudler v. Pfaudler Co., 114 Misc. 477, 186 N.Y.S. 725, affirmed without opinion 197 App.Div. 921, 188 N.Y.S. 946; Freed v. Loew's Inc., 175 Misc. 616, 24 N.Y.S.2d 679. The words in the statute "portrait or picture" of a person require more than a mere picture of a scene suggested by a play. They require a clear representation of a person whether by photograph, statute, imitation or word painting. They require a representation of a person at least approaching likeness.

In the photoplay and in its press exploitation book the defendant states that "Yankee Doodle Dandy" is based on the story of George M. Cohan or that it is the life story of George M. Cohan. These statements do not suggest that Mary in appearance, personality, character, mannerism or action resembles the plaintiff or represents the plaintiff.

Under a picture showing Mary and Cagney in a box it is stated "Mr. and Mrs. George M. Cohan as portrayed by Joan Leslie and James Cagney, appearing in Warner Bros. 'Yankee Doodle Dandy' the star spangled story of America's number one showman George M. Cohan." This reference to Mr. and Mrs. George M. Cohan does represent that the fictional Mary is the wife of Cohan but it does not represent that she is the plaintiff. In view of the fact that the picture does not disclose any divorce and gives the impression that Mary was the only Mrs. Cohan, it can not be said that plaintiff is portrayed in that picture.

The motion picture does not sufficiently portray or picture the plaintiff to justify the conclusion that the defendant violated any right of privacy afforded her by the Civil Rights Law.

The defendant accordingly is entitled to a decree dismissing the complaint.

Questions

1. Does "the fact that the picture does not disclose any divorce" serve to negate identification with plaintiff, or does it rather place plaintiff in a "false light"? See the discussion of "false light" privacy actions in the next chapter. Since plaintiff had remarried, could she claim that the motion picture was defamatory?

2. Would the result have been different if the "facts" contained in the defendant's motion picture had instead been presented in book form in what purported to be a serious biography of George M. Cohan?

TOSCANI v. HERSEY

Supreme Court, Appellate Division, First Department, 1946.
271 App.Div. 445, 65 N.Y.S.2d 814.

CALLAHAN, JUSTICE. This appeal presents the question of the sufficiency of two causes of action in plaintiff's complaint which attempt to set forth claims for damages under Section 51 of the Civil Rights Law. The "Fourth" cause of action refers to a novel published by appellant, and the "Fifth" cause of action to a written play published by him, both of which bore the title: "A Bell for Adano." For the purpose of this appeal we may consider the causes of action attacked as if they were one, for the same legal question is presented as to each.

Section 50 of the Civil Rights Law provides: "A person, firm or corporation that uses for advertising purposes, or for the purposes of trade, the name, portrait or picture of any living person without having first obtained the written consent of such person * * * is guilty of a misdemeanor."

Section 51 of the same law, in so far as material, reads as follows: "Any person whose name, portrait or picture is used within the state for advertising purposes or for the purposes of trade without the written consent [of said person] first obtained * * * may * * * sue and recover damages for any injuries sustained by reason of such use * *."

The gravamen of the causes of action attacked is that in the novel and play referred to, the events and acts narrated in describing the central figure of the story purport to relate to a person fictitiously called "Major Victor Joppolo," who is described as the senior civil affairs officer of the Allied Military Government in a town in Sicily, which is likewise fictitiously called Adano. The events and acts so narrated are alleged by plaintiff to relate, in the main, to events and acts of and concerning him, and that he was in fact the senior civil affairs officer of the Allied Military Government in the town of Licata, Sicily, during its occupation by the Allied Armies of World War II.

Plaintiff calls this narration a "portrayal" of the plaintiff, and an exploitation of his acts, life and personality, and says that such a portrayal constitutes a violation of the statute. * * *

Sections 50 and 51 were considered and construed in Binns v. Vitagraph Co. of America, 210 N.Y. 51, 103 N.E. 1108, L.R.A.1915C, 839, Ann.Cas.1915B, 1024. In that case a moving picture was published based on true occurrences in the life of one John Binns, who had been a radio operator on a steamship, and had been the first to use wireless to broadcast distress signals at sea. The picture was largely fictional in form, but the name of John Binns was used in the scenario, and in advertisements of the picture, and an actor was made up to look like and impersonate Binns.

The court held that the statute had been violated and that Binns had a cause of action under the Civil Rights Law. The court pointed out that the statute was, in part at least, penal, and should be construed accordingly. It further pointed out that not every use of the name, portrait or picture of a living person was prohibited, but only those for trade purposes. It found that in the case before it the moving picture was not that of a current event, but largely a product of the imagination, and that it was actionable.

In the course of its opinion in the Binns case, supra, the court, in discussing the effect of the use of an actor to portray Binns, said (210 N.Y. p. 57, 103 N.E. 1110): "A picture within the meaning of the statute is not necessarily a photograph of the living person, but includes any representation of such person. The picture represented by the defendant to be a true picture of the plaintiff, and exhibited to the public as such, was intended to be, and it was, a representation of plaintiff. The defendant is in no position to say that the picture does not represent the plaintiff, or that it was an actual picture of a person made up to look like and impersonate the plaintiff."

The plaintiff in the present action relies largely on the statement found in the first sentence of the paragraph quoted to support his "Fourth" and "Fifth" causes of action. He says that it indicates a construction of the statute by the Court of Appeals sufficiently broad to support a cause of action based on a word portrayal of the events in the life of a living person, even where fictitious names appear and no picture or similar likeness is used. In other words, he says that "portrait or picture," as used in the statute, has been construed to include any representation of a living person which would include one in words or substance describing events that would be recognizable as acts and events of and concerning a living person.

We do not place any such construction on the statement found in the opinion in the Binns case, supra, nor upon the statute itself. Considered in the light of the facts involved in the Binns case, supra, and the questions that were being discussed, the statement relied on was merely a holding that where the name of a living person is used in advertising for trade purposes, coupled with a picture of a person represented to be a likeness of that named person, there has been a violation of the statute, even though the person posing for the picture was not in fact the person named. But, in the present case, no living person was named, and no picture or other similar likeness of anybody was used.

Giving the language used in Section 51 its ordinary meaning, we find that it was not intended to give a living person a cause of action for damages based on the mere portrayal of acts and events concerning a person designated fictitiously in a novel or play merely because the actual experiences of the living person had been similar to the acts and events so narrated. To so construe the statute would broaden its scope far beyond anything warranted by the meaning that would ordinarily be ascribed to the words "name, portrait or picture," especially when they are considered in the light of the history of the statute.

The order so far as appealed from should be reversed with $20 costs and disbursements to the defendant-appellant and the motion to dismiss the "Fourth" and "Fifth" causes of action granted, with leave to the defendant-appellant to answer within twenty days after service of the order with notice of entry thereof.

Order reversed with $20 costs and disbursements to the defendant-appellant and the motion to dismiss the fourth and fifth causes of action granted, with leave to the defendant-appellant to answer within twenty days after service of order, with notice of entry thereof. Order filed.

MARTIN, P.J., and TOWNLEY and GLENNON, JJ., concur.

DORE, J., dissents and votes to affirm.

DORE, JUSTICE (dissenting).

The language of the statute, Civil Rights Law, § 50, is in the disjunctive: the cause of action may be based on the use for trade purposes of (1) the name *or* (2) portrait *or* (3) picture of a person without his consent.

The Court of Appeals construing the meaning of this statute has expressly held that a picture is not necessarily a photograph "but includes *any* representation of such person". Italics mine. Binns v. Vitagraph Co. of America, 210 N.Y. 51, 57, 103 N.E. 1108, 1110, L.R.A.1915C, 839, Ann.Cas.1915B, 1024. Reason as well as authority supports the construction. A person may be pictured or portrayed through the medium of words as well as through other art media such as paintings or sculpture.

This does not mean, as suggested, that it may be a violation of the statute for a writer to base a novel or play on *events* that occurred in the life of any living person. Basing the novel or play on certain events is one thing. Reproducing or portraying in fiction for trade purposes a living person as the chief character in a play without his consent is quite another. For the purpose of this appeal we must assume as true all the facts alleged in the fourth and fifth causes of action challenged by the motion to dismiss. The pleadings allege that plaintiff was the senior civil affairs officer whose person is portrayed for trade purposes without his consent and the reference is not merely to casual or incidental events in plaintiff's life, but the portrayal of his person is the primary subject matter of both novel and play. Defendant has capitalized on plaintiff's identity in fiction for his own commercial trade purposes without plaintiff's consent.

Special Term correctly held the causes of action sufficient and denied the motion to dismiss.

Accordingly, I dissent and vote to affirm.

Questions

1. Is the court correct in rejecting the plaintiff's argument that a "word portrayal" should be regarded as the equivalent of a "portrait or picture"

within the meaning of the New York statute? Recall Walt Disney Productions v. The Air Pirates, supra.

2. Under the court's construction of the New York statute would the result have been different if the defendant had produced a motion picture rather than a live stage play? Would the fact that there then would have been "a person posing [as the plaintiff] for the picture" have constituted a violation of the statute? Would the court have found for the defendant, in any event, if the plaintiff's true name were not used in the motion picture? Would such a result have been justified given (as Justice Dore points out) the disjunctive structure of the statute?

BERNSTEIN v. NATIONAL BROADCASTING CO.

United States District Court, District of Columbia, 1955.
129 F.Supp. 817.

[Earlier and later portions of this opinion are set forth at p. 710 supra.]

(2) The admitted facts show there was no publication by defendant of the program as the plaintiff's prior history. Not only was there no identification of plaintiff by name in either the telecast or defendant's advertisements thereof, but he was doubly insulated from identification by designation of the television character as "Dave Crouch" and his own trial as "Charles Harris." Except to one already familiar with the facts or one who had stumbled on the reported court decision or the old newspaper items, there was nothing to link Charles Harris with any Charles Bernstein, much less plaintiff. To one who viewed the telecast not already aware of plaintiff's past or Miss Strayer's connection with him, the only link between Dave Crouch and Charles S. Bernstein of Front Royal, Virginia, and the District of Columbia was the alleged physical resemblance of the actor to the Charles Bernstein of *twenty years before*.[1] This is too tenuous a thread on which to permit a jury to hang identification, with consequent liability for invasion of privacy.

Plaintiff argues there were three categories of people as to whom there was identification: first, those who knew about the incidents of plaintiff's past life; second, those who remembered the newspaper articles twenty years before and were able to connect them with the broadcast; and third, those who did not know of Mr. Bernstein's past life but, as the result of the telecast, learned about it "because they were told by other people."

As to persons who already knew the facts of plaintiff's life there was no invasion of plaintiff's privacy by defendant. Although the telecast may have revived their memories, it revealed nothing they did

---

1. If taken literally, the court finds incredible plaintiff's statement ("Answer of Plaintiff to Information Requested by Defendant," filed December 10, 1954) that seventeen named persons in Washington, Front Royal, and Philadelphia, who had no knowledge of his past life, "as a result of the telecast" identified plaintiff as the person whose life story was portrayed. If plaintiff means that as the result of the telecast third persons who knew the basis of the television play identified him to the named persons, this is credible; but it is not the basis of an action against the defendant.

not already know. The gist of an action for invasion of privacy is a wrongful disclosure *by the defendant.* The identification of plaintiff to viewers of the telecast was not by act of the defendant, but by use of their own thought processes. If these people were so thoughtless as to harass plaintiff with calls, as he contends, such harassment was the product of their own deduction and lack of tact and consideration for plaintiff. Persons who recalled the newspaper articles and connected them with plaintiff are indistinguishable from the first group, for the identification to them was through their own mental operations.[2]

As to the third category, those who did not know of Mr. Bernstein's past life but, as the result of the telecast, learned about it "because they were told by other people," counsel for plaintiff very frankly admitted, "We are right in the open spaces." He cited in support of his position a number of cases holding that the author of a defamation is responsible for its repetition by another if the defamation is uttered or published under such circumstances as to time, place, and condition that a repetition or secondary publication is the natural and probable consequence of the original defamation, and for the damage resulting therefrom. The rule varies in different jurisdictions.

But in defamation, there can, of course, be no repetition of a defamatory statement unless the statement is first made. Hence, none of the cited cases deal with an attempt to remedy the absence of proof of publication by defendant, an essential element, by proof of repetition of the statement by third persons. Similarly, in invasion of privacy, where defendant has published facts in such a way that there has been no disclosure to persons not already aware of them, proof of disclosure or identification by third persons to others who lacked prior knowledge cannot be used as a substitute for proof of original disclosure by defendant. In estimating the extent of the injury caused by an invasion of privacy, as in assessing damages for defamation, foreseeable repetition by third persons to whom the defendant disclosed plaintiff's

---

2. Plaintiff has cited to the court many cases involving slander or libel in which it was held that the author of a defamatory statement is liable for damage to the reputation of complainant, even though the latter was not named, if reasonable people knowing some of the circumstances would take the libel complained of to relate to complainant. It is to be remembered that the gist of an action for defamation is the damage to complainant's reputation in the eyes of third persons. It is therefore unimportant whether the identification was completed or merely set in motion by the author of the defamatory statement; whereas in an action for invasion of privacy the gist of the action is the damage to plaintiff's feelings resulting from a wrongful disclosure by defendant. The one invasion of privacy case cited on this point is Walcher v. Loew's, Inc., D.C.Mo., 1948, 129 F.Supp. 815, in which plaintiff, a former Army nurse stationed on Corregidor, sued defendant for damages resulting from exhibition of the motion picture "They Were Expendable," which had been publicized widely, both in book and picture form, as based on the true experiences of actual people, although fictitious names were used. Included was the story of a romantic attachment of an Army nurse for a Naval lieutenant. This case is distinguishable on its facts from the case at bar. There, plaintiff alleged the picture was released for exhibition *after* she had become identified and known to the general public as the character portrayed in the book, and the affairs alleged to have been disclosed were of an inherently private nature. In this case, it is alleged that identification was made by persons who viewed the program in the light of their own knowledge of plaintiff's life, and the affairs alleged to have been disclosed were matters of public record.

private affairs is a factor to be considered. But such evidence is admissible only on the issue of damages, after proof of commission of the tort by the defendant.

The identification by third persons who communicated their own knowledge of the facts on which "The Big Story" was based, would be an original publication by them, for which they—not defendant—would be liable, if such disclosure be wrongful. The same is true of the alleged identification of plaintiff by virtue of the news item in the Washington Daily News of January 18, 1952. If there was identification by the News, the defendant is not chargeable with the act of the newspaper company.[3] The court holds there are no facts on which the court could permit a jury to find identification by defendant, assuming every allegation by plaintiff to be true.

Questions

1. If the news item in the Washington Daily News of January 18, 1952 constituted a "key" which served to identify plaintiff in defendant's broadcast, is the court correct in concluding that "defendant is not chargeable with the act of the newspaper company"? Is it significant that defendant did not refer in its broadcast to the newspaper article?

2. Did the use of reporter Martha Strayer's true name in defendant's broadcast create a "key" by which plaintiff could be identified?

3. Is there an invasion of privacy if that which is disclosed was previously known by all who could identify the plaintiff as the one referred to in the disclosure? May not the plaintiff, in such circumstances suffer an (additional) injury, of the type protected by the right of privacy, by reason of the disclosure? If so, is it then important that the only ones who could recognize Bernstein in N.B.C.'s broadcast were those who previously knew of his participation in the events depicted? Suppose such persons were able to recognize Bernstein only because of their prior knowledge, but nevertheless by reason of the N.B.C. broadcast were made aware of certain facts about Bernstein of which they were previously unaware—should this constitute an invasion of privacy? Should it matter whether such previously unknown "facts" were not in fact true? Should it matter whether or not such facts related to intimate, private acts of the plaintiff?

4. Can there ever be an identification of a given individual (whether or not his true name is used) without extrinsic information that relates the person depicted to such individual? Should it matter when such extrinsic information is obtained?

C. FIRST AMENDMENT DEFENSE

COX BROADCASTING CORP. v. COHN

Supreme Court of the United States, 1975.
420 U.S. 469, 95 S.Ct. 1029, 43 L.Ed.2d 328.

---

3. One news item in one paper on the day of the telecast cannot be held a basis for finding general public identification prior to defendant's telecast, such as was alleged in the Walcher case, supra.

Mr. Justice White delivered the opinion of the Court.

The issue before us in this case is whether consistently with the First and Fourteenth Amendments a State may extend a cause of action for damages for invasion of privacy caused by the publication of the name of a deceased rape victim which was publicly revealed in connection with the prosecution of the crime.

I

In August 1971, appellee's 17-year-old-daughter was the victim of a rape and did not survive the incident. Six youths were soon indicted for murder and rape. Although there was substantial press coverage of the crime and of subsequent developments, the identity of the victim was not disclosed pending trial, perhaps because of Ga.Code Ann. § 26–9901 [1] which makes it a misdemeanor to publish or broadcast the name or identity of a rape victim. In April 1972, some eight months later, the six defendants appeared in court. Five pled guilty to rape or attempted rape, the charge of murder having been dropped. The guilty pleas were accepted by the court, and the trial of the defendant pleading not guilty was set for a later date.

In the course of the proceedings that day, appellant Wassell,[2] a reporter covering the incident for his employer, learned the name of the victim from an examination of the indictments which were made available for his inspection in the courtroom.[3] That the name of the

---

1. "It shall be unlawful for any news media or any other person to print and publish, broadcast, televise, or disseminate through any other medium of public dissemination or cause to be printed and published, broadcast, televised, or disseminated in any newspaper, magazine, periodical or other publication published in this State or through any radio or television broadcast originating in the State the name or identity of any female who may have been raped or upon whom an assault with intent to commit rape may have been made. Any person or corporation violating the provisions of this section shall, upon conviction, be punished as for a misdemeanor."

Three other States have similar statutes. See Fla.Stat.Ann. §§ 794.03, 794.04; S.C. Code § 16–81; Wis.Stat.Ann. § 942.02. The Wisconsin Supreme Court upheld the constitutionality of the Wisconsin statute in State v. Evjue, 253 Wis. 146, 33 N.W.2d 305 (1948). The South Carolina statute was involved in Nappier v. Jefferson Standard Life Insurance Co., 322 F.2d 502, 505 (C.A.4 1963), but no constitutional challenge to the statute was made. In Hunter v. Washington Post, 102 The Daily Washington L.Rptr. 1561 (1974), the D.C. Superior Court denied the defendant's motion for judgment on the pleadings based upon constitutional grounds in an action brought for invasion of privacy resulting from the defendant's publication identifying the plaintiff as a rape victim and giving her name, age, and address.

2. Wassell was employed at the time in question as a news staff reporter for WSB–TV and had been so employed for the prior nine years. His function was to investigate newsworthy stories and make televised news reports. He was assigned the coverage of the trial of the young men accused of the rape and murder of Cynthia Cohn on the morning of April 10, 1972, the day it began, and had not been involved with the story previously. He was present during the entire hearing that day except for the first 30 minutes. App., at 16–17.

3. Wassell has described the way in which he obtained the information reported in the broadcast as follows:

"The information on which I prepared the said report was obtained from several sources. First, by personally attending and taking notes of the said trial and the subsequent transfer of four of the six defendants to the Fulton County Jail, I obtained personal knowledge of the events that transpired during the trial of this action and the said

victim appears in the indictments and that the indictments were public records available for inspection are not disputed.[4] Later that day, Wassell broadcast over the facilities of station WSB–TV, a television station owned by appellant Cox Broadcasting Corporation, a news report concerning the court proceedings. The report named the victim of the crime and was repeated the following day.[5]

In May 1972, appellee brought an action for money damages against appellants, relying on § 26–9901 and claiming that his right to privacy had been invaded by the television broadcasts giving the name of his deceased daughter. Appellants admitted the broadcasts but claimed that they were privileged under both state law and the First and Fourteenth Amendments. The trial court, rejecting appellants' constitutional claims and holding that the Georgia statute gave a civil remedy to those injured by its violation, granted summary judgment to appellee as to liability, with the determination of damages to await trial by jury.

On appeal, the Georgia Supreme Court, in its initial opinion, held that the trial court had erred in construing § 26–9901 to extend a civil cause of action for invasion of privacy and thus found is unnecessary to consider the constitutionality of the statute. 231 Ga. 60, 200 S.E.2d 127 (1973). The court went on to rule, however, that the complaint stated a cause of action "for the invasion of appellee's right of privacy, or for the

---

transfer of the defendants. Such personal observation and notes were the primary and almost exclusive source of the information upon which the said news report was based. Secondly, during a recess of the said trial, I approached the clerk of the court, who was sitting directly in front of the bench, and requested to see a copy of the indictments. In open court, I was handed the indictments, both the murder and the rape indictments, and was allowed to examine fully this document. As is shown by the said indictments * * * the name of the said Cynthia Cohn appears in clear type. Moreover, no attempt was made by the clerk or anyone else to withhold the name and identity of the victim from me or from anyone else and the said indictments apparently were available for public inspection upon request." App., at 17–18.

4. The indictments are in pertinent part as follows:

"THE GRAND JURORS selected, chosen and sworn for the County of Fulton * * * in the name and behalf of the citizens of Georgia, charge and accuse [the defendants] with the offense of:—

"RAPE

"for that said accused, in the County of Fulton and State of Georgia, on the 18th day of August, 1971 did have carnal knowledge of the person of Cynthia Leslie Cohn, a female, forcibly and against her will * *." App., at 22–24.

"THE GRAND JURORS selected, chosen and sworn for the County of Fulton * * * in the name and behalf of the citizens of Georgia, charge and accuse [the defendants] with the offense of:—

"MURDER

"for that said accused, in the County of Fulton and State of Georgia, on the 18th day of August, 1971 did while in the commission of the offense of Rape, a felony, upon the person of Cynthia Leslie Cohn, a female human being, cause her death by causing her to suffocate * * *." App., at 24–25.

5. The relevant portion of the transcript of the televised report reads as follows:

"Six youths went on trial today for the murder-rape of a teenaged girl.

"The six Sandy Springs High School boys were charged with murder and rape in the death of seventeen year old Cynthia Cohn following a drinking party last August 18th.

"The tragic death of the high school girl shocked the entire Sandy Springs community. Today the six boys had their day in court.

"* * * *." App., at 19–20.

tort of public disclosure"—a "common law tort exist[ing] in this jurisdiction without the help of the statute that the trial judge in this case relied on." 231 Ga., at 62, 200 S.E.2d, at 130. Although the privacy invaded was not that of the deceased victim, the father was held to have stated a claim for invasion of his own privacy by reason of the publication of his daughter's name. The court explained, however, that liability did not follow as a matter of law and that summary judgment was improper; whether the public disclosure of the name actually invaded appellee's "zone of privacy," and if so, to what extent, were issues to be determined by the trier of fact. Also, "in formulating such an issue for determination by the fact-finder, it is reasonable to require the appellee to prove that the appellants invaded his privacy with wilful or negligent disregard for the fact that reasonable men would find the invasion highly offensive." 231 Ga., at 64, 200 S.E.2d, at 131. The Georgia Supreme Court did agree with the trial court, however, that the First and Fourteenth Amendments did not, as a matter of law, require judgment for appellants. The court concurred with the statement in Briscoe v. Reader's Digest Association, Inc., 4 Cal.3d 529, 541, 93 Cal.Rptr. 866, 874, 483 P.2d 34, 42 (1971), that "the rights guaranteed by the First Amendment do not require total abrogation of the right to privacy. The goals sought by each may be achieved with a minimum of intrusion upon the other."

Upon motion for rehearing the Georgia court countered the argument that the victim's name was a matter of public interest and could be published with impunity by relying on § 26–9901 as an authoritative declaration of state policy that the name of a rape victim was not a matter of public concern. This time the court felt compelled to determine the constitutionality of the statute and sustained it as a "legitimate limitation on the right of freedom of expression contained in the First Amendment." The court could discern "no public interest or general concern about the identity of the victim of such a crime as will make the right to disclose the identity of the victim rise to the level of First Amendment protection." 231 Ga., at 68–69, 200 S.E.2d, at 133–134.

We postponed decision as to our jurisdiction over this appeal to the hearing on the merits. 415 U.S. 912, 94 S.Ct. 1406, 39 L.Ed.2d 466 (1974). We conclude that the Court has jurisdiction and reverse the judgment of the Georgia Supreme Court.

* * *

III

Georgia stoutly defends both § 26–9901 and the State's common law privacy action challenged here. Her claims are not without force, for powerful arguments can be made, and have been made, that however it may be ultimately defined, there *is* a zone of privacy surrounding every individual, a zone within which the State may protect him from intrusion by the press, with all its attendant publicity.[15] Indeed, the central thesis of the root article by Warren and Brandeis, The Right of Privacy, 4 Harv.L.Rev. 193, 196 (1890), was that the press was overstepping its prerogatives by publishing essentially private information and that there should be a remedy for the alleged abuses.[16]

More compellingly, the century has experienced a strong tide running in favor of the so-called right of privacy. In 1967, we noted that "[i]t has been said that a 'right of privacy' has been recognized at common law in 30 States plus the District of Columbia and by statute in four States." Time, Inc. v. Hill, 385 U.S. 374, 383 n. 7, 87 S.Ct. 534, 539, 17 L.Ed.2d 456 (1967). We there cited the 1964 edition of Prosser's Law of Torts. The 1971 edition of that same source states that "[i]n one form or another, the right of privacy is by this time recognized and accepted in all but a very few jurisdictions." Prosser, id. (4th ed. 1971), at 804 (footnote omitted). Nor is it irrelevant here that the right of privacy is no recent arrival in the jurisprudence of Georgia, which has embraced the right in some form since 1905 when the Georgia Supreme Court decided the leading case of Pavesich v. New England Life Ins. Co., 122 Ga. 190, 50 S.E. 68 (1905).

These are impressive credentials for a right of privacy,[17] but we should recognize that we do not have at issue here an action for the

---

15. See Emerson, The System of Freedom of Expression, 544–562 (1970); Konvitz, Privacy and the Law: A Philosophical Prelude, 31 Law & Contemp.Prob. 272 (1966); Bloustein, Privacy as an Aspect of Human Dignity: An Answer to Dean Prosser, 39 N.Y.U.L.Rev. 962 (1964).

16. "Of the desirability—indeed of the necessity—of some such protection [of the right of privacy], there can, it is believed, be no doubt. The press is overstepping in every direction the obvious bounds of propriety and of decency. Gossip is no longer the resource of the idle and of the vicious, but has become a trade, which is pursued with industry as well as effrontery. To satisfy a prurient taste the details of sexual relations are spread broadcast in the columns of the daily papers. To occupy the indolent, column upon column is filled with idle gossip, which can only be procured by intrusion upon the domestic circle. The intensity and complexity of life, attendant upon advancing civilization, have rendered necessary some retreat from the world, and man, under the refining influence of culture, has become more sensitive to publicity, so that solitude and privacy have become more essential to the individual; but modern enterprise and invention have, through invasions upon his privacy, subjected him to mental pain and distress, far greater than could be inflicted by mere bodily injury. Nor is the harm wrought by such invasions confined to the suffering of those who may be made the subjects of journalistic or other enterprise. In this, as in other branches of commerce, the supply creates the demand. Each crop of unseemly gossip, thus harvested, becomes the seed of more, and, in direct proportion to its circulation, results in a lowering of social standards and of morality. Even gossip apparently harmless, when widely and persistently circulated, is potent for evil. It both belittles and perverts. It belittles by inverting the relative importance of things, thus dwarfing the thoughts and aspirations of a people. When personal gossip attains the dignity of print, and crowds the space available for matters of real interest to the community, what wonder that the ignorant and thoughtless mistake its relative importance. Easy of comprehension, appealing to that weak side of human nature which is never wholly cast down by the misfortunes and frailties of our neighbors, no one can be surprised that it usurps the place of interest in brains capable of other things. Triviality destroys at once robustness of thought and delicacy of feeling. No enthusiasm can flourish, no generous impulse can survive under its blighting influence."

17. See also Time, Inc. v. Hill, supra, 385 U.S., at 404, 87 S.Ct., at 550 (opinion of Harlan, J.), 385 U.S., at 412–415, 87 S.Ct., at 554–556 (opinion of Fortas, J.).

invasion of privacy involving the appropriation of one's name or photograph, a physical or other tangible intrusion into a private area, or a publication of otherwise private information that is also false although perhaps not defamatory. The version of the privacy tort now before us—termed in Georgia "the tort of public disclosure," 231 Ga., at 62, 200 S.E.2d, at 130—is that in which the plaintiff claims the right to be free from unwanted publicity about his private affairs, which, although wholly true, would be offensive to a person of ordinary sensibilities. Because the gravamen of the claimed injury is the publication of information, whether true or not, the dissemination of which is embarrassing or otherwise painful to an individual, it is here that claims of privacy most directly confront the constitutional freedoms of speech and press. The face-off is apparent, and the appellants urge upon us the broad holding that the press may not be made criminally or civilly liable for publishing information that is neither false nor misleading but absolutely accurate, however damaging it may be to reputation or individual sensibilities.

It is true that in defamation actions, where the protected interest is personal reputation, the prevailing view is that truth is a defense;[18] and the message of New York Times v. Sullivan, 376 U.S. 254, 94 S.Ct. 710, 11 L.Ed.2d 686 (1964); Garrison v. Louisiana, 379 U.S. 64, 85 S.Ct. 209, 13 L.Ed.2d 125 (1964); Curtis Publishing Co. v. Butts, 388 U.S. 130, 87 S.Ct. 1975, 18 L.Ed.2d 1094 (1967), and like cases is that the defense of truth is constitutionally required where the subject of the publication is a public official or public figure. What is more, the defamed public official or public figure must prove not only that the publication is false but that it was knowingly so or was circulated with reckless disregard for its truth or falsity. Similarly, where the interest at issue is privacy rather than reputation and the right claimed is to be free from the publication of false or misleading information about one's affairs, the target of the publication must prove knowing or reckless falsehood where the materials published, although assertedly private, are "matters of public interest." Time, Inc. v. Hill, supra, 385 U.S., at 387–388, 87 S.Ct., at 541–542.[19]

The Court has nevertheless carefully left open the question whether the First and Fourteenth Amendments require that truth be recog-

---

18. See American Law Institute, Restatement of Torts (Second) § 582 (Tentative Draft No. 20) (April 25, 1974); Prosser, Handbook of the Law of Torts § 116 (4th ed. 1971). Under the common law, truth was not a complete defense to prosecutions for criminal libel, although it was in civil actions. Several jurisdictions in this country have provided by statute, however, that the defense of truth in civil actions requires a showing that the publication was made for good motives or for justifiable ends. See id., at 796–797.

19. In another "false light" invasion of privacy case before us this Term, Cantrell v. Forest City Publishing Co., 419 U.S. 245, 95 S.Ct. 465, 42 L.Ed.2d 419 (1974), we observed that we had, in that case, "no occasion to consider whether a State may constitutionally apply a more relaxed standard of liability for a publisher or broadcaster of false statements injurious to a private individual under a false-light theory of invasion of privacy, or whether the constitutional standard announced in Time, Inc. v. Hill applies to all false-light cases. Cf. Gertz v. Welch, Inc., 418 U.S. 323, 94 S.Ct. 2997, 41 L.Ed.2d 789."

nized as a defense in a defamation action brought by a private person as distinguished from a public official or public figure. *Garrison* held that where criticism is of a public official and his conduct of public business, "the interest in private reputation is overborne by the larger public interest, secured by the Constitution, in the dissemination of truth," 379 U.S., at 72–73, 85 S.Ct., at 215 (footnote omitted), but recognized that "different interests may be involved where purely private libels, totally unrelated to public affairs, are concerned; therefore, nothing we say today is to be taken as intimating any views as to the impact of the constitutional guarantees in the discrete area of purely private libels." Id., at 72 n. 8, 85 S.Ct., at 215. In similar fashion, Time v. Hill, supra, expressly saved the question whether truthful publication of very private matters unrelated to public affairs could be constitutionally proscribed. 385 U.S., at 383, n. 7, 87 S.Ct., at 539.

Those precedents, as well as other considerations, counsel similar caution here. In this sphere of collision between claims of privacy and those of the free press, the interests on both sides are plainly rooted in the traditions and significant concerns of our society. Rather than address the broader question whether truthful publications may ever be subjected to civil or criminal liability consistently with the First and Fourteenth Amendments, or to put it another way, whether the State may ever define and protect an area of privacy free from unwanted publicity in the press, it is appropriate to focus on the narrower interface between press and privacy that this case presents, namely, whether the State may impose sanctions on the accurate publication of the name of a rape victim obtained from public records—more specifically, from judicial records which are maintained in connection with a public prosecution and which themselves are open to public inspection. We are convinced that the State may not do so.

In the first place, in a society in which each individual has but limited time and resources with which to observe at first hand the operations of his government, he relies necessarily upon the press to bring to him in convenient form the facts of those operations. Great responsibility is accordingly placed upon the news media to report fully and accurately the proceedings of government, and official records and documents open to the public are the basic data of governmental operations. Without the information provided by the press most of us and many of our representatives would be unable to vote intelligently or to register opinions on the administration of government generally. With respect to judicial proceedings in particular, the function of the press serves to guarantee the fairness of trials and to bring to bear the beneficial effects of public scrutiny upon the administration of justice. See Sheppard v. Maxwell, 384 U.S. 333, 350, 86 S.Ct. 1507, 1515, 16 L.Ed.2d 600 (1966).

Appellee has claimed in this litigation that the efforts of the press have infringed his right to privacy by broadcasting to the world the fact that his daughter was a rape victim. The commission of crime, prosecutions resulting from it, and judicial proceedings arising from the prosecutions, however, are without question events of legitimate concern to the public and consequently fall within the responsibility of the press to report the operations of government.

The special protected nature of accurate reports of judicial proceedings has repeatedly been recognized. This Court, in an opinion written by Mr. Justice Douglas, has said:

> A trial is a public event. What transpires in the court room is public property. If a transcript of the court proceedings had been published, we suppose none would claim that the judge could punish the publisher for contempt. And we see no difference though the conduct of the attorneys, of the jury, or even of the judge himself, may have reflected on the court. *Those who see and hear what transpired can report it with impunity.* There is no special perquisite of the judiciary which enables it, as distinguished from other institutions of democratic government, to suppress, edit, or censor events which transpire in proceedings before it. Craig v. Harney, 331 U.S. 367, 374, 67 S.Ct. 1249, 1254, 91 L.Ed. 1546 (1947) (emphasis added).

See also Sheppard v. Maxwell, supra, 384 U.S., at 362–363, 86 S.Ct., at 1522; Estes v. Texas, 381 U.S. 532, 541–542, 85 S.Ct. 1628, 1632–1633, 14 L.Ed.2d 543 (1965); Pennekamp v. Florida, 328 U.S. 331, 66 S.Ct. 1029, 90 L.Ed. 1295 (1946); Bridges v. California, 314 U.S. 252, 62 S.Ct. 190, 86 L.Ed. 192 (1941).

The developing law surrounding the tort of invasion of privacy recognizes a privilege in the press to report the events of judicial proceedings. The Warren and Brandeis article, supra, noted that the proposed new right would be limited in the same manner as actions for libel and slander where such a publication was a privileged communication: "the right to privacy is not invaded by any publication made in a court of justice * * * and (at least in many jurisdictions) reports of any such proceedings would in some measure be accorded a like privilege." [20]

The Restatement of Torts, § 867, embraced an action for privacy.[21] Tentative Draft No. 13 of the Restatement, Second, Torts, §§ 652A–652E, divides the privacy tort into four branches;[22] and with respect to the wrong of giving unwanted publicity about private life, the commentary to § 652D states that "[t]here is no liability when the defendant merely gives further publicity to information about the plaintiff which is already public. Thus there is no liability for giving publicity to facts

---

20. Warren & Brandeis, supra, at 216–217.

21. American Law Institute, Restatement of Torts § 867 (1939).

22. American Law Institute, Restatement, Second, Torts, §§ 652A–652E (Tentative Draft No. 13) (April 27, 1967). The four branches are "unreasonable intrusion upon the seclusion of another" (§ 652B), "appropriation of the other's name or likeness" (§ 652C), "unreasonable publicity given to the other's private life" (§ 652D), and "publicity which unreasonably places the other in a false light before the public" (§ 652E). See § 652A. The same categorization is suggested in Prosser, Handbook of the Law of Torts, supra, § 117; Prosser, Privacy, 48 Cal.L.Rev. 383 (1960).

about the plaintiff's life which are matters of public record * * *."[23] The same is true of the separate tort of physically or otherwise intruding upon the seclusion or private affairs of another. Section 652B, Comment c, provides that "there is no liability for examination of a public record concerning the plaintiff, or of documents which the plaintiff is required to keep and make available for public inspection."[24] According to this draft, ascertaining and publishing the contents of public records are simply not within the reach of these kinds of privacy actions.[25]

Thus even the prevailing law of invasion of privacy generally recognizes that the interests in privacy fade when the information involved already appears on the public record. The conclusion is compelling when viewed in terms of the First and Fourteenth Amendments and in light of the public interest in a vigorous press. The Georgia cause of action for invasion of privacy through public disclosure of the name of a rape victim imposes sanctions on pure expression—the content of a publication—and not conduct or a combination of speech and nonspeech elements that might otherwise be open to regulation or prohibition. See United States v. O'Brien, 391 U.S. 367, 376–377, 88 S.Ct. 1673, 1678–1679, 20 L.Ed.2d 672 (1968). The publication of truthful information available on the public record contains none of the indicia of those limited categories of expression, such as "fighting" words, which "are no essential part of any exposition of ideas, and are of such slight social value as a step to truth that any benefit that may be derived from them is clearly outweighed by the social interest in order and morality." Chaplinsky v. New Hampshire, 315 U.S. 568, 572, 62 S.Ct. 766, 769, 86 L.Ed. 1031 (1942) (footnote omitted).

By placing the information in the public domain on official court records, the State must be presumed to have concluded that the public interest was thereby being served. Public records by their very nature are of interest to those concerned with the administration of government, and a public benefit is performed by the reporting of the true contents of the records by the media. The freedom of the press to

---

23. Restatement, Second, Torts (Tentative Draft No. 13), supra, Comment c, at 114.

24. Restatement, Second, Torts (Tentative Draft No. 13), supra, at 104.

25. See also Prosser, Handbook of the Law of Torts, supra, at 810–811. For decisions emphasizing as a defense to actions claiming invasion of privacy the fact that the information in question was derived from official records available to the public, see Hubbard v. Journal Publishing Co., 69 N.M. 473, 368 P.2d 147 (1962) (information regarding sexual assault by a boy upon his younger sister derived from official juvenile-court records open to public inspection); Edmiston v. Time, Inc., 257 F.Supp. 22 (S.D.N.Y.1966) (fair and true report of court opinion); Bell v. Courier-Journal & Louisville Times Co., 402 S.W.2d 84 (Ky.1966); Lamont v. Commissioner of Motor Vehicles, 269 F.Supp. 880 (S.D.N.Y.) aff'd 386 F.2d 449 (2d Cir.1967), cert. denied, 391 U.S. 915, 88 S.Ct. 1811, 20 L.Ed.2d 654 (1968); Frith v. Associated Press, 176 F.Supp. 671 (D.C.S.C.1959); Meetze v. Associated Press, 230 S.C. 330, 95 S.E.2d 606 (1956); Thompson v. Curtis Publishing Co., 193 F.2d 953 (3d Cir. 1952); Garner v. Triangle Publications, 97 F.Supp. 546 (S.D.N.Y.1951); Berg v. Minneapolis Star & Tribune Co., 79 F.Supp. 957 (D.C.Minn.1948).

publish that information appears to us to be of critical importance to our type of government in which the citizenry is the final judge of the proper conduct of public business. In preserving that form of government the First and Fourteenth Amendments command nothing less than that the States may not impose sanctions for the publication of truthful information contained in official court records open to public inspection.

We are reluctant to embark on a course that would make public records generally available to the media but forbid their publication if offensive to the sensibilities of the supposed reasonable man. Such a rule would make it very difficult for the press to inform their readers about the public business and yet stay within the law. The rule would invite timidity and self-censorship and very likely lead to the suppression of many items that would otherwise be put into print and that should be made available to the public. At the very least, the First and Fourteenth Amendments will not allow exposing the press to liability for truthfully publishing information released to the public in official court records. If there are privacy interests to be protected in judicial proceedings, the States must respond by means which avoid public documentation or other exposure of private information. Their political institutions must weigh the interests in privacy with the interests of the public to know and of the press to publish.[26] Once true information is disclosed in public court documents open to public inspection, the press cannot be sanctioned for publishing it. In this instance as in others reliance must rest upon the judgment of those who decide what to publish or broadcast. See Miami Herald Publishing Co. v. Tornillo, supra, 418 U.S., at 258, 94 S.Ct., at 2840.

Appellant Wassell based his televised report upon notes taken during the court proceedings and obtained the name of the victim from the indictments handed to him at his request during a recess in the hearing. Appellee has not contended that the name was obtained in an improper fashion or that it was not on an official court document open to public inspection. Under these circumstances, the protection of freedom of the press provided by the First and Fourteenth Amendments bars the State of Georgia from making appellants' broadcast the basis of civil liability.[27]

Reversed.

* * *

MR. JUSTICE DOUGLAS, concurring in the judgment.

26. We mean to imply nothing about any constitutional questions which might arise from a state policy not allowing access by the public and press to various kinds of official records, such as records of juvenile-court proceedings.

27. Appellants have contended that whether they derived the information in question from public records or instead through their own investigation, the First and Fourteenth Amendments bar any sanctions from being imposed by the State because of the publication. Because appellant has prevailed on more limited grounds, we need not address this broader challenge to

I agree * * * in the reversal of the Georgia court.* On the merits, the case for me is on all fours with New Jersey State Lottery Comm'n v. United States, 491 F.2d 219 (3d Cir.1974), remanded, 420 U.S. 371, 95 S.Ct. 941, 43 L.Ed.2d 260 (1975). For the reasons I stated in my dissent from our disposition of that case, there is no power on the part of Government to suppress or penalize the publication of "news of the day."

Questions

1. Does *Cox* stand for the proposition that the public disclosure of matter from any "public record" is immune under the First Amendment from right of privacy liability, or does it apply only to matter contained in a "judicial record"?

2. Does the *Cox* immunity apply to all matters contained in a judicial record, or only to such matters as are contemporaneous, and therefore "news"?

3. May the *Cox* immunity be claimed only by newspapers and news broadcasters, or does it apply to all media communications? Does it apply to motion pictures? Does it matter whether the motion picture is a dramatized motion picture photoplay rather than a documentary?

4. As a matter of state law, did the plaintiff have standing to sue for the invasion of privacy of his deceased daughter? See question 3 following Melvin v. Reid, supra.

Collateral Reference

Hill, *Defamation and Privacy Under the First Amendment*, 76 Columbia L.Rev. 1205 (1976).

BRISCOE v. READER'S DIGEST ASSOCIATION

Supreme Court of California, 1971.
4 Cal.3d 529, 93 Cal.Rptr. 866.

PETERS, JUSTICE. Plaintiff Marvin Briscoe filed suit against defend-

the validity of § 26–9901 and of Georgia's right of action for public disclosure.

* While I join in the narrow result reached by the Court, I write separately to emphasize that I would ground that result upon a far broader proposition, namely, that the First Amendment, made applicable to the States through the Fourteenth, prohibits the use of state law "to impose damages for merely discussing public affairs * * *." New York Times Co. v. Sullivan, 376 U.S. 254, 295, 84 S.Ct. 710, 734, 11 L.Ed.2d 686 (1964) (Black, J., concurring). See also Cantrell v. Forest City Publishing Co., 419 U.S. 245, 254, 255, 95 S.Ct. 465, 471, 42 L.Ed.2d 419 (1974) (Douglas, J., dissenting); Gertz v. Robert Welch, Inc., 418 U.S. 323, 355, 94 S.Ct. 2997, 3014, 41 L.Ed.2d 789 (1974) (Douglas, J., dissenting); Time, Inc. v. Hill, 385 U.S. 374, 398, 87 S.Ct. 534, 547, 17 L.Ed.2d 456 (1967) (Black, J., concurring); id., at 401, 87 S.Ct., at 548 (Douglas, J., concurring); Garrison v. Louisiana, 379 U.S. 64, 80, 85 S.Ct. 209, 218, 13 L.Ed.2d 125 (1964) (Douglas, J., concurring). In this context, of course, "public affairs" must be broadly construed—indeed, the term may be said to embrace "any matter of sufficient general interest to prompt media coverage * * *." Gertz v. Robert Welch, Inc., 418 U.S., at 357 n. 6, 94 S.Ct., at 3016 (Douglas, J., dissenting). By its now-familiar process of balancing and accommodating First Amendment freedoms with state or individual interests, the Court raises a spectre of liability which must inevitably induce self-censorship by the media, thereby inhibiting the rough-and-tumble discourse which the First Amendment so clearly protects.

ant Reader's Digest Association, alleging that defendant had willfully and maliciously invaded his privacy by publishing an article which disclosed truthful but embarrassing private facts about plaintiff's past life. A demurrer was sustained without leave to amend, and plaintiff has appealed from the ensuing judgment. Thus, we are presented simply with a pleading problem—does the complaint state a cause of action?

The allegations of the complaint may be summarized as follows: On December 15, 1956, plaintiff and another man hijacked a truck in Danville, Kentucky. "[I]mmediately subsequent to said incident, plaintiff abandoned his life of shame and became entirely rehabilitated and has thereafter at all times lived an exemplary, virtuous and honorable life * * * he has assumed a place in respectable society and made many friends who were not aware of the incident in his earlier life."

"The Big Business of Hijacking," published by defendant 11 years after the hijacking incident, commences with a picture whose caption reads, "Today's highwaymen are looting trucks at a rate of more than $100 million a year. But the truckers have now declared all-out war." The article describes various truck thefts and the efforts being made to stop such thefts. Dates ranging from 1965 to the time of publication are mentioned throughout the article, but none of the described thefts is itself dated.

One sentence in the article refers to plaintiff: "Typical of many beginners, Marvin Briscoe and [another man] stole a 'valuable-looking' truck in Danville, Ky., and then fought a gun battle with the local police, only to learn that they had hijacked four bowling-pin spotters." There is nothing in the article to indicate that the hijacking occurred in 1956.

As the result of defendant's publication,[1] plaintiff's 11-year-old daughter, as well as his friends, for the first time learned of this incident. They thereafter scorned and abandoned him.

Conceding the truth of the facts published in defendant's article, plaintiff claims that the public disclosure of these private facts has humiliated him and exposed him to contempt and ridicule. Conceding that the *subject* of the article may have been "newsworthy," he contends that the use of his *name* was not, and that the defendant has thus invaded his right to privacy.

The concept of a legal right to privacy was first developed by Warren and Brandeis in their landmark law review article, The Right to Privacy (1890) 4 Harv.L.Rev. 193. Warren and Brandeis characterized the right to privacy as the individual's "right of determining, ordinarily, to what extent his thoughts, sentiments, and emotions shall

---

1. The article was a condensed version of an article which originally appeared in the December 10, 1967, issue of Chicago's American Magazine, published by the Chicago American Publishing Company. It is not alleged that this first publication injured plaintiff. Defendant concedes that this first publication does not absolve it from responsibility.

be communicated to others." (Id., at p. 198; see also A. Westin, Privacy and Freedom (1967) p. 7; Gross, The Concept of Privacy (1967) 42 N.Y.U.L.Rev. 34, 35–36.)[2] Try as they might, Warren and Brandeis had a difficult time tracing a right of privacy to the common law. In many respects a person had less privacy in the small community of the 18th century than he did in the urbanizing late 19th century or he does today in the modern metropolis. Extended family networks, primary group relationships, and rigid communal mores served to expose an individual's every deviation from the norm and to straitjacket him in a vise of backyard gossip. Yet Warren and Brandeis perceived that it was mass exposure to public gaze, as opposed to backyard gossip, which threatened to deprive men of the right of "scratching wherever one itches." (Westin, Science, Privacy, and Freedom: Issues and Proposals for the 1970's (1966) 66 Colum.L.Rev. 1003, 1025.)

Acceptance of the right to privacy has grown with the increasing capability of the mass media and electronic devices with their capacity to destroy an individual's anonymity, intrude upon his most intimate activities, and expose his most personal characteristics to public gaze.

In a society in which multiple, often conflicting role performances are demanded of each individual, the original etymological meaning of the word "person"—mask—[3] has taken on new meaning. Men fear exposure not only to those closest to them; much of the outrage underlying the asserted right to privacy is a reaction to exposure to persons known only through business or other secondary relationships. The claim is not so much one of total secrecy as it is of the right to *define* one's circle of intimacy—to choose who shall see beneath the quotidian mask. Loss of control over which "face" one puts on may result in literal loss of self-identity (Westin, supra, at p. 1023; cf. Fried, Privacy (1968) 77 Yale L.J. 475), and is humiliating beneath the gaze of those whose curiosity treats a human being as an object.

A common law right to privacy, based on Warren and Brandeis' article, is now recognized in at least 36 states. (Prosser, Law of Torts (3d ed. 1964) at pp. 831–832; Commonwealth v. Wiseman (1969) 356 Mass. 251, 249 N.E.2d 610, cert. denied (1970) 398 U.S. 960, 90 S.Ct. 2165, 2 L.Ed.2d 546; Hamberger v. Eastman (1964) 106 N.H. 107, 206 A.2d 239; Rugg v. McCarty (Colo.1970) 476 P.2d 753; Fergerstrom v. Hawaiian Ocean View Estates (Hawaii 1968) 441 P.2d 141; Apodaca v. Miller (1968) 79 N.M. 160, 441 P.2d 200.) California has recognized the right to privacy for 40 years. (Melvin v. Reid (1931) 112 Cal.App. 285, 297 P. 91.)

2. Although other ways in which the word "privacy" is used—to indicate an interest in mental repose, physical solitude, or autonomy—are weaker senses of the word (Gross, supra, at pp. 36–39), the "right of privacy" has also served as a general rallying point for those concerned about "deep intrusions on human dignity by those in possession of economic or governmental power." (Havighurst, Foreward (1966) 31 Law & Contemp.Prob. 251, 252.)

3. Webster's New International Dictionary (2d ed. 1958) at p. 1827.

The right to keep information private was bound to clash with the right to disseminate information to the public. We early noted the potential conflict between freedom of the press and the right of privacy (Gill v. Curtis Publishing Co., 38 Cal.2d 273, 277–278, 239 P.2d 630; Gill v. Hearst Publishing Co., 40 Cal.2d 224, 228, 253 P.2d 441), as did Warren and Brandeis themselves, who suggested that the right should not apply to matters of "public or general interest." (Warren and Brandeis, supra, 4 Harv.L.Rev. 193, 214.)[4] The instant case, pitting a rehabilitated felon's right to anonymity against a magazine's right to identify him, compels us to consider the character of these competing interests.

The central purpose of the First Amendment "is to give to every voting member of the body politic the fullest possible participation in the understanding of those problems with which the citizens of a self-governing society must deal. * * * "[5] (A. Meiklejohn, Political Freedom: The Constitutional Powers of the People (1960) p. 75.) Nor is freedom of the press confined to comment upon public affairs and those persons who have voluntarily sought the public spotlight. "Freedom of discussion * * * must embrace all issues about which information is needed or appropriate to enable the members of society to cope with the exigencies of their period. * * * " (Thornhill v. Alabama (1940) 310 U.S. 88, 102, 60 S.Ct. 736, 744, 84 L.Ed. 1093; see Time, Inc. v. Hill (1967) 385 U.S. 374, 388, 87 S.Ct. 534, 17 L.Ed.2d 456.) The scope of the privilege thus extends to almost all reporting of recent events, even though it involves the publication of a purely private individual's name or likeness. (See, e.g., Metter v. Los Angeles Examiner, 35 Cal.App.2d 304, 95 P.2d 491; Coverstone v. Davies, 38 Cal.2d 315, 239 P.2d 876.)[6]

Particularly deserving of First Amendment protection are reports of "hot news," items of possible immediate public concern or interest. The need for constitutional protection is much greater under these circumstances, where deadlines must be met and quick decisions made,

---

4. One writer suggests that the First Amendment's scope is so great as to "swallow the tort." (See Kalven, Privacy in Tort Law—Were Warren and Brandeis Wrong? (1966) 31 Law & Contemp.Prob. 326.) Most commentators place greater emphasis on the right to privacy. (See Bloustein, Privacy, Tort Law, and the Constitution: Is Warren and Brandeis' Tort Petty and Unconstitutional as Well? (1968) 46 Tex.L.Rev. 611; see also Nimmer, The Right to Speak from TIMES to TIME: First Amendment Theory Applied to Libel and Misapplied to Privacy (1968) 56 Cal.L.Rev. 935.)

5. Almost any truthful commentary on public officials or public affairs, no matter how serious the invasion of privacy, will be privileged. By volunteering his services for public office the official (as opposed to the ordinary employee) waives much of his right to privacy.

Other individuals who voluntarily seek the public eye are also subject to fair comment and criticism. (Prosser, Law of Torts, supra, at p. 844.) Because discussion of such figures is not so vital to the maintenance of our self-governing democracy as is discussion of public officials and public affairs, such figures may have greater protection from media exposure or untruths. (See Curtis Publishing Co. v. Butts (1967) 388 U.S. 130, 155, 87 S.Ct. 1975, 18 L.Ed.2d 1094.)

6. The publisher need not intend to educate the public. "The line between * * * informing and * * * entertaining is too elusive * * *. Everyone is familiar with instances of propaganda through fiction. What is one man's amusement, teaches another's doctrine. * * * " (Winters v. New York (1948) 333 U.S. 507, 510, 68 S.Ct. 665, 667, 92 L.Ed. 840.)

than in cases where more considered editorial judgments are possible. (Rosenbloom v. Metromedia, Inc. (3d Cir.1969) 415 F.2d 892, 895–896.)[7] Most factual reporting concerns current events. For example, in Time, Inc. v. Hill, supra, 385 U.S. 374, 383–384, fn. 7, 87 S.Ct. 534, 17 L.Ed.2d 456, the court cited 22 cases in which the right of privacy gave way to the right of the press to publish matters of public interest. Seventeen of these 22 cases (77.3 percent) involved events which had occurred quite recently.[8]

There can be no doubt that reports of current criminal activities are the legitimate province of a free press. The circumstances under which crimes occur, the techniques used by those outside the law, the tragedy that may befall the victims—these are vital bits of information for people coping with the exigencies of modern life. Reports of these events may also promote the values served by the constitutional guarantee of a public trial. Although a case is not to be "tried in the papers," reports regarding a crime or criminal proceedings may encourage unknown witnesses to come forward with useful testimony and friends or relatives to come to the aid of the victim.[9]

It is also generally in the social interest to identify adults currently charged with the commission of a crime. While such an identification

---

7. This is not to say, however, that *all* factual reports of current events have been held absolutely privileged. (See, e.g., Commonwealth v. Wiseman, supra, 356 Mass. 251, 249 N.E.2d 610 [film showing conditions in mental hospital, including naked inmates, forced feedings, masturbation, sadism; individuals identifiable]; Lambert v. Dow Chemical Company (La.App.1968) 215 So.2d 673 [identified picture of plaintiff's unsightly wounds]; Daily Times Democrat v. Graham (1964) 276 Ala. 380, 162 So.2d 474 [identifiable picture of plaintiff with dress blown above her waist]; Harms v. Miami Daily News, Inc. (Fla.App.1961) 127 So.2d 715 [phone number of woman identified as having sexy voice]; Tribune Review Publishing Company v. Thomas (3d Cir.1958) 254 F.2d 883 [picture of criminal defendant in courthouse]; In re Mack (1956) 386 Pa. 251, 126 A.2d 679, cert. denied 352 U.S. 1002, 77 S.Ct. 559, 1 L.Ed.2d 547 [picture of convicted murderer in courthouse just prior to sentencing]; Barber v. Time, Inc. (1942) 348 Mo. 1199, 159 S.W.2d 291 [name and picture of woman with humiliating disease]; cf. Tollefson v. Price (1967) 247 Or. 398, 430 P.2d 990 [advertising that plaintiff owed business debts]; Trammell v. Citizens News Co., Inc. (1941) 285 Ky. 529, 148 S.W.2d 708 [advertising that plaintiff owed business debts]; York v. Story (9th Cir.1963) 324 F.2d 450, cert. denied 376 U.S. 939, 84 S.Ct. 794, 1 L.Ed.2d 659 [indecent photos of plaintiff in poses induced by police officer].)

8. Another of these cases (Thompson v. Curtis Publishing Co. (3d Cir.1952) 193 F.2d 953) clearly involved voluntary waiver. In Samuel v. Curtis Pub. Co. (N.D.Cal.1954) 122 F.Supp. 327, a photograph of plaintiff restraining a would-be suicide was republished two years after the event. The court found that there was nothing offensive or discreditable to a reasonable man in the photograph. In Miller v. National Broadcasting Company (D.Del.1957) 157 F.Supp. 240, plaintiff was presently incarcerated, and would not be heard to complain of a dramatic reenactment of his crime four years later. Of the 22 cases cited, only Barbieri v. News-Journal Company (Del. 1963) 189 A.2d 773, which explicitly rejects our landmark decision of Melvin v. Reid, supra, 112 Cal.App. 285, 297 P. 91, and Smith v. Doss (1948) 251 Ala. 250, 37 So.2d 118, is the recall of past events involving nonpublic figures at issue. In the latter case the spectacular disappearance of plaintiff's father, who was thought murdered, the accusation of an innocent man, and the discovery 25 years later of the facts (the father had deserted his family) was said to be so imprinted on the community's collective history that publication was privileged.

9. We express no opinion, however, regarding the propriety of pretrial court orders, designed to ensure a fair trial, to the effect that parties and their counsel may not comment on a case to the news media.

may not presume guilt, it may legitimately put others on notice that the named individual is suspected of having committed a crime. Naming the suspect may also persuade eye witnesses and character witnesses to testify. For these reasons, while the suspect or offender obviously does not consent to public exposure, his right to privacy must give way to the overriding social interest.

In general, therefore, truthful reports of *recent* crimes and the names of suspects or offenders will be deemed protected by the First Amendment.[10]

The instant case, however, compels us to consider whether reports of the facts of *past* crimes and the identification of *past* offenders serve these same public-interest functions.

We have no doubt that reports of the facts of past crimes are newsworthy. Media publication of the circumstances under which crimes were committed in the past may prove educational in the same way that reports of current crimes do. The public has a strong interest in enforcing the law, and this interest is served by accumulating and disseminating data cataloguing the reasons men commit crimes, the methods they use, and the ways in which they are apprehended. Thus in an article on truck hijackings, Reader's Digest certainly had the right to report the *facts* of plaintiff's criminal act.

However, identification of the *actor* in reports of long past crimes usually serves little independent public purpose. Once legal proceedings have terminated, and a suspect or offender has been released, identification of the individual will not usually aid the administration of justice. Identification will no longer serve to bring forth witnesses or obtain succor for victims. Unless the individual has reattracted the

---

10. We do not mean to imply that the First Amendment gives the media the unmitigated right to publish the identity of suspected offenders or victims. In some jurisdictions, for example, the Legislature has decided that the rehabilitative goals of the juvenile law are so important as to override the right of the press to identify juvenile defendants. (See, e.g., Virgin Islands Code, title 5, § 2511; Fla.Stat. § 801.-14, F.S.A. (sex offenses only).) In many other states the rights of the press to report juvenile proceedings are limited. In In re Gault (1967) 387 U.S. 1, 25, 87 S.Ct. 1428, 18 L.Ed.2d 527, the United States Supreme Court gave implicit approval to such restrictions on First Amendment rights. (See also Government of Virgin Islands v. Brodhurst (D.C.1968) 285 F.Supp. 831, holding the Virgin Islands statute prohibiting the naming of juvenile defendants constitutional as against a First Amendment challenge; Geis, Publication of the Names of Juvenile Felons (1962) 23 Mont.L.Rev. 141.)

Similarly, some states have prohibited the naming of rape victims in news reports. (Fla.Stat. § 794.03, F.S.A.; Ga.Code Ann. § 26–2105; S.C.Code Ann. § 16–81; Wis. Stats.Ann. § 942.02.) The Wisconsin statute has been held constitutional. (State v. Evjue (1948) 253 Wis. 146, 33 N.W.2d 305 (holding that the minimum social value of publication is outweighed by the encouragement given to victims to complain to the police once their privacy is guaranteed).) In Nappier v. Jefferson Standard Life Insurance Company (4th Cir.1963) 322 F.2d 502, the South Carolina statute was not only upheld, following the reasoning of *Evjue,* but also was extended to apply to *any* identification of the victims (in this case televising a picture of their well-known business truck with a report that it belonged to the victims). We of course express no opinion on these matters.

public eye to himself in some independent fashion, the only public "interest" that would usually be served is that of curiosity.

There may be times, of course, when an event involving private citizens may be so unique as to capture the imagination of all. In such cases—e.g., the behavior of the passengers on the sinking *Titanic*, the heroism of Nathan Hale, the horror of the Saint Valentine's Day Massacre—purely private individuals may by an accident of history lose their privacy regarding that incident for all time. There need be no "reattraction" of the public eye because the public interest never wavered. An individual whose name is fixed in the public's memory, such as that of the political assassin, never becomes an anonymous member of the community again. But in each case it is for the trier of fact to determine whether the individual's infamy is such that he has never left the public arena; we cannot do so as a matter of law.

The Restatement of Torts some time ago balanced the considerations relevant here, concluding that criminals "are the objects of legitimate public interest during a period of time after their conduct * * * has brought them to the public attention; until they have reverted to the lawful and unexciting life led by the great bulk of the community, they are subject to the privileges which publishers have to satisfy the curiosity of the public as to their leaders, heroes, villains and victims." (§ 867, com. c.) Where a man has reverted to that "lawful and unexciting life" led by others, the Restatement implies that he no longer need "satisfy the curiosity of the public."

Another factor militating in favor of protecting the individual's privacy here is the state's interest in the integrity of the rehabilitative process. Our courts recognized this issue four decades ago in Melvin v. Reid, supra, 112 Cal.App. 285, 297 P. 91. There, plaintiff had been a prostitute. She was charged with murder and acquitted after a long and very public trial. She thereafter abandoned her life of shame, married, and assumed a place in respectable society, making many friends who were not aware of the incidents of her earlier life.

Seven years after the trial defendants made a movie based entirely on Mrs. Melvin's early life. They used only facts found in the public record, and did not falsify or create false innuendoes regarding that period of her life. Defendants used Mrs. Melvin's true maiden name in the film.

The Court of Appeal, in a decision cited ceaselessly since, held that the *subject* of the film was protected. No cause of action accrues from the use of "incidents of a life * * * so public as to be spread upon a public record," the court reasoned, since these matters "cease to be private." (112 Cal.App. at pp. 290–291, 297 P. at p. 93.) The court took a different view of defendants' use of Mrs. Melvin's *name*. Although that, too, had been spread upon a public record, the court held that defendants' use of plaintiff's name was improper. The lapse of time between the incidents in issue and the making of the film was a relevant, but not conclusive, factor to the court.[11] Rather, the Court of Appeal emphasized that "[o]ne of the major objectives of society * * * and of the administration of our penal system, is the rehabilitation of the fallen and the reformation of the criminal. * * * Where a person has * * * rehabilitated himself, we, as right-thinking members of society, should permit him to continue in the path of rectitude rather than throw him back into a life of shame or crime. Even the thief on the cross was permitted to repent during the hours of his final agony." (112 Cal.App. at p. 292, 297 P. at p. 93.) The plaintiff was held to have stated a cause of action for invasion of privacy.

One of the premises of the rehabilitative process is that the rehabilitated offender can rejoin that great bulk of the community from which he has been ostracized for his anti-social acts. In return for becoming a "new man," he is allowed to melt into the shadows of obscurity.[12]

We are realistic enough to recognize that men are curious about the inner sanctums of their neighbors—that the public will create its heroes and villains. We must also be realistic enough to realize that full disclosure of one's inner thoughts, intimate personal characteristics, and past life is neither the rule nor the norm in these United States. We have developed a variegated panoply of professional listeners to whom we confidentially "reveal all"; otherwise we keep our own counsel. The masks we wear may be stripped away upon the occurrence of some event of public interest. But just as the risk of exposure is a concomitant of urban life, so too is the expectation of anonymity regained. It would be a crass legal fiction to assert that a matter once public never becomes private again.[13] Human forgetfulness over time puts today's "hot" news in tomorrow's dusty archives. In a nation of

---

11. See Note, The Right of Privacy: Normative-Descriptive Confusion in the Defense of Newsworthiness (1963) 30 U.Chi.L. Rev. 722, 733–734.

12. The purpose of the indeterminate sentence law in California (Pen.Code, § 1168), for example, is "to put before the prisoner great incentive to well-doing * *." (In re Lee, 177 Cal. 690, 692, 171 P. 958, 959; Grasso v. McDonough Power Equipment, Inc., 264 Cal.App.2d 597, 600, 70 Cal. Rptr. 458, 460.) The indeterminate sentence law in theory "affords a person convicted of crime the opportunity to *minimize* the term of imprisonment by rehabilitating himself in such manner that he may again become a useful member of society, * * *." (People v. Wade, 266 Cal.App.2d 918, 928, 72 Cal.Rptr. 538, 544; italics added.)

13. "A public figure * * * can be so far removed from his former position in the public eye, that the publisher will no longer enjoy the prophylactic treatment accorded him when he deals with those persons who truly are public officials or public figures.

* * *" (Johnston v. Time, Inc. (M.D.N.C. 1970) 321 F.Supp. 837 [former professional basketball player no longer a public figure, had regained right to privacy].) "[I]t is erroneous * * * to assume that privacy, though lost for a certain time or in a certain context, goes forever unprotected * * *." (Spahn v. Julian Messner, Inc. (1966) 18 N.Y.2d 324, 328, 274 N.Y.S.2d 877, 879, 221 N.E.2d 543, 545; accord, Leverton v. Curtis Pub. Co. (3d Cir.1951) 192 F.2d 974; Mau v. Rio Grande Oil, Inc. (N.D.Cal.1939) 28 F.Supp. 845; see Note, supra, 30 U.Chi.L. Rev. 722, 726–727.)

In Time, Inc. v. Hill, supra, 385 U.S. 374, 87 S.Ct. 534, 17 L.Ed.2d 456, plaintiffs had been held hostage in their own home by escaped criminals three years prior to publication of the article in Life magazine. Their plight had been fully reported at the time. The court did not even question whether that previously publicly reported event remained public; the Hills were assumed to have a right to privacy concerning the event.

200 million people there is ample opportunity for all but the most infamous to begin a new life.

Plaintiff is a man whose last offense took place 11 years before, who has paid his debt to society, who has friends and an 11-year-old daughter who were unaware of his early life—a man who has assumed a position in "respectable" society. Ideally, his neighbors should recognize his present worth and forget his past life of shame. But men are not so divine as to forgive the past trespasses of others, and plaintiff therefore endeavored to reveal as little as possible of his past life. Yet, as if in some bizarre canyon of echoes, petitioner's past life pursues him through the pages of Reader's Digest, now published in 13 languages and distributed in 100 nations, with a circulation in California alone of almost 2,000,000 copies.

In a nation built upon the free dissemination of ideas, it is always difficult to declare that something may not be published.[14] But the great general interest in an unfettered press may at times be outweighed by other great societal interests.[15] As a people we have come to recognize that one of these societal interests is that of protecting an individual's right to privacy. The right to know and the right to have others *not* know are, simplistically considered, irreconcilable. But the rights guaranteed by the First Amendment do not require total abrogation of the right to privacy. The goals sought by each may be achieved with a minimum of intrusion upon the other.

In Time, Inc. v. Hill, supra, 385 U.S. 374, 383, 87 S.Ct. 534, 17 L.Ed.2d 456, the United States Supreme Court considered some of these same balancing problems with regard to a different form of invasion of privacy, that of placing the individual in a false light in the public eye. The New York statute construed in *Time* did not create a right of action for the truthful report of newsworthy people or events.[16] The

---

14. Judicial attempts at defining what constitutes "news" are fraught with oversimplification. Thus news has been defined as the "report of recent occurrences" (Jenkins v. News Syndicate Co., Inc. (N.Y.Sup.Ct.1926) 128 Misc. 284, 285, 219 N.Y.S. 196) or as all factual reports with "that indefinable quality of interest, which attracts public attention." (Associated Press v. International News Service (2d Cir.1917) 245 F. 244, 248, affirmed, 248 U.S. 215, 39 S.Ct. 68, 63 L.Ed. 211.)

15. The notion of balancing competing interests is not foreign to First Amendment controversies. The extent to which government may proscribe advocacy of the use of force or violation of law has long occupied the attention of the judiciary. (See, e.g., Schenck v. United States (1919) 249 U.S. 47, 52, 39 S.Ct. 247, 63 L.Ed. 470 [Holmes' adumbration of the "clear and present danger" test]; Whitney v. California (1927) 274 U.S. 357, 47 S.Ct. 641, 71 L.Ed. 1095; Dennis v. United States (1951) 341 U.S. 494, 507, 71 S.Ct. 857, 95 L.Ed. 1137.) In Brandenburg v. Ohio (1969) 395 U.S. 444, 447, 89 S.Ct. 1827, 1829, 23 L.Ed.2d 430, the United States Supreme Court held that such proscription would be allowed only where "such advocacy is directed to inciting or producing imminent lawless action and is likely to incite or produce such action."

In Roth v. United States (1957) 354 U.S. 476, 485, 77 S.Ct. 1304, 1309, 1 L.Ed.2d 1498, the court held that obscene utterances *" 'are of such slight social value as a step to truth that any benefit that may be derived from them is clearly outweighed by the social interest in order and morality.' "* (See also cases cited supra, fns. 7 and 10; Wright, Defamation, Privacy, and the Public's Right to Know: A National Problem and a New Approach (1968) 46 Tex.L.Rev. 630, 633.)

16. New York does not recognize a common law right to privacy. Its statutory

Supreme Court stated, however, that "[t]his limitation to newsworthy persons and events does not of course foreclose an interpretation * * * to allow damages where 'Revelations may be so intimate and so unwarranted in view of the victim's position as to outrage the community's notions of decency.' * * * ". (385 U.S. at p. 383, fn. 7, 87 S.Ct. at p. 539.) Thus a truthful publication is constitutionally protected if (1) it is newsworthy and (2) it does not reveal facts so offensive as to shock the community's notions of decency.

We have previously set forth criteria for determining whether an incident is newsworthy. We consider "[1] the social value of the facts published, [2] the depth of the article's intrusion into ostensibly private affairs, and [3] the extent to which the party voluntarily acceded to a position of public notoriety. [Citations.]" (Kapellas v. Kofman, 1 Cal.3d 20, 36, 81 Cal.Rptr. 360, 370, 459 P.2d 912, 922.)

On the assumed set of facts before us we are convinced that a jury could reasonably find that plaintiff's identity as a former hijacker was not newsworthy. First, as discussed above, a jury could find that publication of plaintiff's identity in connection with incidents of his past life was in this case of minimal social value. There was no independent reason whatsoever for focusing public attention on Mr. Briscoe as an individual at this time. A jury could certainly find that Mr. Briscoe had once again become an anonymous member of the community. Once legal proceedings have concluded, and particularly once the individual has reverted to the lawful and unexciting life led by the rest of the community, the public's interest in knowing is less compelling.

Second, a jury might find that revealing one's criminal past for all to see is grossly offensive to most people in America. Certainly a criminal background is kept even more hidden from others than a humiliating disease (Barber v. Time, Inc., supra, 348 Mo. 1199, 159 S.W.2d 291) or the existence of business debts (Trammell v. Citizens News Co., Inc., supra, 285 Ky. 529, 148 S.W.2d 708; Tollefson v. Price, supra, 247 Or. 398, 430 P.2d 990).[17] The consequences of revelation in this case—ostracism, isolation, and the alienation of one's family— make all too clear just how deeply offensive to most persons a prior

right to privacy provides no relief for the publication of truthful but embarrassing private facts so long as the reports concern newsworthy persons or events. (Spahn v. Julian Messner, Inc., supra, 18 N.Y.2d 324, 328, 274 N.Y.S.2d 877, 221 N.E.2d 543, vacated on other grounds, 387 U.S. 239, 87 S.Ct. 1706, 18 L.Ed.2d 744, judgment affirmed 21 N.Y.2d 124, 286 N.Y.S.2d 832, 233 N.E.2d 840, appeal dismissed (1968) 393 U.S. 1046, 89 S.Ct. 676, 21 L.Ed.2d 600.)

17. The instant case must be contrasted with the situation in Time, Inc. v. Hill, supra, 385 U.S. 374, 87 S.Ct. 534, 17 L.Ed.2d 456; most people would not consider their former momentary status as a hostage of escaped criminals to be so offensive or discreditable as to render the disclosure of this fact outrageous. (Cf. Melvin v. Reid, supra, 112 Cal.App. 285, 297 P. 91; Mau v. Rio Grande Oil, Inc., supra, D.C., 28 F.Supp. 845, 846; Binns v. Vitagraph Co. (1913) 210 N.Y. 51, 103 N.E. 1108.) Compare Commonwealth v. Wiseman, supra, 356 Mass. 251, 249 N.E.2d 610, limiting public access to defendant's film on Bridgewater Hospital (Titicut Follies) because the film invaded the inmates' right to privacy by showing scenes of forced feeding, masturbation, etc.

crime is and thus how hidden the former offender must keep the knowledge of his prior indiscretion.

Third, in no way can plaintiff be said to have voluntarily consented to the publicity accorded him here. He committed a crime. He was punished. He was rehabilitated. And he became, for 11 years, an obscure and law-abiding citizen. His every effort was to forget and have others forget that he had once hijacked a truck.

Finally, the interest at stake here are not merely those of publication and privacy alone, for the state has a compelling interest in the efficacy of penal systems in rehabilitating criminals and returning them as productive and law-abiding citizens to the society whence they came. A jury might well find that a continuing threat that the rehabilitated offender's old identity will be resurrected by the media is counter-productive to the goals of this correctional process.

Mindful that "the balance is always weighted in favor of free expression" (Liberty Lobby, Inc. v. Pearson (1968) 129 U.S.App.D.C. 74, 390 F.2d 489, 491), and that we must not chill First Amendment freedoms through uncertainty,[18] we find it reasonable to require a plaintiff to prove, in each case, that the publisher invaded his privacy with reckless disregard for the fact that reasonable men would find the invasion highly offensive.[19]

We do not hold today that plaintiff must prevail in his action. It is for the trier of fact to determine (1) whether plaintiff had become a rehabilitated member of society, (2) whether identifying him as a former criminal would be highly offensive and injurious to the reasonable man, (3) whether defendant published this information with a reckless disregard for its offensiveness, and (4) whether any independent justification for printing plaintiff's identity existed. We hold today only that, as pleaded, plaintiff has stated a valid cause of action, sustaining the demurrer to plaintiff's complaint was improper, and that the ensuing judgment must therefore be reversed.

Plaintiff also claims that defendant's article placed him in a false light in the public eye by implying that his criminal activity was of recent vintage. He refers to the words "today" and "now" in the

---

18. Because the categories with which we deal—private and public, newsworthy and nonnewsworthy—have no clear profile, there is a temptation to balance interests in ad hoc fashion in each case. Yet history teaches us that such a process leads too often to discounting society's stake in First Amendment rights. (See Nimmer, supra, 56 Cal.L.Rev. 935, 939–941.) We therefore strive for as much predictability as possible within our system of case-by-case adjudication, lest we unwittingly chill First Amendment freedoms. "One steers clear of a barbed wire fence * * * he stays even farther away if he is not sure exactly where the fence is. * * *" (Wright, supra, 46 Tex.L.Rev. 630, 634.)

However, there is little uncertainty here. A publisher does have every reason to know, *before* publication, that identification of a man as a former criminal will be highly offensive to the individual involved. It does not require close reading of "Les Miserables" or "The Scarlet Letter" to know that men are haunted by the fear of disclosure of their past and destroyed by the exposure itself.

19. In alleging malice and willfulness in his complaint, plaintiff has complied with this initial requirement.

opening caption to the article, and the numerous recent dates mentioned, and contends that these imply to the reasonable man that the incident described took place recently.

We have previously stated that a "false light" cause of action "is in substance equivalent to * * * [a] libel claim, and should meet the same requirements of the libel claim * * * including proof of malice (cf. Time, Inc. v. Hill (1967) 385 U.S. 374, 87 S.Ct. 534, 17 L.Ed.2d 456) and fulfillment of the requirements of section 48a [of the Civil Code]. (See Werner v. Times-Mirror Co., 193 Cal.App.2d 111, 122–123, 14 Cal.Rptr. 208.)" (Kapellas v. Kofman, supra, 1 Cal.3d 20, 35, fn. 16, 81 Cal.Rptr. 360, 459 P.2d 912.)[20]

Plaintiff here alleged malice, but at no time complied with the requirements of section 48a. It would therefore be possible for him to amend his complaint to state a cause of action based on a "false light" theory only if he alleged special damages.

Defendant demurred specially as well as generally to plaintiff's complaint. The trial court sustained defendant's demurrer without leave to amend in general terms, contrary to Code of Civil Procedure, section 472d. Under such circumstances we must assume that the court ruled only on the general demurrer and not on the special demurrer. (Weinstock v. Eissler, 224 Cal.App.2d 212, 237, 36 Cal.Rptr. 537; Stowe v. Fritzie Hotels, Inc., 44 Cal.2d 416, 425, 282 P.2d 890.)

The judgment is reversed and the cause is remanded to the trial court with directions to overrule the general demurrer and to rule upon the points presented by the special demurrer. Appellant shall recover costs on appeal.

WRIGHT, C.J., and McCOMB, TOBRINER, MOSK, BURKE and SULLIVAN, JJ., concur.

Questions

1. Would the rule articulated in Cox Broadcasting Corp. v. Cohn, supra, have been applicable to the decision in *Briscoe* had *Cox* been decided first?

2. Should the public disclosure of private facts which are *not* a matter of public record carry a First Amendment immunity from right of privacy liability? If so, under what circumstances? Does the *Briscoe* opinion articulate a satisfactory standard in this regard? What does it mean to publish information "with a reckless disregard for its offensiveness"? Does this mean that if the information would be offensive to a person of ordinary sensibilities, and if the defendant knew (or reasonably should have known) such to be the case, but nevertheless published it, then no First Amendment immunity may be claimed? Does not such a standard effectively vitiate any First Amendment privilege? Does it simply mean that the defendant published the information with "good"

---

20. Section 48a requires a libelled individual, within 20 days of learning of the publication, to advise the publisher specifically what statements he claims to be libelous and to request that the statements be corrected. Recovery of general damages is possible only if the section is complied with and if the publisher fails to correct the libelous statement.

motives and without ill-will against the plaintiff? Does not such a standard effectively vitiate the right of privacy as a tort? Is the use of a "reckless disregard" standard in this context an unfortunate application of the *New York Times* defamation standard to the law of privacy, where it makes no sense? Does not any disclosure of private facts result in embarrassment or humiliation to the subject, and therefore does not any decision to make such a disclosure involve a "disregard" as to whether the disclosure will result in such embarrassment or humiliation? When does such a "disregard" become "reckless"? What might constitute an "independent justification for printing plaintiff's identity"?

Collateral References

Comment, Accommodation of Privacy Interests and First Amendment Rights in Public Disclosure Cases, 124 U.Pa.L.Rev. 1385 (1976).

Emerson, *Right of Privacy and Freedom of the Press*, 14 Harv.C.R.L.Rev. 329 (1979).

Posner, *Privacy, Secrecy and Reputation*, 28 Buffalo L.Rev. 1 (1979).

VIRGIL v. TIME, INC.
United States Court of Appeals, Ninth Circuit, 1975.
527 F.2d 1122

Before MERRILL and CHOY, CIRCUIT JUDGES, and EAST, DISTRICT JUDGE.

MERRILL, CIRCUIT JUDGE:

This suit was brought in California state courts by appellee, Virgil, complaining of a violation of his right of privacy. It was removed to federal court by appellant, Time, Incorporated, on grounds of diversity. This interlocutory appeal, taken pursuant to 28 U.S.C. § 1292(b), is from an order of the district court denying the motion of appellant for a summary judgment.

The facts are stated by the district court in its memorandum decision as follows:

> The complaint is based upon an article that appeared in the February 22, 1971, issue of *Sports Illustrated* magazine [owned by appellant], entitled "The Closest Thing to Being Born." The article concerned the sport of body surfing as practiced at the "Wedge," a public beach near Newport Beach, California, reputed to be the world's most dangerous site for body surfing. The article attempted to describe and explore the character of the unique breed of man who enjoys meeting the extreme hazards of body surfing at the Wedge. Plaintiff is well known as a constant frequenter of the Wedge and is acknowledged by body surfers there to be the most daredevil of them all. He was extensively interviewed by Thomas Curry Kirkpatrick, the author of the article, and much of the information obtained from these interviews was used in the *Sports Illustrated* story. Photographs showing plaintiff surfing and lying on the public beach were taken and used to illustrate the article.
>
> Plaintiff admits that he willingly gave interviews to Kirkpatrick and that he knew that his name and activities as a body surfer might be used in

connection with a forthcoming article in *Sports Illustrated*. But plaintiff now alleges that he "revoked all consent" upon learning that the article was not confined solely to testimonials to his undoubted physical prowess.

The article complained of was written by Kirkpatrick, a *Sports Illustrated* staff writer. In the summer of 1969 he received authorization from the senior editor of the magazine to do a story about the Wedge and the men who surf there. He was supplied with names and information about prominent body surfers, including the plaintiff, by the Beverly Hills bureau of Time, Inc. He began researching the article that summer, and contacted many surfers at the Wedge. Through these sources Kirkpatrick heard about the plaintiff and his daredevil attitude toward body surfing and life in general. He returned to the Newport Beach area the following summer to complete his research. It was during this period that Kirkpatrick first met the plaintiff and conducted several interviews with him.

The photographs complained of were taken by a local freelance photographer who was commissioned by the defendants to photograph the Wedge and the body surfers. The photographer arranged, through one of the surfers, to have a group of surfers, including the plaintiff, come to the Wedge to have their pictures taken in connection with the article.

Before publication the Kirkpatrick article was checked and researched by another *Sports Illustrated* staff member. For that purpose the checker telephoned the plaintiff's home and verified some of the information with the plaintiff's wife. The checker also talked to the plaintiff concerning the article, at which point for the first time, the plaintiff indicated his desire not to be mentioned in the article at all, and that he wanted to stop the story. While not disputing the truth of the article or the accuracy of the statements about him which it contained, and while admitting that he had known that his picture was being taken, the plaintiff indicated that he thought the article was going to be limited to his prominence as a surfer at the Wedge, and that he did not know that it would contain references to some rather bizarre incidents in his life that were not directly related to surfing.

In spite of the plaintiff's expressed opposition to the article, the article was published following its approval by the editorial staff and legal counsel for *Sports Illustrated*. In its published form, the article is eleven pages long and contains approximately 7,000 words. The article refers by name to many people who surf at the Wedge, and concludes in the last two pages with an account of the plaintiff's daredevil feats at the Wedge and a series of anecdotes about him that emphasize the psychological characteristics which presumably explain the reckless disregard for his own safety which his surfing demonstrates.

Along with the photographs of the plaintiff, he complains of these references to incidents in his private, or non-surfing, life.[1]

1. E.g.: "He is somewhat of a mystery to most of the regular personnel, partly because he is quiet and withdrawn, usually absent from their get-togethers, and partly because he is considered to be somewhat abnormal."

"Virgil's carefree style at the Wedge appears to have emanated from some escapades in his younger days, such as the time at a party when a young lady approached him and asked where she might find an ashtray. 'Why, my dear, right here,' said Virgil, taking her lighted cigarette and extinguishing it in his mouth. He also won a small bet one time by burning a hole in a dollar bill that was resting on the back of

The district court concluded that * * * the [privacy tort] alleged by plaintiff was that of public disclosure of embarrassing private facts. We agree.³

The most recent definition of this tort and discussion of its elements is that to be found in The American Law Institute Restatement (Second) of Torts (Tentative Draft No. 21, 1975). Section 652D gives a new name to the tort, "Publicity Given to Private Life." The black letter reads:

> One who gives publicity to a matter concerning the private life of another is subject to liability to the other for unreasonable invasion of his privacy, if the matter publicized is of a kind which
>
> (a) would be highly offensive to a reasonable person, and
>
> (b) is not of legitimate concern to the public.

With respect to "publicity" comment b reads in part:

> "Publicity," as it is used in this Section, differs from "publication," as that term is used in § 577 in connection with liability for defamation. "Publication," in that sense, is a word of art, which includes any communi-

his hand. In the process he also burned two holes in his wrist."

The article quoted a statement Virgil made to the author about a trip to Mammoth Mountain: "'I quit my job, left home and moved to Mammoth Mountain. At the ski lodge there one night I dove headfirst down a flight of stairs—just because. Because why? Well, there were these chicks all around. I thought it would be groovy. Was I drunk? I think I might have been.'"

The article quotes Virgil as saying: "Every summer I'd work construction and dive off billboards to hurt myself or drop loads of lumber on myself to collect unemployment compensation so I could surf at the Wedge. Would I fake injuries? No, I wouldn't fake them. I'd be damn injured. But I would recover. I guess I used to live a pretty reckless life. I think I might have been drunk most of the time.'"

Again quoting Virgil, the author relates: "'I love tuna fish. Eat it all the time. I do what feels good. That's the way I live my life. If it makes me feel good, whether it's against the law or not, I do it. I'm not sure a lot of the things I've done weren't pure lunacy.' Cherilee [plaintiff's wife] says, 'Mike also eats spiders and other insects and things.'"

Virgil was further quoted as saying, "'I've always been determined to find a sport I could be the best in. I was always aggressive as a kid. You know, competitive, mean. Real mean. I bit off the cheek of a Negro in a six-against-30 gang fight. They had tire irons with them. But that was a long time ago. At the Wedge, there are a lot of individualists.'"

The article notes: "Perhaps because most of his time was spent engaged in such activity, Virgil never learned how to read."

A photo caption reads: "Mike Virgil, the wild man of the Wedge, thinks it possible his brain is being slowly destroyed."

3. While the district court also determined that the "false light" theory applied, Virgil has expressly abandoned this theory on appeal. In the complaint appellee included other claims that can be regarded as dismissed from the case:

(A.) Intentional infliction of emotional distress. Under California law this is found only in cases of extreme or outrageous conduct, State Rubbish Collectors Association v. Siliznoff, 38 Cal.2d 330, 240 P.2d 282 (1952). Such conduct, apart from the invasion of privacy by the publication of private facts, is not present here, and the case is thus best treated on the basis of the publication tort only.

(B.) Intrusion into private areas. It is clear that Kirkpatrick did not intrude on appellee's solitude and that all interviews were freely given.

(C.) Libel. Virgil expressly denies that this is a libel action.

(D.) Publication of the photograph. Under California law one who voluntarily adopts a pose in public view waives any right of privacy in so far as that particular pose is concerned, Gill v. Hearst Publishing Co., 40 Cal.2d 224, 253 P.2d 441 (1953).

cation by the defendant to a third person. "Publicity," on the other hand, means that the matter is made public, by communicating it to the public at large, or to so many persons that the matter must be regarded as substantially certain to become one of public knowledge. The difference is not one of the means of communication, which may be oral, written, or by any other means. It is one of communication which reaches, or is sure to reach the public.

Thus it is not an invasion of the right of privacy, within the rule stated in this Section, to communicate a fact concerning the plaintiff's private life to a single person, or even to a small group of persons. On the other hand, any publication in a newspaper or a magazine, even of small circulation, or in a handbill distributed to a large number of persons, or any broadcast over the radio, or statement made in an address to a large audience, is sufficient to give publicity within the meaning of the term as it is used in this Section. The distinction, in other words, is one between private and public communication.

With respect to "private life," comment c reads in part:

The rule stated in this Section applies only to publicity given to matters concerning the private, as distinguished from the public, life of the individual. There is no liability when the defendant merely gives further publicity to information about the plaintiff which is already public. * * *

Likewise there is no liability for giving further publicity to what the plaintiff himself leaves open to the public eye.

It is argued that by voluntary disclosure of the facts to Kirkpatrick, knowing that he proposed to write an article including information about appellant, appellant had himself rendered public the facts disclosed. We cannot agree.

* * * The question, then, is whether the information disclosed was public rather than private—whether it was generally known and, if not, whether the disclosure by appellant can be said to have been to the public at large.

Talking freely to someone is not in itself, under comment c, making public the substance of the talk. There is an obvious and substantial difference between the disclosure of private facts to an individual—a disclosure that is selective and based on a judgment as to whether knowledge by that person would be felt to be objectionable—and the disclosure of the same facts to the public at large. * * *

Talking freely to a member of the press, knowing the listener to be a member of the press, is not then in itself making public. Such communication can be said to anticipate that what is said will be made public since making public is the function of the press, and accordingly such communication can be construed as a consent to publicize. Thus if publicity results it can be said to have been consented to. However, if consent is withdrawn prior to the act of publicizing, the consequent publicity is without consent.

We conclude that the voluntary disclosure to Kirkpatrick did not in itself constitute a making public of the facts disclosed.

Appellant contends that since Virgil has not denied the truth of the statements made in the article, the publication was privileged under the First Amendment. The law has not yet gone so far.

* * *

The Supreme Court, [in Cox Broadcasting Corp. v. Cohn] then, has not held in accordance with the contentions of appellant. Instead it has expressly declined to reach the issue presented. That issue seems to us to be whether, despite California's recognition and the recognition elsewhere given, this tortious violation of privacy is, as a tort to be written out of the law. It seems to us to contemplate the further question whether the private individual is hereafter to be able to enjoy a private life save with leave of the press; whether (at least so far as the press is concerned) the concept of "private facts" continues to have meaning.

To hold that privilege extends to all true statements would seem to deny the existence of "private" facts, for if facts be facts—that is, if they be true—they would not (at least to the press) be private, and the press would be free to publicize them to the extent it sees fit. The extent to which areas of privacy continue to exist, then, would appear to be based not on rights bestowed by law but on the taste and discretion of the press. We cannot accept this result.

To test the validity of such a rule we might start with the public's right to know under the First Amendment. Does the spirit of the Bill of Rights require that individuals be free to pry into the unnewsworthy private affairs of their fellowmen? In our view it does not. In our view fairly defined areas of privacy must have the protection of law if the quality of life is to continue to be reasonably acceptable. The public's right to know is, then, subject to reasonable limitations so far as concerns the private facts of its individual members.

If the public has no right to know, can it yet be said that the press has a constitutional right to inquire and to inform? In our view it cannot. It is because the public has a right to know that the press has a function to inquire and to inform. The press, then, cannot be said to have any right to give information greater than the extent to which the public is entitled to have information.

We conclude that unless it be privileged as newsworthy (a subject we discuss next), the publicizing of private facts is not protected by the First Amendment.

The privilege to publicize newsworthy matters is included in the definition of the tort set out in Restatement (Second) of Torts § 652D (Tenative Draft No. 21, 1975). Liability may be imposed for an invasion of privacy only if "the matter publicized is of a kind which * * * is not of legitimate concern to the public." While the Restatement does not so emphasize, we are satisfied that this provision is one of constitutional dimension delimiting the scope of the tort and that the extent of the privilege thus is controlled by federal rather than state law.

Restatement comment casts light on the nature of matter that "is not of legitimate concern to the public." The privilege extends to * * * "giving information to the public for purposes of education, amusement or enlightenment, where the public may reasonably be expected to have a legitimate interest in what is published," comment h.

That this privilege extends to private facts is made clear by comment f. It is emphasized, however, that the privilege is not unlimited. The comment states:

> In determining what is a matter of legitimate public interest, account must be taken of the customs and conventions of the community; and in the last analysis what is proper becomes a matter of the community mores. The line is to be drawn when the publicity ceases to be the giving of information to which the public is entitled, and becomes a morbid and sensational prying into private lives for its own sake, with which a reasonable member of the public, with decent standards, would say that he had no concern. * * *

In our judgment such a standard for newsworthiness does not offend the First Amendment; by the extreme limits it imposes in defining the tort [11] it avoids unduly limiting the breathing space needed by the press for the exercise of effective editorial judgment. See Miami Herald Publishing Co. v. Tornillo, 418 U.S. 241, 94 S.Ct. 2831, 41 L.Ed.2d 730 (1974). The definition of the "line to be drawn" is not as clear as one would wish, but it expresses the distinction between that which is of legitimate public interest and that which is not as well as we could do. * * *

We move, then, to the question whether, with such a standard to be applied, the district court correctly ruled that factual issues remained to be resolved on trial. Here appellant makes a vigorous attack upon the order appealed from. Appellant contends: "A press which must depend upon a governmental determination as to what facts are of 'public interest' in order to avoid liability for their truthful publication is not free at all. * * * [However,] protection of the editor's discretion need not result in a rule which abdicates all responsibility to the press. A constitutional rule can be fashioned which protects all the interests involved. This goal is achieved by providing a privilege for truthful publications which is defeasible only when the court concludes as a matter of law that the truthful publication complained of constitutes a clear abuse of the editor's constitutional discretion to publish and discuss subjects and facts which in his judgment are matters of public interest."

* * *

The final question, then, is whether in application of the standard for newsworthiness taken from the Restatement, jury questions are presented.

---

11. We do not intend that "morbid and sensational" be taken too literally. This language is not, in our view, to be regarded as a statement of a prerequisite, but rather as illustrative of the degree of offensiveness which should be present.

We may concede, arguendo, that the privilege to publicize newsworthy matter would, as matter of law, extend to the general subject of the article here in question: body surfing at the Wedge. While not hot news of the day, this subject quite properly can be regarded as of general public interest.

However, accepting that it is, as matter of law, in the public interest to know about some area of activity, it does not necessarily follow that it is in the public interest to know private facts about the persons who engage in that activity. The fact that they engage in an activity in which the public can be said to have a general interest does not render every aspect of their lives subject to public disclosure. Most persons are connected with some activity, vocational or avocational, as to which the public can be said as matter of law to have a legitimate interest or curiosity. To hold as matter of law that private facts as to such persons are also within the area of legitimate public interest could indirectly expose everyone's private life to public view. Limitations, then, remain to be imposed and at this point factual questions are presented respecting the state of community mores.

Among the questions so presented here are: Whether (and, if so, to what extent), private facts respecting Virgil, as a prominent member of the group engaging in body surfing at the Wedge, are matters in which the public has a legitimate interest; whether the identity of Virgil as the one to whom such facts apply is matter in which the public has a legitimate interest. (Additional questions, related not to privilege but to other elements of the tort are: whether, for reasons other than the voluntary and knowing communication to Kirkpatrick, the facts had become matter of public knowledge; if not, whether the publicizing of these facts would prove highly offensive to a reasonable person—one of ordinary sensibilities.)

On these questions the function of the court on motion for summary judgment is to decide whether, on the record, reasonable minds could differ. If in the judgment of the court reasonable minds could not differ, and the answer on which reasonable minds agree favors invocation of the privilege, then summary judgment for the appellant would be proper.

We have no way of knowing whether, in denying summary judgment, the court had in mind matters we have here discussed. * * * We think, on balance, the desirable remand would be one that invites reconsideration of the motion in the light of our views here expressed.

The order denying summary judgment is vacated and the case is remanded for reconsideration of the motion in the light of the views here expressed.

No costs are allowed to either party.

Question

Are you satisfied with the court's (and the Restatement's) definition of "legitimate public interest"? Can you suggest a standard that is more explicit than the rather vague one of whether "a reasonable member of the public, with decent standards, would say that [the matter is one as to which] he had no concern"? Should any distinction be made on the issue of First Amendment privilege as between the various items concerning the plaintiff contained in footnote 1?

Chapter Fifteen

RIGHT OF PRIVACY—FALSE LIGHT

A. NATURE OF THE INJURY

RESTATEMENT (SECOND) OF TORTS, § 652E

"Publicity Placing Person In False Light

One who gives publicity to a matter concerning another that places the other before the public in a false light is subject to liability to the other for invasion of his privacy, if

(a) the false light in which the other was placed would be highly offensive to a reasonable person, and

(b) the actor had knowledge of or acted in reckless disregard as to the falsity of the publicized matter and the false light in which the other would be placed."

KERBY v. HAL ROACH STUDIOS

District Court of Appeal, Second District, Division 3, California, 1942.
53 Cal.App.2d 207, 127 P.2d 577.

SHAW, JUSTICE pro tem. The plaintiff appeals from a judgment of nonsuit. No question is raised regarding the sufficiency of the complaint to present her case; hence we do not review its allegations.

The salient facts shown by the evidence are as follows: The plaintiff is an actress, concert singer, and monologist of many years' experience, both in the United States and Europe. For many years she has been and now is engaged in collecting American folk-lore, including legends, stories and songs, and in presenting them to the public on concert programs. Her character is conceded to be good. Defendant corporation is engaged in the business of producing motion pictures and defendant Seltzer is the head of its publicity department. In March, 1939, a motion picture which the corporation had produced was on exhibition in Los Angeles in the theater mentioned in the letter hereinafter set forth. For the purpose of advertising that picture the defendants caused a letter bearing plaintiff's name as apparent signer to be prepared, handwritten in a feminine hand and then reproduced mechanically on pink stationery, and also caused 1,000 copies of the letter so reproduced to be enclosed in pink envelopes, addressed in a feminine hand and sent by mail to 1,000 men householders selected by the mailing agency which addressed the envelopes. The date of mailing was March 8, 1939. All of this was done without plaintiff's knowledge or consent. The letter so sent reads as follows:

Dearest:

Don't breathe it to a soul, but I'm back in Los Angeles and more curious than ever to see you. Remember how I cut up about a year ago? Well, I'm raring to go again, and believe me I'm in the mood for fun.

Let's renew our *a*quaintanceship and I promise you an evening you won't forget. Meet me in front of Warners Downtown Theatre at 7th and Hill on Thursday. Just look for a girl with a gleam in her eye, a smile on her lips and mischief on her mind!

> Fondly,
> Your ectoplasmic playmate,
> Marion Kerby.

At the time this letter was sent plaintiff was a resident of Los Angeles. At that time and during all of the year 1939 her name and address were listed in the Los Angeles City Directory and in the Los Angeles telephone directory, and she was the only person of that name so listed. The name at the end of this letter, in addition to being that of plaintiff, was also the name of the chief character in two works of fiction previously published and of the chief feminine character in the moving picture above mentioned.

The effects of the sending of this letter in the manner and to the persons above described are not depicted in the record except by an excluded offer of proof and a showing that plaintiff had a large number of telephone calls and a personal visit in regard to it; but no evidence and little imagination and knowledge of human nature are necessary to enable anyone to understand what results should be expected. It could not but lead to misunderstandings between husbands and their wives who saw the letter and put the worst interpretation on it; it would arouse the expectations of lonesome males who were interested in the promised evening; and it must result in telephone calls and other communications from both irate wives and lonesome males and perhaps also from aggrieved but innocent husbands. It would also necessarily affect adversely the reputation of plaintiff with all who might read the letter and suppose her capable of writing and sending it. Apparently the defendants had no foresight in these matters, but they cannot for that reason escape the natural and probable consequences of their acts. The effect of all this on plaintiff does appear; she became terribly excited, nervous, unhappy; she had a feeling of disgrace and anguish; she was heartsick and didn't care what happened, whether she had the rest of a career or not; in the case of a lady caller plaintiff was afraid of being shot. Whereas she had fifteen paid engagements in the twelve months immediately preceding the publication, she had only two in seventeen months thereafter, but the evidence does not certainly show that this was due to the sending of the letter.

Does the law refuse all redress to one who has been thus grievously imposed upon and subjected to embarrassment, humiliation and scorn, merely to satisfy the desire of some business concern for publicity? We think not. Plaintiff rests her appeal here for redress upon her right of privacy and we think it may be so supported. The law regarding privacy is of somewhat recent development. In some states the right of privacy is not yet recognized as a justiciable right. But in California it has been accepted as a right the breach of which gives rise to a cause of action. (Melvin v. Reid, 1931, 112 Cal.App. 285, 297 P. 91, 92, where the law on this subject is quite fully discussed.) The case at bar differs in its facts from that just cited and from any other to which our attention has been called in which the right of privacy has been recognized and enforced, but that fact does not necessarily require us to hold that plaintiff has no right of action here. New sets of facts are continually arising to which, accepted legal principles must be applied, and the novelty of the factual situation is not an unscalable barrier to such application of the law. As stated in Melvin v. Reid, supra, quoting from another case, "The right of privacy has been defined as the right to live one's life in seclusion, without being subjected to unwarranted

Appearing in the original *Topper* motion picture: Topper (Roland Young), George Kirby (Cary Grant), and Marion Kirby (Constance Bennett).

and undesired publicity. In short, it is the right to be let alone." The court further said in Melvin v. Reid: "The right to pursue and obtain happiness is guaranteed to all by the fundamental law of our state. This right by its very nature includes the right to live free from the unwarranted attack of others upon one's liberty, property, and reputation. Any person living a life of rectitude has that right to happiness which includes a freedom from unnecessary attacks on his character, social standing, or reputation."

Here the plaintiff was, without her consent, plucked from her regular routine of life and thrust before the world, or at least 1,000 of its persons, as the author of a letter not written by her and of a nature to at least cast doubt on her moral character, and this was done in a manner to call down on her a train of highly undesirable consequences. This constituted as strong an invasion of the right of privacy as any of those described in the cases. As stated in Pavesich v. New England Life Ins. Co., 1905, 122 Ga. 190, 50 S.E. 68, 69 L.R.A. 101, 113, 106 Am.St.Rep. 104, 126, 2 Ann.Cas. 561, the right of privacy includes protection against "mortifying notoriety," unless some legal justification for its infliction exists. The desire to advertise a business constitutes no such justification. * * *

In Melvin v. Reid, 1931, supra, 112 Cal.App. 285, 297 P. 91, are listed certain qualifications and limitations of the right of privacy, but the present case does not come within any of them. The plaintiff's position as an actress and concert singer might have afforded justification for some sorts of publicity regarding her greater than that to which persons not so engaged must submit, but it in no wise justified the acts done by the defendants here.

Respondent contends that there is "nothing salacious, suggestive or immoral about the letter." Without going that far, a letter written and circulated as was this one might invade the right of privacy, but we cannot accede to this contention in all respects. To understand the full scope of the imputations made by the sending of the letter we must bear in mind all the circumstances of its sending. Plaintiff's name was signed at the end of it and this constituted an assertion that she had written it. It was handwritten in a feminine hand and on such stationery as women use in private correspondence, thus negativing any idea that it was a matter of business or anything but a personal communication to the addressee. It was sent to 1,000 male householders selected by the mailing agency. It may reasonably be inferred that many of these householders would be married and that few, if any, of them would have a personal acquaintance with plaintiff. The letter itself is of somewhat doubtful implications. While it does not directly assert or invite an improper relation between the writer and the person of the opposite sex to whom it is addressed, no great amount of imagination is necessary to read such a meaning into it, and it is easy to see how the wife of an addressee, if she saw the letter, might have done so. But apart from this, and giving the letter the most innocent meaning its words will reasonably bear, no modest woman of fine feelings and sensibilities would write such a letter as this to men whom she did not know. To suggest that a woman has written such a letter under such circumstances is to impute to her a laxness of character, a coarseness of moral fibre and a willingness to scrape acquaintance for no good purpose; and to spread such imputations abroad, as defendants have done, is as much an invasion of the right of privacy as was the publication of true but derogatory statements in Melvin v. Reid, 1931, supra, 112 Cal.App. 285, 297 P. 91.

Defendants also contend that the letter "is plainly an advertisement and should have been so regarded by any reasonable person," advancing in support of this contention the claim that it was printed and that it fixed no time for the meeting proposed. The exact method by which the letter was reproduced does not appear, but the evidence does show that it was first typewritten, then handwritten by a woman clerk, and that the longhand letter was turned over to an engraving plant by which an engraved plate was made. It is a matter of judicial notice that by such methods prints can be made which, in the absence of close inspection, will pass for original handwriting, and we cannot assume that this letter was obviously a printed one. There is nothing in its words to refer to the motion picture or to warn any reader that it was merely an advertisement or other work of fiction. As to the rendezvous, the letter proposed that it be in the evening "on Thursday." The recipient would easily understand this to mean the next Thursday after receipt of the letter, and this would not be so vague as to make it obvious that frustration would meet any attempt to keep the appointment.

As already indicated, the letter was circulated by defendants for the purpose of advertising a moving picture, and as far as appears they had no intent to refer therein to plaintiff and did not know of her existence, although they might easily have discovered it. These facts, which are stressed by defendants, tend to show want of malice, and might avert an award of punitive damages, but they constitute no defense to plaintiff's action. The letter did, in fact, refer to plaintiff in clear and definite fashion, and would reasonably have been so understood by anyone who knew of her existence. The wrong complained of is the invasion of plaintiff's right of privacy, and such an invasion is no less real or damaging because the invader supposed he was in other territory. The case bears considerable analogy, both as to the right invaded and the nature of the injury inflicted, to one of libel. It is well established that inadvertence or mistake affords no defense to a charge of libel, where the defamatory publication does, in fact, refer to the plaintiff. Davis v. Hearst, 1911, 160 Cal. 143, 155, 116 P. 530; Taylor v. Hearst, (1895) 107 Cal. 262, 270, 40 P. 392; Restatement, Torts, §§ 564, 579, and comment; Peck v. Tribune Co., 1909, 214 U.S. 185, 29 S.Ct. 554, 53 L.Ed. 960, 16 Ann.Cas. 1075; Corrigan v. Bobbs-Merrill Co., 1920, 228 N.Y. 58, 63, 126 N.E. 260, 262, 10 A.L.R. 662, 666. "The question is not so much who was aimed at as who was hit." Corrigan v. Bobbs-Merrill Co., supra.

The letter complained of here might very well have formed the basis of a charge of libel. It appears to come fully within the definition of libel in section 45 of the Civil Code. A libel need not be a statement directly referring to a person and stating something defamatory about him. It may as well be accomplished by falsely putting words into the mouth or attaching them to the pen of the person defamed and thus imputing to such person a willingness to use them, where the mere fact of having uttered or used the words would produce any of the results enumerated in section 45, supra. Karjavainean v. MacFadden Publications, 1940, 305 Mass. 573, 26 N.E.2d 538; Ben-Oliel v. Press Pub. Co., 1929, 251 N.Y. 250, 167 N.E. 432, 434; Gershwin v. Ethical Pub. Co., 1937, 166 Misc. 39, 1 N.Y.S.2d 904; D'Altomonte v. New York Herald Co., 1913, 154 App.Div. 453, 139 N.Y.S. 200, 202, approved on this point in 208 N.Y. 596, 102 N.E. 1101.

We do not, however, rest our decision on the ground of libel, for several reasons. The appellant has not sought to uphold her action as one for libel, and the complaint, while possibly sufficient to charge a libel, is not so labeled and was obviously not drawn for that purpose. The record does not show whether or not plaintiff complied with the statute (Stats.1871–72 p. 533; Deering's Gen.Laws, 1937, Act 4317) requiring a bond for costs to be filed in an action for libel or slander, but the facts above recited imbue us with a strong suspicion that she did not; and if such be the case her action, if for libel, would be subject to dismissal on its return to the lower court, unless such bond were filed. Williams v. Superior Court, 1935, 7 Cal.App.2d 436, 45 P.2d 1027; Bried v. Superior Court, 1938, 11 Cal.2d 351, 354, 79 P.2d 1091.

The judgment is reversed.

SCHAUER, P.J., and SHINN, J., concurred.

Questions

1. Since Miss Kerby could not recover for libel, is it not an evasion of the policy considerations which require the posting of a bond in a libel action to permit her to recover on the same facts by substituting the label "privacy" for that of "libel"?

2. Suppose that in fact Miss Kerby had written the letter to one particular person, and the defendant then reproduced the letter and made it public. Would this constitute libel? Would it constitute invasion of privacy?

3. Does the false light form of invasion of privacy require representations which are defamatory? Are any purported facts which actually are untrue sufficient to constitute a "false light"? What is the underlying rationale for the false light form of invasion of privacy? Is it intended to protect the subject's reputation, or does it have some other rationale? Recall your answer to this question when you consider Time, Inc. v. Hill, p. 792 infra.

STRICKLER v. NATIONAL BROADCASTING CO.
United States District Court, Southern District of California, Central Division, 1958.
167 F.Supp. 68.

WESTOVER, DISTRICT JUDGE. Plaintiff, a commander on active duty with the United States Navy, during October, 1956 was a passenger on a commercial air liner flying from Honolulu to San Francisco. While on such flight the air liner developed engine trouble and was forced to make an emergency landing. Plaintiff and other passengers and members of the crew were rescued by a Coast Guard cutter.

In 1957 defendants caused the name, identity and the aforesaid experiences of plaintiff to be depicted in dramatized form on a television program telecast over stations in Los Angeles and San Francisco and over numerous television stations affiliated with the defendant National Broadcasting Company, Inc. throughout the United States.

Plaintiff, claiming such telecasts were made in violation of his right of privacy and without his consent, filed the complaint at bar, setting forth nine causes of action. The First, Fifth, Sixth and Seventh Causes of Action are based on alleged invasion of the right of privacy upon non-statutory causes of action under the laws of California, Illinois, Florida and Pennsylvania.

The Third and Ninth Causes of Action allege invasion of the right of privacy, based upon the statutes of New York and Virginia.

The Second, Fourth and Eighth Causes of Action are based upon a claimed right to publicity.

The matter now comes before the court on a motion to dismiss. Plaintiff alleges in his first cause of action that the telecast, in depicting plaintiff's experiences in the emergency landing and evacuation, vividly and cruelly revived in the public mind and in his mind the terrible and horrifying experiences which he had begun to forget prior to such telecasts.

The complaint alleges the television program portrayed plaintiff in the highly personal and private act of praying during the course of emergency landing; that it showed him out of uniform and wearing a so-called Hawaiian shirt; that the television program repeatedly depicted plaintiff as smoking a pipe and cigarettes, and that the program did not indicate the valuable assistance given by him in the evacuation of the occupants of the plane. Plaintiff claims he was placed in a false position by the telecasts and has experienced humiliation, embarrassment and great mental pain and suffering.

A cause of action predicated upon invasion of privacy is a tort action. It is settled law that an action in tort is governed by the law of the jurisdiction where the tort occurred. Loranger v. Nadeau, 215 Cal. 362, 10 P.2d 63, 84 A.L.R. 1264. Plaintiff contends the tort was committed not only in California but was committed in every State where the telecast was shown. The problem is stated by Judge Goodrich of the Third Circuit in Leverton v. Curtis Publishing Co., 192 F.2d 974, at page 975, as follows:

> * * * Where was the right of privacy invaded, for instance: Alabama where the plaintiff lived, Pennsylvania where the Saturday Evening Post was published, or every state in the Union to which the Post goes? If so, is there a separate lawsuit for each invasion? Does recovery in one action for one invasion preclude suit in some other state for another invasion? * * *

Defendant, in contending there is only one State in which the action could be maintained, to-wit, California, relies primarily upon the case of Bernstein v. National Broadcasting Company, D.C., 129 F.Supp. 817, 825. * * *

We are of the opinion the rule in California should be the one laid down in the Bernstein case, to-wit: that the cause of action should be determined by the law of the jurisdiction where plaintiff sustained the injury. According to the allegations of plaintiff's complaint, he is a resident of California. As a consequence, the alleged causes of action in all States other than California must be dismissed. * * *

Defendant contends the First Cause of Action should * * * be dismissed. Inasmuch as this is a diversity case and plaintiff has a cause of action in California only, the Court must apply California law, California being the place of the alleged invasion of privacy.

The rule relative to a cause of action based on the right of privacy in California is set out in the case of Gill v. Hearst Publishing Co., 40 Cal.2d 224, at page 229, 253 P.2d 441, at page 444:

> * * *, the right of privacy is determined by the norm of the ordinary man; that is to say, the alleged objectionable publication must appear offensive in the light of "ordinary sensibilities." 41 Am.Jur., Privacy sec. 12, p. 934. As has been said: " * * * liability exists only if the defendant's conduct was such that he should have realized that it would be offensive to persons of ordinary sensibilities. It is only where the intrusion has gone beyond the limits of decency that liability accrues * * * ".

Defendant contends the allegations contained in the First Cause of Action of plaintiff's complaint, i.e., that plaintiff was depicted in the highly personal and private act of praying; that he was depicted out of uniform wearing a Hawaiian shirt, and that the program failed to indicate plaintiff assisted in any manner whatsoever in said emergency landing and evacuation, and that the television program repeatedly depicted plaintiff as smoking a pipe and cigarettes when, in fact, plaintiff did not smoke either pipe or cigarettes, is not in itself such as would be offensive to a person of ordinary sensibilities.

Defendants further contend the question of offensiveness is a question of law for the court, and that the court can review the allegations of offensiveness and as a matter of law determine whether or not they are of such a character as to be offensive to persons of ordinary sensibilities. However, the authorities do not sustain defendants' contention.

In Leverton v. Curtis Publishing Co., supra, 192 F.2d 974 at page 976, the Court says:

> * * * We find no help in any of the reported cases or views expressed by the essay writers in answering the question whether this answer is one for the fact-finding body to make. * * *

Judge Hamlin of the United States District Court for the Northern District of California, in Samuel v. Curtis Publishing Co., 122 F.Supp. 327, 328, stated:

> * * *, and whether there has been such an offensive invasion of privacy is *to some extent* * a question of law, * * *

The Supreme Court of California has, however, established the rule that such a question is one of fact. In Gill v. Curtis Publishing Co., 38 Cal.2d 273, at page 280, 239 P.2d 630, at page 635, the Court says:

> * * * If the test is, as defendants claim, what an ordinary man would consider such, then it is a question for the trier of fact rather than one of law.

Defendants' motion to dismiss the First Cause of Action of the complaint is denied.

RESTATEMENT (SECOND) OF TORTS; § 652E

Comment c:

Highly offensive to a reasonable person. The rule stated in this Section applies only when the publicity given to the plaintiff has placed him in a false light before the public, of a kind that would be highly offensive to a reasonable person. In other words, it applies only when the defendant knows that the plaintiff, as a reasonable man, would be justified in the eyes of the community in feeling seriously offended and aggrieved by the publicity. Complete and perfect accuracy in published reports concerning any individual is seldom attainable by any reasonable effort, and most minor errors, such as a wrong address for his home, or a mistake in the date when he entered his employment, or similar unimportant details of his career, would not in the absence of special circumstances give any serious offense to a reasonable person. The plaintiff's privacy is not invaded when the unimportant false statements are made, even when they are made deliberately. It is only when there is such a major misrepresentation of his character, history, activities or beliefs that serious offense may reasonably be expected to be taken by a reasonable man in his position, that there is a cause of action for invasion of privacy.

Question

Is the decision in *Strickler* in accordance with Comment c of Restatement (Second) § 652E? Recall Kelly v. Loew's Inc., supra.

* Emphasis supplied.

SPAHN v. JULIAN MESSNER, INC.

Court of Appeals of New York, 1966.
18 N.Y.2d 324, 274 N.Y.S.2d 877, 221 N.E.2d 543, vacated 387 U.S. 239, 87 S.Ct. 1706, 18 L.Ed.2d 744.

KEATING, JUDGE. To the knowing and the novice alike, the name Warren Spahn brings to mind one of professional baseball's great left-handed pitchers.

Each year, millions of people attend various ball parks throughout the country, hoping to root their team on to victory. National network systems transmit the games into homes and offices and huge sums are expended by advertisers for the attention of audiences attracted to the sport. Each Fall at World Series time, commerce and political programs equally are brought close to a standstill while a large part of the national attention is otherwise diverted.

The size of the audience attracted to each game, whether in person or by transmission, is the profession's bread and butter. The individual player's income will frequently be a direct reflection of his popularity and ability to attract an audience. Professional privacy is thus the very antithesis of the player's need and goal.

With this background, the plaintiff, Warren Spahn, seeks an injunction and damages for the defendants' unauthorized publication of a fictitious biography of his life.

The action is predicated on section 51 of the Civil Rights Law, Consol.Laws, c. 6, which authorizes the double remedy where a person's "name, portrait or picture is used within this state for advertising or for the purposes of trade" without that person's written consent. Its enactment may be traced directly to this court's opinion in Roberson v. Rochester Folding Box Co., 171 N.Y. 538, 545, 64 N.E. 442, 443, 59 L.R.A. 478, wherein we denied the existence of a legal right to privacy in New York but said that "The legislative body could very well interfere and arbitrarily provide that no one should be permitted for his own selfish purpose to use the picture or the name of another for advertising purposes without his consent." In Rhodes v. Sperry & Hutchinson Co., 193 N.Y. 223, 85 N.E. 1097, 34 L.R.A.,N.S., 1143, affd. sub nom. Sperry & Hutchinson Co. v. Rhodes, 220 U.S. 502, 31 S.Ct. 490, 55 L.Ed. 561, the statute enacted as a result of *Roberson* was held constitutional against claims that it deprived persons of liberty and property without due process of law and that it impaired the obligations of contract.

Over the years since the statute's enactment in 1903, its social desirability and remedial nature have led to its being given a liberal construction consonant with its over-all purpose (Flores v. Mosler Safe Co., 7 N.Y.2d 276, 280–281, 196 N.Y.S.2d 975, 977–979, 164 N.E.2d 853, 854–856; Lahiri v. Daily Mirror, 162 Misc. 776, 779, 295 N.Y.S. 382, 385). But at the same time, ever mindful that the written word or picture is involved, courts have engrafted exceptions and restrictions onto the statute to avoid any conflict with the free dissemination of thoughts, ideas, newsworthy events, and matters of public interest.

One of the clearest exceptions to the statutory prohibition is the rule that a public figure, whether he be such by choice or involuntarily, is subject to the often searching beam of publicity and that, in balance with the legitimate public interest, the law affords his privacy little protection (Koussevitzky v. Allen, Towne & Heath, 188 Misc. 479, 68 N.Y.S.2d 779, affd. 272 App.Div. 759, 69 N.Y.S.2d 432; Goelet v. Confidential, Inc., 5 A.D.2d 226, 171 N.Y.S.2d 223; see Hofstadter and Horowitz, The Right of Privacy, § 6.5 et seq.).

But it is erroneous to confuse privacy with "personality" or to assume that privacy, though lost for a certain time or in a certain context, goes forever unprotected (Binns v. Vitagraph Co., 210 N.Y. 51, 103 N.E. 1108, L.R.A. 1915C, 839; Hill v. Hayes, 15 N.Y.2d 986, 260 N.Y.S.2d 7, 207 N.E.2d 604, affg. 18 A.D.2d 485, 240 N.Y.S.2d 286). Thus it may be appropriate to say that the plaintiff here, Warren Spahn, is a public personality and that, insofar as his professional career is involved, he is substantially without a right to privacy. That is not to say, however, that his "personality" may be fictionalized and that, as fictionalized, it may be exploited for the defendants' commercial benefit through the medium of an unauthorized biography.

The factual reporting of newsworthy persons and events is in the public interest and is protected. The fictitious is not. This is the heart of the cases in point (Hill v. Hayes, 15 N.Y.2d 986, 260 N.Y.S.2d 7, 207 N.E.2d 604, supra; Koussevitzky v. Allen, Towne & Heath, 188 Misc. 479, 68 N.Y.S.2d 779, affd. 272 App.Div. 759, 69 N.Y.S.2d 432, supra; Goelet v. Confidential, Inc., 5 A.D.2d 226, 171 N.Y.S.2d 223, supra; Youssoupoff v. Columbia Broadcasting System, 19 A.D.2d 865, 244 N.Y.S.2d 1).

The plaintiff's status as a public figure makes him newsworthy and thus places his biography outside the protection afforded by the statute. But the plaintiff does not seek an injunction and damages for the unauthorized publication of his biography. He seeks only to restrain the publication of that which *purports to be his biography.*

In the present case, the findings of fact go far beyond the establishment of minor errors in an otherwise accurate biography (see Koussevitzky v. Allen, Towne & Heath, 188 Misc. 479, 484, 68 N.Y.S.2d 779, 783–784, supra.) They establish "dramatization, imagined dialogue, manipulated chronologies, and fictionalization of events" (opinion of the Appellate Division, 23 A.D.2d 216, 221, 260 N.Y.S.2d 451, 455). In the language of Justice Markowitz, who presided at the trial, "the record unequivocally establishes that the book publicizes areas of Warren Spahn's personal and private life, albeit inaccurate and distorted, and consists of a host, a preponderant percentage, of factual errors, distortions and fanciful passages" (43 Misc.2d 219, 232, 250 N.Y.S.2d 529, 542). A sufficient number of specific instances of falsification are set forth in that opinion to make repetition here unnecessary.

* * *

We thus conclude that the defendants' publication of a fictitious biography of the plaintiff constitutes an unauthorized exploitation of his personality for purposes of trade and that it is proscribed by Sec. 51 of the Civil Rights Law.

The order appealed from should be affirmed.

Order affirmed.

DESMOND, C.J., and FULD, VAN VOORHIS, BURKE, SCLEIPPI and BERGAN, JJ., concur.

[A subsequent proceeding in this case, after remand from the Supreme Court of the United States, is set forth at p. 816 infra.]

Question

Does "dramatization" or "fictionalization" necessarily constitute "false light"? Is the New York statute, as applied in this case, merely an expression of the false light doctrine as developed in the common law privacy cases?

B. FIRST AMENDMENT DEFENSE

TIME, INC. v. HILL

Supreme Court of the United States, 1967.
385 U.S. 374, 87 S.Ct. 534, 17 L.Ed.2d 456.

MR. JUSTICE BRENNAN delivered the opinion of the Court.

The question in this case is whether appellant, publisher of Life Magazine, was denied constitutional protections of speech and press by the application by the New York courts of §§ 50–51 of the New York Civil Rights Law to award appellee damages on allegations that Life falsely reported that a new play portrayed an experience suffered by appellee and his family.

The article appeared in Life in February 1955. It was entitled "True Crime Inspires Tense Play," with the sub-title, "The ordeal of a family trapped by convicts gives Broadway a new thriller. 'The Desperate Hours.'" The text of the article reads as follows:

> Three years ago Americans all over the country read about the desperate ordeal of the James Hill family, who were held prisoners in their home outside Philadelphia by three escaped convicts. Later they read about it in Joseph Hayes's novel, *The Desperate Hours,* inspired by the family's experience. Now they can see the story re-enacted in Hayes's Broadway play based on the book, and next year will see it in his movie, which has been filmed but is being held up until the play has a chance to pay off.
>
> The play, directed by Robert Montgomery and expertly acted, is a heart-stopping account of how a family rose to heroism in a crisis. *Life* photographed the play during its Philadelphia tryout, transported some of the actors to the actual house where the Hills were besieged. On the next page scenes from the play are re-enacted on the site of the crime.

The pictures on the ensuing two pages included an enactment of the son being "roughed up" by one of the convicts, entitled "brutish

Sec. B   **FIRST AMENDMENT DEFENSE**   793

FEVERISH FATHER cleverly foists off unloaded gun on the leader (Paul Newman), saves his son and family.

DARING DAUGHTER (Patricia Peardon) bites hand of youngest convict (George Grizzard), makes him drop gun.

The above photographs, with the indicated captions, appeared in Life Magazine.

(Cornell Capa, Life Magazine © 1965 Time Inc.)

convict," a picture of the daughter biting the hand of a convict to make him drop a gun, entitled "daring daughter," and one of the father throwing his gun through the door after a "brave try" to save his family is foiled.

The James Hill referred to in the article is the appellee. He and his wife and five children involuntarily became the subjects of a front-page news story after being held hostage by three escaped convicts in their suburban, Whitemarsh, Pennsylvania, home for 19 hours on September 11–12, 1952. The family was released unharmed. In an interview with newsmen after the convicts departed, appellee stressed that the convicts had treated the family courteously, had not molested them, and had not been at all violent. The convicts were thereafter apprehended in a widely publicized encounter with the police which resulted in the killing of two of the convicts. Shortly thereafter the family moved to Connecticut. The appellee discouraged all efforts to keep them in the public spotlight through magazine articles or appearances on television.

In the spring of 1953, Joseph Hayes' novel, The Desperate Hours, was published. The story depicted the experience of a family of four held hostage by three escaped convicts in the family's suburban home. But, unlike Hill's experience, the family of the story suffer violence at the hands of the convicts; the father and son are beaten and the daughter subjected to a verbal sexual insult.

The book was made into a play, also entitled The Desperate Hours, and it is Life's article about the play which is the subject of appellee's action. The complaint sought damages under §§ 50–51 on allegations that the Life article was intended to, and did, give the impression that the play mirrored the Hill family's experience, which, to the knowledge of defendant " * * * was false and untrue." Appellant's defense was that the article was "a subject of legitimate news interest," "a subject of general interest and of value and concern to the public" at the time of publication, and that it was "published in good faith without any malice whatsoever. * * *" A motion to dismiss the complaint for substantially these reasons was made at the close of the case and was denied by the trial judge on the ground that the proofs presented a jury question as to the truth of the article.

The jury awarded appellee $50,000 compensatory and $25,000 punitive damages. On appeal the Appellate Division of the Supreme Court ordered a new trial as to damages but sustained the jury verdict of liability. The court said as to liability:

> Although the play was fictionalized, *Life's* article portrayed it as a re-enactment of the Hills' experience. It is an inescapable conclusion that this was done to advertise and attract further attention to the play, and to increase present and future magazine circulation as well. It is evident that the article cannot be characterized as a mere dissemination of news, nor even an effort to supply legitimate newsworthy information in which the

public had, or might have a proper interest. 18 App.Div.2d 485, 489, 240 N.Y.S.2d 286, 290.

At the new trial on damages, a jury was waived and the court awarded $30,000 compensatory damages without punitive damages.[1]

The New York Court of Appeals affirmed the Appellate Division "on the majority and concurring opinions at the Appellate Division," two judges dissenting. 15 N.Y.2d 986, 207 N.E.2d 604. * * *

We reverse and remand the case to the Court of Appeals for further proceedings not inconsistent with this opinion.

I.

Since the reargument, we have had the advantage of an opinion of the Court of Appeals of New York which has materially aided us in our understanding of that court's construction of the statute. It is the opinion of Judge Keating for the court in Spahn v. Julian Messner, Inc., 18 N.Y.2d 324, 221 N.E.2d 543 (1966). * * *

Although "Right of Privacy" is the caption of §§ 50–51, the term nowhere appears in the text of the statute itself. The text of the statute appears to proscribe only * * * the appropriation and use in advertising or to promote the sale of goods, of another's name, portrait or picture without his consent.[2] An application of that limited scope would present different questions of violation of the constitutional protections for speech and press. Compare Valentine v. Chrestensen, 316 U.S. 52, with New York Times Co. v. Sullivan, 376 U.S. 254, 265–266.

The New York courts have, however, construed the statute to operate much more broadly. In *Spahn* the Court of Appeals stated that "Over the years since the statute's enactment in 1903, its social desirability and remedial nature have led to its being given a liberal construction consonant with its over-all purpose. * * * " 18 N.Y.2d, at 327, 221 N.E.2d, at 544. Specifically, it has been held in some circumstances to authorize a remedy against the press and other communications media which publish the names, pictures, or portraits of people without their consent. Reflecting the fact, however, that such applications may raise serious questions of conflict with the constitutional protections for speech and press, decisions under the statute have tended to limit the statute's application. "[E]ver mindful that the written word or picture is involved, courts have engrafted exceptions and restrictions onto the statute to avoid any conflict with the free

---

1. Initially, appellee's wife was joined in the action, and was awarded $75,000 compensatory and $25,000 punitive damages by the jury. However, her action was apparently dismissed by stipulation prior to remand, because the action has since proceeded solely upon appellee's judgment.

2. Utah's statute was modeled on New York's and, following early New York decisions, the Utah Supreme Court has construed it to afford a cause of action only in such cases. Donahue v. Warner Bros. Pictures Dist. Corp., 2 Utah 2d 256, 272 P.2d 177 (1954).

dissemination of thoughts, ideas, newsworthy events, and matters of public interest." Id., 18 N.Y.2d, at 328, 221 N.E.2d, at 544–545.

In the light of questions that counsel were asked to argue on reargument,[3] it is particularly relevant that the Court of Appeals made crystal clear in the *Spahn* opinion that truth is a complete defense in actions under the statute based upon reports of newsworthy people or events. The opinion states: "The factual reporting of newsworthy persons and events is in the public interest and is protected." 18 N.Y.2d, at 328, 221 N.E.2d, at 545.[4] Constitutional questions which might arise if truth were not a defense are therefore of no concern. Cf. Garrison v. Louisiana, 379 U.S. 64, 72–75.

But although the New York statute affords "little protection" to the "privacy" of a newsworthy person, "whether he be such by choice or involuntarily"[5] the statute gives him a right of action when his name, picture, or portrait is the subject of a "fictitious" report or article.[6]

---

3. "Upon reargument, counsel are requested to discuss in their further briefs and oral arguments, in addition to the other issues, the following questions:

"(1) Is the truthful presentation of a newsworthy item ever actionable under the New York statute as construed or on its face? If so, does appellant have standing to challenge that aspect of the statute?

"(2) Should the *per curiam* opinion of the New York Court of Appeals be read as adopting the following portion of the concurring opinion in the Appellate Division?

"'However, if it can be clearly demonstrated that the newsworthy item is presented, not for the purpose of disseminating news, but rather for the sole purpose of increasing circulation, then the rationale for exemption from section 51 no longer exists and the exemption should not apply. In such circumstances the privilege to use one's name should not be granted even though a true account of the event be given—let alone when the account is sensationalized and fictionalized.'" 384 U.S. 995.

4. This limitation to newsworthy persons and events does not of course foreclose an interpretation of the statute to allow damages where "Revelations may be so intimate and so unwarranted in view of the victim's position as to outrage the community's notions of decency." Sidis v. F-R Pub. Corp., 113 F.2d 806, 809 (C.A.2d Cir.), cert. denied, 311 U.S. 711 (1940). Cf. Garner v. Triangle Pubs., Inc., 97 F.Supp. 546, 550 (D.C.S.D.N.Y.1951); Restatement, Torts § 867, comment d (1939). See id., illust. 6. This case presents no question whether truthful publication of such matter could be constitutionally proscribed.

It has been said that a "right of privacy" has been recognized at common law in 30 States plus the District of Columbia and by statute in four States. See Prosser, Law of Torts 831–832 (3d ed. 1964). Professor Kalven notes, however, that since Warren and Brandeis championed an action against the press for public disclosure of truthful but private details about the individual which caused emotional upset to him, "it has been agreed that there is a generous privilege to serve the public interest in news. * * * What is at issue, it seems to me, is whether the claim of privilege is not so overpowering as virtually to swallow the tort. What can be left of the vaunted new right after the claims of privilege have been confronted?" Kalven, "Privacy and Tort Law—Were Warren and Brandeis Wrong?" 31 Law & Contemp.Prob., 326, 335–336 (1966). * * *

5. "One of the clearest exceptions to the statutory prohibition is the rule that a public figure, whether he be such by choice or involuntarily, is subject to the often searching beam of publicity and that, in balance with the legitimate public interest, the law affords his privacy little protection," *Spahn*, supra, at 328, 221 N.E.2d, at 545.

6. Binns v. Vitagraph Co., 210 N.Y. 51, 103 N.E. 1108 (1913); Youssoupoff v. Columbia Broadcasting System, Inc., 19 App. Div.2d 865, 244 N.Y.S.2d 1 (1963); Sutton v. Hearst Corp., 277 App.Div. 155, 98 N.Y.S.2d 233 (1950); Koussevitzky v. Allen, Towne & Heath, Inc., 188 Misc. 479, 68 N.Y.S.2d 779, 272 App.Div. 759, 69 N.Y.S.2d 432 (1947); Lahiri v. Daily Mirror, Inc., 162 Misc. 776, 295 N.Y.Supp. 382 (1937). The doctrine of

Spahn points up the distinction. *Spahn* was an action under the statute brought by the well-known professional baseball pitcher, Warren Spahn. He sought an injunction and damages against the unauthorized publication of what purported to be a biography of his life. The trial judge had found that "the record unequivocally establishes that the book publicizes areas of Warren Spahn's personal and private life, albeit inaccurate and distorted, and consists of a host, a preponderant percentage, of factual errors, distortions and fanciful passages. * * *" 43 Misc.2d 219, 232, 250 N.Y.S.2d 529, 542. The Court of Appeals sustained the holding that in these circumstances the publication was proscribed by § 51 of the Civil Rights Law and was not within the exceptions and restrictions for newsworthy events engrafted onto the statute. The Court of Appeals said:

> But it is erroneous to confuse privacy with "personality" or to assume that privacy, though lost for a certain time or in a certain context, goes forever unprotected. * * * Thus it may be appropriate to say that the plaintiff here, Warren Spahn, is a public personality and that, insofar as his professional career is involved, he is substantially without a right to privacy. That is not to say, however, that his "personality" may be fictionalized and that, as fictionalized, it may be exploited for the defendants' commercial benefit through the medium of an unauthorized biography. *Spahn,* supra, at 328, 221 N.E.2d at 545.

As the instant case went to the jury, appellee, too, was regarded to be a newsworthy person "substantially without a right to privacy" insofar as his hostage experience was involved, but to be entitled to his action insofar as that experience was "fictionalized" and "exploited for the defendants' commercial benefit." "Fictionalization," the *Spahn* opinion states, "is the heart of the cases in point." 18 N.Y.2d, at 328, 221 N.E.2d, at 545.

"fictionalization" has been applied where there is no statute. See, e.g., Leverton v. Curtis Pub. Co., 192 F.2d 974 (C.A.3d Cir. 1951); Hazlitt v. Fawcett Pubs., 116 F.Supp. 538 (D.C.Conn.1953); Garner v. Triangle Pubs., Inc., 97 F.Supp. 546 (D.C.S.D. N.Y.1951). Commentators have likened the interest protected in those "privacy" cases which focus upon the falsity of the matter to that protected in cases of libel and slander—injury to the reputation. See Prosser, Privacy, 48 Calif.L.Rev. 383, 398–401 (1960); Wade, Defamation and the Right of Privacy, 15 Vand.L.Rev. 1093 (1962). But see Bloustein, Privacy As An Aspect of Human Dignity: An Answer to Dean Prosser, 39 N.Y.U.L.Rev. 962, 991–993 (1964). Many "right of privacy" cases could in fact have been brought as "libel per quod" actions, and several have been brought on both grounds. See, e.g., Hazlitt v. Fawcett Pubs., supra; Freeman v. Busch Jewelry Co., 98 F.Supp. 963 (D.C.N.D.Ga.1951); Peay v. Curtis Pub. Co., 78 F.Supp. 305 (D.C.D.C.1948); Foster-Milburn Co. v. Chinn, 134 Ky. 424, 120 S.W. 364 (1909). Although not usually thought of in terms of "right of privacy," all libel cases concern public exposure by false matter, but the primary harm being compensated is damage to reputation. In the "right of privacy" cases the primary damage is the mental distress from having been exposed to public view, although injury to reputation may be an element bearing upon such damage. See *Wade,* supra, at 1124. Moreover, as *Spahn* illustrates, the published matter need not be defamatory, on its face or otherwise, and might even be laudatory and still warrant recovery. Our decision today is not to be taken to decide any constitutional questions which may be raised in "libel per quod" actions involving publication of matters of public interest, or in libel actions where the plaintiff is not a public official. Nor do we intimate any view whether the Constitution limits state power to sanction publication of matter obtained by an intrusion into a protected area, for example, through the use of electronic listening devices.

The opinion goes on to say that the "establishment of minor errors in an otherwise accurate" report does not prove "fictionalization." Material and substantial falsification is the test. However, it is not clear whether proof of knowledge of the falsity or that the article was prepared with reckless disregard for the truth is also required. In New York Times Co. v. Sullivan, 376 U.S. 254, we held that the Constitution delimits a State's power to award damages for libel in actions brought by public officials against critics of their official conduct. Factual error, content defamatory of official reputation, or both are insufficient for an award of damages for false statements unless actual malice—knowledge that the statements are false or in reckless disregard of the truth—is alleged and proved. The *Spahn* opinion reveals that the defendant in that case relied on *New York Times* as the basis of an argument that application of the statute to the publication of a substantially fictitious biography would run afoul of the constitutional guarantees. The Court of Appeals held that *New York Times* had no application. The court, after distinguishing the cases on the ground that *Spahn* did not deal with public officials or official conduct, then says, "The free speech which is encouraged and essential to the operation of a healthy government is something quite different from an individual's attempt to enjoin the publication of a fictitious biography of him. No public interest is served by protecting the dissemination of the latter. We perceive no constitutional infirmities in this respect." 18 N.Y.2d, at 329, 221 N.E.2d, at 546.

If this is meant to imply that proof of knowing or reckless falsity is not essential to a constitutional application of the statute in these cases, we disagree with the Court of Appeals.[7] We hold that the constitutional protections for speech and press preclude the application of the New York statute to redress false reports of matters of public interest in the absence of proof that the defendant published the report with knowledge of its falsity or in reckless disregard of the truth.

The guarantees for speech and press are not the preserve of political expression or comment upon public affairs, essential as those are to healthy government. One need only pick up any newspaper or magazine to comprehend the vast range of published matter which exposes persons to public view, both private citizens and public officials. Exposure of the self to others in varying degrees is a concomitant of life in a civilized community. The risk of this exposure is an essential incident of life in a society which places a primary value on freedom of speech and of press. "Freedom of discussion, if it would fulfill its historic function in this nation, must embrace all issues about which information is needed or appropriate to enable the members of society to cope with the exigencies of their period." Thornhill v. Alabama, 310 U.S. 88, 102. "No suggestion can be found in the Constitution that the

---

7. Of course *Spahn* is not before us and we in no wise imply any view of the merits of the judgment or remedy afforded the plaintiff in that case. Our reliance is solely on Judge Keating's opinion as an aid to understanding the construction placed on the statute by the New York courts.

freedom there guaranteed for speech and the press bears an inverse ratio to the timeliness and importance of the ideas seeking expression." Bridges v. California, 314 U.S. 252, 269. We have no doubt that the subject of the Life article, the opening of a new play linked to an actual incident, is a matter of public interest. "The line between the informing and the entertaining is too elusive for the protection of * * * [freedom of the press]." Winters v. New York, 333 U.S. 507, 510. Erroneous statement is no less inevitable in such a case than in the case of comment upon public affairs, and in both, if innocent or merely negligent, " * * * it must be protected if the freedoms of expression are to have the 'breathing space' that they 'need * * * to survive'. * * * " New York Times Co. v. Sullivan, supra, at 271–272. As James Madison said, "Some degree of abuse is inseparable from the proper use of every thing; and in no instance is this more true than in that of the press." 4 Elliot's Debates on the Federal Constitution 571 (1876 ed.). We create a grave risk of serious impairment of the indispensable service of a free press in a free society if we saddle the press with the impossible burden of verifying to a certainty the facts associated in news articles with a person's name, picture or portrait, particularly as related to nondefamatory matter. Even negligence would be a most elusive standard, especially when the content of the speech itself affords no warning of prospective harm to another through falsity. A negligence test would place on the press the intolerable burden of guessing how a jury might assess the reasonableness of steps taken by it to verify the accuracy of every reference to a name, picture or portrait.

In this context, sanctions against either innocent or negligent misstatement would present a grave hazard of discouraging the press from exercising the constitutional guarantees. Those guarantees are not for the benefit of the press so much as for the benefit of all of us. A broadly defined freedom of the press assures the maintenance of our political system and an open society. Fear of large verdicts in damage suits for innocent or merely negligent misstatement, even fear of the expense involved in their defense, must inevitably cause publishers to "steer * * * wider of the unlawful zone," New York Times Co. v. Sullivan, 376 U.S., at 279; see also Speiser v. Randall, 357 U.S. 513, 526; Smith v. California, 361 U.S. 147, 153–154; and thus "create the danger that the legitimate utterance will be penalized." Speiser v. Randall, supra, at 526.

But the constitutional guarantees can tolerate sanctions against *calculated* falsehood without significant impairment of their essential function. We held in *New York Times* that calculated falsehood enjoyed no immunity in the case of alleged defamation of a public official concerning his official conduct. Similarly, calculated falsehood should enjoy no immunity in the situation here presented us. What we said in Garrison v. Louisiana, supra, at 75, is equally applicable:

> The use of calculated falsehood * * * would put a different cast on the constitutional question. Although honest utterance, even if inaccurate, may further the fruitful exercise of the right of free speech, it does not

follow that the lie, knowingly and deliberately published * * * should enjoy a like immunity. * * * For the use of the known lie as a tool is at once at odds with the premises of democratic government and with the orderly manner in which economic, social, or political change is to be effected. Calculated falsehood falls into that class of utterances which "are no essential part of any exposition of ideas, and are of such slight social value as a step to truth that any benefit that may be derived from them is clearly outweighed by the social interest in order and morality. * * *" Chaplinsky v. New Hampshire, 315 U.S. 568, 572. Hence the knowingly false statement and the false statement made with reckless disregard of the truth, do not enjoy constitutional protection.

We find applicable here the standard of knowing or reckless falsehood, not through blind application of New York Times Co. v. Sullivan, relating solely to libel actions by public officials, but only upon consideration of the factors which arise in the particular context of the application of the New York statute in cases involving private individuals. This is neither a libel action by a private individual nor a statutory action by a public official. Therefore, although the First Amendment principles pronounced in *New York Times* guide our conclusion, we reach that conclusion only by applying these principles in this discrete context. It therefore serves no purpose to distinguish the facts here from those in *New York Times*. Were this a libel action, the distinction which has been suggested between the relative opportunities of the public official and the private individual to rebut defamatory charges might be germane. And the additional state interest in the protection of the individual against damage to his reputation would be involved. Cf. Rosenblatt v. Baer, 383 U.S. 75, 91 (Stewart, J., concurring). Moreover, a different test might be required in a statutory action by a public official, as opposed to a libel action by a public official or a statutory action by a private individual. Different considerations might arise concerning the degree of "waiver" of the protection the State might afford. But the question whether the same standard should be applicable both to persons voluntarily and involuntarily thrust into the public limelight is not here before us.

II.

Turning to the facts of the present case, the proofs reasonably would support either a jury finding of innocent or merely negligent misstatement by Life, or a finding that Life portrayed the play as a re-enactment of the Hill family's experience reckless of the truth or with actual knowledge that the portrayal was false. The relevant testimony is as follows:

Joseph Hayes, author of the book, also wrote the play. The story theme was inspired by the desire to write about "true crime" and for years before writing the book, he collected newspaper clippings of stories of hostage incidents. His story was not shaped by any single incident, but by several, including incidents which occurred in California, New York, and Detroit. He said that he did not consciously portray any member of the Hill family, or the Hill family's experience, although admitting that "in a very direct way" the Hill experience "triggered" the writing of the book and the play.

The Life article was prepared at the direction and under the supervision of its entertainment editor, Prideaux. He learned of the production of the play from a news story. The play's director, Robert Montgomery, later suggested to him that its interesting stage setting would make the play a worthwhile subject for an article in Life. At about the same time Prideaux ran into a friend of author Hayes, a free-lance photographer, who told Prideaux in casual conversation that the play had a "substantial connection with a true-life incident of a family being held by escaped convicts near Philadelphia." As the play was trying out in Philadelphia, Prideaux decided to contact the author. Hayes confirmed that an incident somewhat similar to the play had occurred in Philadelphia, and agreed with Prideaux to find out whether the former Hill residence would be available for the shooting of pictures for a Life article. Prideaux then met with Hayes in Philadelphia where he saw the play and drove with Hayes to the former Hill residence to test its suitability for a picture story. Neither then nor thereafter did Prideaux question Hayes about the extent to which the play was based on the Hill incident. "A specific question of that nature was never asked, but a discussion of the play itself, what the play was about, in the light of my own knowledge of what the true incident was about, confirmed in my mind beyond any doubt that there was a relationship, and Mr. Hayes' presence at this whole negotiation was tacit proof of that."

Prideaux sent photographers to the Hill residence for location photographs of scenes of the play enacted in the home, and proceeded to construct the text of the article. In his "story file" were several news clippings about the Hill incident which revealed its nonviolent character, and a New York Times article by Hayes in which he stated that the play "was based on various news stories," mentioning incidents in New York, California, Detroit and Philadelphia.

Prideaux's first draft made no mention of the Hill name except for the caption of one of the photographs. The text related that a true story of a suburban Philadelphia family had "sparked off" Hayes to write the novel, that the play was a "somewhat fictionalized" account of the family's heroism in time of crisis. Prideaux's research assistant, whose task it was to check the draft for accuracy, put a question mark over the words "somewhat fictionalized." Prideaux testified that the question mark "must have been" brought to his attention, although he did not recollect having seen it. The draft was also brought before the copy editor, who, in the presence of Prideaux, made several changes in emphasis and substance. The first sentence was changed to focus on the Hill incident, using the family's name; the novel was said to have been "inspired" by that incident, and the play was referred to as a "re-enactment." The words "somewhat fictionalized" were deleted.

Prideaux labeled as "emphatically untrue" defense counsel's suggestion during redirect examination that from the beginning he knew that the play had no relationship to the Hill incident apart from being a hostage incident. Prideaux admitted that he knew the play was "between a little bit and moderately fictionalized," but stated that he thought beyond doubt that the important quality, the "heart and soul" of the play, was the Hill incident.

The jury might reasonably conclude from this evidence—particularly that the New York Times article was in the story file, that the copy editor deleted "somewhat fictionalized" after the research assistant questioned its accuracy, and that Prideaux admitted that he knew the play was "between a little bit and moderately fictionalized"—that Life knew the falsity of, or was reckless of the truth in, stating in the article that "the story re-enacted" the Hill family's experience. On the other hand, the jury might reasonably predicate a finding of innocent or only negligent misstatement on the testimony that a statement was made to Prideaux by the free-lance photographer that linked the play to an incident in Philadelphia, that the author Hayes cooperated in arranging for the availability of the former Hill home, and that Prideaux thought beyond doubt that the "heart and soul" of the play was the Hill incident.[8]

III.

We do not think, however, that the instructions confined the jury to a verdict of liability based on a finding that the statements in the article were made with knowledge of their falsity or in reckless disregard of the truth. The jury was instructed that liability could not be found under §§ 50–51 "merely because of some incidental mistake of fact, or some incidental incorrect statement," and that a verdict of liability could rest only on findings that (1) Life published the article, "not to disseminate news, but was using plaintiffs' names, in connection with a fictionalized episode as to plaintiffs' relationship to The Desperate Hours" * * *

The court also instructed the jury that an award of punitive damages was justified if the jury found that the appellant falsely connected appellee to the play "knowingly or through failure to make a reasonable investigation," adding "You do not need to find that there was any actual ill will or personal malice toward the plaintiffs if you find a reckless or wanton disregard of the plaintiffs' rights."

Appellee argues that the instructions to determine whether Life "altered or changed" the true facts, and whether, apart from incidental errors, the article was a "substantial fiction" or a "fictionalized version" were tantamount to instructions that the jury must find that Life knowingly falsified the facts. We do not think that the instructions

---

8. Where either result finds reasonable support in the record it is for the jury, not for this Court, to determine whether there was knowing or reckless falsehood. Cf. New York Times Co. v. Sullivan, supra, 284–285.

bear that interpretation, particularly in light of the marked contrast in the instructions on compensatory and punitive damages. The element of "knowingly" is mentioned only in the instruction that punitive damages must be supported by a finding that Life falsely connected the Hill family with the play "knowingly or through failure to make a reasonable investigation." Moreover, even as to punitive damages, the instruction that such damages were justified on the basis of "failure to make a reasonable investigation" is an instruction that proof of negligent misstatement is enough, and we have rejected the test of negligent misstatement as inadequate. * * *

The requirement that the jury also find that the article was published "for trade purposes," as defined in the charge, cannot save the charge from constitutional infirmity. "That books, newspapers, and magazines are published and sold for profit does not prevent them from being a form of expression whose liberty is safeguarded by the First Amendment." Joseph Burstyn, Inc. v. Wilson, 343 U.S. 495, 501–502; see New York Times Co. v. Sullivan, 376 U.S., at 266; Smith v. California, 361 U.S. 147, 150; cf. Ex parte Jackson, 96 U.S. 727, 733; Grosjean v. American Press Co., 297 U.S. 233; Lovell v. Griffin, 303 U.S. 444.

IV.

The appellant argues that the statute should be declared unconstitutional on its face if construed by the New York courts to impose liability without proof of knowing or reckless falsity.[9] Such a declaration would not be warranted even if it were entirely clear that this had previously been the view of the New York courts. The New York Court of Appeals, as the *Spahn* opinion demonstrates, has been assiduous in construing the statute to avoid invasion of the constitutional protections of speech and press. We, therefore, confidently expect that the New York courts will apply the statute consistently with the constitutional command. Any possible difference with us as to the thrust of the constitutional command is narrowly limited in this case to the failure of the trial judge to instruct the jury that a verdict of liability could be predicated only on a finding of knowing or reckless falsity in the publication of the Life article.

The judgment of the Court of Appeals is set aside and the case is remanded for further proceedings not inconsistent with this opinion.

It is so ordered.

MR. JUSTICE BLACK, with whom MR. JUSTICE DOUGLAS joins, concurring.

* * *

---

9. Appellant further contends that the threat of criminal penalty invalidates the statute. However, there have been only two cases of criminal proceedings under the statute and both resulted in dismissal. People v. Charles Scribner's Sons, 205 Misc. 818, 130 N.Y.S.2d 514 (1954); People v. McBride & Co., 159 Misc. 5, 288 N.Y.Supp. 501 (1936). There is therefore little realistic threat of prosecution. Cf. United States v. Raines, 362 U.S. 17, 20–24 (1960).

I acquiesce in the application here of the narrower constitutional view of *New York Times* with the belief that this doctrine too is bound to pass away as its application to new cases proves its inadequacy to protect freedom of the press from destruction in libel cases and other cases like this one. The words "malicious" and particularly "reckless disregard of the truth" can never serve as effective substitutes for the First Amendment words: " * * * make no law * * * abridging the freedom of speech, or of the press. * * * "

Mr. Justice Douglas, concurring.

As intimated in my separate opinion in Rosenblatt v. Baer, 383 U.S. 75, 88, and in the opinion of my Brother Black in the same case, id., at 94, state action to abridge freedom of the press is barred by the First and Fourteenth Amendments where the discussion concerns matters in the public domain. The episode around which this book was written had been news of the day for some time. The most that can be said is that the novel, the play, and the magazine article revived that interest. A fictionalized treatment of the event is, in my view, as much in the public domain as would be a watercolor of the assassination of a public official. It seems to me irrelevant to talk of any right of privacy in this context. Here a private person is catapulted into the news by events over which he had no control. He and his activities are then in the public domain as fully as the matters at issue in New York Times Co. v. Sullivan, 376 U.S. 254. Such privacy as a person normally has ceases when his life has ceased to be private. * * *

Mr. Justice Harlan, concurring in part and dissenting in part.

While I find much with which I agree in the opinion of the Court, I am constrained to express my disagreement with its view of the proper standard of liability to be applied on remand. Were the jury on retrial to find negligent rather than, as the Court requires, reckless or knowing "fictionalization," I think that federal constitutional requirements would be met.

I.

The Court's opinion demonstrates that the fictionalization doctrine upon which New York premises liability is one would strip newsworthy material, otherwise protected, of its constitutional shield upon a mere showing of substantial falsity. * * *

Like the Court, I consider that only a narrow problem is presented by these facts. To me this is not "privacy" litigation in its truest sense. See Prosser, Law of Torts § 112; Silver, Privacy and the First Amendment, 34 Ford.L.Rev. 553; but see Bloustein, Privacy as an Aspect of Human Dignity: An Answer to Dean Prosser, 39 N.Y.U.L.Rev. 962. No claim is made that there was any intrusion upon the Hills' solitude or private affairs in order to obtain information for publication. The power of a State to control and remedy such intrusion for newsgathering purposes cannot be denied, cf. Mapp v. Ohio, 367 U.S. 643, but is not here asserted. Similarly it may be strongly contended that certain facts are of such limited public interest and so intimate and potentially embarrassing to an individual that the State may exercise its power to deter publication. Feeney v. Young, 191 App.Div. 501, 181 N.Y.Supp. 481; see Sidis v. F–R Pub. Corp., 113 F.2d 806, 808. But the instructions to the jury, the opinions in the New York appellate courts, and indeed the arguments advanced by both sides before this Court all recognize that the theme of the article in question was a perfectly proper one and that an article of this type could have been prepared without liability. Winters v. New York, 333 U.S. 507, 510. The record is replete with articles commenting on the genesis of The Desperate Hours, one of which was prepared by the author himself and used by appellee to demonstrate the supposed falsity of the Life piece. Finally no claim is made that appellant published the article to advance a commercial interest in the play. There is no evidence to show that Time, Inc., had any financial interest in the production or even that the article was published as an advertisement. Thus the question whether a State may apply more stringent limitations to the use of the personality in "purely commercial advertising" is not before the Court. See Valentine v. Chrestensen, 316 U.S. 52.

II.

Having come this far in step with the Court's opinion, I must part company with its sweeping extension of the principles of New York Times Co. v. Sullivan, 376 U.S. 254. * * *

[A] State should be free to hold the press to a duty of making a reasonable investigation of the underlying facts and limiting itself to "fair comment"[10] on the materials so gathered. Theoretically, of course, such a rule might slightly limit press discussion of matters touching individuals like Mr. Hill. But, from a pragmatic standpoint, until now the press, at least in New York, labored under the more exacting handicap of the existing New York privacy law and has certainly remained robust. Other professional activity of great social value is carried on under a duty of reasonable care and there is no reason to suspect the press would be less hardy than medical practitioners or attorneys for example. The "freedom of the press" guaranteed by the First Amendment, and as reflected in the Fourteenth, cannot be

---

10. A negligence standard has been applied in libel actions both where the underlying facts are alleged to be libelous, Layne v. Tribune Co., 108 Fla. 177, 146 So. 234, and where comment is the subject of the action, Clancy v. Daily News Corp., 202 Minn. 1, 277 N.W. 264. Similarly the press should not be constitutionally insulated from privacy actions brought by parties in the position of Mr. Hill when reasonable care has not been taken in ascertaining or communicating the underlying facts or where the publisher has not kept within the traditional boundaries of "fair comment" with relation to underlying facts and honest opinion. See Prosser, Law of Torts § 110, at 815–816. Similar standards of reasonable investigation and presentation have long been applied in misrepresentation cases. See, e.g., International Products Co. v. Erie Railroad Co., 244 N.Y. 331, 155 N.E. 662; Nash v. Minnesota Title Insurance & Trust Co., 163 Mass. 574, 40 N.E. 1039. Under such a standard the fact that the publication involved in this case was not defamatory would enter into a determination of the amount of care which would have been reasonable in the preparation of the article.

thought to insulate all press conduct from review and responsibility for harm inflicted. The majority would allow sanctions against such conduct only when it is morally culpable. I insist that it can also be reached when it creates a severe risk of irremediable harm to individuals involuntarily exposed to it and powerless to protect themselves against it. I would remand the case to the New York courts for possible retrial under that principle.

A constitutional doctrine which relieves the press of even this minimal responsibility in cases of this sort seems to me unnecessary and ultimately harmful to the permanent good health of the press itself. If the *New York Times* case has ushered in such a trend it will prove in its long-range impact to have done a disservice to the true values encompassed in the freedoms of speech and press.

MR. JUSTICE FORTAS, with whom THE CHIEF JUSTICE and MR. JUSTICE CLARK, join, dissenting.

The Court's holding here is exceedingly narrow. It declines to hold that the New York "Right of Privacy" statute is unconstitutional. I agree. The Court concludes, however, that the instructions to the jury in this case were fatally defective because they failed to advise the jury that a verdict for the plaintiffs could be predicated only on a finding of knowing or reckless falsity in the publication of the Life article. Presumably, the appellee is entitled to a new trial. If he can stand the emotional and financial burden, there is reason to hope that he will recover damages for the reckless and irresponsible assault upon himself and his family which this article represents. But he has litigated this case for 11 years. He should not be subjected to the burden of a new trial without significant cause. This does not exist. Perhaps the purpose of the decision here is to indicate that this Court will place insuperable obstacles in the way of recovery by persons who are injured by reckless and heedless assaults provided they are in print, and even though they are totally divorced from fact. If so, I should think that the Court would cast its decision in constitutional terms. Short of that purpose, with which I would strongly disagree, there is no reason here to order a new trial. The instructions in this case are acceptable even within the principles today announced by the Court. * * * The gravamen of the court's charge, repeated *three times* in virtually the same words, was the following:

> It is for you to determine whether, in publishing the article, the defendant Time, Incorporated *altered* or *changed* the true facts concerning plaintiffs' relationship to The Desperate Hours, so that the article, as published, constituted substantially fiction or a *fictionalized version* for trade purposes. * * * (Emphasis supplied.)

The jury was also instructed that "Before the plaintiffs can be entitled to a verdict * * * you must find that the statements concerning the plaintiffs in the article *constituted fiction,* as compared with news, or matters which were newsworthy." (Emphasis supplied.) With all respect, I submit that this is close enough to this Court's insistence upon "knowing or reckless falsity" as to render a reversal arbitrary and unjustified. If the defendant *altered* or *changed* the true facts so that the article as published was a *fictionalized* version, this, in my judgment, was a knowing or reckless falsity. "Alteration" or "change" denotes a positive act—not a negligent or inadvertent happening. "Fictionalization" and "fiction" to the ordinary mind mean so departing from fact and reality as to be *deliberately* divorced from the fact—not merely in detail but in general and pervasive impact. The English language is not so esoteric as to permit serious consequences to turn upon a supposed difference between the instructions to the jury and this Court's formulation. Nor is the First Amendment in such delicate health that it requires or permits this kind of surgery, the net effect of which is not only an individual injustice, but an encouragement to recklessness and careless readiness to ride roughshod over the interests of others. * * *

This Court cannot and should not refuse to permit under state law the private citizen who is aggrieved by the type of assault which we have here and which is not within the specially protected core of the First Amendment to recover compensatory damages for recklessly inflicted invasion of his rights.

Accordingly, I would affirm.

Questions

1. The opinion in *Time* appears to be primarily if not exclusively concerned with the freedom of the press. Would the doctrine of *Time* be equally applicable if the motion picture and stage productions of "The Desperate Hours" had identified the Hill family, and if the producers of such productions rather than Time, Inc. had been the defendants?

2. Should the result have been different if the acknowledgement that the play was "somewhat fictionalized" had been retained in the Life article? Could it then be said that the Hill family was placed in a "false light"?

3. Is the rule of *Time* limited to "public figures" as is the libel rule under *New York Times* and *Gertz*? Is it limited to "newsworthy" persons? Does the mere fact that a person is mentioned in a news article conclusively establish that he is "newsworthy"? If not, what standard should be applied in determining newsworthiness? Cf. Cantrell v. Forest City Publishing Co., 419 U.S. 245, 250, 95 S.Ct. 465, 469, 42 L.Ed.2d 419 (1974), wherein the Supreme Court suggested the possibility of "a more relaxed standard of liability for a publisher or broadcaster of false statements injurious *to a private individual* under a false-light theory of invasion of privacy * * * " (emphasis added).

4. Is the exclusion of liability without fault, and the limitation on damages, as articulated in Gertz v. Robert Welch, Inc., supra with reference to defamation, now to be read as a gloss on Time, Inc. v. Hill with reference to false light invasion of privacy?

5. How does the "false light" branch of privacy conceptually relate to the "private facts" branch? How does it relate to defamation? Was the *Time* Court correct in applying what is essentially the *New York Times* defamation rule to false light privacy invasion? See the Note which immediately follows.

Collateral References

Kalven, *The Reasonable Man and the First Amendment: Hill, Butts, and Walker,* 1967 Sup.Ct.Rev. 267.

Franklin, *A Constitutional Problem in Privacy Protection: Legal Inhibitions on Reporting of Fact,* 16 Stan.Law Rev. 107 (1963).

Bloustein, *Privacy, Tort Law and the Constitution: Is Warren and Brandeis' Tort Petty and Unconstitutional as Well?,* 46 Tex.Law Rev. 611 (1968).

Green, *Continuing the Privacy Discussion: A Response to Judge Wright and President Bloustein,* 46 Tex.Law Rev. 750 (1968).

Note *

Was the Supreme Court, in Time, Inc. v. Hill, correct in applying virtually the same rule to privacy as it did to defamation in the *New York Times* case? I think the Court was in error, and that the error derives from the superficial similarity between defamation and the particular form of privacy invasion presented by the *Time* case.

It is necessary to recall first Dean Prosser's classic categorization of the four types of privacy cases. He lists these as:

1. Intrusion upon the plaintiff's seclusion or solitude, or into his private affairs.

2. Public disclosure of embarrassing private facts about the plaintiff.

3. Publicity which places the plaintiff in a false light in the public eye.

4. Appropriation, for the defendant's advantage, of the plaintiff's name or likeness.[1]

We may put to one side those forms of privacy invasion which Dean Prosser labels as "intrusion" and "appropriation." Intrusion does not raise first amendment difficulties since its perpetration does not involve speech or other expression. It occurs by virtue of the physical or mechanical observation of the

---

* This is an extract from Nimmer, The Right to Speak From *Times* to *Time:* First Amendment Theory Applied to Libel and Misapplied to Privacy, 56 Cal.Law Rev. 935 (1968).

1. Prosser, Privacy, 48 Calif.L.Rev. 383, 389 (1960). Essentially the same categorization is to be found in W. Prosser, Handbook of the Law of Torts § 112, at 832–44 (3d ed. 1964), and in Restatement (Second) of Torts § 652A (Tent.Draft No. 13, 1967), for which Dean Prosser was the Reporter. The considerable number of cases which have adopted the Prosser categorization are collected in Bloustein, Privacy as An Aspect of Human Dignity: An Answer to Dean Prosser, 39 N.Y.U.L.Rev. 962, 964 n. 10 (1964), and in Wade, Defamation and the Right of Privacy, 15 Vand.L.Rev. 1093, 1095 n. 13 (1962).

This is not the place to explore the substantive differences between the right of privacy as developed at common law and under the New York statute. Such differences, however, are not as great as is sometimes assumed. See Spahn v. Julian Messner, Inc., 43 Misc.2d 219, 250 N.Y.S.2d 529 (Sup.Ct.1964), aff'd, 23 App.Div.2d 216, 260 N.Y.S.2d 451 (1965), affirmed 18 N.Y.2d 234, 221 N.E.2d 543, 274 N.Y.S.2d 877 (1966), vacated and remanded, 387 U.S. 239 (1967). For the purpose of delineating the line between the interest in privacy and that in free speech it is not necessary to dwell upon such substantive differences as exist.

private affairs of another,[2] and not by the publication [3] of such observations. The appropriation form of privacy invasion probably also does not raise first amendment problems, although here speech and other expression is involved. [See Chapter Sixteen, Par. C.] * * *

The difficult first amendment questions in the privacy area are found only when a publication comes under either the "public disclosure of embarrassing private facts" or "false light" labels.

The Court in *Time* emphasized that it was dealing only with a false light type case, and that it was not deciding the question of constitutional sanction for truthful publication of matters " 'so intimate and so unwarranted in view of the victim's position as to outrage the community's notions of decency.' " But the first amendment implications of the false light privacy cases cannot be understood standing alone. There must first be an understanding of the proper weight to be accorded the right of free speech as applied to the type of privacy case with which the Court said it was not dealing, that which involves questions of the public disclosure of embarrassing private facts. It is necessary to understand the manner in which the interest to be protected in such cases differs from the interest to be protected by the defamation torts.

The crucial distinction between privacy and defamation when private facts are disclosed relates to the markedly different interests that are to be protected by the right of privacy on the one hand, and defamation on the other. No defamation action would lie by reason of the publication of embarrassing private facts in view of the defense of truth. Defamation protects a man's interest in his reputation. Reputation is by definition a matter of public knowledge. Injury in a defamation action arises not by the act of bringing an alleged fact to public knowledge, but by the effect on a person's reputation which results from the disclosure of such fact. The right of privacy protects not reputation, but the interest in maintaining the privacy of certain facts. Public disclosure of such facts can create injury regardless of whether such disclosure affects the subject's reputation. The injury is to man's interest in maintaining a haven from society's searching eye.[4] Professor Bloustein in a thoughtful article has stated the distinction well: "The gravamen of a defamation action is engendering a false opinion about a person, whether in the mind of one other

---

2. See Restatement (Second) of Torts, § 652B, comment b at 103 (Tent.Draft No. 13, 1967).

3. Id. comment a.

4. This concept has been a recurring one. Judge Cooley spoke of the right "to be left alone," T. Cooley, A Treatise on the Law of Torts 29 (2d ed. 1888). Consider, however, the explication of the Cooley phrase in Konvitz, Privacy and the Law: A Philosophical Prelude, 31 Law & Contemp. Prob. 272, 279 (1966). Warren and Brandeis in their seminal article found that a necessary concomitant of the interest in an "inviolate personality" was the right of an individual to determine "to what extent his thoughts, sentiments, and emotions shall be communicated to others." Warren & Brandeis, The Right to Privacy, 4 Harv.L.Rev. 193, 198 (1890). Some years later Mr. Justice Brandeis in his dissent to Olmstead v. United States, 277 U.S. 438, 478 (1928) returned to the same theme: "The makers of our Constitution undertook to secure conditions favorable to the pursuit of happiness. They recognized the significance of man's spiritual nature, of his feeling and of his intellect. * * * They sought to protect Americans in their beliefs, their thoughts, their emotions and their sensations. They conferred as against the Government, the right to be let alone—the most comprehensive of rights and the right most valued by civilized men." A variation of the theme recently reached fruition in Griswold v. Connecticut, 381 U.S. 479 (1965), although in the context of a constitutional shield, essentially unrelated to the tort action sword here under scrutiny.

person or many people. The gravamen in the public disclosure [privacy] cases is degrading a person by laying his life open to public view."[5]

Granting this distinction, how does it bear upon whether the first amendment definitional balance applied in defamation actions should be found applicable in privacy actions? Prima facie it might be argued that greater first amendment protection should be afforded to privacy-invading publications than to defamatory publications, since the right of privacy (at least when dealing with the public disclosure of private facts) deals with matters admittedly true while defamation involves matters found to be false. Truth, it may be argued, deserves greater freedom than falsity. But this overly facile approach will not bear analysis. For the reasons set forth below, I would suggest that the privacy definitional balance should give a lesser scope to the first amendment privilege than is recognized under the *Times* definitional balance for defamation. Indeed, with some diffidence, and subject to qualifications set forth below, I would go so far as to deny completely the application of the first amendment privilege to the public disclosure of embarrassing private facts.

I make two important qualifications to the foregoing thesis. First, I intend to deal here only with the public disclosure of embarrassing *private* facts, that is, with facts which but for the defendant's disclosure would not have been known to members of the public. Some privacy cases go beyond this limitation in that the defendant incurs liability by disclosing to a larger segment of the public that which was already known to some smaller public segment.[6] For our present purposes it is irrelevant whether as a matter of tort law this is or is not a desirable extension of the tort right of privacy. The point here is that the suggested exclusion of the first amendment from privacy cases goes only to those cases in which truly private matters are revealed. If a particular speech does not deal with private matters, then however one might characterize the

---

5. Bloustein, supra note 67, at 981. See also Warren and Brandeis, supra note 73, at 197: "The principle on which the law of defamation rests, covers, however, a radically different class of effects from those for which attention is now asked. It deals only with damage to reputation, with the injury done to the individual in his external relations to the community, by lowering him in the estimation of his fellows. The matter published * * * must, in order to be actionable, have a direct tendency to injure him in his intercourse with others * * * the effect of the publication upon his estimate of himself and upon his own feelings not forming an essential element in the cause of action."

A number of cases have recognized the distinction between the interests to be protected by the right of privacy and the tort of defamation. See, e.g., Themo v. New England Newspaper Publishing Co., 306 Mass. 54, 57, 27 N.E.2d 753, 755 (1940): "The fundamental difference between a right of privacy and a right to freedom from defamation is that the former directly concerns one's own peace of mind, while the latter concerns primarily one's reputation. * * * *" Accord, Reed v. Real Detective Publishing Co., 63 Ariz. 294, 306, 162 P.2d 133, 139 (1945); Kelly v. Johnson Publishing Co., 160 Cal.App.2d 718, 721, 325 P.2d 659, 661 (1958); Fairfield v. American Photocopy Equipment Co., 138 Cal.App.2d 82, 86, 291 P.2d 194, 197 (1955); Continental Optical Co. v. Reed, 119 Ind.App. 643, 647–48, 86 N.E.2d 306, 308 (1949); Brink v. Griffith, 65 Wash.2d 253, 255, 396 P.2d 793, 796 (1964).

6. E.g., Strickler v. National Broadcasting Co., 167 F.Supp. 68 (S.D.Cal.1958); Daily Times Democrat v. Graham, 276 Ala. 380, 162 So.2d 474 (1964); Cason v. Baskin, 159 Fla. 31, 30 So.2d 635 (1947); Gautier v. Pro-Football, Inc., 304 N.Y. 354, 360, 107 N.E.2d 485, 489 (1952): "So, one attending a public event such as a professional football game * * * may be [televised] as part of the general audience, but may not be picked out of a crowd alone, thrust upon the screen and unduly featured for public view." But Prosser states that a privacy action will not lie unless the facts disclosed to the public are private, not theretofore publicly known nor matters of public record. W. Prosser, Handbook of the Law of Torts, § 112, at 836 (3d ed. 1964). See also Kalven, Privacy in Tort Law—Were Warren and Brandeis Wrong?, 31 Law & Contemp.Prob. 326, 333 (1966).

interest which competes with the right of free speech, it seems obvious that it is not an interest in privacy.[7]

The second important qualification I make is that the public disclosure of an *embarrassing* private fact should be without first amendment protection only if the disclosure is embarrassing but not defamatory. If a disclosure adversely affects the subject's reputation, then the policy reasons which support the right of speech when reputations are attacked [8] outweigh the privacy considerations.

Notwithstanding these qualifications, there remains a significant privacy area having to do with truly private facts,[9] the disclosure of which, although noninjurious to the subject's reputation, is nevertheless highly embarrassing or otherwise offensive to the subject.[10] The thesis here suggested is that there are greater speech values in a reputation-injuring statement than in a nondefamatory (or "pure") privacy-invading statement; consequently the definitional balance should more severely restrict speech in the case of the pure privacy-invading statement than in the case of defamation.

Where the injury is to reputation, the important consideration is the underlying rationale that the cure for injury due to speech should not be abridgment of that speech but rather "more speech." Reputations which can be injured by false statements can be rehabilitated by further speech which establishes the truth. But this rationale does not apply to invasions of privacy; when publication invades privacy the injury arises from the mere fact of publication, and further speech cannot remedy the injury. Suppose that a nude photograph of a young lady is surreptitiously obtained and published in a newspaper or magazine.[11] Assume further that the publication in no way imputes the cooperation of the young lady in making or publishing the

---

7. One may speak of a protectible interest in personality, or in human dignity, or in individuality, but though such phrases may have some utility in shaping tort law, they are not capable of constituting well-defined interests which can usefully counter the interest in free speech in striking a definitional balance.

8. See the Note which follows New York Times v. Sullivan, supra.

9. "Private facts" are not necessarily facts known only to the subject himself. They are facts which, though known to the immediate participants, are unknown to any substantial number of casual observers, i.e., to the "public."

10. Plaintiff recovered, or the cause of action was recognized, in the following privacy cases: Mau v. Rio Grande Oil, Inc., 28 F.Supp. 845 (N.D.Cal.1939) (plaintiff, an innocent victim of robbery and shooting, depicted on a radio program which reenacted the events); Bazemore v. Savannah Hospital, 171 Ga. 257, 155 S.E. 194 (1930) (publication of nude photographs of plaintiff's malformed child taken in defendant's hospital); McAndrews v. Roy, 131 So.2d 256 (La. Ct.App.1961) (plaintiff undertook treatment at defendant's health studio, and defendant thereafter published "before and after" photographs of plaintiff); Barber v. Time, Inc., 348 Mo. 1199, 159 S.W.2d 291 (1942) (publication of photograph of plaintiff in bed while under hospital treatment for a rare noncontagious ailment, together with an accompanying article identifying plaintiff by name); Griffin v. Medical Society, 11 N.Y.S.2d 109 (Sup.Ct.1939) (publication of plaintiff's photographs made by his physicians before and after treatment); see Feeney v. Young, 191 App.Div. 510, 181 N.Y.S. 481 (1920) (plaintiff permitted motion picture film to be made of her giving birth under a cesarean section operation, but only for the purpose of exhibiting the film to medical societies. Upon public exhibition of the film, held that testimony as to the content of the film should have been admissible, contrary to the ruling below.)

11. For similar but not identical facts, see Meyers v. U.S. Camera Publishing Corp., 9 Misc.2d 765, 167 N.Y.S.2d 771 (City Ct.1957); Myers v. Afro-American Publishing Co., 168 Misc. 429, 5 N.Y.S.2d 223 (Sup. Ct.1938), affirmed mem., 225 App.Div. 838, 7 N.Y.S.2d 662 (1938) (libel action). The two nude plaintiffs Myers were not the same person.

photograph, so that no element of defamation exists. The young lady's privacy injury arises from the mere fact of publication. No amount of further speech can cure the injury—the indignity and humiliation which arose from the initial publication. The fact is that unlike injury arising from defamation, "more speech" is irrelevant in mitigating the injury due to an invasion of privacy.

Moreover, while it has been argued above that the basic rationale for speech justifies first amendment immunity for defamatory statements,[12] this same rationale does not justify immunizing privacy-invading speech. First, speech necessary for an effective and meaningful democratic dialogue by and large does not require references to the intimate activities of named individuals.[13] This is to be contrasted with defamation where a fruitful dialogue may often require references to named individuals that reflect adversely upon the reputations of such individuals. Second, to a society that values privacy, it is difficult to conclude that the right to invade another man's privacy is a necessary function of self-expression or fulfillment. Again this is to be contrasted with defamation where the right to attack another man's reputation may properly be thought of as a valid exercise of self-expression. Finally, the "safety-valve" function does not operate here as it does in the realm of defamation. To permit an attack on a man's reputation may forestall the resort to physical violence. It is to be doubted, however, that the ability to publicly expose intimate activities serves as a sublimation for physical force. This is admittedly a rough-hewn guess as to the psychological forces at work, but I think most readers will agree with the conclusion.

Now return to the *Time* decision in which the Court limited its holding to the false light privacy cases. Since these, like defamation and unlike the private facts disclosures, deal with false statements, was the Court justified in this context in reaching a definitional balance which approximates the defamation balance? The Court fell into error by reason of its failure to pierce the superficial similarity between false light invasion of privacy and defamation, and by its failure to formulate a doctrine which rationally relates the false light cases to the underlying interest in privacy. The heart of the problem of finding a conceptual base for the false light privacy cases lies in the erroneous assumption that the untrue representations in a false light case are necessarily defamatory (or reputation-injuring) in nature.

It is true that this assertion can be supported by some of the authorities. Dean Prosser has expressed the view that in the false light cases "[t]he interest protected is clearly that of reputation, with the same overtones of mental distress as in defamation,"[14] and Professor Kalven, in denying any rational conceptual base for the false light cases, has rhetorically asked: "If the

---

12. See footnote 8, supra.

13. Remember that we do not here speak of reputation-injuring speech.

14. Prosser, Privacy, 48 Calif.L.Rev. 383, 400 (1960). Dean Prosser does state earlier that the false light "need not necessarily be a defamatory one," id., but in view of the statement quoted in the text, this must be understood as meaning that the false statement may be actionable although it does not meet all of the technical requirements for liability under the law of defamation. He later enlarges upon this point in expressing concern that the false light cases may be "capable of swallowing up and engulfing the whole law of public defamation. * * * If that turns out to be the case, it may well be asked, what of the numerous restrictions and limitations which have hedged defamation about for many years, in the interest of freedom of the press and discouragement of trivial and extortionate claims? Are they of so little consequence that they may be circumvented in so casual and cavalier a fashion?" Id. at 401. See also Restatement (Second) of Torts § 652E, special note at 122 (Tent. Draft No. 13, 1967).

statement is not offensive enough to the reasonable man to be defamatory, how does it become offensive enough to the reasonable man to be an invasion of privacy?"[15] If Dean Prosser and Professor Kalven are correct in concluding that the untrue statements in false light privacy cases are necessarily reputation injuring, then the *Time* decision was correct in finding the definitional balance for false light privacy actions to be essentially the same as that for defamation. If a false statement will not constitute a cause of action for libel, why should a plaintiff be able to circumvent the limitations built into the law of defamation by labeling his action one for invasion of privacy?

But the underlying premise is wrong. An untrue statement may in the same way as a public disclosure of embarrassing private facts constitute an invasion of privacy without in any manner constituting an injury to the subject's reputation. Once the false light cases are understood as a logical, even a necessary, extension of the private facts cases, the fallacy of equating the false light cases to defamation actions becomes apparent. The injury to the plaintiff's peace of mind which results from the public disclosure of private facts may be just as real where that which is disclosed is not true. It would be absurd to hold that the publication of an intimate fact creates liability, but that the defendant is immunized from liability (though the injury to plaintiff's peace of mind is no less) if the intimate "fact" publicly disclosed turns out not to be true, thus putting a premium on falsehood. The sensibilities of the young lady whose nude photo is published would be no less offended if it turned out that her face were superimposed upon someone else's nude body. The resulting humiliation would have nothing to do with truth or falsity. The unwarranted disclosure of intimate "facts" is no less offensive and hence no less deserving of protection merely because such "facts" are not true.

It should follow, then, that those false light cases which if true would fall into the public disclosure of embarrassing private facts branch of privacy should be regarded as conceptually indistinguishable from the latter category. If, as argued above, first amendment immunity is not properly applicable to the latter, it likewise should not be applied to the former. This conclusion must be subject to qualifications similar to those expressed with reference to the public disclosure of embarrassing private facts. If the untrue statements in a false light case are not as to matters which *if true* would be private, then the interest in privacy is by hypothesis nonexistent and therefore cannot counterbalance any opposing interest in free speech. Such a publication may nevertheless be offensive, and tortious under the law of privacy,[16] but the tort defense of

---

15. Kalven, Privacy in Tort Law—Were Warren and Brandeis Wrong?, 31 Law and Contemp.Prob. 326, 340 (1966).

16. E.g., Strickler v. National Broadcasting Co., 167 F.Supp. 68 (S.D.Cal.1958) (plaintiff alleging false depiction on a television program of his conduct on a commercial airliner in praying, wearing a Hawaiian shirt rather than his Naval uniform, smoking, and failing to assist in an emergency landing, held to state a cause of action); Fairfield v. American Photocopy Equipment Co., 138 Cal.App.2d 82, 291 P.2d 194 (1955) (plaintiff's name listed among "thousands of leading law firms" that use defendant's machines, when in fact the plaintiff had found the machine unsatisfactory and had returned it); Battaglia v. Adams, 164 So.2d 195 (Fla.1964) (Richard Nixon held to have a right to privacy to prevent unauthorized use of his name on the Florida presidential primary ballot); Spahn v. Julian Messner, Inc., 43 Misc.2d 219, 250 N.Y.S.2d 529 (Sup.Ct. 1964), affirmed 23 App.Div.2d 216, 260 N.Y. S.2d 451 (1965), affirmed 18 N.Y.2d 234, 221 N.E.2d 543, 274 N.Y.S.2d 877 (1966), vacated and remanded, 387 U.S. 239 (1967) ("embarrassing distortion" of the plaintiff's war record so as to make him out to be a wartime hero); Goldberg v. Ideal Publishing Corp., 210 N.Y.S.2d 938 (Sup.Ct.1960) (views on sexual freedom falsely ascribed to the plaintiff, a rabbi).

newsworthiness may carry with it the force of first amendment privilege without being met by the countervailing force of the interest in privacy.[17]

Moreover, if a particular statement not only constitutes an invasion of privacy but also injures the subject's reputation and is therefore prima facie defamatory (subject to the defense of truth), then the *Times* definitional balance for defamation should be applicable. If the first amendment protects such defamatory statements, the right to make them may not be abridged under state law even if the state law gives a "privacy" rather than a "defamation" label to such abridgment. As "libel can claim no talismanic immunity from constitutional limitations,"[18] neither can the talisman of "privacy" vitiate the constitutional protection for speech values contained in defamatory speech, even if that same speech also invades privacy.[19] This may seem to lead to an odd result. That is, one may obtain judicial redress if a statement merely invades one's privacy, but if it goes farther and both invades privacy and is detrimental to reputation, then (at least if one is a public figure) he may be precluded by the first amendment from a judicial remedy. But such a result is not so odd as might at first appear. If a reputation-injuring statement contains speech values not to be found in a privacy-invading statement, those values remain even if the statement combines reputation-injuring and privacy-invading elements. The defense of such values justifies weighing the definitional balance so as to afford first amendment protection where the speech combines both such elements.

The foregoing qualifications would not require first amendment protection for all false light privacy cases. Dean Prosser and Professor Kalven to the contrary, there are many false light cases in which there is no reputation interest to be protected, but only the interest in protecting against embarrassment and humiliation which results from the public disclosure of factually

---

17. It is possible to argue that false light cases which do not deal with matters which if true would be private should have the same exemption from the first amendment as should false light cases where the statement if true would relate to private areas of conduct. If a nude photograph which is false in the sense that the plaintiff's face has been superimposed upon the nude body of another will constitute an invasion of privacy not subject to a first amendment privilege if the setting purports to be the privacy of the plaintiff's bedroom, should the defendant's liability be any less if the setting is falsely depicted as a busy downtown thoroughfare? Despite this seemingly arbitrary distinction, I would submit that the definitional balance should shift when that which is depicted purports to deal in matters open to the public, and that in such circumstances the rule adopted in *Times* as restated in *Time* may properly be applied. As with any definition balance, this rule will produce certain fringe absurdities, such as that suggested above, but it is nevertheless necessary in order to preserve the necessary breathing space for press and speech. If a publication purports to relate to a private aspect of conduct, then regardless of whether it is true or false, the publisher is on notice that he is invading the privacy of another. But if the conduct allegedly occurred in public, then to make the publisher's liability under the law of *privacy* turn absolutely on whether the statement is true or false would be to inhibit publication of that which the publisher may in good faith believe to be both true and nonprivate, and thus to stifle much that may be of legitimate public interest. At this point, on balance it seems preferable to adopt the rule which vitiates the first amendment privilege only in the event of knowing falsity or reckless conduct.

18. New York Times Co. v. Sullivan, 376 U.S. 254, 269 (1964).

19. This is roughly analogous to the decisions in Sears, Roebuck & Co. v. Stiffel Co., 376 U.S. 225 (1964) and Compco Corp. v. Day-Brite Lighting, Inc., 376 U.S. 234 (1964) wherein the Court held that if a design may be freely appropriated under the federal patent and copyright laws, such appropriation may not be rendered actionable under the state law of unfair competition.

untrue, but purportedly private facts.[20] Indeed, Time, Inc. v. Hill is itself a case in point. The defendant falsely reported that in a private setting—within their own home—the son of the Hill family was " 'roughed up' by one of the convicts * * * the daughter [bit] the hand of a convict to make him drop a gun * * * and * * * the father [threw] his gun through the door after a 'brave try' to save his family [and was] foiled." In fact the convicts had treated the Hill family courteously, had not molested them, and there had been no violence. The Hill family was indeed depicted in a false light, and in such a manner that a trier of fact might well find it to be offensive to persons of "ordinary sensibilities." But, surely, nothing in such depiction was injurious to the reputation of any of the Hill family. A report of brutal treatment at the hand of criminals and a brave attempt to resist the criminals is hardly calculated to hold the victims up to public contempt, ridicule, and obloquy. It is submitted, then, that the Court in *Time* was wrong in applying to false light privacy cases in general, and to the particular case before it, a rule which can be justified only when the particular false light case contains defamatory elements, or does not purport to relate to public matters.

The fact that what allegedly happened to the Hill family was news should not in the name of the first amendment justify an obliteration of society's commitment to the values of privacy.[21] The reporting of intimate private matters, whether or not they are true, may pander to the public curiosity, but if the report does not reflect on the subject's reputation it cannot be said that the public interest, or that the factors which form the underlying rationale for freedom of speech, requires reporting the name or other identification of the subject of such private matters.[22] In such circumstances the public's interest in

20. For example, in Spahn v. Julian Messner, Inc., 43 Misc.2d 219, 250 N.Y.S.2d 529 (Sup.Ct.1964), aff'd, 23 App.Div.2d 216, 260 N.Y.S.2d 451 (1965), affirmed 18 N.Y.2d 234, 221 N.E.2d 543, 274 N.Y.S.2d 877 (1966), vacated and remanded, 387 U.S. 239 (1967), the plaintiff complained inter alia of the false depiction of the following: An alleged conversation between the plaintiff and his father's physician in which the latter tries to persuade the plaintiff that he bears no guilt for his father's illness; a fictitious scene depicting plaintiff's reunion with his fiancee upon his surprise return from Europe; other scenes depicting the plaintiff's deeply personal relationship with members of his immediate family and his introspective thoughts. See cases cited note 16 supra for other instances of false light cases in which the offensively false statements do not disparage reputation.

21. The earlier newspaper reports should not detract from the private nature of the matters reported unless such newspaper accounts were made with the plaintiff's cooperation. A related and overlapping defense in privacy cases is based upon the plaintiff's status as a "public figure." See Restatement (Second) of Torts § 652F, comments *c* and *d* at 128–29 (Tent.Draft No. 13, 1967), which suggests that "to some reasonable extent" the privilege to report activities of public figures extends even as to "facts about the individual which would otherwise be purely private." Some decisions have seemed to regard this as an absolute privilege to report the private aspects of a celebrated figure's private life. See Sidis v. F–R Publishing Corp., 113 F.2d 806 (2d Cir.1940); Peay v. Curtis Publishing Co., 78 F.Supp. 305 (D.D.C.1948); Reed v. Real Detective Pub. Co., 61 Ariz. 511, 162 P.2d 133 (1945). Note that Warren and Brandeis qualified the right of privacy, so that "to whatever degree and in whatever connection a man's life has ceased to be private * * * to that extent the protection is to be withdrawn." If the thesis of this article is accepted then the plaintiff's status as a public figure should not affect his claim of a right of privacy as to nondefamatory matters which are truly private. The justification for the "public figure" limitation under the *Times* rule in limiting his right of action for defamation—i.e., the fact that a public figure is in a position to invoke the self-help of "more speech," is not applicable to privacy where more speech is irrelevant.

22. This may be subject to a further qualification. If a news story is reputation-injuring (and therefore privileged) as to one individual, such privilege should not be negated by the fact that recounting the reputation-injuring events (whether true or

news reporting is sufficiently served by an account of the event itself without identification of persons innocently involved.[23]

SPAHN v. JULIAN MESSNER, INC.
Court of Appeals of New York, 1967.
21 N.Y.2d 124, 286 N.Y.S.2d 832, 233 N.E.2d 840.

[An earlier opinion in this case is set forth at p. 790 supra.]

KEATING, JUDGE. Again before us is this appeal by the defendant—author, Milton Shapiro, and his publisher, the defendant Julian Messner, Inc., from an order of the Appellate Division (First Department) unanimously affirming a judgment of the Supreme Court (MARKOWITZ, J.) enjoining the publication and dissemination of the book "The Warren Spahn Story" and awarding the plaintiff $10,000 in damages.

On July 7, 1967, in conformance with the mandate of the Supreme Court of the United States, we vacated our prior order of affirmance (18 N.Y.2d 324, 274 N.Y.S.2d 877, 221 N.E.2d 543) and ordered that the case be set down for reargument in light of Time, Inc. v. Hill, 385 U.S. 374, 87 S.Ct. 534, 17 L.Ed.2d 456.

Upon reconsideration of the appeal, we adhere to our original determination and again affirm the order appealed from.

Little purpose would be served hereby repeating the discussion of sections 50 and 51 of the Civil Rights Law, Consol.Laws, c. 6, found in our original opinion or the extensive discussion of the area found in the Supreme Court opinion of Time, Inc. v. Hill (supra). The difficulty which the Supreme Court found with our construction of sections 50 and 51 was the intimation in our original opinion in this case that the standards outlined by the court in New York Times Co. v. Sullivan, 376 U.S. 254, 84 S.Ct. 710, 11 L.Ed.2d 686, were applicable only to actions brought under the statute by public officials with regard to publications about their official conduct. Since this case involved neither a public official nor a publication relating to official conduct we did not consider the merits of the appellants' arguments under New York Times Co. v. Sullivan (supra).

The remand of this appeal by the Supreme Court gives us an opportunity to construe the statute so as to preserve its constitutionali-

---

false, but subject to the *Times* doctrine if false) will necessarily identify an innocent participant in the events reported. Thus, reporting that a named individual raped his sister will, if he has only one sister, necessarily identify and therefore invade the privacy of the sister. See Hubbard v. Journal Pub. Co., 69 N.M. 473, 368 P.2d 147 (1962); Franklin, A Constitutional Problem in Privacy Protection: Legal Inhibitions on Reporting of Fact, 16 Stan.L.Rev. 107, 117, 134 (1963).

23. This principle has received limited recognition on a statutory level in those states which by law prohibit the naming of a female victim of a sexual offense. See Fla.Stat. § 794.03 (1965); Ga.Code Ann. § 26–2105 (1953); S.C.Code Ann. § 16–81 (1962); Wis.Stat.Ann. § 942.02 (1958); Franklin, supra note 95, at 121–28. See also Barber v. Time, Inc., 348 Mo. 1199, 1206, 159 S.W.2d 291, 295 (1942): "It was not necessary to state plaintiff's name in order to give medical information to the public as to the symptoms, nature, causes or results of her ailment."

ty (People v. Epton, 19 N.Y.2d 496, cert. den. 281 N.Y.S.2d 9, 227 N.E.2d 829) and to review the appeal in light of the standards set forth in New York Times Co. v. Sullivan (supra) and Time, Inc. v. Hill, 385 U.S. 374, 87 S.Ct. 534, 17 L.Ed.2d 456 (supra).

We hold in conformity with our policy of construing sections 50 and 51 so as to fully protect free speech, that, before recovery by a public figure may be had for an unauthorized presentation of his life, it must be shown, in addition to the other requirements of the statute, that the presentation is infected with material and substantial falsification and that the work was published with knowledge of such falsification or with a reckless disregard for the truth.

An examination of the undisputed findings of fact below as well as the defendants' own admission that "[i]n writing this biography, the author used the literary techniques of invented dialogue, imaginary incidents, and attributed thoughts and feelings" (brief for appellants, p. 10) clearly indicates that the test of New York Times Co. v. Sullivan (supra) and Time, Inc. v. Hill (supra) has been met here.

The Trial Judge found gross errors of fact and "all-pervasive distortions, inaccuracies, invented dialogue, and the narration of happenings out of context" (43 Misc.2d 219, 230, 250 N.Y.S.2d 529, 541). These findings were unanimously affirmed by the Appellate Division. The court wrote: "[I]t is conceded that use was made of imaginary incidents, manufactured dialogue and a manipulated chronology. In short, defendants made no effort and had no intention to follow the facts concerning plaintiff's life, except in broad outline and to the extent that the facts readily supplied a dramatic portrayal attractive to the juvenile reader. This liberty * * * was exercised with respect to plaintiff's childhood, his relationship with his father, the courtship of his wife, important events during their marriage, and his military experience." (23 A.D.2d 216, 219, 260 N.Y.S.2d 451, 454.)

Exactly how it may be argued that the "all-pervasive" use of imaginary incidents—incidents which the author knew did not take place—invented dialogue—dialogue which the author knew had never occurred—and attributed thoughts and feelings—thoughts and feelings which were likewise the figment of the author's imagination—can be said not to constitute knowing falsity is not made clear by the defendants. Indeed, the arguments made here are, in essence, not a denial of knowing falsity but a justification for it.

Thus the defendants argue that the literary techniques used in the instant biography are customary for children's books. To quote from their brief (p. 11): "The use of manufactured dialogue was characterized as 'mandatory' by a noted critic, teacher and author of children's books. She explained that the dialogue is 'created, and based on probable facts and possible dialogue, which the biographer, through his association with his subject, through the vast amount of research that is necessary, can assume might have happened. It's not a falsification in that sense of the word at all'. Basically a juvenile biography 'has to be a lively story to catch a youngster away from television and all other distractions. * * * You cannot make it straight narrative. It can't list a great many facts or details which you can find in an encyclopedia or "Who's Who".'"

Even if we were to accept this explanation as a defense to this kind of action (cf. note, 67 Col.L.Rev. 926, 942), the defendants could not succeed here. The author of "The Warren Spahn Story" had virtually no association with the subject. He admitted that he never interviewed Mr. Spahn, any member of his family, or any baseball player who knew Spahn. Moreover, the author did not even attempt to obtain information from the Milwaukee Braves, the team for which Mr. Spahn toiled for almost two decades. The extent of Mr. Shapiro's "vast amount of research" in the case at bar amounted, primarily, to nothing more than newspaper and magazine clippings, the authenticity of which the author rarely, if ever, attempted to check out.*

To hold that this research effort entitles the defendants to publish the kind of knowing fictionalization presented here would amount to granting a literary license which is not only unnecessary to the protection of free speech but destructive of an individual's right—albeit a limited one in the case of a public figure—to be free of the commercial exploitation of his name and personality.

That the defendants realize the weakness of their position is evidenced by the stress which they place upon what must be regarded as a purely technical defect—the failure of the plaintiff to allege in his complaint knowing falsity or reckless disregard for the truth. In addition to the fact that a motion was made to conform the pleading to the proof, the defendants do not allege any prejudice as a result of the defective pleading. Indeed, the defendants relied on New York Times Co. v. Sullivan in the trial court and do not allege that they were denied an opportunity to tailor their proof to that defense. Under these circumstances the defective pleading does not warrant reversal (Himoff Ind. Corp. v. Srybnik, 19 N.Y.2d 273, 279, 279 N.Y.S.2d 31, 35, 225 N.E.2d 756, 759; Diemer v. Diemer, 8 N.Y.2d 206, 203 N.Y.S.2d 829, 168 N.E.2d 654; see, also, Van Gaasbeck v. Webatuck Cent. School Dist., 21 N.Y.2d 239, 287 N.Y.S.2d 77, 234 N.E.2d 243, decided herewith).

For the reasons stated the order appealed from should be affirmed, with costs.

BERGAN, JUDGE (dissenting).

---

* Even when some effort was made to check out these sources, the results were ignored if they interfered with the fictionalization of Mr. Spahn's life. Thus, the author was informed by the Department of the Army that Mr. Spahn did not earn the Bronze Star in combat during World War II, although he was informed that the records were not absolutely accurate and that, if Mr. Spahn said he won the Bronze Star, it was likely that he did. Mr. Shapiro depicted Mr. Spahn as a Bronze Star winner even though he admitted that Mr. Spahn never stated that he had won the Bronze Star nor had he ever been quoted as saying so.

Had the Supreme Court agreed with our decision at 18 N.Y.2d 324, 274 N.Y.S.2d 877, 221 N.E.2d 543, upholding the constitutional validity of sections 50 and 51 of the Civil Rights Law as applied to Spahn's case, it would normally have affirmed in due course. Instead, it remanded the case back here for further consideration in view of Time, Inc. v. Hill, 385 U.S. 374, 87 S.Ct. 534, 17 L.Ed.2d 456.

This seems to imply that on the present record the court disagrees with our earlier determination to sustain the statute against the argument of defendants that, as invoked by Spahn, it invades the constitutionally protected freedom of the press.

Of course, the converse is also true, that the court could have reversed on the present record if it could see that the case could not be re-examined according to different criteria. But it could not necessarily see that and would then leave it open to the State court to re-examine.

Therefore, one alternative open to us is to remit the case to the trial court to examine and decide the right of plaintiff to recover on showing "calculated falsehood" against which "the constitutional guarantees can tolerate sanctions" (Hill, p. 389, 87 S.Ct. p. 543); or a " 'reckless disregard of the truth' " (id., p. 390, 87 S.Ct. p. 543) which is treated similarly. (See, further, New York Times Co. v. Sullivan, 376 U.S. 254, 84 S.Ct. 710, 11 L.Ed.2d 686; Garrison v. State of Louisiana, 379 U.S. 64, 85 S.Ct. 209, 13 L.Ed.2d 125.)

These specific criteria were neither pleaded nor established on this record which essentially rests on an asserted violation of the statute by an actionable invasion of privacy in fictionalized biographical material relating to plaintiff.

The theory of the case, as presented, was that fictionalization relating to plaintiff's life was itself actionable under the statute as the New York courts have construed it. (See, e.g., Binns v. Vitagraph Co. of America, 210 N.Y. 51, 103 N.E. 1108; Goelet v. Confidential, Inc., 5 A.D.2d 226, 171 N.Y.S.2d 223; Koussevitzky v. Allen, Towne & Heath, 188 Misc. 479, 68 N.Y.S.2d 779, affd. 272 App.Div. 759, 69 N.Y.S.2d 432.)

The case was not based, therefore, on a consideration of "reckless disregard of the truth" or "calculated falsehood" in the sense the Supreme Court used these terms. If, upon re-examination it were found that the material complained of was merely "innocent or negligent" in writing and publication, it would seem then to be necessary to give judgment for defendants (Hill, 385 U.S. p. 389, 87 S.Ct. p. 543). There seems to be no suggestion that the publication would be proved on a further examination to be more than that.

Even though the fictionalized parts were literally not true, the writer seems to have regarded the fiction as consistent with Spahn's life and possible or even likely. As to certain dialogue complained of, for example, both sides stipulated in the record that it "was written by the author to interpret what he thought the facts were".

The direction of movement of the cases interpreting the constitutionally shielded freedom of the press suggests that the protection to defendants should now be more broadly based than either the narrow grounds that would rest on the *Hill* criteria, or those laid down by our prior decisions. It does not seem probable, reading *Hill* and *New York Times* together, that fiction alone concerning a public figure, actionable under the New York statute as construed, is any longer actionable.

Spahn is a public figure by his own choice. He is not a public official coming literally within *New York Times* or *Garrison*, but the right to print and publish material about a public figure rests on similar policy considerations even though they are not chosen at elections after public debate on their merits. A vast area of public discussion would be closed off if the press could speak much less freely of public figures than of public officials.

At least no good reason exists for imposing sharp discrimination. The material complained of here is not much more a "purely private defamation" than writing false statements about State officers (*Garrison*, supra, 379 U.S. p. 76, 85 S.Ct. p. 216).

Therefore, it should be held that as to a public figure willingly playing that role, the New York privacy statute gives no protection against fictionalization not shown to hurt him and not shown designed to hurt him. There is, in the term "calculated falsehood", as used in *New York Times* and *Hill*, some of the traditional common-law overtones of meaning in the sense of wrongful injury.

To a fictionalized account of a public figure it is difficult to apply precisely the criteria of *Hill* or *New York Times*. All fiction is false in the literal sense that it is imagined rather than actual. It is, of course, "calculated" because the author knows he is writing fiction and not fact; and it is more than a "reckless" disregard for truth. Fiction is the conscious antithesis of truth.

These categorical assignments do not quite accurately encompass the situation of which Spahn complains and on which defendants claim their constitutional privilege to write and print. This can be met by holding that fiction concerning a public figure, if not actually damaging, is not actionable. There may be other situations in which a broader application of the privilege would be required, but this will meet the needs of the present case. The New York privacy statute should no longer be construed as creating a valid action in Spahn's case.

The order should be reversed.

VAN VOORHIS, BURKE and SCILEPPI, JJ., concur with KEATING, J.

BERGAN, J., dissents and votes to reverse in a separate opinion in which FULD, C.J., concurs.

BREITEL, J., taking no part.

Order affirmed.

LEOPOLD v. LEVIN

Supreme Court of Illinois, 1970.
45 Ill.2d 434, 259 N.E.2d 250.

WARD, JUSTICE. Nathan F. Leopold, Jr., the plaintiff, brought an action in the circuit court of Cook County, which was in the nature of a suit alleging a violation of the right of privacy. The defendants included: the author, publishers and several local distributors of a novel and a play, entitled "Compulsion," and the producer, distributor and Chicago area exhibitors of a related motion picture of the same name. The trial court granted the plaintiff's motion for a summary judgment on the question of liability and reserved the issue as to the amount of damages. The defendants appealed to this court but on the plaintiff's motion the appeal was dismissed on the ground that the judgment was interlocutory and, hence, unappealable. When remanded, the case was assigned to a different judge of the circuit court for pretrial consideration on the question of damages. The defendants at that point contested the judgment which had been entered by the predecessor judge. After extended proceedings the succeeding judge vacated the summary judgment in favor of the plaintiff and granted the motions of the defendants for summary judgment and judgment on the pleadings. A direct appeal has been taken by the plaintiff to this court as a constitutional question is involved.

In 1924, Richard Loeb, who is deceased, and Nathan F. Leopold, Jr., the plaintiff, pleaded guilty to the murder and kidnapping for ransom of a 14-year-old boy, Bobby Franks. Following a presentence proceeding, each was given consecutive prison sentences of life and 99 years. The luridness of the crime, the background of the defendants, their representation by the most prominent criminal advocate of the day, the "trial," and its denouement attracted international notoriety. Public interest in the crime and its principals did not wane with the passage of time and the case became an historical *cause celèbre*.

The novel "Compulsion" was first published in hardcover in October 1956. The author was the defendant Meyer Levin, who had been a fellow student of Loeb and Leopold and who had served as a reporter for a Chicago newspaper at the time of the crime. All concerned in this appeal agree that the basic framework of the novel, as well as of the subsequently produced movie, was factually provided by the kidnapping and murder of Bobby Franks, the events leading to the apprehension of Leopold and Loeb, and their prosecution. However, as the author himself, in the foreword of the book, wrote: "Though the action is taken from reality, it must be recognized that thoughts and emotions described in the characters come from within the author, as he imagines them to belong to the personages in the case he has chosen." And, "I follow known events. Some scenes are, however, total interpolations, and some of my personages have no correspondence to persons in the case in question. This will be recognized as the method of the historical novel. I suppose *Compulsion* may be called a contemporary historical novel or a documentary novel, as distinguished from a *roman à clef.* [That is, a novel drawing upon actual occurrences or real persons under the guise of fiction."]

Neither the name of Loeb or Leopold appear in the foreword, and fictitious names are used in the novel itself for all persons who may have been involved in the case. However, the names of Loeb and the plaintiff were used in advertising the novel. Illustrative of this, on the paper jacket to the hardcover edition it was said: "This book is a novel suggested by what is possibly the most famous and certainly one of the most shocking crimes ever committed in America—the Leopold-Loeb murder case." On the page preceding the title page of the paperback edition of "Compulsion", which was first published in 1958, the following appeared: "In his novel based upon the Leopold-Loeb case, Meyer Levin seeks to discover the psychological motivation behind this monstrous deed." The back cover of the paperback noted that " 'Compulsion' is a spellbinding fictionalized account of one of the most famous and shocking crimes of our age—the Leopold-Loeb murder case."

The case had been of interest to other authors. For example, in 1957, a novel, "Nothing But The Night," by James Yaffe was published. It bore a fictionalized resemblance to the Leopold-Loeb case, but had a different locale and no reference was apparently made in the advertising of it to the actual case. In the same year a factual account of the life and crimes of Leopold and Loeb by Maureen McKernan, entitled, "The Amazing Crime and Trial of Leopold and Loeb" was published and widely advertised. In 1957, too, an account of the kidnapping, murder and prosecution written by the plaintiff for compensation appeared in serialized form for several weeks in a Chicago newspaper. Story captions included: "Leopold Tells Own Story—How It Felt To Be A Killer"; "Leopold Arrested; Time For Him To Use Alibi"; "Darrow Makes Masterful Plea For Understanding." He was granted parole in 1958 and that year his autobiographical story, "Life Plus 99 Years," which included a description of his detection and prosecution and their personal consequences, was published. It was given extensive publicity.

The motion picture "Compulsion" was released in April, 1959. Several major characters in the film, including the one corresponding to the appellant, were styled to resemble actual persons in the case. Fictitious names were used, though, and no photographs of the appellant or any other person connected with the case appeared in the movie or in any material used to promote the film. The promotional material did refer to the crime. In a brochure prepared for movie exhibitors, entitled "Vital Statistics," 20th Century Fox Film Corporation, a defendant, outlined the likenesses and differences between the movie and the actual events, and declared: "It should be made clear emphatically that 'Compulsion' is not an effort to reproduce the crime of Leopold and Loeb, nor their trial. The screenplay was taken from a recognized work of fiction 'suggested' by the Leopold-Loeb case, but neither the author of the book nor the producer of the film has attempted anything but to tell a dramatic story. * * * The picture is in no way a documentary and its makers have attempted only to translate the book into terms of good dramaturgy." One motion picture exhibitor, the Woods Theatre in Chicago, owned by a defendant here, in advertising the movie used a photographic enlargement of the back cover of the paperback book edition of "Compulsion" in which the plaintiff's name was used, as has been described. It displayed also a blow-up or enlargement of portions of reviews given the movie in which the plaintiff's name had been mentioned. His name also was introduced during personal, radio and television interviews in various cities by certain of the defendants in the course of their promotion of the motion picture.

The plaintiff acknowledges that a documentary account of the Leopold-Loeb case would be a constitutionally protected expression, since the subject events are matters of public record. Also constitutionally protected, the plaintiff continues, would be a completely fictional work inspired by the case if matters such as the locale would be changed and if there would be no promotional identification with the plaintiff. Leopold's claim is that the constitutional assurances of free speech and press do not permit an invasion of his privacy through the exploitation of his name, likeness and personality for commercial gain in "knowingly fictionalized accounts" of his private life and through the appropriation of his name and likeness in the advertising materials. Denying him redress would deprive him, he argues, of his right to pursue and obtain happiness guaranteed by section 1 of article II of the constitution of Illinois, S.H.A.

While the question of a right of privacy has not until now been considered by this court, such a right has been recognized in other courts of this State. * * *

We agree that there should be recognition of a right of privacy, a right many years ago described in a limited fashion by Judge Cooley with utter simplicity as the right "to be let alone." Privacy is one of the sensitive and necessary human values and undeniably there are circumstances under which it should enjoy the protection of law. However, we must hold here that the plaintiff did not have a legally protected right of privacy. Considerations which in our judgment require this conclusion include: the liberty of expression constitutionally assured in a matter of public interest, as the one here; the enduring public attention to the plaintiff's crime and prosecution, which remain an American *cause celèbre;* and the plaintiff's consequent and continuing status as a public figure.

It has been expressly recognized by the Supreme Court that books, as well as newspapers and magazines, are normally a form of expression protected by the first amendment and that their protection is not affected by the circumstances that the publications are sold for profit. (Time, Inc. v. Hill, 385 U.S. 374, 397, 87 S.Ct. 534, 17 L.Ed.2d 456, 472, and cases there cited.) Pertinently, too, the Supreme Court earlier declared in Joseph Burstyn, Inc. v. Wilson, 343 U.S. 495, 501–502, 72 S.Ct. 777, 780, 96 L.Ed. 1098, 1105–1106: "It cannot be doubted that motion pictures are a significant medium for the communication of ideas. They may affect public attitudes and behavior in a variety of ways, ranging from direct espousal of a political or social doctrine to the subtle shaping of thought which characterizes all artistic expression. The importance of motion pictures as an organ of public opinion is not lessened by the fact that they are designed to entertain as well as to inform. As was said in Winters v. People of State of New York, 1948, 333 U.S. 507, 510, 68 S.Ct. 665, 667, 92 L.Ed. 840 [847]: 'The line between the informing and the entertaining is too elusive for the protection of that basic right [a free press]. Everyone is familiar with instances of propaganda through fiction. What is one man's amusement, teaches another's doctrine.' It is urged that motion pictures do not fall within the First Amendment's aegis because their production, distribution, and exhibition is a large-scale business conducted for private profit. We cannot agree. That books, newspapers, and magazines are published and sold for profit does not prevent them from being a form of expression whose liberty is safeguarded by the First Amendment. We fail to see why operation for profit should have any different effect in the case of motion pictures. * * * For the foregoing reasons, we conclude that expression by means of motion pictures is included within the free speech and free press guaranty of the First and Fourteenth Amendments."

In Time, Inc. v. Hill, the Supreme Court for the first time had occasion to consider directly the effect of the constitutional guarantees for speech and press upon the rights of privacy. There, as will be seen, the right of privacy when involved with the publication of a matter of public interest was viewed narrowly and cautiously by the court. That decisional attitude toward publication is consistent with other first amendment holdings of the court in recent years, especially in the areas of libel and obscenity, where the announced objective was to insure "uninhibited, robust and wide-open" discussion of legitimate public issues or to protect published materials unless they are "utterly without redeeming social value." E.g. (libel) New York Times Co. v. Sullivan (1964), 376 U.S. 254, 270, 84 S.Ct. 710, 11 L.Ed.2d 686, 701; Curtis Publishing Co. v. Butts (1967), 388 U.S. 130, 87 S.Ct. 1975, 18 L.Ed.2d 1094; (obscenity) A Book Named "John Cleland's Memoirs of a Woman of Pleasure" v. Attorney General (1966), 383 U.S. 413, 418, 419, 86 S.Ct. 975, 16 L.Ed.2d 1, 5, 6; Redrup v. New York (1967), 386 U.S. 767, 87 S.Ct. 1414, 18 L.Ed.2d 515.

It is of importance here, too, that the plaintiff became and remained a public figure because of his criminal conduct in 1924. No right of privacy attached to matters associated with his participation in that completely publicized crime. (See Prosser, Law of Torts, 3rd ed. (1964), sec. 112; Restatement of the Law of Torts, § 867, Comment c.) The circumstances of the crime and the prosecution etched a deep public impression which the passing of time did not extinguish. A strong curiosity and social and news interest in the crime, the prosecution, and Leopold remained. (Consider: Bernstein v. National Broadcasting Co., D.C.C., 129 F.Supp. 817, 835; Estill v. Hearst Publishing Co. (7th Cir.), 186 F.2d 1017; Restatement of the Law of Torts, § 867, Comment c.) It is of some relevance, too, in this consideration, that the plaintiff himself certainly did not appear to seek retirement from public attention. The publication of the autobiographical story and other writings and his providing interviews unquestionably contributed to the continuing public interest in him and the crime. Having encouraged public attention " 'he cannot at his whim withdraw the events of his life from public scrutiny.' " Estate of Hemingway v. Random House, Inc., 23 N.Y.2d 341, 352, 296 N.Y.S.2d 771, 782, 244 N.E.2d 250, 258.

A carefully narrowed argument of the plaintiff appears to be that the defendants through "knowingly fictionalized accounts" caused the public to identify the plaintiff with inventions or fictionalized episodes in the book and motion picture which were so offensive and unwarranted as to "outrage the community's notions of decency." (Sidis v. F–R Pub. Corp. (2d Cir.), 113 F.2d 806, 809; see, Time, Inc. v. Hill, 385 U.S. at 382, 383, 87 S.Ct. 534, 17 L.Ed.2d at 464, n. 7.) However, the core of the novel and film and their dominating subjects were a part of the plaintiff's life which he had caused to be placed in public view. The novel and film were derived from the notorious crime, a matter of public record and interest, in which the plaintiff had been a central figure. Further, as the trial court appeared to do, we consider that the fictionalized aspects of the book and motion picture were reasonably comparable to, or conceivable from facts of record from which they were drawn, or minor in offensiveness when viewed in the light of such facts. *Sidis,* upon which the plaintiff bottomed this argument of outraging "the community's notions of decency," involved the publishing of a "profile" of a one-time prodigy. A magazine article disclosed his undistinguished achievement as an adult and described some of his eccentricities. The court held the publication proper but in a dictum observed: "Revelations may be so intimate and so unwarranted in view of the victim's position as to outrage the community's notions of decency." Even if one were to accept the validity of the dictum for the purpose of discussing it, the genesis of the fictionalized episodes in "Compulsion," as we have observed, can be traced in a substantial way to the exposed conduct of Leopold. Argument that the community's notions of decency were outraged here must be regarded as fanciful.

The contention that a right of privacy was violated by an appropriation, without consent, of the plaintiff's name and likeness for the commercial gain of the defendants through their advertisements must also fail. The circumstances here obviously are distinguishable from those in cases such as Eick v. Perk Dog Food Co., [347 Ill.App. 293, 106 N.E.2d 742 (1952)] which the plaintiff cites. There, as has been noted, a likeness, i.e., a photograph of a girl who was clearly not a public figure, was "appropriated" to promote a purely commercial product.

Unlike here, no question of freedom of expression was presented. The reference to the plaintiff in the advertising material concerned the notorious crime to which he had pleaded guilty. His participation was a matter of public and, even, of historical record. That conduct was without benefit of privacy.

We consider that Time, Inc. v. Hill, 385 U.S. 374, 87 S.Ct. 534, 17 L.Ed.2d 456, to which reference has been made, does not support the plaintiff's positions. * * * It is clear that *Time, Inc.* involved a situation essentially dissimilar from the one here. The case involved what was claimed to be a false but purportedly factual account of the Hill incident. Here, the motion picture, play and novel, while "suggested" by the crime of the plaintiff, were evidently fictional and dramatized materials and they were not represented to be otherwise. They were substantially creative works of fiction and would not be subject to the "knowing or reckless falsity" or actual malice standards discussed in Time, Inc. v. Hill, where the court considered an untrue but supposedly factual magazine account. Consider: Privacy, Defamation and the First Amendment: The Implications of Time, Inc. v. Hill, 67 Columbia L.Rev. 926, 944; Right of Privacy v. Free Press: Suggested Resolution of Conflicting Values, 28 Ind.L.J. 179, 184–187; Spahn v. Julian Messner, Inc., 21 N.Y.2d 124, 286 N.Y.S.2d 832, 233 N.E.2d 840, 845 (dissenting opinion); Donahue v. Warner Bros. Pictures Distributing Corp., 2 Utah 2d 256, 272 P.2d 177, 182.

Spahn v. Julian Messner, Inc., 21 N.Y.2d 124, 286 N.Y.S.2d 832, 233 N.E.2d 840, which is offered as authority by the plaintiff, is basically irrelevant to the questions posed by "Compulsion." There, a publication which was offered as a biography of Warren Spahn, the well known baseball pitcher, contained much false material concerning his private life. A judgment under the New York privacy statute in favor of Spahn, a public figure, was upheld and the case was apparently settled, though the Supreme Court had noted "probable jurisdiction" and placed the case on its summary calendar. It is unnecessary to consider the validity of the holding because of the clear dissimilarity between "Compulsion" and a biography of Spahn. .* * *

We conclude that the judgment of the circuit court of Cook County which vacated the summary judgment for the plaintiff on the issue of liability and granted summary judgment and judgment on the pleadings in favor of the defendants was proper. Accordingly, the judgment is affirmed.

Judgment affirmed.

KLUCZYNSKI, J., took no part in the consideration or decision of this case.

Questions

1. Is the manner in which the *Spahn* court applied the rule of Time, Inc. v. Hill in conflict with the manner in which the *Leopold* case applied the same

rule? Are the cases distinguishable on the ground that the *Leopold* defendants' motion picture, play and novel "were evidently fictional and dramatized materials and they were not represented to be otherwise"?

2. May it be argued that Leopold waived his right of privacy (even as to fictionalized accounts of his life) in a way that Spahn did not?

Collateral Reference

Silver, *Libel, the "Higher Truths" of Art, and the First Amendment*, 126 U.Pa.L.Rev. 1065 (1978).

Chapter Sixteen

RIGHT OF PUBLICITY

A. THE NATURE OF THE INJURY

HAELAN LABORATORIES, INC. v. TOPPS CHEWING GUM, INC.

United States Court of Appeals, Second Circuit, 1953.
202 F.2d 866.

FRANK, CIRCUIT JUDGE. After a trial without a jury, the trial judge dismissed the complaint on the merits.[1] The plaintiff maintains that defendant invaded plaintiff's exclusive right to use the photographs of leading baseball-players. Probably because the trial judge ruled against plaintiff's legal contentions, some of the facts were not too clearly found.

1. So far as we can now tell, there were instances of the following kind:

(a). The plaintiff, engaged in selling chewing-gum, made a contract with a ball-player providing that plaintiff for a stated term should have the exclusive right to use the ball-player's photograph in connection with the sales of plaintiff's gum; the ball-player agreed not to grant any other gum manufacturer a similar right during such term; the contract gave plaintiff an option to extend the term for a designated period.

(b). Defendant, a rival chewing-gum manufacturer, knowing of plaintiff's contract, deliberately induced the ball-player to authorize defendant, by a contract with defendant, to use the player's photograph in connection with the sales of defendant's gum either during the original or extended term of plaintiff's contract, and defendant did so use the photograph.

Defendant argues that, even if such facts are proved, they show no actionable wrong, for this reason: The contract with plaintiff was no more than a release by the ball-player to plaintiff of the liability which,

---

[1] Plaintiff abandoned its appeal from the dismissal of that part of the complaint asserting unfair competition and trade-mark infringement. Defendant has abandoned its cross-appeal from the dismissal of its counterclaim.

absent the release, plaintiff would have incurred in using the ball-player's photograph, because such a use, without his consent, would be an invasion of his right of privacy under Section 50 and Section 51 of the New York Civil Rights Law; this statutory right of privacy is personal, not assignable; therefore, plaintiff's contract vested in plaintiff no "property" right or other legal interest which defendant's conduct invaded.

Both parties agree, and so do we, that, on the facts here, New York "law" governs. And we shall assume, for the moment, that, under the New York decisions, defendant correctly asserts that any such contract between plaintiff and a ball-player, in so far as it merely authorized plaintiff to use the player's photograph, created nothing but a release of liability. On that basis, were there no more to the contract, plaintiff would have no actionable claim against defendant. But defendant's argument neglects the fact that, in the contract, the ball-player also promised not to give similar releases to others. If defendant, knowing of the contract, deliberately induced the ball-player to break that promise, defendant behaved tortiously.[2] See, e.g., Hornstein v. Podwitz, 254 N.Y. 443, 173 N.E. 674, 84 A.L.R. 1; 6 Corbin, Contracts (1951) Sec. 1470.

Some of defendant's contracts were obtained by it through its agent, Players Enterprise, Inc.; others were obtained by Russell Publishing Co., acting independently, and were then assigned by Russell to defendant. Since Players acted as defendant's agent, defendant is liable for any breach of plaintiff's contracts thus induced by Players. However, as Russell did not act as defendant's agent when Russell, having knowledge of plaintiff's contract with a player, by subsequently contracting with that player, induced a breach of plaintiff's contract, defendant is not liable for any breach so induced; nor did there arise such a liability against defendant for such an induced breach when defendant became the assignee of one of those Russell contracts.

2. The foregoing covers the situations where defendant, by itself or through its agent, induced breaches. But in those instances where Russell induced the breach, we have a different problem; and that problem also confronts us in instances—alleged in one paragraph of the complaint and to which the trial judge in his opinion also (although not altogether clearly) refers—where defendant, "with knowledge of plaintiff's exclusive rights," used a photograph of a ball-player without his consent during the term of his contract with plaintiff.[3]

With regard to such situations, we must consider defendant's contention that none of plaintiff's contracts created more than a release of liability, because a man has no legal interest in the publication of his

---

2. Defendant is also liable if he thus induced any player to breach his contract to renew.

3. On the remand, the judge should make findings on this subject, on the basis of the evidence now in the record and such additional evidence as the parties may introduce.

picture other than his right of privacy, *i.e.*, a personal and nonassignable right not to have his feelings hurt by such a publication.

A majority of this court rejects this contention. We think that, in addition to and independent of that right of privacy (which in New York derives from statute), a man has a right in the publicity value of his photograph, *i.e.*, the right to grant the exclusive privilege of publishing his picture, and that such a grant may validly be made "in gross," *i.e.*, without an accompanying transfer of a business or of anything else. Whether it be labelled a "property" right is immaterial; for here, as often elsewhere, the tag "property" simply symbolizes the fact that courts enforce a claim which has pecuniary worth.

This right might be called a "right of publicity." For it is common knowledge that many prominent persons (especially actors and ballplayers), far from having their feelings bruised through public exposure of their likenesses, would feel sorely deprived if they no longer received money for authorizing advertisements, popularizing their countenances, displayed in newspapers, magazines, busses, trains and subways. This right of publicity would usually yield them no money unless it could be made the subject of an exclusive grant which barred any other advertiser from using their pictures.

We think the New York decisions recognize such a right. See, e.g., Wood v. Lucy, Lady Duff Gordon, 222 N.Y. 88, 118 N.E. 214; Madison Square Garden Corp. v. Universal Pictures Co., 255 App.Div. 459, 465, 7 N.Y.S.2d 845; Cf. Liebig's Extract of Meat Co. v. Liebig Extract Co., 2 Cir., 180 F. 688.

We think Pekas Co., Inc. v. Leslie, 52 N.Y.L.J.1864, decided in 1915 by Justice Greenbaum sitting in the Supreme Court Term, is not controlling since—apart from a doubt as to whether an opinion of that court must be taken by us as an authoritative exposition of New York law—the opinion shows that the judge had his attention directed by plaintiff exclusively to Sections 50 and 51 of the New York statute, and, accordingly, held that the right of privacy was "purely personal and not assignable" because "rights for outraged feelings are no more assignable than would be a claim arising from a libelous utterance." We do not agree with Hanna Mfg. Co. v. Hillerich & Bradsby Co., 5 Cir., 78 F.2d 763, 101 A.L.R. 484; see adverse comments on that decision in 36 Col.Law Rev. (1936) 502, 49 Harv.Law Rev. (1936) 496, and 45 Yale L.J. (1936) 520.[4]

We said above that defendant was not liable for a breach of any of plaintiff's contracts induced by Russell, and did not become thus liable (for an induced breach) when there was assigned to defendant a contract between Russell and a ball-player, although Russell, in making that contract, knowingly induced a breach of a contract with plaintiff. But plaintiff, in its capacity as exclusive grantee of a player's "right of

---

4. It should be noted that the Hanna case was a pre-Erie-Tompkins decision, which, although it discussed the New York decisions, did not purport to decide authoritatively the New York "law" on the subject.

Sec. A   THE NATURE OF THE INJURY   831

publicity," has a valid claim against defendant if defendant used that player's photograph during the term of plaintiff's grant and with knowledge of it. It is no defense to such a claim that defendant is the assignee of a subsequent contract between that player and Russell, purporting to make a grant to Russell or its assignees. For the prior grant to plaintiff renders that subsequent grant invalid during the period of the grant (including an exercised option) to plaintiff, but not thereafter.[5]

3. We must remand to the trial court for a determination (on the basis of the present record and of further evidence introduced by either party) of these facts: (1) the date and contents of each of plaintiff's contracts and whether plaintiff exercised its option to renew; (2) defendant's or Players' conduct with respect to each such contract.

Of course, if defendant made a contract with a ball-player which was not executed—or which did not authorize defendant to use the player's photograph—until the expiration of the original or extended term of plaintiff's contract with that player, or which did not induce a breach of the agreement to renew, then defendant did no legal wrong to plaintiff. The same is true of instances where neither defendant nor Players induced a breach of plaintiff's contract, and defendant did not use the player's photograph until after the expiration of such original or extended or option term.

If, upon further exploration of the facts, the trial court, in the light of our opinion, concludes that defendant is liable, it will, of course, ascertain damages and decide what equitable relief is justified.

Reversed and remanded.

SWAN, CHIEF JUDGE (concurring in part).

I agree that the cause should be reversed and remanded, and I concur in so much of the opinion as deals with the defendant's liability for intentionally inducing a ball-player to breach a contract which gave plaintiff the exclusive privilege of using his picture.

ON DEFENDANT'S PETITION FOR REHEARING

Per Curiam. 1. In our original opinion, footnote 1, we said that defendant had "abandoned its cross-appeal from dismissal of its counterclaim." But we are now satisfied that defendant had preserved its cross-appeal on the issue of impairment of its own contract rights. Therefore, if plaintiff induced breaches of exclusive agreements which defendant had made with ball-players, defendant is entitled to relief against plaintiff. Accordingly, we add the following to our mandate as additional items for determination by the trial court: (3) The date and contents of each of defendant's contracts under which defendant claims,

---

5. Since plaintiff asserts that, in all instances, defendant acted with knowledge of plaintiff's contracts, we need not consider whether and how far defendant would be liable to plaintiff, absent such knowledge, when, during the term of plaintiff's contract, defendant used a player's photograph without inducing a breach of that contract.

and whether defendant exercised its option to renew, and (4) plaintiff's conduct with respect to each such contract.

2. The last sentence under point 2 of our opinion might suggest that, as long as one of the parties had a contract with a ball-player giving it exclusive rights, any subsequent contract made between that player and the other party before expiration of the prior rights is necessarily invalid. This point appears to require further clarification. Certainly, if the terms of one party's contract provide that its rights shall go into effect only upon expiration of a prior grantee's exclusive rights, the later grant would become fully effective at the time of such expiration. Indeed, in this situation no tort has been committed. However, the problem becomes more complex where the subsequent contract, by its terms, purports to go into effect before termination of any prior exclusive rights. Where the party soliciting such a subsequent contract knows of the prior rights and actually proceeds to use the grant given in violation thereof, its contract is tainted with illegality and is utterly invalid. See Reiner v. North American Newspaper Alliance, 259 N.Y. 250, 181 N.E. 561, 83 A.L.R. 23. Hence such a contract would convey no rights even if it ran beyond the duration of the other party's prior rights. But where the subsequent solicitor treated its contract as if it became effective only upon expiration of any prior rights and made no effort to use the grant before then, that grant would bloom into full force as soon as the earlier rights expired. The same is true if the subsequent grantee did not know at the time he entered into his contract that the ball-player had already given exclusive rights to another party. The validity of one party's contracts beyond the expiration date of prior exclusive rights given the other will thus depend on the district court's findings of fact as to the considerations we have pointed out. * * *

Note *

The Right of Publicity

Although the concept of privacy which Warren and Brandeis evolved fulfilled the demands of Beacon Street in 1890, it may seriously be doubted that the application of this concept satisfactorily meets the contemporary needs of Broadway and Hollywood. Warren and Brandeis were concerned with the preservation of privacy against a press "overstepping in every direction the obvious bounds of propriety and of decency," and in which "to satisfy a prurient taste the details of sexual relations are spread broadcast in the columns of the daily papers."[1] Without in any way implying that the right of privacy is less important today, it is suggested that the doctrine, first developed to protect the sensibilities of nineteenth century Brahmin Boston, is not adequate to meet the demands of the second half of the twentieth century, particularly with respect to the advertising, motion picture, television, and radio industries. Well known

---

* This is an extract from Nimmer, The Right of Publicity, 19 Law and Contemporary Problems 203 (1954).

1. Warren and Brandeis, The Right to Privacy, 4 Harv.L.Rev. 193, 196 (1890).

personalities connected with these industries do not seek the "solitude and privacy" [2] which Brandeis and Warren sought to protect. Indeed, privacy is the one thing they do "not want, or need." [3] Their concern is rather with publicity, which may be regarded as the reverse side of the coin of privacy. However, although the well known personality does not wish to hide his light under a bushel of privacy, neither does he wish to have his name, photograph, and likeness reproduced and publicized without his consent or without remuneration to him. With the tremendous strides in communications, advertising, and entertainment techniques, the public personality has found that the use of his name, photograph, and likeness has taken on a pecuniary value undreamed of at the turn of the century. Often, however, this important value (which will be referred to in this article as publicity value) cannot be legally protected either under a privacy theory or under any other traditional legal theory. Recently a few cases have begun to indicate that publicity values are emerging as a legally cognizable right protectible without resort to the more traditional legal theories. This tendency reached its culmination in Haelan Laboratories, Inc. v. Topps Chewing Gum, Inc.[4] where the Court of Appeals for the Second Circuit in an opinion written by Judge Jerome Frank expressly recognized a "right of publicity." This article will attempt to outline the inadequacy of traditional legal theories in protecting publicity values, and will then discuss the probable substance of and limitations on the right of publicity, followed by an examination of the extent of judicial recognition thus far accorded to this new right.

Inadequacy of Privacy

Those persons and enterprises in the entertainment and allied industries wishing to control but not prohibit the use by others of their own or their employees' names and portraits will find, for the reasons indicated below, that the right of privacy is generally an unsatisfactory means of assuring such control.

Waiver by Celebrities. It is generally the person who has achieved the somewhat ephemeral status of "celebrity" who must cope with the unauthorized use by others of his name and portrait, since the fact of his fame makes such use commercially attractive to others. Yet, when such a person seeks to invoke the right of privacy to protect himself from such unauthorized use, he finds that by the very fact of his being a celebrity "he has dedicated his life to the public and thereby waived his right to privacy." [5] Some courts find this waiver to be absolute so that even aspects of the celebrity's private life which he has never made public no longer command the protection of the law of privacy.[6] Most courts, however, have adopted the more limited waiver which Warren and Brandeis suggested when they wrote: "to whatever degree and in whatever connection a man's life has ceased to be private * * * to that extent the protection is to be withdrawn." [7] Thus the fact that an actor has waived his right of privacy with respect to his professional life, does not mean that he has no right of privacy in connection with his private life. This doctrine

---

2. Warren and Brandeis, supra note 8, at 196.

3. Gautier v. Pro-Football, 304 N.Y. 354, 361, 107 N.E.2d 485, 489 (1952).

4. This case is set forth supra.

5. Leon R. Yankwich, Chief Judge, United States District Court for the Southern District of California, in his article, The Right of Privacy, 27 Notre Dame Law. 499 (1952).

6. See Peay v. Curtis Publishing Co., 78 F.Supp. 305 (D.D.C.1948); and Reed v. Real Detective Publishing Co., 162 P.2d 133 (Sup. Ct.Ariz.1945).

7. Warren and Brandeis, supra note 8, at 215.

permits the celebrity to maintain the privacy of his non-professional life, but it does not protect him from the appropriation by others of the valuable use of his name and portrait, showing him in the capacity or role which he has made famous. Thus it was held in O'Brien v. Pabst Sales Co.[8] that the plaintiff could not invoke the right of privacy to prevent the defendant from using his photograph in football uniform on a calendar because the plaintiff, having been the most publicized football player of the year 1938–1939, had thereby surrendered his right of privacy. Again, in Martin v. F.I.Y. Theatre Co.,[9] the plaintiff, an actress, brought an action for invasion of privacy on the ground that the defendant had without plaintiff's permission placed a photograph of her on the front of defendant's burlesque theatre, although plaintiff was not appearing in the theatre. The court found for defendant on the ground that the plaintiff as an actress had previously surrendered her right of privacy.[10] Similarly in Paramount Pictures, Inc. v. Leader Press, Inc.[11] it was held that motion picture stars in the employ of the plaintiff had waived their right to privacy so that the defendant could with impunity make and sell posters bearing the names and portraits of the Paramount stars. * * *

Although the doctrine of waiver in privacy cases is not always[12] nor uniformly[13] applied, it nevertheless presents a very real obstacle to the protection by a well known personality of the publicity values which often constitute an important part of his assets.

Offensive Use. It is reported that Warren and Brandeis first became interested in the problem of privacy and decided to write their article as a direct result of a Boston newspaper's practice of reporting in lurid detail the activities of Samuel Warren and his wife.[14] Thus, the doctrine of privacy was evolved as a means of preventing offensive (as distinguished from nonoffensive) publicity. To this day most courts recognize the rule of the Restatement of Torts that in a privacy action "liability exists only if the defendant's conduct was such that he should have realized that it would be offensive to persons of ordinary sensibilities. It is only where the intrusion has gone beyond the limits of decency that liability accrues."[15]

In attempting to control and profit from the use of publicity values connected with the use of his name, photograph, and likeness, the well known personality will usually find it difficult to invoke such protection under the

---

8. 124 F.2d 167 (5th Cir.1941).

9. 1 Ohio Supp. 19, 10 Ohio Ops. 338 (1938).

10. A similar factual situation occurred in Loftus v. Greenwich Lithographing Co., 192 App.Div. 251, 182 N.Y.S. 428 (1st Dep't 1920), where plaintiff's right of privacy under the New York statute was upheld. The issue of waiver apparently was not raised. Cf. Sinclair v. Postal Telegraph and Cable Co., 72 N.Y.S.2d 841 (1935); Semler v. Ultem Publications, 170 Misc. 551, 9 N.Y.S.2d 319 (N.Y.City Ct.1938); Lane v. F.W. Woolworth Co., 171 Misc. 66, 11 N.Y.S.2d 199 (Sup.Ct.1939); and Young v. Greneker Studios, 175 Misc. 1027, 26 N.Y.S.2d 357 (Sup. Ct.1941).

11. 24 F.Supp. 1004 (W.D.Okla.1938), reversed on other grounds, 106 F.2d 229 (10th Cir.1939).

12. For an example of an almost complete rejection of the waiver theory, see Pavesich v. New England Life Ins. Co., 122 Ga. 190, 50 S.E. 68 (1904).

13. Within New York state there would appear to be a lack of consistency in applying the doctrine of waiver. Thus, compare Jansen v. Hilo Packing Co., 202 Misc. 900, 118 N.Y.S.2d 162 (Sup.Ct.1952); Oma v. Hillman Periodical Inc., 281 App.Div. 240, 118 N.Y.S.2d 720 (1st Dep't 1953); and Redmond v. Columbia Pictures Corp., 277 N.Y. 707, 14 N.E.2d 636 (1938).

14. Mason, Brandeis, A Free Man's Life 70 (1946).

15. Restatement, Torts § 867, comment d (1939). See also Yankwich, The Right of Privacy, 27 Notre Dame Law. 499, 506 (1952).

right of privacy for the reason that usually such publicity cannot be considered such as "would be offensive to persons of ordinary sensibilities" or as an intrusion "beyond the limits of decency." Situations may of course occur where exploitation of a plaintiff's publicity values will prove humiliating or embarrassing to him,[16] but in most situations one who has achieved such prominence as to give a publicity value to the use of his name, photograph, and likeness cannot honestly claim that he is humiliated or offended by their use before the public. The fact that he wishes to be paid for such use does not indicate that use without payment is so offensive as to give a right of action in privacy. * *

Even in those jurisdictions where it is held that a cause of action in privacy is stated despite the fact that use of the plaintiff's name, photograph or likeness was done in a non-offensive manner, the person wishing to be paid for the publicity value of such use will find himself effectively circumvented by the rule of damages. Thus, in Cason v. Baskin,[17] the defendant Marjorie Kinnan Rawlings in her book *Cross Creek* depicted the plaintiff, using plaintiff's real first name. The court held that plaintiff had stated a cause of action in privacy but because "there was no mental anguish—no loss of friends—no loss of respect to the community—no loss of character or reputation," the court refused to award plaintiff any damages. Thus even if a plaintiff can establish a cause of action in privacy for non-offensive use of his publicity values, he will not succeed in recovering any damages if he cannot show an offensive use. * *

Therefore since a defendant may well exploit for his own gain the publicity values of a plaintiff without presenting such publicity in an offensive manner, it follows that in such instances a plaintiff will usually be unable to protect his publicity values under a privacy theory.

Non-assignable. In most jurisdictions it is well established that a right of privacy is a personal right rather than a property right and consequently is not assignable.[18] The publicity value of a prominent person's name and portrait is greatly restricted if this value cannot be assigned to others. Moreover, persons willing to pay for such publicity values will usually demand that in return for payment they obtain an exclusive right. Yet since the right of privacy is non-assignable, any agreement purporting to grant the right to use the grantor's name and portrait (as in connection with a commercial endorsement or tie-up) is construed as constituting merely a release as to the purchaser and as not granting the purchaser any right which he can enforce as against a third party. Thus, if a prominent motion picture actress should grant to a bathing suit manufacturer the right to use her name and portrait in connection with its product and if subsequently a competitive manufacturer should use the same

---

16. For example, in Sinclair v. Postal Telegraph and Cable Co., 72 N.Y.S.2d 841 (1935), the defendant used a photograph of the plaintiff (an actor) which had been taken in connection with a motion picture photoplay in which plaintiff appeared. Defendant's use of the photo made it appear that plaintiff was notifying his "enthusiastic admirers" by telegraph that he was about to appear in a motion picture at a given theatre. Plaintiff brought an action under the New York privacy act arguing that defendant's use of his photograph was humiliating to plaintiff in that it put him in an undignified light, in the same manner as an attorney would appear if he telegraphed his friends requesting that they attend a court room where he was about to participate in a case. Plaintiff recovered.

17. 159 Fla. 31, 30 So.2d 635 (1947).

18. Hanna Manufacturing Co. v. Hillerich & Bradsby, 78 F.2d 763 (5th Cir.1935); Note, 45 Yale L.J. 520 (1936); see Haelan Laboratories v. Topps Chewing Gum, 202 F.2d 866 (2d Cir.1953).

actress's name and portrait in connection with its product, the first manufacturer cannot claim any right of action on a privacy theory against its competitor since the first manufacturer cannot claim to "own" the actress's right of privacy. Assuming the second manufacturer acted with the consent of the actress, it is possible that the first manufacturer would have a cause of action for breach of contract against the actress, but this would present a remedy in damages only and in some instances even recovery of damages might be doubtful. Therefore, if a prominent person is found merely to have a personal right of privacy and not a property right of publicity, the important publicity values which he has developed are greatly circumscribed and thereby reduced in value.

Limited to Human Beings. It is common knowledge that animals often develop important publicity values. Thus, it is obvious that the use of the name and portrait of the dog Lassie in connection with dog food would constitute a valuable asset. Yet an unauthorized use of this name could not be prevented under a right of privacy theory, since it has been expressly held that the right of privacy "does not cover the case of a dog or a photograph of a dog." [19] Not only animals but business enterprises as well are unprotected under the right of privacy.[20] Yet as in the case of animals so also with business enterprises, the economic realities are such that the use of a business name may have a considerable publicity value. * * *

Inadequacy of Unfair Competition

If the well known personality finds that misappropriation of his publicity values cannot be effectively prevented under a privacy theory, he will usually find no greater relief under the traditional theory of unfair competition.

Competition Requirement. The absence of competition between the plaintiff and defendant is in a number of jurisdictions an effective defense to an unfair competition action.[21] In such jurisdictions, it is obvious that publicity values are not effectively protected, since a person's publicity values may be profitably exploited in non-competitive fields. Thus, a chewing gum company which includes in its packages pictures of prominent baseball players could hardly be characterized as in competition with the players. Even with respect to business or other enterprises (as distinguished from personalities) which, as has been indicated supra, cannot invoke the right of privacy, the defense of no competition will effectively prevent a successful unfair competition action for misappropriation of the enterprise's publicity values. Thus, in Vassar College v. Loose-Wiles Biscuit Co.,[22] the defendant manufactured chocolates which it sold in a package labeled "Vassar Chocolates," and upon which there appeared a seal closely resembling the seal of the plaintiff college and a picture of a young lady wearing a mortarboard. The court rendered judgment for the

---

19. Lawrence v. Ylla, 184 Misc. 807, 55 N.Y.S.2d 343 (Sup.Ct.1945).

20. Shubert v. Columbia Pictures Corp., 189 Misc. 734, 72 N.Y.S.2d 851 (Sup.Ct. 1947); Gautier v. Pro-Football, 278 App.Div. 531, 106 N.Y.S.2d 553 (1st Dep't 1951), aff'd, 304 N.Y. 354, 107 N.E.2d 485 (1952); Maysville Transit Co. v. Ort, 296 Ky. 524, 177 S.W.2d 364 (1943).

[But note Sec. 397, New York General Business Law enacted by L.1961 c. 438.]

21. E.g., Women's Mutual Benefit Society v. Catholic Society Feminine, 304 Mass. 349, 23 N.E.2d 886 (1939); Acme Screen Co. v. Pebbles, 159 Okl. 116, 14 P.2d 366 (1932); Scutt v. Bassett, 86 Cal.App.2d 373, 194 P.2d 781 (1948). See Riggs Optical Co. v. Riggs, 132 Neb. 26, 270 N.W. 667 (1937).

22. 197 Fed. 982 (W.D.Mo.1912).

defendant, holding that no unfair competition could be established since the parties were not in competition. Yet, it can hardly be doubted that the defendant was trading on the publicity values established by the plaintiff. * *

Passing Off Requirement. It is generally recognized that "the essence of unfair competition consists in the palming off of the goods or business of one person as that of another." [23]

This requirement of passing off (or palming off), which is probably more universally recognized than the requirement of competition discussed supra, serves to limit further the protection available for publicity values under the theory of unfair competition. Publicity values of a person or firm may be profitably appropriated and exploited without the necessity of any imputation that such person or firm is connected with the exploitation undertaken by the appropriator. That is to say, publicity values may be usefully appropriated without the necessity of passing off, and therefore without violating the traditional theory of unfair competition. Thus in Paramount Pictures, Inc. v. Leader Press [24] the defendant manufactured and sold to theatre exhibitors advertising accessories (posters, etc.) relating to plaintiff's motion pictures; these accessories were valuable and salable by reason of their containing and exploiting the publicity values inherent in both plaintiff's motion pictures and in the actors employed by plaintiff. The Court of Appeals for the Tenth Circuit found that the above practice did not constitute unfair competition since there was no passing off of the advertising accessories of the defendant as those of the plaintiff.[25]

The commercial "tie up," as distinguished from the commercial endorsement,[26] presents another instance in which publicity values may be appropriated without the necessity of passing off. Advertisements, almost regardless of their nature, will increase their reader appeal by including the name and portrait of a prominent personality or a well known enterprise, although there is no "passing off" that such personality or enterprise produces or endorses the product being advertised.

No Assignment in Gross. The pecuniary worth of publicity values will be greatly diminished if not totally destroyed if these values cannot be effectively sold. Yet, under the theory of unfair competition, an assignee cannot acquire the right to use a name except as an incident to his purchase of the business and good will in connection with which the name has been used.[27] Therefore, if the potential purchaser of publicity values must rely upon the law of unfair competition to protect his investment, he will be unwilling to purchase publicity values unconnected with a business. This in effect means that the sale of publicity values will usually be effectively blocked, since the potential seller of publicity values generally has established such value not in connection with his own business but rather through the rendering of personal services for another; he will therefore be unable to sell the business in connection with which his

---

23. American Broadcasting Co. v. Wahl Co., 36 F.Supp. 167, 168 (S.D.N.Y.1940). The leading case on this point is Howe Scale Co. v. Wyckoff, Seamans & Benedict, 198 U.S. 118 (1905).

24. 106 F.2d 229 (10th Cir.1939).

25. However, the court found for the plaintiff on the theories of disparagement and inducing breach of a contract.

26. The commercial "tie-up" presents the name and portrait of an actor or other celebrity within the context of an advertisement without necessarily indicating that the actor endorses the product advertised.

27. Fisk v. Fisk, 3 F.2d 7 (8th Cir.1924).

name has achieved fame. Furthermore, even if the potential seller has achieved fame through his own business, if he can only sell his publicity values as an incident to the sale of his business, he will ordinarily prefer not to enter such a transaction.

Unfair Competition Extended. In recent years there has been a marked tendency in a number of jurisdictions to take a broader view of the scope of unfair competition. Many courts have rejected the defense of lack of competition between the parties. Some other courts no longer require a showing of passing off in order to establish an action in unfair competition. However, even in those jurisdictions which have permitted recovery in the absence of either competition or passing off, the doctrine would generally not appear to be so far extended as to permit recovery where *both* competition and passing off are absent. Thus, in International News Service v. Associated Press,[28] a case usually cited by those courts which have extended the doctrine of unfair competition, I.N.S. appropriated news gathered by the Associated Press, and although there was no passing off in that I.N.S. did not represent the appropriated news as emanating from Associated Press, there was, of course, the element of competition between the two major news services. * * * The language contained in Metropolitan Opera Ass'n v. Wagner-Nichols Recorder Corp.,[29] however, goes so far as to indicate that relief might be granted although both competition and passing off were not established. This is dicta, however, since the court found as a matter of fact the existence of both competition and passing off.[30] The danger of protecting publicity values on an unfair competition theory in the absence of both competition and passing off is indicated by further language found in the *Metropolitan* case. The court stated that the law of unfair competition rests on the principle that "property rights of commercial value are to be and will be protected from any form of unfair invasion or infringement and from any form of commercial immorality, and a court of equity will penetrate and restrain every guise resorted to by the wrongdoer. The courts have thus recognized that in the complex pattern of modern business relationships, persons in theoretically non-competitive fields may, by unethical business practices, inflict as severe and reprehensible injuries upon others as can direct competitors." It will be seen from the above passage that under this view (i.e., discarding the requirements of competition and passing off) the scope of unfair competition covers "any form of commercial immorality," and "unethical business practices." If this loose standard were in fact applied by the courts, the already uncertain field of unfair competition would be reduced to a chaos of complete uncertainty, since what lawyer or business man could predict with any degree of certainty where the courts would find that properly aggressive business practices leave off and "commercial immorality" and "unethical business practices" begin? True, publicity values might be protected under such a broad theory, but in doing so the courts would

---

28. This case is set forth supra.

29. 101 N.Y.S.2d 483 (Sup.Ct.1950).

30. In this case the defendant recorded radio broadcasts of the Metropolitan Opera and made phonograph records therefrom which it sold to the public. Defendant advertised and sold the records as records of broadcast Metropolitan Opera performances. The court found that competition existed due to the fact that Columbia Records, Inc. joined the Metropolitan Association as a plaintiff in the case (Columbia having contracted for the phonograph rights in the Metropolitan performances). Furthermore, the court found that the element of passing off existed since an inference could be drawn that the activities of the defendant misled the public into believing that the recordings were made with the cooperation of the Metropolitan Opera Association.

be adopting a standard which by its uncertainty could prove highly detrimental to orderly commercial intercourse. It is suggested that publicity values can be adequately protected under the right of publicity discussed infra, without going to the extremes indicated above.

Inadequacy of Other Theories

Publicity values may to a limited extent be protected by contract,[31] but such protection extends, of course, only to the parties to such contracts. The inadequacy of the contract theory in protecting publicity values is illustrated in Corliss v. E.W. Walker Co.,[32] in which plaintiff's deceased husband had his portrait taken by a photographer who agreed by contract not to furnish prints of the photograph to anyone other than plaintiff and plaintiff's husband. Thereafter the defendant purchased a print of the photograph from the photographer and inserted it in a biographical sketch of the deceased husband. The plaintiff sought to obtain an injunction against the use of the photograph, and the court granted the defendant's motion to dissolve the injunction on the ground that defendant was not a party to the contract between the plaintiff's husband and the photographer, and therefore defendant was not bound thereby. However, if the plaintiff can establish a contract restricting use of the publicity values and if defendant although not a party to the contract can be shown to have induced breach of the contract, then relief may be obtained.[33] Thus if A purchases the right to use B's publicity values under contract in which B agrees not to grant the right to use such publicity values to anyone else, and if thereafter C induces B to grant to him the same publicity values and thereby causes B to breach his contract with A, C will be liable to A for the tort of inducing breach of contract. However, if C having thus acquired the publicity rights from B in turn assigns these rights to D, D in using such publicity rights will not be liable to A for the tort of inducing breach of contract since D merely benefited from the breach of the contract but did not induce it,[34] and D will not be liable for breach of contract since he was not a party to the contract between A and B. Thus even in the limited situations where appropriation of publicity values involves a breach of contract, a person who is not a party to the contract and who has not induced its breach may not be prevented from using the publicity values on either a contract theory or a theory of inducing breach of contract. * * *

Substance of and Limitations on the Right of Publicity

The substance and direction of the right of publicity has to some extent been indicated by adjudicated cases which will be discussed later.[35] Before examining the somewhat fragmentary outline embodied in existing case law, it might be well first to attempt some perspective as to the fundamental elements necessary to a workable and socially useful right of publicity. From such a perspective, the meaning and continuity of existing case law will be more apparent.

The substance of the right of publicity must be largely determined by two considerations: first, the economic reality of pecuniary values inherent in

31. See Wood v. Lucy, Lady Duff Gordon, 222 N.Y. 88, 118 N.E. 214 (1917).

32. 64 Fed. 280 (C.C.D.Mass.1894).

33. Paramount Pictures v. Leader Press, 106 F.2d 229 (10th Cir.1939).

34. Haelan Laboratories v. Topps Chewing Gum supra.

35. [Omitted from this extract.]

publicity and, second, the inadequacy of traditional legal theories in protecting such publicity values. It is an unquestioned fact that the use of a prominent person's name, photograph or likeness (i.e., his publicity values) in advertising a product or in attracting an audience is of great pecuniary value. This is attested to by the now pervasive trade practice of paying well known personalities considerable sums for the right thus to use such publicity values. It is also unquestionably true that in most instances a person achieves publicity values of substantial pecuniary worth only after he has expended considerable time, effort, skill, and even money. It would seem to be a first principle of Anglo-American jurisprudence, an axiom of the most fundamental nature, that every person is entitled to the fruit of his labors unless there are important countervailing public policy considerations. Yet, because of the inadequacy of traditional legal theories discussed supra, persons who have long and laboriously nurtured the fruit of publicity values may be deprived of them, unless judicial recognition is given to what is here referred to as the right of publicity—that is, the right of each person to control and profit from the publicity values which he has created or purchased.

The nature of the inadequacy of the traditional legal theories dictates in large measure the substance of the right of publicity. The right of publicity must be recognized as a property (not a personal) right, and as such capable of assignment and subsequent enforcement by the assignee. Furthermore, appropriation of publicity values should be actionable regardless of whether the defendant has used the publicity in a manner offensive to the sensibilities of the plaintiff. Usually the use will be non-offensive, since such a use is more valuable to the defendant as well as to the plaintiff. Likewise, the measure of damages should be computed in terms of the value of the publicity appropriated by defendant rather than, as in privacy, in terms of the injury sustained by the plaintiff. There must be no waiver of the right by reason of the plaintiff being a well known personality. Indeed, the right usually becomes important only when the plaintiff (or potential plaintiff) has achieved in some degree, a celebrated status. Moreover, since animals, inanimate objects, and business and other institutions all may be endowed with publicity values, the human owners of these non-human entities should have a right of publicity (although no right of privacy) in such property, and this right should exist (unlike unfair competition) regardless of whether the defendant is in competition with the plaintiff, and regardless of whether he is passing off his own products as those of the plaintiff.

It is not possible to set forth here in any detail the necessary limitations on the right of publicity which only the unhurried occurrence of actual cases will clearly establish. Yet some few suggestions can be made. In privacy cases there is a tendency by some courts to confuse or at least fail to distinguish between the defense of waiver by a well known personality and the defense of "news" or public interest.[36] Although, as indicated supra, the defense of waiver by celebrities should not be recognized in a publicity action, the defense of public interest should be no less effective in a publicity action than in a privacy action. Where use of a person's name, photograph, or likeness is made in the dissemination of news or in a manner required by the public interest, that person should not be able to complain of the infringement of his right of publicity.

36. E.g., Gautier v. Pro-Football, 304 N.Y. 354, 107 N.E.2d 485 (1952); Smith v. Suratt, 7 Alaska 416 (1926).

The question will be raised as to whether there is an infringement of the right of publicity when defendant appropriates the plaintiff's publicity values and uses them, but not for purposes of trade or advertising. It may be argued that since publicity values are useful mainly in connection with trade and advertising, this presents a convenient place to draw the line between wrongful infringement of the right of publicity and proper exercise of freedom of expression. However, in view of the holding in Gautier v. Pro-Football [37] that only that portion of a television broadcast containing the "commercial" may be said to be for purposes of trade or advertising,[38] if the right of publicity were restricted to uses for purposes of trade or advertising, there might be no protection against appropriation of publicity values on television programs. Probably it would be wiser not to inject any arbitrary limitation on the scope of the right of publicity, relying instead on the limitation imposed by the rule of damages. In most instances, the use of publicity values for purposes other than for trade or advertising will be of no great value to the defendant and consequently will result in small or nominal damages for the plaintiff. It may also be suggested that the right of publicity should be limited to those persons having achieved the status of a "celebrity," as it is only such persons who possess publicity values which require protection from appropriation. Here too, however, it would probably be preferable not to impose an arbitrary limit on the right but rather to rely upon the rule of damages. It is impractical to attempt to draw a line as to which persons have achieved the status of celebrity and which have not; it should rather be held that every person has the property right of publicity, but that the damages which a person may claim for infringement of the right will depend upon the value of the publicity appropriated which in turn will depend in great measure upon the degree of fame attained by the plaintiff. Thus, the right of publicity accorded to each individual "may have much or little, or only a nominal value," but the right should be available to everyone.

It may also be argued that the right of publicity should be limited to protection against appropriation of one's portrait but should not protect against appropriation of one's name.[39] However, the use of a name may in itself carry considerable publicity value, and there would seem to be no reason to exclude such appropriation from the protection of the right of publicity.

Recognition of the Right of Publicity

It would be premature to state that the right of publicity has as yet received any substantial degree of judicial recognition. Yet, even before Judge Jerome Frank's recent express application of the right in Haelan Laboratories v. Topps Chewing Gum Inc., a number of cases have indicated a judicial willingness to extend protection to publicity values which would not be protectable under the traditional legal theories discussed supra.

[The remainder of the article, containing a discussion of cases bearing upon the right of publicity, is omitted.]

37. 304 N.Y. 354, 107 N.E.2d 485 (1952).

38. Note, however, that the program telecast in the *Gautier* case was a sports event, with plaintiff's animal act appearing only during the half time.

39. Haelan Laboratories v. Topps Chewing Gum, 202 F.2d 866 (2d Cir.1953) indicates that the right of publicity may be limited to the protection of the publicity value of one's photograph.

Collateral References

Gordon, *Right of Property in Name, Likeness, Personality and History,* 55 Northwestern Law Rev. 553 (1960).

Treece, *Commercial Exploitation of Names, Likenesses and Personal Histories,* 51 Tex.L.Rev. 637 (1973).

RESTATEMENT (SECOND) OF TORTS, § 652C

Comment:

    a. The interest protected by the rule stated in this Section is the interest of the individual in the exclusive use of his own identity, in so far as it is represented by his name or likeness, and in so far as the use may be of benefit to him or to others. Although the protection of his personal feelings against mental distress is an important factor leading to a recognition of the rule, the right created by it is in the nature of a property right, for the exercise of which an exclusive license may be given to a third person, which will entitle the licensee to maintain an action to protect it.

    b. How invaded. The common form of invasion of privacy under the rule here stated is the appropriation and use of the plaintiff's name or likeness to advertise the defendant's business or product, or for some similar commercial purpose. Apart from statute, however, the rule stated is not limited to commercial appropriation. It applies also when the defendant makes use of the plaintiff's name or likeness for his own purposes and benefit, even though the use is not a commercial one, and even though the benefit sought to be obtained is not a pecuniary one. Statutes in some states have, however, limited the liability to commercial uses of the name or likeness.

Question

Does the foregoing right as formulated in the Restatement (Second) of Torts differ from the right of public as proposed in the foregoing article? In what manner?

CALIFORNIA CIVIL CODE SEC. 3344

    (a) Any person who knowingly uses another's name, voice, signature, photograph, or likeness, in any manner, on or in products, merchandise, or goods, or for purposes of advertising or selling, or soliciting purchases of, products, merchandise, goods or services, without such person's prior consent, or, in the case of a minor, the prior consent of his parent or legal guardian, shall be liable for any damages sustained by the person or persons injured as a result thereof. In addition, in any action brought under this section, the person who violated the section shall be liable to the injured party or parties in an amount equal to the greater of seven hundred fifty dollars ($750) or the actual damages suffered by him or her as a result of the unauthorized use, and any profits from the unauthorized use that are attributable to the use and are not taken into account in computing the actual damages. In establishing such profits, the injured party or parties are required to present proof only of the gross revenue attributable to such use, and the person who violated this section is required to prove his or her deductible expenses. Punitive damages may also be awarded to the injured party or parties. The prevailing party in any action under this section shall also be entitled to attorney's fees and costs.

(b) As used in this section, "photograph" means any photograph or photographic reproduction, still or moving, or any videotape or live television transmission, of any person, such that the person is readily identifiable.

(1) A person shall be deemed to be readily identifiable from a photograph when one who views the photograph with the naked eye can reasonably determine that the person depicted in the photograph is the same person who is complaining of its unauthorized use.

(2) If the photograph includes more than one person so identifiable, then the person or persons complaining of the use shall be represented as individuals rather than solely as members of a definable group represented in the photograph. A definable group includes, but is not limited to, the following examples: a crowd at any sporting event, a crowd in any street or public building, the audience at any theatrical or stage production, a glee club, or a baseball team.

(3) A person or persons shall be considered to be represented as members of a definable group if they are represented in the photograph solely as a result of being present at the time the photograph was taken and have not been singled out as individuals in any manner.

(c) Where a photograph or likeness of an employee of the person using the photograph or likeness appearing in the advertisement or other publication prepared by or in behalf of the user is only incidental, and not essential, to the purpose of the publication in which it appears, there shall arise a rebuttable presumption affecting the burden of producing evidence that the failure to obtain the consent of the employee was not a knowing use of the employee's photograph or likeness.

(d) For purposes of this section, a use of a name, voice, signature, photograph, or likeness in connection with any news, public affairs, or sports broadcast or account, or any political campaign, shall not constitute a use for which consent is required under subdivision (a).

(e) The use of a name, voice, signature, photograph, or likeness in a commercial medium shall not constitute a use for which consent is required under subdivision (a) solely because the material containing such use is commercially sponsored or contains paid advertising. Rather it shall be a question of fact whether or not the use of the person's name, voice, signature, photograph, or likeness was so directly connected with the commercial sponsorship or with the paid advertising as to constitute a use for which consent is required under subdivision (a).

(f) Nothing in this section shall apply to the owners or employees of any medium used for advertising, including, but not limited to, newspapers, magazines, radio and television networks and stations, cable television systems, billboards, and transit ads, by whom any advertisement or solicitation in violation of this section is published or disseminated, unless it is established that such owners or employees had knowledge of the unauthorized use of the person's name, voice, signature, photograph, or likeness as prohibited by this section.

(g) The remedies provided for in this section are cumulative and shall be in addition to any others provided for by law.

HISTORY: A.B. 826, approved and filed November 22, 1971, as amended by SB 613, approved and filed September 30, 1984.

Questions

1. Would a motion picture which dramatized the life of a well-known personality constitute a violation of Sec. 3344? What if the motion picture were broadcast by television, with the customary insertion of commercial messages? Does Sec. 3344(d) indicate by negative implication that such a broadcast would violate Sec. 3344(a)? What is the impact of Sec. 3344(e)? What is the significance of the fact that there is no counterpart in California Civil Code Section 3344 (relating to living persons) to California Civil Code Section 990(n)(1) (p. 857 infra) (relating to deceased persons)?

2. What is the significance of whether the persons complaining are "represented as individuals rather than solely as members of a definable group" within the meaning of Sec. 3344(b)(2)? If a person within a group is individually identifiable, but has not been "singled out" in any manner, does he have a cause of action? Compare Secs. 3344(b)(2) and 3344(b)(3).

FACTORS ETC., INC. v. PRO ARTS, INC.

United States Court of Appeals, Second Circuit, 1978.
579 F.2d 215.

Before WATERMAN, INGRAHAM and MANSFIELD, CIRCUIT JUDGES.

INGRAHAM, CIRCUIT JUDGE:

Plaintiffs-Appellees, Factors Etc., Inc. (Factors) and Boxcar Enterprises, Inc. (Boxcar), sued Defendants-Appellants, Pro Arts, Inc. (Pro Arts) and Stop and Shop Companies, Inc. (Stop and Shop), for injunctive relief and damages based upon defendants' alleged misappropriation and unauthorized use of the name and likeness of Elvis Presley (Presley). The trial court granted the plaintiffs' preliminary injunction upon its findings that the exclusive right to market Presley memorabilia survived the death of Presley, and the Presley poster printed by defendants allegedly in derogation of this right was not privileged as the publication of a newsworthy event. This is an interlocutory appeal pursuant to 28 U.S.C.A. § 1292(a)(1).

Because the facts are not in dispute, we need not describe them in detail. During Presley's career as an entertainer, Colonel Tom Parker (Parker) served as his close friend, mentor and personal manager. This professional relationship between the two parties began on March 26,

1956, with the execution of the first contract between them. Parker immediately began the task of creating the "Elvis persona." In so doing, both he and Presley capitalized upon the marketing of merchandise bearing the Elvis name and likeness. Parker directed this effort until Presley's death, a task reflected by the numerous extensions of the contract between the two parties.[1]

Boxcar Enterprises, a Tennessee corporation controlled by Presley and Parker,[2] was the vehicle through which the commercial Elvis Presley rights were marketed. Boxcar sublicensed other companies to do the actual manufacturing and distributing of each specific item, receiving royalties from the sales.[3]

On August 16, 1977, Elvis Presley died suddenly and unexpectedly. His father, Vernon Presley, was appointed executor of his estate. On August 18, 1977, two days after Presley's death, Boxcar granted Factors the exclusive license to exploit commercially the name and likeness of Elvis Presley. Factors paid Boxcar $100,000 on execution of the agreement against a guarantee of $150,000. Vernon Presley, as executor of the estate, signed the agreement licensing Factors, at the same time warranting that Boxcar was the sole and exclusive owner of the commercial Elvis Presley rights.[4] The agreement was also approved by Parker.

Immediately following Presley's death, Pro Arts decided that it too wanted a share in the market for Elvis Presley memorabilia. It purchased the copyright in the photograph of Presley from a staff photographer of the Atlanta (Georgia) Journal. On August 19, 1977, three days after his death, Pro Arts published a poster using the photograph and filed an application for registration of copyright. The poster is entitled "IN MEMORY" and below the photograph of Presley the poster bears the dates "1935–1977."

On the same day that the poster was published, Pro Arts began to market it. One of its first customers was co-defendant Stop and Shop Companies, which thereafter sold the poster through its Bradlees Stores Division in the Southern District of New York. On August 24, 1977, five days after its poster was placed on the market, Pro Arts notified

---

1. At the time of his death, Presley was operating under an agreement with Parker, who was doing business as "All Star Shows." The agreement was executed on May 25, 1963, and was thereafter extended several times. The last extension occurred on January 22, 1976, and granted merchandising rights to Parker for another seven years.

2. Parker owned 56% of the shares; Presley and Tom Dishkin, President of Boxcar, each owned 22%.

3. When Boxcar licensed a merchandising item, Presley received 20% of the royalties, Parker received 20%, and Dishkin received 10%. The remaining 50% went to Boxcar.

4. Contemporaneous with this agreement, Vernon Presley wrote to Parker, asking him to "carry on according to the same terms and conditions as stated in the contractual agreement [between Presley and Parker] dated January 22, 1976" (See n. 1, supra).

The disputed Pro Arts poster

Boxcar Enterprises that it was offering "a memorial 'Elvis' poster to meet the public demand." When Factors was informed of the letter, it replied to Pro Arts claiming the exclusive right to manufacture, sell and distribute all merchandise utilizing the name and likeness of Elvis Presley. Factors also warned Pro Arts that if it did not discontinue sale of the poster, it would be subject to a lawsuit for injunctive relief, damages and an accounting. * * *

Upon the filing of the complaint in this action, the district judge entered an "order to show cause" requiring Pro Arts to show cause why an injunction should not issue against it. * * * On October 13, 1977, the New York court filed an opinion and order of preliminary injunction against Pro Arts. The injunction restrained Pro Arts during the pendency of the action from manufacturing, selling or distributing (1) any more copies of the poster labeled "IN MEMORY * * * 1935–1977," (2) any other posters, reproductions or copies containing any likeness of Elvis Presley, and (3) utilizing for commercial profit in any manner or form the name or likeness of Elvis Presley. The order also denied Pro Arts' motion to dismiss, stay or transfer. Pro Arts has duly perfected this interlocutory appeal from the order. * * *

We now proceed to the determination of the principal issue in this case—whether or not the preliminary injunction was improvidently granted. In order to be granted a preliminary injunction under Rule 65(a), Fed.R.Civ.P., the movant must make " 'a clear showing of either (1) probable success on the merits *and* possible irreparable injury, *or* (2) sufficiently serious questions going to the merits to make them a fair ground for litigation *and* a balance of hardships tipping decidedly toward the party requesting the preliminary relief.' " Triebwasser & Katz v. American Tel. & Tel. Co., 535 F.2d 1356, 1358 (2d Cir.1976) (emphasis in original), *quoting* Sonesta International Hotels Corp. v. Wellington Assoc., 483 F.2d 247, 250 (2d Cir.1973). The trial court employed the first prong of the test, finding that Factors had demonstrated probable success on the merits and possible irreparable injury. Because Pro Arts does not challenge the trial court's finding of possible irreparable harm, we need only address the first of the two requirements, that of probable success on the merits.

In concluding that Factors would likely prevail on the merits at trial, the court found that Elvis Presley exercised his right of publicity during his lifetime by giving Parker the exclusive authority to exploit his image through Boxcar Enterprises. This exclusive authority survived Presley's death, after which it was validly assigned to Factors. For this reason Pro Arts was enjoined from manufacturing, distributing, selling or otherwise profiting from merchandise bearing the name or likeness of the late Elvis Presley.

It is beyond cavil that the grant or denial of preliminary injunctive relief " 'will not be disturbed [on appeal] unless there is an abuse of [the trial court's] discretion * * * or unless there is a clear mistake of law.' " New York v. Nuclear Regulatory Commission, 550 F.2d 745, 751 (2d

Cir.1977), quoting Triebwasser & Katz v. American Tel. & Tel. Co., 535 F.2d at 1358. On appeal, Pro Arts alleges two errors of law on the part of the trial court. According to Pro Arts, the trial court erred first in concluding that the right of publicity could survive the death of the celebrity. Second, Pro Arts argues that even if the right did so survive, Pro Arts was privileged, as a matter of law, in printing and distributing its "memorial poster" of Presley, because the poster celebrated a newsworthy event.

The first issue, the duration of the so-called "right of publicity," is one of state law, more specifically the law of the State of New York. Because of the dearth of New York case law in this area, however, we have sought assistance from federal court decisions interpreting and applying New York law, as well as decisions from courts of other states.

As the district court noted, much confusion shrouds the so-called "right of publicity," largely because it has often been discussed under the rubric "right of privacy." As Dean Prosser has stated, the right of privacy embraces "four distinct kinds of invasion of four different interests of the plaintiff, which are tied together by the common name, but otherwise have almost nothing in common except that each represents an interference with the right of the plaintiff 'to be let alone.'" W. Prosser, Torts 804 (4th ed. 1971). Prosser has classified the four species of this tort as (1) intrusion upon the plaintiff's physical solitude or seclusion, id. at 807, (2) public disclosure of private facts, id. at 809, (3) false light in the public eye, id. at 812, and (4) appropriation of plaintiff's name or likeness for defendant's benefit, id. at 804.

The fourth type, appropriation of plaintiff's name or likeness for defendant's benefit, has in recent years acquired the label, "right of publicity." The distinguishing feature of this branch of the tort is that it involves the use of plaintiff's protected right for defendant's direct commercial advantage. The nature of the remedy also separates the right of publicity from the other three species of the tort. To protect his interest with respect to the first three, the injured party attempts to minimize the intrusion or publication of the damaging matter. In contrast, the right of publicity plaintiff does not necessarily object to the commercial exploitation—so long as the exploitation is at his behest and he is receiving the profits. This point was recently underscored by the Supreme Court in Zacchini v. Scripps-Howard Broadcasting Co., 433 U.S. 562, 97 S.Ct. 2849, 53 L.Ed.2d 965 (1977). According to the Court, the interest protected:

> is closely analogous to the goals of patent and copyright law, focusing on the right of the individual to reap the reward of his endeavors and having little to do with protecting feeling or reputation.

Id. at 573, 97 S.Ct. at 2856.

> [The rationale is thus] "one of preventing unjust enrichment by the theft of good will. No social purpose is served by having the defendant get free some aspect of the plaintiff that would have market value and for which he would normally pay."

Id. at 576, 97 S.Ct. at 2857, quoting Kalven, Privacy in Tort Law—Were Warren and Brandeis Wrong? 31 Law & Contemp.Prob. 326, 331 (1966).

The State of New York provides a statutory right for the protection of a *living* person from commercial exploitation of his name and picture by others without his written consent. This statutory right, also called a "right of privacy," is predicated upon the classic right of privacy's theoretical basis which is to prevent injury to feelings. Price v. Hal Roach Studios, Inc., 400 F.Supp. 836, 843 (S.D.N.Y.1975); Lombardo v. Doyle, Dane & Bernbach, 58 A.D.2d 620, 396 N.Y.S.2d 661 (1977). In Haelan Laboratories, Inc. v. Topps Chewing Gum, Inc., 202 F.2d 866 (2d Cir.), cert. denied, 346 U.S. 816, 74 S.Ct. 26, 98 L.Ed. 343 (1953), we recognized that the right of publicity exists independent from the statutory right of privacy and that it can be validly transferred by its owner:

> We think that, in addition to and independent of that right of privacy (which in New York derives from statute), a man has a right in the publicity value of his photograph, i.e., the right to grant the exclusive privilege of publishing his picture, and that such a grant may validly be made "in gross," i.e., without an accompanying transfer of a business or of anything else. Whether it be labelled a "property" right is immaterial; for here, as often elsewhere, the tag "property" simply symbolizes the fact that courts enforce a claim which has pecuniary worth.

Id. at 868.

Since the landmark *Haelan Laboratories, Inc.* case, several decisions by courts applying New York law have labeled the right of publicity as a valid transferable property right, see, e.g., Price v. Hal Roach Studios, Inc., 400 F.Supp. at 844; Groucho Marx Productions, Inc. v. Playboy Enterprises, Inc., No. 77–1782 (S.D.N.Y. Dec. 30, 1977); Lombardo v. Doyle, Dane & Bernbach, 58 A.D.2d 620, 396 N.Y.S.2d 661 (1977), as well as recent decisions by courts applying the law of other states, see, e.g., Cepeda v. Swift & Co., 415 F.2d 1205, 1206 (8th Cir.1969); Memphis Development Foundation v. Factors, Etc., Inc., 441 F.Supp. 1323, 1329 (W.D.Tenn.1977).

There can be no doubt that Elvis Presley assigned to Boxcar a valid property right, the exclusive authority to print, publish and distribute his name and likeness. In so doing, he carved out a separate intangible property right for himself, the right to a certain percentage of the royalties which would be realized by Boxcar upon exploitation of Presley's likeness and name. The identification of this exclusive right belonging to Boxcar as a transferable property right compels the conclusion that the right survives Presley's death. The death of Presley, who was merely the beneficiary of an income interest in Boxcar's exclusive right, should not in itself extinguish Boxcar's property right. Instead, the income interest, continually produced from Boxcar's exclusive right of commercial exploitation, should inure to Presley's estate at death like any other intangible property right. To hold that the right did not survive Presley's death, would be to grant competitors of

Factors, such as Pro Arts, a windfall in the form of profits from the use of Presley's name and likeness. At the same time, the exclusive right purchased by Factors and the financial benefits accruing to the celebrity's heirs would be rendered virtually worthless.

Though no New York court has directly addressed this issue,[10] the only two cases on point agree with our conclusion that the right of publicity should survive the celebrity's death. See Memphis Development Foundation v. Factors, Etc., Inc., 441 F.Supp. 1323 (W.D.Tenn. 1977); Price v. Hal Roach Studios, Inc., 400 F.Supp. 836 (S.D.N.Y.1975). Of these two cases the *Price* case is particularly persuasive since it is a decision of a United States District Court purportedly applying New York law. *Price* involved a dispute over the ownership of the commercial right to use the names and likenesses of Stanley Laurel and Oliver Hardy ("Laurel and Hardy") following the death of the renowned comedians. The exclusive right to exploit the comedy team commercially was assigned to co-plaintiff Larry Harmon Pictures Corporation by Stan Laurel during his lifetime, by Oliver Hardy's widow and sole heir under Hardy's will, Lucille Hardy Price, and by Laurel and Hardy's production company, Laurel and Hardy Feature Productions. Several years later, when the *Price* defendants sought to utilize the name and likenesses of Laurel and Hardy, the owners sued. The district court held that the deaths of the actors did not extinguish the right of publicity held by the grantee of the right. This conclusion was found to be inherent in the distinction between the right of publicity and the right of privacy:

> Since the theoretical basis for the classic right of privacy, and of the statutory right in New York, is to prevent injury to feelings, death is a logical conclusion to any such claim. In addition, based upon the same theoretical foundation, such a right of privacy is not assignable during life. When determining the scope of the right of publicity, however, one must take into account the purely commercial nature of the protected right. Courts and commentators have done just that in recognizing the right of publicity as assignable. There appears to be no logical reason to terminate this right upon death of the person protected.

400 F.Supp. at 844. In sum, we hold that Boxcar's exclusive right to exploit the Presley name and likeness, because exercised during Presley's life, survived his death.[11] The right was therefore validly transferred to Factors following Presley's death.

Pro Arts' final argument is that even if Factors possesses the exclusive right to distribute Presley memorabilia, this right does not prevent Pro Arts from publishing what it terms a "memorial poster"

---

10. We do note, however, dicta from a recent appellate division opinion, Lombardo v. Doyle, Dane & Bernbach, 58 A.D.2d 620, 396 N.Y.S.2d 661 (2d Dept.1977), to the effect that "while a cause of action under the Civil Rights Law is not assignable during one's lifetime and terminates at death, the right to publicity, e.g., the property right to one's name, photograph and image is under no such inhibition."

11. Because the right was exploited during Presley's life, we need not, and therefore do not, decide whether the right would survive the death of the celebrity if not exploited during the celebrity's life.

commemorating a newsworthy event. In support of this argument, Pro Arts cites Paulsen v. Personality Posters, Inc., 59 Misc.2d 444, 299 N.Y.S.2d 501 (Sup.Ct.1968), a case arising out of the bogus presidential candidacy of the television comedian Pat Paulsen. Paulsen sued defendant for publishing and distributing a poster of Paulsen with the legend "FOR PRESIDENT." The court refused to enjoin sale of the poster because Paulsen's choice of the political arena for satire made him "newsworthy" in the First Amendment sense. We cannot accept Pro Arts contention that the legend "IN MEMORY * * *" placed its poster in the same category as one picturing a presidential candidate, albeit a mock candidate. We hold, therefore, that Pro Arts' poster of Presley was not privileged as celebrating a newsworthy event.

In conclusion we hold that the district court did not abuse its discretion in granting the injunction since Factors has demonstrated a strong likelihood of success on the merits at trial. Factors possesses the exclusive right to print and distribute Elvis Presley memorabilia, a right which was validly transferred to it from Boxcar following Presley's death. Pro Arts infringed this right by printing and distributing the Elvis Presley poster, a poster whose publication was not privileged as a newsworthy event.

We affirm the action of the district court and remand for further proceedings.

Questions

1. Recall that the court in *Haelan* concluded that whether the right of publicity is "labelled a 'property' right is immaterial; for here, as often elsewhere, the tag 'property' simply symbolizes the fact that courts enforce a claim which has pecuniary worth." Does the conclusion in *Factors* that the difference between the interests protected in a right of privacy action and in a right of publicity action justifies holding that the latter but not the former may be both assignable and descendible, although both such rights have "pecuniary worth", indicate that the label "property" may be appropriate in a publicity action but not in a privacy action? In what other contexts might a "property" label be significant? Is it relevant on the question of whether a written consent to be depicted is binding in the absence of consideration?

2. Is there any limitation on the duration of the right of publicity following the subject's death? One company advertises T-shirts bearing the portraits of Bach, Beethoven, Mozart, Thoreau, Dostoevsky, Shakespeare, etc. See The New Republic, September 30, 1978, p. 42. If the heirs of any of the above could be identified, would they have a cause of action? Does this raise First Amendment issues? See Zacchini v. Scripps-Howard Broadcasting Co., infra. Could a court, without legislative direction, impose a time limit on the right of publicity? Might a court analogize to the law of copyright, and hold that the right of publicity terminates fifty years after the death of the subject? See Lugosi v. Universal Pictures, 25 Cal.3d 813, 847; 160 Cal.Rptr. 323, 603 P.2d 425 (1979) (Bird, C.J., dissenting). Is this like a court determining a period which constitutes laches by looking to a comparable statute of limitations period? See Holmberg v. Armbrecht, 327 U.S. 392 (1946); Russell v. Todd, 309 U.S. 280 (1940); International Telephone and Telegraph Corp. v. General

Telephone and Electronics Corp., 518 F.2d 913 (9th Cir.1975); Kimberly Corp. v. Hartley Pen Co., 237 F.2d 294 (9th Cir.1956).

3. If a celebrity does not exploit his right of publicity during his lifetime, should such right be held to terminate upon his death?

Collateral References

Felcher and Rubin, *The Descendibility of the Right of Publicity: Is There Commercial Life After Death?* 89 Yale L.J. 1125 (1980).

Comment, *Transfer of the Right of Publicity: Dracula's Progeny and Privacy's Stepchild,* 22 U.C.L.A.L.Rev. 1103 (1975).

Comment, *Community Property Interests in the Right of Publicity: Some and/or Fortune,* 25 U.C.L.A.L.Rev. 1095 (1978).

Note

Descendibility of the Right of Publicity

Following the Second Circuit's affirmance of the preliminary injunction in the *Pro Arts* case, another right of publicity action involving the use of Elvis Presley's name and likeness arose in the Sixth Circuit. In Memphis Development Foundation v. Factors Etc., Inc., 616 F.2d 956 (6th Cir.1980) once again acting as assignee of Elvis Presley's right of publicity, Factors Etc. sought to prevent the sale of Presley statuettes. In this diversity action, the Sixth Circuit Court of Appeals applied Tennessee law, the place of Presley's domicile. In doing so, the Court concluded that (despite the absence of any state cases on the issue) the right of publicity is not descendible under Tennessee law. In the meantime Factors Etc. had prevailed at trial in its action against *Pro Arts*. However, when this case returned to the Second Circuit Court of Appeals, the district court's holding of liability was reversed on the ground that the proper choice of right of publicity law was that of Tennessee, Presley's domicile and place of business. The Second Circuit reasoned that Pro Arts must prevail since (following the *Memphis Development* decision) under Tennessee law the right of publicity is not descendible. This despite the fact that the Second Circuit Court of Appeals recognized that under New York law the right of publicity is descendible. Factors Etc., Inc. v. Pro Arts, Inc., 652 F.2d 278 (2d Cir.1981), cert. denied 456 U.S. 927, 102 S.Ct. 1973, 72 L.Ed.2d 442 (1982). Following this flurry of federal court concern with the status of Tennessee publicity law, the Tennessee legislature enacted a law explicitly providing that the right of publicity is descendible in Tennessee.[1]

The courts, applying the law of two other states, also found the right of publicity to be descendible. Martin Luther King, Jr., Center For Social Change, Inc. v. American Heritage Products, Inc., 694 F.2d 674 (11th Cir.1983), incorporating opinion of Georgia Supreme Court, 250 Ga. 135, 296 S.D.2d 697 (1982) (Martin Luther King, Jr.'s right of publicity held descendible); Estate of Presley v. Russen, 513 F.Supp. 1339 (D.N.J.1981) (Elvis Presley's right of publicity held descendible).

It was in California that the descendibility issue was most extensively fought. In Lugosi v. Universal Pictures, 25 Cal.3d 813, 160 Cal.Rptr. 323, 603

---

1. Tennessee Statutes, Title 47, "Commercial Instruments and Transactions", Chapter 25, "Trade Practices", Section 1103(b).

P.2d 425 (1979) the widow and son of the actor Bela Lugosi claimed that Universal had infringed the late actor's right of publicity by licensing the sale of T-shirts and various other items of merchandise bearing the face of Bela Lugosi in his most famous role, that of the vampire Dracula. Universal had produced the film *Dracula,* starring Mr. Lugosi, but his contract with Universal had not expressly authorized such merchandising. The Supreme Court of California ruled for Universal, holding that Bela Lugosi's right of publicity did not descend to his heirs upon his death. But the opinion in which the court reached this conclusion was wrapped in considerable ambiguity. In a case decided two days later, Guglielmi v. Spelling-Goldberg Productions, 25 Cal.3d 860, 160 Cal.Rptr. 352, 603 P.2d 454 (1979) the California Supreme Court described its earlier decision as follows: "In Lugosi v. Universal Pictures we hold that the right of publicity protects against the unauthorized use of one's name, likeness or personality, but that the right is not descendible and expires upon the death of the person so protected." The *Lugosi* opinion itself, however, arguably did not deny descendibility in such absolute terms. In support of the *Guglielmi* interpretation is the fact that the court in *Lugosi* seemed to equate the right of publicity with other branches of the law of privacy, in which the right is clearly a personal one, and dies with the subject. This view of the right of publicity as merely one subdivision of the right of privacy was attributed in the *Lugosi* opinion to Professor Prosser's influential article *Privacy,* 48 Cal.L. Rev. 383 (1960). For reasons discussed in the first *Factors* opinion, and in this writer's article in Law and Contemporary Problems, both set forth supra, Prosser's lumping of right of publicity (which he called "misappropriation") with right of privacy is, to say the least, most questionable. Those branches of the right of privacy dealing with disclosure of intimate private facts and depiction in a false light are intended to guard against personal feelings of embarrassment and humiliation. Such feelings do indeed die with the subject. But the value created in the commercial use of a well-known personality's name and likeness, protected by the right of publicity, may be transferred (under *Haelan*) precisely because such value is not personal to the subject. For the same reason such value continues even after the subject's death, and hence should not be regarded as without legal protection merely because the subject has died. See the excellent discussion of the right of publicity in Chief Justice Bird's dissenting opinion in *Lugosi,* 25 Cal.3d at 828. But if in one part of the *Lugosi* opinion the majority confused the right of publicity with the right of privacy, in other parts of the opinion the majority confused the right of publicity with unfair competition. The court's opinion states: "Lugosi could have created during his lifetime through the commercial exploitation of his name, face and/or likeness in connection with the operation of any kind of business or the sale of any kind of product or service a general acceptance and good will for such business product or service among the public, the effect of which would have been to impress upon such business product or service with a secondary meaning, protectible under the law of unfair competition." 25 Cal.3d at 818. Building upon this premise, the *Lugosi* court apparently [2]

---

2. But note the following puzzling passage in *Lugosi:* "However, even on the above assumption, whether Lugosi's heirs would have succeeded to such property depends entirely how it was managed before Lugosi died. Lugosi may have sold the property and spent the consideration before he died, or sold it for installment payments and/or royalties due after his death, in which latter event such payments and/or royalties would, of course, be a part of his estate." 25 Cal.3d at 820. Is the court there suggesting that the heirs would, in any event, be limited to contract claims owed the estate? Probably the court simply means that to the extent that Lugosi

concluded that the right of publicity would be descendible, but only as regards those activities involving his name and/or likeness as to which Bela Lugosi exercised his right of publicity during his lifetime, and then, only if such activities were sufficiently pervasive as to establish a secondary meaning.[3] To apply the passing off concept of unfair competition in general, and secondary meaning in particular, to the right of publicity would seem to be entirely inappropriate. Such concepts are intended to protect against public confusion, and have nothing to do with the underlying rationale for the right of publicity. See the discussion at p. 842 supra. California has now discarded the notion that one must exercise his or her right of publicity during the subject's lifetime in order for the right to descend. See California Civil Code Section 990, set forth below.[4] But by reason of *Lugosi*, has that concept now infected the common law right of publicity as applied in other states? Compare the question raised in footnote 11 of the *Factors* opinion at p. 850 supra, with the apparent misreading of *Factors* in Hicks v. Casablanca Records at p. 871 infra.

CALIFORNIA CIVIL CODE SEC. 990

(a) Any person who uses a deceased personality's name, voice,

divested himself of his entire right of publicity during his lifetime, the heirs would be limited to such consideration for the divestment which was still due and owing by contract to Lugosi or his estate. But if the right of publicity only descends as regards those uses of name and/or likeness which were exploited during the subject's lifetime, would there be any claims which might descend which were not already the subject of an assignment, for which only a contract claim might be asserted?

3. In Groucho Marx Productions, Inc. v. Day and Night Co., Inc., 689 F.2d 317 (2d Cir.1982) the court held that California right of publicity law should be applied, even though the allegedly infringing acts of using the Marx Brothers characters in a play had occurred in New York. This for the reason that the Marx Brothers were California residents at the times of their respective deaths, and prior thereto had conveyed their respective rights of publicity in California. Thus called upon to construe the meaning of *Lugosi*, the *Groucho Marx* court considered whether Lugosi's heirs could have claimed a descendible right of publicity if during his lifetime Bela Lugosi had established a company to market "Lugosi as Dracula" T-shirts. The Second Circuit concluded that there were three possible readings of *Lugosi*. Applying the above quoted statement from *Guglielmi*, the answer would be that "the heirs would have had no right of publicity that could prevent others from marketing Lugosi's likeness, even on T-shirts." Alternatively, the heirs "might have had a right of publicity that could prevent others from marketing his likeness on T-shirts, but not on any other product." The third possible reading of *Lugosi* according to the Second Circuit was that, given such a T-shirt business during Lugosi's lifetime, his heirs "might have had a right of publicity that could prevent others from profiting in any way from the use of his likeness." The Second Circuit rejected the third alternative, and concluded that "at most, California would recognize a descendible right of publicity that would have enabled the heirs to prevent others from using Lugosi's name and likeness on T-shirts or any other product he had promoted during his life."

4. While California has by statute reversed the judicial rule denying or limiting descendability of the right of publicity, as this work goes to press it appears that New York has moved in the opposite direction. The Second Circuit's recognition (applying diversity jurisdiction) of a New York common law right of publicity, and its further recognition that such right is descendable, has been rendered questionable, if not outright overruled by the highest authority on New York law, the New York Court of Appeals. In Stephano v. News Group Publications, Inc., 64 N.Y.2d 174, 485 N.Y.S.2d 220, 474 N.E.2d 580 (1984) it was held that the right of publicity is recognized in New York as a part of the Civil Rights Law (the so-called right of privacy statute), and not under the common law. On the issue of descendability under the Civil Rights Law, the Court of Appeals stated: "In view of the fact that the plaintiff is asserting his own right of publicity we need not consider whether the statute would also control assignment, transfer or descent of publicity rights * * *"

signature, photograph, or likeness, in any manner, on or in products, merchandise, or goods, or for purposes of advertising or selling, or soliciting purchases of, products, merchandise, goods, or services, without prior consent from the person or persons specified in subdivision (c), shall be liable for any damages sustained by the person or persons injured as a result thereof. In addition, in any action brought under this section, the person who violated the section shall be liable to the injured party or parties in an amount equal to the greater of seven hundred and fifty dollars ($750) or the actual damages suffered by the injured party or parties, as a result of the unauthorized use, and any profits from the unauthorized use that are attributable to the use and are not taken into account in computing the actual damages. In establishing these profits, the injured party or parties shall be required to present proof only of the gross revenue attributable to the use and the person who violated the section is required to prove his or her deductible expenses. Punitive damages may also be awarded to the injured party or parties. The prevailing party or parties in any action under this section shall also be entitled to attorneys' fees and costs.

(b) The rights recognized under this section are property rights, freely transferable, in whole or in part, by contract or by means of trust or testamentary documents, whether the transfer occurs before the death of the deceased personality, by the deceased personality or his or her transferees, or, after the death of the deceased personality, by the person or persons in whom such rights vest under this section or the transferees of that person or persons.

(c) The consent required by this section shall be exercisable by the person or persons to whom such right of consent (or portion thereof) has been transferred in accordance with subdivision (b), or if no such transfer has occurred, then by the person or persons to whom such right of consent (or portion thereof) has passed in accordance with subdivision (d).

(d) Subject to subdivisions (b) and (c), after the death of any person, the rights under this section shall belong to the following person or persons and may be exercised, on behalf of and for the benefit of all of those persons, by those persons who, in the aggregate, are entitled to more than a one-half interest in such rights:

(1) The entire interest in those rights belong to the surviving spouse of the deceased personality unless there are any surviving children or grandchildren of the deceased personality, in which case one-half of the entire interest in those rights belong to the surviving spouse.

(2) The entire interest in those rights belong to the surviving children of the deceased personality and to the surviving children of any dead child of the deceased personality unless the deceased personality has a surviving spouse, in which case the ownership of a one-half interest in rights is divided among the surviving children and grandchildren.

(3) If there is no surviving spouse, and no surviving children or grandchildren, then the entire interest in those rights belong to the surviving parent or parents of the deceased personality.

(4) The rights of the deceased personality's children and grandchildren are in all cases divided among them and exercisable on a per stirpes basis according to the number of the deceased personality's children represented; the share of the children of a dead child of a deceased personality can be exercised only by the action of a majority of them. For the purposes of this section, "per stirpes" is defined as it is defined in Section 240 of the Probate Code.

(e) If any deceased personality does not transfer his or her rights under this section by contract, or by means of a trust or testamentary document, and there are no surviving persons as described in subdivision (d), then the rights set forth in subdivision (a) shall terminate.

(f)(1) A successor-in-interest to the rights of a deceased personality under this section or a licensee thereof may not recover damages for a use prohibited by this section that occurs before the successor-in-interest or licensee registers a claim of the rights under paragraph (2).

(2) Any person claiming to be a successor-in-interest to the rights of a deceased personality under this section or a licensee thereof may register that claim with the Secretary of State on a form prescribed by the Secretary of State and upon payment of a fee of ten dollars ($10). The form shall be verified and shall include the name and date of death of the deceased personality, the name and address of the claimant, the basis of the claim, and the rights claimed.

(3) Upon receipt and after filing of any document under this section, the Secretary of State may microfilm or reproduce by other techniques any of the filings or documents and destroy the original filing or document. The microfilm or other reproduction of any document under the provision of this section shall be admissible in any court of law. The microfilm or other reproduction of any document may be destroyed by the Secretary of State 50 years after the death of the personality named therein.

(4) Claims registered under this subdivision shall be public records.

(g) No action shall be brought under this section by reason of any use of a deceased personality's name, voice, signature, photograph, or likeness occurring after the expiration of 50 years from the death of the deceased personality.

(h) As used in this section, "deceased personality" means any natural person whose name, voice, signature, photograph, or likeness has commercial value at the time of his or her death, whether or not during the lifetime of that natural person the person used his or her name, voice, signature, photograph, or likeness on or in products, merchandise or goods, or for purposes of advertising or selling, or solicitation of purchase of, products, merchandise, goods or service. A "deceased personality" shall include, without limitation, any such natural person who has died within 50 years prior to January 1, 1985.

(i) As used in this section, "photograph" means any photograph or photographic reproduction, still or moving, or any videotape or live television transmission, of any person, such that the deceased personality is readily identifiable. A deceased personality shall be deemed to be readily identifiable from a photograph when one who views the photograph with the naked eye can reasonably determine who the person depicted in the photograph is.

(j) For purposes of this section, a use of a name, voice, signature, photograph, or likeness in connection with any news, public affairs, or sports broadcast or account, or any political campaign, shall not constitute a use for which consent is required under subdivision (a).

(k) The use of a name, voice, signature, photograph, or likeness in a commercial medium shall not constitute a use for which consent is required under subdivision (a) solely because the material containing such use is commercially sponsored or contains paid advertising. Rather it shall be a question of fact whether or not the use of the deceased personality's name, voice, signature, photograph, or likeness was so directly connected with the commercial sponsorship or with the paid advertising as to constitute a use for which consent is required under subdivision (a).

(*l*) Nothing in this section shall apply to the owners or employees of any medium used for advertising, including, but not limited to, newspapers, magazines, radio and television networks and stations, cable television systems, billboards, and transit ads, by whom any advertisement or solicitation is violation of this section is published or disseminated, unless it is established that such owners or employees had knowledge of the unauthorized use of the deceased personality's name, voice, signature, photograph, or likeness as prohibited by this section.

(m) The remedies provided for in this section are cumulative and shall be in addition to any others provided for by law.

(n) This section shall not apply to the use of a deceased personality's name, voice, signature, photograph, or likeness, in any of the following instances:

(1) A play, book, magazine, newspaper, musical composition, film, radio or television program, other than an advertisement or commercial announcement not exempt under paragraph (4).

(2) Material that is of political or newsworthy value.

(3) Single and original works of fine art.

(4) An advertisement or commercial announcement for a use permitted by paragraph (1), (2), or (3).

Questions

1. Is the California rule of descendibility, including the registration requirement, significant with respect to right of publicity actions brought in other states? What is the applicable conflicts of law rule? See the discussion in the Note at p. 852 supra.

2. Section 990(d) is patterned after the successor class for termination rights under the Copyright Act. Wherein does the class under Section 990(d) differ from the similar class under Section 304(c)(2) of the Copyright Act?

3. Of what significance is the fact that the word "knowingly" in Section 3344(a) (p. 842 supra) is omitted from the otherwise similarly worded Section 990(a).

B. FIRST AMENDMENT DEFENSE

ZACCHINI V. SCRIPPS–HOWARD BROADCASTING CO.

Supreme Court of the United States, 1977.
433 U.S. 562, 97 S.Ct. 2849, 53 L.Ed.2d 965.

MR. JUSTICE WHITE delivered the opinion of the Court.

Petitioner, Hugo Zacchini, is an entertainer. He performs a "human cannonball" act in which he is shot from a cannon into a net some 200 feet away. Each performance occupies some 15 seconds. In August and September 1972, petitioner was engaged to perform his act on a regular basis at the Geauga County Fair in Burton, Ohio. He performed in a fenced area, surrounded by grandstands, at the fair grounds. Members of the public attending the fair were not charged a separate admission fee to observe his act.

On August 30, a freelance reporter for Scripps-Howard Broadcasting Co. the operator of a television broadcasting station and respondent in this case, attended the fair. He carried a small movie camera. Petitioner noticed the reporter and asked him not to film the performance. The reporter did not do so on that day; but on the instructions of the producer of respondent's daily newscast, he returned the following day and videotaped the entire act. This film clip, approximately 15 seconds in length, was shown on the 11 o'clock news program that night, together with favorable commentary.[1]

Petitioner then brought this action for damages, alleging that he is "engaged in the entertainment business," that the act he performs is one "invented by his father and * * * performed only by his family for the last fifty years," that respondent "showed and commercialized the

---

1. The script of the commentary accompanying the film clip read as follows:

"This * * * now * * * is the story of a *true spectator* sport * * * the sport of human cannonballing * * * in fact, the great *Zacchini* is about the only human cannonball around, these days * * * just happens that, *where* he is, is the Great Geauga County Fair, in Burton * * * and believe me, although it's not a *long* act, it's a thriller * * * and you really need to see it *in person* * * * to appreciate it. * * *" (Emphasis in original.) App. 12.

Hugo Zacchini performing his *human cannonball* act

film of his act without his consent," and that such conduct was an "unlawful appropriation of plaintiff's professional property." App. 4–5. Respondent answered and moved for summary judgment, which was granted by the trial court.

The Court of Appeals of Ohio reversed. The majority held that petitioner's complaint stated a cause of action for conversion and for infringement of a common-law copyright, and one judge concurred in the judgment on the ground that the complaint stated a cause of action for appropriation of petitioner's "right of publicity" in the film of his act. All three judges agreed that the First Amendment did not privilege the press to show the entire performance on a news program without compensating petitioner for any financial injury he could prove at trial.

Like the concurring judge in the Court of Appeals, the Supreme Court of Ohio rested petitioner's cause of action under state law on his "right to the publicity value of his performance." 47 Ohio St.2d 224, 351 N.E.2d 454, 455 (1976). The opinion syllabus, to which we are to look for the rule of law used to decide the case, declared first that one may not use for his own benefit the name or likeness of another, whether or not the use or benefit is a commercial one, and second that respondent would be liable for the appropriation, over petitioner's objection and in the absence of license or privilege, of petitioner's right to the publicity value of his performance. Ibid. The court nevertheless gave judgment for respondent because, in the words of the syllabus:

> A TV station has a privilege to report in its newscasts matters of legitimate public interest which would otherwise be protected by an individual's right of publicity, unless the actual intent of the TV station was to appropriate the benefit of the publicity for some non-privileged private use, or unless the actual intent was to injure the individual. Ibid.

We granted certiorari, 429 U.S. 1037, 50 L.Ed.2d 747, 97 S.Ct. 730 (1977), to consider an issue unresolved by this Court: whether the First and Fourteenth Amendments immunized respondent from damages for its alleged infringement of petitioner's state-law "right of publicity." Pet for Cert 2. Insofar as the Ohio Supreme Court held that the First and Fourteenth Amendments of the United States Constitution required judgment for respondent, we reverse the judgment of that court.

I

If the judgment below rested on an independent and adequate state ground, the writ of certiorari should be dismissed as improvidently granted, Wilson v. Loew's Inc., 355 U.S. 597, 2 L.Ed.2d 519, 78 S.Ct. 526 (1958), for "[o]ur only power over state judgments is to correct them to the extent that they incorrectly adjudge federal rights. And our power is to correct wrong judgments, not to revise opinions. We are not permitted to render an advisory opinion, and if the same judgment would be rendered by the state court after we corrected its views of federal laws, our review could amount to nothing more than an advisory opinion." Herb v. Pitcairn, 324 U.S. 117, 125–126, 89 L.Ed. 789, 65 S.Ct. 459 (1945). We are confident, however, that the judgment below did not rest on an adequate and independent state ground and that we have jurisdiction to decide the federal issue presented in this case.

There is no doubt that petitioner's complaint was grounded in state law and that the right of publicity which petitioner was held to possess was a right arising under Ohio law. It is also clear that respondent's claim of constitutional privilege was sustained. The source of this privilege was not identified in the syllabus. It is clear enough from the opinion of the Ohio Supreme Court, which we are permitted to consult for understanding of the syllabus, Perkins v. Benguet Consolidated Mining Co., 342 U.S. 437, 441–443, 96 L.Ed. 485, 72 S.Ct. 413, 47 O.O. 216, 63 O.L.A. 146 (1952), that in adjudicating the crucial question of whether respondent had a privilege to film and televise petitioner's performance, the court placed principal reliance on Time, Inc. v. Hill, 385 U.S. 374, 17 L.Ed.2d 456, 87 S.Ct. 534 (1967), a case involving First Amendment limitations on state tort actions. It construed the principle of that case, along with that of New York Times Co. v. Sullivan, 376 U.S. 254, 11 L.Ed.2d 686, 84 S.Ct. 710, 95 A.L.R.2d 1412 (1964), to be that "the press has a privilege to report matters of legitimate public interest even though such reports might intrude on matters otherwise private," and concluded, therefore, that the press is also "privileged when an individual seeks to publicly exploit his talents while keeping the benefits private." 47 Ohio St.2d, at 234, 351 N.E.2d, at 461. The privilege thus exists in cases "where appropriation of a right of publicity is claimed." The court's opinion also referred to Draft 21 of the relevant portion of Restatement (Second) of Torts (1975), which was understood to make room for reasonable press appropriations by limiting the reach of the right of privacy rather than by creating a privileged invasion. The court preferred the notion of privilege over the Restatement's formulation, however, reasoning that "since the gravamen of the issue in this case is not whether the degree of intrusion is reasonable, but whether *First Amendment principles* require that the right of privacy give way to the public right to be informed of matters of public interest and concern, the concept of privilege seems the more useful and appropriate one." 47 Ohio St.2d, at 234 n. 5, 351 N.E.2d at 461 n. 5. (Emphasis added.)

Had the Ohio court rested its decision on both state and federal grounds, either of which would have been dispositive, we would have had no jurisdiction. Fox Film Corp. v. Muller, 296 U.S. 207, 80 L.Ed. 158, 56 S.Ct. 183 (1935); Enterprise Irrigation Dist. v. Farmers Mutual Canal Co., 243 U.S. 157, 164, 61 L.Ed. 644, 37 S.Ct. 318 (1917). But the opinion, like the syllabus, did not mention the Ohio Constitution, citing instead this Court's First Amendment cases as controlling. It appears to us that the decision rested solely on federal grounds. That the Ohio court might have, but did not, invoke state law does not foreclose jurisdiction here. Steele v. Louisville & Nashville R. Co., 323 U.S. 192, 197 n. 1, 89 L.Ed. 173, 65 S.Ct. 226 (1944); Indiana ex rel. Anderson v.

Brand, 303 U.S. 95, 98, 82 L.Ed. 685, 58 S.Ct. 443, 113 A.L.R. 1482 (1938).

Even if the judgment in favor of respondent must nevertheless be understood as ultimately resting on Ohio law, it appears that at the very least the Ohio court felt compelled by what it understood to be federal constitutional considerations to construe and apply its own law in the manner it did. In this event, we have jurisdiction and should decide the federal issue; for if the state court erred in its understanding of our cases and of the First and Fourteenth Amendments, we should so declare, leaving the state court free to decide the privilege issue solely as a matter of Ohio law. Perkins v. Benguet Consolidated Mining Co., supra. If the Supreme Court of Ohio "held as it did because it felt under compulsion of federal law as enunciated by this Court so to hold, it should be relieved of that compulsion. It should be free to decide * * these suits according to its own local law." Missouri ex rel. Southern R. Co. v. Mayfield, 340 U.S. 1, 5, 95 L.Ed. 3, 71 S.Ct. 1 (1950).

II

The Ohio Supreme Court held that respondent is constitutionally privileged to include in its newscasts matters of public interest that would otherwise be protected by the right of publicity, absent an intent to injure or to appropriate for some nonprivileged purpose. If under this standard respondent had merely reported that petitioner was performing at the fair and described or commented on his act, with or without showing his picture on television, we would have a very different case. But petitioner is not contending that his appearance at the fair and his performance could not be reported by the press as newsworthy items. His complaint is that respondent filmed his entire act and displayed that film on television for the public to see and enjoy. This, he claimed, was an appropriation of his professional property. The Ohio Supreme Court agreed that petitioner had "a right of publicity" that gave him "personal control over commercial display and exploitation of his personality and the exercise of his talents."[4] This right of "exclusive control over the publicity given to his performances" was said to be such a "valuable part of the benefit which may be attained by his talents and efforts" that it was entitled to legal protection. It was also observed, or at least expressly assumed, that

---

4. The court relied on Housh v. Peth, 165 Ohio St. 35, 133 N.E.2d 340, 341 (1956), the syllabus of which held:

"An actionable invasion of the right of privacy is the unwarranted appropriation or exploitation of one's personality, the publicizing of one's private affairs with which the public has no legitimate concern, or the wrongful intrusion into one's private activities in such a manner as to outrage or cause mental suffering, shame or humiliation to a person of ordinary sensibilities."

The court also indicated that the applicable principles of Ohio law were those set out in Restatement (Second) § 652C of Torts (Tent Draft No. 13, 1967), and the comments thereto, portions of which were stated in the footnotes of the opinion. Also, referring to the right as the "right of publicity," the court quoted approvingly from Haelan Laboratories, Inc. v. Topps Chewing Gum, Inc., 202 F.2d 866, 868 (C.A.2 1953).

petitioner had not abandoned his rights by performing under the circumstances present at the Geauga County Fair Grounds.

The Ohio Supreme Court nevertheless held that the challenged invasion was privileged, saying that the press "must be accorded broad latitude in its choice of how much it presents of each story or incident, and of the emphasis to be given to such presentation. No fixed standard which would bar the press from reporting or depicting either an entire occurrence or an entire discrete part of a public performance can be formulated which would not unduly restrict the 'breathing room' in reporting which freedom of the press requires." 47 Ohio St.2d, at 235, 351 N.E.2d, at 461. Under this view, respondent was thus constitutionally free to film and display petitioner's entire act.[5]

The Ohio Supreme Court relied heavily on Time, Inc. v. Hill, 385 U.S. 374, 17 L.Ed.2d 456, 87 S.Ct. 534 (1967), but that case does not mandate a media privilege to televise a performer's entire act without his consent. Involved in Time, Inc. v. Hill was a claim under the New York "Right of Privacy" statute [6] that Life Magazine, in the course of reviewing a new play, had connected the play with a long-past incident involving petitioner and his family and had falsely described their experience and conduct at that time. The complaint sought damages for humiliation and suffering flowing from these nondefamatory falsehoods that allegedly invaded Hill's privacy. The Court held, however, that the opening of a new play linked to an actual incident was a matter of public interest and that Hill could not recover without showing that the Life report was knowingly false or was published with reckless disregard for the truth—the same rigorous standard that had been applied in New York Times Co. v. Sullivan, 376 U.S. 254, 11 L.Ed.2d 686, 84 S.Ct. 710, 95 A.L.R.2d 1412 (1964).

Time, Inc. v. Hill, which was hotly contested and decided by a divided Court, involved an entirely different tort from the "right of publicity" recognized by the Ohio Supreme Court. As the opinion reveals in Time, Inc. v. Hill, the Court was steeped in the literature of privacy law and was aware of the developing distinctions and nuances in this branch of the law. The Court, for example, cited W. Prosser,

---

5. The court's explication was as follows:

"The proper standard must necessarily be whether the matters reported were of public interest, and if so, the press will be liable for appropriation of a performer's right of publicity only if its actual intent was not to report the performance, but, rather, to appropriate the performance for some other private use, or if the actual intent was to injure the performer. It might also be the case that the press would be liable if it recklessly disregarded contract rights existing between the plaintiff and a third person to present the performance to the public, but that question is not presented here." 47 Ohio St.2d, at 235, 351 N.E.2d, at 461.

6. Section 51 of the New York Civil Rights Law provides an action for injunction and damages for invasion of the "right of privacy" granted by § 50 (McKinney 1976):

"A person, firm or corporation that uses for advertising purposes, or for the purposes of trade, the name, portrait or picture of any living person without having first obtained the written consent of such person, or if a minor of his or her parent or guardian, is guilty of a misdemeanor."

Law of Torts 831–832 (3d ed. 1964), and the same author's well-known article, Privacy, 48 Calif.L.Rev. 383 (1960), both of which divided privacy into four distinct branches.[7] The Court was aware that it was adjudicating a "false light" privacy case involving a matter of public interest, not a case involving "intrusion," 385 U.S. at 384–385, n. 9, 17 L.Ed.2d 456, 87 S.Ct. 534, "appropriation" of a name or likeness for the purposes of trade, id., at 381, 17 L.Ed.2d 456, 87 S.Ct. 534, or "private details" about a non-newsworthy person or event, id., at 383 n. 7, 17 L.Ed.2d 456, 87 S.Ct. 534. It is also abundantly clear that Time, Inc. v. Hill did not involve a performer, a person with a name having commercial value, or any claim to a "right of publicity." This discrete kind of "appropriation" case was plainly identified in the literature cited by the Court[8] and had been adjudicated in the reported cases.[9]

The differences between these two torts are important. First, the State's interests in providing a cause of action in each instance are different. "The interest protected" in permitting recovery for placing the plaintiff in a false light "is clearly that of reputation, with the same overtones of mental distress as in defamation." Prosser, supra, 48 Calif.L.Rev., at 400. By contrast, the State's interest in permitting a

---

7. "The law of privacy comprises four distinct kinds of invasion of four different interests of the plaintiff, which are tied together by the common name, but otherwise have almost nothing in common except that each represents an interference with the right of the plaintiff * * * 'to be let alone.'" Prosser, Privacy, 48 Calif.L.Rev., at 389. Thus, according to Prosser, some courts had recognized a cause of action for "intrusion" upon the plaintiff's seclusion or solitude; public disclosure of "private facts" about the plaintiff's personal life; publicity that places the plaintiff in a "false light" in the public eye; and "appropriation" of the plaintiff's name or likeness for commercial purposes. One may be liable for "appropriation" if he "pirate[s] the plaintiff's identity for some advantage of his own." Id., at 403.

8. See, for example, W. Prosser, Law of Torts 842 (3d ed. 1964); Bloustein, Privacy as an Aspect of Human Dignity: An Answer to Dean Prosser, 39 N.Y.U.L.Rev. 962, 986–991 (1964); Kalven, Privacy in Tort Law—Were Warren and Brandeis Wrong?, 31 Law & Contemp.Prob. 326, 331 (1966).

9. E.g., Ettore v. Philco Television Broadcasting Corp., 229 F.2d 481 (C.A.3), cert. denied, 351 U.S. 926, 100 L.Ed. 1456, 76 S.Ct. 783 (1956); Sharkey v. National Broadcasting Co., 93 F.Supp. 986 (S.D.N.Y. 1950); Pittsburgh Athletic Co. v. KQV Broadcasting Co., 24 F.Supp. 490 (W.D.Pa. 1938); Twentieth Century Sporting Club, Inc. v. Transradio Press Service, 165 Misc. 71, 300 N.Y.S. 159 (1937); Hogan v. A.S. Barnes & Co., 114 U.S.P.Q. 314 (Pa.Ct.C.P. 1957); Myers v. U.S. Camera Publishing Corp., 9 Misc.2d 765, 167 N.Y.S.2d 771 (1957). The cases prior to 1961 are helpfully reviewed in Gordon, Right of Property in Name, Likeness, Personality and History, 55 Nw.U.L.Rev. 553 (1960).

Ettore v. Philco Television Broadcasting Corp., supra, involved a challenge to television exhibition of a film made of a prize fight that had occurred some time ago. Judge Biggs, writing for the Court of Appeals, said:

"There are, speaking very generally, two polar types of cases. One arises when some accidental occurrence rends the veil of obscurity surrounding an average person and makes him, arguably, newsworthy. The other type involves the appropriation of the performance or production of a professional performer or entrepreneur. Between the two extremes are many gradations, most involving strictly commercial exploitation of some aspect of an individual's personality, such as his name or picture." 229 F.2d, at 486.

" * * * The fact is that, if a performer performs for hire, a curtailment, without consideration, of his right to control his performance is a wrong to him. Such a wrong vitally affects his livelihood, precisely as a trade libel, for example, affects the earnings of a corporation. If the artistry of the performance be used as a criterion, every judge perforce must turn himself into a literary, theatrical or sports critic." Id., at 490.

"right of publicity" is in protecting the proprietary interest of the individual in his act in part to encourage such entertainment.[10] As we later note, the State's interest is closely analogous to the goals of patent and copyright law focusing on the right of the individual to reap the reward of his endeavors and having little to do with protecting feelings or reputation. Second, the two torts differ in the degree to which they intrude on dissemination of information to the public. In "false light" cases the only way to protect the interests involved is to attempt to minimize publication of the damaging matter, while in "right of publicity" cases the only question is who gets to do the publishing. An entertainer such as petitioner usually has no objection to the widespread publication of his act as long as he gets the commercial benefit of such publication. Indeed, in the present case petitioner did not seek to enjoin the broadcast of his act; he simply sought compensation for the broadcast in the form of damages.

Nor does it appear that our later cases, such as Rosenbloom v. Metromedia, Inc., 403 U.S. 29, 29 L.Ed.2d 296, 91 S.Ct. 1811 (1971); Gertz v. Robert Welch, Inc., 418 U.S. 323, 41 L.Ed.2d 789, 94 S.Ct. 2997 (1974); and Time, Inc. v. Firestone, 424 U.S. 448, 47 L.Ed.2d 154, 96 S.Ct. 958 (1976), require or furnish substantial support for the Ohio court's privilege ruling. These cases, like *New York Times*, emphasize the protection extended to the press by the First Amendment in defamation cases, particularly when suit is brought by a public official or a public figure. None of them involve an alleged appropriation by the press of a right of publicity existing under state law.

Moreover, Time, Inc. v. Hill, *New York Times, Metromedia, Gertz,* and *Firestone* all involved the reporting of events; in none of them was there an attempt to broadcast or publish an entire act for which the performer ordinarily gets paid. It is evident, and there is no claim here to the contrary, that petitioner's state-law right of publicity would not serve to prevent respondent from reporting the newsworthy facts about petitioner's act.[11] Wherever the line in particular situations is to be

---

10. The Ohio Supreme Court expressed the view "that plaintiff's claim is one for invasion of the right of privacy by appropriation, and should be considered as such." 47 Ohio St.2d, at 226, 351 N.E.2d, at 456. It should be noted, however, that the case before us is more limited than the broad category of lawsuits that may arise under the heading of "appropriation." Petitioner does not merely assert that some general use, such as advertising, was made of his name or likeness; he relies on the much narrower claim that respondent televised an entire act that he ordinarily gets paid to perform.

11. W. Prosser, Law of Torts 806–807 (4th ed. 1971), generalizes on the cases:

"The New York courts were faced very early with the obvious fact that newspapers and magazines, to say nothing of radio, television and motion pictures are by no means philanthropic institutions, but are operated for profit. As against the contention that everything published by these agencies must necessarily be 'for purposes of trade,' they were compelled to hold that there must be some closer and more direct connection, beyond the mere fact that the newspaper itself is sold; and that the presence of advertising matter in adjacent columns, or even the duplication of a news item for the purpose of advertising the publication itself, does not make any difference. Any other conclusion would in all probability have been an unconstitutional interference with the freedom of the press. Accordingly, it has been held that the mere incidental mention of the plaintiff's name in a book or a motion picture is not an

drawn between media reports that are protected and those that are not, we are quite sure that the First and Fourteenth Amendments do not immunize the media when they broadcast a performer's entire act without his consent. The Constitution no more prevents a State from requiring respondent to compensate petitioner for broadcasting his act on television than it would privilege respondent to film and broadcast a copyrighted dramatic work without liability to the copyright owner, Copyrights Act, 90 Stat. 2541 (1976); cf. Kalem Co. v. Harper Bros., 222 U.S. 55, 56 L.Ed. 92, 32 S.Ct. 20 (1911); Manners v. Morosco, 252 U.S. 317, 64 L.Ed. 590, 40 S.Ct. 335 (1920), or to film and broadcast a prize fight, Ettore v. Philco Television Broadcasting Corp., 229 F.2d 481 (C.A.3), cert. denied, 351 U.S. 926, 100 L.Ed. 1456, 76 S.Ct. 783 (1956); or a baseball game, Pittsburgh Athletic Co. v. KQV Broadcasting Co., 24 F.Supp. 490 (W.D.Pa.1938), where the promoters or the participants had other plans for publicizing the event. There are ample reasons for reaching this conclusion.

The broadcast of a film of petitioner's entire act poses a substantial threat to the economic value of that performance. As the Ohio court recognized, this act is the product of petitioner's own talents and energy, the end result of much time, effort, and expense. Much of its economic value lies in the "right of exclusive control over the publicity given to his performance"; if the public can see the act free on television, it will be less willing to pay to see it at the fair.[12] The effect of a public broadcast of the performance is similar to preventing petitioner from charging an admission fee. "The rationale for [protecting the right of publicity] is the straightforward one of preventing unjust enrichment by the theft of good will. No social purpose is served by having the defendant get free some aspect of the plaintiff that would have market value and for which he would normally pay." Kalven, Privacy in Tort Law—Were Warren and Brandeis Wrong?, 31 Law & Contemp.Prob. 326, 331 (1966). Moreover, the broadcast of petitioner's entire performance, unlike the unauthorized use of another's name for purposes of trade or the incidental use of a name or picture by the press, goes to the heart of petitioner's ability to earn a living as an entertainer. Thus, in this case, Ohio has recognized what may be the strongest case for a "right of publicity"—involving, not the appropriation of an entertainer's reputation to enhance the attractiveness of a commercial product, but the appropriation of the very activity by which the entertainer acquired his reputation in the first place.

invasion of his privacy; nor is the publication of a photograph or a newsreel in which he incidentally appears." (Footnotes omitted.)

Compare Restatement (Second) of Torts § 652C, Comment *d* (Tent Draft No. 22, 1976).

12. It is possible, of course, that respondent's news broadcast increased the value of petitioner's performance by stimulating the public's interest in seeing the act live. In these circumstances, petitioner would not be able to prove damages and thus would not recover. But petitioner has alleged that the broadcast injured him to the extent of $25,000, App. 5, and we think the State should be allowed to authorize compensation of this injury if proved.

Of course, Ohio's decision to protect petitioner's right of publicity here rests on more than a desire to compensate the performer for the time and effort invested in his act; the protection provides an economic incentive for him to make the investment required to produce a performance of interest to the public. This same consideration underlies the patent and copyright laws long enforced by this Court. As the Court stated in Mazer v. Stein, 347 U.S. 201, 219, 98 L.Ed. 630, 74 S.Ct. 460 (1954):

> The economic philosophy behind the clause empowering Congress to grant patents and copyrights is the conviction that encouragement of individual effort by personal gain is the best way to advance public welfare through the talents of authors and inventors in "Science and useful Arts." Sacrificial days devoted to such creative activities deserve rewards commensurate with the services rendered.

These laws perhaps regard the "reward to the owner [as] a secondary consideration," United States v. Paramount Pictures, 334 U.S. 131, 158, 92 L.Ed. 1260, 68 S.Ct. 915 (1948), but they were "intended definitely to grant valuable, enforceable rights" in order to afford greater encouragement to the production of works of benefit to the public. Washingtonian Publishing Co. v. Pearson, 306 U.S. 30, 36, 83 L.Ed. 470, 59 S.Ct. 397 (1939). The Constitution does not prevent Ohio from making a similar choice here in deciding to protect the entertainer's incentive in order to encourage the production of this type of work. Cf. Goldstein v. California, 412 U.S. 546, 37 L.Ed.2d 163, 93 S.Ct. 2303 (1973); Kewanee Oil Co. v. Bicron Corp., 416 U.S. 470, 40 L.Ed.2d 315, 94 S.Ct. 1879, 69 O.O.2d 235 (1974).[13]

---

13. *Goldstein* involved a California statute outlawing "record piracy"—the unauthorized duplication of recordings of performances by major musical artists. Petitioners there launched a multifaceted constitutional attack on the statute, but they did not argue that the statute violated the First Amendment. In rejecting this broad-based constitutional attack, the Court concluded:

> "The California statutory scheme evidences a legislative policy to prohibit 'tape piracy' and 'record piracy,' conduct that may adversely affect the continued production of new recordings, a large industry in California. Accordingly, the State has, by statute, given to recordings the attributes of property. *No restraint has been placed on the use of an idea or concept;* rather, petitioners and other individuals remain free to record the same compositions in precisely the same manner and with the same personnel as appeared on the original recording.

> "Until and unless Congress takes further action with respect to recordings * *, the California statute may be enforced against acts of piracy such as those which occurred in the present case." 412 U.S., at 571, 37 L.Ed.2d 163, 93 S.Ct. 2303. (Emphasis added.)

We note that Federal District Courts have rejected First Amendment challenges to the federal copyright law on the ground that "no restraint [has been] placed on the use of an idea or concept." United States v. Bodin, 375 F.Supp. 1265, 1267 (W.D.Okl. 1974). See also Walt Disney Productions v. Air Pirates, 345 F.Supp. 108, 115–116 (N.D. Cal.1972) (citing Nimmer, Does Copyright Abridge The First Amendment Guarantees of Free Speech and Press?, 17 U.C.L.A.L. Rev. 1180 (1970), who argues that copyright law does not abridge the First Amendment because it does not restrain the communication of ideas or concepts); Robert Stigwood Group Ltd. v. O'Reilly, 346 F.Supp. 376 (Conn.1972) (also relying on Nimmer, supra). Of course this case does not involve a claim that respondent would be prevented by petitioner's "right of publicity" from staging or filming its own "human cannonball" act.

In *Kewanee* this Court upheld the constitutionality of Ohio's trade-secret law, al-

There is no doubt that entertainment, as well as news, enjoys First Amendment protection. It is also true that entertainment itself can be important news. Time, Inc. v. Hill. But it is important to note that neither the public nor respondent will be deprived of the benefit of petitioner's performance as long as his commercial stake in his act is appropriately recognized. Petitioner does not seek to enjoin the broadcast of his performance; he simply wants to be paid for it. Nor do we think that a state-law damages remedy against respondent would represent a species of liability without fault contrary to the letter or spirit of Gertz v. Robert Welch, Inc., 418 U.S. 323, 41 L.Ed.2d 789, 94 S.Ct. 2997 (1974). Respondent knew exactly that petitioner objected to televising his act, but nevertheless displayed the entire film.

We conclude that although the State of Ohio may as a matter of its own law privilege the press in the circumstances of this case, the First and Fourteenth Amendments do not require it to do so.

Reversed.

MR. JUSTICE POWELL, with whom MR. JUSTICE BRENNAN and MR. JUSTICE MARSHALL join, dissenting.

Disclaiming any attempt to do more than decide the narrow case before us, the Court reverses the decision of the Supreme Court of Ohio based on repeated incantation of a single formula: "A performer's entire act." The holding today is summed up in one sentence:

> Wherever the line in particular situations is to be drawn between media reports that are protected and those that are not, we are quite sure that the First and Fourteenth Amendments do not immunize the media when they broadcast a performer's entire act without his consent. Ante, at 574–575, 53 L.Ed.2d 975.

I doubt that this formula provides a standard clear enough even for resolution of this case.[1] In any event, I am not persuaded that the

---

though again no First Amendment claim was presented. Citing *Goldstein,* the Court stated:

"Just as the States may exercise regulatory power over writings so may the States regulate with respect to discoveries. States may hold diverse viewpoints in protecting intellectual property relating to invention as they do in protecting the intellectual property relating to the subject matter of copyright. The only limitation on the States is that in regulating the area of patents and copyrights they do not conflict with the operation of the laws in this area passed by Congress * * *." 416 U.S. at 479, 40 L.Ed.2d 315, 94 S.Ct. 1879, 69 O.O.2d 235.

Although recognizing that the trade-secret law resulted in preventing the public from gaining certain information, the Court emphasized that the law had "a decidedly beneficial effect on society," id., at 485, 40 L.Ed.2d 315, 94 S.Ct. 1879, 69 O.O.2d 235, and that without it, "organized scientific and technological research could become fragmented, and society, as a whole, would suffer." Id., at 486, 40 L.Ed.2d 315, 94 S.Ct. 1879, 69 O.O.2d 235.

1. Although the record is not explicit, it is unlikely that the "act" commenced abruptly with the explosion that launched petitioner on his way, ending with the landing in the net a few seconds later. One may assume that the actual firing was preceded by some fanfare, possibly stretching over several minutes, to heighten the audience's anticipation: introduction of the performer, description of the uniqueness and danger, last-minute checking of the apparatus, and entry into the cannon, all accompanied by suitably ominous commentary from the master of ceremonies. If this is found to be the case on remand, then respondent could not be said to have appropriated the "entire

Court's opinion is appropriately sensitive to the First Amendment values at stake, and I therefore dissent.

Although the Court would draw no distinction, ante, at 575, 53 L.Ed.2d 975–976, I do not view respondent's action as comparable to unauthorized commercial broadcasts of sporting events, theatrical performances, and the like where the broadcaster keeps the profits. There is no suggestion here that respondent made any such use of the film. Instead, it simply reported on what petitioner concedes to be a newsworthy event, in a way hardly surprising for a television station—by means of film coverage. The report was part of an ordinary daily news program, consuming a total of 15 seconds. It is a routine example of the press fulfilling the informing function so vital to our system.

The Court's holding that the station's ordinary news report may give rise to substantial liability [2] has disturbing implications, for the decision could lead to a degree of media selfcensorship. Cf. Smith v. California, 361 U.S. 147, 150–154, 4 L.Ed.2d 205, 80 S.Ct. 215, 14 O.O.2d 459 (1959). Hereafter, whenever a television news editor is unsure whether certain film footage received from a camera crew might be held to portray an "entire act," [3] he may decline coverage—even of clearly newsworthy events—or confine the broadcast to watered-down verbal reporting, perhaps with an occasional still picture. The public is then the loser. This is hardly the kind of news reportage that the First Amendment is meant to foster. See generally Miami Herald Publishing Co. v. Tornillo, 418 U.S. 241, 257–258, 41 L.Ed.2d 730, 94 S.Ct. 2831 (1974); Time, Inc. v. Hill, 385 U.S. 374, 389, 17 L.Ed.2d 456, 87 S.Ct. 534 (1967); New York Times Co. v. Sullivan, 376 U.S. 254, 270–272, 279, 11 L.Ed.2d 686, 84 S.Ct. 710, 95 A.L.R.2d 1412 (1964).

In my view the First Amendment commands a different analytical starting point from the one selected by the Court. Rather than begin with a quantitative analysis of the performer's behavior—is this or is this not his entire act?—we should direct initial attention to the actions of the news media: what use did the station make of the film footage?

---

act" in its 15-second newsclip—and the Court's opinion then would afford no guidance for resolution of the case. Moreover, in future cases involving different performances, similar difficulties in determining just what constitutes the "entire act" are inevitable.

2. At some points the Court seems to acknowledge that the reason for recognizing a cause of action asserting a "right of publicity" is to prevent unjust enrichment. See, e.g., ante, at 576, 53 L.Ed.2d 976. But the remainder of the opinion inconsistently accepts a measure of damages based not on the defendant's enhanced profits but on harm to the plaintiff regardless of any gain to the defendant. See, e.g., ante, at 575 n. 12, 53 L.Ed.2d 976. Indeed, in this case there is no suggestion that respondent's television station gained financially by showing petitioner's flight (although it no doubt received its normal advertising revenue for the news program—revenue it would have received no matter which news items appeared). Nevertheless, in the unlikely event that petitioner can prove that his income was somehow reduced as a result of the broadcast, respondent will apparently have to compensate him for the difference.

3. Such doubts are especially likely to arise when the editor receives film footage of an event at a local fair, a circus, a sports competition of limited duration (e.g., the winning effort in a ski-jump competition), or a dramatic production made up of short skits, to offer only a few examples.

When a film is used, as here, for a routine portion of a regular news program, I would hold that the First Amendment protects the station from a "right of publicity" or "appropriation" suit, absent a strong showing by the plaintiff that the news broadcast was a subterfuge or cover for private or commercial exploitation.[4]

I emphasize that this is "reappropriation" suit, rather than one of the other varieties of "right of privacy" tort suits identified by Dean Prosser in his classic article. Prosser, Privacy, 48 Calif.L.Rev. 383 (1960). In those other causes of action the competing interests are considerably different. The plaintiff generally seeks to avoid any sort of public exposure, and the existence of constitutional privilege is therefore less likely to turn on whether the publication occurred in a news broadcast or in some other fashion. In a suit like the one before us, however, the plaintiff does not complain about the fact of exposure to the public, but rather about its timing or manner. He welcomes some publicity, but seeks to retain control over means and manner as a way to maximize for himself the monetary benefits that flow from such publication. But having made the matter public—having chosen, in essence, to make it newsworthy—he cannot, consistent with the First Amendment, complain of routine news reportage. Cf. Gertz v. Robert Welch, Inc., 418 U.S. 323, 339–348, 351–352, 94 S.Ct. 2997, 41 L.Ed.2d 789 (1974) (clarifying the different liability standards appropriate in defamation suits, depending on whether or not the plaintiff is a public figure).

Since the film clip here was undeniably treated as news and since there is no claim that the use was subterfuge, respondent's actions were constitutionally privileged. I would affirm.

Mr. Justice Stevens, dissenting.

The Ohio Supreme Court held that respondent's telecast of the "human cannonball" was a privileged invasion of petitioner's common-law "right of publicity" because respondent's actual intent was neither (a) to appropriate the benefit of the publicity for a private use, nor (b) to injure petitioner.[*]

---

4. This case requires no detailed specification of the standards for identifying a subterfuge, since there is no claim here that respondent's news use was anything but bona fide. Cf. 47 Ohio St.2d 224, 351 N.E.2d 454 (the standards suggested by the Supreme Court of Ohio, quoted ante, at 565, 53 L.Ed.2d 970). I would point out, however, that selling time during a news broadcast to advertisers in the customary fashion does not make for "commercial exploitation" in the sense intended here. See W. Prosser, Law of Torts 806–807 (4th ed. 1971). Cf. New York Times Co. v. Sullivan, 376 U.S. 254, 266, 11 L.Ed.2d 686, 84 S.Ct. 710, 95 A.L.R.2d 1412 (1964).

* Paragraph 3 of the court's syllabus, 47 Ohio St.2d 224, 351 N.E.2d 454, 455, reads as follows:

"A TV station has a privilege to report in its newscasts matters of legitimate public interest which would otherwise be protected by an individual's right of publicity, unless the actual intent of the TV station was to appropriate the benefit of the publicity for some nonprivileged private use, or unless the actual intent was to injure the individual."

In its opinion, the court described the "proper standard" in language which I read as defining the boundaries of a common-law tort:

Sec. B   FIRST AMENDMENT DEFENSE   871

As I read the state court's explanation of the limits on the concept of privilege, they define the substantive reach of a common-law tort rather than anything I recognize as a limit on a federal constitutional right. The decision was unquestionably influenced by the Ohio court's proper sensitivity to First Amendment principles, and to this Court's cases construing the First Amendment; indeed, I must confess that the opinion can be read as resting entirely on federal constitutional grounds. Nevertheless, the basis of the state court's action is sufficiently doubtful that I would remand the case to that court for clarification of its holding before deciding the federal constitutional issue.

Questions

1. If the defendant had not appropriated the plaintiff's "entire act", but had only reproduced his name and picture for merchandising purposes (e.g., on a T-shirt), would the defendant have a stronger or weaker First Amendment defense? Does the *Zacchini* opinion suggest that the First Amendment would be more available in the case of an advertising use? Cf. Bates v. Arizona, 433 U.S. 350 (1977).

2. Does *Zacchini* suggest by negative implication that the First Amendment would preclude a right of publicity claim by one who was neither "a performer" or "a person with a name having commercial value"?

3. Is there a contradiction between the court's description of the interest protected in false light privacy cases as "clearly that of reputation", and its reference to Time, Inc. v. Hill as involving "nondefamatory falsehoods"?

4. Should the availability of the First Amendment as a defense in right of publicity action vary as between (1) a depiction of the plaintiff performing his "act"; (2) the use of the plaintiff's photograph or likeness on merchandise; (3) the use of the plaintiff's photograph or likeness in advertising the sale of merchandise or services; (4) the use of the plaintiff's photograph or likeness on posters; (5) the depiction of the plaintiff in a dramatized account of his life or career?

5. Does Mr. Justice Powell articulate a workable standard? What constitutes a "routine" portion of a "regular" news program?

HICKS v. CASABLANCA RECORDS

United States District Court, Southern District of New York, 1978.
464 F.Supp. 426.

PIERCE, DISTRICT JUDGE.

Plaintiffs, the heir and assignees of the late Agatha Christie, seek an order enjoining the defendant movie producers, Casablanca Records,

"The proper standard must necessarily be whether the matters reported were of public interest, and if so, the press will be liable for appropriation of a performer's right of publicity only if its actual intent was not to report the performance, but, rather, to appropriate the performance for some other private use, or if the actual intent was to injure the performer. It might also be the case that the press would be liable if it recklessly disregarded contract rights existing between the plaintiff and a third person to present the performance to the public, but that question is not presented here." Id., at 235, 351 N.E.2d, at 461.

Filmworks, First Artist and Warner Brothers (hereinafter referred to as the "movie case") from distributing or showing the motion picture "Agatha". Plaintiffs, in a related case, similarly seek an order enjoining defendant publisher, Ballantine Books (hereinafter referred to as the "book case") from distributing or making the book *Agatha* available to the public.

The defendants in both cases oppose the plaintiff's applications for injunctive relief, and have separately moved to dismiss plaintiffs' claims on the ground that they fail to state claims upon which relief could be granted pursuant to Rule 12(b)(6) Fed.R.Civ.P.[1]

Background

Plaintiffs' decedent and assignor was the late Dame Agatha Christie, one of the best-known mystery writers in modern times. Her career spanned five decades until her death in 1976, and culminated in the production of scores of mystery novels; not the least famous of which are *Murder on the Orient Express* and the short story, "Witness for the Prosecution." Although Mrs. Christie attempted to shun publicity with respect to her personal life, professionally, she cultivated the name "Agatha Christie" in such a way as to make it almost synonymous with mystery novels.[2] Thus, during her life, she agreed to the use of her name in connection with various motion pictures and plays based on her works. Upon her death, the rights in her works descended to plaintiff, Rosalind Christie Hicks, Mrs. Christie's sole legatee, and plaintiffs, Agatha Christie, Ltd., and William Collins Sons & Co., Ltd., her assignees.

In the winter of 1977, defendants in the movie case began the filming of a movie entitled, "Agatha" which, like the book in the related case, presents a fictionalized account of a true incident which occurred during the life of Mrs. Christie. The book is scheduled for distribution shortly. Although both the movie and the book are entitled "Agatha", it is not disputed by defendants in either case that both concern the late mystery writer.

Plaintiffs, in seeking preliminary injunctions, have asserted their right to recover on the basis of the recently developing law of the right of publicity.[3]

It appears that on or about December 4, 1926, Mrs. Christie, then married to Colonel Archibald Christie, disappeared from her home in England. This disappearance was widely-publicized and, although a major effort was launched to find her, everyone was at a loss to explain

---

1. * * * [T]his opinion addresses the motions to dismiss made by the defendants in each case, and plaintiffs' motions for preliminary injunction made in each.

2. See Defendant's Exhibit, Agatha Christie, An Autobiography, at 269.

3. During the past ten months, other courts in this circuit have been asked to resolve issues involving this nascent right. See, e.g., Ali v. Playgirl, Inc., et al., 78 Civ. 445 (S.D.N.Y.1978); Price, et al. v. Worlddivision Enterprises, Inc., 455 F.Supp. 252 (S.D.N.Y.1978); and Factors Etc., Inc. v. Creative Card Co., 444 F.Supp. 279, Factors Etc., Inc. v. Pro Arts, Inc., 444 F.Supp. 288, aff'd, 579 F.2d 215 (2d Cir.1978).

her disappearance. However, eleven days after she was reported missing, Mrs. Christie reappeared, but her true whereabouts and the reasons for her disappearance are, to this day, a mystery.

In view of the death of Mrs. Christie, the public may never know the facts surrounding this incident, but should the defendants prevail herein, the public will have a fictionalized account of this disappearance as set forth in the movie and in the book.[4] In each instance, Mrs. Christie is portrayed as an emotionally unstable woman, who, during her eleven-day disappearance, engages in a sinister plot to murder her husband's mistress, in an attempt to regain the alienated affections of her husband. Given this portrayal of their decedent and assignor, plaintiffs, mindful of the personal nature of defamation and privacy actions, bring the instant actions alleging unfair competition and infringement of the right of publicity.

DISCUSSION

This Circuit has recently addressed the parameters of the right of publicity in Factors Etc., Inc., et al. v. Pro Arts, Inc., et al., 579 F.2d 215 (2d Cir.1978) [hereinafter cited as *Factors*]. In *Factors*, the Court found that the right of publicity, i.e., the right in the publicity value of one's name or likeness, is a valid property right which is transferable and capable of surviving the death of the owner. Id. at 3651–52. However, the Court went on to state that this interest survives only if it is found that the owner "exploited" the right during his or her lifetime. Id. at 3654 n. 11; *accord*, Guglielmi v. Spelling-Goldberg Prods., 140 Cal.Rptr. 775 (1977).[5] While the *Factors* opinion does not define "exploitation", it would appear that a party claiming the right must establish that the decedent acted in such a way as to evidence his or her own recognition of the extrinsic commercial value of his or her name or likeness, and manifested that recognition in some overt manner, e.g., making an *inter vivos* transfer of the rights in the name, (*Factors*), or posing for bubble gum cards (see Haelan Laboratories, Inc. v. Topps Chewing Gum, Inc., 202 F.2d 866 (2d Cir.), cert. denied, 346 U.S. 816 (1953)).

In applying the *Factors* analysis to the cases at bar, this Court finds that plaintiffs have established that Mrs. Christie "exploited" her name during her lifetime. The plaintiffs have established that Mrs. Christie assigned rights to her literary works to plaintiff, Agatha Christie Ltd., and also bequeathed similar rights by testamentary disposition.[6] The

---

4. Defendants thus would be able to distribute both the novel and the movie without the consent of the plaintiffs.

5. See also, Price v. Hal Roach Studios, Inc., 400 F.Supp. 836 (S.D.N.Y.1975).

6. The Court notes here that defendants allege that this assignment is not sufficient to constitute "exploitation" because, as they interpret *Factors*, the Second Circuit requires that the grantor of the right must have exercised that right independently of the thing for which the grantor was known. They argue that the omission by the *Factors'* Court of any reference to assignments of movie rights made by the late Elvis Presley, the subject grantor in that case, supports their contention that the exploitation must take the form of merchandise or some such other product. See *Factors*, supra.

Court finds that this evidence, when considered together with evidence of contracts entered into by Mrs. Christie for the use of her name during her lifetime in connection with movies and plays based on her books, sufficiently establishes "exploitation". Thus, it seems clear that her right of publicity survived her death and was properly transferred to the plaintiffs as her heirs and assignees.

However, unlike the *Factors* case, our inquiry here does not end upon this finding that plaintiffs possess valid property rights. Here, the Court is faced with the novel and rather complex question of "whether the right of publicity attaches where the name or likeness is used in connection with a book or movie?" The question is novel in view of the fact that more so than posters, bubble gum cards, or some other such "merchandise", books and movies are vehicles through which ideas and opinions are disseminated and, as such, have enjoyed certain constitutional protections, not generally accorded "merchandise." It is complex because this Court is unaware of any other cases presenting a similar fact pattern or similar constitutional question with respect to this issue of right of publicity. Thus, in a search of guidance to resolve the issue presented herein, the Court has looked to cases involving the right of privacy pursuant to § 51 of the New York Civil Rights Act (McKinney 1976). While the right of publicity is not statutory, and both the rights of privacy and of publicity are intertwined due to the similarity between the nature of the interests protected by each (see W. Prosser, Torts 804 (4th ed. 1971)) and as a result of earlier interpretations of these rights (see generally for a discussion thereof, Ali v. Playgirl, Inc., [447 F.Supp. 723] (S.D.N.Y. 1978)), it would appear that judicial interpretations with respect to the limits of the right of privacy could be helpful in determining the limitations, if any, to be placed on the right of publicity. Cf. *Factors*, supra, at 3654 (for a discussion of the constitutional defense of "fair comment.").

The New York privacy statute, Civil Rights Law § 51, provides in pertinent part:

> Any person whose name, portrait or picture is used within this state for advertising purposes or for the purposes of trade without the written consent first obtained * * * may maintain an equitable action * * *.

In interpreting this provision, the New York State Supreme Court, Appellate Division, has held that:

> engrafted upon [the statute are] certain privileged uses or exemptions * * * [i.e.] matters of news, history, biography, and other factual subjects of public interest despite the necessary references to the names, portraits, identities, or histories of living persons." Spahn v. Julian Messner, Inc., 23

Since the "omission" could have resulted from the failure of plaintiffs to produce such evidence in the trial court, this Court does not attach the same significance to it as do defendants.

App.Div.2d 216, 219, 260 N.Y.S.2d 451, 453 (1st Dep't 1965) [hereinafter cited as *Spahn*].[7]

This Court finds that the same privileges and exemptions "engrafted" upon the privacy statute are engrafted upon the right of publicity.

In addressing defendants' argument that the book *Agatha* is a biography protected under *Spahn,* this Court, while noting that the affidavit of the author of the book details her investigation with respect to the "facts" surrounding the disappearance, finds the book to be fiction, not biography. Indeed, defendant Ballantine Books' use of the word "novel" on the cover of the book, as well as the notable absence of any cited source or reference material therein, belie its contention that the book is a biography. Moreover, the only "facts" contained in the book appear to be the names of Mrs. Christie, her husband, her daughter, and Ms. Neeley; and that Mrs. Christie disappeared for eleven days. The remainder is mainly conjecture, surmise, and fiction. Accordingly, the Court finds that the defendants in both cases cannot avail themselves of the biography privilege in connection with the book or movie. Further since the book and the movie treat these few scant facts about the disappearance of Mrs. Christie as mere appendages to the main body of their fictional accounts, neither can be considered privileged as "fair comment" (see Hill, Defamation and Privacy under the First Amendment, 76 Col.L.Rev. 1205, 1277 (1976) [hereinafter cited as Hill]); or as "newsworthy" (see *Factors,* supra); or historical (see *Spahn,* supra.)

Thus, finding none of the *Spahn* privileges available to the defendants herein, the Court must next inquire as to whether the movie or the novel, as fictionalizations, are entitled to any constitutional protection. In so doing, it is noted that other courts, in addressing the scope of first amendment protections of speech, have engaged in a balancing test between society's interest in the speech for which protection is sought and the societal, commercial or governmental interests seeking to restrain such speech. See generally, Miller v. California, 413 U.S. 15 (1973); Near v. Minnesota, 283 U.S. 697 (1931); Nimmer, The Right to Speak from *Times* to *Time*; First Amendment Theory Applied to Libel and Misapplied to Privacy, 56 Calif.L.Rev. 935 (1968). And unless there appears to be some countervailing legal or policy reason, courts have found the exercise of the right of speech to be protected. Thus, for instance, such a balancing test was employed by the Supreme Court in New York Times v. Sullivan, 376 U.S. 254 (1964) with respect to the law of defamation in relation to public figures. There, the Court found that speech, even though false, was protected unless it was shown that it was published "with knowledge that it was false or with reckless disregard of whether it was false or not." Id. at 280. Here, this Court is of the opinion that the interests in the speech sought to be protected,

---

7. Aff'd, 18 N.Y.2d 324, 274 N.Y.S.2d 877, 221 N.E.2d 543 (1966), judgment vacated and remanded in light of Time, Inc. v. Hill, 385 U.S. 374 (1967), 387 U.S. 239 (1967), aff'd on remand, 21 N.Y.2d 124, 286 N.Y.S.2d 832, 233 N.E.2d 840 (1967), appeal dismissed, 393 U.S. 1046 (1969).

i.e., the movie and the novel, should be protected and that there are no countervailing legal or policy grounds against such protection. *Accord, Hill,* supra, at 1299.

In support of this position, resort is again made to cases in the privacy field, of which two are found to be particularly relevant: *Spahn,* cited supra, and University of Notre Dame Du-Lac v. Twentieth Century-Fox Film Corp., 22 App.Div.2d 452, 256 N.Y.S.2d 301 (1965), aff'd upon the opinion of the Appellate Division, 15 N.Y.2d 940, 259 N.Y.S.2d 832, 207 N.E.2d 508 (1965) [hereinafter cited as *Notre Dame*]. The *Spahn* case, like the book case here, involved the distribution of a book which was presented by the defendant as being a biography of the well-known baseball player Warren Spahn. However, presented in the book were deliberate falsifications of events represented to be true, manufactured dialogue, and erroneous statistical data. Defendant argued that this material was presented in an effort to make the book more attractive to youngsters. Plaintiff sued on the ground that the book constituted a violation of his right of privacy under § 51. The New York Court of Appeals agreed, stating:

> We hold in conformity with our policy of construing sections 50 and 51 so as to fully protect free speech, that, before recovery by a public figure may be had for an unauthorized presentation of his life it must be shown, in addition to the other requirements of the statute, that the presentation is infected *with material and substantial falsification * * * or with a reckless disregard for the truth.* Spahn v. Julian Messner, Inc., 21 N.Y.2d 124, 127, 286 N.Y.S.2d 832, 834, 233 N.E.2d 840 (1967) (emphasis supplied).

> To hold that this research effort [on the part of the author] entitled the defendants to publish the kind of knowing fictionalization presented here would amount to granting a literary license which is not only unnecessary to the protection of free speech but destructive of an individual's right, albeit a limited one in the case of a public figure, to be free of the commercial exploitation of his name * * *. Id. at 129, 286 N.Y.S.2d at 836.

The *Notre Dame* case involved the distribution of a movie, entitled, "John Golfarb, Please Come Home" which satirized modern-day events, people, and institutions, including a football team, identified as that of Notre Dame. Notre Dame University and its president, Father Hesburg, brought suit against the defendant pursuant to the New York Civil Rights Act and the common law on unfair competition. The Appellate Division, in denying the relief requested, stated:

> Motion pictures, as well as books, are "a significant medium for the communication of ideas"; their importance "as an organ of public opinion is not lessened by the fact that they are designed to entertain as well as to inform"; and like books, they are a constitutionally protected form of expression notwithstanding that "their production, distribution and exhibition is a large-scale business conducted for private profit [citations omitted]." *Notre Dame,* supra, at 457, 256 N.Y.S.2d at 306.

And by way of dicta, the Court stated:

> Defendants argue that injunctive relief would violate the First Amendment, but that is an issue we do not reach. It is permissible to express

praise or derision of a college's athletic activities in a journal of news or opinion. If such a journal, a novel and a photoplay are on a parity in law as media of expression, extension of the doctrine of unfair competition to interdict praise or derision by means of the novel or photoplay would seem without justification. Social cost may properly be considered in these matters * * * and the granting of an injunction in this case would outlaw large areas heretofore deemed permissible subject matter for literature and the arts * * *. Id.[8]

In applying the holdings of these two cases to those at bar, it would appear that the later decided *Spahn* case—which curiously did not cite *Notre Dame*—would dictate the result herein. However, upon closer scrutiny of *Spahn,* this Court is of the opinion that the *Spahn* holding should be and was intended to be limited to its facts, and that the result here should follow the holding in the *Notre Dame* case. See *Hill,* supra, at 1301 n. 447. The Court reaches this conclusion based on the very language of the New York Court of Appeals' decision in *Spahn.* In essence, the Court in *Spahn* stressed the fact that the lower court had found that the defendant had engaged in deliberate falsifications of the circumstances surrounding the life of plaintiff and that such falsifications, which the reader might accept as true, were capable of presenting plaintiff in a false light. Spahn v. Julian Messner, Inc., 18 N.Y.2d 324, 328, 274 N.Y.S.2d 877, 880, 221 N.E.2d 543 (1966) (citing opinion of the Appellate Division, 23 App.Div.2d 216, 221, 260 N.Y.S.2d 451, 455 (1965) and citing the trial justice, 43 Misc.2d 219, 232, 250 N.Y.S.2d 529, 542 (1964)). Thus, the Court of Appeals in *Spahn* balanced the plaintiff's privacy rights against the first amendment protection of fictionalization *qua* falsification and, after finding there to be no such protection, held for the plaintiff. Id. See also Time, Inc. v. Hill, 385 U.S. 374 (1967). Conversely, in the *Notre Dame* case, the Appellate Division, as affirmed by the New York Court of Appeals, found that the defendant had not represented the events in the movie to be true and that a viewer of the film would certainly know that the circumstances involved therein were fictitious; thus, finding for the defendants.

It is clear from the review of these two cases that the absence or presence of deliberate falsifications or an attempt by a defendant to present the disputed events as true, determines whether the scales in this balancing process, shall tip in favor of or against protection of the speech at issue. Since the cases at bar are more factually similar to the *Notre Dame* case, i.e., there were no deliberate falsifications alleged by plaintiffs,[9] and the reader of the novel in the book case, by the presence of the word "novel", would know that the work was fictitious, this Court finds that the first amendment protection usually accorded

---

8. Defendants' point to the developing literary genre involving fictionalization of the lives of deceased figures, e.g., *Burr* by Gore Vidal, to buttress their argument that if plaintiffs prevail publishers may be unable to publish such books.

9. A copy of the movie script was furnished to plaintiffs; they have not alleged any deliberate falsifications by defendants.

novels and movies outweighs whatever publicity rights plaintiffs may possess and for this reason their complaints must be dismissed.

Accordingly, the Court finds that the right of publicity does not attach here, where a fictionalized account of an event in the life of a public figure is depicted in a novel or a movie, and in such novel or movie it is evident to the public that the events so depicted are fictitious. * * *

Accordingly, plaintiffs' motion for a preliminary injunction in the movie case is denied for failure to establish likelihood of success on the merits (see Sonesta Int'l Hotels Corp. v. Wellington Assocs., 483 F.2d 247 (2d Cir.1973)); defendant Casablanca Records, First Artists and Warner Brothers' motion to dismiss is granted; defendant Ballantine Books' motion to dismiss in the book case is granted; plaintiffs' cross-motion for a preliminary injunction therein is denied for the same reasons set forth with respect to the movie case (id.).

The foregoing shall constitute the Court's findings of fact and conclusions of law in accordance with Rule 52(a) Fed.R.Civ.P.

So Ordered.

Questions

1. The *Hicks* opinion states that decision turns on "the absence or presence of deliberate falsifications *or* an attempt by a defendant to present the disputed events as true * * *" (emphasis added). Did the court mean "and" rather than "or"?

2. The *Hicks* court found it significant that in the *Notre Dame* case "the defendant had not represented the events in the movie to be true and that a viewer of the film would certainly know that the circumstances involved therein were fictitious". What if a work is presented as fiction but the characters depicted are known to be actual, not fictitious? Isn't the audience often left in doubt as to whether particular events as depicted are factual or fictitious? Some such events might be presumed to be fictitious (such as the Notre Dame team playing football in Saudi Arabia in the *John Golfarb* film), but this would not be clear as to many, perhaps most of the events. Would a reader or viewer of "Agatha" conclude that simply because the book is presented as a "novel" it therefore follows that all of the events shown to have occurred during Mrs. Christie's eleven day disappearance were fictitious?

3. Although falsity is a relevant issue in both defamation and false light privacy actions should it be regarded as irrelevant in a right of publicity action? Might the result reached by the court nevertheless be justified on the ground that the right of publicity only extends to unauthorized merchandising, not to factual or even fictionalized biographies? Does this represent an acceptable definitional balance for invoking a First Amendment defense in a right of publicity action?

Collateral References

Silver, *Libel, the "Higher Truths" of Art, and the First Amendment*, 126 U.Pa.L.Rev. 1065 (1978).

Hoffman, *Limitations on the Right of Publicity*, 28 Bull.Copr.Soc'y 111 (1980).

GUGLIELMI v. SPELLING–GOLDBERG PRODUCTIONS

Supreme Court of California, 1979.
25 Cal.3d 860, 160 Cal.Rptr. 352, 603 P.2d 454.

BIRD, C.J., Concurring.—This court must decide whether the use of a deceased celebrity's name and likeness in a fictional film exhibited on television constitutes an actionable infringement of that person's right of publicity. It is clear that appellant's action cannot be maintained. Therefore, the trial court properly dismissed his complaint.

* * *

In his complaint, appellant alleges that Rudolpho Guglielmi, also known as Rudolph Valentino, was his paternal uncle. * * * Appellant alleges that he inherited this right of publicity under Valentino's will, following Valentino's death in 1926.

On November 23, 1975, respondents exhibited on the television network owned by American Broadcasting Companies, Inc., a film entitled *Legend of Valentino: A Romantic Fiction*. Appellant alleges that "[s]aid film purports to represent a portion of the life of Rudolph Valentino and employs the name, likeness and personality of Rudolph Valentino." However, appellant asserts that while the principal character is identified as Valentino, the film is "a work of fiction about the life and loves of an Italian actor who became Hollywood's first romantic screen star and who died at the height of his fame." Hence, the film is a "fictionalized version of Rudolph Valentino's life." Appellant alleges that respondents knew that the film did not truthfully portray Valentino's life, and that the film was made without Valentino's or appellant's consent. Appellant contends that respondents also used Valentino's name, likeness and personality in advertising the film "to solicit and to sell commercial sponsorship exhibited in conjunction with the exhibition of said film and to solicit viewers for the exhibition of said film."

* * *

Appellant contends that the Valentino film is not entitled to the cloak of constitutional protection because respondents incorporated Valentino's name and likeness in: (1) a work of fiction, (2) for financial gain, (3) knowing that such film falsely portrayed Valentino's life. The critical issue is whether the presence of these factors, individually or collectively, sufficiently outweighs any protection this expression would otherwise enjoy under the United States and California Constitutions.

* * *

The First Amendment and article I, section 2 of the California Constitution serve "to preserve an uninhibited marketplace of ideas" and to repel efforts to limit the " 'uninhibited, robust and wide-open' debate on public issues." (Red Lion Broadcasting Co. v. FCC, supra, 395 U.S. at p. 390 [23 L.Ed.2d at p. 389]; Gertz v. Robert Welch, Inc. (1974) 418 U.S. 323, 340 [41 L.Ed.2d 789, 805, 94 S.Ct. 2997].) These rights are essential in a democratic system of government. Free speech is also guaranteed because of our fundamental respect for individual development and self-realization. The right to self-expression is inherent in any political system which respects individual dignity. * * *

* * *

It is clear that works of fiction are constitutionally protected in the same manner as political treatises and topical news stories. Using fiction as a vehicle, commentaries on our values, habits, customs, laws, prejudices, justice, heritage and future are frequently expressed. What may be difficult to communicate or understand when factually reported may be poignant and powerful if offered in satire, science fiction or parable. Indeed, Dickens and Dostoevski may well have written more trenchant and comprehensive commentaries on their times than any factual recitation could ever yield. Such authors are no less entitled to express their views than the town crier with the daily news or the philosopher with his discourse on the nature of justice. Even the author who creates distracting tales for amusement is entitled to constitutional protection. (See Berlin v. E.C. Publications, Inc. (2d Cir.1964) 329 F.2d 541, 545; Hill, supra, 76 Colum.L.Rev. at p. 1308.)

Thus, no distinction may be drawn in this context between fictional and factual accounts of Valentino's life. Respondents' election of the former as the mode for their views does not diminish the constitutional protection afforded speech. * * *

* * *

Contemporary events, symbols and people are regularly used in fictional works. Fiction writers may be able to more persuasively, or more accurately, express themselves by weaving into the tale persons or events familiar to their readers. The choice is theirs. No author should be forced into creating mythological worlds or characters wholly divorced from reality. The right of publicity derived from public prominence does not confer a shield to ward off caricature, parody and satire. Rather, prominence invites creative comment. Surely, the range of free expression would be meaningfully reduced if prominent persons in the present and recent past were forbidden topics for the imaginations of authors of fiction.[12]

* * *

No such constitutional dichotomy exists in this area between truthful and fictional accounts. They have equal constitutional stature and each is as likely to fulfill the objectives underlying the constitutional guarantees of free expression. * * * Moreover, in defamation cases, the concern is with defamatory lies masquerading as truth. In contrast, the author who denotes his work as fiction proclaims his literary license and indifference to "the facts." There is no pretense. All fiction, by definition, eschews an obligation to be faithful to historical truth. Every fiction writer knows his creation is in some sense "false." That is the nature of the art. Therefore, where fiction is the medium— as alleged by appellant in this case and as evident in the film's title, *A*

---

12. For example, Garry Trudeau, creator of the satiric cartoon strip "Doonesbury," regularly fictionalizes events and dialogue involving prominent political figures. It cannot be seriously maintained that one such satirized notable could successfully pursue an action for an infringement on his right of publicity based on such use.

Romantic Fiction —it is meaningless to charge that the author "knew" his work was false.

* * *

A cause of action for the appropriation of Valentino's right of publicity through the use of his name and likeness in respondents' film may not be maintained. The trial court properly sustained the demurrer and dismissed the complaint.

* * *

In contrast, the facts underlying Lugosi v. Universal Pictures * * * are substantially different than those in the present case. *Lugosi* involved the use of Bela Lugosi's likeness in connection with the sale of such commercial products "as plastic toy pencil sharpeners, soap products, target games, candy dispensers and beverage stirring rods." * * * These objects, unlike motion pictures, are not vehicles through which ideas and opinions are regularly disseminated. * * *

Question

Should a First Amendment defense be available as against a right of publicity claim whenever the subject's name or likeness is used in what Chief Justice Bird refers to as "vehicles through which ideas and opinions are regularly disseminated"? What constitutes such a "vehicle"? Recall the poster in Factors Etc., Inc. v. Pro Arts, Inc., p. 846 supra. Is not a poster a vehicle for the dissemination of ideas and opinions? By reason of First Amendment considerations, should the right of publicity be limited to the use of the subject's name or likeness on or in connection with the sale of "useful articles," as that phrase is defined in Section 101 of the Copyright Act?

EASTWOOD v. SUPERIOR COURT

Court of Appeal, Second District, Division 7, California, 1983.
149 Cal.App.3d 409, 198 Cal.Rptr. 342.

THOMPSON, ASSOCIATE JUSTICE.

In this proceeding in mandate, we inquire into the propriety of the respondent court's ruling sustaining without leave to amend the general demurrer of the real party in interest, National Enquirer, Inc. (Enquirer), to the second cause of action of the complaint of petitioner, Clint Eastwood (Eastwood), for commercial appropriation of the right of publicity. We consider whether the unauthorized use of a celebrity's name, photograph, or likeness on the cover of a publication and in related telecast advertisements, in connection with a published nondefamatory article, which is false but presented as true, constitutes an actionable infringement of that person's right of publicity under both the common law and Civil Code section 3344, subdivision (a). We have determined that such use constitutes commercial exploitation and is not privileged or protected by constitutional considerations or expressly exempted as a news account under Civil Code section 3344, subdivision (d). Accordingly, we have concluded that the respondent court improperly sustained the general demurrer to the second cause of action without leave to amend.

Clint Eastwood in Love Triangle

Superstar Clint Eastwood's been swept off his feet by sexy 23-year-old singer Tanya Tucker — and now he's locked in a romantic triangle with Tanya and his longtime love Sondra Locke.

What's more, sources say the two gals will fight to the bitter end to land the two-fisted movie tough guy for keeps.

And Clint himself is torn between his two dazzling beauties.

"Clint loves both Tanya and Sondra," said a close friend of the 50-year-old actor. "He can't decide between Sondra, a woman he knows will always love him, and Tanya, who's like a bubbly fresh bottle of champagne."

He's Torn Between Tanya Tucker and His Longtime Gal

The romantic tug-of-war started in late February, after Clint and 34-year-old Sondra, who's starred in almost all of Eastwood's movies since they fell in love, had a huge argument over marriage.

"Clint and Sondra were having serious problems," said a source close to the rugged superstar. "Sondra was pressing him to take a walk down the aisle — but Clint felt that was more like walking a plank. He's already had one miserable marriage.

"After that nasty fight at Clint's Carmel, Calif., home, Sondra stormed out and went back to her own place in Los Angeles — and Clint took off for the World Cup ski races in Aspen, Colo.

"Clint ran into Tanya his very first night in Aspen at a party for the competitors and celebrities attending. He was immediately smitten with her.

"Throughout the whole 10 days they shared fun-filled and romantic evenings. They were constantly in each other's arms.

"Clint told me, 'Tanya is terrific! She makes me feel 20 years younger. She's beautiful, intelligent, bubbly — and she knows how to use her charms to get what she wants. I love that kind of woman. She makes my head spin'"

The cuddling couple turned heads at Chisholm's Saloon, a popular Aspen country and western club.

"Clint and Tanya walked arm in arm," revealed a friend of Tanya. "Then they sat at a table alone, held hands and gazed at each other romantically. They laughed and smiled, and were very lovey-dovey."

And three nights later at Andre's, an Aspen restaurant and disco, an eyewitness reported, "They were dancing cheek to cheek, kissing and hugging as if they were the only people in the room."

After 10 days in Aspen with Tanya, Clint returned to his Carmel home — only to find Sondra anxious to make up with him.

"Sondra was there waiting on his doorstep," said the source close to Clint. "She was determined to patch up their relationship.

"She was virtually on her hands and knees, begging him to keep her. Sondra vowed she wouldn't pressure him into marriage, and took the blame for everything. But Clint acted totally oblivious to Sondra's pleas. He was walking on cloud nine.

"Sondra sensed that something was wrong.

"She knew another woman had to have entered his life."

Clint's close friend added, "She suspects that he was with another woman while he was away."

But a source close to Sondra confided. "Sondra's weathered all the curves and bumps so far, and she's not about to give Clint up!"

Tanya won't give up her he-man, either, an acquaintance said.

"She's in love. Tanya fell head over heels for Clint, and hasn't stopped talking about him since she's been home in Los Angeles.

"Tanya is so in love with Clint that she would battle Sondra to the end."

Added a close friend of the singer, "This is her first serious relationship since she broke up with Glen Campbell, and she isn't the kind of girl who'll let a man like Clint slip through her fingers. She told me, 'I've never been so happy in my life! Clint's wonderful. He makes me feel like a real woman.'

"'I'm determined to make this new relationship last.'"

Clint's and Tanya's incredibly busy show biz schedules are keeping them apart at the moment, but sources say they're in almost constant touch.

"They're always talking on the phone, and Tanya has made plans to make the 300-mile trip to visit Clint in Carmel soon," said Tanya's close friend.

However, while Tanya is temporarily out of Clint's arms, Sondra is seeing him whenever possible.

"Clint is doing somersaults in his mind," the actor's close friend revealed. "He told me when he's with one he can't help thinking about the other. When he was with Tanya in Aspen, he confessed to me, he was thinking about Sondra and his love for her.

"And when Clint and Sondra are together, he's told me that Tanya is constantly on his mind.

"He daydreams about their enchanted evenings together in Aspen."

"Now he's got two women dueling over him. Tanya means a lot to him but he left his wife for Sondra.

"We're all waiting anxiously to see which girl he chooses."

— CHARLES PARMITER

SKIING BUDDIES Clint and Tanya at a celebrity tournament in Sun Valley, Idaho, in 1979. Now the sultry songstress — also pictured at left — is battling Clint's longtime steady for his affections.

TAKING A BACKSEAT? Clint's longtime lady Sondra Locke — with him here in the 1977 movie "The Gauntlet" — has a rival.

The National Enquirer article concerning plaintiff.

Facts and Proceedings Below

The facts before this court as set forth in the petition of Eastwood and the return of the Enquirer are not in substantial dispute.

Eastwood, a well-known motion picture actor, filed a complaint containing two causes of action against the Enquirer. The gist of the first cause of action is for false light invasion of privacy. The second cause of action is for invasion of privacy through the commercial appropriation of name, photograph and likeness under both the common law and Civil Code section 3344.

The following pertinent facts emerge from the allegations of the first cause of action. The Enquirer publishes a weekly newspaper known as the "National Enquirer" which enjoys wide circulation and is read by a great number of people. In its April 13, 1982 edition of the National Enquirer, the Enquirer published a 600-word article about Eastwood's romantic involvement with two other celebrities, singer Tanya Tucker and actress Sondra Locke. On the cover of this edition appeared the pictures of Eastwood and Tucker above the caption "Clint Eastwood in Love Triangle with Tanya Tucker."

The article is headlined "Clint Eastwood in Love Triangle" and appears on page 48 of this edition. Eastwood alleges the article is false and in this regard alleges:

(a) The offending article falsely states that Eastwood "loves" Tucker and that Tucker means a lot to him.

(b) The offending article falsely states that Eastwood was, in late February, 1982, swept off his feet and immediately smitten by Tucker; that Tucker makes his head spin; that Tucker used her charms to get what she wanted from Eastwood; and that Eastwood now daydreams about their supposedly enchanted evenings together.

(c) The offending article falsely states that Eastwood and Tucker, in late February, 1982, shared 10 fun-filled romantic evenings together; were constantly, during that period, in each other's arms; publicly "cuddled" and publicly gazed romantically at one another; and publicly kissed and hugged.

(d) The offending article falsely states that Eastwood is locked in a romantic triangle involving Tucker and Sondra Locke ("Locke"); is torn between Locke and Tucker; can't decide between Locke and Tucker; is involved in a romantic tug-of-war involving Locke and Tucker; that Locke and Tucker are dueling over him; that Tucker is battling Locke for his affections; and that when he is with Locke, Tucker is constantly on his mind.

(e) The offending article falsely states that, in or about late February of 1982, there were serious problems in Eastwood's relationship with Locke; that he and Locke at that time had a huge argument over marriage; that he and Locke had a nasty fight; and that Locke stormed out of his presence.

(f) The offending article falsely states that after his supposed romantic interlude with Tucker, Locke camped at his doorstep and, while on hands and knees, begged Eastwood to "keep her", vowing that she wouldn't pressure him into marriage; but that Eastwood acted oblivious to her pleas.

Eastwood further asserts that Enquirer "published the offending article maliciously, willfully and wrongfully, with the intent to injure and disgrace Eastwood, either knowing that the statements therein contained were false or with reckless disregard of * * * their * * * falsity." Enquirer used Eastwood's name and photograph without his consent or permission. As a consequence thereof, Eastwood alleges that he has suffered mental anguish and emotional distress and seeks both compensatory and punitive damages.

The second cause of action of the complaint incorporates all the allegations of the first cause of action concerning the status of Enquirer and the falsity of the article. It does not, however, incorporate the allegation that the article was published with knowledge or in reckless disregard of its falsity.

Additionally, Eastwood alleges that the Enquirer made a telecast advertisement in which it featured Eastwood's name and photograph and mentioned prominently the subject article. Moreover, Eastwood alleges that the telecast advertisements as well as the cover of the April 13 publication were calculated to promote the sales of the Enquirer. Eastwood asserts that the unauthorized use of his name and photograph has damaged him in his right to control the commercial exploitation of his name, photograph and likeness, in addition to injuring his feelings and privacy. Eastwood seeks damages under both the common law and Civil Code section 3344.

Enquirer did not challenge the legal sufficiency of the first cause of action for invasion of privacy by placing Eastwood in a false light in the public eye.

Enquirer demurred to the second cause of action for invasion of privacy through appropriation of name, photograph and likeness on the basis it failed to state a cause of action on two grounds: (1) Eastwood's name and photograph were not used to imply an endorsement of the Enquirer; and (2) Eastwood's name and photograph were used in connection with a news account.

The respondent court sustained the general demurrers of Enquirer without leave to amend, and this petition followed. We granted an alternative writ.

Issues

This petition poses two basic issues: (1) Has Eastwood stated a cause of action for commercial appropriation of the right of publicity under either the common law or Civil Code section 3344? (2) Is the conduct of the Enquirer privileged so as not to constitute an infringement of Eastwood's right of publicity?

Discussion

In order to put the issues raised by these proceedings into proper focus, we consider first the framework of Eastwood's complaint against the Enquirer.

California has long recognized a common law right of privacy (see, e.g., Melvin v. Reid (1931) 112 Cal.App. 285, 297 P. 91), which provides protection against four distinct categories of invasion (see Kapellas v. Kofman (1969) 1 Cal.3d 20, 35, fn. 16, 81 Cal.Rptr. 360, 459 P.2d 912). These four distinct torts identified by Dean Prosser [5] and grouped under the privacy rubric are: (1) intrusion upon the plaintiff's seclusion or solitude, or into his private affairs; (2) public disclosure of embarrassing private facts about the plaintiff; (3) publicity which places the plaintiff in a false light in the public eye; and (4) appropriation, for the defendant's advantage, of the plaintiff's name or likeness. (See Lugosi v. Universal Pictures (1979) 25 Cal.3d 813, 819, 160 Cal.Rptr. 323, 603 P.2d 425; Weinstein, *Commercial Appropriation of Name or Likeness: Section 3344 and the Common Law* (1977) 52 L.A.Bar J. 430; Note, *Commercial Appropriation of an Individual's Name, Photograph or Likeness: A New Remedy for Californians* (1972) 3 Pac.L.J. 651, 655–656.)

Moreover, the fourth category of invasion of privacy, namely, appropriation, "has been *complemented* legislatively by Civil Code section 3344, adopted in 1971." (Lugosi v. Universal Pictures, supra, 25 Cal.3d at p. 819, fn. 6, 160 Cal.Rptr. 323, 603 P.2d 425.) [6] (Emphasis added.)

Civil Code section 3344, subdivision (a), provides in pertinent part as follows: "Any person who knowingly uses another's name, photograph, or likeness, in any manner, for purposes of advertising products, merchandise, goods, or services, or for purposes of solicitation of purchases of products * * * without such person's prior consent * * * shall be liable for any damages sustained by the person * * * injured as a result thereof."

Eastwood has framed his complaint against Enquirer on the third and fourth branches of the right of privacy. His first cause of action, which is not at issue here, rests on the theory that the subject publication placed him in a false light in the public eye. The focus of

---

5. Prosser, *Privacy* (1960) 48 Cal.L.Rev. 383, 384.

6. This is the correct characterization, in contrast to Johnson v. Harcourt, Brace, Jovanovich (1974) 43 Cal.App.3d 880, 894, 118 Cal.Rptr. 370, where the court stated that Civil Code section 3344, subdivision (a), "codifies" the law of appropriation of name and likeness for commercial purposes. The differences between the common law and statutory actions are: (1) Section 3344, subdivision (a) requires a *knowing* use whereas under case law, mistake and inadvertence are not a defense against commercial appropriation (see Fairfield v. American Photocopy Equipment Co. (1955) 138 Cal.App.2d 82, 87, 291 P.2d 194); and (2) Section 3344, subdivision (g) expressly provides that its remedies are cumulative and in addition to any provided for by law. (See Note, *Commercial Appropriation of an Individual's Name, Photograph or Likeness: A New Remedy For Californians* (1972) 3 Pac.L.J. 651, 659–661.)

this tort is the falsity of the published article. His second cause of action, which is at issue here, rests on alternative theories. One is the common law action of commercial appropriation. The other is the statutory remedy provided in Civil Code section 3344, subdivision (a), for the knowing use, without consent, of another's name, photograph or likeness for the purposes of advertising or solicitation of purchases.

A common law cause of action for appropriation of name or likeness may be pleaded by alleging (1) the defendant's use of the plaintiff's identity; (2) the appropriation of plaintiff's name or likeness to defendant's advantage, commercially or otherwise; (3) lack of consent; and (4) resulting injury. (See Prosser, *Law of Torts* (4th ed. 1971) § 117, pp. 804–807; Witkin, *Cal.Procedure* (2d ed. 1971) Pleading, § 606, p. 2244.)

In addition, to plead the statutory remedy provided in Civil Code section 3344, there must also be an allegation of a knowing use of the plaintiff's name, photograph or likeness for purposes of advertising or solicitation of purchases. (See Weinstein, *Commercial Appropriation*, supra, 52 L.A.Bar J. at pp. 430–433.) Furthermore, recent judicial construction of section 3344 has imposed an additional requirement. A "direct" connection must be alleged between the use and the commercial purpose. (See Johnson v. Harcourt, Brace, Jovanovich, Inc., supra, 43 Cal.App.3d at p. 895, 118 Cal.Rptr. 370.)

The *Johnson* court held that the use of a magazine article about plaintiff's finding a large sum of money in defendant's textbook was not "so directly connected with the sale" of the textbook that it fell within the purview of section 3344, subdivision (a). (Ibid.) The court reasoned: "The article must be viewed in the context in which it was republished. It was only used as an educational tool in an English textbook. It is obvious that the article was not a primary reason for the textbook; nor was it a substantial factor in the students' purchases of the book." (Ibid.; see Weinstein, *Commercial Appropriation*, supra, 52 L.A.Bar J. at p. 439.)

Here, Eastwood has alleged that the Enquirer employed his name, photograph and likeness on the front page of the subject publication and in related telecast advertisements, without his prior consent, for the purpose of promoting the sales of the Enquirer. Therefore, Eastwood states an actionable claim in his second cause of action under either the common law or section 3344, or both, if two conditions are satisfied: (1) Enquirer's use of Eastwood's name, photograph and likeness constitutes an appropriation for commercial purposes, and (2) Enquirer's conduct constitutes an impermissible infringement of Eastwood's right of publicity.

I

Eastwood Has Stated Facts Showing An Appropriation of His Right of Publicity for Commercial Purposes

Enquirer argues, citing Fairfield v. American Photocopy Equipment Co., supra, 138 Cal.App.2d 82, 291 P.2d 194 and Williams v.

Weisser (1969) 273 Cal.App.2d 726, 78 Cal.Rptr. 542, that the failure of Eastwood to allege the appearance of an "endorsement" of the Enquirer is fatal to stating a cause of action for commercial appropriation.

California law has not imposed any requirement that the unauthorized use or publication of a person's name or picture be suggestive of an endorsement or association with the injured person. Enquirer's reliance on the *Fairfield* and *Williams* cases is therefore misplaced. * *

Moreover, the appearance of an "endorsement" is not the *sine qua non* of a claim for commercial appropriation. * * *

Further, Enquirer contends that under *Lugosi* an appropriation of name and likeness for commercial purposes can only be shown by Eastwood, if their use has impressed the Enquirer with a secondary meaning. We disagree.

In Lugosi v. Universal Pictures, which involved an action by the heirs of Bela Lugosi for commercial appropriation of his right of publicity, our Supreme Court held that the right of publicity, which is the legally protected interest a person has to control the commercial exploitation of his name, photograph or likeness, is not descendible and expires upon the death of the person so protected. (25 Cal.3d at pp. 819, 824, 160 Cal.Rptr. 323, 603 P.2d 425; see Guglielmi v. Spelling-Goldberg Productions (1979) 25 Cal.3d 860, 861, 160 Cal.Rptr. 352, 603 P.2d 454.) Contrary to the Enquirer's position that the impression of a secondary meaning is a prerequisite to a claim for commercial appropriation, Lugosi recognized that the right of publicity includes not only the power to control the exploitation of one's personality through licensing agreements, but also the right to obtain relief, both injunctive and/or for damages, when a third party appropriates one's name and likeness for commercial purposes without permission. (25 Cal.3d at p. 819, 160 Cal.Rptr. 323, 603 P.2d 425.)

Furthermore, to illustrate the import of *Lugosi*, we offer the following example: Henry Ford, during his lifetime, could have given a license to General Motors to use his name to endorse a "Buick" automobile. This would have constituted an assignment of his right of publicity. However, this assignment would have expired upon the death of Henry Ford and his name would have been in the marketplace for anyone to use. (Id., at pp. 822–823, 160 Cal.Rptr. 323, 603 P.2d 425.) On the other hand, if Henry Ford had used his name as the name for a particular automobile so that his name acquired a secondary meaning, i.e., the use of the name "Ford" meant a particular automobile, it would be protectable as property under the law of unfair competition. (Id., at p. 818, 160 Cal.Rptr. 323, 603 P.2d 425.) Notwithstanding these contrasting uses, Henry Ford could elect not to exercise his right of publicity and "protect it from invasion by others by a suit for injunction and/or damages." (Id., at p. 819, 160 Cal.Rptr. 323, 603 P.2d 425.)

Moreover, apart from its inconsistency with the common law, Enquirer's suggested limitation of the scope of actionable commercial appropriation is at odds with the clear language of Civil Code section 3344. The statute imposes liability on a person "who knowingly uses another name, photograph, or likeness, *in any manner* * * *." This broad language does not admit of the Enquirer's suggested limitation.

We therefore find that Enquirer's argument is without merit.

Turning to whether the Enquirer has commercially exploited Eastwood's name, photograph or likeness, we note that one of the primary purposes of advertising is to motivate a decision to purchase a particular product or service.

The first step toward selling a product or service is to attract the consumers' attention. Because of a celebrity's audience appeal, people respond almost automatically to a celebrity's name or picture. Here, the Enquirer used Eastwood's personality and fame on the cover of the subject publication and in related telecast advertisements. To the extent their use attracted the readers' attention, the Enquirer gained a commercial advantage. Furthermore, the Enquirer used Eastwood's personality in the context of an alleged news account, entitled "Clint Eastwood in Love Triangle with Tanya Tucker" to generate maximum curiosity and the necessary motivation to purchase the newspaper.

Moreover, the use of Eastwood's personality in the context of a news account, allegedly false but presented as true, provided the Enquirer with a ready-made "scoop"—a commercial advantage over its competitors which it would otherwise not have.

Absent a constitutional or statutory proscription, we find that Eastwood can show that such use is a subterfuge or cover-up for commercial exploitation. (See Note, *"Right of Publicity" Tort Actions* (1977) 91 Harv.L.Rev. 208, 213.)

We therefore conclude that Eastwood has sufficiently alleged that the Enquirer has commercially exploited his name, photograph, and likeness under both the common law and section 3344, subdivision (a).

II

ENQUIRER'S CONDUCT MAY CONSTITUTE AN INFRINGEMENT OF
EASTWOOD'S RIGHT OF PUBLICITY

Enquirer argues that Eastwood's second cause of action fails to state an actionable claim under California law because the use of his name and photograph in the telecast advertisements, the cover page, and the story is expressly exempted from liability as a news account under the provisions of Civil Code section 3344, subdivision (d).

Civil Code section 3344, subdivision (d) provides inter alia that "[f]or purposes of this section, a use of a name, photograph or likeness in connection with any news * * * shall not constitute a use for purposes of advertising or solicitation."

While the issue raised by the Enquirer's argument solely involves the statutory remedy of Civil Code section 3344, subdivision (a), its resolution will necessarily determine Eastwood's ability to maintain a cause of action for commercial appropriation under the common law. The reason is that implicit in this issue are major constitutional questions which we must confront and determine. Publication of matters in the public interest, which rests on the right of the public to know, and the freedom of the press to tell it, cannot ordinarily be actionable. (See Coverstone v. Davies (1952) 38 Cal.2d 315, 323, 239 P.2d 876; Carlisle v. Fawcett Publications, Inc. (1962) 201 Cal.App.2d 733, 745–746, 20 Cal.Rptr. 405; Stryker v. Republic Pictures Corp. (1951) 108 Cal.App.2d 191, 194, 238 P.2d 670.)

In Carlisle v. Fawcett Publications, Inc., supra, the court defined "matters in the public interest" as follows: "The privilege of printing an account of happenings and of enlightening the public as to matters of interest is not restricted to current events; magazines and books, radio and television may legitimately inform and entertain the public with the reproduction of past events, travelogues and biographies." (Id., 201 Cal.App.2d at p. 746, 20 Cal.Rptr. 405.)

Hence we are called upon to determine the boundaries of Eastwood's ability to control the commercial exploitation of his personality in the publication field. This determination will necessitate a weighing of the private interest of the right of publicity against matters of public interest calling for constitutional protection, and a consideration of the character of these competing interests.

Freedom of the press is constitutionally guaranteed, and the publication of daily news is an acceptable and necessary function in the life of the community. (Gill v. Hearst Publishing Co. (1953) 40 Cal.2d 224, 228, 253 P.2d 441; Carlisle v. Fawcett Publications, Inc., supra, 201 Cal.App.2d at p. 746, 20 Cal.Rptr. 405.) The scope of the privilege extends to almost all reporting of recent events even though it involves the publication of a purely private person's name or likeness. (See, e.g., Coverstone v. Davis, supra, 38 Cal.2d 315, 323, 239 P.2d 876; Metter v. Los Angeles Examiner (1939) 35 Cal.App.2d 304, 312, 95 P.2d 491.)

Moreover, "there is a public interest which attaches to people who, by their accomplishments, mode of living, professional standing or calling, create a legitimate and widespread attention to their activities. Certainly, the accomplishments and way of life of those who have achieved a marked reputation or notoriety by appearing before the public such as actors * * * may legitimately be mentioned and discussed in print * * *." (Carlisle v. Fawcett Publications, Inc., supra, 201 Cal.App.2d at p. 746, 20 Cal.Rptr. 405.) Thus, a celebrity has relinquished "'a part of his right of privacy to the extent that the public has a legitimate interest in his doings, affairs or character.'" (Id., at p. 747, 20 Cal.Rptr. 405.)

Yet absolute protection of the press in the case at bench requires a total sacrifice of the competing interest of Eastwood in controlling the commercial exploitation of his personality. Often considerable money, time and energy are needed to develop the ability in a person's name or likeness to attract attention and evoke a desired response in a particular consumer market. (See Lugosi v. Universal Pictures, supra, 25 Cal.3d at p. 824, 160 Cal.Rptr. 323, 603 P.2d 425; Nimmer, *Right of Publicity* (1954) 19 Law & Contemp.Prob., 203, 216.) Thus, a proper accommodation between these competing concerns must be defined, since "the rights guaranteed by the First Amendment do not require total abrogation of the right to privacy" (Briscoe v. Reader's Digest Association, Inc. (1971) 4 Cal.3d 529, 541, 93 Cal.Rptr. 866, 483 P.2d 34), and in the case at bench, the right of publicity (see, e.g., Zacchini v. Scripps-Howard Broadcasting Co. (1977) 433 U.S. 562, 574–575, 97 S.Ct. 2849, 2856–57, 53 L.Ed.2d 965.)

Ordinarily, only two branches of the law of privacy, namely, public disclosure and false light, create tension with the First Amendment, because of their intrusion on the dissemination of information to the public. (See, e.g., Briscoe v. Reader's Digest Association, Inc., supra, 4 Cal.3d at p. 534, 93 Cal.Rptr. 866, 483 P.2d 34; Kapellas v. Kofman, supra, 1 Cal.3d 20, 35–36, 81 Cal.Rptr. 360, 459 P.2d 912; Prosser, *Torts*, supra, § 118 at p. 827; Note, *Triangulating the Limits on the Tort of Invasion of Privacy: The Development of the Remedy in Light of the Expansion of Constitutional Privilege* (1976) 3 Hastings Constitutional Law Quarterly 543, fn. 1.) Normally, in a commercial appropriation case involving the right of publicity, the only question is who gets to do the publishing, since the celebrity is primarily concerned with whether he gets the commercial benefit of such publication. (See, e.g., Zacchini v. Scripps-Howard Broadcasting Co., supra, 433 U.S. at p. 573, 97 S.Ct. at p. 2856.)

All fiction is false in the literal sense that it is imagined rather than actual. However, works of fiction are constitutionally protected in the same manner as topical new stories. (See Cohen v. California, supra, 403 U.S. 15, 25, 91 S.Ct. 1780, 1788, 29 L.Ed.2d 284; Katzev v. County of Los Angeles (1959) 52 Cal.2d 360, 365, 341 P.2d 310.)

Therefore, since Eastwood asserts that the alleged news account is entirely false, and is a cover-up or subterfuge for commercial appropriation of his name and likeness, we must consider First Amendment limitations.

We have no doubt that the subject of the Enquirer article—the purported romantic involvements of Eastwood with other celebrities—is a matter of public concern, which would generally preclude the imposition of liability. (See, e.g., Briscoe v. Reader's Digest Association, Inc., supra, 4 Cal.3d at pp. 535–536, 93 Cal.Rptr. 866, 483 P.2d 34; Carlisle v. Fawcett Publications, Inc., supra, 201 Cal.App.2d at pp. 746–747, 20 Cal.Rptr. 405.) However, Eastwood argues that the article, and thereby the related advertisements, are not entitled to either constitutional protection or exemption from liability as a news account because the article is a calculated falsehood.

Since New York Times v. Sullivan (1964) 376 U.S. 254, 279–280, 84 S.Ct. 710, 725–26, 11 L.Ed.2d 686, it is clear that the First Amendment generally precludes the imposition of liability upon a publisher for its expressive activities, except upon a finding of fault. Thus, our analysis must determine whether Eastwood has alleged the kinds of fault and the appropriate standard that may constitutionally warrant liability in this case. (See Hill, *Defamation and Privacy Under the First Amendment* (1976) 76 Columbia L.Rev. 1205, 1254–1255.)

In actions where the fault involves defamatory statements, the cases have focused on the status of plaintiff to determine the standard of fault necessary to impose liability on a media defendant. For example, in the case of a public official or public figure, the Supreme Court established the rule that a plaintiff may not recover except upon showing that the defendant published defamatory statements with *actual malice* (hereafter "scienter"), i.e., either with knowledge of their falsity or with reckless disregard for the truth. (See Curtis Publishing Co. v. Butts, and its companion, Associated Press v. Walker (1967) 388 U.S. 130, 162, 87 S.Ct. 1975, 1995, 18 L.Ed.2d 1094; New York Times Co. v. Sullivan, supra, 376 U.S. at pp. 279–280, 84 S.Ct. at pp. 725–26.[8]) However, in defamation actions brought by private individuals, the Supreme Court has allowed any appropriate standard of fault less than scienter to be used, short of liability without fault. (See, e.g., Time, Inc. v. Firestone (1976) 424 U.S. 448, 96 S.Ct. 958, 47 L.Ed.2d 154; Gertz v. Robert Welch, Inc. (1974) 418 U.S. 323, 347, 94 S.Ct. 2997, 3010, 41 L.Ed.2d 789.) Thus, a private-party plaintiff may sue for negligent publication of defamatory falsehoods. (*Gertz*, at pp. 347–350, 94 S.Ct. at pp. 3010–12.)

Similarly, in privacy actions involving deliberate fictionalization presented as truth, the cases have focused on the materials published to determine the standard of fault required to impose liability on a publisher. For example, where the materials published, although assertedly private and nondefamatory, are matters of public interest, the target of the publication must prove knowing or reckless falsehood. (See, e.g., Cox Broadcasting Corp. v. Cohn (1975) 420 U.S. 469, 490, 95 S.Ct. 1029, 1043, 43 L.Ed.2d 328; Cantrell v. Forest City Publishing Co. (1974) 419 U.S. 245, 250–251, 95 S.Ct. 465, 469, 42 L.Ed.2d 419; Time, Inc. v. Hill (1966) 385 U.S. 374, 379, 387–388, 87 S.Ct. 534, 537, 541–42, 17 L.Ed.2d 456.)

Moreover, the standard of scienter, whether in a defamation or privacy case, reflects the Supreme Court's recognition that while a calculated falsehood has no constitutional value, such statements are inevitable in the continuing debate on public issues and thus, the fruitful exercise of the freedoms of speech and press requires "breathing space" for speech that matters. (Gertz v. Robert Welch, Inc., supra, 418 U.S. at pp. 339–343, 94 S.Ct. at pp. 3006–08; Time, Inc. v. Hill, supra, 385 U.S. at pp. 387–391, 87 S.Ct. at pp. 541–43; New York Times Co. v. Sullivan, supra, 376 U.S. at pp. 279–280, 84 S.Ct. at pp. 725–26.)

---

8. Prosser criticized the use of the term "actual malice," and would substitute for it the word "scienter." (Prosser, *Torts,* supra, § 118, p. 821.) We find this suggestion helpful, and shall use "scienter" in place of "actual malice."

Accordingly, we conclude whether the focus is on the status of Eastwood, or upon the materials published in the Enquirer article, scienter of the alleged calculated falsehood is the proper standard of fault to impose liability on the Enquirer, contrary to the position of Eastwood, that calculated falsehood alone is enough.

Enquirer contends, however, that it is the manifest character of the article which is determinative as to whether it is news under section 3344, subdivision (d). Enquirer argues that the statute, by its terms, refers only to generic categories; it does not distinguish between news accounts that are true or false. Thus, whether an article is a news account does not turn on the truth or falsity of its content. We disagree.

The spacious interest in an unfettered press is not without limitation. This privilege is subject to the qualification that it shall not be so exercised as to abuse the rights of individuals. Hence, in defamation cases, the concern is with defamatory lies masquerading as truth. (See, e.g., New York Times Co. v. Sullivan, supra, 376 U.S. at pp. 279–280, 84 S.Ct. at pp. 725–26.) Similarly, in privacy cases, the concern is with nondefamatory lies masquerading as truth. (See, e.g., Time, Inc. v. Hill, supra, 385 U.S. at pp. 390–391, 87 S.Ct. at pp. 543–44.) Accordingly, we do not believe that the Legislature intended to provide an exemption from liability for a knowing or reckless falsehood under the canopy of "news." We therefore hold that Civil Code section 3344, subdivision (d), as it pertains to news, does not provide an exemption for a knowing or reckless falsehood.

Moreover, wherever the line in a particular situation is to be drawn between news accounts that are protected and those that are not, we are quite sure that the First Amendment does not immunize Enquirer when the entire article is allegedly false. (See, e.g., Zacchini v. Scripps-Howard Broadcasting Co., supra, 433 U.S. at pp. 574–575, 97 S.Ct. at pp. 2856–57.)

Finally, Enquirer contends that falsity is the predicate, not for commercial appropriation, but for false light claims. We disagree.

As noted earlier, all fiction is literally false, but enjoys constitutional protection.

However, the deliberate fictionalization of Eastwood's personality constitutes commercial exploitation, and becomes actionable when it is presented to the reader as if true with the requisite scienter.[10] (See, e.g., Spahn v. Julian Messner (1967) 21 N.Y.2d 124, 286 N.Y.S.2d 832, 233 N.E.2d 840; Hill, supra, 76 Columbia L.Rev. at pp. 1306–1307.)

Here, Eastwood failed to incorporate from his first cause of action that the article was published with knowledge or in reckless disregard

---

10. Although the issue is unsettled under California common law, we see no constitutional barrier to imposing damages under section 3344, subdivision (a) measured not only by the harm done to the plaintiff but additionally by the benefit enjoyed by defendant.

of its falsity. Accordingly, we find that such failure renders the second cause of action insufficient to make the Enquirer's expressive conduct actionable under the common law or Civil Code section 3344, subdivision (a).

Manifestly, such defect is capable of being cured by amendment. (See Tate v. Superior Court (1963) 213 Cal.App.2d 238, 251, 28 Cal.Rptr. 548.) Thus, where it appears that the trial court has made a ruling which deprives a party of the opportunity to plead his cause of action or defense, relief by mandamus may be appropriate to prevent a needless and expensive trial and reversal. (Ibid.)

Let a peremptory writ of mandamus issue requiring the respondent court to set aside its order sustaining the demurrer to Eastwood's second cause of action without leave to amend, and to grant Eastwood leave to amend his second cause of action.

SCHAUER, P.J., and JOHNSON, J., concur.

Questions

1. Should "actual malice" (or what the court in the instant case refers to as "scienter") negate a First Amendment defense in a right of publicity action even as against a newspaper? Does this create an unacceptable "chilling effect" on the news media? Should a First Amendment defense in a right of publicity action as against the news media be lost if the use of the subject's name or likeness is "knowingly false," but not lost if the use is found to be with a "reckless disregard" of the truth?

2. Would the court have reached the same result if the cause of action had arisen after enactment of the amendment to Cal. Civil Code Sec. 3344?

Appendix A

THE CONSTITUTIONAL PROVISION RESPECTING COPYRIGHT

The Congress shall have Power * * * To Promote the Progress of Science and useful Arts, by securing for limited Times to Authors and Inventors the exclusive Right to their respective Writings and Discoveries. (U.S. Const. Art. I, § 8.)

Appendix B

THE COPYRIGHT ACT OF 1976 [1]

Public Law 94–553, 94th Congress, 90 Stat. 2541

TITLE 1—GENERAL REVISION OF COPYRIGHT LAW

Sec. 101. Title 17 of the United States Code, entitled "Copyrights", is hereby amended in its entirety to read as follows:

Title 17—Copyrights

Chap.		Sec.
1.	Subject Matter and Scope of Copyright	101
2.	Copyright Ownership and Transfer	201
3.	Duration of Copyright	301
4.	Copyright Notice, Deposit, and Registration	401
5.	Copyright Infringement and Remedies	501
6.	Manufacturing Requirements and Importation	601
7.	Copyright Office	701
8.	Copyright Royalty Tribunal	801

CHAPTER 1.—SUBJECT MATTER AND SCOPE OF COPYRIGHT

Sec.
- 101. Definitions.
- 102. Subject Matter of Copyright: In General.
- 103. Same: Compilations and Derivative Works.
- 104. Same: National Origin.
- 105. Same: United States Government Works.
- 106. Exclusive Rights in Copyrighted Works.
- 107. Limitations on Exclusive Rights: Fair Use.
- 108. Same: Reproduction by Libraries and Archives.
- 109. Same: Effect of Transfer of Particular Copy or Phonorecord.
- 110. Same: Exemption of Certain Performances and Displays.
- 111. Same: Secondary Transmissions.
- 112. Same: Ephemeral Recordings.
- 113. Scope of Exclusive Rights in Pictorial, Graphic, and Sculptural Works.

---

1. The Act of August 5, 1977 (Pub.L. No. 95–94), amended Section 708(c). The Act of December 12, 1980 (Pub.L. No. 96–517), amended Sections 101 and 117. The Act of Oct. 4, 1984 (Pub.L. 98–450) amended Sections 109 and 115.

Sec.
114. Scope of Exclusive Rights in Sound Recordings.
115. Scope of Exclusive Rights in Nondramatic Musical Works: Compulsory License for Making and Distributing Phonorecords.
116. Same: Public Performances by Means of Coin-operated Phonorecord Players.
117. Limitations on Exclusive Rights: Computer Programs.
118. Scope of Exclusive Rights: Use of Certain Works in Connection With Noncommercial Broadcasting.

Sec. 101. Definitions

As used in this title, the following terms and their variant forms mean the following:

An "anonymous work" is a work on the copies or phonorecords of which no natural person is identified as author.

"Audiovisual works" are works that consist of a series of related images which are intrinsically intended to be shown by the use of machines or devices such as projectors, viewers, or electronic equipment, together with accompanying sounds, if any, regardless of the nature of the material objects, such as films or tapes, in which the works are embodied.

The "best edition" of a work is the edition, published in the United States at any time before the date of deposit, that the Library of Congress determines to be most suitable for its purposes.

A person's "children" are that person's immediate offspring, whether legitimate or not, and any children legally adopted by that person.

A "collective work" is a work, such as a periodical issue, anthology, or encyclopedia, in which a number of contributions, constituting separate and independent works in themselves, are assembled into a collective whole.

A "compilation" is a work formed by the collection and assembling of preexisting materials or of data that are selected, coordinated, or arranged in such a way that the resulting work as a whole constitutes an original work of authorship. The term "compilation" includes collective works.

"Copies" are material objects, other than phonorecords, in which a work is fixed by any method now known or later developed, and from which the work can be perceived, reproduced, or otherwise communicated, either directly or with the aid of a machine or device. The term "copies" includes the material object, other than a phonorecord, in which the work is first fixed.

"Copyright owner", with respect to any one of the exclusive rights comprised in a copyright, refers to the owner of that particular right.

A work is "created" when it is fixed in a copy or phonorecord for the first time; where a work is prepared over a period of time, the portion of it that has been fixed at any particular time constitutes the work as of that time, and where the work has been prepared in different versions, each version constitutes a separate work.

A "derivative work" is a work based upon one or more preexisting works, such as a translation, musical arrangement, dramatization, fictionalization, motion picture version, sound recording, art reproduction, abridgment, condensation, or any other form in which a work may be recast, transformed or adapted. A work consisting of editorial revisions, annotations, elaborations, or other modifications which, as a whole, represent an original work of authorship, is a "derivative work".

A "device", "machine", or "process" is one now known or later developed.

To "display" a work means to show a copy of it, either directly or by means of a film, slide, television image, or any other device or process or, in the case of a motion picture or other audiovisual work, to show individual images nonsequentially.

A work is "fixed" in a tangible medium of expression when its embodiment in a copy or phonorecord, by or under the authority of the author, is sufficiently permanent or stable to permit it to be perceived, reproduced, or otherwise communicated for a period of more than transitory duration. A work consisting of sounds, images, or both, that are being transmitted, is "fixed" for purposes of this title if a fixation of the work is being made simultaneously with its transmission.

The terms "including" and "such as" are illustrative and not limitative.

A "joint work" is a work prepared by two or more authors with the intention that their contributions be merged into inseparable or interdependent parts of a unitary whole.

"Literary works" are works, other than audiovisual works, expressed in words, numbers, or other verbal or numerical symbols or indicia, regardless of the nature of the material objects, such as books, periodicals, manuscripts, phonorecords, film, tapes, disks, or cards, in which they are embodied.

"Motion pictures" are audiovisual works consisting of a series of related images which, when shown in succession, impart an impression of motion, together with accompanying sounds, if any.

To "perform" a work means to recite, render, play, dance, or act it, either directly or by means of any device or process or, in the case of a motion picture or other audiovisual work, to show its images in any sequence or to make the sounds accompanying it audible.

"Phonorecords" are material objects in which sounds, other than those accompanying a motion picture or other audiovisual work, are fixed by any method now known or later developed, and from which the sounds can be perceived, reproduced, or otherwise communicated, either directly or with the aid of a machine or device. The term "phonorecords" includes the material object in which the sounds are first fixed.

"Pictorial, graphic, and sculptural works" include two-dimensional and three-dimensional works of fine, graphic, and applied art, photographs, prints and art reproductions, maps, globes, charts, technical drawings, diagrams, and models. Such works shall include works of artistic craftsmanship insofar as their form but not their mechanical or utilitarian aspects are concerned; the design of a useful article, as defined in this section, shall be considered a pictorial, graphic, or sculptural work only if, and only to the extent that, such design incorporates pictorial, graphic, or sculptural features that can be identified separately from, and are capable of existing independently of, the utilitarian aspects of the article.

A "pseudonymous work" is a work on the copies or phonorecords of which the author is identified under a fictitious name.

"Publication" is the distribution of copies or phonorecords of a work to the public by sale or other transfer of ownership, or by rental, lease, or lending. The offering to distribute copies or phonorecords to a group of persons for purposes of further distribution, public performance, or public display, constitutes publication. A public performance or display of a work does not of itself constitute publication.

To perform or display a work "publicly" means—

(1) to perform or display it at a place open to the public or at any place where a substantial number of persons outside of a normal circle of a family and its social acquaintances is gathered; or

(2) to transmit or otherwise communicate a performance or display of the work to a place specified by clause (1) or to the public, by means of any device or process, whether the members of the public capable of receiving the performance or display receive it in the same place or in separate places and at the same time or at different times.

"Sound recordings" are works that result from the fixation of a series of musical, spoken, or other sounds, but not including the sounds accompanying a motion picture or other audiovisual work, regardless of the nature of the material objects, such as disks, tapes, or other phonorecords, in which they are embodied.

"State" includes the District of Columbia and the Commonwealth of Puerto Rico, and any territories to which this title is made applicable by an Act of Congress.

A "transfer of copyright ownership" is an assignment, mortgage, exclusive license, or any other conveyance, alienation, or hypothecation of a copyright or of any of the exclusive rights comprised in a copyright, whether or not it is limited in time or place of effect, but not including a nonexclusive license.

A "transmission program" is a body of material that, as an aggregate, has been produced for the sole purpose of transmission to the public in sequence and as a unit.

To "transmit" a performance or display is to communicate it by any device or process whereby images or sounds are received beyond the place from which they are sent.

The "United States", when used in a geographical sense, comprises the several States, the District of Columbia and the Commonwealth of Puerto Rico, and the organized territories under the jurisdiction of the United States Government.

A "useful article" is an article having an intrinsic utilitarian function that is not merely to portray the appearance of the article or to convey information. An article that is normally a part of a useful article is considered a "useful article".

The author's "widow" or "widower" is the author's surviving spouse under the law of the author's domicile at the time of his or her death, whether or not the spouse has later remarried.

A "work of the United States Government" is a work prepared by an officer or employee of the United States Government as part of that person's official duties.

A "work made for hire" is—

(1) a work prepared by an employee within the scope of his or her employment; or

(2) a work specially ordered or commissioned for use as a contribution to a collective work, as a part of a motion picture or other audiovisual work, as a translation, as a supplementary work, as a compilation, as an instructional text, as a test, as answer material for a test, or as an atlas, if the parties expressly agree in a written instrument signed by them that the work shall be considered a work made for hire. For the purpose of the foregoing sentence, a "supplementary work" is a work prepared for publication as a secondary adjunct to a work by another author for the purpose of introducing, concluding, illustrating, explaining, revising, commenting upon, or assisting in the use of the other work, such as forewords, afterwords, pictorial illustrations, maps, charts, tables, editorial notes, musical arrangements, answer material for tests, bibliographies, appendixes, and indexes, and an "instructional text" is a literary, pictorial, or graphic work prepared for publication and with the purpose of use in systematic instructional activities.

A "computer program" is a set of statements or instructions to be used directly or indirectly in a computer in order to bring about a certain result.[2]

2. Section 101 as amended by the Act of December 12, 1980, Pub.L. No. 96–517.

Sec. 102. Subject Matter of Copyright: In General

(a) Copyright protection subsists, in accordance with this title, in original works of authorship fixed in any tangible medium of expression, now known or later developed, from which they can be perceived, reproduced, or otherwise communicated, either directly or with the aid of a machine or device. Works of authorship include the following categories:

(1) literary works;

(2) musical works, including any accompanying words;

(3) dramatic works, including any accompanying music;

(4) pantomimes and choreographic works;

(5) pictorial, graphic, and sculptural works;

(6) motion pictures and other audiovisual works; and

(7) sound recordings.

(b) In no case does copyright protection for an original work of authorship extend to any idea, procedure, process, system, method of operation, concept, principle, or discovery, regardless of the form in which it is described, explained, illustrated, or embodied in such work.

Sec. 103. Subject Matter of Copyright: Compilations and Derivative Works

(a) The subject matter of copyright as specified by section 102 includes compilations and derivative works, but protection for a work employing preexisting material in which copyright subsists does not extend to any part of the work in which such material has been used unlawfully.

(b) The copyright in a compilation or derivative work extends only to the material contributed by the author of such work, as distinguished from the preexisting material employed in the work, and does not imply any exclusive right in the preexisting material. The copyright in such work is independent of, and does not affect or enlarge the scope, duration, ownership, or subsistence of, any copyright protection in the preexisting material.

Sec. 104. Subject Matter of Copyright: National Origin

(a) **Unpublished Works.** The works specified by sections 102 and 103, while unpublished, are subject to protection under this title without regard to the nationality or domicile of the author.

(b) **Published Works.** The works specified by sections 102 and 103, when published, are subject to protection under this title if—

(1) on the date of first publication, one or more of the authors is a national or domiciliary of the United States, or is a national, domiciliary, or sovereign authority of a foreign nation that is a party to a copyright treaty to which the United States is also a party, or is a stateless person, wherever that person may be domiciled; or

(2) the work is first published in the United States or in a foreign nation that, on the date of first publication, is a party to the Universal Copyright Convention; or

(3) the work is first published by the United Nations or any of its specialized agencies, or by the Organization of American States; or

(4) the work comes within the scope of a Presidential proclamation. Whenever the President finds that a particular foreign nation extends, to works by authors who are nationals or domiciliaries of the United States or to works that are first published in the United States, copyright protection on substantially the same basis as that on which the foreign nation extends protection to works of its own nationals and domiciliaries and works first published in that nation, the President may by proclamation extend protection under this title to works of which one or more of the authors is, on the date of first publication, a national, domiciliary, or sovereign authority of that nation, or which was first published in that nation. The President may revise, suspend, or revoke any such proclamation or impose any conditions or limitations on protection under a proclamation.

Sec. 105. Subject Matter of Copyright: United States Government Works

Copyright protection under this title is not available for any work of the United States Government, but the United States Government is not precluded from receiving and holding copyrights transferred to it by assignment, bequest, or otherwise.

Sec. 106. Exclusive Rights in Copyrighted Works

Subject to sections 107 through 118, the owner of copyright under this title has the exclusive rights to do and to authorize any of the following:

(1) to reproduce the copyrighted work in copies or phonorecords;

(2) to prepare derivative works based upon the copyrighted work;

(3) to distribute copies or phonorecords of the copyrighted work to the public by sale or other transfer of ownership, or by rental, lease, or lending;

(4) in the case of literary, musical, dramatic, and choreographic works, pantomimes, and motion pictures and other audiovisual works, to perform the copyrighted work publicly; and

(5) in the case of literary, musical, dramatic, and choreographic works, pantomimes, and pictorial, graphic, or sculptural works, including the individual images of a motion picture or other audiovisual work, to display the copyrighted work publicly.

Sec. 107. Limitations on Exclusive Rights: Fair Use

Notwithstanding the provisions of section 106, the fair use of a copyrighted work, including such use by reproduction in copies or phonorecords or by any other means specified by that section, for purposes such as criticism, comment, news reporting, teaching (including multiple copies for classroom use), scholarship, or research, is not an infringement of copyright. In determining whether the use made of a work in any particular case is a fair use the factors to be considered shall include—

(1) the purpose and character of the use, including whether such use is of a commercial nature or is for nonprofit educational purposes;

(2) the nature of the copyrighted work;

(3) the amount and substantiality of the portion used in relation to the copyrighted work as a whole; and

(4) the effect of the use upon the potential market for or value of the copyrighted work.

Sec. 108. Limitations on Exclusive Rights: Reproduction by Libraries and Archives

(a) Notwithstanding the provisions of section 106, it is not an infringement of copyright for a library or archives, or any of its employees acting within the scope of their employment, to reproduce no more than one copy or phonorecord of a work, or to distribute such copy or phonorecord, under the conditions specified by this section, if—

(1) the reproduction or distribution is made without any purpose of direct or indirect commercial advantage;

(2) the collections of the library or archives are (i) open to the public, or (ii) available not only to researchers affiliated with the library or archives or with the institution of which it is a part, but also to other persons doing research in a specialized field; and

(3) the reproduction or distribution of the work includes a notice of copyright.

(b) The rights of reproduction and distribution under this section apply to a copy or phonorecord of an unpublished work duplicated in facsimile form solely for purposes of preservation and security or for deposit for research use in another library or archives of the type described by clause (2) of subsection (a), if the copy or phonorecord reproduced is currently in the collections of the library or archives.

(c) The right of reproduction under this section applies to a copy or phonorecord of a published work duplicated in facsimile form solely for the purpose of replacement of a copy or phonorecord that is damaged, deteriorating, lost, or stolen, if the library or archives has, after a reasonable effort, determined that an unused replacement cannot be obtained at a fair price.

(d) The rights of reproduction and distribution under this section apply to a copy, made from the collection of a library or archives where the user makes his or her request or from that of another library or archives, of no more than one article or other contribution to a copyrighted collection or periodical issue, or to a copy or phonorecord of a small part of any other copyrighted work, if—

(1) the copy or phonorecord becomes the property of the user, and the library or archives has had no notice that the copy or phonorecord would be used for any purpose other than private study, scholarship, or research; and

(2) the library or archives displays prominently, at the place where orders are accepted, and includes on its order form, a warning of copyright in accordance with requirements that the Register of Copyrights shall prescribe by regulation.

(e) The rights of reproduction and distribution under this section apply to the entire work, or to a substantial part of it, made from the collection of a library or archives where the user makes his or her request or from that of another library or archives, if the library or archives has first determined, on the basis of a reasonable investigation, that a copy, or phonorecord of the copyrighted work cannot be obtained at a [f]air price, if—

(1) the copy or phonorecord becomes the property of the user, and the library or archives has had no notice that the copy or phonorecord would be used for any purpose other than private study, scholarship, or research; and

(2) the library or archives displays prominently, at the place where orders are accepted, and includes on its order form, a warning of copyright in accordance with requirements that the Register of Copyrights shall prescribe by regulation.

(f) Nothing in this section—

(1) shall be construed to impose liability for copyright infringement upon a library or archives or its employees for the unsupervised use of reproducing equipment located on its premises: *Provided,* That such equipment displays a notice that the making of a copy may be subject to the copyright law;

(2) excuses a person who uses such reproducing equipment or who requests a copy or phonorecord under subsection (d) from liability for copyright infringement for any such act, or for any later use of such copy or phonorecord, if it exceeds fair use as provided by section 107;

(3) shall be construed to limit the reproduction and distribution by lending of a limited number of copies and excerpts by a library or archives of an audiovisual news program, subject to clauses (1), (2), and (3) of subsection (a); or

(4) in any way affects the right of fair use as provided by section 107, or any contractual obligations assumed at any time by the library or archives when it obtained a copy or phonorecord of a work in its collections.

(g) The rights of reproduction and distribution under this section extend to the isolated and unrelated reproduction or distribution of a single copy or phonorecord of the same material on separate occasions, but do not extend to cases where the library or archives, or its employee—

(1) is aware or has substantial reason to believe that it is engaging in the related or concerted reproduction or distribution of multiple copies or phonorecords of the same material, whether made on one occasion or over a period of time, and whether intended for aggregate use by one or more individuals or for separate use by the individual members of a group; or

(2) engages in the systematic reproduction or distribution of single or multiple copies or phonorecords of material described in subsection (d): *Provided,* That nothing in this clause prevents a library or archives from participating in interlibrary arrangements that do not have, as their purpose or effect, that the library or archives receiving such copies or phonorecords for distribution does so in such aggregate quantities as to substitute for a subscription to or purchase of such work.

(h) The rights of reproduction and distribution under this section do not apply to a musical work, a pictorial, graphic or sculptural work, or a motion picture or other audiovisual work other than an audiovisual work dealing with news, except that no such limitation shall apply with respect to rights granted by subsections (b) and (c), or with respect to pictorial or graphic works published as illustrations, diagrams, or similar adjuncts to works of which copies are reproduced or distributed in accordance with subsections (d) and (e).

(i) Five years from the effective date of this Act, and at five-year intervals thereafter, the Register of Copyrights, after consulting with representatives of authors, book and periodical publishers, and other owners of copyrighted materials, and with representatives of library users and librarians, shall submit to the Congress a report setting forth the extent to which this section has achieved the intended statutory balancing of the rights of creators, and the needs of users. The report should also describe any problems that may have arisen, and present legislative or other recommendations, if warranted.

Sec. 109. Limitations on Exclusive Rights: Effect of Transfer of Particular Copy or Phonorecord

(a) Notwithstanding the provisions of section 106(3), the owner of a particular copy or phonorecord lawfully made under this title, or any person authorized by such owner, is entitled, without the authority of the copyright owner, to sell or otherwise dispose of the possession of that copy or phonorecord.

(b)(1) Notwithstanding the provisions of subsection (a), unless authorized by the owners of copyright in the sound recording and in the musical works embodied therein, the owners of a particular phonorecord may not, for purposes of direct or indirect commercial advantage, dispose of, or authorize the disposal of, the possession of that phonorecord by rental, lease, or lending, or by any other act or practice in the nature of rental, lease, or lending. Nothing in the preceding sentence shall apply to the rental, lease, or lending of a phonorecord for nonprofit purposes by a nonprofit library or nonprofit education institution.

(2) Nothing in this subsection shall affect any provision of the antitrust laws. For purposes of the preceding sentence, "antitrust laws" has the meaning given that term in the first section of the Clayton Act and includes section 5 of the Federal Trade Commission Act to the extent that section relates to unfair methods of competition.

(3) Any person who distributes a phonorecord in violation of clause (1) is an infringer of copyright under section 501 of this title and is subject to the remedies set forth in sections 502, 503, 504, 505, and 509. Such violation shall not be a criminal offense under section 506 or cause such person to be subject to the criminal penalties set forth in section 2319 of title 18.

(c) Notwithstanding the provisions of section 106(5), the owner of a particular copy lawfully made under this title, or any person authorized by such owner, is entitled, without the authority of the copyright owner, to display that copy publicly, either directly or by the projection of no more than one image at a time, to viewers present at the place where the copy is located.

(d) The privileges prescribed by subsections (a) and (b) do not, unless authorized by the copyright owner, extend to any person who has acquired possession of the copy or phonorecord from the copyright owner, by rental, lease, loan, or otherwise, without acquiring ownership of it.[3]

Sec. 110. Limitations on Exclusive Rights: Exemption of Certain Performances and Displays

Notwithstanding the provisions of section 106, the following are not infringements of copyright:

(1) performance or display of a work by instructors or pupils in the course of face-to-face teaching activities of a nonprofit educational institution, in a classroom or similar place devoted to instruction, unless, in the case of a motion picture or other audiovisual work, the performance, or the display of individual images, is given by means of a

---

3. Subsections (b) and (c) of section 109 were redesignated as subsections (c) and (d) and subsection (b) was added by section 2 of P.L. 98–450, 98 Stat. 1727, the "Record Rental Amendment of 1984," effective October 4, 1984. In addition, section 4 of P.L. 98–450 provided that "* * * (b) The provisions of section 109(b) of title 17, United States Code, as added by section 2 of this Act, shall not affect the right of an owner of a particular phonorecord of a sound recording, who acquired such ownership before the date of the enactment of this Act, to dispose of the possession of that particular phonorecord on or after such date of enactment in any manner permitted by section 109 of title 17, United States Code, as in effect on the day before the date of the enactment of this Act. (c) The amendments made by this Act shall not apply to rentals, leasings, lendings (or acts or practices in the nature of rentals, leasings, or lendings) occurring after the date which is five years after the date of the enactment of this Act."

copy that was not lawfully made under this title, and that the person responsible for the performance knew or had reason to believe was not lawfully made;

(2) performance of a nondramatic literary or musical work or display of a work, by or in the course of a transmission, if—

(A) the performance or display is a regular part of the systematic instructional activities of a governmental body or a nonprofit educational institution; and

(B) the performance or display is directly related and of material assistance to the teaching content of the transmission; and

(C) the transmission is made primarily for—

(i) reception in classrooms or similar places normally devoted to instruction, or

(ii) reception by persons to whom the transmission is directed because their disabilities or other special circumstances prevent their attendance in classrooms or similar places normally devoted to instruction, or

(iii) reception by officers or employees of governmental bodies as a part of their official duties or employment;

(3) performance of a nondramatic literary or musical work or of a dramatico-musical work of a religious nature, or display of a work, in the course of services at a place of worship or other religious assembly;

(4) performance of a nondramatic literary or musical work otherwise than in a transmission to the public, without any purpose of direct or indirect commercial advantage and without payment of any fee or other compensation for the performance to any of its performers, promoters, or organizers, if—

(A) there is no direct or indirect admission charge; or

(B) the proceeds, after deducting the reasonable costs of producing the performance, are used exclusively for educational, religious, or charitable purposes and not for private financial gain, except where the copyright owner has served notice of objection to the performance under the following conditions;

(i) the notice shall be in writing and signed by the copyright owner or such owner's duly authorized agent; and

(ii) the notice shall be served on the person responsible for the performance at least seven days before the date of the performance, and shall state the reasons for the objection; and

(iii) the notice shall comply, in form, content, and manner of service, with requirements that the Register of Copyrights shall prescribe by regulation;

(5) communication of a transmission embodying a performance or display of a work by the public reception of the transmission on a single

receiving apparatus of a kind commonly used in private homes, unless—

(A) a direct charge is made to see or hear the transmission; or

(B) the transmission thus received is further transmitted to the public;

(6) performance of a nondramatic musical work by a governmental body or a nonprofit agricultural or horticultural organization, in the course of an annual agricultural or horticultural fair or exhibition conducted by such body or organization; the exemption provided by this clause shall extend to any liability for copyright infringement that would otherwise be imposed on such body or organization, under doctrines of vicarious liability or related infringement, for a performance by a concessionnaire, business establishment, or other person at such fair or exhibition, but shall not excuse any such person from liability for the performance;

(7) performance of a nondramatic musical work by a vending establishment open to the public at large without any direct or indirect admission charge, where the sole purpose of the performance is to promote the retail sale of copies or phonorecords of the work, and the performance is not transmitted beyond the place where the establishment is located and is within the immediate area where the sale is occurring;

(8) performance of a nondramatic literary work, by or in the course of a transmission specifically designed for and primarily directed to blind or other handicapped persons who are unable to read normal printed material as a result of their handicap, or deaf or other handicapped persons who are unable to hear the aural signals accompanying a transmission of visual signals, if the performance is made without any purpose of direct or indirect commercial advantage and its transmission is made through the facilities of: (i) a governmental body; or (ii) a noncommercial educational broadcast station (as defined in section 397 of title 47); or (iii) a radio subcarrier authorization (as defined in 47 CFR 73.293–73.295 and 73.593–73.595); or (iv) a cable system (as defined in section 111(f)).

(9) performance on a single occasion of a dramatic literary work published at least ten years before the date of the performance, by or in the course of a transmission specifically designed for and primarily directed to blind or other handicapped persons who are unable to read normal printed material as a result of their handicap, if the performance is made without any purpose of direct or indirect commercial advantage and its transmission is made through the facilities of a radio subcarrier authorization referred to in clause (8)(iii), *Provided,* That the provisions of this clause shall not be applicable to more than one performance of the same work by the same performers or under the auspices of the same organization.

(10)[4] notwithstanding paragraph 4 above, the following is not an infringement of copyright: performance of a nondramatic literary or musical work in the course of a social function which is organized and promoted by a nonprofit veterans' organization or a nonprofit fraternal organization to which the general public is not invited, but not including the invitees of the organizations, if the proceeds from the performance, after deducting the reasonable costs of producing the performance, are used exclusively for charitable purposes and not for financial gain. For purposes of this section the social functions of any college or university fraternity or sorority shall not be included unless the social function is held solely to raise funds for a specific charitable purpose.

Sec. 111. Limitations on Exclusive Rights: Secondary Transmissions

(a) Certain Secondary Transmissions Exempted. The secondary transmission of a primary transmission embodying a performance or display of a work is not an infringement of copyright if—

(1) the secondary transmission is not made by a cable system, and consists entirely of the relaying, by the management of a hotel, apartment house, or similar establishment, of signals transmitted by a broadcast station licensed by the Federal Communications Commission, within the local service area of such station, to the private lodgings of guests or residents of such establishment, and no direct charge is made to see or hear the secondary transmission; or

(2) the secondary transmission is made solely for the purpose and under the conditions specified by clause (2) of section 110; or

(3) the secondary transmission is made by any carrier who has no direct or indirect control over the content or selection of the primary transmission or over the particular recipients of the secondary transmission, and whose activities with respect to the secondary transmission consist solely of providing wires, cables, or other communications channels for the use of others: *Provided,* That the provisions of this clause extend only to the activities of said carrier with respect to secondary transmissions and do not exempt from liability the activities of others with respect to their own primary or secondary transmissions; or

(4) the secondary transmission is not made by a cable system but is made by a governmental body, or other nonprofit organization, without any purpose of direct or indirect commercial advantage, and without charge to the recipients of the secondary transmission other than assessments necessary to defray the actual and reasonable costs of maintaining and operating the secondary transmission service.

(b) Secondary Transmission of Primary Transmission to Controlled Group. Notwithstanding the provisions of subsections (a) and (c), the secondary transmission to the public of a primary transmission

---

4. Section 110(10) was added by Pub.L. 97–366, 96 Stat. 1759, effective November 24, 1982.

embodying a performance or display of a work is actionable as an act of infringement under section 501, and is fully subject to the remedies provided by sections 502 through 506 and 509, if the primary transmission is not made for reception by the public at large but is controlled and limited to reception by particular members of the public: *Provided,* however, That such secondary transmission is not actionable as an act of infringement if—

(1) the primary transmission is made by a broadcast station licensed by the Federal Communications Commission; and

(2) the carriage of the signals comprising the secondary transmission is required under the rules, regulations, or authorizations of the Federal Communications Commission; and

(3) the signal of the primary transmitter is not altered or changed in any way by the secondary transmitter.

(c) Secondary Transmissions by Cable Systems.

(1) Subject to the provisions of clauses (2), (3), and (4) of this subsection, secondary transmissions to the public by a cable system of a primary transmission made by a broadcast station licensed by the Federal Communications Commission or by an appropriate governmental authority of Canada or Mexico and embodying a performance or display of a work shall be subject to compulsory licensing upon compliance with the requirements of subsection (d) where the carriage of the signals comprising the secondary transmission is permissible under the rules, regulations, or authorizations of the Federal Communications Commission.

(2) Notwithstanding the provisions of clause (1) of this subsection, the willful or repeated secondary transmission to the public by a cable system of a primary transmission made by a broadcast station licensed by the Federal Communications Commission or by an appropriate governmental authority of Canada or Mexico and embodying a performance or display of a work is actionable as an act of infringement under section 501, and is fully subject to the remedies provided by sections 502 through 506 and 509, in the following cases:

(A) where the carriage of the signals comprising the secondary transmission is not permissible under the rules, regulations, or authorizations of the Federal Communications Commission; or

(B) where the cable system has not recorded the notice specified by subsection (d) and deposited the statement of account and royalty fee required by subsection (d).

(3) Notwithstanding the provisions of clause (1) of this subsection and subject to the provisions of subsection (e) of this section, the secondary transmission to the public by a cable system of a primary transmission made by a broadcast station licensed by the Federal Communications Commission or by an appropriate governmental authority of Canada or Mexico and embodying a performance or display of a work is actionable as an act of infringement under section 501, and is

fully subject to the remedies provided by sections 502 through 506 and sections 509 and 510, if the content of the particular program in which the performance or display is embodied, or any commercial advertising or station announcements transmitted by the primary transmitter during, or immediately before or after, the transmission of such program, is in any way willfully altered by the cable system through changes, deletions, or additions, except for the alteration, deletion, or substitution of commercial advertisements performed by those engaged in television commercial advertising market research: *Provided,* That the research company has obtained the prior consent of the advertiser who has purchased the original commercial advertisement, the television station broadcasting that commercial advertisement, and the cable system performing the secondary transmission: *And provided further,* That such commercial alteration, deletion, or substitution is not performed for the purpose of deriving income from the sale of that commercial time.

(4) Notwithstanding the provisions of clause (1) of this subsection, the secondary transmission to the public by a cable system of a primary transmission made by a broadcast station licensed by an appropriate governmental authority of Canada or Mexico and embodying a performance or display of a work is actionable as an act of infringement under section 501, and is fully subject to the remedies provided by sections 502 through 506 and section 509, if (A) with respect to Canadian signals, the community of the cable system is located more than 150 miles from the United States-Canadian border and is also located south of the forty-second parallel of latitude, or (B) with respect to Mexican signals, the secondary transmission is made by a cable system which received the primary transmission by means other than direct interception of a free space radio wave emitted by such broadcast television station, unless prior to April 15, 1976, such cable system was actually carrying, or was specifically authorized to carry, the signal of such foreign station on the system pursuant to the rules, regulations, or authorizations of the Federal Communications Commission.

(d) Compulsory License for Secondary Transmissions by Cable Systems.

(1) For any secondary transmission to be subject to compulsory licensing under subsection (c), the cable system shall, at least one month before the date of the commencement of operations of the cable system or within one hundred and eighty days after the enactment of this Act, whichever is later, and thereafter within thirty days after each occasion on which the ownership or control or the signal carriage complement of the cable system changes, record in the Copyright Office a notice including a statement of the identity and address of the person who owns or operates the secondary transmission service or has power to exercise primary control over it, together with the name and location of the primary transmitter or primary transmitters whose signals are regularly carried by the cable system, and thereafter, from time to time, such further information as the Register of Copyrights, after

consultation with the Copyright Royalty Tribunal (if and when the Tribunal has been constituted), shall prescribe by regulation to carry out the purpose of this clause.

(2) A cable system whose secondary transmissions have been subject to compulsory licensing under subsection (c) shall, on a semiannual basis, deposit with the Register of Copyrights, in accordance with requirements that the Register shall, after consultation with the Copyright Royalty Tribunal (if and when the Tribunal has been constituted), prescribe by regulation—

(A) a statement of account, covering the six months next preceding, specifying the number of channels on which the cable system made secondary transmissions to its subscribers, the names and locations of all primary transmitters whose transmissions were further transmitted by the cable system, the total number of subscribers, the gross amounts paid to the cable system for the basic service of providing secondary transmissions of primary broadcast transmitters, and such other data as the Register of Copyrights may, after consultation with the Copyright Royalty Tribunal (if and when the Tribunal has been constituted), from time to time prescribe by regulation. Such statement shall also include a special statement of account covering any nonnetwork television programming that was carried by the cable system in whole or in part beyond the local service area of the primary transmitter, under rules, regulations, or authorizations of the Federal Communications Commission permitting the substitution or addition of signals under certain circumstances, together with logs showing the times, dates, stations, and programs involved in such substituted or added carriage; and

(B) except in the case of a cable system whose royalty is specified in subclause (C) or (D), a total royalty fee for the period covered by the statement, computed on the basis of specified percentages of the gross receipts from subscribers to the cable service during said period for the basic service of providing secondary transmissions of primary broadcast transmitters, as follows:

(i) 0.675 of 1 per centum of such gross receipts for the privilege of further transmitting any nonnetwork programming of a primary transmitter in whole or in part beyond the local service area of such primary transmitter, such amount to be applied against the fee, if any, payable pursuant to paragraphs (ii) through (iv);

(ii) 0.675 of 1 per centum of such gross receipts for the first distant signal equivalent;

(iii) 0.425 of 1 per centum of such gross receipts for each of the second, third, and fourth distant signal equivalents;

(iv) 0.2 of 1 per centum of such gross receipts for the fifth distant signal equivalent and each additional distant signal equivalent thereafter; and in computing the amounts payable under paragraph (ii) through (iv), above, any fraction of a distant signal equivalent shall be computed at its fractional value and, in the case of any cable system located partly within and partly without the local service area of a primary transmitter, gross receipts shall be limited to those gross receipts derived from subscribers located without the local service area of such primary transmitter; and

(C) if the actual gross receipts paid by subscribers to a cable system for the period covered by the statement for the basic service of providing secondary transmissions of primary broadcast transmitters total $80,000 or less, gross receipts of the cable system for the purpose of this subclause shall be computed by subtracting from such actual gross receipts the amount by which $80,000 exceeds such actual gross receipts, except that in no case shall a cable system's gross receipts be reduced to less than $3,000. The royalty fee payable under this subclause shall be 0.5 of 1 per centum, regardless of the number of distant signal equivalents, if any; and

(D) if the actual gross receipts paid by subscribers to a cable system for the period covered by the statement, for the basic service of providing secondary transmissions of primary broadcast transmitters, are more than $80,000 but less than $160,000, the royalty fee payable under this subclause shall be (i) 0.5 of 1 per centum of any gross receipts up to $80,000; and (ii) 1 per centum of any gross receipts in excess of $80,000 but less than $160,000, regardless of the number of distant signal equivalents, if any.

(3) The Register of Copyrights shall receive all fees deposited under this section and, after deducting the reasonable costs incurred by the Copyright Office under this section, shall deposit the balance in the Treasury of the United States, in such manner as the Secretary of the Treasury directs. All funds held by the Secretary of the Treasury shall be invested in interest-bearing United States securities for later distribution with interest by the Copyright Royalty Tribunal as provided by this title. The Register shall submit to the Copyright Royalty Tribunal, on a semi-annual basis, a compilation of all statements of account covering the relevant six-month period provided by clause (2) of this subsection.

(4) The royalty fees thus deposited shall, in accordance with the procedures provided by clause (5), be distributed to those among the following copyright owners who claim that their works were the subject of secondary transmissions by cable systems during the relevant semi-annual period:

(A) any such owner whose work was included in a secondary transmission made by a cable system of a nonnetwork television program in whole or in part beyond the local service area of the primary transmitter; and

(B) any such owner whose work was included in a secondary transmission identified in a special statement of account deposited under clause (2)(A); and

(C) any such owner whose work was included in nonnetwork programming consisting exclusively of aural signals carried by a cable system in whole or in part beyond the local service area of the primary transmitter of such programs.

(5) The royalty fees thus deposited shall be distributed in accordance with the following procedures:

(A) During the month of July in each year, every person claiming to be entitled to compulsory license fees for secondary transmissions shall file a claim with the Copyright Royalty Tribunal, in accordance with requirements that the Tribunal shall prescribe by regulation. Notwithstanding any provisions of the antitrust laws, for purposes of this clause any claimants may agree among themselves as to the proportionate division of compulsory licensing fees among them, may lump their claims together and file them jointly or as a single claim, or may designate a common agent to receive payment on their behalf.

(B) After the first day of August of each year, the Copyright Royalty Tribunal shall determine whether there exists a controversy concerning the distribution of royalty fees. If the Tribunal determines that no such controversy exists, it shall, after deducting its reasonable administrative costs under this section, distribute such fees to the copyright owners entitled, or to their designated agents. If the Tribunal finds the existence of a controversy, it shall, pursuant to chapter 8 of this title, conduct a proceeding to determine the distribution of royalty fees.

(C) During the pendency of any proceeding under this subsection, the Copyright Royalty Tribunal shall withhold from distribution an amount sufficient to satisfy all claims with respect to which a controversy exists, but shall have discretion to proceed to distribute any amounts that are not in controversy.

(e) **Nonsimultaneous Secondary Transmissions by Cable Systems.**

(1) Notwithstanding those provisions of the second paragraph of subsection (f) relating to nonsimultaneous secondary transmissions by a cable system, any such transmissions are actionable as an act of infringement under section 501, and are fully subject to the remedies provided by sections 502 through 506 and sections 509 and 510, unless—

(A) the program on the videotape is transmitted no more than one time to the cable system's subscribers; and

(B) the copyrighted program, episode, or motion picture videotape, including the commercials contained within such program, episode, or picture, is transmitted without deletion or editing; and

(C) an owner or officer of the cable system (i) prevents the duplication of the videotape while in the possession of the system, (ii) prevents unauthorized duplication while in the possession of the facility making the videotape for the system if the system owns or controls the facility, or takes reasonable precautions to prevent such duplication if it does not own or control the facility, (iii) takes adequate precautions to prevent duplication while the tape is being transported, and (iv) subject to clause (2), erases or destroys, or causes the erasure or destruction of, the videotape; and

(D) within forty-five days after the end of each calendar quarter, an owner or officer of the cable system executes an affidavit attesting (i) to the steps and precautions taken to prevent duplication of the videotape, and (ii) subject to clause (2), to the erasure or destruction of all videotapes made or used during such quarter; and

(E) such owner or officer places or causes each such affidavit, and affidavits received pursuant to clause (2)(C), to be placed in a file, open to public inspection, at such system's main office in the community where the transmission is made or in the nearest community where such system maintains an office; and

(F) the nonsimultaneous transmission is one that the cable system would be authorized to transmit under the rules, regulations, and authorizations of the Federal Communications Commission in effect at the time of the nonsimultaneous transmission if the transmission had been made simultaneously, except that this subclause shall not apply to inadvertent or accidental transmissions.

(2) If a cable system transfers to any person a videotape of a program nonsimultaneously transmitted by it, such transfer is actionable as an act of infringement under section 501, and is fully subject to the remedies provided by sections 502 through 506 and 509, except that, pursuant to a written, nonprofit contract providing for the equitable sharing of the costs of such videotape and its transfer, a videotape nonsimultaneously transmitted by it, in accordance with clause (1), may be transferred by one cable system in Alaska to another system in Alaska, by one cable system in Hawaii permitted to make such nonsimultaneous transmissions to another such cable system in Hawaii, or by one cable system in Guam, the Northern Mariana Islands, or the Trust Territory of the Pacific Islands, to another cable system in any of those three territories, if—

(A) each such contract is available for public inspection in the offices of the cable systems involved, and a copy of such contract is filed, within thirty days after such contract is entered into, with the Copyright Office (which Office shall make each such contract available for public inspection); and

(B) the cable system to which the videotape is transferred complies with clause (1)(A), (B), (C)(i), (iii), and (iv), and (D) through (F); and

(C) such system provides a copy of the affidavit required to be made in accordance with clause (1)(D) to each cable system making a previous nonsimultaneous transmission of the same videotape.

(3) This subsection shall not be construed to supersede the exclusivity protection provisions of any existing agreement, or any such agreement hereafter entered into, between a cable system and a television broadcast station in the area in which the cable system is located, or a network with which such station is affiliated.

(4) As used in this subsection, the term "videotape", and each of its variant forms, means the reproduction of the images and sounds of a program or programs broadcast by a television broadcast station licensed by the Federal Communications Commission, regardless of the nature of the material objects, such as tapes or films, in which the reproduction is embodied.

(f) Definitions. As used in this section, the following terms and their variant forms mean the following:

A "primary transmission" is a transmission made to the public by the transmitting facility whose signals are being received and further transmitted by the secondary transmission service, regardless of where or when the performance or display was first transmitted.

A "secondary transmission" is the further transmitting of a primary transmission simultaneously with the primary transmission, or nonsimultaneously with the primary transmission if by a "cable system" not located in whole or in part within the boundary of the forty-eight contiguous States, Hawaii, or Puerto Rico: *Provided, however,* That a nonsimultaneous further transmission by a cable system located in Hawaii of a primary transmission shall be deemed to be a secondary transmission if the carriage of the television broadcast signal comprising such further transmission is permissible under the rules, regulations, or authorizations of the Federal Communications Commission.

A "cable system" is a facility, located in any State, Territory, Trust Territory, or Possession, that in whole or in part receives signals transmitted or programs broadcast by one or more television broadcast stations licensed by the Federal Communications Commission, and makes secondary transmissions of such signals or programs by wires, cables, or other communications channels to subscribing members of the public who pay for such service. For purposes of determining the royalty fee under subsection (d)(2), two or more cable systems in contiguous communities under common ownership or control or operating from one headend shall be considered as one system.

The "local service area of a primary transmitter", in the case of a television broadcast station, comprises the area in which such station is entitled to insist upon its signal being retransmitted by a cable system pursuant to the rules, regulations, and authorizations of the Federal Communications Commission in effect on April 15, 1976, or in the case of a television broadcast station licensed by an appropriate governmental authority of Canada or Mexico, the area in which it would be entitled to insist upon its signal being retransmitted if it were a television broadcast station subject to such rules, regulations, and authorizations. The "local service area of a primary transmitter", in the case of a radio broadcast station, comprises the primary service area of such station, pursuant to the rules and regulations of the Federal Communications Commission.

A "distant signal equivalent" is the value assigned to the secondary transmission of any nonnetwork television programing carried by a cable system in whole or in part beyond the local service area of the primary transmitter of such programing. It is computed by assigning a value of one to each independent station and a value of one-quarter to each network station and noncommercial educational station for the nonnetwork programing so carried pursuant to the rules, regulations, and authorizations of the Federal Communications Commission. The foregoing values for independent, network, and noncommercial educational stations are subject, however, to the following exceptions and limitations. Where the rules and regulations of the Federal Communications Commission require a cable system to omit the further transmission of a particular program and such rules and regulations also permit the substitution of another program embodying a performance or display of a work in place of the omitted transmission, or where such rules and regulations in effect on the date of enactment of this Act permit a cable system, at its election, to effect such deletion and substitution of a nonlive program or to carry additional programs not transmitted by primary transmitters within whose local service area the cable system is located, no value shall be assigned for the substituted or additional program; where the rules, regulations, or authorizations of the Federal Communications Commission in effect on the date of enactment of this Act permit a cable system, at its election, to omit the further transmission of a particular program and such rules, regulations, or authorizations also permit the substitution of another program embodying a performance or display of a work in place of the omitted transmission, the value assigned for the substituted or additional program shall be, in the case of a live program, the value of one full distant signal equivalent multiplied by a fraction that has as its numerator the number of days in the year in which such substitution occurs and as its denominator the number of days in the year. In the case of a station carried pursuant to the late-night or specialty programing rules of the Federal Communications Commission, or a station carried on a part-time basis where full-time carriage is not possible because the cable system lacks the activated channel capacity to retransmit on a full-time basis all signals which it is authorized to carry, the values for independent, network, and noncommercial educational stations set forth above, as the case may be, shall be multiplied by a fraction which is equal to the ratio of the broadcast hours of such station carried by the cable system to the total broadcast hours of the station.

A "network station" is a television broadcast station that is owned or operated by, or affiliated with, one or more of the television networks in the United States providing nationwide transmissions, and that transmits a substantial part of the programing supplied by such networks for a substantial part of that station's typical broadcast day.

An "independent station" is a commercial television broadcast station other than a network station.

A "noncommercial educational station" is a television station that is a noncommercial educational broadcast station as defined in section 397 of title 47.

Sec. 112. Limitations on Exclusive Rights: Ephemeral Recordings

(a) Notwithstanding the provisions of section 106, and except in the case of a motion picture or other audiovisual work, it is not an infringement of copyright for a transmitting organization entitled to transmit to the public a performance or display of a work, under a license or transfer of the copyright or under the limitations on exclusive rights in sound recordings specified by section 114(a), to make no more than one copy or phonorecord of a particular transmission program embodying the performance or display, if—

(1) the copy or phonorecord is retained and used solely by the transmitting organization that made it, and no further copies or phonorecords are reproduced from it; and

(2) the copy or phonorecord is used solely for the transmitting organization's own transmissions within its local service area, or for purposes of archival preservation or security; and

(3) unless preserved exclusively for archival purposes, the copy or phonorecord is destroyed within six months from the date the transmission program was first transmitted to the public.

(b) Notwithstanding the provisions of section 106, it is not an infringement of copyright for a governmental body or other nonprofit organization entitled to transmit a performance or display of a work, under section 110(2) or under the limitations on exclusive rights in sound recordings specified by section 114(a), to make no more than thirty copies or phonorecords of a particular transmission program embodying the performance or display, if—

(1) no further copies or phonorecords are reproduced from the copies or phonorecords made under this clause; and

(2) except for one copy or phonorecord that may be preserved exclusively for archival purposes, the copies or phonorecords are destroyed within seven years from the date the transmission program was first transmitted to the public.

(c) Notwithstanding the provisions of section 106, it is not an infringement of copyright for a governmental body or other nonprofit organization to make for distribution no more than one copy or phonorecord, for each transmitting organization specified in clause (2) of this subsection, of a particular transmission program embodying a performance of a nondramatic musical work of a religious nature, or of a sound recording of such a musical work, if—

(1) there is no direct or indirect charge for making or distributing any such copies or phonorecords; and

(2) none of such copies or phonorecords is used for any performance other than a single transmission to the public by a transmitting organization entitled to transmit to the public a performance of the work under a license or transfer of the copyright; and

(3) except for one copy or phonorecord that may be preserved exclusively for archival purposes, the copies or phonorecords are all destroyed within one year from the date the transmission program was first transmitted to the public.

(d) Notwithstanding the provisions of section 106, it is not an infringement of copyright for a governmental body or other nonprofit organization entitled to transmit a performance of a work under section 110(8) to make no more than ten copies or phonorecords embodying the performance, or to permit the use of any such copy or phonorecord by any governmental body or nonprofit organization entitled to transmit a performance of a work under section 110(8), if—

(1) any such copy or phonorecord is retained and used solely by the organization that made it, or by a governmental body or nonprofit organization entitled to transmit a performance of a work under section 110(8), and no further copies or phonorecords are reproduced from it; and

(2) any such copy or phonorecord is used solely for transmissions authorized under section 110(8), or for purposes of archival preservation or security; and

(3) the governmental body or nonprofit organization permitting any use of any such copy or phonorecord by any governmental body or nonprofit organization under this subsection does not make any charge for such use.

(e) The transmission program embodied in a copy or phonorecord made under this section is not subject to protection as a derivative work under this title except with the express consent of the owners of copyright in the preexisting works employed in the program.

Sec. 113. Scope of Exclusive Rights in Pictorial, Graphic, and Sculptural Works

(a) Subject to the provisions of subsections (b) and (c) of this section, the exclusive right to reproduce a copyrighted pictorial, graphic, or sculptural work in copies under section 106 includes the right to reproduce the work in or on any kind of article, whether useful or otherwise.

(b) This title does not afford, to the owner of copyright in a work that portrays a useful article as such, any greater or lesser rights with respect to the making, distribution, or display of the useful article so portrayed than those afforded to such works under the law, whether title 17 or the common law or statutes of a State, in effect on December 31, 1977, as held applicable and construed by a court in an action brought under this title.

(c) In the case of a work lawfully reproduced in useful articles that have been offered for sale or other distribution to the public, copyright does not include any right to prevent the making, distribution, or display of pictures or photographs of such articles in connection with advertisements or commentaries related to the distribution or display of such articles, or in connection with news reports.

Sec. 114. Scope of Exclusive Rights in Sound Recordings

(a) The exclusive rights of the owner of copyright in a sound recording are limited to the rights specified by clauses (1), (2), and (3) of section 106, and do not include any right of performance under section 106(4).

(b) The exclusive right of the owner of copyright in a sound recording under clause (1) of section 106 is limited to the right to duplicate the sound recording in the form of phonorecords, or of copies of motion pictures and other audiovisual works, that directly or indirectly recapture the actual sounds fixed in the recording. The exclusive right of the owner of copyright in a sound recording under clause (2) of section 106 is limited to the right to prepare a derivative work in which the actual sounds fixed in the sound recording are rearranged, remixed, or otherwise altered in sequence or quality. The exclusive rights of the owner of copyright in a sound recording under clauses (1) and (2) of section 106 do not extend to the making or duplication of another sound recording that consists entirely of an independent fixation of other sounds, even though such sounds imitate or simulate those in the copyrighted sound recording. The exclusive rights of the owner of copyright in a sound recording under clauses (1), (2), and (3) of section 106 do not apply to sound recordings included in educational television and radio programs (as defined in section 397 of title 47) distributed or transmitted by or through public broadcasting entities (as defined by section 118(g)): *Provided*, That copies or phonorecords of said programs are not commercially distributed by or through public broadcasting entities to the general public.

(c) This section does not limit or impair the exclusive right to perform publicly, by means of a phonorecord, any of the works specified by section 106(4).

(d) On January 3, 1978, the Register of Copyrights, after consulting with representatives of owners of copyrighted materials, representatives of the broadcasting, recording, motion picture, entertainment industries, and arts organizations, representatives of organized labor and performers of copyrighted materials, shall submit to the Congress a report setting forth recommendations as to whether this section should be amended to provide for performers and copyright owners of copyrighted material any performance rights in such material. The report should describe the status of such rights in foreign countries, the views of major interested parties, and specific legislative or other recommendations, if any.

Sec. 115. Scope of Exclusive Rights in Nondramatic Musical Works: Compulsory License for Making and Distributing Phonorecords

In the case of nondramatic musical works, the exclusive rights provided by clauses (1) and (3) of section 106, to make and to distribute phonorecords of such works, are subject to compulsory licensing under the conditions specified by this section.

(a) Availability and Scope of Compulsory License.

(1) When phonorecords of a nondramatic musical work have been distributed to the public in the United States under the authority of the copyright owner, any other person may, by complying with the provisions of this section, obtain a compulsory license to make and distribute phonorecords of the work. A person may obtain a compulsory license only if his or her primary purpose in making phonorecords is to distribute them to the public for private use. A person may not obtain a compulsory license for use of the work in the making of phonorecords duplicating a sound recording fixed by another, unless: (i) such sound recording was fixed lawfully; and (ii) the making of the phonorecords was authorized by the owner of copyright in the sound recording or, if the sound recording was fixed before February 15, 1972, by any person who fixed the sound recording pursuant to an express license from the owner of the copyright in the musical work or pursuant to a valid compulsory license for use of such work in a sound recording.

(2) A compulsory license includes the privilege of making a musical arrangement of the work to the extent necessary to conform it to the style or manner of interpretation of the performance involved, but the arrangement shall not change the basic melody or fundamental character of the work, and shall not be subject to protection as a derivative work under this title, except with the express consent of the copyright owner.

(b) Notice of Intention To Obtain Compulsory License.

(1) Any person who wishes to obtain a compulsory license under this section shall, before or within thirty days after making, and before distributing any phonorecords of the work, serve notice of intention to do so on the copyright owner. If the registration or other public records of the Copyright Office do not identify the copyright owner and include an address at which notice can be served, it shall be sufficient

to file the notice of intention in the Copyright Office. The notice shall comply, in form, content, and manner of service, with requirements that the Register of Copyrights shall prescribe by regulation.

(2) Failure to serve or file the notice required by clause (1) forecloses the possibility of a compulsory license and, in the absence of a negotiated license, renders the making and distribution of phonorecords actionable as acts of infringement under section 501 and fully subject to the remedies provided by sections 502 through 506 and 509.

(c) Royalty Payable Under Compulsory License.

(1) To be entitled to receive royalties under a compulsory license, the copyright owner must be identified in the registration or other public records of the Copyright Office. The owner is entitled to royalties for phonorecords made and distributed after being so identified, but is not entitled to recover for any phonorecords previously made and distributed.

(2) Except as provided by clause (1), the royalty under a compulsory license shall be payable for every phonorecord made and distributed in accordance with the license. For this purpose, a phonorecord is considered "distributed" if the person exercising the compulsory license has voluntarily and permanently parted with its possession. With respect to each work embodied in the phonorecord, the royalty shall be either two and three-fourths cents, or one-half of one cent per minute of playing time or fraction thereof, whichever amount is larger.

(3) A compulsory license under this section includes the right of the maker of a phonorecord of a nondramatic musical work under subsection (a)(1) to distribute or authorize distribution of such phonorecord by rental, lease, or lending (or by acts or practices in the nature of rental, lease, or lending). In addition to any royalty payable under clause (2) and chapter 8 of this title, a royalty shall be payable by the compulsory licensee for every act of distribution of a phonorecord by or in the nature of rental, lease, or lending, by or under the authority of the compulsory licensee. With respect to each nondramatic musical work embodied in the phonorecord, the royalty shall be a proportion of the revenue received by the compulsory licensee from every such act of distribution of the phonorecord under this clause equal to the proportion of the revenue received by the compulsory licensee from distribution of the phonorecord under clause (2) that is payable by a compulsory licensee under that clause and under chapter 8. The Register of Copyrights shall issue regulations to carry out the purpose of this clause.[5]

(4) Royalty payments shall be made on or before the twentieth day of each month and shall include all royalties for the month next preceding. Each monthly payment shall be made under oath and shall

---

5. Section 115(c)(3) as amended by the Act of October 4, 1984, Pub.L. 98–450 (98 Stat. 1727). See footnote 3, p. 905 supra.

comply with requirements that the Register of Copyrights shall prescribe by regulation. The Register shall also prescribe regulations under which detailed cumulative annual statements of account, certified by a certified public accountant, shall be filed for every compulsory license under this section. The regulations covering both the monthly and the annual statements of account shall prescribe the form, content, and manner of certification with respect to the number of records made and the number of records distributed.

(5) If the copyright owner does not receive the monthly payment and the monthly and annual statements of account when due, the owner may give written notice to the licensee that, unless the default is remedied within thirty days from the date of the notice, the compulsory license will be automatically terminated. Such termination renders either the making or the distribution, or both, of all phonorecords for which the royalty has not been paid, actionable as acts of infringement under section 501 and fully subject to the remedies provided by sections 502 through 506 and 509.

Sec. 116. Scope of Exclusive Rights in Nondramatic Musical Works: Public Performances by Means of Coin-operated Phonorecord Players

(a) Limitation on Exclusive Right. In the case of a nondramatic musical work embodied in a phonorecord, the exclusive right under clause (4) of section 106 to perform the work publicly by means of a coin-operated phonorecord player is limited as follows:

(1) The proprietor of the establishment in which the public performance takes place is not liable for infringement with respect to such public performance unless—

(A) such proprietor is the operator of the phonorecord player; or

(B) such proprietor refuses or fails, within one month after receipt by registered or certified mail of a request, at a time during which the certificate required by clause (1)(C) of subsection (b) is not affixed to the phonorecord player, by the copyright owner, to make full disclosure, by registered or certified mail, of the identity of the operator of the phonorecord player.

(2) The operator of the coin-operated phonorecord player may obtain a compulsory license to perform the work publicly on that phonorecord player by filing the application, affixing the certificate, and paying the royalties provided by subsection (b).

(b) Recordation of Coin-Operated Phonorecord Player, Affixation of Certificate, and Royalty Payable Under Compulsory License.

(1) Any operator who wishes to obtain a compulsory license for the public performance of works on a coin-operated phonorecord player shall fulfill the following requirements:

(A) Before or within one month after such performances are made available on a particular phonorecord player, and during the month of January in each succeeding year that such performances are made available on that particular phonorecord player, the operator shall file in the Copyright Office, in accordance with requirements that the Register of Copyrights, after consultation with the Copyright Royalty Tribunal (if and when the Tribunal has been constituted), shall prescribe by regulation, an application containing the name and address of the operator of the phonorecord player and the manufacturer and serial number or other explicit identification of the phonorecord player, and deposit with the Register of Copyrights a royalty fee for the current calendar year of $8 for that particular phonorecord player. If such performances are made available on a particular phonorecord player for the first time after July 1 of any year, the royalty fee to be deposited for the remainder of that year shall be $4.

(B) Within twenty days of receipt of an application and a royalty fee pursuant to subclause (A), the Register of Copyrights shall issue to the applicant a certificate for the phonorecord player.

(C) On or before March 1 of the year in which the certificate prescribed by subclause (B) of this clause is issued, or within ten days after the date of issue of the certificate, the operator shall affix to the particular phonorecord player, in a position where it can be readily examined by the public, the certificate, issued by the Register of Copyrights under subclause (B), of the latest application made by such operator under subclause (A) of this clause with respect to that phonorecord player.

(2) Failure to file the application, to affix the certificate, or to pay the royalty required by clause (1) of this subsection renders the public performance actionable as an act of infringement under section 501 and fully subject to the remedies provided by sections 502 through 506 and 509.

(c) Distribution of Royalties.

(1) The Register of Copyrights shall receive all fees deposited under this section and, after deducting the reasonable costs incurred by the Copyright Office under this section, shall deposit the balance in the Treasury of the United States, in such manner as the Secretary of the Treasury directs. All funds held by the Secretary of the Treasury shall be invested in interest-bearing United States securities for later distribution with interest by the Copyright Royalty Tribunal as provided by this title. The Register shall submit to the Copyright Royalty Tribunal, on an annual basis, a detailed statement of account covering all fees received for the relevant period provided by subsection (b).

(2) During the month of January in each year, every person claiming to be entitled to compulsory license fees under this section for performances during the preceding twelve-month period shall file a claim with the Copyright Royalty Tribunal, in accordance with requirements that the Tribunal shall prescribe by regulation. Such claim

shall include an agreement to accept as final, except as provided in section 810 of this title, the determination of the Copyright Royalty Tribunal in any controversy concerning the distribution of royalty fees deposited under subclause (A) of subsection (b)(1) of this section to which the claimant is a party. Notwithstanding any provisions of the antitrust laws, for purposes of this subsection any claimants may agree among themselves as to the proportionate division of compulsory licensing fees among them, may lump their claims together and file them jointly or as a single claim, or may designate a common agent to receive payment on their behalf.

(3) After the first day of October of each year, the Copyright Royalty Tribunal shall determine whether there exists a controversy concerning the distribution of royalty fees deposited under subclause (A) of subsection (b)(1). If the Tribunal determines that no such controversy exists, it shall, after deducting its reasonable administrative costs under this section, distribute such fees to the copyright owners entitled, or to their designated agents. If it finds that such a controversy exists, it shall, pursuant to chapter 8 of this title, conduct a proceeding to determine the distribution of royalty fees.

(4) The fees to be distributed shall be divided as follows:

(A) to every copyright owner not affiliated with a performing rights society, the pro rata share of the fees to be distributed to which such copyright owner proves entitlement.

(B) to the performing rights societies, the remainder of the fees to be distributed in such pro rata shares as they shall by agreement stipulate among themselves, or, if they fail to agree, the pro rata share to which such performing rights societies prove entitlement.

(C) during the pendency of any proceeding under this section, the Copyright Royalty Tribunal shall withhold from distribution an amount sufficient to satisfy all claims with respect to which a controversy exists, but shall have discretion to proceed to distribute any amounts that are not in controversy.

(5) The Copyright Royalty Tribunal shall promulgate regulations under which persons who can reasonably be expected to have claims may, during the year in which performances take place, without expense to or harassment of operators or proprietors of establishments in which phonorecord players are located, have such access to such establishments and to the phonorecord players located therein and such opportunity to obtain information with respect thereto as may be reasonably necessary to determine, by sampling procedures or otherwise, the proportion of contribution of the musical works of each such person to the earnings of the phonorecord players for which fees shall have been deposited. Any person who alleges that he or she has been denied the access permitted under the regulations prescribed by the Copyright Royalty Tribunal may bring an action in the United States District Court for the District of Columbia for the cancellation of the compulsory license of the phonorecord player to which such access has

been denied, and the court shall have the power to declare the compulsory license thereof invalid from the date of issue thereof.

(d) Criminal Penalties. Any person who knowingly makes a false representation of a material fact in an application filed under clause (1)(A) of subsection (b), or who knowingly alters a certificate issued under clause (1)(B) of subsection (b) or knowingly affixes such a certificate to a phonorecord player other than the one it covers, shall be fined not more than $2,500.

(e) Definitions. As used in this section, the following terms and their variant forms mean the following:

(1) A "coin-operated phonorecord player" is a machine or device that—

(A) is employed solely for the performance of nondramatic musical works by means of phonorecords upon being activated by insertion of coins, currency, tokens, or other monetary units or their equivalent;

(B) is located in an establishment making no direct or indirect charge for admission;

(C) is accompanied by a list of the titles of all the musical works available for performance on it, which list is affixed to the phonorecord player or posted in the establishment in a prominent position where it can be readily examined by the public; and

(D) affords a choice of works available for performance and permits the choice to be made by the patrons of the establishment in which it is located.

(2) An "operator" is any person who, alone or jointly with others:

(A) owns a coin-operated phonorecord player; or

(B) has the power to make a coin-operated phonorecord player available for placement in an establishment for purposes of public performance; or

(C) has the power to exercise primary control over the selection of the musical works made available for public performance on a coin-operated phonorecord player.

(3) A "performing rights society" is an association or corporation that licenses the public performance of nondramatic musical works on behalf of the copyright owners, such as the American Society of Composers, Authors and Publishers, Broadcast Music, Inc., and SESAC, Inc.

Sec. 117. Limitations on Exclusive Rights: Computer Programs

Notwithstanding the provisions of § 106, it is not an infringement for the owner of a copy of a computer program to make or authorize the making of another copy or adaptation of that computer program provided:

(1) that such a new copy or adaptation is created as an essential step in the utilization of the computer program in conjunction with a machine and that it is used in no other manner, or

(2) that such new copy or adaptation is for archival purposes only and that all archival copies are destroyed in the event that continued possession of the computer program should cease to be rightful.

Any exact copies prepared in accordance with the provisions of this section may be leased, sold, or otherwise transferred, along with the copy from which such copies were prepared, only as part of the lease, sale, or other transfer of all rights in the program. Adaptations so prepared may be transferred only with the authorization of the copyright owner.[6]

Sec. 118. Scope of Exclusive Rights: Use of Certain Works in Connection With Noncommercial Broadcasting

(a) The exclusive rights provided by section 106 shall, with respect to the works specified by subsection (b) and the activities specified by subsection (d), be subject to the conditions and limitations prescribed by this section.

(b) Not later than thirty days after the Copyright Royalty Tribunal has been constituted in accordance with section 802, the Chairman of the Tribunal shall cause notice to be published in the Federal Register of the initiation of proceedings for the purpose of determining reasonable terms and rates of royalty payments for the activities specified by subsection (d) with respect to published nondramatic musical works and published pictorial, graphic, and sculptural works during a period beginning as provided in clause (3) of this subsection and ending on December 31, 1982. Copyright owners and public broadcasting entities shall negotiate in good faith and cooperate fully with the Tribunal in an effort to reach reasonable and expeditious results. Notwithstanding any provision of the antitrust laws, any owners of copyright in works specified by this subsection and any public broadcasting entities, respectively, may negotiate and agree upon the terms and rates of royalty payments and the proportionate division of fees paid among various copyright owners, and may designate common agents to negotiate, agree to, pay, or receive payments.

---

6. Section 117 as amended by the Act of December 12, 1980, Pub.L. 96-517 (94 Stat. 3015). Prior to this amendment, Section 117 read as follows:

§ 117. **Scope of Exclusive Rights: Use in Conjunction With Computers and Similar Information Systems**

Notwithstanding the provisions of sections 106 through 116 and 118, this title does not afford to the owner of copyright in a work any greater or lesser rights with respect to the use of the work in conjunction with automatic systems capable of storing, processing, retrieving, or transferring information, or in conjunction with any similar device, machine, or process, than those afforded to works under the law, whether title 17 or the common law or statutes of a State, in effect on December 31, 1977, as held applicable and construed by a court in an action brought under this title.

(1) Any owner of copyright in a work specified in this subsection or any public broadcasting entity may, within one hundred and twenty days after publication of the notice specified in this subsection, submit to the Copyright Royalty Tribunal proposed licenses covering such activities with respect to such works. The Copyright Royalty Tribunal shall proceed on the basis of the proposals submitted to it as well as any other relevant information. The Copyright Royalty Tribunal shall permit any interested party to submit information relevant to such proceedings.

(2) License agreements voluntarily negotiated at any time between one or more copyright owners and one or more public broadcasting entities shall be given effect in lieu of any determination by the Tribunal: *Provided,* That copies of such agreements are filed in the Copyright Office within thirty days of execution in accordance with regulations that the Register of Copyrights shall prescribe.

(3) Within six months, but not earlier than one hundred and twenty days, from the date of publication of the notice specified in this subsection the Copyright Royalty Tribunal shall make a determination and publish in the Federal Register a schedule of rates and terms which, subject to clause (2) of this subsection, shall be binding on all owners of copyright in works specified by this subsection and public broadcasting entities, regardless of whether or not such copyright owners and public broadcasting entities have submitted proposals to the Tribunal. In establishing such rates and terms the Copyright Royalty Tribunal may consider the rates for comparable circumstances under voluntary license agreements negotiated as provided in clause (2) of this subsection. The Copyright Royalty Tribunal shall also establish requirements by which copyright owners may receive reasonable notice of the use of their works under this section, and under which records of such use shall be kept by public broadcasting entities.

(4) With respect to the period beginning on the effective date of this title and ending on the date of publication of such rates and terms, this title shall not afford to owners of copyright or public broadcasting entities any greater or lesser rights with respect to the activities specified in subsection (d) as applied to works specified in this subsection than those afforded under the law in effect on December 31, 1977, as held applicable and construed by a court in an action brought under this title.

(c) The initial procedure specified in subsection (b) shall be repeated and concluded between June 30 and December 31, 1982, and at five-year intervals thereafter, in accordance with regulations that the Copyright Royalty Tribunal shall prescribe.

(d) Subject to the transitional provisions of subsection (b)(4), and to the terms of any voluntary license agreements that have been negotiated as provided by subsection (b)(2), a public broadcasting entity may, upon compliance with the provisions of this section, including the rates and terms established by the Copyright Royalty Tribunal under subsection (b)(3), engage in the following activities with respect to published nondramatic musical works and published pictorial, graphic, and sculptural works:

(1) performance or display of a work by or in the course of a transmission made by a noncommercial educational broadcast station referred to in subsection (g); and

(2) production of a transmission program, reproduction of copies or phonorecords of such a transmission program, and distribution of such copies or phonorecords, where such production, reproduction, or distribution is made by a nonprofit institution or organization solely for the purpose of transmissions specified in clause (1); and

(3) the making of reproductions by a governmental body or a nonprofit institution of a transmission program simultaneously with its transmission as specified in clause (1), and the performance or display of the contents of such program under the conditions specified by clause (1) of section 110, but only if the reproductions are used for performances or displays for a period of no more than seven days from the date of the transmission specified in clause (1), and are destroyed before or at the end of such period. No person supplying, in accordance with clause (2), a reproduction of a transmission program to governmental bodies or nonprofit institutions under this clause shall have any liability as a result of failure of such body or institution to destroy such reproduction: *Provided,* That it shall have notified such body or institution of the requirement for such destruction pursuant to this clause: *And provided further,* That if such body or institution itself fails to destroy such reproduction it shall be deemed to have infringed.

(e) Except as expressly provided in this subsection, this section shall have no applicability to works other than those specified in subsection (b).

(1) Owners of copyright in nondramatic literary works and public broadcasting entities may, during the course of voluntary negotiations, agree among themselves, respectively, as to the terms and rates of royalty payments without liability under the anti-trust laws. Any such terms and rates of royalty payments shall be effective upon filing in the Copyright Office, in accordance with regulations that the Register of Copyrights shall prescribe.

(2) On January 3, 1980, the Register of Copyrights, after consulting with authors and other owners of copyright in nondramatic literary works and their representatives, and with public broadcasting entities and their representatives, shall submit to the Congress a report setting forth the extent to which voluntary licensing arrangements have been reached with respect to the use of nondramatic literary works by such broadcast stations. The report should also describe any problems that may have arisen, and present legislative or other recommendations, if warranted.

(f) Nothing in this section shall be construed to permit, beyond the limits of fair use as provided by section 107, the unauthorized dramatization of a nondramatic musical work, the production of a transmission program drawn to any substantial extent from a published compilation of pictorial, graphic, or sculptural works, or the unauthorized use of any portion of an audiovisual work.

(g) As used in this section, the term "public broadcasting entity" means a noncommercial educational broadcast station as defined in section 397 of title 47 and any nonprofit institution or organization engaged in the activities described in clause (2) of subsection (d).

CHAPTER 2.—COPYRIGHT OWNERSHIP AND TRANSFER

Sec.
201. Ownership of Copyright.
202. Ownership of Copyright as Distinct from Ownership of Material Object.
203. Termination of Transfers and Licenses Granted by the Author.
204. Execution of Transfers of Copyright Ownership.
205. Recordation of Transfers and Other Documents.

Sec. 201. Ownership of Copyright

(a) **Initial Ownership.** Copyright in a work protected under this title vests initially in the author or authors of the work. The authors of a joint work are coowners of copyright in the work.

(b) **Works Made for Hire.** In the case of a work made for hire, the employer or other person for whom the work was prepared is considered the author for purposes of this title, and, unless the parties have expressly agreed otherwise in a written instrument signed by them, owns all of the rights comprised in the copyright.

(c) **Contributions to Collective Works.** Copyright in each separate contribution to a collective work is distinct from copyright in the collective work as a whole, and vests initially in the author of the contribution. In the absence of an express transfer of the copyright or of any rights under it, the owner of copyright in the collective work is presumed to have acquired only the privilege of reproducing and distributing the contribution as part of that particular collective work, any revision of that collective work, and any later collective work in the same series.

(d) **Transfer of Ownership.**

(1) The ownership of a copyright may be transferred in whole or in part by any means of conveyance or by operation of law, and may be bequeathed by will or pass as personal property by the applicable laws of intestate succession.

(2) Any of the exclusive rights comprised in a copyright, including any subdivision of any of the rights specified by section 106, may be transferred as provided by clause (1) and owned separately. The owner of any particular exclusive right is entitled, to the extent of that right,

to all of the protection and remedies accorded to the copyright owner by this title.

(e) **Involuntary Transfer.** When an individual author's ownership of a copyright, or of any of the exclusive rights under a copyright, has not previously been transferred voluntarily by that individual author, no action by any governmental body or other official or organization purporting to seize, expropriate, transfer, or exercise rights of ownership with respect to the copyright, or any of the exclusive rights under a copyright, shall be given effect under this title, except as provided under title 11.[7]

Sec. 202. Ownership of Copyright as Distinct from Ownership of Material Object

Ownership of a copyright, or of any of the exclusive rights under a copyright, is distinct from ownership of any material object in which the work is embodied. Transfer of ownership of any material object, including the copy or phonorecord in which the work is first fixed, does not of itself convey any rights in the copyrighted work embodied in the object; nor, in the absence of an agreement, does transfer of ownership of a copyright or of any exclusive rights under a copyright convey property rights in any material object.

Sec. 203. Termination of Transfers and Licenses Granted by the Author

(a) **Conditions for Termination.** In the case of any work other than a work made for hire, the exclusive or nonexclusive grant of a transfer or license of copyright or of any right under a copyright, executed by the author on or after January 1, 1978, otherwise than by will, is subject to termination under the following conditions:

(1) In the case of a grant executed by one author, termination of the grant may be effected by that author or, if the author is dead, by the person or persons who, under clause (2) of this subsection, own and are entitled to exercise a total of more than one-half of that author's termination interest. In the case of a grant executed by two or more authors of a joint work, termination of the grant may be effected by a majority of the authors who executed it; if any of such authors is dead, the termination interest of any such author may be exercised as a unit by the person or persons who, under clause (2) of this subsection, own and are entitled to exercise a total of more than one-half of that author's interest.

(2) Where an author is dead, his or her termination interest is owned, and may be exercised, by his widow or her widower and his or her children or grandchildren as follows:

(A) the widow or widower owns the author's entire termination interest unless there are any surviving children or grandchildren of the

---

7. Section 201(e) as amended by the Act of November 6, 1978, Pub.L. 95–598, 92 Stat. 2676.

author, in which case the widow or widower owns one-half of the author's interest;

(B) the author's surviving children, and the surviving children of any dead child of the author, own the author's entire termination interest unless there is a widow or widower, in which case the ownership of one-half of the author's interest is divided among them;

(C) the rights of the author's children and grandchildren are in all cases divided among them and exercised on a per stirpes basis according to the number of such author's children represented; the share of the children of a dead child in a termination interest can be exercised only by the action of a majority of them.

(3) Termination of the grant may be effected at any time during a period of five years beginning at the end of thirty-five years from the date of execution of the grant; or, if the grant covers the right of publication of the work, the period begins at the end of thirty-five years from the date of publication of the work under the grant or at the end of forty years from the date of execution of the grant, whichever term ends earlier.

(4) The termination shall be effected by serving an advance notice in writing, signed by the number and proportion of owners of termination interests required under clauses (1) and (2) of this subsection, or by their duly authorized agents, upon the grantee or the grantee's successor in title.

(A) The notice shall state the effective date of the termination, which shall fall within the five-year period specified by clause (3) of this subsection, and the notice shall be served not less than two or more than ten years before that date. A copy of the notice shall be recorded in the Copyright Office before the effective date of termination, as a condition to its taking effect.

(B) The notice shall comply, in form, content, and manner of service, with requirements that the Register of Copyrights shall prescribe by regulation.

(5) Termination of the grant may be effected notwithstanding any agreement to the contrary, including an agreement to make a will or to make any future grant.

(b) Effect of Termination. Upon the effective date of termination, all rights under this title that were covered by the terminated grants revert to the author, authors, and other persons owning termination interests under clauses (1) and (2) of subsection (a), including those owners who did not join in signing the notice of termination under clause (4) of subsection (a), but with the following limitations:

(1) A derivative work prepared under authority of the grant before its termination may continue to be utilized under the terms of the grant after its termination, but this privilege does not extend to the preparation after the termination of other derivative works based upon the copyrighted work covered by the terminated grant.

(2) The future rights that will revert upon termination of the grant become vested on the date the notice of termination has been served as provided by clause (4) of subsection (a). The rights vest in the author, authors, and other persons named in, and in the proportionate shares provided by, clauses (1) and (2) of subsection (a).

(3) Subject to the provisions of clause (4) of this subsection, a further grant, or agreement to make a further grant, of any right covered by a terminated grant is valid only if it is signed by the same number and proportion of the owners, in whom the right has vested under clause (2) of this subsection, as are required to terminate the grant under clauses (1) and (2) of subsection (a). Such further grant or agreement is effective with respect to all of the persons in whom the right it covers has vested under clause (2) of this subsection, including those who did not join in signing it. If any person dies after rights under a terminated grant have vested in him or her, that person's legal representatives, legatees, or heirs at law represent him or her for purposes of this clause.

(4) A further grant, or agreement to make a further grant, of any right covered by a terminated grant is valid only if it is made after the effective date of the termination. As an exception, however, an agreement for such a further grant may be made between the persons provided by clause (3) of this subsection and the original grantee or such grantee's successor in title, after the notice of termination has been served as provided by clause (4) of subsection (a).

(5) Termination of a grant under this section affects only those rights covered by the grants that arise under this title, and in no way affects rights arising under any other Federal, State, or foreign laws.

(6) Unless and until termination is effected under this section, the grant, if it does not provide otherwise, continues in effect for the term of copyright provided by this title.

Sec. 204. Execution of Transfers of Copyright Ownership

(a) A transfer of copyright ownership, other than by operation of law, is not valid unless an instrument of conveyance, or a note or memorandum of the transfer, is in writing and signed by the owner of the rights conveyed or such owner's duly authorized agent.

(b) A certificate of acknowledgement is not required for the validity of a transfer, but is prima facie evidence of the execution of the transfer if—

(1) in the case of a transfer executed in the United States, the certificate is issued by a person authorized to administer oaths within the United States; or

(2) in the case of a transfer executed in a foreign country, the certificate is issued by a diplomatic or consular officer of the United States, or by a person authorized to administer oaths whose authority is proved by a certificate of such an officer.

Sec. 205. Recordation of Transfers and Other Documents

(a) Conditions for Recordation. Any transfer of copyright ownership or other document pertaining to a copyright may be recorded in the Copyright Office if the document filed for recordation bears the actual signature of the person who executed it, or if it is accompanied by a sworn or official certification that it is a true copy of the original, signed document.

(b) Certificate of Recordation. The Register of Copyrights shall, upon receipt of a document as provided by subsection (a) and of the fee provided by section 708, record the document and return it with a certificate of recordation.

(c) Recordation as Constructive Notice. Recordation of a document in the Copyright Office gives all persons constructive notice of the facts stated in the recorded document, but only if—

(1) the document, or material attached to it, specifically identifies the work to which it pertains so that, after the document is indexed by the Register of Copyrights, it would be revealed by a reasonable search under the title or registration number of the work; and

(2) registration has been made for the work.

(d) Recordation as Prerequisite to Infringement Suit. No person claiming by virtue of a transfer to be the owner of copyright or of any exclusive right under a copyright is entitled to institute an infringement action under this title until the instrument of transfer under which such person claims has been recorded in the Copyright Office, but suit may be instituted after such recordation on a cause of action that arose before recordation.

(e) Priority Between Conflicting Transfers. As between two conflicting transfers, the one executed first prevails if it is recorded, in the manner required to give constructive notice under subsection (c), within one month after its execution in the United States or within two months after its execution outside the United States, or at any time before recordation in such manner of the later transfer. Otherwise the later transfer prevails if recorded first in such manner, and if taken in good faith, for valuable consideration or on the basis of a binding promise to pay royalties, and without notice of the earlier transfer.

(f) Priority Between Conflicting Transfer of Ownership and Nonexclusive License. A nonexclusive license, whether recorded or not, prevails over a conflicting transfer of copyright ownership if the license is evidenced by a written instrument signed by the owner of the rights licensed or such owner's duly authorized agent, and if—

(1) the license was taken before execution of the transfer; or

(2) the license was taken in good faith before recordation of the transfer and without notice of it.

CHAPTER 3.—DURATION OF COPYRIGHT

Sec.
301. Preemption with Respect to Other Laws.
302. Duration of Copyright: Works Created on or after January 1, 1978.
303. Same: Works Created but not Published or Copyrighted before January 1, 1978.
304. Same: Subsisting Copyrights.
305. Same: Terminal Date.

Sec. 301. Preemption with Respect to Other Laws

(a) On and after January 1, 1978, all legal or equitable rights that are equivalent to any of the exclusive rights within the general scope of copyright as specified by section 106 in works of authorship that are fixed in a tangible medium of expression and come within the subject matter of copyright as specified by sections 102 and 103, whether created before or after that date and whether published or unpublished, are governed exclusively by this title. Thereafter, no person is entitled to any such right or equivalent right in any such work under the common law or statutes of any State.

(b) Nothing in this title annuls or limits any rights or remedies under the common law or statutes of any State with respect to—

(1) subject matter that does not come within the subject matter of copyright as specified by sections 102 and 103, including works of authorship not fixed in any tangible medium of expression; or

(2) any cause of action arising from undertakings commenced before January 1, 1978; or

(3) activities violating legal or equitable rights that are not equivalent to any of the exclusive rights within the general scope of copyright as specified by section 106.

(c) With respect to sound recordings fixed before February 15, 1972, any rights or remedies under the common law or statutes of any State shall not be annulled or limited by this title until February 15, 2047. The preemptive provisions of subsection (a) shall apply to any such rights and remedies pertaining to any cause of action arising from undertakings commenced on and after February 15, 2047. Notwithstanding the provisions of section 303, no sound recording fixed before February 15, 1972, shall be subject to copyright under this title before, on, or after February 15, 2047.

(d) Nothing in this title annuls or limits any rights or remedies under any other Federal statute.

Sec. 302. Duration of Copyright: Works Created on or after January 1, 1978

(a) **In General.** Copyright in a work created on or after January 1, 1978, subsists from its creation and, except as provided by the following subsections, endures for a term consisting of the life of the author and fifty years after the author's death.

(b) Joint Works. In the case of a joint work prepared by two or more authors who did not work for hire, the copyright endures for a term consisting of the life of the last surviving author and fifty years after such last surviving author's death.

(c) Anonymous Works, Pseudonymous Works, and Works Made for Hire. In the case of an anonymous work, a pseudonymous work, or a work made for hire, the copyright endures for a term of seventy-five years from the year of its first publication, or a term of one hundred years from the year of its creation, whichever expires first. If, before the end of such term, the identity of one or more of the authors of an anonymous or pseudonymous work is revealed in the records of a registration made for that work under subsections (a) or (d) of section 408, or in the records provided by this subsection, the copyright in the work endures for the term specified by subsection (a) or (b), based on the life of the author or authors whose identity has been revealed. Any person having an interest in the copyright in an anonymous or pseudonymous work may at any time record, in records to be maintained by the Copyright Office for that purpose, a statement identifying one or more authors of the work; the statement shall also identify the person filing it, the nature of that person's interest, the source of the information recorded, and the particular work affected, and shall comply in form and content with requirements that the Register of Copyrights shall prescribe by regulation.

(d) Records Relating to Death of Authors. Any person having an interest in a copyright may at any time record in the Copyright Office a statement of the date of death of the author of the copyrighted work, or a statement that the author is still living on a particular date. The statement shall identify the person filing it, the nature of that person's interest, and the source of the information recorded, and shall comply in form and content with requirements that the Register of Copyrights shall prescribe by regulation. The Register shall maintain current records of information relating to the death of authors of copyrighted works, based on such recorded statements and, to the extent the Register considers practicable, on data contained in any of the records of the Copyright Office or in other reference sources.

(e) Presumption as to Author's Death. After a period of seventy-five years from the year of first publication of a work, or a period of one hundred years from the year of its creation, whichever expires first, any person who obtains from the Copyright Office a certified report that the records provided by subsection (d) disclose nothing to indicate that the author of the work is living, or died less than fifty years before, is entitled to the benefit of a presumption that the author has been dead for at least fifty years. Reliance in good faith upon this presumption shall be a complete defense to any action for infringement under this title.

Sec. 303. Duration of Copyright: Works Created but not Published or Copyrighted Before January 1, 1978

Copyright in a work created before January 1, 1978, but not theretofore in the public domain or copyrighted, subsists from January 1, 1978, and endures for the term provided by section 302. In no case, however, shall the term of copyright in such a work expire before December 31, 2002; and, if the work is published on or before December 31, 2002, the term of copyright shall not expire before December 31, 2027.

Sec. 304. Duration of Copyright: Subsisting Copyrights

(a) **Copyrights in Their First Term on January 1, 1978.** Any copyright, the first term of which is subsisting on January 1, 1978, shall endure for twenty-eight years from the date it was originally secured: *Provided,* That in the case of any posthumous work or of any periodical, cyclopedic, or other composite work upon which the copyright was originally secured by the proprietor thereof, or of any work copyrighted by a corporate body (otherwise than as assignee or licensee of the individual author) or by an employer for whom such work is made for hire, the proprietor of such copyright shall be entitled to a renewal and extension of the copyright in such work for the further term of forty-seven years when application for such renewal and extension shall have been made to the Copyright Office and duly registered therein within one year prior to the expiration of the original term of copyright: *And provided further,* That in the case of any other copyrighted work, including a contribution by an individual author to a periodical or to a cyclopedic or other composite work, the author of such work, if still living, or the widow, widower, or children of the author, if the author be not living, or if such author, widow, widower, or children be not living, then the author's executors, or in the absence of a will, his or her next of kin shall be entitled to a renewal and extension of the copyright in such work for a further term of forty-seven years when application for such renewal and extension shall have been made to the Copyright Office and duly registered therein within one year prior to the expiration of the original term of copyright: *And provided further,* That in default of the registration of such application for renewal and extension, the copyright in any work shall terminate at the expiration of twenty-eight years from the date copyright was originally secured.

(b) **Copyrights in Their Renewal Term or Registered for Renewal Before January 1, 1978.** The duration of any copyright, the renewal term of which is subsisting at any time between December 31, 1976, and December 31, 1977, inclusive, or for which renewal registration is made between December 31, 1976, and December 31, 1977, inclusive, is extended to endure for a term of seventy-five years from the date copyright was originally secured.

(c) **Termination of Transfers and Licenses Covering Extended Renewal Term.** In the case of any copyright subsisting in either its first or renewal term on January 1, 1978, other than a copyright in a work made for hire, the exclusive or nonexclusive grant of a transfer or license of the renewal copyright or any right under it, executed before January 1, 1978, by any of the persons designated by the second proviso of subsection (a) of this section, otherwise than by will, is subject to termination under the following conditions:

(1) In the case of a grant executed by a person or persons other than the author, termination of the grant may be effected by the surviving person or persons who executed it. In the case of a grant executed by one or more of the authors of the work, termination of the grant may be effected, to the extent of a particular author's share in the ownership of the renewal copyright, by the author who executed it or, if such author is dead, by the person or persons who, under clause (2) of this subsection, own and are entitled to exercise a total of more than one-half of that author's termination interest.

(2) Where an author is dead, his or her termination interest is owned, and may be exercised, by his widow or her widower and his or her children or grandchildren as follows:

(A) the widow or widower owns the author's entire termination interest unless there are any surviving children or grandchildren of the author, in which case the widow or widower owns one-half of the author's interest;

(B) the author's surviving children, and the surviving children of any dead child of the author, own the author's entire termination interest unless there is a widow or widower, in which case the ownership of one-half of the author's interest is divided among them;

(C) the rights of the author's children and grandchildren are in all cases divided among them and exercised on a per stirpes basis according to the number of such author's children represented; the share of the children of a dead child in a termination interest can be exercised only by the action of a majority of them.

(3) Termination of the grant may be effected at any time during a period of five years beginning at the end of fifty-six years from the date copyright was originally secured, or beginning on January 1, 1978, whichever is later.

(4) The termination shall be effected by serving an advance notice in writing upon the grantee or the grantee's successor in title. In the case of a grant executed by a person or persons other than the author, the notice shall be signed by all of those entitled to terminate the grant under clause (1) of this subsection, or by their duly authorized agents. In the case of a grant executed by one or more of the authors of the work, the notice as to any one author's share shall be signed by that author or his or her duly authorized agent or, if that author is dead, by the number and proportion of the owners of his or her termination interest required under clauses (1) and (2) of this subsection, or by their duly authorized agents.

(A) The notice shall state the effective date of the termination, which shall fall within the five-year period specified by clause (3) of this subsection, and the notice shall be served not less than two or more than ten years before that date. A copy of the notice shall be recorded in the Copyright Office before the effective date of termination, as a condition to its taking effect.

(B) The notice shall comply, in form, content, and manner of service, with requirements that the Register of Copyrights shall prescribe by regulation.

(5) Termination of the grant may be effected notwithstanding any agreement to the contrary, including an agreement to make a will or to make any future grant.

(6) In the case of a grant executed by a person or persons other than the author, all rights under this title that were covered by the terminated grant revert, upon the effective date of termination, to all of those entitled to terminate the grant under clause (1) of this subsection. In the case of a grant executed by one or more of the authors of the work, all of a particular author's rights under this title that were covered by the terminated grant revert, upon the effective date of termination, to that author or, if that author is dead, to the persons owning his or her termination interest under clause (2) of this subsection, including those owners who did not join in signing the notice of termination under clause (4) of this subsection. In all cases the reversion of rights is subject to the following limitations:

(A) A derivative work prepared under authority of the grant before its termination may continue to be utilized under the terms of the grant after its termination, but this privilege does not extend to the preparation after the termination of other derivative works based upon the copyrighted work covered by the terminated grant.

(B) The future rights that will revert upon termination of the grant become vested on the date the notice of termination has been served as provided by clause (4) of this subsection.

(C) Where the author's rights revert to two or more persons under clause (2) of this subsection, they shall vest in those persons in the proportionate shares provided by that clause. In such a case, and subject to the provisions of subclause (D) of this clause, a further grant, or agreement to make a further grant, of a particular author's share with respect to any right covered by a terminated grant is valid only if it is signed by the same number and proportion of the owners, in whom the right has vested under this clause, as are required to terminate the grant under clause (2) of this subsection. Such further grant or agreement is effective with respect to all of the persons in whom the right it covers has vested under this subclause, including those who did not join in signing it. If any person dies after rights under a terminated grant have vested in him or her, that person's legal representatives, legatees, or heirs at law represent him or her for purposes of this subclause.

(D) A further grant, or agreement to make a further grant, of any right covered by a terminated grant is valid only if it is made after the effective date of the termination. As an exception, however, an agreement for such a further grant may be made between the author or any of the persons provided by the first sentence of clause (6) of this subsection, or between the persons provided by subclause (C) of this clause, and the original grantee or such grantee's successor in title, after the notice of termination has been served as provided by clause (4) of this subsection.

(E) Termination of a grant under this subsection affects only those rights covered by the grant that arise under this title, and in no way affects rights arising under any other Federal, State, or foreign laws.

(F) Unless and until termination is effected under this subsection, the grant, if it does not provide otherwise, continues in effect for the remainder of the extended renewal term.

Sec. 305. Duration of Copyright: Terminal Date

All terms of copyright provided by sections 302 through 304 run to the end of the calendar year in which they would otherwise expire.

CHAPTER 4.—COPYRIGHT NOTICE, DEPOSIT, AND REGISTRATION

Sec.
401. Notice of Copyright: Visually Perceptible Copies.
402. Same: Phonorecords of Sound Recordings.
403. Same: Publications Incorporating United States Government Works.
404. Same: Contributions to Collective Works.
405. Same: Omission of Notice.
406. Same: Error in Name or Date.
407. Deposit of Copies or Phonorecords for Library of Congress.
408. Copyright Registration in General.
409. Application for Copyright Registration.
410. Registration of Claim and Issuance of Certificate.
411. Registration as Prerequisite to Infringement Suit.
412. Registration as Prerequisite to Certain Remedies for Infringement.

Sec. 401. Notice of Copyright: Visually Perceptible Copies

(a) **General Requirement.** Whenever a work protected under this title is published in the United States or elsewhere by authority of the copyright owner, a notice of copyright as provided by this section shall be placed on all publicly distributed copies from which the work can be visually perceived, either directly or with the aid of a machine or device.

(b) **Form of Notice.** The notice appearing on the copies shall consist of the following three elements:

(1) the symbol © (the letter C in a circle), or the word "Copyright", or the abbreviation "Copr."; and

(2) the year of first publication of the work; in the case of compilations or derivative works incorporating previously published material,

the year date of first publication of the compilation or derivative work is sufficient. The year date may be omitted where a pictorial, graphic, or sculptural work, with accompanying text matter, if any, is reproduced in or on greeting cards, postcards, stationery, jewelry, dolls, toys, or any useful articles; and

(3) the name of the owner of copyright in the work, or an abbreviation by which the name can be recognized, or a generally known alternative designation of the owner.

(c) **Position of Notice.** The notice shall be affixed to the copies in such manner and location as to give reasonable notice of the claim of copyright. The Register of Copyrights shall prescribe by regulation, as examples, specific methods of affixation and positions of the notice on various types of works that will satisfy this requirement, but these specifications shall not be considered exhaustive.

Sec. 402. Notice of Copyright: Phonorecords of Sound Recordings

(a) **General Requirement.** Whenever a sound recording protected under this title is published in the United States or elsewhere by authority of the copyright owner, a notice of copyright as provided by this section shall be placed on all publicly distributed phonorecords of the sound recording.

(b) **Form of Notice.** The notice appearing on the phonorecords shall consist of the following three elements:

(1) the symbol ℗ (the letter P in a circle); and

(2) the year of first publication of the sound recording; and

(3) the name of the owner of copyright in the sound recording, or an abbreviation by which the name can be recognized, or a generally known alternative designation of the owner; if the producer of the sound recording is named on the phonorecord labels or containers, and if no other name appears in conjunction with the notice, the producer's name shall be considered a part of the notice.

(c) **Position of Notice.** The notice shall be placed on the surface of the phonorecord, or on the phonorecord label or container, in such manner and location as to give reasonable notice of the claim of copyright.

Sec. 403. Notice of Copyright: Publications Incorporating United States Government Works

Whenever a work is published in copies or phonorecords consisting preponderantly of one or more works of the United States Government, the notice of copyright provided by sections 401 or 402 shall also include a statement identifying, either affirmatively or negatively, those portions of the copies or phonorecords embodying any work or works protected under this title.

Sec. 404. Notice of Copyright: Contributions to Collective Works

(a) A separate contribution to a collective work may bear its own notice of copyright, as provided by sections 401 through 403. However, a single notice applicable to the collective work as a whole is sufficient to satisfy the requirements of sections 401 through 403 with respect to the separate contributions it contains (not including advertisements inserted on behalf of persons other than the owner of copyright in the collective work), regardless of the ownership of copyright in the contributions and whether or not they have been previously published.

(b) Where the person named in a single notice applicable to a collective work as a whole is not the owner of copyright in a separate contribution that does not bear its own notice, the case is governed by the provisions of section 406(a).

Sec. 405. Notice of Copyright: Omission of Notice

(a) **Effect of Omission on Copyright.** The omission of the copyright notice prescribed by sections 401 through 403 from copies or phonorecords publicly distributed by authority of the copyright owner does not invalidate the copyright in a work if—

(1) the notice has been omitted from no more than a relatively small number of copies or phonorecords distributed to the public; or

(2) registration for the work has been made before or is made within five years after the publication without notice, and a reasonable effort is made to add notice to all copies or phonorecords that are distributed to the public in the United States after the omission has been discovered; or

(3) the notice has been omitted in violation of an express requirement in writing that, as a condition of the copyright owner's authorization of the public distribution of copies or phonorecords, they bear the prescribed notice.

(b) **Effect of Omission on Innocent Infringers.** Any person who innocently infringes a copyright, in reliance upon an authorized copy or phonorecord from which the copyright notice has been omitted, incurs no liability for actual or statutory damages under section 504 for any infringing acts committed before receiving actual notice that registration for the work has been made under section 408, if such person proves that he or she was misled by the omission of notice. In a suit for infringement in such a case the court may allow or disallow recovery of any of the infringer's profits attributable to the infringement, and may enjoin the continuation of the infringing undertaking or may require, as a condition or permitting the continuation of the infringing undertaking, that the infringer pay the copyright owner a reasonable license fee in an amount and on terms fixed by the court.

(c) **Removal of Notice.** Protection under this title is not affected by the removal, destruction, or obliteration of the notice, without the authorization of the copyright owner, from any publicly distributed copies or phonorecords.

Sec. 406. Notice of Copyright: Error in Name or Date

(a) **Error in Name.** Where the person named in the copyright notice on copies or phonorecords publicly distributed by authority of the copyright owner is not the owner of copyright, the validity and ownership of the copyright are not affected. In such a case, however, any person who innocently begins an undertaking that infringes the copyright has a complete defense to any action for such infringement if such person proves that he or she was misled by the notice and began the undertaking in good faith under a purported transfer or license from the person named therein, unless before the undertaking was begun—

(1) registration for the work had been made in the name of the owner of copyright; or

(2) a document executed by the person named in the notice and showing the ownership of the copyright had been recorded.

The person named in the notice is liable to account to the copyright owner for all receipts from transfers or licenses purportedly made under the copyright by the person named in the notice.

(b) **Error in Date.** When the year date in the notice on copies or phonorecords distributed by authority of the copyright owner is earlier than the year in which publication first occurred, any period computed from the year of first publication under section 302 is to be computed from the year in the notice. Where the year date is more than one year later than the year in which publication first occurred, the work is considered to have been published without any notice and is governed by the provisions of section 405.

(c) **Omission of Name or Date.** Where copies or phonorecords publicly distributed by authority of the copyright owner contain no name or no date that could reasonably be considered a part of the notice, the work is considered to have been published without any notice and is governed by the provisions of section 405.

Sec. 407. Deposit of Copies or Phonorecords for Library of Congress

(a) Except as provided by subsection (c), and subject to the provisions of subsection (e), the owner of copyright or of the exclusive right of publication in a work published with notice of copyright in the United States shall deposit, within three months after the date of such publication—

(1) two complete copies of the best edition; or

(2) if the work is a sound recording, two complete phonorecords of the best edition, together with any printed or other visually perceptible material published with such phonorecords.

Neither the deposit requirements of this subsection nor the acquisition provisions of subsection (e) are conditions of copyright protection.

(b) The required copies or phonorecords shall be deposited in the Copyright Office for the use or disposition of the Library of Congress. The Register of Copyrights shall, when requested by the depositor and upon payment of the fee prescribed by section 708, issue a receipt for the deposit.

(c) The Register of Copyrights may by regulation exempt any categories of material from the deposit requirements of this section, or require deposit of only one copy or phonorecord with respect to any categories. Such regulations shall provide either for complete exemption from the deposit requirements of this section, or for alternative forms of deposit aimed at providing a satisfactory archival record of a work without imposing practical or financial hardships on the depositor, where the individual author is the owner of copyright in a pictorial, graphic, or sculptural work and (i) less than five copies of the work have been published, or (ii) the work has been published in a limited edition consisting of numbered copies, the monetary value of which would make the mandatory deposit of two copies of the best edition of the work burdensome, unfair, or unreasonable.

(d) At any time after publication of a work as provided by subsection (a), the Register of Copyrights may make written demand for the required deposit on any of the persons obligated to make the deposit under subsection (a). Unless deposit is made within three months after the demand is received, the person or persons on whom the demand was made are liable—

(1) to a fine of not more than $250 for each work; and

(2) to pay into a specially designated fund in the Library of Congress the total retail price of the copies or phonorecords demanded, or, if no retail price has been fixed, the reasonable cost of the Library of Congress of acquiring them; and

(3) to pay a fine of $2,500, in addition to any fine or liability imposed under clauses (1) and (2), if such person willfully or repeatedly fails or refuses to comply with such a demand.

(e) With respect to transmission programs that have been fixed and transmitted to the public in the United States but have not been published, the Register of Copyrights shall, after consulting with the Librarian of Congress and other interested organizations and officials, establish regulations governing the acquisition, through deposit or otherwise, of copies or phonorecords of such programs for the collections of the Library of Congress.

(1) The Librarian of Congress shall be permitted, under the standards and conditions set forth in such regulations, to make a fixation of a transmission program directly from a transmission to the public, and to reproduce one copy or phonorecord from such fixation for archival purposes.

(2) Such regulations shall also provide standards and procedures by which the Register of Copyrights may make written demand, upon the

owner of the right of transmission in the United States, for the deposit of a copy or phonorecord of a specific transmission program. Such deposit may, at the option of the owner of the right of transmission in the United States, be accomplished by gift, by loan for purposes of reproduction, or by sale at a price not to exceed the cost of reproducing and supplying the copy or phonorecord. The regulations established under this clause shall provide reasonable periods of not less than three months for compliance with a demand, and shall allow for extensions of such periods and adjustments in the scope of the demand or the methods for fulfilling it, as reasonably warranted by the circumstances. Willful failure or refusal to comply with the conditions prescribed by such regulations shall subject the owner of the right of transmission in the United States to liability for an amount, not to exceed the cost of reproducing and supplying the copy or phonorecord in question, to be paid into a specially designated fund in the Library of Congress.

(3) Nothing in this subsection shall be construed to require the making or retention, for purposes of deposit, of any copy or phonorecord of an unpublished transmission program, the transmission of which occurs before the receipt of a specific written demand as provided by clause (2).

(4) No activity undertaken in compliance with regulations prescribed under clauses (1) or (2) of this subsection shall result in liability if intended solely to assist in the acquisition of copies or phonorecords under this subsection.

Sec. 408. Copyright Registration in General

(a) **Registration Permissive.** At any time during the subsistence of copyright in any published or unpublished work, the owner of copyright or of any exclusive right in the work may obtain registration of the copyright claim by delivering to the Copyright Office the deposit specified by this section, together with the application and fee specified by sections 409 and 708. Subject to the provisions of section 405(a), such registration is not a condition of copyright protection.

(b) **Deposit for Copyright Registration.** Except as provided by subsection (c), the material deposited for registration shall include—

(1) in the case of an unpublished work, one complete copy or phonorecord;

(2) in the case of a published work, two complete copies or phonorecords of the best edition;

(3) in the case of a work first published outside the United States, one complete copy or phonorecord as so published;

(4) in the case of a contribution to a collective work, one complete copy or phonorecord of the best edition of the collective work.

Copies or phonorecords deposited for the Library of Congress under section 407 may be used to satisfy the deposit provisions of this section, if they are accompanied by the prescribed application and fee, and by any additional identifying material that the Register may, by regulation, require. The Register shall also prescribe regulations establishing requirements under which copies or phonorecords acquired for the Library of Congress under subsection (e) of section 407, otherwise than by deposit, may be used to satisfy the deposit provisions of this section.

(c) Administrative Classification and Optional Deposit.

(1) The Register of Copyrights is authorized to specify by regulation the administrative classes into which works are to be placed for purposes of deposit and registration, and the nature of the copies or phonorecords to be deposited in the various classes specified. The regulations may require or permit, for particular classes, the deposit of identifying material instead of copies or phonorecords, the deposit of only one copy or phonorecord where two would normally be required, or a single registration for a group of related works. This administrative classification of works has no significance with respect to the subject matter of copyright or the exclusive rights provided by this title.

(2) Without prejudice to the general authority provided under clause (1), the Register of Copyrights shall establish regulations specifically permitting a single registration for a group of works by the same individual author, all first published as contributions to periodicals, including newspapers, within a twelve-month period, on the basis of a single deposit, application, and registration fee, under all of the following conditions—

(A) if each of the works as first published bore a separate copyright notice, and the name of the owner of copyright in the work, or an abbreviation by which the name can be recognized, or a generally known alternative designation of the owner was the same in each notice; and

(B) if the deposit consists of one copy of the entire issue of the periodical, or of the entire section in the case of a newspaper, in which each contribution was first published; and

(C) if the application identifies each work separately, including the periodical containing it and its date of first publication.

(3) As an alternative to separate renewal registrations under subsection (a) of section 304, a single renewal registration may be made for a group of works by the same individual author, all first published as contributions to periodicals, including newspapers, upon the filing of a single application and fee, under all of the following conditions:

(A) the renewal claimant or claimants, and the basis of claim or claims under section 304(a), is the same for each of the works; and

(B) the works were all copyrighted upon their first publication, either through separate copyright notice and registration or by virtue of a general copyright notice in the periodical issue as a whole; and

(C) the renewal application and fee are received not more than twenty-eight or less than twenty-seven years after the thirty-first day of

December of the calendar year in which all of the works were first published; and

(D) the renewal application identifies each work separately, including the periodical containing it and its date of first publication.

(d) Corrections and Amplifications. The Register may also establish, by regulation, formal procedures for the filing of an application for supplementary registration, to correct an error in a copyright registration or to amplify the information given in a registration. Such application shall be accompanied by the fee provided by section 708, and shall clearly identify the registration to be corrected or amplified. The information contained in a supplementary registration augments but does not supersede that contained in the earlier registration.

(e) **Published Edition of Previously Registered Work.** Registration for the first published edition of a work previously registered in unpublished form may be made even though the work as published is substantially the same as the unpublished version.

Sec. 409. Application for Copyright Registration

The application for copyright registration shall be made on a form prescribed by the Register of Copyrights and shall include—

(1) the name and address of the copyright claimant;

(2) in the case of a work other than an anonymous or pseudonymous work, the name and nationality or domicile of the author or authors, and, if one or more of the authors is dead, the dates of their deaths;

(3) if the work is anonymous or pseudonymous, the nationality or domicile of the author or authors;

(4) in the case of a work made for hire, a statement to this effect;

(5) if the copyright claimant is not the author, a brief statement of how the claimant obtained ownership of the copyright;

(6) the title of the work, together with any previous or alternative titles under which the work can be identified;

(7) the year in which creation of the work was completed;

(8) if the work has been published, the date and nation of its first publication;

(9) in the case of a compilation or derivative work, an identification of any preexisting work or works that it is based on or incorporates, and a brief, general statement of the additional material covered by the copyright claim being registered;

(10) in the case of a published work containing material of which copies are required by section 601 to be manufactured in the United States, the names of the persons or organizations who performed the processes specified by subsection (c) of section 601 with respect to that material, and the places where those processes were performed; and

(11) any other information regarded by the Register of Copyrights as bearing upon the preparation or identification of the work or the existence, ownership, or duration of the copyright.

Sec. 410. Registration of Claim and Issuance of Certificate

(a) When, after examination, the Register of Copyrights determines that, in accordance with the provisions of this title, the material deposited constitutes copyrightable subject matter and that the other legal and formal requirements of this title have been met, the Register shall register the claim and issue to the applicant a certificate of registration under the seal of the Copyright Office. The certificate shall contain the information given in the application, together with the number and effective date of the registration.

(b) In any case in which the Register of Copyrights determines that, in accordance with the provisions of this title, the material deposited does not constitute copyrightable subject matter or that the claim is invalid for any other reason, the Register shall refuse registration and shall notify the applicant in writing of the reasons for such refusal.

(c) In any judicial proceedings the certificate of a registration made before or within five years after first publication of the work shall constitute prima facie evidence of the validity of the copyright and of the facts stated in the certificate. The evidentiary weight to be accorded the certificate of a registration made thereafter shall be within the discretion of the court.

(d) The effective date of a copyright registration is the day on which an application, deposit, and fee, which are later determined by the Register of Copyrights or by a court of competent jurisdiction to be acceptable for registration, have all been received in the Copyright Office.

Sec. 411. Registration as Prerequisite to Infringement Suit

(a) Subject to the provisions of subsection (b), no action for infringement of the copyright in any work shall be instituted until registration of the copyright claim has been made in accordance with this title. In any case, however, where the deposit, application, and fee required for registration have been delivered to the Copyright Office in proper form and registration has been refused, the applicant is entitled to institute an action for infringement if notice thereof, with a copy of the complaint, is served on the Register of Copyrights. The Register may, at his or her option, become a party to the action with respect to the issue of registrability of the copyright claim by entering an appearance within sixty days after such service, but the Register's failure to become a party shall not deprive the court of jurisdiction to determine that issue.

(b) In the case of a work consisting of sounds, images, or both, the first fixation of which is made simultaneously with its transmission, the copyright owner may, either before or after such fixation takes place, institute an action for infringement under section 501, fully subject to the remedies provided by sections 502 through 506 and sections 509 and 510, if, in accordance with requirements that the Register of Copyrights shall prescribe by regulation, the copyright owner—

(1) serves notice upon the infringer, not less than ten or more than thirty days before such fixation, identifying the work and the specific time and source of its first transmission, and declaring an intention to secure copyright in the work; and

(2) makes registration for the work within three months after its first transmission.

Sec. 412. Registration as Prerequisite to Certain Remedies for Infringement

In any action under this title, other than an action instituted under section 411(b), no award of statutory damages or of attorney's fees, as provided by sections 504 and 505, shall be made for—

(1) any infringement of copyright in an unpublished work commenced before the effective date of its registration; or

(2) any infringement of copyright commenced after first publication of the work and before the effective date of its registration, unless such registration is made within three months after the first publication of the work.

CHAPTER 5.—COPYRIGHT INFRINGEMENT AND REMEDIES

Sec.
501. Infringement of Copyright.
502. Remedies for Infringement: Injunctions.
503. Same: Impounding and Disposition of Infringing Articles.
504. Same: Damages and Profits.
505. Same: Costs and Attorney's Fees.
506. Criminal Offenses.
507. Limitations on Actions.
508. Notification of Filing and Determination of Actions.
509. Seizure and Forfeiture.
510. Remedies for Alteration of Programing by Cable Systems.

Sec. 501. Infringement of Copyright

(a) Anyone who violates any of the exclusive rights of the copyright owner as provided by sections 106 through 118, or who imports copies or phonorecords into the United States in violation of section 602, is an infringer of the copyright.

(b) The legal or beneficial owner of an exclusive right under a copyright is entitled, subject to the requirements of sections 205(d) and 411, to institute an action for any infringement of that particular right committed while he or she is the owner of it. The court may require such owner to serve written notice of the action with a copy of the complaint upon any person shown, by the records of the Copyright Office or otherwise, to have or claim an interest in the copyright, and shall require that such notice be served upon any person whose interest is likely to be affected by a decision in the case. The court may require the joinder, and shall permit the intervention, of any person having or claiming an interest in the copyright.

(c) For any secondary transmission by a cable system that embodies a performance or a display of a work which is actionable as an act of infringement under subsection (c) of section 111, a television broadcast station holding a copyright or other license to transmit or perform the same version of that work shall, for purposes of subsection (b) of this section, be treated as a legal or beneficial owner if such secondary transmission occurs within the local service area of that television station.

(d) For any secondary transmission by a cable system that is actionable as an act of infringement pursuant to section 111(c)(3), the following shall also have standing to sue: (i) the primary transmitter whose transmission has been altered by the cable system; and (ii) any broadcast station within whose local service area the secondary transmission occurs.

Sec. 502. Remedies for Infringement: Injunctions

(a) Any court having jurisdiction of a civil action arising under this title may, subject to the provisions of section 1498 of title 28, grant temporary and final injunctions on such terms as it may deem reasonable to prevent or restrain infringement of a copyright.

(b) Any such injunction may be served anywhere in the United States on the person enjoined; it shall be operative throughout the United States and shall be enforceable, by proceedings in contempt or otherwise, by any United States court having jurisdiction of that person. The clerk of the court granting the injunction shall, when requested by any other court in which enforcement of the injunction is sought, transmit promptly to the other court a certified copy of all the papers in the case on file in such clerk's office.

Sec. 503. Remedies for Infringement: Impounding and Disposition of Infringing Articles

(a) At any time while an action under this title is pending, the court may order the impounding, on such terms as it may deem reasonable, of all copies or phonorecords claimed to have been made or used in violation of the copyright owner's exclusive rights, and of all plates, molds, matrices, masters, tapes, film negatives, or other articles by means of which such copies or phonorecords may be reproduced.

(b) As part of a final judgment or decree, the court may order the destruction or other reasonable disposition of all copies or phonorecords found to have been made or used in violation of the copyright owner's exclusive rights, and of all plates, molds, matrices, masters, tapes, film negatives, or other articles by means of which such copies or phonorecords may be reproduced.

Sec. 504. Remedies for Infringement: Damages and Profits

(a) In General. Except as otherwise provided by this title, an infringer of copyright is liable for either—

(1) the copyright owner's actual damages and any additional profits of the infringer, as provided by subsection (b); or

(2) statutory damages, as provided by subsection (c).

(b) Actual Damages and Profits. The copyright owner is entitled to recover the actual damages suffered by him or her as a result of the infringement, and any profits of the infringer that are attributable to the infringement and are not taken into account in computing the actual damages. In establishing the infringer's profits, the copyright owner is required to present proof only of the infringer's gross revenue, and the infringer is required to prove his or her deductible expenses and the elements of profit attributable to factors other than the copyrighted work.

(c) Statutory Damages.

(1) Except as provided by clause (2) of this subsection, the copyright owner may elect, at any time before final judgment is rendered, to recover, instead of actual damages and profits, an award of statutory damages for all infringements involved in the action, with respect to any one work, for which any one infringer is liable individually, or for which any two or more infringers are liable jointly and severally, in a sum of not less than $250 or more than $10,000 as the court considers just. For the purposes of this subsection, all the parts of a compilation or derivative work constitute one work.

(2) In a case where the copyright owner sustains the burden of proving, and the court finds, that infringement was committed willfully, the court in its discretion may increase the award of statutory damages to a sum of not more than $50,000. In a case where the infringer sustains the burden of proving, and the court finds, that such infringer was not aware and had no reason to believe that his or her acts constituted an infringement of copyright, the court in its discretion may reduce the award of statutory damages to a sum of not less than $100. The court shall remit statutory damages in any case where an infringer believed and had reasonable grounds for believing that his or her use of the copyrighted work was a fair use under section 107, if the infringer was: (i) an employee or agent of a nonprofit educational institution, library, or archives acting within the scope of his or her employment who, or such institution, library, or archives itself, which infringed by reproducing the work in copies or phonorecords; or (ii) a public broadcasting entity which or a person who, as a regular part of the nonprofit activities of a public broadcasting entity (as defined in subsection (g) of section 118) infringed by performing a published

nondramatic literary work or by reproducing a transmission program embodying a performance of such a work.

Sec. 505. Remedies for Infringement: Costs and Attorney's Fees

In any civil action under this title, the court in its discretion may allow the recovery of full costs by or against any party other than the United States or an officer thereof. Except as otherwise provided by this title, the court may also award a reasonable attorney's fee to the prevailing party as part of the costs.

Sec. 506. Criminal Offenses

(a) [8] **Criminal Infringement.** Any person who infringes a copyright willfully and for purposes of commercial advantage or private financial gain shall be punished as provided in section 2319 of title 18.[9]

(b) Forfeiture and Destruction. When any person is convicted of any violation of subsection (a), the court in its judgment of conviction shall, in addition to the penalty therein prescribed, order the forfeiture and destruction or other disposition of all infringing copies or phonorecords and all implements, devices, or equipment used in the manufacture of such infringing copies or phonorecords.

---

8. Section 506(a) as amended by the Act of May 24, 1982 (Pub.L. 97–180).

9. 18 U.S.C. Section 2319 (Act of May 24, 1982—Pub.L. 97–180) reads as follows:

"§ 2319. **Criminal infringement of a copyright**

"(a) Whoever violates section 506(a) (relating to criminal offenses) of title 17 shall be punished as provided in subsection (b) of this section and such penalties shall be in addition to any other provisions of title 17 or any other law.

"(b) Any person who commits an offense under subsection (a) of this section—

"(1) shall be fined not more than $250,000 or imprisoned for not more than five years, or both, if the offense—

"(A) involves the reproduction or distribution, during any one-hundred-and-eighty-day period, of at least one thousand phonorecords or copies infringing the copyright in one or more sound recordings;

"(B) involves the reproduction or distribution, during any one-hundred-and-eighty-day period, of at least sixty-five copies infringing the copyright in one or more motion pictures or other audiovisual works; or

"(C) is a second or subsequent offense under either of subsection (b)(1) or (b)(2) of this section, where a prior offense involved a sound recording, or a motion picture or other audiovisual work;

"(2) shall be fined not more than $250,000 or imprisoned for not more than two years, or both, if the offense—

"(A) involves the reproduction or distribution, during any one-hundred-and-eighty-day period of more than one hundred but less than one thousand phonorecords or copies infringing the copyright in one or more sound recordings; or

"(B) involves the reproduction or distribution, during any one-hundred-and-eighty-day period, of more than seven but less than sixty-five copies infringing the copyright in one or more motion pictures or other audiovisual works; and

"(3) shall be fined not more than $25,000 or imprisoned for not more than one year, or both, in any other case.

"(c) As used in this section—

"(1) the terms 'sound recording', 'motion picture', 'audiovisual work', 'phonorecord', and 'copies' have, respectively, the meanings set forth in section 101 (relating to definitions) of title 17; and

"(2) the terms 'reproduction' and 'distribution' refer to the exclusive rights of a copyright owner under clauses (1) and (3) respectively of section 106 (relating to exclusive rights in copyrighted works), as limited by sections 107 through 118, of title 17."

(c) **Fraudulent Copyright Notice.** Any person who, with fraudulent intent, places on any article a notice of copyright or words of the same purport that such person knows to be false, or who, with fraudulent intent, publicly distributes or imports for public distribution any article bearing such notice or words that such person knows to be false, shall be fined not more than $2,500.

(d) **Fraudulent Removal of Copyright Notice.** Any person who, with fraudulent intent, removes or alters any notice of copyright appearing on a copy of a copyrighted work shall be fined not more than $2,500.

(e) **False Representation.** Any person who knowingly makes a false representation of a material fact in the application for copyright registration provided for by section 409, or in any written statement filed in connection with the application, shall be fined not more than $2,500.

Sec. 507. Limitations on Actions

(a) **Criminal Proceedings.** No criminal proceeding shall be maintained under the provisions of this title unless it is commenced within three years after the cause of action arose.

(b) **Civil Actions.** No civil action shall be maintained under the provisions of this title unless it is commenced within three years after the claim accrued.

Sec. 508. Notification of Filing and Determination of Actions

(a) Within one month after the filing of any action under this title, the clerks of the courts of the United States shall send written notification to the Register of Copyrights setting forth, as far as is shown by the papers filed in the court, the names and addresses of the parties and the title, author, and registration number of each work involved in the action. If any other copyrighted work is later included in the action by amendment, answer, or other pleading, the clerk shall also send a notification concerning it to the Register within one month after the pleading is filed.

(b) Within one month after any final order or judgment is issued in the case, the clerk of the court shall notify the Register of it, sending with the notification a copy of the order or judgment together with the written opinion, if any, of the court.

(c) Upon receiving the notifications specified in this section, the Register shall make them a part of the public records of the Copyright Office.

Sec. 509. Seizure and Forfeiture

(a) All copies or phonorecords manufactured, reproduced, distributed, sold, or otherwise used, intended for use, or possessed with intent to use in violation of section 506(a), and all plates, molds, matrices, masters, tapes, film negatives, or other articles by means of which such copies or phonorecords may be reproduced, and all electronic, mechanical, or other devices for manufacturing, reproducing, or assembling such copies or phonorecords may be seized and forfeited to the United States.

(b) The applicable procedures relating to (i) the seizure, summary and judicial forfeiture, and condemnation of vessels, vehicles, merchandise, and baggage for violations of the customs laws contained in title 19, (ii) the disposition of such vessels, vehicles, merchandise, and baggage or the proceeds from the sale thereof, (iii) the remission or mitigation of such forfeiture, (iv) the compromise of claims, and (v) the award of compensation to informers in respect of such forfeitures, shall apply to seizures and forfeitures incurred, or alleged to have been incurred, under the provisions of this section, insofar as applicable and not inconsistent with the provisions of this section; except that such duties as are imposed upon any office or employee of the Treasury Department or any other person with respect to the seizure and forfeiture of vessels, vehicles, merchandise; and baggage under the provisions of the customs laws contained in title 19 shall be performed with respect to seizure and forfeiture of all articles described in subsection (a) by such officers, agents, or other persons as may be authorized or designated for that purpose by the Attorney General.

Sec. 510. Remedies for Alteration of Programing by Cable Systems

(a) In any action filed pursuant to section 111(c)(3), the following remedies shall be available:

(1) Where an action is brought by a party identified in subsections (b) or (c) of section 501, the remedies provided by sections 502 through 505, and the remedy provided by subsection (b) of this section; and

(2) When an action is brought by a party identified in subsection (d) of section 501, the remedies provided by sections 502 and 505, together with any actual damages suffered by such party as a result of the infringement, and the remedy provided by subsection (b) of this section.

(b) In any action filed pursuant to section 111(c)(3), the court may decree that, for a period not to exceed thirty days, the cable system shall be deprived of the benefit of a compulsory license for one or more distant signals carried by such cable system.

CHAPTER 6.—MANUFACTURING REQUIREMENTS AND IMPORTATION

Sec.
601. Manufacture, Importation, and Public Distribution of Certain Copies.
602. Infringing Importation of Copies or Phonorecords.
603. Importation Prohibitions: Enforcement and Disposition of Excluded Articles.

Sec. 601. Manufacture, Importation, and Public Distribution of Certain Copies

(a) [10] Prior to July 1, 1986, and except as provided by subsection (b), the importation into or public distribution in the United States of copies of a work consisting preponderantly of nondramatic literary material that is in the English language and is protected under this title is prohibited unless the portions consisting of such material have been manufactured in the United States or Canada.

(b) The provisions of subsection (a) do not apply—

(1) where, on the date when importation is sought or public distribution in the United States is made, the author of any substantial part of such material is neither a national nor a domiciliary of the United States or, if such author is a national of the United States, he or she has been domiciled outside the United States for a continuous period of at least one year immediately preceding that date; in the case of a work made for hire, the exemption provided by this clause does not apply unless a substantial part of the work was prepared for an employer or other person who is not a national or domiciliary of the United States or a domestic corporation or enterprise;

(2) where the United States Customs Service is presented with an import statement issued under the seal of the Copyright Office, in which case a total of no more than two thousand copies of any one such work shall be allowed entry; the import statement shall be issued upon request to the copyright owner or to a person designated by such owner at the time of registration for the work under section 408 or at any time thereafter;

(3) where importation is sought under the authority or for the use, other than in schools, of the Government of the United States or of any State or political subdivision of a State;

(4) where importation, for use and not for sale, is sought—

(A) by any person with respect to no more than one copy of any work at any one time;

(B) by any person arriving from outside the United States, with respect to copies forming part of such person's personal baggage; or

(C) by an organization operated for scholarly, educational, or religious purposes and not for private gain, with respect to copies intended to form a part of its library;

(5) where the copies are reproduced in raised characters for the use of the blind; or

(6) where, in addition to copies imported under clauses (3) and (4) of this subsection, no more than two thousand copies of any one such

---

10. Section 601(a) as amended by the Act of July 13, 1982 (Pub.L. 97–215). The amendment struck "1982" and inserted "1986" in lieu thereof.

work, which have not been manufactured in the United States or Canada, are publicly distributed in the United States; or

(7) where, on the date when importation is sought or public distribution in the United States is made—

(A) the author of any substantial part of such material is an individual and receives compensation for the transfer or license of the right to distribute the work in the United States; and

(B) the first publication of the work has previously taken place outside the United States under a transfer or license granted by such author to a transferee or licensee who was not a national or domiciliary of the United States or a domestic corporation or enterprise; and

(C) there has been no publication of an authorized edition of the work of which the copies were manufactured in the United States; and

(D) the copies were reproduced under a transfer or license granted by such author or by the transferee or licensee of the right of first publication as mentioned in subclause (B), and the transferee or the licensee of the right of reproduction was not a national or domiciliary of the United States or a domestic corporation or enterprise.

(c) The requirement of this section that copies be manufactured in the United States or Canada is satisfied if—

(1) in the case where the copies are printed directly from type that has been set, or directly from plates made from such type, the setting of the type and the making of the plates have been performed in the United States or Canada; or

(2) in the case where the making of plates by a lithographic or photoengraving process is a final or intermediate step preceding the printing of the copies, the making of the plates has been performed in the United States or Canada; and

(3) in any case, the printing or other final process of producing multiple copies and any binding of the copies have been performed in the United States or Canada.

(d) Importation or public distribution of copies in violation of this section does not invalidate protection for a work under this title. However, in any civil action or criminal proceeding for infringement of the exclusive rights to reproduce and distribute copies of the work, the infringer has a complete defense with respect to all of the nondramatic literary material comprised in the work and any other parts of the work in which the exclusive rights to reproduce and distribute copies are owned by the same person who owns such exclusive rights in the nondramatic literary material, if the infringer proves—

(1) that copies of the work have been imported into or publicly distributed in the United States in violation of this section by or with the authority of the owner of such exclusive rights; and

(2) that the infringing copies were manufactured in the United States or Canada in accordance with the provisions of subsection (c); and

(3) that the infringement was commenced before the effective date of registration for an authorized edition of the work, the copies of which have been manufactured in the United States or Canada in accordance with the provisions of subsection (c).

(e) In any action for infringement of the exclusive rights to reproduce and distribute copies of a work containing material required by this section to be manufactured in the United States or Canada, the copyright owner shall set forth in the complaint the names of the persons or organizations who performed the processes specified by subsection (c) with respect to that material, and the places where those processes were performed.

Sec. 602. Infringing Importation of Copies or Phonorecords

(a) Importation into the United States, without the authority of the owner of copyright under this title, of copies or phonorecords of a work that have been acquired outside the United States is an infringement of the exclusive right to distribute copies or phonorecords under section 106, actionable under section 501. This subsection does not apply to—

(1) importation of copies or phonorecords under the authority or for the use of the Government of the United States or of any State or political subdivision of a State, but not including copies or phonorecords for use in schools, or copies of any audiovisual work imported for purposes other than archival use;

(2) importation, for the private use of the importer and not for distribution, by any person with respect to no more than one copy or phonorecord of any one work at any one time, or by any person arriving from outside the United States with respect to copies or phonorecords forming part of such person's personal baggage; or

(3) importation by or for an organization operated for scholarly, educational, or religious purposes and not for private gain, with respect to no more than one copy of an audiovisual work solely for its archival purposes, and no more than five copies or phonorecords of any other work for its library lending or archival purposes, unless the importation of such copies or phonorecords is part of an activity consisting of systematic reproduction or distribution, engaged in by such organization in violation of the provisions of section 108(g)(2).

(b) In a case where the making of the copies or phonorecords would have constituted an infringement of copyright if this title had been applicable, their importation is prohibited. In a case where the copies or phonorecords were lawfully made, the United States Customs Service has no authority to prevent their importation unless the provisions of section 601 are applicable. In either case, the Secretary of the Treasury is authorized to prescribe, by regulation, a procedure under which any person claiming an interest in the copyright in a particular work may, upon payment of a specified fee, be entitled to notification by the Customs Service of the importation of articles that appear to be copies or phonorecords of the work.

Sec. 603. Importation Prohibitions: Enforcement and Disposition of Excluded Articles

(a) The Secretary of the Treasury and the United States Postal Service shall separately or jointly make regulations for the enforcement of the provisions of this title prohibiting importation.

(b) These regulations may require, as a condition for the exclusion of articles under section 602—

(1) that the person seeking exclusion obtain a court order enjoining importation of the articles; or

(2) that the person seeking exclusion furnish proof, of a specified nature and in accordance with prescribed procedures, that the copyright in which such person claims an interest is valid and that the importation would violate the prohibition in section 602; the person seeking exclusion may also be required to post a surety bond for any injury that may result if the detention or exclusion of the articles proves to be unjustified.

(c) Articles imported in violation of the importation prohibitions of this title are subject to seizure and forfeiture in the same manner as property imported in violation of the customs revenue laws. Forfeited articles shall be destroyed as directed by the Secretary of the Treasury or the court, as the case may be; however, the articles may be returned to the country of export whenever it is shown to the satisfaction of the Secretary of the Treasury that the importer had no reasonable grounds for believing that his or her acts constituted a violation of law.

CHAPTER 7.—COPYRIGHT OFFICE

Sec.
701. The Copyright Office: General Responsibilities and Organization.
702. Copyright Office Regulations.
703. Effective Date of Actions in Copyright Office.
704. Retention and Disposition of Articles Deposited in Copyright Office.
705. Copyright Office Records: Preparation, Maintenance, Public Inspection, and Searching.
706. Copies of Copyright Office Records.
707. Copyright Office Forms and Publications.
708. Copyright Office Fees.
709. Delay in Delivery Caused by Disruption of Postal or Other Services.
710. Reproduction for Use of the Blind and Physically Handicapped: Voluntary Licensing Forms and Procedures.

Sec. 701. The Copyright Office: General Responsibilities and Organization

(a) All administrative functions and duties under this title, except as otherwise specified, are the responsibility of the Register of Copyrights as director of the Copyright Office of the Library of Congress. The Register of Copyrights, together with the subordinate officers and employees of the Copyright Office, shall be appointed by the Librarian of Congress, and shall act under the Librarian's general direction and supervision.

(b) The Register of Copyrights shall adopt a seal to be used on and after January 1, 1978, to authenticate all certified documents issued by the Copyright Office.

(c) The Register of Copyrights shall make an annual report to the Librarian of Congress of the work and accomplishments of the Copyright Office during the previous fiscal year. The annual report of the Register of Copyrights shall be published separately and as a part of the annual report of the Librarian of Congress.

(d) Except as provided by section 706(b) and the regulations issued thereunder, all actions taken by the Register of Copyrights under this title are subject to the provisions of the Administrative Procedure Act of June 11, 1946, as amended (c. 324, 60 Stat. 237, title 5, United States Code, Chapter 5, Subchapter II and Chapter 7).

Sec. 702. Copyright Office Regulations

The Register of Copyrights is authorized to establish regulations not inconsistent with law for the administration of the functions and duties made the responsibility of the Register under this title. All regulations established by the Register under this title are subject to the approval of the Librarian of Congress.

Sec. 703. Effective Date of Actions in Copyright Office

In any case in which time limits are prescribed under this title for the performance of an action in the Copyright Office, and in which the last day of the prescribed period falls on a Saturday, Sunday, holiday, or other nonbusiness day within the District of Columbia or the Federal Government, the action may be taken on the next succeeding business day, and is effective as of the date when the period expired.

Sec. 704. Retention and Disposition of Articles Deposited in Copyright Office

(a) Upon their deposit in the Copyright Office under sections 407 and 408, all copies, phonorecords, and identifying material, including those deposited in connection with claims that have been refused registration, are the property of the United States Government.

(b) In the case of published works, all copies, phonorecords, and identifying material deposited are available to the Library of Congress for its collections, or for exchange or transfer to any other library. In the case of unpublished works, the Library is entitled, under regulations that the Register of Copyrights shall prescribe, to select any deposits for its collections or for transfer to the National Archives of the United States or to a Federal records center, as defined in section 2901 of title 44.

(c) The Register of Copyrights is authorized, for specific or general categories of works, to make a facsimile reproduction of all or any part of the material deposited under section 408, and to make such reproduction a part of the Copyright Office records of the registration, before transferring such material to the Library of Congress as provided by subsection (b), or before destroying or otherwise disposing of such material as provided by subsection (d).

(d) Deposits not selected by the Library under subsection (b), or identifying portions or reproductions of them, shall be retained under the control of the Copyright Office, including retention in Government storage facilities, for the longest period considered practicable and desirable by the Register of Copyrights and the Librarian of Congress. After that period it is within the joint discretion of the Register and the Librarian to order their destruction or other disposition; but, in the case of unpublished works, no deposit shall be knowingly or intentionally destroyed or otherwise disposed of during its term of copyright unless a facsimile reproduction of the entire deposit has been made a part of the Copyright Office records as provided by subsection (c).

(e) The depositor of copies, phonorecords, or identifying material under section 408, or the copyright owner of record, may request retention, under the control of the Copyright Office, of one or more of such articles for the full term of copyright in the work. The Register of Copyrights shall prescribe, by regulation, the conditions under which such requests are to be made and granted, and shall fix the fee to be charged under section 708(a)(11) if the request is granted.

Sec. 705. Copyright Office Records: Preparation, Maintenance, Public Inspection, and Searching

(a) The Register of Copyrights shall provide and keep in the Copyright Office records of all deposits, registrations, recordations, and other actions taken under this title, and shall prepare indexes of all such records.

(b) Such records and indexes, as well as the articles deposited in connection with completed copyright registrations and retained under the control of the Copyright Office, shall be open to public inspection.

(c) Upon request and payment of the fee specified by section 708, the Copyright Office shall make a search of its public records, indexes, and deposits, and shall furnish a report of the information they disclose with respect to any particular deposits, registrations, or recorded documents.

Sec. 706. Copies of Copyright Office Records

(a) Copies may be made of any public records or indexes of the Copyright Office; additional certificates of copyright registration and copies of any public records or indexes may be furnished upon request and payment of the fees specified by section 708.

(b) Copies or reproductions of deposited articles retained under the control of the Copyright Office shall be authorized or furnished only under the conditions specified by the Copyright Office regulations.

Sec. 707. Copyright Office Forms and Publications

(a) **Catalog of Copyright Entries.** The Register of Copyrights shall compile and publish at periodic intervals catalogs of all copyright registrations. These catalogs shall be divided into parts in accordance with the various classes of works, and the Register has discretion to determine, on the basis of practicability and usefulness, the form and frequency of publication of each particular part.

(b) **Other Publications.** The Register shall furnish, free of charge upon request, application forms for copyright registration and general informational material in connection with the functions of the Copyright Office. The Register also has the authority to publish compilations of information, bibliographies, and other material he or she considers to be of value to the public.

(c) **Distribution of Publications.** All publications of the Copyright Office shall be furnished to depository libraries as specified under section 1905 of title 44, and, aside from those furnished free of charge, shall be offered for sale to the public at prices based on the cost of reproduction and distribution.

Sec. 708. Copyright Office Fees

(a) The following fees shall be paid to the Register of Copyrights:

(1) on filing each application for registration of a copyright claim or a supplementary registration under section 408, including the issuance of a certificate of registration, $10;

(2) on filing each application for registration of a claim to renewal of a subsisting copyright in its first term under section 304(a), including the issuance of a certificate of registration if registration is made, $6;

(3) for the issuance of a receipt for a deposit under section 407, $2;

(4) for the recordation, as provided by section 205, of a transfer of copyright ownership or other document of six pages or less, covering no more than one title, $10; for each page over six and each title over one, 50 cents additional;

(5) for the filing, under section 115(b), of a notice of intention to make phonorecords, $6;

(6) for the recordation, under section 302(c), of a statement revealing the identity of an author of an anonymous or pseudonymous work, or for the recordation, under section 302(d), of a statement relating to the death of an author, $10 for a document of six pages or less, covering no more than one title; for each page over six and for each title over one, $1 additional;

(7) for the issuance, under section 601, of an import statement, $3;

(8) for the issuance, under section 706, of an additional certificate of registration, $4;

(9) for the issuance of any other certification, $4; the Register of Copyrights has discretion, on the basis of their cost, to fix the fees for preparing copies of Copyright Office records, whether they are to be certified or not;

(10) for the making and reporting of a search as provided by section 705, and for any related services, $10 for each hour or fraction of an hour consumed;

(11) for any other special services requiring a substantial amount of time or expense, such fees as the Register of Copyrights may fix on the basis of the cost of providing the service.[11]

(b) The fees prescribed by or under this section are applicable to the United States Government and any of its agencies, employees, or officers, but the Register of Copyrights has discretion to waive the requirement of this subsection in occasional or isolated cases involving relatively small amounts.

(c) All fees received under this section shall be deposited by the Register of Copyrights in the Treasury of the United States and shall be credited to the appropriation for necessary expenses of the Copyright Office. The Register may, in accordance with regulations that he or she shall prescribe, refund any sum paid by mistake or in excess of the fee required by this section.[12]

Sec. 709. Delay in Delivery Caused by Disruption of Postal or Other Services

In any case in which the Register of Copyrights determines, on the basis of such evidence as the Register may by regulation require, that a deposit, application, fee, or any other material to be delivered to the Copyright Office by a particular date, would have been received in the Copyright Office in due time except for a general disruption or suspension of postal or other transportation or communications services, the actual receipt of such material in the Copyright Office within one month after the date on which the Register determines that the disruption or suspension of such services has terminated, shall be considered timely.

Sec. 710. Reproduction for Use of the Blind and Physically Handicapped: Voluntary Licensing Forms and Procedures

The Register of Copyrights shall, after consultation with the Chief of the Division for the Blind and Physically Handicapped and other appropriate officials of the Library of Congress, establish by regulation standardized forms and procedures by which, at the time applications

---

11. Section 708(a) as amended by the Act of October 25, 1982, Pub.L. 97-366, 96 Stat. 1759, effective November 24, 1982.

12. Section 708(c) as amended by the Act of August 5, 1977, Pub.L. No. 95-94, and as further amended by the Act of October 25, 1982, Pub.L. 97-366.

covering certain specified categories of nondramatic literary works are submitted for registration under section 408 of this title, the copyright owner may voluntarily grant to the Library of Congress a license to reproduce the copyrighted work by means of Braille or similar tactile symbols, or by fixation of a reading of the work in a phonorecord, or both, and to distribute the resulting copies or phonorecords solely for the use of the blind and physically handicapped and under limited conditions to be specified in the standardized forms.

CHAPTER 8.—COPYRIGHT ROYALTY TRIBUNAL

Sec.
801. Copyright Royalty Tribunal: Establishment and Purpose.
802. Membership of the Tribunal.
803. Procedures of the Tribunal.
804. Institution and Conclusion of Proceedings.
805. Staff of the Tribunal.
806. Administrative Support of the Tribunal.
807. Deduction of Costs of Proceedings.
808. Reports.
809. Effective Date of Final Determinations.
810. Judicial Review.

Sec. 801. Copyright Royalty Tribunal: Establishment and Purpose

(a) There is hereby created an independent Copyright Royalty Tribunal in the legislative branch.

(b) Subject to the provisions of this chapter, the purposes of the Tribunal shall be—

(1) to make determinations concerning the adjustment of reasonable copyright royalty rates as provided in sections 115 and 116, and to make determinations as to reasonable terms and rates of royalty payments as provided in section 118. The rates applicable under sections 115 and 116 shall be calculated to achieve the following objectives:

(A) To maximize the availability of creative works to the public;

(B) To afford the copyright owner a fair return for his creative work and the copyright user a fair income under existing economic conditions;

(C) To reflect the relative roles of the copyright owner and the copyright user in the product made available to the public with respect to relative creative contribution, technological contribution, capital investment, cost, risk, and contribution to the opening of new markets for creative expression and media for their communication;

(D) To minimize any disruptive impact on the structure of the industries involved and on generally prevailing industry practices.

(2) to make determinations concerning the adjustment of the copyright royalty rates in section 111 solely in accordance with the following provisions:

(A) The rates established by section 111(d)(2)(B) may be adjusted to reflect (i) national monetary inflation or deflation or (ii) changes in the average rates charged cable subscribers for the basic service of providing secondary transmissions to maintain the real constant dollar level of the royalty fee per subscriber which existed as of the date of enactment of this Act: *Provided,* That if the average rates charged cable system subscribers for the basic service of providing secondary transmissions are changed so that the average rates exceed national monetary inflation, no change in the rates established by section 111(d)(2)(B) shall be permitted: *And provided further,* That no increase in the royalty fee shall be permitted based on any reduction in the average number of distant signal equivalents per subscriber. The Commission may consider all factors relating to the maintenance of such level of payments including, as an extenuating factor, whether the cable industry has been restrained by subscriber rate regulating authorities from increasing the rates for the basic service of providing secondary transmissions.

(B) In the event that the rules and regulations of the Federal Communications Commission are amended at any time after April 15, 1976, to permit the carriage by cable systems of additional television broadcast signals beyond the local service area of the primary transmitters of such signals, the royalty rates established by section 111(d)(2)(B) may be adjusted to insure that the rates for the additional distant signal equivalents resulting from such carriage are reasonable in the light of the changes effected by the amendment to such rules and regulations. In determining the reasonableness of rates proposed following an amendment of Federal Communications Commission rules and regulations, the Copyright Royalty Tribunal shall consider, among other factors, the economic impact on copyright owners and users: *Provided,* That no adjustment in royalty rates shall be made under this subclause with respect to any distant signal equivalent or fraction thereof represented by (i) carriage of any signal permitted under the rules and regulations of the Federal Communications Commission in effect on April 15, 1976, or the carriage of a signal of the same type (that is, independent, network, or noncommercial educational) substituted for such permitted signal, or (ii) a television broadcast signal first carried after April 15, 1976, pursuant to an individual waiver of the rules and regulations of the Federal Communications Commission, as such rules and regulations were in effect on April 15, 1976.

(C) In the event of any change in the rules and regulations of the Federal Communications Commission with respect to syndicated and sports program exclusivity after April 15, 1976, the rates established by section 111(d)(2)(B) may be adjusted to assure that such rates are reasonable in light of the changes to such rules and regulations, but any such adjustment shall apply only to the affected television broadcast signals carried on those systems affected by the change.

(D) The gross receipts limitations established by section 111(d)(2)(C) and (D) shall be adjusted to reflect national monetary inflation or deflation or changes in the average rates charged cable system subscribers for the basic service of providing secondary transmissions to maintain the real constant dollar value of the exemption provided by such section; and the royalty rate specified therein shall not be subject to adjustment; and

(3) to distribute royalty fees deposited with the Register of Copyrights under sections 111 and 116, and to determine, in cases where controversy exists, the distribution of such fees.

(c) As soon as possible after the date of enactment of this Act, and no later than six months following such date, the President shall publish a notice announcing the initial appointments provided in section 802, and shall designate an order of seniority among the initially-appointed commissioners for purposes of section 802(b).

Sec. 802. Membership of the Tribunal

(a) The Tribunal shall be composed of five commissioners appointed by the President with the advice and consent of the Senate for a term of seven years each; of the first five members appointed, three shall be designated to serve for seven years from the date of the notice specified in section 801(c), and two shall be designated to serve for five years from such date, respectively. Commissioners shall be compensated at the highest rate now or hereafter prescribe[d] for grade 18 of the General Schedule pay rates (5 U.S.C. 5332).

(b) Upon convening the commissioners shall elect a chairman from among the commissioners appointed for a full seven-year term. Such chairman shall serve for a term of one year. Thereafter, the most senior commissioner who has not previously served as chairman shall serve as chairman for a period of one year, except that, if all commissioners have served a full term as chairman, the most senior commissioner who has served the least number of terms as chairman shall be designated as chairman.

(c) Any vacancy in the Tribunal shall not affect its powers and shall be filled, for the unexpired term of the appointment, in the same manner as the original appointment was made.

Sec. 803. Procedures of the Tribunal

(a) The Tribunal shall adopt regulations, not inconsistent with law, governing its procedure and methods of operation. Except as otherwise provided in this chapter, the Tribunal shall be subject to the provisions of the Administrative Procedure Act of June 11, 1946, as amended (c. 324, 60 Stat. 237, title 5, United States Code, chapter 5, subchapter II and chapter 7).

(b) Every final determination of the Tribunal shall be published in the Federal Register. It shall state in detail the criteria that the Tribunal determined to be applicable to the particular proceeding, the various facts that it found relevant to its determination in that proceeding, and the specific reasons for its determination.

Sec. 804. Institution and Conclusion of Proceedings

(a) With respect to proceedings under section 801(b)(1) concerning the adjustment of royalty rates as provided in sections 115 and 116, and with respect to proceedings under section 801(b)(2)(A) and (D)—

(1) on January 1, 1980, the Chairman of the Tribunal shall cause to be published in the Federal Register notice of commencement of proceedings under this chapter; and

(2) during the calendar years specified in the following schedule, any owner or user of a copyrighted work whose royalty rates are specified by this title, or by a rate established by the Tribunal, may file a petition with the Tribunal declaring that the petitioner requests an adjustment of the rate. The Tribunal shall make a determination as to whether the applicant has a significant interest in the royalty rate in which an adjustment is requested. If the Tribunal determines that the petitioner has a significant interest, the Chairman shall cause notice of this determination, with the reasons therefor, to be published in the Federal Register, together with notice of commencement of proceedings under this chapter.

(A) In proceedings under section 801(b)(2)(A) and (D), such petition may be filed during 1985 and in each subsequent fifth calendar year.

(B) In proceedings under section 801(b)(1) concerning the adjustment of royalty rates as provided in section 115, such petition may be filed in 1987 and in each subsequent tenth calendar year.

(C) In proceedings under section 801(b)(1) concerning the adjustment of royalty rates under section 116, such petition may be filed in 1990 and in each subsequent tenth calendar year.

(b) With respect to proceedings under subclause (B) or (C) of section 801(b)(2), following an event described in either of those subsections, any owner or user of a copyrighted work whose royalty rates are specified by section 111, or by a rate established by the Tribunal, may, within twelve months, file a petition with the Tribunal declaring that the petitioner requests an adjustment of the rate. In this event the Tribunal shall proceed as in subsection (a)(2), above. Any change in royalty rates made by the Tribunal pursuant to this subsection may be reconsidered in 1980, 1985, and each fifth calendar year thereafter, in accordance with the provisions in section 801(b)(2)(B) or (C), as the case may be.

(c) With respect to proceedings under section 801(b)(1), concerning the determination of reasonable terms and rates of royalty payments as provided in section 118, the Tribunal shall proceed when and as provided by that section.

(d) With respect to proceedings under section 801(b)(3), concerning the distribution of royalty fees in certain circumstances under sections 111 or 116, the Chairman of the Tribunal shall, upon determination by the Tribunal that a controversy exists concerning such distribution, cause to be published in the Federal Register notice of commencement of proceedings under this chapter.

(e) All proceedings under this chapter shall be initiated without delay following publication of the notice specified in this section, and the Tribunal shall render its final decision in any such proceeding within one year from the date of such publication.

Sec. 805. Staff of the Tribunal

(a) The Tribunal is authorized to appoint and fix the compensation of such employees as may be necessary to carry out the provisions of this chapter, and to prescribe their functions and duties.

(b) The Tribunal may procure temporary and intermittent services to the same extent as is authorized by section 3109 of title 5.

Sec. 806. Administrative Support of the Tribunal

(a) The Library of Congress shall provide the Tribunal with necessary administrative services, including those related to budgeting, accounting, financial reporting, travel, personnel, and procurement. The Tribunal shall pay the Library for such services, either in advance or by reimbursement from the funds of the Tribunal, at amounts to be agreed upon between the Librarian and the Tribunal.

(b) The Library of Congress is authorized to disburse funds for the Tribunal, under regulations prescribed jointly by the Librarian of Congress and the Tribunal and approved by the Comptroller General. Such regulations shall establish requirements and procedures under which every voucher certified for payment by the Library of Congress under this chapter shall be supported with a certification by a duly authorized officer or employee of the Tribunal, and shall prescribe the responsibilities and accountability of said officers and employees of the Tribunal with respect to such certifications.

Sec. 807. Deduction of Costs of Proceedings

Before any funds are distributed pursuant to a final decision in a proceeding involving distribution of royalty fees, the Tribunal shall assess the reasonable costs of such proceeding.

Sec. 808. Reports

In addition to its publication of the reports of all final determinations as provided in section 803(b), the Tribunal shall make an annual report to the President and the Congress concerning the Tribunal's work during the preceding fiscal year, including a detailed fiscal statement of account.

Sec. 809. Effective Date of Final Determinations

Any final determination by the Tribunal under this chapter shall become effective thirty days following its publication in the Federal Register as provided in section 803(b), unless prior to that time an appeal has been filed pursuant to section 810, to vacate, modify, or correct such determination, and notice of such appeal has been served on all parties who appeared before the Tribunal in the proceeding in question. Where the proceeding involves the distribution of royalty fees under sections 111 or 116, the Tribunal shall, upon the expiration of such thirty-day period, distribute any royalty fees not subject to an appeal filed pursuant to section 810.

Sec. 810. Judicial Review

Any final decision of the Tribunal in a proceeding under section 801(b) may be appealed to the United States Court of Appeals, within thirty days after its publication in the Federal Register by an aggrieved party. The judicial review of the decision shall be had, in accordance with chapter 7 of title 5, on the basis of the record before the Tribunal. No court shall have jurisdiction to review a final decision of the Tribunal except as provided in this section.

TRANSITIONAL AND SUPPLEMENTARY PROVISIONS

SEC. 102. This Act becomes effective on January 1, 1978, except as otherwise expressly provided by this Act, including provisions of the first section of this Act. The provisions of sections 118, 304(b), and chapter 8 of title 17, as amended by the first section of this Act, take effect upon enactment of this Act.

SEC. 103. This Act does not provide copyright protection for any work that goes into the public domain before January 1, 1978. The exclusive rights, as provided by section 106 of title 17 as amended by the first section of this Act, to reproduce a work in phonorecords and to distribute phonorecords of the work, do not extend to any nondramatic musical work copyrighted before July 1, 1909.

SEC. 104. All proclamations issued by the President under section 1(e) or 9(b) of title 17 as it existed on December 31, 1977, or under previous copyright statutes of the United States, shall continue in force until terminated, suspended, or revised by the President.

SEC. 105. (a)(1) Section 505 of title 44 is amended to read as follows:

§ 505. Sale of Duplicate Plates

The Public Printer shall sell, under regulations of the Joint Committee on Printing to persons who may apply, additional or duplicate stereotype or electrotype plates from which a Government publication is printed, at a price not to exceed the cost of composition, the metal, and making to the Government, plus 10 per centum, and the full amount of the price shall be paid when the order is filed.

(2) The item relating to section 505 in the sectional analysis at the beginning of chapter 5 of title 44, is amended to read as follows:

"505. Sale of Duplicate Plates."

(b) Section 2113 of title 44 is amended to read as follows:

§ 2113. Limitation on Liability

When letters and other intellectual productions (exclusive of patented material, published works under copyright protection, and unpublished works for which copyright registration has been made) come into the custody or possession of the Administrator of General Services, the United States or its agents are not liable for infringement of copyright or analogous rights arising out of use of the materials for display, inspection, research, reproduction, or other purposes.

(c) In section 1498(b) of title 28, the phrase "section 101(b) of title 17" is amended to read "section 504(c) of title 17".

(d) Section 543(a)(4) of the Internal Revenue Code of 1954, as amended, is amended by striking out "(other than by reason of section 2 or 6 thereof)".

(e) Section 3202(a) of title 39 is amended by striking out clause (5). Section 3206 of title 39 is amended by deleting the words "subsections (b) and (c)" and inserting "subsection (b)" in subsection (a), and by deleting subsection (c). Section 3206(d) is renumbered (c).

(f) Subsection (a) of section 290(e) of title 15 is amended by deleting the phrase "section 8" and inserting in lieu thereof the phrase "section 105".

(g) Section 131 of title 2 is amended by deleting the phrase "deposit to secure copyright," and inserting in lieu thereof the phrase "acquisition of material under the copyright law,".

SEC. 106. In any case where, before January 1, 1978, a person has lawfully made parts of instruments serving to reproduce mechanically a copyrighted work under the compulsory license provisions of section 1(e) of title 17 as it existed on December 31, 1977, such person may continue to make and distribute such parts embodying the same mechanical reproduction without obtaining a new compulsory license under the terms of section 115 of title 17 as amended by the first section of this Act. However, such parts made on or after January 1, 1978, constitute phonorecords and are otherwise subject to the provisions of said section 115.

SEC. 107. In the case of any work in which an ad interim copyright is subsisting or is capable of being secured on December 31, 1977, under section 22 of title 17 as it existed on that date, copyright protection is hereby extended to endure for the term or terms provided by section 304 of title 17 as amended by the first section of this Act.

SEC. 108. The notice provisions of sections 401 through 403 of title 17 as amended by the first section of this Act apply to all copies or phonorecords publicly distributed on or after January 1, 1978. However, in the case of a work published before January 1, 1978, compliance with the notice provisions of title 17 either as it existed on December 31, 1977, or as amended by the first section of this Act, is adequate with respect to copies publicly distributed after December 31, 1977.

SEC. 109. The registration of claims to copyright for which the required deposit, application, and fee were received in the Copyright Office before January 1, 1978, and the recordation of assignments of copyright or other instruments received in the Copyright Office before January 1, 1978, shall be made in accordance with title 17 as it existed on December 31, 1977.

SEC. 110. The demand and penalty provisions of section 14 of title 17 as it existed on December 31, 1977, apply to any work in which copyright has been secured by publication with notice of copyright on or before that date, but any deposit and registration made after that date in response to a demand under that section shall be made in accordance with the provisions of title 17 as amended by the first section of this Act.

SEC. 111. Section 2318 of title 18 of the United States Code is amended to read as follows:

§ 2318. Transportation, Sale or Receipt of Phonograph Records Bearing Forged or Counterfeit Labels

(a) Whoever knowingly and with fraudulent intent transports, causes to be transported, receives, sells, or offers for sale in interstate or foreign commerce any phonograph record, disk, wire, tape, film, or other article on which sounds are recorded, to which or upon which is stamped, pasted, or affixed any forged or counterfeited label, knowing the label to have been falsely made, forged, or counterfeited shall be fined not more than $10,000 or imprisoned for not more than one year, or both, for the first such offense and shall be fined not more than $25,000 or imprisoned for not more than two years, or both, for any subsequent offense.

(b) When any person is convicted of any violation of subsection (a), the court in its judgment of conviction shall, in addition to the penalty therein prescribed, order the forfeiture and destruction or other disposition of all counterfeit labels and all articles to which counterfeit labels have been affixed or which were intended to have had such labels affixed.

(c) Except to the extent they are inconsistent with the provisions of this title, all provisions of section 509, title 17, United States Code, are applicable to violations of subsection (a).

SEC. 112. All causes of action that arose under title 17 before January 1, 1978, shall be governed by title 17 as it existed when the cause of action arose.

SEC. 113. (a) The Librarian of Congress (hereinafter referred to as the "Librarian") shall establish and maintain in the Library of Congress a library to be known as the American Television and Radio Archives (hereinafter referred to as the "Archives"). The purpose of the Archives shall be to preserve a permanent record of the television and radio programs which are the heritage of the people of the United States and to provide access to such programs to historians and scholars without encouraging or causing copyright infringement.

(1) The Librarian, after consultation with interested organizations and individuals, shall determine and place in the Archives such copies and phonorecords of television and radio programs transmitted to the public in the United States and in other countries which are of present or potential public or cultural interest, historical significance, cognitive value, or otherwise worthy of preservation, including copies and phonorecords of published and unpublished transmission programs—

(A) acquired in accordance with sections 407 and 408 of title 17 as amended by the first section of this Act; and

(B) transferred from the existing collections of the Library of Congress; and

(C) given to or exchanged with the Archives by other libraries, archives, organizations, and individuals; and

(D) purchased from the owner thereof.

(2) The Librarian shall maintain and publish appropriate catalogs and indexes of the collections of the Archives, and shall make such collections available for study and research under the conditions prescribed under this section.

(b) Notwithstanding the provisions of section 106 of title 17 as amended by the first section of this Act, the Librarian is authorized with respect to a transmission program which consists of a regularly scheduled newscast or on-the-spot coverage of news events and, under standards and conditions that the Librarian shall prescribe by regulation—

(1) to reproduce a fixation of such a program, in the same or another tangible form, for the purposes of preservation or security or for distribution under the conditions of clause (3) of this subsection; and

(2) to compile, without abridgment or any other editing, portions of such fixations according to subject matter, and to reproduce such compilations for the purpose of clause (1) of this subsection; and

(3) to distribute a reproduction made under clause (1) or (2) of this subsection—

(A) by loan to a person engaged in research; and

(B) for deposit in a library or archives which meets the requirements of section 108(a) of title 17 as amended by the first section of this Act,

in either case for use only in research and not for further reproduction or performance.

(c) The Librarian or any employee of the Library who is acting under the authority of this section shall not be liable in any action for copyright infringement committed by any other person unless the Librarian or such employee knowingly participated in the act of infringement committed by such person. Nothing in this section shall be construed to excuse or limit liability under title 17 as amended by the first section of this Act for any act not authorized by that title or this section, or for any act performed by a person not authorized to act under that title or this section.

(d) This section may be cited as the "American Television and Radio Archives Act".

SEC. 114. There are hereby authorized to be appropriated such funds as may be necessary to carry out the purposes of this Act.

SEC. 115. If any provision of title 17, as amended by the first section of this Act, is declared unconstitutional, the validity of the remainder of this title is not affected.

Approved October 19, 1976.*

LEGISLATIVE HISTORY:

HOUSE REPORTS: No. 94–1476 (Comm. on the Judiciary) and No. 94–1733 (Comm. of Conference).

SENATE REPORT: No. 94–473 (Comm. on the Judiciary).

CONGRESSIONAL RECORD, Vol. 122 (1976):

Feb. 6, 16–19, considered and passed Senate.

Sept. 22, considered and passed Senate, amended.

Sept. 30, Senate and House agreed to conference report.

---

* The Semiconductor Chip Protection Act of 1984, Public Law No. 98–620 was approved on November 8, 1984 and added to Title 17 of the United States Code as Chapter 9. This law is analyzed in Chapter 18 of *Nimmer on Copyright*.

Appendix C

THE COPYRIGHT ACT OF 1909 AS INCORPORATED IN THE UNITED STATES CODE

Title 17—Copyrights [1]

Chap.		Sec.
1.	Registration of Copyright	1
2.	Infringement Proceedings	101
3.	Copyright Office	201

CHAPTER 1—REGISTRATION OF COPYRIGHT

Sec.
1. Exclusive rights as to copyrighted works.
2. Rights of author or proprietor of unpublished work.
3. Protection of component parts of work copyrighted; composite works or periodicals.
4. All writings of author included.
5. Classification of works for registration.
6. Registration of prints and labels.
7. Copyright on compilations of works in public domain or of copyrighted works; subsisting copyrights not affected.
8. Copyright not to subsist in works in public domain, or published prior to July 1, 1909, and not already copyrighted, or Government publica-

---

1. Act of July 30, 1947 (61 Stat. 652). The enacting clause provides that Title 17 of the United States Code entitled "Copyrights" is codified and enacted into positive law and may be cited as "Title 17, U.S.C., Sec. —". The Act of April 27, 1948 (62 Stat. 202) amended sections 211 and 215. The Act of June 25, 1948 (62 Stat. 869) repealed sections 101(f), 102, 103, 110 and 111; however, see sections 1338, 1440 and 2072 (Title 28, United States Code) and the Federal Rules of Civil Procedure. The Act of June 3, 1949 (63 Stat. 153) amended sections 16, 22, 23 and 215. The Act of October 31, 1951 (65 Stat. 710) amended sections 3, 8, 112 and 114, and struck out the items of the analysis of chapter 2 relating to the repealed sections. The Act of July 17, 1952 (66 Stat. 752) amended section 1(c). The Act of April 13, 1954 (68 Stat. 52) added section 216. The Act of August 31, 1954 (68 Stat. 1030) amended sections 9, 16 and 19. The Act of March 29, 1956 (70 Stat. 63) amended section 13. The Act of September 7, 1957 (71 Stat. 633), amended section 115. The Act of Sept. 7, 1962 (79 Stat. 606) amended section 21. The Act of October 15, 1971 (85 Stat. 391) amended sections 1, 5, 19, 20, 26, and 101. The Act of December 31, 1974 (88 Stat. 1873) amended section 104.

Sec.

tions; publication by Government of copyrighted material.
9. Authors or proprietors, entitled; aliens.
10. Publication of work with notice.
11. Registration of claim and issuance of certificate.
12. Works not reproduced for sale.
13. Deposit of copies after publication; action or proceeding for infringement.
14. Same; failure to deposit; demand; penalty.
15. Same; postmaster's receipt; transmission by mail without cost.
16. Mechanical work to be done in United States.
17. Affidavit to accompany copies.
18. Making false affidavit.
19. Notice; form.
20. Same; place of application of; one notice in each volume or number of newspaper or periodical.
21. Same; effect of accidental omission from copy or copies.
22. Ad interim protection of book or periodical published abroad.
23. Same; extension to full term.
24. Duration; renewal and extension.
25. Renewal of copyrights registered in Patent Office under repealed law.
26. Terms defined.
27. Copyright distinct from property in object copyrighted; effect of sale of object, and of assignment of copyright.
28. Assignments and bequests.
29. Same; executed in foreign country; acknowledgment and certificate.
30. Same; record.
31. Same; certificate of record.
32. Same; use of name of assignee in notice.

Sec. 1. Exclusive Rights as to Copyrighted Works

Any person entitled thereto, upon complying with the provisions of this title, shall have the exclusive right:

(a) To print, reprint, publish, copy, and vend the copyrighted work;

(b) To translate the copyrighted work into other languages or dialects, or make any other version thereof, if it be a literary work; to dramatize it if it be a nondramatic work; to convert it into a novel or other nondramatic work if it be a drama; to arrange or adapt it if it be a musical work; to complete, execute, and finish it if it be a model or design for a work of art;

(c) [2] To deliver, authorize the delivery of, read, or present the copyrighted work in public for profit if it be a lecture, sermon, address or similar production, or other nondramatic literary work; to make or procure the making of any transcription or record thereof by or from which, in whole or in part, it may in any manner or by any method be exhibited, delivered, presented, produced, or reproduced; and to play or perform it in public for profit, and to exhibit, represent, produce, or

---

2. Section 1(c) as amended by the Act of July 17, 1952 (66 Stat. 752), effective January 1, 1953.

reproduce it in any manner or by any method whatsoever. The damages for the infringement by broadcast of any work referred to in this subsection shall not exceed the sum of $100 where the infringing broadcaster shows that he was not aware that he was infringing and that such infringement could not have been reasonably foreseen; and

(d) To perform or represent the copyrighted work publicly if it be a drama or, if it be a dramatic work and not reproduced in copies for sale, to vend any manuscript or any record whatsoever thereof; to make or to procure the making of any transcription or record thereof by or from which, in whole or in part, it may in any manner or by any method be exhibited, performed, represented, produced, or reproduced; and to exhibit, perform, represent, produce, or reproduce it in any manner or by any method whatsoever; and

(e) To perform the copyrighted work publicly for profit if it be a musical composition; and for the purpose of public performance for profit, and for the purposes set forth in subsection (a) hereof, to make any arrangement or setting of it or of the melody of it in any system of notation or any form of record in which the thought of an author may be recorded and from which it may be read or reproduced: *Provided,* That the provisions of this title, so far as they secure copyright controlling the parts of instruments serving to reproduce mechanically the musical work, shall include only compositions published and copyrighted after July 1, 1909, and shall not include the works of a foreign author or composer unless the foreign state or nation of which such author or composer is a citizen or subject grants, either by treaty, convention, agreement, or law, to citizens of the United States similar rights. And as a condition of extending the copyright control to such mechanical reproductions, that whenever the owner of a musical copyright has used or permitted or knowingly acquiesced in the use of the copyrighted work upon the parts of instruments serving to reproduce mechanically the musical work, any other person may make similar use of the copyrighted work upon the payment to the copyright proprietor of a royalty of 2 cents on each such part manufactured, to be paid by the manufacturer thereof; and the copyright proprietor may require, and if so the manufacturer shall furnish, a report under oath on the 20th day of each month on the number of parts of instruments manufactured during the previous month serving to reproduce mechanically said musical work, and royalties shall be due on the parts manufactured during any month upon the 20th of the next succeeding month. The payment of the royalty provided for by this section shall free the articles or devices for which such royalty has been paid from further contribution to the copyright except in case of public performance for profit. It shall be the duty of the copyright owner, if he uses the musical composition himself for the manufacture of parts of instruments serving to reproduce mechanically the musical work, or licenses others to do so, to file notice thereof, accompanied by a recording fee, in the copyright office, and any failure to file such notice shall be a complete defense to any suit, action, or proceeding for any infringement of such copyright.

In case of failure of such manufacturer to pay to the copyright proprietor within thirty days after demand in writing the full sum of royalties due at said rate at the date of such demand, the court may award taxable costs to the plaintiff and a reasonable counsel fee, and the court may, in its discretion, enter judgment therein for any sum in addition over the amount found to be due as royalty in accordance with the terms of this title, not exceeding three times such amount.

The reproduction or rendition of a musical composition by or upon coin-operated machines shall not be deemed a public performance for profit unless a fee is charged for admission to the place where such reproduction or rendition occurs.

(f) [3] To produce and distribute to the public by sale or other transfer of ownership, or by rental, lease, or lending, reproductions of the copyrighted work if it be a sound recording: *Provided,* That the exclusive right of the owner of a copyright in a sound recording to reproduce it is limited to the right to duplicate the sound recording in a tangible form that directly or indirectly recaptures the actual sounds fixed in the recording: *Provided further,* That this right does not extend to the making or duplication of another sound recording that is an independent fixation of other sounds, even though such sounds imitate or simulate those in the copyrighted sound recording; or to the reproductions made by transmitting organizations exclusively for their own use.

Sec. 2. Rights of Author or Proprietor of Unpublished Work

Nothing in this title shall be construed to annul or limit the right of the author or proprietor of an unpublished work, at common law or in equity, to prevent the copying, publication, or use of such unpublished work without his consent, and to obtain damages therefor.

Sec. 3. Protection of Component Parts of Work Copyrighted; Composite Works or Periodicals

The copyright provided by this title shall protect all the copyrightable component parts of the work copyrighted, and all matter therein in which copyright is already subsisting, but without extending the duration or scope of such copyright. The copyright upon composite works or periodicals shall give to the proprietor thereof all the rights in respect thereto which he would have if each part were individually copyrighted under this title.

Sec. 4. All Writings of Author Included

The works for which copyright may be secured under this title

---

3. Subsection (f) was added by the Act of October 15, 1971 (85 Stat. 391), effective February 15, 1972. See Sec. 5(n), n1.

shall include all the writings of an author.

Sec. 5. Classification of Works for Registration

The application for registration shall specify to which of the following classes the work in which copyright is claimed belongs:

(a) Books, including composite and cyclopedic works, directories, gazetteers, and other compilations.

(b) Periodicals, including newspapers.

(c) Lectures, sermons, addresses (prepared for oral delivery).

(d) Dramatic or dramatico-musical compositions.

(e) Musical compositions.

(f) Maps.

(g) Works of art; models or designs for works of art.

(h) Reproductions of a work of art.

(i) Drawings or plastic works of a scientific or technical character.

(j) Photographs.

(k) Prints and pictorial illustrations including prints or labels used for articles of merchandise.

(l) Motion-picture photoplays.

(m) Motion pictures other than photoplays.

(n) Sound recordings.[4]

The above specifications shall not be held to limit the subject matter of copyright as defined in section 4 of this title, nor shall any error in classification invalidate or impair the copyright protection secured under this title.

Sec. 6. Registration of Prints and Labels

Commencing July 1, 1940, the Register of Copyrights is charged with the registration of claims to copyright properly presented, in all prints and labels published in connection with the sale or advertisement of articles of merchandise, including all claims to copyright in prints and labels pending in the Patent Office and uncleared at the

---

4. Subsection (n) was added by the Act of October 15, 1971 (85 Stat. 391). Sec. 3 of said Act reads as follows:

This Act shall take effect four months after its enactment [date of enactment: October 15, 1971] except that section 2 of this Act [amending Sec. 101(e)] shall take effect immediately upon its enactment. The provisions of title 17, United States Code, as amended by section 1 of this Act, shall apply only to sound recordings fixed, published, and copyrighted on and after the effective date of this Act and before January 1, 1975, and nothing in title 17, United States Code, as amended by section 1 of this Act, shall be applied retroactively or be construed as affecting in any way any rights with respect to sound recordings fixed before the effective date of this Act.

Sec. 101 of the Act of December 31, 1974 (88 Stat. 1873) amended Sec. 3 of the Act of October 15, 1971 by striking out the words "and before January 1, 1975". The effect of this amendment was to make Sec. 5(n) of the Copyright Act applicable to all sound recordings fixed, published and copyrighted on and after February 15, 1972.

close of business June 30, 1940. There shall be paid for registering a claim of copyright in any such print or label not a trade-mark $6, which sum shall cover the expense of furnishing a certificate of such registration, under the seal of the Copyright Office, to the claimant of copyright.

Sec. 7. Copyright on Compilations of Works in Public Domain or of Copyrighted Works; Subsisting Copyrights Not Affected

Compilations or abridgments, adaptations, arrangements, dramatizations, translations, or other versions of works in the public domain or of copyrighted works when produced with the consent of the proprietor of the copyright in such works, or works republished with new matter, shall be regarded as new works subject to copyright under the provisions of this title; but the publication of any such new works shall not affect the force or validity of any subsisting copyright upon the matter employed or any part thereof, or be construed to imply an exclusive right to such use of the original works, or to secure or extend copyright in such original works.

Sec. 8. Copyright Not to Subsist in Works in Public Domain, or Published Prior to July 1, 1909, and not Already Copyrighted, or Government Publications; Publication by Government of Copyrighted Material

No copyright shall subsist in the original text of any work which is in the public domain, or in any work which was published in this country or any foreign country prior to July 1, 1909, and has not been already copyrighted in the United States, or in any publication of the United States Government, or any reprint, in whole or in part, thereof: *Provided,* That copyright may be secured by the Postmaster General on behalf of the United States in the whole or any part of the publications authorized by section 2506 of title 39.

The publication or republication by the Government, either separately or in a public document, of any material in which copyright is subsisting shall not be taken to cause any abridgment or annulment of the copyright or to authorize any use or appropriation of such copyright material without the consent of the copyright proprietor.

Sec. 9. Authors or Proprietors, Entitled: Aliens [5]

The author or proprietor of any work made the subject of copyright by this title, or his executors, administrators, or assigns, shall have copyright for such work under the conditions and for the terms specified in this title: *Provided, however,* That the copyright secured by this title shall extend to the work of an author or proprietor who is a citizen or subject of a foreign state or nation only under the conditions described in subsections (a), (b), or (c) below:

---

[5]. Section 9 as amended by the Act of August 31, 1954 (68 Stat. 1030), effective September 16, 1955.

(a) When an alien author or proprietor shall be domiciled within the United States at the time of the first publication of his work; or

(b) When the foreign state or nation of which such author or proprietor is a citizen or subject grants, either by treaty, convention, agreement, or law, to citizens of the United States the benefit of copyright on substantially the same basis as to its own citizens, or copyright protection, substantially equal to the protection secured to such foreign author under this title or by treaty; or when such foreign state or nation is a party to an international agreement which provides for reciprocity in the granting of copyright, by the terms of which agreement the United States may, at its pleasure, become a party thereto.

The existence of the reciprocal conditions aforesaid shall be determined by the President of the United States, by proclamation made from time to time, as the purposes of this title may require: *Provided,* That whenever the President shall find that the authors, copyright owners, or proprietors of works first produced or published abroad and subject to copyright or to renewal of copyright under the laws of the United States, including works subject to ad interim copyright, are or may have been temporarily unable to comply with the conditions and formalities prescribed with respect to such works by the copyright laws of the United States, because of the disruption or suspension of facilities essential for such compliance, he may by proclamation grant such extension of time as he may deem appropriate for the fulfillment of such conditions or formalities by authors, copyright owners, or proprietors who are citizens of the United States or who are nationals of countries which accord substantially equal treatment in this respect to authors, copyright owners, or proprietors who are citizens of the United States: *Provided further,* That no liability shall attach under this title for lawful uses made or acts done prior to the effective date of such proclamation in connection with such works, or in respect to the continuance for one year subsequent to such date of any business undertaking or enterprise lawfully undertaken prior to such date involving expenditure or contractual obligation in connection with the exploitation, production, reproduction, circulation, or performance of any such work.

The President may at any time terminate any proclamation authorized herein or any part thereof or suspend or extend its operation for such period or periods of time as in his judgment the interests of the United States may require.

(c) When the Universal Copyright Convention, signed at Geneva on September 6, 1952, shall be in force [6] between the United States of America and the foreign state or nation of which such author is a citizen or subject, or in which the work was first published. Any work to which copyright is extended pursuant to this subsection shall be exempt from the following provisions of this title: (1) The requirement

---

6. The Universal Copyright Convention came into force on September 16, 1955.

in section 1(e) that a foreign state or nation must grant to United States citizens mechanical reproduction rights similar to those specified therein; (2) the obligatory deposit requirements of the first sentence of section 13; (3) the provisions of sections 14, 16, 17, and 18; (4) the import prohibitions of section 107, to the extent that they are related to the manufacturing requirements of section 16; and (5) the requirements of sections 19 and 20: *Provided, however,* That such exemptions shall apply only if from the time of first publication all the copies of the work published with the authority of the author or other copyright proprietor shall bear the symbol © accompanied by the name of the copyright proprietor and the year of first publication placed in such manner and location as to give reasonable notice of claim of copyright.

Upon the coming into force of the Universal Copyright Convention in a foreign state or nation as hereinbefore provided, every book or periodical of a citizen or subject thereof in which ad interim copyright was subsisting on the effective date of said coming into force shall have copyright for twenty-eight years from the date of first publication abroad without the necessity of complying with the further formalities specified in section 23 of this title.

The provisions of this subsection shall not be extended to works of an author who is a citizen of, or domiciled in the United States of America regardless of place of first publication, or to works first published in the United States.

Sec. 10. Publication of Work With Notice

Any person entitled thereto by this title may secure copyright for his work by publication thereof with the notice of copyright required by this title; and such notice shall be affixed to each copy thereof published or offered for sale in the United States by authority of the copyright proprietor, except in the case of books seeking ad interim protection under section 22 of this title.

Sec. 11. Registration of Claim and Issuance of Certificate

Such person may obtain registration of his claim to copyright by complying with the provisions of this title, including the deposit of copies, and upon such compliance the Register of Copyrights shall issue to him the certificates provided for in section 209 of this title.

Sec. 12. Works Not Reproduced for Sale

Copyright may also be had of the works of an author, of which copies are not reproduced for sale, by the deposit, with claim of copyright, of one complete copy of such work if it be a lecture or similar production or a dramatic, musical, or dramatico-musical composition; of a title and description, with one print taken from each scene or act, if the work be a motion-picture photoplay; of a photographic print if the work be a photograph; of a title and description, with not less than two prints taken from different sections of a complete motion picture, if the work be a motion picture other than a photoplay; or of a photograph or other identifying reproduction thereof, if it be a work of art or a plastic work or drawing. But the privilege of registration of copyright secured hereunder shall not exempt the copyright proprietor from the deposit of copies, under sections 13 and 14 of this title, where the work is later reproduced in copies for sale.

Sec. 13. Deposit of Copies After Publication; Action or Proceeding for Infringement [7]

After copyright has been secured by publication of the work with the notice of copyright as provided in section 10 of this title, there shall be promptly deposited in the Copyright Office or in the mail addressed to the Register of Copyrights, Washington, District of Columbia, two complete copies of the best edition thereof then published, or if the work is by an author who is a citizen or subject of a foreign state or nation and has been published in a foreign country, one complete copy of the best edition then published in such foreign country, which copies or copy, if the work be a book or periodical, shall have been produced in accordance with the manufacturing provisions specified in section 16 of this title; or if such work be a contribution to a periodical, for which contribution special registration is requested, one copy of the issue or issues containing such contribution; or if the work belongs to a class specified in subsections (g), (h), (i) or (k) of section 5 of this title, and if the Register of Copyrights determines that it is impracticable to deposit copies because of their size, weight, fragility, or monetary value he may permit the deposit of photographs or other identifying reproductions in lieu of copies of the work as published under such rules and regulations as he may prescribe with the approval of the Librarian of Congress; or if the work is not reproduced in copies for sale there shall be deposited the copy, print, photograph, or other identifying reproduction provided by section 12 of this title, such copies or copy, print, photograph, or other reproduction to be accompanied in each case by a claim of copyright. No action or proceeding shall be maintained for infringement of copyright in any work until the provisions of this title with respect to the deposit of copies and registration of such work shall have been complied with.

Sec. 14. Same; Failure to Deposit; Demand; Penalty

Should the copies called for by section 13 of this title not be promptly deposited as provided in this title, the Register of Copyrights may at any time after the publication of the work, upon actual notice, require the proprietor of the copyright to deposit them, and after the said demand shall have been made, in default of the deposit of copies of the work within three months from any part of the United States, except an outlying territorial possession of the United States, or within six months from any outlying territorial possession of the United States, or from any foreign country, the proprietor of the copyright shall be liable to a fine of $100 and to pay to the Library of Congress

---

7. Section 13 as amended by the Act of March 29, 1956 (70 Stat. 63).

twice the amount of the retail price of the best edition of the work, and the copyright shall become void.

Sec. 15. Same; Postmaster's Receipt; Transmission by Mail Without Cost

The postmaster to whom are delivered the articles deposited as provided in sections 12 and 13 of this title shall, if requested, give a receipt therefor and shall mail them to their destination without cost to the copyright claimant.

Sec. 16. Mechanical Work To Be Done in United States [8]

Of the printed book or periodical specified in section 5, subsections (a) and (b), of this title, except the original text of a book or periodical of foreign origin in a language or languages other than English, the text of all copies accorded protection under this title, except as below provided, shall be printed from type set within the limits of the United States, either by hand or by the aid of any kind of typesetting machine, or from plates made within the limits of the United States from type set therein, or, if the text be produced by lithographic process, or photoengraving process, then by a process wholly performed within the limits of the United States, and the printing of the text and binding of the said book shall be performed within the limits of the United States; which requirements shall extend also to the illustrations within a book consisting of printed text and illustrations produced by lithographic process, or photoengraving process, and also to separate lithographs or photoengravings, except where in either case the subjects represented are located in a foreign country and illustrate a scientific work or reproduce a work of art: *Provided, however,* That said requirements shall not apply to works in raised characters for the use of the blind, or to books or periodicals of foreign origin in a language or languages other than English, or to works printed or produced in the United States by any other process than those above specified in this section, or to copies of books or periodicals, first published abroad in the English language, imported into the United States within five years after first publication in a foreign state or nation up to the number of fifteen hundred copies of each such book or periodical if said copies shall contain notice of copyright in accordance with sections 10, 19, and 20 of this title and if ad interim copyright in said work shall have been obtained pursuant to section 22 of this title prior to the importation into the United States of any copy except those permitted by the provisions of section 107 of this title: *Provided further,* That the provisions of this section shall not affect the right of importation under the provisions of section 107 of this title.

Sec. 17. Affidavit to Accompany Copies

In the case of the book the copies so deposited shall be accompanied

---

8. Section 16 as amended by the Act of August 31, 1954 (68 Stat. 1030), effective September 16, 1955.

by an affidavit under the official seal of any officer authorized to administer oaths within the United States, duly made by the person claiming copyright or by his duly authorized agent or representative residing in the United States, or by the printer who has printed the book, setting forth that the copies deposited have been printed from type set within the limits of the United States or from plates made within the limits of the United States from type set therein; or, if the text be produced by lithographic process, or photoengraving process, that such process was wholly performed within the limits of the United States and that the printing of the text and binding of the said book have also been performed within the limits of the United States. Such affidavit shall state also the place where and the establishment or establishments in which such type was set or plates were made or lithographic process, or photoengraving process or printing and binding were performed and the date of the completion of the printing of the book or the date of publication.

Sec. 18. Making False Affidavit

Any person who, for the purpose of obtaining registration of a claim to copyright, shall knowingly make a false affidavit as to his having complied with the above conditions shall be deemed guilty of a misdemeanor, and upon conviction thereof shall be punished by a fine of not more than $1,000, and all of his rights and privileges under said copyright shall thereafter be forfeited.

Sec. 19. Notice; Form [9]

The notice of copyright required by section 10 of this title shall consist either of the word "Copyright," the abbreviation "Copr.," or the symbol ©, accompanied by the name of the copyright proprietor, and if the work be a printed literary, musical, or dramatic work, the notice shall include also the year in which the copyright was secured by publication. In the case, however, of copies of works specified in subsections (f) to (k), inclusive, of section 5 of this title, the notice may consist of the letter C enclosed within a circle, thus ©, accompanied by the initials, monogram, mark, or symbol of the copyright proprietor: *Provided*, That on some accessible portion of such copies or of the margin, back, permanent base, or pedestal, or of the substance on which such copies shall be mounted, his name shall appear. But in the case of works in which copyright was subsisting on July 1, 1909, the notice of copyright may be either in one of the forms prescribed herein or may consist of the following words: "Entered according to Act of Congress, in the year _____, by A.B., in the office of the Librarian of Congress, at Washington, D.C.," or, at his option, the word "Copyright," together with the year the copyright was entered and the name of the party by whom it was taken out; thus, "Copyright, 19——, by A.B."

---

9. Section 19 as amended by the Act of August 31, 1954 (68 Stat. 1030), effective September 16, 1955, and by the Act of October 15, 1971 (85 Stat. 391), effective February 15, 1972. See Sec. 5(n), n1.

In the case of reproductions of works specified in subsection (n) of section 5 of this title, the notice shall consist of the symbol ℗ (the letter P in a circle), the year of first publication of the sound recording, and the name of the owner of copyright in the sound recording, or an abbreviation by which the name can be recognized, or a generally known alternative designation of the owner: *Provided,* That if the producer of the sound recording is named on the labels or containers of the reproduction, and if no other name on the labels or containers of the reproduction, and if no other name appears in conjunction with the notice, his name shall be considered a part of the notice.

Sec. 20. Same; Place of Application of; One Notice in Each Volume or Number of Newspaper or Periodical [10]

The notice of copyright shall be applied, in the case of a book or other printed publication, upon its title page or the page immediately following, or if a periodical either upon the title page or upon the first page of text of each separate number or under the title heading, or if a musical work either upon its title page or the first page of music, or if a sound recording on the surface of reproductions thereof or on the label or container in such manner and location as to give reasonable notice to the claim of copyright. One notice of copyright in each volume or in each number of a newspaper or periodical published shall suffice.

Sec. 21. Same; Effect of Accidental Omission from Copy or Copies

Where the copyright proprietor has sought to comply with the provisions of this title with respect to notice, the omission by accident or mistake of the prescribed notice from a particular copy or copies shall not invalidate the copyright or prevent recovery for infringement against any person who, after actual notice of the copyright, begins an undertaking to infringe it, but shall prevent the recovery of damages against an innocent infringer who has been misled by the omission of the notice; and in a suit for infringement no permanent injunction shall be had unless the copyright proprietor shall reimburse to the innocent infringer his reasonable outlay innocently incurred if the court, in its discretion, shall so direct.

Sec. 22. Ad Interim Protection of Book or Periodical Published Abroad [11]

In the case of a book or periodical first published abroad in the English language, the deposit in the Copyright Office, not later than six months after its publication abroad, of one complete copy of the foreign edition, with a request for the reservation of the copyright and a statement of the name and nationality of the author and of the copyright proprietor and of the date of publication of the said book or

---

10. Section 20 as amended by the Act of October 15, 1971 (85 Stat. 391), effective February 15, 1972. See Sec. 5(n), n1.

11. Section 22 as amended by the Act of June 3, 1949 (63 Stat. 153).

periodical, shall secure to the author or proprietor an ad interim copyright therein, which shall have all the force and effect given to copyright by this title, and shall endure until the expiration of five years after the date of first publication abroad.

Sec. 23. Same; Extension to Full Term [12]

Whenever within the period of such ad interim protection an authorized edition of such books or periodicals shall be published within the United States, in accordance with the manufacturing provisions specified in section 16 of this title, and whenever the provisions of this title as to deposit of copies, registration, filing of affidavits, and the printing of the copyright notice shall have been duly complied with, the copyright shall be extended to endure in such book or periodical for the term provided in this title.

Sec. 24. Duration; Renewal and Extension

The copyright secured by this title shall endure for twenty-eight years from the date of first publication, whether the copyrighted work bears the author's true name or is published anonymously or under an assumed name: *Provided,* That in the case of any posthumous work or of any periodical, cyclopedic, or other composite work upon which the copyright was originally secured by the proprietor thereof, or of any work copyrighted by a corporate body (otherwise than as assignee or licensee of the individual author) or by an employer for whom such work is made for hire, the proprietor of such copyright shall be entitled to a renewal and extension of the copyright in such work for the further term of twenty-eight years when application for such renewal and extension shall have been made to the copyright office and duly registered therein within one year prior to the expiration of the original term of copyright: *And provided further,* That in the case of any other copyrighted work, including a contribution by an individual author to a periodical or to a cyclopedic or other composite work, the author of such work, if still living, or the widow, widower, or children of the author, if the author be not living, or if such author, widow, widower, or children be not living, then the author's executors, or in the absence of a will, his next of kin shall be entitled to a renewal and extension of the copyright in such work for a further term of twenty-eight years when application for such renewal and extension shall have been made to the copyright office and duly registered therein within one year prior to the expiration of the original term of copyright: *And provided further,* That in default of the registration of such application for renewal and extension, the copyright in any work shall determine at the expiration of twenty-eight years from first publication.

Sec. 25. Renewal of Copyrights Registered in Patent Office Under Repealed Law

Subsisting copyrights originally registered in the Patent Office prior to July 1, 1940, under section 3 of the act of June 18, 1874, shall

---

12. Section 23 as amended by the Act of June 3, 1949 (63 Stat. 153).

be subject to renewal in behalf of the proprietor upon application made to the Register of Copyrights within one year prior to the expiration of the original term of twenty-eight years.

Sec. 26. Terms Defined [13]

In the interpretation and construction of this title "the date of publication" shall in the case of a work of which copies are reproduced for sale or distribution be held to be the earliest date when copies of the first authorized edition were placed on sale, sold, or publicly distributed by the proprietor of the copyright or under his authority, and the word "author" shall include an employer in the case of works made for hire. For the purposes of this section and sections 10, 11, 13, 14, 21, 101, 106, 109, 209, 215, but not for any other purpose, a reproduction of a work described in subsection 5(n) shall be considered to be a copy thereof. "Sound recordings" are works that result from the fixation of a series of musical, spoken, or other sounds, but not including the sounds accompanying a motion picture. "Reproductions of sound recordings" are material objects in which sounds other than those accompanying a motion picture are fixed by any method now known or later developed, and from which the sounds can be perceived, reproduced, or otherwise communicated, either directly or with the aid of a machine or device, and include the "parts of instruments serving to reproduce mechanically the musical work," "mechanical reproductions," and "interchangeable parts, such as discs or tapes for use in mechanical music-producing machines" referred to in sections 1(e) and 101(e) of this title.

Sec. 27. Copyright Distinct from Property in Object Copyrighted; Effect of Sale of Object, and of Assignment of Copyright

The copyright is distinct from the property in the material object copyrighted, and the sale or conveyance, by gift or otherwise, of the material object shall not of itself constitute a transfer of the copyright, nor shall the assignment of the copyright constitute a transfer of the title to the material object; but nothing in this title shall be deemed to forbid, prevent, or restrict the transfer of any copy of a copyrighted work the possession of which has been lawfully obtained.

Sec. 28. Assignments and Bequests

Copyright secured under this title or previous copyright laws of the United States may be assigned, granted, or mortgaged by an instrument in writing signed by the proprietor of the copyright, or may be bequeathed by will.

Sec. 29. Same; Executed in Foreign Country; Acknowledgment and Certificate

Every assignment of copyright executed in a foreign country shall

---

[13]. Section 26 as amended by the Act of October 15, 1971 (85 Stat. 391), effective February 15, 1972. See Sec. 5(n), n1.

be acknowledged by the assignor before a consular officer or secretary of legation of the United States authorized by law to administer oaths or perform notarial acts. The certificate of such acknowledgment under the hand and official seal of such consular officer or secretary of legation shall be prima facie evidence of the execution of the instrument.

Sec. 30. Same; Record

Every assignment of copyright shall be recorded in the copyright office within three calendar months after its execution in the United States or within six calendar months after its execution without the limits of the United States, in default of which it shall be void as against any subsequent purchaser or mortgagee for a valuable consideration, without notice, whose assignment has been duly recorded.

Sec. 31. Same; Certificate of Record

The Register of Copyrights shall, upon payment of the prescribed fee, record such assignment, and shall return it to the sender with a certificate of record attached under seal of the copyright office, and upon the payment of the fee prescribed by this title he shall furnish to any person requesting the same a certified copy thereof under the said seal.

Sec. 32. Same; Use of Name of Assignee in Notice

When an assignment of the copyright in a specified book or other work has been recorded the assignee may substitute his name for that of the assignor in the statutory notice of copyright prescribed by this title.

CHAPTER 2—INFRINGEMENT PROCEEDINGS [14]

Sec.
101. Infringement:
    (a) Injunction.
    (b) Damages and profits; amounts; other remedies.
    (c) Impounding during action.
    (d) Destruction of infringing copies and plates.
    (e) Interchangeable parts for use in mechanical music-producing machines.
104. Willful infringement for profit.
105. Fraudulent notice of copyright, or removal or alteration of notice.
106. Importation of article bearing false notice or piratical copies of copyrighted work.
107. Importation, during existence of copyright, of piratical copies, or of copies not produced in accordance with section 16 of this title.
108. Forfeiture and destruction of articles prohibited importation.

---

[14]. Sections 101(f), 102, 103, 110 and 111 were repealed by the Act of June 25, 1948 (62 Stat. 869), effective September 1, 1948. However, see sections 1338, 1440 and 2072 (Title 28, United States Code), appearing infra and the Federal Rules of Civil Procedure.

Sec.
109. Importation of prohibited articles; regulations; proof of deposit of copies by complainants.
112. Injunctions; service and enforcement.
113. Transmission of certified copies of papers for enforcement of injunction by other court.
114. Review of orders, judgments, or decrees.
115. Limitations.
    (a) Criminal Proceedings.
    (b) Civil Actions.
116. Costs; attorney's fees.

Sec. 101. Infringement

If any person shall infringe the copyright in any work protected under the copyright laws of the United States such person shall be liable:

(a) **Injunction**—To an injunction restraining such infringement:

(b) **Damages and Profits; Amount; Other Remedies**—To pay to the copyright proprietor such damages as the copyright proprietor may have suffered due to the infringement, as well as all the profits which the infringer shall have made from such infringement, and in proving profits the plaintiff shall be required to prove sales only, and the defendant shall be required to prove every element of cost which he claims, or in lieu of actual damages and profits, such damages as to the court shall appear to be just, and in assessing such damages the court may, in its discretion, allow the amounts as hereinafter stated, but in case of a newspaper reproduction of a copyrighted photograph, such damages shall not exceed the sum of $200 nor be less than the sum of $50, and in the case of the infringement of an undramatized or nondramatic work by means of motion pictures, where the infringer shall show that he was not aware that he was infringing, and that such infringement could not have been reasonably foreseen, such damages shall not exceed the sum of $100; and in the case of an infringement of a copyrighted dramatic or dramatico-musical work by a maker of motion pictures and his agencies for distribution thereof to exhibitors, where such infringer shows that he was not aware that he was infringing a copyrighted work, and that such infringements could not reasonably have been foreseen, the entire sum of such damages recoverable by the copyright proprietor from such infringing maker and his agencies for the distribution to exhibitors of such infringing motion picture shall not exceed the sum of $5,000 nor be less than $250, and such damages shall in no other case exceed the sum of $5,000 nor be less than the sum of $250, and shall not be regarded as a penalty. But the foregoing exceptions shall not deprive the copyright proprietor of any other remedy given him under this law, nor shall the limitation as to the amount of recovery apply to infringements occurring after the actual notice to a defendant, either by service of process in a suit or other written notice served upon him.

First. In the case of a painting, statue, or sculpture, $10 for every infringing copy made or sold by or found in the possession of the infringer or his agents or employees;

Second. In the case of any work enumerated in section 5 of this title, except a painting, statue, or sculpture, $1 for every infringing copy made or sold by or found in the possession of the infringer or his agents or employees;

Third. In the case of a lecture, sermon, or address, $50 for every infringing delivery;

Fourth. In the case of a dramatic or dramatico-musical or a choral or orchestral composition, $100 for the first and $50 for every subsequent infringing performance; in the case of other musical compositions $10 for every infringing performance;

(c) Impounding During Action—To deliver up on oath, to be impounded during the pendency of the action, upon such terms and conditions as the court may prescribe, all articles alleged to infringe a copyright;

(d) Destruction of Infringing Copies and Plates—To deliver up on oath for destruction all the infringing copies or devices, as well as all plates, molds, matrices, or other means for making such infringing copies as the court may order.

(e) Interchangeable Parts for Use in Mechanical Music-Producing Machines[15]—Interchangeable parts, such as discs or tapes for use in mechanical music-producing machines adapted to reproduce copyrighted musical works, shall be considered copies of the copyrighted musical works which they serve to reproduce mechanically for the purpose of this section 101 and sections 106 and 109 of this title, and the unauthorized manufacture, use, or sale of such interchangeable parts shall constitute an infringement of the copyrighted work rendering the infringer liable in accordance with all provisions of this title dealing with infringements of copyright and, in a case of willful infringement for profit, to criminal prosecution pursuant to section 104 of this title. Whenever any person, in the absence of a license agreement, intends to use a copyrighted musical composition upon the parts of instruments serving to reproduce mechanically the musical work, relying upon the compulsory license provision of this title, he shall serve notice of such intention, by registered mail, upon the copyright proprietor at his last address disclosed by the records of the copyright office, sending to the copyright office a duplicate of such notice.

Sec. 104. Willful Infringement for Profit [16]

(a) Except as provided in subsection (b), any person who willfully and for profit shall infringe any copyright secured by this title, or who shall knowingly and willfully aid or abet such infringement, shall be

---

15. Section 101(e) as amended by the Act of October 15, 1971 (85 Stat. 391).

16. Section 104 as amended by the Act of December 31, 1974 (88 Stat. 1873).

deemed guilty of a misdemeanor, and upon conviction thereof shall be punished by imprisonment for not exceeding one year or by a fine of not less than $100 nor more than $1,000, or both, in the discretion of the court: *Provided, however,* That nothing in this title shall be so construed as to prevent the performance of religious or secular works such as oratorios, cantatas, masses, or octavo choruses by public schools, church choirs, or vocal societies, rented, borrowed, or obtained from some public library, public school, church choir, school choir, or vocal society, provided the performance is given for charitable or educational purposes and not for profit.

(b) Any person who willfully and for profit shall infringe any copyright provided by section 1(f) of this title, or who should knowingly and willfully aid or abet such infringement, shall be fined not more than $25,000 or imprisoned not more than one year, or both, for the first offense and shall be fined not more than $50,000 or imprisoned not more than two years, or both, for any subsequent offense.

Sec. 105. Fraudulent Notice of Copyright, or Removal or Alteration of Notice

Any person who, with fraudulent intent, shall insert or impress any notice of copyright required by this title, or words of the same purport, in or upon any uncopyrighted article, or with fraudulent intent shall remove or alter the copyright notice upon any article duly copyrighted shall be guilty of a misdemeanor, punishable by a fine of not less than $100 and not more than $1,000. Any person who shall knowingly issue or sell any article bearing a notice of United States copyright which has not been copyrighted in this country, or who shall knowingly import any article bearing such notice or words of the same purport, which has not been copyrighted in this country, shall be liable to a fine of $100.

Sec. 106. Importation of Article Bearing False Notice or Piratical Copies of Copyrighted Work

The importation into the United States of any article bearing a false notice of copyright when there is no existing copyright thereon in the United States, or of any piratical copies of any work copyrighted in the United States, is prohibited.

Sec. 107. Importation, During Existence of Copyright, of Piratical Copies, or of Copies Not Produced in Accordance With Section 16 of This Title

During the existence of the American copyright in any book the importation into the United States of any piratical copies thereof or of any copies thereof (although authorized by the author or proprietor) which have not been produced in accordance with the manufacturing provisions specified in section 16 of this title, or any plates of the same not made from type set within the limits of the United States, or any copies thereof produced by lithographic or photoengraving process not performed within the limits of the United States, in accordance with the provisions of section 16 of this title, is prohibited: *Provided, however,* That, except as regards piratical copies, such prohibition shall not apply:

(a) To works in raised characters for the use of the blind.

(b) To a foreign newspaper or magazine, although containing matter copyrighted in the United States printed or reprinted by authority of the copyright proprietor, unless such newspaper or magazine contains also copyright matter printed or reprinted without such authorization.

(c) To the authorized edition of a book in a foreign language or languages of which only a translation into English has been copyrighted in this country.

(d) To any book published abroad with the authorization of the author or copyright proprietor when imported under the circumstances stated in one of the four subdivisions following, that is to say:

First. When imported, not more than one copy at one time, for individual use and not for sale; but such privilege of importation shall not extend to a foreign reprint of a book by an American author copyrighted in the United States.

Second. When imported by the authority or for the use of the United States.

Third. When imported, for use and not for sale, not more than one copy of any such book in any one invoice, in good faith by or for any society or institution incorporated for educational, literary, philosophical, scientific, or religious purposes, or for the encouragement of the fine arts, or for any college, academy, school, or seminary of learning, or for any State, school, college, university, or free public library in the United States.

Fourth. When such books form parts of libraries or collections purchased en bloc for the use of societies, institutions, or libraries designated in the foregoing paragraph, or form parts of the libraries or personal baggage belonging to persons or families arriving from foreign countries and are not intended for sale: *Provided,* That copies imported as above may not lawfully be used in any way to violate the rights of the proprietor of the American copyright or annul or limit the copyright protection secured by this title, and such unlawful use shall be deemed an infringement of copyright.

Sec. 108. Forfeiture and Destruction of Articles Prohibited Importation

Any and all articles prohibited importation by this title which are brought into the United States from any foreign country (except in the mails) shall be seized and forfeited by like proceedings as those provided by law for the seizure and condemnation of property imported into the United States in violation of the customs revenue laws. Such articles when forfeited shall be destroyed in such manner as the Secretary of the Treasury or the court, as the case may be, shall direct: *Provided, however,* That all copies of authorized editions of copyright books imported in the mails or otherwise in violation of the provisions of this title may be exported and returned to the country of export whenever it is shown to the satisfaction of the Secretary of the Treasury, in a written application, that such importation does not involve willful negligence or fraud.

Sec. 109. Importation of Prohibited Articles; Regulations; Proof of Deposit of Copies by Complainants

The Secretary of the Treasury and the Postmaster General are hereby empowered and required to make and enforce individually or jointly such rules and regulations as shall prevent the importation into the United States of articles prohibited importation by this title, and may require, as conditions precedent to exclusion of any work in which copyright is claimed, the copyright proprietor or any person claiming actual or potential injury by reason of actual or contemplated importations of copies of such work to file with the Post Office Department or the Treasury Department a certificate of the Register of Copyrights that the provisions of section 13 of this title have been fully complied with, and to give notice of such compliance to postmasters or to customs officers at the ports of entry in the United States in such form and accompanied by such exhibits as may be deemed necessary for the practical and efficient administration and enforcement of the provisions of sections 106 and 107 of this title.

Sec. 112. Injunctions; Service and Enforcement [17]

Any court mentioned in section 1338 of Title 28 or judge thereof shall have power, upon complaint filed by any party aggrieved, to grant injunctions to prevent and restrain the violation of any right secured by this title, according to the course and principles of courts of equity, on such terms as said court or judge may deem reasonable. Any injunction that may be granted restraining and enjoining the doing of anything forbidden by this title may be served on the parties against whom such injunction may be granted anywhere in the United States, and shall be operative throughout the United States and be enforceable by proceedings in contempt or otherwise by any other court or judge possessing jurisdiction of the defendants.

Sec. 113. Transmission of Certified Copies of Papers for Enforcement of Injunction by Other Court

The clerk of the court, or judge granting the injunction, shall, when required so to do by the court hearing the application to enforce said injunction, transmit without delay to said court a certified copy of all the papers in said cause that are on file in his office.

---

17. Sections 112 and 114 as amended by the Act of October 31, 1951 (65 Stat. 710).

Sec. 114. Review of Orders, Judgments, or Decrees [18]

The orders, judgments, or decrees of any court mentioned in section 1338 of Title 28 arising under the copyright laws of the United States may be reviewed on appeal in the manner and to the extent now provided by law for the review of cases determined in said courts, respectively.

Sec. 115. Limitations [19]

(a) **Criminal Proceedings**—No criminal proceedings shall be maintained under the provisions of this title unless the same is commenced within three years after the cause of action arose.

(b) **Civil Actions**—No civil action shall be maintained under the provisions of this title unless the same is commenced within three years after the claim accrued.

Sec. 116. Costs; Attorney's Fees

In all actions, suits, or proceedings under this title, except when brought by or against the United States or any officer thereof, full costs shall be allowed, and the court may award to the prevailing party a reasonable attorney's fee as part of the costs.

CHAPTER 3—COPYRIGHT OFFICE

Sec.
- 201. Copyright office; preservation of records.
- 202. Register, assistant register, and subordinates.
- 203. Same; deposit of moneys received; reports.
- 204. Same; bond.
- 205. Same; annual report.
- 206. Seal of copyright office.
- 207. Rules for registration of claims.
- 208. Record books in copyright office.
- 209. Certificates of registration; effect as evidence; receipt for copies deposited.
- 210. Catalog of copyright entries: effect as evidence.
- 211. Same; distribution and sale; disposal of proceeds.
- 212. Records and works deposited in copyright office open to public inspection; taking copies of entries.
- 213. Disposition of articles deposited in office.
- 214. Destruction of articles deposited in office remaining undisposed of; removal of by author or proprietor; manuscripts of unpublished works.
- 215. Fees.
- 216. When the day for taking action falls on Saturday, Sunday, or a holiday.[20]

---

18. Ibid.
19. Section 115 as amended by the Act of September 7, 1957 (71 Stat. 633), effective September 7, 1958.
20. Section 216 was added by the Act of April 13, 1954 (68 Stat. 52).

Sec. 201. Copyright Office; Preservation of Records

All records and other things relating to copyrights required by law to be preserved shall be kept and preserved in the copyright office, Library of Congress, District of Columbia, and shall be under the control of the register of copyrights, who shall, under the direction and supervision of the Librarian of Congress, perform all the duties relating to the registration of copyrights.

Sec. 202. Register, Assistant Register, and Subordinates

There shall be appointed by the Librarian of Congress a Register of Copyrights, and one Assistant Register of Copyrights, who shall have authority during the absence of the Register of Copyrights to attach the copyright office seal to all papers issued from the said office and to sign such certificates and other papers as may be necessary. There shall also be appointed by the Librarian such subordinate assistants to the register as may from time to time be authorized by law.

Sec. 203. Same; Deposit of Moneys Received; Reports

The Register of Copyrights shall make daily deposits in some bank in the District of Columbia, designated for this purpose by the Secretary of the Treasury as a national depository, of all moneys received to be applied as copyright fees, and shall make weekly deposits with the Secretary of the Treasury, in such manner as the latter shall direct, of all copyright fees actually applied under the provisions of this title, and annual deposits of sums received which it has not been possible to apply as copyright fees or to return to the remitters, and shall also make monthly reports to the Secretary of the Treasury and to the Librarian of Congress of the applied copyright fees for each calendar month, together with a statement of all remittances received, trust funds on hand, moneys refunded, and unapplied balances.

Sec. 204. Same; Bond

The Register of Copyrights shall give bond to the United States in the sum of $20,000, in form to be approved by the General Counsel for the Department of the Treasury and with sureties satisfactory to the Secretary of the Treasury, for the faithful discharge of his duties.

Sec. 205. Same; Annual Report

The Register of Copyrights shall make an annual report to the Librarian of Congress, to be printed in the annual report on the Library of Congress, of all copyright business for the previous fiscal year, including the number and kind of works which have been deposited in the copyright office during the fiscal year, under the provisions of this title.

Sec. 206. Seal of Copyright Office

The seal used in the copyright office on July 1, 1909, shall be the seal of the copyright office, and by it all papers issued from the copyright office requiring authentication shall be authenticated.

Sec. 207. Rules for Registration of Claims [21]

Subject to the approval of the Librarian of Congress, the Register of Copyrights shall be authorized to make rules and regulations for the registration of claims to copyright as provided by this title.

Sec. 208. Record Books in Copyright Office

The Register of Copyrights shall provide and keep such record books in the copyright office as are required to carry out the provisions of this title, and whenever deposit has been made in the copyright office of a copy of any work under the provisions of this title he shall make entry thereof.

Sec. 209. Certificate of Registration; Effect as Evidence; Receipt for Copies Deposited

In the case of each entry the person recorded as the claimant of the copyright shall be entitled to a certificate of registration under seal of the copyright office, to contain the name and address of said claimant, the name of the country of which the author of the work is a citizen or subject, and when an alien author domiciled in the United States at the time of said registration, then a statement of that fact, including his place of domicile, the name of the author (when the records of the copyright office shall show the same), the title of the work which is registered for which copyright is claimed, the date of the deposit of the copies of such work, the date of publication if the work has been reproduced in copies for sale, or publicly distributed, and such marks as to class designation and entry number as shall fully identify the entry. In the case of a book, the certificate shall also state the receipt of the affidavit, as provided by section 17 of this title, and the date of the completion of the printing, or the date of the publication of the book, as stated in the said affidavit. The Register of Copyrights shall prepare a printed form for the said certificate, to be filled out in each case as above provided for in the case of all registrations made after July 1, 1909, and in the case of all previous registrations so far as the copyright office record books shall show such facts, which certificate, sealed with the seal of the copyright office, shall, upon payment of the prescribed fee, be given to any person making application for the same. Said certificate shall be admitted in any court as prima facie evidence of the facts stated therein. In addition to such certificate the register of

---

21. Published in the Federal Register and Title 37 of the Code of Federal Regulations. See infra, for the current regulations.

copyrights shall furnish, upon request, without additional fee, a receipt for the copies of the work deposited to complete the registration.

Sec. 210. Catalog of Copyright Entries; Effect as Evidence

The Register of Copyrights shall fully index all copyright registrations and assignments and shall print at periodic intervals a catalog of the titles of articles deposited and registered for copyright, together with suitable indexes, and at stated intervals shall print complete and indexed catalog for each class of copyright entries, and may thereupon, if expedient, destroy the original manuscript catalog cards containing the titles included in such printed volumes and representing the entries made during such intervals. The current catalog of copyright entries and the index volumes herein provided for shall be admitted in any court as prima facie evidence of the facts stated therein as regards any copyright registration.

Sec. 211. Same; Distribution and Sale; Disposal of Proceeds [22]

The said printed current catalogs as they are issued shall be promptly distributed by the Superintendent of Documents to the collectors of customs of the United States and to the postmasters of all exchange offices of receipt of foreign mails, in accordance with revised list of such collectors of customs and postmasters prepared by the Secretary of the Treasury and the Postmaster General, and they shall also be furnished in whole or in part to all parties desiring them at a price to be determined by the Register of Copyrights for each part of the catalog not exceeding $25 for the complete yearly catalog of copyright entries. The consolidated catalogs and indexes shall also be supplied to all persons ordering them at such prices as may be fixed by the Register of Copyrights, and all subscriptions for the catalogs shall be received by the Superintendent of Documents, who shall forward the said publications; and the moneys thus received shall be paid into the Treasury of the United States and accounted for under such laws and Treasury regulations as shall be in force at the time.

Sec. 212. Records and Works Deposited in Copyright Office Open to Public Inspection; Taking Copies of Entries

The record books of the copyright office, together with the indexes to such record books, and all works deposited and retained in the copyright office, shall be open to public inspection; and copies may be taken of the copyright entries actually made in such record books, subject to such safeguards and regulations as shall be prescribed by the Register of Copyrights and approved by the Librarian of Congress.

Sec. 213. Disposition of Articles Deposited in Office

Of the articles deposited in the copyright office under the provisions of the copyright laws of the United States, the Librarian of

---

22. Section 211 as amended by the Act of April 27, 1948 (62 Stat. 202) effective May 27, 1948.

Congress shall determine what books and other articles shall be transferred to the permanent collections of the Library of Congress, including the law library, and what other books or articles shall be placed in the reserve collections of the Library of Congress for sale or exchange, or be transferred to other governmental libraries in the District of Columbia for use therein.

Sec. 214. Destruction of Articles Deposited in Office Remaining Undisposed of; Removal of by Author or Proprietor; Manuscripts of Unpublished Works

Of any articles undisposed of as above provided, together with all titles and correspondence relating thereto, the Librarian of Congress and the Register of Copyrights jointly shall, at suitable intervals, determine what of these received during any period of years it is desirable or useful to preserve in the permanent files of the copyright office, and, after due notice as hereinafter provided, may within their discretion cause the remaining articles and other things to be destroyed: *Provided,* That there shall be printed in the Catalog of Copyright Entries from February to November, inclusive, a statement of the years of receipt of such articles and a notice to permit any author, copyright proprietor, or other lawful claimant to claim and remove before the expiration of the month of December of that year anything found which relates to any of his productions deposited or registered for copyright within the period of years stated, not reserved or disposed of as provided for in this title. No manuscript of an unpublished work shall be destroyed during its term of copyright without specific notice to the copyright proprietor of record, permitting him to claim and remove it.

Sec. 215. Fees [23]

The Register of Copyrights shall receive, and the persons to whom the services designated are rendered shall pay, the following fees:

For the registration of a claim to copyright in any work, $6; which fee shall include a certificate of registration under seal for each work registered: *Provided,* That only one registration fee shall be required in the case of several volumes of the same book published and deposited at the same time: *And provided further,* That with respect to works of foreign origin, in lieu of payment of the copyright fee of $6 together with one copy of the work and application, the foreign author or proprietor may at any time within six months from the date of first publication abroad deposit in the Copyright Office an application for registration and two copies of the work which shall be accompanied by a catalog card in form and content satisfactory to the Register of Copyrights.

For recording the renewal of copyright and issuance of certificate therefor, $4.

---

[23]. Section 215 as amended by the Act of April 27, 1948 (62 Stat. 202), effective May 27, 1948, and the Act of June 3, 1949 (63 Stat. 153), and as further amended by Public Law 89-297 effective November 26, 1965.

For every additional certificate of registration, $2.

For certifying a copy of an application for registration of copyright, and for all other certifications, $3.

For recording every assignment, agreement, power of attorney, or other paper not exceeding six pages, $5; for each additional page or less, 50 cents; for each title over one in the paper recorded, 50 cents additional.

For recording a notice of use, $2, for each notice of not more than five titles; and 50 cents for each additional title.

For any requested search of Copyright Office records, or weeks deposited, or services rendered in connection therewith, $5 for each hour of time consumed.

Sec. 216. When the Day for Taking Action Falls on Saturday, Sunday, or a Holiday [24]

When the last day for making any deposit or application, or the paying any fee, or for delivering any other material to the Copyright Office falls on Saturday, Sunday, or a holiday within the District of Columbia, such action may be taken on the next succeeding business day.

24. Section 216 was added by the Act of April 13, 1954 (68 Stat. 52).

Appendix D

PARALLEL REFERENCE TABLES SHOWING DISPOSITION OF SECTIONS OF ACT OF MARCH 4, 1909, AS AMENDED (IN 1947) IN TITLE 17, UNITED STATES CODE (PRE-1978)

Act of Mar. 4, 1909, as amended	Title 17, U.S.C.	Act of Mar. 4, 1909, as amended	Title 17, U.S.C.	Title 17, U.S.C.	Act of Mar. 4, 1909, as amended	Title 17, U.S.C.	Act of Mar. 4, 1909, as amended
1	1	33	109	1	1	¹101	25
2	2.	34	¹110	2	2	¹102	26
3	3	35	¹111	3	3	¹103	27
4	4	36	112	4	4	104	28
5	5	37	113	5	5	105	29
6	7	38	114	6	(²)	106	30
7	8	39	115	7	6	107	31
8	9	40	116	8	³7	108	32
9	10	41	27	9	8	109	33
10	11	42	28	10	9	¹110	34
11	12	43	29	11	10	¹111	35
12	13	44	30	12	11	112	36
13	14	45	31	13	12	113	37
14	15	46	32	14	13	114	38
15	16	47	201	15	14	115	39
16	17	48	202	16	15	116	40
17	18	49	203	17	16	201	47
18	19	50	204	18	17	202	48
19	20	51	205	19	18	203	49
20	21	52	206	20	19	204	50
21	22	53	207	21	20	205	51
22	23	54	208	22	21	206	52
23	24	55	209	23	22	207	53
24	Omitted	56	210	24	23	208	54
25	¹101	57	211	25	(⁴)	209	55
26	¹102	58	212	26	62	210	56
27	¹103	59	213	27	41	211	57
28	104	60	214	28	42	212	58
29	105	61	215	29	43	213	59
30	106	62	26	30	44	214	60
31	107	63	Omitted	31	45	215	61
32	108	64	Omitted	32	46		

[1042]

1. Sections 101(f), 102, 103, 110 and 111 were repealed by the Act of June 25, 1948 (62 Stat. 869).

2. This was § 3 of Act of July 31, 1939 (53 Stat. 1142).

3. A portion of § 1 of Act of Jan. 27, 1938 (52 Stat. 6) is also included.

4. This was § 4 of the Act of July 31, 1939 (53 Stat. 1142).

Appendix E

FAIR USE

HARPER & ROW, PUBLISHERS, INC. v. NATION ENTERPRISES*

Supreme Court of the United States, 1985.
— U.S. —, 105 S.Ct. 2218, — L.Ed.2d —.

JUSTICE O'CONNOR delivered the opinion of the Court.

This case requires us to consider to what extent the "fair use" provision of the Copyright Revision Act of 1976, 17 U.S.C. § 107 (hereinafter the Copyright Act), sanctions the unauthorized use of quotations from a public figure's unpublished manuscript. In March 1979, an undisclosed source provided The Nation magazine with the unpublished manuscript of "A Time to Heal: The Autobiography of Gerald R. Ford." Working directly from the purloined manuscript, an editor of The Nation produced a short piece entitled "The Ford Memoirs—Behind the Nixon Pardon." The piece was timed to "scoop" an article scheduled shortly to appear in Time magazine. Time had agreed to purchase the exclusive right to print prepublication excerpts from the copyright holders, Harper & Row Publishers, Inc. (hereinafter Harper & Row) and Reader's Digest Association, Inc. (hereinafter Reader's Digest). As a result of The Nation article, Time canceled its agreement. Petitioners brought a successful copyright action against The Nation. On appeal, the Second Circuit reversed the lower court's finding of infringement, holding that The Nation's act was sanctioned as a "fair use" of the copyrighted material. We granted certiorari, 467 U.S. —, — S.Ct. —, — L.Ed.2d — (1984), and we now reverse.

I

In February 1977, shortly after leaving the White House, former President Gerald R. Ford contracted with petitioners Harper & Row and The Reader's Digest, to publish his as yet unwritten memoirs. The memoirs were to contain "significant hitherto unpublished material" concerning the Watergate crisis, Mr. Ford's pardon of former President Nixon and "Mr. Ford's reflections on this period of history, and the morality and personalities involved." App. to Pet. for Cert. C–14—C–15. In addition to the right to publish the Ford memoirs in book form, the

---

* Because this case was decided on May 20, 1985, just before this work went to press, it was necessary to place the case in the appendix.

1000

agreement gave petitioners the exclusive right to license prepublication excerpts, known in the trade as "first serial rights." Two years later, as the memoirs were nearing completion, petitioners negotiated a prepublication licensing agreement with Time, a weekly news magazine. Time agreed to pay $25,000, $12,500 in advance and an additional $12,500 at publication, in exchange for the right to excerpt 7,500 words from Mr. Ford's account of the Nixon pardon. The issue featuring the excerpts was timed to appear approximately one week before shipment of the full length book version to bookstores. Exclusivity was an important consideration; Harper & Row instituted procedures designed to maintain the confidentiality of the manuscript, and Time retained the right to renegotiate the second payment should the material appear in print prior to its release of the excerpts.

Two to three weeks before the Time article's scheduled release, an unidentified person secretly brought a copy of the Ford manuscript to Victor Navasky, editor of The Nation, a political commentary magazine. Mr. Navasky knew that his possession of the manuscript was not authorized and that the manuscript must be returned quickly to his "source" to avoid discovery. 557 F.Supp. 1067, 1069 (SDNY 1983). He hastily put together what he believed was "a real hot news story" composed of quotes, paraphrases and facts drawn exclusively from the manuscript. Ibid. Mr. Navasky attempted no independent commentary, research or criticism, in part because of the need for speed if he was to "make news" by "publish[ing] in advance of publication of the Ford book." App. 416–417. The 2,250 word article, reprinted in the Appendix to this opinion, appeared on April 3, 1979. As a result of The Nation's article, Time canceled its piece and refused to pay the remaining $12,500.

Petitioners brought suit in the District Court for the Southern District of New York, alleging conversion, tortious interference with contract and violations of the Copyright Act. After a 6-day bench trial, the District Judge found that "A Time to Heal" was protected by copyright at the time of The Nation publication * * * The District Court rejected respondents' argument that The Nation's piece was a "fair use" sanctioned by § 107 of the Act. * * * Although certain elements of the Ford memoir, such as historical facts and memoranda, were not *per se* copyrightable, the District Court held that it was "the totality of these facts and memoranda collected together with Ford's reflections that made them of value to The Nation, [and] this * * * totality * * * is protected by the copyright laws." Id., at 1072–1073. The court awarded actual damages of $12,500.

A divided panel of the Court of Appeals for the Second Circuit reversed. The majority recognized that Mr. Ford's verbatim "reflections" were original "expression" protected by copyright. But it held that the District Court had erred in assuming the "coupling [of these reflections] with uncopyrightable fact transformed that information into a copyrighted 'totality.'" 723 F.2d 195, 205 (1983). * * *

II

* * *

Creation of a nonfiction work, even a compilation of pure fact, entails originality. See, e.g., Schroeder v. William Morrow & Co., 566 F.2d 3 (CA7 1977) (copyright in gardening directory); cf. Burrow-Giles Lithographic Co. v. Sarony, 111 U.S. 53, 58, 4 S.Ct. 279, 281, 28 L.Ed. 349 (1884) (originator of a photograph may claim copyright in his work). The copyright holders of "A Time to Heal" complied with the relevant statutory notice and registration procedures. See §§ 106, 401, 408; App. to Pet. for Cert. C–20. Thus there is no dispute that the unpublished manuscript of "A Time to Heal," as a whole, was protected by § 106 from unauthorized reproduction. Nor do respondents dispute that verbatim copying of excerpts of the manuscript's original form of expression would constitute infringement unless excused as fair use. See 1 M. Nimmer, Nimmer on Copyright § 2.11[B], p. 2–159 (1984) (hereinafter Nimmer). Yet copyright does not prevent subsequent users from copying from a prior author's work those constituent elements that are not original—for example, quotations borrowed under the rubric of fair use from other copyrighted works, facts, or materials in the public domain—as long as such use does not unfairly appropriate the author's original contributions. Ibid.; A. Latman Fair Use of Copyrighted Works (1958), reprinted as Study No. 14 in Copyright Law Revision Studies Nos. 14–16, Prepared for the Senate Committee on the Judiciary, 86th Cong., 2d Sess., 7 (1960) (hereinafter Latman). Perhaps the controversy between the lower courts in this case over copyrightability is more aptly styled a dispute over whether The Nation's appropriation of unoriginal and uncopyrightable elements encroached on the originality embodied in the work as a whole. Especially in the realm of factual narrative, the law is currently unsettled regarding the ways in which uncopyrightable elements combine with the author's original contributions to form protected expression. Compare Wainwright Securities Inc. v. Wall Street Transcript Corp., 558 F.2d 91 (CA2 1977) (protection accorded author's analysis, structuring of material and marshaling of facts), with Hoehling v. Universal City Studios, Inc., 618 F.2d 972 (CA2 1980) (limiting protection to ordering and choice of words). See, e.g., 1 Nimmer § 2.11[D], at 2–164–2–165.

We need not reach these issues, however, as the Nation has admitted to lifting verbatim quotes of the author's original language totalling between 300 and 400 words and constituting some 13% of The Nation article. In using generous verbatim excerpts of Mr. Ford's unpublished manuscript to lend authenticity to its account of the forthcoming memoirs, The Nation effectively arrogated to itself the right of first publication, an important marketable subsidiary right. For the reasons set forth below, we find that this use of the copyrighted manuscript, even stripped to the verbatim quotes conceded by The Nation to be copyrightable expression, was not a fair use within the meaning of the Copyright Act.

III

A

Fair use was traditionally defined as "a privilege in others than the owner of the copyright to use the copyrighted material in a reasonable manner without his consent." H. Ball, Law of Copyright and Literary Property 260 (1944) (hereinafter Ball). The statutory formulation of the defense of fair use in the Copyright Act of 1976 reflects the intent of Congress to codify the common-law doctrine. 3 Nimmer § 13.05. Section 107 requires a case-by-case determination whether a particular use is fair, and the statute notes four nonexclusive factors to be considered. This approach was "intended to restate the [pre-existing] judicial doctrine of fair use, not to change, narrow, or enlarge it in any way." H.R.Rep. No. 94–1476, p. 66 (1976) (hereinafter House Report).

* * * Professor Latman, in a study of the doctrine of fair use commissioned by Congress for the revision effort, see Sony Corp. v. Universal City Studios, Inc., 464 U.S., at 462-463, n. 9, 104 S.Ct., at —, n. 9 (dissenting opinion), summarized prior law as turning on the "importance of the material copied or performed from the point of view of the reasonable copyright owner. In other words, would the reasonable copyright owner have consented to the use?" Latman 15.[3]

As early as 1841, Justice Story, gave judicial recognition to the doctrine in a case that concerned the letters of another former President, George Washington.

> "[A] reviewer may fairly cite largely from the original work, if his design be really and truly to use the passages for the purposes of fair and reasonable criticism. On the other hand, it is as clear, that if he thus cites the most important parts of the work, with a view, not to criticise, but to supersede the use of the original work, and substitute the review for it, such a use will be deemed in law a piracy." Folsom v. Marsh, 9 F. Cas. 342, 344–345 (No. 4,901) (CC Mass.)

As Justice Story's hypothetical illustrates, the fair use doctrine has always precluded a use that "supersede[s] the use of the original." Ibid. Accord S.Rep. No. 94–473, p. 65 (1975) (hereinafter Senate Report).

Perhaps because the fair use doctrine was predicated on the author's implied consent to "reasonable and customary" use when he released his work for public consumption, fair use traditionally was not recognized as

---

3. Professor Nimmer notes, "[perhaps] no more precise guide can be stated than Joseph McDonald's clever paraphrase of the Golden Rule: 'Take not from others to such an extent and in such a manner that you would be resentful if they so took from you.'" 3 Nimmer § 13.05[A], at 13–66, quoting McDonald, Non-infringing Uses, 9 Bull. Copyright Soc. 466, 467 (1962). This "equitable rule of reason," Sony Corp. v. Universal City Studios, Inc., 464 U.S., at 448, 104 S.Ct., at —, "permits courts to avoid rigid application of the copyright statute when, on occasion, it would stifle the very creativity which that law is designed to foster." Iowa State University Research Foundation, Inc. v. American Broadcasting Cos., 621 F.2d 57, 60 (CA2 1980). See generally, L. Seltzer, Exemptions and Fair Use in Copyright 18–48 (1978).

a defense to charges of copying from an author's as yet unpublished works. Under common-law copyright, "the property of the author * * * in his intellectual creation [was] absolute until he voluntarily part[ed] with the same." American Tobacco Co. v. Werckmeister, 207 U.S. 284, 299, 28 S.Ct. 72, 77, 52 L.Ed. 208 (1907); 2 Nimmer § 8.23, at 8–273. This absolute rule, however, was tempered in practice by the equitable nature of the fair use doctrine. * * *

Though the right of first publication, like the other rights enumerated in § 106 is expressly made subject to the fair use provision of § 107, fair use analysis must always be tailored to the individual case. Id., at 65; 3 Nimmer § 13.05[A]. * * * First publication is inherently different from other § 106 rights in that only one person can be the first publisher; as the contract with Time illustrates, the commercial value of the right lies primarily in exclusivity. Because the potential damage to the author from judicially enforced "sharing" of the first publication right with unauthorized users of his manuscript is substantial, the balance of equities in evaluating such a claim of fair use inevitably shifts.

* * *

* * * We conclude that the unpublished nature of a work is "[a] key, though not necessarily determinative, factor" tending to negate a defense of fair use. Senate Report, at 64. See 3 Nimmer § 13.05, at 13–62, n. 2; W. Patry, The Fair Use Privilege in Copyright Law 125 (1985) (hereinafter Patry).

We also find unpersuasive respondents' argument that fair use may be made of a soon-to-be-published manuscript on the ground that the author has demonstrated he has no interest in nonpublication. This argument assumes that the unpublished nature of copyrighted material is only relevant to letters or other confidential writings not intended for dissemination. It is true that common-law copyright was often enlisted in the service of personal privacy. See Brandeis & Warren, The Right to Privacy, 4 Harv.L.Rev. 193, 198–199 (1890). In its commercial guise, however, an author's right to choose when he will publish is no less deserving of protection. The period encompassing the work's initiation, its preparation, and its grooming for public dissemination is a crucial one for any literary endeavor. The Copyright Act, which accords the copyright owner the "right to control the first public distribution" of his work, House Report, at 62, echos the common law's concern that the author or copyright owner retain control throughout this critical stage. See generally Comment, The Stage of Publication as a "Fair Use" Factor: Harper & Row, Publishers v. Nation Enterprises, 58 St. John's L.Rev. 597 (1984). The obvious benefit to author and public alike of assuring authors the leisure to develop their ideas free from fear of expropriation outweighs any short term "news value" to be gained from premature publication of the author's expression. See Goldstein, Copyright and the First Amendment, 70 Colum.L.Rev. 983, 1004–1006 (1970) (The absolute protection the common law accorded to soon-to-be published works "[was] justified by [its] brevity and expedience"). The author's control of first public distribution implicates not only his personal interest in creative control but his property interest in exploitation of prepublication rights, which are valuable in themselves and serve as a valuable adjunct to publicity and marketing. See Belushi v. Woodward, 598 F.Supp. 36 (DC 1984) (successful marketing depends on coordination of serialization and release to public); Marks, Subsidiary Rights and Permissions, in What Happens in Book Publishing 230 (C. Grannis ed. 1967) (exploitation of subsidiary rights is necessary to financial success of new books). Under ordinary circumstances, the author's right to control the first public appearance of his undisseminated expression will outweigh a claim of fair use.

B

Respondents, however, contend that First Amendment values require a different rule under the circumstances of this case. The thrust of the decision below is that "[t]he scope of [fair use] is undoubtedly wider when the information conveyed relates to matters of high public concern." * * * In respondents' view, not only the facts contained in Mr. Ford's memoirs, but "the precise manner in which [he] expressed himself was as newsworthy as what he had to say." Brief for Respondents 38–39. Respondents argue that the public's interest in learning this news as fast as possible outweighs the right of the author to control its first publication.

The Second Circuit noted, correctly, that copyright's idea/expression dichotomy "strike[s] a definitional balance between the First Amendment and the Copyright Act by permitting free communication of facts while still protecting an author's expression." 723 F.2d, at 203.

No author may copyright his ideas or the facts he narrates. 17 U.S.C. § 102(b). See, e.g., New York Times Co. v. United States, 403 U.S. 713, 726, n.*, 91 S.Ct. 2140, 2147, n.*, 29 L.Ed.2d 822 (1971) (Brennan, J., concurring) (Copyright laws are not restrictions on freedom of speech as copyright protects only form of expression and not the ideas expressed); 1 Nimmer § 1.10[B][2]. As this Court long ago observed: "[T]he news element—the information respecting current events contained in the literary production—is not the creation of the writer, but is a report of matters that ordinarily are *publici juris;* it is the history of the day." International News Service v. Associated Press, 248 U.S. 215, 234, 39 S.Ct. 68, 70, 63 L.Ed. 211 (1918). But copyright assures those who write and publish factual narratives such as "A Time to Heal" that that they may at least enjoy the right to market the original expression contained therein as just compensation for their investment. Cf. Zacchini v. Scripps-Howard Broadcasting Co., 433 U.S. 562, 575, 97 S.Ct. 2849, 2857, 53 L.Ed.2d 965 (1977).

Respondents' theory, however, would expand fair use to effectively destroy any expectation of copyright protection in the work of a public figure. Absent such protection, there would be little incentive to create or profit in financing such memoirs and the public would be denied an important source of significant historical information. The promise of copyright would be an empty one if it could be avoided merely by dubbing the infringement a fair use "news report" of the book. See Wainwright Securities Inc. v. Wall Street Transcript Corp., 558 F.2d 91 (CA2 1977), cert. denied, 434 U.S. 1014, 98 S.Ct. 730, 54 L.Ed.2d 759 (1978).

* * * Where an author and publisher have invested extensive resources in creating an original work and are poised to release it to the public, no legitimate aim is served by preempting the right of first publication. The fact that the words the author has chosen to clothe his narrative may of themselves be "newsworthy" is not an independent justification for unauthorized copying of the author's expression prior to publication. To paraphrase another recent Second Circuit decision:

> "[Respondent] possessed an unfettered right to use any factual information revealed in [the memoirs] for the purpose of enlightening its audience, but it can claim no need to 'bodily appropriate' [Mr. Ford's] 'expression' of that information by utilizing portions of the actual [manuscript]. The public interest in the free flow of information is assured by the law's refusal to recognize a valid copyright in facts. The fair use doctrine is not a license for corporate theft, empowering a court to ignore a copyright whenever it determines the underlying work contains material of possible public importance." Iowa State University Research Foundation, Inc. v. American Broadcasting Cos., Inc., 621 F.2d 57, 61 (1980) (citations omitted).

* * *

In our haste to disseminate news, it should not be forgotten that the Framers intended copyright itself to be the engine of free expression. By establishing a marketable right to the use of one's expression, copyright supplies the economic incentive to create and disseminate ideas. * * *

It is fundamentally at odds with the scheme of copyright to accord lesser rights in those works that are of greatest importance to the public. Such a notion ignores the major premise of copyright and injures author and public alike. "[T]o propose that fair use be imposed whenever the 'social value [of dissemination] * * * outweighs any detriment to the artist,' would be to propose depriving copyright owners of their right in the property precisely when they encounter those users who could afford to pay for it." Gordon, Fair Use as Market Failure: A Structural and Economic Analysis of the *Betamax* Case and its Predecessors, 82 Colum.L.Rev. 1600, 1615 (1982). And as one commentator has noted: "If every volume that was in the public interest could be pirated away by a competing publisher, * * * the public [soon] would have nothing worth reading." Sobel, Copyright and the First Amendment: A Gathering Storm?, 19 ASCAP Copyright Law Symposium 43, 78 (1971). See generally Comment, Copyright and the First Amendment; Where Lies the Public Interest?, 59 Tulane L.Rev. 133 (1984).

Moreover, freedom of thought and expression "includes both the right to speak freely and the right to refrain from speaking at all."

Wooley v. Maynard, 430 U.S. 705, 714, 97 S.Ct. 1428, 1435, 51 L.Ed.2d 752 (1977) (Burger, C. J.). We do not suggest this right not to speak would sanction abuse of the copyright owner's monopoly as an instrument to suppress facts. But in the words of New York's Chief Judge Fuld:

> "The essential thrust of the First Amendment is to prohibit improper restraints on the *voluntary* public expression of ideas; it shields the man who wants to speak or publish when others wish him to be quiet. There is necessarily, and within suitably defined areas, a concomitant freedom *not* to speak publicly, one which serves the same ultimate end as freedom of speech in its affirmative aspect." Estate of Hemingway v. Random House, 23 N.Y.2d 341, 348, 244 N.E.2d 250, 255 (1968).

Courts and commentators have recognized that copyright, and the right of first publication in particular, serve this countervailing First Amendment value. See Schnapper v. Foley, 215 U.S.App.D.C. 59, 667 F.2d 102 (1981), cert. denied, 455 U.S. 948, 102 S.Ct. 1448, 71 L.Ed.2d 661 (1982); 1 Nimmer § 1.10[B], at 1–70, n. 24; Patry 140–142.

In view of the First Amendment protections already embodied in the Copyright Act's distinction between copyrightable expression and uncopyrightable facts and ideas, and the latitude for scholarship and comment traditionally afforded by fair use, we see no warrant for expanding the doctrine of fair use to create what amounts to a public figure exception to copyright. Whether verbatim copying from a public figure's manuscript in a given case is or is not fair must be judged according to the traditional equities of fair use.

IV

* * * Thus whether The Nation article constitutes fair use under § 107 must be reviewed in light of the principles discussed above. The factors enumerated in the section are not meant to be exclusive: "[S]ince the doctrine is an equitable rule of reason, no generally applicable definition is possible, and each case raising the question must be decided on its own facts." House Report, at 65. * * *

Purpose of the Use. The Second Circuit correctly identified news reporting as the general purpose of The Nation's use. News reporting is one of the examples enumerated in § 107 to "give some idea of the sort of activities the courts might regard as fair use under the circumstances." Senate Report, at 61. * * * The fact that an article arguably is "news" and therefore a productive use is simply one factor in a fair use analysis.

We agree with the Second Circuit that the trial court erred in fixing on whether the information contained in the memoir was actually new to the public. As Judge Meskill wisely noted, "[c]ourts should be chary of deciding what is and what is not news." 723 F.2d, at 215 (Meskill, J., dissenting). Cf., Gertz v. Robert Welch, Inc., 418 U.S. 323, 345–346, 94 S.Ct. 2997, 3009–3010, 41 L.Ed.2d 789 (1974). "The issue is not what constitutes 'news,' but whether a claim of newsreporting is a valid fair use defense to an infringement of *copyrightable expression.*" Patry 119.

The Nation has every right to seek to be the first to publish information. But the Nation went beyond simply reporting uncopyrightable information and actively sought to exploit the headline value of its infringement, making a "news event" out of its unauthorized first publication of a noted figure's copyrighted expression.

The fact that a publication was commercial as opposed to non-profit is a separate factor that tends to weigh against a finding of fair use. "[E]very commercial use of copyrighted material is presumptively an unfair exploitation of the monopoly privilege that belongs to the owner of the copyright." Sony Corp. v. Universal City Studios, Inc., 464 U.S., at 451, 104 S.Ct., at —. In arguing that the purpose of news reporting is not purely commercial, The Nation misses the point entirely. The crux of the profit/nonprofit distinction is not whether the sole motive of the use is monetary gain but whether the user stands to profit from exploitation of the copyrighted material without paying the customary price. See Roy Export Co. Establishment v. Columbia Broadcasting System, Inc., 503 F.Supp., at 1144; 3 Nimmer § 13.05[A][1], at 13–71, n. 25.3.

In evaluating character and purpose we cannot ignore The Nation's stated purpose of scooping the forthcoming hardcover and Time abstracts. * * * Also relevant to the "character" of the use is "the propriety of the defendant's conduct." 3 Nimmer § 13.05[A], at 13–72. "Fair use presupposes 'good faith' and 'fair dealing.'" Time Inc. v. Bernard Geis Associates, 293 F.Supp. 130, 146 (SDNY 1968), quoting Schulman, Fair Use and the Revision of the Copyright Act, 53 Iowa L.Rev. 832 (1968). The trial court found that the Nation knowingly exploited a purloined manuscript. * * *

Nature of the Copyrighted Work. Second, the Act directs attention to the nature of the copyrighted work. "A Time to Heal" may be characterized as an unpublished historical narrative or autobiography. The law generally recognizes a greater need to disseminate factual works than works of fiction or fantasy. See Gorman, Fact or Fancy? The Implications for Copyright, 29 J. Copyright Soc. 560, 561 (1982).

> "[E]ven within the field of fact works, there are gradations as to the relative proportion of fact and fancy. One may move from sparsely embellished maps and directories to elegantly written biography. The extent to which one must permit expressive language to be copied, in order to assure dissemination of the underlying facts, will thus vary from case to case." Id., at 563.

Some of the briefer quotes from the memoir are arguably necessary adequately to convey the facts; for example, Mr. Ford's characterization of the White House tapes as the "smoking gun" is perhaps so integral to the idea expressed as to be inseparable from it. Cf. 1 Nimmer § 1.10[C]. But The Nation did not stop at isolated phrases and instead excerpted subjective descriptions and portraits of public figures whose power lies in the author's individualized expression. Such use, focusing on the most expressive elements of the work, exceeds that necessary to disseminate the facts.

* * *

Amount and Substantiality of the Portion Used. * * * In absolute terms, the words actually quoted were an insubstantial portion of "A Time to Heal." The district court, however, found that "[T]he Nation took what was essentially the heart of the book." 557 F.Supp., at 1072. We believe the Court of Appeals erred in overruling the district judge's evaluation of the qualitative nature of the taking. See, e.g., Roy Export Co. Establishment v. Columbia Broadcasting System, Inc., supra, at 1145 (taking of 55 seconds out of one hour and twenty-nine minute film deemed qualitatively substantial). A Time editor described the chapters on the pardon as "the most interesting and moving parts of the entire manuscript." Reply Brief for Petitioners 16, n. 8. The portions actually quoted were selected by Mr. Navasky as among the most powerful passages in those chapters. * * *

As the statutory language indicates, a taking may not be excused merely because it is insubstantial with respect to the *infringing* work. As Judge Learned Hand cogently remarked, "[N]o plagiarist can excuse the wrong by showing how much of his work he did not pirate." Sheldon v. Metro-Goldwyn Pictures Corp., 81 F.2d 49, 56 (CA2), cert. denied, 298 U.S. 669, 56 S.Ct. 835, 80 L.Ed. 1392 (1936). Conversely, the fact that a substantial portion of the infringing work was copied verbatim is evidence of the qualitative value of the copied material, both to the originator and to the plagiarist who seeks to profit from marketing someone else's copyrighted expression.

Stripped to the verbatim quotes, the direct takings from the unpublished manuscript constitute at least 13% of the infringing article. See Meeropol v. Nizer, 560 F.2d 1061, 1071 (CA2 1977) (copyrighted letters constituted less than 1% of infringing work but were prominently featured). The Nation article is structured around the quoted excerpts which serve as its dramatic focal points. See Appendix, infra. In view of the expressive value of the excerpts and their key role in the infringing work, we cannot agree with the Second Circuit that the "magazine took a meager, indeed an infinitesimal amount of Ford's original language." 723 F.2d, at 209.

Effect on the Market. Finally, the Act focuses on "the effect of the use upon the potential market for or value of the copyrighted work." This last factor is undoubtedly the single most important element of fair use. See 3 Nimmer § 13.05[A], at 13–76, and cases cited therein. "Fair use, when properly applied, is limited to copying by others which does not materially impair the marketability of the work which is copied." 1 Nimmer § 1.10[D], at 1–87. The trial court found not merely a potential but an actual effect on the market. Time's cancellation of its projected serialization and its refusal to pay the $12,500 were the direct effect of the infringement. The Court of Appeals rejected this fact finding as clearly erroneous, noting that the record did not establish a causal relation between Time's nonperformance and respondents' unauthorized publication of Mr. Ford's *expression* as opposed to the facts taken from the memoirs. We disagree. Rarely will a case of copyright infringement present such clear cut evidence of actual damage. Petitioners assured Time that there would be no other authorized publication of *any* portion of the unpublished manuscript prior to April 23, 1979. *Any* publication of material from chapters 1 and 3 would permit Time to renegotiate its final payment. Time cited The Nation's article, which contained verbatim quotes from the unpublished manuscript, as a reason for its nonperformance. With respect to apportionment of profits flowing from a copyright infringement, this Court has held that an infringer who commingles infringing and noninfringing elements "must abide the consequences, inless he can make a separation of the profits so as to assure to the injured party all that justly belongs to him." Sheldon v. Metro-Goldwyn Pictures Corp., 309 U.S. 390, 406, 60 S.Ct. 681, 687, 84 L.Ed. 825 (1940). Cf. 17 U.S.C. § 504(b) (the infringer is required to prove elements of profits attributable to other than the infringed work). Similarly, once a copyrightholder establishes with reasonable probability the existence of a causal connection between the infringement and a loss of revenue, the burden properly shifts to the infringer to show that this damage would have occurred had there been no taking of copyrighted expression. See 3 Nimmer § 14.02, pp. 14–7—14–8.1. Petitioners established a prima facie case of actual damage that respondent failed to rebut. See Stevens Linen Associates, Inc. v. Mastercraft Corp., 656 F.2d 11, 15 (CA2 1981). The trial court properly awarded actual damages and accounting of profits. See 17 U.S.C. § 504(b).

More important, to negate fair use one need only show that if the challenged use "should become widespread, it would adversely affect the *potential* market for the copyrighted work." Sony Corp. v. Universal City Studios, Inc., 464 U.S., at 451, 104 S.Ct., at — (emphasis added); *id.,* at 484, and n. 36 (collecting cases) (dissenting opinion). This inquiry must take account not only of harm to the original but also of harm to the market for derivative works. See Iowa State University Research Foundation, Inc. v. American Broadcasting Cos., 621 F.2d 57 (CA2 1980); Meeropol v. Nizer, supra, at 1070; Roy Export v. Columbia Broadcasting System, Inc., 503 F.Supp., at 1146. "If the defendant's work adversely affects the value of any of the rights in the copyrighted work (in this case the adaptation [and serialization] right) the use is not fair." 3 Nimmer § 13.05[B], at 13–77—13–78 (footnote omitted).

It is undisputed that the factual material in the balance of The Nation's article, besides the verbatim quotes at issue here, was drawn exclusively from the chapters on the pardon. The excerpts were employed as featured episodes in a story about the Nixon pardon—precisely the use petitioners had licensed to Time. The borrowing of these verbatim quotes from the unpublished manuscript lent The Nation's piece a special air of authenticity—as Navasky expressed it, the reader would know it was Ford speaking and not The Nation. App. 300c. Thus it directly competed for a share of the market for prepublication excerpts. The Senate Report states:

> "With certain special exceptions * * * a use that supplants any part of the normal market for a copyrighted work would ordinarily be considered an infringement." Senate Report, at 65.

Placed in a broader perspective, a fair use doctrine that permits extensive prepublication quotations from an unreleased manuscript without the copyright owner's consent poses substantial potential for damage to the marketability of first serialization rights in general. "Isolated instances of minor infringements, when multiplied many times, become in the aggregate a major inroad on copyright that must be prevented." Ibid.

* * *

The Nation conceded that its verbatim copying of some 300 words of direct quotation from the Ford manuscript would constitute an infringement unless excused as a fair use. Because we find that The Nation's use of these verbatim excerpts from the unpublished manuscript was not a fair use, the judgment of the Court of Appeals is reversed and remanded for further proceedings consistent with this opinion.

* * *

JUSTICE BRENNAN, joined by JUSTICE WHITE and JUSTICE MARSHALL, filed a dissenting opinion.

APPENDIX TO OPINION OF THE COURT

The portions of The Nation article which were copied verbatim from "A Time to Heal," excepting quotes from government documents and quotes attributed by Ford to third persons, are identified in bold face in the text. See n. 7, ante, at ——. The corresponding passages in the Ford manuscript are footnoted.

THE FORD MEMOIRS BEHIND THE NIXON PARDON

In his memoirs, *A Time To Heal,* which Harper & Row will publish in late May or early June, former President Gerald R. Ford says that the idea of giving a blanket pardon to Richard M. Nixon was raised before Nixon resigned from the Presidency by Gen. Alexander Haig, who was then the White House chief of staff.

Ford also writes that, but for a misunderstanding, he might have selected Ronald Reagan as his 1976 running mate, that Washington lawyer Edward Bennett Williams, a Democrat, was his choice for head of the Central Intelligence Agency, that Nixon was the one who first proposed Rockefeller for Vice President, and that he regretted his "cowardice"[1] in allowing Rockefeller to remove himself from Vice Presidential contention. Ford also describes his often prickly relations with Henry Kissinger.

---

1. I was angry at myself for showing cowardice in not saying to the ultra-conservatives, "It's going to be Ford and Rockefeller, whatever the consequences." p. 496.

The Nation obtained the 655-page typescript before publication. Advance excerpts from the book will appear in *Time* in mid-April and in *The Reader's Digest* thereafter. Although the initial print order has not been decided, the figure is tentatively set at 50,000; it could change, depending upon the public reaction to the serialization.

Ford's account of the Nixon pardon contains significant new detail on the negotiations and considerations that surrounded it. According to Ford's version, the subject was first broached to him by General Haig on August 1, 1974, a week before Nixon resigned. General Haig revealed that the newly transcribed White House tapes were the equivalent of the "smoking gun"[2] and that Ford should prepare himself to become President.

Ford was deeply hurt by Haig's revelation: "Over the past several months Nixon had repeatedly assured me that he was not involved in Watergate, that the evidence would prove his innocence, that the matter would fade from view."[3] Ford had believed him, but he let Haig explain the President's alternatives.

He could "ride it out"[4] or he could resign, Haig said. He then listed the different ways Nixon might resign and concluded by pointing out that Nixon could agree to leave in return for an agreement that the new President, Ford, would pardon him.[5] Although Ford said it would be improper for him to make any recommendation, he basically agreed with Haig's assessment and adds, "Because of his references to the pardon authority, I did ask Haig about the extent of a President's pardon power."[6]

"It's my understanding from a White House lawyer," Haig replied, "that a President does have authority to grant a pardon even before criminal action has been taken against an individual."

But because Ford had neglected to tell Haig he thought the idea of a resignation conditioned on a pardon was improper, his press aide, Bob Hartmann, suggested that Haig might well have returned to the White House and told President Nixon that he had mentioned the idea and Ford seemed comfortable with it. "Silence implies assent."

Ford then consulted with White House special counsel James St. Clair, who had no advice one way or the other on the matter more than pointing out that he was not the lawyer who had given Haig the opinion on the pardon. Ford also discussed the matter with Jack Marsh, who felt that the mention of a pardon in this context was a "time bomb," and

2. [I]t contained the so-called smoking gun. p. 3.

3. [O]ver the past several months Nixon had repeatedly assured me that he was not involved in Watergate, that the evidence would prove his innocence, that the matter would fade from view. p. 7.

4. The first [option] was that he could try to "ride it out" by letting impeachment take its natural course through the House and the Senate trial, fighting against conviction all the way. p. 4.

5. Finally, Haig said that according to some on Nixon's White House staff, Nixon could agree to leave in return for an agreement that the new President—Gerald Ford—would pardon him. p. 5.

6. Because of his references to pardon authority, I did ask Haig about the extent of a President's pardon power. pp. 5–6.

with Bryce Harlow, who had served six Presidents and who agreed that the mere mention of a pardon "could cause a lot of trouble." [7]

As a result of these various conversations, Vice President Ford called Haig and read him a written statement: "I want you to understand that I have no intention of recommending what the President should do about resigning or not resigning and that nothing we talked about yesterday afternoon should be given any consideration in whatever decision the President may wish to make."

Despite what Haig had told him about the "smoking gun" tapes, Ford told a Jackson, Mich., luncheon audience later in the day that the President was not guilty of an impeachable offense. "Had I said otherwise at that moment," he writes, "the whole house of cards might have collapsed." [8]

In justifying the pardon, Ford goes out of his way to assure the reader that "compassion for Nixon as an individual hadn't prompted my decision at all." [9] Rather, he did it because he had "to get the monkey off my back one way or the other." [10]

The precipitating factor in his decision was a series of secret meetings his general counsel, Phil Buchen, held with Watergate Special Prosecutor Leon Jaworski in the Jefferson Hotel, where they were both staying at the time. Ford attributes Jaworski with providing some "crucial" information [11]—i.e., that Nixon was under investigation in ten separate areas, and that the court process could "take years." [12] Ford cites a memorandum from Jaworski's assistant, Henry S. Ruth Jr., as being especially persuasive. Ruth had written:

"If you decide to recommend indictment I think it is fair and proper to notify Jack Miller and the White House sufficiently in advance so that pardon action could be taken before the indictment." He went on to say: "One can make a strong argument for leniency and if President Ford is so inclined, I think he ought to do it early rather than late."

Ford decided that court proceedings against Nixon might take six years, that Nixon "would not spend time quietly in San Clemente," [13] and "it would be virtually impossible for me to direct public attention on anything else." [14]

---

7. Only after I had finished did [Bryce Harlow] let me know in no uncertain terms that he agreed with Bob and Jack, that the mere mention of the pardon option could cause a lot of trouble in the days ahead. p. 18.

8. During the luncheon I repeated my assertion that the President was not guilty of an impeachable offense. Had I said otherwise at that moment, the whole house of cards might have collapsed. p. 21.

9. But compassion for Nixon as an individual hadn't prompted my decision at all. p. 266.

10. I had to get the monkey off my back one way or another. p. 236.

11. Jaworski gave Phil several crucial pieces of information. p. 246.

12. And if the verdict was Guilty, one had to assume that Nixon would appeal. That process would take years. p. 248.

13. The entire process would no doubt require years: a minimum of two, a maximum of six. And Nixon would not spend time quietly in San Clemente. p. 238.

14. It would be virtually impossible for me to direct public attention on anything else. p. 239.

Buchen, Haig and Henry Kissinger agreed with him. Hartmann was not so sure.

Buchen wanted to condition the pardon on Nixon agreeing to settle the question of who would retain custody and control over the tapes and Presidential papers that might be relevant to various Watergate proceedings, but Ford was reluctant to do that.

At one point a plan was considered whereby the Presidential materials would be kept in a vault at a Federal facility near San Clemente, but the vault would require two keys to open it. One would be retained by the General Services Administration, the other by Richard Nixon.

The White House did, however, want Nixon to make a full confession on the occasion of his pardon or, at a minimum, express true contrition. Ford tells of the negotiation with Jack Miller, Nixon's lawyer, over the wording of Nixon's statement. But as Ford reports Miller's response. Nixon was not likely to yield. "His few meetings with his client had shown him that the former President's ability to discuss Watergate objectively was almost nonexistent." [15]

The statement they really wanted was never forthcoming. As soon as Ford's emissary arrived in San Clemente, he was confronted with an ultimatum by Ron Zeigler, Nixon's former press secretary. "Lets get one thing straight immediately," Zeigler said. "President Nixon is not issuing any statement whatsoever regarding Watergate, whether Jerry Ford pardons him or not." Zeigler proposed a draft, which was turned down on the ground that "no statement would be better than that." [16] They went through three more drafts before they agreed on the statement Nixon finally made, which stopped far short of a full confession.

When Ford aide Benton Becker tried to explain to Nixon that acceptance of a pardon was an admission of guilt, he felt the President wasn't really listening. Instead, Nixon wanted to talk about the Washington Redskins. And when Becker left, Nixon pressed on him some cuff links and a tiepin "out of my own jewelry box."

Ultimately, Ford sums up the philosophy underlying his decision as one he picked up as a student at Yale Law School many years before. "I learned that public policy often took precedence over a rule of law. Although I respected the tenet that no man should be above the law, public policy demanded that I put Nixon—and Watergate—behind us as quickly as possible." [17]

Later, when Ford learned that Nixon's phlebitis had acted up and his health was seriously impaired, he debated whether to pay the ailing

---

15. But [Miller] wasn't optimistic about getting such a statement. His few meetings with his client had shown him that the former President's ability to discuss Watergate objectively was almost nonexistent. p. 246.

16. When Zeigler asked Becker what he thought of it, Becker replied that *no* statement would be better than that. p. 251.

17. Years before, at Yale Law School, I'd learned that public policy often took precedence over a rule of law. Although I respected the tenet that no man should be above the law, public policy demanded that I put Nixon—and Watergate—behind us as quickly as possible. p. 256.

former President a visit. "If I made the trip it would remind everybody of Watergate and the pardon. If I didn't, people would say I lacked compassion." [18] Ford went:

> He was stretched out flat on his back. There were tubes in his nose and mouth, and wires led from his arms, chest and legs to machines with orange lights that blinked on and off. His face was ashen, and I thought I had never seen anyone closer to death.[19]

The manuscript made available to The Nation includes many references to Henry Kissinger and other personalities who played a major role during the Ford years.

On Kissinger. Immediately after being informed by Nixon of his intention to resign, Ford returned to the Executive Office Building and phoned Henry Kissinger to let him know how he felt. "Henry," he said, "I need you. The country needs you. I want you to stay. I'll do everything I can to work with you." [20]

"Sir," Kissinger replied, "it is my job to get along with you and not yours to get along with me."

"We'll get along," Ford said. "I know we'll get along." Referring to Kissinger's joint jobs as Secretary of State and National Security Adviser to the President, Ford said, "I don't want to make any change. I think it's worked out well, so let's keep it that way." [21]

Later Ford did make the change and relieved Kissinger of his responsibilities as National Security Adviser at the same time that he fired James Schlesinger as Secretary of Defense. Shortly thereafter, he reports, Kissinger presented him with a "draft" letter of resignation, which he said Ford could call upon at will if he felt he needed it to quiet dissent from conservatives who objected to Kissinger's role in the firing of Schlesinger.

On John Connally. When Ford was informed that Nixon wanted him to replace Agnew, he told the President he had "no ambition to hold office after January 1977." [22] Nixon replied that that was good since his own choice for his running mate in 1976 was John Connally. "He'd be excellent," observed Nixon. Ford says he had "no problem with that."

---

18. My staff debated whether or not I ought to visit Nixon at the Long Beach Hospital, only half an hour away. If I made the trip, it would remind everyone of Watergate and the pardon. If I didn't, people would say I lacked compassion. I ended their debate as soon as I found out it had begun. Of course I would go. p. 298.

19. He was stretched out flat on his back. There were tubes in his nose and mouth, and wires led from his arms, chest and legs to machines with orange lights that blinked on and off. His face was ashen, and I thought I had never seen anyone closer to death. p. 299.

20. "Henry," I said when he came on the line, "I need you. The country needs you. I want you to stay. I'll do everything I can to work with you." p. 46.

21. "We'll get along," I said. "I know we can get along." We talked about the two hats he wore, as Secretary of State and National Security Advisor to the President. "I don't want to make any change," I said. "I think it's worked out well, so let's keep it that way." p. 46.

22. I told him about my promise to Betty and said that I had no ambitions to hold office after January 1977. p. 155.

On the Decision to Run Again. Ford was, he tells us, so sincere in his intention not to run again that he thought he would announce it and enhance his credibility in the country and the Congress, as well as keep the promise he had made to his wife, Betty.

Kissinger talked him out of it. "You can't do that. It would be disastrous from a foreign policy point of view. For the next two and a half years foreign governments would know that they were dealing with a lame-duck President. All our initiatives would be dead in the water, and I wouldn't be able to implement your foreign policy. It would probably have the same consequences in dealing with the Congress on domestic issues. You can't reassert the authority of the Presidency if you leave yourself hanging out on a dead limb. You've got to be an affirmative President."

On David Kennerly, the White House photographer. Schlesinger was arguing with Kissinger and Ford over the appropriate response to the seizure of the *Mayaguez*. At issue was whether airstrikes against the Cambodians were desirable; Schlesinger was opposed to bombings. Following a lull in the conversation, Ford reports, up spoke the 30-year-old White House photographer, David Kennerly, who had been taking pictures for the last hour.

"Has anyone considered," Kennerly asked, "that this might be the act of a local Cambodian commander who has just taken it into his own hands to stop any ship that comes by?" Nobody, apparently, had considered it, but following several seconds of silence, Ford tells us, the view carried the day. "Massive airstrikes would constitute overkill," Ford decided. "It would be far better to have Navy jets from the Coral Sea make surgical strikes against specific targets." [23]

On Nixon's Character. Nixon's flaw, according to Ford, was "pride." "A terribly proud man," writes Ford, "he detested weakness in other people. I'd often heard him speak disparagingly of those whom he felt to be soft and expedient. (Curiously, he didn't feel that the press was weak. Reporters, he sensed, were his adversaries. He knew they didn't like him, and he responded with reciprocal disdain.)" [24]

Nixon felt disdain for the Democratic leadership of the House, whom he also regarded as weak. According to Ford, "His pride and personal contempt for weakness had overcome his ability to tell the difference between right and wrong," [25] all of which leads Ford to wonder whether Nixon had known in advance about Watergate.

23. Subjectively, I felt that what Kennerly had said made a lot of sense. Massive airstrikes would constitute overkill. It would be far better to have Navy jets from the *Coral Sea* make surgical strikes against specific targets in the vicinity of Kompong Som. p. 416.

24. In Nixon's case, that flaw was pride. A terribly proud man, he detested weakness in other people. I'd often heard him speak disparagingly of those whom he felt to be soft and expedient. (Curiously, he didn't feel that the press was weak. Reporters, he sensed, were his adversaries. He knew they didn't like him, and he responded with reciprocal disdain.) p. 53.

25. His pride and personal contempt for weakness had overcome his ability to tell the difference between right and wrong. p. 54.

On hearing Nixon's resignation speech, which Ford felt lacked an adequate plea for forgiveness, he was persuaded that "Nixon was out of touch with reality." [26]

In February of last year, when *The Washington Post* obtained and printed advance excerpts from H. R. Haldeman's memoir, *The Ends of Power,* on the eve of its publication by Times Books, *The New York Times* called *The Post's* feat "a second-rate burglary."

The Post disagreed, claiming that its coup represented "first-rate enterprise" and arguing that it had burglarized nothing, that publication of the Haldeman memoir came under the Fair Comment doctrine long recognized by the courts, and that "There is a fundamental journalistic principle here—a First Amendment principle that was central to the Pentagon Papers case."

In the issue of *The Nation* dated May 5, 1979, our special Spring Books number, we will discuss some of the ethical problems raised by the issue of disclosure.

Questions

1. The Supreme Court found it unnecessary to decide the issues of copyrightability which had largely concerned the district court (557 F.Supp. 1067 (S.D.N.Y. 1983)) and the court of appeals (723 F.2d 195 (2d Cir.1983)). Judge Owen in the district court acknowledged that historical facts and memoranda prepared by others are not *per se* copyrightable. He concluded, however, that President Ford's "revelations as to his state of mind while involved in governmental affairs of the highest consequence" were copyrightable. He further concluded that "it is the totality of these facts and memoranda collected together with Ford's reflections * * * that is protected by the copyright laws." 557 F.Supp. at 1072–1073.

a. Should facts *per se* gain a copyrightable status simply because they are "collected together with" copyrightable elements?

b. Should "revelations" as to President Ford's "state of mind" be regarded as uncopyrightable fact or copyrightable expression? Clearly the words used by Ford to describe his views of Henry Kissinger are copyrightable, but are the views themselves, apart from the words in which they are expressed, also copyrightable? Should it make any difference in this regard whether the author of the book disclosing those views is President Ford himself in his memoirs, or a third party who disclosed such views in a Ford biography?

c. Is there any theory under which President Ford might be able to claim copyright in statements made by others as reported in his memoirs?

d. To what extent should the Section 105 prohibition on copyright in any work of the United States Government affect the issues in this case?

e. Does paraphrasing of copyrightable expression constitute infringement? Should it make any difference whether the work which is paraphrased is itself factual or fictional?

26. The speech lasted fifteen minutes, and at the end I was convinced Nixon was out of touch with reality. p. 57.

f. Was there substantial similarity in the selection and arrangement of the noncopyrightable facts and idea as between the two works? If so, should this in itself constitute copyright infringement?

2. When, if ever, should the unpublished status of the plaintiff's work negate the defendant's claim of fair use? Should it extend beyond those works which the plaintiff wishes to remain forever (or indefinitely) unpublished, such as letters and diaries? If the plaintiff intends to publish in the near future, so that no privacy interest may be asserted, is the Court correct in nevertheless finding that the leisure to develop ideas and to engage in marketing plans outweighs any fair use claim?

3. Does the Section 107 reference to "news reporting" inevitably mean that the courts must define what constitutes "news" in applying the fair use privilege?

4. Is the Supreme Court correct in concluding that to follow the Court of Appeals rule whereby copying 300 words verbatim (out of a total of some 200,000 words) was regarded as fair use would mean that public figures would have "little incentive to create or profit in financing such memoirs and the public would be denied an important source of significant historical information"? Is the Supreme Court's conclusion correct in this case because the 300 words were of such qualitative (if not quantitative) importance?

5. In determining the quantum of copying, should it matter that the 300 verbatim words were not contained consecutively in either plaintiff's or defendant's works, but were dispersed throughout each of the works, a line or two at a time?

6. In evaluating the fourth fair use factor under Section 107, is it significant whether *Time Magazine* cancelled its agreement with Harper and Row because of the Nation's publication of the 300 verbatim words, or whether, alternatively, it was the publication of the facts contained in the Nation article which caused the cancellation, and that this would have occurred even if there had been no verbatim copying? Does the Court effectively meet this issue by its discussion of the apportionment of profits?

7. If the manuscript furnished to the Nation had not been "purloined," would the Court have held the 300 word copy to be fair use? Should this bear upon the fair use issue? Would it have been better for the law of copyright if this case had been tried and decided on a misappropriation theory à la International News Service v. Associated Press, supra at p. 524? Would such a cause of action lie under these facts? What about preemption?

Index

References are to Pages

ABANDONMENT
Definition of, 132.

ADAPTATION RIGHT
Defined, 208n.

ADVERTISEMENTS
Copyrightability of, 2–7.

APPROPRIATION
See Privacy, Right of; Publicity, Right of.

ARCHITECTURAL PLANS
See Copyrightability.

ART, WORKS OF
Applied art, 56–74.
Definition, 59.
Exhibition as publication, 158–161.
Judicial standard, 5.
Mass production of, 58–59.
Reproductions of, 17–19.
Writings, as, 60.

ASCAP (American Society of Composers, Authors, Publishers)
Founding of, 229–230.

ASSIGNMENTS
See Publicity, Right of; Renewal of Copyright; Transfers of Copyright, generally.

ATTORNEY'S FEE
See Damages.

AUTHOR
Defined, 1.

AUTHORS' MORAL RIGHTS
Generally, 479–523.
Author's name,
　Prevent use of, right to,
　　False attribution, 509–513.
　　Truthful attribution, 503–509.
　Require use of, right to, 513–520.
California Art Preservation Act, 497–498.
Distortion, 480–496.
Droit moral, definition of, 479.
Enumerated, 479.
"Joint work theory," 490.
Lanham Act, 493–496, 513–520.

AUTHORS' MORAL RIGHTS—Cont'd
Remake rights, 498–503.
New York Artists' Authorship Rights Act, 498.
United States, recognition, 479, 484–485, 492–493, 495.

AUTHOR'S NAME
See Authors' Moral Rights.

B.M.I. (Broadcast Music, Inc.)
Performing rights society, 230.

BELT BUCKLES
Copyrightability of, 69–74.

"BETAMAX DECISION"
See Videotape recording.

CABLE TELEVISION
Secondary transmission, 226–228.

CALIFORNIA ART PRESERVATION ACT
Summarized, 497–498.

CALIFORNIA RESALE ROYALTIES ACT
Provisions of, 521–522.

CARICATURE
See Defamation.

CHARACTERS
Comic book and cartoon, 80–85.
Comic book vs. literary, 84.
Copyrightability, 74–93.
Unfair competition, 559–565.

CLASSROOM USE
See Fair Use, Photocopying by teachers.

COLLECTIVE WORKS
Definition of, 96–97.

COMMON LAW COPYRIGHT
Definition of, 32–33.

COMPILATION
Definition of, 96.

COMPULSORY LICENSES
Royalty tribunal, 449–450.

COMPUTER PROGRAMS
Copyrightability, 115–126.

CONSTITUTION
Basis for copyright, 8, 14.
Copyright, basis for, 25, 81n.
Copyright provision, 894.

CONTESTS
Copyrightability, 113–115.

CONTU
Commission on New Technological Uses, Report of, 118–126.

COPY, THE RIGHT TO
See Reproduction Right

COPYRIGHT ACTS
Copyright Act of 1909, text of, 972–997.
Copyright Act of 1976, text of, 895–971.
Parallel reference tables showing 1909 Act in United States Code, 998–999.

COPYRIGHT NOTICE
See Notice.

COPYRIGHT ROYALTY TRIBUNAL
See Damages.

COPYRIGHTABILITY
Accounting forms, 108–113.
Advertisements, 2–7.
Applied art, 56–74.
Architectural plans, 113.
Belt buckles, 69–74.
Characters, 74–93.
Computer programs, 115–126.
Constitutional authority, 467.
Contests, 113–115.
Derivative works, 19–24.
Directories, 4, 103–107.
Economic philosophy of, 28–29.
Factual works, 49–56.
Fixation intangible medium, 93–94.
Historical facts, 49–56, 1000–1017.
Letters, 36–37.
Light fixtures, 61–69.
Phonograph records, 13.
Photography, 7–13, 41–49.
Pictorial illustrations, 4–5.
Sound recordings,
    Definition of, 93.
    Federal preemption, 94–95.
Tangible medium of expression, fixation in,
    Generally, 30–40.
Utility, works of, 108–115.

CREATIVITY
Photographs, 47.

DAMAGES
Generally, 431–450.
Actual damages,
    Infringer's profits, relationship to recovery of, 431–432.
Attorney's fee, 445–449.
    Bad faith, 447.
    Moral blame, 449.
    Prevailing party, 447–449.

DAMAGES—Cont'd
Attorney's fee—Cont'd
    Reasonable fee, criteria for, 447–448.
Defamation, 614–616.
Equity, 440.
Expert testimony, 440.
Infringer's profits,
    Generally, 432–441.
    Computation of, 440–441.
"In lieu" damages, 432, 434.
Royalty tribunal, 449–450.
Statutory, 441–445.
    Registration requirement, 445.
Statutory damages, 432.

DEFAMATION
Generally, 595–703.
Care in reporting news, 679–680, 682, 687.
Caricature, 617–621.
Conflicts of law, 610, 716.
Damages, 614–616.
Defamatory communication, definition of, 597–598.
"Equal time" requirements, 596.
Fair comment, 596, 693–694.
First Amendment defense,
    Generally, 640–703.
    Balancing of interests, 640–654.
    Historical documentary, 688–703.
    Matters of public concern, 670, 673–674, 683–684, 687–688, 695–696.
    "Private" persons, 654, 655, 660–661, 665, 668, 670, 688, 696–698.
    Public figure or official,
        Actual malice, 646–647, 658, 672–674, 682, 686, 698–701.
        Public figure, what constitutes, 672–673, 675, 683–684, 689.
        Public figures vs. public officials, 652–653, 657, 660–661, 669–670, 688, 696–701.
Identification,
    Generally, 622–639.
    Disclaimer, 617, 622–623.
    Extrinsic "key," 623, 633.
Injury, nature of, 597–621.
Judicial notice, 616.
Libel and slander, distinguished, 595–596.
Libel "per quod," 595.
Personal habits, 598–600.
Privacy, right to, comparison, 809–810, 812–815.
Privileges, absolute and conditional, 596, 646.
Recipients of alleged defamatory communication,
    Size and composition of group, 598–599.
Reputation, harm to,
    Professional career, 600–617, 634–639.
    Tendency vs. actual, 597.
Scienter standard, 891–892.
Standard of determination, 597–598.

DEFAMATION—Cont'd
States, ability to set standards,
    Liability for defamation of private individual, 666–667, 702–703.
    Punitive damages, 668–670.
Strict liability, 666–667, 678–679, 681–682.
Truth as defense, 596, 694, 756–757.

DERIVATIVE WORKS
    Generally, 95–108.
Definition of, 96.
Originality, 19–24.
Publication of, 161–170.
Renewal of copyright, 263–276.

DIRECTORIES
Copyrightability, 4, 18, 103–107.

DISPLAY RIGHT
    Generally, 238–239.
Paintings, 239.
Performance right compared, 239.
Reproduction right compared, 239.

DISTRIBUTION RIGHT
    Generally, 208–214.
First sale doctrine, 209–214.

DROIT DE SUITE
Nature of, 520–523.

DROIT MORAL
See Author's Moral Rights.

DURATION OF COPYRIGHT
    Generally, 240–245.
Anonymous or pseudonymous works, 240, 242–243.
Common law copyright, 243–244.
Creation of work, 240.
Joint works, 241.
Public domain, 241.
Works made for hire, 240–242.
Works obtaining statutory copyright under 1909 Act, 244–245.

EUROPEAN PRINCIPLES
Droit de suite (rights in resale proceeds), 520–523.
Droit moral (moral rights), 479–520.

FACTUAL WORKS
Copyrightability, 49–56.

FAIR USE
    Generally, 90–91, 346, 348, 366–426, 1000–1018.
Amount used, 1009.
Comic book character, 374–378, 428.
Contributory infringement, 421–425.
Factors to be considered, 366–368.
Innocent intent, 387.
Issue of fact, 366.
Library photocopying, 392–406.
Market, effect upon, 1009–1011.
Music, 378–389.
Parody, burlesque or satire, 368–385.
Photocopying by teachers,
    Brevity, 390.
    Cumulative effect test, 391–392.

FAIR USE—Cont'd
Photocopying by teachers—Cont'd
    Guidelines, 389–392.
    Spontaneity, 390–391.
    Teacher use, 390.
Time-shifting, 408.
    Authorized, 411–412.
    Unauthorized, 412–415.
    Unpublished manuscript, quotation from, 1000–1018.
Videotape recording, 407–426.

FALSE LIGHT
See Privacy, Right of.

FEDERAL PREEMPTION
    Generally, 451–478.
Current copyright act,
    Legislative history, 475–478.
Federal copyright statute vs. state proscription of record piracy, 459–475.
Misappropriation doctrine, 475–478.
Pre-1978 status, 451–475.
Tangible medium of expression, fixation in, 32–33.
Unfair competition, 451–459.

FINE ART
Statutory definition, 301–302.

FIRST AMENDMENT
    See also, Defamation; Privacy, Right of; Publicity, Right to.
Fair use, 1005–1007.
Relationship to copyright, 27.

FIRST SALE DOCTRINE
See Distribution Right.

FIXATION IN TANGIBLE MEDIUM
Definition of, 118.

FORFEITURE
Definition of, 132.

FORMALITIES
    See also, Manufacturing Clause; Notice; Registration and Deposit.
Generally, 171–196.

IDEAS
Protection of,
    Expression, 27.

IDEAS, PROTECTION OF
Confidential relationship, breach of, 582.
Express or implied contract,
    Generally, 566–594.
    Elements of, 588.
    First Amendment, 580.
    "Implied in fact" vs. "implied-in-law," 572–573.
    Novelty, 579, 581, 588.
    Opportunity to reject terms, 574.
    Release form negating contractual relationship, 591, 594.
    Substantial similarity requirement, 581.
Moral ideas, 580.
Property theory, 580, 582.

IMPLIED COPYRIGHT LICENSE
Generally, 19–24.

INFRINGEMENT ACTIONS
    See also, Fair Use.
    Generally, 316–430.
Contributory infringement, 421–425.
Deposit, effect of failure to deposit copies, 186–191.
Fair use, 90–91.
First Amendment defense, 426–430.
    Generally, 359.
    Copyright Act, constitutionality of, 427–429.
First sale doctrine, 209–214.
Innocent intent, 387.
Jurisdiction, 316–322.
Plagiarism or copying,
    Generally, 322–366.
    Access, 322–331, 358, 362.
    Similarity, 322–328, 331–366.
        Extrinsic test vs. intrinsic test, 354–356, 359.
        Ideas vs. expression of ideas, 352–359.
        Unity of idea and expression, 356–358.
Similarity,
    Ideas vs. expression of ideas,
        Generally, 362–366.
"Striking Similarity," definition of, 328.
Tests, 88–89.

INTRUSION
See Privacy, Right of.

LANHAM ACT
See Authors' Moral Rights.

LIBEL
See Defamation.

LIBRARY PHOTOCOPYING
See Fair Use.

LIGHT FIXTURES
Copyrightability, 61–69.

LITERARY WORKS
Definition of, 117–118.

MANUFACTURING CLAUSE
Copyright Act of 1909, pp. 194–195.
Copyright Act of 1976, pp. 193–194.

MISAPPROPRIATION
    See also, Unfair Competition.
Federal preemption issues, 475–478.

NEW YORK ARTISTS' AUTHORSHIP RIGHTS ACT
Summarized, 498.

NEWS
Unfair competition, 524–542.

NIXON PARDON
Ford memoirs, publication of, 1000–1018.

NOTICE
    Generally, 171–186.

NOTICE—Cont'd
Compilations, 174–180.
Date, significance of, 180.
Foreign publication, 181–186.
Incorrect owner, effect of, 180–181.
Omission of,
    "Relatively small number" distributed, 173.
Phonorecords, 171–172, 180.
Rationale for, 171.
Significance under current Act of requirements under 1909 Act, 173–174.

NOVELTY
See Originality.

ORIGINALITY
    Generally, 1–30.
Definition of,
    Judicial, 15–16.
    Undefined in 1909 Act.
Directories, 4, 18.
Maps, 18.
Novelty, distinguished from, 24–30.

PAINTING
Display right, 239.

"PALMING OFF"
Defined, 516.

PARODY
See Fair Use.

PATENTS
Compared with copyright 14–18, 26–27.
Federal preemption of state unfair competition laws, 451–459.

PERFORMANCE RIGHT
    See also, Display Right.
    Generally, 214–238.
ASCAP, 229–239.
    Antitrust problems, 231.
    General license, 230.
B.M.I., 230.
Educational institution, 224.
"Musical" vs. "dramatico-musical" works, 234.
Performance,
    Definition of, 218.
Performing rights societies, 229–238.
Profit requirement, 221–224.
    "Commercial advantage," 224.
Public requirement, 214–216.
    Composition of audience, 214–215.
    Dispersed audience, 215.
Publicly,
    Definition of, 219–220.
Secondary transmission, 225–229.
    Under 1909 Act, 225–228.
    Under 1976 Act, 228–229.
Video cassettes, 216–221.

INDEX

PERFORMANCES
Publication, 150–158.

PHONORECORDS
Compulsory license, 449–450.
Copyrightability, 13.
Notice of copyright, 171–172, 180.
Piracy, state effort to proscribe, 459–475.
Publication, 140–149.
Royalty tribunal, 449–450.

PHOTOCOPYING
See Fair Use.

PHOTOGRAPHS
Copyrightability, 7–13, 41–49.
Creativity, 47.
Publicity, right of, 843.

PLAGIARISM
See Infringement Actions.

PLAYER PIANO
Piano roll, 197–202, 468–469.

PRIVACY, RIGHT OF
Generally, 542.
Appropriation, 825–826.
Conflict of law, 715–718.
Defamation compared, 809–810.
False light,
    Generally, 781–827.
    Elements, 781.
    Fictional biography, 791–792, 818–820.
    Fictionalization, 791–792, 796–798, 806–807, 818–820, 825.
    First Amendment defense,
        Generally, 792–827.
    Injury, nature of, 781–792.
    Knowing or reckless falsehood, 798–804.
    Newsworthy material, 804, 807.
    Ordinary sensibilities test, 784–786, 788–789.
First Amendment issues, 688–703.
Motion pictures, 821–824.
Public disclosure of private facts,
    Generally, 704–780.
    Celebrities, waiver by, 833–834.
    Consent to publish, withdrawal of, 773–774.
    Elements, 704, 707–708.
    First Amendment defense,
        Generally, 751–780.
        Newsworthy events, 764–765, 777.
    Identification, 742–751.
    Mistaken identity, 734–735.
    Name, use of, 708–709.
    Nature of injury, 704–742.
    Non-assignable, 835–836.
    Offensiveness, 704, 729–730, 732–734, 834–835.
    Ordinary sensibilities test, 723–725, 728–730, 732–734.
    Privilege or waiver as to prior disclosure, effect of, 722–723.

PRIVACY, RIGHT OF—Cont'd
Public disclosure of private facts—Cont'd
    Public or general interest test, 723–725, 773–780.
    Public record, public disclosure of matters contained therein, 709–710, 756–761.
    Public vs. private, 729–733.
    Survival of action, 710.
    Time lapse, effect of, 710–711, 713–714, 718–720, 723, 761–773, 824–825.
    Waiver by celebrities, 833–834.
    Waiver of right by public appearance, 729–733.
Public figures, 735–742.
Publicity, right of, compared, 833–836.
Truth, not necessarily a defense, 810–815.
Types of cases, 808, 848, 885.
Underlying rationale, 808–815.
Waiver of, 614.

PUBLIC DOMAIN
Forfeiture of copyright, 135.

PUBLIC FIGURE
See Defamation, First Amendment defense.

PUBLICATION
Generally, 127–170.
Abandonment, 132.
Art exhibitions, 158–161.
Definition of, 129.
Derivative works, 161–170.
Forfeiture, 132–140.
General versus limited, 130–140, 157.
Performances, 150–158.
Phonorecords, distribution of, 140–149.
Significance of, 127–129.
    Occurring on or after January 1, 1978, pp. 127–128.
    Occurring prior to January 1, 1978, pp. 128–129.

PUBLICITY, RIGHT OF
Generally, 828–893.
Appropriation, 848, 860, 864, 881–893.
Assignability, 851.
Biography, 871–878.
Contract theory, compared, 839.
Defined, 842–844.
Exploitation of right during lifetime, lack of, 852, 873–874, 879–881.
Falsification, 875–881.
First Amendment defense,
    Generally, 858–893.
    "Actual malice," 893.
    Balancing test, 874–878.
    "Reckless disregard of the truth", 893.
Historical evolution, 832–833.
Inadequacy of other doctrines, 833–842.
Injury, nature of, 828–858.
News broadcast of performance, 858–871.
Newsworthy event, 850–851.
Privacy, right of, compared, 833–836.
Recognition of, 830–831, 841.
Substance and limitations, 839–841.

PUBLICITY, RIGHT OF—Cont'd
Survival, 852–858.
Time limit, 851–852.
Unfair competition, compared, 836–839.
Vehicles of dissemination, 878–881.

RECORD PIRACY
State effort to proscribe, 459–475.

REGISTRATION AND DEPOSIT
  Generally, 186–193.
Constructive notice, 191.
Damages,
  Attorney's fee, relationship and requirement, 449.
  Prerequisite, 445.
Delay, penalty for, 189–190, 192–193.
Delay in deposit, effect of, 186–191.
Deposit, distinguished from registration, 192–193.
Five year cut off date on prima facie evidence of validity, 191.
Mandamus to obtain registration, 191.
Prompt deposit, meaning of, 187–189.
Register's authority to demand deposit, 189.
Unpublished works, 190.

REMEDIES
See Damages.

RENEWAL OF COPYRIGHT
  Generally, 245–276.
Assignability, 253–276.
Assignment of renewal interest prior to vesting, 253–263.
  Wife and children vs. assignee, 262.
  Will beneficiary vs. assignee, 262.
Children as claimants, 248–253.
  Illegitimate children, 251–253.
Claimants, 247–253.
Derivative works, 263–276.
Proprietor, 253.
Rationale of, 245–247.
"Tying arrangements" provision of Sherman Act, 262.

REPRODUCTION RIGHT
  Generally, 197–208, 301–302.
Compulsory license,
    Generally, 205–208.
  Adaptation right, 206–207.
  Juke box operators, 206.
  Nondramatic musical works, 205–206.
  Notice of intent to obtain, 206–208.
  Radio stations, 206.
  Royalties, 207–208.
  Sound recordings, 205–206.
Computer, input to, 202.
Copying,
  Copy of a copy, 205.
  Definition of "copy", 199–202.
  Ephemeral copies, 202.
Exclusivity of right, 205.
Photograph, 203–205.

RESALE RIGHTS
California Resale Royalties Act, 521–522.
Droit de suite, nature of, 520–523.

RIGHTS OF COPYRIGHT OWNER
Enumerated, 197.
Waiver of, 197.

SATIRE
See Fair Use.

"SCIENCE AND USEFUL ARTS"
Meaning of, 29–30.

SLANDER
See Defamation.

SOUND RECORDINGS
  See also, Copyrightability.
Definition of, 93.
Pre-February 15, 1972 recordings, exclusion from federal protection, 93–95.
Record piracy, 95.

SPEECHES
Publication, 150–158.

TANGIBLE MEDIUM OF EXPRESSION
Fixation in, 30–40.

TELEVISION BROADCASTS
Fixation in tangible medium of expression, 30–31.

"TIME SHIFTING"
Definition of, 408.

TITLES
Unfair competition, 542–559.

TRANSFERS OF COPYRIGHT
  Generally, 277–315.
Book rights,
  Hardcover and paperback, 288–289.
Definition of, 288.
Determination of media, 302–313.
  Television rights, 302–308.
Employment for hire,
  Constitutional limitations, 277–278.
Indivisibility under current Act, abolition of, 288–289.
Indivisibility under 1909 Act,
    Generally, 278–288.
  Assignment vs. license, 278–281.
  Right to claim copyright, 280–281.
  Standing to sue, 280.
  Post-recordation assignment, 297.
  Presumptions, 302.
Recordation, 289–297.
  Bona fide purchaser, 291–292.
Sequel rights, 308–313.
Tangible object, copyright distinct from, 297–302.
Termination of transfers and nonexclusive licenses, 313–314.

UNFAIR COMPETITION
  See also, Federal Preemption.

UNFAIR COMPETITION—Cont'd
    Generally, 524–565.
Characters, 559–565.
    Names and nicknames, 565.
    Sequels, 559.
    Sexually explicit portrayal, 561–564.
    Uniform, trademark implications, 561–563.
Misappropriation doctrine, 475–478, 541–542, 1002.
News, 524–542.
Palming off, 541.
Right of publicity, compared, 836–839.
Secondary meaning, 459.
Titles,
    Generally, 542–559.
    Confusion, likelihood of, 552–559.
    Copyright,
        Effect of obtaining, 550–551.
        Expiration, effect of, 548–549.
    Lanham Act, provisions of, 555.
    Lapse of time, 551–552, 554.
    Reverse confusion, 557–558.

UNFAIR COMPETITION—Cont'd
Titles—Cont'd
    Secondary meaning, 542–548, 551–557.
    Trademark implications, 550–551.

"USEFUL ARTICLE"
Definition of, 67.

UTILITY, WORKS OF
Copyrightability, 108–115.

VEND, THE RIGHT TO
See Distribution Right, generally.

VIDEO CASSETTES
    See also, Performance Right.
Rental, 216–221.

VIDEOTAPE RECORDING
Fair use issues, 407–426.

WORKS OF AUTHORSHIP
    Generally, 40–126.
Writings, compared with, 40.

WRITINGS
Works of authorship, compared with, 40.

†

KF 2993 .N54 1985

DATE DUE		
DEC 1 7 1992		